SHOWCASE PRESENTS

SUPERGIRL

VOLUME ONE

Dan DiDio Senior VP-Executive Editor

Mort Weisinger Editor-original series

Bob Harras and Bob Joy Editors-collected edition

Robbin Brosterman Senior Art Director

Paul Levitz President & Publisher

Georg Brewer VP-Design & DC Direct Creative

Richard Bruning Senior VP-Creative Director

Patrick Caldon Executive VP-Finance & Operations

Chris Caramalis VP-Finance

John Cunningham VP-Marketing

Terri Cunningham VP-Managing Editor

Alison Gill VP-Manufacturing

David Hyde VP-Publicity

Hank Kanalz VP-General Manager, WildStorm

Jim Lee Editorial Director-WildStorm

Paula Lowitt Senior VP-Business & Legal Affairs

MaryEllen McLaughlin VP-Advertising & Custom Publishing

John Nee Senior VP-Business Development

Gregory Noveck Senior VP-Creative Affairs

Sue Pohja VP-Book Trade Sales

Steve Rotterdam Senior VP-Sales & Marketing

Cheryl Rubin Senior VP-Brand Management

Jeff Trojan VP-Business Development, DC Direct

Bob Wayne VP-Sales

Cover art by Curt Swan and Stan Kaye.
Front cover color by Drew Moore.
Cover reconstruction by Dale Crain.

TABLE OF CONTENTS

SUPERMAN #123
AUGUST 1958
COVER ART: CURT SWAN AND STAN KAYE

5

THE THREE MAGIC WISHES: THE GIRL OF STEEL
WRITER: OTTO BINDER
PENCILLER: DICK SPRANG
INKER: STAN KAYE

6

DC COMICS HOUSE AD ANNOUNCING THE FIRST APPEARANCE OF SUPERGIRL IN ACTION COMICS
ARTIST: AL PLASTINO

32

ACTION COMICS #252
MAY 1959
COVER ART: CURT SWAN AND STAN KAYE

33

THE SUPERGIRL FROM KRYPTON!
WRITER: OTTO BINDER
ARTIST: AL PLASTINO

34

ACTION COMICS #253
JUNE 1959

THE SECRET OF THE SUPER-ORPHAN!
WRITER: OTTO BINDER
ARTIST: JIM MOONEY

42

ACTION COMICS #254
JULY 1959

SUPERGIRL'S FOSTER PARENTS!
WRITER: OTTO BINDER
ARTIST: JIM MOONEY

50

ACTION COMICS #255
AUGUST 1959

SUPERGIRL VISITS THE 21ST CENTURY!
WRITER: OTTO BINDER
ARTIST: JIM MOONEY

58

ACTION COMICS #256
SEPTEMBER 1959

THE GREAT SUPERGIRL MIRAGE!
WRITER: OTTO BINDER
ARTIST: JIM MOONEY

65

SUPERMAN'S PAL JIMMY OLSEN #40
OCTOBER 1959

JIMMY OLSEN, SUPERGIRL'S PAL!
WRITER: OTTO BINDER
PENCILLER: CURT SWAN
INKER: GEORGE KLEIN

72

ACTION COMICS #257
OCTOBER 1959

THE THREE MAGIC WISHES!
WRITER: OTTO BINDER
ARTIST: JIM MOONEY

81

ACTION COMICS #258
NOVEMBER 1959
COVER ART: CURT SWAN AND STAN KAYE

89

SUPERGIRL'S FAREWELL TO EARTH!
WRITER: OTTO BINDER
ARTIST: JIM MOONEY

90

ACTION COMICS #259
DECEMBER 1959

THE CAVE-GIRL OF STEEL!
WRITER: OTTO BINDER
ARTIST: JIM MOONEY

98

SUPERMAN'S GIRL FRIEND LOIS LANE #14
JANUARY 1960

LOIS LANE'S SECRET ROMANCE!
WRITER: UNKNOWN
ARTIST: KURT SCHAFFENBERGER

105

ACTION COMICS #260
JANUARY 1960
COVER ART: CURT SWAN AND STAN KAYE

114

MIGHTY MAID!
WRITER: OTTO BINDER
ARTIST: AL PLASTINO

115

THE GIRL SUPERBABY!
WRITER: OTTO BINDER
ARTIST: JIM MOONEY

127

ACTION COMICS #261
FEBRUARY 1960

SUPERGIRL'S SUPER PET!
WRITER: JERRY SIEGEL
ARTIST: JIM MOONEY

135

ACTION COMICS #262
MARCH 1960
COVER ART: CURT SWAN AND STAN KAYE

143

SUPERGIRL'S GREATEST VICTORY!
WRITER: OTTO BINDER
ARTIST: JIM MOONEY

144

SUPERBOY #80
APRIL 1960
COVER ART: CURT SWAN AND STAN KAYE
156

SUPERBOY MEETS SUPERGIRL!
WRITER: OTTO BINDER
PENCILLER: CURT SWAN
INKER: GEORGE KLEIN
157

ACTION COMICS #263
APRIL 1960

SUPERGIRL'S DARKEST DAY!
WRITER: OTTO BINDER
ARTIST: JIM MOONEY
166

ACTION COMICS #264
MARCH 1960

SUPERGIRL GETS ADOPTED!
WRITER: JERRY SIEGEL
ARTIST: JIM MOONEY
178

ACTION COMICS #265
JUNE 1960
COVER ART: CURT SWAN AND STAN KAYE
190

THE DAY SUPERGIRL REVEALED HERSELF!
WRITER: JERRY SIEGEL
ARTIST: JIM MOONEY
191

SUPERMAN'S PAL JIMMY OLSEN #46
JULY 1960
COVER ART: CURT SWAN AND STAN KAYE
204

JIMMY OLSEN, ORPHAN!
WRITER: JERRY SIEGEL
PENCILLER: CURT SWAN
INKER: GEORGE KLEIN
205

ACTION COMICS #266
JULY 1960
COVER ART: CURT SWAN AND STAN KAYE
214

THE WORLD'S MIGHTIEST CAT!
WRITER: JERRY SIEGEL
ARTIST: JIM MOONEY
215

SUPERMAN #139
AUGUST 1960

THE UNTOLD STORY OF RED KRYPTONITE!
WRITER: OTTO BINDER
PENCILLER: CURT SWAN
INKER: GEORGE KLEIN
228

ACTION COMICS #267
AUGUST 1960

THE THREE SUPER-HEROES!
WRITER: JERRY SIEGEL
ARTIST: JIM MOONEY
237

ACTION COMICS #268
SEPTEMBER 1960

THE MYSTERY SUPERGIRL!
WRITER: JERRY SIEGEL
ARTIST: JIM MOONEY
250

SUPERMAN #140
OCTOBER 1960

PART I: THE SON OF BIZARRO!
PART II: THE ORPHAN BIZARRO!
PART III: THE BIZARRO SUPERGIRL!
WRITER: OTTO BINDER
ARTIST: WAYNE BORING
263

ACTION COMICS #269
OCTOBER 1960

SUPERGIRL'S FIRST ROMANCE!
WRITER: JERRY SIEGEL
ARTIST: JIM MOONEY
289

ACTION COMICS #270
NOVEMBER 1960
COVER ART: CURT SWAN AND STAN KAYE
301

THE OLD MAN OF METROPOLIS!
WRITER: OTTO BINDER
PENCILLER: CURT SWAN
INKER: JOHN FORTE
302

SUPERGIRL'S BUSIEST DAY!
WRITER: JERRY SIEGEL
ARTIST: JIM MOONEY
312

ADVENTURE COMICS #278
NOVEMBER 1960
COVER ART: CURT SWAN AND STAN KAYE
325

SUPERGIRL IN SMALLVILLE!
WRITER: OTTO BINDER
ARTIST: AL PLASTINO
326

ACTION COMICS #271
DECEMBER 1960

SUPERGIRL'S FORTRESS OF SOLITUDE!
WRITER: JERRY SIEGEL
ARTIST: JIM MOONEY
338

ACTION COMICS #272
JANUARY 1961

THE SECOND SUPERGIRL!
WRITER: OTTO BINDER
ARTIST: JIM MOONEY

351

ACTION COMICS #273
FEBRUARY 1961

THE SUPERGIRL OF TWO WORLDS!
WRITER: OTTO BINDER
ARTIST: JIM MOONEY

364

PICK A NEW HAIRSTYLE FOR LINDA (SUPERGIRL) LEE!
ARTIST: JIM MOONEY

377

SUPERMAN'S PAL JIMMY OLSEN #51
MARCH 1961

THE GIRL WITH GREEN HAIR!
WRITER: OTTO BINDER
PENCILLER: CURT SWAN
INKER: GEORGE KLEIN

378

ACTION COMICS #274
MARCH 1961

SUPERGIRL'S THREE TIME TRIPS!
WRITER: JERRY SIEGEL
ARTIST: JIM MOONEY

387

SUPERMAN #144
APRIL 1961
COVER ART: CURT SWAN AND STAN KAYE

400

THE ORPHANS OF SPACE!
WRITER: JERRY SIEGEL
ARTIST: AL PLASTINO

401

ACTION COMICS #275
APRIL 1961

MA AND PA KENT ADOPT SUPERGIRL!
WRITER: JERRY SIEGEL
ARTIST: JIM MOONEY

409

ACTION COMICS #276
MAY 1961
COVER ART: CURT SWAN AND STAN KAYE

422

THE WAR BETWEEN SUPERGIRL AND THE SUPERMEN EMERGENCY SQUAD!
WRITER: ROBERT BERNSTEIN
ARTIST: WAYNE BORING

423

SUPERGIRL'S THREE SUPER GIRL-FRIENDS!
WRITER: JERRY SIEGEL
ARTIST: JIM MOONEY

437

ACTION COMICS #277
JUNE 1961
COVER ART: CURT SWAN AND STAN KAYE

449

THE BATTLE OF THE SUPER-PETS!
WRITER: JERRY SIEGEL
ARTIST: JIM MOONEY

450

ACTION COMICS #278
JULY 1961

THE UNKNOWN SUPERGIRL!
WRITER: JERRY SIEGEL
ARTIST: JIM MOONEY

463

ACTION COMICS #279
AUGUST 1961

SUPERGIRL'S SECRET ENEMY!
WRITER: JERRY SIEGEL
ARTIST: JIM MOONEY

476

ACTION COMICS #280
SEPTEMBER 1961

TRAPPED IN KANDOR!
WRITER: JERRY SIEGEL
ARTIST: JIM MOONEY

488

ACTION COMICS #281
OCTOBER 1961

THE SECRET OF THE TIME BARRIER!
WRITER: JERRY SIEGEL
ARTIST: JIM MOONEY

500

DID YOU VOTE FOR SUPERGIRL'S NEW HAIRSTYLE?
ARTIST: JIM MOONEY

512

ACTION COMICS #282
NOVEMBER 1961

THE SUPERGIRL OF TOMORROW!
WRITER: JERRY SIEGEL
ARTIST: JIM MOONEY

513

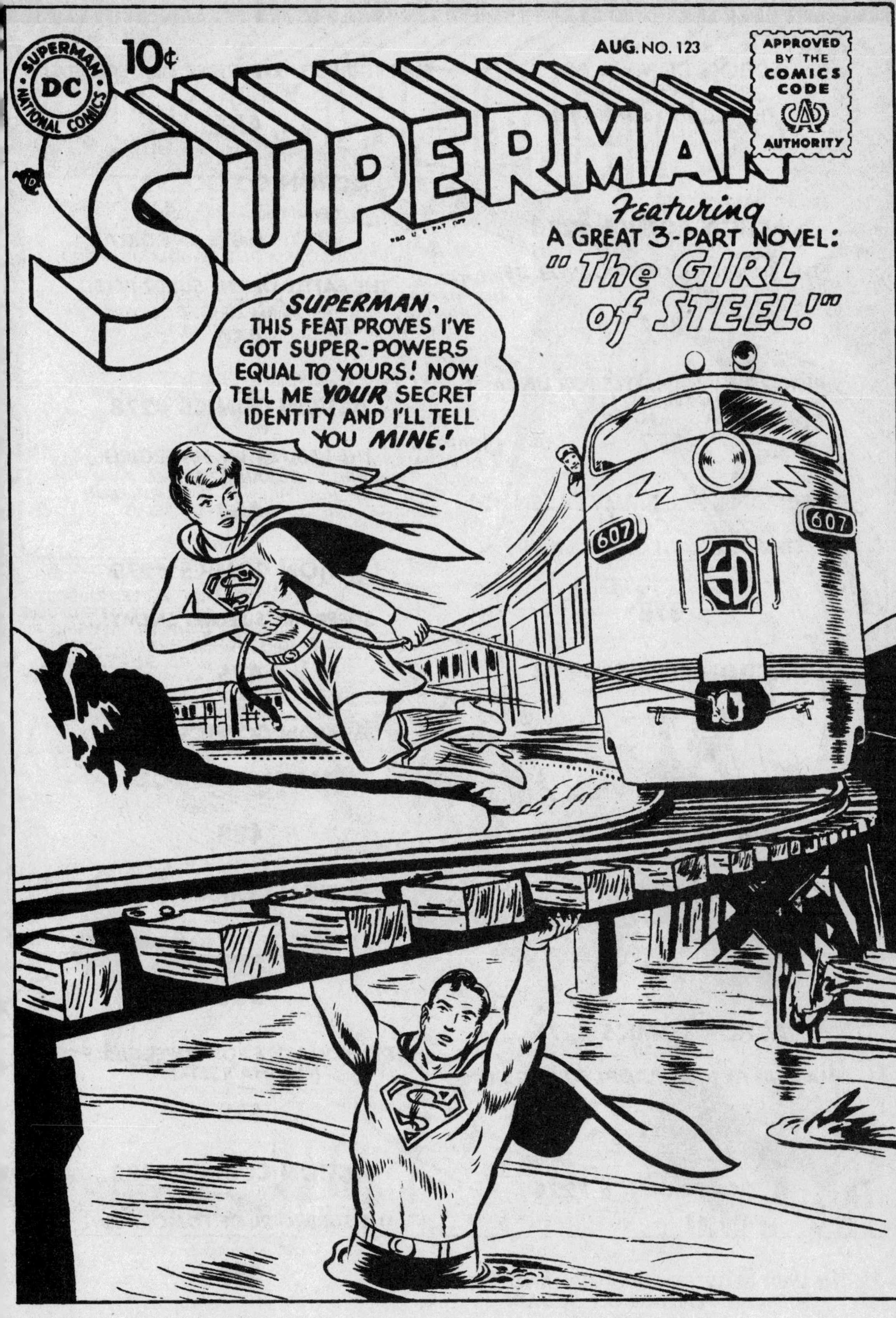
SUPERMAN NATIONAL COMICS DC
10¢
AUG. NO. 123
APPROVED BY THE COMICS CODE AUTHORITY
SUPERMAN
Featuring
A GREAT 3-PART NOVEL:
"The GIRL of STEEL!"
SUPERMAN, THIS FEAT PROVES I'VE GOT SUPER-POWERS EQUAL TO YOURS! NOW TELL ME YOUR SECRET IDENTITY AND I'LL TELL YOU MINE!
607
607

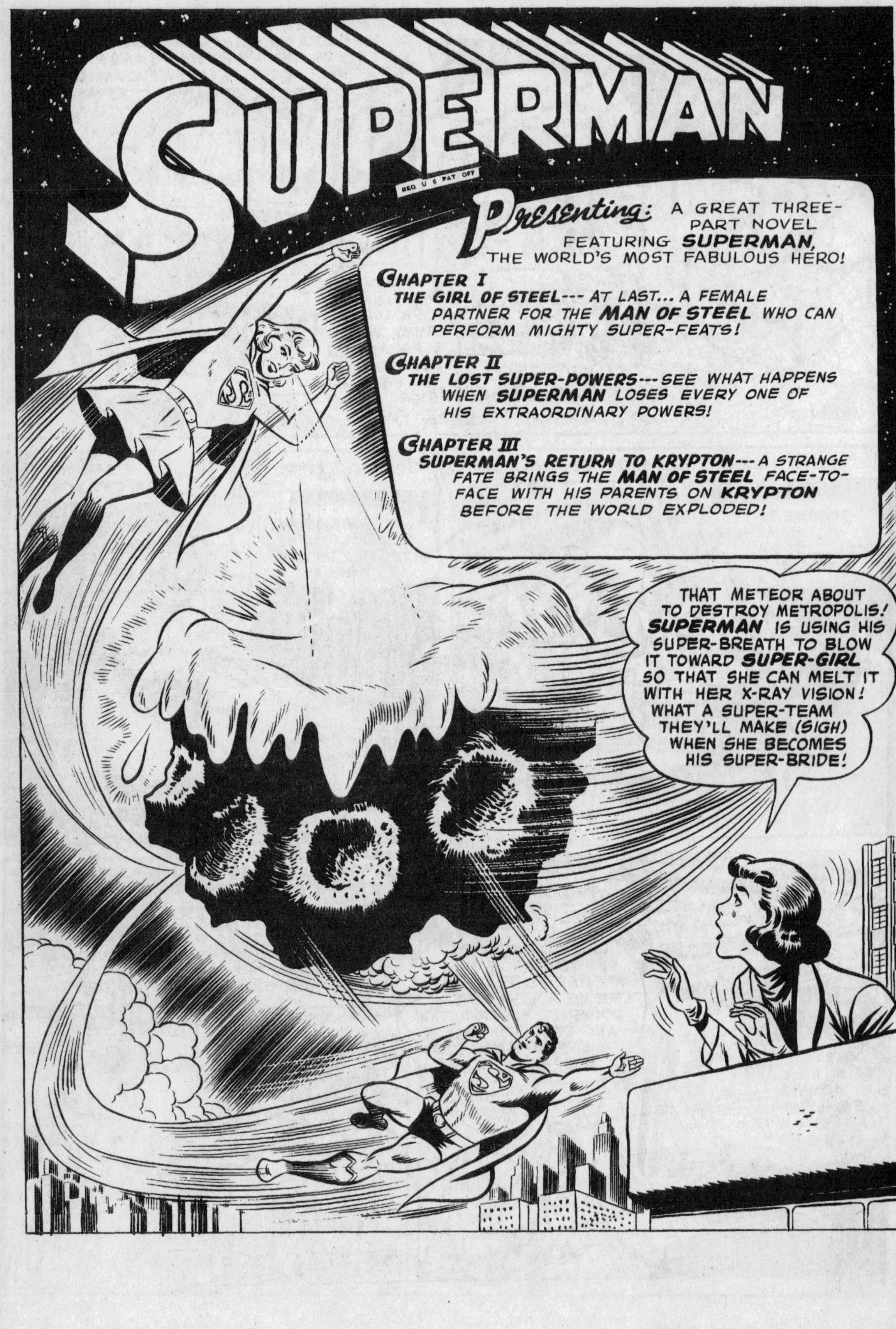
SUPERMAN
REG U S PAT OFF
Presenting: A GREAT THREE-PART NOVEL FEATURING SUPERMAN, THE WORLD'S MOST FABULOUS HERO!
CHAPTER I
THE GIRL OF STEEL--- AT LAST... A FEMALE PARTNER FOR THE MAN OF STEEL WHO CAN PERFORM MIGHTY SUPER-FEATS!
CHAPTER II
THE LOST SUPER-POWERS--- SEE WHAT HAPPENS WHEN SUPERMAN LOSES EVERY ONE OF HIS EXTRAORDINARY POWERS!
CHAPTER III
SUPERMAN'S RETURN TO KRYPTON--- A STRANGE FATE BRINGS THE MAN OF STEEL FACE-TO-FACE WITH HIS PARENTS ON KRYPTON BEFORE THE WORLD EXPLODED!
THAT METEOR ABOUT TO DESTROY METROPOLIS! SUPERMAN IS USING HIS SUPER-BREATH TO BLOW IT TOWARD SUPER-GIRL SO THAT SHE CAN MELT IT WITH HER X-RAY VISION! WHAT A SUPER-TEAM THEY'LL MAKE (SIGH) WHEN SHE BECOMES HIS SUPER-BRIDE!

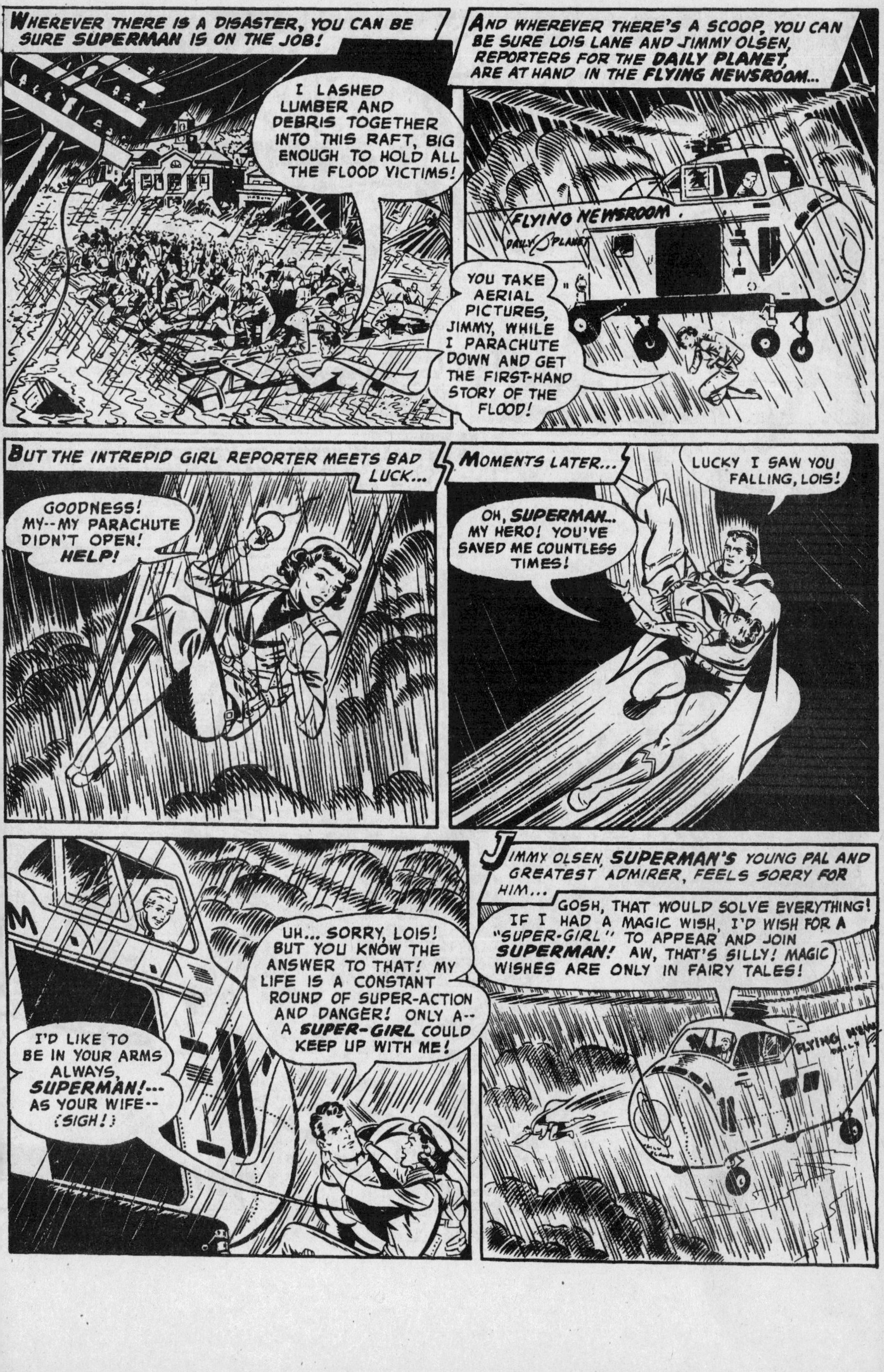
WHEREVER THERE IS A DISASTER, YOU CAN BE SURE SUPERMAN IS ON THE JOB!
I LASHED LUMBER AND DEBRIS TOGETHER INTO THIS RAFT, BIG ENOUGH TO HOLD ALL THE FLOOD VICTIMS!
AND WHEREVER THERE'S A SCOOP, YOU CAN BE SURE LOIS LANE AND JIMMY OLSEN, REPORTERS FOR THE DAILY PLANET, ARE AT HAND IN THE FLYING NEWSROOM...
FLYING NEWSROOM
DAILY PLANET
YOU TAKE AERIAL PICTURES, JIMMY, WHILE I PARACHUTE DOWN AND GET THE FIRST-HAND STORY OF THE FLOOD!
BUT THE INTREPID GIRL REPORTER MEETS BAD LUCK...
GOODNESS! MY--MY PARACHUTE DIDN'T OPEN! HELP!
MOMENTS LATER...
LUCKY I SAW YOU FALLING, LOIS!
OH, SUPERMAN... MY HERO! YOU'VE SAVED ME COUNTLESS TIMES!
I'D LIKE TO BE IN YOUR ARMS ALWAYS, SUPERMAN!--- AS YOUR WIFE-- (SIGH!)
UH... SORRY, LOIS! BUT YOU KNOW THE ANSWER TO THAT! MY LIFE IS A CONSTANT ROUND OF SUPER-ACTION AND DANGER! ONLY A-- A SUPER-GIRL COULD KEEP UP WITH ME!
JIMMY OLSEN, SUPERMAN'S YOUNG PAL AND GREATEST ADMIRER, FEELS SORRY FOR HIM...
GOSH, THAT WOULD SOLVE EVERYTHING! IF I HAD A MAGIC WISH, I'D WISH FOR A "SUPER-GIRL" TO APPEAR AND JOIN SUPERMAN! AW, THAT'S SILLY! MAGIC WISHES ARE ONLY IN FAIRY TALES!

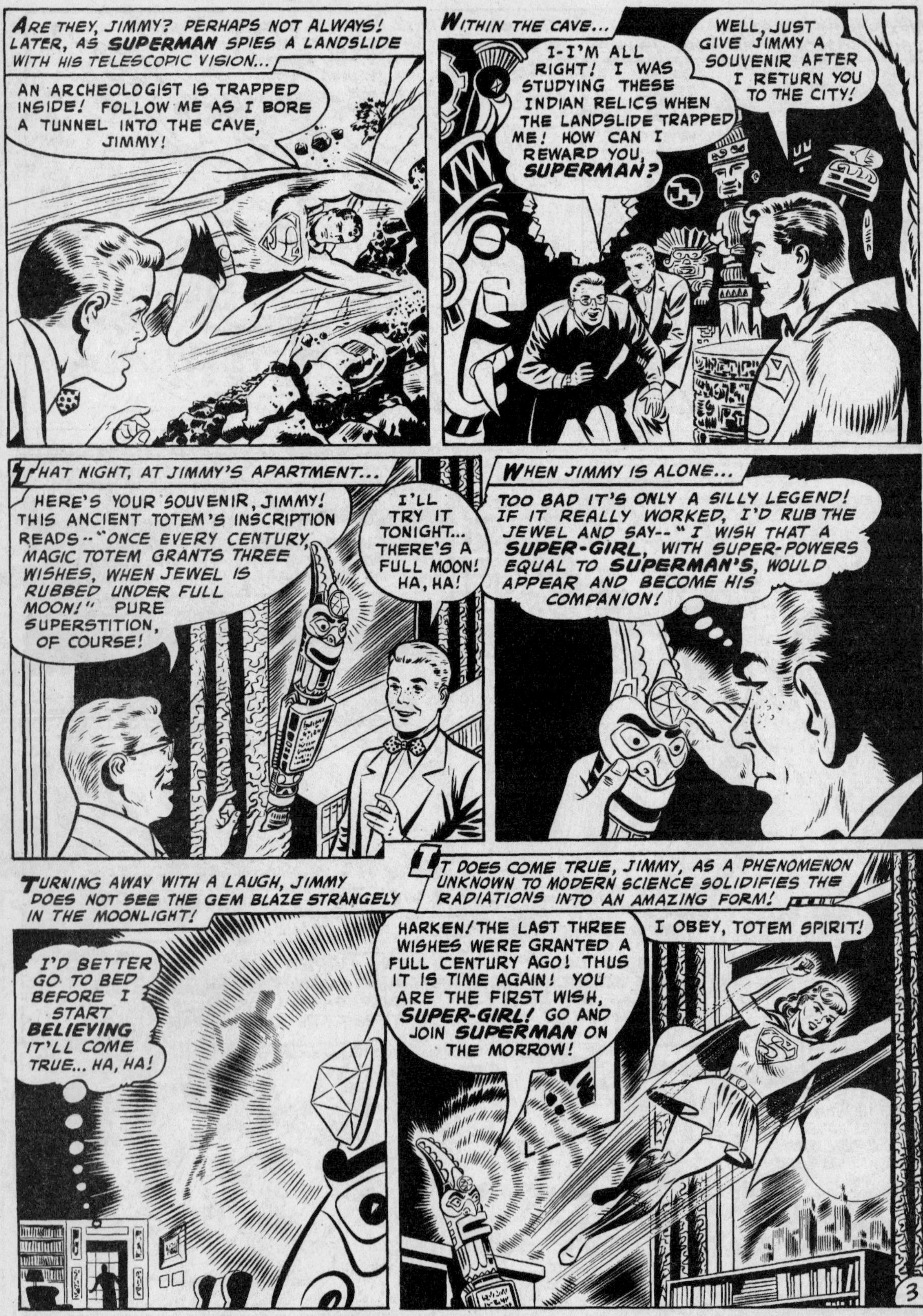
ARE THEY, JIMMY? PERHAPS NOT ALWAYS! LATER, AS SUPERMAN SPIES A LANDSLIDE WITH HIS TELESCOPIC VISION...
AN ARCHEOLOGIST IS TRAPPED INSIDE! FOLLOW ME AS I BORE A TUNNEL INTO THE CAVE, JIMMY!
WITHIN THE CAVE...
I-I'M ALL RIGHT! I WAS STUDYING THESE INDIAN RELICS WHEN THE LANDSLIDE TRAPPED ME! HOW CAN I REWARD YOU, SUPERMAN?
WELL, JUST GIVE JIMMY A SOUVENIR AFTER I RETURN YOU TO THE CITY!
THAT NIGHT, AT JIMMY'S APARTMENT...
HERE'S YOUR SOUVENIR, JIMMY! THIS ANCIENT TOTEM'S INSCRIPTION READS--"ONCE EVERY CENTURY, MAGIC TOTEM GRANTS THREE WISHES, WHEN JEWEL IS RUBBED UNDER FULL MOON!" PURE SUPERSTITION, OF COURSE!
I'LL TRY IT TONIGHT... THERE'S A FULL MOON! HA, HA!
WHEN JIMMY IS ALONE...
TOO BAD IT'S ONLY A SILLY LEGEND! IF IT REALLY WORKED, I'D RUB THE JEWEL AND SAY--"I WISH THAT A SUPER-GIRL, WITH SUPER-POWERS EQUAL TO SUPERMAN'S, WOULD APPEAR AND BECOME HIS COMPANION!
TURNING AWAY WITH A LAUGH, JIMMY DOES NOT SEE THE GEM BLAZE STRANGELY IN THE MOONLIGHT!
I'D BETTER GO TO BED BEFORE I START BELIEVING IT'LL COME TRUE... HA, HA!
IT DOES COME TRUE, JIMMY, AS A PHENOMENON UNKNOWN TO MODERN SCIENCE SOLIDIFIES THE RADIATIONS INTO AN AMAZING FORM!
HARKEN! THE LAST THREE WISHES WERE GRANTED A FULL CENTURY AGO! THUS IT IS TIME AGAIN! YOU ARE THE FIRST WISH, SUPER-GIRL! GO AND JOIN SUPERMAN ON THE MORROW!
I OBEY, TOTEM SPIRIT!
3

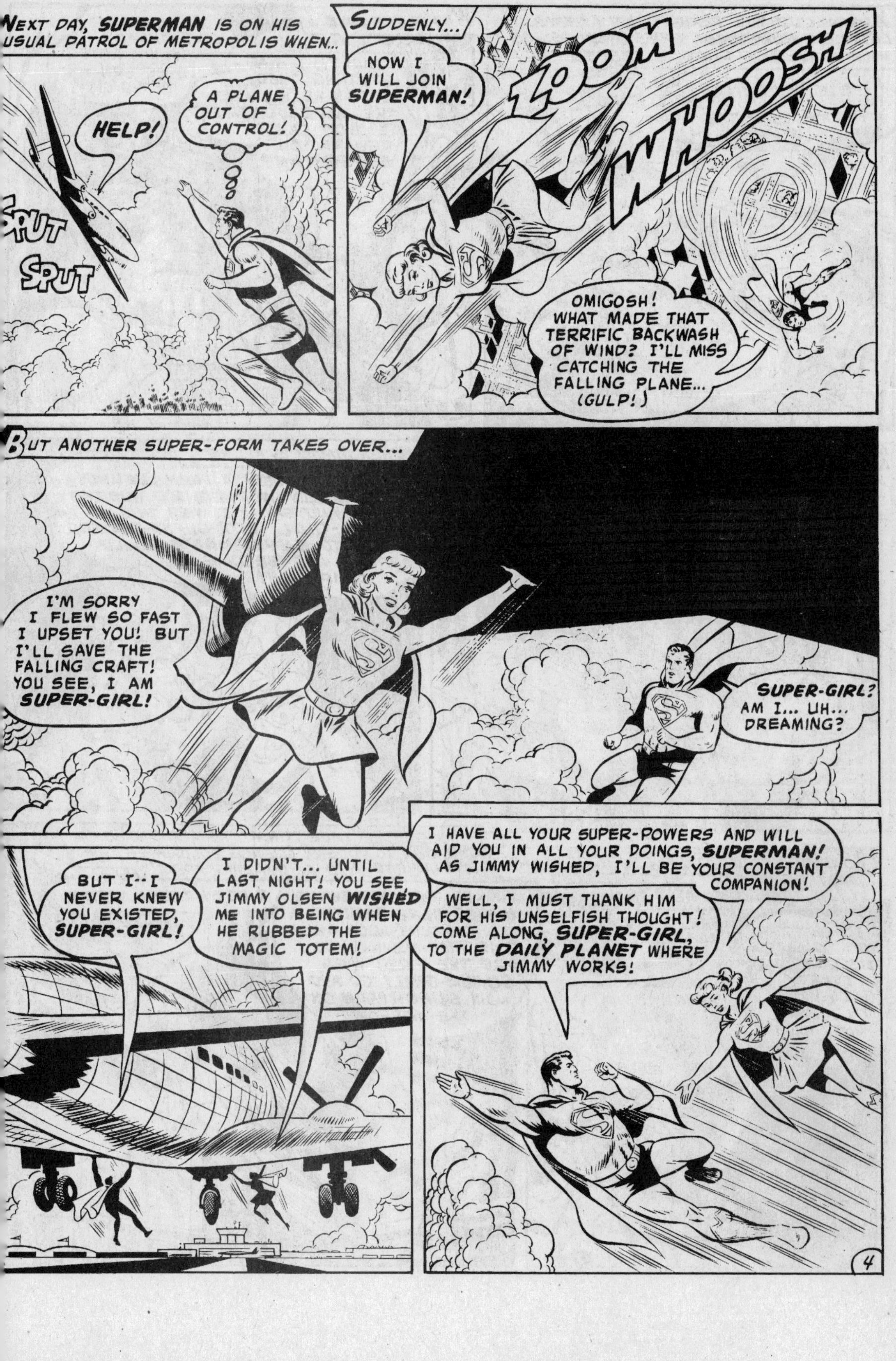
NEXT DAY, SUPERMAN IS ON HIS USUAL PATROL OF METROPOLIS WHEN...
HELP!
A PLANE OUT OF CONTROL!
SPUT
SPUT
SUDDENLY...
NOW I WILL JOIN SUPERMAN!
ZOOM
WHOOSH
OMIGOSH! WHAT MADE THAT TERRIFIC BACKWASH OF WIND? I'LL MISS CATCHING THE FALLING PLANE... (GULP!)
BUT ANOTHER SUPER-FORM TAKES OVER...
I'M SORRY I FLEW SO FAST I UPSET YOU! BUT I'LL SAVE THE FALLING CRAFT! YOU SEE, I AM SUPER-GIRL!
SUPER-GIRL? AM I... UH... DREAMING?
BUT I--I NEVER KNEW YOU EXISTED, SUPER-GIRL!
I DIDN'T... UNTIL LAST NIGHT! YOU SEE JIMMY OLSEN WISHED ME INTO BEING WHEN HE RUBBED THE MAGIC TOTEM!
I HAVE ALL YOUR SUPER-POWERS AND WILL AID YOU IN ALL YOUR DOINGS, SUPERMAN! AS JIMMY WISHED, I'LL BE YOUR CONSTANT COMPANION!
WELL, I MUST THANK HIM FOR HIS UNSELFISH THOUGHT! COME ALONG, SUPER-GIRL, TO THE DAILY PLANET WHERE JIMMY WORKS!
4

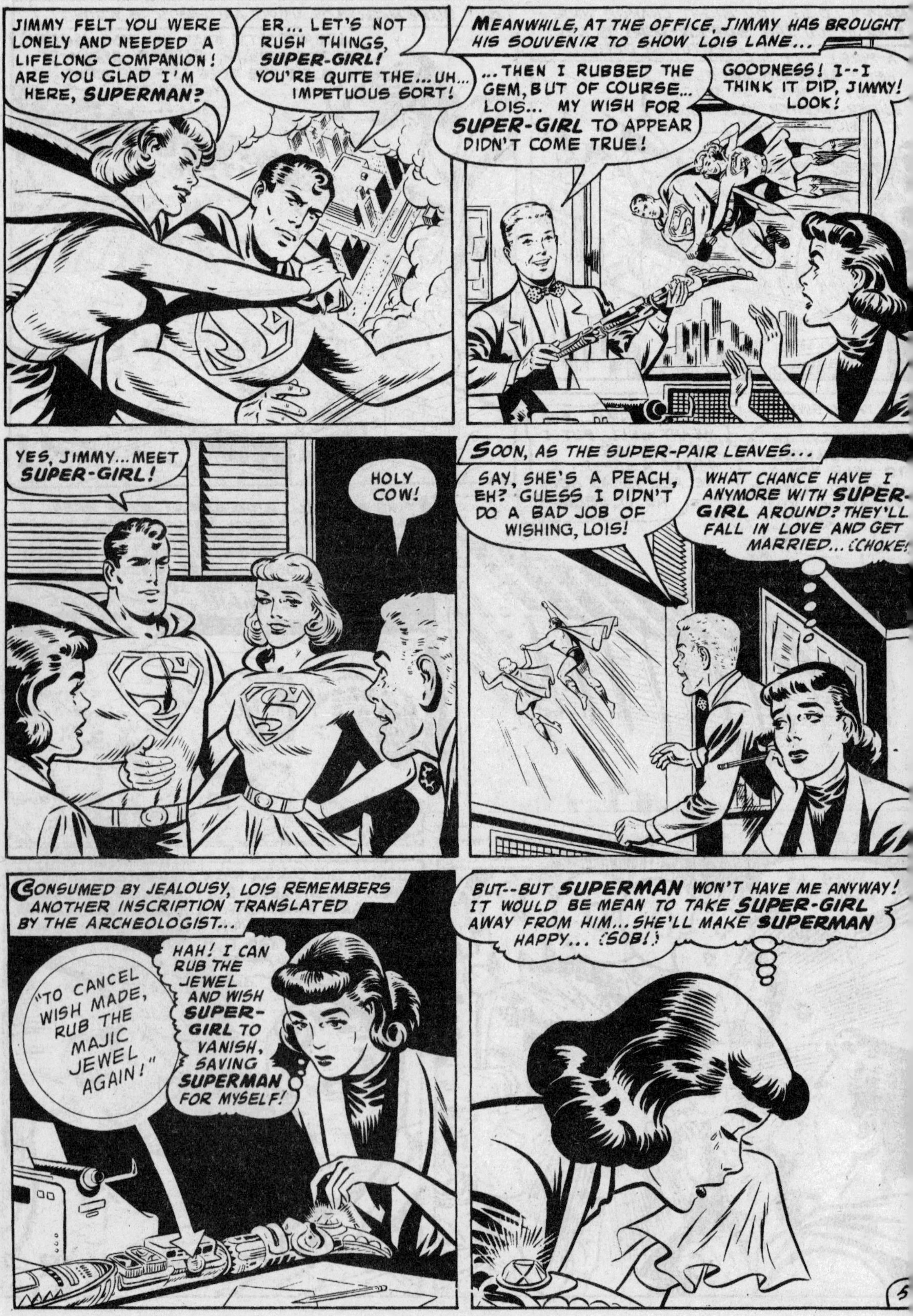
JIMMY FELT YOU WERE LONELY AND NEEDED A LIFELONG COMPANION! ARE YOU GLAD I'M HERE, SUPERMAN?
ER... LET'S NOT RUSH THINGS, SUPER-GIRL! YOU'RE QUITE THE... UH... IMPETUOUS SORT!
MEANWHILE, AT THE OFFICE, JIMMY HAS BROUGHT HIS SOUVENIR TO SHOW LOIS LANE...
...THEN I RUBBED THE GEM, BUT OF COURSE... LOIS... MY WISH FOR SUPER-GIRL TO APPEAR DIDN'T COME TRUE!
GOODNESS! I--I THINK IT DID, JIMMY! LOOK!
YES, JIMMY... MEET SUPER-GIRL!
HOLY COW!
SOON, AS THE SUPER-PAIR LEAVES...
SAY, SHE'S A PEACH, EH? GUESS I DIDN'T DO A BAD JOB OF WISHING, LOIS!
WHAT CHANCE HAVE I ANYMORE WITH SUPER-GIRL AROUND? THEY'LL FALL IN LOVE AND GET MARRIED... (CHOKE!
CONSUMED BY JEALOUSY, LOIS REMEMBERS ANOTHER INSCRIPTION TRANSLATED BY THE ARCHEOLOGIST...
"TO CANCEL WISH MADE, RUB THE MAJIC JEWEL AGAIN!"
HAH! I CAN RUB THE JEWEL AND WISH SUPER-GIRL TO VANISH, SAVING SUPERMAN FOR MYSELF!
BUT--BUT SUPERMAN WON'T HAVE ME ANYWAY! IT WOULD BE MEAN TO TAKE SUPER-GIRL AWAY FROM HIM... SHE'LL MAKE SUPERMAN HAPPY... (SOB!)
5

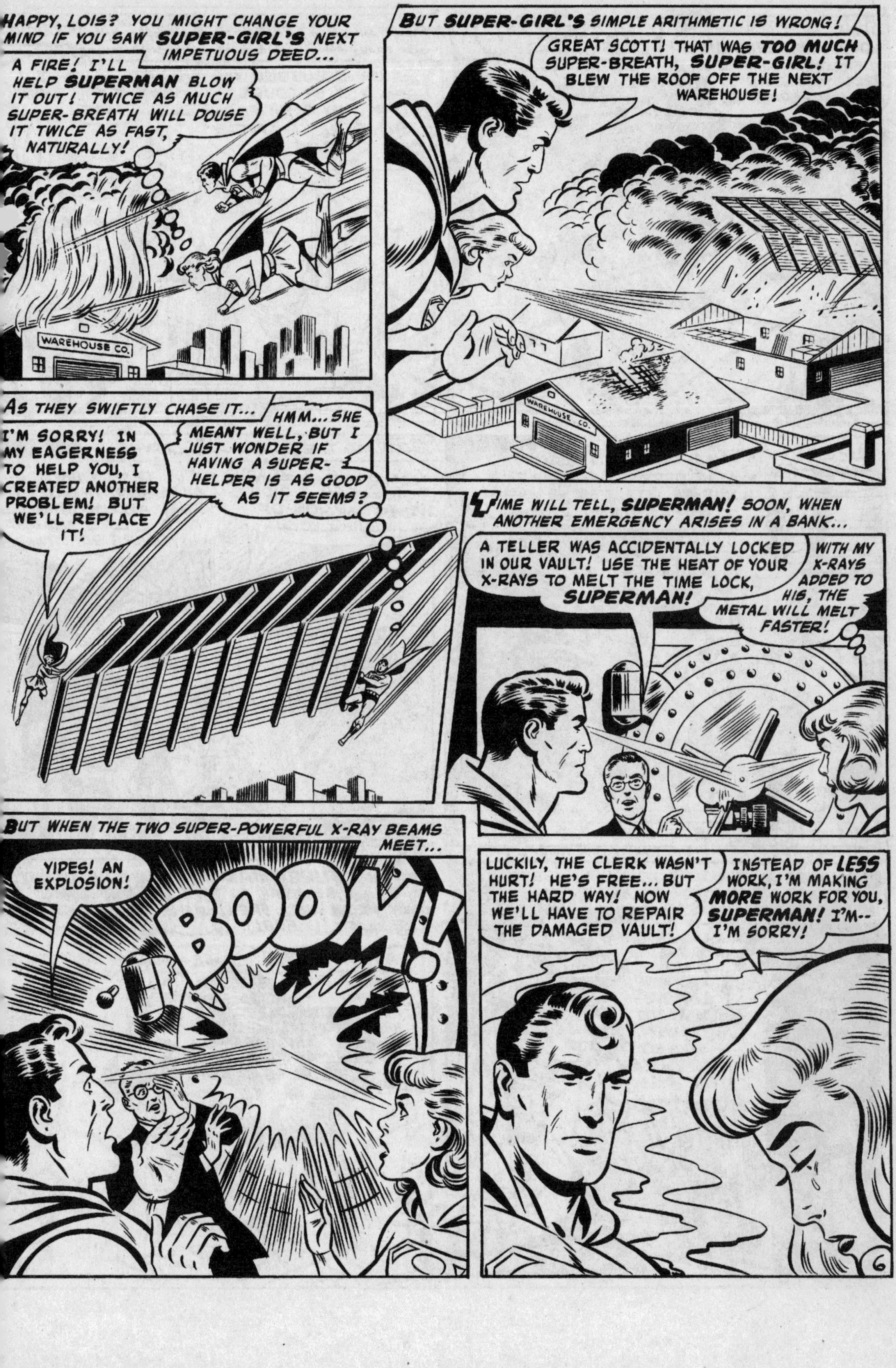
HAPPY, LOIS? YOU MIGHT CHANGE YOUR MIND IF YOU SAW SUPER-GIRL'S NEXT IMPETUOUS DEED...
A FIRE! I'LL HELP SUPERMAN BLOW IT OUT! TWICE AS MUCH SUPER-BREATH WILL DOUSE IT TWICE AS FAST, NATURALLY!
WAREHOUSE CO.
BUT SUPER-GIRL'S SIMPLE ARITHMETIC IS WRONG!
GREAT SCOTT! THAT WAS TOO MUCH SUPER-BREATH, SUPER-GIRL! IT BLEW THE ROOF OFF THE NEXT WAREHOUSE!
WAREHOUSE CO.
AS THEY SWIFTLY CHASE IT...
I'M SORRY! IN MY EAGERNESS TO HELP YOU, I CREATED ANOTHER PROBLEM! BUT WE'LL REPLACE IT!
HMM... SHE MEANT WELL, BUT I JUST WONDER IF HAVING A SUPER-HELPER IS AS GOOD AS IT SEEMS?
TIME WILL TELL, SUPERMAN! SOON, WHEN ANOTHER EMERGENCY ARISES IN A BANK...
A TELLER WAS ACCIDENTALLY LOCKED IN OUR VAULT! USE THE HEAT OF YOUR X-RAYS TO MELT THE TIME LOCK, SUPERMAN!
WITH MY X-RAYS ADDED TO HIS, THE METAL WILL MELT FASTER!
BUT WHEN THE TWO SUPER-POWERFUL X-RAY BEAMS MEET...
YIPES! AN EXPLOSION!
BOOM!
LUCKILY, THE CLERK WASN'T HURT! HE'S FREE... BUT THE HARD WAY! NOW WE'LL HAVE TO REPAIR THE DAMAGED VAULT!
INSTEAD OF LESS WORK, I'M MAKING MORE WORK FOR YOU, SUPERMAN! I'M-- I'M SORRY!
6

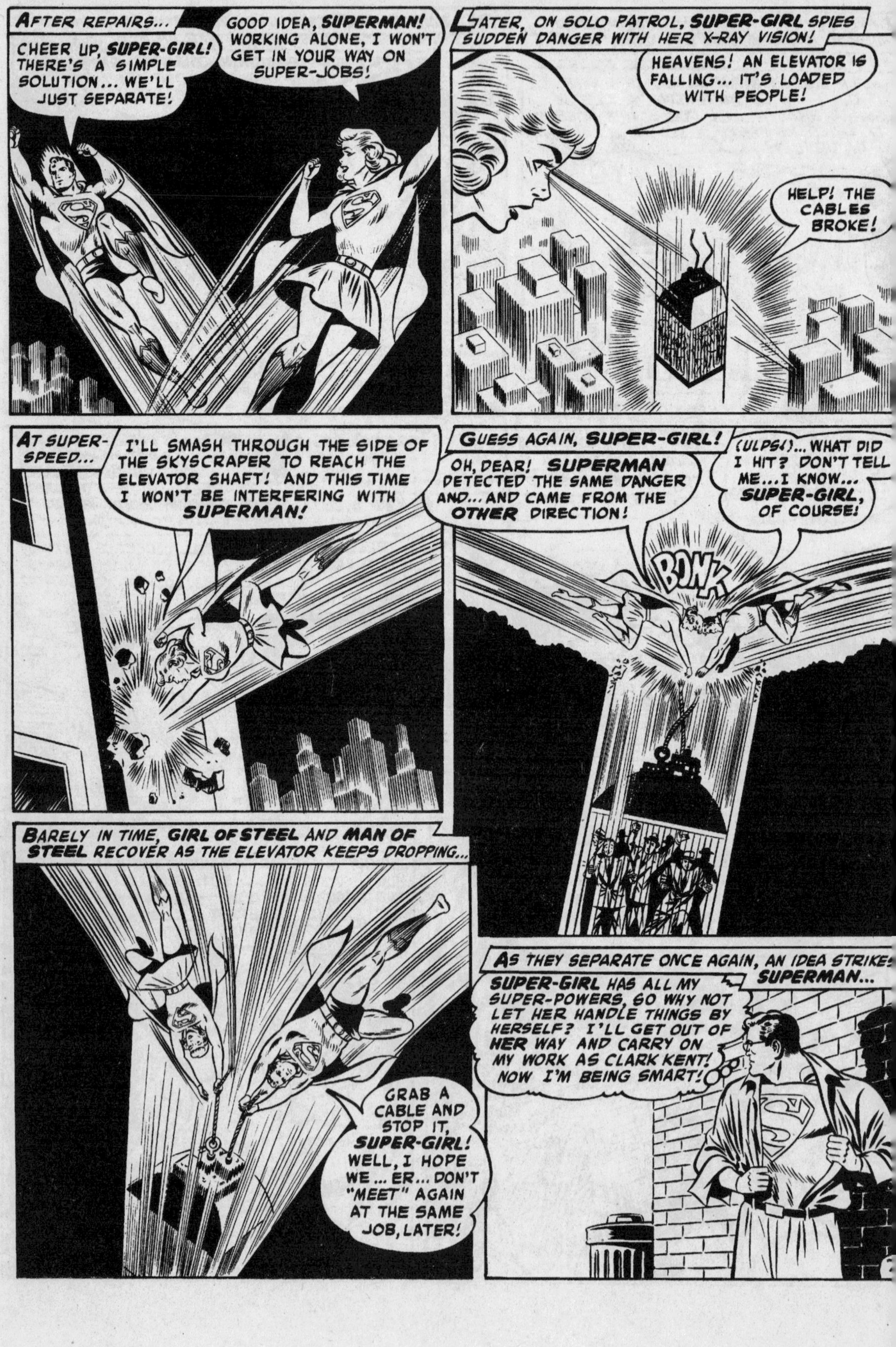
AFTER REPAIRS...
CHEER UP, SUPER-GIRL! THERE'S A SIMPLE SOLUTION... WE'LL JUST SEPARATE!
GOOD IDEA, SUPERMAN! WORKING ALONE, I WON'T GET IN YOUR WAY ON SUPER-JOBS!
LATER, ON SOLO PATROL, SUPER-GIRL SPIES SUDDEN DANGER WITH HER X-RAY VISION!
HEAVENS! AN ELEVATOR IS FALLING... IT'S LOADED WITH PEOPLE!
HELP! THE CABLES BROKE!
AT SUPER-SPEED...
I'LL SMASH THROUGH THE SIDE OF THE SKYSCRAPER TO REACH THE ELEVATOR SHAFT! AND THIS TIME I WON'T BE INTERFERING WITH SUPERMAN!
GUESS AGAIN, SUPER-GIRL!
OH, DEAR! SUPERMAN DETECTED THE SAME DANGER AND... AND CAME FROM THE OTHER DIRECTION!
(ULPS!)... WHAT DID I HIT? DON'T TELL ME... I KNOW... SUPER-GIRL, OF COURSE!
BONK
BARELY IN TIME, GIRL OF STEEL AND MAN OF STEEL RECOVER AS THE ELEVATOR KEEPS DROPPING...
GRAB A CABLE AND STOP IT, SUPER-GIRL! WELL, I HOPE WE... ER... DON'T "MEET" AGAIN AT THE SAME JOB, LATER!
AS THEY SEPARATE ONCE AGAIN, AN IDEA STRIKES SUPERMAN...
SUPER-GIRL HAS ALL MY SUPER-POWERS, SO WHY NOT LET HER HANDLE THINGS BY HERSELF? I'LL GET OUT OF HER WAY AND CARRY ON MY WORK AS CLARK KENT! NOW I'M BEING SMART!

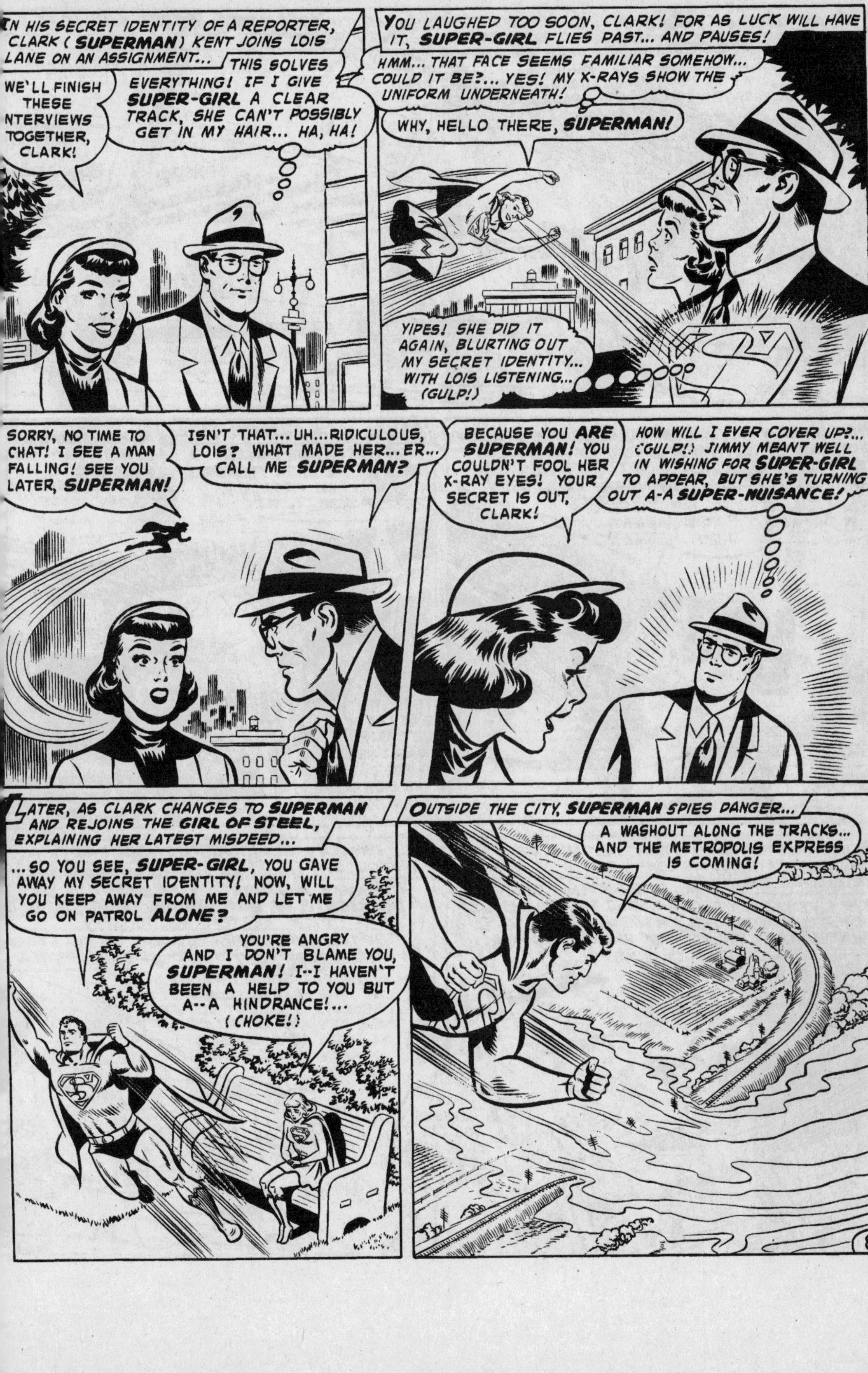
IN HIS SECRET IDENTITY OF A REPORTER, CLARK (SUPERMAN) KENT JOINS LOIS LANE ON AN ASSIGNMENT...
WE'LL FINISH THESE INTERVIEWS TOGETHER, CLARK!
THIS SOLVES EVERYTHING! IF I GIVE SUPER-GIRL A CLEAR TRACK, SHE CAN'T POSSIBLY GET IN MY HAIR... HA, HA!
YOU LAUGHED TOO SOON, CLARK! FOR AS LUCK WILL HAVE IT, SUPER-GIRL FLIES PAST... AND PAUSES!
HMM... THAT FACE SEEMS FAMILIAR SOMEHOW... COULD IT BE?... YES! MY X-RAYS SHOW THE UNIFORM UNDERNEATH!
WHY, HELLO THERE, SUPERMAN!
YIPES! SHE DID IT AGAIN, BLURTING OUT MY SECRET IDENTITY... WITH LOIS LISTENING... (GULP!)
SORRY, NO TIME TO CHAT! I SEE A MAN FALLING! SEE YOU LATER, SUPERMAN!
ISN'T THAT... UH... RIDICULOUS, LOIS? WHAT MADE HER... ER... CALL ME SUPERMAN?
BECAUSE YOU ARE SUPERMAN! YOU COULDN'T FOOL HER X-RAY EYES! YOUR SECRET IS OUT, CLARK!
HOW WILL I EVER COVER UP?... (GULP!) JIMMY MEANT WELL IN WISHING FOR SUPER-GIRL TO APPEAR, BUT SHE'S TURNING OUT A-A SUPER-NUISANCE!
LATER, AS CLARK CHANGES TO SUPERMAN AND REJOINS THE GIRL OF STEEL, EXPLAINING HER LATEST MISDEED...
...SO YOU SEE, SUPER-GIRL, YOU GAVE AWAY MY SECRET IDENTITY! NOW, WILL YOU KEEP AWAY FROM ME AND LET ME GO ON PATROL ALONE?
YOU'RE ANGRY AND I DON'T BLAME YOU, SUPERMAN! I--I HAVEN'T BEEN A HELP TO YOU BUT A--A HINDRANCE!... (CHOKE!)
OUTSIDE THE CITY, SUPERMAN SPIES DANGER...
A WASHOUT ALONG THE TRACKS... AND THE METROPOLIS EXPRESS IS COMING!
8

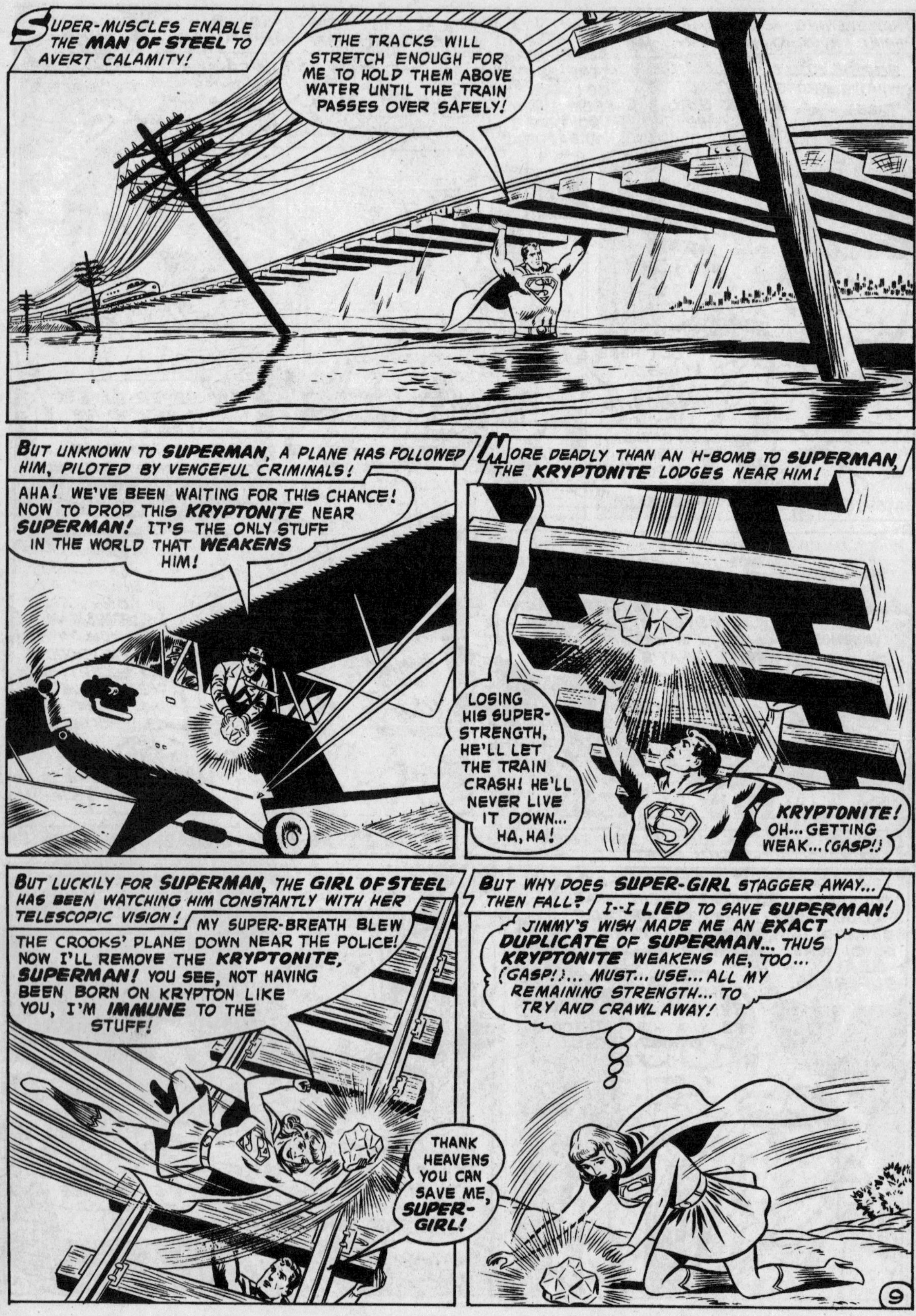
SUPER-MUSCLES ENABLE THE MAN OF STEEL TO AVERT CALAMITY!
THE TRACKS WILL STRETCH ENOUGH FOR ME TO HOLD THEM ABOVE WATER UNTIL THE TRAIN PASSES OVER SAFELY!
BUT UNKNOWN TO SUPERMAN, A PLANE HAS FOLLOWED HIM, PILOTED BY VENGEFUL CRIMINALS!
AHA! WE'VE BEEN WAITING FOR THIS CHANCE! NOW TO DROP THIS KRYPTONITE NEAR SUPERMAN! IT'S THE ONLY STUFF IN THE WORLD THAT WEAKENS HIM!
MORE DEADLY THAN AN H-BOMB TO SUPERMAN, THE KRYPTONITE LODGES NEAR HIM!
LOSING HIS SUPER-STRENGTH, HE'LL LET THE TRAIN CRASH! HE'LL NEVER LIVE IT DOWN... HA, HA!
KRYPTONITE! OH... GETTING WEAK... (GASP!)
BUT LUCKILY FOR SUPERMAN, THE GIRL OF STEEL HAS BEEN WATCHING HIM CONSTANTLY WITH HER TELESCOPIC VISION!
MY SUPER-BREATH BLEW THE CROOKS' PLANE DOWN NEAR THE POLICE! NOW I'LL REMOVE THE KRYPTONITE, SUPERMAN! YOU SEE, NOT HAVING BEEN BORN ON KRYPTON LIKE YOU, I'M IMMUNE TO THE STUFF!
THANK HEAVENS YOU CAN SAVE ME, SUPER-GIRL!
BUT WHY DOES SUPER-GIRL STAGGER AWAY... THEN FALL?
I--I LIED TO SAVE SUPERMAN! JIMMY'S WISH MADE ME AN EXACT DUPLICATE OF SUPERMAN... THUS KRYPTONITE WEAKENS ME, TOO... (GASP!)... MUST... USE... ALL MY REMAINING STRENGTH... TO TRY AND CRAWL AWAY!
9

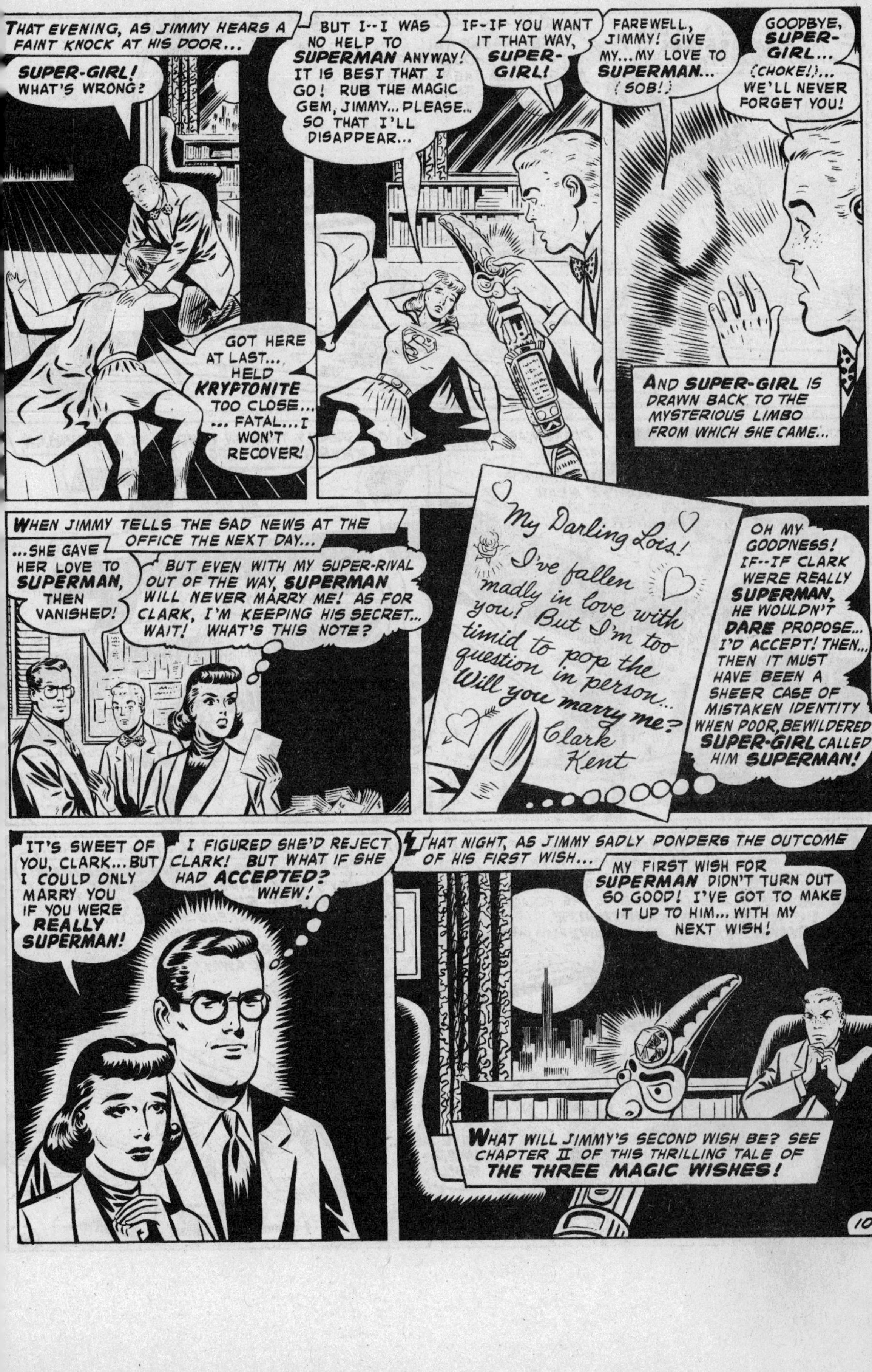
THAT EVENING, AS JIMMY HEARS A FAINT KNOCK AT HIS DOOR...
SUPER-GIRL! WHAT'S WRONG?
GOT HERE AT LAST... HELD KRYPTONITE TOO CLOSE... ...FATAL...I WON'T RECOVER!
BUT I--I WAS NO HELP TO SUPERMAN ANYWAY! IT IS BEST THAT I GO! RUB THE MAGIC GEM, JIMMY...PLEASE.. SO THAT I'LL DISAPPEAR...
IF-IF YOU WANT IT THAT WAY, SUPER-GIRL!
FAREWELL, JIMMY! GIVE MY...MY LOVE TO SUPERMAN... (SOB!)
GOODBYE, SUPER-GIRL... (CHOKE!)... WE'LL NEVER FORGET YOU!
AND SUPER-GIRL IS DRAWN BACK TO THE MYSTERIOUS LIMBO FROM WHICH SHE CAME...
WHEN JIMMY TELLS THE SAD NEWS AT THE OFFICE THE NEXT DAY...
...SHE GAVE HER LOVE TO SUPERMAN, THEN VANISHED!
BUT EVEN WITH MY SUPER-RIVAL OUT OF THE WAY, SUPERMAN WILL NEVER MARRY ME! AS FOR CLARK, I'M KEEPING HIS SECRET... WAIT! WHAT'S THIS NOTE?
My Darling Lois! I've fallen madly in love with you! But I'm too timid to pop the question in person... Will you marry me? Clark Kent
OH MY GOODNESS! IF--IF CLARK WERE REALLY SUPERMAN, HE WOULDN'T DARE PROPOSE... I'D ACCEPT! THEN... THEN IT MUST HAVE BEEN A SHEER CASE OF MISTAKEN IDENTITY WHEN POOR, BEWILDERED SUPER-GIRL CALLED HIM SUPERMAN!
IT'S SWEET OF YOU, CLARK...BUT I COULD ONLY MARRY YOU IF YOU WERE REALLY SUPERMAN!
I FIGURED SHE'D REJECT CLARK! BUT WHAT IF SHE HAD ACCEPTED? WHEW!
THAT NIGHT, AS JIMMY SADLY PONDERS THE OUTCOME OF HIS FIRST WISH...
MY FIRST WISH FOR SUPERMAN DIDN'T TURN OUT SO GOOD! I'VE GOT TO MAKE IT UP TO HIM... WITH MY NEXT WISH!
WHAT WILL JIMMY'S SECOND WISH BE? SEE CHAPTER II OF THIS THRILLING TALE OF THE THREE MAGIC WISHES!
10

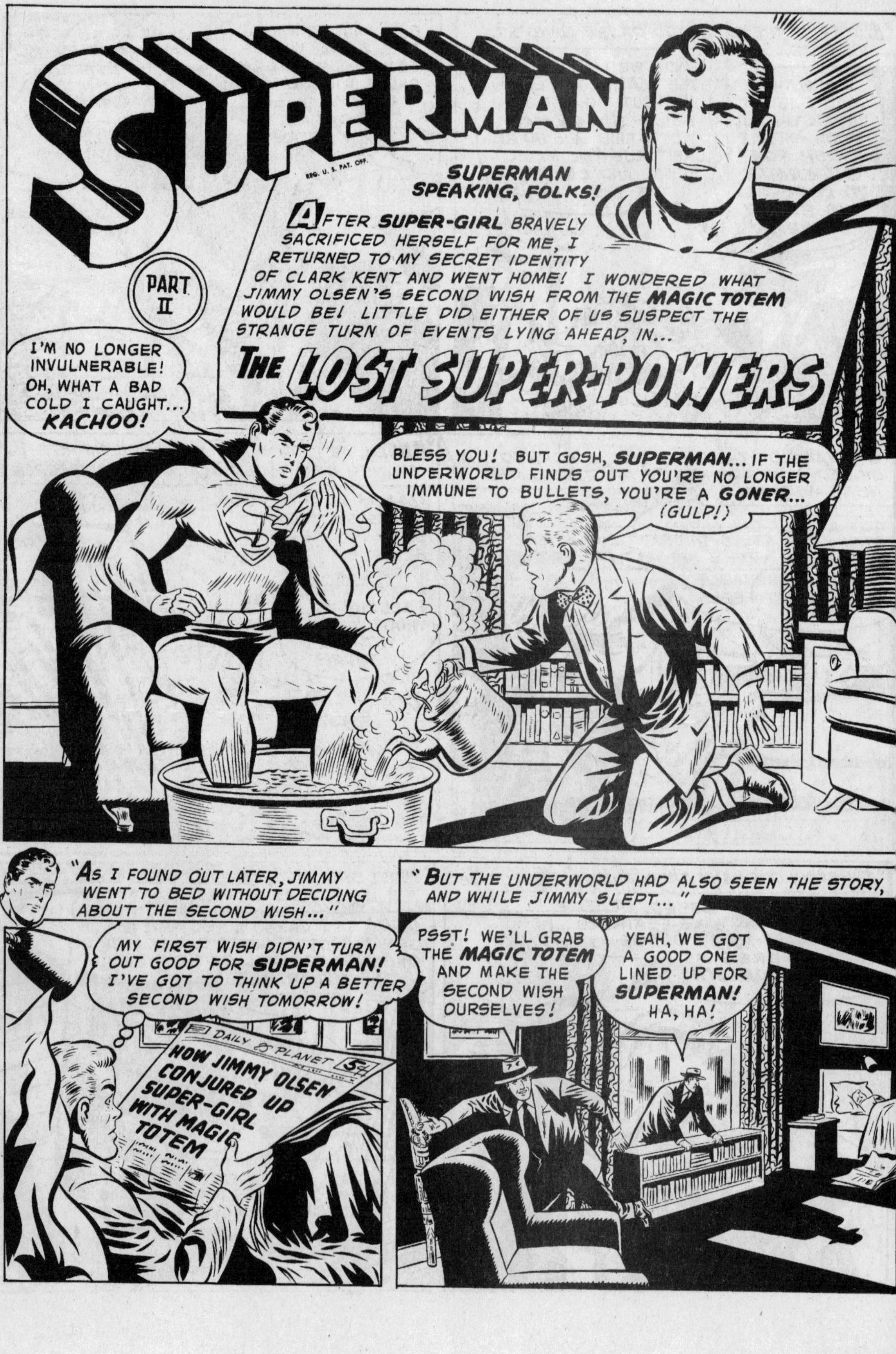
SUPERMAN
REG. U.S. PAT. OFF.
PART II
SUPERMAN SPEAKING, FOLKS!
AFTER SUPER-GIRL BRAVELY SACRIFICED HERSELF FOR ME, I RETURNED TO MY SECRET IDENTITY OF CLARK KENT AND WENT HOME! I WONDERED WHAT JIMMY OLSEN'S SECOND WISH FROM THE MAGIC TOTEM WOULD BE! LITTLE DID EITHER OF US SUSPECT THE STRANGE TURN OF EVENTS LYING AHEAD, IN...
THE LOST SUPER-POWERS
I'M NO LONGER INVULNERABLE! OH, WHAT A BAD COLD I CAUGHT... KACHOO!
BLESS YOU! BUT GOSH, SUPERMAN... IF THE UNDERWORLD FINDS OUT YOU'RE NO LONGER IMMUNE TO BULLETS, YOU'RE A GONER... (GULP!)
"AS I FOUND OUT LATER, JIMMY WENT TO BED WITHOUT DECIDING ABOUT THE SECOND WISH..."
MY FIRST WISH DIDN'T TURN OUT GOOD FOR SUPERMAN! I'VE GOT TO THINK UP A BETTER SECOND WISH TOMORROW!
DAILY PLANET 5¢
HOW JIMMY OLSEN CONJURED UP SUPER-GIRL WITH MAGIC TOTEM
"BUT THE UNDERWORLD HAD ALSO SEEN THE STORY, AND WHILE JIMMY SLEPT..."
PSST! WE'LL GRAB THE MAGIC TOTEM AND MAKE THE SECOND WISH OURSELVES!
YEAH, WE GOT A GOOD ONE LINED UP FOR SUPERMAN! HA, HA!

"LATER, IN THE BACKYARD OF THE GANG'S HIDEOUT..."

I RUB THE MAGIC JEWEL UNDER THE FULL MOON AND... I WISH FOR SUPERMAN TO LOSE ALL HIS SUPER-POWERS!

NOW WE'LL BURY THE MAGIC TOTEM! WITHOUT HIS X-RAY VISION-- SUPERMAN WON'T FIND IT... SO HE CAN'T RUB THE MAGIC JEWEL AND CANCEL THE WISH! HA, HA!

BUT WHAT IF ONLY... ER... GOOD WISHES COME TRUE, NOT BAD ONES? WILL SUPERMAN REALLY LOSE HIS POWERS?

WE'LL MAKE SURE TOMORROW-- BY TAILING SUPERMAN!

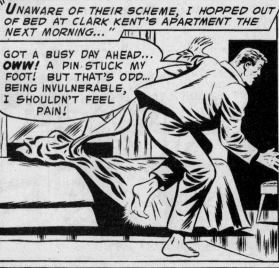

"UNAWARE OF THEIR SCHEME, I HOPPED OUT OF BED AT CLARK KENT'S APARTMENT THE NEXT MORNING..."

GOT A BUSY DAY AHEAD... OWW! A PIN STUCK MY FOOT! BUT THAT'S ODD... BEING INVULNERABLE, I SHOULDN'T FEEL PAIN!

"THEN, AS I TOOK MY USUAL BOILING HOT SHOWER THAT WOULD SCALD NORMAL PEOPLE..."

YIPES! MY SKIN SEEMS ON FIRE! BUT I--I USED TO BE ABLE TO DIVE INTO MOLTEN LAVA WITHOUT FEELING IT! WHAT'S WRONG WITH ME TODAY?

"MY BEWILDERMENT GREW DURING MY SETTING-UP EXERCISES..."

OOF! I ALWAYS TOSSED THESE AROUND LIKE FEATHERS... BUT NOW I CAN'T BUDGE THEM! WHERE'S MY SUPER-STRENGTH?

1000 lbs.

"MOST SHOCKING, WHEN I TRIED TO LEAP FROM THE WINDOW AS USUAL..."

UGH! I-I CAN'T FLY, EITHER! GREAT SCOTT... THERE'S ONLY ONE ANSWER TO ALL THIS... ONE HORRIBLE ANSWER!

CRASH!

2

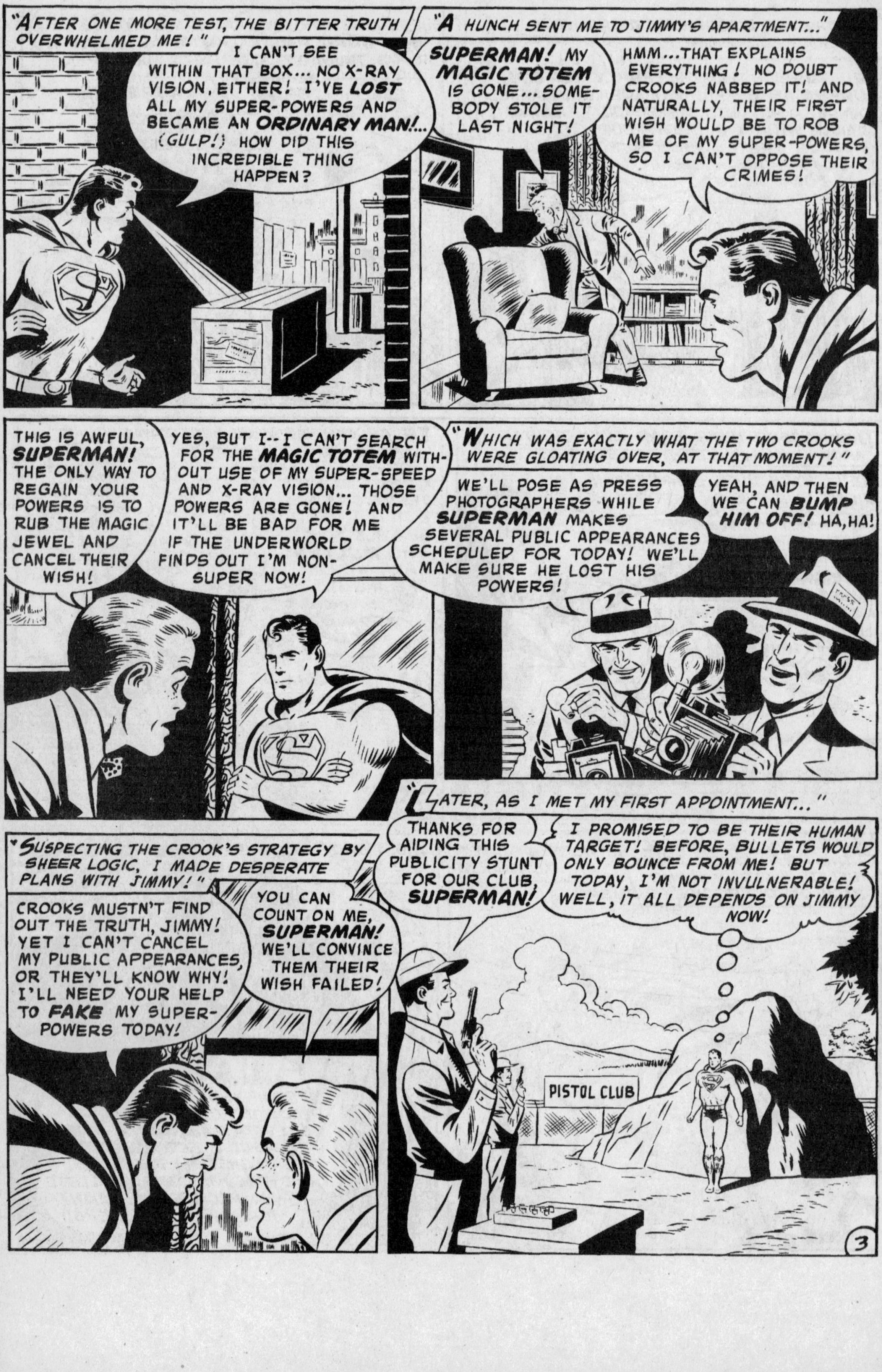
"AFTER ONE MORE TEST, THE BITTER TRUTH OVERWHELMED ME!"
I CAN'T SEE WITHIN THAT BOX... NO X-RAY VISION, EITHER! I'VE LOST ALL MY SUPER-POWERS AND BECAME AN ORDINARY MAN!... (GULP!) HOW DID THIS INCREDIBLE THING HAPPEN?
"A HUNCH SENT ME TO JIMMY'S APARTMENT..."
SUPERMAN! MY MAGIC TOTEM IS GONE... SOMEBODY STOLE IT LAST NIGHT!
HMM...THAT EXPLAINS EVERYTHING! NO DOUBT CROOKS NABBED IT! AND NATURALLY, THEIR FIRST WISH WOULD BE TO ROB ME OF MY SUPER-POWERS, SO I CAN'T OPPOSE THEIR CRIMES!
THIS IS AWFUL, SUPERMAN! THE ONLY WAY TO REGAIN YOUR POWERS IS TO RUB THE MAGIC JEWEL AND CANCEL THEIR WISH!
YES, BUT I-- I CAN'T SEARCH FOR THE MAGIC TOTEM WITHOUT USE OF MY SUPER-SPEED AND X-RAY VISION... THOSE POWERS ARE GONE! AND IT'LL BE BAD FOR ME IF THE UNDERWORLD FINDS OUT I'M NON-SUPER NOW!
"WHICH WAS EXACTLY WHAT THE TWO CROOKS WERE GLOATING OVER, AT THAT MOMENT!"
WE'LL POSE AS PRESS PHOTOGRAPHERS WHILE SUPERMAN MAKES SEVERAL PUBLIC APPEARANCES SCHEDULED FOR TODAY! WE'LL MAKE SURE HE LOST HIS POWERS!
YEAH, AND THEN WE CAN BUMP HIM OFF! HA, HA!
"SUSPECTING THE CROOK'S STRATEGY BY SHEER LOGIC, I MADE DESPERATE PLANS WITH JIMMY!"
CROOKS MUSTN'T FIND OUT THE TRUTH, JIMMY! YET I CAN'T CANCEL MY PUBLIC APPEARANCES, OR THEY'LL KNOW WHY! I'LL NEED YOUR HELP TO FAKE MY SUPER-POWERS TODAY!
YOU CAN COUNT ON ME, SUPERMAN! WE'LL CONVINCE THEM THEIR WISH FAILED!
"LATER, AS I MET MY FIRST APPOINTMENT..."
THANKS FOR AIDING THIS PUBLICITY STUNT FOR OUR CLUB, SUPERMAN!
I PROMISED TO BE THEIR HUMAN TARGET! BEFORE, BULLETS WOULD ONLY BOUNCE FROM ME! BUT TODAY, I'M NOT INVULNERABLE! WELL, IT ALL DEPENDS ON JIMMY NOW!
PISTOL CLUB
3

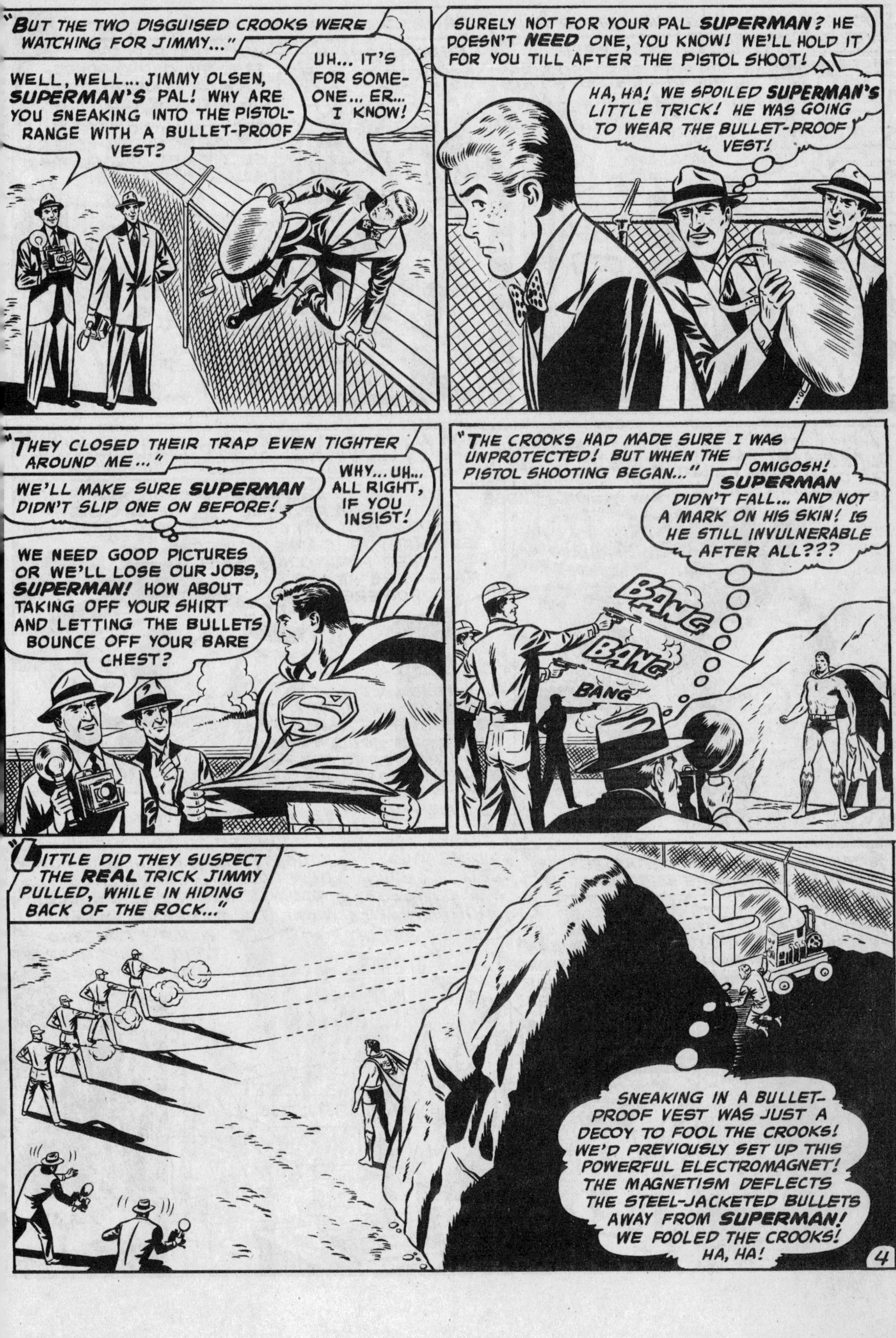
"BUT THE TWO DISGUISED CROOKS WERE WATCHING FOR JIMMY..."
WELL, WELL... JIMMY OLSEN, SUPERMAN'S PAL! WHY ARE YOU SNEAKING INTO THE PISTOL-RANGE WITH A BULLET-PROOF VEST?
UH... IT'S FOR SOME-ONE... ER... I KNOW!
SURELY NOT FOR YOUR PAL SUPERMAN? HE DOESN'T NEED ONE, YOU KNOW! WE'LL HOLD IT FOR YOU TILL AFTER THE PISTOL SHOOT!
HA, HA! WE SPOILED SUPERMAN'S LITTLE TRICK! HE WAS GOING TO WEAR THE BULLET-PROOF VEST!
"THEY CLOSED THEIR TRAP EVEN TIGHTER AROUND ME..."
WE'LL MAKE SURE SUPERMAN DIDN'T SLIP ONE ON BEFORE!
WHY... UH... ALL RIGHT, IF YOU INSIST!
WE NEED GOOD PICTURES OR WE'LL LOSE OUR JOBS, SUPERMAN! HOW ABOUT TAKING OFF YOUR SHIRT AND LETTING THE BULLETS BOUNCE OFF YOUR BARE CHEST?
"THE CROOKS HAD MADE SURE I WAS UNPROTECTED! BUT WHEN THE PISTOL SHOOTING BEGAN..."
OMIGOSH! SUPERMAN DIDN'T FALL... AND NOT A MARK ON HIS SKIN! IS HE STILL INVULNERABLE AFTER ALL???
BANG
BANG
BANG
"LITTLE DID THEY SUSPECT THE REAL TRICK JIMMY PULLED, WHILE IN HIDING BACK OF THE ROCK..."
SNEAKING IN A BULLET-PROOF VEST WAS JUST A DECOY TO FOOL THE CROOKS! WE'D PREVIOUSLY SET UP THIS POWERFUL ELECTROMAGNET! THE MAGNETISM DEFLECTS THE STEEL-JACKETED BULLETS AWAY FROM SUPERMAN! WE FOOLED THE CROOKS! HA, HA!
4

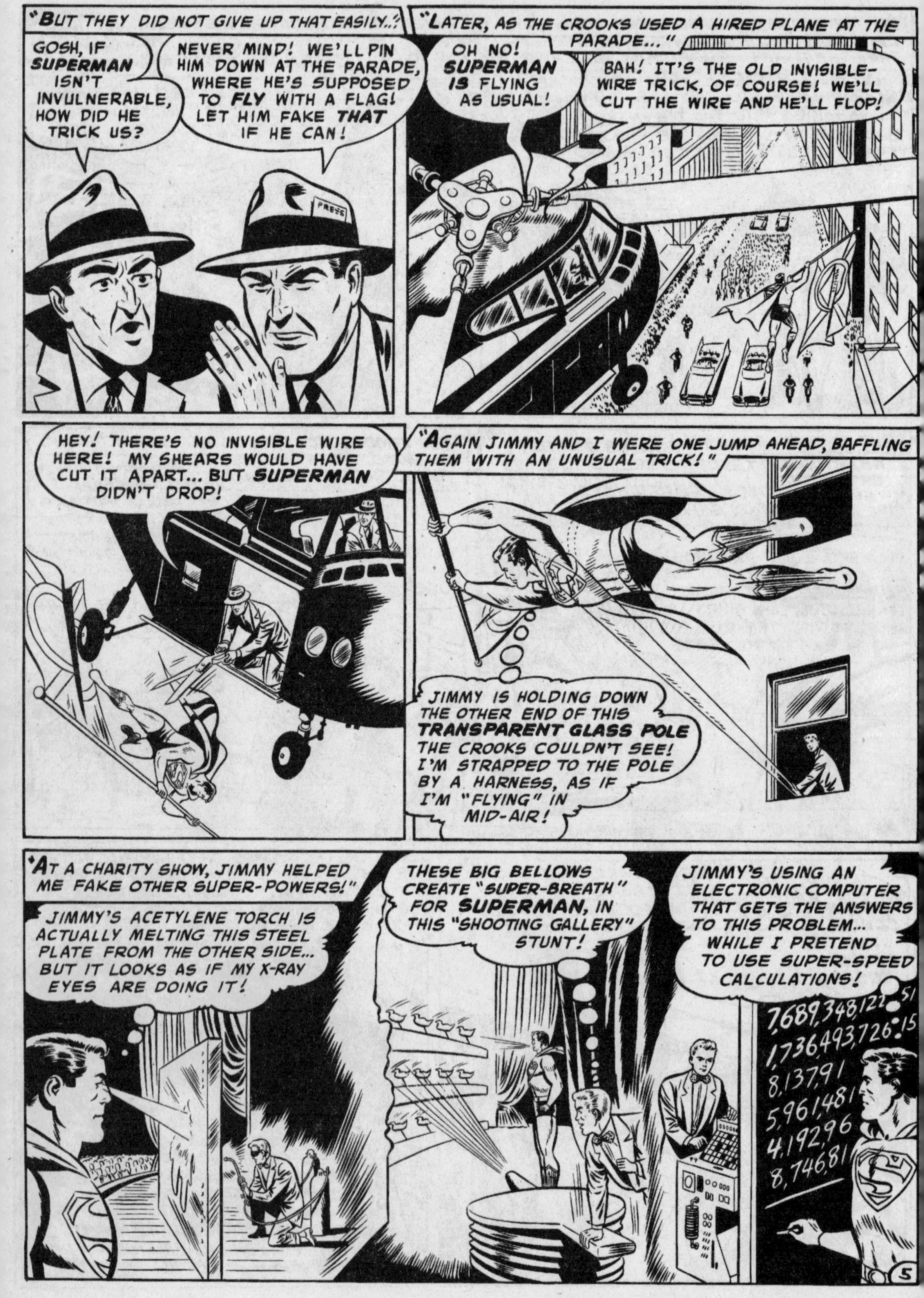
"BUT THEY DID NOT GIVE UP THAT EASILY..."
GOSH, IF SUPERMAN ISN'T INVULNERABLE, HOW DID HE TRICK US?
NEVER MIND! WE'LL PIN HIM DOWN AT THE PARADE, WHERE HE'S SUPPOSED TO FLY WITH A FLAG! LET HIM FAKE THAT IF HE CAN!
PRESS
"LATER, AS THE CROOKS USED A HIRED PLANE AT THE PARADE..."
OH NO! SUPERMAN IS FLYING AS USUAL!
BAH! IT'S THE OLD INVISIBLE-WIRE TRICK, OF COURSE! WE'LL CUT THE WIRE AND HE'LL FLOP!
HEY! THERE'S NO INVISIBLE WIRE HERE! MY SHEARS WOULD HAVE CUT IT APART... BUT SUPERMAN DIDN'T DROP!
"AGAIN JIMMY AND I WERE ONE JUMP AHEAD, BAFFLING THEM WITH AN UNUSUAL TRICK!"
JIMMY IS HOLDING DOWN THE OTHER END OF THIS TRANSPARENT GLASS POLE THE CROOKS COULDN'T SEE! I'M STRAPPED TO THE POLE BY A HARNESS, AS IF I'M "FLYING" IN MID-AIR!
"AT A CHARITY SHOW, JIMMY HELPED ME FAKE OTHER SUPER-POWERS!"
JIMMY'S ACETYLENE TORCH IS ACTUALLY MELTING THIS STEEL PLATE FROM THE OTHER SIDE... BUT IT LOOKS AS IF MY X-RAY EYES ARE DOING IT!
THESE BIG BELLOWS CREATE "SUPER-BREATH" FOR SUPERMAN, IN THIS "SHOOTING GALLERY" STUNT!
JIMMY'S USING AN ELECTRONIC COMPUTER THAT GETS THE ANSWERS TO THIS PROBLEM... WHILE I PRETEND TO USE SUPER-SPEED CALCULATIONS!
7,689,348,122.51
1,736,493,726.15
8,137,91
5,961,481
4,192,96
8,746,81
5

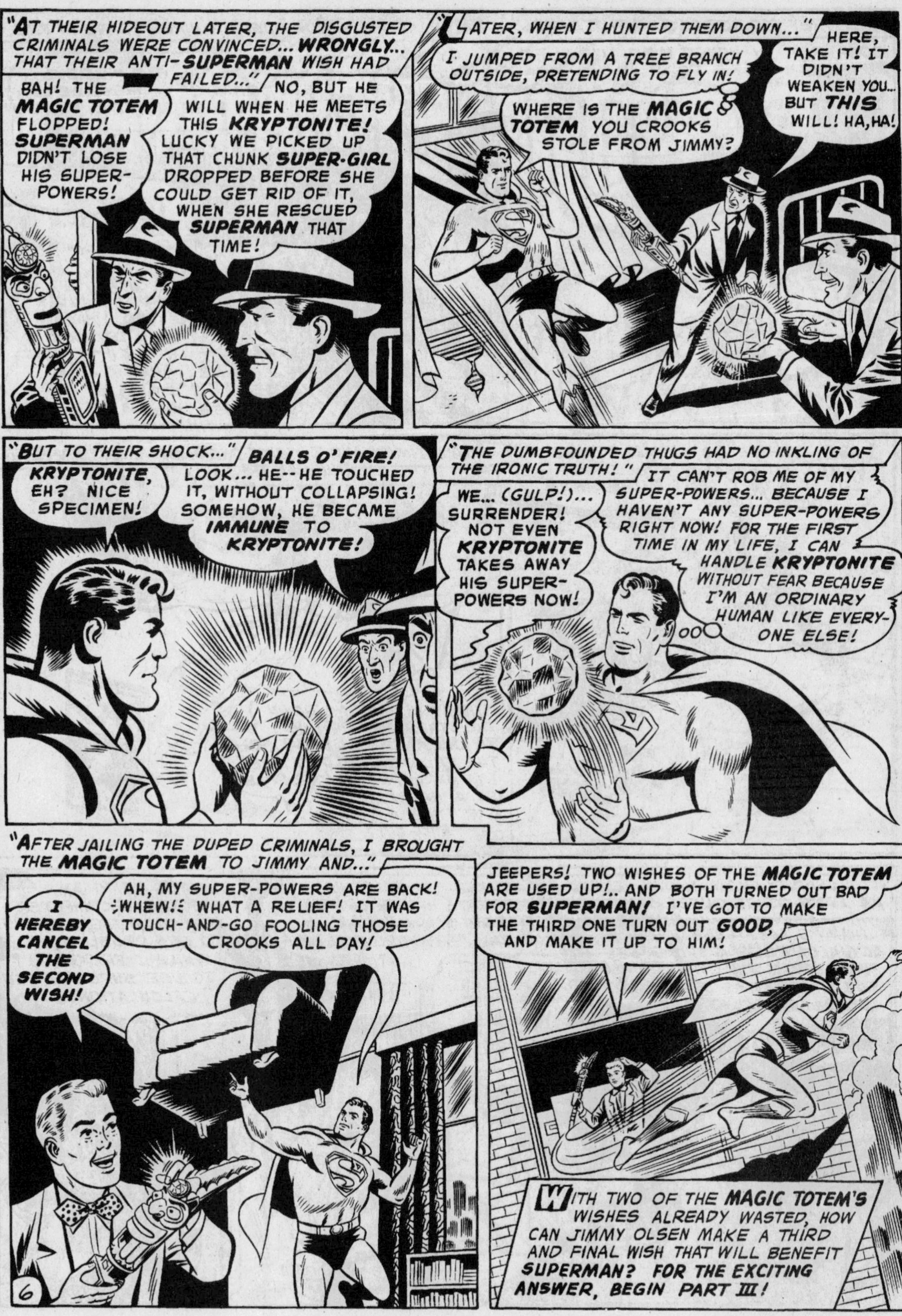
"AT THEIR HIDEOUT LATER, THE DISGUSTED CRIMINALS WERE CONVINCED... WRONGLY... THAT THEIR ANTI-SUPERMAN WISH HAD FAILED..."
BAH! THE MAGIC TOTEM FLOPPED! SUPERMAN DIDN'T LOSE HIS SUPER-POWERS!
NO, BUT HE WILL WHEN HE MEETS THIS KRYPTONITE! LUCKY WE PICKED UP THAT CHUNK SUPER-GIRL DROPPED BEFORE SHE COULD GET RID OF IT, WHEN SHE RESCUED SUPERMAN THAT TIME!
"LATER, WHEN I HUNTED THEM DOWN..."
I JUMPED FROM A TREE BRANCH OUTSIDE, PRETENDING TO FLY IN!
WHERE IS THE MAGIC TOTEM YOU CROOKS STOLE FROM JIMMY?
HERE, TAKE IT! IT DIDN'T WEAKEN YOU... BUT THIS WILL! HA, HA!
"BUT TO THEIR SHOCK..."
KRYPTONITE, EH? NICE SPECIMEN!
BALLS O' FIRE! LOOK... HE--HE TOUCHED IT, WITHOUT COLLAPSING! SOMEHOW, HE BECAME IMMUNE TO KRYPTONITE!
"THE DUMBFOUNDED THUGS HAD NO INKLING OF THE IRONIC TRUTH!"
WE... (GULP!)... SURRENDER! NOT EVEN KRYPTONITE TAKES AWAY HIS SUPER-POWERS NOW!
IT CAN'T ROB ME OF MY SUPER-POWERS... BECAUSE I HAVEN'T ANY SUPER-POWERS RIGHT NOW! FOR THE FIRST TIME IN MY LIFE, I CAN HANDLE KRYPTONITE WITHOUT FEAR BECAUSE I'M AN ORDINARY HUMAN LIKE EVERY-ONE ELSE!
"AFTER JAILING THE DUPED CRIMINALS, I BROUGHT THE MAGIC TOTEM TO JIMMY AND..."
I HEREBY CANCEL THE SECOND WISH!
AH, MY SUPER-POWERS ARE BACK! WHEW! WHAT A RELIEF! IT WAS TOUCH-AND-GO FOOLING THOSE CROOKS ALL DAY!
6
JEEPERS! TWO WISHES OF THE MAGIC TOTEM ARE USED UP!.. AND BOTH TURNED OUT BAD FOR SUPERMAN! I'VE GOT TO MAKE THE THIRD ONE TURN OUT GOOD, AND MAKE IT UP TO HIM!
WITH TWO OF THE MAGIC TOTEM'S WISHES ALREADY WASTED, HOW CAN JIMMY OLSEN MAKE A THIRD AND FINAL WISH THAT WILL BENEFIT SUPERMAN? FOR THE EXCITING ANSWER, BEGIN PART III!

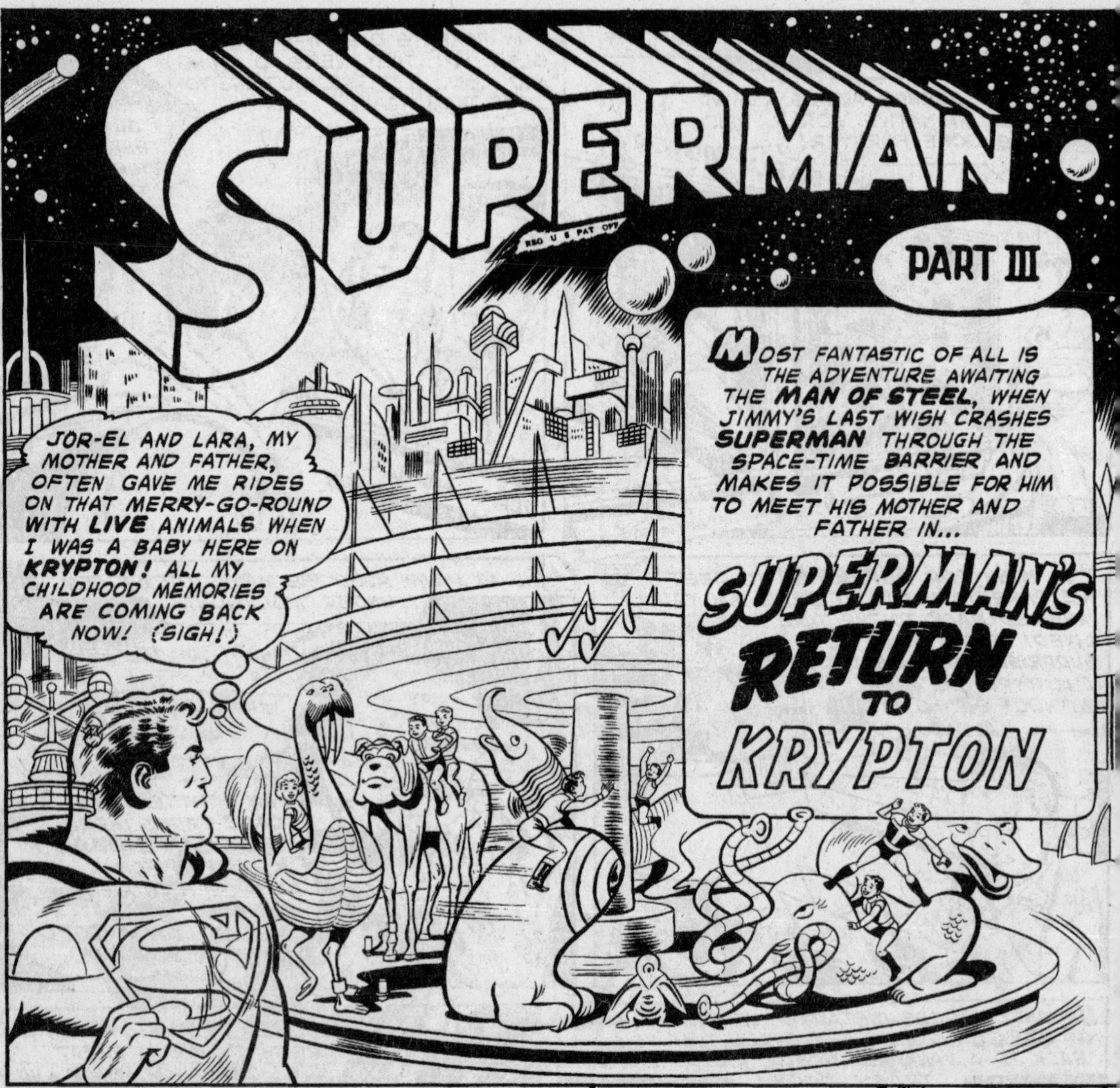
SUPERMAN
REG. U.S. PAT. OFF.
PART III
MOST FANTASTIC OF ALL IS THE ADVENTURE AWAITING THE MAN OF STEEL, WHEN JIMMY'S LAST WISH CRASHES SUPERMAN THROUGH THE SPACE-TIME BARRIER AND MAKES IT POSSIBLE FOR HIM TO MEET HIS MOTHER AND FATHER IN...
SUPERMAN'S RETURN TO KRYPTON
JOR-EL AND LARA, MY MOTHER AND FATHER, OFTEN GAVE ME RIDES ON THAT MERRY-GO-ROUND WITH LIVE ANIMALS WHEN I WAS A BABY HERE ON KRYPTON! ALL MY CHILDHOOD MEMORIES ARE COMING BACK NOW! (SIGH!)

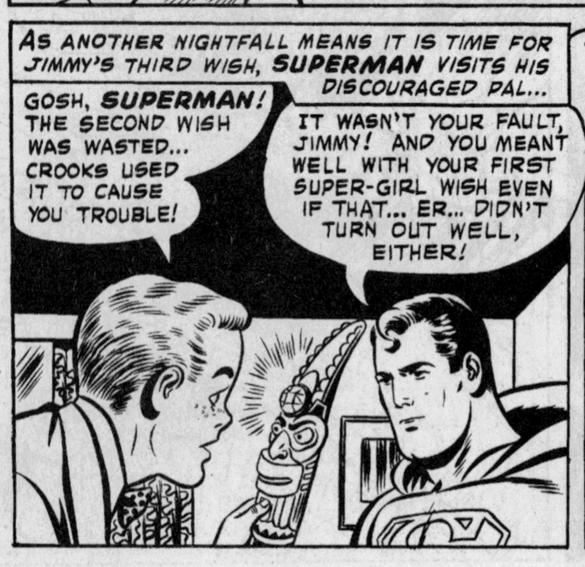
AS ANOTHER NIGHTFALL MEANS IT IS TIME FOR JIMMY'S THIRD WISH, SUPERMAN VISITS HIS DISCOURAGED PAL...
GOSH, SUPERMAN! THE SECOND WISH WAS WASTED... CROOKS USED IT TO CAUSE YOU TROUBLE!
IT WASN'T YOUR FAULT, JIMMY! AND YOU MEANT WELL WITH YOUR FIRST SUPER-GIRL WISH EVEN IF THAT... ER... DIDN'T TURN OUT WELL, EITHER!

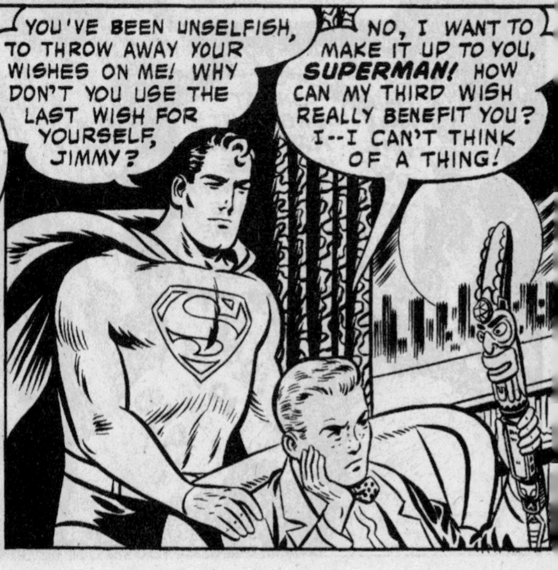
YOU'VE BEEN UNSELFISH, TO THROW AWAY YOUR WISHES ON ME! WHY DON'T YOU USE THE LAST WISH FOR YOURSELF, JIMMY?
NO, I WANT TO MAKE IT UP TO YOU, SUPERMAN! HOW CAN MY THIRD WISH REALLY BENEFIT YOU? I--I CAN'T THINK OF A THING!

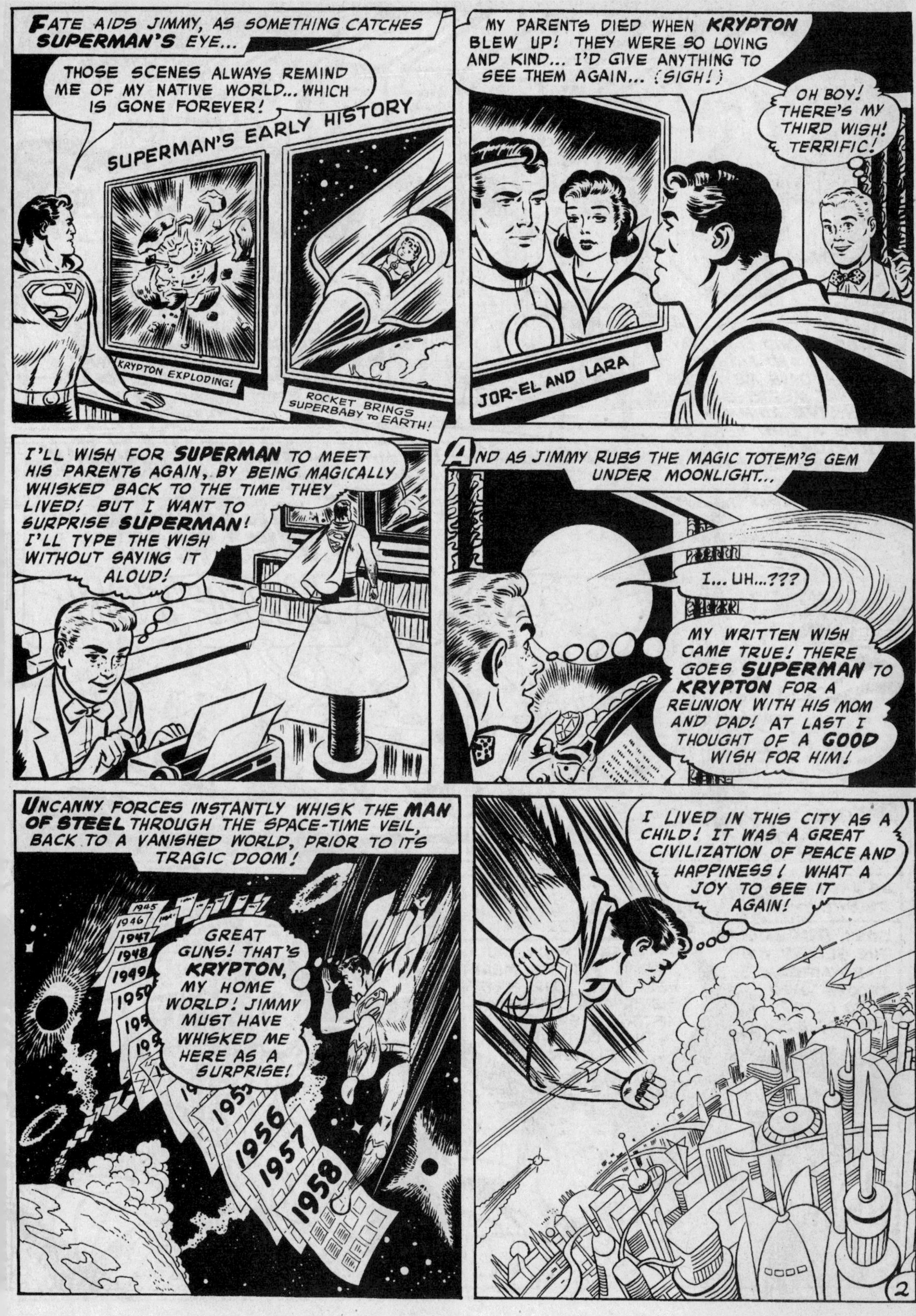
FATE AIDS JIMMY, AS SOMETHING CATCHES SUPERMAN'S EYE...
THOSE SCENES ALWAYS REMIND ME OF MY NATIVE WORLD... WHICH IS GONE FOREVER!
SUPERMAN'S EARLY HISTORY
KRYPTON EXPLODING!
ROCKET BRINGS SUPERBABY TO EARTH!
MY PARENTS DIED WHEN KRYPTON BLEW UP! THEY WERE SO LOVING AND KIND... I'D GIVE ANYTHING TO SEE THEM AGAIN... (SIGH!)
OH BOY! THERE'S MY THIRD WISH! TERRIFIC!
JOR-EL AND LARA
I'LL WISH FOR SUPERMAN TO MEET HIS PARENTS AGAIN, BY BEING MAGICALLY WHISKED BACK TO THE TIME THEY LIVED! BUT I WANT TO SURPRISE SUPERMAN! I'LL TYPE THE WISH WITHOUT SAYING IT ALOUD!
AND AS JIMMY RUBS THE MAGIC TOTEM'S GEM UNDER MOONLIGHT...
I... UH...???
MY WRITTEN WISH CAME TRUE! THERE GOES SUPERMAN TO KRYPTON FOR A REUNION WITH HIS MOM AND DAD! AT LAST I THOUGHT OF A GOOD WISH FOR HIM!
UNCANNY FORCES INSTANTLY WHISK THE MAN OF STEEL THROUGH THE SPACE-TIME VEIL, BACK TO A VANISHED WORLD, PRIOR TO ITS TRAGIC DOOM!
1945
1946
1947
1948
1949
1956
1957
1958
GREAT GUNS! THAT'S KRYPTON, MY HOME WORLD! JIMMY MUST HAVE WHISKED ME HERE AS A SURPRISE!
I LIVED IN THIS CITY AS A CHILD! IT WAS A GREAT CIVILIZATION OF PEACE AND HAPPINESS! WHAT A JOY TO SEE IT AGAIN!
2

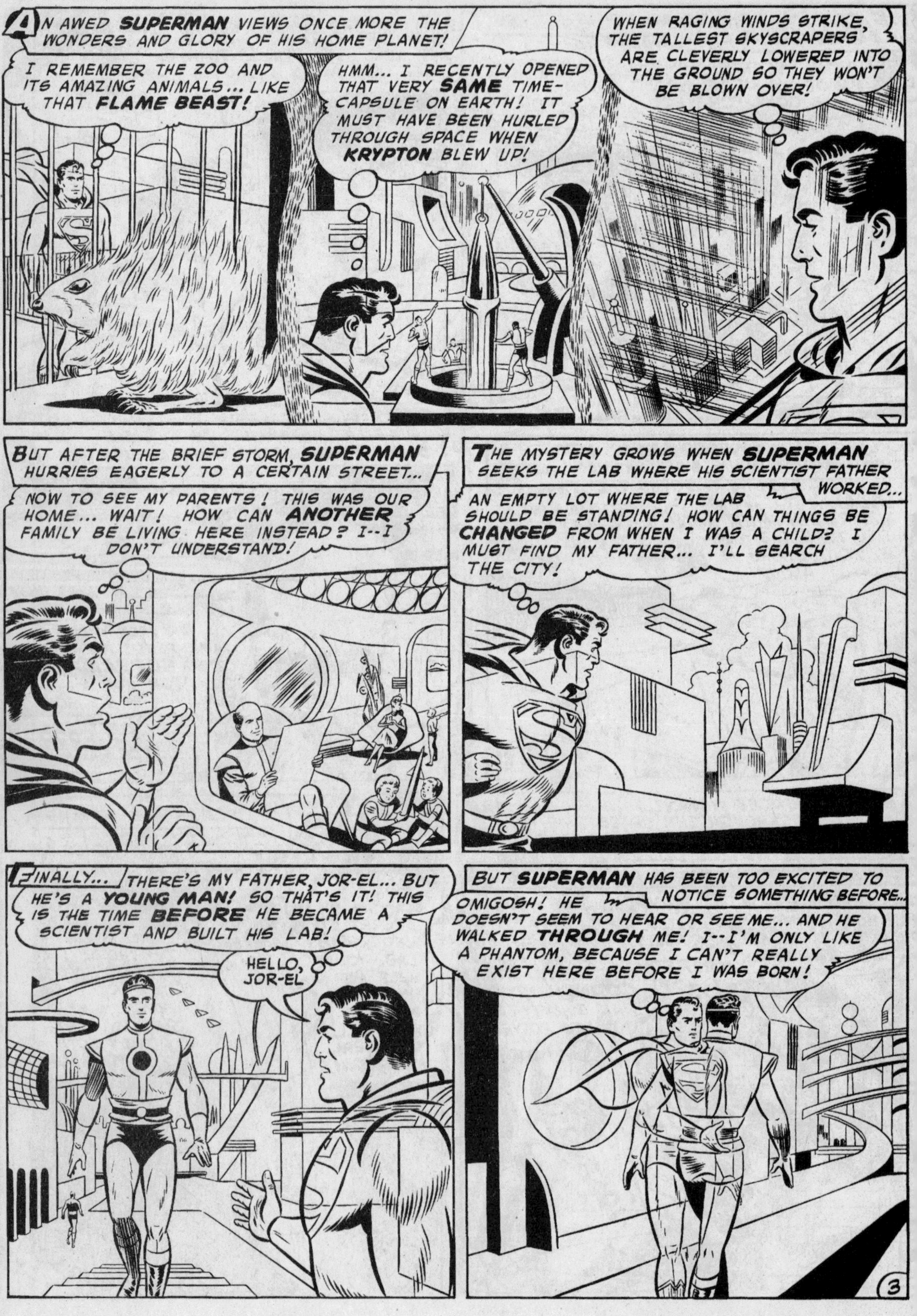
AN AWED SUPERMAN VIEWS ONCE MORE THE WONDERS AND GLORY OF HIS HOME PLANET!
I REMEMBER THE ZOO AND ITS AMAZING ANIMALS... LIKE THAT FLAME BEAST!
HMM... I RECENTLY OPENED THAT VERY SAME TIME-CAPSULE ON EARTH! IT MUST HAVE BEEN HURLED THROUGH SPACE WHEN KRYPTON BLEW UP!
WHEN RAGING WINDS STRIKE, THE TALLEST SKYSCRAPERS ARE CLEVERLY LOWERED INTO THE GROUND SO THEY WON'T BE BLOWN OVER!
BUT AFTER THE BRIEF STORM, SUPERMAN HURRIES EAGERLY TO A CERTAIN STREET...
NOW TO SEE MY PARENTS! THIS WAS OUR HOME... WAIT! HOW CAN ANOTHER FAMILY BE LIVING HERE INSTEAD? I--I DON'T UNDERSTAND!
THE MYSTERY GROWS WHEN SUPERMAN SEEKS THE LAB WHERE HIS SCIENTIST FATHER WORKED...
AN EMPTY LOT WHERE THE LAB SHOULD BE STANDING! HOW CAN THINGS BE CHANGED FROM WHEN I WAS A CHILD? I MUST FIND MY FATHER... I'LL SEARCH THE CITY!
FINALLY...
THERE'S MY FATHER, JOR-EL... BUT HE'S A YOUNG MAN! SO THAT'S IT! THIS IS THE TIME BEFORE HE BECAME A SCIENTIST AND BUILT HIS LAB!
HELLO, JOR-EL
BUT SUPERMAN HAS BEEN TOO EXCITED TO NOTICE SOMETHING BEFORE...
OMIGOSH! HE DOESN'T SEEM TO HEAR OR SEE ME... AND HE WALKED THROUGH ME! I--I'M ONLY LIKE A PHANTOM, BECAUSE I CAN'T REALLY EXIST HERE BEFORE I WAS BORN!
3

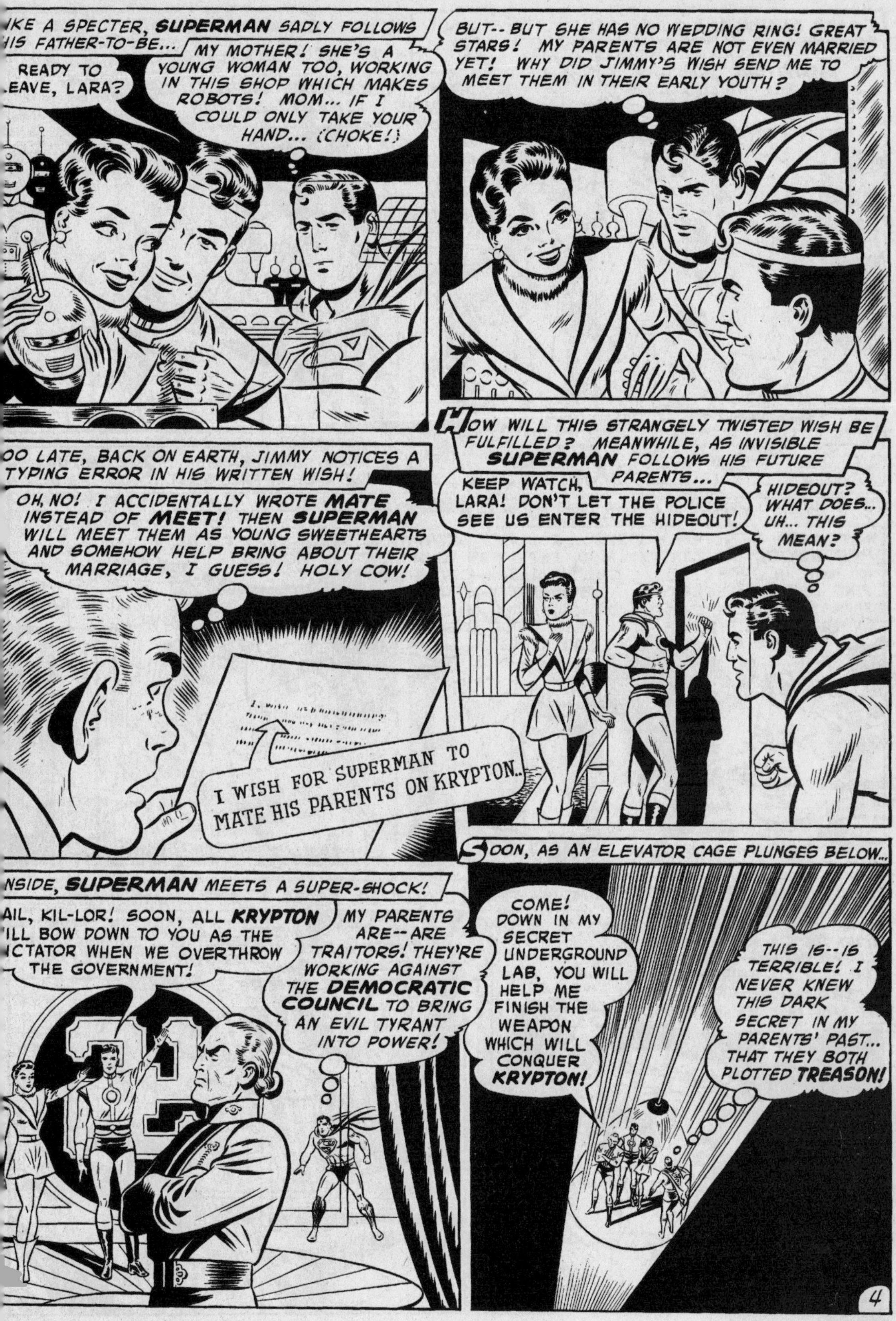
IKE A SPECTER, SUPERMAN SADLY FOLLOWS IS FATHER-TO-BE...
READY TO EAVE, LARA?
MY MOTHER! SHE'S A YOUNG WOMAN TOO, WORKING IN THIS SHOP WHICH MAKES ROBOTS! MOM... IF I COULD ONLY TAKE YOUR HAND... (CHOKE!)
BUT-- BUT SHE HAS NO WEDDING RING! GREAT STARS! MY PARENTS ARE NOT EVEN MARRIED YET! WHY DID JIMMY'S WISH SEND ME TO MEET THEM IN THEIR EARLY YOUTH?
OO LATE, BACK ON EARTH, JIMMY NOTICES A TYPING ERROR IN HIS WRITTEN WISH!
OH, NO! I ACCIDENTALLY WROTE MATE INSTEAD OF MEET! THEN SUPERMAN WILL MEET THEM AS YOUNG SWEETHEARTS AND SOMEHOW HELP BRING ABOUT THEIR MARRIAGE, I GUESS! HOLY COW!
I WISH FOR SUPERMAN TO MATE HIS PARENTS ON KRYPTON..
HOW WILL THIS STRANGELY TWISTED WISH BE FULFILLED? MEANWHILE, AS INVISIBLE SUPERMAN FOLLOWS HIS FUTURE PARENTS...
KEEP WATCH, LARA! DON'T LET THE POLICE SEE US ENTER THE HIDEOUT!
HIDEOUT? WHAT DOES... UH... THIS MEAN?
NSIDE, SUPERMAN MEETS A SUPER-SHOCK!
AIL, KIL-LOR! SOON, ALL KRYPTON ILL BOW DOWN TO YOU AS THE CTATOR WHEN WE OVERTHROW THE GOVERNMENT!
MY PARENTS ARE--ARE TRAITORS! THEY'RE WORKING AGAINST THE DEMOCRATIC COUNCIL TO BRING AN EVIL TYRANT INTO POWER!
SOON, AS AN ELEVATOR CAGE PLUNGES BELOW...
COME! DOWN IN MY SECRET UNDERGROUND LAB, YOU WILL HELP ME FINISH THE WEAPON WHICH WILL CONQUER KRYPTON!
THIS IS--IS TERRIBLE! I NEVER KNEW THIS DARK SECRET IN MY PARENTS' PAST... THAT THEY BOTH PLOTTED TREASON!
4

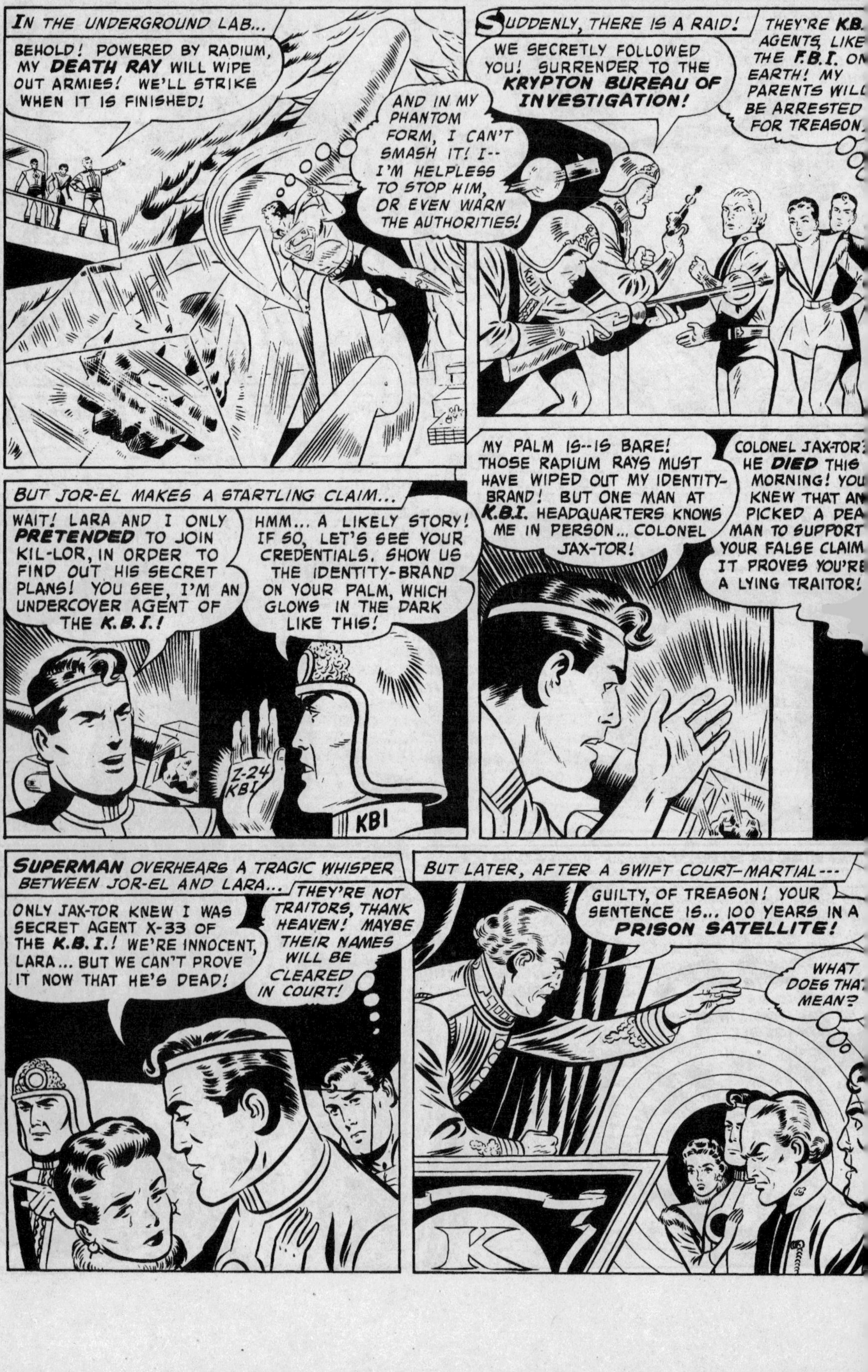
IN THE UNDERGROUND LAB...
BEHOLD! POWERED BY RADIUM, MY DEATH RAY WILL WIPE OUT ARMIES! WE'LL STRIKE WHEN IT IS FINISHED!
AND IN MY PHANTOM FORM, I CAN'T SMASH IT! I-- I'M HELPLESS TO STOP HIM, OR EVEN WARN THE AUTHORITIES!
SUDDENLY, THERE IS A RAID!
WE SECRETLY FOLLOWED YOU! SURRENDER TO THE KRYPTON BUREAU OF INVESTIGATION!
THEY'RE K.B. AGENTS, LIKE THE F.B.I. ON EARTH! MY PARENTS WILL BE ARRESTED FOR TREASON
KBI
BUT JOR-EL MAKES A STARTLING CLAIM...
WAIT! LARA AND I ONLY PRETENDED TO JOIN KIL-LOR, IN ORDER TO FIND OUT HIS SECRET PLANS! YOU SEE, I'M AN UNDERCOVER AGENT OF THE K.B.I.!
HMM... A LIKELY STORY! IF SO, LET'S SEE YOUR CREDENTIALS. SHOW US THE IDENTITY-BRAND ON YOUR PALM, WHICH GLOWS IN THE DARK LIKE THIS!
Z-24 KBI
KBI
MY PALM IS--IS BARE! THOSE RADIUM RAYS MUST HAVE WIPED OUT MY IDENTITY-BRAND! BUT ONE MAN AT K.B.I. HEADQUARTERS KNOWS ME IN PERSON... COLONEL JAX-TOR!
COLONEL JAX-TOR? HE DIED THIS MORNING! YOU KNEW THAT AN PICKED A DEA MAN TO SUPPORT YOUR FALSE CLAIM IT PROVES YOU'RE A LYING TRAITOR!
SUPERMAN OVERHEARS A TRAGIC WHISPER BETWEEN JOR-EL AND LARA...
ONLY JAX-TOR KNEW I WAS SECRET AGENT X-33 OF THE K.B.I.! WE'RE INNOCENT, LARA... BUT WE CAN'T PROVE IT NOW THAT HE'S DEAD!
THEY'RE NOT TRAITORS, THANK HEAVEN! MAYBE THEIR NAMES WILL BE CLEARED IN COURT!
BUT LATER, AFTER A SWIFT COURT-MARTIAL---
GUILTY, OF TREASON! YOUR SENTENCE IS... 100 YEARS IN A PRISON SATELLITE!
WHAT DOES THAT MEAN?
K

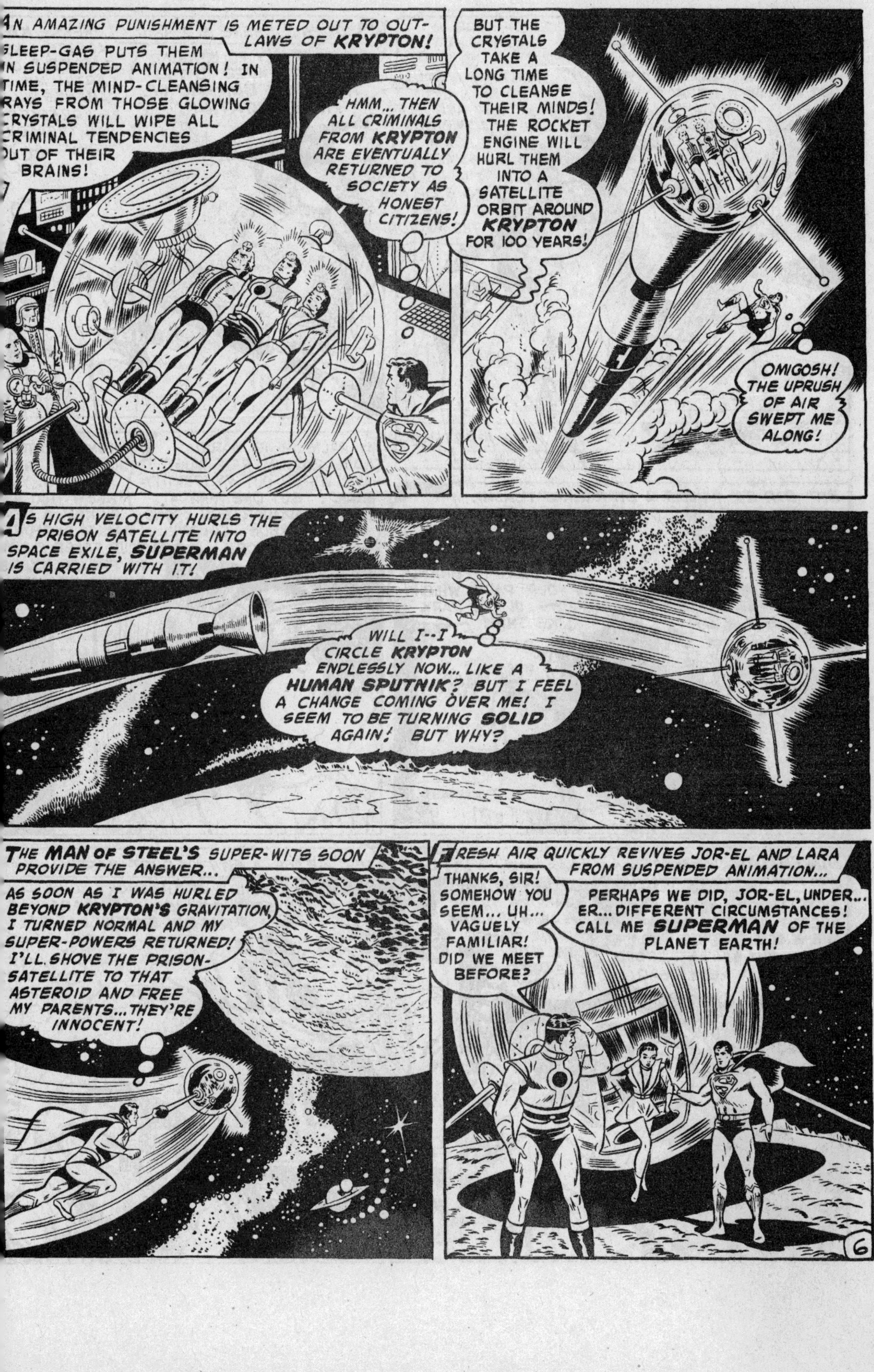
AN AMAZING PUNISHMENT IS METED OUT TO OUT-LAWS OF KRYPTON!
SLEEP-GAS PUTS THEM IN SUSPENDED ANIMATION! IN TIME, THE MIND-CLEANSING RAYS FROM THOSE GLOWING CRYSTALS WILL WIPE ALL CRIMINAL TENDENCIES OUT OF THEIR BRAINS!
HMM... THEN ALL CRIMINALS FROM KRYPTON ARE EVENTUALLY RETURNED TO SOCIETY AS HONEST CITIZENS!
BUT THE CRYSTALS TAKE A LONG TIME TO CLEANSE THEIR MINDS! THE ROCKET ENGINE WILL HURL THEM INTO A SATELLITE ORBIT AROUND KRYPTON FOR 100 YEARS!
OMIGOSH! THE UPRUSH OF AIR SWEPT ME ALONG!
AS HIGH VELOCITY HURLS THE PRISON SATELLITE INTO SPACE EXILE, SUPERMAN IS CARRIED WITH IT!
WILL I--I CIRCLE KRYPTON ENDLESSLY NOW... LIKE A HUMAN SPUTNIK? BUT I FEEL A CHANGE COMING OVER ME! I SEEM TO BE TURNING SOLID AGAIN! BUT WHY?
THE MAN OF STEEL'S SUPER-WITS SOON PROVIDE THE ANSWER...
AS SOON AS I WAS HURLED BEYOND KRYPTON'S GRAVITATION, I TURNED NORMAL AND MY SUPER-POWERS RETURNED! I'LL SHOVE THE PRISON-SATELLITE TO THAT ASTEROID AND FREE MY PARENTS... THEY'RE INNOCENT!
FRESH AIR QUICKLY REVIVES JOR-EL AND LARA FROM SUSPENDED ANIMATION...
THANKS, SIR! SOMEHOW YOU SEEM... UH... VAGUELY FAMILIAR! DID WE MEET BEFORE?
PERHAPS WE DID, JOR-EL, UNDER... ER... DIFFERENT CIRCUMSTANCES! CALL ME SUPERMAN OF THE PLANET EARTH!
6

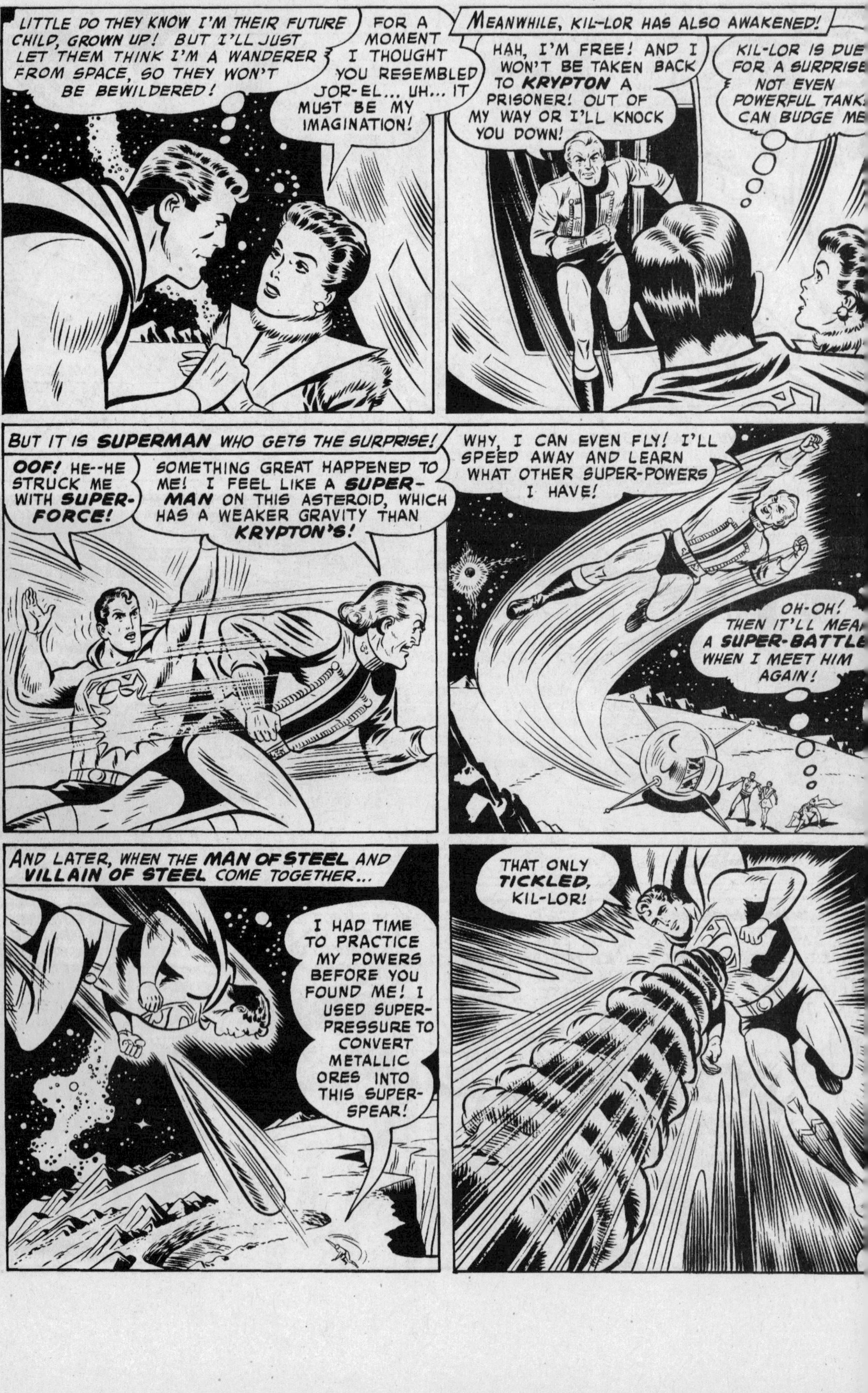
LITTLE DO THEY KNOW I'M THEIR FUTURE CHILD, GROWN UP! BUT I'LL JUST LET THEM THINK I'M A WANDERER FROM SPACE, SO THEY WON'T BE BEWILDERED!
FOR A MOMENT I THOUGHT YOU RESEMBLED JOR-EL... UH... IT MUST BE MY IMAGINATION!
MEANWHILE, KIL-LOR HAS ALSO AWAKENED!
HAH, I'M FREE! AND I WON'T BE TAKEN BACK TO KRYPTON A PRISONER! OUT OF MY WAY OR I'LL KNOCK YOU DOWN!
KIL-LOR IS DUE FOR A SURPRISE NOT EVEN POWERFUL TANK CAN BUDGE ME
BUT IT IS SUPERMAN WHO GETS THE SURPRISE!
OOF! HE--HE STRUCK ME WITH SUPER-FORCE!
SOMETHING GREAT HAPPENED TO ME! I FEEL LIKE A SUPER-MAN ON THIS ASTEROID, WHICH HAS A WEAKER GRAVITY THAN KRYPTON'S!
WHY, I CAN EVEN FLY! I'LL SPEED AWAY AND LEARN WHAT OTHER SUPER-POWERS I HAVE!
OH-OH! THEN IT'LL MEA A SUPER-BATTLE WHEN I MEET HIM AGAIN!
AND LATER, WHEN THE MAN OF STEEL AND VILLAIN OF STEEL COME TOGETHER...
I HAD TIME TO PRACTICE MY POWERS BEFORE YOU FOUND ME! I USED SUPER-PRESSURE TO CONVERT METALLIC ORES INTO THIS SUPER-SPEAR!
THAT ONLY TICKLED, KIL-LOR!

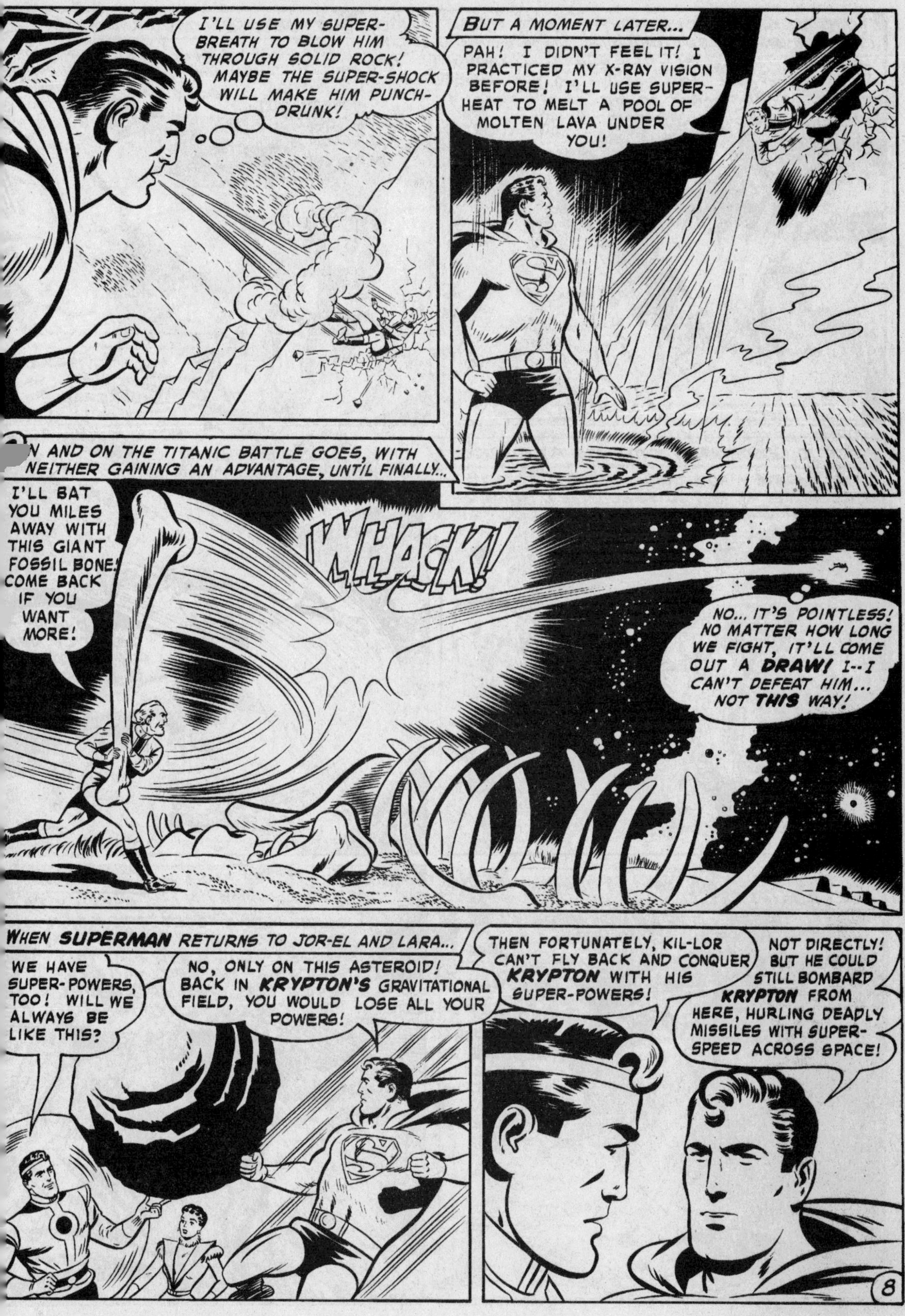
I'LL USE MY SUPER-BREATH TO BLOW HIM THROUGH SOLID ROCK! MAYBE THE SUPER-SHOCK WILL MAKE HIM PUNCH-DRUNK!
BUT A MOMENT LATER...
PAH! I DIDN'T FEEL IT! I PRACTICED MY X-RAY VISION BEFORE! I'LL USE SUPER-HEAT TO MELT A POOL OF MOLTEN LAVA UNDER YOU!
ON AND ON THE TITANIC BATTLE GOES, WITH NEITHER GAINING AN ADVANTAGE, UNTIL FINALLY...
I'LL BAT YOU MILES AWAY WITH THIS GIANT FOSSIL BONE! COME BACK IF YOU WANT MORE!
WHACK!
NO... IT'S POINTLESS! NO MATTER HOW LONG WE FIGHT, IT'LL COME OUT A DRAW! I--I CAN'T DEFEAT HIM... NOT THIS WAY!
WHEN SUPERMAN RETURNS TO JOR-EL AND LARA...
WE HAVE SUPER-POWERS, TOO! WILL WE ALWAYS BE LIKE THIS?
NO, ONLY ON THIS ASTEROID! BACK IN KRYPTON'S GRAVITATIONAL FIELD, YOU WOULD LOSE ALL YOUR POWERS!
THEN FORTUNATELY, KIL-LOR CAN'T FLY BACK AND CONQUER KRYPTON WITH HIS SUPER-POWERS!
NOT DIRECTLY! BUT HE COULD STILL BOMBARD KRYPTON FROM HERE, HURLING DEADLY MISSILES WITH SUPER-SPEED ACROSS SPACE!
8

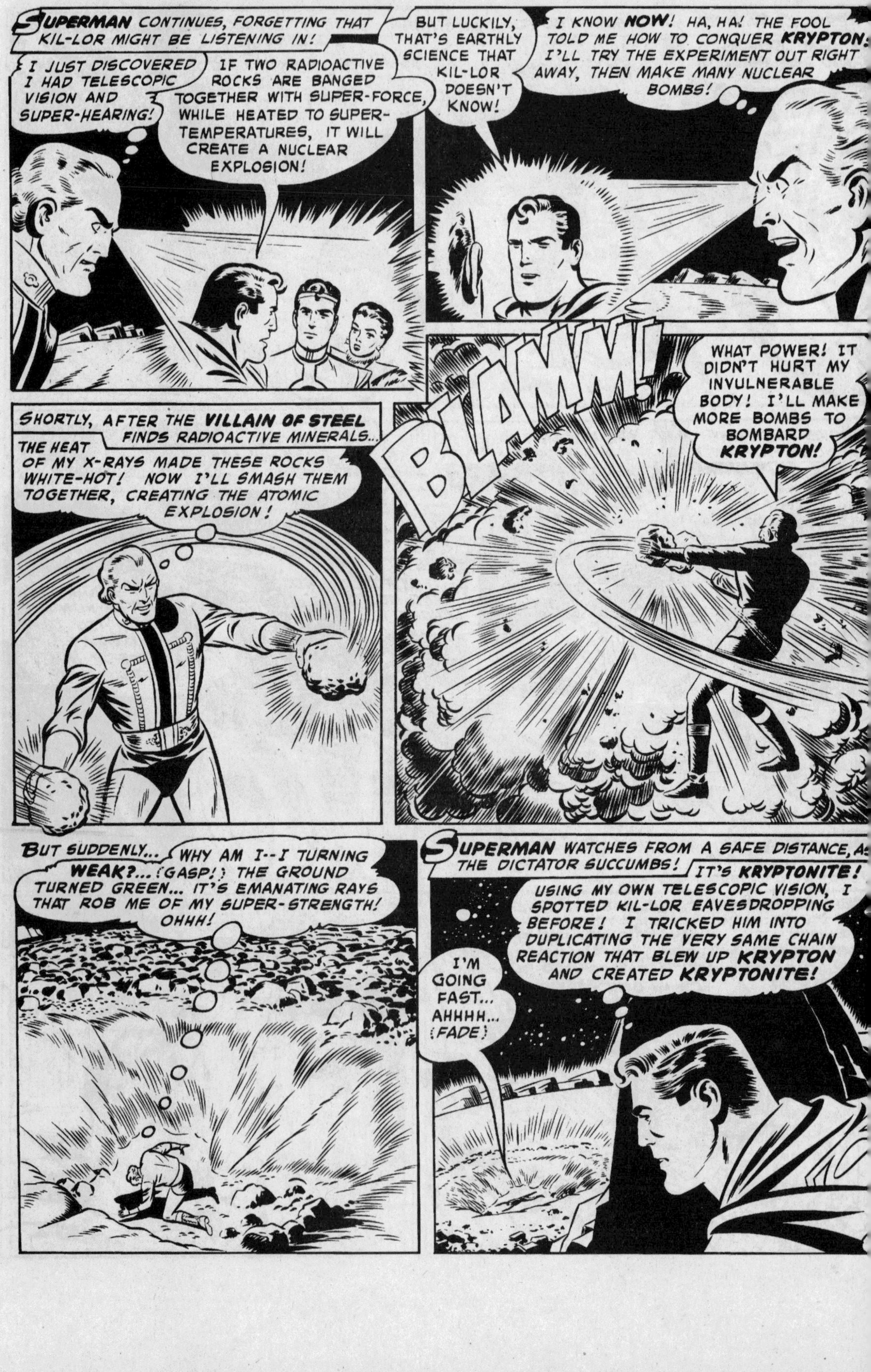
SUPERMAN CONTINUES, FORGETTING THAT KIL-LOR MIGHT BE LISTENING IN!
I JUST DISCOVERED I HAD TELESCOPIC VISION AND SUPER-HEARING!
IF TWO RADIOACTIVE ROCKS ARE BANGED TOGETHER WITH SUPER-FORCE, WHILE HEATED TO SUPER-TEMPERATURES, IT WILL CREATE A NUCLEAR EXPLOSION!
BUT LUCKILY, THAT'S EARTHLY SCIENCE THAT KIL-LOR DOESN'T KNOW!
I KNOW NOW! HA, HA! THE FOOL TOLD ME HOW TO CONQUER KRYPTON! I'LL TRY THE EXPERIMENT OUT RIGHT AWAY, THEN MAKE MANY NUCLEAR BOMBS!
SHORTLY, AFTER THE VILLAIN OF STEEL FINDS RADIOACTIVE MINERALS...
THE HEAT OF MY X-RAYS MADE THESE ROCKS WHITE-HOT! NOW I'LL SMASH THEM TOGETHER, CREATING THE ATOMIC EXPLOSION!
BLAMM!
WHAT POWER! IT DIDN'T HURT MY INVULNERABLE BODY! I'LL MAKE MORE BOMBS TO BOMBARD KRYPTON!
BUT SUDDENLY...
WHY AM I--I TURNING WEAK?... (GASP!) THE GROUND TURNED GREEN... IT'S EMANATING RAYS THAT ROB ME OF MY SUPER-STRENGTH! OHHH!
SUPERMAN WATCHES FROM A SAFE DISTANCE, AS THE DICTATOR SUCCUMBS!
IT'S KRYPTONITE! USING MY OWN TELESCOPIC VISION, I SPOTTED KIL-LOR EAVESDROPPING BEFORE! I TRICKED HIM INTO DUPLICATING THE VERY SAME CHAIN REACTION THAT BLEW UP KRYPTON AND CREATED KRYPTONITE!
I'M GOING FAST... AHHHH... (FADE)

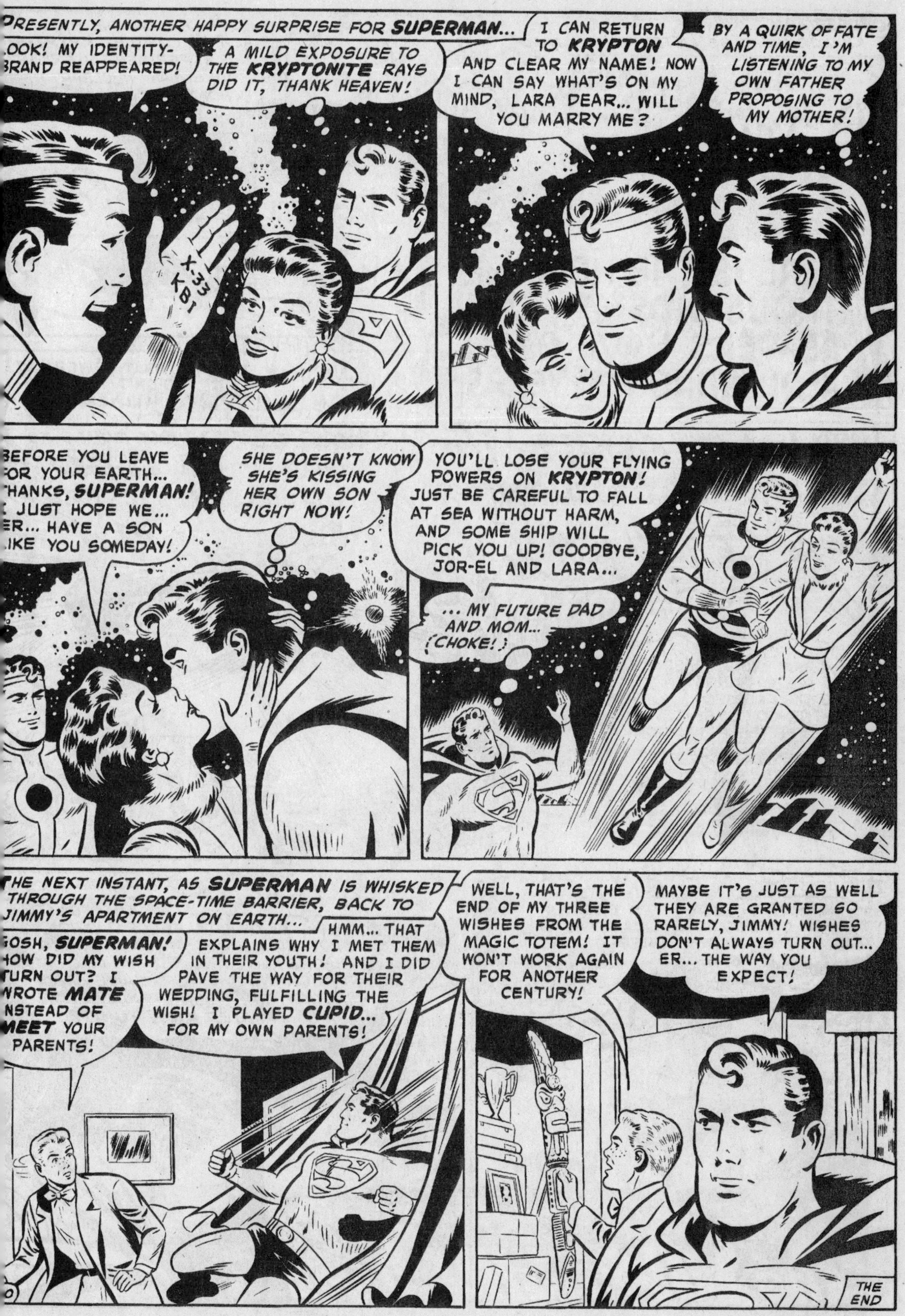
PRESENTLY, ANOTHER HAPPY SURPRISE FOR SUPERMAN...
LOOK! MY IDENTITY-BRAND REAPPEARED!
A MILD EXPOSURE TO THE KRYPTONITE RAYS DID IT, THANK HEAVEN!
X-33 KBI
I CAN RETURN TO KRYPTON AND CLEAR MY NAME! NOW I CAN SAY WHAT'S ON MY MIND, LARA DEAR... WILL YOU MARRY ME?
BY A QUIRK OF FATE AND TIME, I'M LISTENING TO MY OWN FATHER PROPOSING TO MY MOTHER!
BEFORE YOU LEAVE FOR YOUR EARTH... THANKS, SUPERMAN! I JUST HOPE WE... ER... HAVE A SON LIKE YOU SOMEDAY!
SHE DOESN'T KNOW SHE'S KISSING HER OWN SON RIGHT NOW!
YOU'LL LOSE YOUR FLYING POWERS ON KRYPTON! JUST BE CAREFUL TO FALL AT SEA WITHOUT HARM, AND SOME SHIP WILL PICK YOU UP! GOODBYE, JOR-EL AND LARA...
... MY FUTURE DAD AND MOM... (CHOKE!)
THE NEXT INSTANT, AS SUPERMAN IS WHISKED THROUGH THE SPACE-TIME BARRIER, BACK TO JIMMY'S APARTMENT ON EARTH...
GOSH, SUPERMAN! HOW DID MY WISH TURN OUT? I WROTE MATE INSTEAD OF MEET YOUR PARENTS!
HMM... THAT EXPLAINS WHY I MET THEM IN THEIR YOUTH! AND I DID PAVE THE WAY FOR THEIR WEDDING, FULFILLING THE WISH! I PLAYED CUPID... FOR MY OWN PARENTS!
WELL, THAT'S THE END OF MY THREE WISHES FROM THE MAGIC TOTEM! IT WON'T WORK AGAIN FOR ANOTHER CENTURY!
MAYBE IT'S JUST AS WELL THEY ARE GRANTED SO RARELY, JIMMY! WISHES DON'T ALWAYS TURN OUT... ER... THE WAY YOU EXPECT!
THE END

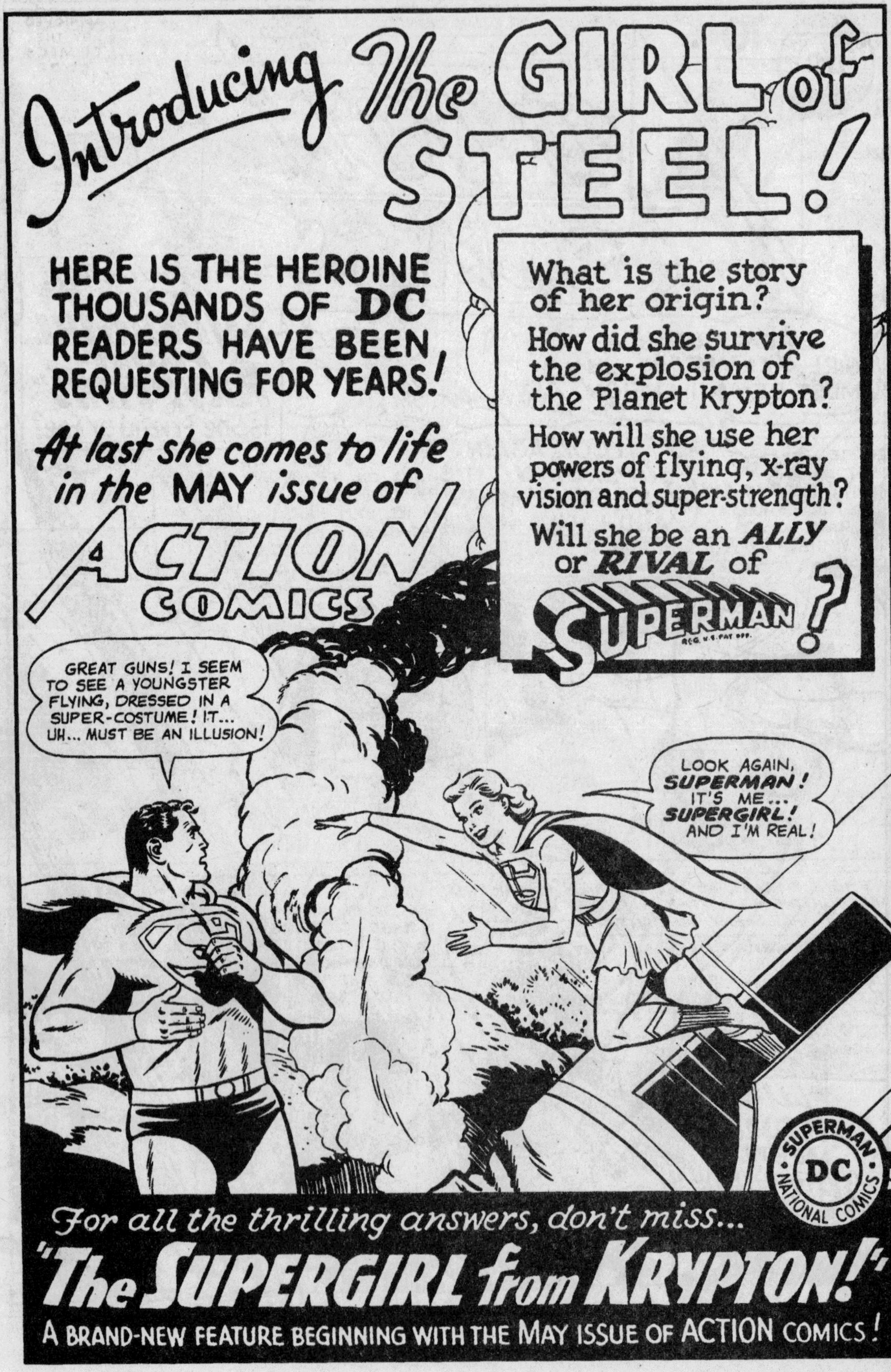
Introducing The GIRL of STEEL!
HERE IS THE HEROINE THOUSANDS OF DC READERS HAVE BEEN REQUESTING FOR YEARS!
At last she comes to life in the MAY issue of ACTION COMICS
What is the story of her origin?
How did she survive the explosion of the Planet Krypton?
How will she use her powers of flying, x-ray vision and super-strength?
Will she be an ALLY or RIVAL of SUPERMAN?
GREAT GUNS! I SEEM TO SEE A YOUNGSTER FLYING, DRESSED IN A SUPER-COSTUME! IT... UH... MUST BE AN ILLUSION!
LOOK AGAIN, SUPERMAN! IT'S ME... SUPERGIRL! AND I'M REAL!
SUPERMAN DC NATIONAL COMICS
For all the thrilling answers, don't miss...
"The SUPERGIRL from KRYPTON!"
A BRAND-NEW FEATURE BEGINNING WITH THE MAY ISSUE OF ACTION COMICS!

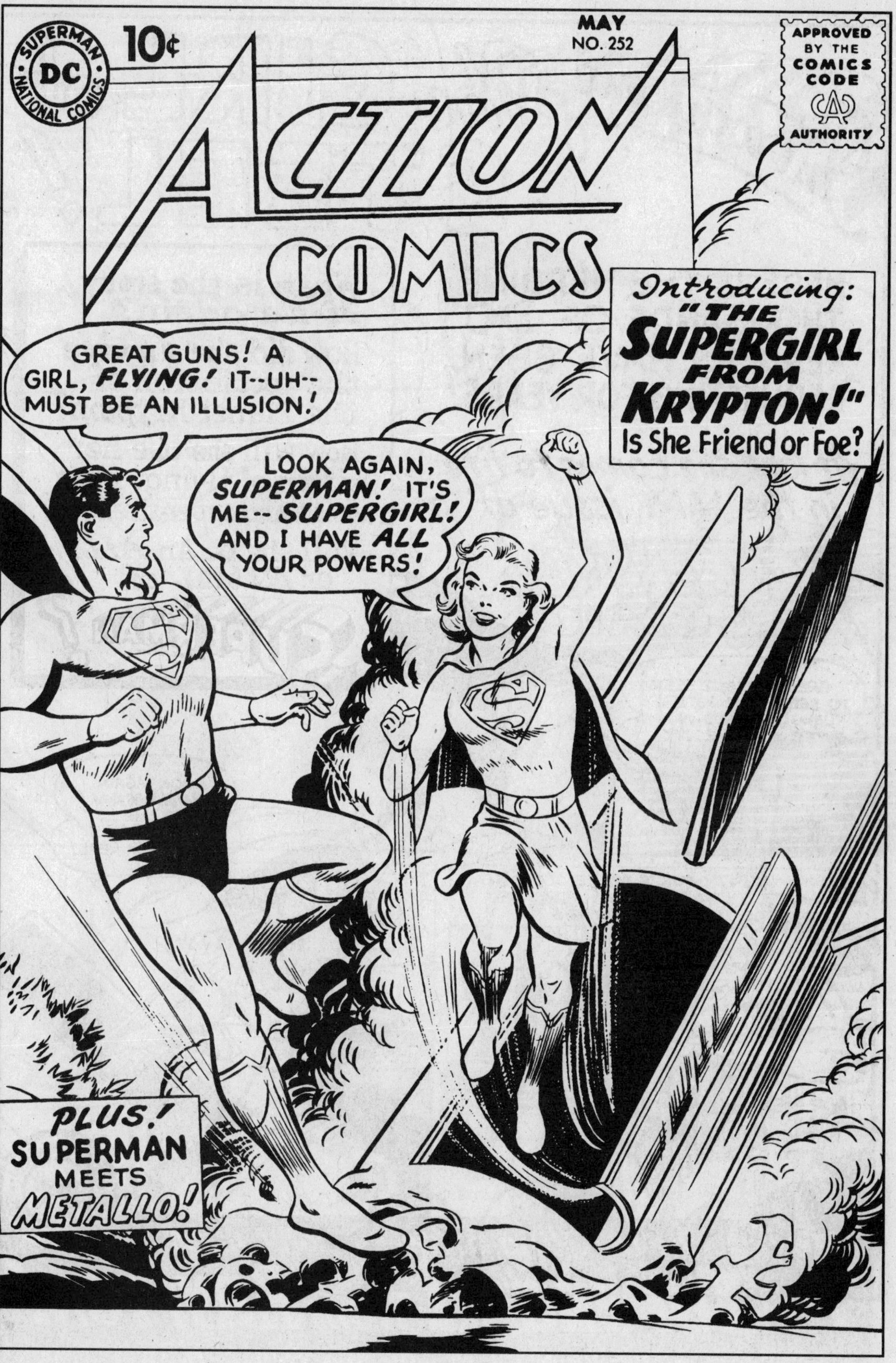
SUPERMAN DC NATIONAL COMICS
10¢
MAY
NO. 252
APPROVED BY THE COMICS CODE AUTHORITY
ACTION COMICS
Introducing: "THE SUPERGIRL FROM KRYPTON!" Is She Friend or Foe?
GREAT GUNS! A GIRL, FLYING! IT--UH--MUST BE AN ILLUSION!
LOOK AGAIN, SUPERMAN! IT'S ME--SUPERGIRL! AND I HAVE ALL YOUR POWERS!
PLUS! SUPERMAN MEETS METALLO!

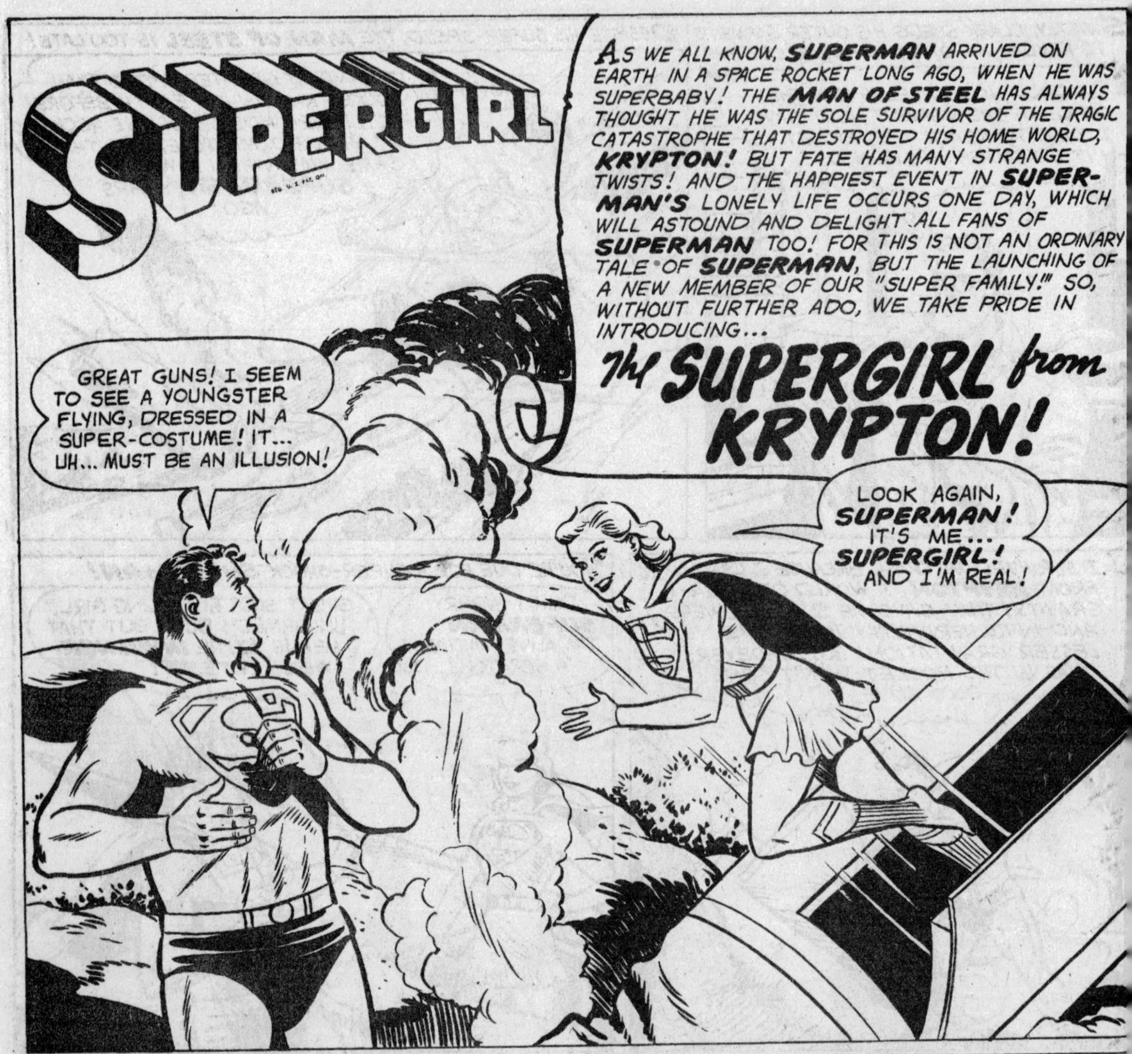
SUPERGIRL
AS WE ALL KNOW, SUPERMAN ARRIVED ON EARTH IN A SPACE ROCKET LONG AGO, WHEN HE WAS SUPERBABY! THE MAN OF STEEL HAS ALWAYS THOUGHT HE WAS THE SOLE SURVIVOR OF THE TRAGIC CATASTROPHE THAT DESTROYED HIS HOME WORLD, KRYPTON! BUT FATE HAS MANY STRANGE TWISTS! AND THE HAPPIEST EVENT IN SUPERMAN'S LONELY LIFE OCCURS ONE DAY, WHICH WILL ASTOUND AND DELIGHT ALL FANS OF SUPERMAN TOO! FOR THIS IS NOT AN ORDINARY TALE OF SUPERMAN, BUT THE LAUNCHING OF A NEW MEMBER OF OUR "SUPER FAMILY!" SO, WITHOUT FURTHER ADO, WE TAKE PRIDE IN INTRODUCING...
The SUPERGIRL from KRYPTON!
GREAT GUNS! I SEEM TO SEE A YOUNGSTER FLYING, DRESSED IN A SUPER-COSTUME! IT... UH... MUST BE AN ILLUSION!
LOOK AGAIN, SUPERMAN! IT'S ME... SUPERGIRL! AND I'M REAL!

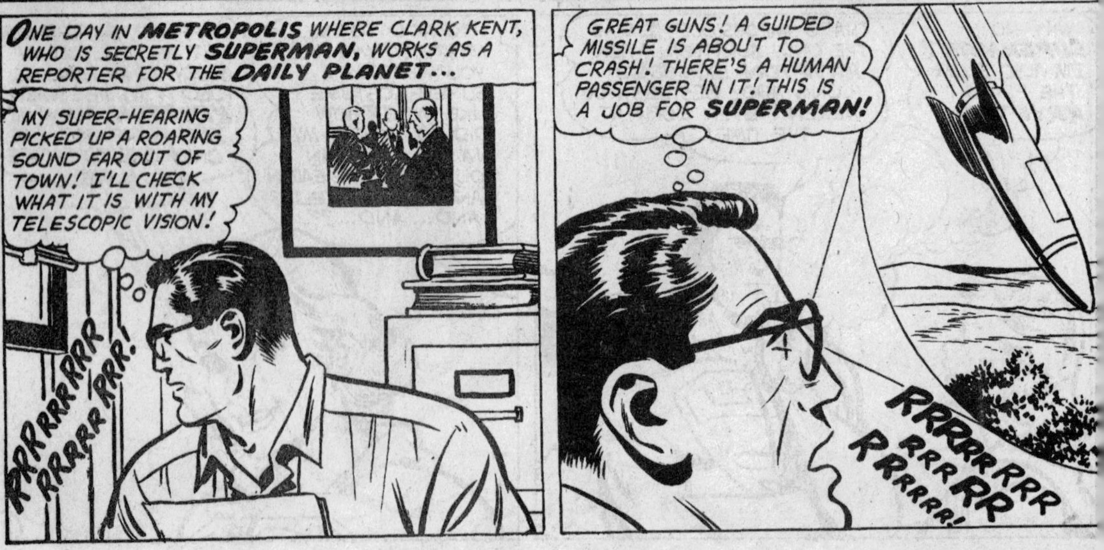
ONE DAY IN METROPOLIS WHERE CLARK KENT, WHO IS SECRETLY SUPERMAN, WORKS AS A REPORTER FOR THE DAILY PLANET...
MY SUPER-HEARING PICKED UP A ROARING SOUND FAR OUT OF TOWN! I'LL CHECK WHAT IT IS WITH MY TELESCOPIC VISION!
RRRRRRRRR RRRRRRRR!
GREAT GUNS! A GUIDED MISSILE IS ABOUT TO CRASH! THERE'S A HUMAN PASSENGER IN IT! THIS IS A JOB FOR SUPERMAN!
RRRRRRRRR RRRRRR RRrrrrr!

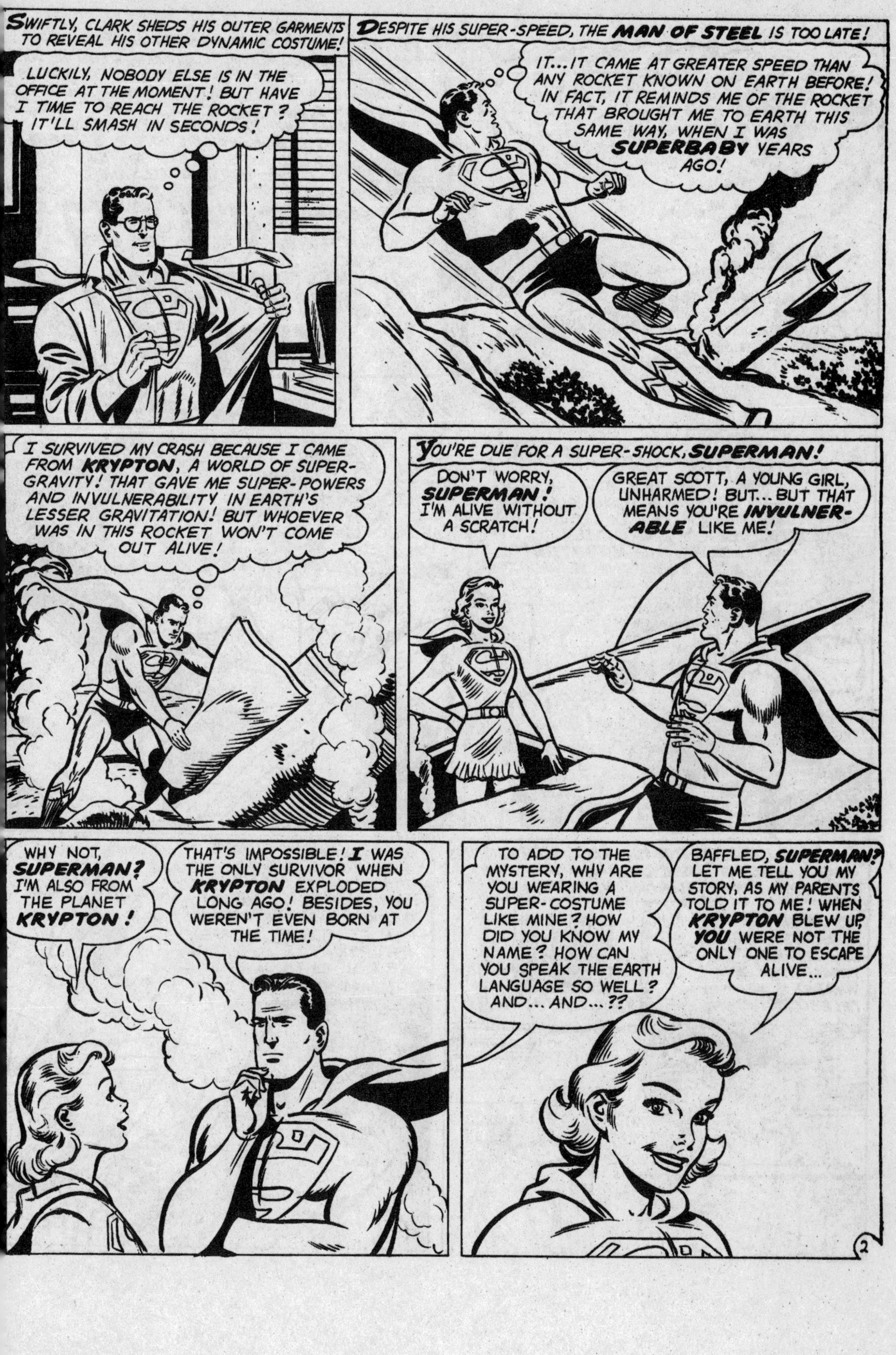
SWIFTLY, CLARK SHEDS HIS OUTER GARMENTS TO REVEAL HIS OTHER DYNAMIC COSTUME!
LUCKILY, NOBODY ELSE IS IN THE OFFICE AT THE MOMENT! BUT HAVE I TIME TO REACH THE ROCKET? IT'LL SMASH IN SECONDS!
DESPITE HIS SUPER-SPEED, THE MAN OF STEEL IS TOO LATE!
IT...IT CAME AT GREATER SPEED THAN ANY ROCKET KNOWN ON EARTH BEFORE! IN FACT, IT REMINDS ME OF THE ROCKET THAT BROUGHT ME TO EARTH THIS SAME WAY, WHEN I WAS SUPERBABY YEARS AGO!
I SURVIVED MY CRASH BECAUSE I CAME FROM KRYPTON, A WORLD OF SUPER-GRAVITY! THAT GAVE ME SUPER-POWERS AND INVULNERABILITY IN EARTH'S LESSER GRAVITATION! BUT WHOEVER WAS IN THIS ROCKET WON'T COME OUT ALIVE!
YOU'RE DUE FOR A SUPER-SHOCK, SUPERMAN!
DON'T WORRY, SUPERMAN! I'M ALIVE WITHOUT A SCRATCH!
GREAT SCOTT, A YOUNG GIRL, UNHARMED! BUT...BUT THAT MEANS YOU'RE INVULNERABLE LIKE ME!
WHY NOT, SUPERMAN? I'M ALSO FROM THE PLANET KRYPTON!
THAT'S IMPOSSIBLE! I WAS THE ONLY SURVIVOR WHEN KRYPTON EXPLODED LONG AGO! BESIDES, YOU WEREN'T EVEN BORN AT THE TIME!
TO ADD TO THE MYSTERY, WHY ARE YOU WEARING A SUPER-COSTUME LIKE MINE? HOW DID YOU KNOW MY NAME? HOW CAN YOU SPEAK THE EARTH LANGUAGE SO WELL? AND... AND...??
BAFFLED, SUPERMAN? LET ME TELL YOU MY STORY, AS MY PARENTS TOLD IT TO ME! WHEN KRYPTON BLEW UP, YOU WERE NOT THE ONLY ONE TO ESCAPE ALIVE...
2

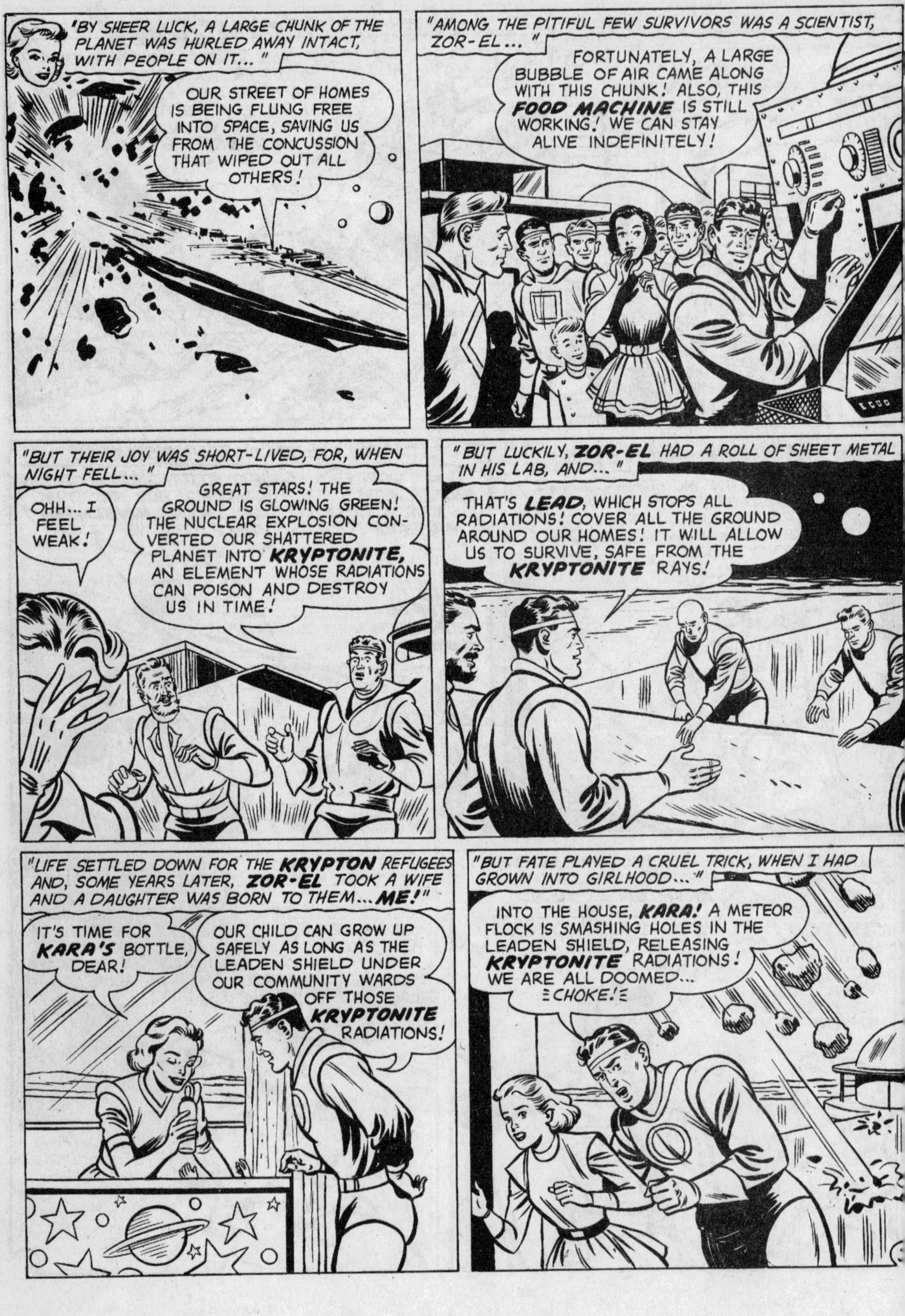
"BY SHEER LUCK, A LARGE CHUNK OF THE PLANET WAS HURLED AWAY INTACT, WITH PEOPLE ON IT..."
OUR STREET OF HOMES IS BEING FLUNG FREE INTO SPACE, SAVING US FROM THE CONCUSSION THAT WIPED OUT ALL OTHERS!
"AMONG THE PITIFUL FEW SURVIVORS WAS A SCIENTIST, ZOR-EL..."
FORTUNATELY, A LARGE BUBBLE OF AIR CAME ALONG WITH THIS CHUNK! ALSO, THIS FOOD MACHINE IS STILL WORKING! WE CAN STAY ALIVE INDEFINITELY!
"BUT THEIR JOY WAS SHORT-LIVED, FOR, WHEN NIGHT FELL..."
OHH... I FEEL WEAK!
GREAT STARS! THE GROUND IS GLOWING GREEN! THE NUCLEAR EXPLOSION CONVERTED OUR SHATTERED PLANET INTO KRYPTONITE, AN ELEMENT WHOSE RADIATIONS CAN POISON AND DESTROY US IN TIME!
"BUT LUCKILY, ZOR-EL HAD A ROLL OF SHEET METAL IN HIS LAB, AND..."
THAT'S LEAD, WHICH STOPS ALL RADIATIONS! COVER ALL THE GROUND AROUND OUR HOMES! IT WILL ALLOW US TO SURVIVE, SAFE FROM THE KRYPTONITE RAYS!
"LIFE SETTLED DOWN FOR THE KRYPTON REFUGEES AND, SOME YEARS LATER, ZOR-EL TOOK A WIFE AND A DAUGHTER WAS BORN TO THEM... ME!"
IT'S TIME FOR KARA'S BOTTLE, DEAR!
OUR CHILD CAN GROW UP SAFELY AS LONG AS THE LEADEN SHIELD UNDER OUR COMMUNITY WARDS OFF THOSE KRYPTONITE RADIATIONS!
"BUT FATE PLAYED A CRUEL TRICK, WHEN I HAD GROWN INTO GIRLHOOD..."
INTO THE HOUSE, KARA! A METEOR FLOCK IS SMASHING HOLES IN THE LEADEN SHIELD, RELEASING KRYPTONITE RADIATIONS! WE ARE ALL DOOMED... CHOKE!

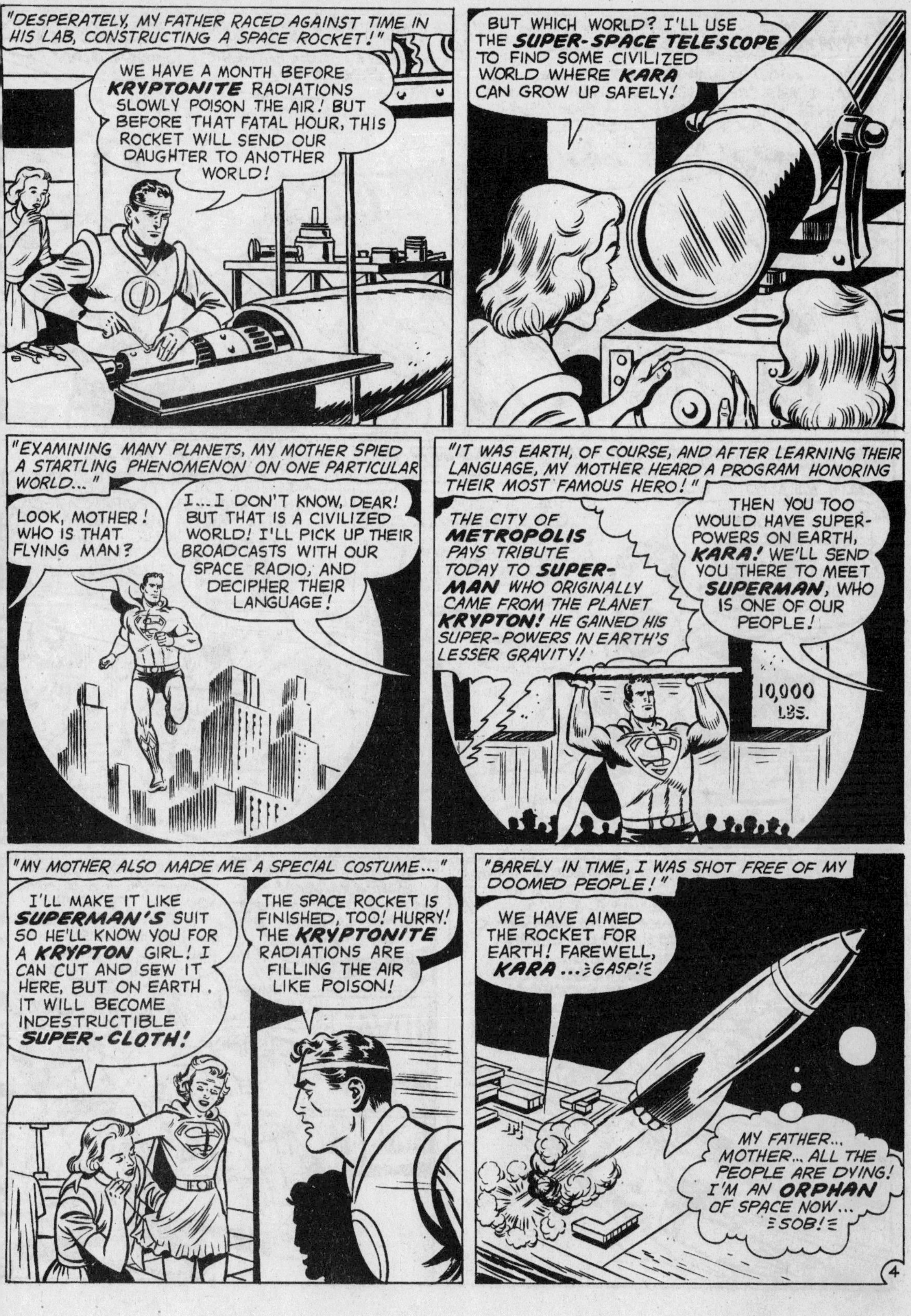
"DESPERATELY, MY FATHER RACED AGAINST TIME IN HIS LAB, CONSTRUCTING A SPACE ROCKET!"
WE HAVE A MONTH BEFORE KRYPTONITE RADIATIONS SLOWLY POISON THE AIR! BUT BEFORE THAT FATAL HOUR, THIS ROCKET WILL SEND OUR DAUGHTER TO ANOTHER WORLD!
BUT WHICH WORLD? I'LL USE THE SUPER-SPACE TELESCOPE TO FIND SOME CIVILIZED WORLD WHERE KARA CAN GROW UP SAFELY!
"EXAMINING MANY PLANETS, MY MOTHER SPIED A STARTLING PHENOMENON ON ONE PARTICULAR WORLD..."
LOOK, MOTHER! WHO IS THAT FLYING MAN?
I... I DON'T KNOW, DEAR! BUT THAT IS A CIVILIZED WORLD! I'LL PICK UP THEIR BROADCASTS WITH OUR SPACE RADIO, AND DECIPHER THEIR LANGUAGE!
"IT WAS EARTH, OF COURSE, AND AFTER LEARNING THEIR LANGUAGE, MY MOTHER HEARD A PROGRAM HONORING THEIR MOST FAMOUS HERO!"
THE CITY OF METROPOLIS PAYS TRIBUTE TODAY TO SUPERMAN WHO ORIGINALLY CAME FROM THE PLANET KRYPTON! HE GAINED HIS SUPER-POWERS IN EARTH'S LESSER GRAVITY!
THEN YOU TOO WOULD HAVE SUPER-POWERS ON EARTH, KARA! WE'LL SEND YOU THERE TO MEET SUPERMAN, WHO IS ONE OF OUR PEOPLE!
10,000 LBS.
"MY MOTHER ALSO MADE ME A SPECIAL COSTUME..."
I'LL MAKE IT LIKE SUPERMAN'S SUIT SO HE'LL KNOW YOU FOR A KRYPTON GIRL! I CAN CUT AND SEW IT HERE, BUT ON EARTH IT WILL BECOME INDESTRUCTIBLE SUPER-CLOTH!
THE SPACE ROCKET IS FINISHED, TOO! HURRY! THE KRYPTONITE RADIATIONS ARE FILLING THE AIR LIKE POISON!
"BARELY IN TIME, I WAS SHOT FREE OF MY DOOMED PEOPLE!"
WE HAVE AIMED THE ROCKET FOR EARTH! FAREWELL, KARA ... GASP!
MY FATHER... MOTHER... ALL THE PEOPLE ARE DYING! I'M AN ORPHAN OF SPACE NOW... SOB!
4

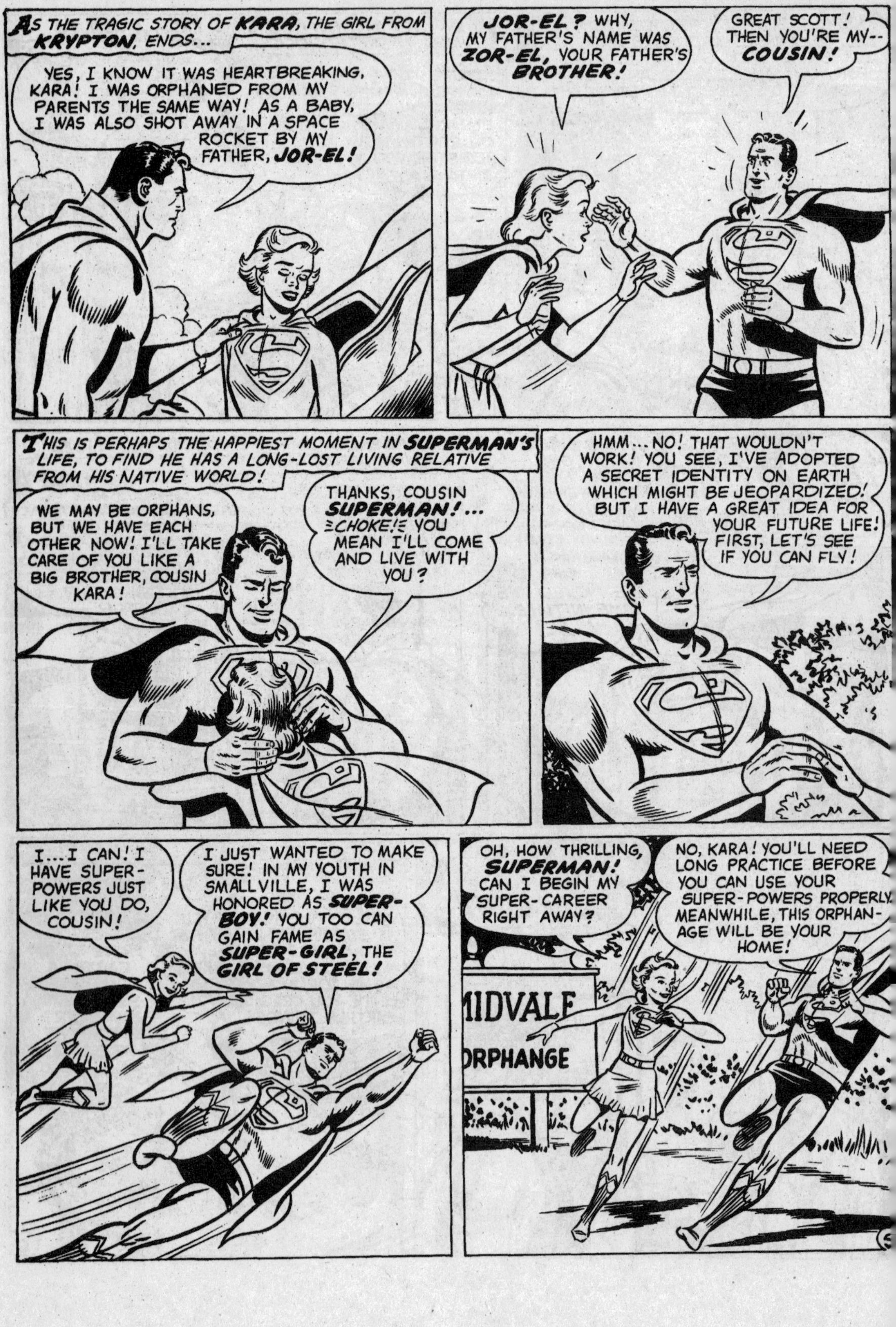
AS THE TRAGIC STORY OF KARA, THE GIRL FROM KRYPTON, ENDS...
YES, I KNOW IT WAS HEARTBREAKING, KARA! I WAS ORPHANED FROM MY PARENTS THE SAME WAY! AS A BABY, I WAS ALSO SHOT AWAY IN A SPACE ROCKET BY MY FATHER, JOR-EL!
JOR-EL? WHY, MY FATHER'S NAME WAS ZOR-EL, YOUR FATHER'S BROTHER!
GREAT SCOTT! THEN YOU'RE MY-- COUSIN!
THIS IS PERHAPS THE HAPPIEST MOMENT IN SUPERMAN'S LIFE, TO FIND HE HAS A LONG-LOST LIVING RELATIVE FROM HIS NATIVE WORLD!
WE MAY BE ORPHANS, BUT WE HAVE EACH OTHER NOW! I'LL TAKE CARE OF YOU LIKE A BIG BROTHER, COUSIN KARA!
THANKS, COUSIN SUPERMAN!... CHOKE! YOU MEAN I'LL COME AND LIVE WITH YOU?
HMM... NO! THAT WOULDN'T WORK! YOU SEE, I'VE ADOPTED A SECRET IDENTITY ON EARTH WHICH MIGHT BE JEOPARDIZED! BUT I HAVE A GREAT IDEA FOR YOUR FUTURE LIFE! FIRST, LET'S SEE IF YOU CAN FLY!
I...I CAN! I HAVE SUPER-POWERS JUST LIKE YOU DO, COUSIN!
I JUST WANTED TO MAKE SURE! IN MY YOUTH IN SMALLVILLE, I WAS HONORED AS SUPER-BOY! YOU TOO CAN GAIN FAME AS SUPER-GIRL, THE GIRL OF STEEL!
OH, HOW THRILLING, SUPERMAN! CAN I BEGIN MY SUPER-CAREER RIGHT AWAY?
NO, KARA! YOU'LL NEED LONG PRACTICE BEFORE YOU CAN USE YOUR SUPER-POWERS PROPERLY. MEANWHILE, THIS ORPHAN-AGE WILL BE YOUR HOME!
MIDVALE
ORPHANGE

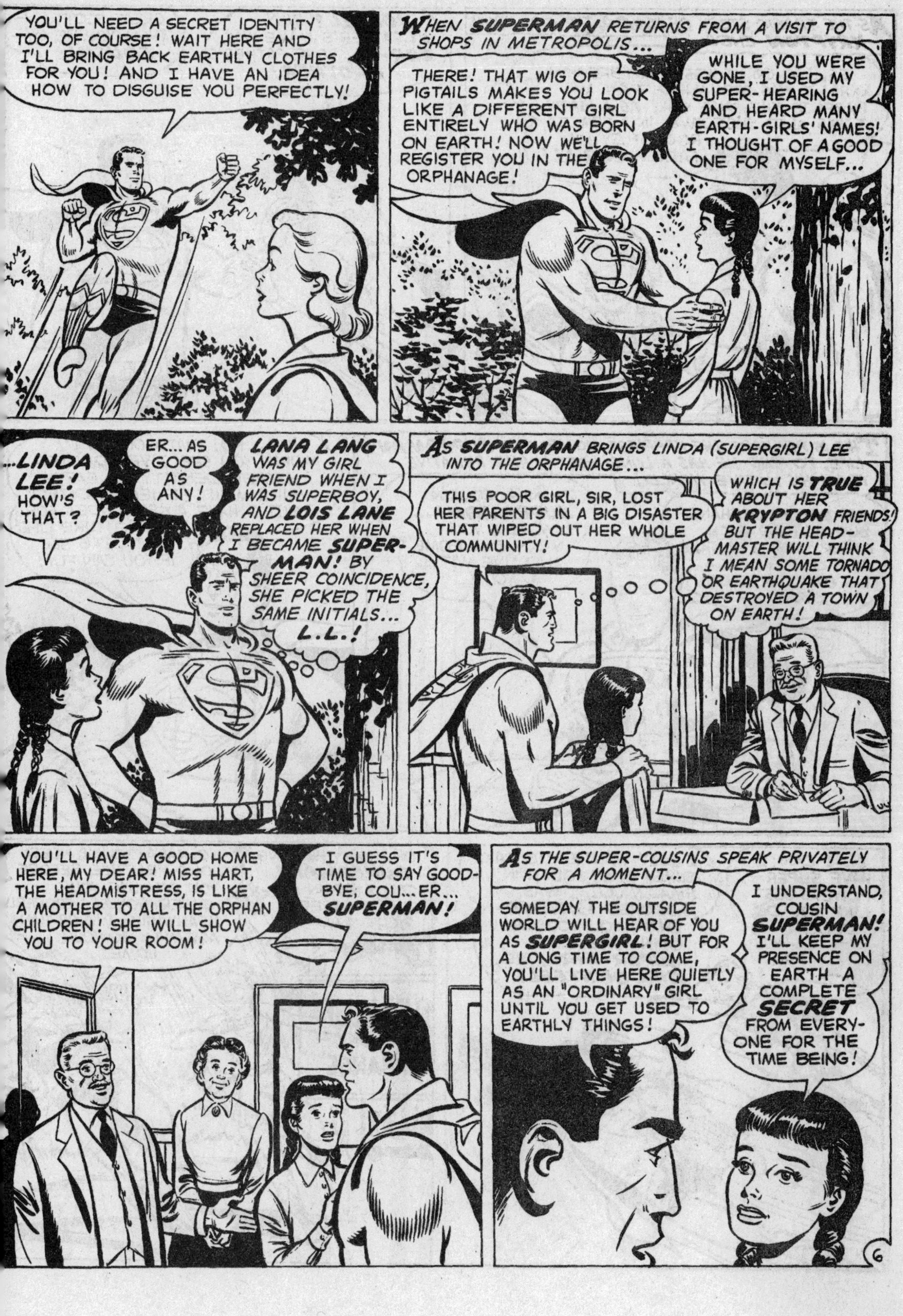
YOU'LL NEED A SECRET IDENTITY TOO, OF COURSE! WAIT HERE AND I'LL BRING BACK EARTHLY CLOTHES FOR YOU! AND I HAVE AN IDEA HOW TO DISGUISE YOU PERFECTLY!
WHEN SUPERMAN RETURNS FROM A VISIT TO SHOPS IN METROPOLIS...
THERE! THAT WIG OF PIGTAILS MAKES YOU LOOK LIKE A DIFFERENT GIRL ENTIRELY WHO WAS BORN ON EARTH! NOW WE'LL REGISTER YOU IN THE ORPHANAGE!
WHILE YOU WERE GONE, I USED MY SUPER-HEARING AND HEARD MANY EARTH-GIRLS' NAMES! I THOUGHT OF A GOOD ONE FOR MYSELF...
...LINDA LEE! HOW'S THAT?
ER... AS GOOD AS ANY!
LANA LANG WAS MY GIRL FRIEND WHEN I WAS SUPERBOY, AND LOIS LANE REPLACED HER WHEN I BECAME SUPERMAN! BY SHEER COINCIDENCE, SHE PICKED THE SAME INITIALS... L.L.!
AS SUPERMAN BRINGS LINDA (SUPERGIRL) LEE INTO THE ORPHANAGE...
THIS POOR GIRL, SIR, LOST HER PARENTS IN A BIG DISASTER THAT WIPED OUT HER WHOLE COMMUNITY!
WHICH IS TRUE ABOUT HER KRYPTON FRIENDS! BUT THE HEADMASTER WILL THINK I MEAN SOME TORNADO OR EARTHQUAKE THAT DESTROYED A TOWN ON EARTH!
YOU'LL HAVE A GOOD HOME HERE, MY DEAR! MISS HART, THE HEADMISTRESS, IS LIKE A MOTHER TO ALL THE ORPHAN CHILDREN! SHE WILL SHOW YOU TO YOUR ROOM!
I GUESS IT'S TIME TO SAY GOOD-BYE, COU... ER... SUPERMAN!
AS THE SUPER-COUSINS SPEAK PRIVATELY FOR A MOMENT...
SOMEDAY THE OUTSIDE WORLD WILL HEAR OF YOU AS SUPERGIRL! BUT FOR A LONG TIME TO COME, YOU'LL LIVE HERE QUIETLY AS AN "ORDINARY" GIRL UNTIL YOU GET USED TO EARTHLY THINGS!
I UNDERSTAND, COUSIN SUPERMAN! I'LL KEEP MY PRESENCE ON EARTH A COMPLETE SECRET FROM EVERYONE FOR THE TIME BEING!
6

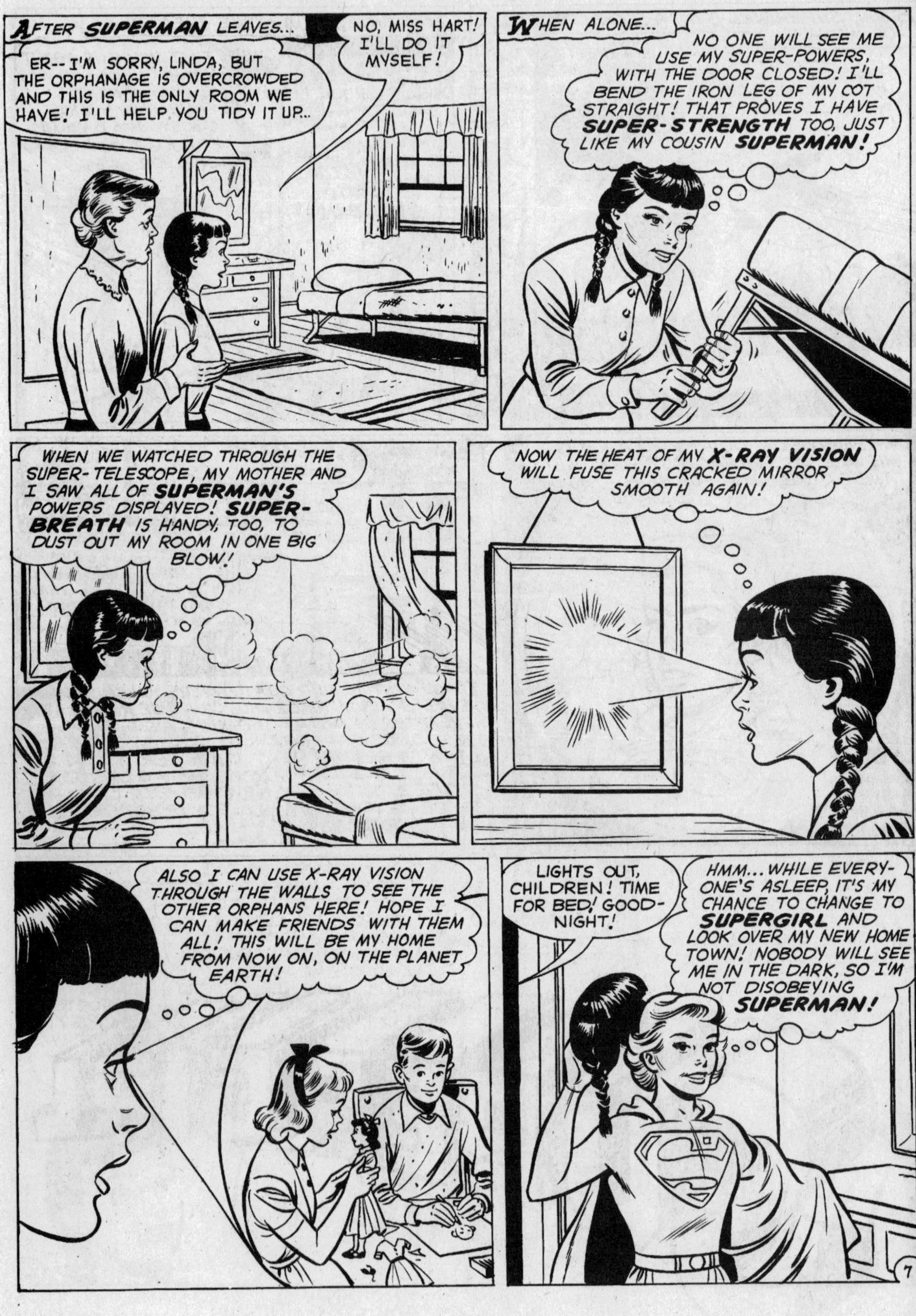
AFTER SUPERMAN LEAVES...
ER-- I'M SORRY, LINDA, BUT THE ORPHANAGE IS OVERCROWDED AND THIS IS THE ONLY ROOM WE HAVE! I'LL HELP YOU TIDY IT UP..
NO, MISS HART! I'LL DO IT MYSELF!
WHEN ALONE...
NO ONE WILL SEE ME USE MY SUPER-POWERS, WITH THE DOOR CLOSED! I'LL BEND THE IRON LEG OF MY COT STRAIGHT! THAT PROVES I HAVE SUPER-STRENGTH TOO, JUST LIKE MY COUSIN SUPERMAN!
WHEN WE WATCHED THROUGH THE SUPER-TELESCOPE, MY MOTHER AND I SAW ALL OF SUPERMAN'S POWERS DISPLAYED! SUPER-BREATH IS HANDY, TOO, TO DUST OUT MY ROOM IN ONE BIG BLOW!
NOW THE HEAT OF MY X-RAY VISION WILL FUSE THIS CRACKED MIRROR SMOOTH AGAIN!
ALSO I CAN USE X-RAY VISION THROUGH THE WALLS TO SEE THE OTHER ORPHANS HERE! HOPE I CAN MAKE FRIENDS WITH THEM ALL! THIS WILL BE MY HOME FROM NOW ON, ON THE PLANET EARTH!
LIGHTS OUT, CHILDREN! TIME FOR BED! GOOD-NIGHT!
HMM... WHILE EVERY-ONE'S ASLEEP, IT'S MY CHANCE TO CHANGE TO SUPERGIRL AND LOOK OVER MY NEW HOME TOWN! NOBODY WILL SEE ME IN THE DARK, SO I'M NOT DISOBEYING SUPERMAN!
7

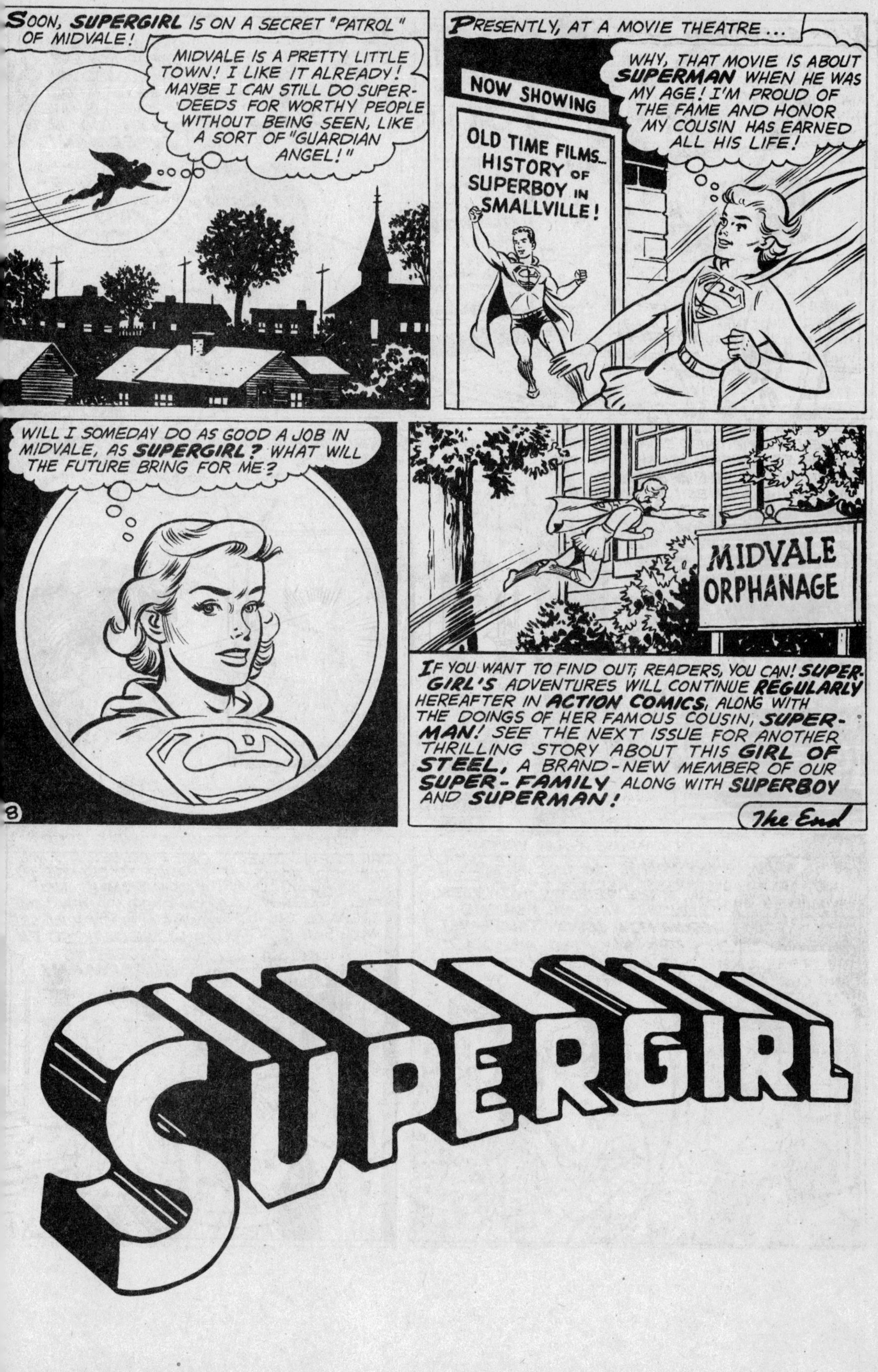
SOON, SUPERGIRL IS ON A SECRET "PATROL" OF MIDVALE!
MIDVALE IS A PRETTY LITTLE TOWN! I LIKE IT ALREADY! MAYBE I CAN STILL DO SUPER-DEEDS FOR WORTHY PEOPLE WITHOUT BEING SEEN, LIKE A SORT OF "GUARDIAN ANGEL!"
PRESENTLY, AT A MOVIE THEATRE...
NOW SHOWING
OLD TIME FILMS... HISTORY OF SUPERBOY IN SMALLVILLE!
WHY, THAT MOVIE IS ABOUT SUPERMAN WHEN HE WAS MY AGE! I'M PROUD OF THE FAME AND HONOR MY COUSIN HAS EARNED ALL HIS LIFE!
WILL I SOMEDAY DO AS GOOD A JOB IN MIDVALE, AS SUPERGIRL? WHAT WILL THE FUTURE BRING FOR ME?
8
MIDVALE ORPHANAGE
IF YOU WANT TO FIND OUT, READERS, YOU CAN! SUPERGIRL'S ADVENTURES WILL CONTINUE REGULARLY HEREAFTER IN ACTION COMICS, ALONG WITH THE DOINGS OF HER FAMOUS COUSIN, SUPERMAN! SEE THE NEXT ISSUE FOR ANOTHER THRILLING STORY ABOUT THIS GIRL OF STEEL, A BRAND-NEW MEMBER OF OUR SUPER-FAMILY ALONG WITH SUPERBOY AND SUPERMAN!
The End

SUPERGIRL

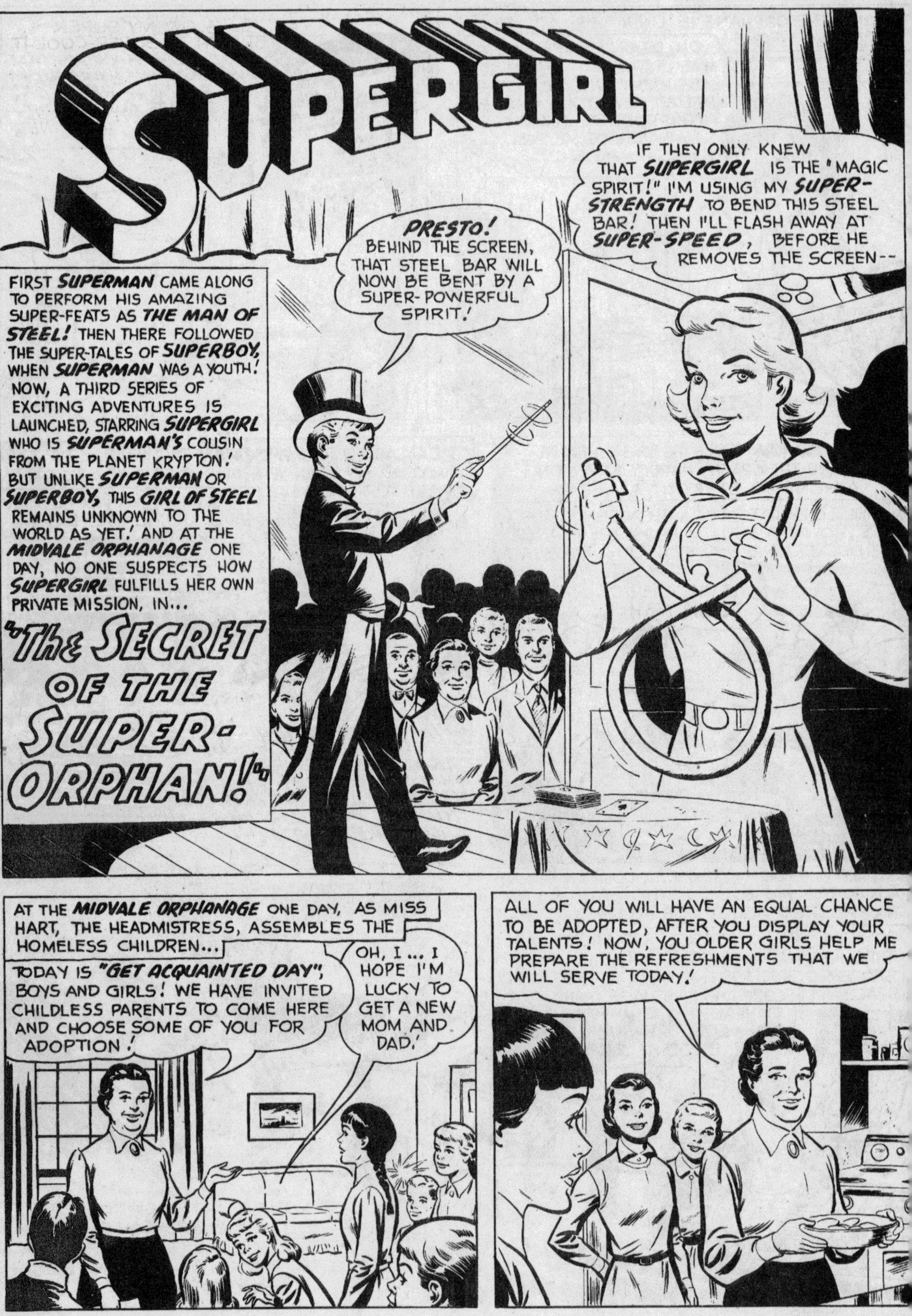
SUPERGIRL
FIRST SUPERMAN CAME ALONG TO PERFORM HIS AMAZING SUPER-FEATS AS THE MAN OF STEEL! THEN THERE FOLLOWED THE SUPER-TALES OF SUPERBOY, WHEN SUPERMAN WAS A YOUTH! NOW, A THIRD SERIES OF EXCITING ADVENTURES IS LAUNCHED, STARRING SUPERGIRL WHO IS SUPERMAN'S COUSIN FROM THE PLANET KRYPTON! BUT UNLIKE SUPERMAN OR SUPERBOY, THIS GIRL OF STEEL REMAINS UNKNOWN TO THE WORLD AS YET! AND AT THE MIDVALE ORPHANAGE ONE DAY, NO ONE SUSPECTS HOW SUPERGIRL FULFILLS HER OWN PRIVATE MISSION, IN...
"The SECRET OF THE SUPER-ORPHAN!"
PRESTO! BEHIND THE SCREEN, THAT STEEL BAR WILL NOW BE BENT BY A SUPER-POWERFUL SPIRIT!
IF THEY ONLY KNEW THAT SUPERGIRL IS THE "MAGIC SPIRIT!" I'M USING MY SUPER-STRENGTH TO BEND THIS STEEL BAR! THEN I'LL FLASH AWAY AT SUPER-SPEED, BEFORE HE REMOVES THE SCREEN--
AT THE MIDVALE ORPHANAGE ONE DAY, AS MISS HART, THE HEADMISTRESS, ASSEMBLES THE HOMELESS CHILDREN...
TODAY IS "GET ACQUAINTED DAY", BOYS AND GIRLS! WE HAVE INVITED CHILDLESS PARENTS TO COME HERE AND CHOOSE SOME OF YOU FOR ADOPTION!
OH, I ... I HOPE I'M LUCKY TO GET A NEW MOM AND DAD!
ALL OF YOU WILL HAVE AN EQUAL CHANCE TO BE ADOPTED, AFTER YOU DISPLAY YOUR TALENTS! NOW, YOU OLDER GIRLS HELP ME PREPARE THE REFRESHMENTS THAT WE WILL SERVE TODAY!

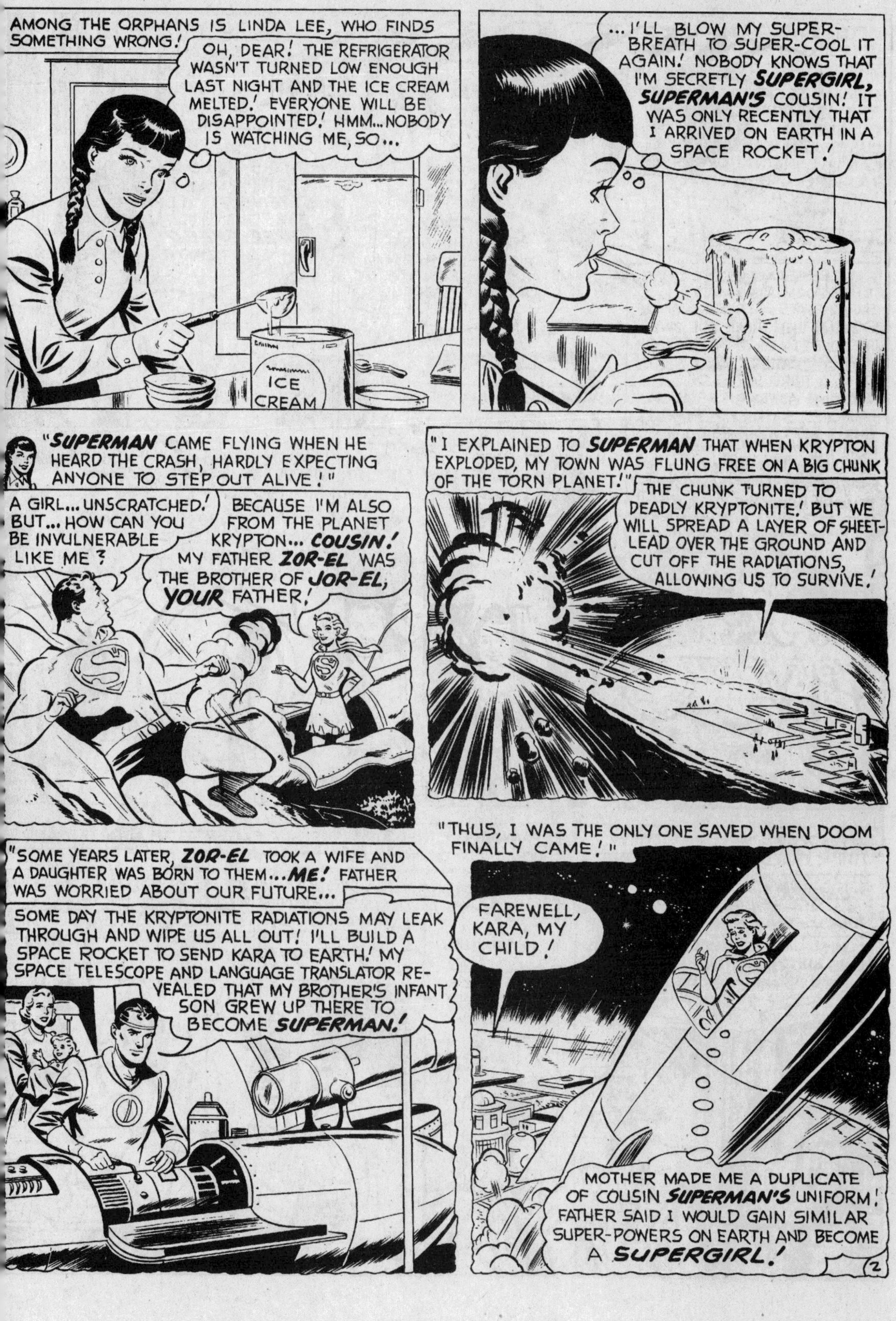
AMONG THE ORPHANS IS LINDA LEE, WHO FINDS SOMETHING WRONG!
OH, DEAR! THE REFRIGERATOR WASN'T TURNED LOW ENOUGH LAST NIGHT AND THE ICE CREAM MELTED! EVERYONE WILL BE DISAPPOINTED! HMM...NOBODY IS WATCHING ME, SO...
ICE CREAM
...I'LL BLOW MY SUPER-BREATH TO SUPER-COOL IT AGAIN! NOBODY KNOWS THAT I'M SECRETLY SUPERGIRL, SUPERMAN'S COUSIN! IT WAS ONLY RECENTLY THAT I ARRIVED ON EARTH IN A SPACE ROCKET!
"SUPERMAN CAME FLYING WHEN HE HEARD THE CRASH, HARDLY EXPECTING ANYONE TO STEP OUT ALIVE!"
A GIRL...UNSCRATCHED! BUT...HOW CAN YOU BE INVULNERABLE LIKE ME?
BECAUSE I'M ALSO FROM THE PLANET KRYPTON... COUSIN! MY FATHER ZOR-EL WAS THE BROTHER OF JOR-EL, YOUR FATHER!
"I EXPLAINED TO SUPERMAN THAT WHEN KRYPTON EXPLODED, MY TOWN WAS FLUNG FREE ON A BIG CHUNK OF THE TORN PLANET!"
THE CHUNK TURNED TO DEADLY KRYPTONITE! BUT WE WILL SPREAD A LAYER OF SHEET-LEAD OVER THE GROUND AND CUT OFF THE RADIATIONS, ALLOWING US TO SURVIVE!
"SOME YEARS LATER, ZOR-EL TOOK A WIFE AND A DAUGHTER WAS BORN TO THEM...ME! FATHER WAS WORRIED ABOUT OUR FUTURE...
SOME DAY THE KRYPTONITE RADIATIONS MAY LEAK THROUGH AND WIPE US ALL OUT! I'LL BUILD A SPACE ROCKET TO SEND KARA TO EARTH! MY SPACE TELESCOPE AND LANGUAGE TRANSLATOR REVEALED THAT MY BROTHER'S INFANT SON GREW UP THERE TO BECOME SUPERMAN!
"THUS, I WAS THE ONLY ONE SAVED WHEN DOOM FINALLY CAME!"
FAREWELL, KARA, MY CHILD!
MOTHER MADE ME A DUPLICATE OF COUSIN SUPERMAN'S UNIFORM! FATHER SAID I WOULD GAIN SIMILAR SUPER-POWERS ON EARTH AND BECOME A SUPERGIRL!
2

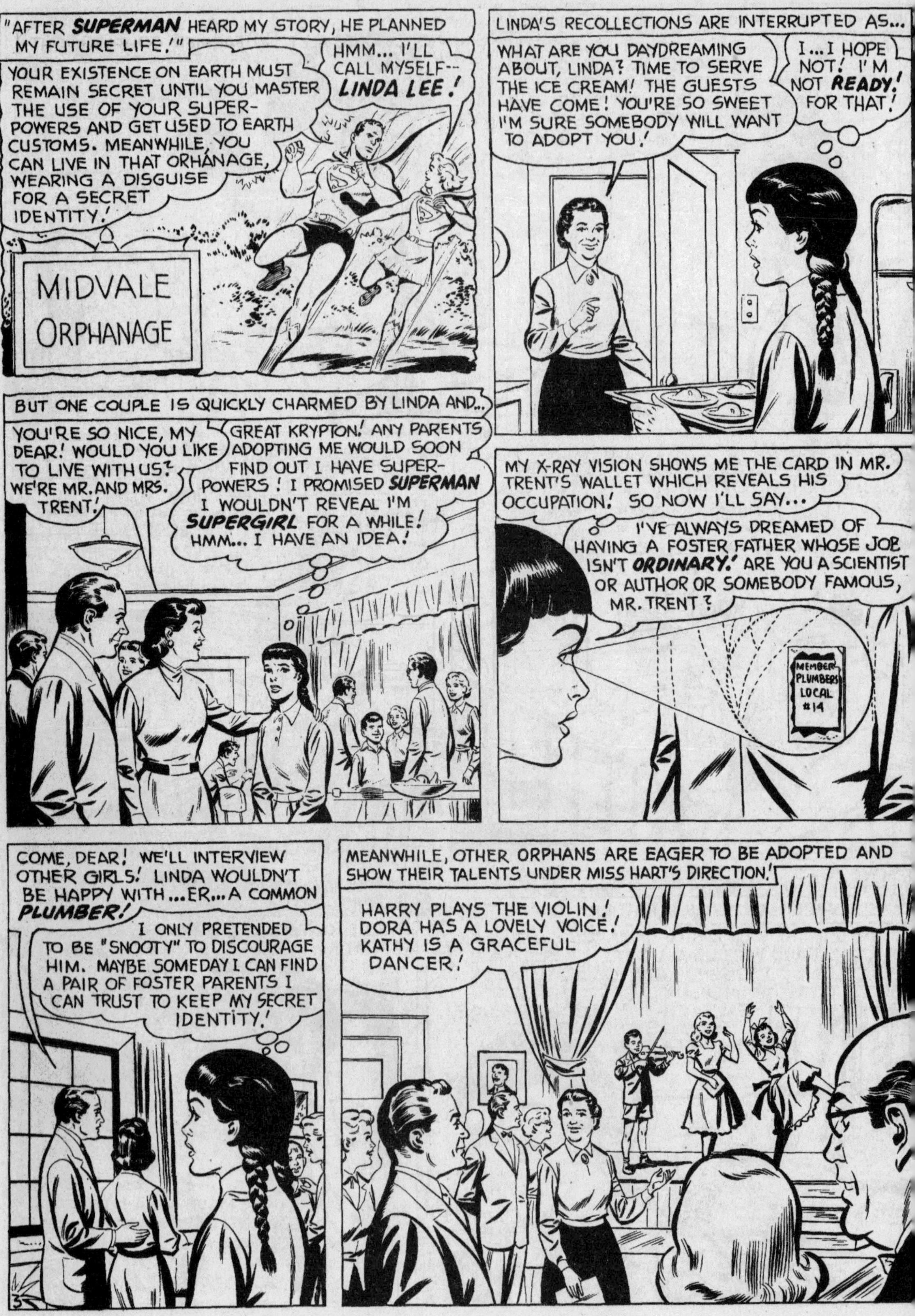
"AFTER SUPERMAN HEARD MY STORY, HE PLANNED MY FUTURE LIFE!"
YOUR EXISTENCE ON EARTH MUST REMAIN SECRET UNTIL YOU MASTER THE USE OF YOUR SUPER-POWERS AND GET USED TO EARTH CUSTOMS. MEANWHILE, YOU CAN LIVE IN THAT ORHANAGE, WEARING A DISGUISE FOR A SECRET IDENTITY!
HMM... I'LL CALL MYSELF-- LINDA LEE!
MIDVALE ORPHANAGE
LINDA'S RECOLLECTIONS ARE INTERRUPTED AS...
WHAT ARE YOU DAYDREAMING ABOUT, LINDA? TIME TO SERVE THE ICE CREAM! THE GUESTS HAVE COME! YOU'RE SO SWEET I'M SURE SOMEBODY WILL WANT TO ADOPT YOU!
I...I HOPE NOT! I'M NOT READY! FOR THAT!
BUT ONE COUPLE IS QUICKLY CHARMED BY LINDA AND...
YOU'RE SO NICE, MY DEAR! WOULD YOU LIKE TO LIVE WITH US? WE'RE MR. AND MRS. TRENT!
GREAT KRYPTON! ANY PARENTS ADOPTING ME WOULD SOON FIND OUT I HAVE SUPER-POWERS! I PROMISED SUPERMAN I WOULDN'T REVEAL I'M SUPERGIRL FOR A WHILE! HMM... I HAVE AN IDEA!
MY X-RAY VISION SHOWS ME THE CARD IN MR. TRENT'S WALLET WHICH REVEALS HIS OCCUPATION! SO NOW I'LL SAY...
I'VE ALWAYS DREAMED OF HAVING A FOSTER FATHER WHOSE JOB ISN'T ORDINARY! ARE YOU A SCIENTIST OR AUTHOR OR SOMEBODY FAMOUS, MR. TRENT?
MEMBER PLUMBERS LOCAL #14
COME, DEAR! WE'LL INTERVIEW OTHER GIRLS! LINDA WOULDN'T BE HAPPY WITH...ER...A COMMON PLUMBER!
I ONLY PRETENDED TO BE "SNOOTY" TO DISCOURAGE HIM. MAYBE SOMEDAY I CAN FIND A PAIR OF FOSTER PARENTS I CAN TRUST TO KEEP MY SECRET IDENTITY!
3
MEANWHILE, OTHER ORPHANS ARE EAGER TO BE ADOPTED AND SHOW THEIR TALENTS UNDER MISS HART'S DIRECTION!
HARRY PLAYS THE VIOLIN! DORA HAS A LOVELY VOICE! KATHY IS A GRACEFUL DANCER!

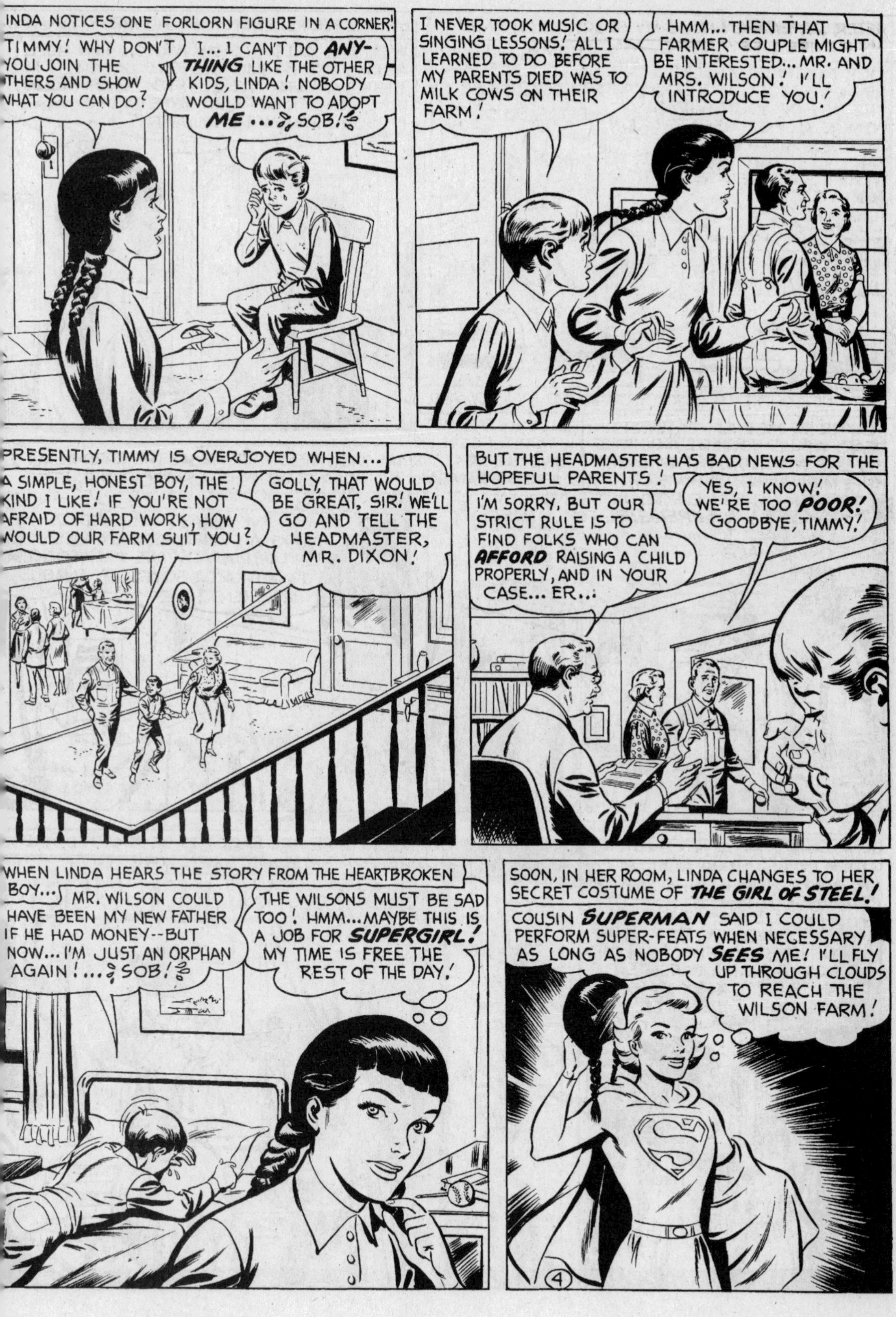
INDA NOTICES ONE FORLORN FIGURE IN A CORNER!
TIMMY! WHY DON'T YOU JOIN THE THERS AND SHOW HAT YOU CAN DO?
I... I CAN'T DO ANY-THING LIKE THE OTHER KIDS, LINDA! NOBODY WOULD WANT TO ADOPT ME... SOB!
I NEVER TOOK MUSIC OR SINGING LESSONS! ALL I LEARNED TO DO BEFORE MY PARENTS DIED WAS TO MILK COWS ON THEIR FARM!
HMM... THEN THAT FARMER COUPLE MIGHT BE INTERESTED... MR. AND MRS. WILSON! I'LL INTRODUCE YOU!
PRESENTLY, TIMMY IS OVERJOYED WHEN...
A SIMPLE, HONEST BOY, THE KIND I LIKE! IF YOU'RE NOT AFRAID OF HARD WORK, HOW WOULD OUR FARM SUIT YOU?
GOLLY, THAT WOULD BE GREAT, SIR! WE'LL GO AND TELL THE HEADMASTER, MR. DIXON!
BUT THE HEADMASTER HAS BAD NEWS FOR THE HOPEFUL PARENTS!
I'M SORRY, BUT OUR STRICT RULE IS TO FIND FOLKS WHO CAN AFFORD RAISING A CHILD PROPERLY, AND IN YOUR CASE... ER...!
YES, I KNOW! WE'RE TOO POOR! GOODBYE, TIMMY!
WHEN LINDA HEARS THE STORY FROM THE HEARTBROKEN BOY...
MR. WILSON COULD HAVE BEEN MY NEW FATHER IF HE HAD MONEY--BUT NOW... I'M JUST AN ORPHAN AGAIN!... SOB!
THE WILSONS MUST BE SAD TOO! HMM... MAYBE THIS IS A JOB FOR SUPERGIRL! MY TIME IS FREE THE REST OF THE DAY!
SOON, IN HER ROOM, LINDA CHANGES TO HER SECRET COSTUME OF THE GIRL OF STEEL!
COUSIN SUPERMAN SAID I COULD PERFORM SUPER-FEATS WHEN NECESSARY AS LONG AS NOBODY SEES ME! I'LL FLY UP THROUGH CLOUDS TO REACH THE WILSON FARM!
4

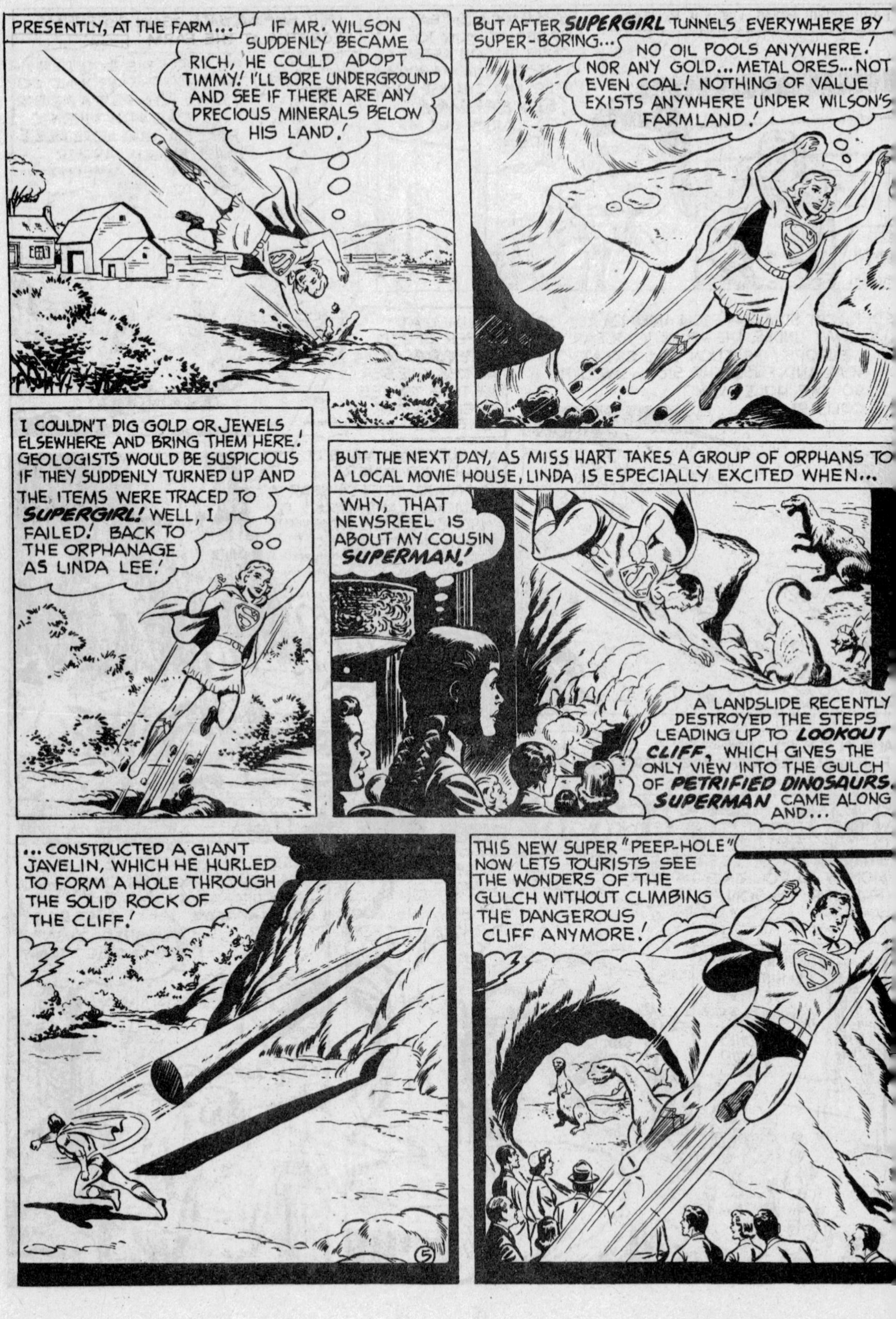
PRESENTLY, AT THE FARM...
IF MR. WILSON SUDDENLY BECAME RICH, HE COULD ADOPT TIMMY! I'LL BORE UNDERGROUND AND SEE IF THERE ARE ANY PRECIOUS MINERALS BELOW HIS LAND!
BUT AFTER SUPERGIRL TUNNELS EVERYWHERE BY SUPER-BORING...
NO OIL POOLS ANYWHERE! NOR ANY GOLD... METAL ORES... NOT EVEN COAL! NOTHING OF VALUE EXISTS ANYWHERE UNDER WILSON'S FARMLAND!
I COULDN'T DIG GOLD OR JEWELS ELSEWHERE AND BRING THEM HERE! GEOLOGISTS WOULD BE SUSPICIOUS IF THEY SUDDENLY TURNED UP AND THE ITEMS WERE TRACED TO SUPERGIRL! WELL, I FAILED! BACK TO THE ORPHANAGE AS LINDA LEE!
BUT THE NEXT DAY, AS MISS HART TAKES A GROUP OF ORPHANS TO A LOCAL MOVIE HOUSE, LINDA IS ESPECIALLY EXCITED WHEN...
WHY, THAT NEWSREEL IS ABOUT MY COUSIN SUPERMAN!
A LANDSLIDE RECENTLY DESTROYED THE STEPS LEADING UP TO LOOKOUT CLIFF, WHICH GIVES THE ONLY VIEW INTO THE GULCH OF PETRIFIED DINOSAURS. SUPERMAN CAME ALONG AND...
...CONSTRUCTED A GIANT JAVELIN, WHICH HE HURLED TO FORM A HOLE THROUGH THE SOLID ROCK OF THE CLIFF!
5
THIS NEW SUPER "PEEP-HOLE" NOW LETS TOURISTS SEE THE WONDERS OF THE GULCH WITHOUT CLIMBING THE DANGEROUS CLIFF ANYMORE!

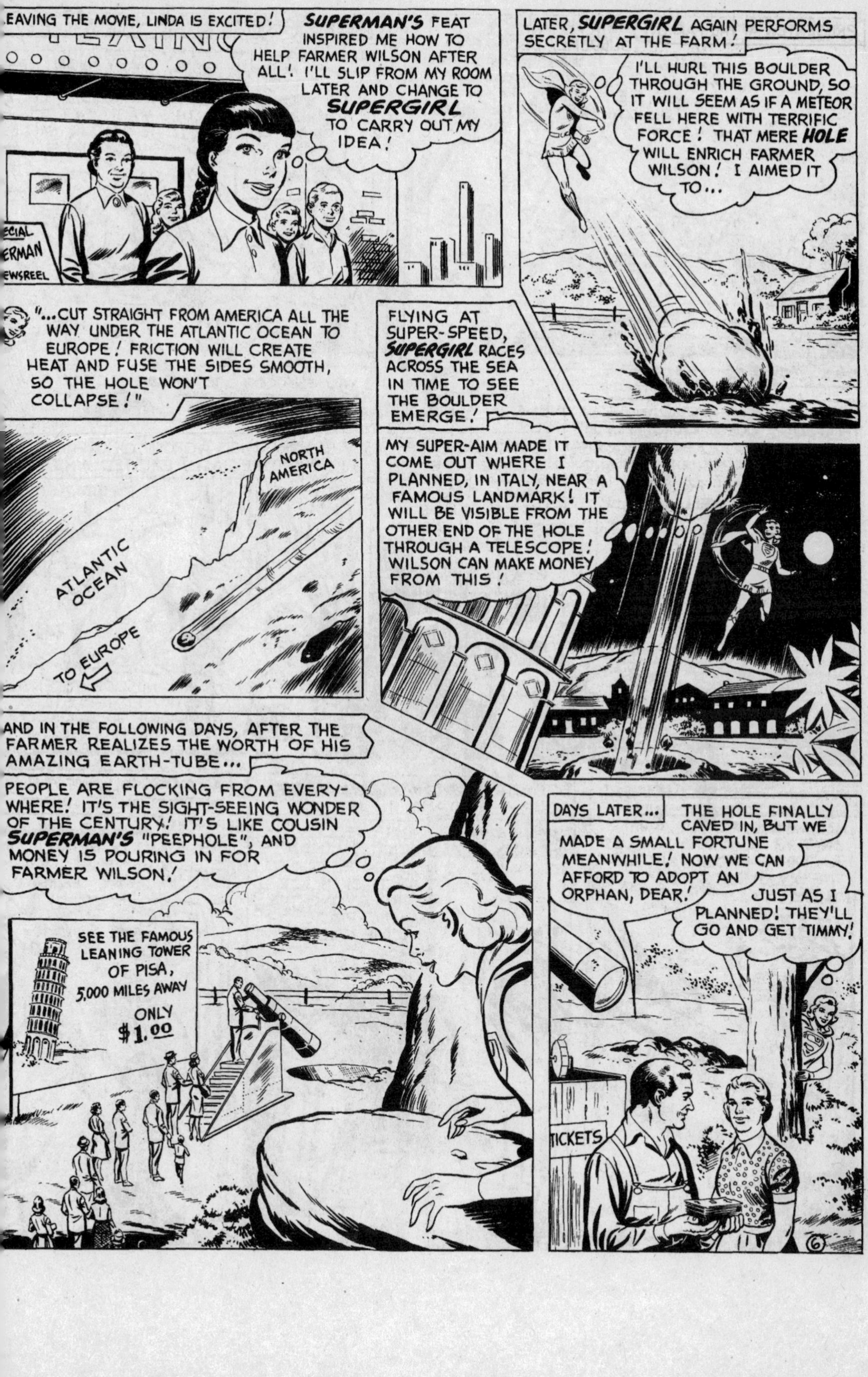
LEAVING THE MOVIE, LINDA IS EXCITED!
SUPERMAN'S FEAT INSPIRED ME HOW TO HELP FARMER WILSON AFTER ALL! I'LL SLIP FROM MY ROOM LATER AND CHANGE TO SUPERGIRL TO CARRY OUT MY IDEA!
ECIAL ERMAN EWSREEL
LATER, SUPERGIRL AGAIN PERFORMS SECRETLY AT THE FARM!
I'LL HURL THIS BOULDER THROUGH THE GROUND, SO IT WILL SEEM AS IF A METEOR FELL HERE WITH TERRIFIC FORCE! THAT MERE HOLE WILL ENRICH FARMER WILSON! I AIMED IT TO...
"...CUT STRAIGHT FROM AMERICA ALL THE WAY UNDER THE ATLANTIC OCEAN TO EUROPE! FRICTION WILL CREATE HEAT AND FUSE THE SIDES SMOOTH, SO THE HOLE WON'T COLLAPSE!"
NORTH AMERICA
ATLANTIC OCEAN
TO EUROPE
FLYING AT SUPER-SPEED, SUPERGIRL RACES ACROSS THE SEA IN TIME TO SEE THE BOULDER EMERGE!
MY SUPER-AIM MADE IT COME OUT WHERE I PLANNED, IN ITALY, NEAR A FAMOUS LANDMARK! IT WILL BE VISIBLE FROM THE OTHER END OF THE HOLE THROUGH A TELESCOPE! WILSON CAN MAKE MONEY FROM THIS!
AND IN THE FOLLOWING DAYS, AFTER THE FARMER REALIZES THE WORTH OF HIS AMAZING EARTH-TUBE...
PEOPLE ARE FLOCKING FROM EVERYWHERE! IT'S THE SIGHT-SEEING WONDER OF THE CENTURY! IT'S LIKE COUSIN SUPERMAN'S "PEEPHOLE", AND MONEY IS POURING IN FOR FARMER WILSON!
SEE THE FAMOUS LEANING TOWER OF PISA, 5,000 MILES AWAY
ONLY $1.00
DAYS LATER...
THE HOLE FINALLY CAVED IN, BUT WE MADE A SMALL FORTUNE MEANWHILE! NOW WE CAN AFFORD TO ADOPT AN ORPHAN, DEAR!
JUST AS I PLANNED! THEY'LL GO AND GET TIMMY!
TICKETS
6

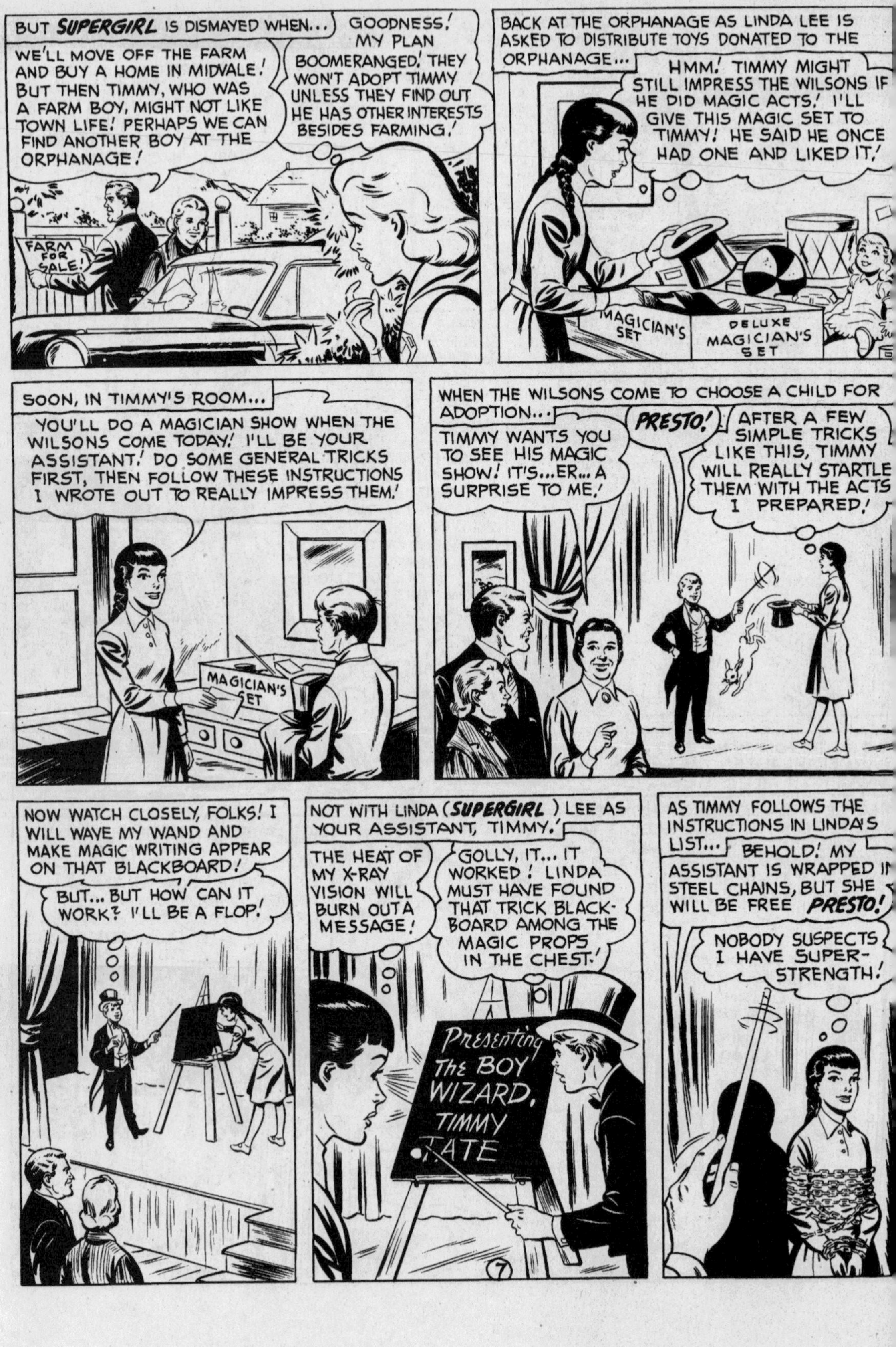
BUT SUPERGIRL IS DISMAYED WHEN...
WE'LL MOVE OFF THE FARM AND BUY A HOME IN MIDVALE! BUT THEN TIMMY, WHO WAS A FARM BOY, MIGHT NOT LIKE TOWN LIFE! PERHAPS WE CAN FIND ANOTHER BOY AT THE ORPHANAGE!
GOODNESS! MY PLAN BOOMERANGED! THEY WON'T ADOPT TIMMY UNLESS THEY FIND OUT HE HAS OTHER INTERESTS BESIDES FARMING!
FARM FOR SALE!
BACK AT THE ORPHANAGE AS LINDA LEE IS ASKED TO DISTRIBUTE TOYS DONATED TO THE ORPHANAGE...
HMM! TIMMY MIGHT STILL IMPRESS THE WILSONS IF HE DID MAGIC ACTS! I'LL GIVE THIS MAGIC SET TO TIMMY! HE SAID HE ONCE HAD ONE AND LIKED IT!
MAGICIAN'S SET
DELUXE MAGICIAN'S SET
SOON, IN TIMMY'S ROOM...
YOU'LL DO A MAGICIAN SHOW WHEN THE WILSONS COME TODAY! I'LL BE YOUR ASSISTANT! DO SOME GENERAL TRICKS FIRST, THEN FOLLOW THESE INSTRUCTIONS I WROTE OUT TO REALLY IMPRESS THEM!
MAGICIAN'S SET
WHEN THE WILSONS COME TO CHOOSE A CHILD FOR ADOPTION...
TIMMY WANTS YOU TO SEE HIS MAGIC SHOW! IT'S...ER...A SURPRISE TO ME!
PRESTO!
AFTER A FEW SIMPLE TRICKS LIKE THIS, TIMMY WILL REALLY STARTLE THEM WITH THE ACTS I PREPARED!
NOW WATCH CLOSELY, FOLKS! I WILL WAVE MY WAND AND MAKE MAGIC WRITING APPEAR ON THAT BLACKBOARD!
BUT... BUT HOW CAN IT WORK? I'LL BE A FLOP!
NOT WITH LINDA (SUPERGIRL) LEE AS YOUR ASSISTANT, TIMMY!
THE HEAT OF MY X-RAY VISION WILL BURN OUT A MESSAGE!
GOLLY, IT... IT WORKED! LINDA MUST HAVE FOUND THAT TRICK BLACK-BOARD AMONG THE MAGIC PROPS IN THE CHEST!
Presenting The BOY WIZARD, TIMMY TATE
7
AS TIMMY FOLLOWS THE INSTRUCTIONS IN LINDA'S LIST...
BEHOLD! MY ASSISTANT IS WRAPPED IN STEEL CHAINS, BUT SHE WILL BE FREE PRESTO!
NOBODY SUSPECTS I HAVE SUPER-STRENGTH!

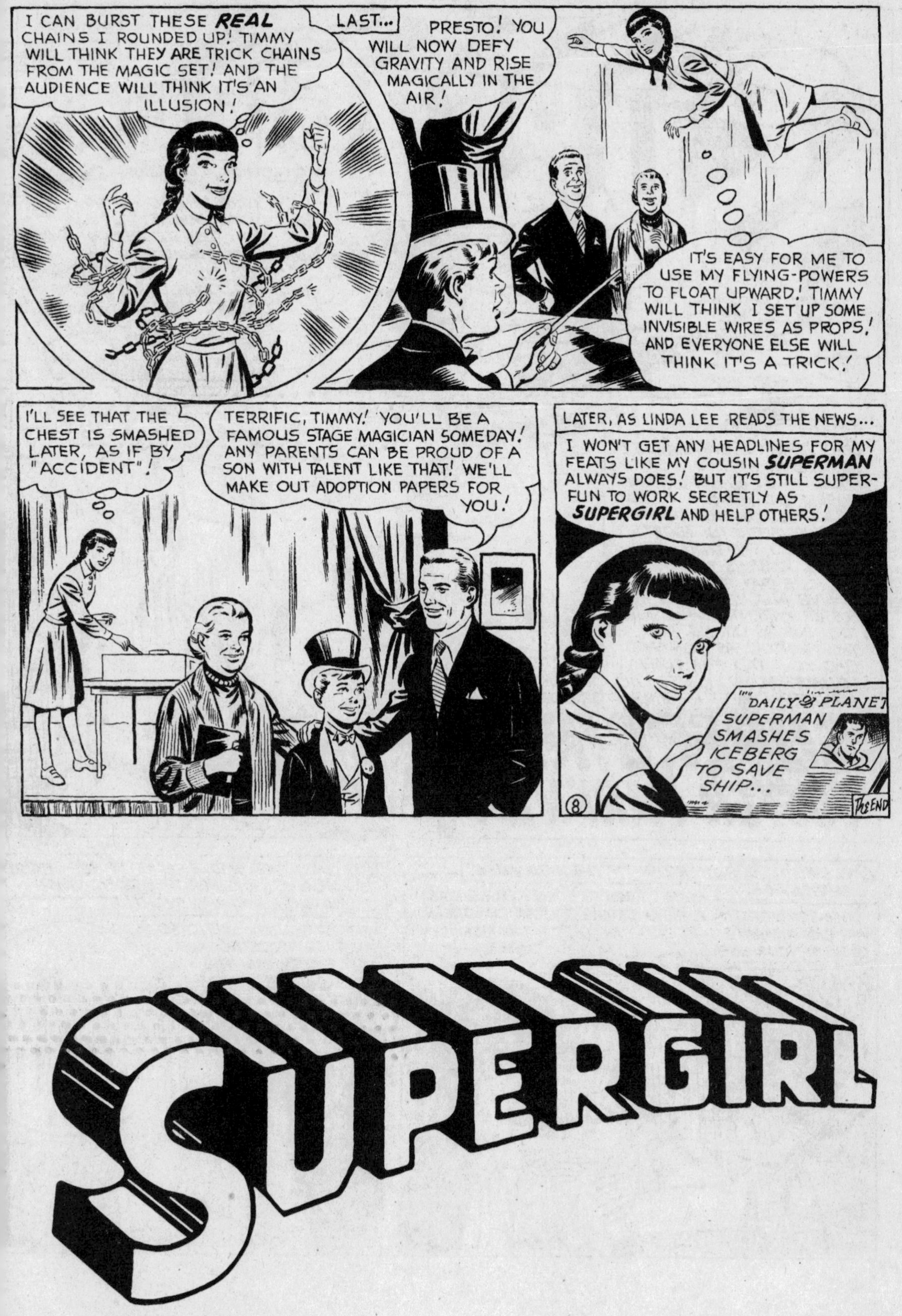
I CAN BURST THESE **REAL** CHAINS I ROUNDED UP! TIMMY WILL THINK THEY ARE TRICK CHAINS FROM THE MAGIC SET! AND THE AUDIENCE WILL THINK IT'S AN ILLUSION!
LAST...
PRESTO! YOU WILL NOW DEFY GRAVITY AND RISE MAGICALLY IN THE AIR!
IT'S EASY FOR ME TO USE MY FLYING-POWERS TO FLOAT UPWARD! TIMMY WILL THINK I SET UP SOME INVISIBLE WIRES AS PROPS! AND EVERYONE ELSE WILL THINK IT'S A TRICK!
I'LL SEE THAT THE CHEST IS SMASHED LATER, AS IF BY "ACCIDENT"!
TERRIFIC, TIMMY! YOU'LL BE A FAMOUS STAGE MAGICIAN SOMEDAY! ANY PARENTS CAN BE PROUD OF A SON WITH TALENT LIKE THAT! WE'LL MAKE OUT ADOPTION PAPERS FOR YOU!
LATER, AS LINDA LEE READS THE NEWS...
I WON'T GET ANY HEADLINES FOR MY FEATS LIKE MY COUSIN **SUPERMAN** ALWAYS DOES! BUT IT'S STILL SUPER-FUN TO WORK SECRETLY AS **SUPERGIRL** AND HELP OTHERS!
DAILY PLANET
SUPERMAN SMASHES ICEBERG TO SAVE SHIP...
8
THE END

SUPERGIRL

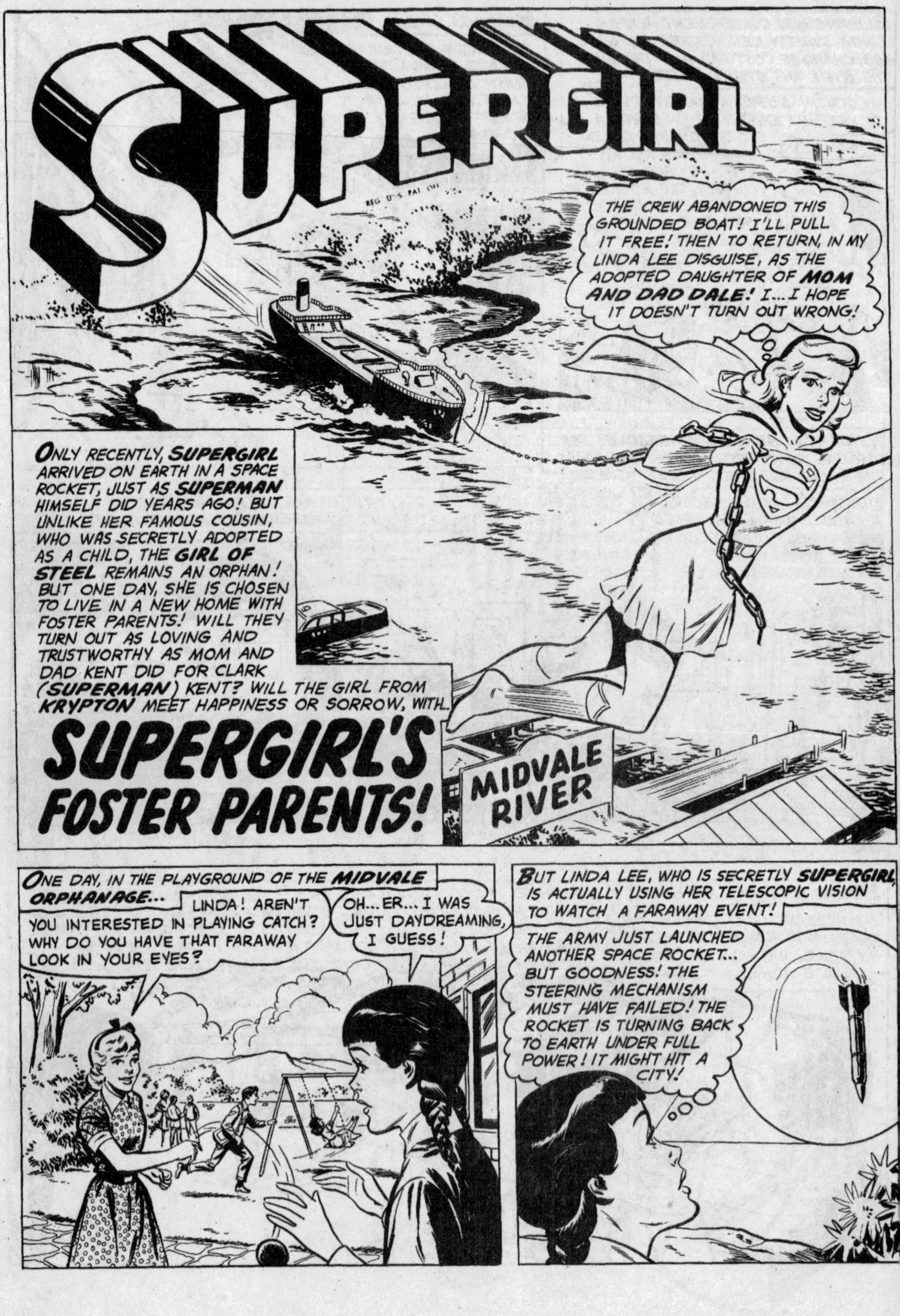
SUPERGIRL
REG. U.S. PAT. OFF.
THE CREW ABANDONED THIS GROUNDED BOAT! I'LL PULL IT FREE! THEN TO RETURN, IN MY LINDA LEE DISGUISE, AS THE ADOPTED DAUGHTER OF MOM AND DAD DALE! I...I HOPE IT DOESN'T TURN OUT WRONG!
ONLY RECENTLY, SUPERGIRL ARRIVED ON EARTH IN A SPACE ROCKET, JUST AS SUPERMAN HIMSELF DID YEARS AGO! BUT UNLIKE HER FAMOUS COUSIN, WHO WAS SECRETLY ADOPTED AS A CHILD, THE GIRL OF STEEL REMAINS AN ORPHAN! BUT ONE DAY, SHE IS CHOSEN TO LIVE IN A NEW HOME WITH FOSTER PARENTS! WILL THEY TURN OUT AS LOVING AND TRUSTWORTHY AS MOM AND DAD KENT DID FOR CLARK (SUPERMAN) KENT? WILL THE GIRL FROM KRYPTON MEET HAPPINESS OR SORROW, WITH...
SUPERGIRL'S FOSTER PARENTS!
MIDVALE RIVER
ONE DAY, IN THE PLAYGROUND OF THE MIDVALE ORPHANAGE...
LINDA! AREN'T YOU INTERESTED IN PLAYING CATCH? WHY DO YOU HAVE THAT FARAWAY LOOK IN YOUR EYES?
OH...ER...I WAS JUST DAYDREAMING, I GUESS!
BUT LINDA LEE, WHO IS SECRETLY SUPERGIRL, IS ACTUALLY USING HER TELESCOPIC VISION TO WATCH A FARAWAY EVENT!
THE ARMY JUST LAUNCHED ANOTHER SPACE ROCKET... BUT GOODNESS! THE STEERING MECHANISM MUST HAVE FAILED! THE ROCKET IS TURNING BACK TO EARTH UNDER FULL POWER! IT MIGHT HIT A CITY!

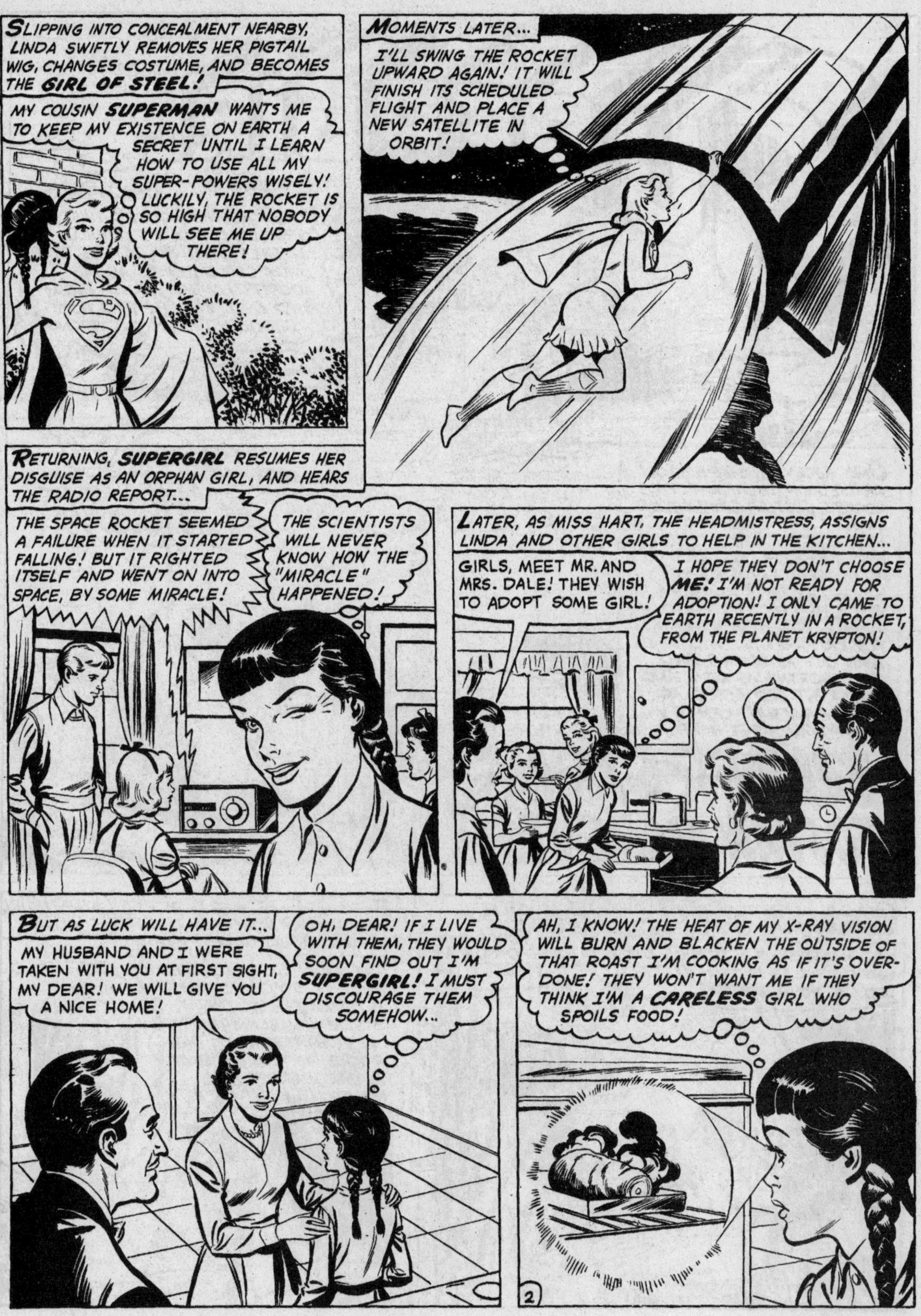
SLIPPING INTO CONCEALMENT NEARBY, LINDA SWIFTLY REMOVES HER PIGTAIL WIG, CHANGES COSTUME, AND BECOMES THE GIRL OF STEEL!
MY COUSIN SUPERMAN WANTS ME TO KEEP MY EXISTENCE ON EARTH A SECRET UNTIL I LEARN HOW TO USE ALL MY SUPER-POWERS WISELY! LUCKILY, THE ROCKET IS SO HIGH THAT NOBODY WILL SEE ME UP THERE!
MOMENTS LATER...
I'LL SWING THE ROCKET UPWARD AGAIN! IT WILL FINISH ITS SCHEDULED FLIGHT AND PLACE A NEW SATELLITE IN ORBIT!
RETURNING, SUPERGIRL RESUMES HER DISGUISE AS AN ORPHAN GIRL, AND HEARS THE RADIO REPORT...
THE SPACE ROCKET SEEMED A FAILURE WHEN IT STARTED FALLING! BUT IT RIGHTED ITSELF AND WENT ON INTO SPACE, BY SOME MIRACLE!
THE SCIENTISTS WILL NEVER KNOW HOW THE "MIRACLE" HAPPENED!
LATER, AS MISS HART, THE HEADMISTRESS, ASSIGNS LINDA AND OTHER GIRLS TO HELP IN THE KITCHEN...
GIRLS, MEET MR. AND MRS. DALE! THEY WISH TO ADOPT SOME GIRL!
I HOPE THEY DON'T CHOOSE ME! I'M NOT READY FOR ADOPTION! I ONLY CAME TO EARTH RECENTLY IN A ROCKET, FROM THE PLANET KRYPTON!
BUT AS LUCK WILL HAVE IT...
MY HUSBAND AND I WERE TAKEN WITH YOU AT FIRST SIGHT, MY DEAR! WE WILL GIVE YOU A NICE HOME!
OH, DEAR! IF I LIVE WITH THEM, THEY WOULD SOON FIND OUT I'M SUPERGIRL! I MUST DISCOURAGE THEM SOMEHOW...
AH, I KNOW! THE HEAT OF MY X-RAY VISION WILL BURN AND BLACKEN THE OUTSIDE OF THAT ROAST I'M COOKING AS IF IT'S OVER-DONE! THEY WON'T WANT ME IF THEY THINK I'M A CARELESS GIRL WHO SPOILS FOOD!
2

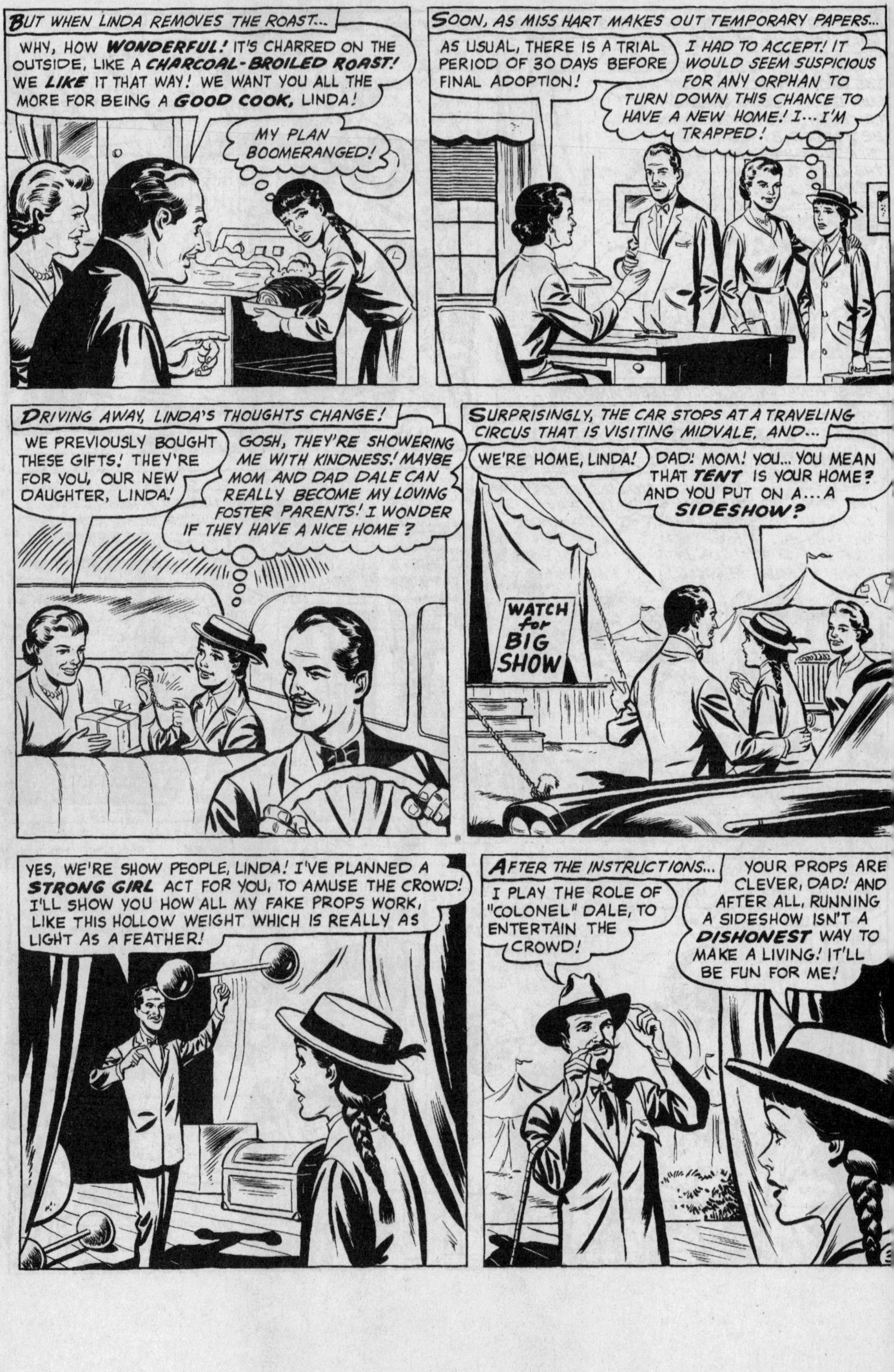
BUT WHEN LINDA REMOVES THE ROAST...
WHY, HOW WONDERFUL! IT'S CHARRED ON THE OUTSIDE, LIKE A CHARCOAL-BROILED ROAST! WE LIKE IT THAT WAY! WE WANT YOU ALL THE MORE FOR BEING A GOOD COOK, LINDA!
MY PLAN BOOMERANGED!
SOON, AS MISS HART MAKES OUT TEMPORARY PAPERS...
AS USUAL, THERE IS A TRIAL PERIOD OF 30 DAYS BEFORE FINAL ADOPTION!
I HAD TO ACCEPT! IT WOULD SEEM SUSPICIOUS FOR ANY ORPHAN TO TURN DOWN THIS CHANCE TO HAVE A NEW HOME! I... I'M TRAPPED!
DRIVING AWAY, LINDA'S THOUGHTS CHANGE!
WE PREVIOUSLY BOUGHT THESE GIFTS! THEY'RE FOR YOU, OUR NEW DAUGHTER, LINDA!
GOSH, THEY'RE SHOWERING ME WITH KINDNESS! MAYBE MOM AND DAD DALE CAN REALLY BECOME MY LOVING FOSTER PARENTS! I WONDER IF THEY HAVE A NICE HOME?
SURPRISINGLY, THE CAR STOPS AT A TRAVELING CIRCUS THAT IS VISITING MIDVALE, AND...
WE'RE HOME, LINDA!
DAD! MOM! YOU... YOU MEAN THAT TENT IS YOUR HOME? AND YOU PUT ON A... A SIDESHOW?
WATCH for BIG SHOW
YES, WE'RE SHOW PEOPLE, LINDA! I'VE PLANNED A STRONG GIRL ACT FOR YOU, TO AMUSE THE CROWD! I'LL SHOW YOU HOW ALL MY FAKE PROPS WORK, LIKE THIS HOLLOW WEIGHT WHICH IS REALLY AS LIGHT AS A FEATHER!
AFTER THE INSTRUCTIONS...
I PLAY THE ROLE OF "COLONEL" DALE, TO ENTERTAIN THE CROWD!
YOUR PROPS ARE CLEVER, DAD! AND AFTER ALL, RUNNING A SIDESHOW ISN'T A DISHONEST WAY TO MAKE A LIVING! IT'LL BE FUN FOR ME!

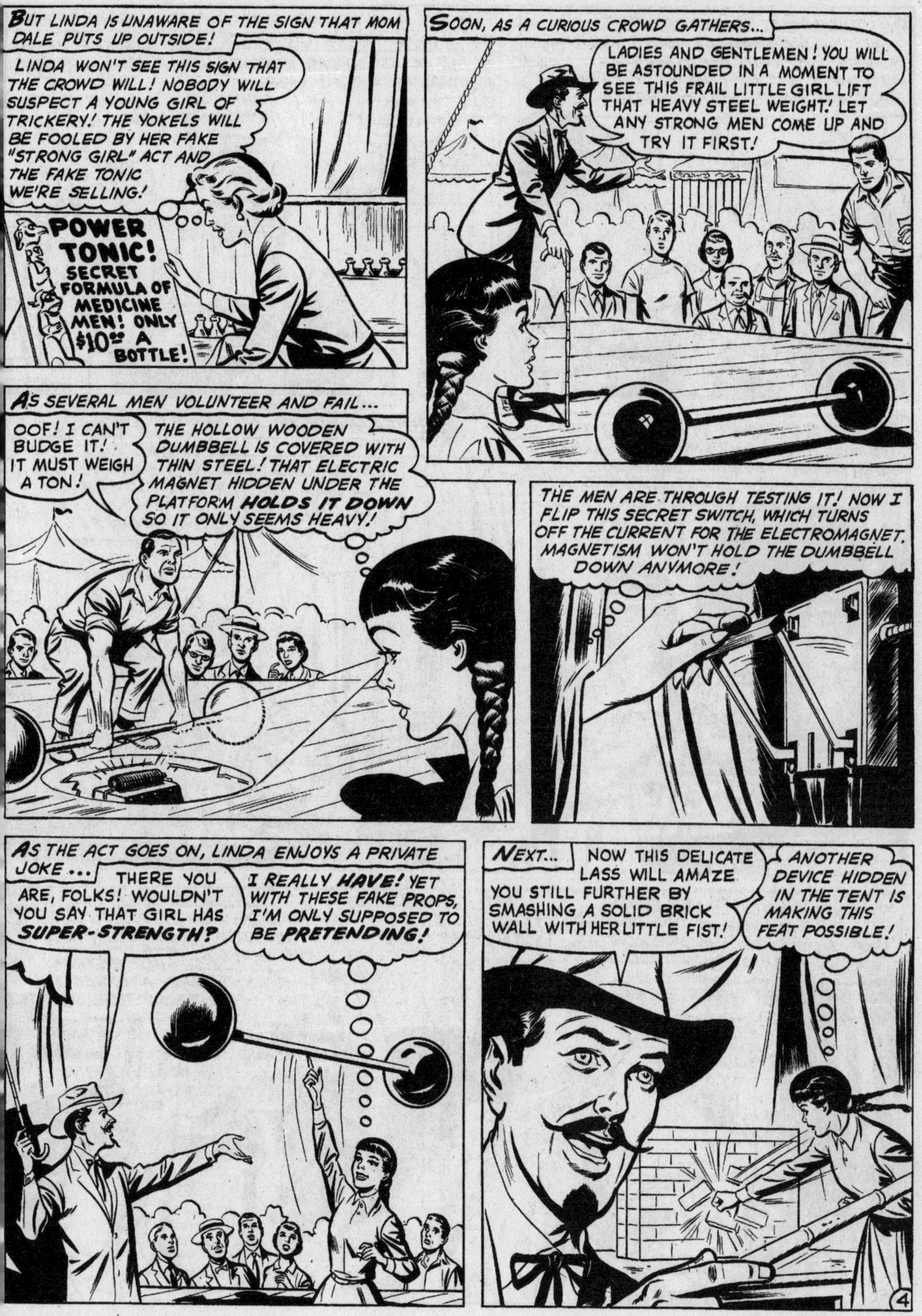
BUT LINDA IS UNAWARE OF THE SIGN THAT MOM DALE PUTS UP OUTSIDE!
LINDA WON'T SEE THIS SIGN THAT THE CROWD WILL! NOBODY WILL SUSPECT A YOUNG GIRL OF TRICKERY! THE YOKELS WILL BE FOOLED BY HER FAKE "STRONG GIRL" ACT AND THE FAKE TONIC WE'RE SELLING!
POWER TONIC! SECRET FORMULA OF MEDICINE MEN! ONLY $10.00 A BOTTLE!
SOON, AS A CURIOUS CROWD GATHERS...
LADIES AND GENTLEMEN! YOU WILL BE ASTOUNDED IN A MOMENT TO SEE THIS FRAIL LITTLE GIRL LIFT THAT HEAVY STEEL WEIGHT! LET ANY STRONG MEN COME UP AND TRY IT FIRST!
AS SEVERAL MEN VOLUNTEER AND FAIL...
OOF! I CAN'T BUDGE IT! IT MUST WEIGH A TON!
THE HOLLOW WOODEN DUMBBELL IS COVERED WITH THIN STEEL! THAT ELECTRIC MAGNET HIDDEN UNDER THE PLATFORM HOLDS IT DOWN SO IT ONLY SEEMS HEAVY!
THE MEN ARE THROUGH TESTING IT! NOW I FLIP THIS SECRET SWITCH, WHICH TURNS OFF THE CURRENT FOR THE ELECTROMAGNET. MAGNETISM WON'T HOLD THE DUMBBELL DOWN ANYMORE!
AS THE ACT GOES ON, LINDA ENJOYS A PRIVATE JOKE...
THERE YOU ARE, FOLKS! WOULDN'T YOU SAY THAT GIRL HAS SUPER-STRENGTH?
I REALLY HAVE! YET WITH THESE FAKE PROPS, I'M ONLY SUPPOSED TO BE PRETENDING!
NEXT...
NOW THIS DELICATE LASS WILL AMAZE YOU STILL FURTHER BY SMASHING A SOLID BRICK WALL WITH HER LITTLE FIST!
ANOTHER DEVICE HIDDEN IN THE TENT IS MAKING THIS FEAT POSSIBLE!
4

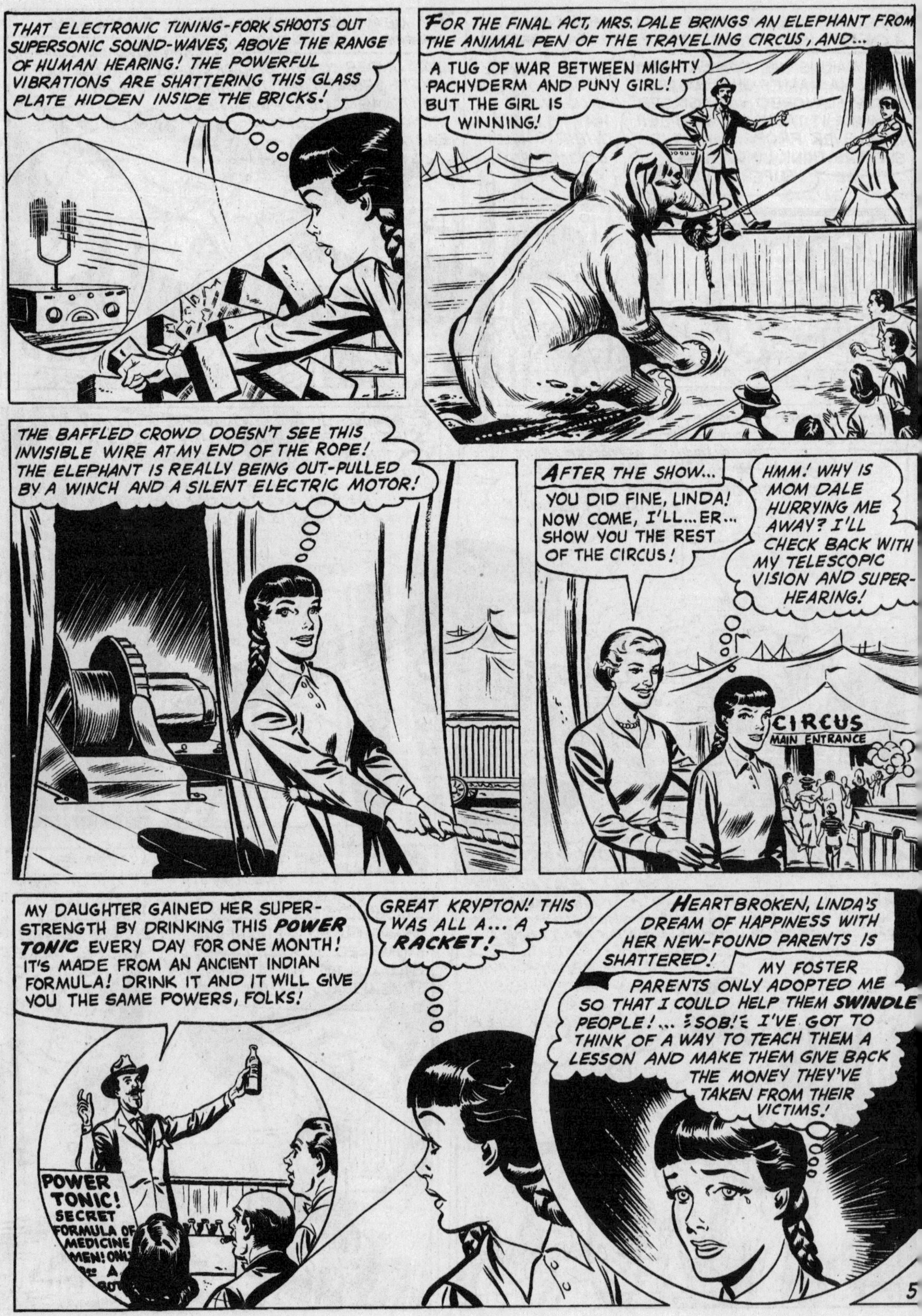
THAT ELECTRONIC TUNING-FORK SHOOTS OUT SUPERSONIC SOUND-WAVES, ABOVE THE RANGE OF HUMAN HEARING! THE POWERFUL VIBRATIONS ARE SHATTERING THIS GLASS PLATE HIDDEN INSIDE THE BRICKS!
FOR THE FINAL ACT, MRS. DALE BRINGS AN ELEPHANT FROM THE ANIMAL PEN OF THE TRAVELING CIRCUS, AND...
A TUG OF WAR BETWEEN MIGHTY PACHYDERM AND PUNY GIRL! BUT THE GIRL IS WINNING!
THE BAFFLED CROWD DOESN'T SEE THIS INVISIBLE WIRE AT MY END OF THE ROPE! THE ELEPHANT IS REALLY BEING OUT-PULLED BY A WINCH AND A SILENT ELECTRIC MOTOR!
AFTER THE SHOW...
YOU DID FINE, LINDA! NOW COME, I'LL...ER... SHOW YOU THE REST OF THE CIRCUS!
HMM! WHY IS MOM DALE HURRYING ME AWAY? I'LL CHECK BACK WITH MY TELESCOPIC VISION AND SUPER-HEARING!
CIRCUS
MAIN ENTRANCE
MY DAUGHTER GAINED HER SUPER-STRENGTH BY DRINKING THIS POWER TONIC EVERY DAY FOR ONE MONTH! IT'S MADE FROM AN ANCIENT INDIAN FORMULA! DRINK IT AND IT WILL GIVE YOU THE SAME POWERS, FOLKS!
POWER TONIC! SECRET FORMULA OF MEDICINE MEN! ONLY
GREAT KRYPTON! THIS WAS ALL A... A RACKET!
HEARTBROKEN, LINDA'S DREAM OF HAPPINESS WITH HER NEW-FOUND PARENTS IS SHATTERED!
MY FOSTER PARENTS ONLY ADOPTED ME SO THAT I COULD HELP THEM SWINDLE PEOPLE!... SOB! I'VE GOT TO THINK OF A WAY TO TEACH THEM A LESSON AND MAKE THEM GIVE BACK THE MONEY THEY'VE TAKEN FROM THEIR VICTIMS!
5

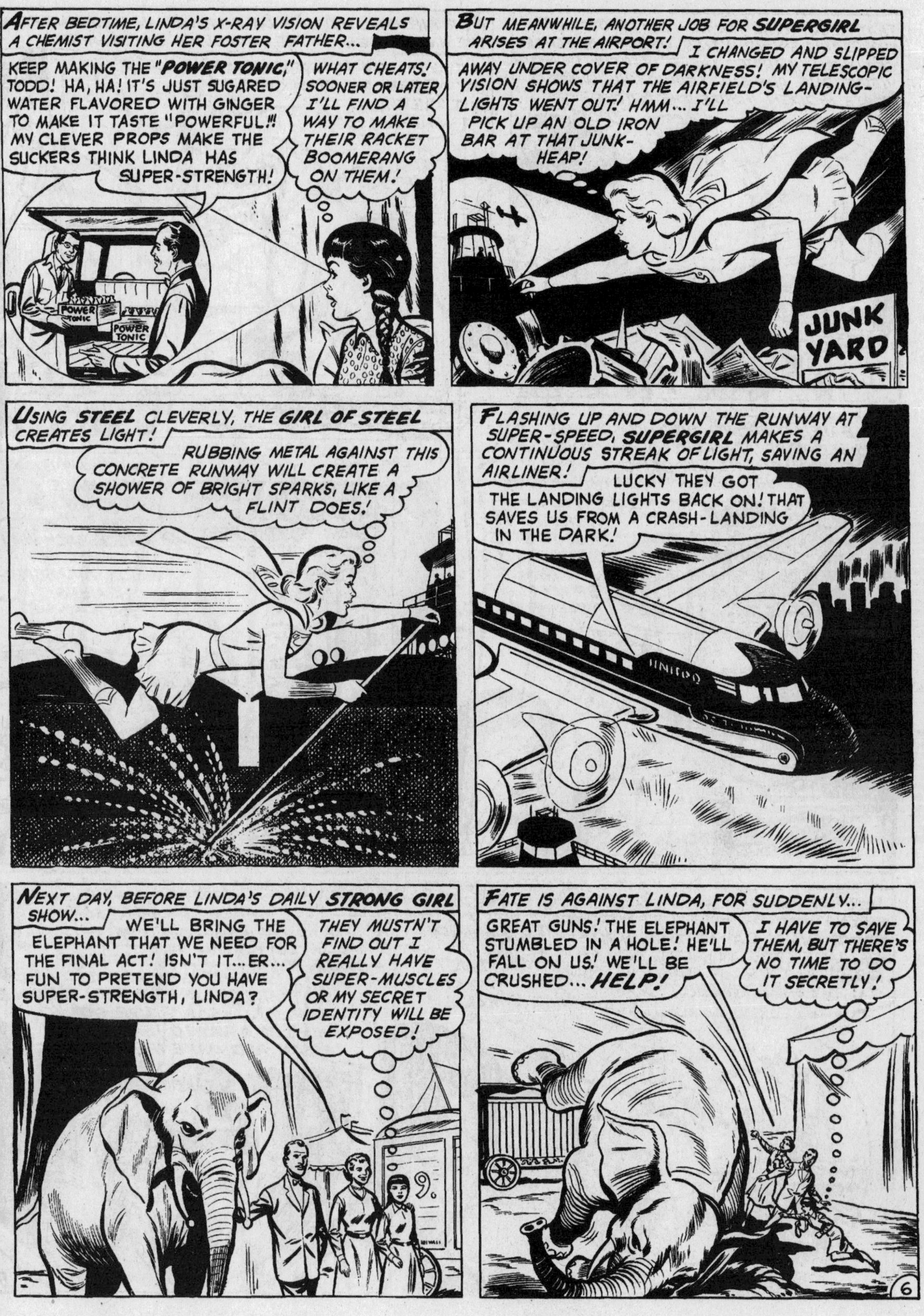
AFTER BEDTIME, LINDA'S X-RAY VISION REVEALS A CHEMIST VISITING HER FOSTER FATHER...
KEEP MAKING THE "POWER TONIC," TODD! HA, HA! IT'S JUST SUGARED WATER FLAVORED WITH GINGER TO MAKE IT TASTE "POWERFUL"!! MY CLEVER PROPS MAKE THE SUCKERS THINK LINDA HAS SUPER-STRENGTH!
WHAT CHEATS! SOONER OR LATER I'LL FIND A WAY TO MAKE THEIR RACKET BOOMERANG ON THEM!
POWER TONIC
POWER TONIC
BUT MEANWHILE, ANOTHER JOB FOR SUPERGIRL ARISES AT THE AIRPORT!
I CHANGED AND SLIPPED AWAY UNDER COVER OF DARKNESS! MY TELESCOPIC VISION SHOWS THAT THE AIRFIELD'S LANDING-LIGHTS WENT OUT! HMM... I'LL PICK UP AN OLD IRON BAR AT THAT JUNK-HEAP!
JUNK YARD
USING STEEL CLEVERLY, THE GIRL OF STEEL CREATES LIGHT!
RUBBING METAL AGAINST THIS CONCRETE RUNWAY WILL CREATE A SHOWER OF BRIGHT SPARKS, LIKE A FLINT DOES!
FLASHING UP AND DOWN THE RUNWAY AT SUPER-SPEED, SUPERGIRL MAKES A CONTINUOUS STREAK OF LIGHT, SAVING AN AIRLINER!
LUCKY THEY GOT THE LANDING LIGHTS BACK ON! THAT SAVES US FROM A CRASH-LANDING IN THE DARK!
UNITED
NEXT DAY, BEFORE LINDA'S DAILY STRONG GIRL SHOW...
WE'LL BRING THE ELEPHANT THAT WE NEED FOR THE FINAL ACT! ISN'T IT...ER... FUN TO PRETEND YOU HAVE SUPER-STRENGTH, LINDA?
THEY MUSTN'T FIND OUT I REALLY HAVE SUPER-MUSCLES OR MY SECRET IDENTITY WILL BE EXPOSED!
FATE IS AGAINST LINDA, FOR SUDDENLY...
GREAT GUNS! THE ELEPHANT STUMBLED IN A HOLE! HE'LL FALL ON US! WE'LL BE CRUSHED... HELP!
I HAVE TO SAVE THEM, BUT THERE'S NO TIME TO DO IT SECRETLY!
6

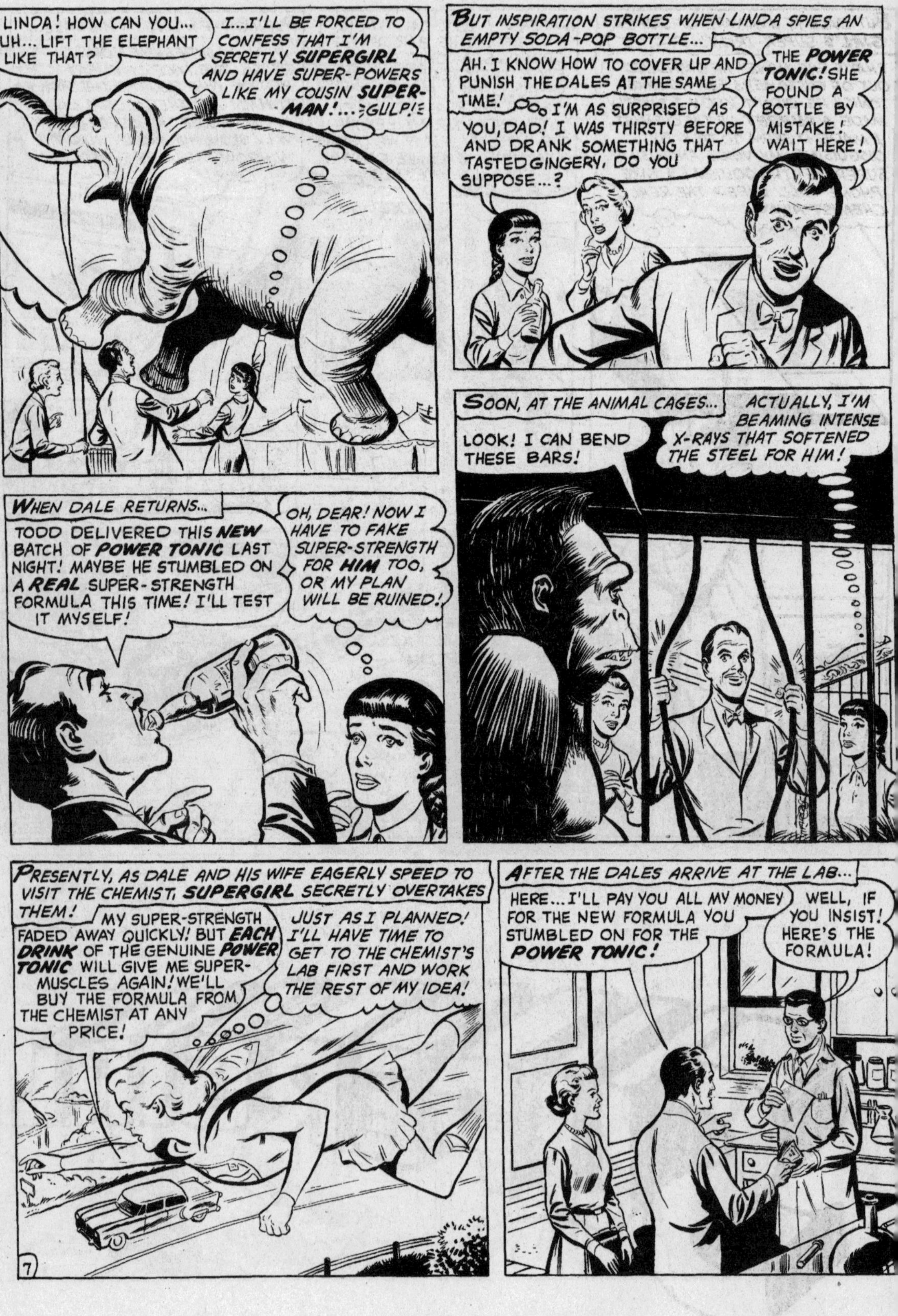
LINDA! HOW CAN YOU... UH... LIFT THE ELEPHANT LIKE THAT?
I...I'LL BE FORCED TO CONFESS THAT I'M SECRETLY SUPERGIRL AND HAVE SUPER-POWERS LIKE MY COUSIN SUPERMAN!... GULP!
BUT INSPIRATION STRIKES WHEN LINDA SPIES AN EMPTY SODA-POP BOTTLE...
AH. I KNOW HOW TO COVER UP AND PUNISH THE DALES AT THE SAME TIME!
I'M AS SURPRISED AS YOU, DAD! I WAS THIRSTY BEFORE AND DRANK SOMETHING THAT TASTED GINGERY. DO YOU SUPPOSE...?
THE POWER TONIC! SHE FOUND A BOTTLE BY MISTAKE! WAIT HERE!
WHEN DALE RETURNS...
TODD DELIVERED THIS NEW BATCH OF POWER TONIC LAST NIGHT! MAYBE HE STUMBLED ON A REAL SUPER-STRENGTH FORMULA THIS TIME! I'LL TEST IT MYSELF!
OH, DEAR! NOW I HAVE TO FAKE SUPER-STRENGTH FOR HIM TOO, OR MY PLAN WILL BE RUINED!
SOON, AT THE ANIMAL CAGES...
LOOK! I CAN BEND THESE BARS!
ACTUALLY, I'M BEAMING INTENSE X-RAYS THAT SOFTENED THE STEEL FOR HIM!
PRESENTLY, AS DALE AND HIS WIFE EAGERLY SPEED TO VISIT THE CHEMIST, SUPERGIRL SECRETLY OVERTAKES THEM!
MY SUPER-STRENGTH FADED AWAY QUICKLY! BUT EACH DRINK OF THE GENUINE POWER TONIC WILL GIVE ME SUPER-MUSCLES AGAIN! WE'LL BUY THE FORMULA FROM THE CHEMIST AT ANY PRICE!
JUST AS I PLANNED! I'LL HAVE TIME TO GET TO THE CHEMIST'S LAB FIRST AND WORK THE REST OF MY IDEA!
7
AFTER THE DALES ARRIVE AT THE LAB...
HERE... I'LL PAY YOU ALL MY MONEY FOR THE NEW FORMULA YOU STUMBLED ON FOR THE POWER TONIC!
WELL, IF YOU INSIST! HERE'S THE FORMULA!

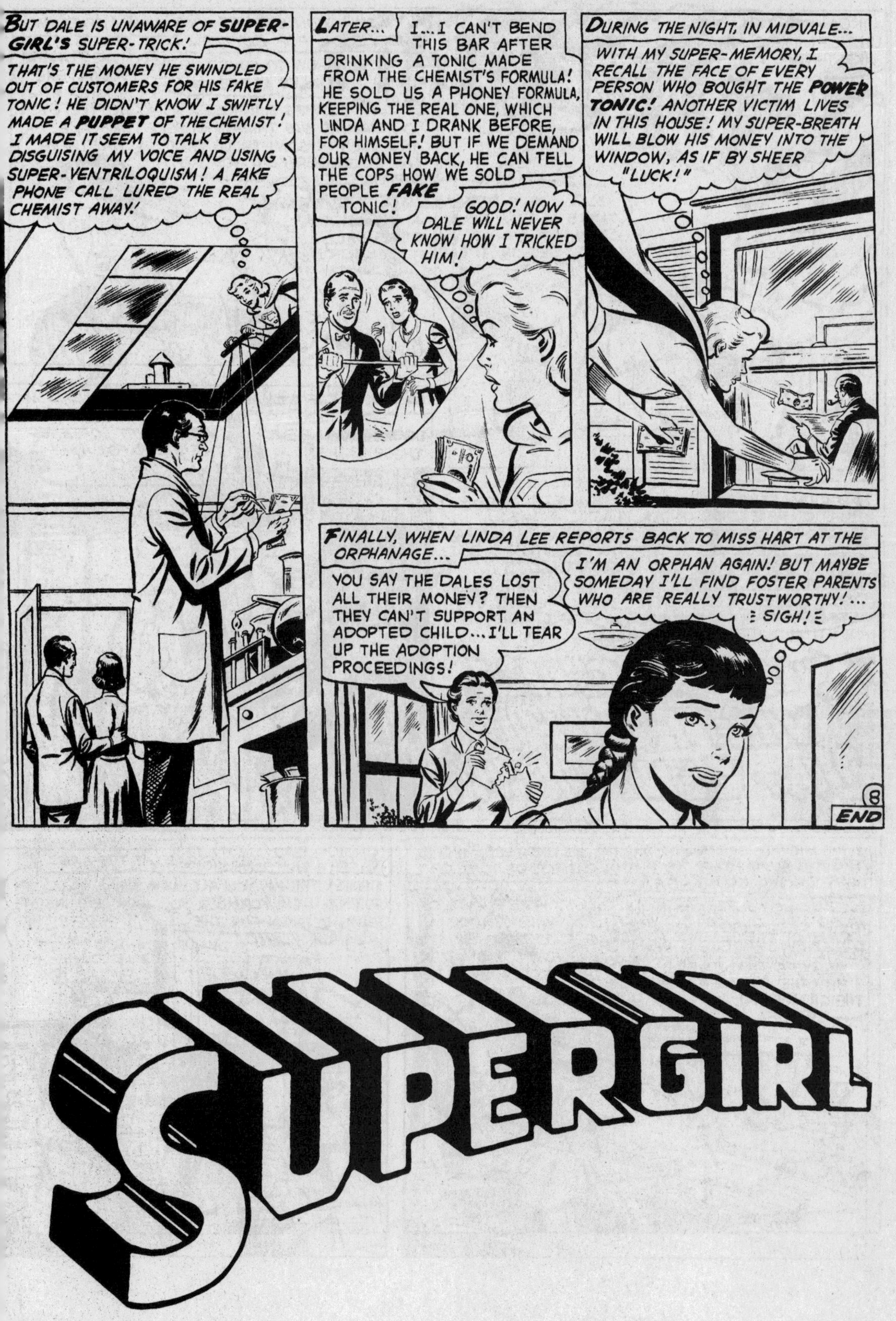
BUT DALE IS UNAWARE OF SUPER-GIRL'S SUPER-TRICK!
THAT'S THE MONEY HE SWINDLED OUT OF CUSTOMERS FOR HIS FAKE TONIC! HE DIDN'T KNOW I SWIFTLY MADE A PUPPET OF THE CHEMIST! I MADE IT SEEM TO TALK BY DISGUISING MY VOICE AND USING SUPER-VENTRILOQUISM! A FAKE PHONE CALL LURED THE REAL CHEMIST AWAY!
LATER...
I... I CAN'T BEND THIS BAR AFTER DRINKING A TONIC MADE FROM THE CHEMIST'S FORMULA! HE SOLD US A PHONEY FORMULA, KEEPING THE REAL ONE, WHICH LINDA AND I DRANK BEFORE, FOR HIMSELF! BUT IF WE DEMAND OUR MONEY BACK, HE CAN TELL THE COPS HOW WE SOLD PEOPLE FAKE TONIC!
GOOD! NOW DALE WILL NEVER KNOW HOW I TRICKED HIM!
DURING THE NIGHT, IN MIDVALE...
WITH MY SUPER-MEMORY, I RECALL THE FACE OF EVERY PERSON WHO BOUGHT THE POWER TONIC! ANOTHER VICTIM LIVES IN THIS HOUSE! MY SUPER-BREATH WILL BLOW HIS MONEY INTO THE WINDOW, AS IF BY SHEER "LUCK!"
FINALLY, WHEN LINDA LEE REPORTS BACK TO MISS HART AT THE ORPHANAGE...
YOU SAY THE DALES LOST ALL THEIR MONEY? THEN THEY CAN'T SUPPORT AN ADOPTED CHILD... I'LL TEAR UP THE ADOPTION PROCEEDINGS!
I'M AN ORPHAN AGAIN! BUT MAYBE SOMEDAY I'LL FIND FOSTER PARENTS WHO ARE REALLY TRUSTWORTHY! ... SIGH!
8
END

SUPERGIRL

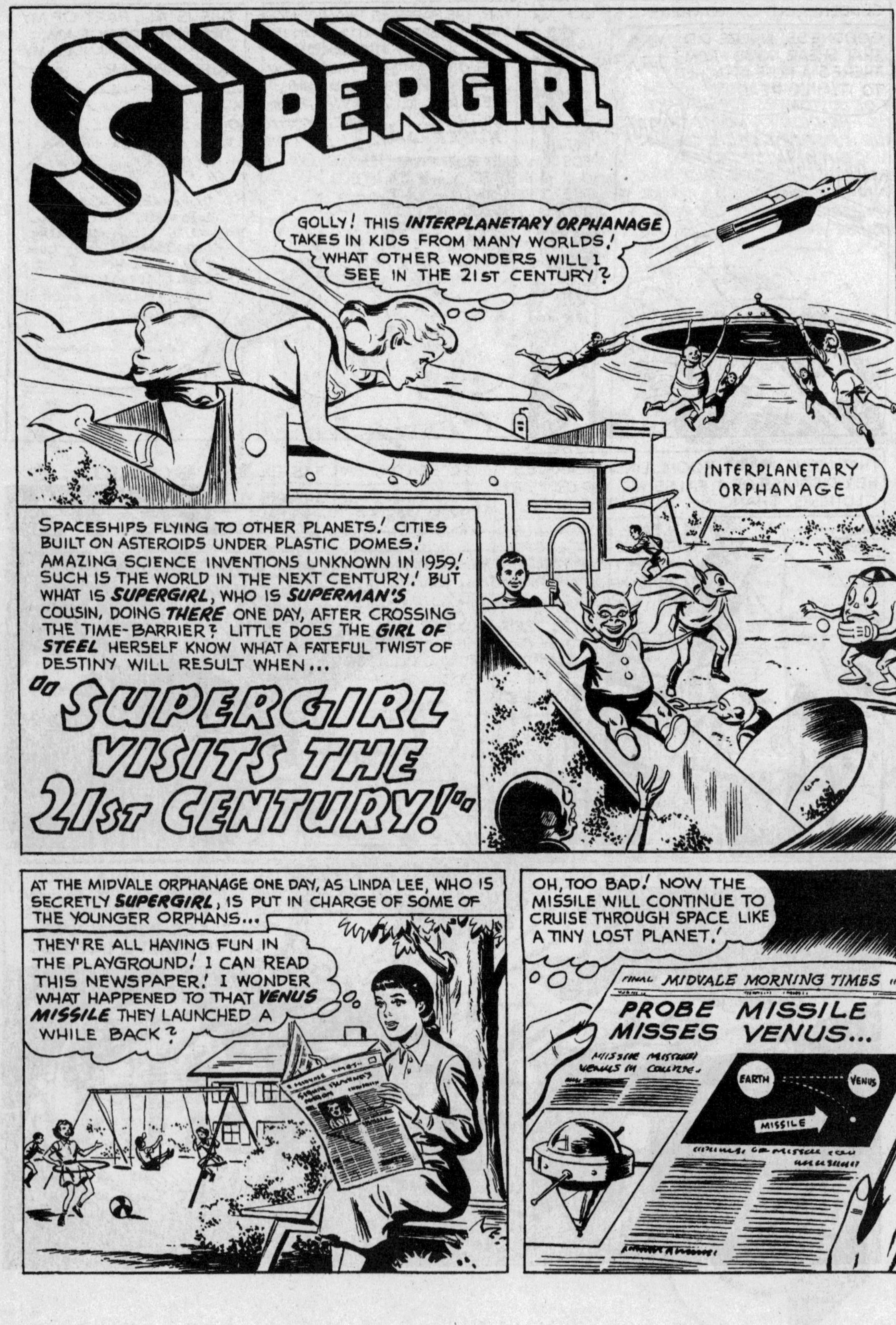
SUPERGIRL
GOLLY! THIS INTERPLANETARY ORPHANAGE TAKES IN KIDS FROM MANY WORLDS! WHAT OTHER WONDERS WILL I SEE IN THE 21ST CENTURY?
INTERPLANETARY ORPHANAGE
SPACESHIPS FLYING TO OTHER PLANETS! CITIES BUILT ON ASTEROIDS UNDER PLASTIC DOMES! AMAZING SCIENCE INVENTIONS UNKNOWN IN 1959! SUCH IS THE WORLD IN THE NEXT CENTURY! BUT WHAT IS SUPERGIRL, WHO IS SUPERMAN'S COUSIN, DOING THERE ONE DAY, AFTER CROSSING THE TIME-BARRIER? LITTLE DOES THE GIRL OF STEEL HERSELF KNOW WHAT A FATEFUL TWIST OF DESTINY WILL RESULT WHEN...
"SUPERGIRL VISITS THE 21ST CENTURY!"
AT THE MIDVALE ORPHANAGE ONE DAY, AS LINDA LEE, WHO IS SECRETLY SUPERGIRL, IS PUT IN CHARGE OF SOME OF THE YOUNGER ORPHANS...
THEY'RE ALL HAVING FUN IN THE PLAYGROUND! I CAN READ THIS NEWSPAPER! I WONDER WHAT HAPPENED TO THAT VENUS MISSILE THEY LAUNCHED A WHILE BACK?
OH, TOO BAD! NOW THE MISSILE WILL CONTINUE TO CRUISE THROUGH SPACE LIKE A TINY LOST PLANET!
FINAL MIDVALE MORNING TIMES
PROBE MISSILE MISSES VENUS...
EARTH
VENUS
MISSILE

SUDDENLY, OUT OF NOWHERE...

GOODNESS! WHERE DID THAT SPEAR COME FROM? THERE'S A NOTE ATTACHED TO IT! I'LL READ IT!

WHI-ZZZZZ! PLUNK!

WHY, THE PAPER IS BLANK! NO, WAIT...THERE'S WRITING ON IT THAT ONLY MY **MICROSCOPIC VISION** CAN SEE! HMM...NOW I KNOW **WHO** HURLED THIS MESSAGE ALL THE WAY FROM METROPOLIS, USING **SUPER-AIM!**

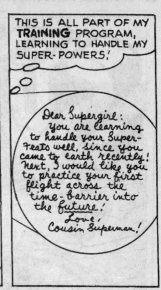

THIS IS ALL PART OF MY **TRAINING** PROGRAM, LEARNING TO HANDLE MY SUPER-POWERS!

Dear Supergirl:
You are learning to handle your Super-feats well, since you came to earth recently! Next, I would like you to practice your first flight across the time-barrier into the future!
Love,
Cousin Superman!

THAT NIGHT, IN HER ROOM, LINDA REMOVES HER DISGUISE OF A FALSE WIG AND ORDINARY CLOTHING, CHANGING TO **SUPERGIRL!**

I'LL LEAVE NOW, WHILE EVERYONE'S ASLEEP! I'LL FLY OUT THE WINDOW INTO THE SKY, PILING ON SUPER-SPEED!

PRESENTLY, FAR FASTER THAN ANY ROCKET...

LIKE COUSIN **SUPERMAN**, I'LL SPEED FASTER THAN LIGHT AND PROPEL MYSELF ACROSS THE TIME-BARRIER! I'LL TRAVEL ABOUT A HUNDRED YEARS AHEAD, INTO THE 21ST CENTURY!

DIZZYING MOMENTS LATER...

I'M IN THE FUTURE, ALL RIGHT! THEY HAVE SPACE TRAVEL NOW! EVEN CITIES HAVE BEEN BUILT ON THOSE ASTEROIDS, UNDER PLASTIC DOMES!

(2)

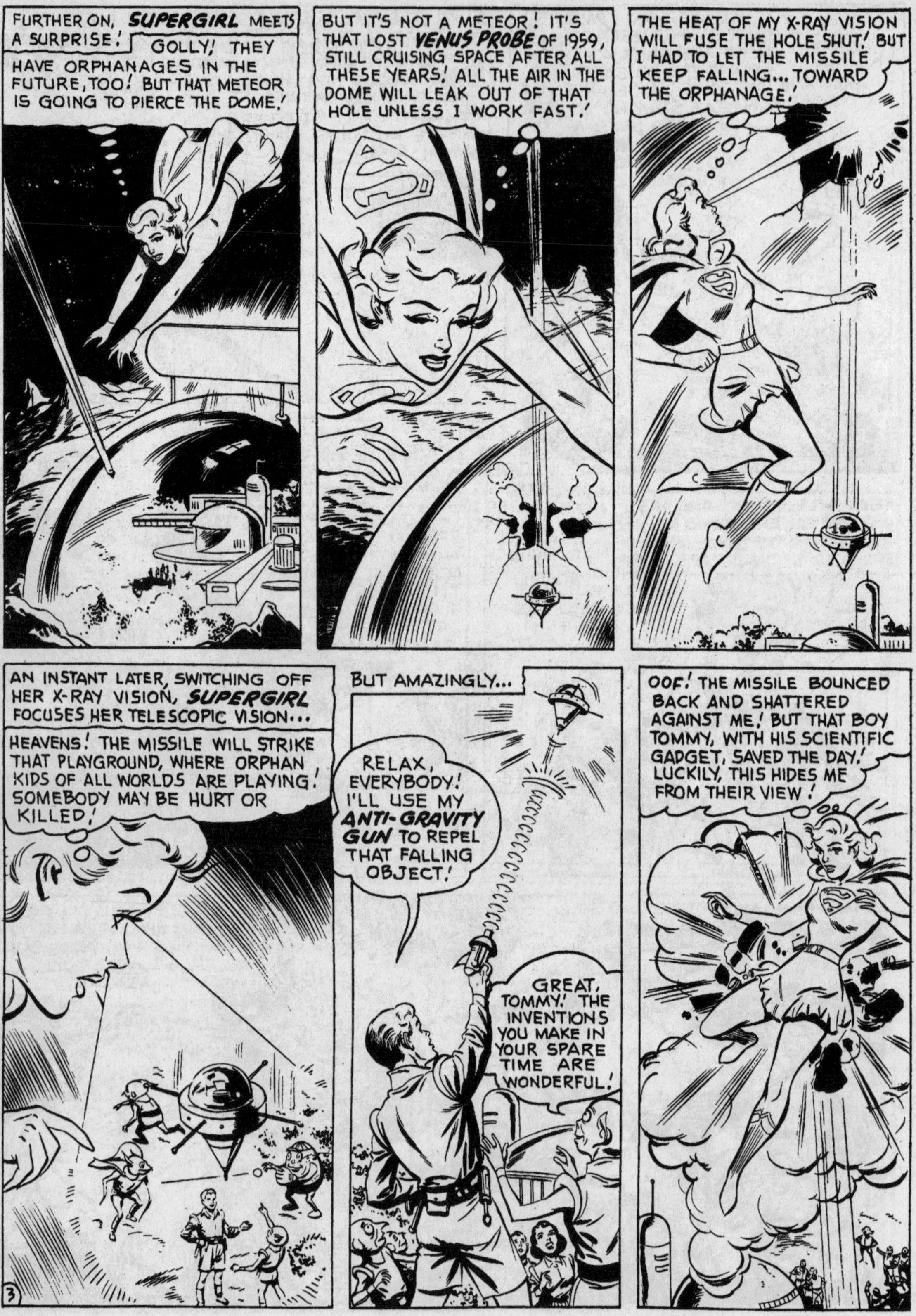
FURTHER ON, SUPERGIRL MEETS A SURPRISE!
GOLLY! THEY HAVE ORPHANAGES IN THE FUTURE, TOO! BUT THAT METEOR IS GOING TO PIERCE THE DOME!
BUT IT'S NOT A METEOR! IT'S THAT LOST VENUS PROBE OF 1959, STILL CRUISING SPACE AFTER ALL THESE YEARS! ALL THE AIR IN THE DOME WILL LEAK OUT OF THAT HOLE UNLESS I WORK FAST!
THE HEAT OF MY X-RAY VISION WILL FUSE THE HOLE SHUT! BUT I HAD TO LET THE MISSILE KEEP FALLING... TOWARD THE ORPHANAGE!
AN INSTANT LATER, SWITCHING OFF HER X-RAY VISION, SUPERGIRL FOCUSES HER TELESCOPIC VISION...
HEAVENS! THE MISSILE WILL STRIKE THAT PLAYGROUND, WHERE ORPHAN KIDS OF ALL WORLDS ARE PLAYING! SOMEBODY MAY BE HURT OR KILLED!
3
BUT AMAZINGLY...
RELAX, EVERYBODY! I'LL USE MY ANTI-GRAVITY GUN TO REPEL THAT FALLING OBJECT!
GREAT, TOMMY! THE INVENTIONS YOU MAKE IN YOUR SPARE TIME ARE WONDERFUL!
OOF! THE MISSILE BOUNCED BACK AND SHATTERED AGAINST ME! BUT THAT BOY TOMMY, WITH HIS SCIENTIFIC GADGET, SAVED THE DAY! LUCKILY, THIS HIDES ME FROM THEIR VIEW!

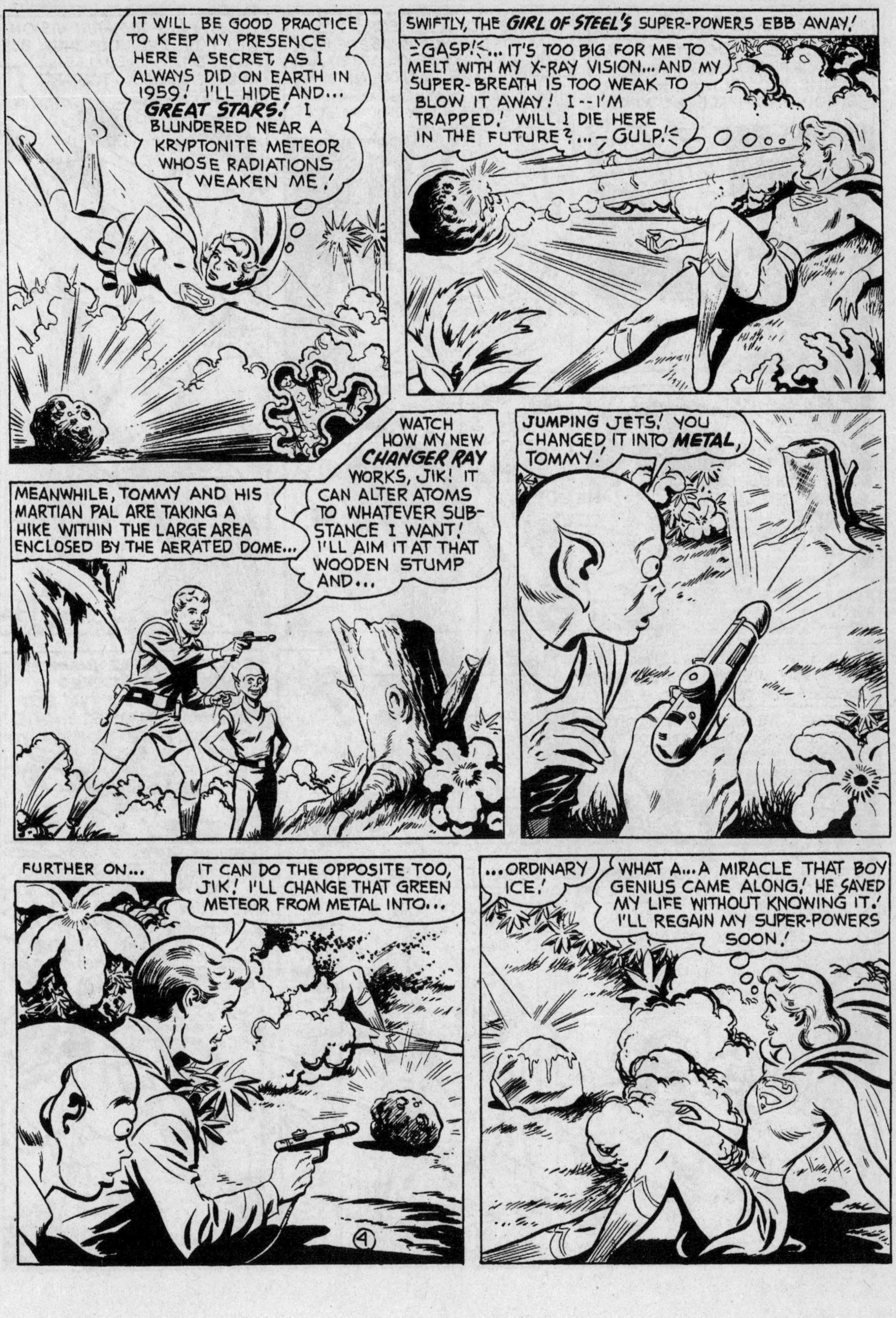
IT WILL BE GOOD PRACTICE TO KEEP MY PRESENCE HERE A SECRET, AS I ALWAYS DID ON EARTH IN 1959! I'LL HIDE AND... GREAT STARS! I BLUNDERED NEAR A KRYPTONITE METEOR WHOSE RADIATIONS WEAKEN ME!
SWIFTLY, THE GIRL OF STEEL'S SUPER-POWERS EBB AWAY!
GASP! ... IT'S TOO BIG FOR ME TO MELT WITH MY X-RAY VISION... AND MY SUPER-BREATH IS TOO WEAK TO BLOW IT AWAY! I--I'M TRAPPED! WILL I DIE HERE IN THE FUTURE? ... GULP!
MEANWHILE, TOMMY AND HIS MARTIAN PAL ARE TAKING A HIKE WITHIN THE LARGE AREA ENCLOSED BY THE AERATED DOME...
WATCH HOW MY NEW CHANGER RAY WORKS, JIK! IT CAN ALTER ATOMS TO WHATEVER SUBSTANCE I WANT! I'LL AIM IT AT THAT WOODEN STUMP AND...
JUMPING JETS! YOU CHANGED IT INTO METAL, TOMMY!
FURTHER ON...
IT CAN DO THE OPPOSITE TOO, JIK! I'LL CHANGE THAT GREEN METEOR FROM METAL INTO...
4
...ORDINARY ICE!
WHAT A...A MIRACLE THAT BOY GENIUS CAME ALONG! HE SAVED MY LIFE WITHOUT KNOWING IT! I'LL REGAIN MY SUPER-POWERS SOON!

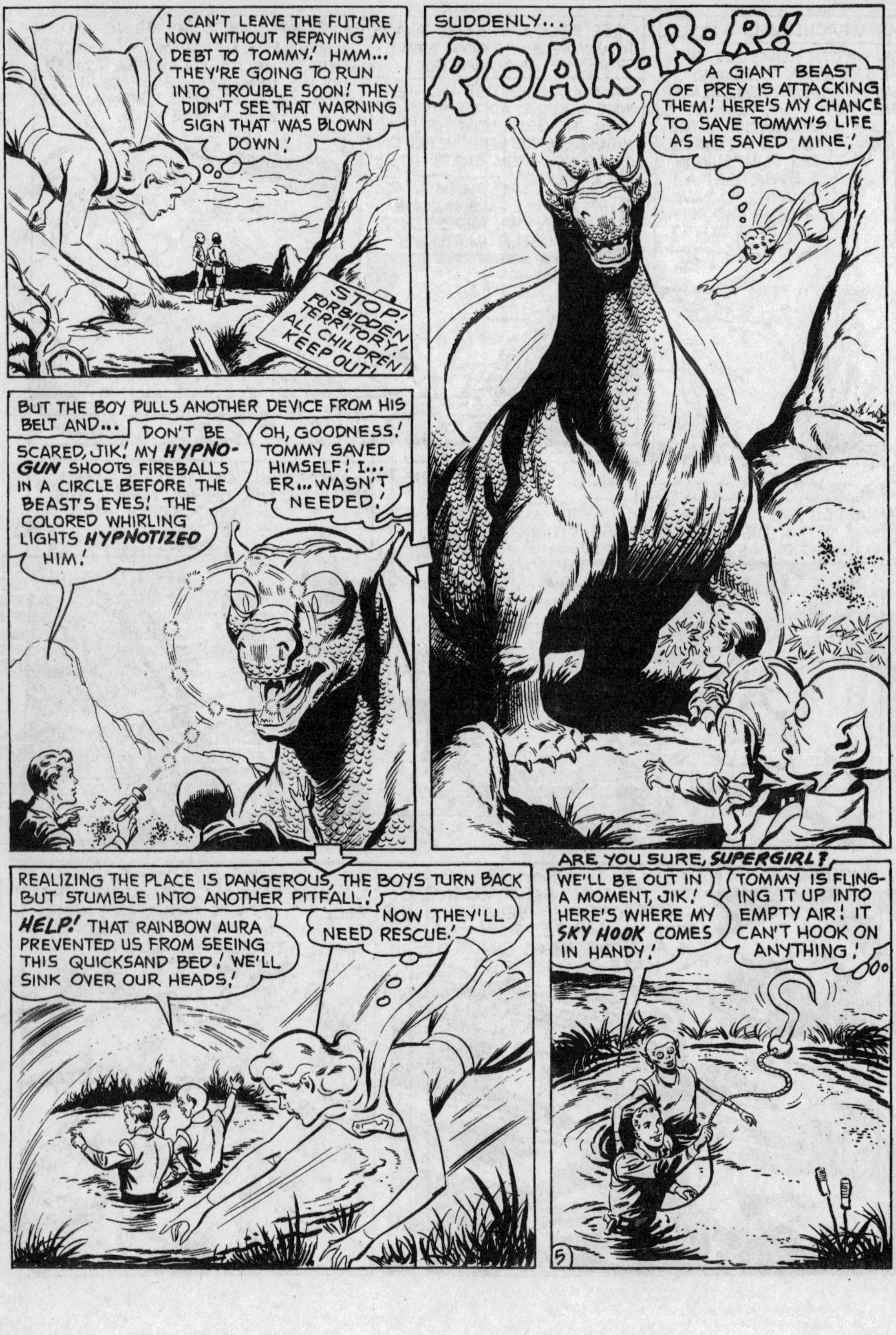
I CAN'T LEAVE THE FUTURE NOW WITHOUT REPAYING MY DEBT TO TOMMY! HMM... THEY'RE GOING TO RUN INTO TROUBLE SOON! THEY DIDN'T SEE THAT WARNING SIGN THAT WAS BLOWN DOWN!
STOP! FORBIDDEN TERRITORY! ALL CHILDREN KEEP OUT!
SUDDENLY...
ROAR-R-R!
A GIANT BEAST OF PREY IS ATTACKING THEM! HERE'S MY CHANCE TO SAVE TOMMY'S LIFE AS HE SAVED MINE!
BUT THE BOY PULLS ANOTHER DEVICE FROM HIS BELT AND...
DON'T BE SCARED, JIK! MY HYPNO-GUN SHOOTS FIREBALLS IN A CIRCLE BEFORE THE BEAST'S EYES! THE COLORED WHIRLING LIGHTS HYPNOTIZED HIM!
OH, GOODNESS! TOMMY SAVED HIMSELF! I... ER... WASN'T NEEDED!
REALIZING THE PLACE IS DANGEROUS, THE BOYS TURN BACK BUT STUMBLE INTO ANOTHER PITFALL!
HELP! THAT RAINBOW AURA PREVENTED US FROM SEEING THIS QUICKSAND BED! WE'LL SINK OVER OUR HEADS!
NOW THEY'LL NEED RESCUE!
ARE YOU SURE, SUPERGIRL?
WE'LL BE OUT IN A MOMENT, JIK! HERE'S WHERE MY SKY HOOK COMES IN HANDY!
TOMMY IS FLINGING IT UP INTO EMPTY AIR! IT CAN'T HOOK ON ANYTHING!
5

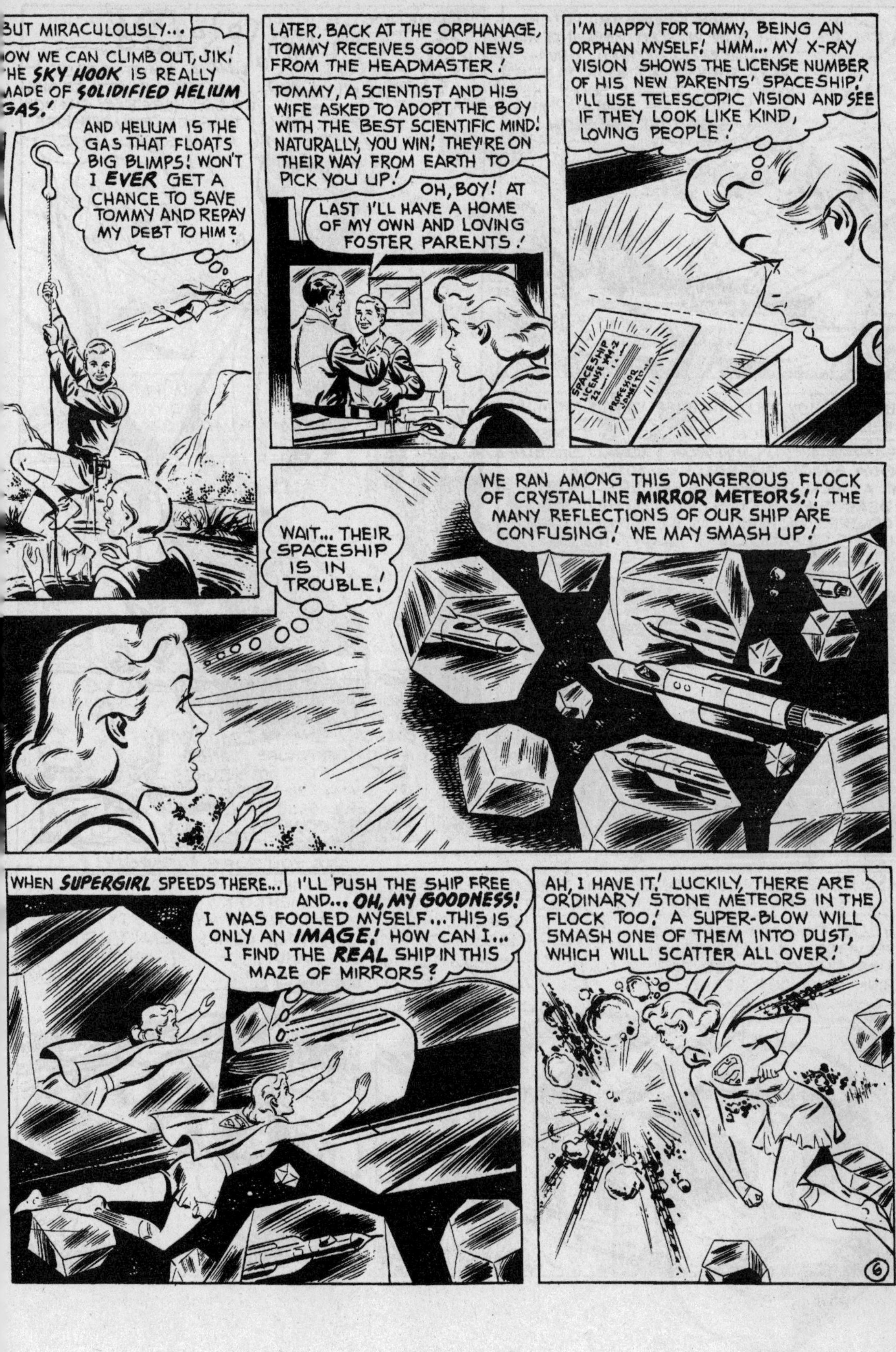
BUT MIRACULOUSLY...
NOW WE CAN CLIMB OUT, JIK! THE SKY HOOK IS REALLY MADE OF SOLIDIFIED HELIUM GAS!
AND HELIUM IS THE GAS THAT FLOATS BIG BLIMPS! WON'T I EVER GET A CHANCE TO SAVE TOMMY AND REPAY MY DEBT TO HIM?
LATER, BACK AT THE ORPHANAGE, TOMMY RECEIVES GOOD NEWS FROM THE HEADMASTER!
TOMMY, A SCIENTIST AND HIS WIFE ASKED TO ADOPT THE BOY WITH THE BEST SCIENTIFIC MIND! NATURALLY, YOU WIN! THEY'RE ON THEIR WAY FROM EARTH TO PICK YOU UP!
OH, BOY! AT LAST I'LL HAVE A HOME OF MY OWN AND LOVING FOSTER PARENTS!
I'M HAPPY FOR TOMMY, BEING AN ORPHAN MYSELF! HMM... MY X-RAY VISION SHOWS THE LICENSE NUMBER OF HIS NEW PARENTS' SPACESHIP! I'LL USE TELESCOPIC VISION AND SEE IF THEY LOOK LIKE KIND, LOVING PEOPLE!
SPACESHIP LICENSE
PROFESSOR
WE RAN AMONG THIS DANGEROUS FLOCK OF CRYSTALLINE MIRROR METEORS!! THE MANY REFLECTIONS OF OUR SHIP ARE CONFUSING! WE MAY SMASH UP!
WAIT... THEIR SPACESHIP IS IN TROUBLE!
WHEN SUPERGIRL SPEEDS THERE...
I'LL PUSH THE SHIP FREE AND... OH, MY GOODNESS! I WAS FOOLED MYSELF...THIS IS ONLY AN IMAGE! HOW CAN I... I FIND THE REAL SHIP IN THIS MAZE OF MIRRORS?
AH, I HAVE IT! LUCKILY, THERE ARE ORDINARY STONE METEORS IN THE FLOCK TOO! A SUPER-BLOW WILL SMASH ONE OF THEM INTO DUST, WHICH WILL SCATTER ALL OVER!
6

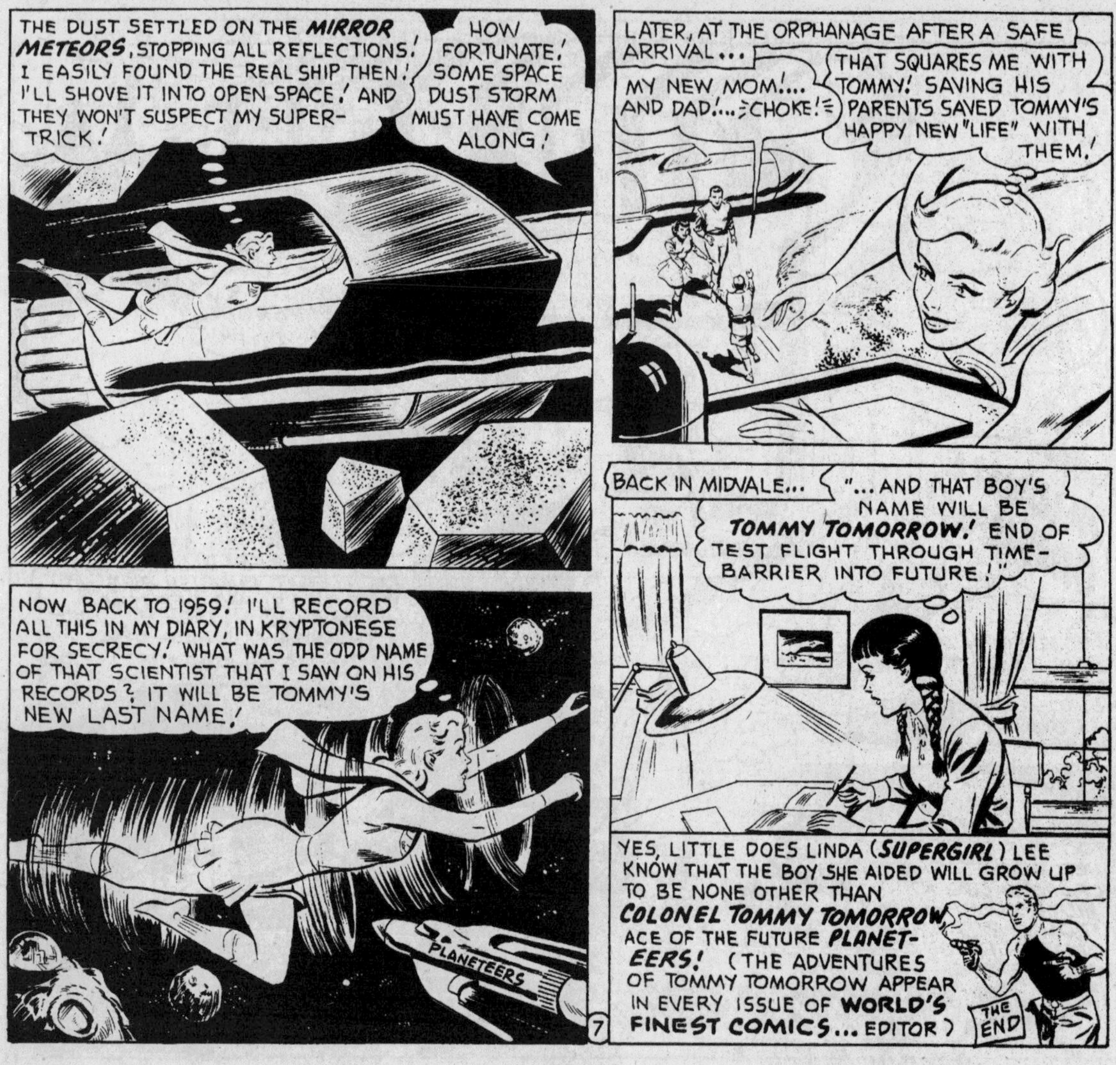
THE DUST SETTLED ON THE MIRROR METEORS, STOPPING ALL REFLECTIONS! I EASILY FOUND THE REAL SHIP THEN! I'LL SHOVE IT INTO OPEN SPACE! AND THEY WON'T SUSPECT MY SUPER-TRICK!
HOW FORTUNATE! SOME SPACE DUST STORM MUST HAVE COME ALONG!
LATER, AT THE ORPHANAGE AFTER A SAFE ARRIVAL...
MY NEW MOM!... AND DAD!... CHOKE!
THAT SQUARES ME WITH TOMMY! SAVING HIS PARENTS SAVED TOMMY'S HAPPY NEW "LIFE" WITH THEM!
NOW BACK TO 1959! I'LL RECORD ALL THIS IN MY DIARY, IN KRYPTONESE FOR SECRECY! WHAT WAS THE ODD NAME OF THAT SCIENTIST THAT I SAW ON HIS RECORDS? IT WILL BE TOMMY'S NEW LAST NAME!
PLANETEERS
7
BACK IN MIDVALE...
"...AND THAT BOY'S NAME WILL BE TOMMY TOMORROW! END OF TEST FLIGHT THROUGH TIME-BARRIER INTO FUTURE!"
YES, LITTLE DOES LINDA (SUPERGIRL) LEE KNOW THAT THE BOY SHE AIDED WILL GROW UP TO BE NONE OTHER THAN COLONEL TOMMY TOMORROW, ACE OF THE FUTURE PLANETEERS! (THE ADVENTURES OF TOMMY TOMORROW APPEAR IN EVERY ISSUE OF WORLD'S FINEST COMICS... EDITOR)
THE END

SUPERGIRL

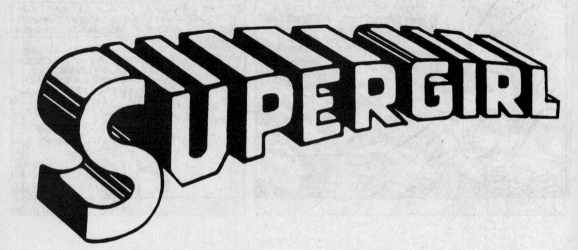

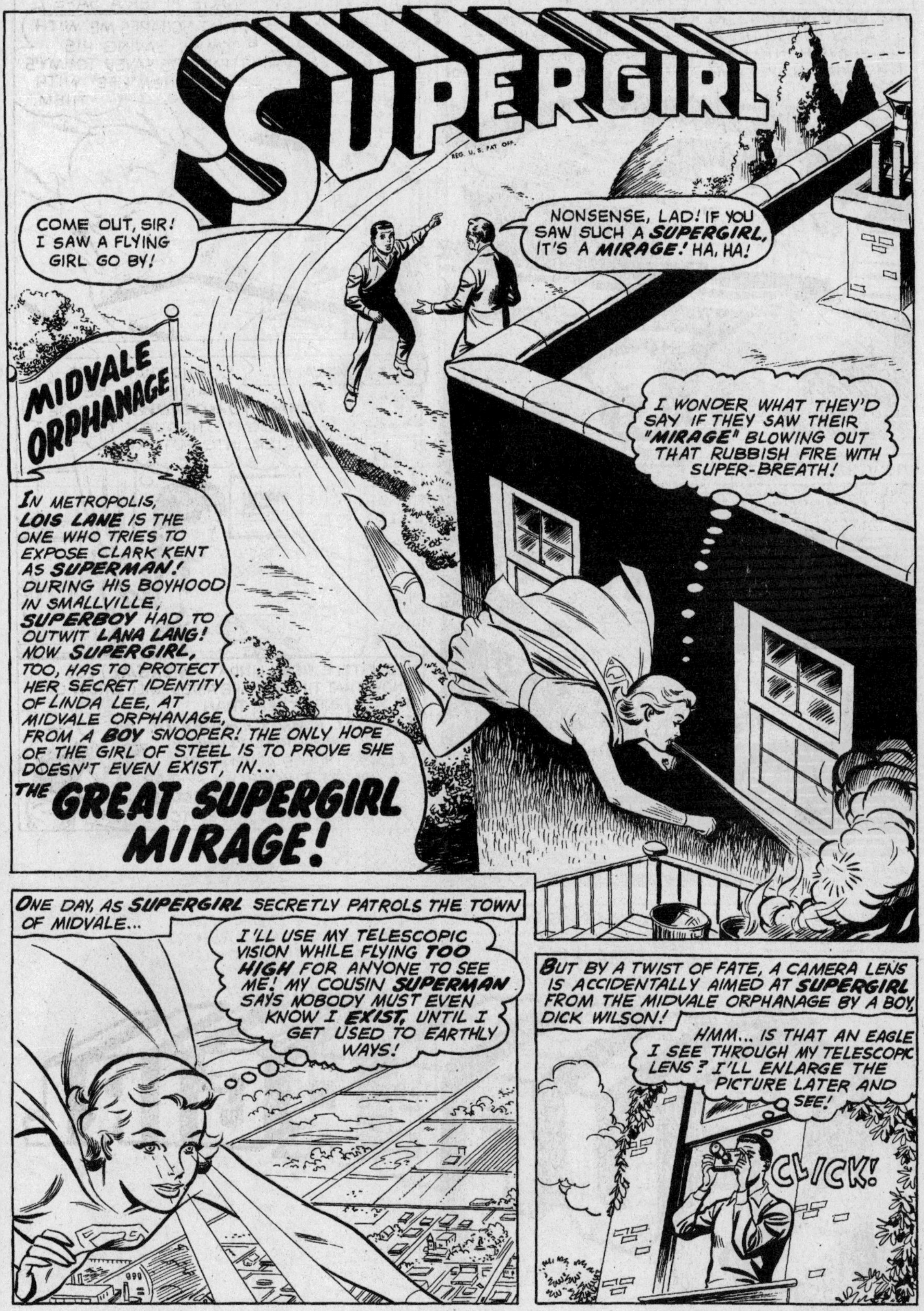
SUPERGIRL
REG. U. S. PAT. OFF.
COME OUT, SIR! I SAW A FLYING GIRL GO BY!
NONSENSE, LAD! IF YOU SAW SUCH A SUPERGIRL, IT'S A MIRAGE! HA, HA!
MIDVALE ORPHANAGE
I WONDER WHAT THEY'D SAY IF THEY SAW THEIR "MIRAGE" BLOWING OUT THAT RUBBISH FIRE WITH SUPER-BREATH!
IN METROPOLIS, LOIS LANE IS THE ONE WHO TRIES TO EXPOSE CLARK KENT AS SUPERMAN! DURING HIS BOYHOOD IN SMALLVILLE, SUPERBOY HAD TO OUTWIT LANA LANG! NOW SUPERGIRL, TOO, HAS TO PROTECT HER SECRET IDENTITY OF LINDA LEE, AT MIDVALE ORPHANAGE, FROM A BOY SNOOPER! THE ONLY HOPE OF THE GIRL OF STEEL IS TO PROVE SHE DOESN'T EVEN EXIST, IN...
THE GREAT SUPERGIRL MIRAGE!
ONE DAY, AS SUPERGIRL SECRETLY PATROLS THE TOWN OF MIDVALE...
I'LL USE MY TELESCOPIC VISION WHILE FLYING TOO HIGH FOR ANYONE TO SEE ME! MY COUSIN SUPERMAN SAYS NOBODY MUST EVEN KNOW I EXIST, UNTIL I GET USED TO EARTHLY WAYS!
BUT BY A TWIST OF FATE, A CAMERA LENS IS ACCIDENTALLY AIMED AT SUPERGIRL FROM THE MIDVALE ORPHANAGE BY A BOY, DICK WILSON!
HMM... IS THAT AN EAGLE I SEE THROUGH MY TELESCOPIC LENS? I'LL ENLARGE THE PICTURE LATER AND SEE!
CLICK!

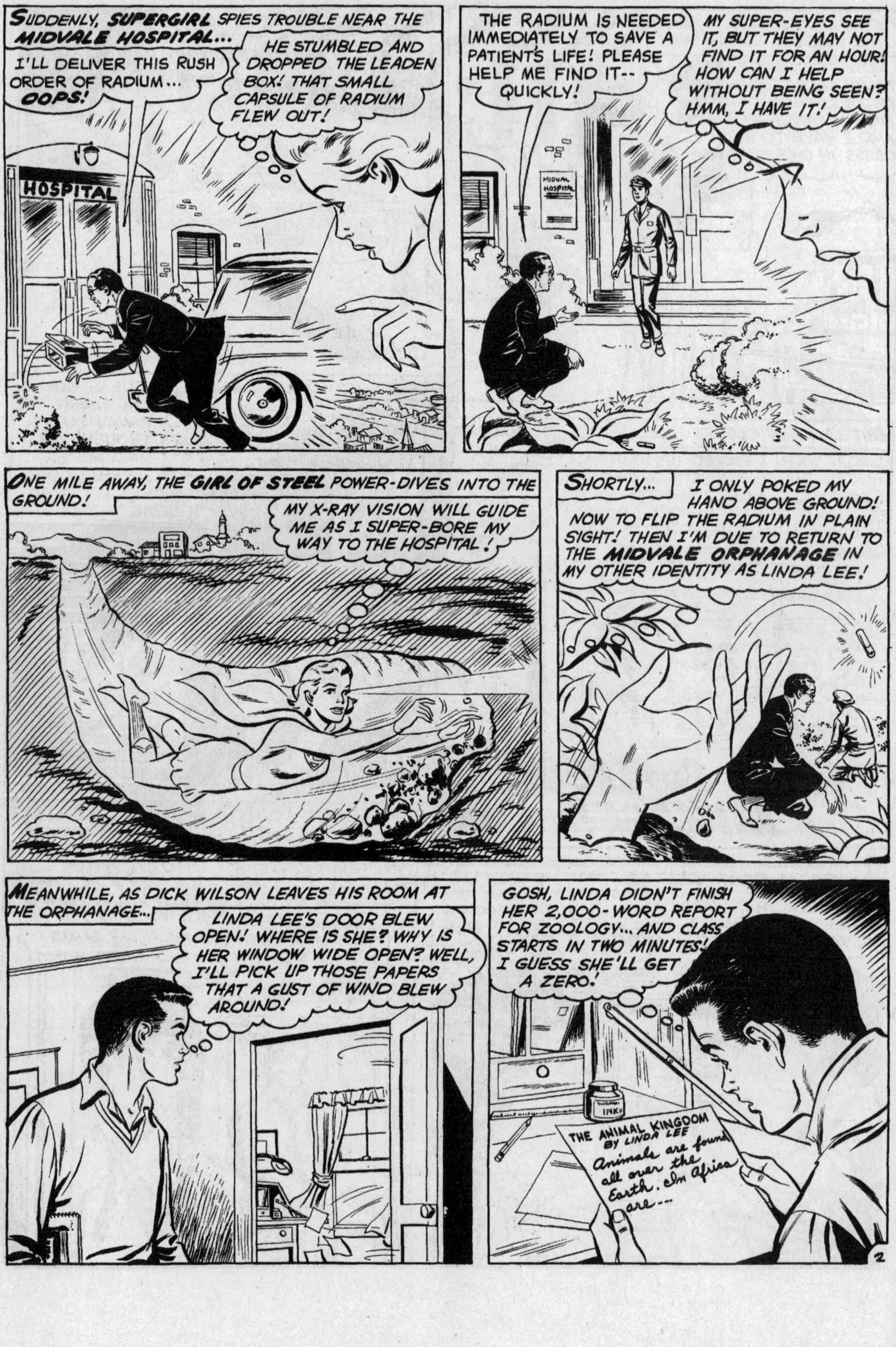
SUDDENLY, SUPERGIRL SPIES TROUBLE NEAR THE MIDVALE HOSPITAL...
I'LL DELIVER THIS RUSH ORDER OF RADIUM... OOPS!
HE STUMBLED AND DROPPED THE LEADEN BOX! THAT SMALL CAPSULE OF RADIUM FLEW OUT!
HOSPITAL
THE RADIUM IS NEEDED IMMEDIATELY TO SAVE A PATIENT'S LIFE! PLEASE HELP ME FIND IT-- QUICKLY!
MY SUPER-EYES SEE IT, BUT THEY MAY NOT FIND IT FOR AN HOUR! HOW CAN I HELP WITHOUT BEING SEEN? HMM, I HAVE IT!
ONE MILE AWAY, THE GIRL OF STEEL POWER-DIVES INTO THE GROUND!
MY X-RAY VISION WILL GUIDE ME AS I SUPER-BORE MY WAY TO THE HOSPITAL!
SHORTLY...
I ONLY POKED MY HAND ABOVE GROUND! NOW TO FLIP THE RADIUM IN PLAIN SIGHT! THEN I'M DUE TO RETURN TO THE MIDVALE ORPHANAGE IN MY OTHER IDENTITY AS LINDA LEE!
MEANWHILE, AS DICK WILSON LEAVES HIS ROOM AT THE ORPHANAGE...
LINDA LEE'S DOOR BLEW OPEN! WHERE IS SHE? WHY IS HER WINDOW WIDE OPEN? WELL, I'LL PICK UP THOSE PAPERS THAT A GUST OF WIND BLEW AROUND!
GOSH, LINDA DIDN'T FINISH HER 2,000-WORD REPORT FOR ZOOLOGY... AND CLASS STARTS IN TWO MINUTES! I GUESS SHE'LL GET A ZERO!
INK
THE ANIMAL KINGDOM BY LINDA LEE
Animals are found all over the Earth. In Africa are...
2

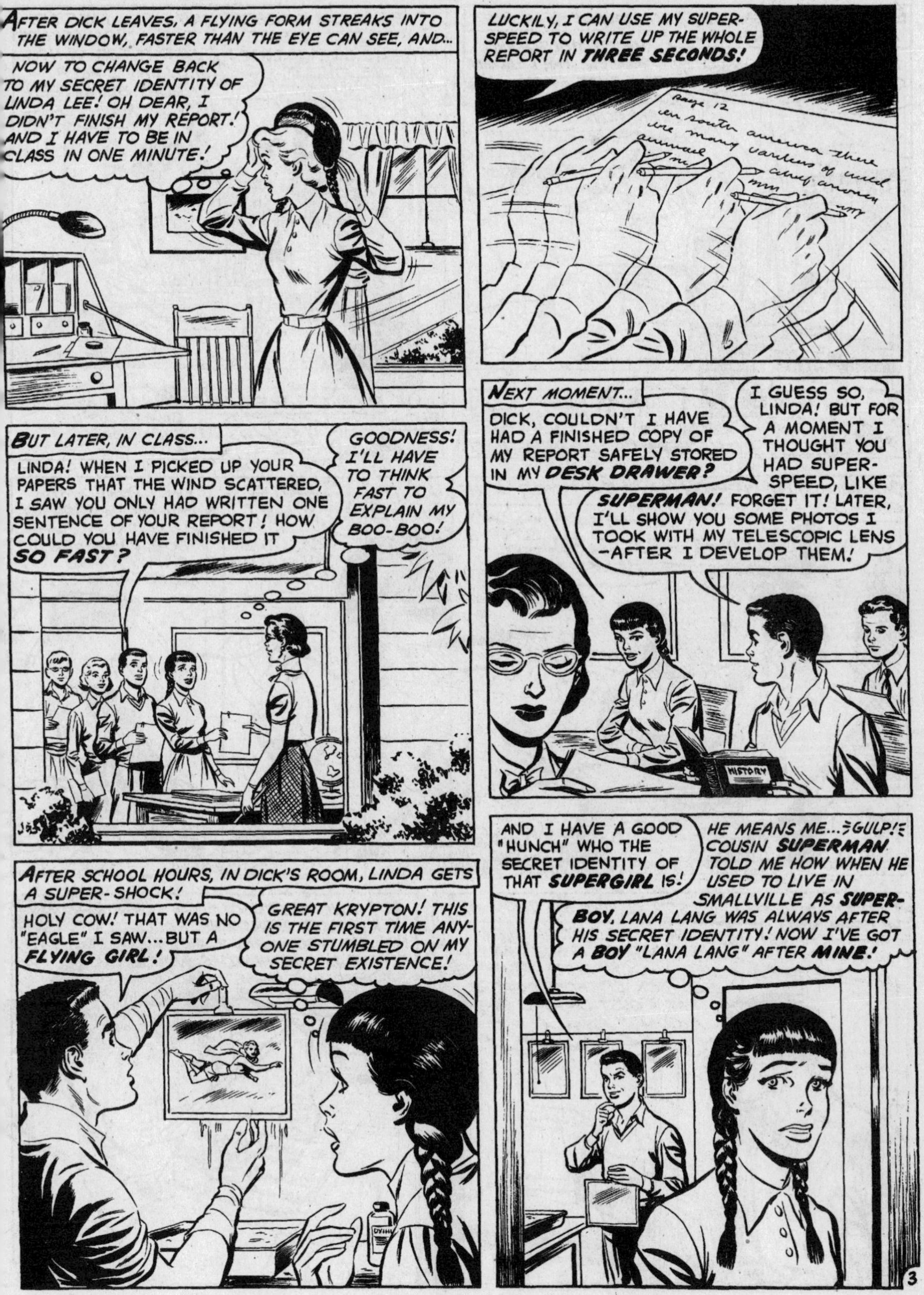
AFTER DICK LEAVES, A FLYING FORM STREAKS INTO THE WINDOW, FASTER THAN THE EYE CAN SEE, AND...
NOW TO CHANGE BACK TO MY SECRET IDENTITY OF LINDA LEE! OH DEAR, I DIDN'T FINISH MY REPORT! AND I HAVE TO BE IN CLASS IN ONE MINUTE!
LUCKILY, I CAN USE MY SUPER-SPEED TO WRITE UP THE WHOLE REPORT IN THREE SECONDS!
BUT LATER, IN CLASS...
LINDA! WHEN I PICKED UP YOUR PAPERS THAT THE WIND SCATTERED, I SAW YOU ONLY HAD WRITTEN ONE SENTENCE OF YOUR REPORT! HOW COULD YOU HAVE FINISHED IT SO FAST?
GOODNESS! I'LL HAVE TO THINK FAST TO EXPLAIN MY BOO-BOO!
NEXT MOMENT...
DICK, COULDN'T I HAVE HAD A FINISHED COPY OF MY REPORT SAFELY STORED IN MY DESK DRAWER?
I GUESS SO, LINDA! BUT FOR A MOMENT I THOUGHT YOU HAD SUPER-SPEED, LIKE SUPERMAN! FORGET IT! LATER, I'LL SHOW YOU SOME PHOTOS I TOOK WITH MY TELESCOPIC LENS -AFTER I DEVELOP THEM!
HISTORY
AFTER SCHOOL HOURS, IN DICK'S ROOM, LINDA GETS A SUPER-SHOCK!
HOLY COW! THAT WAS NO "EAGLE" I SAW...BUT A FLYING GIRL!
GREAT KRYPTON! THIS IS THE FIRST TIME ANYONE STUMBLED ON MY SECRET EXISTENCE!
AND I HAVE A GOOD "HUNCH" WHO THE SECRET IDENTITY OF THAT SUPERGIRL IS!
HE MEANS ME... GULP! COUSIN SUPERMAN TOLD ME HOW WHEN HE USED TO LIVE IN SMALLVILLE AS SUPERBOY, LANA LANG WAS ALWAYS AFTER HIS SECRET IDENTITY! NOW I'VE GOT A BOY "LANA LANG" AFTER MINE!
3

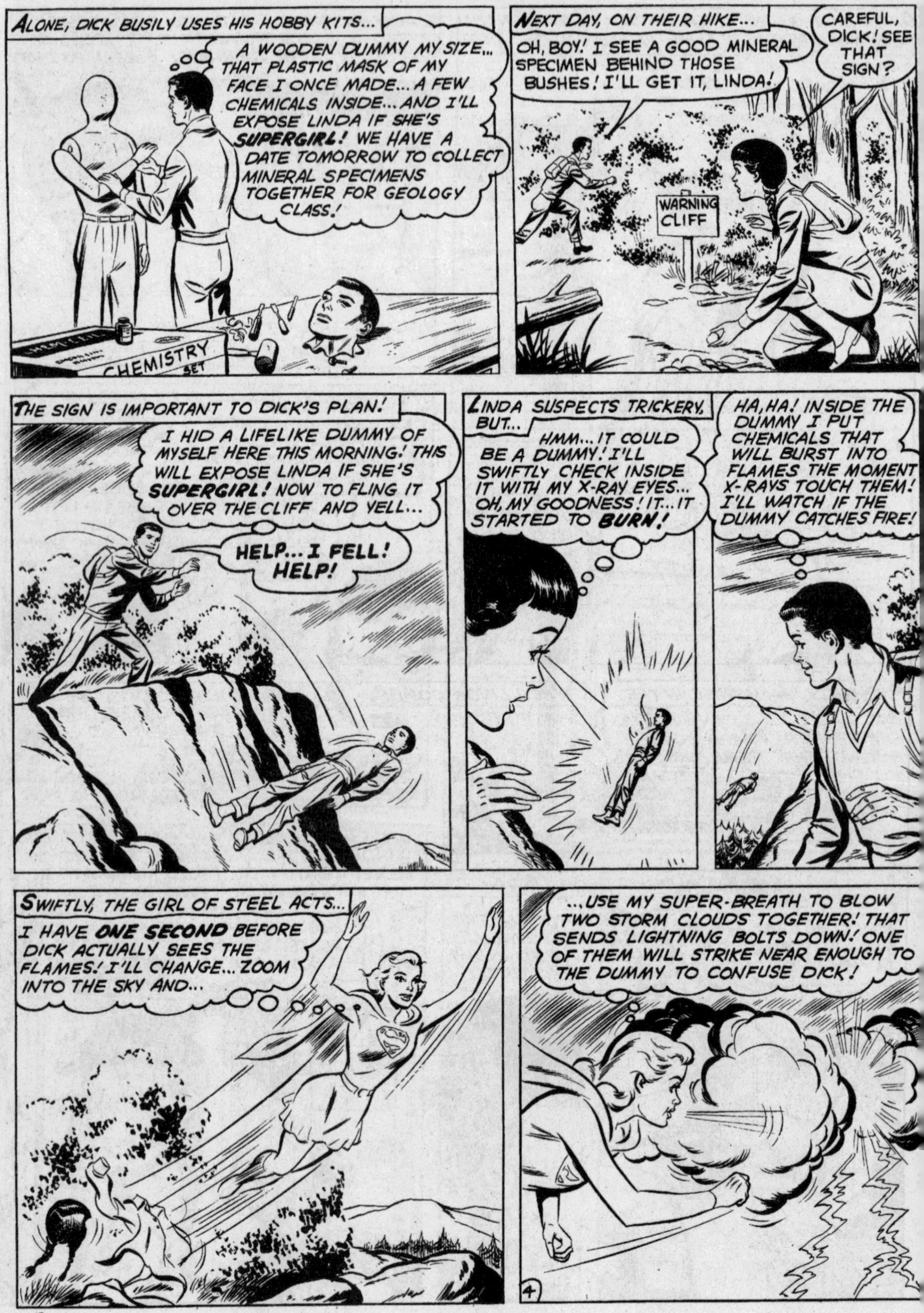
ALONE, DICK BUSILY USES HIS HOBBY KITS...
A WOODEN DUMMY MY SIZE... THAT PLASTIC MASK OF MY FACE I ONCE MADE... A FEW CHEMICALS INSIDE... AND I'LL EXPOSE LINDA IF SHE'S SUPERGIRL! WE HAVE A DATE TOMORROW TO COLLECT MINERAL SPECIMENS TOGETHER FOR GEOLOGY CLASS!
CHEMISTRY SET
NEXT DAY, ON THEIR HIKE...
OH, BOY! I SEE A GOOD MINERAL SPECIMEN BEHIND THOSE BUSHES! I'LL GET IT, LINDA!
CAREFUL, DICK! SEE THAT SIGN?
WARNING CLIFF
THE SIGN IS IMPORTANT TO DICK'S PLAN!
I HID A LIFELIKE DUMMY OF MYSELF HERE THIS MORNING! THIS WILL EXPOSE LINDA IF SHE'S SUPERGIRL! NOW TO FLING IT OVER THE CLIFF AND YELL...
HELP... I FELL! HELP!
LINDA SUSPECTS TRICKERY, BUT...
HMM... IT COULD BE A DUMMY! I'LL SWIFTLY CHECK INSIDE IT WITH MY X-RAY EYES... OH, MY GOODNESS! IT... IT STARTED TO BURN!
HA, HA! INSIDE THE DUMMY I PUT CHEMICALS THAT WILL BURST INTO FLAMES THE MOMENT X-RAYS TOUCH THEM! I'LL WATCH IF THE DUMMY CATCHES FIRE!
SWIFTLY, THE GIRL OF STEEL ACTS...
I HAVE ONE SECOND BEFORE DICK ACTUALLY SEES THE FLAMES! I'LL CHANGE... ZOOM INTO THE SKY AND...
...USE MY SUPER-BREATH TO BLOW TWO STORM CLOUDS TOGETHER! THAT SENDS LIGHTNING BOLTS DOWN! ONE OF THEM WILL STRIKE NEAR ENOUGH TO THE DUMMY TO CONFUSE DICK!
4

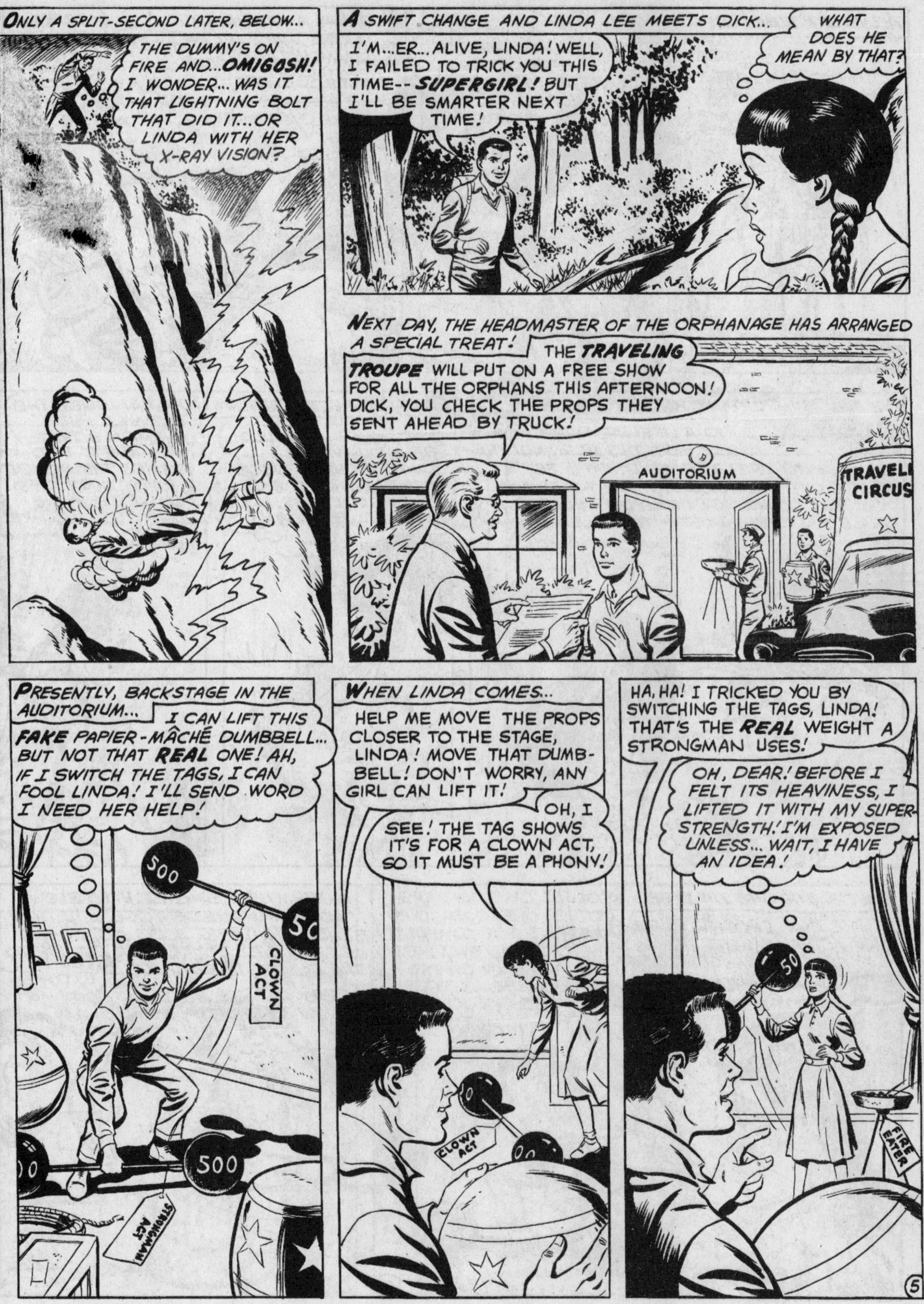
ONLY A SPLIT-SECOND LATER, BELOW...
THE DUMMY'S ON FIRE AND...OMIGOSH! I WONDER... WAS IT THAT LIGHTNING BOLT THAT DID IT...OR LINDA WITH HER X-RAY VISION?
A SWIFT CHANGE AND LINDA LEE MEETS DICK...
I'M...ER...ALIVE, LINDA! WELL, I FAILED TO TRICK YOU THIS TIME-- SUPERGIRL! BUT I'LL BE SMARTER NEXT TIME!
WHAT DOES HE MEAN BY THAT?
NEXT DAY, THE HEADMASTER OF THE ORPHANAGE HAS ARRANGED A SPECIAL TREAT!
THE TRAVELING TROUPE WILL PUT ON A FREE SHOW FOR ALL THE ORPHANS THIS AFTERNOON! DICK, YOU CHECK THE PROPS THEY SENT AHEAD BY TRUCK!
AUDITORIUM
TRAVEL CIRCUS
PRESENTLY, BACKSTAGE IN THE AUDITORIUM...
I CAN LIFT THIS FAKE PAPIER-MÂCHÉ DUMBBELL... BUT NOT THAT REAL ONE! AH, IF I SWITCH THE TAGS, I CAN FOOL LINDA! I'LL SEND WORD I NEED HER HELP!
500
CLOWN ACT
500
STRONGMAN ACT
WHEN LINDA COMES...
HELP ME MOVE THE PROPS CLOSER TO THE STAGE, LINDA! MOVE THAT DUMB-BELL! DON'T WORRY, ANY GIRL CAN LIFT IT!
OH, I SEE! THE TAG SHOWS IT'S FOR A CLOWN ACT, SO IT MUST BE A PHONY!
CLOWN ACT
HA, HA! I TRICKED YOU BY SWITCHING THE TAGS, LINDA! THAT'S THE REAL WEIGHT A STRONGMAN USES!
OH, DEAR! BEFORE I FELT ITS HEAVINESS, I LIFTED IT WITH MY SUPER-STRENGTH! I'M EXPOSED UNLESS... WAIT, I HAVE AN IDEA!
50
FIRE EATER
5

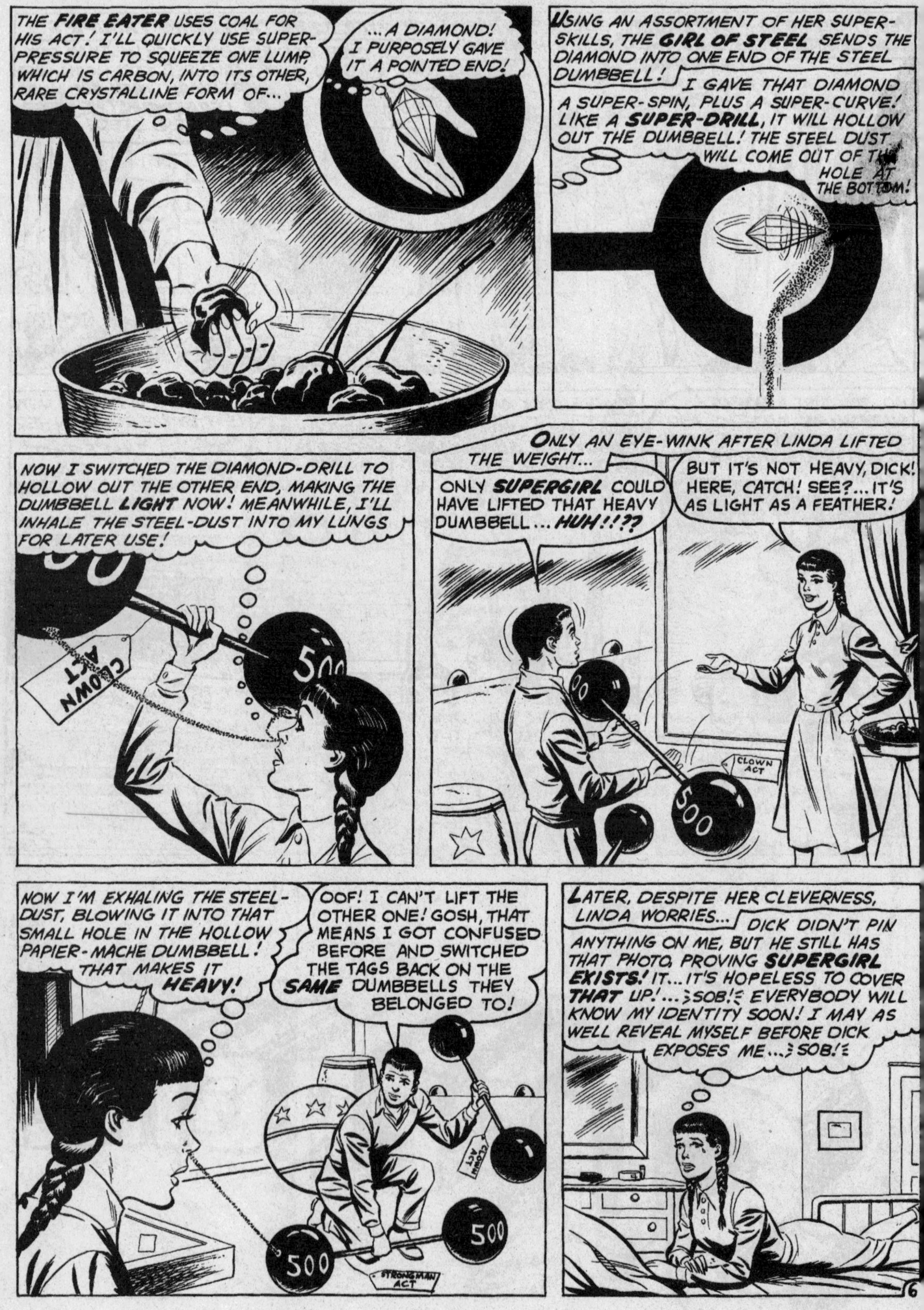
THE FIRE EATER USES COAL FOR HIS ACT! I'LL QUICKLY USE SUPER-PRESSURE TO SQUEEZE ONE LUMP, WHICH IS CARBON, INTO ITS OTHER, RARE CRYSTALLINE FORM OF...
...A DIAMOND! I PURPOSELY GAVE IT A POINTED END!
USING AN ASSORTMENT OF HER SUPER-SKILLS, THE GIRL OF STEEL SENDS THE DIAMOND INTO ONE END OF THE STEEL DUMBBELL!
I GAVE THAT DIAMOND A SUPER-SPIN, PLUS A SUPER-CURVE! LIKE A SUPER-DRILL, IT WILL HOLLOW OUT THE DUMBBELL! THE STEEL DUST WILL COME OUT OF THE HOLE AT THE BOTTOM!
NOW I SWITCHED THE DIAMOND-DRILL TO HOLLOW OUT THE OTHER END, MAKING THE DUMBBELL LIGHT NOW! MEANWHILE, I'LL INHALE THE STEEL-DUST INTO MY LUNGS FOR LATER USE!
CLOWN ACT
500
ONLY AN EYE-WINK AFTER LINDA LIFTED THE WEIGHT...
ONLY SUPERGIRL COULD HAVE LIFTED THAT HEAVY DUMBBELL... HUH!!??
BUT IT'S NOT HEAVY, DICK! HERE, CATCH! SEE?...IT'S AS LIGHT AS A FEATHER!
CLOWN ACT
500
NOW I'M EXHALING THE STEEL-DUST, BLOWING IT INTO THAT SMALL HOLE IN THE HOLLOW PAPIER-MACHE DUMBBELL! THAT MAKES IT HEAVY!
OOF! I CAN'T LIFT THE OTHER ONE! GOSH, THAT MEANS I GOT CONFUSED BEFORE AND SWITCHED THE TAGS BACK ON THE SAME DUMBBELLS THEY BELONGED TO!
CLOWN ACT
500
500
STRONGMAN ACT
LATER, DESPITE HER CLEVERNESS, LINDA WORRIES...
DICK DIDN'T PIN ANYTHING ON ME, BUT HE STILL HAS THAT PHOTO, PROVING SUPERGIRL EXISTS! IT...IT'S HOPELESS TO COVER THAT UP!... SOB! EVERYBODY WILL KNOW MY IDENTITY SOON! I MAY AS WELL REVEAL MYSELF BEFORE DICK EXPOSES ME... SOB!
6

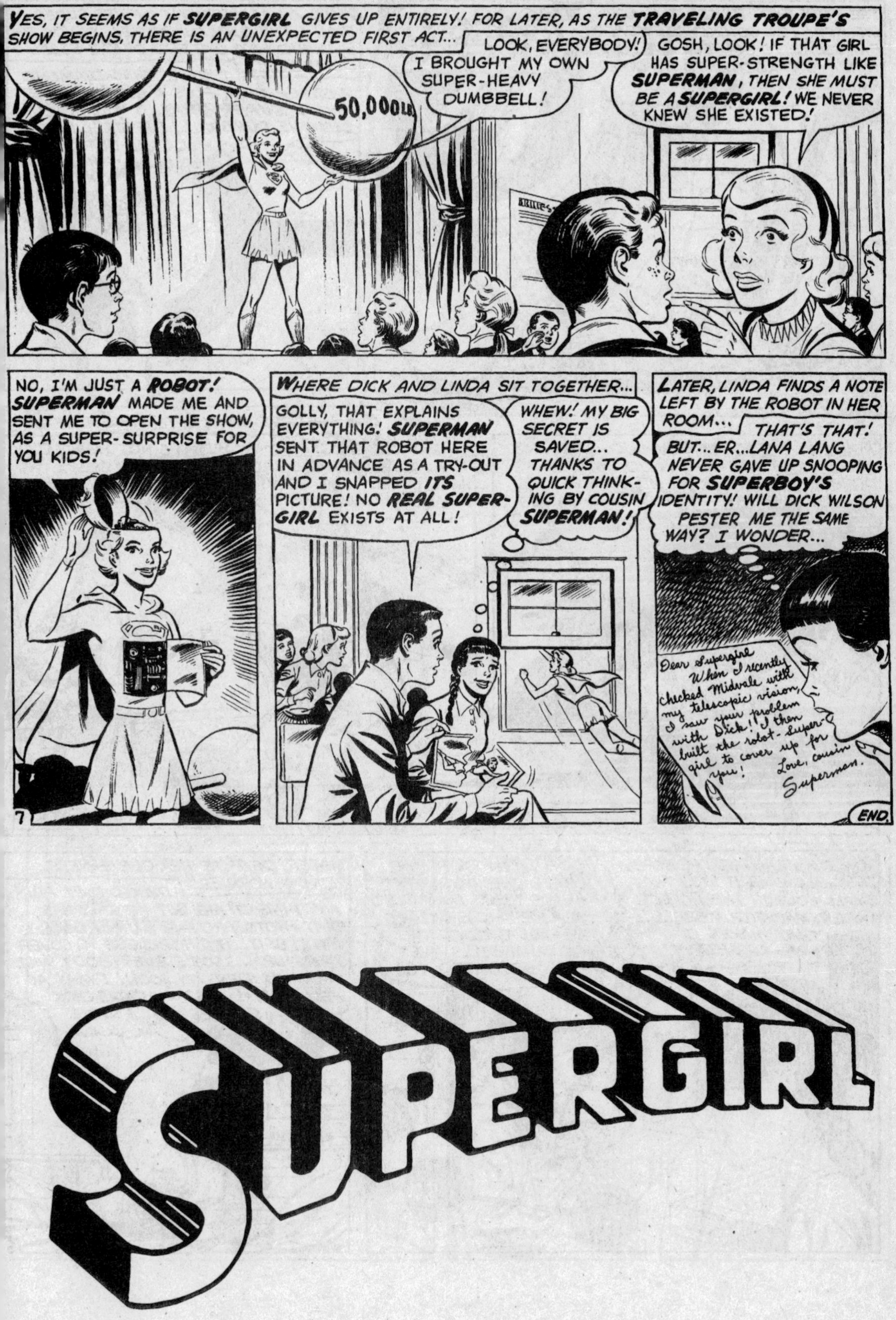
YES, IT SEEMS AS IF SUPERGIRL GIVES UP ENTIRELY! FOR LATER, AS THE TRAVELING TROUPE'S SHOW BEGINS, THERE IS AN UNEXPECTED FIRST ACT...
LOOK, EVERYBODY! I BROUGHT MY OWN SUPER-HEAVY DUMBBELL!
50,000 LB.
GOSH, LOOK! IF THAT GIRL HAS SUPER-STRENGTH LIKE SUPERMAN, THEN SHE MUST BE A SUPERGIRL! WE NEVER KNEW SHE EXISTED!
NO, I'M JUST A ROBOT! SUPERMAN MADE ME AND SENT ME TO OPEN THE SHOW, AS A SUPER-SURPRISE FOR YOU KIDS!
7
WHERE DICK AND LINDA SIT TOGETHER...
GOLLY, THAT EXPLAINS EVERYTHING! SUPERMAN SENT THAT ROBOT HERE IN ADVANCE AS A TRY-OUT AND I SNAPPED ITS PICTURE! NO REAL SUPER-GIRL EXISTS AT ALL!
WHEW! MY BIG SECRET IS SAVED... THANKS TO QUICK THINKING BY COUSIN SUPERMAN!
LATER, LINDA FINDS A NOTE LEFT BY THE ROBOT IN HER ROOM...
THAT'S THAT! BUT... ER... LANA LANG NEVER GAVE UP SNOOPING FOR SUPERBOY'S IDENTITY! WILL DICK WILSON PESTER ME THE SAME WAY? I WONDER...
Dear Supergirl
When I recently checked Midvale with my telescopic vision, I saw your problem with Dick! I then built the robot-Supergirl to cover up for you!
Love, cousin Superman.
END

SUPERGIRL

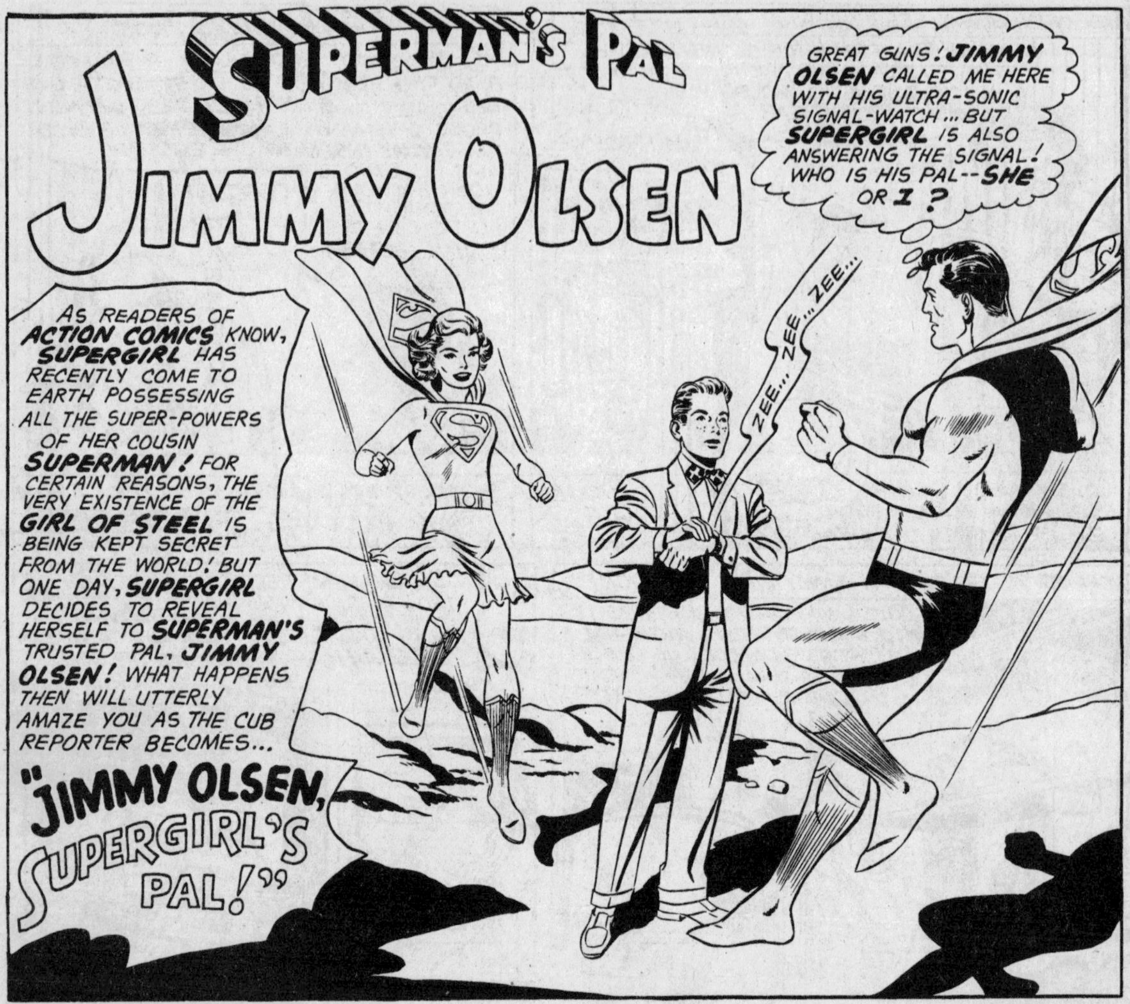
SUPERMAN'S PAL
JIMMY OLSEN
AS READERS OF ACTION COMICS KNOW, SUPERGIRL HAS RECENTLY COME TO EARTH POSSESSING ALL THE SUPER-POWERS OF HER COUSIN SUPERMAN! FOR CERTAIN REASONS, THE VERY EXISTENCE OF THE GIRL OF STEEL IS BEING KEPT SECRET FROM THE WORLD! BUT ONE DAY, SUPERGIRL DECIDES TO REVEAL HERSELF TO SUPERMAN'S TRUSTED PAL, JIMMY OLSEN! WHAT HAPPENS THEN WILL UTTERLY AMAZE YOU AS THE CUB REPORTER BECOMES...
"JIMMY OLSEN, SUPERGIRL'S PAL!"
GREAT GUNS! JIMMY OLSEN CALLED ME HERE WITH HIS ULTRA-SONIC SIGNAL-WATCH ... BUT SUPERGIRL IS ALSO ANSWERING THE SIGNAL! WHO IS HIS PAL--SHE OR I?
ZEE... ZEE... ZEE...

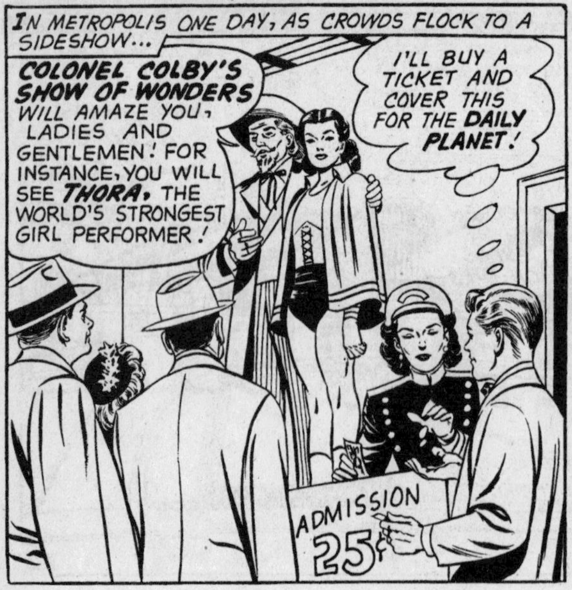
IN METROPOLIS ONE DAY, AS CROWDS FLOCK TO A SIDESHOW...
COLONEL COLBY'S SHOW OF WONDERS WILL AMAZE YOU, LADIES AND GENTLEMEN! FOR INSTANCE, YOU WILL SEE THORA, THE WORLD'S STRONGEST GIRL PERFORMER!
I'LL BUY A TICKET AND COVER THIS FOR THE DAILY PLANET!
ADMISSION 25¢

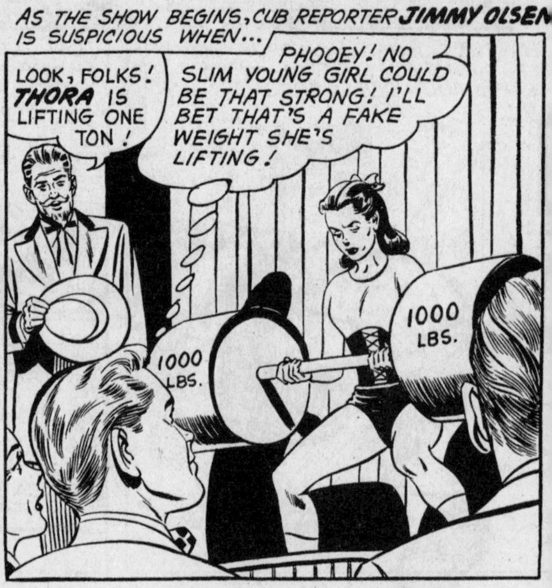
AS THE SHOW BEGINS, CUB REPORTER JIMMY OLSEN IS SUSPICIOUS WHEN...
LOOK, FOLKS! THORA IS LIFTING ONE TON!
PHOOEY! NO SLIM YOUNG GIRL COULD BE THAT STRONG! I'LL BET THAT'S A FAKE WEIGHT SHE'S LIFTING!
1000 LBS.
1000 LBS.

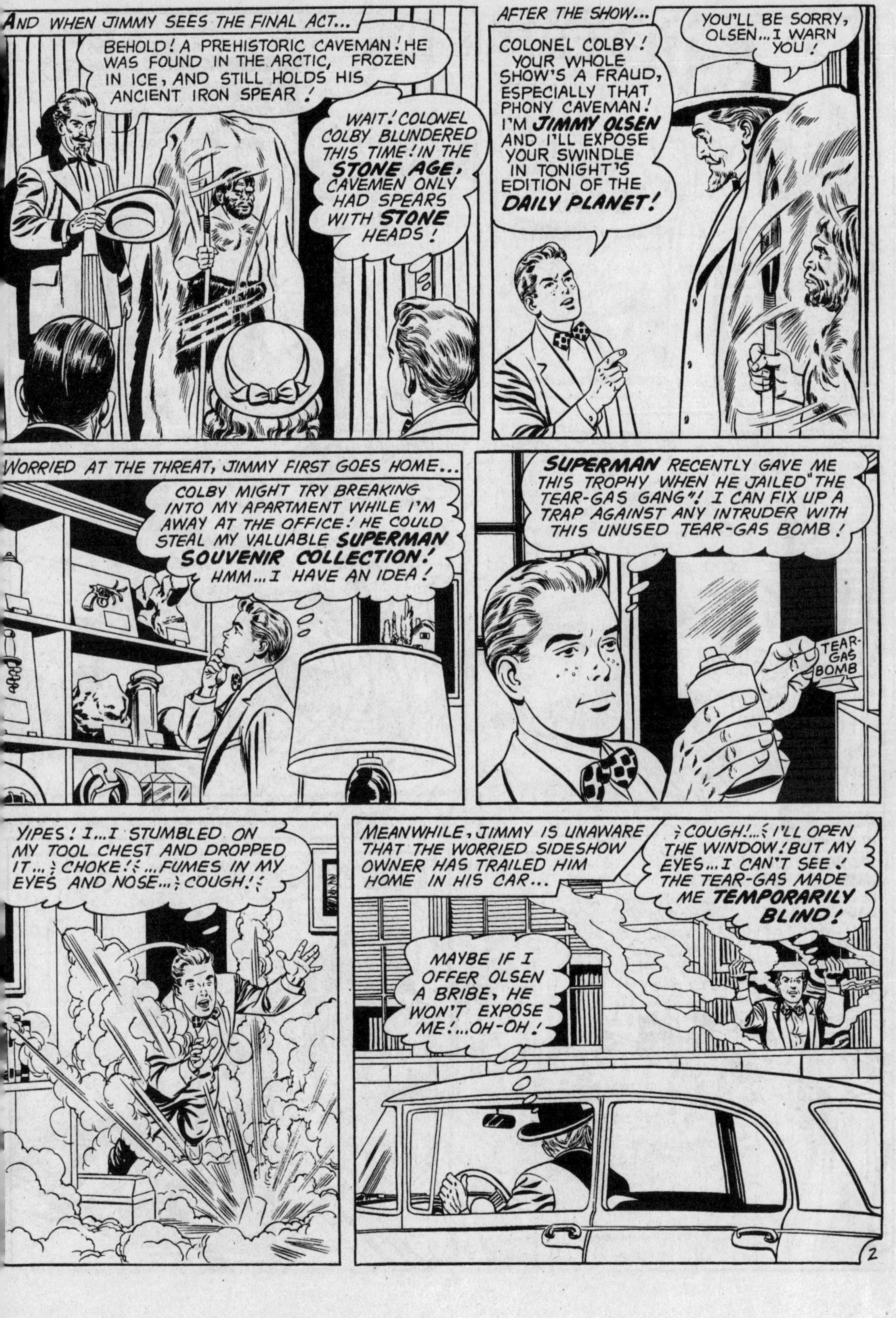
AND WHEN JIMMY SEES THE FINAL ACT...
BEHOLD! A PREHISTORIC CAVEMAN! HE WAS FOUND IN THE ARCTIC, FROZEN IN ICE, AND STILL HOLDS HIS ANCIENT IRON SPEAR!
WAIT! COLONEL COLBY BLUNDERED THIS TIME! IN THE STONE AGE, CAVEMEN ONLY HAD SPEARS WITH STONE HEADS!
AFTER THE SHOW...
COLONEL COLBY! YOUR WHOLE SHOW'S A FRAUD, ESPECIALLY THAT PHONY CAVEMAN! I'M JIMMY OLSEN AND I'LL EXPOSE YOUR SWINDLE IN TONIGHT'S EDITION OF THE DAILY PLANET!
YOU'LL BE SORRY, OLSEN... I WARN YOU!
WORRIED AT THE THREAT, JIMMY FIRST GOES HOME...
COLBY MIGHT TRY BREAKING INTO MY APARTMENT WHILE I'M AWAY AT THE OFFICE! HE COULD STEAL MY VALUABLE SUPERMAN SOUVENIR COLLECTION! HMM... I HAVE AN IDEA!
SUPERMAN RECENTLY GAVE ME THIS TROPHY WHEN HE JAILED "THE TEAR-GAS GANG"! I CAN FIX UP A TRAP AGAINST ANY INTRUDER WITH THIS UNUSED TEAR-GAS BOMB!
TEAR-GAS BOMB
YIPES! I...I STUMBLED ON MY TOOL CHEST AND DROPPED IT... CHOKE! ...FUMES IN MY EYES AND NOSE... COUGH!
MEANWHILE, JIMMY IS UNAWARE THAT THE WORRIED SIDESHOW OWNER HAS TRAILED HIM HOME IN HIS CAR...
COUGH!... I'LL OPEN THE WINDOW! BUT MY EYES... I CAN'T SEE! THE TEAR-GAS MADE ME TEMPORARILY BLIND!
MAYBE IF I OFFER OLSEN A BRIBE, HE WON'T EXPOSE ME!...OH-OH!
2

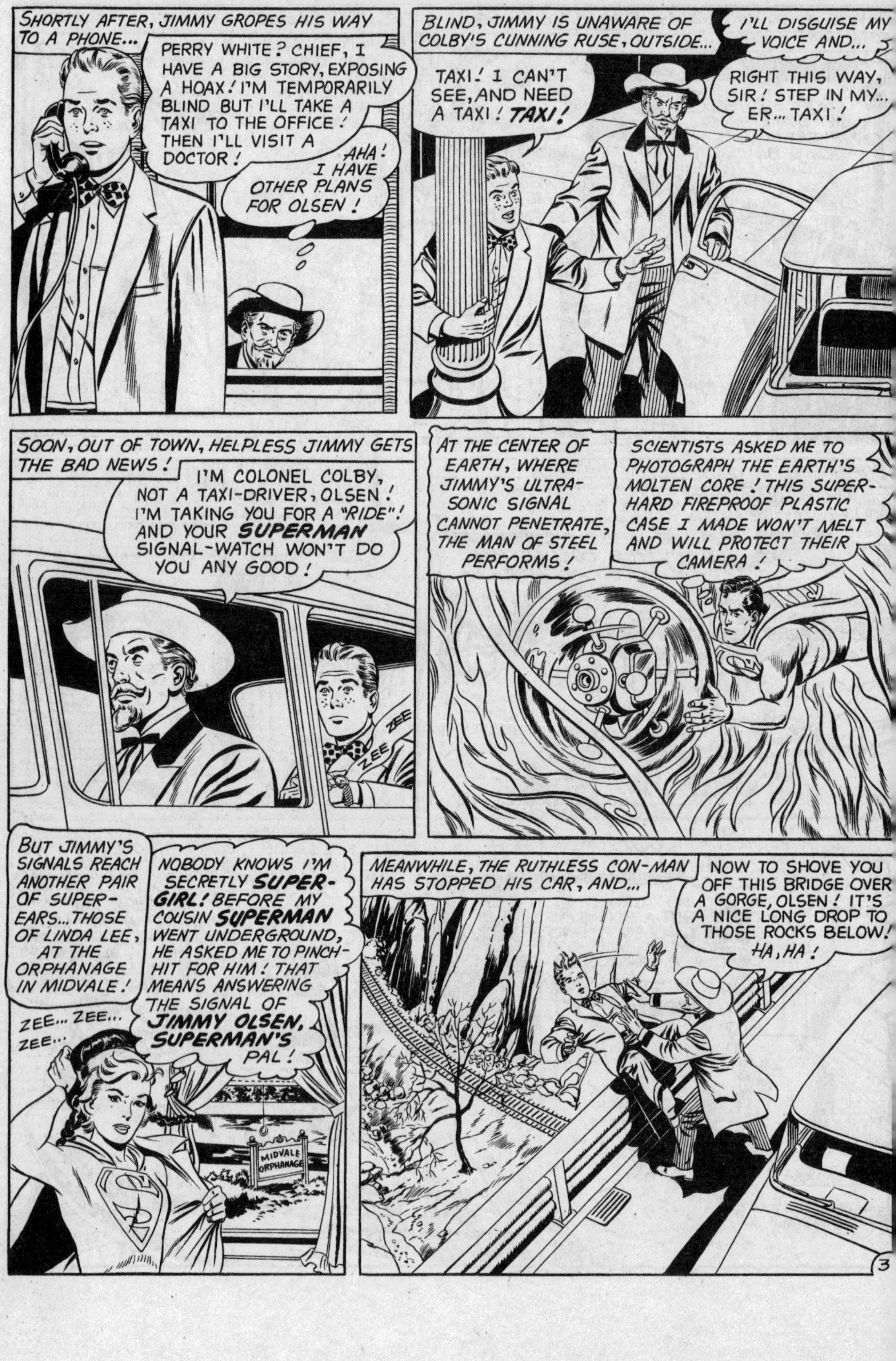
SHORTLY AFTER, JIMMY GROPES HIS WAY TO A PHONE...
PERRY WHITE? CHIEF, I HAVE A BIG STORY, EXPOSING A HOAX! I'M TEMPORARILY BLIND BUT I'LL TAKE A TAXI TO THE OFFICE! THEN I'LL VISIT A DOCTOR!
AHA! I HAVE OTHER PLANS FOR OLSEN!
BLIND, JIMMY IS UNAWARE OF COLBY'S CUNNING RUSE, OUTSIDE...
I'LL DISGUISE MY VOICE AND...
TAXI! I CAN'T SEE, AND NEED A TAXI! TAXI!
RIGHT THIS WAY, SIR! STEP IN MY... ER... TAXI!
SOON, OUT OF TOWN, HELPLESS JIMMY GETS THE BAD NEWS!
I'M COLONEL COLBY, NOT A TAXI-DRIVER, OLSEN! I'M TAKING YOU FOR A "RIDE"! AND YOUR SUPERMAN SIGNAL-WATCH WON'T DO YOU ANY GOOD!
ZEE
ZEE
AT THE CENTER OF EARTH, WHERE JIMMY'S ULTRA-SONIC SIGNAL CANNOT PENETRATE, THE MAN OF STEEL PERFORMS!
SCIENTISTS ASKED ME TO PHOTOGRAPH THE EARTH'S MOLTEN CORE! THIS SUPER-HARD FIREPROOF PLASTIC CASE I MADE WON'T MELT AND WILL PROTECT THEIR CAMERA!
BUT JIMMY'S SIGNALS REACH ANOTHER PAIR OF SUPER-EARS... THOSE OF LINDA LEE, AT THE ORPHANAGE IN MIDVALE!
NOBODY KNOWS I'M SECRETLY SUPER-GIRL! BEFORE MY COUSIN SUPERMAN WENT UNDERGROUND, HE ASKED ME TO PINCH-HIT FOR HIM! THAT MEANS ANSWERING THE SIGNAL OF JIMMY OLSEN, SUPERMAN'S PAL!
ZEE... ZEE... ZEE...
MIDVALE ORPHANAGE
MEANWHILE, THE RUTHLESS CON-MAN HAS STOPPED HIS CAR, AND...
NOW TO SHOVE YOU OFF THIS BRIDGE OVER A GORGE, OLSEN! IT'S A NICE LONG DROP TO THOSE ROCKS BELOW! HA, HA!
3

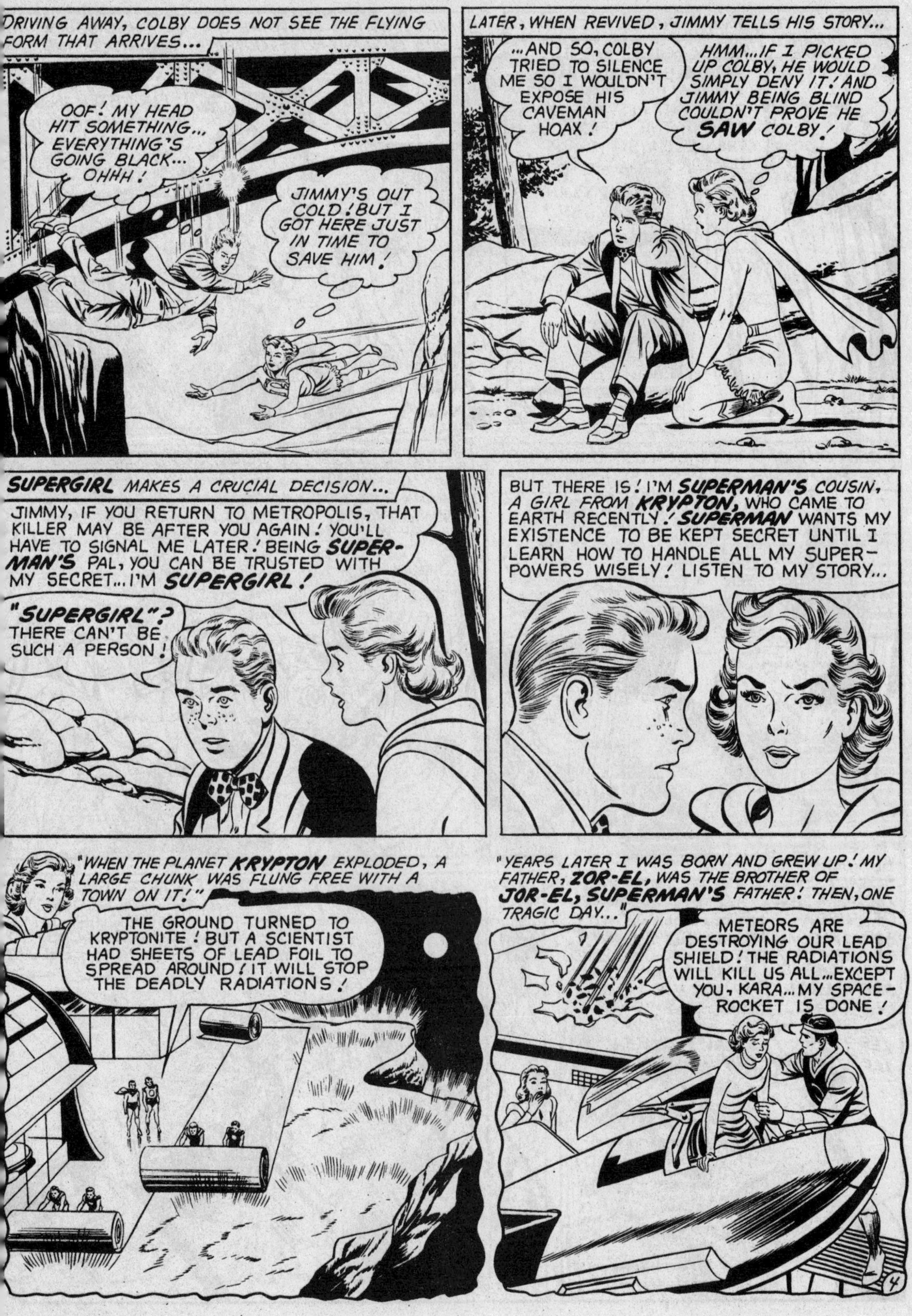
DRIVING AWAY, COLBY DOES NOT SEE THE FLYING FORM THAT ARRIVES...
OOF! MY HEAD HIT SOMETHING... EVERYTHING'S GOING BLACK... OHHH!
JIMMY'S OUT COLD! BUT I GOT HERE JUST IN TIME TO SAVE HIM!
LATER, WHEN REVIVED, JIMMY TELLS HIS STORY...
...AND SO, COLBY TRIED TO SILENCE ME SO I WOULDN'T EXPOSE HIS CAVEMAN HOAX!
HMM...IF I PICKED UP COLBY, HE WOULD SIMPLY DENY IT! AND JIMMY BEING BLIND COULDN'T PROVE HE SAW COLBY!
SUPERGIRL MAKES A CRUCIAL DECISION...
JIMMY, IF YOU RETURN TO METROPOLIS, THAT KILLER MAY BE AFTER YOU AGAIN! YOU'LL HAVE TO SIGNAL ME LATER! BEING SUPERMAN'S PAL, YOU CAN BE TRUSTED WITH MY SECRET...I'M SUPERGIRL!
"SUPERGIRL"? THERE CAN'T BE SUCH A PERSON!
BUT THERE IS! I'M SUPERMAN'S COUSIN, A GIRL FROM KRYPTON, WHO CAME TO EARTH RECENTLY! SUPERMAN WANTS MY EXISTENCE TO BE KEPT SECRET UNTIL I LEARN HOW TO HANDLE ALL MY SUPER-POWERS WISELY! LISTEN TO MY STORY...
"WHEN THE PLANET KRYPTON EXPLODED, A LARGE CHUNK WAS FLUNG FREE WITH A TOWN ON IT!"
THE GROUND TURNED TO KRYPTONITE! BUT A SCIENTIST HAD SHEETS OF LEAD FOIL TO SPREAD AROUND! IT WILL STOP THE DEADLY RADIATIONS!
"YEARS LATER I WAS BORN AND GREW UP! MY FATHER, ZOR-EL, WAS THE BROTHER OF JOR-EL, SUPERMAN'S FATHER! THEN, ONE TRAGIC DAY..."
METEORS ARE DESTROYING OUR LEAD SHIELD! THE RADIATIONS WILL KILL US ALL...EXCEPT YOU, KARA...MY SPACE-ROCKET IS DONE!
4

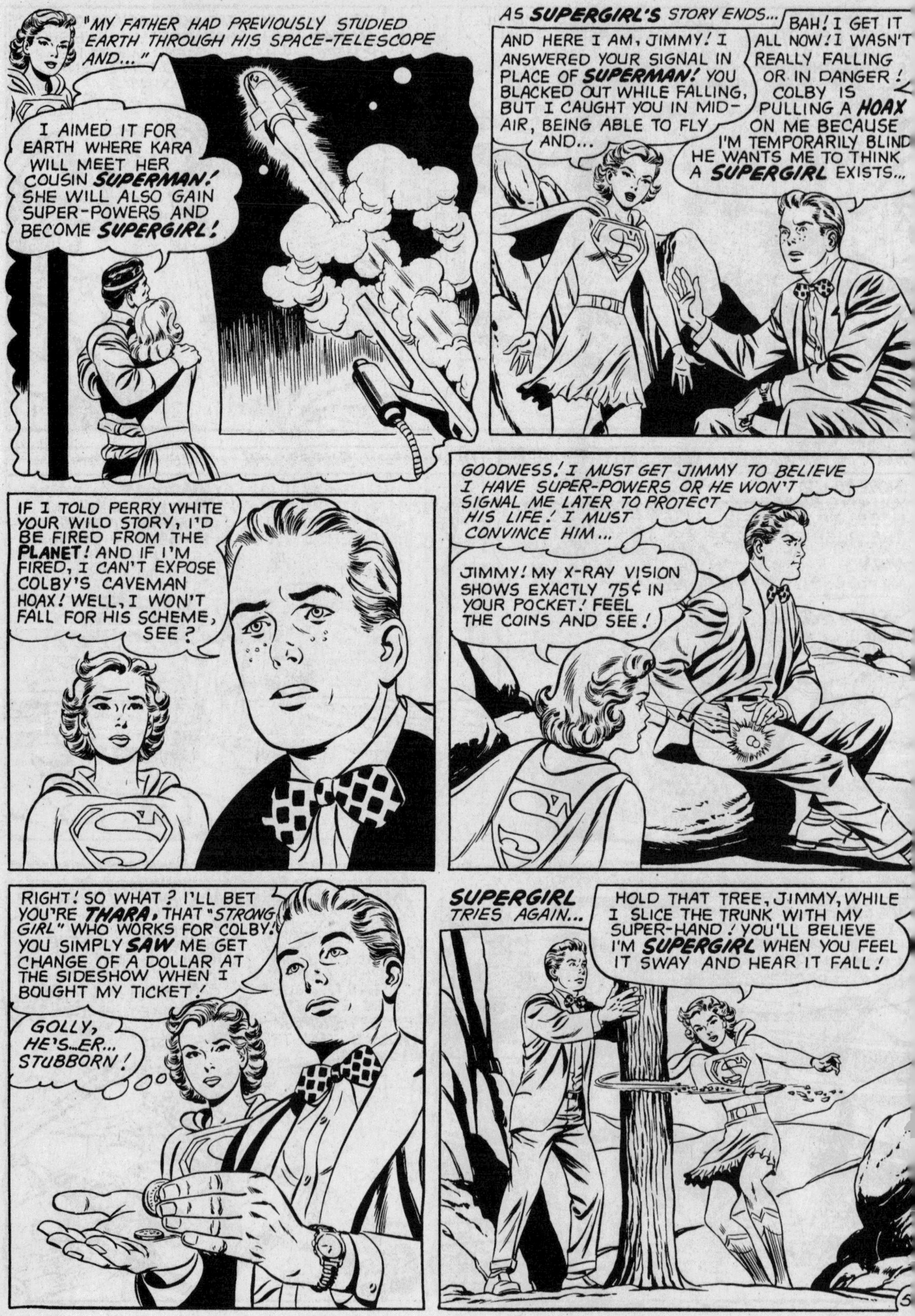
"MY FATHER HAD PREVIOUSLY STUDIED EARTH THROUGH HIS SPACE-TELESCOPE AND..."
I AIMED IT FOR EARTH WHERE KARA WILL MEET HER COUSIN SUPERMAN! SHE WILL ALSO GAIN SUPER-POWERS AND BECOME SUPERGIRL!
AS SUPERGIRL'S STORY ENDS...
AND HERE I AM, JIMMY! I ANSWERED YOUR SIGNAL IN PLACE OF SUPERMAN! YOU BLACKED OUT WHILE FALLING, BUT I CAUGHT YOU IN MID-AIR, BEING ABLE TO FLY AND...
BAH! I GET IT ALL NOW! I WASN'T REALLY FALLING OR IN DANGER! COLBY IS PULLING A HOAX ON ME BECAUSE I'M TEMPORARILY BLIND HE WANTS ME TO THINK A SUPERGIRL EXISTS...
IF I TOLD PERRY WHITE YOUR WILD STORY, I'D BE FIRED FROM THE PLANET! AND IF I'M FIRED, I CAN'T EXPOSE COLBY'S CAVEMAN HOAX! WELL, I WON'T FALL FOR HIS SCHEME, SEE?
GOODNESS! I MUST GET JIMMY TO BELIEVE I HAVE SUPER-POWERS OR HE WON'T SIGNAL ME LATER TO PROTECT HIS LIFE! I MUST CONVINCE HIM...
JIMMY! MY X-RAY VISION SHOWS EXACTLY 75¢ IN YOUR POCKET! FEEL THE COINS AND SEE!
RIGHT! SO WHAT? I'LL BET YOU'RE THARA, THAT "STRONG GIRL" WHO WORKS FOR COLBY! YOU SIMPLY SAW ME GET CHANGE OF A DOLLAR AT THE SIDESHOW WHEN I BOUGHT MY TICKET!
GOLLY, HE'S...ER... STUBBORN!
SUPERGIRL TRIES AGAIN...
HOLD THAT TREE, JIMMY, WHILE I SLICE THE TRUNK WITH MY SUPER-HAND! YOU'LL BELIEVE I'M SUPERGIRL WHEN YOU FEEL IT SWAY AND HEAR IT FALL!
5

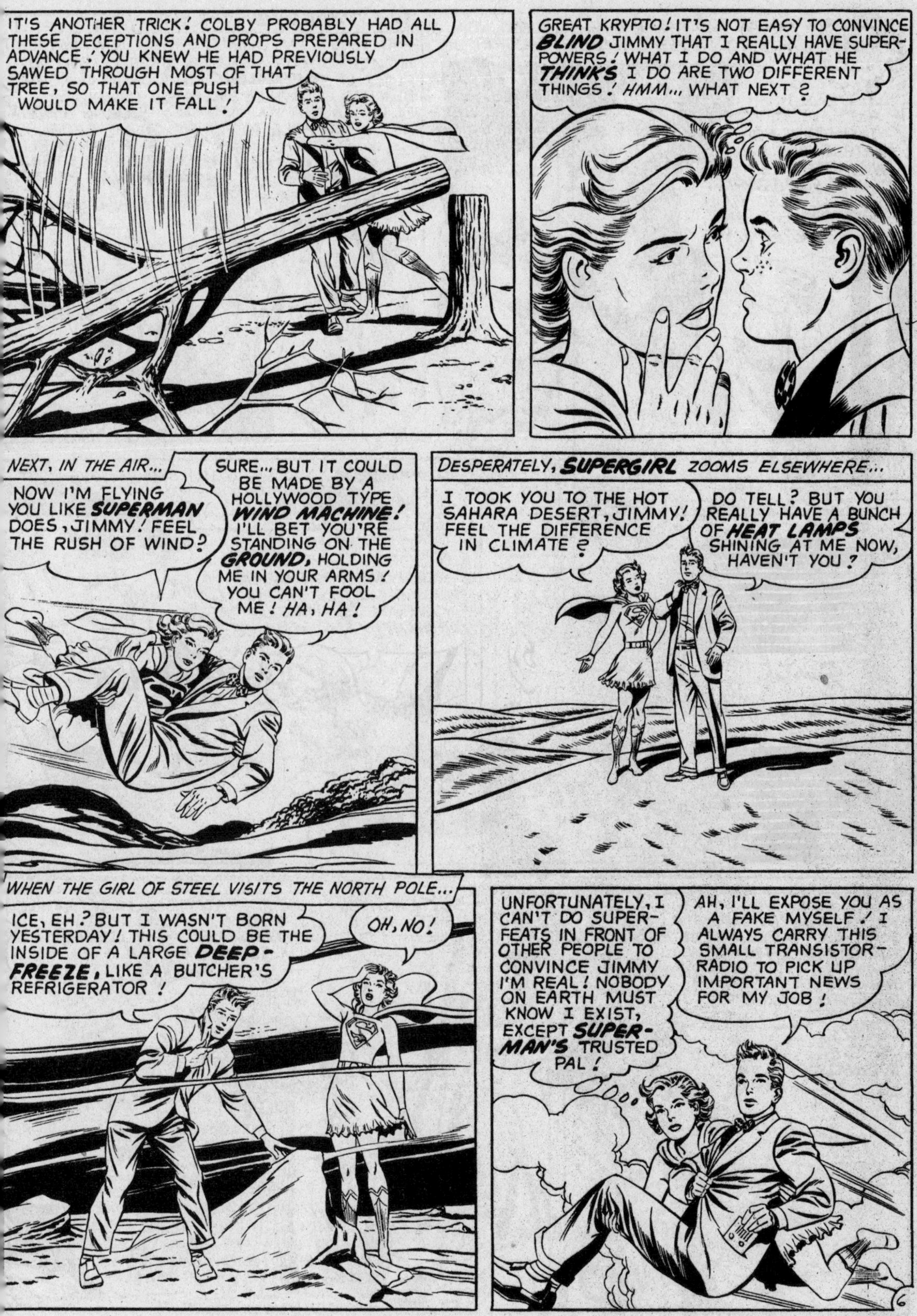
IT'S ANOTHER TRICK! COLBY PROBABLY HAD ALL THESE DECEPTIONS AND PROPS PREPARED IN ADVANCE! YOU KNEW HE HAD PREVIOUSLY SAWED THROUGH MOST OF THAT TREE, SO THAT ONE PUSH WOULD MAKE IT FALL!
GREAT KRYPTO! IT'S NOT EASY TO CONVINCE BLIND JIMMY THAT I REALLY HAVE SUPER-POWERS! WHAT I DO AND WHAT HE THINKS I DO ARE TWO DIFFERENT THINGS! HMM... WHAT NEXT?
NEXT, IN THE AIR...
NOW I'M FLYING YOU LIKE SUPERMAN DOES, JIMMY! FEEL THE RUSH OF WIND?
SURE... BUT IT COULD BE MADE BY A HOLLYWOOD TYPE WIND MACHINE! I'LL BET YOU'RE STANDING ON THE GROUND, HOLDING ME IN YOUR ARMS! YOU CAN'T FOOL ME! HA, HA!
DESPERATELY, SUPERGIRL ZOOMS ELSEWHERE...
I TOOK YOU TO THE HOT SAHARA DESERT, JIMMY! FEEL THE DIFFERENCE IN CLIMATE?
DO TELL? BUT YOU REALLY HAVE A BUNCH OF HEAT LAMPS SHINING AT ME NOW, HAVEN'T YOU?
WHEN THE GIRL OF STEEL VISITS THE NORTH POLE...
ICE, EH? BUT I WASN'T BORN YESTERDAY! THIS COULD BE THE INSIDE OF A LARGE DEEP-FREEZE, LIKE A BUTCHER'S REFRIGERATOR!
OH, NO!
UNFORTUNATELY, I CAN'T DO SUPER-FEATS IN FRONT OF OTHER PEOPLE TO CONVINCE JIMMY I'M REAL! NOBODY ON EARTH MUST KNOW I EXIST, EXCEPT SUPERMAN'S TRUSTED PAL!
AH, I'LL EXPOSE YOU AS A FAKE MYSELF! I ALWAYS CARRY THIS SMALL TRANSISTOR-RADIO TO PICK UP IMPORTANT NEWS FOR MY JOB!
6

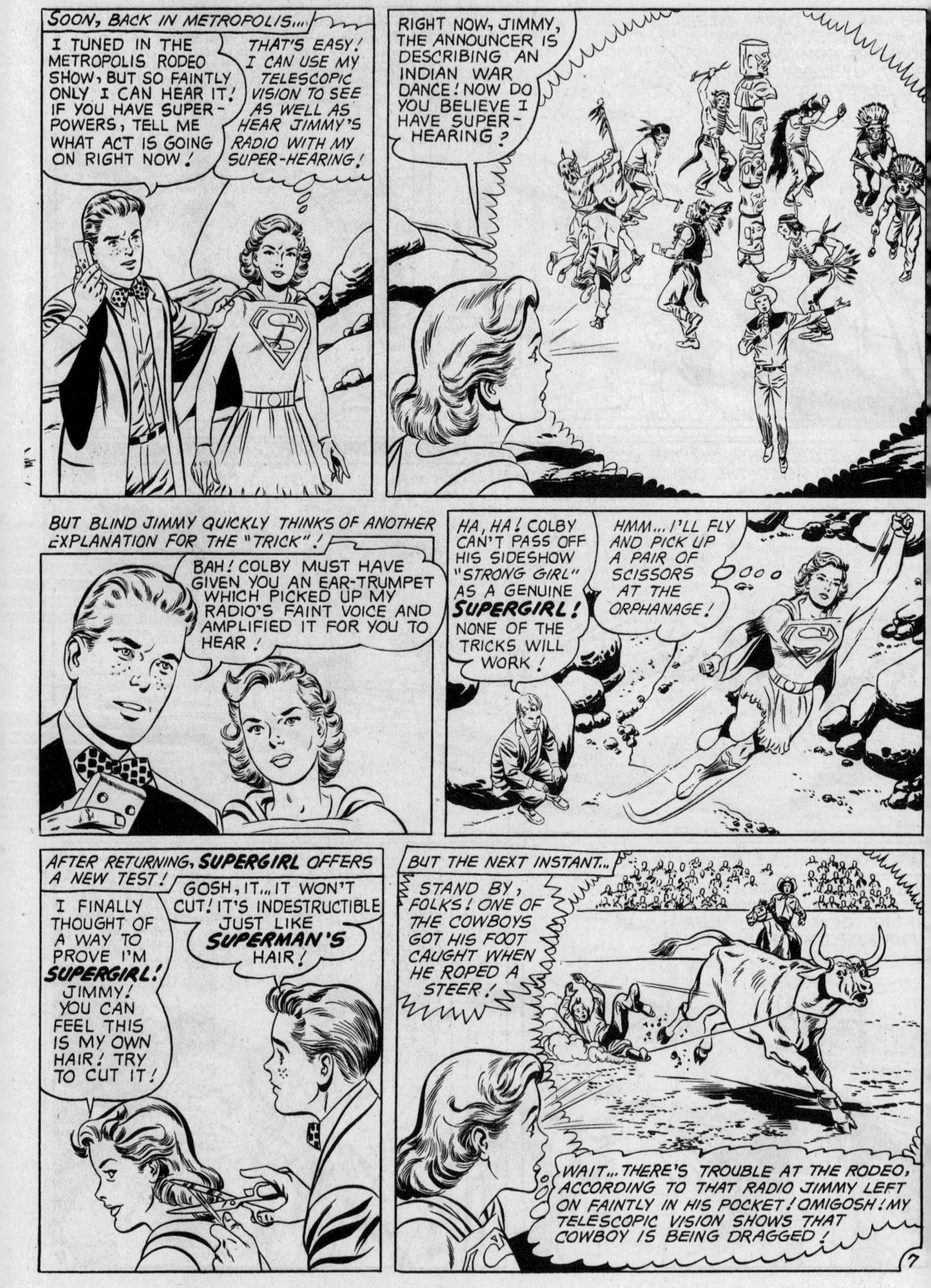
SOON, BACK IN METROPOLIS...
I TUNED IN THE METROPOLIS RODEO SHOW, BUT SO FAINTLY ONLY I CAN HEAR IT! IF YOU HAVE SUPER-POWERS, TELL ME WHAT ACT IS GOING ON RIGHT NOW!
THAT'S EASY! I CAN USE MY TELESCOPIC VISION TO SEE AS WELL AS HEAR JIMMY'S RADIO WITH MY SUPER-HEARING!
RIGHT NOW, JIMMY, THE ANNOUNCER IS DESCRIBING AN INDIAN WAR DANCE! NOW DO YOU BELIEVE I HAVE SUPER-HEARING?
BUT BLIND JIMMY QUICKLY THINKS OF ANOTHER EXPLANATION FOR THE "TRICK"!
BAH! COLBY MUST HAVE GIVEN YOU AN EAR-TRUMPET WHICH PICKED UP MY RADIO'S FAINT VOICE AND AMPLIFIED IT FOR YOU TO HEAR!
HA, HA! COLBY CAN'T PASS OFF HIS SIDESHOW "STRONG GIRL" AS A GENUINE SUPERGIRL! NONE OF THE TRICKS WILL WORK!
HMM... I'LL FLY AND PICK UP A PAIR OF SCISSORS AT THE ORPHANAGE!
AFTER RETURNING, SUPERGIRL OFFERS A NEW TEST!
I FINALLY THOUGHT OF A WAY TO PROVE I'M SUPERGIRL! JIMMY! YOU CAN FEEL THIS IS MY OWN HAIR! TRY TO CUT IT!
GOSH, IT... IT WON'T CUT! IT'S INDESTRUCTIBLE JUST LIKE SUPERMAN'S HAIR!
BUT THE NEXT INSTANT...
STAND BY, FOLKS! ONE OF THE COWBOYS GOT HIS FOOT CAUGHT WHEN HE ROPED A STEER!
WAIT... THERE'S TROUBLE AT THE RODEO, ACCORDING TO THAT RADIO JIMMY LEFT ON FAINTLY IN HIS POCKET! OMIGOSH! MY TELESCOPIC VISION SHOWS THAT COWBOY IS BEING DRAGGED!
7

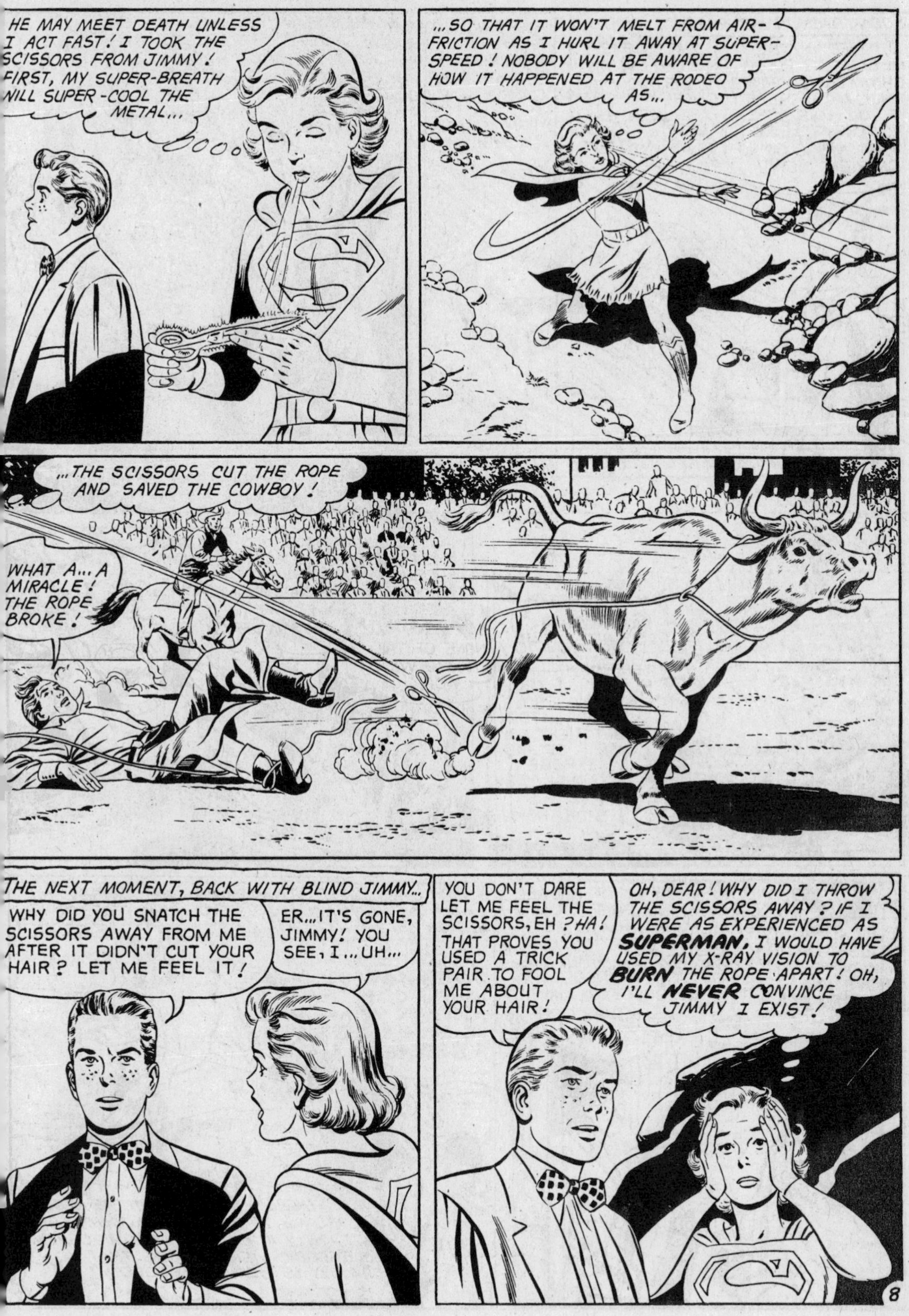
HE MAY MEET DEATH UNLESS I ACT FAST! I TOOK THE SCISSORS FROM JIMMY! FIRST, MY SUPER-BREATH WILL SUPER-COOL THE METAL...
...SO THAT IT WON'T MELT FROM AIR-FRICTION AS I HURL IT AWAY AT SUPER-SPEED! NOBODY WILL BE AWARE OF HOW IT HAPPENED AT THE RODEO AS...
...THE SCISSORS CUT THE ROPE AND SAVED THE COWBOY!
WHAT A...A MIRACLE! THE ROPE BROKE!
THE NEXT MOMENT, BACK WITH BLIND JIMMY...
WHY DID YOU SNATCH THE SCISSORS AWAY FROM ME AFTER IT DIDN'T CUT YOUR HAIR? LET ME FEEL IT!
ER...IT'S GONE, JIMMY! YOU SEE, I...UH...
YOU DON'T DARE LET ME FEEL THE SCISSORS, EH? HA! THAT PROVES YOU USED A TRICK PAIR TO FOOL ME ABOUT YOUR HAIR!
OH, DEAR! WHY DID I THROW THE SCISSORS AWAY? IF I WERE AS EXPERIENCED AS SUPERMAN, I WOULD HAVE USED MY X-RAY VISION TO BURN THE ROPE APART! OH, I'LL NEVER CONVINCE JIMMY I EXIST!
8

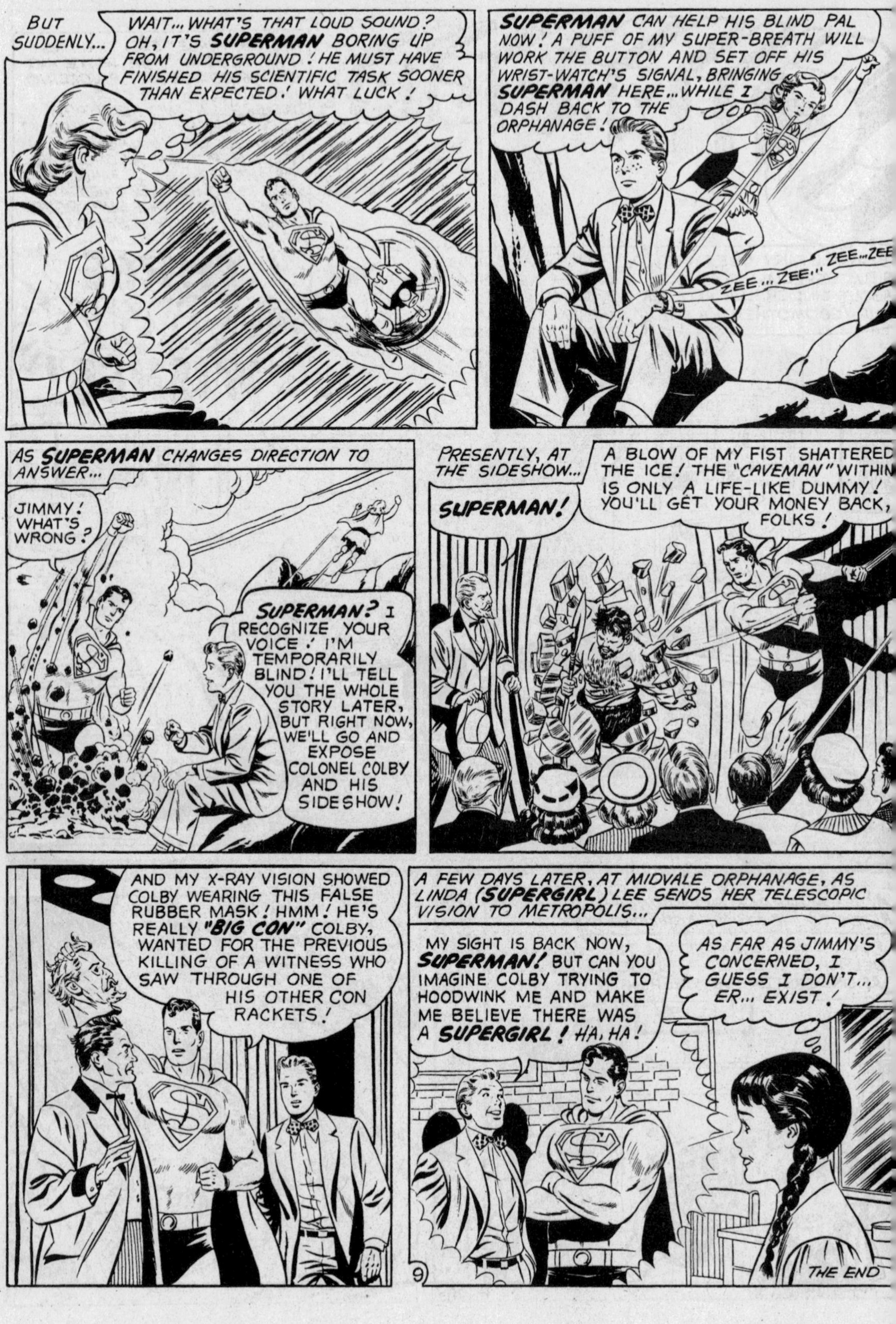
BUT SUDDENLY...
WAIT... WHAT'S THAT LOUD SOUND? OH, IT'S SUPERMAN BORING UP FROM UNDERGROUND! HE MUST HAVE FINISHED HIS SCIENTIFIC TASK SOONER THAN EXPECTED! WHAT LUCK!
SUPERMAN CAN HELP HIS BLIND PAL NOW! A PUFF OF MY SUPER-BREATH WILL WORK THE BUTTON AND SET OFF HIS WRIST-WATCH'S SIGNAL, BRINGING SUPERMAN HERE... WHILE I DASH BACK TO THE ORPHANAGE!
ZEE... ZEE... ZEE... ZEE
AS SUPERMAN CHANGES DIRECTION TO ANSWER...
JIMMY! WHAT'S WRONG?
SUPERMAN? I RECOGNIZE YOUR VOICE! I'M TEMPORARILY BLIND! I'LL TELL YOU THE WHOLE STORY LATER, BUT RIGHT NOW, WE'LL GO AND EXPOSE COLONEL COLBY AND HIS SIDESHOW!
PRESENTLY, AT THE SIDESHOW...
SUPERMAN!
A BLOW OF MY FIST SHATTERED THE ICE! THE "CAVEMAN" WITHIN IS ONLY A LIFE-LIKE DUMMY! YOU'LL GET YOUR MONEY BACK, FOLKS!
AND MY X-RAY VISION SHOWED COLBY WEARING THIS FALSE RUBBER MASK! HMM! HE'S REALLY "BIG CON" COLBY, WANTED FOR THE PREVIOUS KILLING OF A WITNESS WHO SAW THROUGH ONE OF HIS OTHER CON RACKETS!
9
A FEW DAYS LATER, AT MIDVALE ORPHANAGE, AS LINDA (SUPERGIRL) LEE SENDS HER TELESCOPIC VISION TO METROPOLIS...
MY SIGHT IS BACK NOW, SUPERMAN! BUT CAN YOU IMAGINE COLBY TRYING TO HOODWINK ME AND MAKE ME BELIEVE THERE WAS A SUPERGIRL! HA, HA!
AS FAR AS JIMMY'S CONCERNED, I GUESS I DON'T... ER... EXIST!
THE END

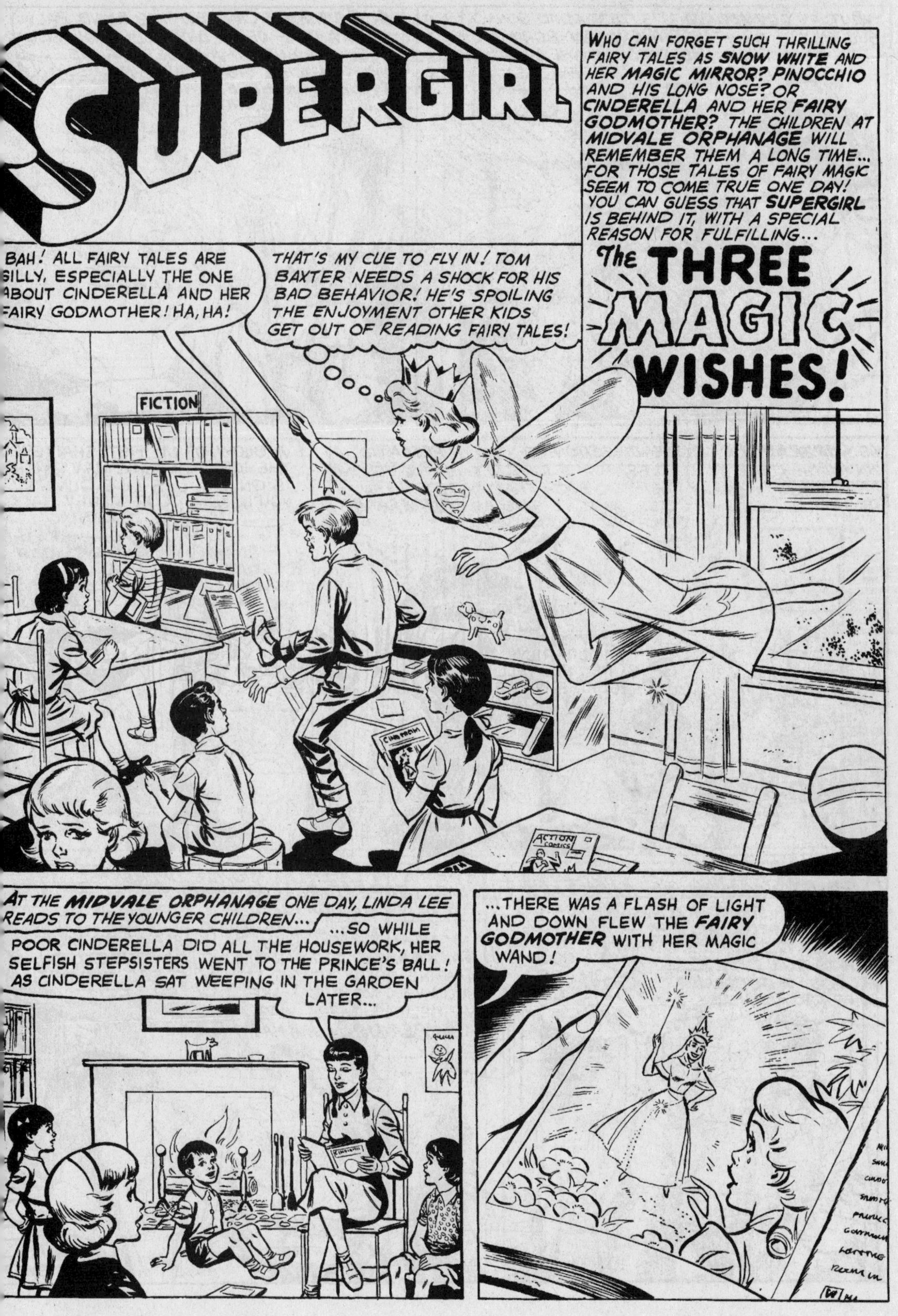
SUPERGIRL
WHO CAN FORGET SUCH THRILLING FAIRY TALES AS SNOW WHITE AND HER MAGIC MIRROR? PINOCCHIO AND HIS LONG NOSE? OR CINDERELLA AND HER FAIRY GODMOTHER? THE CHILDREN AT MIDVALE ORPHANAGE WILL REMEMBER THEM A LONG TIME... FOR THOSE TALES OF FAIRY MAGIC SEEM TO COME TRUE ONE DAY! YOU CAN GUESS THAT SUPERGIRL IS BEHIND IT, WITH A SPECIAL REASON FOR FULFILLING...
The THREE MAGIC WISHES!
BAH! ALL FAIRY TALES ARE SILLY, ESPECIALLY THE ONE ABOUT CINDERELLA AND HER FAIRY GODMOTHER! HA, HA!
THAT'S MY CUE TO FLY IN! TOM BAXTER NEEDS A SHOCK FOR HIS BAD BEHAVIOR! HE'S SPOILING THE ENJOYMENT OTHER KIDS GET OUT OF READING FAIRY TALES!
FICTION
ACTION COMICS
AT THE MIDVALE ORPHANAGE ONE DAY, LINDA LEE READS TO THE YOUNGER CHILDREN...
...SO WHILE POOR CINDERELLA DID ALL THE HOUSEWORK, HER SELFISH STEPSISTERS WENT TO THE PRINCE'S BALL! AS CINDERELLA SAT WEEPING IN THE GARDEN LATER...
...THERE WAS A FLASH OF LIGHT AND DOWN FLEW THE FAIRY GODMOTHER WITH HER MAGIC WAND!

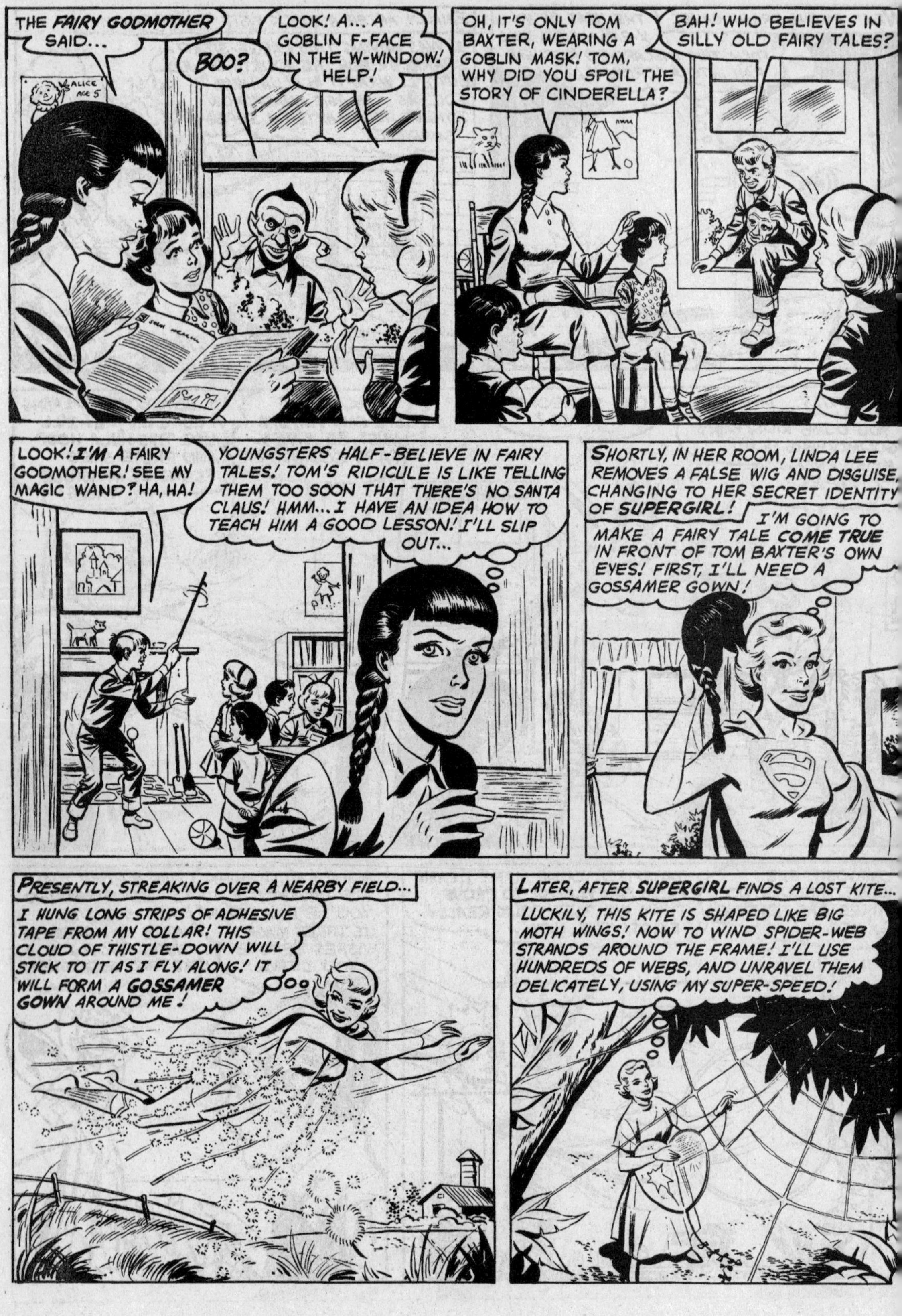
THE FAIRY GODMOTHER SAID...
BOO?
LOOK! A... A GOBLIN F-FACE IN THE W-WINDOW! HELP!
ALICE AGE 5
OH, IT'S ONLY TOM BAXTER, WEARING A GOBLIN MASK! TOM, WHY DID YOU SPOIL THE STORY OF CINDERELLA?
BAH! WHO BELIEVES IN SILLY OLD FAIRY TALES?
LOOK! I'M A FAIRY GODMOTHER! SEE MY MAGIC WAND? HA, HA!
YOUNGSTERS HALF-BELIEVE IN FAIRY TALES! TOM'S RIDICULE IS LIKE TELLING THEM TOO SOON THAT THERE'S NO SANTA CLAUS! HMM... I HAVE AN IDEA HOW TO TEACH HIM A GOOD LESSON! I'LL SLIP OUT...
SHORTLY, IN HER ROOM, LINDA LEE REMOVES A FALSE WIG AND DISGUISE, CHANGING TO HER SECRET IDENTITY OF SUPERGIRL!
I'M GOING TO MAKE A FAIRY TALE COME TRUE IN FRONT OF TOM BAXTER'S OWN EYES! FIRST, I'LL NEED A GOSSAMER GOWN!
PRESENTLY, STREAKING OVER A NEARBY FIELD...
I HUNG LONG STRIPS OF ADHESIVE TAPE FROM MY COLLAR! THIS CLOUD OF THISTLE-DOWN WILL STICK TO IT AS I FLY ALONG! IT WILL FORM A GOSSAMER GOWN AROUND ME!
LATER, AFTER SUPERGIRL FINDS A LOST KITE...
LUCKILY, THIS KITE IS SHAPED LIKE BIG MOTH WINGS! NOW TO WIND SPIDER-WEB STRANDS AROUND THE FRAME! I'LL USE HUNDREDS OF WEBS, AND UNRAVEL THEM DELICATELY, USING MY SUPER-SPEED!

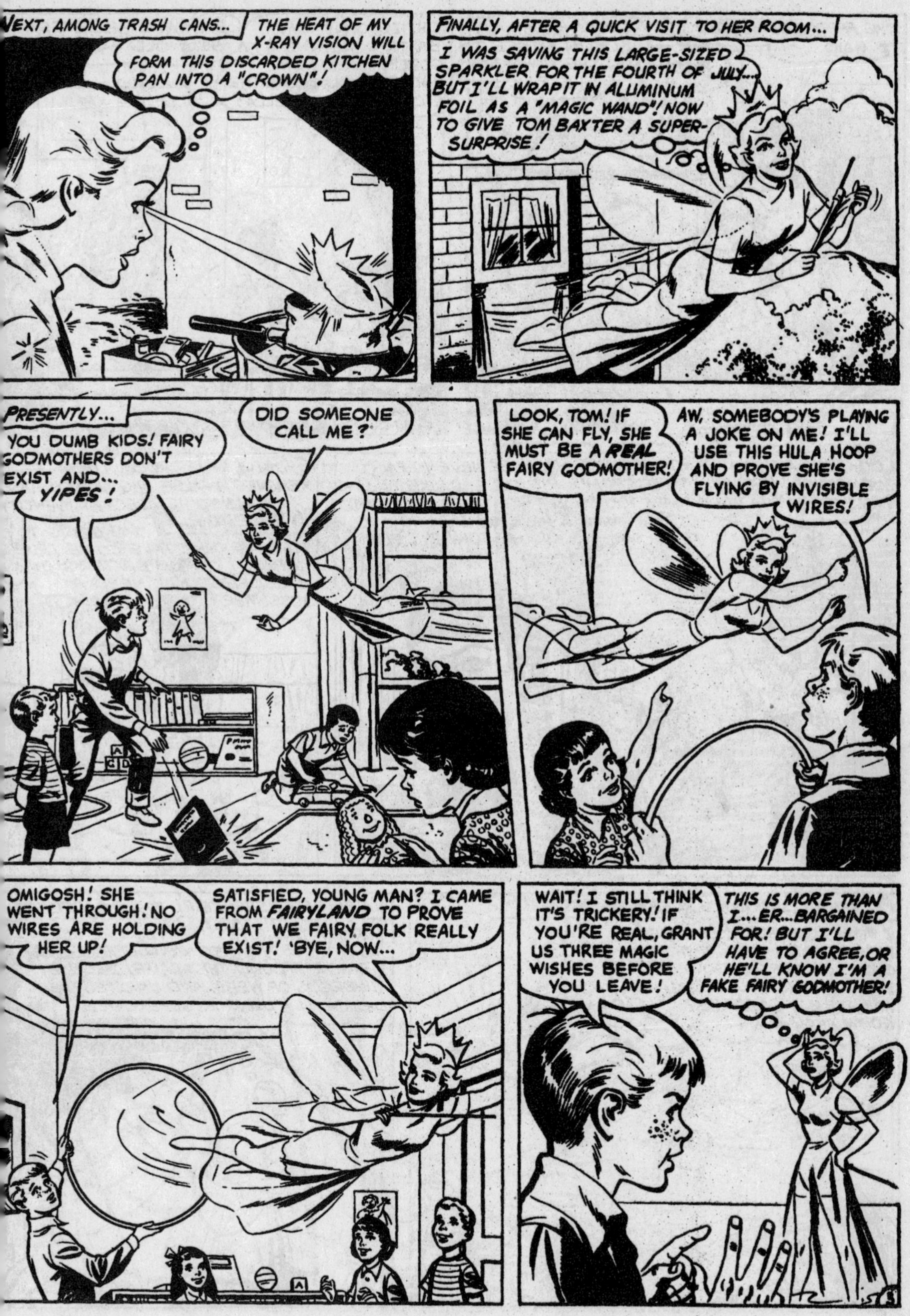
NEXT, AMONG TRASH CANS...
THE HEAT OF MY X-RAY VISION WILL FORM THIS DISCARDED KITCHEN PAN INTO A "CROWN"!
FINALLY, AFTER A QUICK VISIT TO HER ROOM...
I WAS SAVING THIS LARGE-SIZED SPARKLER FOR THE FOURTH OF JULY... BUT I'LL WRAP IT IN ALUMINUM FOIL AS A "MAGIC WAND"! NOW TO GIVE TOM BAXTER A SUPER-SURPRISE!
PRESENTLY...
YOU DUMB KIDS! FAIRY GODMOTHERS DON'T EXIST AND... YIPES!
DID SOMEONE CALL ME?
LOOK, TOM! IF SHE CAN FLY, SHE MUST BE A REAL FAIRY GODMOTHER!
AW, SOMEBODY'S PLAYING A JOKE ON ME! I'LL USE THIS HULA HOOP AND PROVE SHE'S FLYING BY INVISIBLE WIRES!
OMIGOSH! SHE WENT THROUGH! NO WIRES ARE HOLDING HER UP!
SATISFIED, YOUNG MAN? I CAME FROM FAIRYLAND TO PROVE THAT WE FAIRY FOLK REALLY EXIST! 'BYE, NOW...
WAIT! I STILL THINK IT'S TRICKERY! IF YOU'RE REAL, GRANT US THREE MAGIC WISHES BEFORE YOU LEAVE!
THIS IS MORE THAN I...ER...BARGAINED FOR! BUT I'LL HAVE TO AGREE, OR HE'LL KNOW I'M A FAKE FAIRY GODMOTHER!

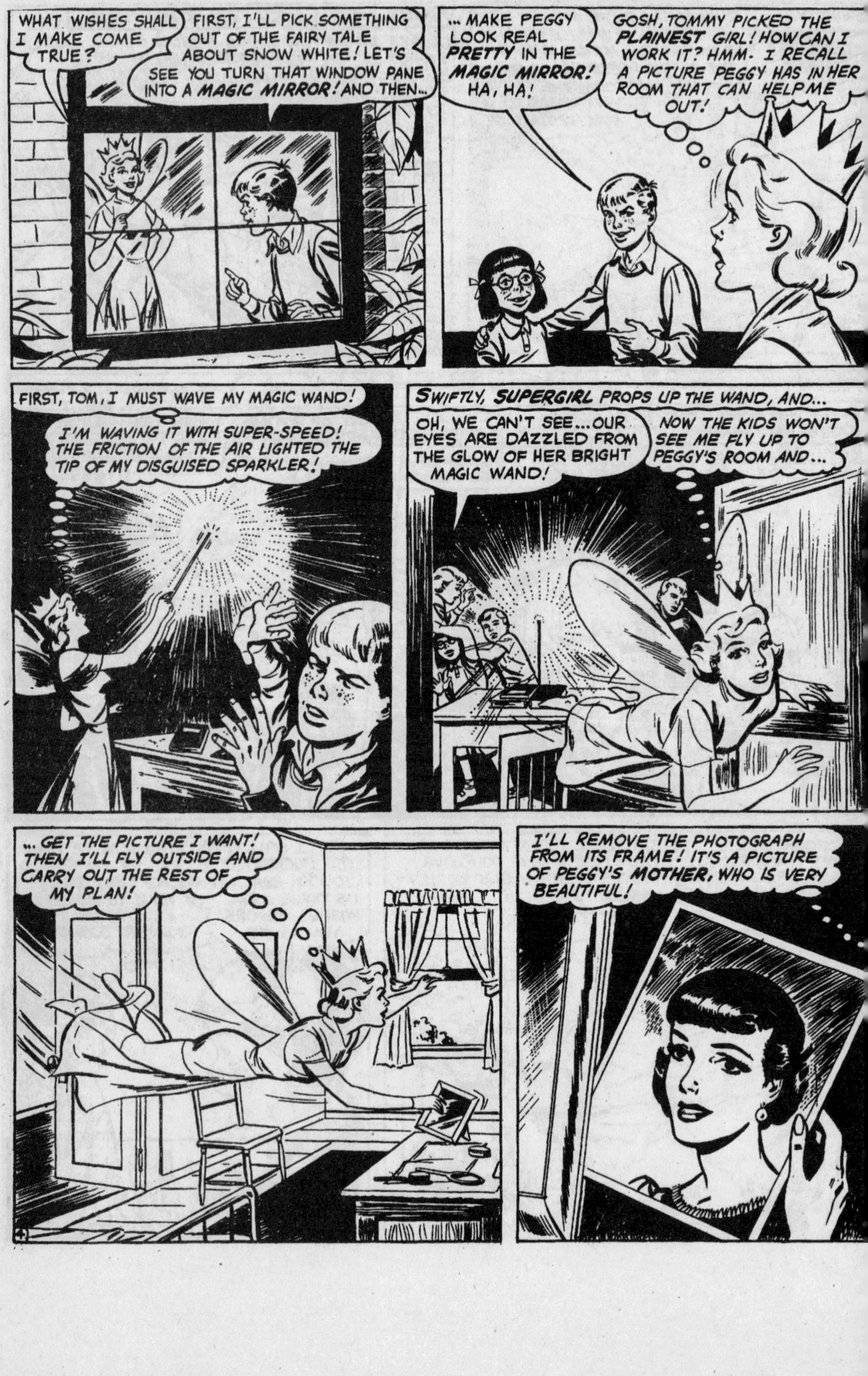
WHAT WISHES SHALL I MAKE COME TRUE?
FIRST, I'LL PICK SOMETHING OUT OF THE FAIRY TALE ABOUT SNOW WHITE! LET'S SEE YOU TURN THAT WINDOW PANE INTO A MAGIC MIRROR! AND THEN...
... MAKE PEGGY LOOK REAL PRETTY IN THE MAGIC MIRROR! HA, HA!
GOSH, TOMMY PICKED THE PLAINEST GIRL! HOW CAN I WORK IT? HMM- I RECALL A PICTURE PEGGY HAS IN HER ROOM THAT CAN HELP ME OUT!
FIRST, TOM, I MUST WAVE MY MAGIC WAND!
I'M WAVING IT WITH SUPER-SPEED! THE FRICTION OF THE AIR LIGHTED THE TIP OF MY DISGUISED SPARKLER!
SWIFTLY, SUPERGIRL PROPS UP THE WAND, AND...
OH, WE CAN'T SEE...OUR EYES ARE DAZZLED FROM THE GLOW OF HER BRIGHT MAGIC WAND!
NOW THE KIDS WON'T SEE ME FLY UP TO PEGGY'S ROOM AND...
... GET THE PICTURE I WANT! THEN I'LL FLY OUTSIDE AND CARRY OUT THE REST OF MY PLAN!
I'LL REMOVE THE PHOTOGRAPH FROM ITS FRAME! IT'S A PICTURE OF PEGGY'S MOTHER, WHO IS VERY BEAUTIFUL!

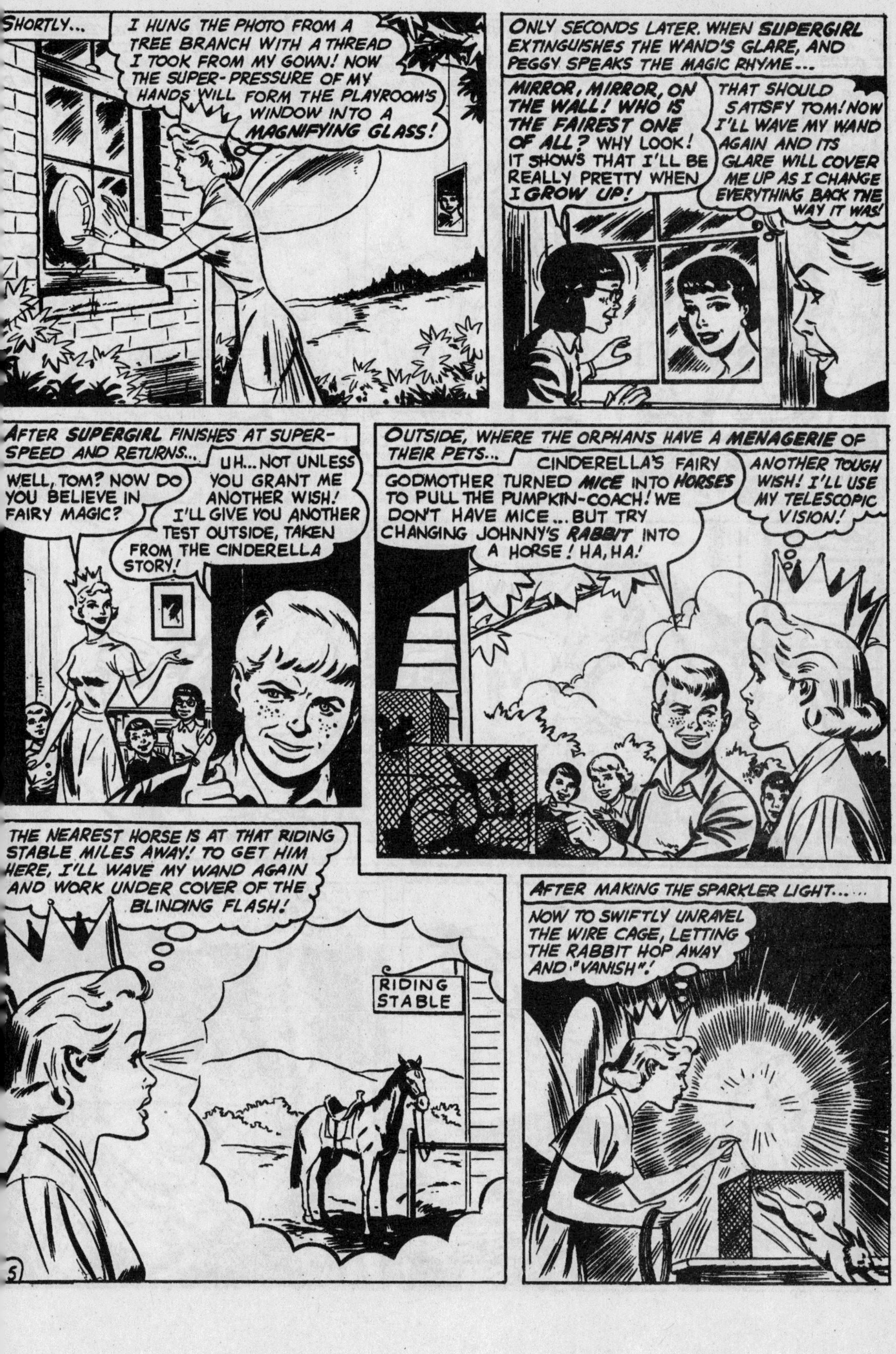
SHORTLY...
I HUNG THE PHOTO FROM A TREE BRANCH WITH A THREAD I TOOK FROM MY GOWN! NOW THE SUPER-PRESSURE OF MY HANDS WILL FORM THE PLAYROOM'S WINDOW INTO A MAGNIFYING GLASS!
ONLY SECONDS LATER. WHEN SUPERGIRL EXTINGUISHES THE WAND'S GLARE, AND PEGGY SPEAKS THE MAGIC RHYME...
MIRROR, MIRROR, ON THE WALL! WHO IS THE FAIREST ONE OF ALL? WHY LOOK! IT SHOWS THAT I'LL BE REALLY PRETTY WHEN I GROW UP!
THAT SHOULD SATISFY TOM! NOW I'LL WAVE MY WAND AGAIN AND ITS GLARE WILL COVER ME UP AS I CHANGE EVERYTHING BACK THE WAY IT WAS!
AFTER SUPERGIRL FINISHES AT SUPER-SPEED AND RETURNS...
WELL, TOM? NOW DO YOU BELIEVE IN FAIRY MAGIC?
UH...NOT UNLESS YOU GRANT ME ANOTHER WISH! I'LL GIVE YOU ANOTHER TEST OUTSIDE, TAKEN FROM THE CINDERELLA STORY!
OUTSIDE, WHERE THE ORPHANS HAVE A MENAGERIE OF THEIR PETS...
CINDERELLA'S FAIRY GODMOTHER TURNED MICE INTO HORSES TO PULL THE PUMPKIN-COACH! WE DON'T HAVE MICE...BUT TRY CHANGING JOHNNY'S RABBIT INTO A HORSE! HA, HA!
ANOTHER TOUGH WISH! I'LL USE MY TELESCOPIC VISION!
THE NEAREST HORSE IS AT THAT RIDING STABLE MILES AWAY! TO GET HIM HERE, I'LL WAVE MY WAND AGAIN AND WORK UNDER COVER OF THE BLINDING FLASH!
RIDING STABLE
5
AFTER MAKING THE SPARKLER LIGHT...
NOW TO SWIFTLY UNRAVEL THE WIRE CAGE, LETTING THE RABBIT HOP AWAY AND "VANISH"!

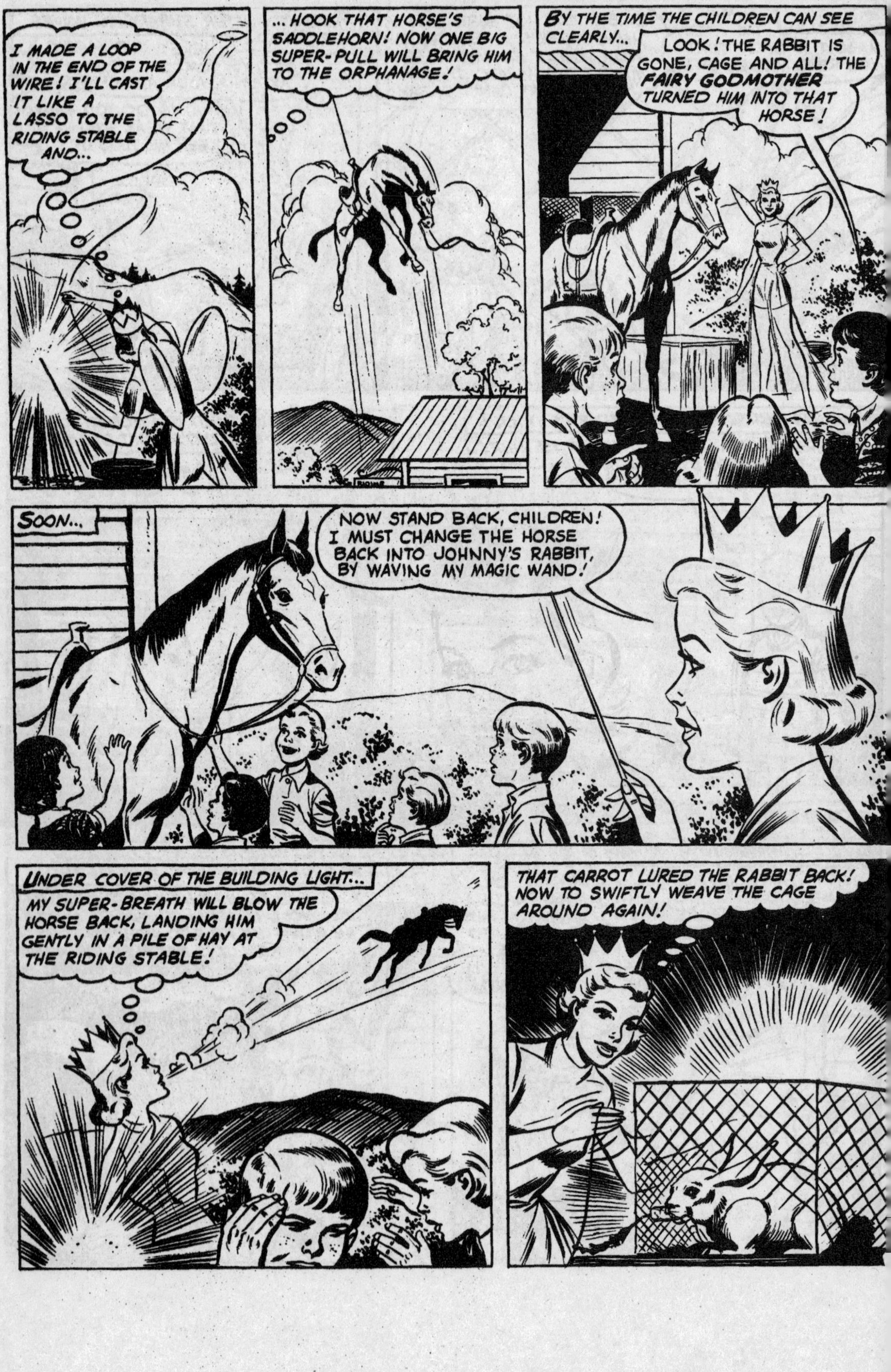
I MADE A LOOP IN THE END OF THE WIRE! I'LL CAST IT LIKE A LASSO TO THE RIDING STABLE AND...
... HOOK THAT HORSE'S SADDLEHORN! NOW ONE BIG SUPER-PULL WILL BRING HIM TO THE ORPHANAGE!
BY THE TIME THE CHILDREN CAN SEE CLEARLY...
LOOK! THE RABBIT IS GONE, CAGE AND ALL! THE FAIRY GODMOTHER TURNED HIM INTO THAT HORSE!
SOON...
NOW STAND BACK, CHILDREN! I MUST CHANGE THE HORSE BACK INTO JOHNNY'S RABBIT, BY WAVING MY MAGIC WAND!
UNDER COVER OF THE BUILDING LIGHT...
MY SUPER-BREATH WILL BLOW THE HORSE BACK, LANDING HIM GENTLY IN A PILE OF HAY AT THE RIDING STABLE!
THAT CARROT LURED THE RABBIT BACK! NOW TO SWIFTLY WEAVE THE CAGE AROUND AGAIN!

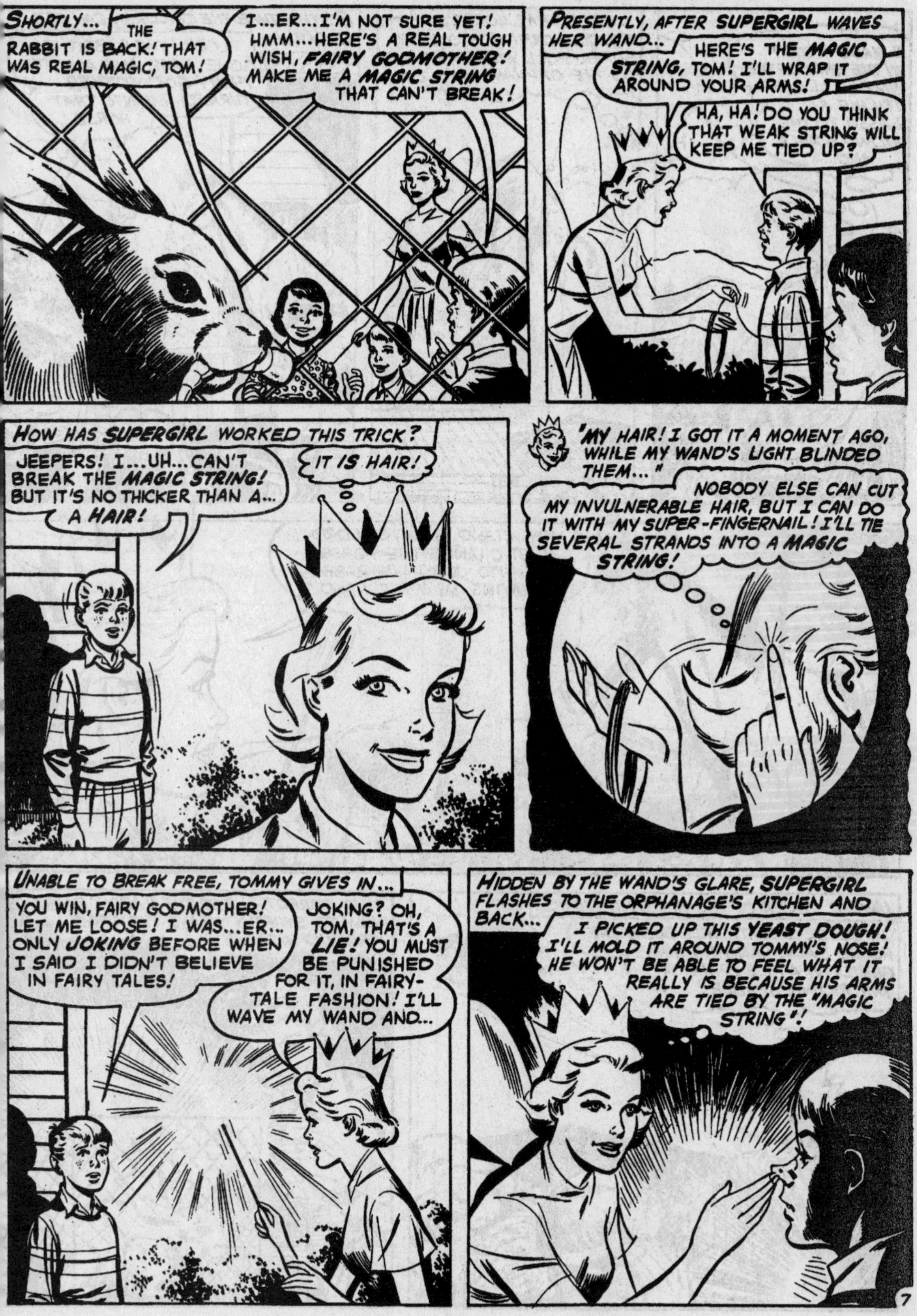
SHORTLY...
THE RABBIT IS BACK! THAT WAS REAL MAGIC, TOM!
I...ER...I'M NOT SURE YET! HMM...HERE'S A REAL TOUGH WISH, FAIRY GODMOTHER! MAKE ME A MAGIC STRING THAT CAN'T BREAK!
PRESENTLY, AFTER SUPERGIRL WAVES HER WAND...
HERE'S THE MAGIC STRING, TOM! I'LL WRAP IT AROUND YOUR ARMS!
HA, HA! DO YOU THINK THAT WEAK STRING WILL KEEP ME TIED UP?
HOW HAS SUPERGIRL WORKED THIS TRICK?
JEEPERS! I...UH...CAN'T BREAK THE MAGIC STRING! BUT IT'S NO THICKER THAN A... A HAIR!
IT IS HAIR!
"MY HAIR! I GOT IT A MOMENT AGO, WHILE MY WAND'S LIGHT BLINDED THEM..."
NOBODY ELSE CAN CUT MY INVULNERABLE HAIR, BUT I CAN DO IT WITH MY SUPER-FINGERNAIL! I'LL TIE SEVERAL STRANDS INTO A MAGIC STRING!
UNABLE TO BREAK FREE, TOMMY GIVES IN...
YOU WIN, FAIRY GODMOTHER! LET ME LOOSE! I WAS...ER... ONLY JOKING BEFORE WHEN I SAID I DIDN'T BELIEVE IN FAIRY TALES!
JOKING? OH, TOM, THAT'S A LIE! YOU MUST BE PUNISHED FOR IT, IN FAIRY-TALE FASHION! I'LL WAVE MY WAND AND...
HIDDEN BY THE WAND'S GLARE, SUPERGIRL FLASHES TO THE ORPHANAGE'S KITCHEN AND BACK...
I PICKED UP THIS YEAST DOUGH! I'LL MOLD IT AROUND TOMMY'S NOSE! HE WON'T BE ABLE TO FEEL WHAT IT REALLY IS BECAUSE HIS ARMS ARE TIED BY THE "MAGIC STRING"!
7

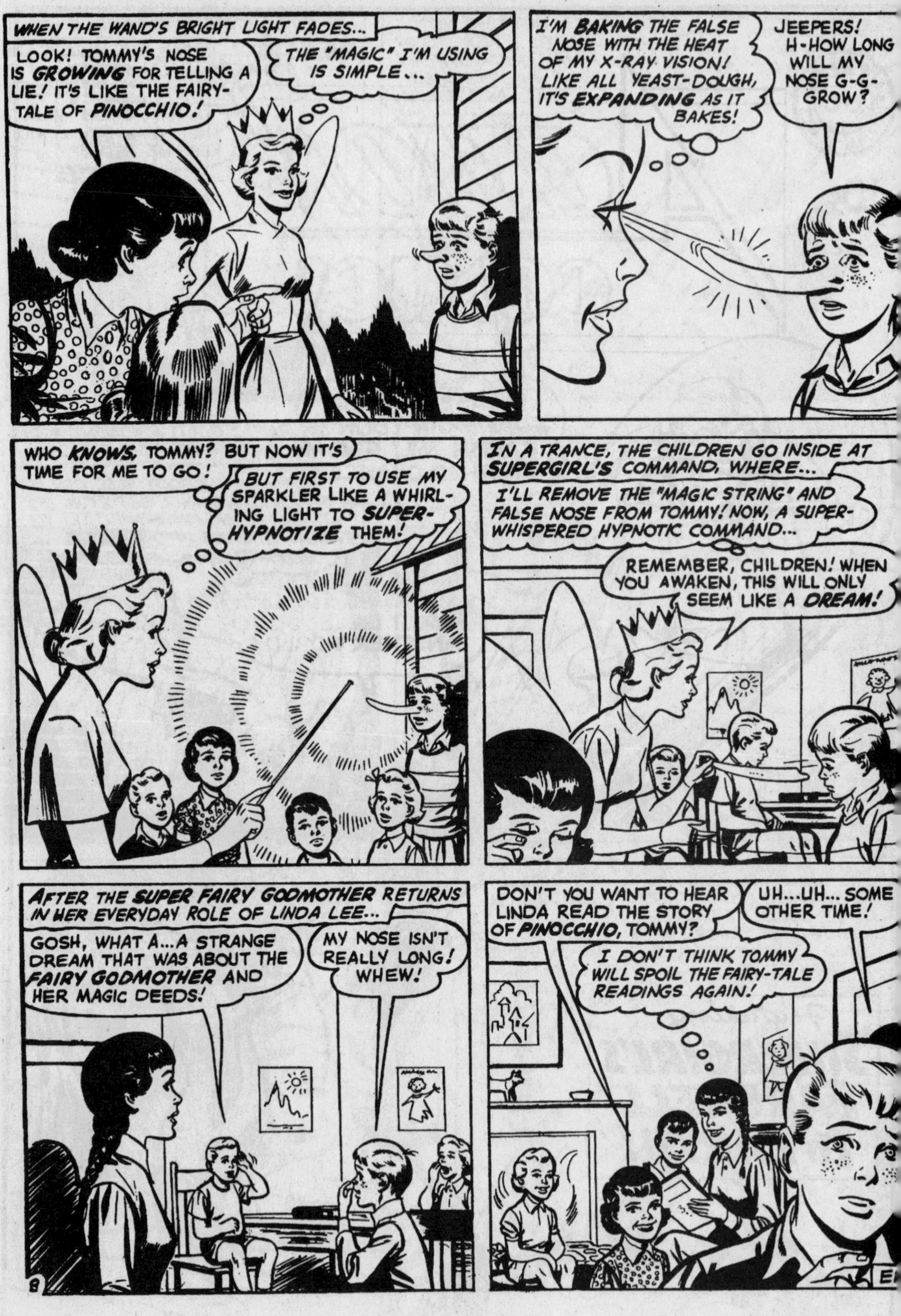
WHEN THE WAND'S BRIGHT LIGHT FADES...
LOOK! TOMMY'S NOSE IS GROWING FOR TELLING A LIE! IT'S LIKE THE FAIRY-TALE OF PINOCCHIO!
THE "MAGIC" I'M USING IS SIMPLE...
I'M BAKING THE FALSE NOSE WITH THE HEAT OF MY X-RAY VISION! LIKE ALL YEAST-DOUGH, IT'S EXPANDING AS IT BAKES!
JEEPERS! H-HOW LONG WILL MY NOSE G-G-GROW?
WHO KNOWS, TOMMY? BUT NOW IT'S TIME FOR ME TO GO!
BUT FIRST TO USE MY SPARKLER LIKE A WHIRLING LIGHT TO SUPER-HYPNOTIZE THEM!
IN A TRANCE, THE CHILDREN GO INSIDE AT SUPERGIRL'S COMMAND, WHERE...
I'LL REMOVE THE "MAGIC STRING" AND FALSE NOSE FROM TOMMY! NOW, A SUPER-WHISPERED HYPNOTIC COMMAND...
REMEMBER, CHILDREN! WHEN YOU AWAKEN, THIS WILL ONLY SEEM LIKE A DREAM!
AFTER THE SUPER FAIRY GODMOTHER RETURNS IN HER EVERYDAY ROLE OF LINDA LEE...
GOSH, WHAT A...A STRANGE DREAM THAT WAS ABOUT THE FAIRY GODMOTHER AND HER MAGIC DEEDS!
MY NOSE ISN'T REALLY LONG! WHEW!
8
DON'T YOU WANT TO HEAR LINDA READ THE STORY OF PINOCCHIO, TOMMY?
UH...UH... SOME OTHER TIME!
I DON'T THINK TOMMY WILL SPOIL THE FAIRY-TALE READINGS AGAIN!

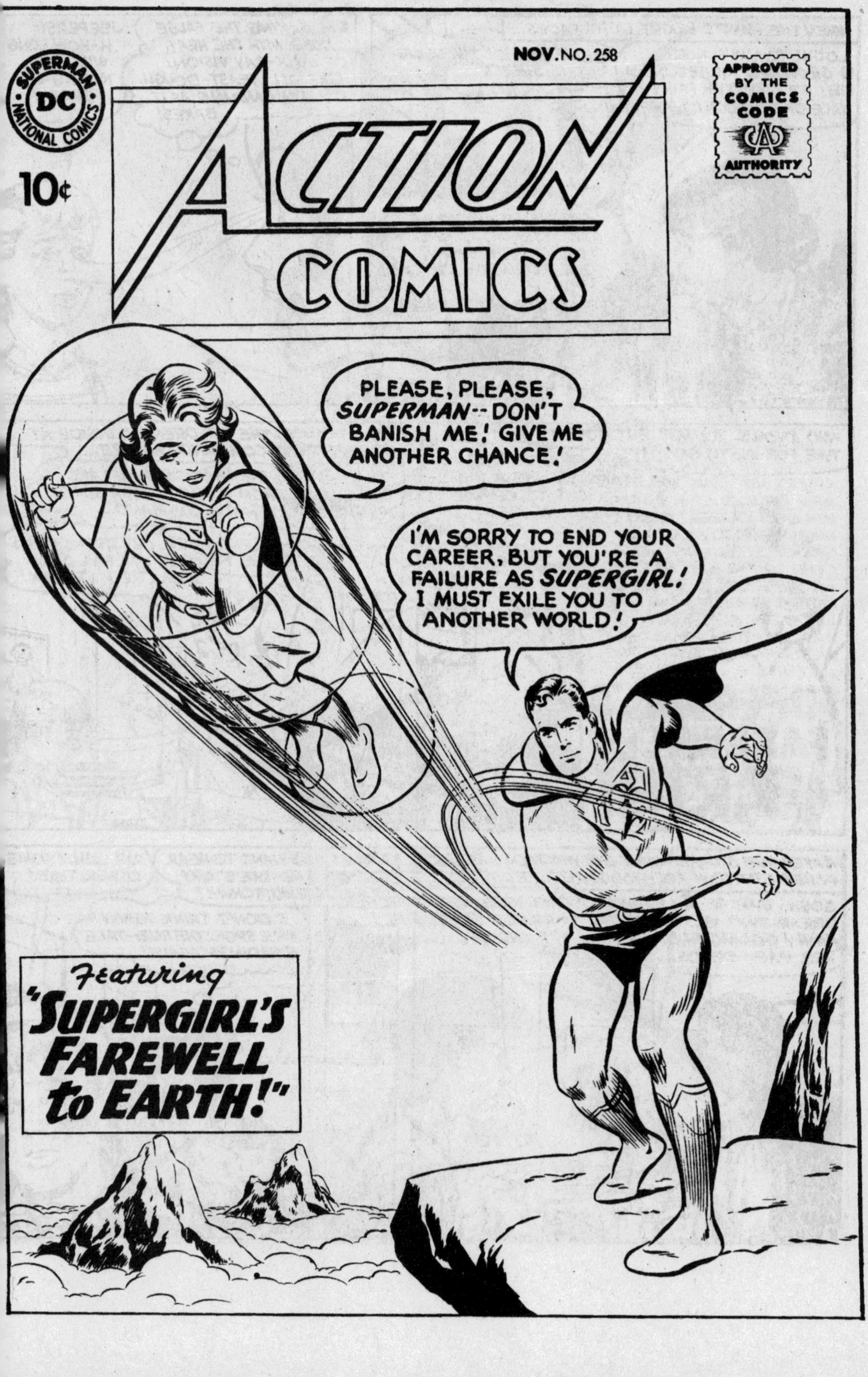
SUPERMAN DC NATIONAL COMICS
10¢
NOV. NO. 258
APPROVED BY THE COMICS CODE AUTHORITY
ACTION COMICS
PLEASE, PLEASE, SUPERMAN-- DON'T BANISH ME! GIVE ME ANOTHER CHANCE!
I'M SORRY TO END YOUR CAREER, BUT YOU'RE A FAILURE AS SUPERGIRL! I MUST EXILE YOU TO ANOTHER WORLD!
Featuring "SUPERGIRL'S FAREWELL to EARTH!"

SUPERGIRL

SUPERMAN EXILED ME TO THIS ASTEROID! I - I'LL HAVE TO LIVE HERE LIKE A...A GIRL ROBINSON CRUSOE!

EVER SINCE *SUPERGIRL* ARRIVED ON EARTH IN A SPACE ROCKET, NOT LONG AGO, *SUPERMAN* HAS AIDED HER IN PLANNING HER OWN CAREER! GREAT FAME SEEMS TO AWAIT THE *GIRL OF STEEL*, JUST AS IT CAME TO THE *MAN OF STEEL*! BUT *SUPERGIRL'S* BUBBLE OF HAPPINESS BURSTS ONE DAY! WHY DOES *SUPERMAN* SUDDENLY TURN AGAINST HER? INCREDIBLE INDEED, IS THE MYSTERY OF...

SUPERGIRL'S FAREWELL to EARTH!

NEAR MIDVALE ORPHANAGE ONE WINDY DAY, AS LINDA LEE TAKES A STROLL THROUGH THE WOODS...

HELP! A GUST OF WIND BLEW THAT DEAD TREE OVER!

IT'S FALLING STRAIGHT TOWARD THOSE KIDS PICKING FLOWERS! THIS IS A JOB FOR *SUPERGIRL*!

BEHIND CONCEALMENT, LINDA SWIFTLY REMOVES A FALSE WIG AND OUTER CLOTHING...

I HAVE TO CHANGE BECAUSE ONLY MY SUPER-COSTUME CAN TAKE THE PUNISHMENT WHEN I GO INTO SUPER-ACTION! MY ORDINARY CLOTHING WOULD GET TORN!

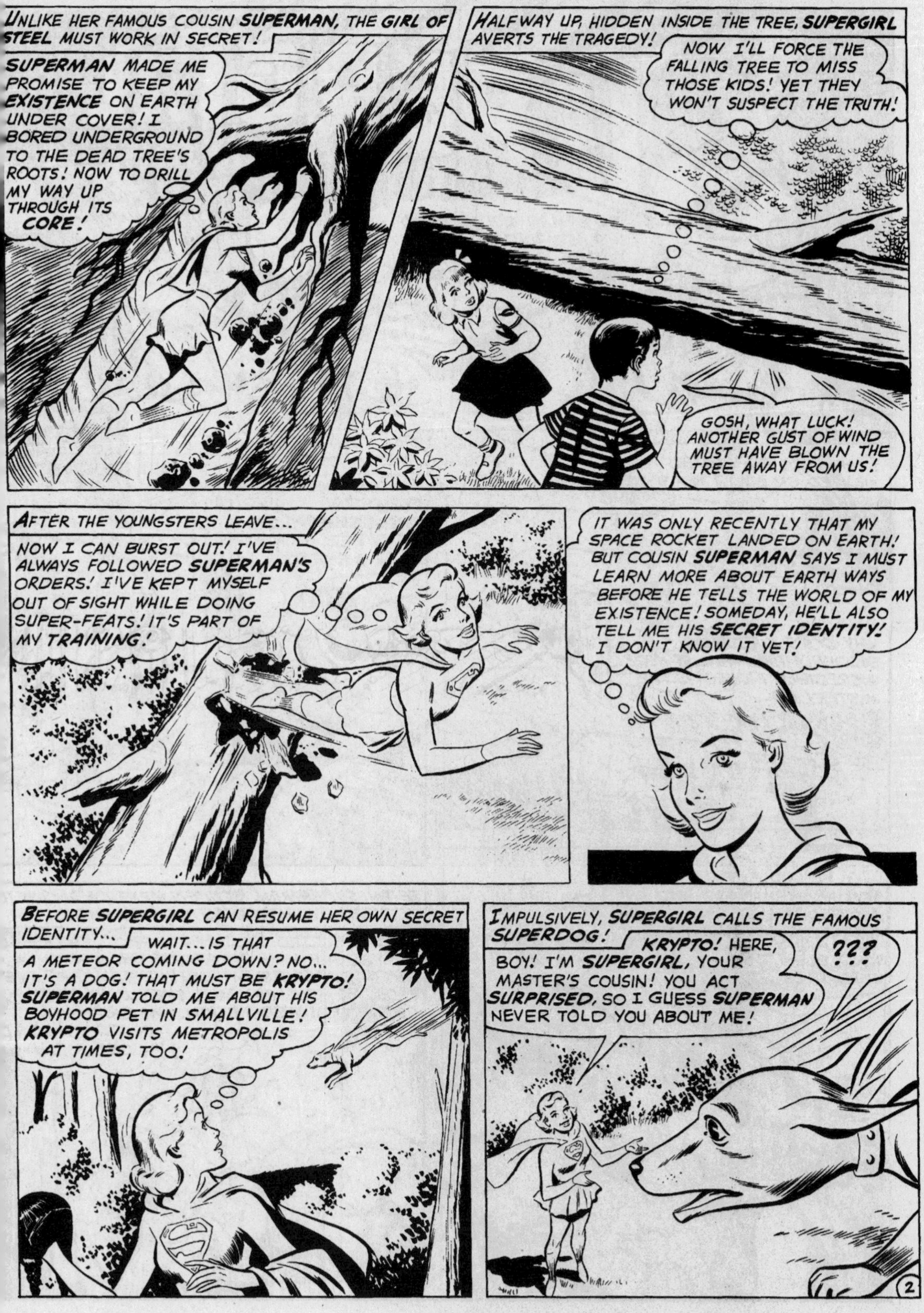
UNLIKE HER FAMOUS COUSIN SUPERMAN, THE GIRL OF STEEL MUST WORK IN SECRET!
SUPERMAN MADE ME PROMISE TO KEEP MY EXISTENCE ON EARTH UNDER COVER! I BORED UNDERGROUND TO THE DEAD TREE'S ROOTS! NOW TO DRILL MY WAY UP THROUGH ITS CORE!
HALFWAY UP, HIDDEN INSIDE THE TREE, SUPERGIRL AVERTS THE TRAGEDY!
NOW I'LL FORCE THE FALLING TREE TO MISS THOSE KIDS! YET THEY WON'T SUSPECT THE TRUTH!
GOSH, WHAT LUCK! ANOTHER GUST OF WIND MUST HAVE BLOWN THE TREE AWAY FROM US!
AFTER THE YOUNGSTERS LEAVE...
NOW I CAN BURST OUT! I'VE ALWAYS FOLLOWED SUPERMAN'S ORDERS! I'VE KEPT MYSELF OUT OF SIGHT WHILE DOING SUPER-FEATS! IT'S PART OF MY TRAINING!
IT WAS ONLY RECENTLY THAT MY SPACE ROCKET LANDED ON EARTH! BUT COUSIN SUPERMAN SAYS I MUST LEARN MORE ABOUT EARTH WAYS BEFORE HE TELLS THE WORLD OF MY EXISTENCE! SOMEDAY, HE'LL ALSO TELL ME HIS SECRET IDENTITY! I DON'T KNOW IT YET!
BEFORE SUPERGIRL CAN RESUME HER OWN SECRET IDENTITY...
WAIT... IS THAT A METEOR COMING DOWN? NO... IT'S A DOG! THAT MUST BE KRYPTO! SUPERMAN TOLD ME ABOUT HIS BOYHOOD PET IN SMALLVILLE! KRYPTO VISITS METROPOLIS AT TIMES, TOO!
IMPULSIVELY, SUPERGIRL CALLS THE FAMOUS SUPERDOG!
KRYPTO! HERE, BOY! I'M SUPERGIRL, YOUR MASTER'S COUSIN! YOU ACT SURPRISED, SO I GUESS SUPERMAN NEVER TOLD YOU ABOUT ME!
???
2

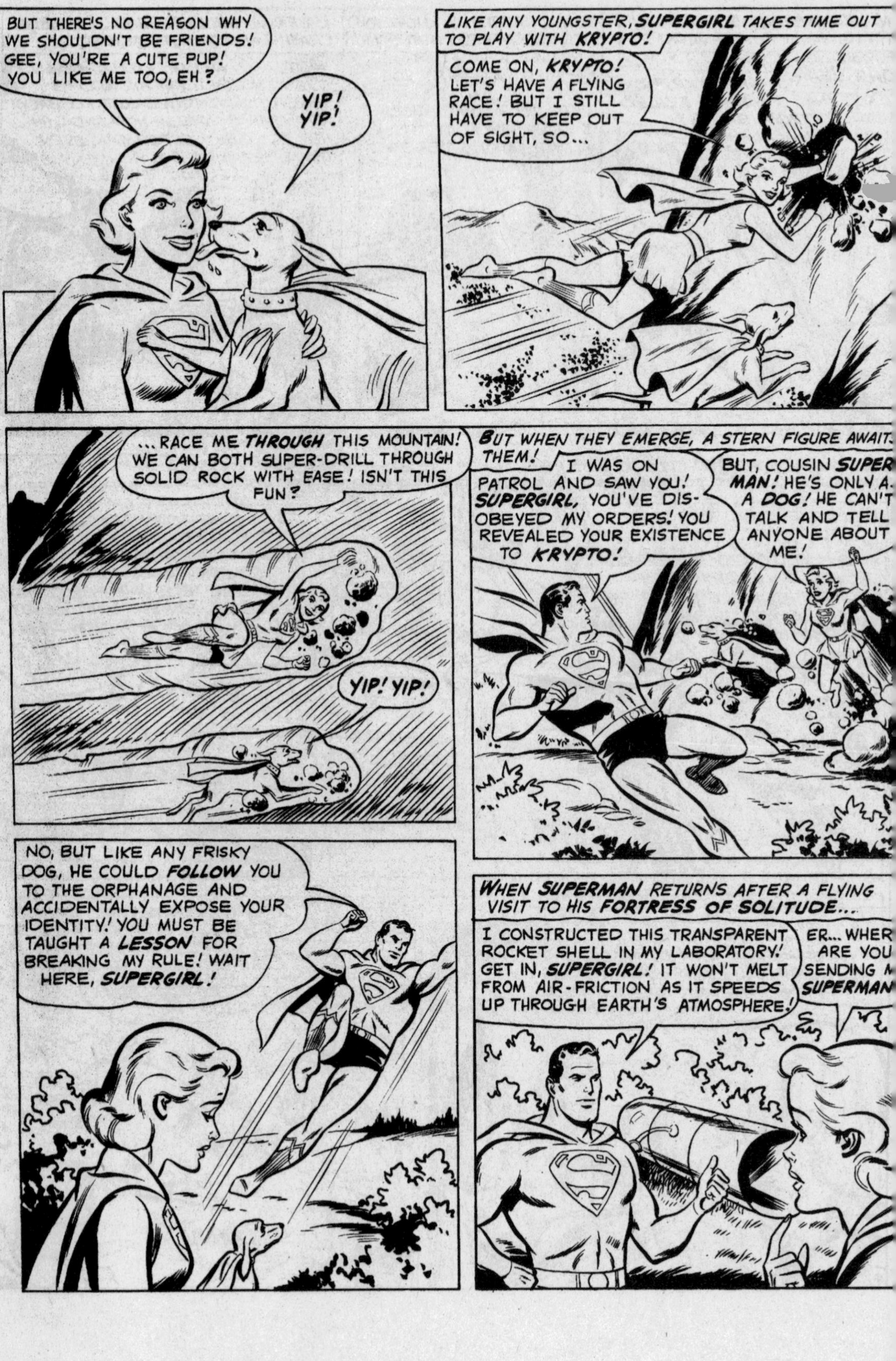
BUT THERE'S NO REASON WHY WE SHOULDN'T BE FRIENDS! GEE, YOU'RE A CUTE PUP! YOU LIKE ME TOO, EH?
YIP! YIP!
LIKE ANY YOUNGSTER, SUPERGIRL TAKES TIME OUT TO PLAY WITH KRYPTO!
COME ON, KRYPTO! LET'S HAVE A FLYING RACE! BUT I STILL HAVE TO KEEP OUT OF SIGHT, SO...
...RACE ME THROUGH THIS MOUNTAIN! WE CAN BOTH SUPER-DRILL THROUGH SOLID ROCK WITH EASE! ISN'T THIS FUN?
YIP! YIP!
BUT WHEN THEY EMERGE, A STERN FIGURE AWAIT THEM!
I WAS ON PATROL AND SAW YOU! SUPERGIRL, YOU'VE DISOBEYED MY ORDERS! YOU REVEALED YOUR EXISTENCE TO KRYPTO!
BUT, COUSIN SUPERMAN! HE'S ONLY A. A DOG! HE CAN'T TALK AND TELL ANYONE ABOUT ME!
NO, BUT LIKE ANY FRISKY DOG, HE COULD FOLLOW YOU TO THE ORPHANAGE AND ACCIDENTALLY EXPOSE YOUR IDENTITY! YOU MUST BE TAUGHT A LESSON FOR BREAKING MY RULE! WAIT HERE, SUPERGIRL!
WHEN SUPERMAN RETURNS AFTER A FLYING VISIT TO HIS FORTRESS OF SOLITUDE...
I CONSTRUCTED THIS TRANSPARENT ROCKET SHELL IN MY LABORATORY! GET IN, SUPERGIRL! IT WON'T MELT FROM AIR-FRICTION AS IT SPEEDS UP THROUGH EARTH'S ATMOSPHERE!
ER... WHER ARE YOU SENDING SUPERMAN

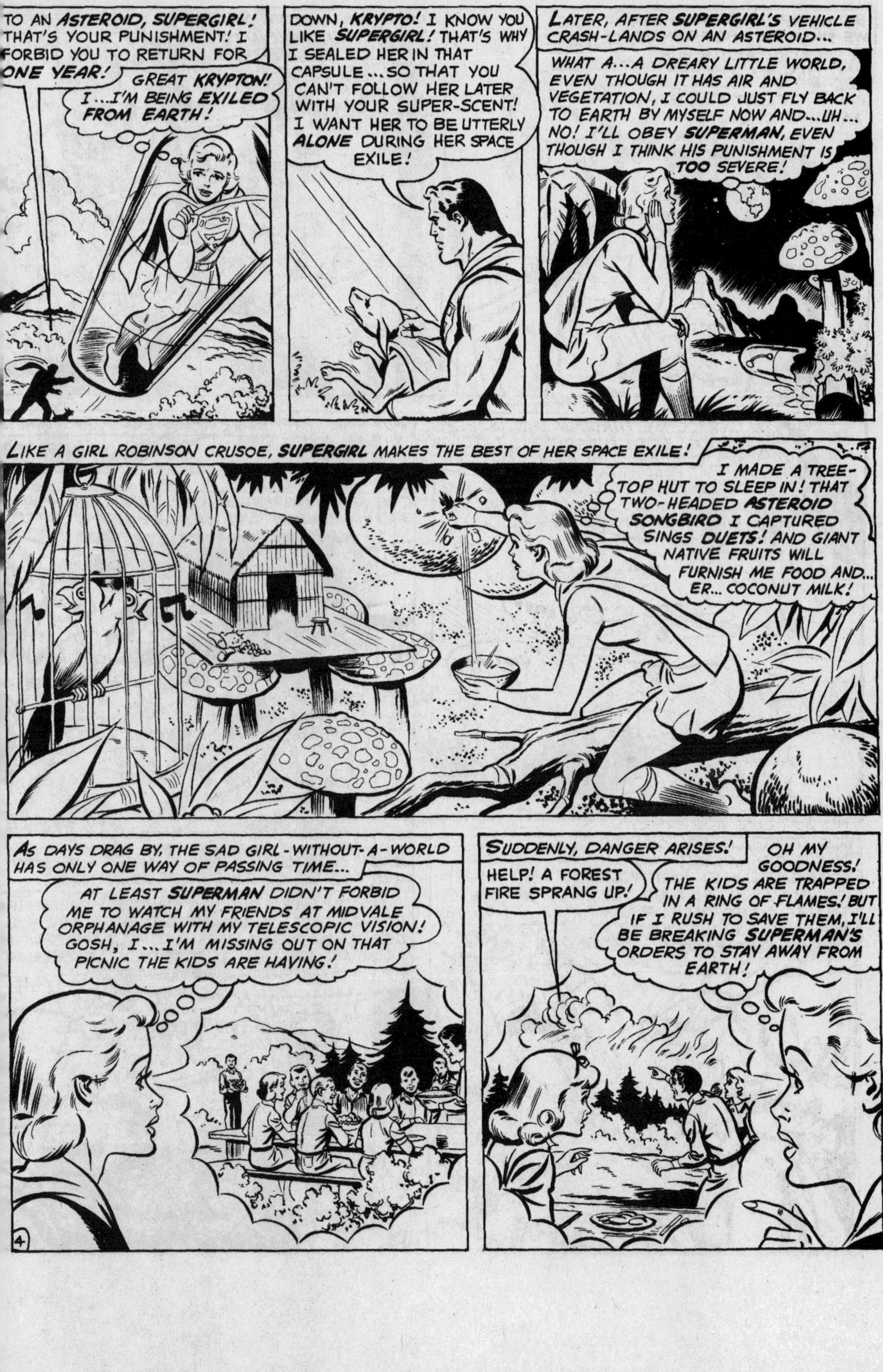
TO AN ASTEROID, SUPERGIRL! THAT'S YOUR PUNISHMENT! I FORBID YOU TO RETURN FOR ONE YEAR!
GREAT KRYPTON! I...I'M BEING EXILED FROM EARTH!
DOWN, KRYPTO! I KNOW YOU LIKE SUPERGIRL! THAT'S WHY I SEALED HER IN THAT CAPSULE...SO THAT YOU CAN'T FOLLOW HER LATER WITH YOUR SUPER-SCENT! I WANT HER TO BE UTTERLY ALONE DURING HER SPACE EXILE!
LATER, AFTER SUPERGIRL'S VEHICLE CRASH-LANDS ON AN ASTEROID...
WHAT A...A DREARY LITTLE WORLD, EVEN THOUGH IT HAS AIR AND VEGETATION, I COULD JUST FLY BACK TO EARTH BY MYSELF NOW AND...UH... NO! I'LL OBEY SUPERMAN, EVEN THOUGH I THINK HIS PUNISHMENT IS TOO SEVERE!
LIKE A GIRL ROBINSON CRUSOE, SUPERGIRL MAKES THE BEST OF HER SPACE EXILE!
I MADE A TREE-TOP HUT TO SLEEP IN! THAT TWO-HEADED ASTEROID SONGBIRD I CAPTURED SINGS DUETS! AND GIANT NATIVE FRUITS WILL FURNISH ME FOOD AND... ER... COCONUT MILK!
AS DAYS DRAG BY, THE SAD GIRL-WITHOUT-A-WORLD HAS ONLY ONE WAY OF PASSING TIME...
AT LEAST SUPERMAN DIDN'T FORBID ME TO WATCH MY FRIENDS AT MIDVALE ORPHANAGE WITH MY TELESCOPIC VISION! GOSH, I...I'M MISSING OUT ON THAT PICNIC THE KIDS ARE HAVING!
4
SUDDENLY, DANGER ARISES!
HELP! A FOREST FIRE SPRANG UP!
OH MY GOODNESS! THE KIDS ARE TRAPPED IN A RING OF FLAMES! BUT IF I RUSH TO SAVE THEM, I'LL BE BREAKING SUPERMAN'S ORDERS TO STAY AWAY FROM EARTH!

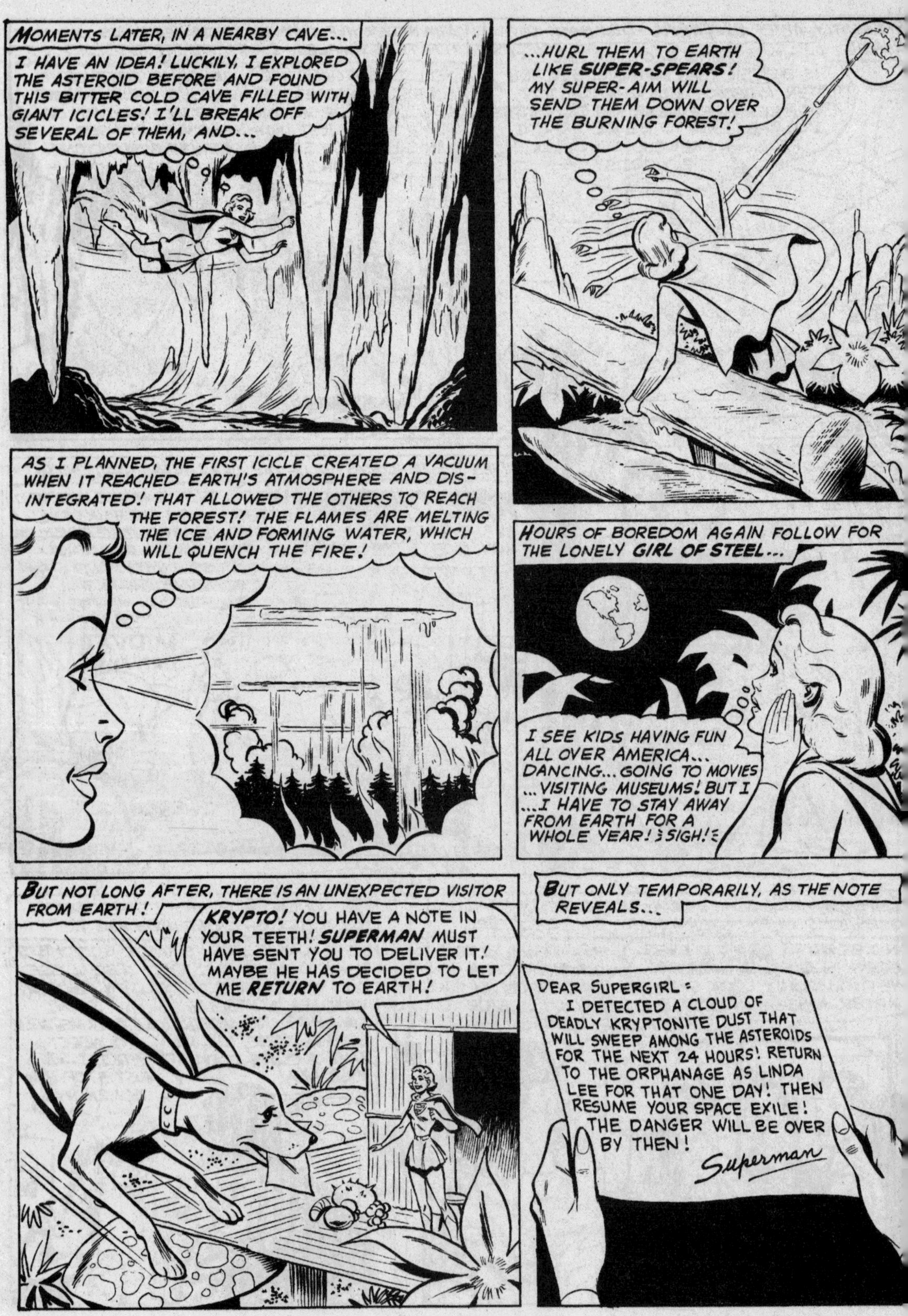
MOMENTS LATER, IN A NEARBY CAVE...
I HAVE AN IDEA! LUCKILY, I EXPLORED THE ASTEROID BEFORE AND FOUND THIS BITTER COLD CAVE FILLED WITH GIANT ICICLES! I'LL BREAK OFF SEVERAL OF THEM, AND...
...HURL THEM TO EARTH LIKE SUPER-SPEARS! MY SUPER-AIM WILL SEND THEM DOWN OVER THE BURNING FOREST!
AS I PLANNED, THE FIRST ICICLE CREATED A VACUUM WHEN IT REACHED EARTH'S ATMOSPHERE AND DISINTEGRATED! THAT ALLOWED THE OTHERS TO REACH THE FOREST! THE FLAMES ARE MELTING THE ICE AND FORMING WATER, WHICH WILL QUENCH THE FIRE!
HOURS OF BOREDOM AGAIN FOLLOW FOR THE LONELY GIRL OF STEEL...
I SEE KIDS HAVING FUN ALL OVER AMERICA... DANCING... GOING TO MOVIES ...VISITING MUSEUMS! BUT I ...I HAVE TO STAY AWAY FROM EARTH FOR A WHOLE YEAR! SIGH!
BUT NOT LONG AFTER, THERE IS AN UNEXPECTED VISITOR FROM EARTH!
KRYPTO! YOU HAVE A NOTE IN YOUR TEETH! SUPERMAN MUST HAVE SENT YOU TO DELIVER IT! MAYBE HE HAS DECIDED TO LET ME RETURN TO EARTH!
BUT ONLY TEMPORARILY, AS THE NOTE REVEALS...
DEAR SUPERGIRL: I DETECTED A CLOUD OF DEADLY KRYPTONITE DUST THAT WILL SWEEP AMONG THE ASTEROIDS FOR THE NEXT 24 HOURS! RETURN TO THE ORPHANAGE AS LINDA LEE FOR THAT ONE DAY! THEN RESUME YOUR SPACE EXILE! THE DANGER WILL BE OVER BY THEN! Superman

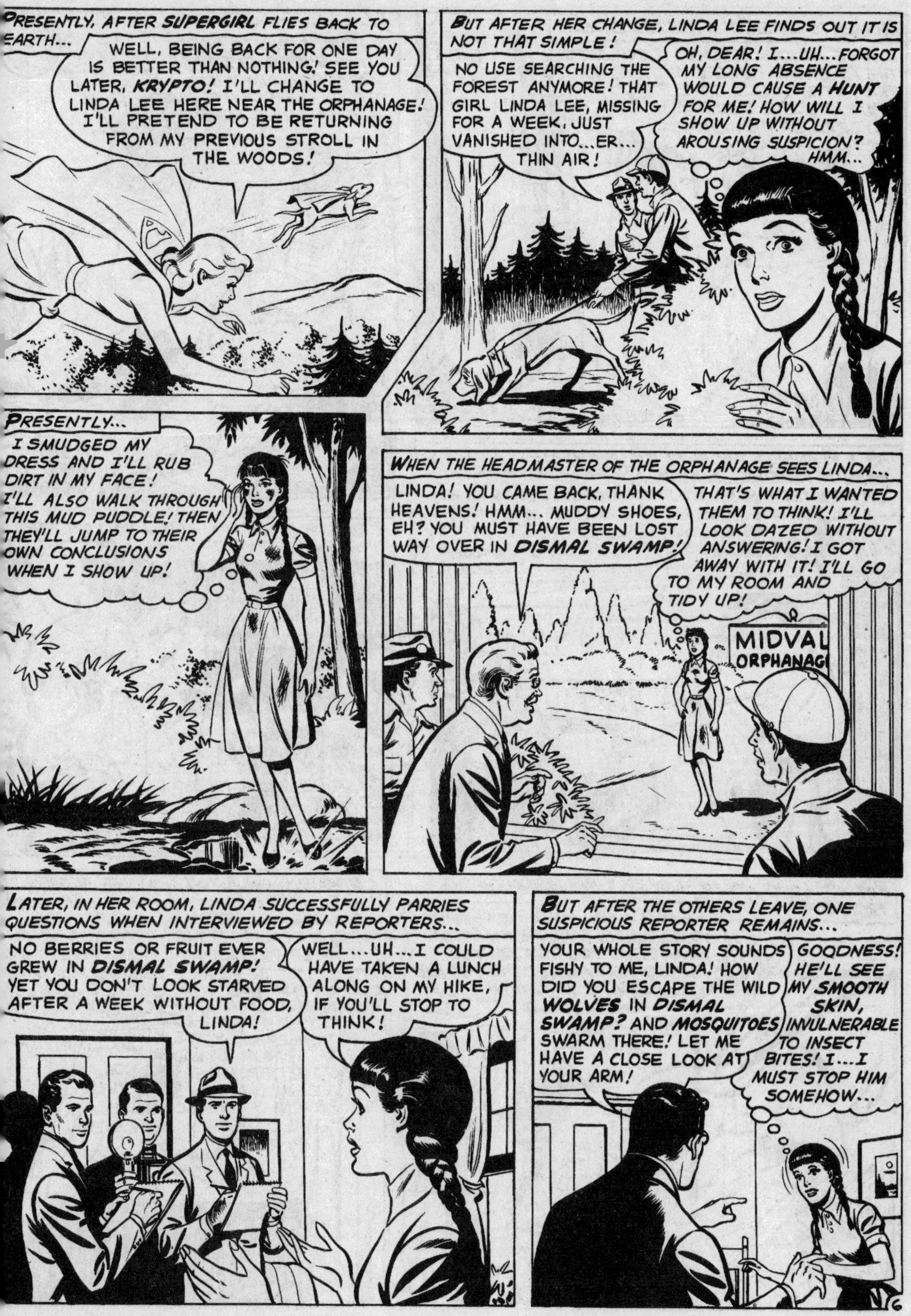
PRESENTLY, AFTER SUPERGIRL FLIES BACK TO EARTH...
WELL, BEING BACK FOR ONE DAY IS BETTER THAN NOTHING! SEE YOU LATER, KRYPTO! I'LL CHANGE TO LINDA LEE HERE NEAR THE ORPHANAGE! I'LL PRETEND TO BE RETURNING FROM MY PREVIOUS STROLL IN THE WOODS!
BUT AFTER HER CHANGE, LINDA LEE FINDS OUT IT IS NOT THAT SIMPLE!
NO USE SEARCHING THE FOREST ANYMORE! THAT GIRL LINDA LEE, MISSING FOR A WEEK, JUST VANISHED INTO...ER... THIN AIR!
OH, DEAR! I...UH...FORGOT MY LONG ABSENCE WOULD CAUSE A HUNT FOR ME! HOW WILL I SHOW UP WITHOUT AROUSING SUSPICION? HMM...
PRESENTLY...
I SMUDGED MY DRESS AND I'LL RUB DIRT IN MY FACE! I'LL ALSO WALK THROUGH THIS MUD PUDDLE! THEN THEY'LL JUMP TO THEIR OWN CONCLUSIONS WHEN I SHOW UP!
WHEN THE HEADMASTER OF THE ORPHANAGE SEES LINDA...
LINDA! YOU CAME BACK, THANK HEAVENS! HMM... MUDDY SHOES, EH? YOU MUST HAVE BEEN LOST WAY OVER IN DISMAL SWAMP!
THAT'S WHAT I WANTED THEM TO THINK! I'LL LOOK DAZED WITHOUT ANSWERING! I GOT AWAY WITH IT! I'LL GO TO MY ROOM AND TIDY UP!
MIDVAL
ORPHANAG
LATER, IN HER ROOM, LINDA SUCCESSFULLY PARRIES QUESTIONS WHEN INTERVIEWED BY REPORTERS...
NO BERRIES OR FRUIT EVER GREW IN DISMAL SWAMP! YET YOU DON'T LOOK STARVED AFTER A WEEK WITHOUT FOOD, LINDA!
WELL...UH...I COULD HAVE TAKEN A LUNCH ALONG ON MY HIKE, IF YOU'LL STOP TO THINK!
BUT AFTER THE OTHERS LEAVE, ONE SUSPICIOUS REPORTER REMAINS...
YOUR WHOLE STORY SOUNDS FISHY TO ME, LINDA! HOW DID YOU ESCAPE THE WILD WOLVES IN DISMAL SWAMP? AND MOSQUITOES SWARM THERE! LET ME HAVE A CLOSE LOOK AT YOUR ARM!
GOODNESS! HE'LL SEE MY SMOOTH SKIN, INVULNERABLE TO INSECT BITES! I...I MUST STOP HIM SOMEHOW...
6

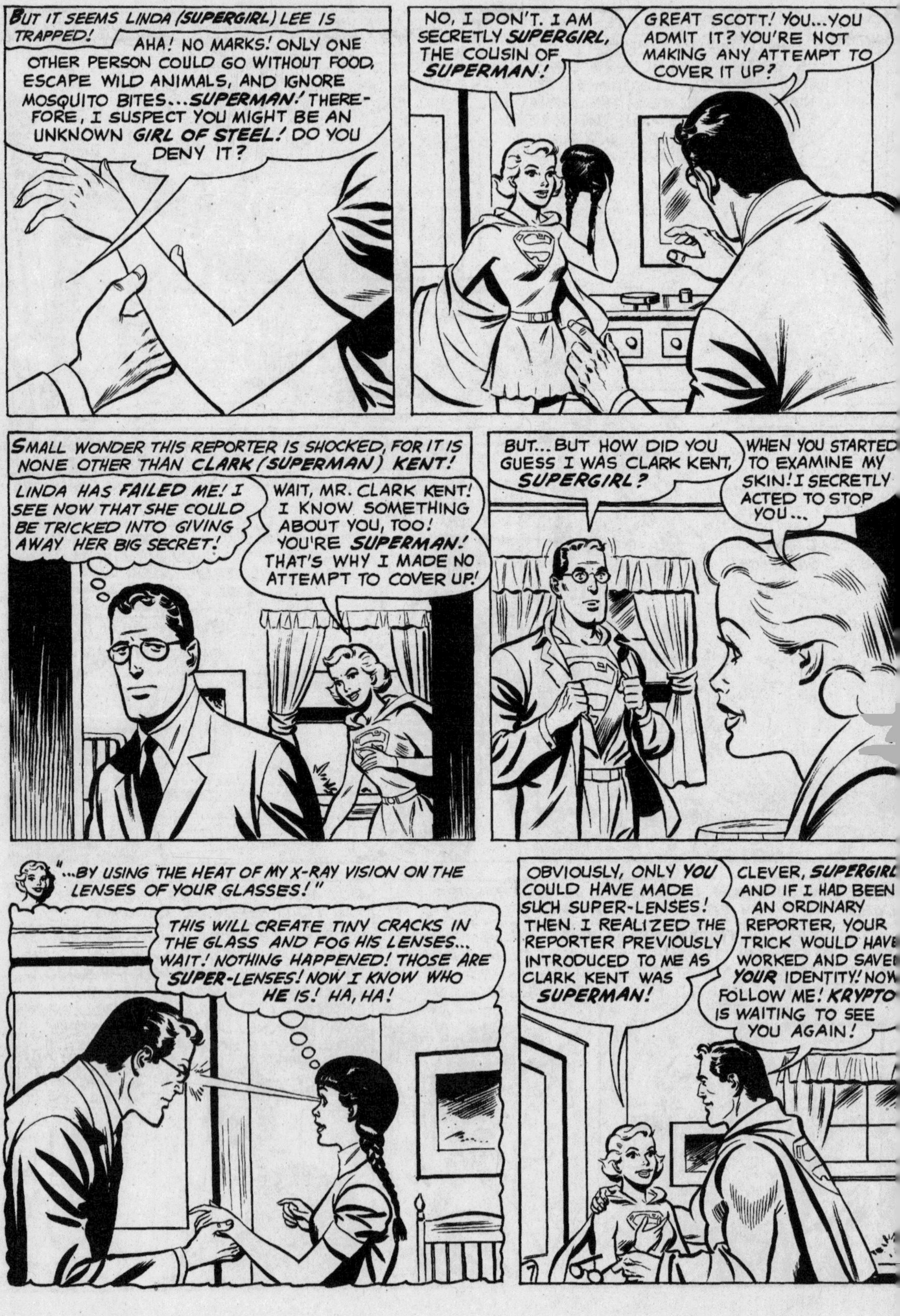
BUT IT SEEMS LINDA (SUPERGIRL) LEE IS TRAPPED!
AHA! NO MARKS! ONLY ONE OTHER PERSON COULD GO WITHOUT FOOD, ESCAPE WILD ANIMALS, AND IGNORE MOSQUITO BITES...SUPERMAN! THEREFORE, I SUSPECT YOU MIGHT BE AN UNKNOWN GIRL OF STEEL! DO YOU DENY IT?
NO, I DON'T. I AM SECRETLY SUPERGIRL, THE COUSIN OF SUPERMAN!
GREAT SCOTT! YOU...YOU ADMIT IT? YOU'RE NOT MAKING ANY ATTEMPT TO COVER IT UP?
SMALL WONDER THIS REPORTER IS SHOCKED, FOR IT IS NONE OTHER THAN CLARK (SUPERMAN) KENT!
LINDA HAS FAILED ME! I SEE NOW THAT SHE COULD BE TRICKED INTO GIVING AWAY HER BIG SECRET!
WAIT, MR. CLARK KENT! I KNOW SOMETHING ABOUT YOU, TOO! YOU'RE SUPERMAN! THAT'S WHY I MADE NO ATTEMPT TO COVER UP!
BUT...BUT HOW DID YOU GUESS I WAS CLARK KENT, SUPERGIRL?
WHEN YOU STARTE TO EXAMINE MY SKIN! I SECRETLY ACTED TO STOP YOU...
"...BY USING THE HEAT OF MY X-RAY VISION ON THE LENSES OF YOUR GLASSES!"
THIS WILL CREATE TINY CRACKS IN THE GLASS AND FOG HIS LENSES... WAIT! NOTHING HAPPENED! THOSE ARE SUPER-LENSES! NOW I KNOW WHO HE IS! HA, HA!
OBVIOUSLY, ONLY YOU COULD HAVE MADE SUCH SUPER-LENSES! THEN I REALIZED THE REPORTER PREVIOUSLY INTRODUCED TO ME AS CLARK KENT WAS SUPERMAN!
CLEVER, SUPERGIRL AND IF I HAD BEEN AN ORDINARY REPORTER, YOUR TRICK WOULD HAVE WORKED AND SAVE YOUR IDENTITY! NOW FOLLOW ME! KRYPTO IS WAITING TO SEE YOU AGAIN!

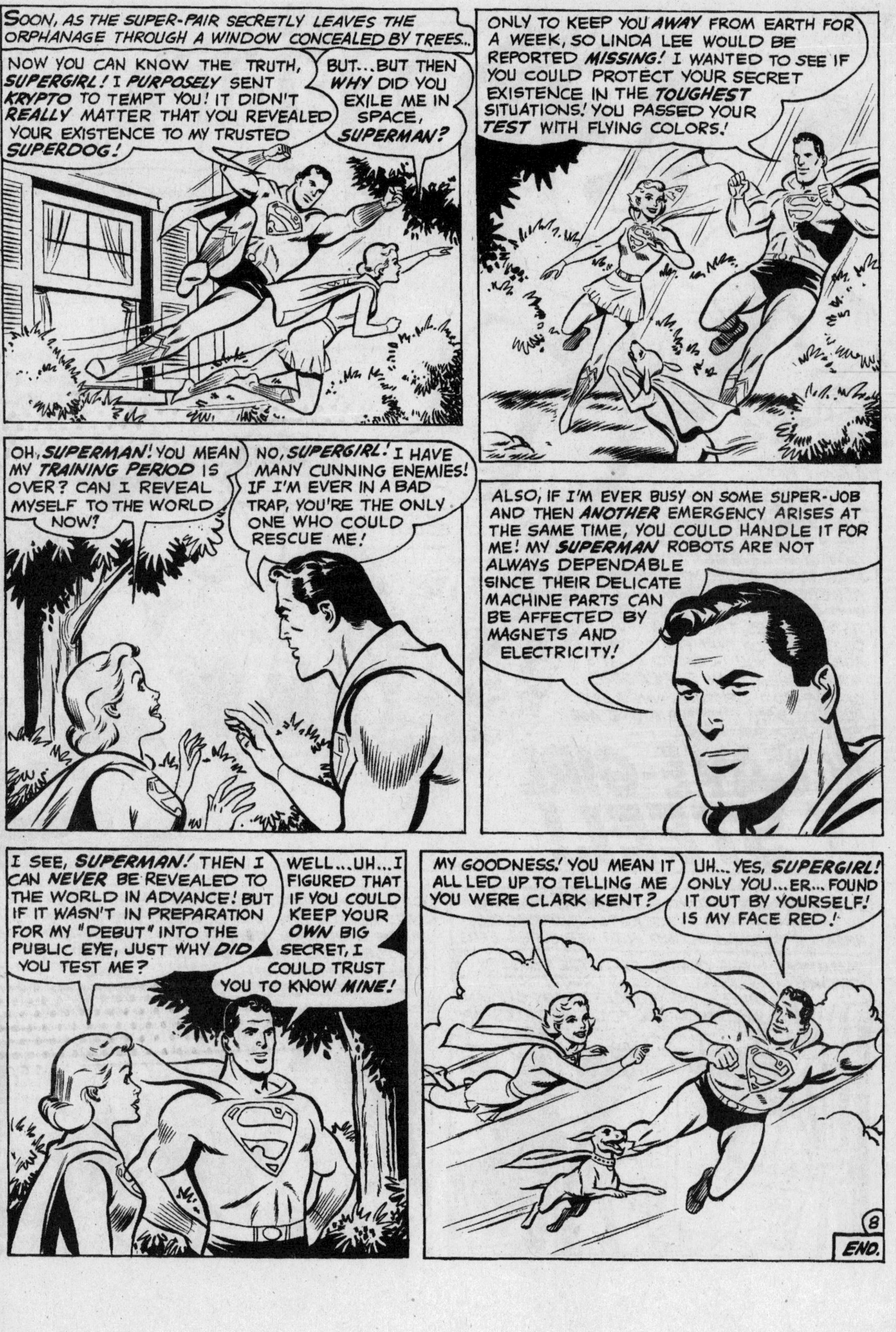
SOON, AS THE SUPER-PAIR SECRETLY LEAVES THE ORPHANAGE THROUGH A WINDOW CONCEALED BY TREES...
NOW YOU CAN KNOW THE TRUTH, SUPERGIRL! I PURPOSELY SENT KRYPTO TO TEMPT YOU! IT DIDN'T REALLY MATTER THAT YOU REVEALED YOUR EXISTENCE TO MY TRUSTED SUPERDOG!
BUT...BUT THEN WHY DID YOU EXILE ME IN SPACE, SUPERMAN?
ONLY TO KEEP YOU AWAY FROM EARTH FOR A WEEK, SO LINDA LEE WOULD BE REPORTED MISSING! I WANTED TO SEE IF YOU COULD PROTECT YOUR SECRET EXISTENCE IN THE TOUGHEST SITUATIONS! YOU PASSED YOUR TEST WITH FLYING COLORS!
OH, SUPERMAN! YOU MEAN MY TRAINING PERIOD IS OVER? CAN I REVEAL MYSELF TO THE WORLD NOW?
NO, SUPERGIRL! I HAVE MANY CUNNING ENEMIES! IF I'M EVER IN A BAD TRAP, YOU'RE THE ONLY ONE WHO COULD RESCUE ME!
ALSO, IF I'M EVER BUSY ON SOME SUPER-JOB AND THEN ANOTHER EMERGENCY ARISES AT THE SAME TIME, YOU COULD HANDLE IT FOR ME! MY SUPERMAN ROBOTS ARE NOT ALWAYS DEPENDABLE SINCE THEIR DELICATE MACHINE PARTS CAN BE AFFECTED BY MAGNETS AND ELECTRICITY!
I SEE, SUPERMAN! THEN I CAN NEVER BE REVEALED TO THE WORLD IN ADVANCE! BUT IF IT WASN'T IN PREPARATION FOR MY "DEBUT" INTO THE PUBLIC EYE, JUST WHY DID YOU TEST ME?
WELL...UH...I FIGURED THAT IF YOU COULD KEEP YOUR OWN BIG SECRET, I COULD TRUST YOU TO KNOW MINE!
MY GOODNESS! YOU MEAN IT ALL LED UP TO TELLING ME YOU WERE CLARK KENT?
UH...YES, SUPERGIRL! ONLY YOU...ER...FOUND IT OUT BY YOURSELF! IS MY FACE RED!
8
END.

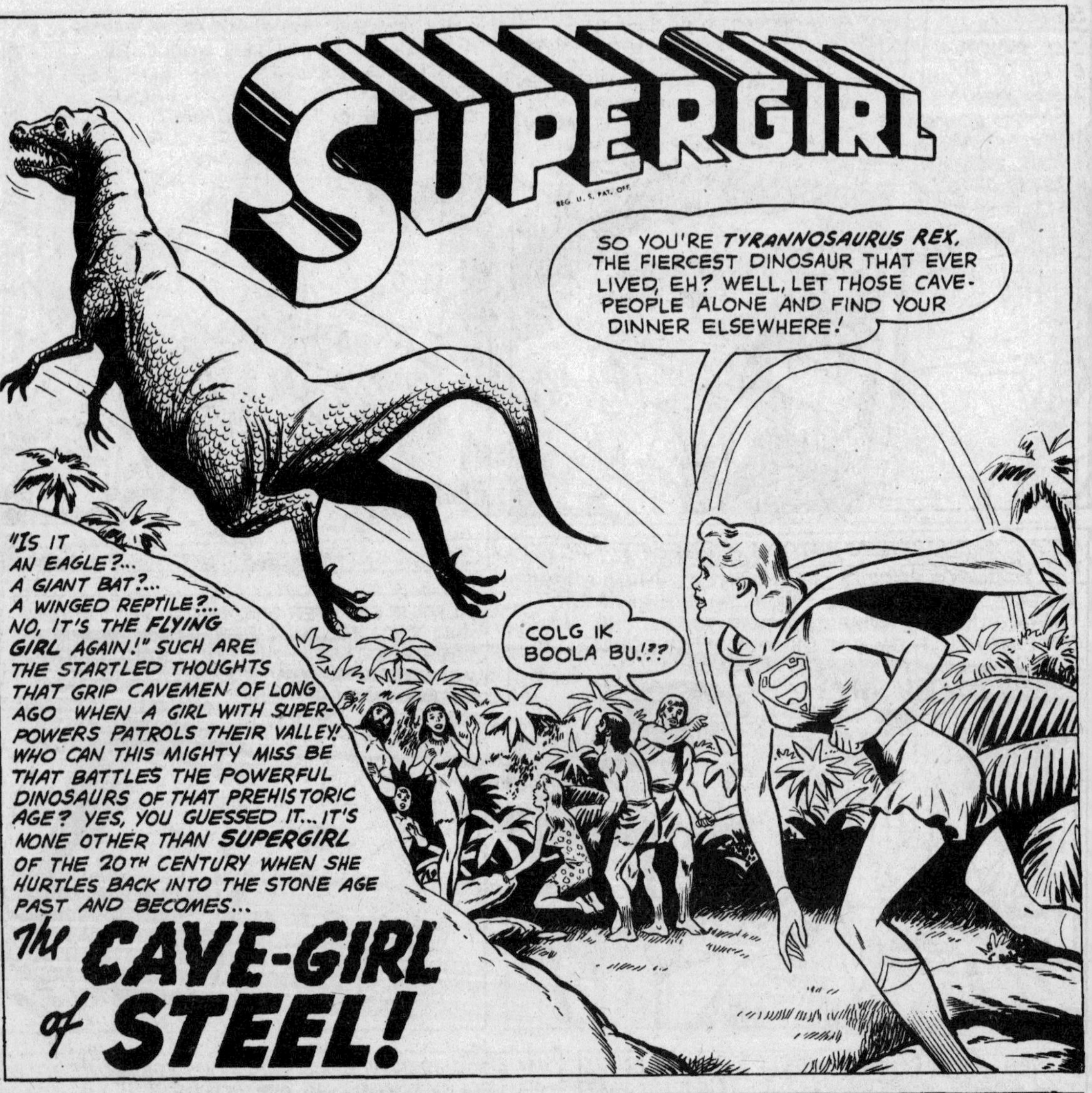
SUPERGIRL
REG. U. S. PAT. OFF.
"IS IT AN EAGLE?... A GIANT BAT?... A WINGED REPTILE?... NO, IT'S THE FLYING GIRL AGAIN!" SUCH ARE THE STARTLED THOUGHTS THAT GRIP CAVEMEN OF LONG AGO WHEN A GIRL WITH SUPER-POWERS PATROLS THEIR VALLEY! WHO CAN THIS MIGHTY MISS BE THAT BATTLES THE POWERFUL DINOSAURS OF THAT PREHISTORIC AGE? YES, YOU GUESSED IT... IT'S NONE OTHER THAN SUPERGIRL OF THE 20TH CENTURY WHEN SHE HURTLES BACK INTO THE STONE AGE PAST AND BECOMES...
The CAVE-GIRL of STEEL!
SO YOU'RE TYRANNOSAURUS REX, THE FIERCEST DINOSAUR THAT EVER LIVED, EH? WELL, LET THOSE CAVE-PEOPLE ALONE AND FIND YOUR DINNER ELSEWHERE!
COLG IK BOOLA BU!??

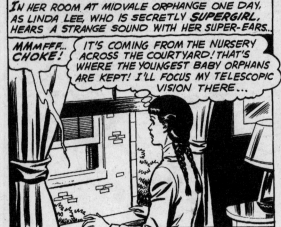

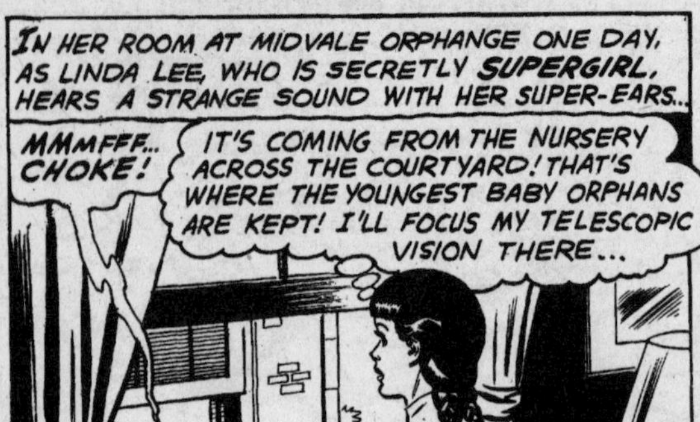
IN HER ROOM AT MIDVALE ORPHANGE ONE DAY, AS LINDA LEE, WHO IS SECRETLY SUPERGIRL, HEARS A STRANGE SOUND WITH HER SUPER-EARS...
MMMFFF... CHOKE!
IT'S COMING FROM THE NURSERY ACROSS THE COURTYARD! THAT'S WHERE THE YOUNGEST BABY ORPHANS ARE KEPT! I'LL FOCUS MY TELESCOPIC VISION THERE...

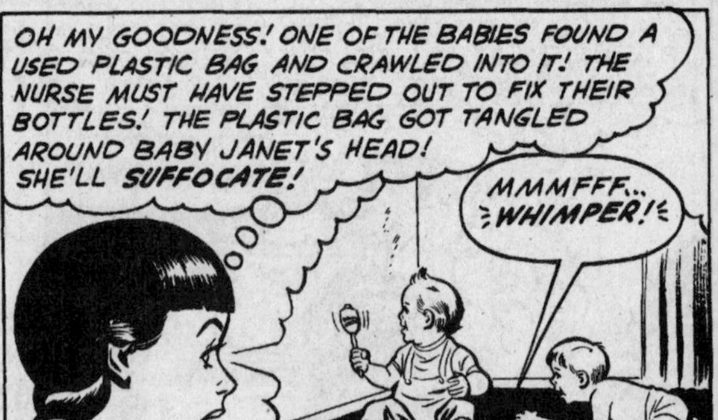
OH MY GOODNESS! ONE OF THE BABIES FOUND A USED PLASTIC BAG AND CRAWLED INTO IT! THE NURSE MUST HAVE STEPPED OUT TO FIX THEIR BOTTLES! THE PLASTIC BAG GOT TANGLED AROUND BABY JANET'S HEAD! SHE'LL SUFFOCATE!
MMMFFF... WHIMPER!

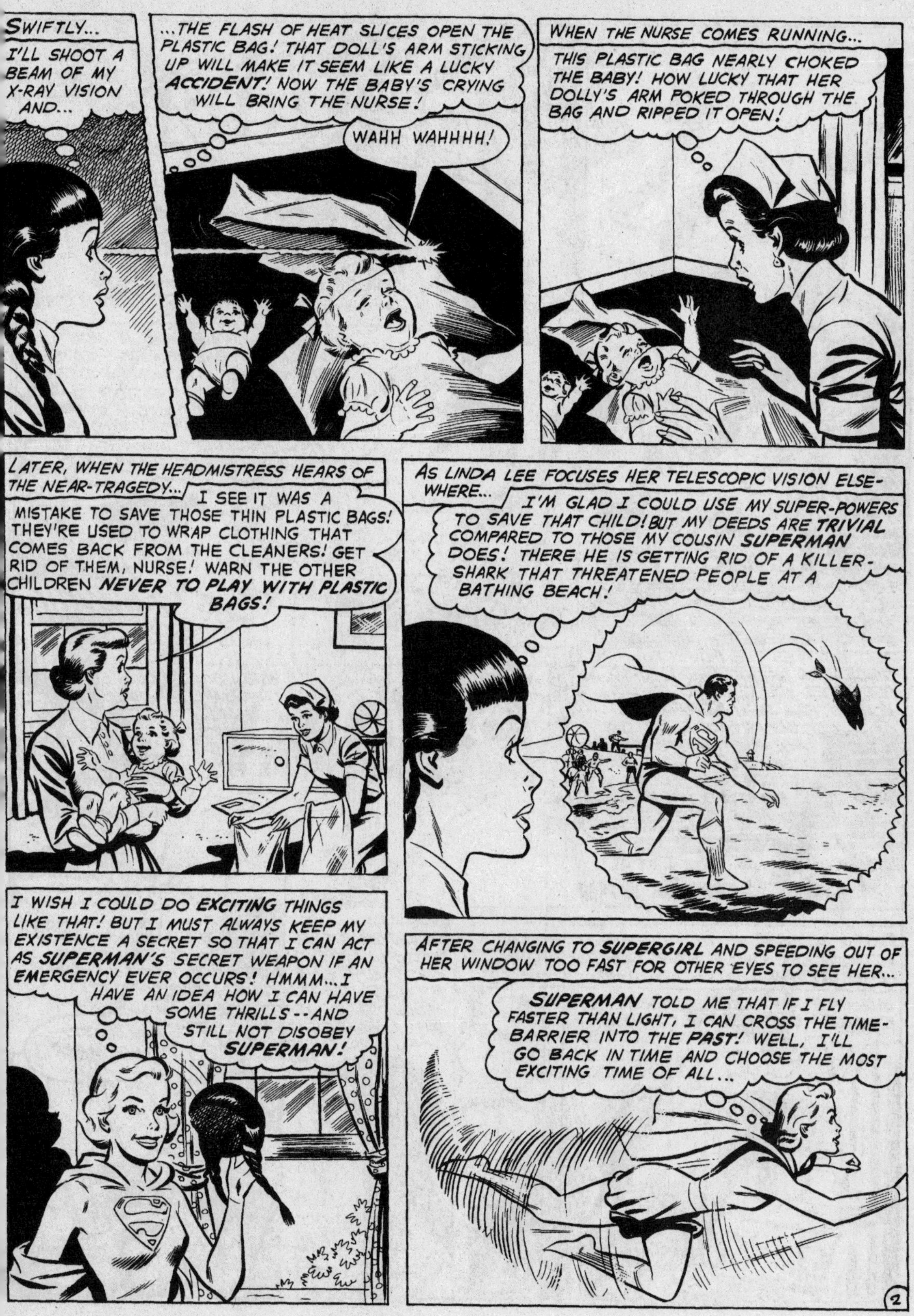
SWIFTLY...
I'LL SHOOT A BEAM OF MY X-RAY VISION AND...
...THE FLASH OF HEAT SLICES OPEN THE PLASTIC BAG! THAT DOLL'S ARM STICKING UP WILL MAKE IT SEEM LIKE A LUCKY ACCIDENT! NOW THE BABY'S CRYING WILL BRING THE NURSE!
WAHH WAHHHH!
WHEN THE NURSE COMES RUNNING...
THIS PLASTIC BAG NEARLY CHOKED THE BABY! HOW LUCKY THAT HER DOLLY'S ARM POKED THROUGH THE BAG AND RIPPED IT OPEN!
LATER, WHEN THE HEADMISTRESS HEARS OF THE NEAR-TRAGEDY...
I SEE IT WAS A MISTAKE TO SAVE THOSE THIN PLASTIC BAGS! THEY'RE USED TO WRAP CLOTHING THAT COMES BACK FROM THE CLEANERS! GET RID OF THEM, NURSE! WARN THE OTHER CHILDREN NEVER TO PLAY WITH PLASTIC BAGS!
AS LINDA LEE FOCUSES HER TELESCOPIC VISION ELSE-WHERE...
I'M GLAD I COULD USE MY SUPER-POWERS TO SAVE THAT CHILD! BUT MY DEEDS ARE TRIVIAL COMPARED TO THOSE MY COUSIN SUPERMAN DOES! THERE HE IS GETTING RID OF A KILLER-SHARK THAT THREATENED PEOPLE AT A BATHING BEACH!
I WISH I COULD DO EXCITING THINGS LIKE THAT! BUT I MUST ALWAYS KEEP MY EXISTENCE A SECRET SO THAT I CAN ACT AS SUPERMAN'S SECRET WEAPON IF AN EMERGENCY EVER OCCURS! HMMM...I HAVE AN IDEA HOW I CAN HAVE SOME THRILLS--AND STILL NOT DISOBEY SUPERMAN!
AFTER CHANGING TO SUPERGIRL AND SPEEDING OUT OF HER WINDOW TOO FAST FOR OTHER EYES TO SEE HER...
SUPERMAN TOLD ME THAT IF I FLY FASTER THAN LIGHT, I CAN CROSS THE TIME-BARRIER INTO THE PAST! WELL, I'LL GO BACK IN TIME AND CHOOSE THE MOST EXCITING TIME OF ALL...
2

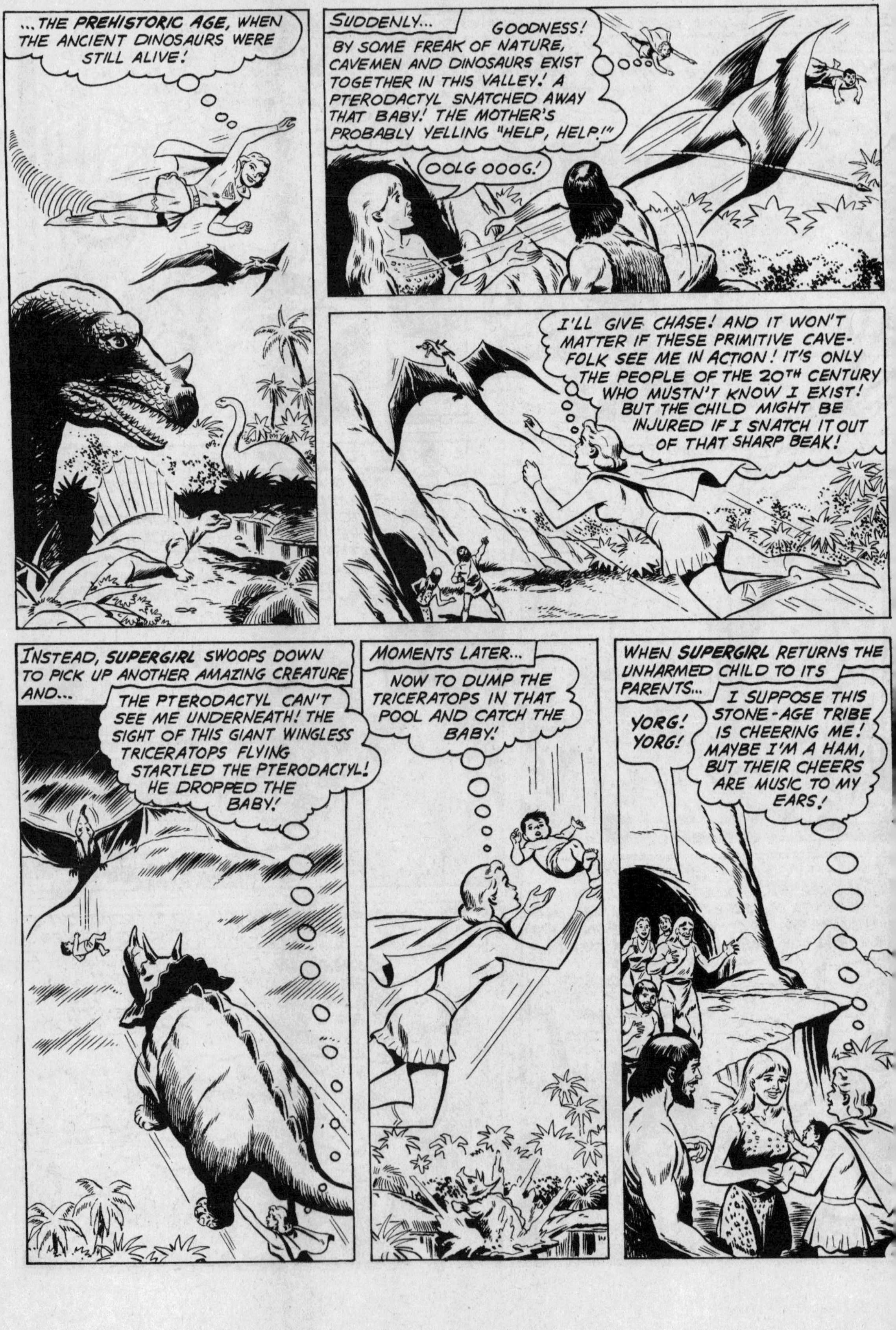
...THE PREHISTORIC AGE, WHEN THE ANCIENT DINOSAURS WERE STILL ALIVE!
SUDDENLY...
GOODNESS! BY SOME FREAK OF NATURE, CAVEMEN AND DINOSAURS EXIST TOGETHER IN THIS VALLEY! A PTERODACTYL SNATCHED AWAY THAT BABY! THE MOTHER'S PROBABLY YELLING "HELP, HELP!"
OOLG OOOG!
I'LL GIVE CHASE! AND IT WON'T MATTER IF THESE PRIMITIVE CAVE-FOLK SEE ME IN ACTION! IT'S ONLY THE PEOPLE OF THE 20TH CENTURY WHO MUSTN'T KNOW I EXIST! BUT THE CHILD MIGHT BE INJURED IF I SNATCH IT OUT OF THAT SHARP BEAK!
INSTEAD, SUPERGIRL SWOOPS DOWN TO PICK UP ANOTHER AMAZING CREATURE AND...
THE PTERODACTYL CAN'T SEE ME UNDERNEATH! THE SIGHT OF THIS GIANT WINGLESS TRICERATOPS FLYING STARTLED THE PTERODACTYL! HE DROPPED THE BABY!
MOMENTS LATER...
NOW TO DUMP THE TRICERATOPS IN THAT POOL AND CATCH THE BABY!
WHEN SUPERGIRL RETURNS THE UNHARMED CHILD TO ITS PARENTS...
YORG! YORG!
I SUPPOSE THIS STONE-AGE TRIBE IS CHEERING ME! MAYBE I'M A HAM, BUT THEIR CHEERS ARE MUSIC TO MY EARS!

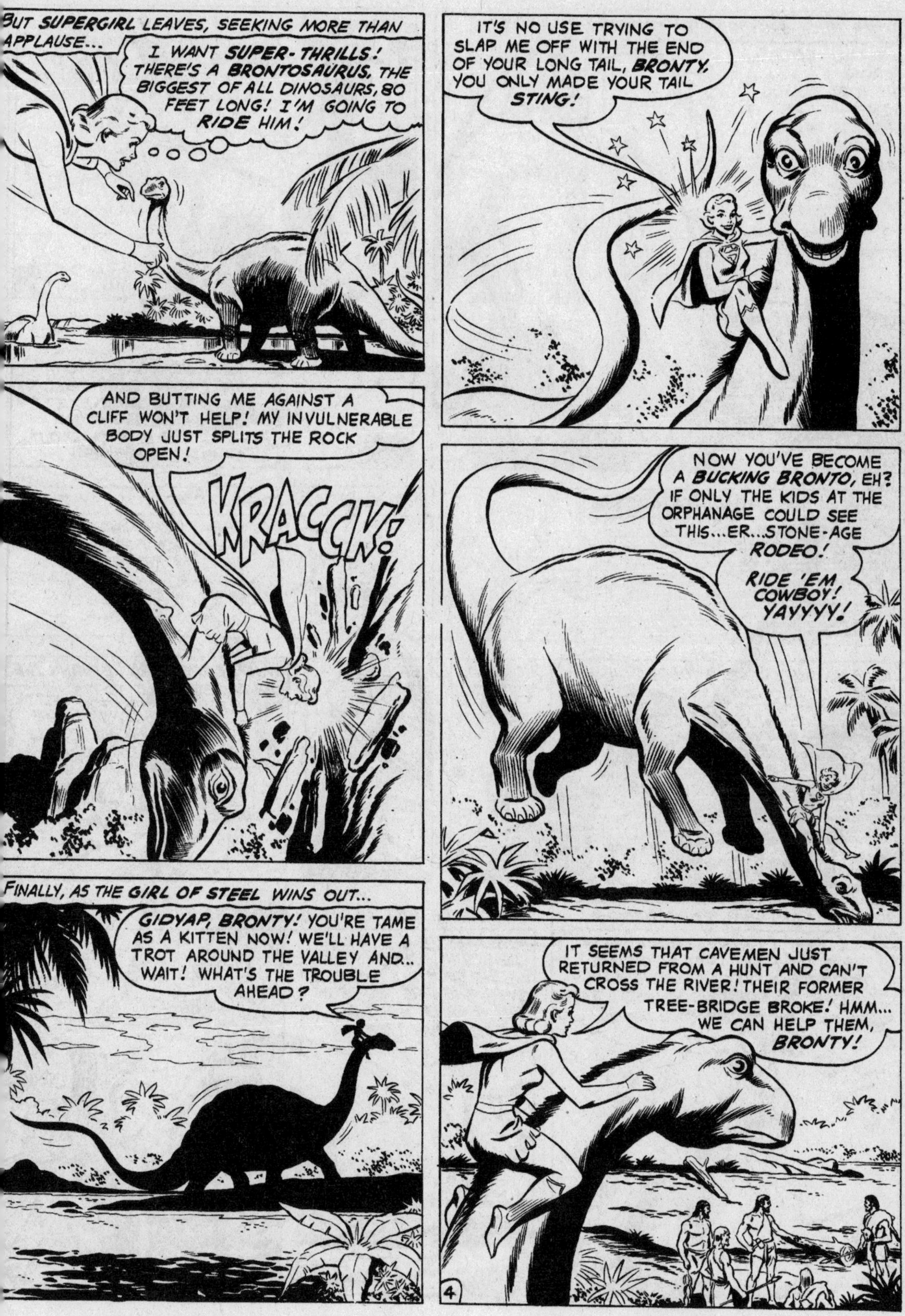
BUT SUPERGIRL LEAVES, SEEKING MORE THAN APPLAUSE...
I WANT SUPER-THRILLS! THERE'S A BRONTOSAURUS, THE BIGGEST OF ALL DINOSAURS, 80 FEET LONG! I'M GOING TO RIDE HIM!
IT'S NO USE TRYING TO SLAP ME OFF WITH THE END OF YOUR LONG TAIL, BRONTY. YOU ONLY MADE YOUR TAIL STING!
AND BUTTING ME AGAINST A CLIFF WON'T HELP! MY INVULNERABLE BODY JUST SPLITS THE ROCK OPEN!
KRACCK!
NOW YOU'VE BECOME A BUCKING BRONTO, EH? IF ONLY THE KIDS AT THE ORPHANAGE COULD SEE THIS...ER...STONE-AGE RODEO!
RIDE 'EM COWBOY! YAYYYY!
FINALLY, AS THE GIRL OF STEEL WINS OUT...
GIDYAP, BRONTY! YOU'RE TAME AS A KITTEN NOW! WE'LL HAVE A TROT AROUND THE VALLEY AND.. WAIT! WHAT'S THE TROUBLE AHEAD?
IT SEEMS THAT CAVEMEN JUST RETURNED FROM A HUNT AND CAN'T CROSS THE RIVER! THEIR FORMER TREE-BRIDGE BROKE! HMM... WE CAN HELP THEM, BRONTY!
4

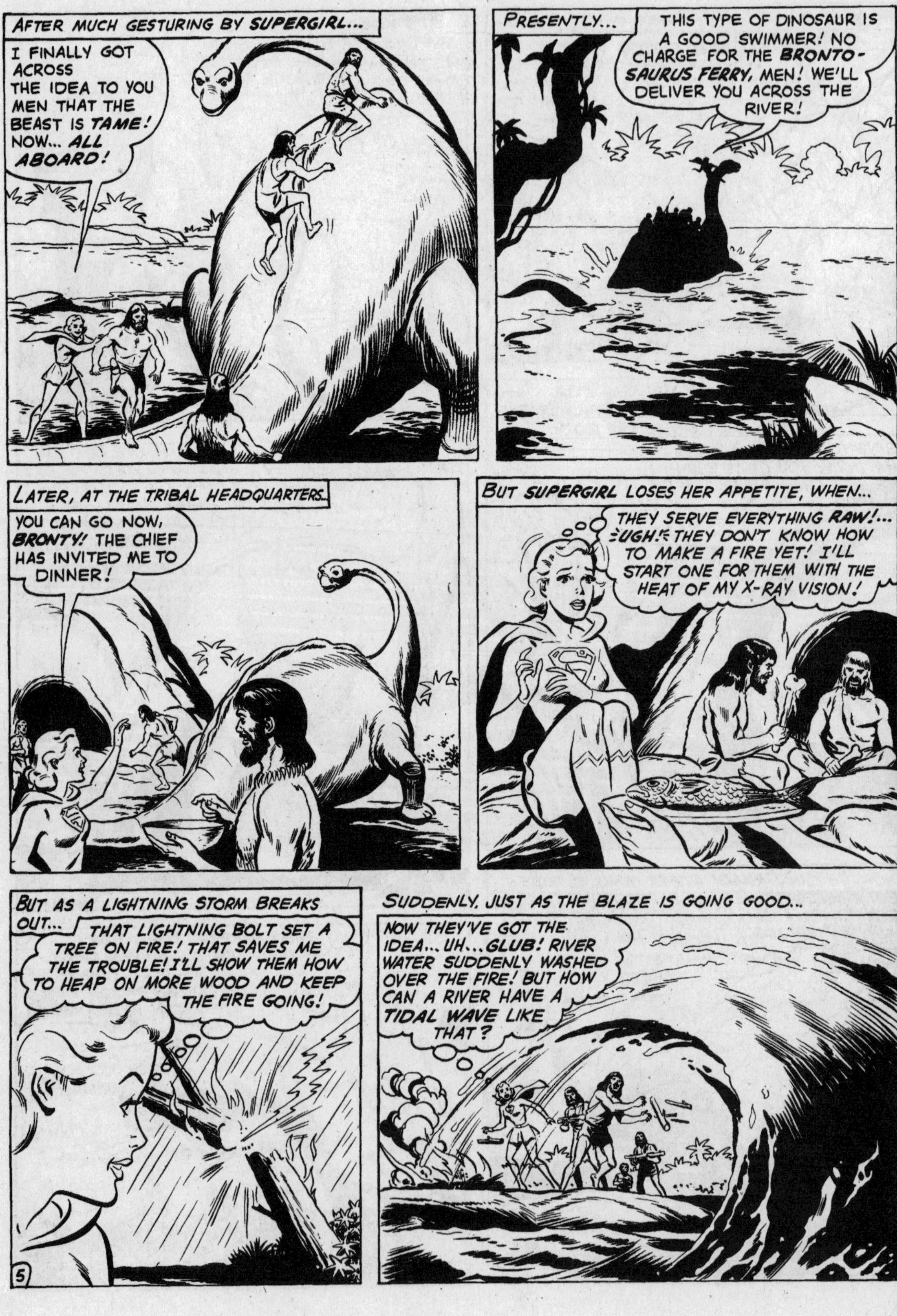
AFTER MUCH GESTURING BY SUPERGIRL...
I FINALLY GOT ACROSS THE IDEA TO YOU MEN THAT THE BEAST IS TAME! NOW... ALL ABOARD!
PRESENTLY...
THIS TYPE OF DINOSAUR IS A GOOD SWIMMER! NO CHARGE FOR THE BRONTOSAURUS FERRY, MEN! WE'LL DELIVER YOU ACROSS THE RIVER!
LATER, AT THE TRIBAL HEADQUARTERS...
YOU CAN GO NOW, BRONTY! THE CHIEF HAS INVITED ME TO DINNER!
BUT SUPERGIRL LOSES HER APPETITE, WHEN...
THEY SERVE EVERYTHING RAW!... UGH! THEY DON'T KNOW HOW TO MAKE A FIRE YET! I'LL START ONE FOR THEM WITH THE HEAT OF MY X-RAY VISION!
BUT AS A LIGHTNING STORM BREAKS OUT...
THAT LIGHTNING BOLT SET A TREE ON FIRE! THAT SAVES ME THE TROUBLE! I'LL SHOW THEM HOW TO HEAP ON MORE WOOD AND KEEP THE FIRE GOING!
5
SUDDENLY, JUST AS THE BLAZE IS GOING GOOD...
NOW THEY'VE GOT THE IDEA... UH... GLUB! RIVER WATER SUDDENLY WASHED OVER THE FIRE! BUT HOW CAN A RIVER HAVE A TIDAL WAVE LIKE THAT?

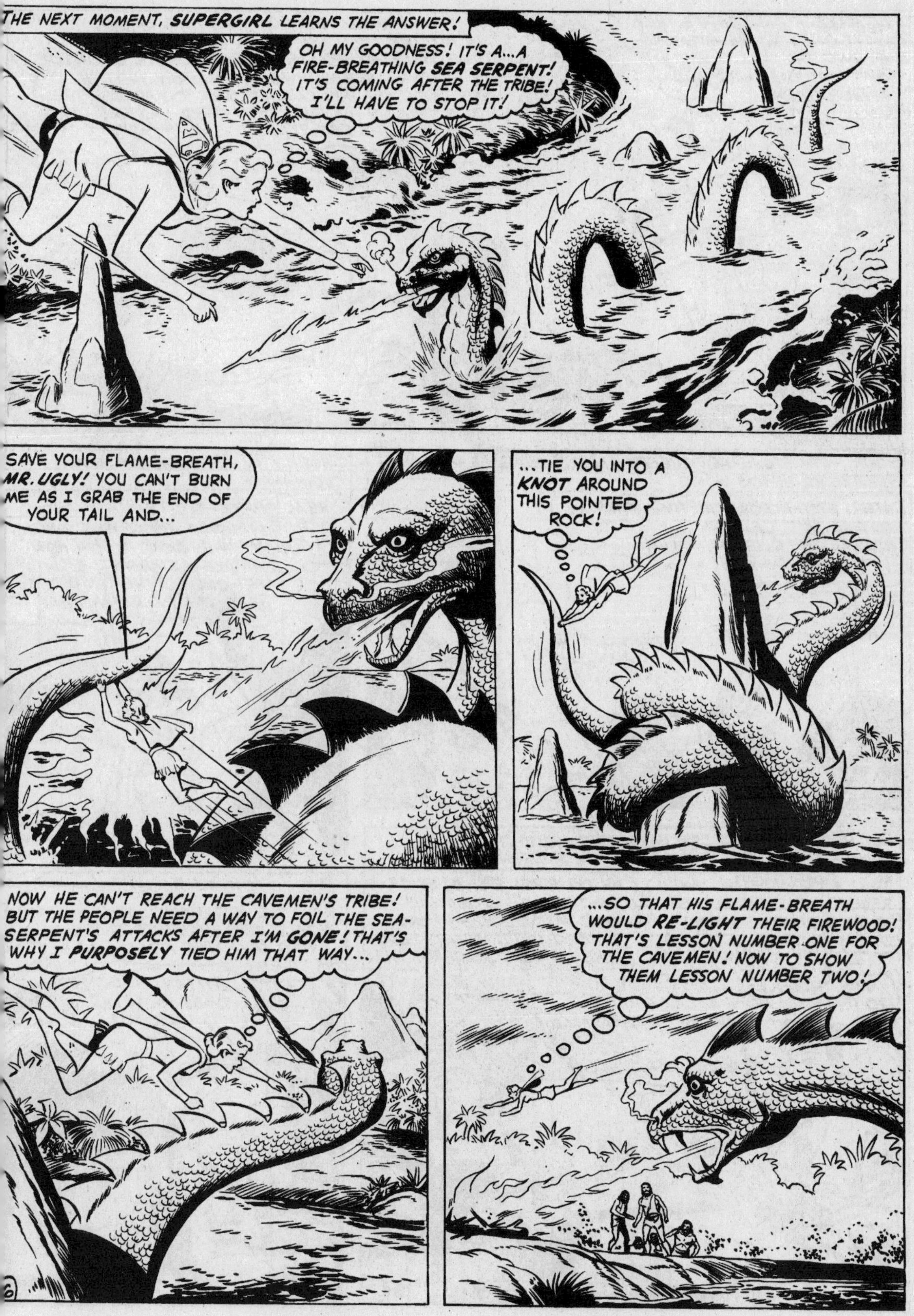
THE NEXT MOMENT, SUPERGIRL LEARNS THE ANSWER!
OH MY GOODNESS! IT'S A...A FIRE-BREATHING SEA SERPENT! IT'S COMING AFTER THE TRIBE! I'LL HAVE TO STOP IT!
SAVE YOUR FLAME-BREATH, MR. UGLY! YOU CAN'T BURN ME AS I GRAB THE END OF YOUR TAIL AND...
...TIE YOU INTO A KNOT AROUND THIS POINTED ROCK!
NOW HE CAN'T REACH THE CAVEMEN'S TRIBE! BUT THE PEOPLE NEED A WAY TO FOIL THE SEA-SERPENT'S ATTACKS AFTER I'M GONE! THAT'S WHY I PURPOSELY TIED HIM THAT WAY...
...SO THAT HIS FLAME-BREATH WOULD RE-LIGHT THEIR FIREWOOD! THAT'S LESSON NUMBER ONE FOR THE CAVEMEN! NOW TO SHOW THEM LESSON NUMBER TWO!

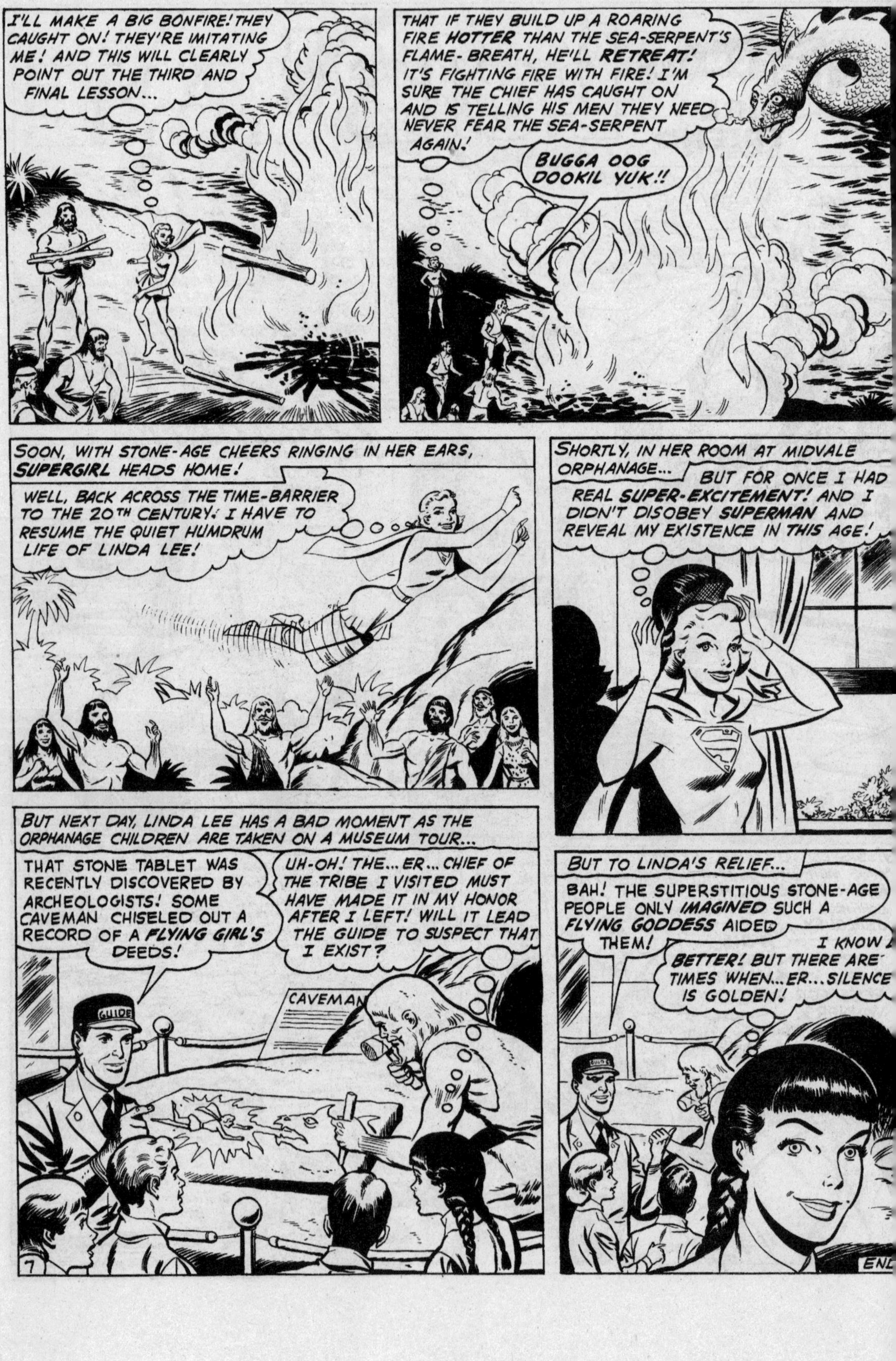
I'LL MAKE A BIG BONFIRE! THEY CAUGHT ON! THEY'RE IMITATING ME! AND THIS WILL CLEARLY POINT OUT THE THIRD AND FINAL LESSON...
THAT IF THEY BUILD UP A ROARING FIRE HOTTER THAN THE SEA-SERPENT'S FLAME-BREATH, HE'LL RETREAT! IT'S FIGHTING FIRE WITH FIRE! I'M SURE THE CHIEF HAS CAUGHT ON AND IS TELLING HIS MEN THEY NEED NEVER FEAR THE SEA-SERPENT AGAIN!
BUGGA OOG DOOKIL YUK!!
SOON, WITH STONE-AGE CHEERS RINGING IN HER EARS, SUPERGIRL HEADS HOME!
WELL, BACK ACROSS THE TIME-BARRIER TO THE 20TH CENTURY! I HAVE TO RESUME THE QUIET HUMDRUM LIFE OF LINDA LEE!
SHORTLY, IN HER ROOM AT MIDVALE ORPHANAGE...
BUT FOR ONCE I HAD REAL SUPER-EXCITEMENT! AND I DIDN'T DISOBEY SUPERMAN AND REVEAL MY EXISTENCE IN THIS AGE!
BUT NEXT DAY, LINDA LEE HAS A BAD MOMENT AS THE ORPHANAGE CHILDREN ARE TAKEN ON A MUSEUM TOUR...
THAT STONE TABLET WAS RECENTLY DISCOVERED BY ARCHEOLOGISTS! SOME CAVEMAN CHISELED OUT A RECORD OF A FLYING GIRL'S DEEDS!
UH-OH! THE... ER... CHIEF OF THE TRIBE I VISITED MUST HAVE MADE IT IN MY HONOR AFTER I LEFT! WILL IT LEAD THE GUIDE TO SUSPECT THAT I EXIST?
CAVEMAN
GUIDE
7
BUT TO LINDA'S RELIEF...
BAH! THE SUPERSTITIOUS STONE-AGE PEOPLE ONLY IMAGINED SUCH A FLYING GODDESS AIDED THEM!
I KNOW
BETTER! BUT THERE ARE TIMES WHEN... ER... SILENCE IS GOLDEN!

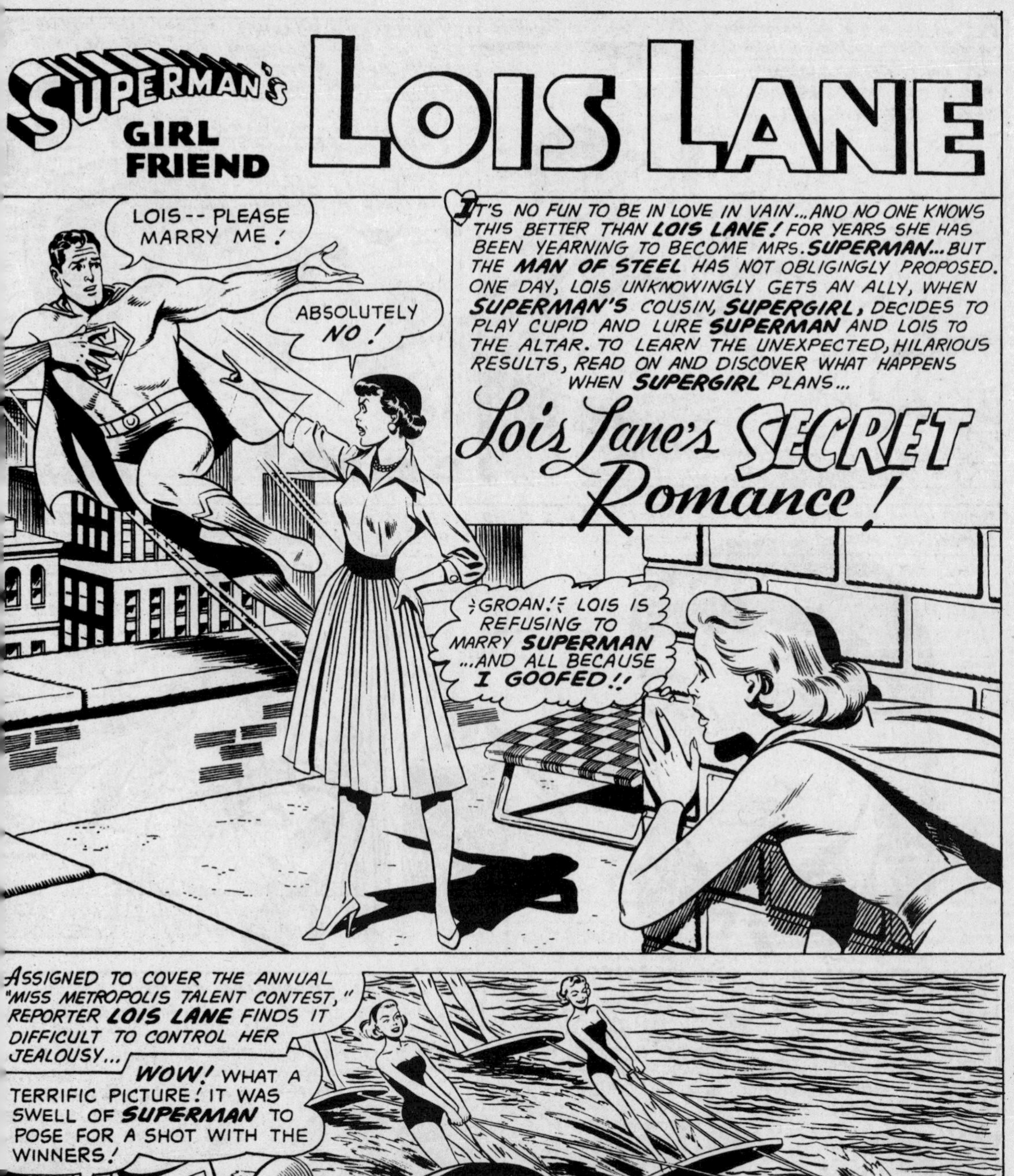
SUPERMAN'S GIRL FRIEND
LOIS LANE
IT'S NO FUN TO BE IN LOVE IN VAIN... AND NO ONE KNOWS THIS BETTER THAN LOIS LANE! FOR YEARS SHE HAS BEEN YEARNING TO BECOME MRS. SUPERMAN... BUT THE MAN OF STEEL HAS NOT OBLIGINGLY PROPOSED. ONE DAY, LOIS UNKNOWINGLY GETS AN ALLY, WHEN SUPERMAN'S COUSIN, SUPERGIRL, DECIDES TO PLAY CUPID AND LURE SUPERMAN AND LOIS TO THE ALTAR. TO LEARN THE UNEXPECTED, HILARIOUS RESULTS, READ ON AND DISCOVER WHAT HAPPENS WHEN SUPERGIRL PLANS...
Lois Lane's SECRET Romance!
LOIS-- PLEASE MARRY ME!
ABSOLUTELY NO!
GROAN! LOIS IS REFUSING TO MARRY SUPERMAN ...AND ALL BECAUSE I GOOFED!!

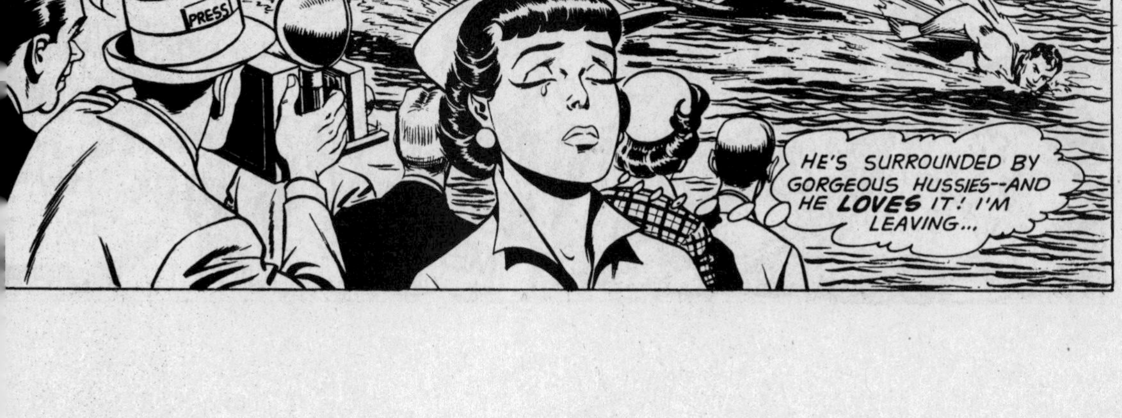
ASSIGNED TO COVER THE ANNUAL "MISS METROPOLIS TALENT CONTEST," REPORTER LOIS LANE FINDS IT DIFFICULT TO CONTROL HER JEALOUSY...
WOW! WHAT A TERRIFIC PICTURE! IT WAS SWELL OF SUPERMAN TO POSE FOR A SHOT WITH THE WINNERS!
PRESS
HE'S SURROUNDED BY GORGEOUS HUSSIES--AND HE LOVES IT! I'M LEAVING...

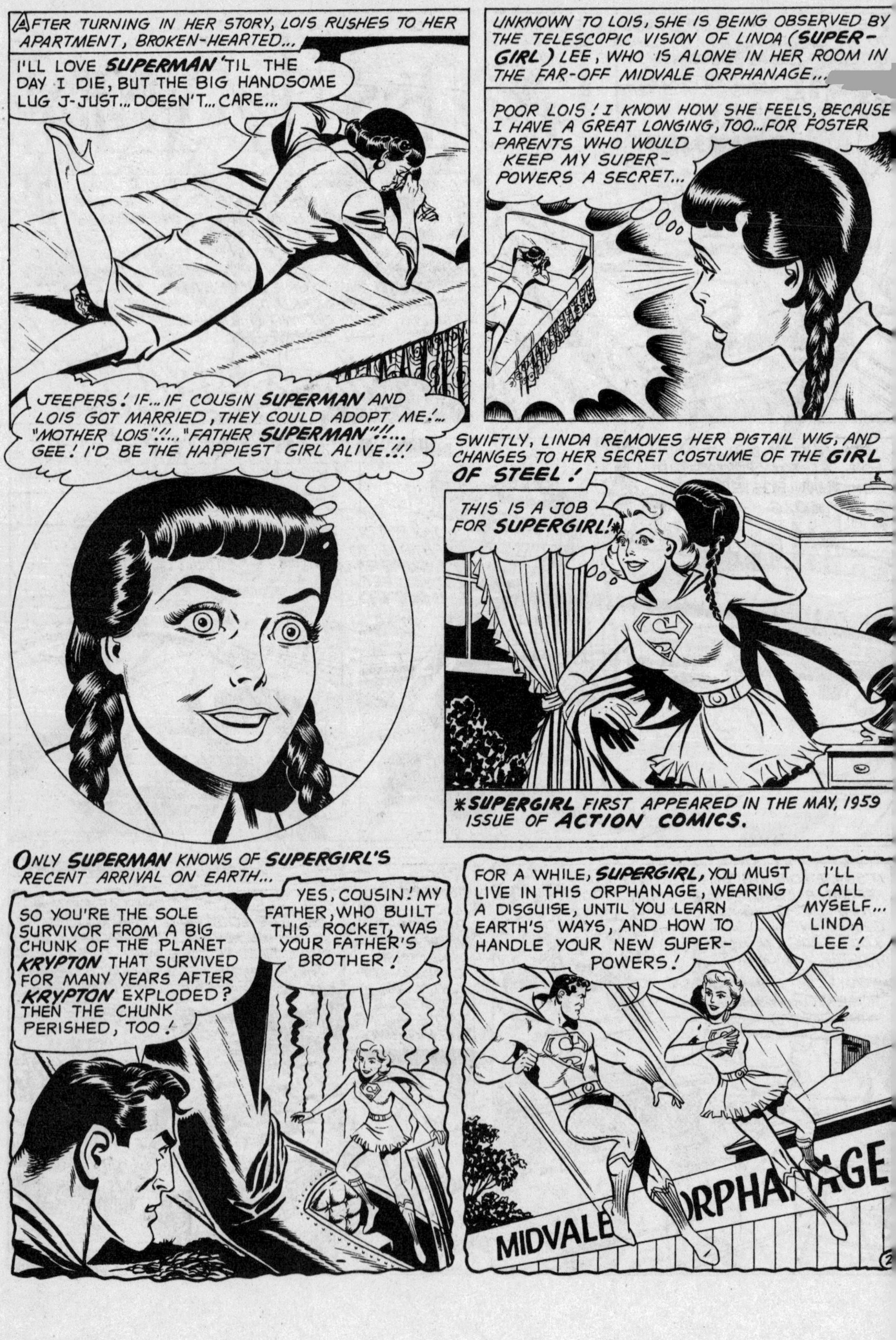
AFTER TURNING IN HER STORY, LOIS RUSHES TO HER APARTMENT, BROKEN-HEARTED...
I'LL LOVE SUPERMAN 'TIL THE DAY I DIE, BUT THE BIG HANDSOME LUG J-JUST... DOESN'T... CARE...
UNKNOWN TO LOIS, SHE IS BEING OBSERVED BY THE TELESCOPIC VISION OF LINDA (SUPER-GIRL) LEE, WHO IS ALONE IN HER ROOM IN THE FAR-OFF MIDVALE ORPHANAGE...
POOR LOIS! I KNOW HOW SHE FEELS, BECAUSE I HAVE A GREAT LONGING, TOO... FOR FOSTER PARENTS WHO WOULD KEEP MY SUPER-POWERS A SECRET...
JEEPERS! IF... IF COUSIN SUPERMAN AND LOIS GOT MARRIED, THEY COULD ADOPT ME!... "MOTHER LOIS"!!... "FATHER SUPERMAN"!!... GEE! I'D BE THE HAPPIEST GIRL ALIVE!!!
SWIFTLY, LINDA REMOVES HER PIGTAIL WIG, AND CHANGES TO HER SECRET COSTUME OF THE GIRL OF STEEL!
THIS IS A JOB FOR SUPERGIRL!*
*SUPERGIRL FIRST APPEARED IN THE MAY, 1959 ISSUE OF ACTION COMICS.
ONLY SUPERMAN KNOWS OF SUPERGIRL'S RECENT ARRIVAL ON EARTH...
SO YOU'RE THE SOLE SURVIVOR FROM A BIG CHUNK OF THE PLANET KRYPTON THAT SURVIVED FOR MANY YEARS AFTER KRYPTON EXPLODED? THEN THE CHUNK PERISHED, TOO!
YES, COUSIN! MY FATHER, WHO BUILT THIS ROCKET, WAS YOUR FATHER'S BROTHER!
FOR A WHILE, SUPERGIRL, YOU MUST LIVE IN THIS ORPHANAGE, WEARING A DISGUISE, UNTIL YOU LEARN EARTH'S WAYS, AND HOW TO HANDLE YOUR NEW SUPER-POWERS!
I'LL CALL MYSELF... LINDA LEE!
MIDVALE ORPHANAGE

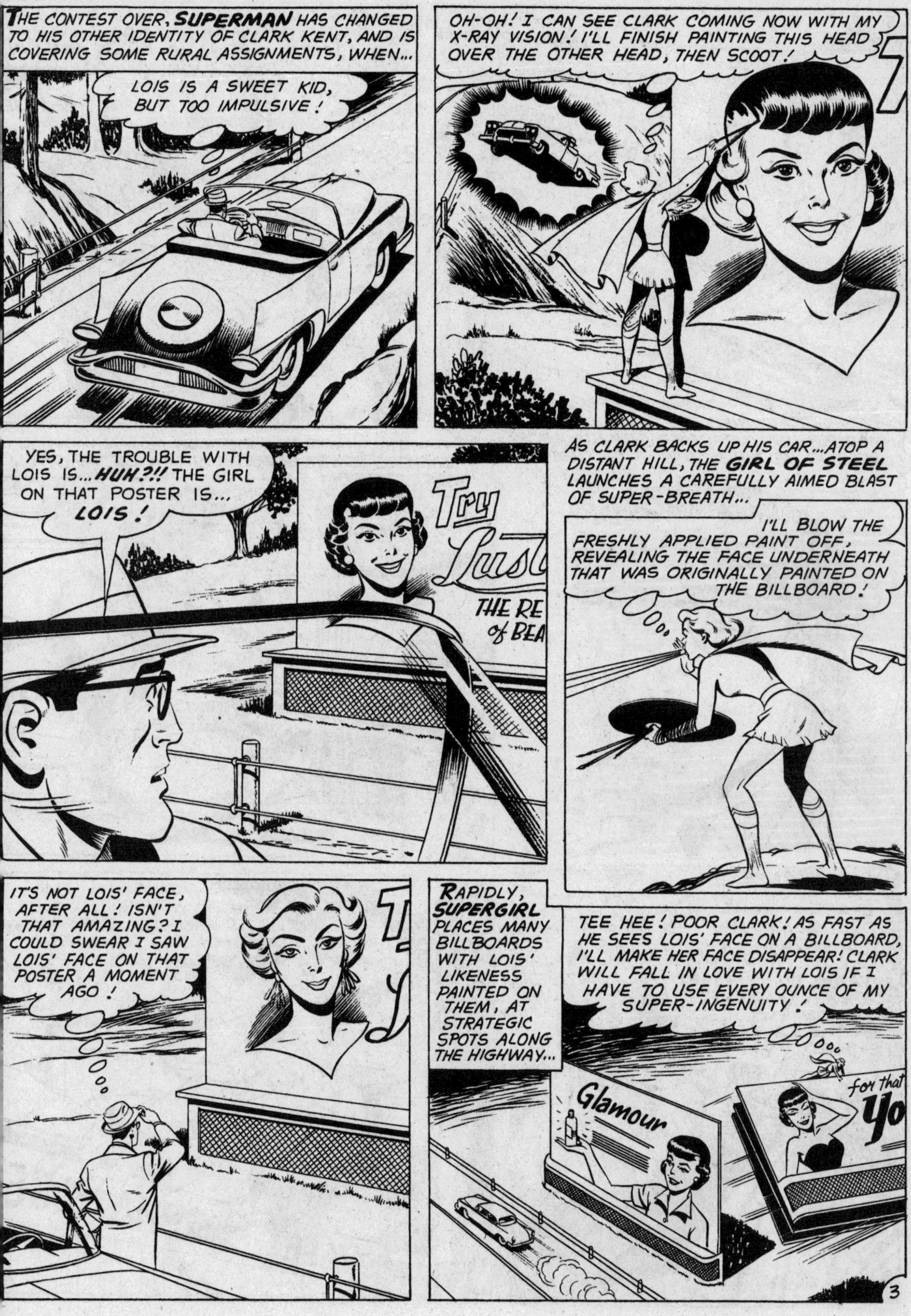
THE CONTEST OVER, SUPERMAN HAS CHANGED TO HIS OTHER IDENTITY OF CLARK KENT, AND IS COVERING SOME RURAL ASSIGNMENTS, WHEN...
LOIS IS A SWEET KID, BUT TOO IMPULSIVE!
OH-OH! I CAN SEE CLARK COMING NOW WITH MY X-RAY VISION! I'LL FINISH PAINTING THIS HEAD OVER THE OTHER HEAD, THEN SCOOT!
YES, THE TROUBLE WITH LOIS IS... HUH?!! THE GIRL ON THAT POSTER IS... LOIS!
Try Lust
THE RE
of BEA
AS CLARK BACKS UP HIS CAR... ATOP A DISTANT HILL, THE GIRL OF STEEL LAUNCHES A CAREFULLY AIMED BLAST OF SUPER-BREATH...
I'LL BLOW THE FRESHLY APPLIED PAINT OFF, REVEALING THE FACE UNDERNEATH THAT WAS ORIGINALLY PAINTED ON THE BILLBOARD!
IT'S NOT LOIS' FACE, AFTER ALL! ISN'T THAT AMAZING? I COULD SWEAR I SAW LOIS' FACE ON THAT POSTER A MOMENT AGO!
RAPIDLY, SUPERGIRL PLACES MANY BILLBOARDS WITH LOIS' LIKENESS PAINTED ON THEM, AT STRATEGIC SPOTS ALONG THE HIGHWAY...
TEE HEE! POOR CLARK! AS FAST AS HE SEES LOIS' FACE ON A BILLBOARD, I'LL MAKE HER FACE DISAPPEAR! CLARK WILL FALL IN LOVE WITH LOIS IF I HAVE TO USE EVERY OUNCE OF MY SUPER-INGENUITY!
Glamour
for that Yo
3

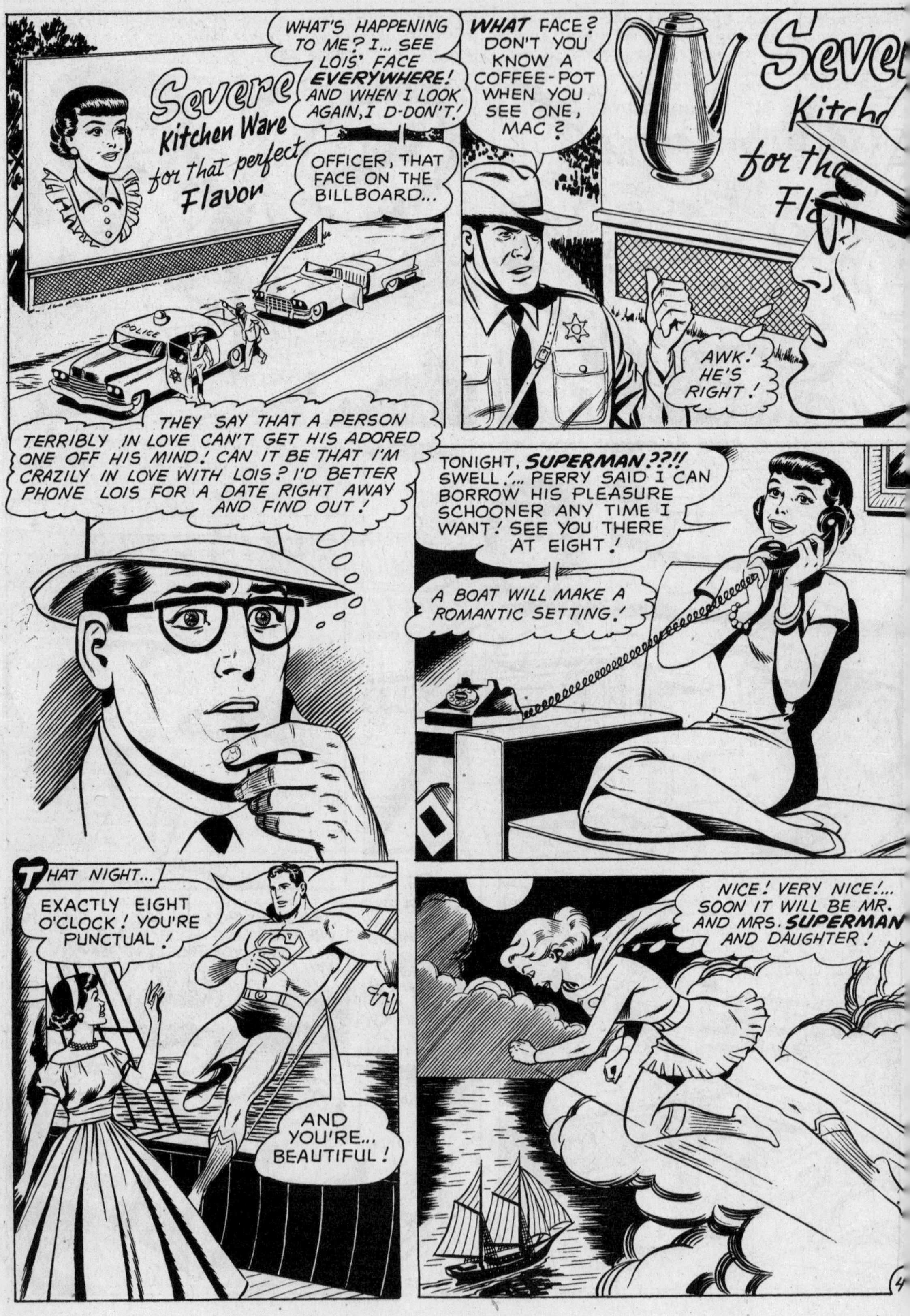
Severe Kitchen Ware for that perfect Flavor
WHAT'S HAPPENING TO ME? I... SEE LOIS' FACE EVERYWHERE! AND WHEN I LOOK AGAIN, I D-DON'T!
OFFICER, THAT FACE ON THE BILLBOARD...
POLICE
WHAT FACE? DON'T YOU KNOW A COFFEE-POT WHEN YOU SEE ONE, MAC?
AWK! HE'S RIGHT!
THEY SAY THAT A PERSON TERRIBLY IN LOVE CAN'T GET HIS ADORED ONE OFF HIS MIND! CAN IT BE THAT I'M CRAZILY IN LOVE WITH LOIS? I'D BETTER PHONE LOIS FOR A DATE RIGHT AWAY AND FIND OUT!
TONIGHT, SUPERMAN??!! SWELL!... PERRY SAID I CAN BORROW HIS PLEASURE SCHOONER ANY TIME I WANT! SEE YOU THERE AT EIGHT!
A BOAT WILL MAKE A ROMANTIC SETTING!
THAT NIGHT...
EXACTLY EIGHT O'CLOCK! YOU'RE PUNCTUAL!
AND YOU'RE... BEAUTIFUL!
NICE! VERY NICE!... SOON IT WILL BE MR. AND MRS. SUPERMAN AND DAUGHTER!

I PREPARED OUR DINNER MYSELF! I'M AFRAID IT DIDN'T TURN OUT VERY WELL, THOUGH!

DON'T BE SO MODEST, LOIS! I'M SURE YOU'RE A FINE COOK!

OVER-HEARING THE CONVERSATION, *SUPERGIRL* STREAKS INTO THE GALLEY AND PREPARES A NEW MEAL AT SUPER-SPEED...

LUCKILY I TOOK A COOKING COURSE AT THE ORPHANAGE! THE HEAT FROM MY X-RAY VISION SHOULD GIVE THE STEAKS A SUPER-TENDER FLAVOR!

OFF SPEEDS THE *GIRL OF STEEL* AGAIN, SO THAT LOIS BELIEVES SHE IS SERVING THE MEAL SHE HERSELF HAD PREPARED...

HMM! IT'S THE MOST DELICIOUS MEAL I EVER ATE!...??... WHAT HAPPENED TO THE LIGHTS, LOIS?

THEY FAILED! I'LL LIGHT THIS CANDELABRA!

DINING BY CANDLE-LIGHT! ;SIGH; HOW ROMANTIC!... I'M GLAD, NOW, THAT I TAMPERED WITH THE BOAT'S WIRING, AT SUPER-SPEED!

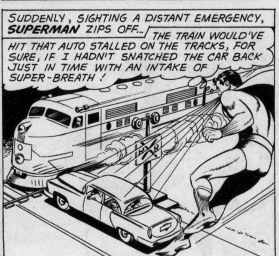

SUDDENLY, SIGHTING A DISTANT EMERGENCY, *SUPERMAN* ZIPS OFF...

THE TRAIN WOULD'VE HIT THAT AUTO STALLED ON THE TRACKS, FOR SURE, IF I HADN'T SNATCHED THE CAR BACK JUST IN TIME WITH AN INTAKE OF SUPER-BREATH!

BUT WHEN *THE MAN OF STEEL* RETURNS...

THE FOOD IS COLD NOW! AND AFTER I WORKED SO HARD TO PLEASE YOU!

I'M SORRY, LOIS! SHALL WE...GO ON DECK?

5

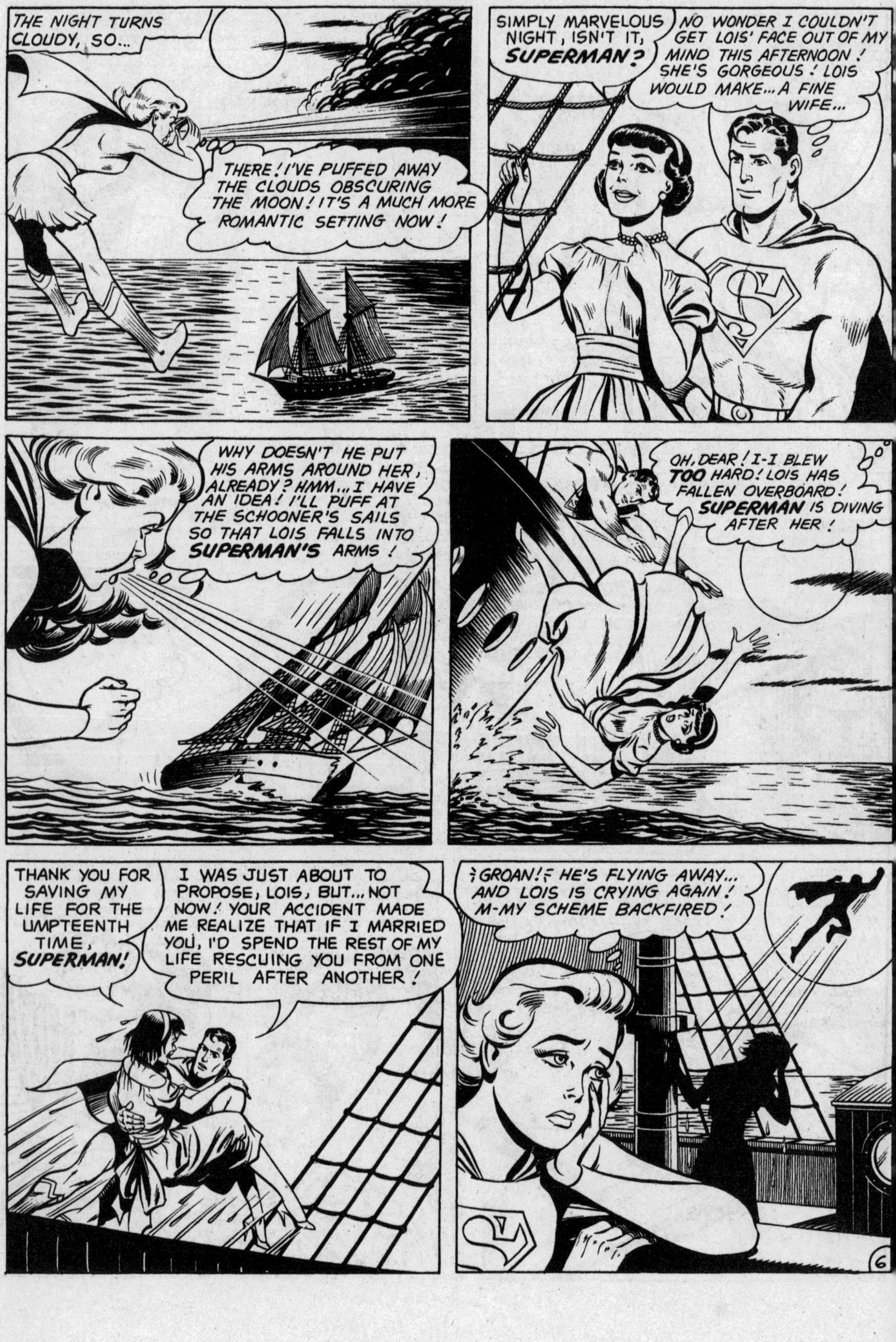
THE NIGHT TURNS CLOUDY, SO...
THERE! I'VE PUFFED AWAY THE CLOUDS OBSCURING THE MOON! IT'S A MUCH MORE ROMANTIC SETTING NOW!
SIMPLY MARVELOUS NIGHT, ISN'T IT, SUPERMAN?
NO WONDER I COULDN'T GET LOIS' FACE OUT OF MY MIND THIS AFTERNOON! SHE'S GORGEOUS! LOIS WOULD MAKE... A FINE WIFE...
WHY DOESN'T HE PUT HIS ARMS AROUND HER, ALREADY? HMM... I HAVE AN IDEA! I'LL PUFF AT THE SCHOONER'S SAILS SO THAT LOIS FALLS INTO SUPERMAN'S ARMS!
OH, DEAR! I-I BLEW TOO HARD! LOIS HAS FALLEN OVERBOARD! SUPERMAN IS DIVING AFTER HER!
THANK YOU FOR SAVING MY LIFE FOR THE UMPTEENTH TIME, SUPERMAN!
I WAS JUST ABOUT TO PROPOSE, LOIS, BUT... NOT NOW! YOUR ACCIDENT MADE ME REALIZE THAT IF I MARRIED YOU, I'D SPEND THE REST OF MY LIFE RESCUING YOU FROM ONE PERIL AFTER ANOTHER!
GROAN! HE'S FLYING AWAY... AND LOIS IS CRYING AGAIN! M-MY SCHEME BACKFIRED!
6

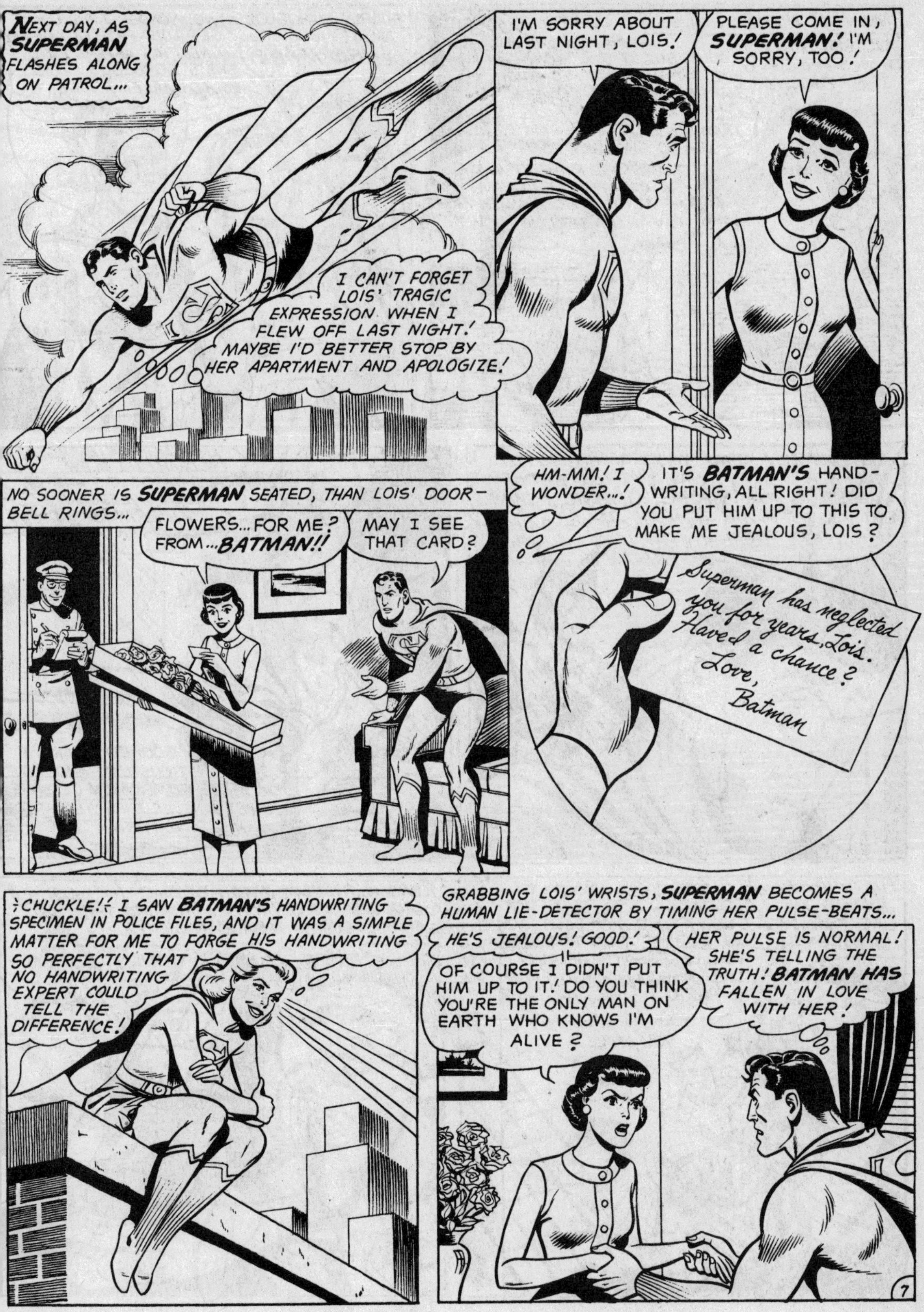
NEXT DAY, AS SUPERMAN FLASHES ALONG ON PATROL...
I CAN'T FORGET LOIS' TRAGIC EXPRESSION WHEN I FLEW OFF LAST NIGHT! MAYBE I'D BETTER STOP BY HER APARTMENT AND APOLOGIZE!
I'M SORRY ABOUT LAST NIGHT, LOIS!
PLEASE COME IN, SUPERMAN! I'M SORRY, TOO!
NO SOONER IS SUPERMAN SEATED, THAN LOIS' DOOR-BELL RINGS...
FLOWERS...FOR ME? FROM...BATMAN!!
MAY I SEE THAT CARD?
HM-MM! I WONDER...!
IT'S BATMAN'S HAND-WRITING, ALL RIGHT! DID YOU PUT HIM UP TO THIS TO MAKE ME JEALOUS, LOIS?
Superman has neglected you for years, Lois. Have I a chance? Love, Batman
CHUCKLE! I SAW BATMAN'S HANDWRITING SPECIMEN IN POLICE FILES, AND IT WAS A SIMPLE MATTER FOR ME TO FORGE HIS HANDWRITING SO PERFECTLY THAT NO HANDWRITING EXPERT COULD TELL THE DIFFERENCE!
GRABBING LOIS' WRISTS, SUPERMAN BECOMES A HUMAN LIE-DETECTOR BY TIMING HER PULSE-BEATS...
HE'S JEALOUS! GOOD!
OF COURSE I DIDN'T PUT HIM UP TO IT! DO YOU THINK YOU'RE THE ONLY MAN ON EARTH WHO KNOWS I'M ALIVE?
HER PULSE IS NORMAL! SHE'S TELLING THE TRUTH! BATMAN HAS FALLEN IN LOVE WITH HER!
7

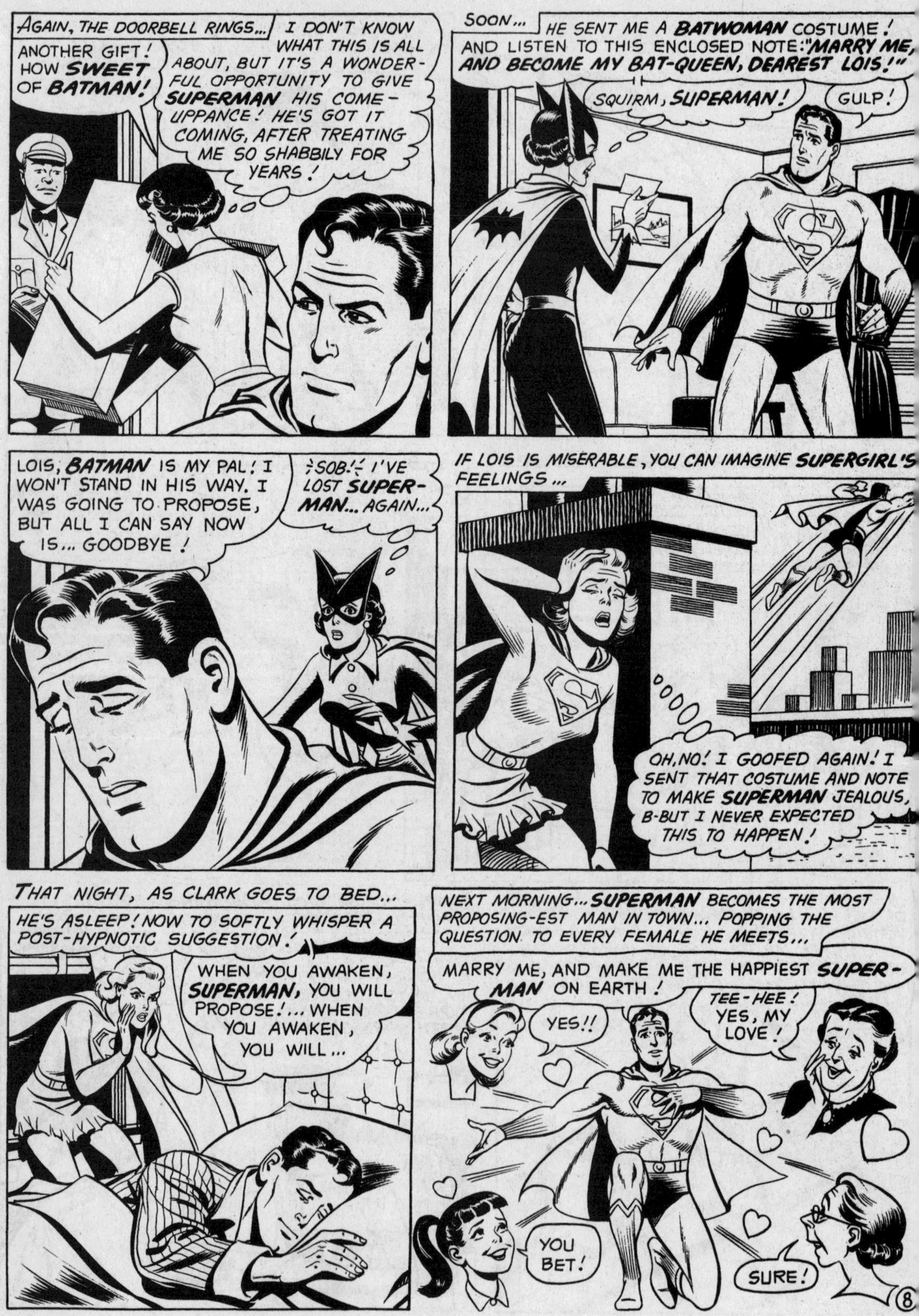
AGAIN, THE DOORBELL RINGS...
ANOTHER GIFT! HOW SWEET OF BATMAN!
I DON'T KNOW WHAT THIS IS ALL ABOUT, BUT IT'S A WONDERFUL OPPORTUNITY TO GIVE SUPERMAN HIS COME-UPPANCE! HE'S GOT IT COMING, AFTER TREATING ME SO SHABBILY FOR YEARS!
SOON...
HE SENT ME A BATWOMAN COSTUME! AND LISTEN TO THIS ENCLOSED NOTE: "MARRY ME, AND BECOME MY BAT-QUEEN, DEAREST LOIS!"
SQUIRM, SUPERMAN!
GULP!
LOIS, BATMAN IS MY PAL! I WON'T STAND IN HIS WAY. I WAS GOING TO PROPOSE, BUT ALL I CAN SAY NOW IS... GOODBYE!
-SOB!- I'VE LOST SUPERMAN... AGAIN...
IF LOIS IS MISERABLE, YOU CAN IMAGINE SUPERGIRL'S FEELINGS...
OH, NO! I GOOFED AGAIN! I SENT THAT COSTUME AND NOTE TO MAKE SUPERMAN JEALOUS, B-BUT I NEVER EXPECTED THIS TO HAPPEN!
THAT NIGHT, AS CLARK GOES TO BED...
HE'S ASLEEP! NOW TO SOFTLY WHISPER A POST-HYPNOTIC SUGGESTION!
WHEN YOU AWAKEN, SUPERMAN, YOU WILL PROPOSE!... WHEN YOU AWAKEN, YOU WILL...
NEXT MORNING... SUPERMAN BECOMES THE MOST PROPOSING-EST MAN IN TOWN... POPPING THE QUESTION TO EVERY FEMALE HE MEETS...
MARRY ME, AND MAKE ME THE HAPPIEST SUPERMAN ON EARTH!
YES!!
TEE-HEE! YES, MY LOVE!
YOU BET!
SURE!
8

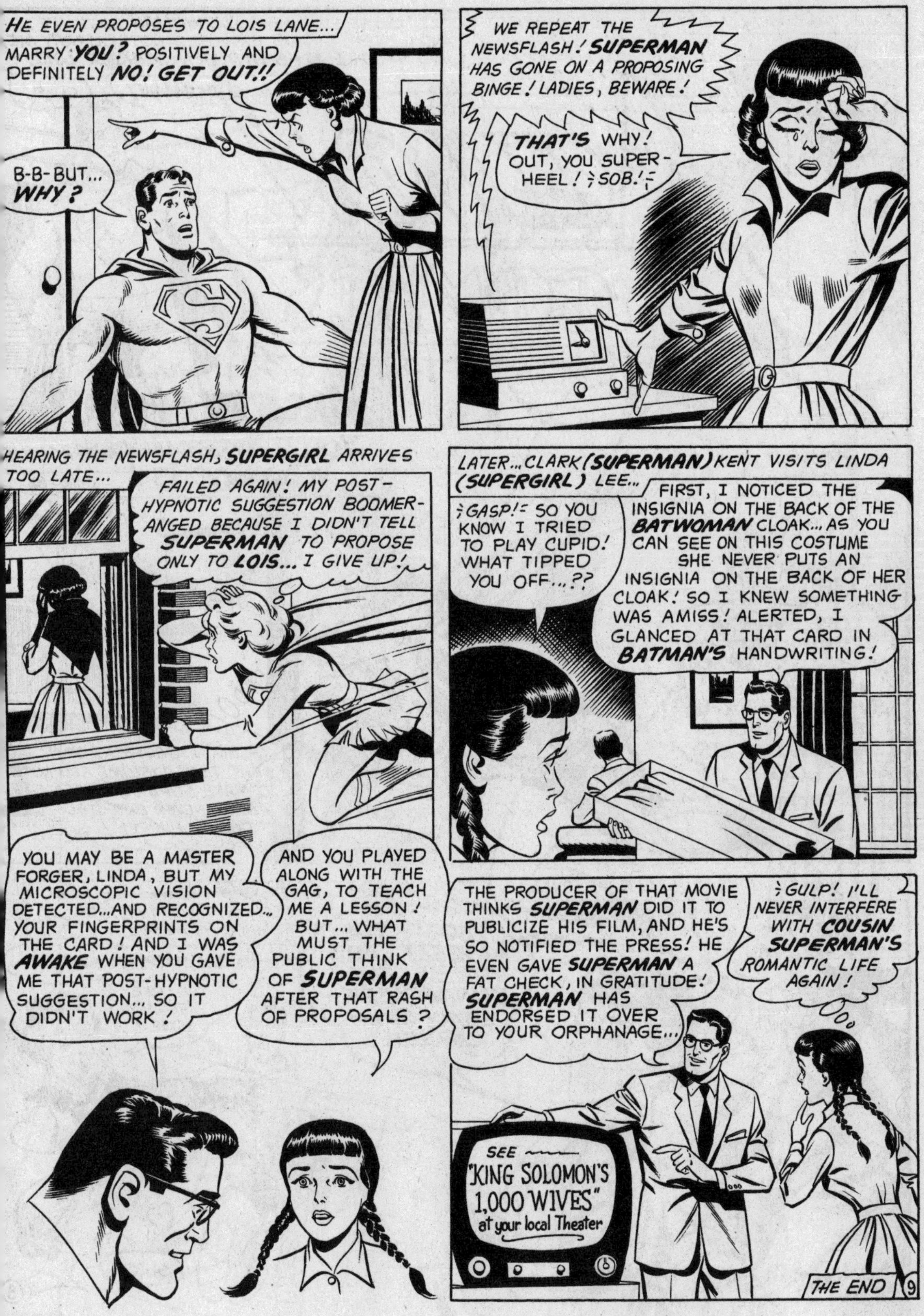
HE EVEN PROPOSES TO LOIS LANE...
MARRY YOU? POSITIVELY AND DEFINITELY NO! GET OUT!!
B-B-BUT... WHY?
WE REPEAT THE NEWSFLASH! SUPERMAN HAS GONE ON A PROPOSING BINGE! LADIES, BEWARE!
THAT'S WHY! OUT, YOU SUPER-HEEL! SOB!
HEARING THE NEWSFLASH, SUPERGIRL ARRIVES TOO LATE...
FAILED AGAIN! MY POST-HYPNOTIC SUGGESTION BOOMERANGED BECAUSE I DIDN'T TELL SUPERMAN TO PROPOSE ONLY TO LOIS... I GIVE UP!
LATER... CLARK (SUPERMAN) KENT VISITS LINDA (SUPERGIRL) LEE...
GASP! SO YOU KNOW I TRIED TO PLAY CUPID! WHAT TIPPED YOU OFF...??
FIRST, I NOTICED THE INSIGNIA ON THE BACK OF THE BATWOMAN CLOAK... AS YOU CAN SEE ON THIS COSTUME SHE NEVER PUTS AN INSIGNIA ON THE BACK OF HER CLOAK! SO I KNEW SOMETHING WAS AMISS! ALERTED, I GLANCED AT THAT CARD IN BATMAN'S HANDWRITING!
YOU MAY BE A MASTER FORGER, LINDA, BUT MY MICROSCOPIC VISION DETECTED...AND RECOGNIZED... YOUR FINGERPRINTS ON THE CARD! AND I WAS AWAKE WHEN YOU GAVE ME THAT POST-HYPNOTIC SUGGESTION... SO IT DIDN'T WORK!
AND YOU PLAYED ALONG WITH THE GAG, TO TEACH ME A LESSON! BUT... WHAT MUST THE PUBLIC THINK OF SUPERMAN AFTER THAT RASH OF PROPOSALS?
THE PRODUCER OF THAT MOVIE THINKS SUPERMAN DID IT TO PUBLICIZE HIS FILM, AND HE'S SO NOTIFIED THE PRESS! HE EVEN GAVE SUPERMAN A FAT CHECK, IN GRATITUDE! SUPERMAN HAS ENDORSED IT OVER TO YOUR ORPHANAGE...
GULP! I'LL NEVER INTERFERE WITH COUSIN SUPERMAN'S ROMANTIC LIFE AGAIN!
SEE "KING SOLOMON'S 1,000 WIVES" at your local Theater
THE END
9

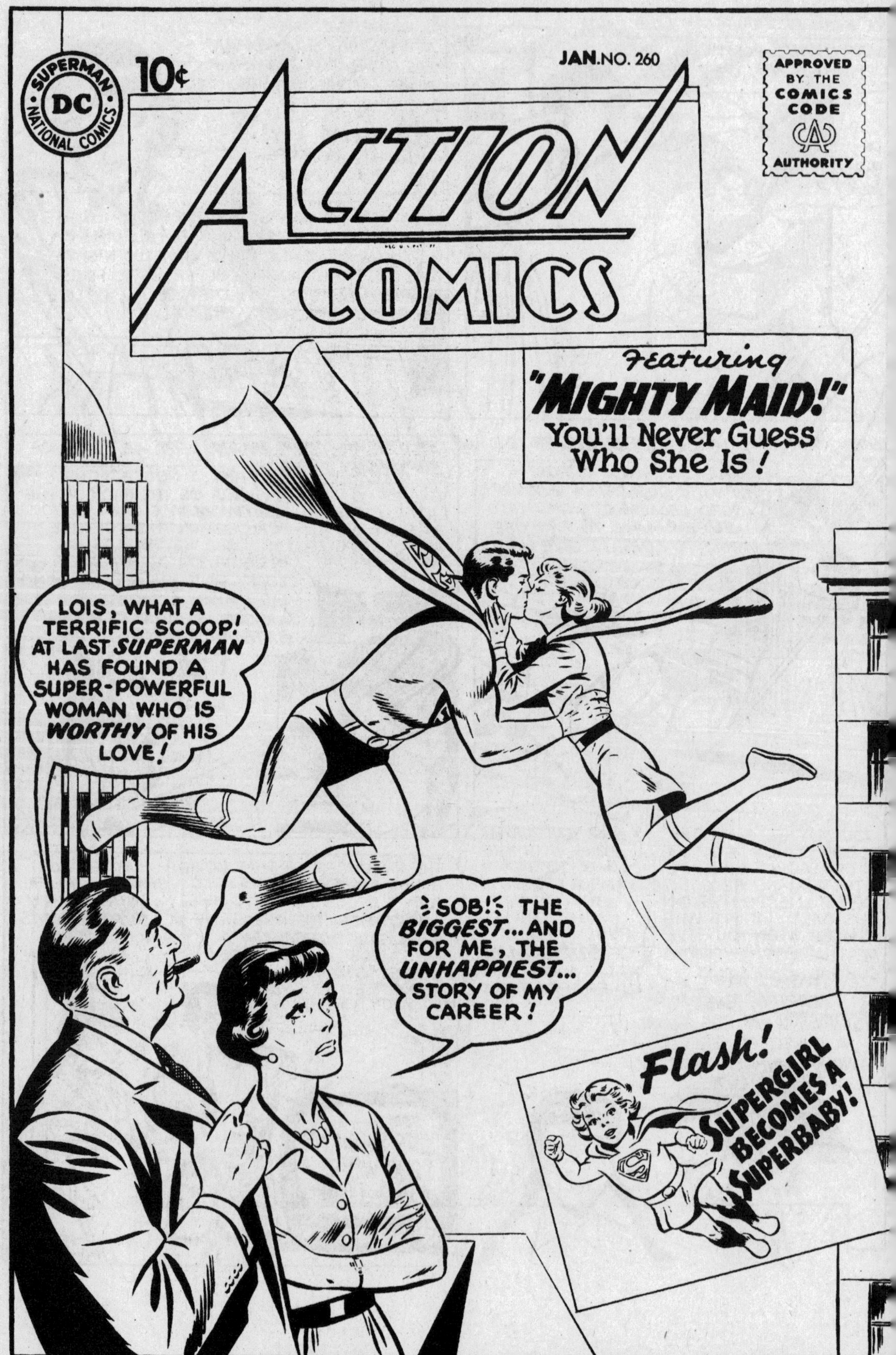
SUPERMAN DC NATIONAL COMICS
10¢
JAN. NO. 260
APPROVED BY THE COMICS CODE AUTHORITY
ACTION COMICS
Featuring "MIGHTY MAID!" You'll Never Guess Who She Is!
LOIS, WHAT A TERRIFIC SCOOP! AT LAST SUPERMAN HAS FOUND A SUPER-POWERFUL WOMAN WHO IS WORTHY OF HIS LOVE!
SOB! THE BIGGEST...AND FOR ME, THE UNHAPPIEST... STORY OF MY CAREER!
Flash! SUPERGIRL BECOMES A SUPERBABY!

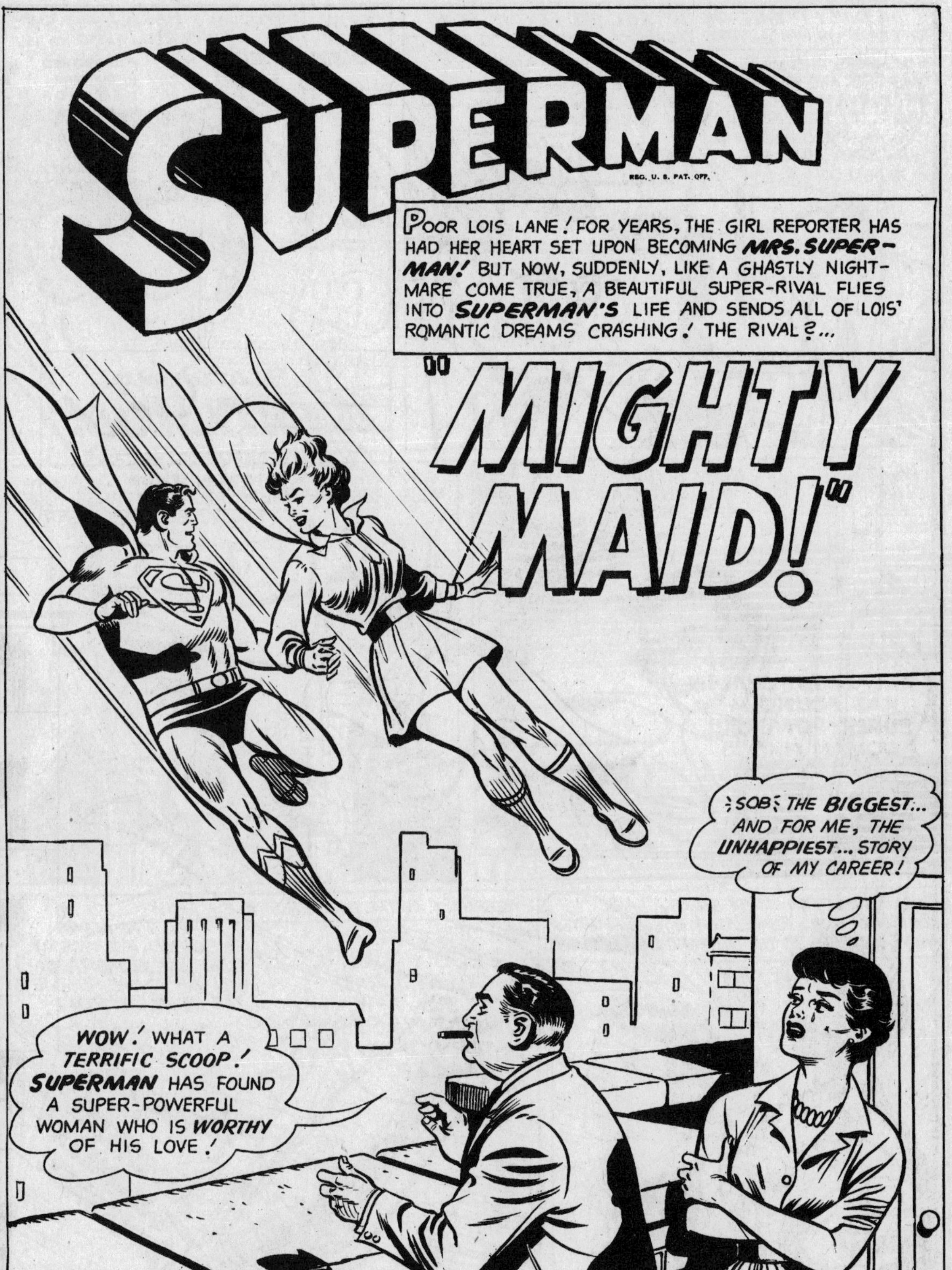
SUPERMAN
REG. U. S. PAT. OFF.
POOR LOIS LANE! FOR YEARS, THE GIRL REPORTER HAS HAD HER HEART SET UPON BECOMING MRS. SUPERMAN! BUT NOW, SUDDENLY, LIKE A GHASTLY NIGHTMARE COME TRUE, A BEAUTIFUL SUPER-RIVAL FLIES INTO SUPERMAN'S LIFE AND SENDS ALL OF LOIS' ROMANTIC DREAMS CRASHING! THE RIVAL?...
"MIGHTY MAID!"
SOB! THE BIGGEST... AND FOR ME, THE UNHAPPIEST... STORY OF MY CAREER!
WOW! WHAT A TERRIFIC SCOOP! SUPERMAN HAS FOUND A SUPER-POWERFUL WOMAN WHO IS WORTHY OF HIS LOVE!

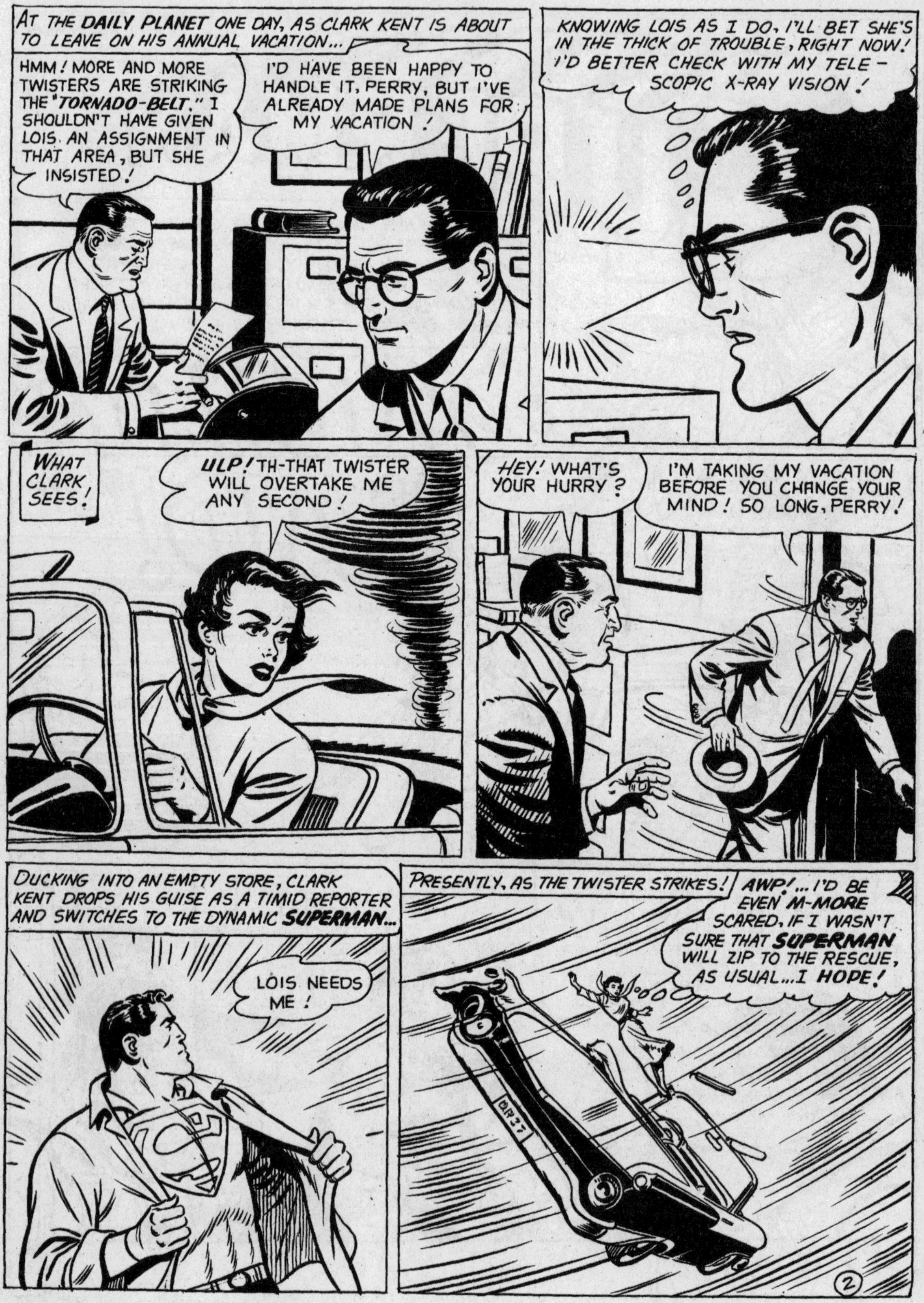
AT THE DAILY PLANET ONE DAY, AS CLARK KENT IS ABOUT TO LEAVE ON HIS ANNUAL VACATION...
HMM! MORE AND MORE TWISTERS ARE STRIKING THE "TORNADO-BELT." I SHOULDN'T HAVE GIVEN LOIS AN ASSIGNMENT IN THAT AREA, BUT SHE INSISTED!
I'D HAVE BEEN HAPPY TO HANDLE IT, PERRY, BUT I'VE ALREADY MADE PLANS FOR MY VACATION!
KNOWING LOIS AS I DO, I'LL BET SHE'S IN THE THICK OF TROUBLE, RIGHT NOW! I'D BETTER CHECK WITH MY TELE-SCOPIC X-RAY VISION!
WHAT CLARK SEES!
ULP! TH-THAT TWISTER WILL OVERTAKE ME ANY SECOND!
HEY! WHAT'S YOUR HURRY?
I'M TAKING MY VACATION BEFORE YOU CHANGE YOUR MIND! SO LONG, PERRY!
DUCKING INTO AN EMPTY STORE, CLARK KENT DROPS HIS GUISE AS A TIMID REPORTER AND SWITCHES TO THE DYNAMIC SUPERMAN...
LOIS NEEDS ME!
PRESENTLY, AS THE TWISTER STRIKES!
AWP!... I'D BE EVEN M-MORE SCARED, IF I WASN'T SURE THAT SUPERMAN WILL ZIP TO THE RESCUE, AS USUAL... I HOPE!
2

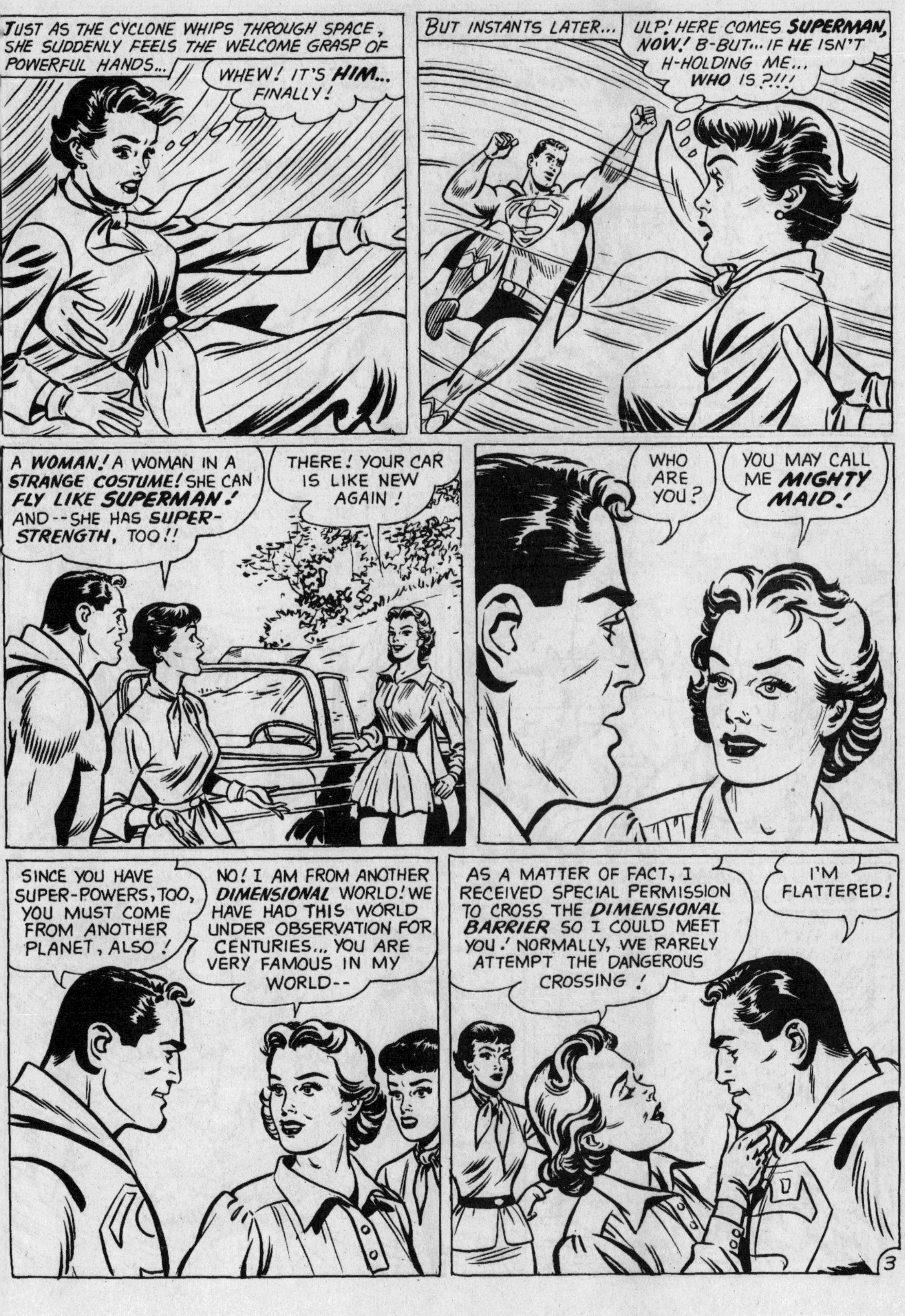
JUST AS THE CYCLONE WHIPS THROUGH SPACE, SHE SUDDENLY FEELS THE WELCOME GRASP OF POWERFUL HANDS...
WHEW! IT'S HIM... FINALLY!
BUT INSTANTS LATER...
ULP! HERE COMES SUPERMAN, NOW! B-BUT... IF HE ISN'T H-HOLDING ME... WHO IS ?!!!
A WOMAN! A WOMAN IN A STRANGE COSTUME! SHE CAN FLY LIKE SUPERMAN! AND--SHE HAS SUPER-STRENGTH, TOO!!
THERE! YOUR CAR IS LIKE NEW AGAIN!
WHO ARE YOU?
YOU MAY CALL ME MIGHTY MAID!
SINCE YOU HAVE SUPER-POWERS, TOO, YOU MUST COME FROM ANOTHER PLANET, ALSO!
NO! I AM FROM ANOTHER DIMENSIONAL WORLD! WE HAVE HAD THIS WORLD UNDER OBSERVATION FOR CENTURIES... YOU ARE VERY FAMOUS IN MY WORLD--
AS A MATTER OF FACT, I RECEIVED SPECIAL PERMISSION TO CROSS THE DIMENSIONAL BARRIER SO I COULD MEET YOU! NORMALLY, WE RARELY ATTEMPT THE DANGEROUS CROSSING!
I'M FLATTERED!
3

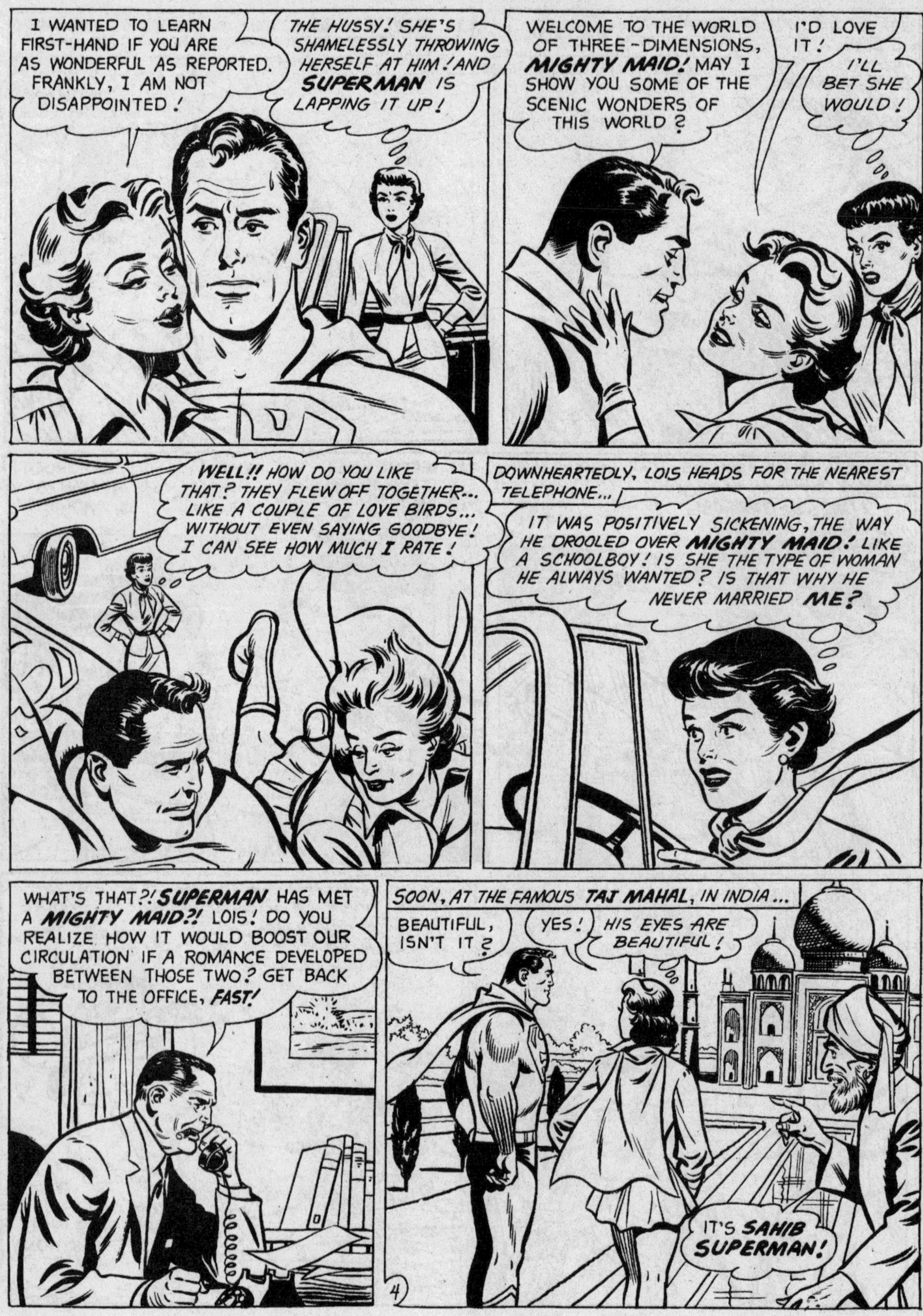
I WANTED TO LEARN FIRST-HAND IF YOU ARE AS WONDERFUL AS REPORTED. FRANKLY, I AM NOT DISAPPOINTED!
THE HUSSY! SHE'S SHAMELESSLY THROWING HERSELF AT HIM! AND SUPERMAN IS LAPPING IT UP!
WELCOME TO THE WORLD OF THREE-DIMENSIONS, MIGHTY MAID! MAY I SHOW YOU SOME OF THE SCENIC WONDERS OF THIS WORLD?
I'D LOVE IT!
I'LL BET SHE WOULD!
WELL!! HOW DO YOU LIKE THAT? THEY FLEW OFF TOGETHER... LIKE A COUPLE OF LOVE BIRDS... WITHOUT EVEN SAYING GOODBYE! I CAN SEE HOW MUCH I RATE!
DOWNHEARTEDLY, LOIS HEADS FOR THE NEAREST TELEPHONE...
IT WAS POSITIVELY SICKENING, THE WAY HE DROOLED OVER MIGHTY MAID! LIKE A SCHOOLBOY! IS SHE THE TYPE OF WOMAN HE ALWAYS WANTED? IS THAT WHY HE NEVER MARRIED ME?
WHAT'S THAT?! SUPERMAN HAS MET A MIGHTY MAID?! LOIS! DO YOU REALIZE HOW IT WOULD BOOST OUR CIRCULATION IF A ROMANCE DEVELOPED BETWEEN THOSE TWO? GET BACK TO THE OFFICE, FAST!
4
SOON, AT THE FAMOUS TAJ MAHAL, IN INDIA...
BEAUTIFUL, ISN'T IT?
YES!
HIS EYES ARE BEAUTIFUL!
IT'S SAHIB SUPERMAN!

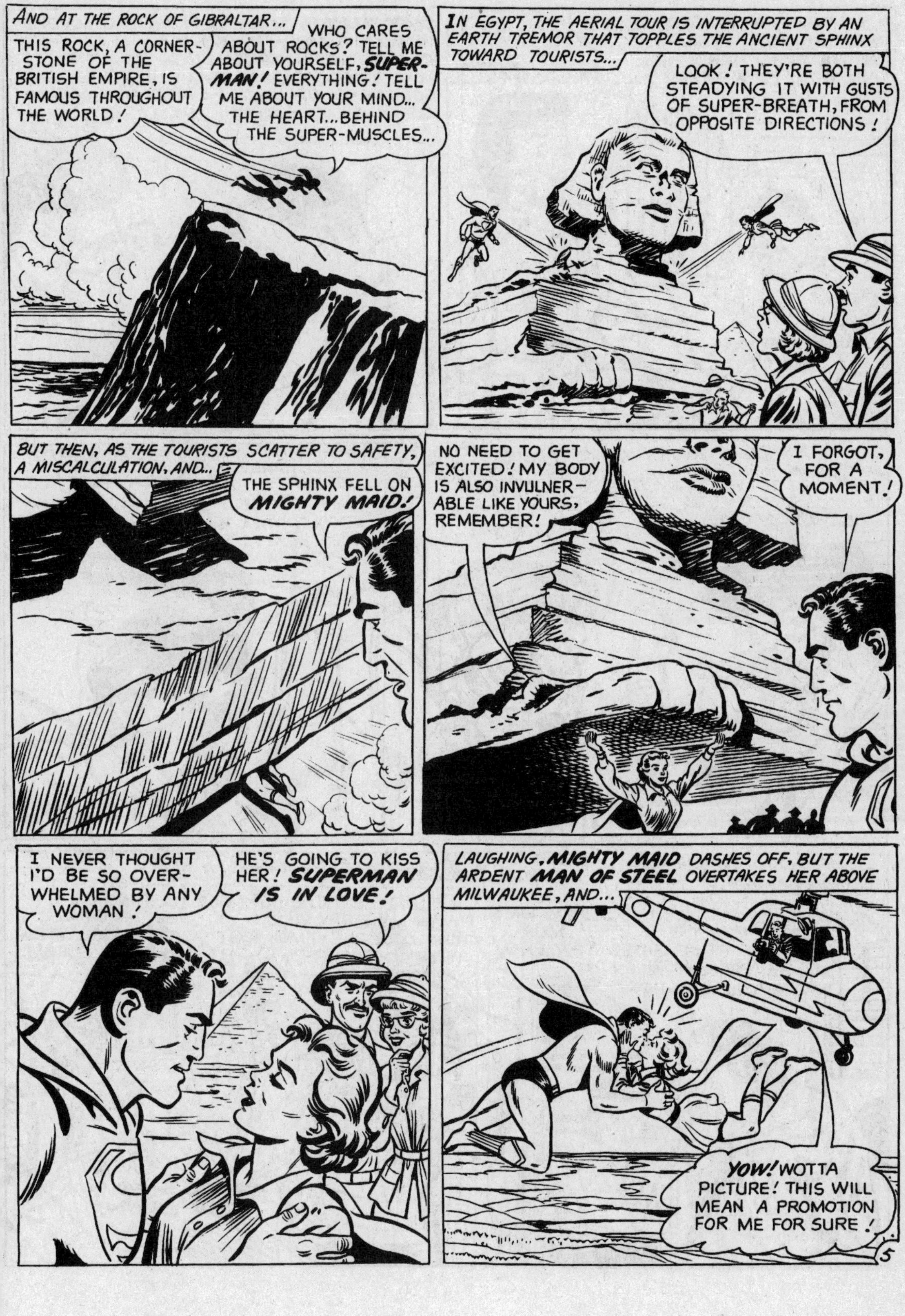
AND AT THE ROCK OF GIBRALTAR...
THIS ROCK, A CORNERSTONE OF THE BRITISH EMPIRE, IS FAMOUS THROUGHOUT THE WORLD!
WHO CARES ABOUT ROCKS? TELL ME ABOUT YOURSELF, SUPERMAN! EVERYTHING! TELL ME ABOUT YOUR MIND... THE HEART...BEHIND THE SUPER-MUSCLES...
IN EGYPT, THE AERIAL TOUR IS INTERRUPTED BY AN EARTH TREMOR THAT TOPPLES THE ANCIENT SPHINX TOWARD TOURISTS...
LOOK! THEY'RE BOTH STEADYING IT WITH GUSTS OF SUPER-BREATH, FROM OPPOSITE DIRECTIONS!
BUT THEN, AS THE TOURISTS SCATTER TO SAFETY, A MISCALCULATION, AND...
THE SPHINX FELL ON MIGHTY MAID!
NO NEED TO GET EXCITED! MY BODY IS ALSO INVULNERABLE LIKE YOURS, REMEMBER!
I FORGOT, FOR A MOMENT!
I NEVER THOUGHT I'D BE SO OVERWHELMED BY ANY WOMAN!
HE'S GOING TO KISS HER! SUPERMAN IS IN LOVE!
LAUGHING, MIGHTY MAID DASHES OFF, BUT THE ARDENT MAN OF STEEL OVERTAKES HER ABOVE MILWAUKEE, AND...
YOW! WOTTA PICTURE! THIS WILL MEAN A PROMOTION FOR ME FOR SURE!
5

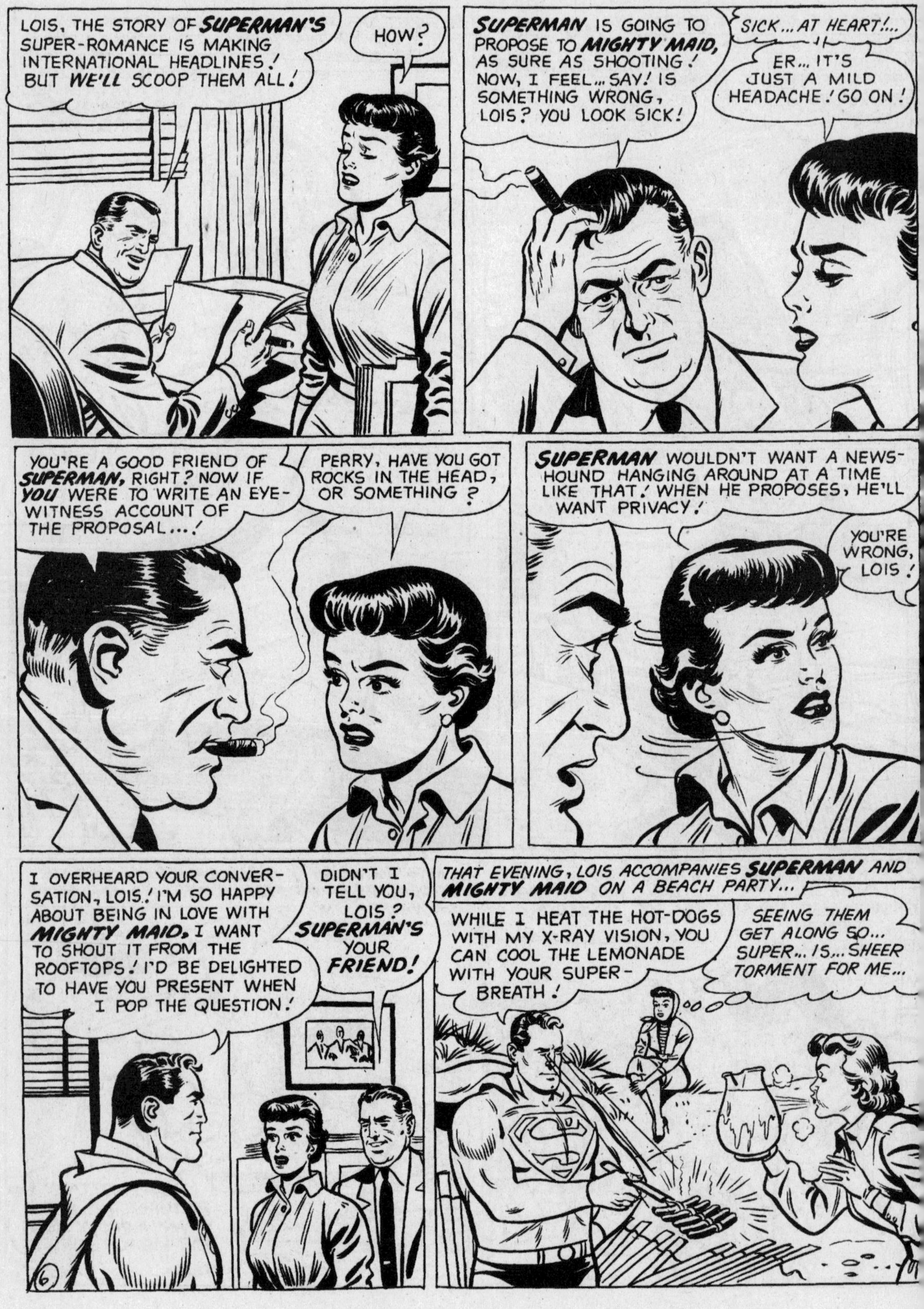
LOIS, THE STORY OF SUPERMAN'S SUPER-ROMANCE IS MAKING INTERNATIONAL HEADLINES! BUT WE'LL SCOOP THEM ALL!
HOW?
SUPERMAN IS GOING TO PROPOSE TO MIGHTY MAID, AS SURE AS SHOOTING! NOW, I FEEL... SAY! IS SOMETHING WRONG, LOIS? YOU LOOK SICK!
SICK... AT HEART!...
ER... IT'S JUST A MILD HEADACHE! GO ON!
YOU'RE A GOOD FRIEND OF SUPERMAN, RIGHT? NOW IF YOU WERE TO WRITE AN EYE-WITNESS ACCOUNT OF THE PROPOSAL...!
PERRY, HAVE YOU GOT ROCKS IN THE HEAD, OR SOMETHING?
SUPERMAN WOULDN'T WANT A NEWS-HOUND HANGING AROUND AT A TIME LIKE THAT! WHEN HE PROPOSES, HE'LL WANT PRIVACY!
YOU'RE WRONG, LOIS!
I OVERHEARD YOUR CONVERSATION, LOIS! I'M SO HAPPY ABOUT BEING IN LOVE WITH MIGHTY MAID, I WANT TO SHOUT IT FROM THE ROOFTOPS! I'D BE DELIGHTED TO HAVE YOU PRESENT WHEN I POP THE QUESTION!
DIDN'T I TELL YOU, LOIS? SUPERMAN'S YOUR FRIEND!
6
THAT EVENING, LOIS ACCOMPANIES SUPERMAN AND MIGHTY MAID ON A BEACH PARTY...
WHILE I HEAT THE HOT-DOGS WITH MY X-RAY VISION, YOU CAN COOL THE LEMONADE WITH YOUR SUPER-BREATH!
SEEING THEM GET ALONG SO... SUPER... IS... SHEER TORMENT FOR ME...

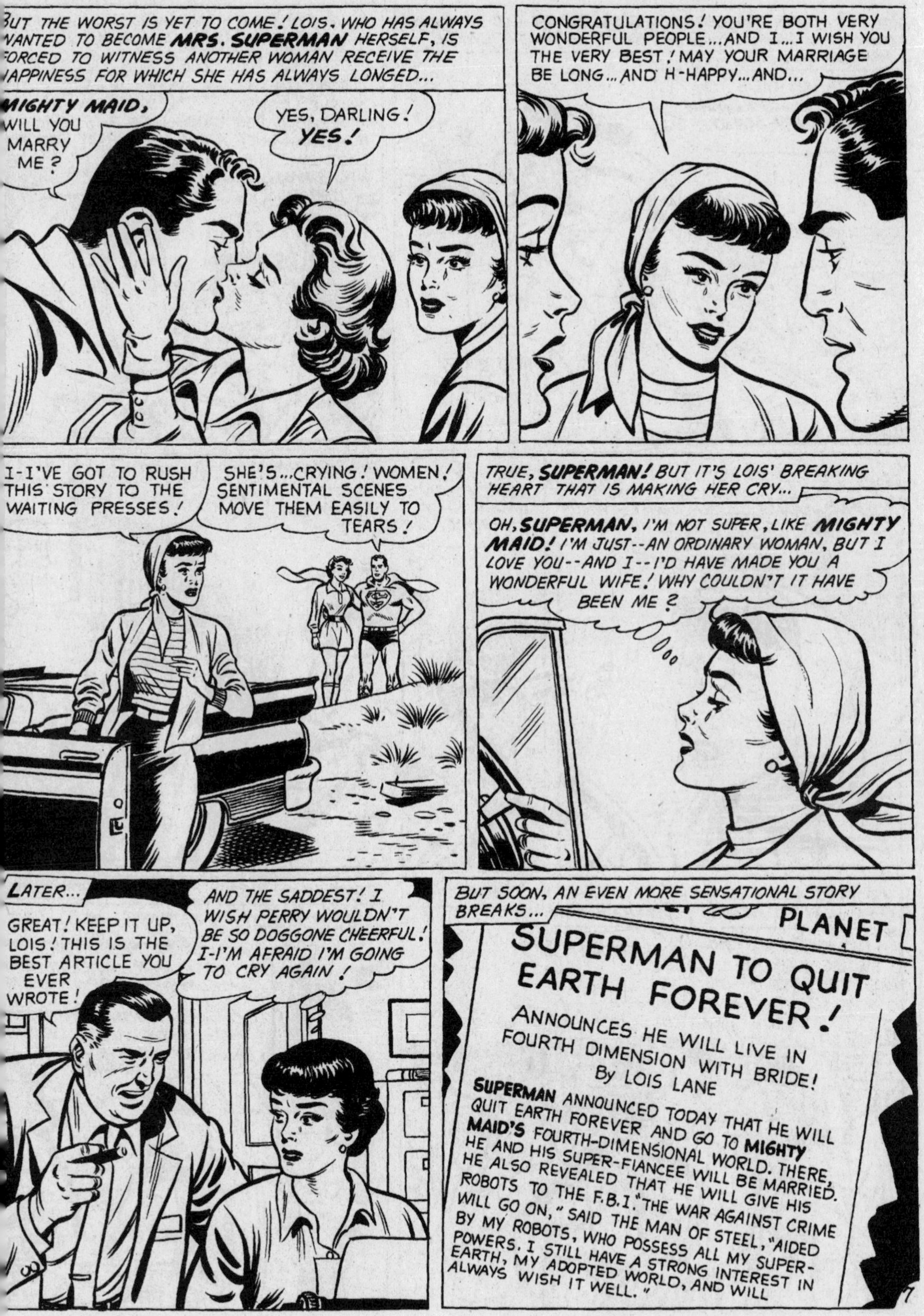
BUT THE WORST IS YET TO COME! LOIS, WHO HAS ALWAYS WANTED TO BECOME MRS. SUPERMAN HERSELF, IS FORCED TO WITNESS ANOTHER WOMAN RECEIVE THE HAPPINESS FOR WHICH SHE HAS ALWAYS LONGED...
MIGHTY MAID, WILL YOU MARRY ME?
YES, DARLING! YES!
CONGRATULATIONS! YOU'RE BOTH VERY WONDERFUL PEOPLE...AND I...I WISH YOU THE VERY BEST! MAY YOUR MARRIAGE BE LONG...AND H-HAPPY...AND...
I-I'VE GOT TO RUSH THIS STORY TO THE WAITING PRESSES!
SHE'S...CRYING! WOMEN! SENTIMENTAL SCENES MOVE THEM EASILY TO TEARS!
TRUE, SUPERMAN! BUT IT'S LOIS' BREAKING HEART THAT IS MAKING HER CRY...
OH, SUPERMAN, I'M NOT SUPER, LIKE MIGHTY MAID! I'M JUST--AN ORDINARY WOMAN, BUT I LOVE YOU--AND I--I'D HAVE MADE YOU A WONDERFUL WIFE! WHY COULDN'T IT HAVE BEEN ME?
LATER...
GREAT! KEEP IT UP, LOIS! THIS IS THE BEST ARTICLE YOU EVER WROTE!
AND THE SADDEST! I WISH PERRY WOULDN'T BE SO DOGGONE CHEERFUL! I-I'M AFRAID I'M GOING TO CRY AGAIN!
BUT SOON, AN EVEN MORE SENSATIONAL STORY BREAKS...
PLANET
SUPERMAN TO QUIT EARTH FOREVER!
ANNOUNCES HE WILL LIVE IN FOURTH DIMENSION WITH BRIDE!
By LOIS LANE
SUPERMAN ANNOUNCED TODAY THAT HE WILL QUIT EARTH FOREVER AND GO TO MIGHTY MAID'S FOURTH-DIMENSIONAL WORLD. THERE, HE AND HIS SUPER-FIANCEE WILL BE MARRIED. HE ALSO REVEALED THAT HE WILL GIVE HIS ROBOTS TO THE F.B.I. "THE WAR AGAINST CRIME WILL GO ON," SAID THE MAN OF STEEL, "AIDED BY MY ROBOTS, WHO POSSESS ALL MY SUPER-POWERS. I STILL HAVE A STRONG INTEREST IN EARTH, MY ADOPTED WORLD, AND WILL ALWAYS WISH IT WELL."
7

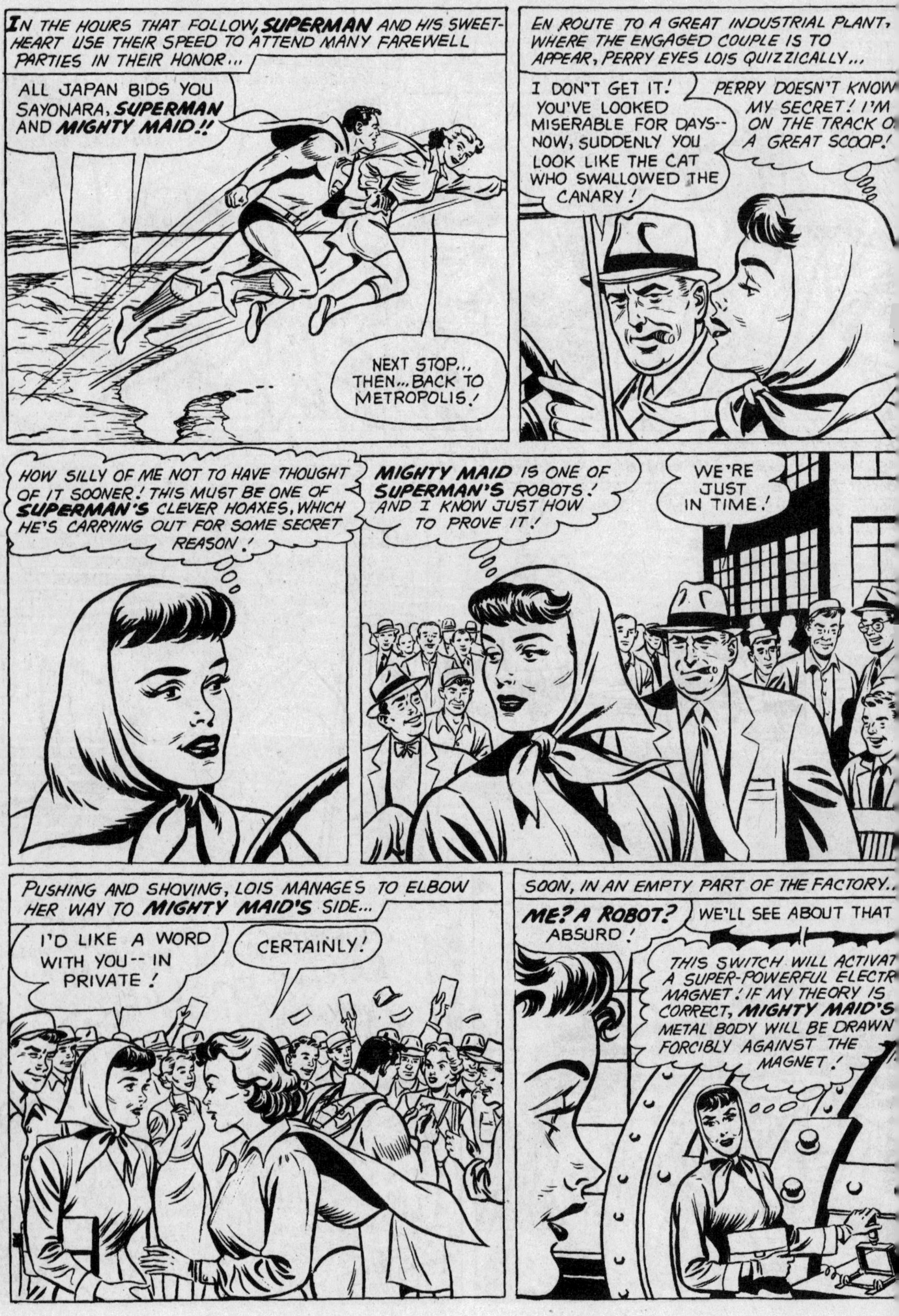
IN THE HOURS THAT FOLLOW, SUPERMAN AND HIS SWEETHEART USE THEIR SPEED TO ATTEND MANY FAREWELL PARTIES IN THEIR HONOR...
ALL JAPAN BIDS YOU SAYONARA, SUPERMAN AND MIGHTY MAID!!
NEXT STOP... THEN... BACK TO METROPOLIS!
EN ROUTE TO A GREAT INDUSTRIAL PLANT, WHERE THE ENGAGED COUPLE IS TO APPEAR, PERRY EYES LOIS QUIZZICALLY...
I DON'T GET IT! YOU'VE LOOKED MISERABLE FOR DAYS-- NOW, SUDDENLY YOU LOOK LIKE THE CAT WHO SWALLOWED THE CANARY!
PERRY DOESN'T KNOW MY SECRET! I'M ON THE TRACK O A GREAT SCOOP!
HOW SILLY OF ME NOT TO HAVE THOUGHT OF IT SOONER! THIS MUST BE ONE OF SUPERMAN'S CLEVER HOAXES, WHICH HE'S CARRYING OUT FOR SOME SECRET REASON!
MIGHTY MAID IS ONE OF SUPERMAN'S ROBOTS! AND I KNOW JUST HOW TO PROVE IT!
WE'RE JUST IN TIME!
PUSHING AND SHOVING, LOIS MANAGES TO ELBOW HER WAY TO MIGHTY MAID'S SIDE...
I'D LIKE A WORD WITH YOU-- IN PRIVATE!
CERTAINLY!
SOON, IN AN EMPTY PART OF THE FACTORY...
ME? A ROBOT? ABSURD!
WE'LL SEE ABOUT THAT
THIS SWITCH WILL ACTIVAT A SUPER-POWERFUL ELECTR MAGNET! IF MY THEORY IS CORRECT, MIGHTY MAID'S METAL BODY WILL BE DRAWN FORCIBLY AGAINST THE MAGNET!

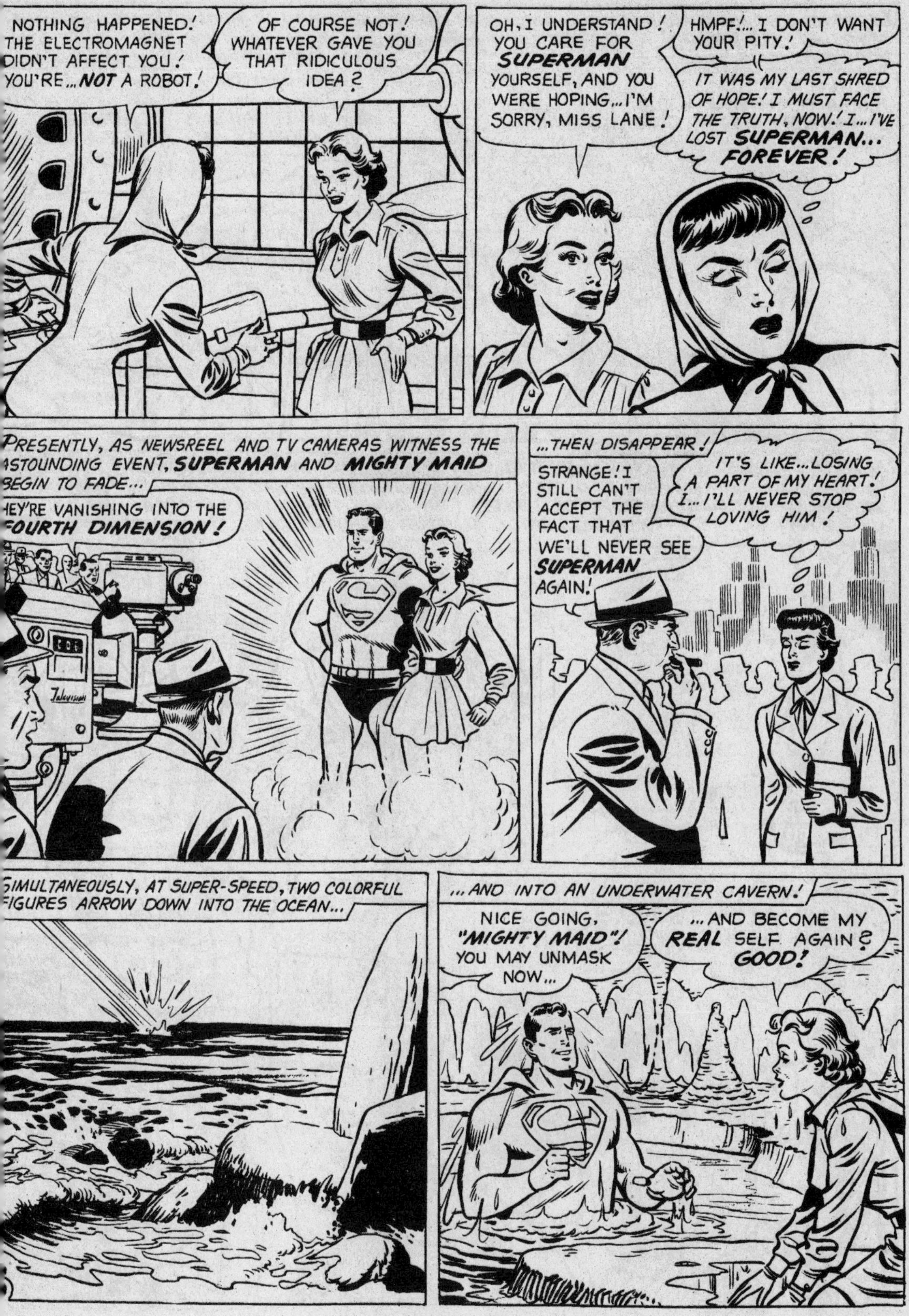
NOTHING HAPPENED! THE ELECTROMAGNET DIDN'T AFFECT YOU! YOU'RE... NOT A ROBOT!
OF COURSE NOT! WHATEVER GAVE YOU THAT RIDICULOUS IDEA?
OH, I UNDERSTAND! YOU CARE FOR SUPERMAN YOURSELF, AND YOU WERE HOPING... I'M SORRY, MISS LANE!
HMPF!... I DON'T WANT YOUR PITY!
IT WAS MY LAST SHRED OF HOPE! I MUST FACE THE TRUTH, NOW! I... I'VE LOST SUPERMAN... FOREVER!
PRESENTLY, AS NEWSREEL AND TV CAMERAS WITNESS THE ASTOUNDING EVENT, SUPERMAN AND MIGHTY MAID BEGIN TO FADE...
HEY'RE VANISHING INTO THE FOURTH DIMENSION!
...THEN DISAPPEAR!
STRANGE! I STILL CAN'T ACCEPT THE FACT THAT WE'LL NEVER SEE SUPERMAN AGAIN!
IT'S LIKE... LOSING A PART OF MY HEART! I... I'LL NEVER STOP LOVING HIM!
SIMULTANEOUSLY, AT SUPER-SPEED, TWO COLORFUL FIGURES ARROW DOWN INTO THE OCEAN...
...AND INTO AN UNDERWATER CAVERN!
NICE GOING, "MIGHTY MAID"! YOU MAY UNMASK NOW...
...AND BECOME MY REAL SELF AGAIN? GOOD!

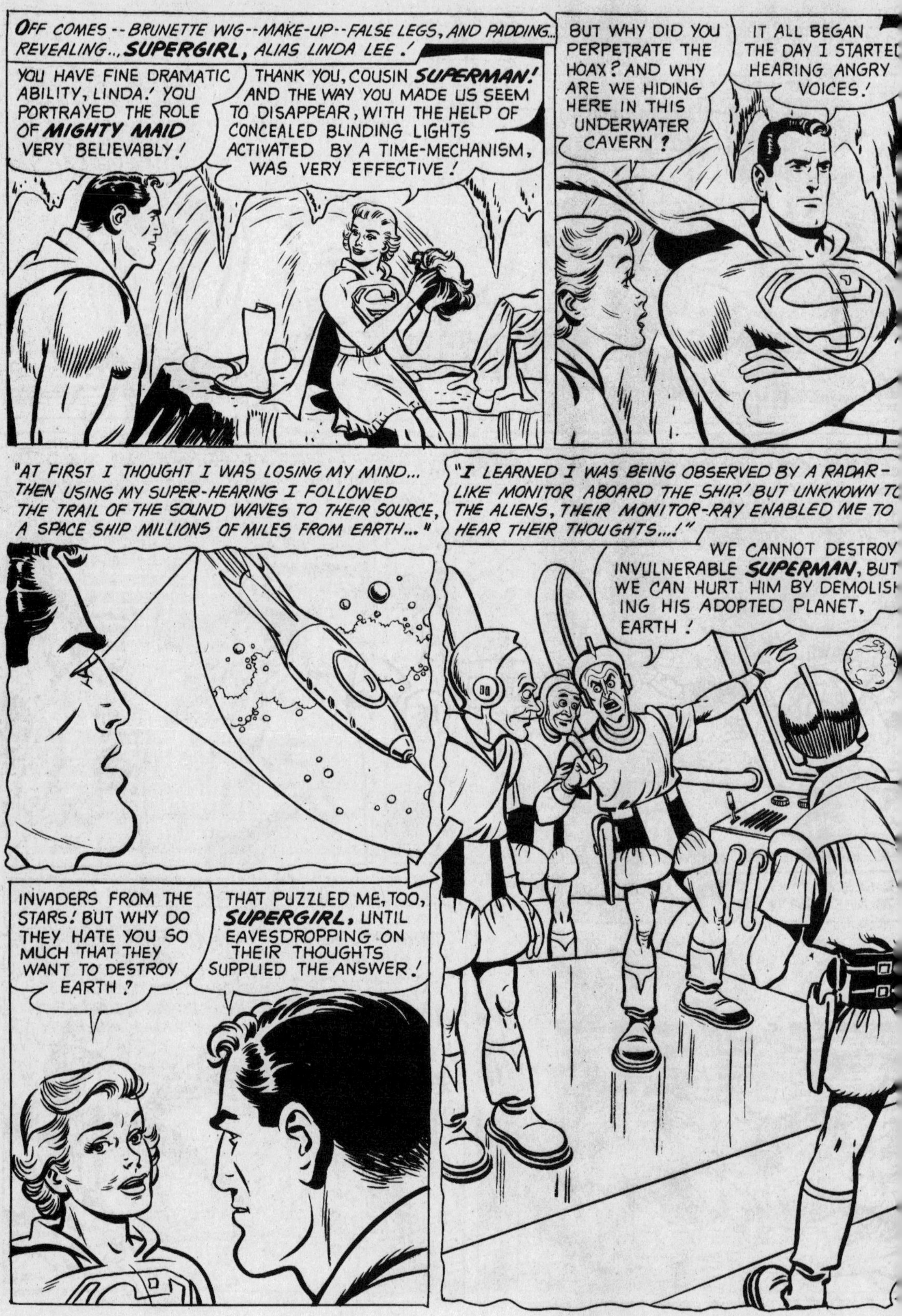
OFF COMES--BRUNETTE WIG--MAKE-UP--FALSE LEGS, AND PADDING... REVEALING..., SUPERGIRL, ALIAS LINDA LEE!
YOU HAVE FINE DRAMATIC ABILITY, LINDA! YOU PORTRAYED THE ROLE OF MIGHTY MAID VERY BELIEVABLY!
THANK YOU, COUSIN SUPERMAN! AND THE WAY YOU MADE US SEEM TO DISAPPEAR, WITH THE HELP OF CONCEALED BLINDING LIGHTS ACTIVATED BY A TIME-MECHANISM, WAS VERY EFFECTIVE!
BUT WHY DID YOU PERPETRATE THE HOAX? AND WHY ARE WE HIDING HERE IN THIS UNDERWATER CAVERN?
IT ALL BEGAN THE DAY I STARTED HEARING ANGRY VOICES!
"AT FIRST I THOUGHT I WAS LOSING MY MIND... THEN USING MY SUPER-HEARING I FOLLOWED THE TRAIL OF THE SOUND WAVES TO THEIR SOURCE, A SPACE SHIP MILLIONS OF MILES FROM EARTH..."
"I LEARNED I WAS BEING OBSERVED BY A RADAR-LIKE MONITOR ABOARD THE SHIP! BUT UNKNOWN TO THE ALIENS, THEIR MONITOR-RAY ENABLED ME TO HEAR THEIR THOUGHTS...!"
WE CANNOT DESTROY INVULNERABLE SUPERMAN, BUT WE CAN HURT HIM BY DEMOLISHING HIS ADOPTED PLANET, EARTH!
INVADERS FROM THE STARS! BUT WHY DO THEY HATE YOU SO MUCH THAT THEY WANT TO DESTROY EARTH?
THAT PUZZLED ME, TOO, SUPERGIRL, UNTIL EAVESDROPPING ON THEIR THOUGHTS SUPPLIED THE ANSWER!

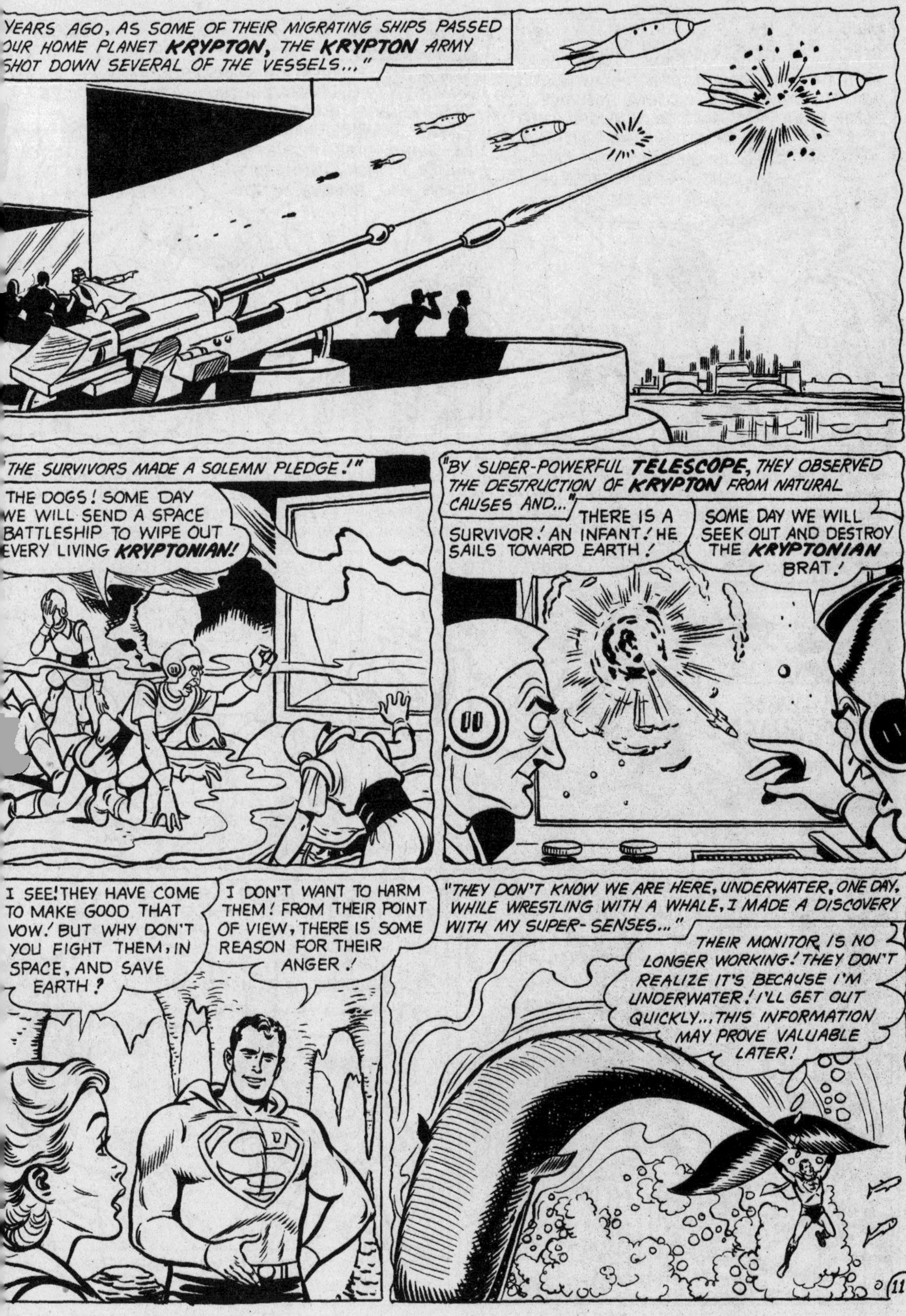
YEARS AGO, AS SOME OF THEIR MIGRATING SHIPS PASSED OUR HOME PLANET KRYPTON, THE KRYPTON ARMY SHOT DOWN SEVERAL OF THE VESSELS..."
"THE SURVIVORS MADE A SOLEMN PLEDGE!"
THE DOGS! SOME DAY WE WILL SEND A SPACE BATTLESHIP TO WIPE OUT EVERY LIVING KRYPTONIAN!
"BY SUPER-POWERFUL TELESCOPE, THEY OBSERVED THE DESTRUCTION OF KRYPTON FROM NATURAL CAUSES AND..."
THERE IS A SURVIVOR! AN INFANT! HE SAILS TOWARD EARTH!
SOME DAY WE WILL SEEK OUT AND DESTROY THE KRYPTONIAN BRAT!
I SEE! THEY HAVE COME TO MAKE GOOD THAT VOW! BUT WHY DON'T YOU FIGHT THEM, IN SPACE, AND SAVE EARTH?
I DON'T WANT TO HARM THEM! FROM THEIR POINT OF VIEW, THERE IS SOME REASON FOR THEIR ANGER!
"THEY DON'T KNOW WE ARE HERE, UNDERWATER. ONE DAY, WHILE WRESTLING WITH A WHALE, I MADE A DISCOVERY WITH MY SUPER-SENSES..."
THEIR MONITOR IS NO LONGER WORKING! THEY DON'T REALIZE IT'S BECAUSE I'M UNDERWATER! I'LL GET OUT QUICKLY... THIS INFORMATION MAY PROVE VALUABLE LATER!
11

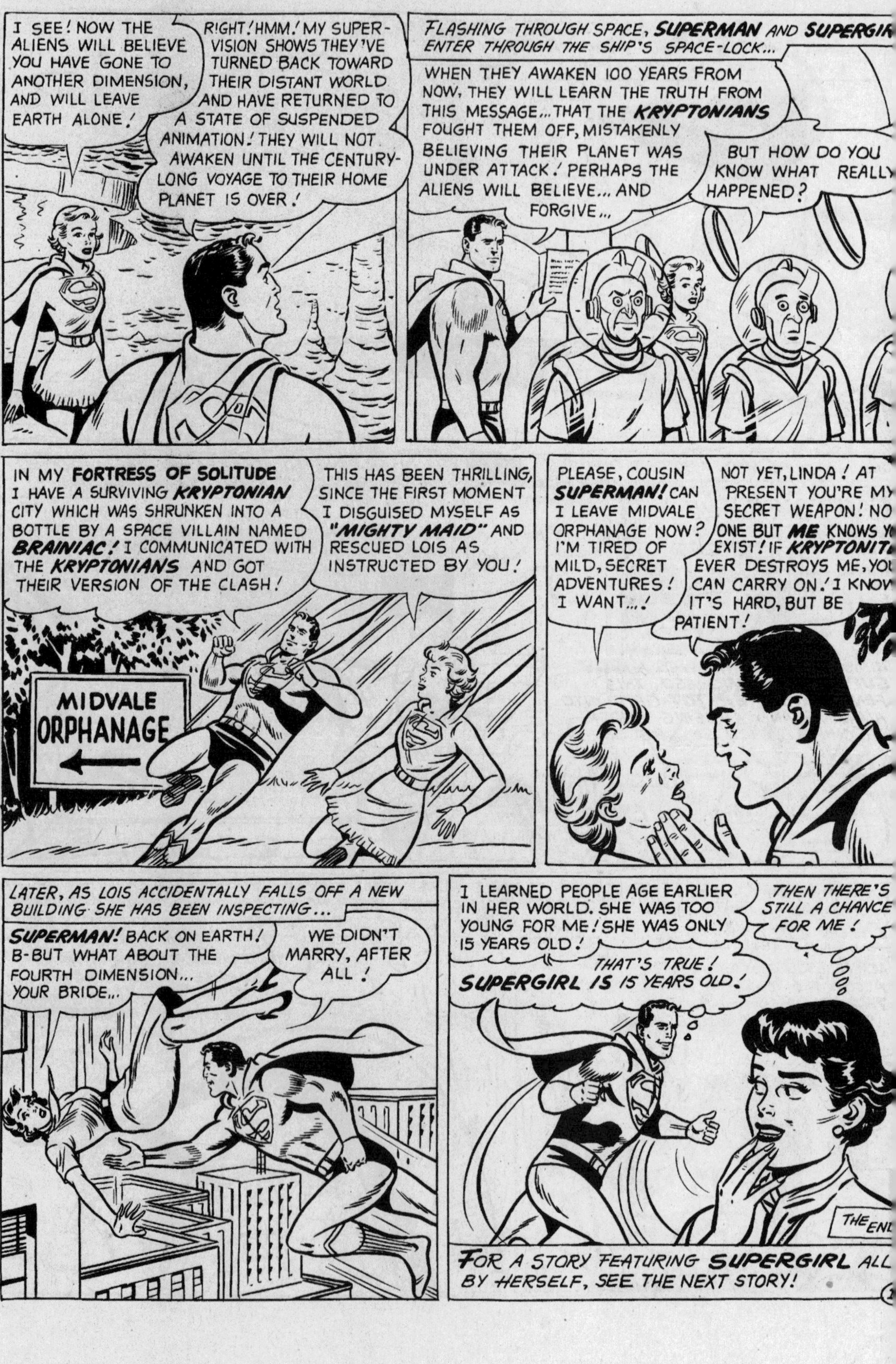
I SEE! NOW THE ALIENS WILL BELIEVE YOU HAVE GONE TO ANOTHER DIMENSION, AND WILL LEAVE EARTH ALONE!
RIGHT! HMM! MY SUPER-VISION SHOWS THEY'VE TURNED BACK TOWARD THEIR DISTANT WORLD AND HAVE RETURNED TO A STATE OF SUSPENDED ANIMATION! THEY WILL NOT AWAKEN UNTIL THE CENTURY-LONG VOYAGE TO THEIR HOME PLANET IS OVER!
FLASHING THROUGH SPACE, SUPERMAN AND SUPERGIR ENTER THROUGH THE SHIP'S SPACE-LOCK...
WHEN THEY AWAKEN 100 YEARS FROM NOW, THEY WILL LEARN THE TRUTH FROM THIS MESSAGE... THAT THE KRYPTONIANS FOUGHT THEM OFF, MISTAKENLY BELIEVING THEIR PLANET WAS UNDER ATTACK! PERHAPS THE ALIENS WILL BELIEVE... AND FORGIVE...
BUT HOW DO YOU KNOW WHAT REALLY HAPPENED?
IN MY FORTRESS OF SOLITUDE I HAVE A SURVIVING KRYPTONIAN CITY WHICH WAS SHRUNKEN INTO A BOTTLE BY A SPACE VILLAIN NAMED BRAINIAC! I COMMUNICATED WITH THE KRYPTONIANS AND GOT THEIR VERSION OF THE CLASH!
THIS HAS BEEN THRILLING, SINCE THE FIRST MOMENT I DISGUISED MYSELF AS "MIGHTY MAID" AND RESCUED LOIS AS INSTRUCTED BY YOU!
MIDVALE ORPHANAGE
PLEASE, COUSIN SUPERMAN! CAN I LEAVE MIDVALE ORPHANAGE NOW? I'M TIRED OF MILD, SECRET ADVENTURES! I WANT...!
NOT YET, LINDA! AT PRESENT YOU'RE MY SECRET WEAPON! NO ONE BUT ME KNOWS YOU EXIST! IF KRYPTONIT EVER DESTROYS ME, YOU CAN CARRY ON! I KNOW IT'S HARD, BUT BE PATIENT!
LATER, AS LOIS ACCIDENTALLY FALLS OFF A NEW BUILDING SHE HAS BEEN INSPECTING...
SUPERMAN! BACK ON EARTH! B-BUT WHAT ABOUT THE FOURTH DIMENSION... YOUR BRIDE...
WE DIDN'T MARRY, AFTER ALL!
I LEARNED PEOPLE AGE EARLIER IN HER WORLD. SHE WAS TOO YOUNG FOR ME! SHE WAS ONLY 15 YEARS OLD!
THEN THERE'S STILL A CHANCE FOR ME!
THAT'S TRUE! SUPERGIRL IS 15 YEARS OLD!
THE END
FOR A STORY FEATURING SUPERGIRL ALL BY HERSELF, SEE THE NEXT STORY!

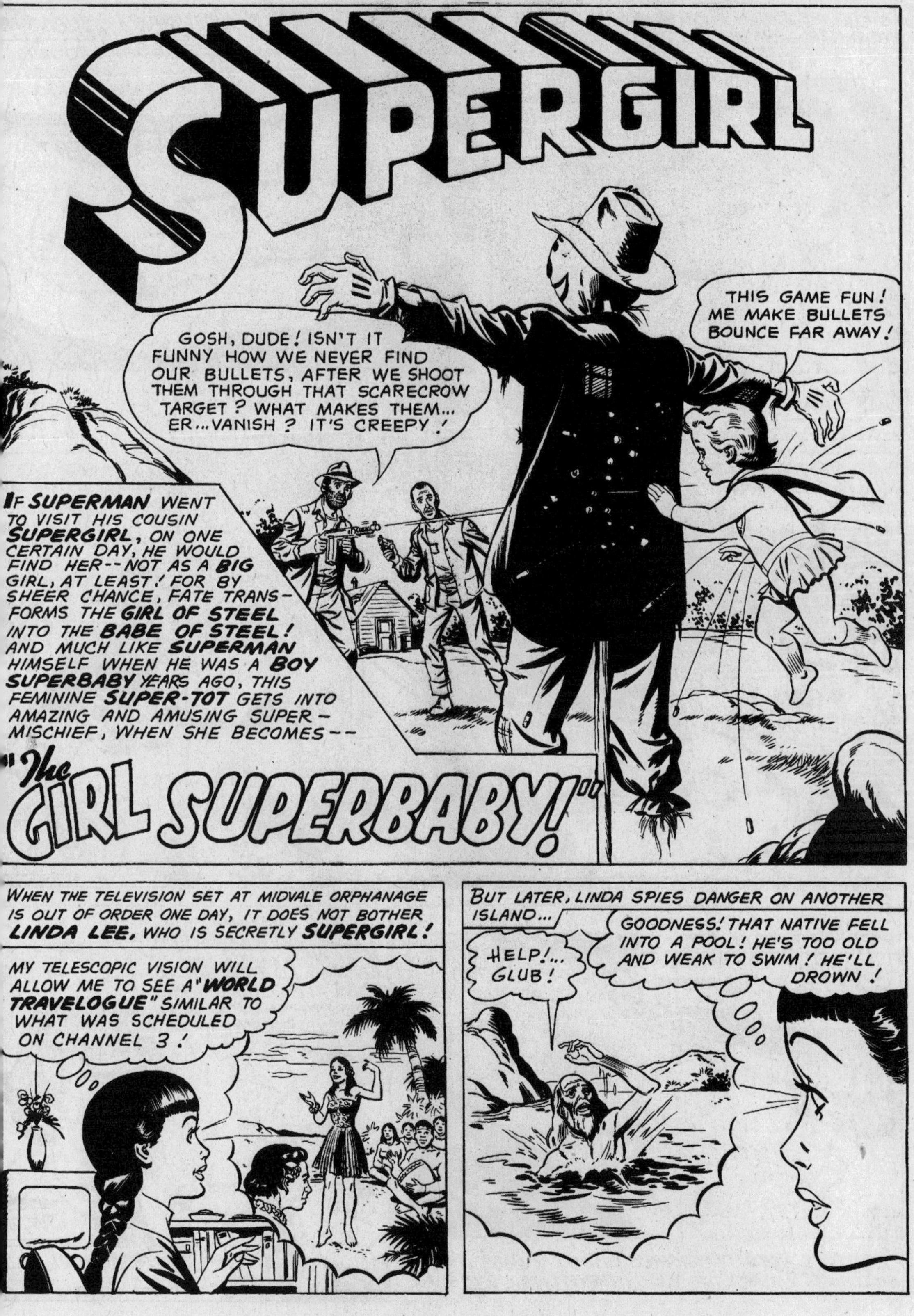
SUPERGIRL
GOSH, DUDE! ISN'T IT FUNNY HOW WE NEVER FIND OUR BULLETS, AFTER WE SHOOT THEM THROUGH THAT SCARECROW TARGET? WHAT MAKES THEM... ER...VANISH? IT'S CREEPY!
THIS GAME FUN! ME MAKE BULLETS BOUNCE FAR AWAY!
IF SUPERMAN WENT TO VISIT HIS COUSIN SUPERGIRL, ON ONE CERTAIN DAY, HE WOULD FIND HER--NOT AS A BIG GIRL, AT LEAST! FOR BY SHEER CHANCE, FATE TRANSFORMS THE GIRL OF STEEL INTO THE BABE OF STEEL! AND MUCH LIKE SUPERMAN HIMSELF WHEN HE WAS A BOY SUPERBABY YEARS AGO, THIS FEMININE SUPER-TOT GETS INTO AMAZING AND AMUSING SUPER-MISCHIEF, WHEN SHE BECOMES--
"The GIRL SUPERBABY!"
WHEN THE TELEVISION SET AT MIDVALE ORPHANAGE IS OUT OF ORDER ONE DAY, IT DOES NOT BOTHER LINDA LEE, WHO IS SECRETLY SUPERGIRL!
MY TELESCOPIC VISION WILL ALLOW ME TO SEE A "WORLD TRAVELOGUE" SIMILAR TO WHAT WAS SCHEDULED ON CHANNEL 3!
BUT LATER, LINDA SPIES DANGER ON ANOTHER ISLAND...
HELP!... GLUB!
GOODNESS! THAT NATIVE FELL INTO A POOL! HE'S TOO OLD AND WEAK TO SWIM! HE'LL DROWN!

SWIFTLY REMOVING A FALSE PIGTAILED WIG AND OUTER GARMENTS... I--IT'S A *JOB* FOR *SUPERGIRL!* BUT SINCE MY COUSIN *SUPERMAN* IS DEPENDING ON ME TO TAKE OVER AS HIS SECRET WEAPON AGAINST CRIME-DOM IF ANYTHING EVER HAPPENS TO *HIM!*...

...MY EXISTENCE ON EARTH MUST BE KEPT *SECRET!* I'LL SUPER-BORE *UNDERGROUND* OUT OF SIGHT! MY X-RAY VISION WILL GUIDE ME TO THE ISLAND!

ONLY MOMENTS LATER... I CAME UP IN THE BOTTOM OF THE POOL! I MUSN'T LET THAT NATIVE SEE ME! I'LL USE MY SUPER-BREATH AND...

...MAKE THE WATER FORM WHAT SEEMS TO BE A NATURAL *GEYSER!* IT WILL FLING HIM ASHORE SAFELY AMONG BUSHES! BUT HOW ODD! I THOUGHT HE WAS AN OLD MAN! HE...UH...LOOKS *YOUNG NOW!*

ASTOUNDINGLY, ON HER WAY BACK BY THE UNDERGROUND ROUTE... UH...W-WHAT'S HAPPENING TO ME? I-I'M *SHRINKING* IN SIZE! *

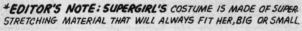

*EDITOR'S NOTE: SUPERGIRL'S COSTUME IS MADE OF SUPER-STRETCHING MATERIAL THAT WILL ALWAYS FIT HER, BIG OR SMALL.

SOON... HEAVENS--I'M GETTING *YOUNG,* TOO! WAIT--THAT OLD MAN SEEMED TO TURN YOUNG, TOO! I'LL COME UP HERE AND CHECK BACK WITH MY TELESCOPIC VISION--

2

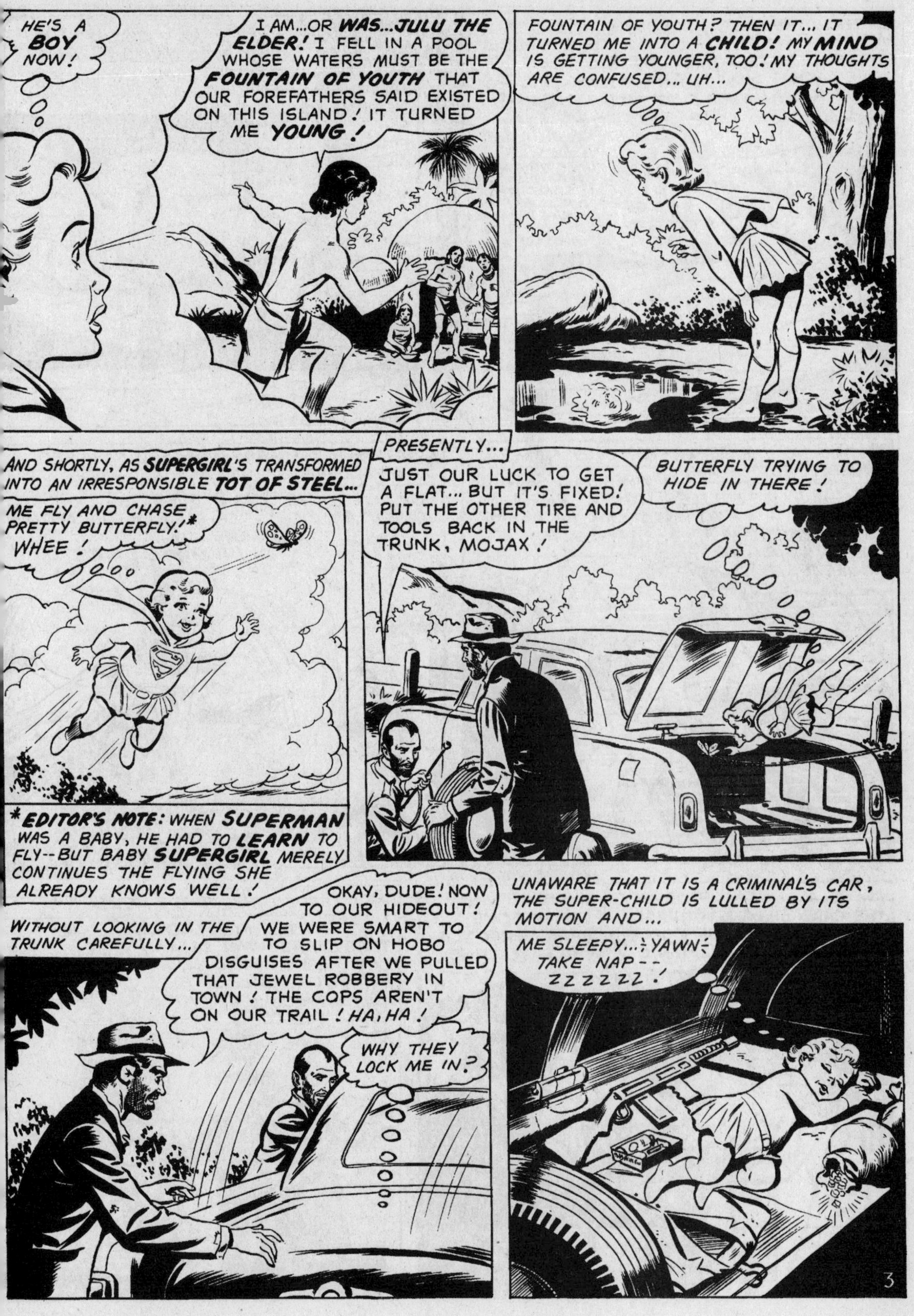
HE'S A BOY NOW!
I AM...OR WAS...JULU THE ELDER! I FELL IN A POOL WHOSE WATERS MUST BE THE FOUNTAIN OF YOUTH THAT OUR FOREFATHERS SAID EXISTED ON THIS ISLAND! IT TURNED ME YOUNG!
FOUNTAIN OF YOUTH? THEN IT... IT TURNED ME INTO A CHILD! MY MIND IS GETTING YOUNGER, TOO! MY THOUGHTS ARE CONFUSED... UH...
AND SHORTLY, AS SUPERGIRL'S TRANSFORMED INTO AN IRRESPONSIBLE TOT OF STEEL...
ME FLY AND CHASE PRETTY BUTTERFLY!* WHEE!
*EDITOR'S NOTE: WHEN SUPERMAN WAS A BABY, HE HAD TO LEARN TO FLY--BUT BABY SUPERGIRL MERELY CONTINUES THE FLYING SHE ALREADY KNOWS WELL!
PRESENTLY...
JUST OUR LUCK TO GET A FLAT... BUT IT'S FIXED! PUT THE OTHER TIRE AND TOOLS BACK IN THE TRUNK, MOJAX!
BUTTERFLY TRYING TO HIDE IN THERE!
WITHOUT LOOKING IN THE TRUNK CAREFULLY...
OKAY, DUDE! NOW TO OUR HIDEOUT! WE WERE SMART TO TO SLIP ON HOBO DISGUISES AFTER WE PULLED THAT JEWEL ROBBERY IN TOWN! THE COPS AREN'T ON OUR TRAIL! HA, HA!
WHY THEY LOCK ME IN?
UNAWARE THAT IT IS A CRIMINAL'S CAR, THE SUPER-CHILD IS LULLED BY ITS MOTION AND...
ME SLEEPY...YAWN TAKE NAP--ZZZZZZ!
3

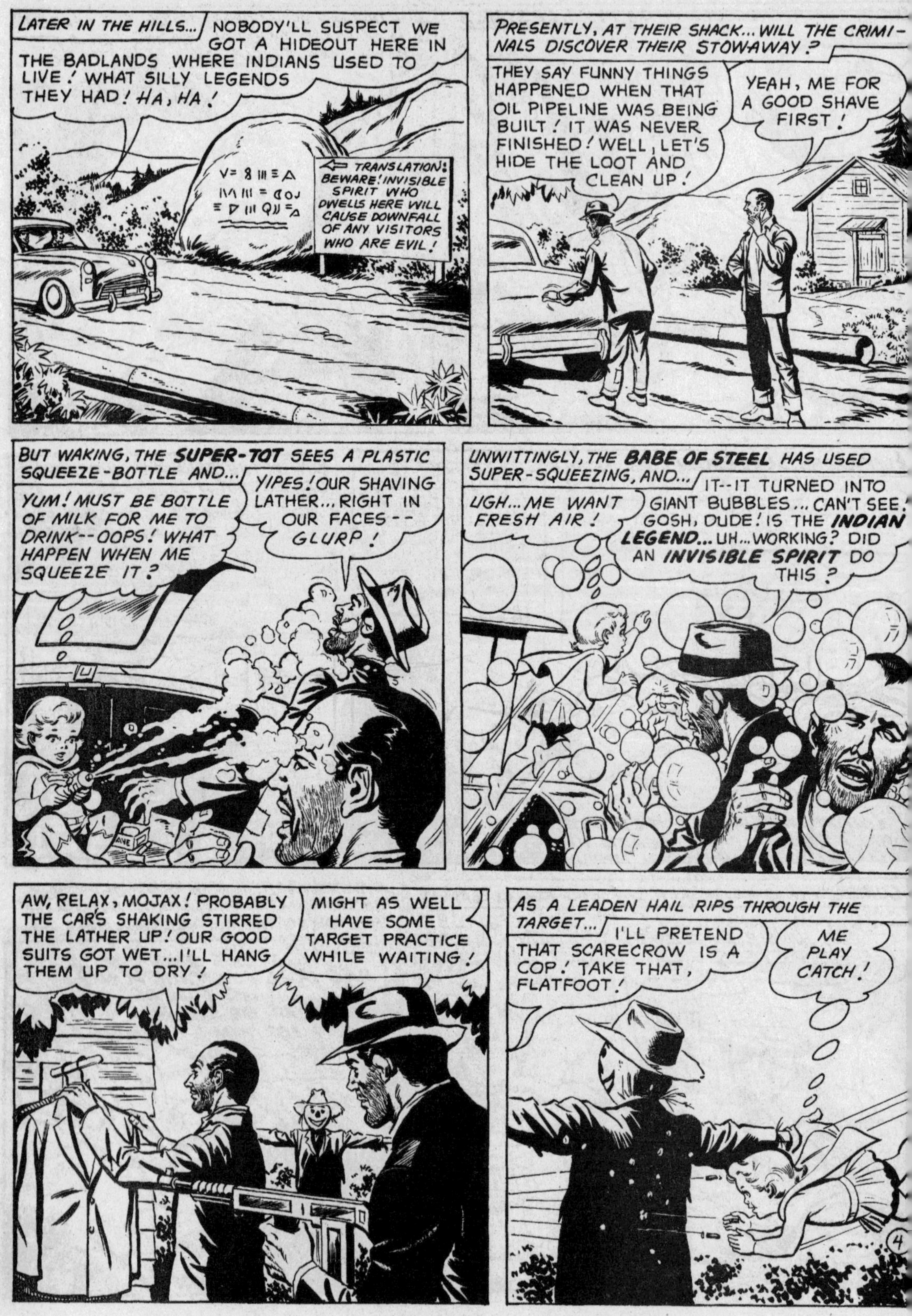
LATER IN THE HILLS...
NOBODY'LL SUSPECT WE GOT A HIDEOUT HERE IN THE BADLANDS WHERE INDIANS USED TO LIVE! WHAT SILLY LEGENDS THEY HAD! HA, HA!
TRANSLATION: BEWARE! INVISIBLE SPIRIT WHO DWELLS HERE WILL CAUSE DOWNFALL OF ANY VISITORS WHO ARE EVIL!
PRESENTLY, AT THEIR SHACK... WILL THE CRIMINALS DISCOVER THEIR STOWAWAY?
THEY SAY FUNNY THINGS HAPPENED WHEN THAT OIL PIPELINE WAS BEING BUILT! IT WAS NEVER FINISHED! WELL, LET'S HIDE THE LOOT AND CLEAN UP!
YEAH, ME FOR A GOOD SHAVE FIRST!
BUT WAKING, THE SUPER-TOT SEES A PLASTIC SQUEEZE-BOTTLE AND...
YUM! MUST BE BOTTLE OF MILK FOR ME TO DRINK--OOPS! WHAT HAPPEN WHEN ME SQUEEZE IT?
YIPES! OUR SHAVING LATHER... RIGHT IN OUR FACES--GLURP!
UNWITTINGLY, THE BABE OF STEEL HAS USED SUPER-SQUEEZING, AND...
UGH... ME WANT FRESH AIR!
IT--IT TURNED INTO GIANT BUBBLES... CAN'T SEE. GOSH, DUDE! IS THE INDIAN LEGEND... UH... WORKING? DID AN INVISIBLE SPIRIT DO THIS?
AW, RELAX, MOJAX! PROBABLY THE CAR'S SHAKING STIRRED THE LATHER UP! OUR GOOD SUITS GOT WET...I'LL HANG THEM UP TO DRY!
MIGHT AS WELL HAVE SOME TARGET PRACTICE WHILE WAITING!
AS A LEADEN HAIL RIPS THROUGH THE TARGET...
I'LL PRETEND THAT SCARECROW IS A COP! TAKE THAT, FLATFOOT!
ME PLAY CATCH!
4

UNDER SUPER-PRESSURE IN THE *TYKE OF STEEL'S* HANDS...

ME MADE BALL! ME BOUNCE IT FROM CLIFF!

BUT THROWN WITH SUPER-FORCE, THE LEADEN BALL SMASHES THROUGH, HEADING FOR A STRANGE RENDEZVOUS WITH FATE!

SMASH!

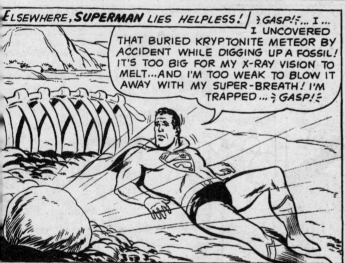

ELSEWHERE, *SUPERMAN* LIES HELPLESS!

≥GASP!≤... I... I UNCOVERED THAT BURIED KRYPTONITE METEOR BY ACCIDENT WHILE DIGGING UP A FOSSIL! IT'S TOO BIG FOR MY X-RAY VISION TO MELT...AND I'M TOO WEAK TO BLOW IT AWAY WITH MY SUPER-BREATH! I'M TRAPPED... ≥GASP!≤

BUT BY THE STRANGE WORKINGS OF DESTINY...

GREAT SCOTT! THAT CHUNK OF LEAD CAME FLYING FROM NOWHERE! AIR FRICTION MADE IT MELT! IT'S DRIPPING AND COVERING THE KRYPTONITE, STOPPING THE DEADLY RADIATIONS!

SUPERMAN IS NEVER TO KNOW WHO REALLY SAVED HIM!

WHAT SUPER-LUCK! IT MUST HAVE BEEN A RARE LEADEN *METEOR* FROM SPACE!

WHERE BALL? IT DIDN'T BOUNCE BACK! GAME SPOILED!

DISAPPOINTED, THE *INFANT OF STEEL* SEEKS OTHER AMUSEMENT AND, WHEN SHE SPIES THE SCARECROW, GETS AN IDEA...

GEE! THIS MAKE NICE *RAG DOLL* FOR ME TO PLAY WITH! BUT IT'S FULL OF HOLES! AH, ME SEE NEW SUIT FOR HIM!

⑤

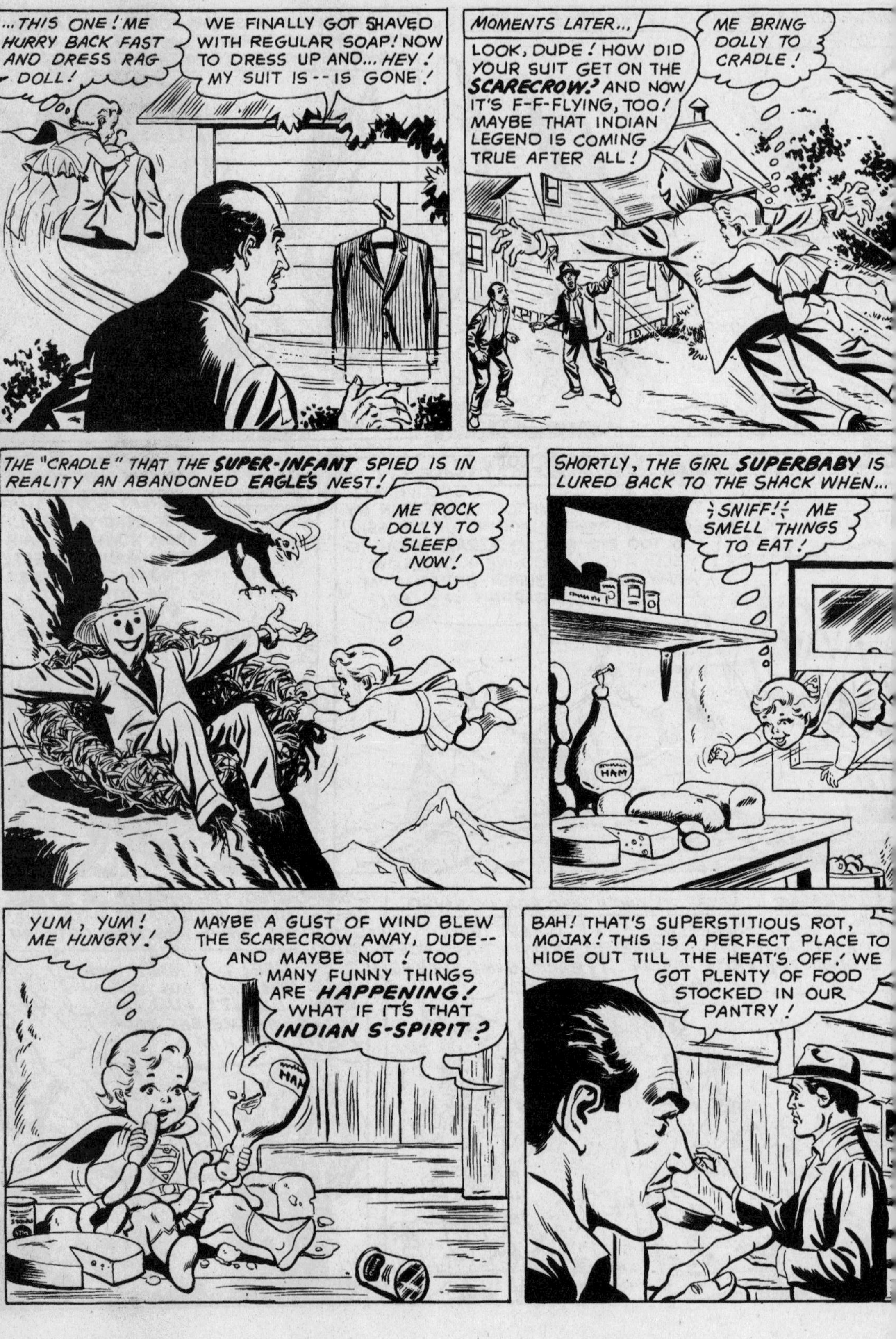
...THIS ONE! ME HURRY BACK FAST AND DRESS RAG DOLL!
WE FINALLY GOT SHAVED WITH REGULAR SOAP! NOW TO DRESS UP AND... HEY! MY SUIT IS--IS GONE!
MOMENTS LATER...
LOOK, DUDE! HOW DID YOUR SUIT GET ON THE SCARECROW? AND NOW IT'S F-F-FLYING, TOO! MAYBE THAT INDIAN LEGEND IS COMING TRUE AFTER ALL!
ME BRING DOLLY TO CRADLE!
THE "CRADLE" THAT THE SUPER-INFANT SPIED IS IN REALITY AN ABANDONED EAGLE'S NEST!
ME ROCK DOLLY TO SLEEP NOW!
SHORTLY, THE GIRL SUPERBABY IS LURED BACK TO THE SHACK WHEN...
SNIFF! ME SMELL THINGS TO EAT!
HAM
YUM, YUM! ME HUNGRY!
MAYBE A GUST OF WIND BLEW THE SCARECROW AWAY, DUDE--AND MAYBE NOT! TOO MANY FUNNY THINGS ARE HAPPENING! WHAT IF IT'S THAT INDIAN S-SPIRIT?
BAH! THAT'S SUPERSTITIOUS ROT, MOJAX! THIS IS A PERFECT PLACE TO HIDE OUT TILL THE HEAT'S OFF! WE GOT PLENTY OF FOOD STOCKED IN OUR PANTRY!

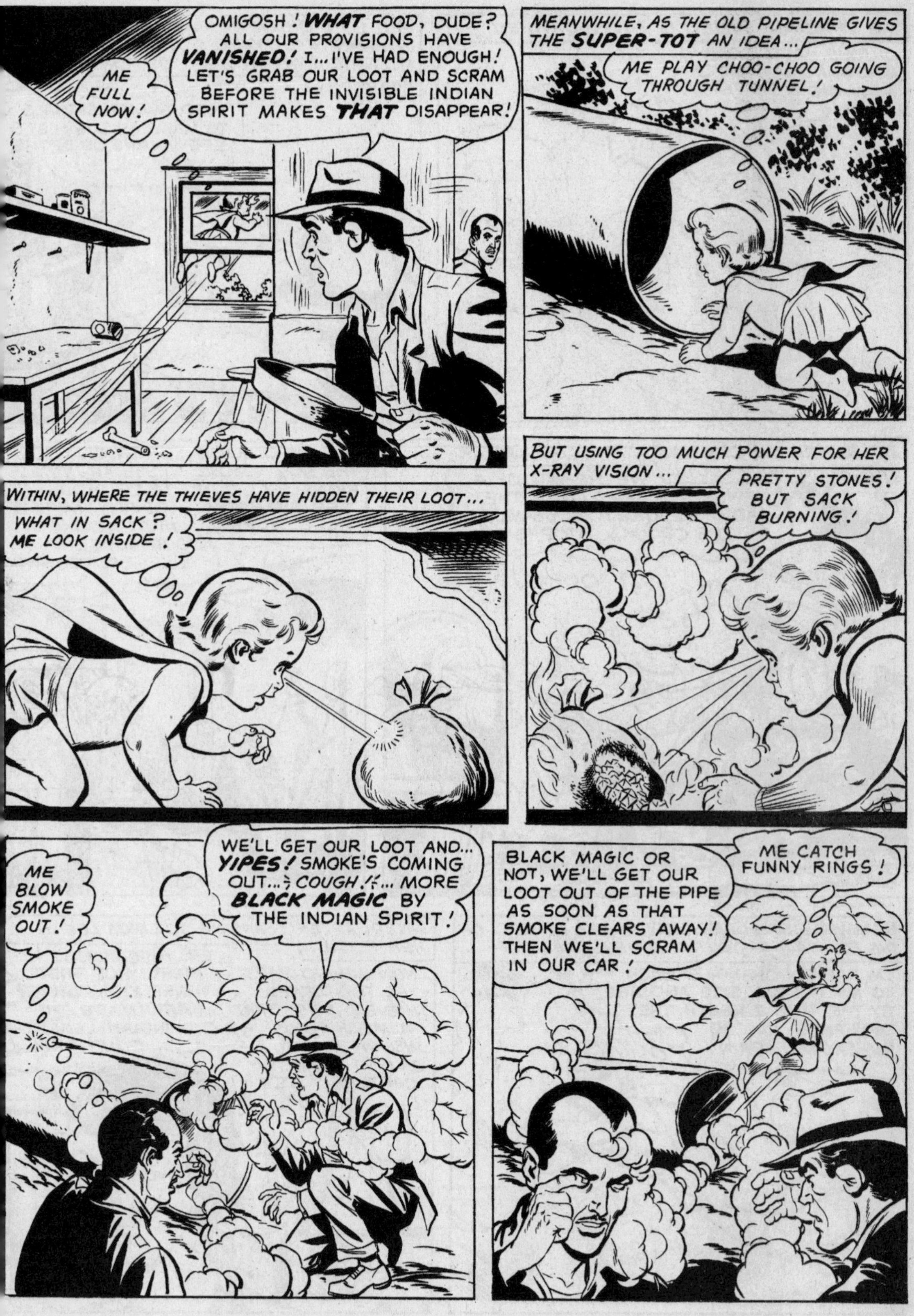
ME FULL NOW!
OMIGOSH! WHAT FOOD, DUDE? ALL OUR PROVISIONS HAVE VANISHED! I...I'VE HAD ENOUGH! LET'S GRAB OUR LOOT AND SCRAM BEFORE THE INVISIBLE INDIAN SPIRIT MAKES THAT DISAPPEAR!
MEANWHILE, AS THE OLD PIPELINE GIVES THE SUPER-TOT AN IDEA...
ME PLAY CHOO-CHOO GOING THROUGH TUNNEL!
WITHIN, WHERE THE THIEVES HAVE HIDDEN THEIR LOOT...
WHAT IN SACK? ME LOOK INSIDE!
BUT USING TOO MUCH POWER FOR HER X-RAY VISION...
PRETTY STONES! BUT SACK BURNING!
ME BLOW SMOKE OUT!
WE'LL GET OUR LOOT AND... YIPES! SMOKE'S COMING OUT... COUGH! ... MORE BLACK MAGIC BY THE INDIAN SPIRIT!
BLACK MAGIC OR NOT, WE'LL GET OUR LOOT OUT OF THE PIPE AS SOON AS THAT SMOKE CLEARS AWAY! THEN WE'LL SCRAM IN OUR CAR!
ME CATCH FUNNY RINGS!

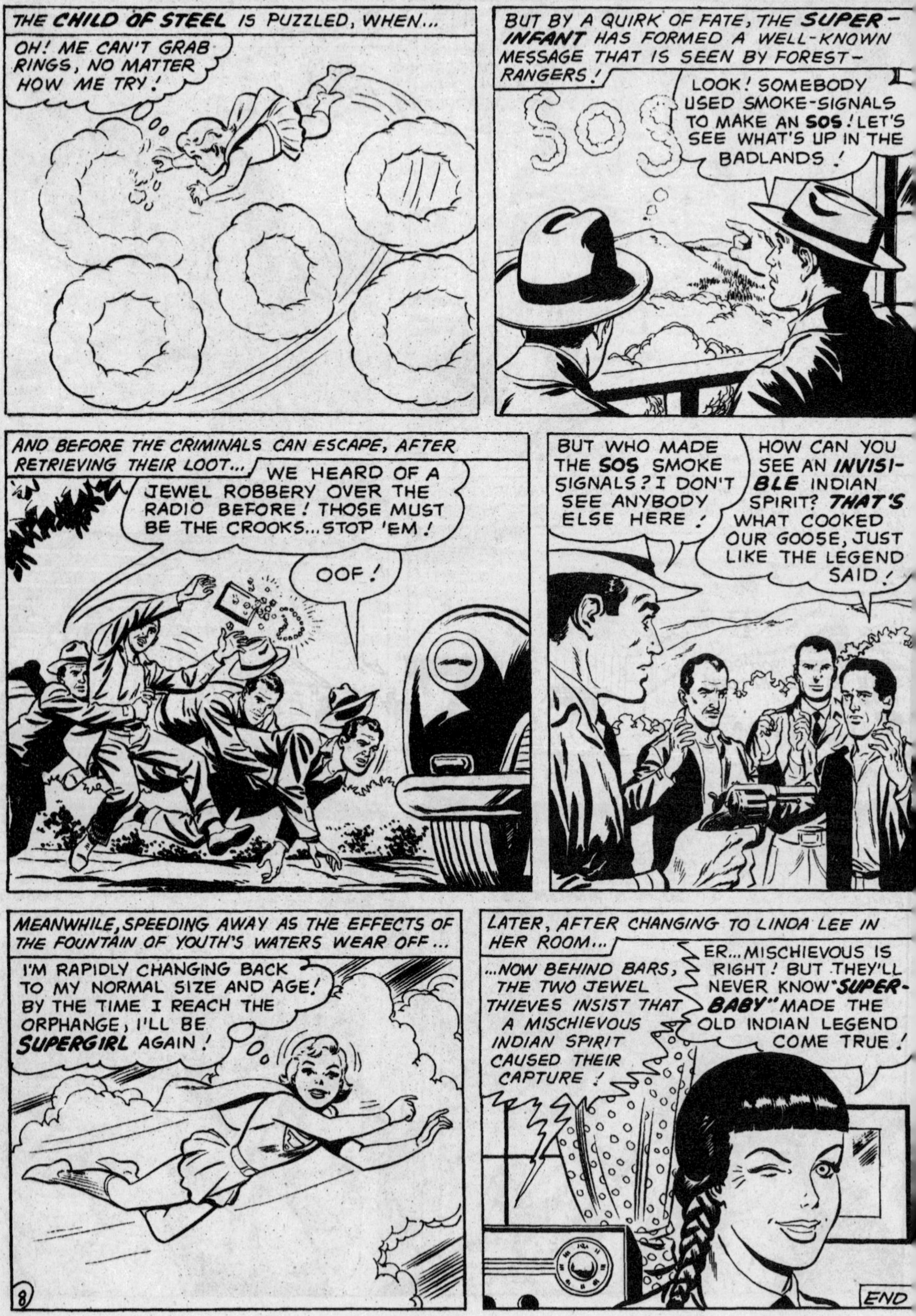
THE CHILD OF STEEL IS PUZZLED, WHEN...
OH! ME CAN'T GRAB RINGS, NO MATTER HOW ME TRY!
BUT BY A QUIRK OF FATE, THE SUPER-INFANT HAS FORMED A WELL-KNOWN MESSAGE THAT IS SEEN BY FOREST-RANGERS!
SOS
LOOK! SOMEBODY USED SMOKE-SIGNALS TO MAKE AN SOS! LET'S SEE WHAT'S UP IN THE BADLANDS!
AND BEFORE THE CRIMINALS CAN ESCAPE, AFTER RETRIEVING THEIR LOOT...
WE HEARD OF A JEWEL ROBBERY OVER THE RADIO BEFORE! THOSE MUST BE THE CROOKS...STOP 'EM!
OOF!
BUT WHO MADE THE SOS SMOKE SIGNALS? I DON'T SEE ANYBODY ELSE HERE!
HOW CAN YOU SEE AN INVISIBLE INDIAN SPIRIT? THAT'S WHAT COOKED OUR GOOSE, JUST LIKE THE LEGEND SAID!
MEANWHILE, SPEEDING AWAY AS THE EFFECTS OF THE FOUNTAIN OF YOUTH'S WATERS WEAR OFF...
I'M RAPIDLY CHANGING BACK TO MY NORMAL SIZE AND AGE! BY THE TIME I REACH THE ORPHANGE, I'LL BE SUPERGIRL AGAIN!
8
LATER, AFTER CHANGING TO LINDA LEE IN HER ROOM...
...NOW BEHIND BARS, THE TWO JEWEL THIEVES INSIST THAT A MISCHIEVOUS INDIAN SPIRIT CAUSED THEIR CAPTURE!
ER...MISCHIEVOUS IS RIGHT! BUT THEY'LL NEVER KNOW "SUPER-BABY" MADE THE OLD INDIAN LEGEND COME TRUE!
END

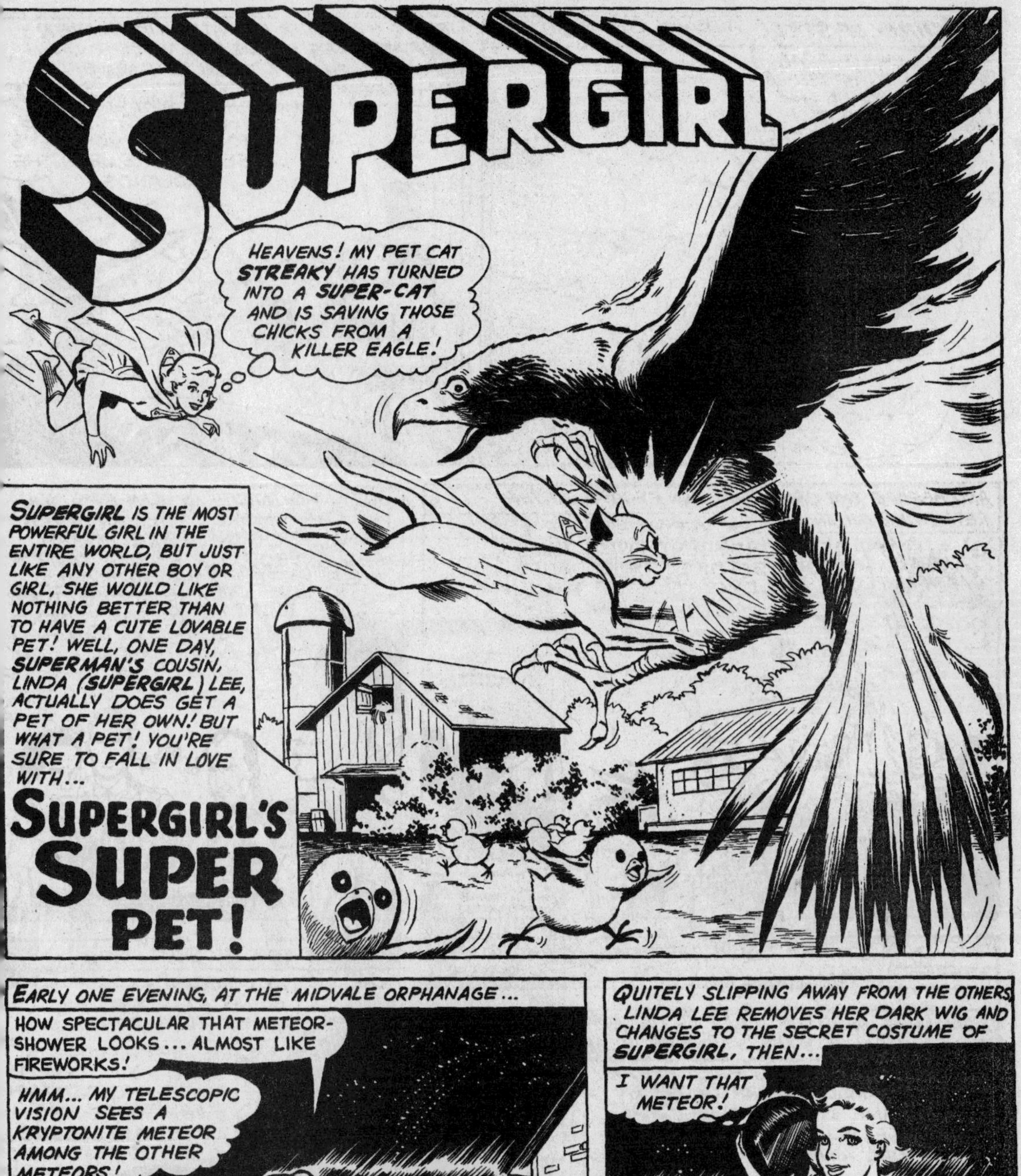
SUPERGIRL
HEAVENS! MY PET CAT STREAKY HAS TURNED INTO A SUPER-CAT AND IS SAVING THOSE CHICKS FROM A KILLER EAGLE!
SUPERGIRL IS THE MOST POWERFUL GIRL IN THE ENTIRE WORLD, BUT JUST LIKE ANY OTHER BOY OR GIRL, SHE WOULD LIKE NOTHING BETTER THAN TO HAVE A CUTE LOVABLE PET! WELL, ONE DAY, SUPERMAN'S COUSIN, LINDA (SUPERGIRL) LEE, ACTUALLY DOES GET A PET OF HER OWN! BUT WHAT A PET! YOU'RE SURE TO FALL IN LOVE WITH...
SUPERGIRL'S SUPER PET!

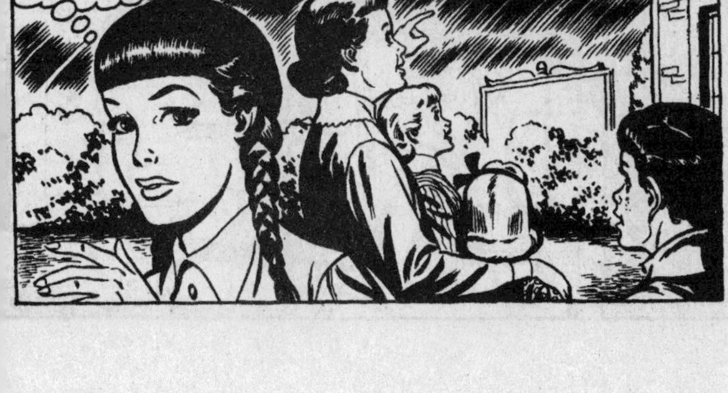
EARLY ONE EVENING, AT THE MIDVALE ORPHANAGE...
HOW SPECTACULAR THAT METEOR-SHOWER LOOKS... ALMOST LIKE FIREWORKS!
HMM... MY TELESCOPIC VISION SEES A KRYPTONITE METEOR AMONG THE OTHER METEORS!

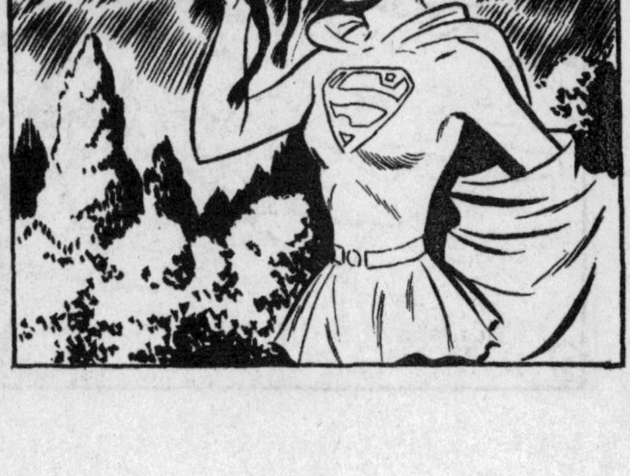
QUITELY SLIPPING AWAY FROM THE OTHERS, LINDA LEE REMOVES HER DARK WIG AND CHANGES TO THE SECRET COSTUME OF SUPERGIRL, THEN...
I WANT THAT METEOR!

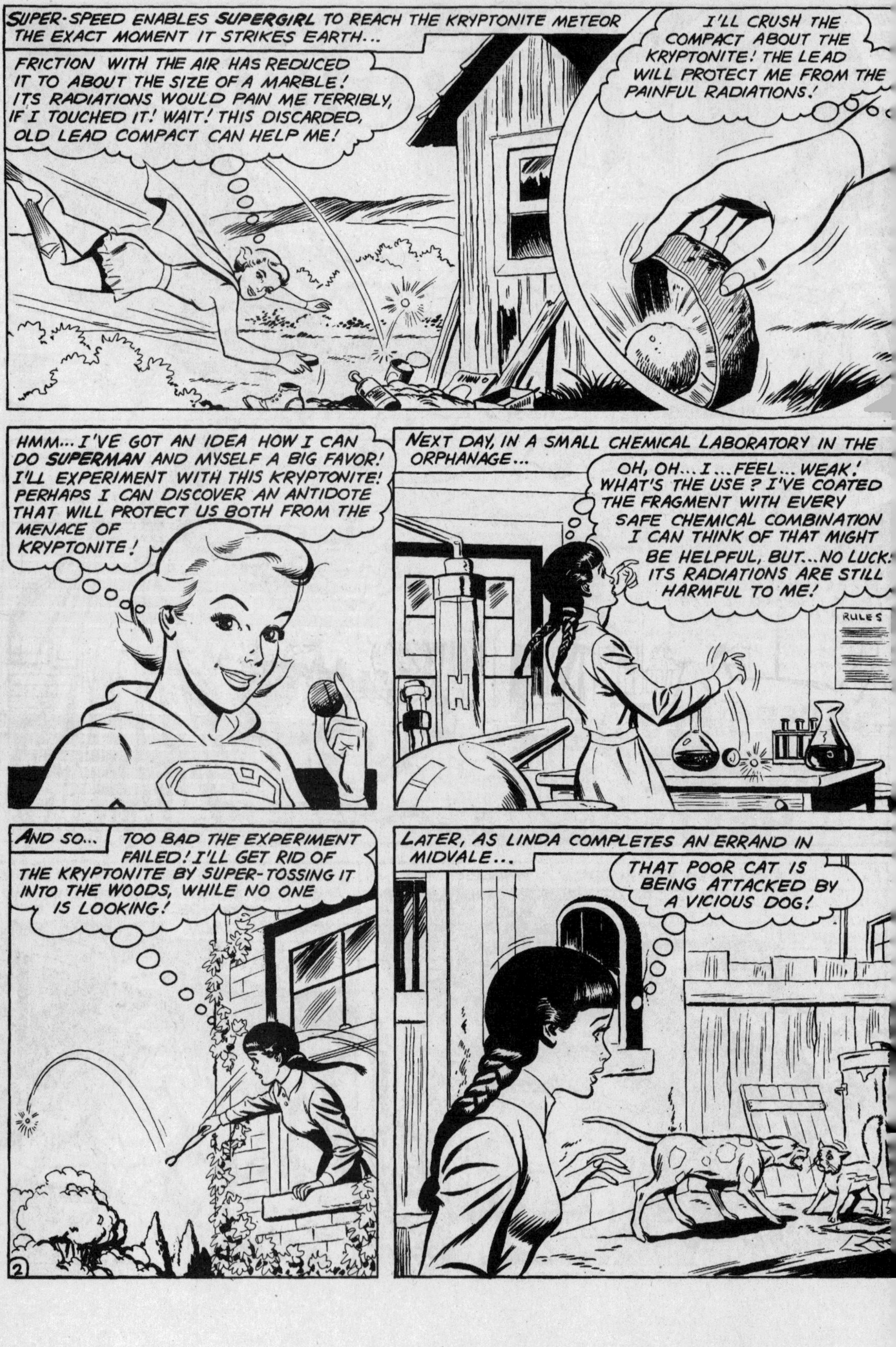
SUPER-SPEED ENABLES SUPERGIRL TO REACH THE KRYPTONITE METEOR THE EXACT MOMENT IT STRIKES EARTH...
FRICTION WITH THE AIR HAS REDUCED IT TO ABOUT THE SIZE OF A MARBLE! ITS RADIATIONS WOULD PAIN ME TERRIBLY, IF I TOUCHED IT! WAIT! THIS DISCARDED, OLD LEAD COMPACT CAN HELP ME!
I'LL CRUSH THE COMPACT ABOUT THE KRYPTONITE! THE LEAD WILL PROTECT ME FROM THE PAINFUL RADIATIONS!
HMM... I'VE GOT AN IDEA HOW I CAN DO SUPERMAN AND MYSELF A BIG FAVOR! I'LL EXPERIMENT WITH THIS KRYPTONITE! PERHAPS I CAN DISCOVER AN ANTIDOTE THAT WILL PROTECT US BOTH FROM THE MENACE OF KRYPTONITE!
NEXT DAY, IN A SMALL CHEMICAL LABORATORY IN THE ORPHANAGE...
OH, OH... I ... FEEL... WEAK! WHAT'S THE USE? I'VE COATED THE FRAGMENT WITH EVERY SAFE CHEMICAL COMBINATION I CAN THINK OF THAT MIGHT BE HELPFUL, BUT...NO LUCK! ITS RADIATIONS ARE STILL HARMFUL TO ME!
RULES
AND SO...
TOO BAD THE EXPERIMENT FAILED! I'LL GET RID OF THE KRYPTONITE BY SUPER-TOSSING IT INTO THE WOODS, WHILE NO ONE IS LOOKING!
2
LATER, AS LINDA COMPLETES AN ERRAND IN MIDVALE...
THAT POOR CAT IS BEING ATTACKED BY A VICIOUS DOG!

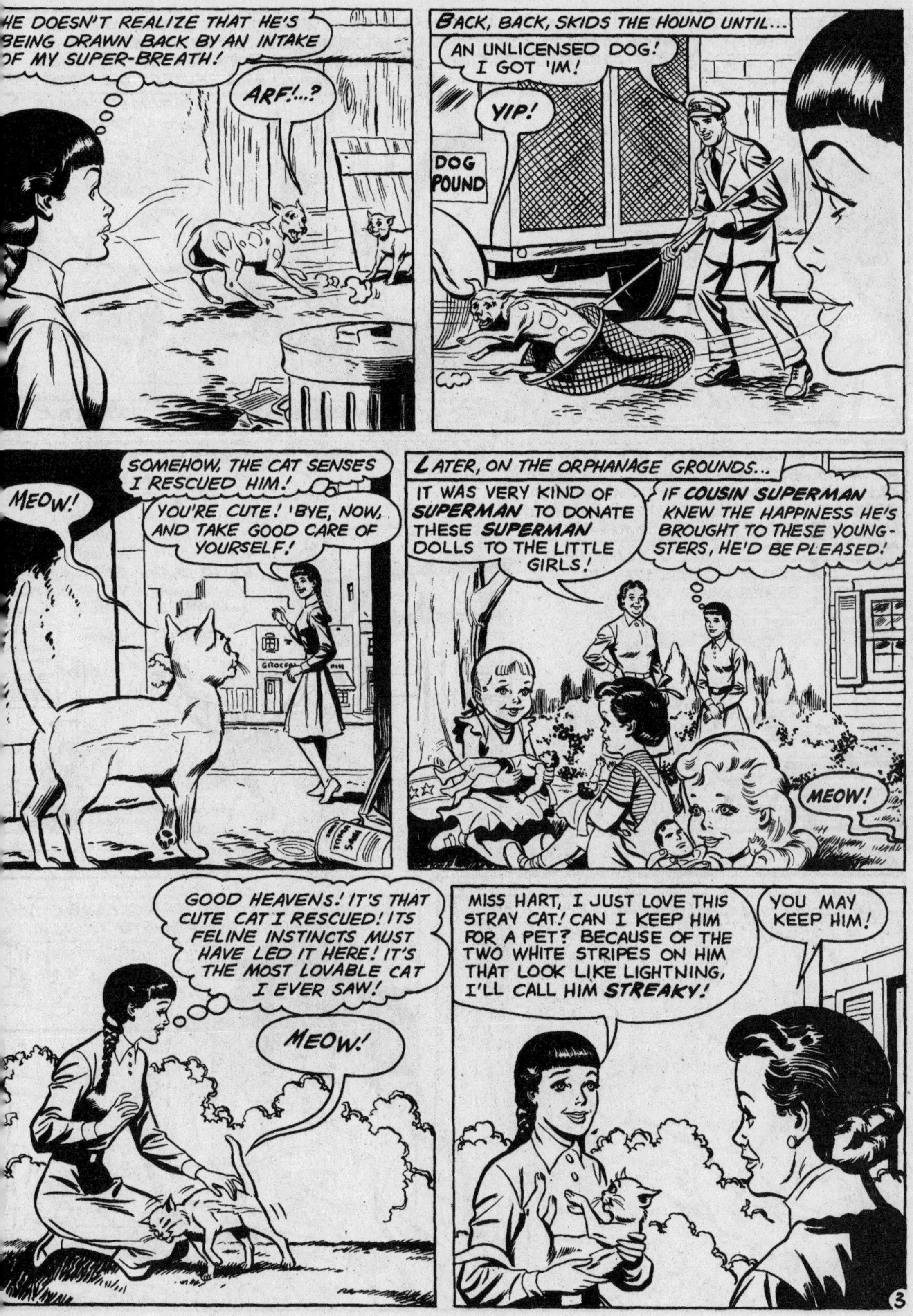
HE DOESN'T REALIZE THAT HE'S BEING DRAWN BACK BY AN INTAKE OF MY SUPER-BREATH!
ARF!..?
BACK, BACK, SKIDS THE HOUND UNTIL...
AN UNLICENSED DOG! I GOT 'IM!
YIP!
DOG POUND
SOMEHOW, THE CAT SENSES I RESCUED HIM!
MEOW!
YOU'RE CUTE! 'BYE, NOW, AND TAKE GOOD CARE OF YOURSELF!
LATER, ON THE ORPHANAGE GROUNDS...
IT WAS VERY KIND OF SUPERMAN TO DONATE THESE SUPERMAN DOLLS TO THE LITTLE GIRLS!
IF COUSIN SUPERMAN KNEW THE HAPPINESS HE'S BROUGHT TO THESE YOUNGSTERS, HE'D BE PLEASED!
MEOW!
GOOD HEAVENS! IT'S THAT CUTE CAT I RESCUED! ITS FELINE INSTINCTS MUST HAVE LED IT HERE! IT'S THE MOST LOVABLE CAT I EVER SAW!
MEOW!
MISS HART, I JUST LOVE THIS STRAY CAT! CAN I KEEP HIM FOR A PET? BECAUSE OF THE TWO WHITE STRIPES ON HIM THAT LOOK LIKE LIGHTNING, I'LL CALL HIM STREAKY!
YOU MAY KEEP HIM!
3

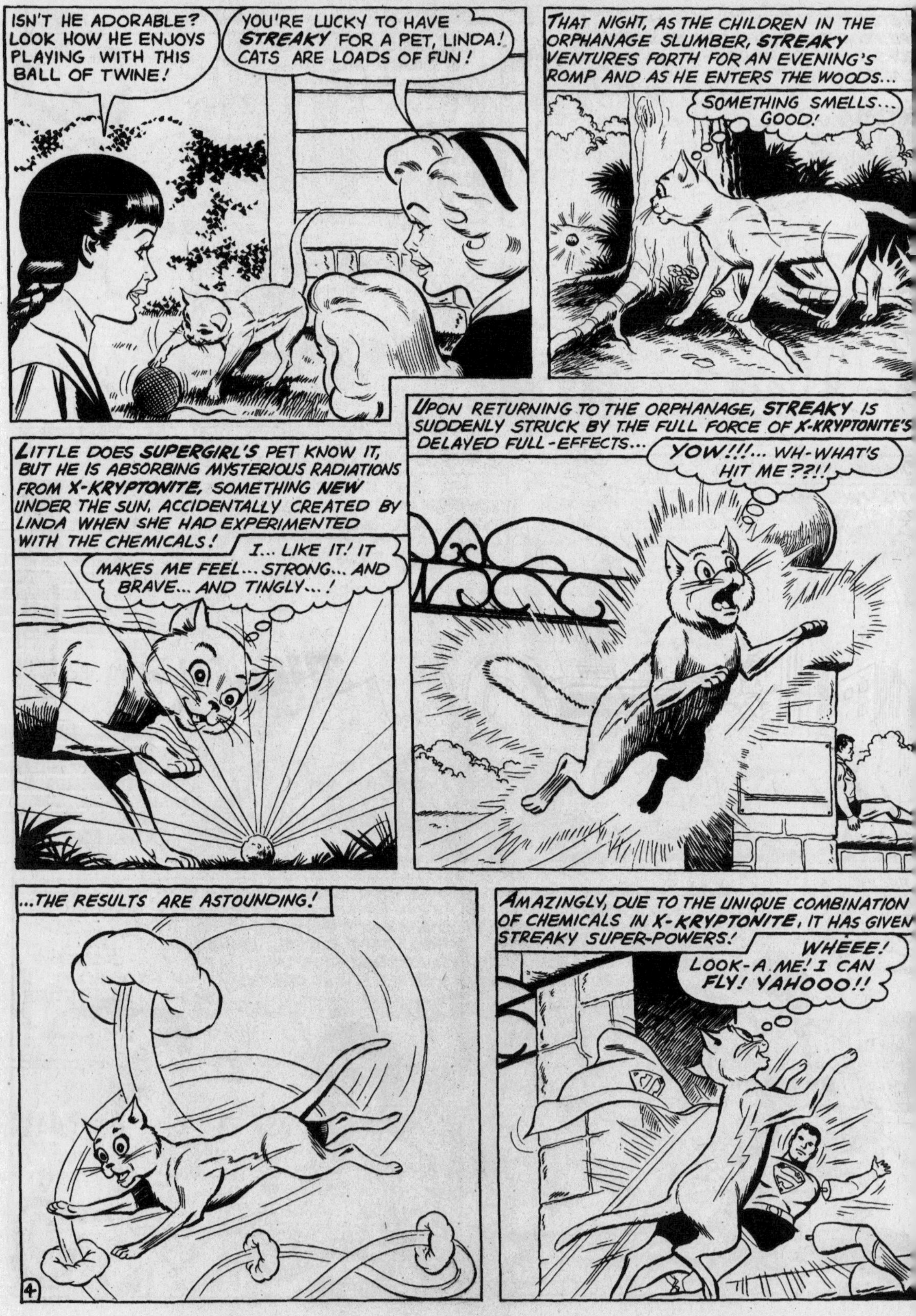
ISN'T HE ADORABLE? LOOK HOW HE ENJOYS PLAYING WITH THIS BALL OF TWINE!
YOU'RE LUCKY TO HAVE STREAKY FOR A PET, LINDA! CATS ARE LOADS OF FUN!
THAT NIGHT, AS THE CHILDREN IN THE ORPHANAGE SLUMBER, STREAKY VENTURES FORTH FOR AN EVENING'S ROMP AND AS HE ENTERS THE WOODS...
SOMETHING SMELLS... GOOD!
LITTLE DOES SUPERGIRL'S PET KNOW IT, BUT HE IS ABSORBING MYSTERIOUS RADIATIONS FROM X-KRYPTONITE, SOMETHING NEW UNDER THE SUN, ACCIDENTALLY CREATED BY LINDA WHEN SHE HAD EXPERIMENTED WITH THE CHEMICALS!
I... LIKE IT! IT MAKES ME FEEL... STRONG... AND BRAVE... AND TINGLY...!
UPON RETURNING TO THE ORPHANAGE, STREAKY IS SUDDENLY STRUCK BY THE FULL FORCE OF X-KRYPTONITE'S DELAYED FULL-EFFECTS...
YOW!!!... WH-WHAT'S HIT ME??!!
...THE RESULTS ARE ASTOUNDING!
4
AMAZINGLY, DUE TO THE UNIQUE COMBINATION OF CHEMICALS IN X-KRYPTONITE, IT HAS GIVEN STREAKY SUPER-POWERS!
WHEEE! LOOK-A ME! I CAN FLY! YAHOOO!!

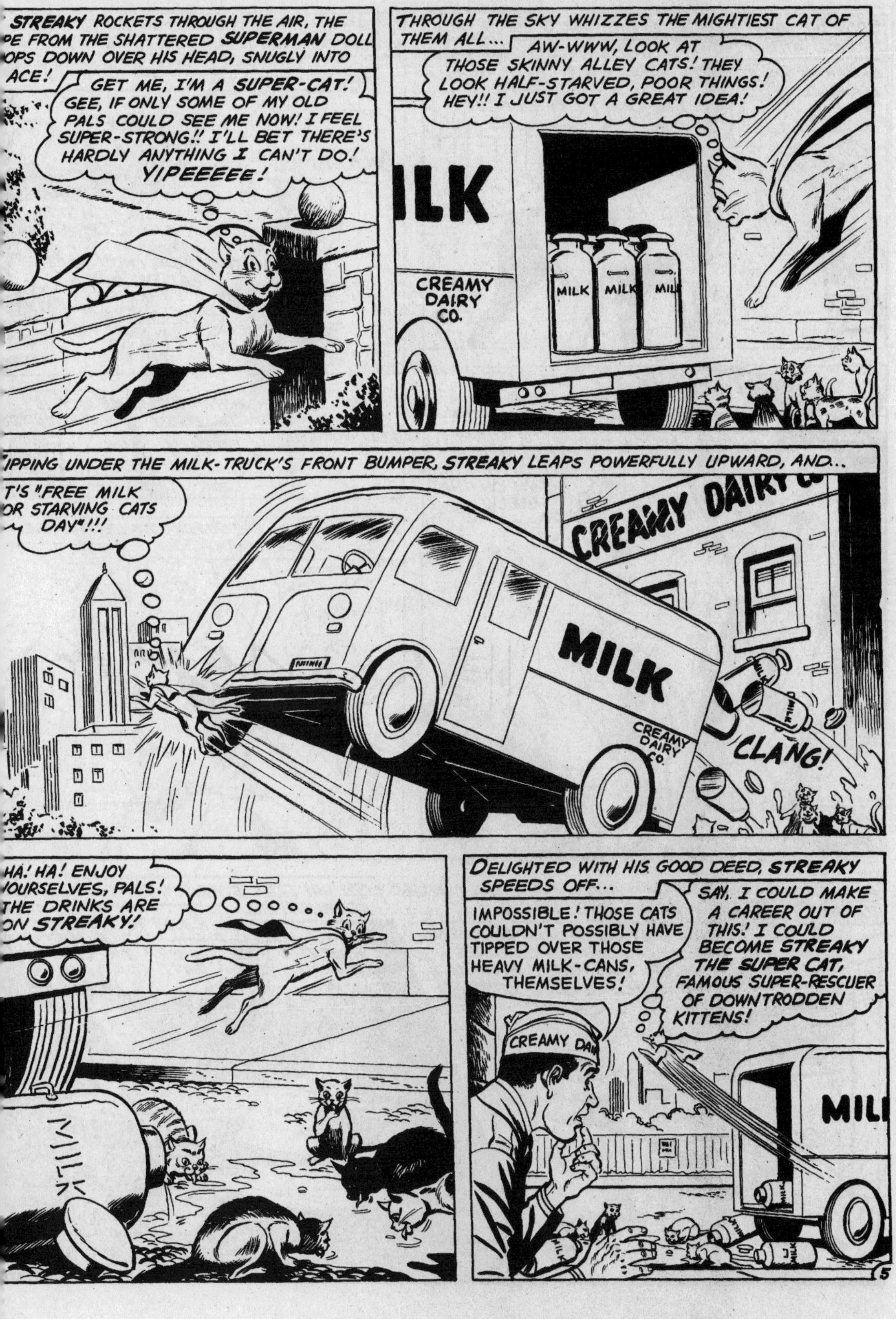
STREAKY ROCKETS THROUGH THE AIR, THE PE FROM THE SHATTERED SUPERMAN DOLL OPS DOWN OVER HIS HEAD, SNUGLY INTO ACE!
GET ME, I'M A SUPER-CAT! GEE, IF ONLY SOME OF MY OLD PALS COULD SEE ME NOW! I FEEL SUPER-STRONG!! I'LL BET THERE'S HARDLY ANYTHING I CAN'T DO! YIPEEEEE!
THROUGH THE SKY WHIZZES THE MIGHTIEST CAT OF THEM ALL...
AW-WWW, LOOK AT THOSE SKINNY ALLEY CATS! THEY LOOK HALF-STARVED, POOR THINGS! HEY!! I JUST GOT A GREAT IDEA!
MILK
CREAMY DAIRY CO.
MILK MILK
IPPING UNDER THE MILK-TRUCK'S FRONT BUMPER, STREAKY LEAPS POWERFULLY UPWARD, AND...
T'S "FREE MILK OR STARVING CATS DAY"!!!
CREAMY DAIRY CO
MILK
CREAMY DAIRY CO.
CLANG!
HA! HA! ENJOY YOURSELVES, PALS! THE DRINKS ARE ON STREAKY!
MILK
DELIGHTED WITH HIS GOOD DEED, STREAKY SPEEDS OFF...
IMPOSSIBLE! THOSE CATS COULDN'T POSSIBLY HAVE TIPPED OVER THOSE HEAVY MILK-CANS, THEMSELVES!
SAY, I COULD MAKE A CAREER OUT OF THIS! I COULD BECOME STREAKY THE SUPER CAT, FAMOUS SUPER-RESCUER OF DOWNTRODDEN KITTENS!
CREAMY DAI
MILI
5

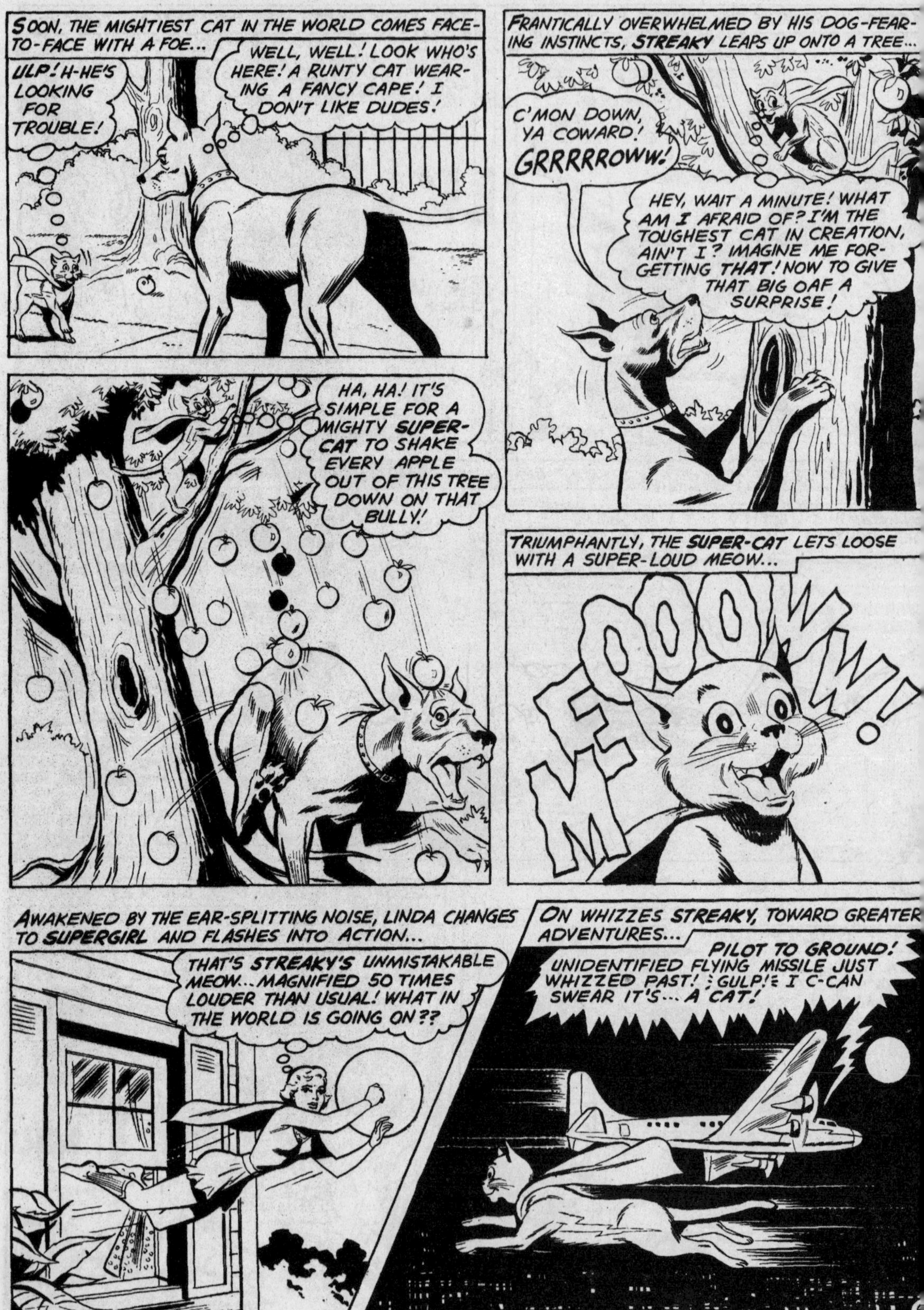
SOON, THE MIGHTIEST CAT IN THE WORLD COMES FACE-TO-FACE WITH A FOE...
ULP! H-HE'S LOOKING FOR TROUBLE!
WELL, WELL! LOOK WHO'S HERE! A RUNTY CAT WEARING A FANCY CAPE! I DON'T LIKE DUDES!
FRANTICALLY OVERWHELMED BY HIS DOG-FEARING INSTINCTS, STREAKY LEAPS UP ONTO A TREE...
C'MON DOWN, YA COWARD! GRRRRROWW!
HEY, WAIT A MINUTE! WHAT AM I AFRAID OF? I'M THE TOUGHEST CAT IN CREATION, AIN'T I? IMAGINE ME FORGETTING THAT! NOW TO GIVE THAT BIG OAF A SURPRISE!
HA, HA! IT'S SIMPLE FOR A MIGHTY SUPER-CAT TO SHAKE EVERY APPLE OUT OF THIS TREE DOWN ON THAT BULLY!
TRIUMPHANTLY, THE SUPER-CAT LETS LOOSE WITH A SUPER-LOUD MEOW...
MEOOOWW!
AWAKENED BY THE EAR-SPLITTING NOISE, LINDA CHANGES TO SUPERGIRL AND FLASHES INTO ACTION...
THAT'S STREAKY'S UNMISTAKABLE MEOW... MAGNIFIED 50 TIMES LOUDER THAN USUAL! WHAT IN THE WORLD IS GOING ON??
ON WHIZZES STREAKY, TOWARD GREATER ADVENTURES...
PILOT TO GROUND! UNIDENTIFIED FLYING MISSILE JUST WHIZZED PAST! GULP! I C-CAN SWEAR IT'S... A CAT!

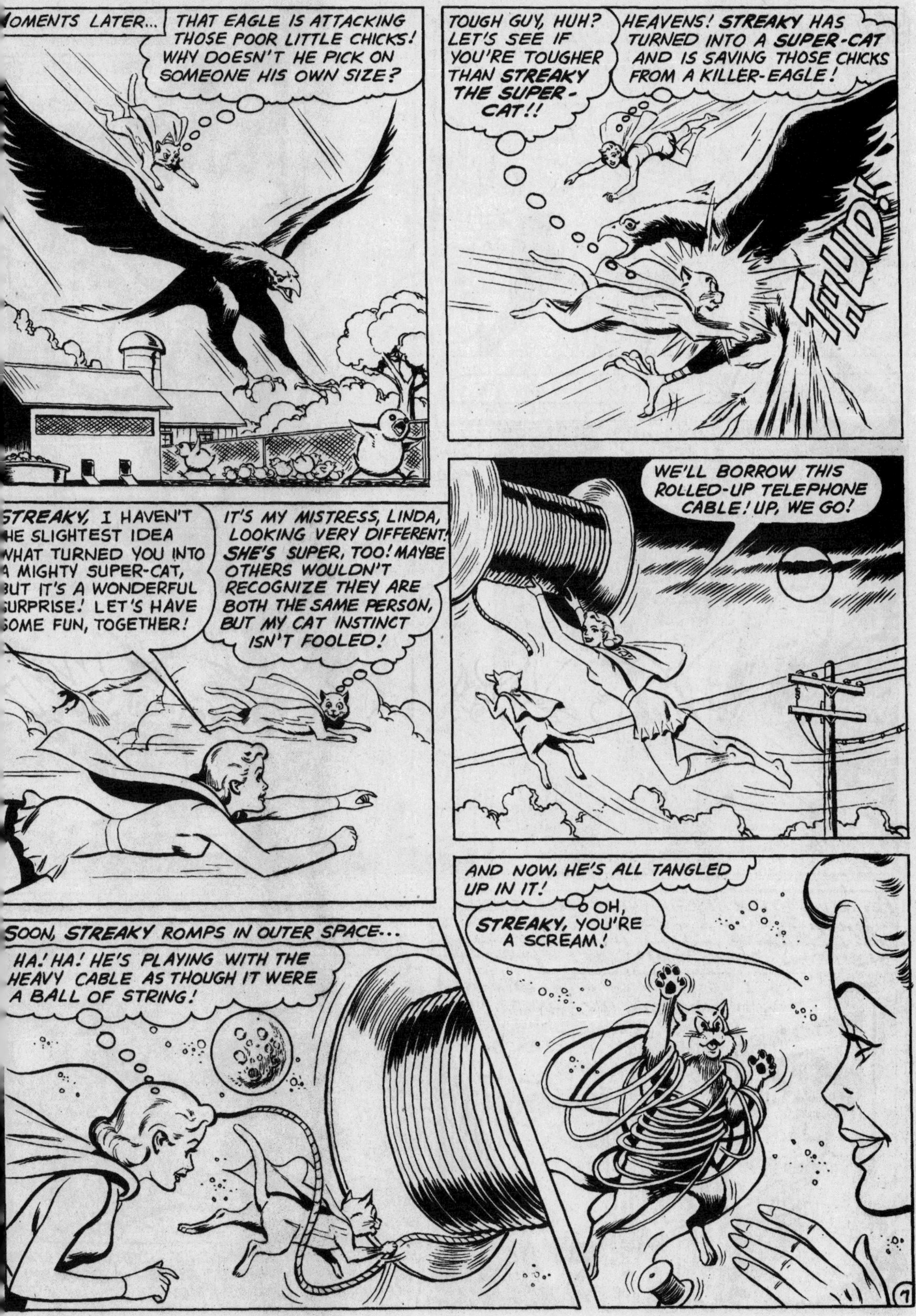
OMENTS LATER...
THAT EAGLE IS ATTACKING THOSE POOR LITTLE CHICKS! WHY DOESN'T HE PICK ON SOMEONE HIS OWN SIZE?
TOUGH GUY, HUH? LET'S SEE IF YOU'RE TOUGHER THAN STREAKY THE SUPER-CAT!!
HEAVENS! STREAKY HAS TURNED INTO A SUPER-CAT AND IS SAVING THOSE CHICKS FROM A KILLER-EAGLE!
THUD!
STREAKY, I HAVEN'T HE SLIGHTEST IDEA WHAT TURNED YOU INTO A MIGHTY SUPER-CAT, BUT IT'S A WONDERFUL SURPRISE! LET'S HAVE SOME FUN, TOGETHER!
IT'S MY MISTRESS, LINDA, LOOKING VERY DIFFERENT! SHE'S SUPER, TOO! MAYBE OTHERS WOULDN'T RECOGNIZE THEY ARE BOTH THE SAME PERSON, BUT MY CAT INSTINCT ISN'T FOOLED!
WE'LL BORROW THIS ROLLED-UP TELEPHONE CABLE! UP, WE GO!
SOON, STREAKY ROMPS IN OUTER SPACE...
HA! HA! HE'S PLAYING WITH THE HEAVY CABLE AS THOUGH IT WERE A BALL OF STRING!
AND NOW, HE'S ALL TANGLED UP IN IT!
OH, STREAKY, YOU'RE A SCREAM!
7

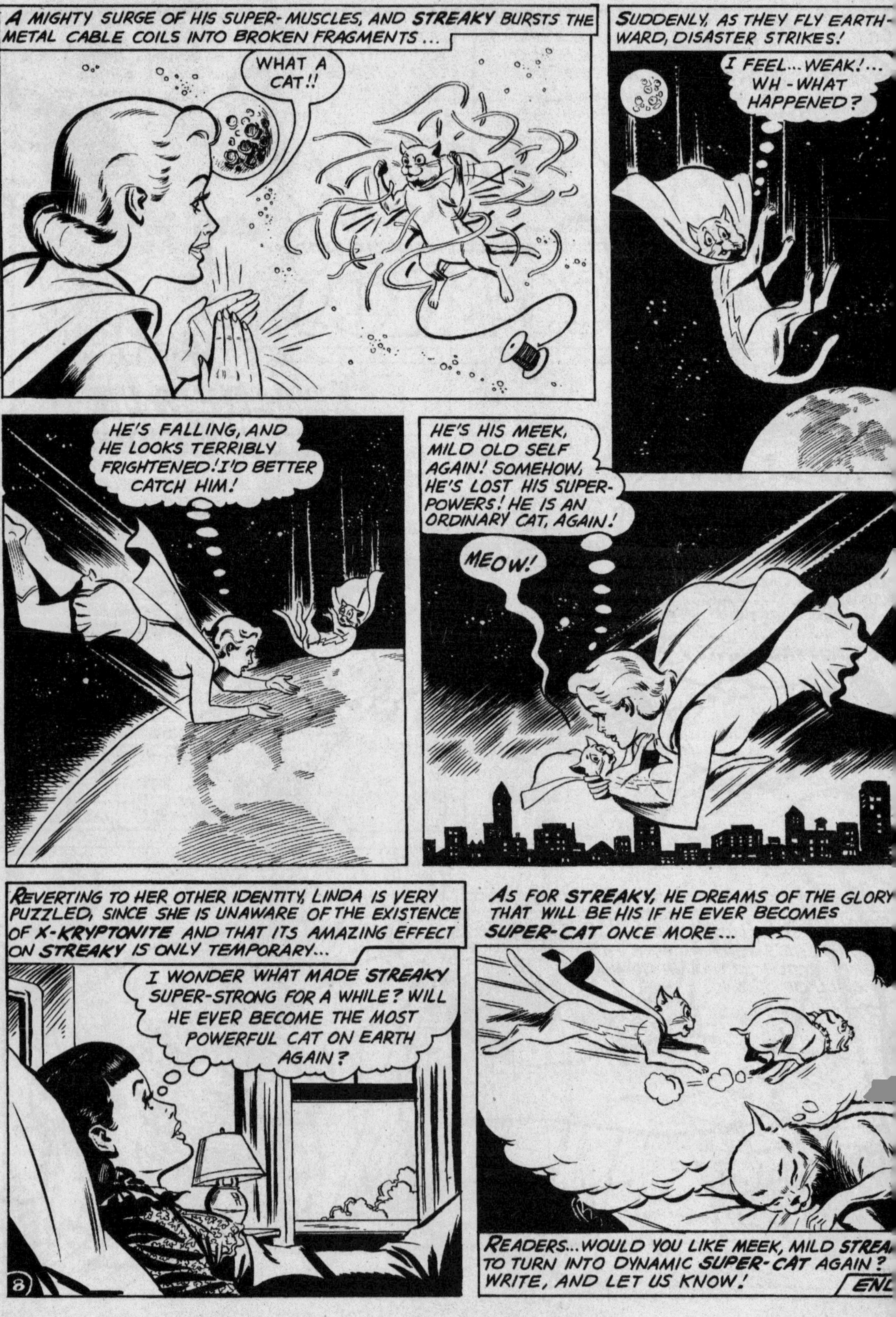
A MIGHTY SURGE OF HIS SUPER-MUSCLES, AND STREAKY BURSTS THE METAL CABLE COILS INTO BROKEN FRAGMENTS...
WHAT A CAT!!
SUDDENLY, AS THEY FLY EARTHWARD, DISASTER STRIKES!
I FEEL...WEAK!... WH-WHAT HAPPENED?
HE'S FALLING, AND HE LOOKS TERRIBLY FRIGHTENED! I'D BETTER CATCH HIM!
HE'S HIS MEEK, MILD OLD SELF AGAIN! SOMEHOW, HE'S LOST HIS SUPER-POWERS! HE IS AN ORDINARY CAT, AGAIN!
MEOW!
REVERTING TO HER OTHER IDENTITY, LINDA IS VERY PUZZLED, SINCE SHE IS UNAWARE OF THE EXISTENCE OF X-KRYPTONITE AND THAT ITS AMAZING EFFECT ON STREAKY IS ONLY TEMPORARY...
I WONDER WHAT MADE STREAKY SUPER-STRONG FOR A WHILE? WILL HE EVER BECOME THE MOST POWERFUL CAT ON EARTH AGAIN?
8
AS FOR STREAKY, HE DREAMS OF THE GLORY THAT WILL BE HIS IF HE EVER BECOMES SUPER-CAT ONCE MORE...
READERS...WOULD YOU LIKE MEEK, MILD STREA
TO TURN INTO DYNAMIC SUPER-CAT AGAIN? WRITE, AND LET US KNOW!

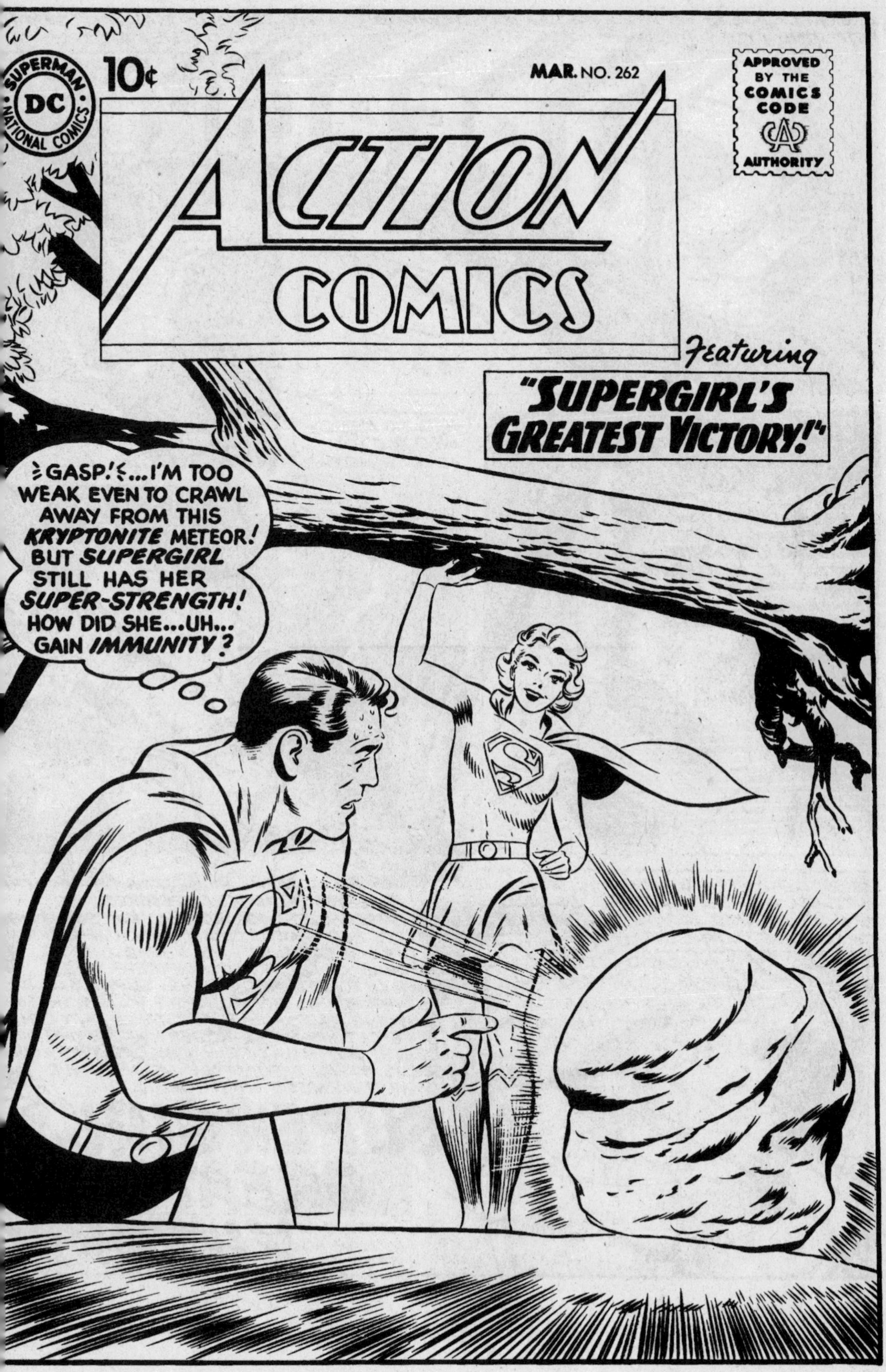
SUPERMAN DC NATIONAL COMICS
10¢
MAR. NO. 262
APPROVED BY THE COMICS CODE AUTHORITY
ACTION COMICS
Featuring
"SUPERGIRL'S GREATEST VICTORY!"
GASP! ...I'M TOO WEAK EVEN TO CRAWL AWAY FROM THIS KRYPTONITE METEOR! BUT SUPERGIRL STILL HAS HER SUPER-STRENGTH! HOW DID SHE...UH... GAIN IMMUNITY?

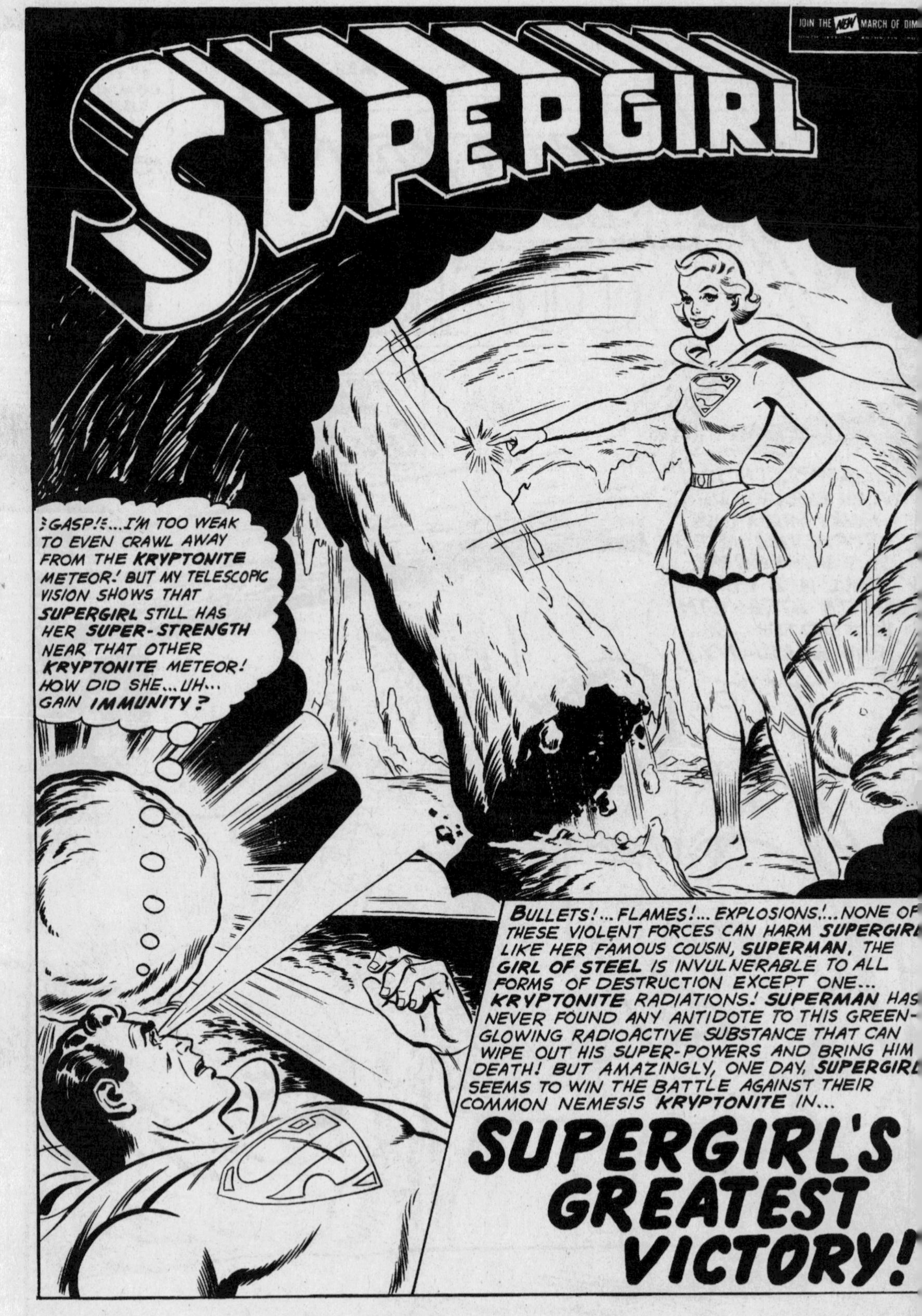
JOIN THE NEW MARCH OF DIM
SUPERGIRL
;GASP!;...I'M TOO WEAK TO EVEN CRAWL AWAY FROM THE KRYPTONITE METEOR! BUT MY TELESCOPIC VISION SHOWS THAT SUPERGIRL STILL HAS HER SUPER-STRENGTH NEAR THAT OTHER KRYPTONITE METEOR! HOW DID SHE...UH... GAIN IMMUNITY?
BULLETS!...FLAMES!...EXPLOSIONS!...NONE OF THESE VIOLENT FORCES CAN HARM SUPERGIRL! LIKE HER FAMOUS COUSIN, SUPERMAN, THE GIRL OF STEEL IS INVULNERABLE TO ALL FORMS OF DESTRUCTION EXCEPT ONE... KRYPTONITE RADIATIONS! SUPERMAN HAS NEVER FOUND ANY ANTIDOTE TO THIS GREEN-GLOWING RADIOACTIVE SUBSTANCE THAT CAN WIPE OUT HIS SUPER-POWERS AND BRING HIM DEATH! BUT AMAZINGLY, ONE DAY, SUPERGIRL SEEMS TO WIN THE BATTLE AGAINST THEIR COMMON NEMESIS KRYPTONITE IN...
SUPERGIRL'S GREATEST VICTORY!

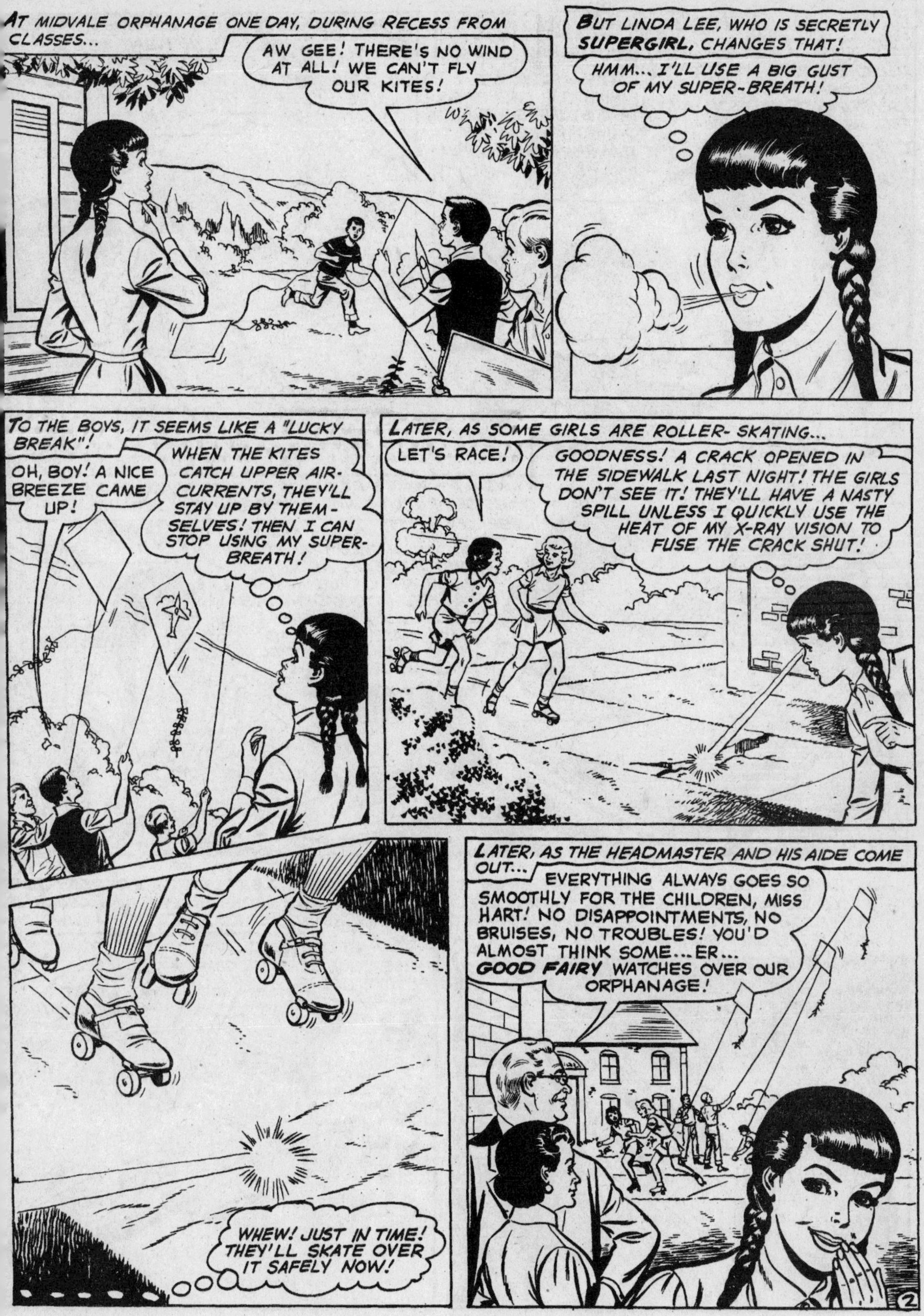
AT MIDVALE ORPHANAGE ONE DAY, DURING RECESS FROM CLASSES...
AW GEE! THERE'S NO WIND AT ALL! WE CAN'T FLY OUR KITES!
BUT LINDA LEE, WHO IS SECRETLY SUPERGIRL, CHANGES THAT!
HMM... I'LL USE A BIG GUST OF MY SUPER-BREATH!
TO THE BOYS, IT SEEMS LIKE A "LUCKY BREAK"!
OH, BOY! A NICE BREEZE CAME UP!
WHEN THE KITES CATCH UPPER AIR-CURRENTS, THEY'LL STAY UP BY THEMSELVES! THEN I CAN STOP USING MY SUPER-BREATH!
LATER, AS SOME GIRLS ARE ROLLER-SKATING...
LET'S RACE!
GOODNESS! A CRACK OPENED IN THE SIDEWALK LAST NIGHT! THE GIRLS DON'T SEE IT! THEY'LL HAVE A NASTY SPILL UNLESS I QUICKLY USE THE HEAT OF MY X-RAY VISION TO FUSE THE CRACK SHUT!
WHEW! JUST IN TIME! THEY'LL SKATE OVER IT SAFELY NOW!
LATER, AS THE HEADMASTER AND HIS AIDE COME OUT...
EVERYTHING ALWAYS GOES SO SMOOTHLY FOR THE CHILDREN, MISS HART! NO DISAPPOINTMENTS, NO BRUISES, NO TROUBLES! YOU'D ALMOST THINK SOME... ER... GOOD FAIRY WATCHES OVER OUR ORPHANAGE!
2

SUDDENLY, AS LINDA'S SUPER-HEARING PICKS UP A LOUD DISTANT SOUND...

I'LL CHECK WITH MY TELESCOPIC VISION...HMM! A *KRYPTONITE* METEOR JUST FELL NEAR THOSE FOREST RANGERS!

WE'LL GET RID OF IT LATER AFTER WE FINISH OUR FIRE PATROL! THAT STUFF IS HARMLESS TO EARTH-PEOPLE BUT IS *DANGEROUS* TO *SUPERMAN*! WE'LL SEND A WARNING TO HIM!

THUD!

LATER... *SUPERMAN* GOT THE WARNING! TO BE SAFE, HE WENT TO HIS *FORTRESS OF SOLITUDE* IN THE ARCTIC! *KRYPTONITE* IS THE ONLY SUBSTANCE IN THE UNIVERSE THAT CAN HARM HIM... OR *ME!*

THAT NIGHT, AS LINDA KEEPS UP HER DIARY...

Thus far all attempts by SUPERMAN and me to find a KRYPTONITE ANTIDOTE have failed! But I must try again or SUPERMAN and I will NEVER be safe!

AS LINDA RE-READS PREVIOUS ENTRIES IN HER DIARY, LITTLE DOES SHE REALIZE HOW *KRYPTONITE* IS SOON TO AFFECT HER LIFE...

AN ATOMIC CHAIN-REACTION BLEW UP THE PLANET *KRYPTON* YEARS AGO! THE FRAGMENTS OF THE PLANET CHANGED INTO RADIOACTIVE GREEN *KRYPTONITE!* I HAVE IT ALL RECORDED HERE IN MY DIARY... I'LL REVIEW IT...

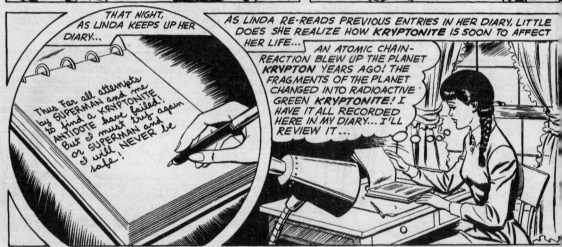

"AFTER I ARRIVED ON EARTH, *SUPERMAN* TOLD ME HOW HE HAD ESCAPED FROM DOOMED *KRYPTON* IN A ROCKET, AS A BABY! HE SEEMED TO BE THE ONLY SURVIVOR..."

"BUT, AS I FOUND OUT LATER, A *KRYPTON-QUAKE* HAD PREVIOUSLY LOOSENED ONE HUGE CHUNK! IT WAS HURLED INTO SPACE INTACT...WITH A *TOWN* ON IT..."

BY COSMIC LUCK, A HUGE BUBBLE OF AIR CAME WITH US!

WE...WE'RE SAVED!

3

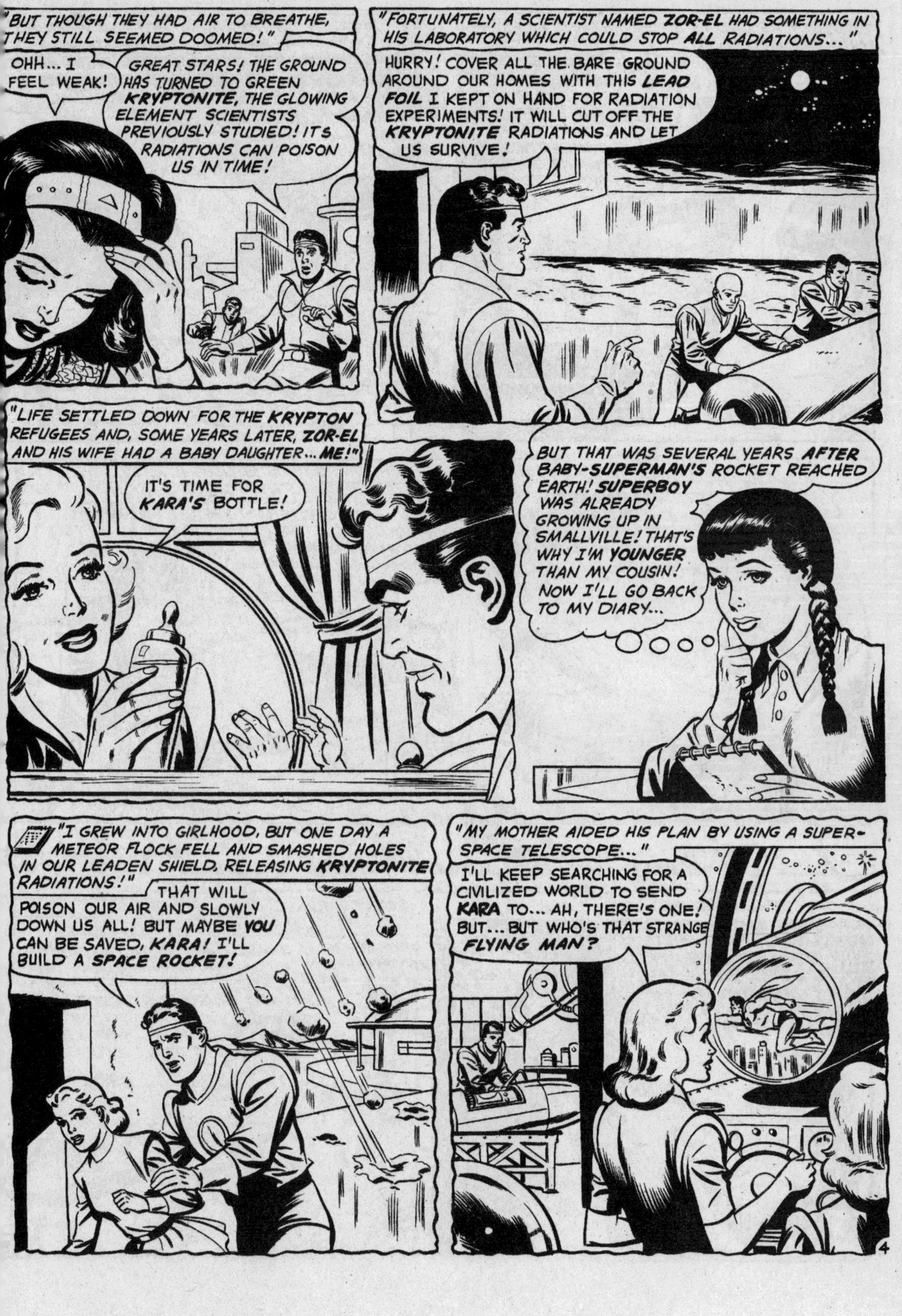
"BUT THOUGH THEY HAD AIR TO BREATHE, THEY STILL SEEMED DOOMED!"
OHH... I FEEL WEAK!
GREAT STARS! THE GROUND HAS TURNED TO GREEN KRYPTONITE, THE GLOWING ELEMENT SCIENTISTS PREVIOUSLY STUDIED! IT'S RADIATIONS CAN POISON US IN TIME!
"FORTUNATELY, A SCIENTIST NAMED ZOR-EL HAD SOMETHING IN HIS LABORATORY WHICH COULD STOP ALL RADIATIONS..."
HURRY! COVER ALL THE BARE GROUND AROUND OUR HOMES WITH THIS LEAD FOIL I KEPT ON HAND FOR RADIATION EXPERIMENTS! IT WILL CUT OFF THE KRYPTONITE RADIATIONS AND LET US SURVIVE!
"LIFE SETTLED DOWN FOR THE KRYPTON REFUGEES AND, SOME YEARS LATER, ZOR-EL AND HIS WIFE HAD A BABY DAUGHTER... ME!"
IT'S TIME FOR KARA'S BOTTLE!
BUT THAT WAS SEVERAL YEARS AFTER BABY-SUPERMAN'S ROCKET REACHED EARTH! SUPERBOY WAS ALREADY GROWING UP IN SMALLVILLE! THAT'S WHY I'M YOUNGER THAN MY COUSIN! NOW I'LL GO BACK TO MY DIARY...
"I GREW INTO GIRLHOOD, BUT ONE DAY A METEOR FLOCK FELL AND SMASHED HOLES IN OUR LEADEN SHIELD, RELEASING KRYPTONITE RADIATIONS!"
THAT WILL POISON OUR AIR AND SLOWLY DOWN US ALL! BUT MAYBE YOU CAN BE SAVED, KARA! I'LL BUILD A SPACE ROCKET!
"MY MOTHER AIDED HIS PLAN BY USING A SUPER-SPACE TELESCOPE..."
I'LL KEEP SEARCHING FOR A CIVILIZED WORLD TO SEND KARA TO... AH, THERE'S ONE! BUT... BUT WHO'S THAT STRANGE FLYING MAN?
4

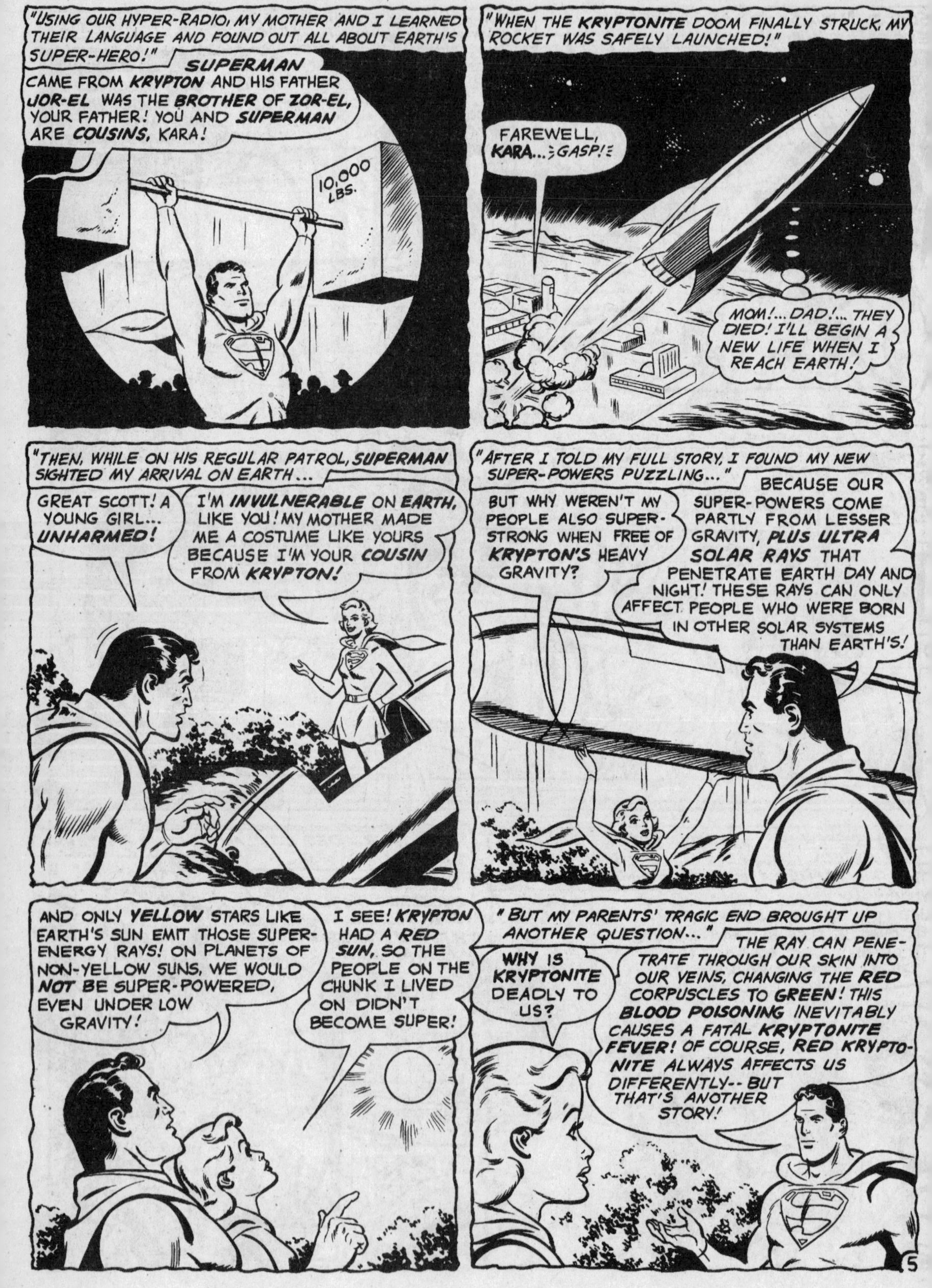
"USING OUR HYPER-RADIO, MY MOTHER AND I LEARNED THEIR LANGUAGE AND FOUND OUT ALL ABOUT EARTH'S SUPER-HERO!"
SUPERMAN CAME FROM KRYPTON AND HIS FATHER JOR-EL WAS THE BROTHER OF ZOR-EL, YOUR FATHER! YOU AND SUPERMAN ARE COUSINS, KARA!
10,000 LBS.
"WHEN THE KRYPTONITE DOOM FINALLY STRUCK, MY ROCKET WAS SAFELY LAUNCHED!"
FAREWELL, KARA... GASP!
MOM!... DAD!... THEY DIED! I'LL BEGIN A NEW LIFE WHEN I REACH EARTH!
"THEN, WHILE ON HIS REGULAR PATROL, SUPERMAN SIGHTED MY ARRIVAL ON EARTH...
GREAT SCOTT! A YOUNG GIRL... UNHARMED!
I'M INVULNERABLE ON EARTH, LIKE YOU! MY MOTHER MADE ME A COSTUME LIKE YOURS BECAUSE I'M YOUR COUSIN FROM KRYPTON!
"AFTER I TOLD MY FULL STORY, I FOUND MY NEW SUPER-POWERS PUZZLING..."
BUT WHY WEREN'T MY PEOPLE ALSO SUPER-STRONG WHEN FREE OF KRYPTON'S HEAVY GRAVITY?
BECAUSE OUR SUPER-POWERS COME PARTLY FROM LESSER GRAVITY, PLUS ULTRA SOLAR RAYS THAT PENETRATE EARTH DAY AND NIGHT! THESE RAYS CAN ONLY AFFECT PEOPLE WHO WERE BORN IN OTHER SOLAR SYSTEMS THAN EARTH'S!
AND ONLY YELLOW STARS LIKE EARTH'S SUN EMIT THOSE SUPER-ENERGY RAYS! ON PLANETS OF NON-YELLOW SUNS, WE WOULD NOT BE SUPER-POWERED, EVEN UNDER LOW GRAVITY!
I SEE! KRYPTON HAD A RED SUN, SO THE PEOPLE ON THE CHUNK I LIVED ON DIDN'T BECOME SUPER!
"BUT MY PARENTS' TRAGIC END BROUGHT UP ANOTHER QUESTION..."
WHY IS KRYPTONITE DEADLY TO US?
THE RAY CAN PENETRATE THROUGH OUR SKIN INTO OUR VEINS, CHANGING THE RED CORPUSCLES TO GREEN! THIS BLOOD POISONING INEVITABLY CAUSES A FATAL KRYPTONITE FEVER! OF COURSE, RED KRYPTONITE ALWAYS AFFECTS US DIFFERENTLY-- BUT THAT'S ANOTHER STORY!
5

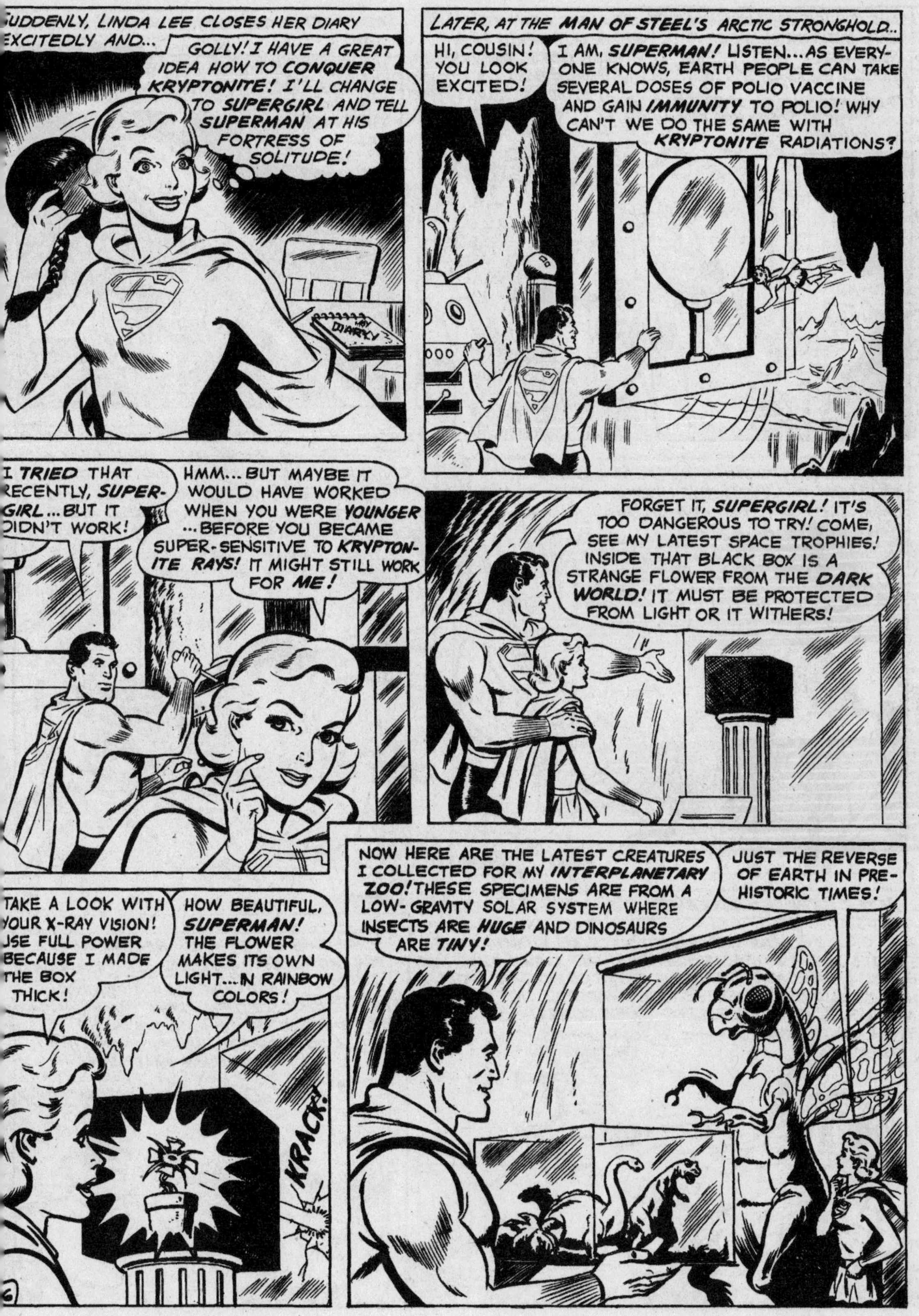
UDDENLY, LINDA LEE CLOSES HER DIARY EXCITEDLY AND...
GOLLY! I HAVE A GREAT IDEA HOW TO CONQUER KRYPTONITE! I'LL CHANGE TO SUPERGIRL AND TELL SUPERMAN AT HIS FORTRESS OF SOLITUDE!
DIARY
LATER, AT THE MAN OF STEEL'S ARCTIC STRONGHOLD...
HI, COUSIN! YOU LOOK EXCITED!
I AM, SUPERMAN! LISTEN...AS EVERYONE KNOWS, EARTH PEOPLE CAN TAKE SEVERAL DOSES OF POLIO VACCINE AND GAIN IMMUNITY TO POLIO! WHY CAN'T WE DO THE SAME WITH KRYPTONITE RADIATIONS?
I TRIED THAT RECENTLY, SUPER-GIRL...BUT IT DIDN'T WORK!
HMM...BUT MAYBE IT WOULD HAVE WORKED WHEN YOU WERE YOUNGER ...BEFORE YOU BECAME SUPER-SENSITIVE TO KRYPTONITE RAYS! IT MIGHT STILL WORK FOR ME!
FORGET IT, SUPERGIRL! IT'S TOO DANGEROUS TO TRY! COME, SEE MY LATEST SPACE TROPHIES! INSIDE THAT BLACK BOX IS A STRANGE FLOWER FROM THE DARK WORLD! IT MUST BE PROTECTED FROM LIGHT OR IT WITHERS!
TAKE A LOOK WITH YOUR X-RAY VISION! USE FULL POWER BECAUSE I MADE THE BOX THICK!
HOW BEAUTIFUL, SUPERMAN! THE FLOWER MAKES ITS OWN LIGHT....IN RAINBOW COLORS!
KRACK!
NOW HERE ARE THE LATEST CREATURES I COLLECTED FOR MY INTERPLANETARY ZOO! THESE SPECIMENS ARE FROM A LOW-GRAVITY SOLAR SYSTEM WHERE INSECTS ARE HUGE AND DINOSAURS ARE TINY!
JUST THE REVERSE OF EARTH IN PREHISTORIC TIMES!

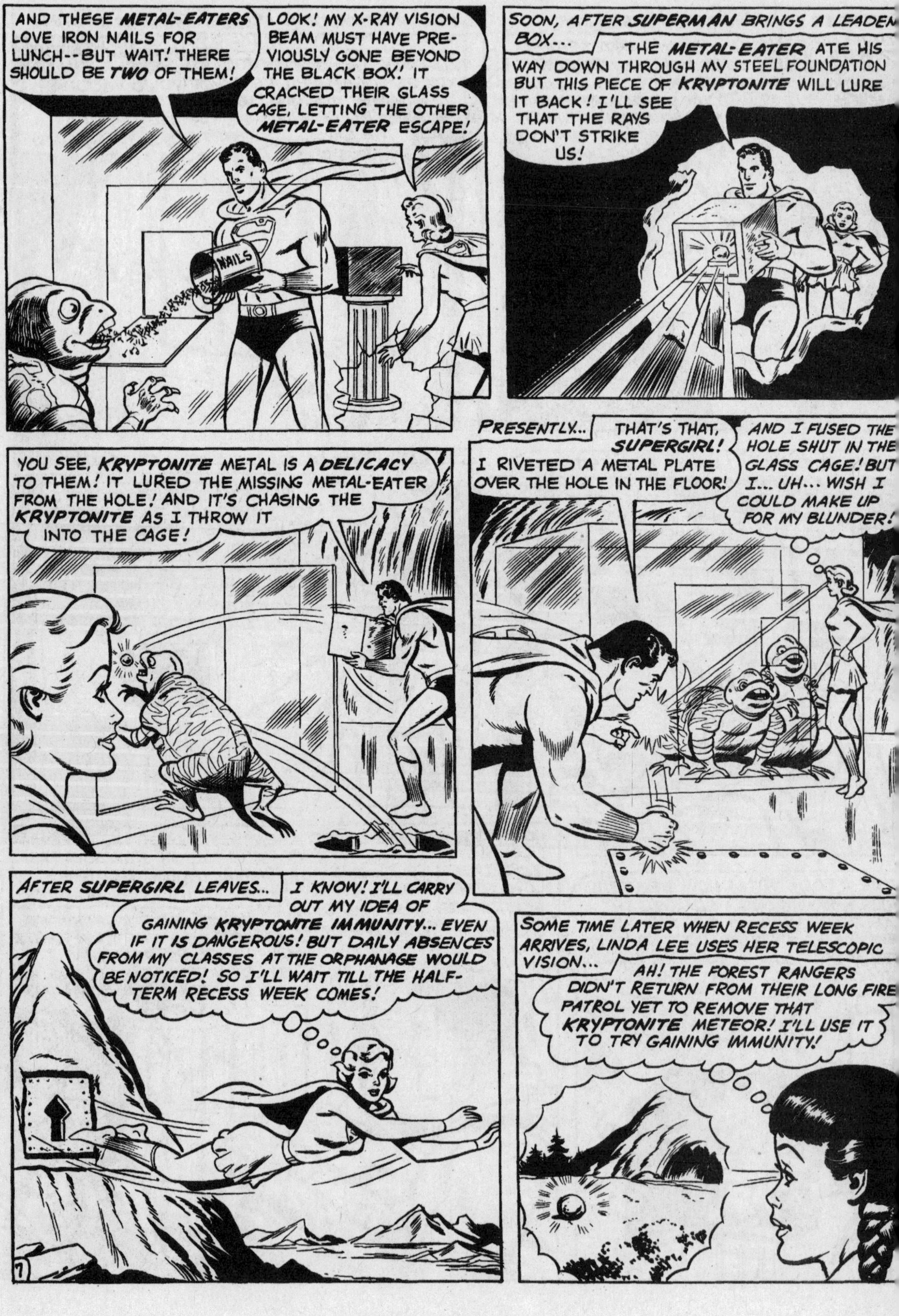
AND THESE METAL-EATERS LOVE IRON NAILS FOR LUNCH--BUT WAIT! THERE SHOULD BE TWO OF THEM!
LOOK! MY X-RAY VISION BEAM MUST HAVE PREVIOUSLY GONE BEYOND THE BLACK BOX! IT CRACKED THEIR GLASS CAGE, LETTING THE OTHER METAL-EATER ESCAPE!
NAILS
SOON, AFTER SUPERMAN BRINGS A LEADEN BOX...
THE METAL-EATER ATE HIS WAY DOWN THROUGH MY STEEL FOUNDATION BUT THIS PIECE OF KRYPTONITE WILL LURE IT BACK! I'LL SEE THAT THE RAYS DON'T STRIKE US!
YOU SEE, KRYPTONITE METAL IS A DELICACY TO THEM! IT LURED THE MISSING METAL-EATER FROM THE HOLE! AND IT'S CHASING THE KRYPTONITE AS I THROW IT INTO THE CAGE!
PRESENTLY...
THAT'S THAT, SUPERGIRL! I RIVETED A METAL PLATE OVER THE HOLE IN THE FLOOR!
AND I FUSED THE HOLE SHUT IN THE GLASS CAGE! BUT I... UH... WISH I COULD MAKE UP FOR MY BLUNDER!
AFTER SUPERGIRL LEAVES...
I KNOW! I'LL CARRY OUT MY IDEA OF GAINING KRYPTONITE IMMUNITY... EVEN IF IT IS DANGEROUS! BUT DAILY ABSENCES FROM MY CLASSES AT THE ORPHANAGE WOULD BE NOTICED! SO I'LL WAIT TILL THE HALF-TERM RECESS WEEK COMES!
7
SOME TIME LATER WHEN RECESS WEEK ARRIVES, LINDA LEE USES HER TELESCOPIC VISION...
AH! THE FOREST RANGERS DIDN'T RETURN FROM THEIR LONG FIRE PATROL YET TO REMOVE THAT KRYPTONITE METEOR! I'LL USE IT TO TRY GAINING IMMUNITY!

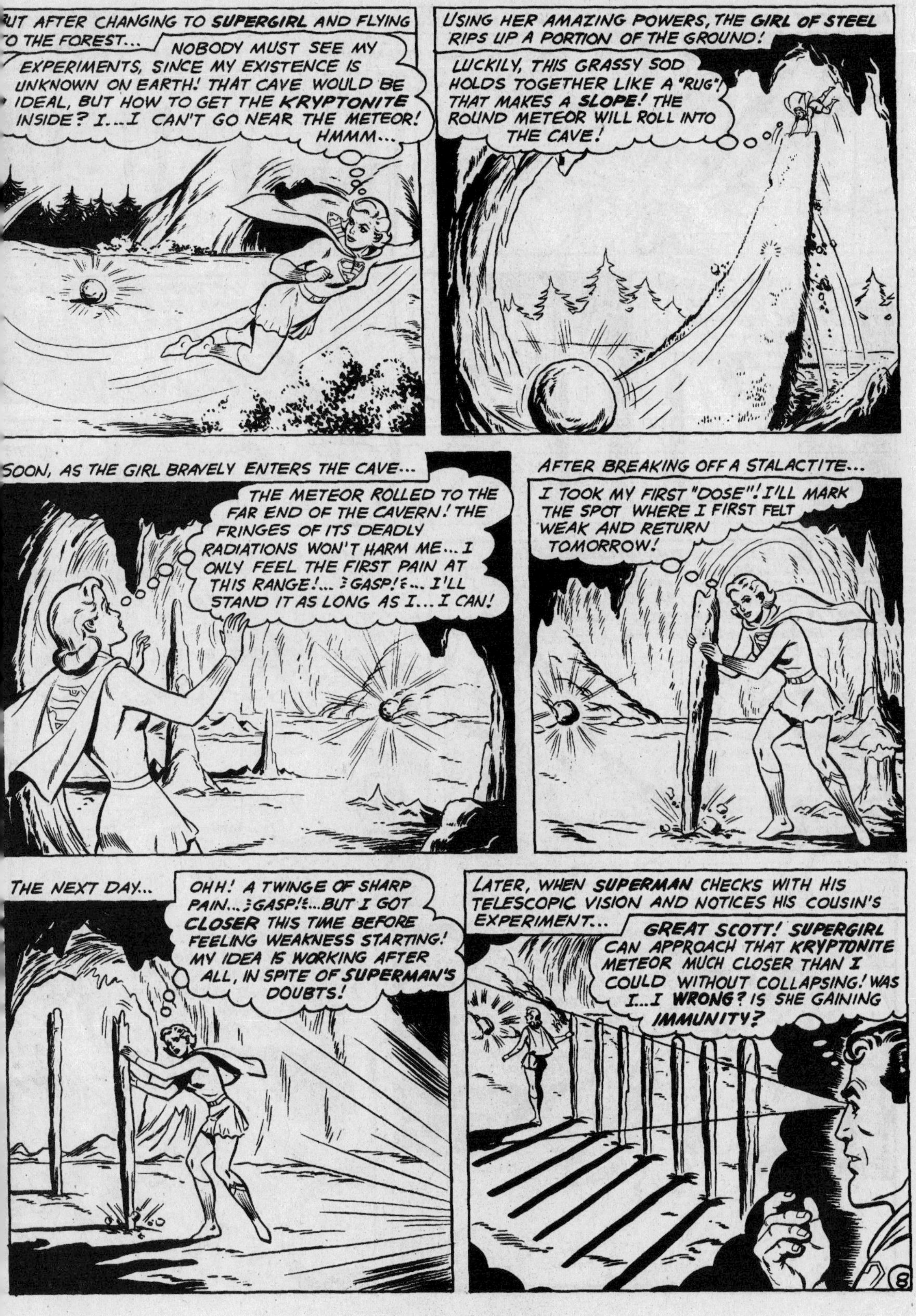
BUT AFTER CHANGING TO SUPERGIRL AND FLYING TO THE FOREST...
NOBODY MUST SEE MY EXPERIMENTS, SINCE MY EXISTENCE IS UNKNOWN ON EARTH! THAT CAVE WOULD BE IDEAL, BUT HOW TO GET THE KRYPTONITE INSIDE? I...I CAN'T GO NEAR THE METEOR! HMMM...
USING HER AMAZING POWERS, THE GIRL OF STEEL RIPS UP A PORTION OF THE GROUND!
LUCKILY, THIS GRASSY SOD HOLDS TOGETHER LIKE A "RUG" THAT MAKES A SLOPE! THE ROUND METEOR WILL ROLL INTO THE CAVE!
SOON, AS THE GIRL BRAVELY ENTERS THE CAVE...
THE METEOR ROLLED TO THE FAR END OF THE CAVERN! THE FRINGES OF ITS DEADLY RADIATIONS WON'T HARM ME... I ONLY FEEL THE FIRST PAIN AT THIS RANGE!... GASP!... I'LL STAND IT AS LONG AS I... I CAN!
AFTER BREAKING OFF A STALACTITE...
I TOOK MY FIRST "DOSE"! I'LL MARK THE SPOT WHERE I FIRST FELT WEAK AND RETURN TOMORROW!
THE NEXT DAY...
OHH! A TWINGE OF SHARP PAIN... GASP!...BUT I GOT CLOSER THIS TIME BEFORE FEELING WEAKNESS STARTING! MY IDEA IS WORKING AFTER ALL, IN SPITE OF SUPERMAN'S DOUBTS!
LATER, WHEN SUPERMAN CHECKS WITH HIS TELESCOPIC VISION AND NOTICES HIS COUSIN'S EXPERIMENT...
GREAT SCOTT! SUPERGIRL CAN APPROACH THAT KRYPTONITE METEOR MUCH CLOSER THAN I COULD WITHOUT COLLAPSING! WAS I...I WRONG? IS SHE GAINING IMMUNITY?
8

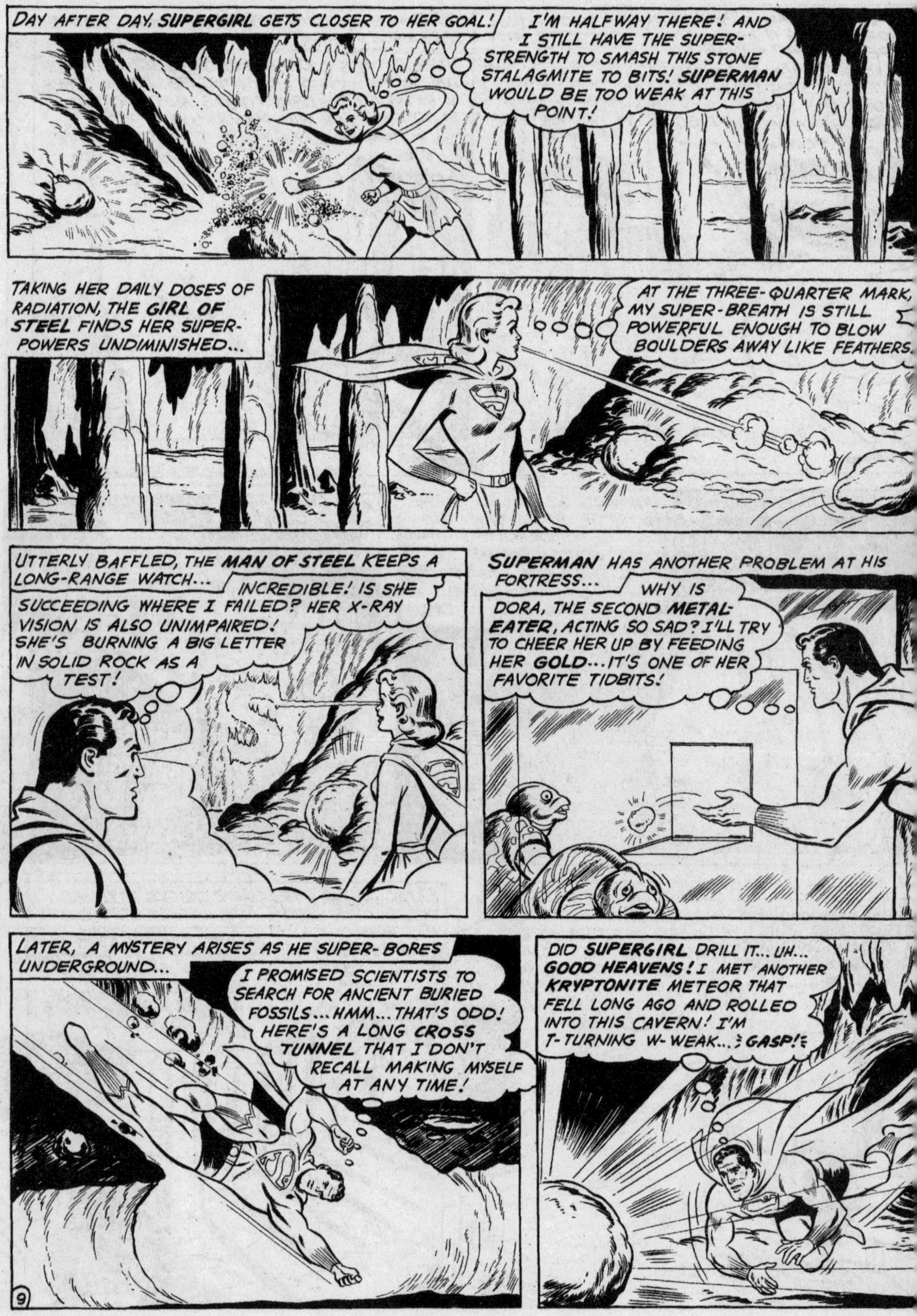
DAY AFTER DAY, SUPERGIRL GETS CLOSER TO HER GOAL!
I'M HALFWAY THERE! AND I STILL HAVE THE SUPER-STRENGTH TO SMASH THIS STONE STALAGMITE TO BITS! SUPERMAN WOULD BE TOO WEAK AT THIS POINT!
TAKING HER DAILY DOSES OF RADIATION, THE GIRL OF STEEL FINDS HER SUPER-POWERS UNDIMINISHED...
AT THE THREE-QUARTER MARK, MY SUPER-BREATH IS STILL POWERFUL ENOUGH TO BLOW BOULDERS AWAY LIKE FEATHERS.
UTTERLY BAFFLED, THE MAN OF STEEL KEEPS A LONG-RANGE WATCH...
INCREDIBLE! IS SHE SUCCEEDING WHERE I FAILED? HER X-RAY VISION IS ALSO UNIMPAIRED! SHE'S BURNING A BIG LETTER IN SOLID ROCK AS A TEST!
SUPERMAN HAS ANOTHER PROBLEM AT HIS FORTRESS...
WHY IS DORA, THE SECOND METAL-EATER, ACTING SO SAD? I'LL TRY TO CHEER HER UP BY FEEDING HER GOLD...IT'S ONE OF HER FAVORITE TIDBITS!
LATER, A MYSTERY ARISES AS HE SUPER-BORES UNDERGROUND...
I PROMISED SCIENTISTS TO SEARCH FOR ANCIENT BURIED FOSSILS...HMM...THAT'S ODD! HERE'S A LONG CROSS TUNNEL THAT I DON'T RECALL MAKING MYSELF AT ANY TIME!
9
DID SUPERGIRL DRILL IT...UH... GOOD HEAVENS! I MET ANOTHER KRYPTONITE METEOR THAT FELL LONG AGO AND ROLLED INTO THIS CAVERN! I'M T-TURNING W-WEAK... GASP!

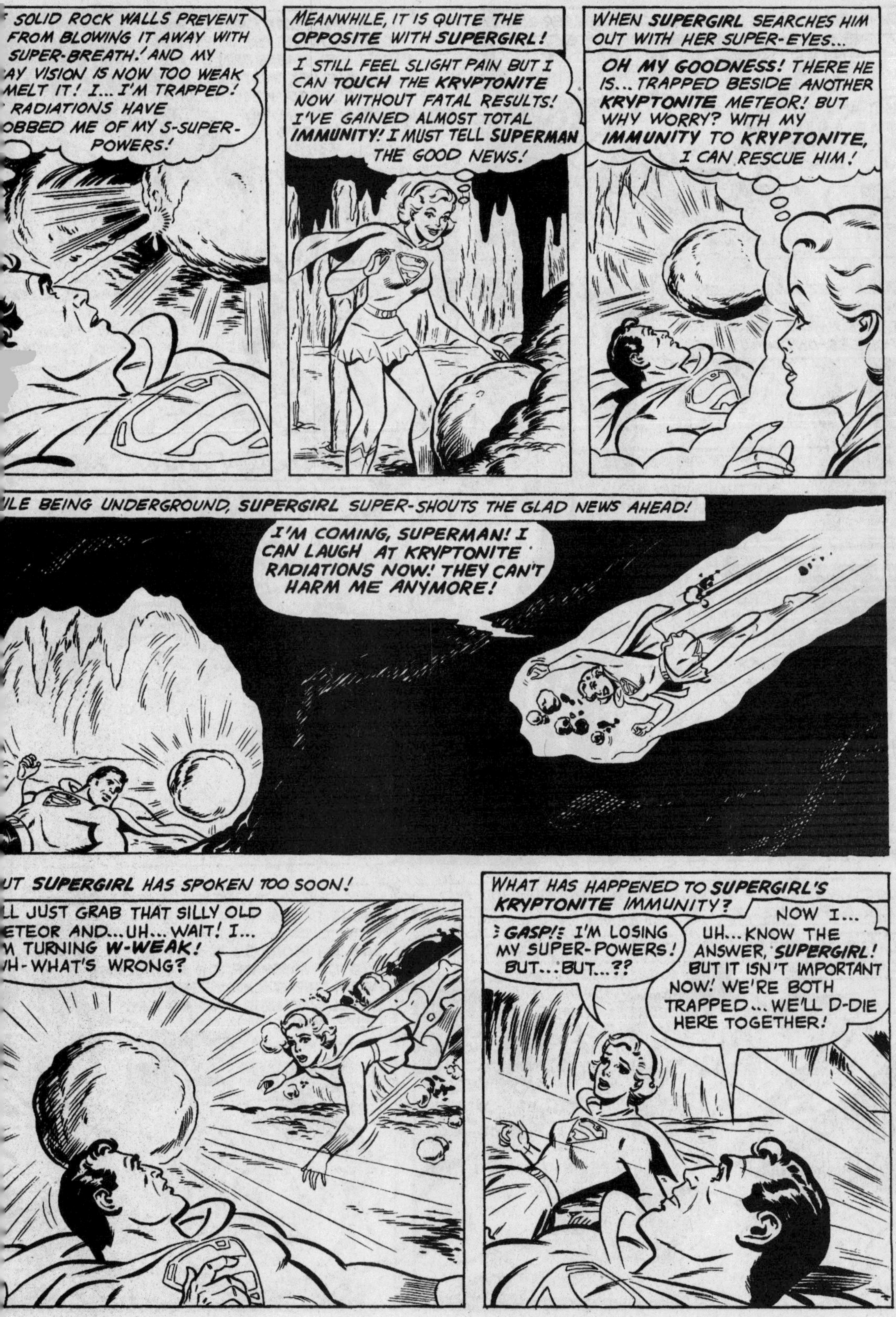
SOLID ROCK WALLS PREVENT FROM BLOWING IT AWAY WITH SUPER-BREATH! AND MY AY VISION IS NOW TOO WEAK MELT IT! I... I'M TRAPPED! RADIATIONS HAVE OBBED ME OF MY S-SUPER-POWERS!
MEANWHILE, IT IS QUITE THE OPPOSITE WITH SUPERGIRL!
I STILL FEEL SLIGHT PAIN BUT I CAN TOUCH THE KRYPTONITE NOW WITHOUT FATAL RESULTS! I'VE GAINED ALMOST TOTAL IMMUNITY! I MUST TELL SUPERMAN THE GOOD NEWS!
WHEN SUPERGIRL SEARCHES HIM OUT WITH HER SUPER-EYES...
OH MY GOODNESS! THERE HE IS... TRAPPED BESIDE ANOTHER KRYPTONITE METEOR! BUT WHY WORRY? WITH MY IMMUNITY TO KRYPTONITE, I CAN RESCUE HIM!
ILE BEING UNDERGROUND, SUPERGIRL SUPER-SHOUTS THE GLAD NEWS AHEAD!
I'M COMING, SUPERMAN! I CAN LAUGH AT KRYPTONITE RADIATIONS NOW! THEY CAN'T HARM ME ANYMORE!
UT SUPERGIRL HAS SPOKEN TOO SOON!
LL JUST GRAB THAT SILLY OLD ETEOR AND... UH... WAIT! I... M TURNING W-WEAK! VH-WHAT'S WRONG?
WHAT HAS HAPPENED TO SUPERGIRL'S KRYPTONITE IMMUNITY?
GASP! I'M LOSING MY SUPER-POWERS! BUT... BUT...??
NOW I... UH... KNOW THE ANSWER, SUPERGIRL! BUT IT ISN'T IMPORTANT NOW! WE'RE BOTH TRAPPED... WE'LL D-DIE HERE TOGETHER!

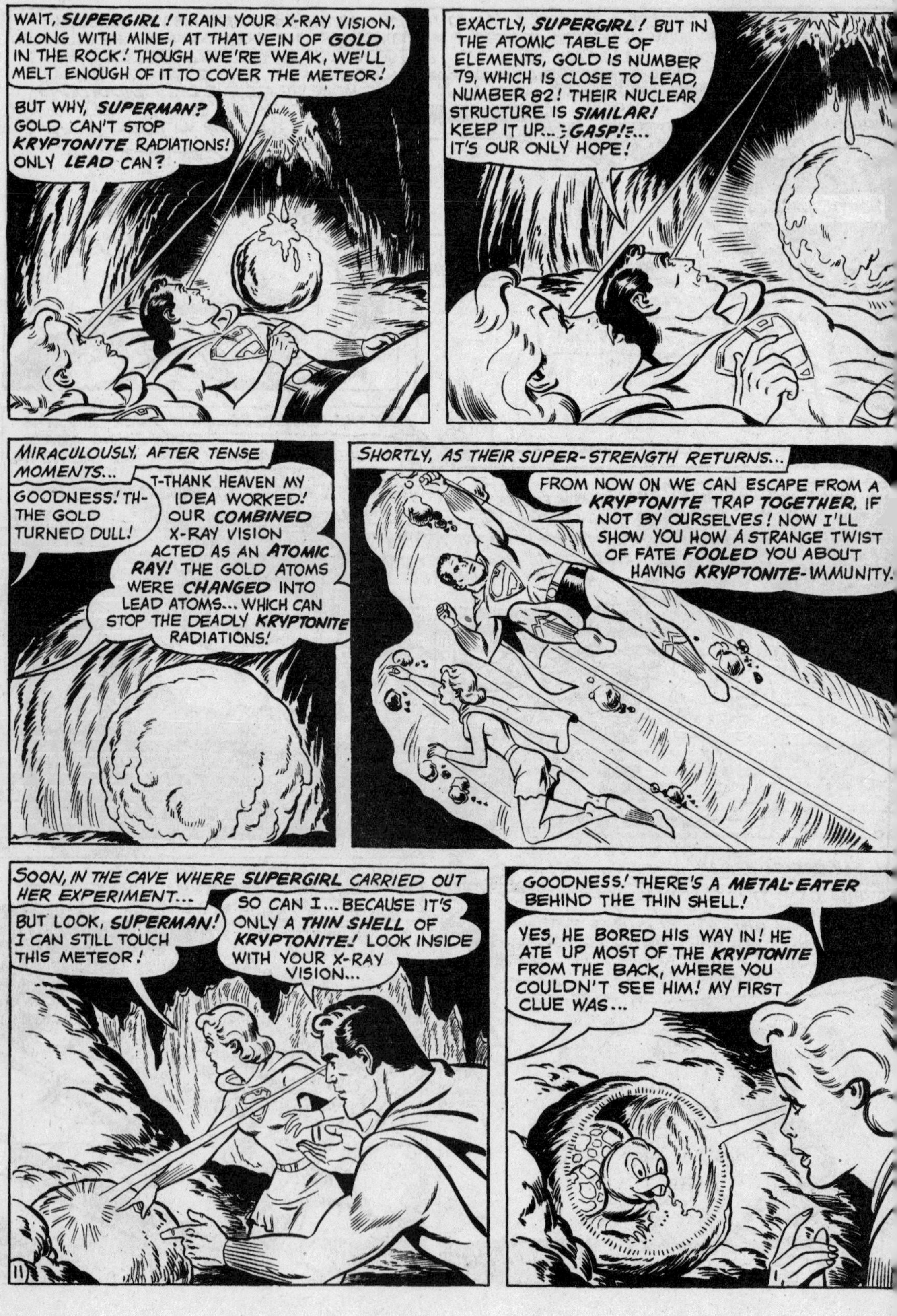
WAIT, SUPERGIRL! TRAIN YOUR X-RAY VISION, ALONG WITH MINE, AT THAT VEIN OF GOLD IN THE ROCK! THOUGH WE'RE WEAK, WE'LL MELT ENOUGH OF IT TO COVER THE METEOR!
BUT WHY, SUPERMAN? GOLD CAN'T STOP KRYPTONITE RADIATIONS! ONLY LEAD CAN?
EXACTLY, SUPERGIRL! BUT IN THE ATOMIC TABLE OF ELEMENTS, GOLD IS NUMBER 79, WHICH IS CLOSE TO LEAD, NUMBER 82! THEIR NUCLEAR STRUCTURE IS SIMILAR! KEEP IT UP... GASP!... IT'S OUR ONLY HOPE!
MIRACULOUSLY, AFTER TENSE MOMENTS...
GOODNESS! TH-THE GOLD TURNED DULL!
T-THANK HEAVEN MY IDEA WORKED! OUR COMBINED X-RAY VISION ACTED AS AN ATOMIC RAY! THE GOLD ATOMS WERE CHANGED INTO LEAD ATOMS... WHICH CAN STOP THE DEADLY KRYPTONITE RADIATIONS!
SHORTLY, AS THEIR SUPER-STRENGTH RETURNS...
FROM NOW ON WE CAN ESCAPE FROM A KRYPTONITE TRAP TOGETHER, IF NOT BY OURSELVES! NOW I'LL SHOW YOU HOW A STRANGE TWIST OF FATE FOOLED YOU ABOUT HAVING KRYPTONITE-IMMUNITY.
SOON, IN THE CAVE WHERE SUPERGIRL CARRIED OUT HER EXPERIMENT...
BUT LOOK, SUPERMAN! I CAN STILL TOUCH THIS METEOR!
SO CAN I... BECAUSE IT'S ONLY A THIN SHELL OF KRYPTONITE! LOOK INSIDE WITH YOUR X-RAY VISION...
11
GOODNESS! THERE'S A METAL-EATER BEHIND THE THIN SHELL!
YES, HE BORED HIS WAY IN! HE ATE UP MOST OF THE KRYPTONITE FROM THE BACK, WHERE YOU COULDN'T SEE HIM! MY FIRST CLUE WAS...

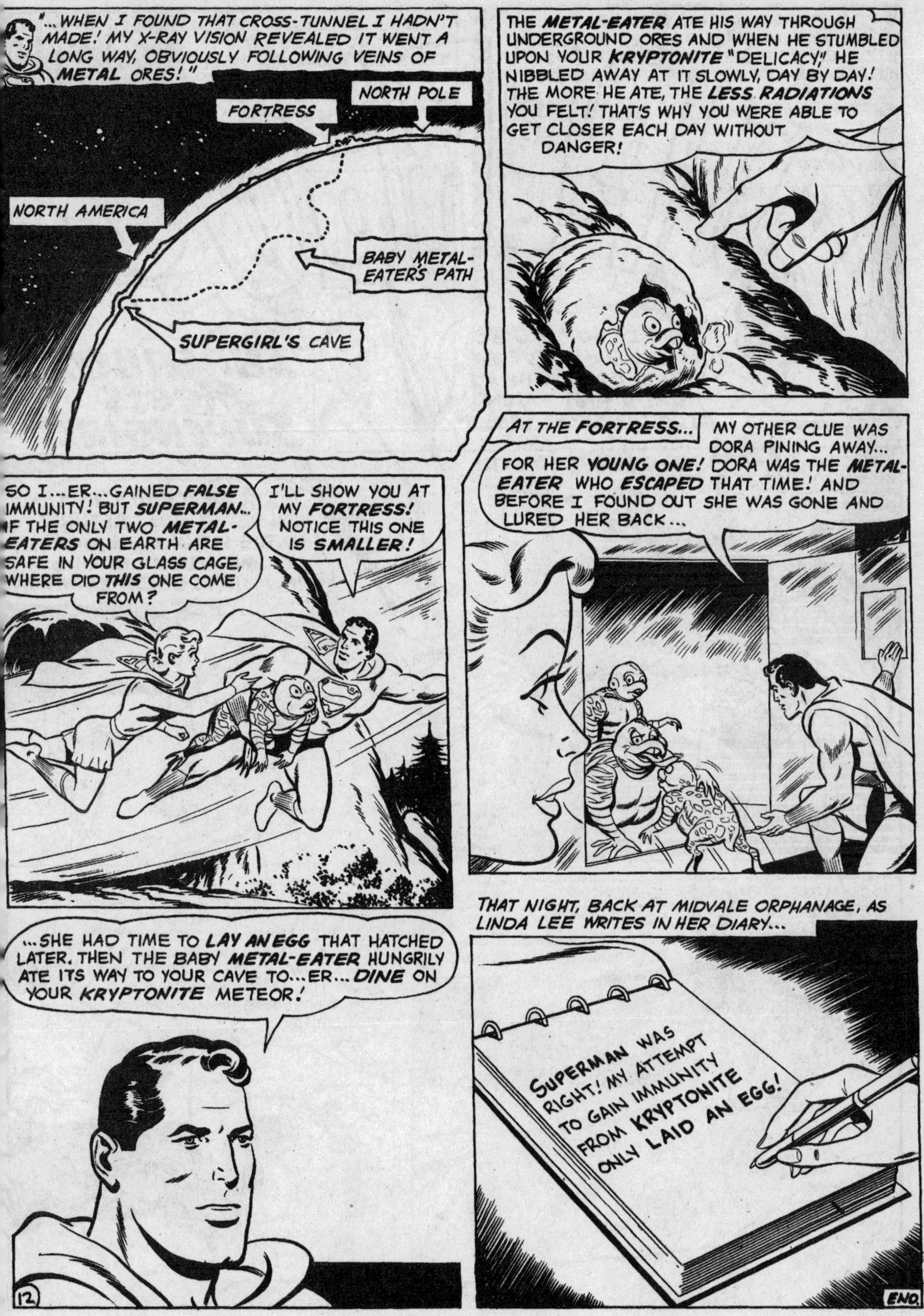
"...WHEN I FOUND THAT CROSS-TUNNEL I HADN'T MADE! MY X-RAY VISION REVEALED IT WENT A LONG WAY, OBVIOUSLY FOLLOWING VEINS OF METAL ORES!"
NORTH POLE
FORTRESS
NORTH AMERICA
BABY METAL-EATER'S PATH
SUPERGIRL'S CAVE
THE METAL-EATER ATE HIS WAY THROUGH UNDERGROUND ORES AND WHEN HE STUMBLED UPON YOUR KRYPTONITE "DELICACY," HE NIBBLED AWAY AT IT SLOWLY, DAY BY DAY! THE MORE HE ATE, THE LESS RADIATIONS YOU FELT! THAT'S WHY YOU WERE ABLE TO GET CLOSER EACH DAY WITHOUT DANGER!
SO I...ER...GAINED FALSE IMMUNITY! BUT SUPERMAN... IF THE ONLY TWO METAL-EATERS ON EARTH ARE SAFE IN YOUR GLASS CAGE, WHERE DID THIS ONE COME FROM?
I'LL SHOW YOU AT MY FORTRESS! NOTICE THIS ONE IS SMALLER!
AT THE FORTRESS...
MY OTHER CLUE WAS DORA PINING AWAY... FOR HER YOUNG ONE! DORA WAS THE METAL-EATER WHO ESCAPED THAT TIME! AND BEFORE I FOUND OUT SHE WAS GONE AND LURED HER BACK...
...SHE HAD TIME TO LAY AN EGG THAT HATCHED LATER. THEN THE BABY METAL-EATER HUNGRILY ATE ITS WAY TO YOUR CAVE TO...ER...DINE ON YOUR KRYPTONITE METEOR!
12
THAT NIGHT, BACK AT MIDVALE ORPHANAGE, AS LINDA LEE WRITES IN HER DIARY...
SUPERMAN WAS RIGHT! MY ATTEMPT TO GAIN IMMUNITY FROM KRYPTONITE ONLY LAID AN EGG!
END

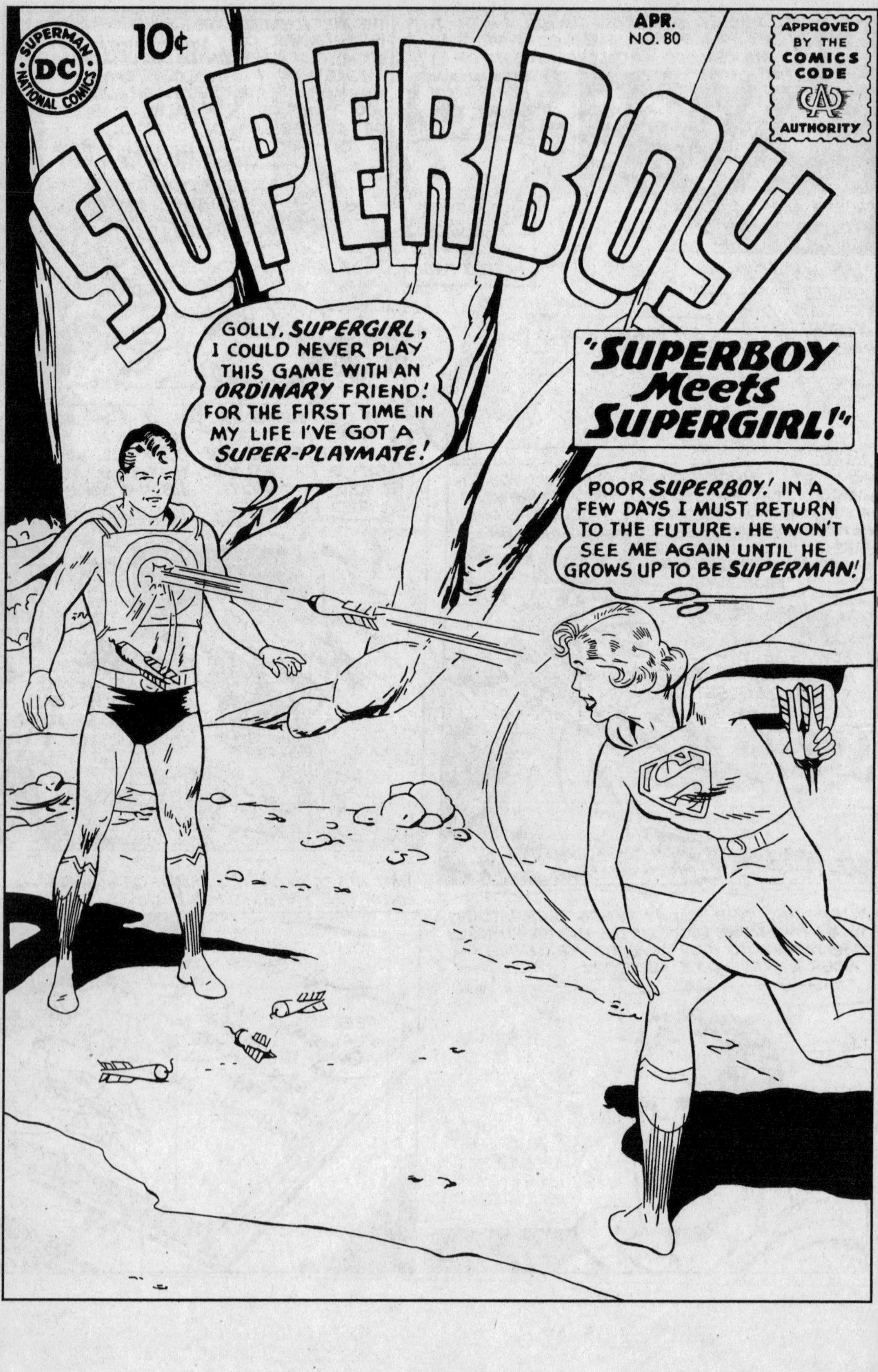
SUPERMAN DC NATIONAL COMICS
10¢
APR.
NO. 80
APPROVED BY THE COMICS CODE AUTHORITY
SUPERBOY
GOLLY, SUPERGIRL, I COULD NEVER PLAY THIS GAME WITH AN ORDINARY FRIEND! FOR THE FIRST TIME IN MY LIFE I'VE GOT A SUPER-PLAYMATE!
"SUPERBOY Meets SUPERGIRL!"
POOR SUPERBOY! IN A FEW DAYS I MUST RETURN TO THE FUTURE. HE WON'T SEE ME AGAIN UNTIL HE GROWS UP TO BE SUPERMAN!

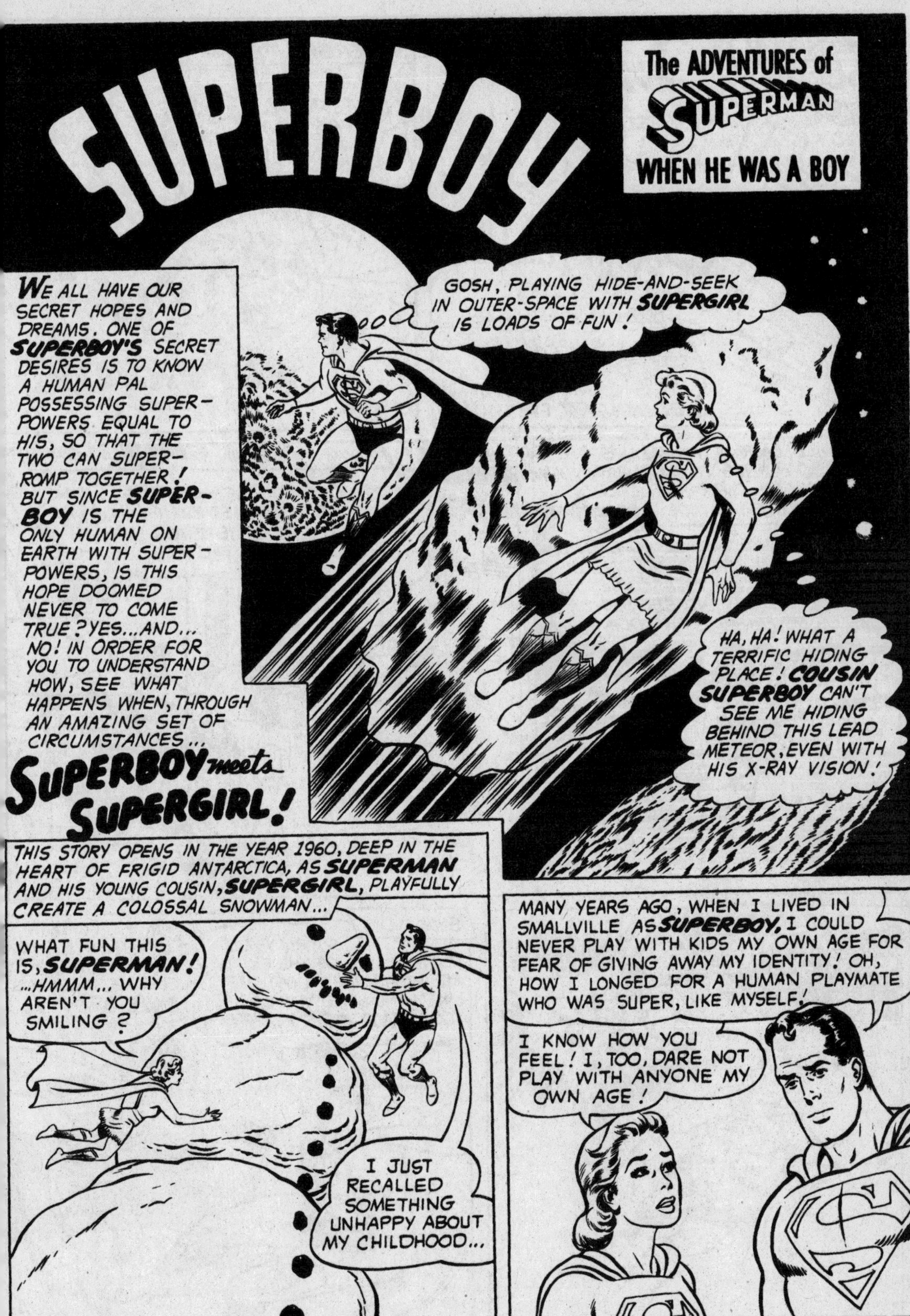
SUPERBOY
The ADVENTURES of SUPERMAN WHEN HE WAS A BOY
WE ALL HAVE OUR SECRET HOPES AND DREAMS. ONE OF SUPERBOY'S SECRET DESIRES IS TO KNOW A HUMAN PAL POSSESSING SUPER-POWERS EQUAL TO HIS, SO THAT THE TWO CAN SUPER-ROMP TOGETHER! BUT SINCE SUPERBOY IS THE ONLY HUMAN ON EARTH WITH SUPER-POWERS, IS THIS HOPE DOOMED NEVER TO COME TRUE? YES...AND... NO! IN ORDER FOR YOU TO UNDERSTAND HOW, SEE WHAT HAPPENS WHEN, THROUGH AN AMAZING SET OF CIRCUMSTANCES...
SUPERBOY meets SUPERGIRL!
GOSH, PLAYING HIDE-AND-SEEK IN OUTER-SPACE WITH SUPERGIRL IS LOADS OF FUN!
HA, HA! WHAT A TERRIFIC HIDING PLACE! COUSIN SUPERBOY CAN'T SEE ME HIDING BEHIND THIS LEAD METEOR, EVEN WITH HIS X-RAY VISION!
THIS STORY OPENS IN THE YEAR 1960, DEEP IN THE HEART OF FRIGID ANTARCTICA, AS SUPERMAN AND HIS YOUNG COUSIN, SUPERGIRL, PLAYFULLY CREATE A COLOSSAL SNOWMAN...
WHAT FUN THIS IS, SUPERMAN! ...HMMM... WHY AREN'T YOU SMILING?
I JUST RECALLED SOMETHING UNHAPPY ABOUT MY CHILDHOOD...
MANY YEARS AGO, WHEN I LIVED IN SMALLVILLE AS SUPERBOY, I COULD NEVER PLAY WITH KIDS MY OWN AGE FOR FEAR OF GIVING AWAY MY IDENTITY! OH, HOW I LONGED FOR A HUMAN PLAYMATE WHO WAS SUPER, LIKE MYSELF!
I KNOW HOW YOU FEEL! I, TOO, DARE NOT PLAY WITH ANYONE MY OWN AGE!

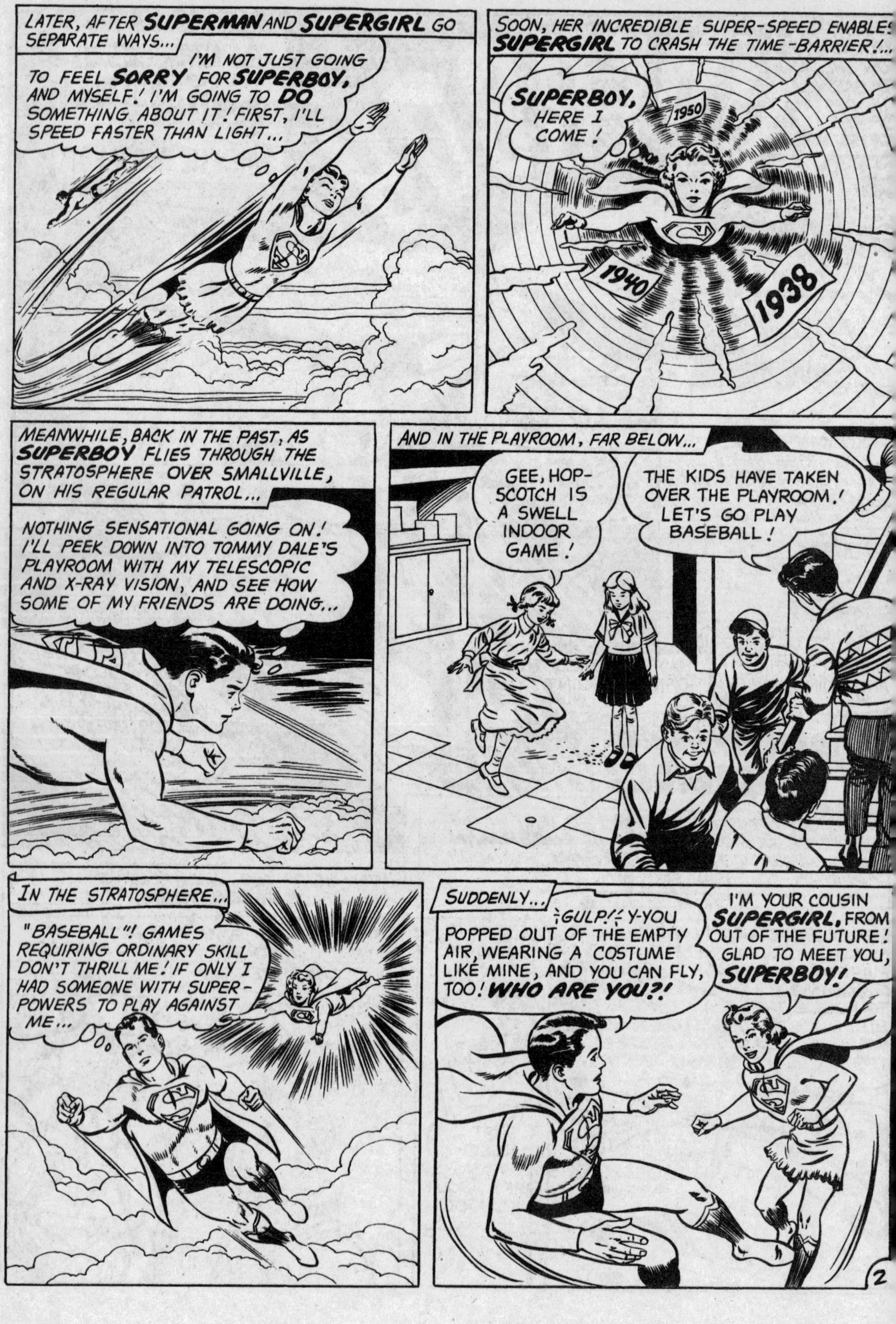
LATER, AFTER SUPERMAN AND SUPERGIRL GO SEPARATE WAYS...
I'M NOT JUST GOING TO FEEL SORRY FOR SUPERBOY, AND MYSELF! I'M GOING TO DO SOMETHING ABOUT IT! FIRST, I'LL SPEED FASTER THAN LIGHT...
SOON, HER INCREDIBLE SUPER-SPEED ENABLES SUPERGIRL TO CRASH THE TIME-BARRIER!...
SUPERBOY, HERE I COME!
1950
1940
1938
MEANWHILE, BACK IN THE PAST, AS SUPERBOY FLIES THROUGH THE STRATOSPHERE OVER SMALLVILLE, ON HIS REGULAR PATROL...
NOTHING SENSATIONAL GOING ON! I'LL PEEK DOWN INTO TOMMY DALE'S PLAYROOM WITH MY TELESCOPIC AND X-RAY VISION, AND SEE HOW SOME OF MY FRIENDS ARE DOING...
AND IN THE PLAYROOM, FAR BELOW...
GEE, HOP-SCOTCH IS A SWELL INDOOR GAME!
THE KIDS HAVE TAKEN OVER THE PLAYROOM! LET'S GO PLAY BASEBALL!
IN THE STRATOSPHERE...
"BASEBALL"! GAMES REQUIRING ORDINARY SKILL DON'T THRILL ME! IF ONLY I HAD SOMEONE WITH SUPER-POWERS TO PLAY AGAINST ME...
SUDDENLY...
¡GULP!¡ Y-YOU POPPED OUT OF THE EMPTY AIR, WEARING A COSTUME LIKE MINE, AND YOU CAN FLY, TOO! WHO ARE YOU?!
I'M YOUR COUSIN SUPERGIRL, FROM OUT OF THE FUTURE! GLAD TO MEET YOU, SUPERBOY!
2

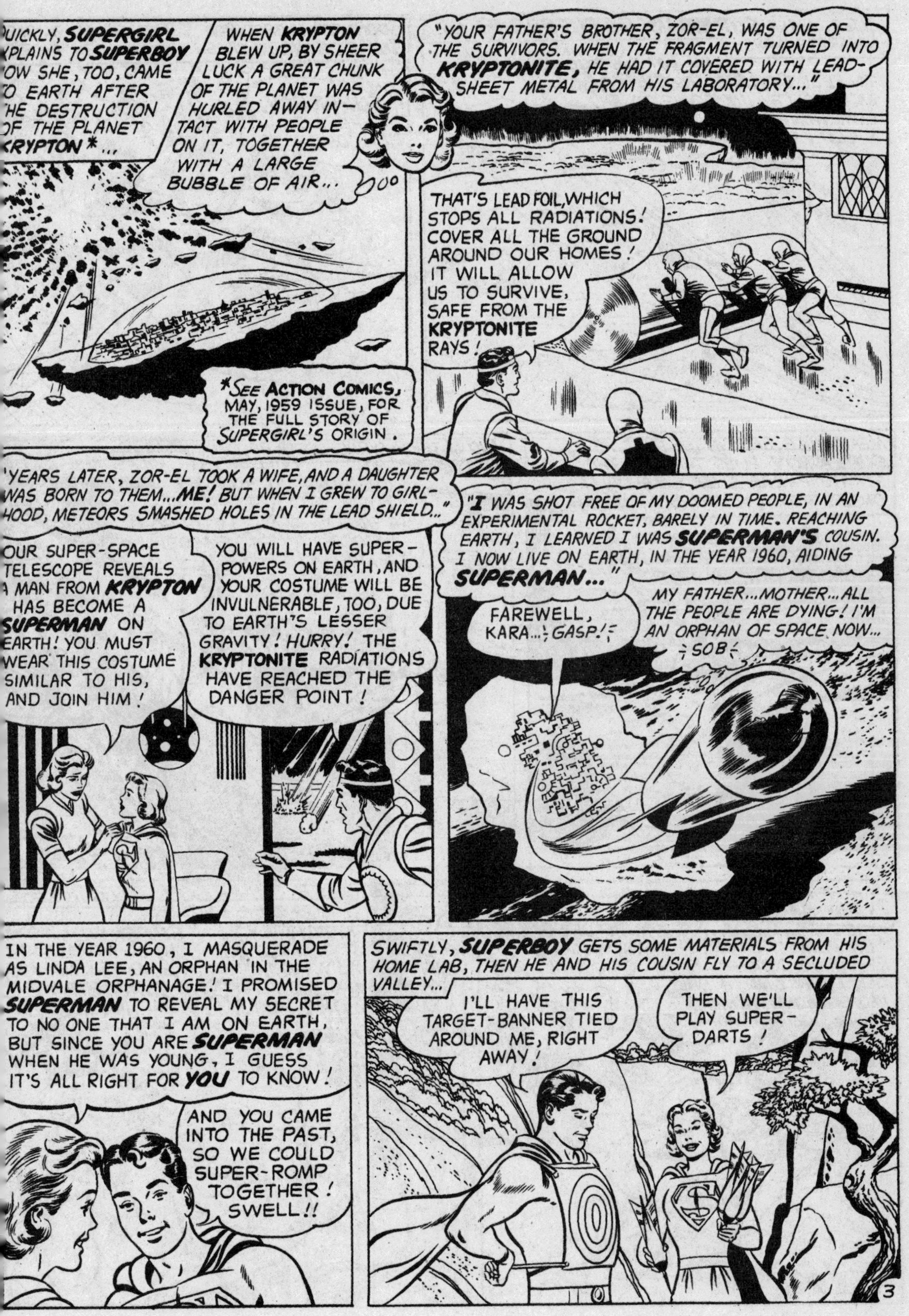
UICKLY, SUPERGIRL XPLAINS TO SUPERBOY OW SHE, TOO, CAME O EARTH AFTER HE DESTRUCTION OF THE PLANET KRYPTON*...
WHEN KRYPTON BLEW UP, BY SHEER LUCK A GREAT CHUNK OF THE PLANET WAS HURLED AWAY INTACT WITH PEOPLE ON IT, TOGETHER WITH A LARGE BUBBLE OF AIR...
*SEE ACTION COMICS, MAY, 1959 ISSUE, FOR THE FULL STORY OF SUPERGIRL'S ORIGIN.
"YOUR FATHER'S BROTHER, ZOR-EL, WAS ONE OF THE SURVIVORS. WHEN THE FRAGMENT TURNED INTO KRYPTONITE, HE HAD IT COVERED WITH LEAD-SHEET METAL FROM HIS LABORATORY..."
THAT'S LEAD FOIL, WHICH STOPS ALL RADIATIONS! COVER ALL THE GROUND AROUND OUR HOMES! IT WILL ALLOW US TO SURVIVE, SAFE FROM THE KRYPTONITE RAYS!
"YEARS LATER, ZOR-EL TOOK A WIFE, AND A DAUGHTER WAS BORN TO THEM...ME! BUT WHEN I GREW TO GIRLHOOD, METEORS SMASHED HOLES IN THE LEAD SHIELD..."
OUR SUPER-SPACE TELESCOPE REVEALS A MAN FROM KRYPTON HAS BECOME A SUPERMAN ON EARTH! YOU MUST WEAR THIS COSTUME SIMILAR TO HIS, AND JOIN HIM!
YOU WILL HAVE SUPER-POWERS ON EARTH, AND YOUR COSTUME WILL BE INVULNERABLE, TOO, DUE TO EARTH'S LESSER GRAVITY! HURRY! THE KRYPTONITE RADIATIONS HAVE REACHED THE DANGER POINT!
"I WAS SHOT FREE OF MY DOOMED PEOPLE, IN AN EXPERIMENTAL ROCKET, BARELY IN TIME. REACHING EARTH, I LEARNED I WAS SUPERMAN'S COUSIN. I NOW LIVE ON EARTH, IN THE YEAR 1960, AIDING SUPERMAN..."
FAREWELL, KARA...GASP!
MY FATHER...MOTHER...ALL THE PEOPLE ARE DYING! I'M AN ORPHAN OF SPACE NOW... SOB
IN THE YEAR 1960, I MASQUERADE AS LINDA LEE, AN ORPHAN IN THE MIDVALE ORPHANAGE! I PROMISED SUPERMAN TO REVEAL MY SECRET TO NO ONE THAT I AM ON EARTH, BUT SINCE YOU ARE SUPERMAN WHEN HE WAS YOUNG, I GUESS IT'S ALL RIGHT FOR YOU TO KNOW!
AND YOU CAME INTO THE PAST, SO WE COULD SUPER-ROMP TOGETHER! SWELL!!
SWIFTLY, SUPERBOY GETS SOME MATERIALS FROM HIS HOME LAB, THEN HE AND HIS COUSIN FLY TO A SECLUDED VALLEY...
I'LL HAVE THIS TARGET-BANNER TIED AROUND ME, RIGHT AWAY!
THEN WE'LL PLAY SUPER-DARTS!
3

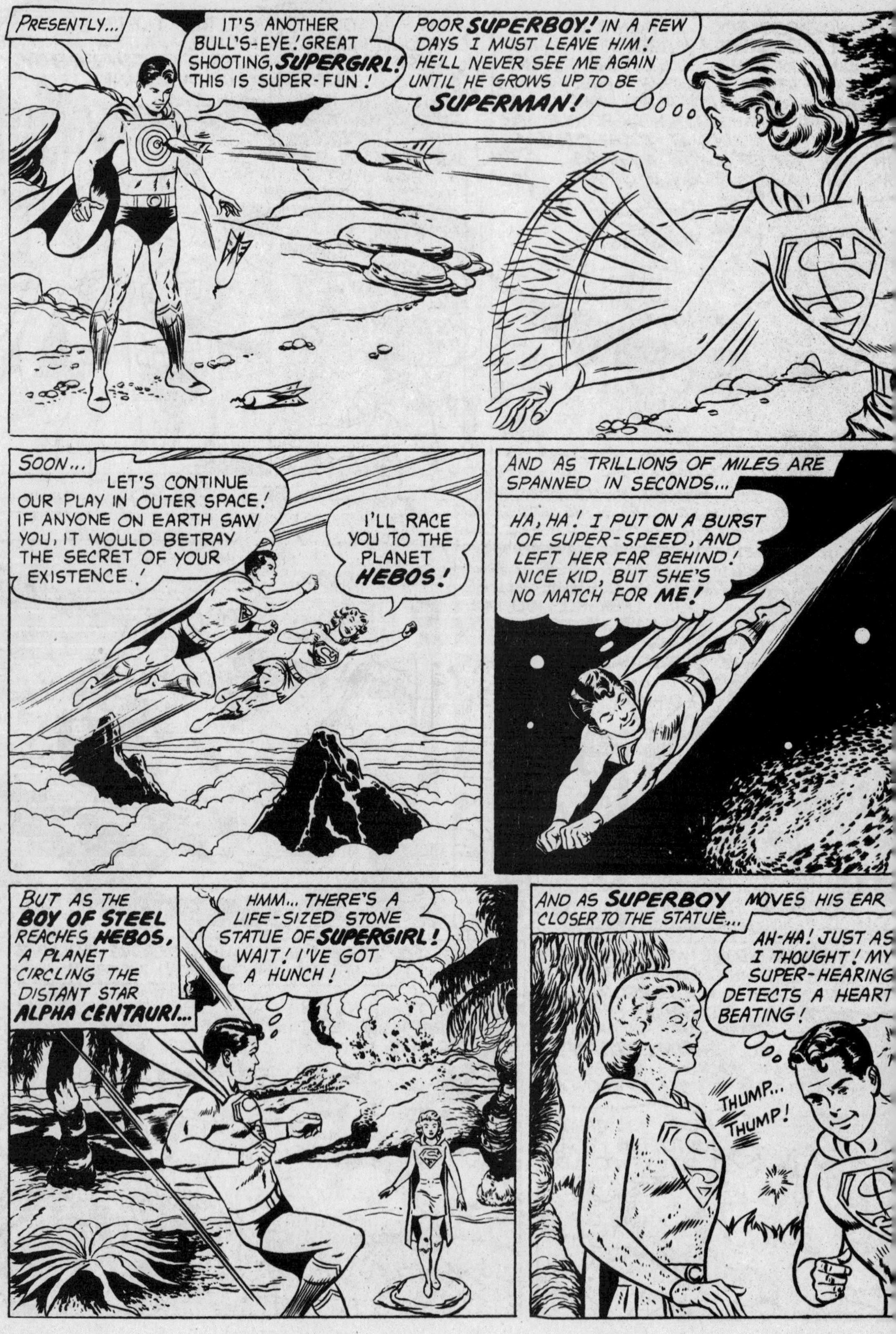
PRESENTLY...
IT'S ANOTHER BULL'S-EYE! GREAT SHOOTING, SUPERGIRL! THIS IS SUPER-FUN!
POOR SUPERBOY! IN A FEW DAYS I MUST LEAVE HIM! HE'LL NEVER SEE ME AGAIN UNTIL HE GROWS UP TO BE SUPERMAN!
SOON...
LET'S CONTINUE OUR PLAY IN OUTER SPACE! IF ANYONE ON EARTH SAW YOU, IT WOULD BETRAY THE SECRET OF YOUR EXISTENCE!
I'LL RACE YOU TO THE PLANET HEBOS!
AND AS TRILLIONS OF MILES ARE SPANNED IN SECONDS...
HA, HA! I PUT ON A BURST OF SUPER-SPEED, AND LEFT HER FAR BEHIND! NICE KID, BUT SHE'S NO MATCH FOR ME!
BUT AS THE BOY OF STEEL REACHES HEBOS, A PLANET CIRCLING THE DISTANT STAR ALPHA CENTAURI...
HMM... THERE'S A LIFE-SIZED STONE STATUE OF SUPERGIRL! WAIT! I'VE GOT A HUNCH!
AND AS SUPERBOY MOVES HIS EAR CLOSER TO THE STATUE...
AH-HA! JUST AS I THOUGHT! MY SUPER-HEARING DETECTS A HEART BEATING!
THUMP... THUMP!

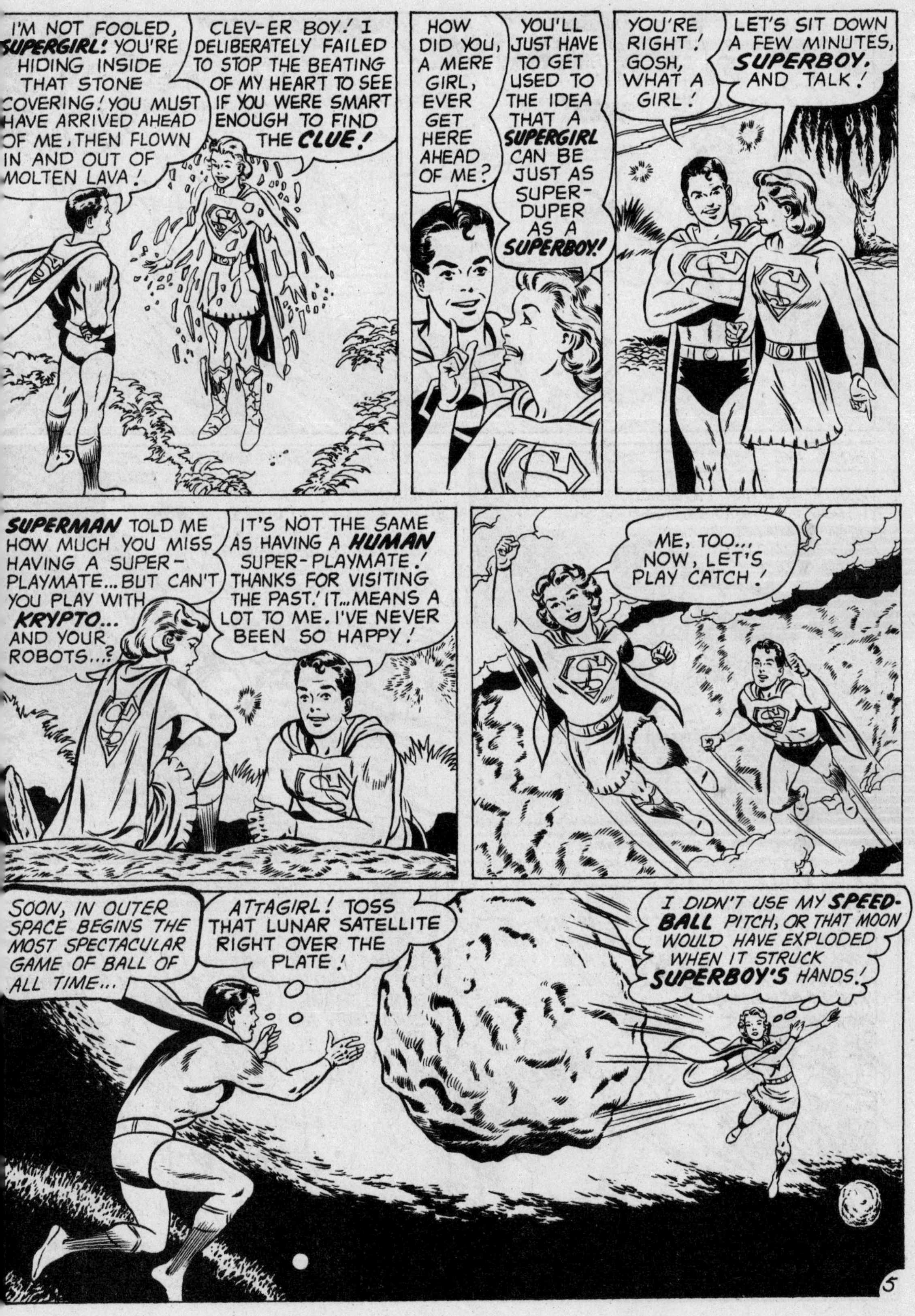
I'M NOT FOOLED, SUPERGIRL! YOU'RE HIDING INSIDE THAT STONE COVERING! YOU MUST HAVE ARRIVED AHEAD OF ME, THEN FLOWN IN AND OUT OF MOLTEN LAVA!
CLEV-ER BOY! I DELIBERATELY FAILED TO STOP THE BEATING OF MY HEART TO SEE IF YOU WERE SMART ENOUGH TO FIND THE CLUE!
HOW DID YOU, A MERE GIRL, EVER GET HERE AHEAD OF ME?
YOU'LL JUST HAVE TO GET USED TO THE IDEA THAT A SUPERGIRL CAN BE JUST AS SUPER-DUPER AS A SUPERBOY!
YOU'RE RIGHT! GOSH, WHAT A GIRL!
LET'S SIT DOWN A FEW MINUTES, SUPERBOY, AND TALK!
SUPERMAN TOLD ME HOW MUCH YOU MISS HAVING A SUPER-PLAYMATE... BUT CAN'T YOU PLAY WITH KRYPTO... AND YOUR ROBOTS...?
IT'S NOT THE SAME AS HAVING A HUMAN SUPER-PLAYMATE! THANKS FOR VISITING THE PAST! IT... MEANS A LOT TO ME. I'VE NEVER BEEN SO HAPPY!
ME, TOO... NOW, LET'S PLAY CATCH!
SOON, IN OUTER SPACE BEGINS THE MOST SPECTACULAR GAME OF BALL OF ALL TIME...
ATTAGIRL! TOSS THAT LUNAR SATELLITE RIGHT OVER THE PLATE!
I DIDN'T USE MY SPEED-BALL PITCH, OR THAT MOON WOULD HAVE EXPLODED WHEN IT STRUCK SUPERBOY'S HANDS!
5

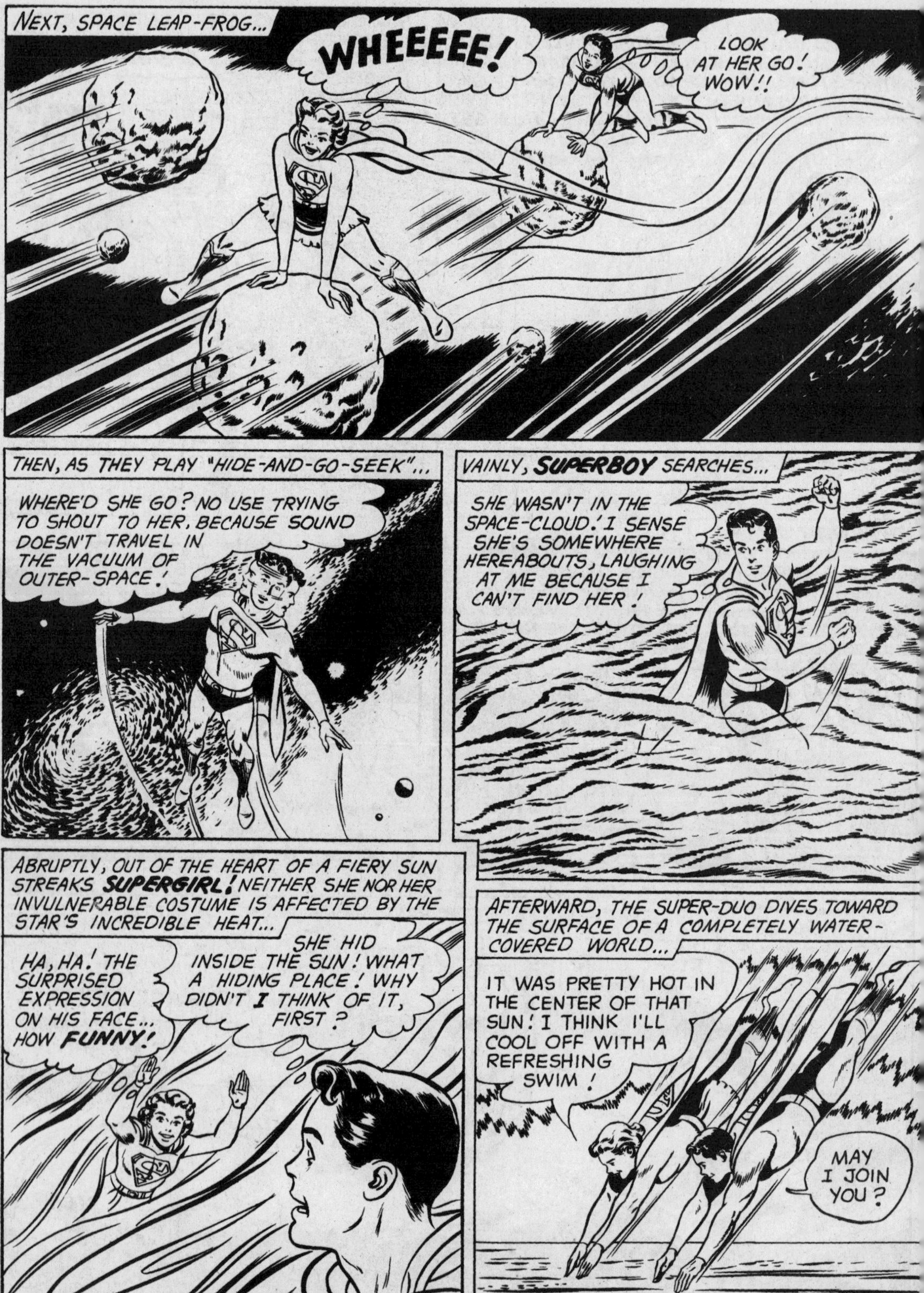
NEXT, SPACE LEAP-FROG...
WHEEEEE!
LOOK AT HER GO! WOW!!
THEN, AS THEY PLAY "HIDE-AND-GO-SEEK"...
WHERE'D SHE GO? NO USE TRYING TO SHOUT TO HER, BECAUSE SOUND DOESN'T TRAVEL IN THE VACUUM OF OUTER-SPACE!
VAINLY, SUPERBOY SEARCHES...
SHE WASN'T IN THE SPACE-CLOUD! I SENSE SHE'S SOMEWHERE HEREABOUTS, LAUGHING AT ME BECAUSE I CAN'T FIND HER!
ABRUPTLY, OUT OF THE HEART OF A FIERY SUN STREAKS SUPERGIRL! NEITHER SHE NOR HER INVULNERABLE COSTUME IS AFFECTED BY THE STAR'S INCREDIBLE HEAT...
HA, HA! THE SURPRISED EXPRESSION ON HIS FACE... HOW FUNNY!
SHE HID INSIDE THE SUN! WHAT A HIDING PLACE! WHY DIDN'T I THINK OF IT, FIRST?
AFTERWARD, THE SUPER-DUO DIVES TOWARD THE SURFACE OF A COMPLETELY WATER-COVERED WORLD...
IT WAS PRETTY HOT IN THE CENTER OF THAT SUN! I THINK I'LL COOL OFF WITH A REFRESHING SWIM!
MAY I JOIN YOU?

SIDE-BY-SIDE, **SUPERBOY** AND **SUPERGIRL** BRAVE THE UNKNOWN WATERS OF A STRANGE AQUA-WORLD, SWIMMING AT SUCH AMAZING SPEED THAT THE WATERS SPLIT AND REAR ABOVE THEM LIKE EERIE, LIQUID MOUNTAINS...

BUT THEN...

LOOK OUT!!

GIANT, TALONED, METAL CLAWS...OUT OF THE DEPTHS!!

WHAT STRANGE, UNKNOWN MENACE IS *THIS*?!!

PRESENTLY, THE ANSWER IS CLEAR...

THE CLAWS ARE BEING OPERATED FROM THAT MERMAN CRAFT!

THEY'RE FISHING! AND THE "CATCH" IS...*US!*

SWIFTLY, THE SUPER-COUSINS FREE THEMSELVES FROM THE CLAWING MENACE WITH A SURGE OF TREMENDOUSLY SUPER-POWERFUL MUSCLES...

WE CAME HERE FOR LAUGHS, NOT TO BE THE MAIN COURSE FOR A MERMAN DINNER!

'BYE-BYE, WATER WORLD! YOU'RE ALL WET!

LATER, AS **SUPERBOY** AND **SUPERGIRL** RETURN HOMEWARD...

TWO STRANGE SPACE SHIPS...HEADING TOWARD EARTH!

ARE THEY FRIENDLY?

AND AS THE RAY-PROJECTORS, AIMED AT EARTH, BEGIN TO GLOW...

DEATH-RAYS! THEY'LL BE FIRED AT ANY MOMENT! IT'S AN INVASION!

IF WE FIGHT BACK, WE MAY DESTROY THOSE SHIPS...AND THE BEINGS INSIDE! BUT ACCORDING TO THE CODE TAUGHT ME BY **SUPERMAN**, WE MUST NEVER WIPE OUT HUMAN LIFE! *WHAT CAN WE DO???*

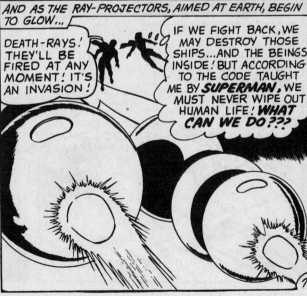

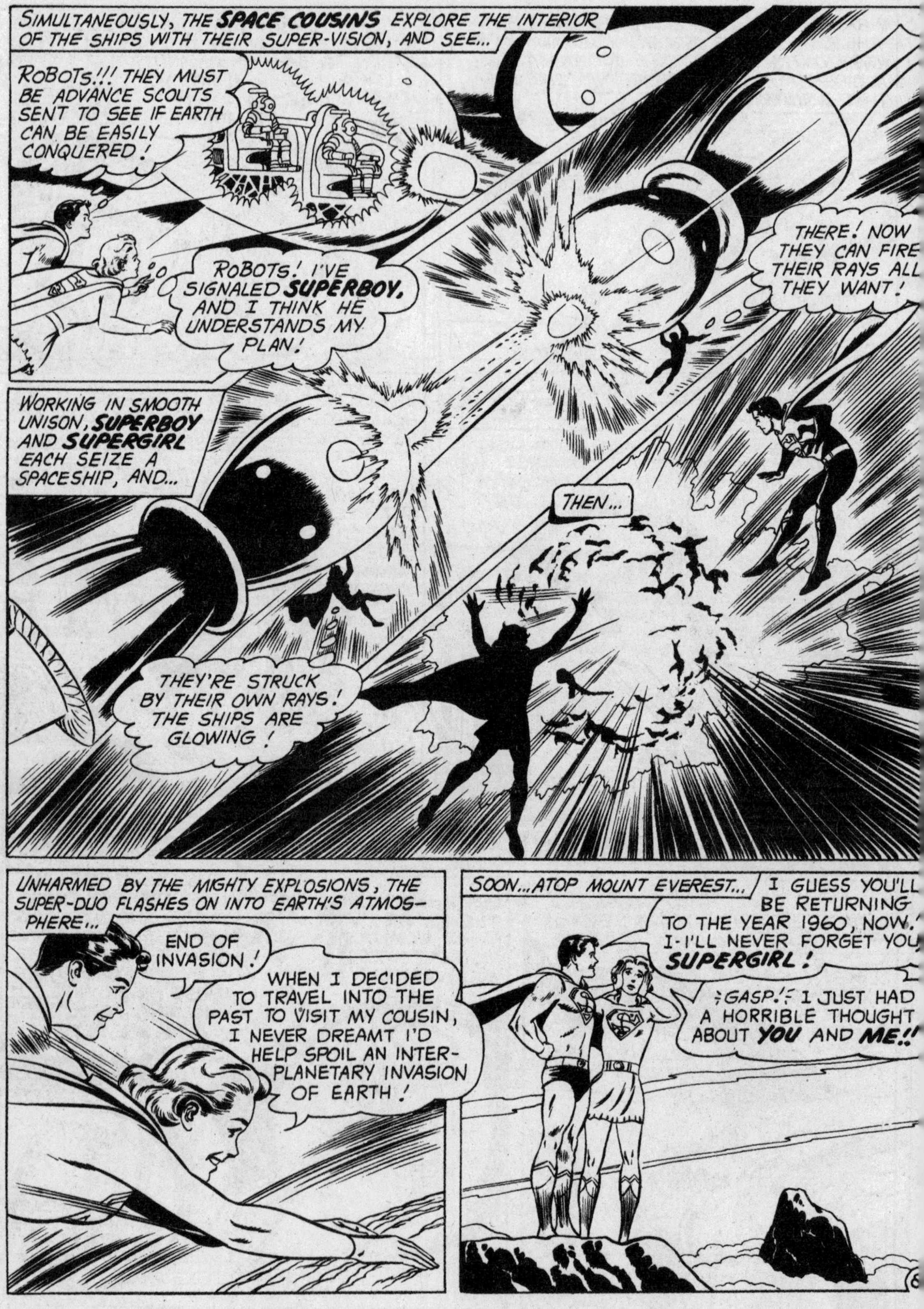
SIMULTANEOUSLY, THE SPACE COUSINS EXPLORE THE INTERIOR OF THE SHIPS WITH THEIR SUPER-VISION, AND SEE...
ROBOTS!!! THEY MUST BE ADVANCE SCOUTS SENT TO SEE IF EARTH CAN BE EASILY CONQUERED!
ROBOTS! I'VE SIGNALED SUPERBOY, AND I THINK HE UNDERSTANDS MY PLAN!
THERE! NOW THEY CAN FIRE THEIR RAYS ALL THEY WANT!
WORKING IN SMOOTH UNISON, SUPERBOY AND SUPERGIRL EACH SEIZE A SPACESHIP, AND...
THEN...
THEY'RE STRUCK BY THEIR OWN RAYS! THE SHIPS ARE GLOWING!
UNHARMED BY THE MIGHTY EXPLOSIONS, THE SUPER-DUO FLASHES ON INTO EARTH'S ATMOSPHERE...
END OF INVASION!
WHEN I DECIDED TO TRAVEL INTO THE PAST TO VISIT MY COUSIN, I NEVER DREAMT I'D HELP SPOIL AN INTER-PLANETARY INVASION OF EARTH!
SOON...ATOP MOUNT EVEREST...
I GUESS YOU'LL BE RETURNING TO THE YEAR 1960, NOW. I-I'LL NEVER FORGET YOU, SUPERGIRL!
GASP! I JUST HAD A HORRIBLE THOUGHT ABOUT YOU AND ME!!

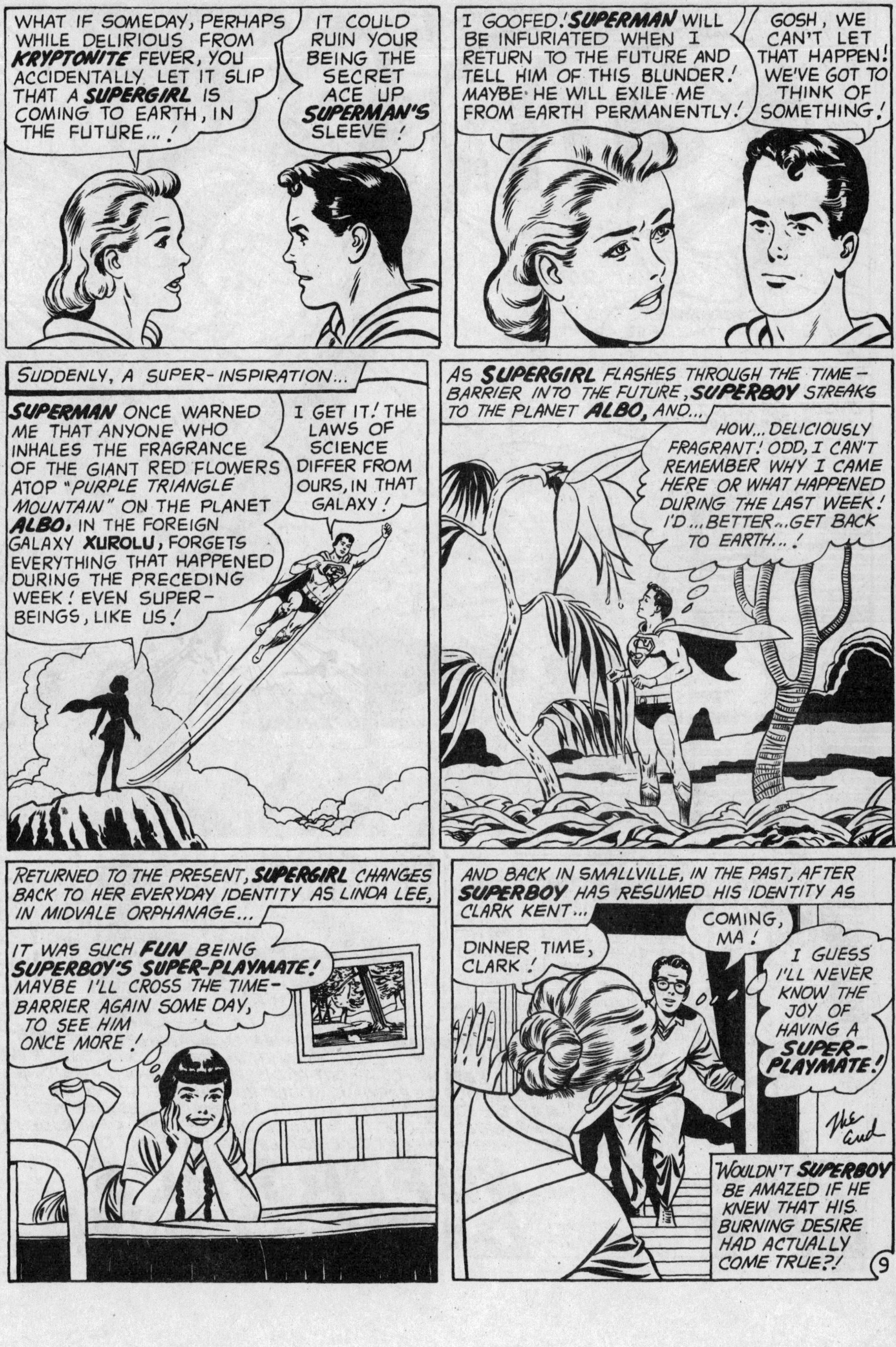
WHAT IF SOMEDAY, PERHAPS WHILE DELIRIOUS FROM KRYPTONITE FEVER, YOU ACCIDENTALLY LET IT SLIP THAT A SUPERGIRL IS COMING TO EARTH, IN THE FUTURE...!
IT COULD RUIN YOUR BEING THE SECRET ACE UP SUPERMAN'S SLEEVE!
I GOOFED! SUPERMAN WILL BE INFURIATED WHEN I RETURN TO THE FUTURE AND TELL HIM OF THIS BLUNDER! MAYBE HE WILL EXILE ME FROM EARTH PERMANENTLY!
GOSH, WE CAN'T LET THAT HAPPEN! WE'VE GOT TO THINK OF SOMETHING!
SUDDENLY, A SUPER-INSPIRATION...
SUPERMAN ONCE WARNED ME THAT ANYONE WHO INHALES THE FRAGRANCE OF THE GIANT RED FLOWERS ATOP "PURPLE TRIANGLE MOUNTAIN" ON THE PLANET ALBO, IN THE FOREIGN GALAXY XUROLU, FORGETS EVERYTHING THAT HAPPENED DURING THE PRECEDING WEEK! EVEN SUPER-BEINGS, LIKE US!
I GET IT! THE LAWS OF SCIENCE DIFFER FROM OURS, IN THAT GALAXY!
AS SUPERGIRL FLASHES THROUGH THE TIME-BARRIER INTO THE FUTURE, SUPERBOY STREAKS TO THE PLANET ALBO, AND...
HOW... DELICIOUSLY FRAGRANT! ODD, I CAN'T REMEMBER WHY I CAME HERE OR WHAT HAPPENED DURING THE LAST WEEK! I'D... BETTER... GET BACK TO EARTH...!
RETURNED TO THE PRESENT, SUPERGIRL CHANGES BACK TO HER EVERYDAY IDENTITY AS LINDA LEE, IN MIDVALE ORPHANAGE...
IT WAS SUCH FUN BEING SUPERBOY'S SUPER-PLAYMATE! MAYBE I'LL CROSS THE TIME-BARRIER AGAIN SOME DAY, TO SEE HIM ONCE MORE!
AND BACK IN SMALLVILLE, IN THE PAST, AFTER SUPERBOY HAS RESUMED HIS IDENTITY AS CLARK KENT...
DINNER TIME, CLARK!
COMING, MA!
I GUESS I'LL NEVER KNOW THE JOY OF HAVING A SUPER-PLAYMATE!
The end
WOULDN'T SUPERBOY BE AMAZED IF HE KNEW THAT HIS BURNING DESIRE HAD ACTUALLY COME TRUE?!
9

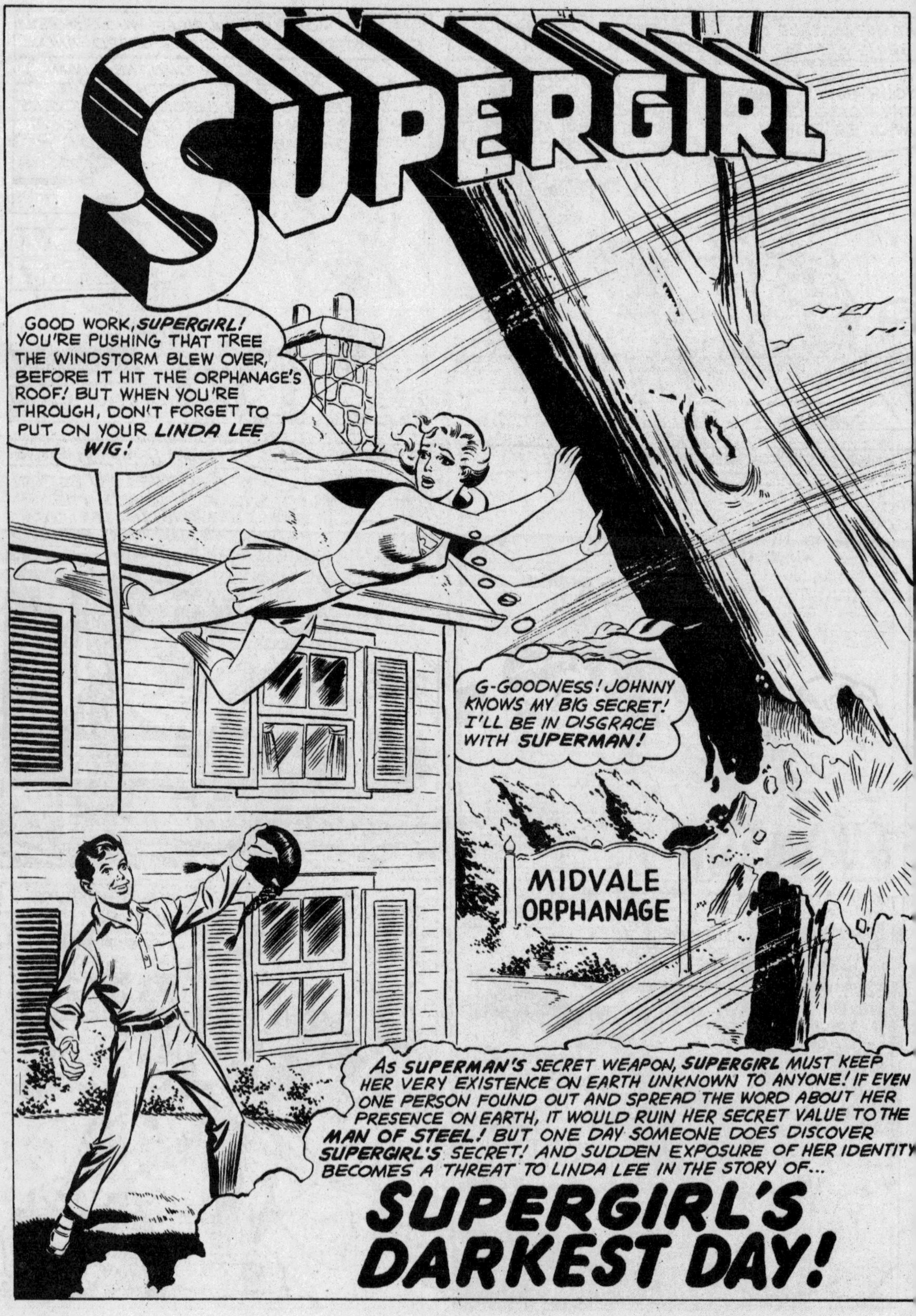
SUPERGIRL
GOOD WORK, SUPERGIRL! YOU'RE PUSHING THAT TREE THE WINDSTORM BLEW OVER, BEFORE IT HIT THE ORPHANAGE'S ROOF! BUT WHEN YOU'RE THROUGH, DON'T FORGET TO PUT ON YOUR LINDA LEE WIG!
G-GOODNESS! JOHNNY KNOWS MY BIG SECRET! I'LL BE IN DISGRACE WITH SUPERMAN!
MIDVALE ORPHANAGE
AS SUPERMAN'S SECRET WEAPON, SUPERGIRL MUST KEEP HER VERY EXISTENCE ON EARTH UNKNOWN TO ANYONE! IF EVEN ONE PERSON FOUND OUT AND SPREAD THE WORD ABOUT HER PRESENCE ON EARTH, IT WOULD RUIN HER SECRET VALUE TO THE MAN OF STEEL! BUT ONE DAY SOMEONE DOES DISCOVER SUPERGIRL'S SECRET! AND SUDDEN EXPOSURE OF HER IDENTITY BECOMES A THREAT TO LINDA LEE IN THE STORY OF...
SUPERGIRL'S DARKEST DAY!

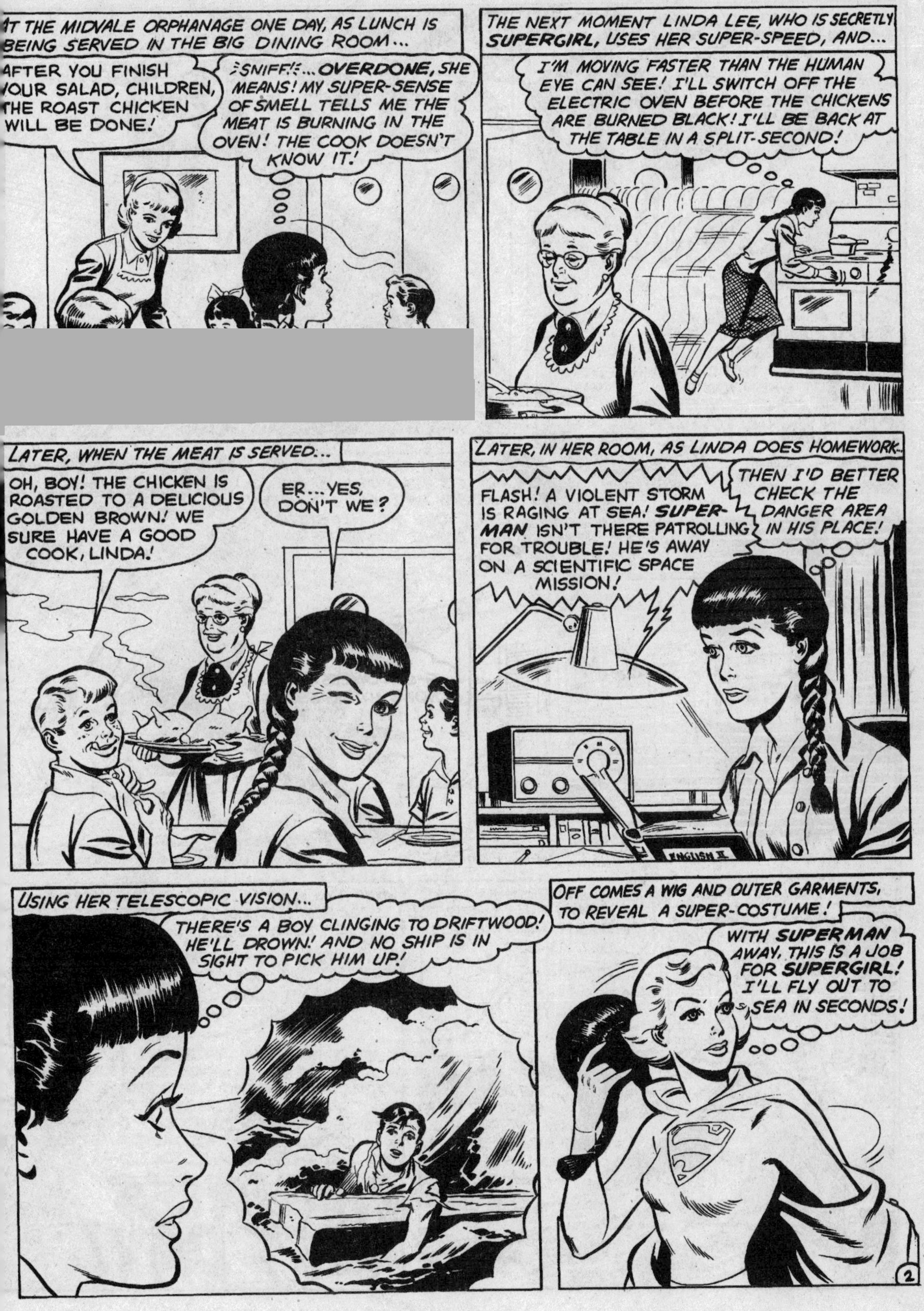
AT THE MIDVALE ORPHANAGE ONE DAY, AS LUNCH IS BEING SERVED IN THE BIG DINING ROOM...
AFTER YOU FINISH YOUR SALAD, CHILDREN, THE ROAST CHICKEN WILL BE DONE!
SNIFF!... OVERDONE, SHE MEANS! MY SUPER-SENSE OF SMELL TELLS ME THE MEAT IS BURNING IN THE OVEN! THE COOK DOESN'T KNOW IT!
THE NEXT MOMENT LINDA LEE, WHO IS SECRETLY SUPERGIRL, USES HER SUPER-SPEED, AND...
I'M MOVING FASTER THAN THE HUMAN EYE CAN SEE! I'LL SWITCH OFF THE ELECTRIC OVEN BEFORE THE CHICKENS ARE BURNED BLACK! I'LL BE BACK AT THE TABLE IN A SPLIT-SECOND!
LATER, WHEN THE MEAT IS SERVED...
OH, BOY! THE CHICKEN IS ROASTED TO A DELICIOUS GOLDEN BROWN! WE SURE HAVE A GOOD COOK, LINDA!
ER... YES, DON'T WE?
LATER, IN HER ROOM, AS LINDA DOES HOMEWORK...
FLASH! A VIOLENT STORM IS RAGING AT SEA! SUPERMAN ISN'T THERE PATROLLING FOR TROUBLE! HE'S AWAY ON A SCIENTIFIC SPACE MISSION!
THEN I'D BETTER CHECK THE DANGER AREA IN HIS PLACE!
ENGLISH II
USING HER TELESCOPIC VISION...
THERE'S A BOY CLINGING TO DRIFTWOOD! HE'LL DROWN! AND NO SHIP IS IN SIGHT TO PICK HIM UP!
OFF COMES A WIG AND OUTER GARMENTS, TO REVEAL A SUPER-COSTUME!
WITH SUPERMAN AWAY, THIS IS A JOB FOR SUPERGIRL! I'LL FLY OUT TO SEA IN SECONDS!
2

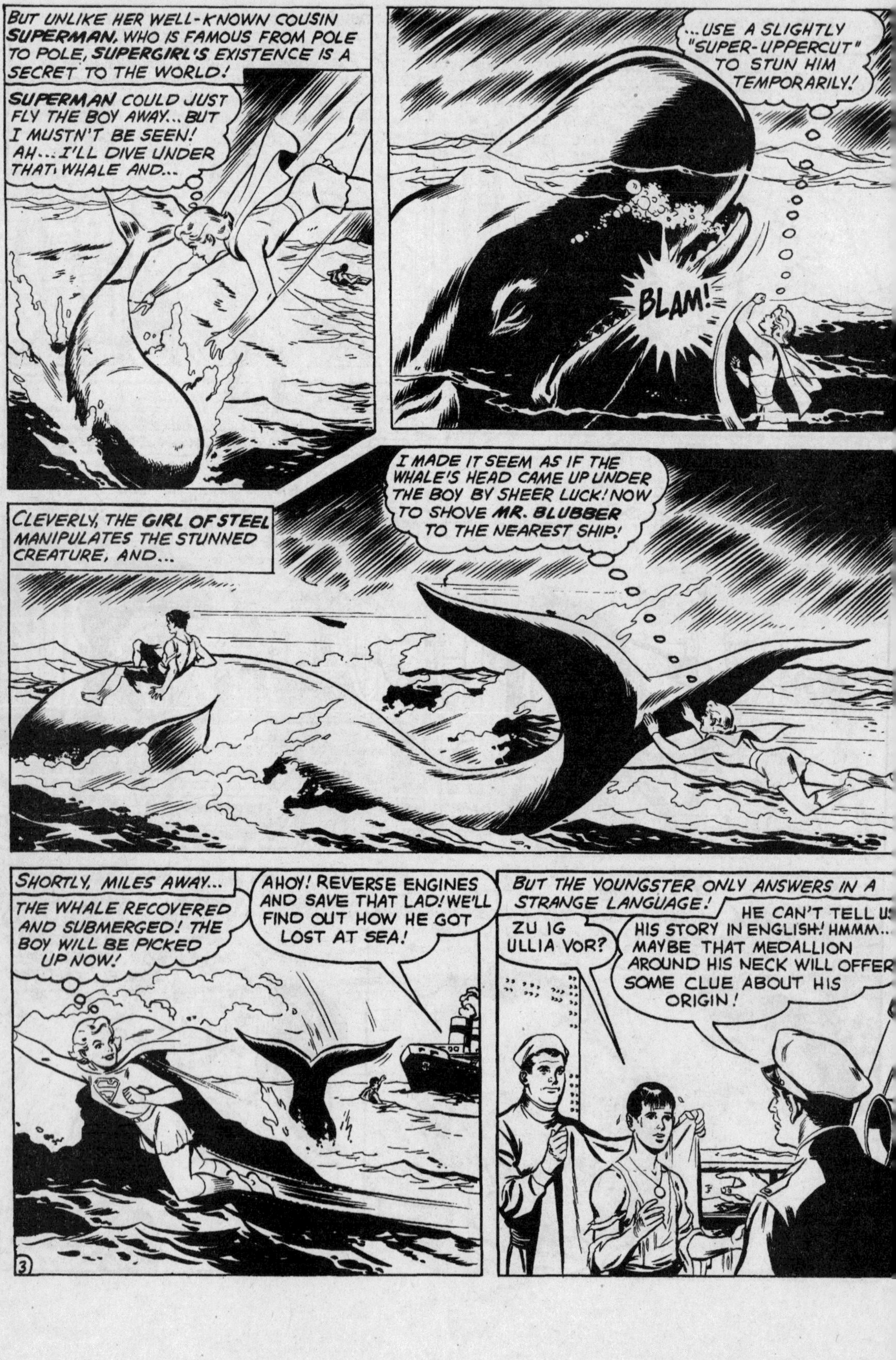
BUT UNLIKE HER WELL-KNOWN COUSIN SUPERMAN. WHO IS FAMOUS FROM POLE TO POLE, SUPERGIRL'S EXISTENCE IS A SECRET TO THE WORLD!
SUPERMAN COULD JUST FLY THE BOY AWAY... BUT I MUSTN'T BE SEEN! AH... I'LL DIVE UNDER THAT WHALE AND...
...USE A SLIGHTLY "SUPER-UPPERCUT" TO STUN HIM TEMPORARILY!
BLAM!
CLEVERLY, THE GIRL OF STEEL MANIPULATES THE STUNNED CREATURE, AND...
I MADE IT SEEM AS IF THE WHALE'S HEAD CAME UP UNDER THE BOY BY SHEER LUCK! NOW TO SHOVE MR. BLUBBER TO THE NEAREST SHIP!
SHORTLY, MILES AWAY...
THE WHALE RECOVERED AND SUBMERGED! THE BOY WILL BE PICKED UP NOW!
AHOY! REVERSE ENGINES AND SAVE THAT LAD! WE'LL FIND OUT HOW HE GOT LOST AT SEA!
3
BUT THE YOUNGSTER ONLY ANSWERS IN A STRANGE LANGUAGE!
ZU IG ULLIA VOR?
HE CAN'T TELL US HIS STORY IN ENGLISH! HMMM... MAYBE THAT MEDALLION AROUND HIS NECK WILL OFFER SOME CLUE ABOUT HIS ORIGIN!

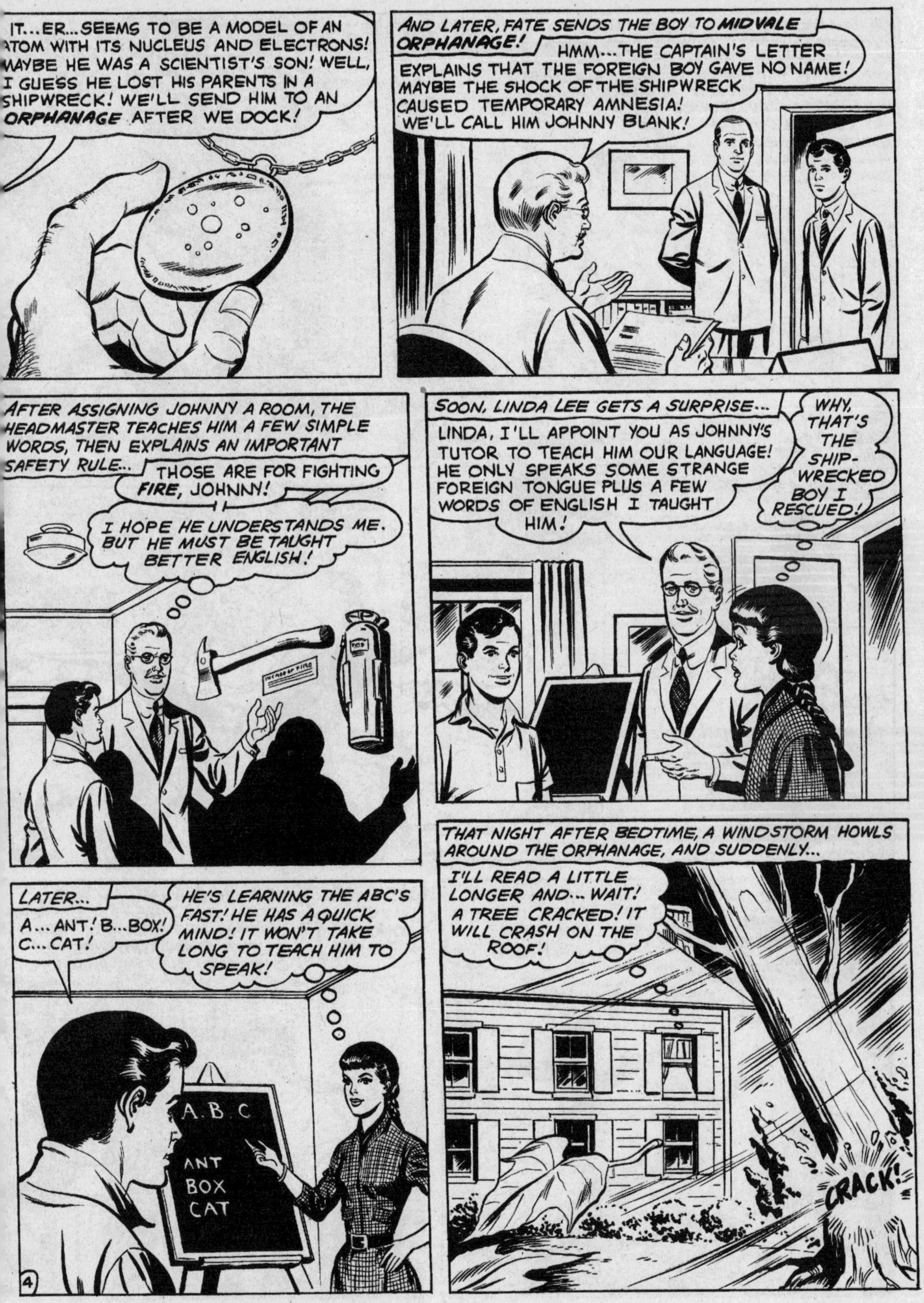
IT...ER...SEEMS TO BE A MODEL OF AN ATOM WITH ITS NUCLEUS AND ELECTRONS! MAYBE HE WAS A SCIENTIST'S SON! WELL, I GUESS HE LOST HIS PARENTS IN A SHIPWRECK! WE'LL SEND HIM TO AN ORPHANAGE AFTER WE DOCK!
AND LATER, FATE SENDS THE BOY TO MIDVALE ORPHANAGE!
HMM...THE CAPTAIN'S LETTER EXPLAINS THAT THE FOREIGN BOY GAVE NO NAME! MAYBE THE SHOCK OF THE SHIPWRECK CAUSED TEMPORARY AMNESIA! WE'LL CALL HIM JOHNNY BLANK!
AFTER ASSIGNING JOHNNY A ROOM, THE HEADMASTER TEACHES HIM A FEW SIMPLE WORDS, THEN EXPLAINS AN IMPORTANT SAFETY RULE...
THOSE ARE FOR FIGHTING FIRE, JOHNNY!
I HOPE HE UNDERSTANDS ME. BUT HE MUST BE TAUGHT BETTER ENGLISH!
SOON, LINDA LEE GETS A SURPRISE...
LINDA, I'LL APPOINT YOU AS JOHNNY'S TUTOR TO TEACH HIM OUR LANGUAGE! HE ONLY SPEAKS SOME STRANGE FOREIGN TONGUE PLUS A FEW WORDS OF ENGLISH I TAUGHT HIM!
WHY, THAT'S THE SHIP-WRECKED BOY I RESCUED!
LATER...
A... ANT! B...BOX! C...CAT!
HE'S LEARNING THE ABC'S FAST! HE HAS A QUICK MIND! IT WON'T TAKE LONG TO TEACH HIM TO SPEAK!
A B C
ANT
BOX
CAT
4
THAT NIGHT AFTER BEDTIME, A WINDSTORM HOWLS AROUND THE ORPHANAGE, AND SUDDENLY...
I'LL READ A LITTLE LONGER AND... WAIT! A TREE CRACKED! IT WILL CRASH ON THE ROOF!
CRACK!

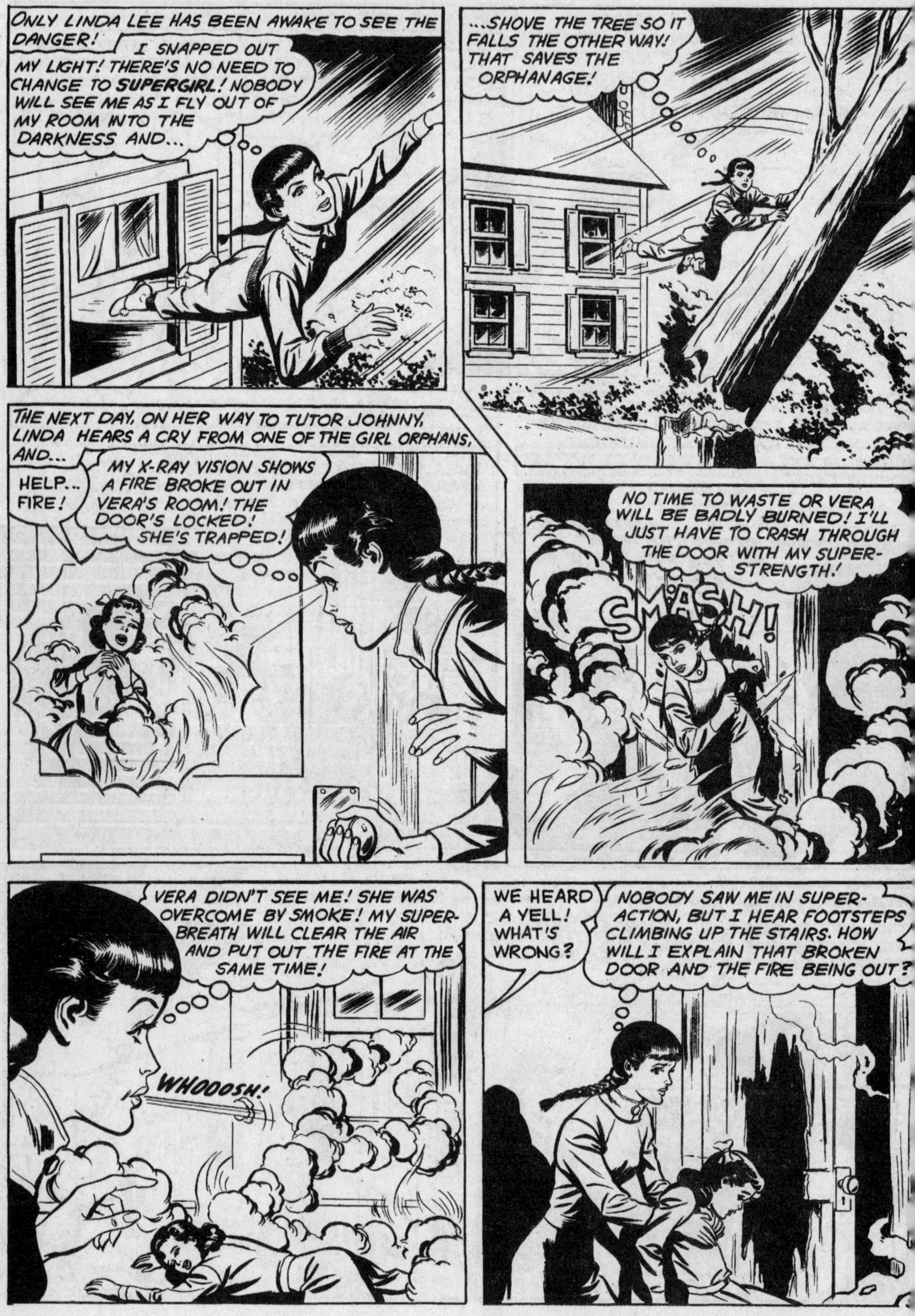
ONLY LINDA LEE HAS BEEN AWAKE TO SEE THE DANGER!
I SNAPPED OUT MY LIGHT! THERE'S NO NEED TO CHANGE TO SUPERGIRL! NOBODY WILL SEE ME AS I FLY OUT OF MY ROOM INTO THE DARKNESS AND...
...SHOVE THE TREE SO IT FALLS THE OTHER WAY! THAT SAVES THE ORPHANAGE!
THE NEXT DAY, ON HER WAY TO TUTOR JOHNNY, LINDA HEARS A CRY FROM ONE OF THE GIRL ORPHANS, AND...
HELP... FIRE!
MY X-RAY VISION SHOWS A FIRE BROKE OUT IN VERA'S ROOM! THE DOOR'S LOCKED! SHE'S TRAPPED!
NO TIME TO WASTE OR VERA WILL BE BADLY BURNED! I'LL JUST HAVE TO CRASH THROUGH THE DOOR WITH MY SUPER-STRENGTH!
SMASH!
VERA DIDN'T SEE ME! SHE WAS OVERCOME BY SMOKE! MY SUPER-BREATH WILL CLEAR THE AIR AND PUT OUT THE FIRE AT THE SAME TIME!
WHOOOSH!
WE HEARD A YELL! WHAT'S WRONG?
NOBODY SAW ME IN SUPER-ACTION, BUT I HEAR FOOTSTEPS CLIMBING UP THE STAIRS. HOW WILL I EXPLAIN THAT BROKEN DOOR AND THE FIRE BEING OUT?

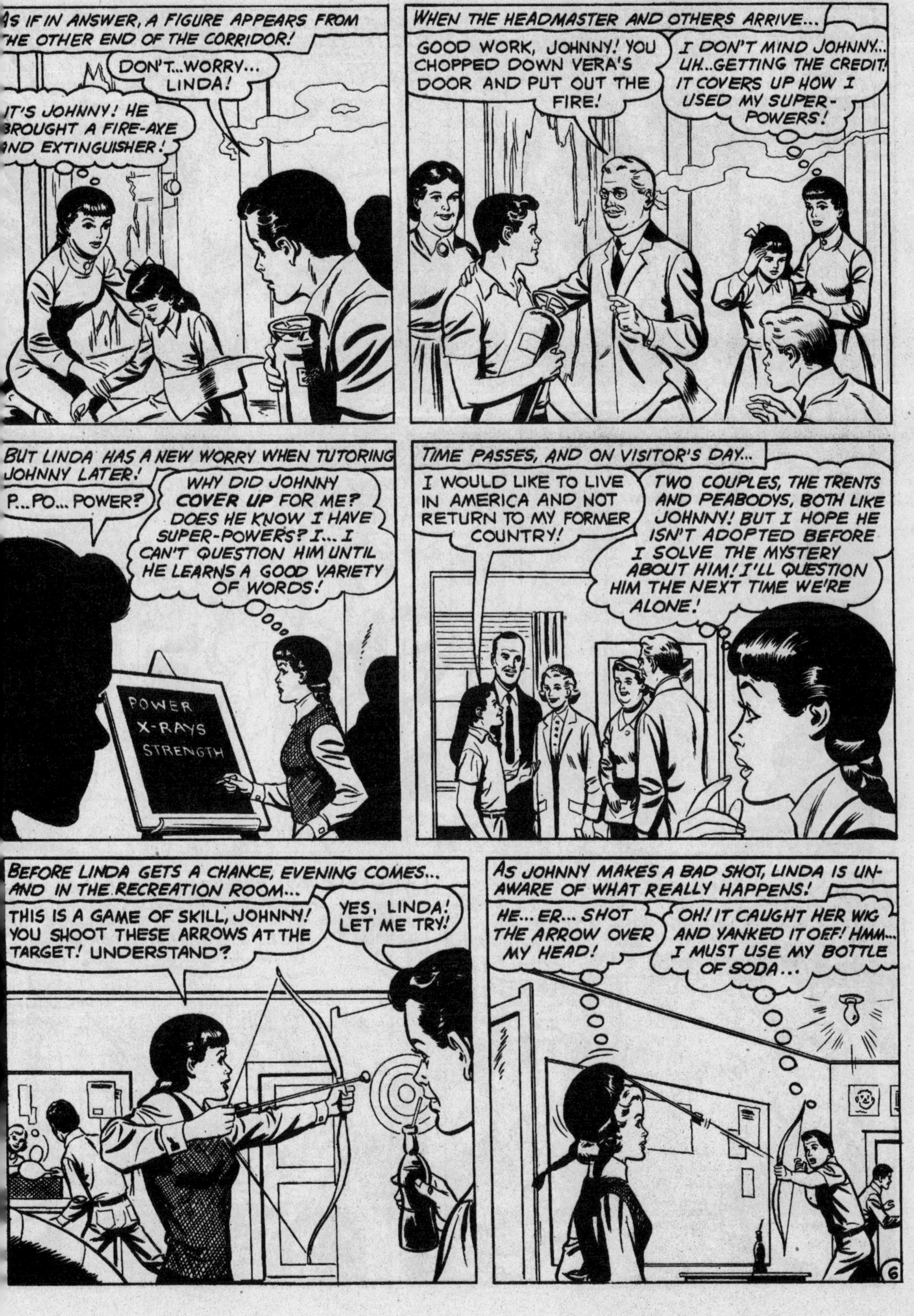
AS IF IN ANSWER, A FIGURE APPEARS FROM THE OTHER END OF THE CORRIDOR!
DON'T...WORRY... LINDA!
IT'S JOHNNY! HE BROUGHT A FIRE-AXE AND EXTINGUISHER!
WHEN THE HEADMASTER AND OTHERS ARRIVE...
GOOD WORK, JOHNNY! YOU CHOPPED DOWN VERA'S DOOR AND PUT OUT THE FIRE!
I DON'T MIND JOHNNY... UH...GETTING THE CREDIT! IT COVERS UP HOW I USED MY SUPER-POWERS!
BUT LINDA HAS A NEW WORRY WHEN TUTORING JOHNNY LATER!
P...PO... POWER?
WHY DID JOHNNY COVER UP FOR ME? DOES HE KNOW I HAVE SUPER-POWERS? I... I CAN'T QUESTION HIM UNTIL HE LEARNS A GOOD VARIETY OF WORDS!
POWER
X-RAYS
STRENGTH
TIME PASSES, AND ON VISITOR'S DAY...
I WOULD LIKE TO LIVE IN AMERICA AND NOT RETURN TO MY FORMER COUNTRY!
TWO COUPLES, THE TRENTS AND PEABODYS, BOTH LIKE JOHNNY! BUT I HOPE HE ISN'T ADOPTED BEFORE I SOLVE THE MYSTERY ABOUT HIM! I'LL QUESTION HIM THE NEXT TIME WE'RE ALONE!
BEFORE LINDA GETS A CHANCE, EVENING COMES... AND IN THE RECREATION ROOM...
THIS IS A GAME OF SKILL, JOHNNY! YOU SHOOT THESE ARROWS AT THE TARGET! UNDERSTAND?
YES, LINDA! LET ME TRY!
AS JOHNNY MAKES A BAD SHOT, LINDA IS UNAWARE OF WHAT REALLY HAPPENS!
HE... ER... SHOT THE ARROW OVER MY HEAD!
OH! IT CAUGHT HER WIG AND YANKED IT OFF! HMM... I MUST USE MY BOTTLE OF SODA...
6

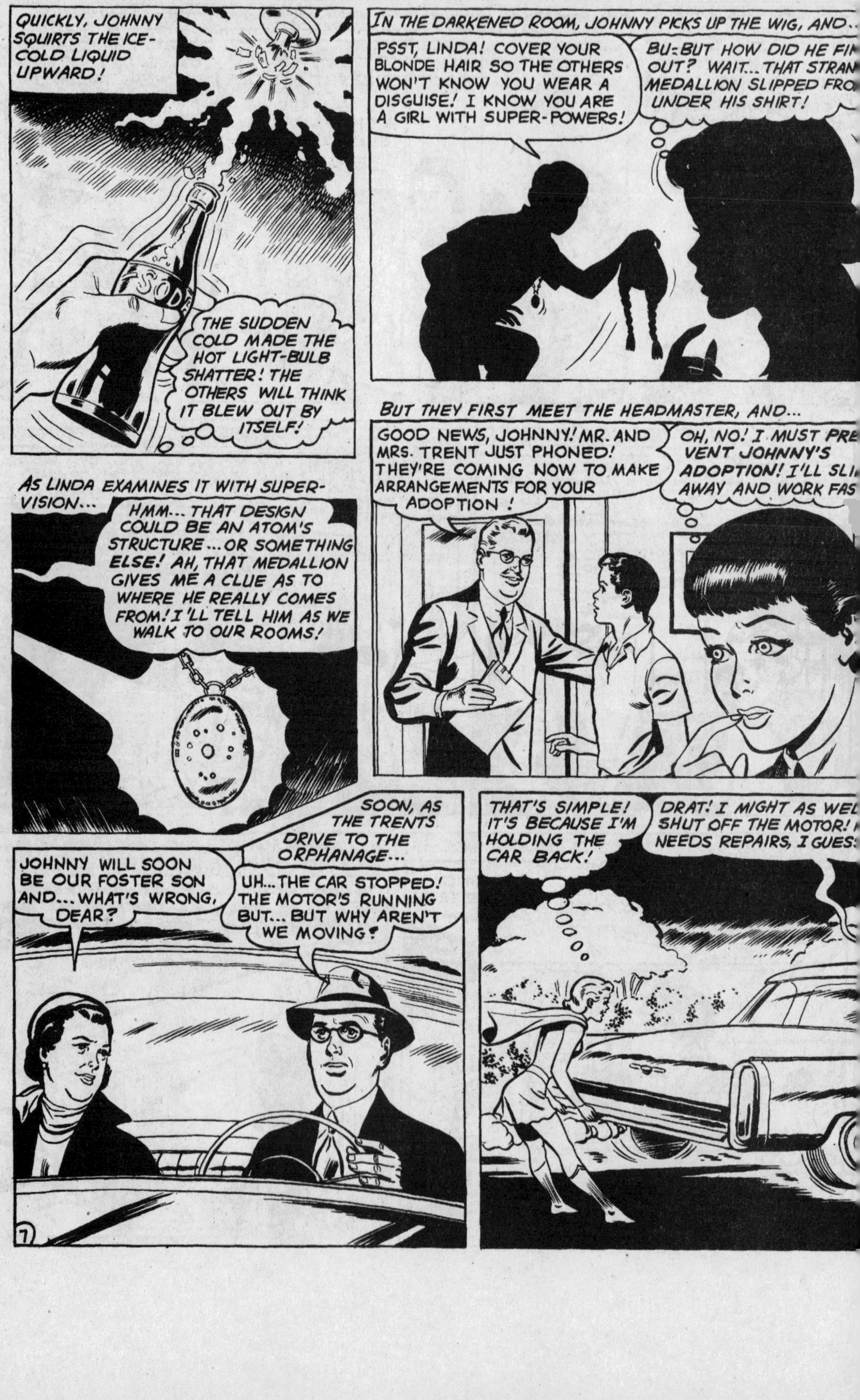
QUICKLY, JOHNNY SQUIRTS THE ICE-COLD LIQUID UPWARD!
SODA
THE SUDDEN COLD MADE THE HOT LIGHT-BULB SHATTER! THE OTHERS WILL THINK IT BLEW OUT BY ITSELF!
IN THE DARKENED ROOM, JOHNNY PICKS UP THE WIG, AND...
PSST, LINDA! COVER YOUR BLONDE HAIR SO THE OTHERS WON'T KNOW YOU WEAR A DISGUISE! I KNOW YOU ARE A GIRL WITH SUPER-POWERS!
BU-BUT HOW DID HE FI OUT? WAIT... THAT STRAN MEDALLION SLIPPED FRO UNDER HIS SHIRT!
AS LINDA EXAMINES IT WITH SUPER-VISION...
HMM... THAT DESIGN COULD BE AN ATOM'S STRUCTURE... OR SOMETHING ELSE! AH, THAT MEDALLION GIVES ME A CLUE AS TO WHERE HE REALLY COMES FROM! I'LL TELL HIM AS WE WALK TO OUR ROOMS!
BUT THEY FIRST MEET THE HEADMASTER, AND...
GOOD NEWS, JOHNNY! MR. AND MRS. TRENT JUST PHONED! THEY'RE COMING NOW TO MAKE ARRANGEMENTS FOR YOUR ADOPTION!
OH, NO! I MUST PRE VENT JOHNNY'S ADOPTION! I'LL SLI AWAY AND WORK FAS
SOON, AS THE TRENTS DRIVE TO THE ORPHANAGE...
JOHNNY WILL SOON BE OUR FOSTER SON AND... WHAT'S WRONG, DEAR?
UH... THE CAR STOPPED! THE MOTOR'S RUNNING BUT... BUT WHY AREN'T WE MOVING?
7
THAT'S SIMPLE! IT'S BECAUSE I'M HOLDING THE CAR BACK!
DRAT! I MIGHT AS WEL SHUT OFF THE MOTOR! NEEDS REPAIRS, I GUES

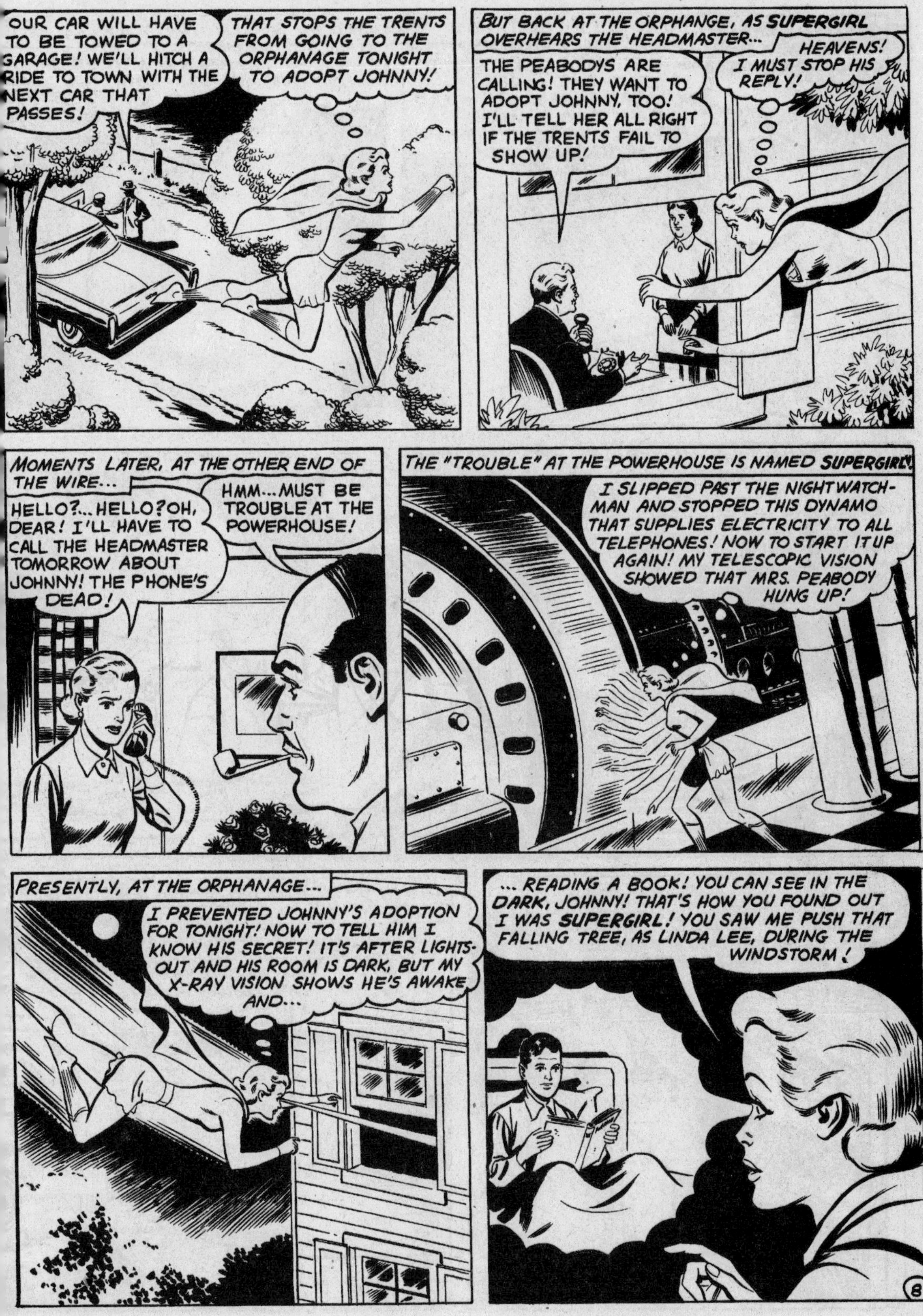
OUR CAR WILL HAVE TO BE TOWED TO A GARAGE! WE'LL HITCH A RIDE TO TOWN WITH THE NEXT CAR THAT PASSES!
THAT STOPS THE TRENTS FROM GOING TO THE ORPHANAGE TONIGHT TO ADOPT JOHNNY!
BUT BACK AT THE ORPHANGE, AS SUPERGIRL OVERHEARS THE HEADMASTER...
THE PEABODYS ARE CALLING! THEY WANT TO ADOPT JOHNNY, TOO! I'LL TELL HER ALL RIGHT IF THE TRENTS FAIL TO SHOW UP!
HEAVENS! I MUST STOP HIS REPLY!
MOMENTS LATER, AT THE OTHER END OF THE WIRE...
HELLO?...HELLO? OH, DEAR! I'LL HAVE TO CALL THE HEADMASTER TOMORROW ABOUT JOHNNY! THE PHONE'S DEAD!
HMM...MUST BE TROUBLE AT THE POWERHOUSE!
THE "TROUBLE" AT THE POWERHOUSE IS NAMED SUPERGIRL!
I SLIPPED PAST THE NIGHTWATCHMAN AND STOPPED THIS DYNAMO THAT SUPPLIES ELECTRICITY TO ALL TELEPHONES! NOW TO START IT UP AGAIN! MY TELESCOPIC VISION SHOWED THAT MRS. PEABODY HUNG UP!
PRESENTLY, AT THE ORPHANAGE...
I PREVENTED JOHNNY'S ADOPTION FOR TONIGHT! NOW TO TELL HIM I KNOW HIS SECRET! IT'S AFTER LIGHTS-OUT AND HIS ROOM IS DARK, BUT MY X-RAY VISION SHOWS HE'S AWAKE AND...
... READING A BOOK! YOU CAN SEE IN THE DARK, JOHNNY! THAT'S HOW YOU FOUND OUT I WAS SUPERGIRL! YOU SAW ME PUSH THAT FALLING TREE, AS LINDA LEE, DURING THE WINDSTORM!
8

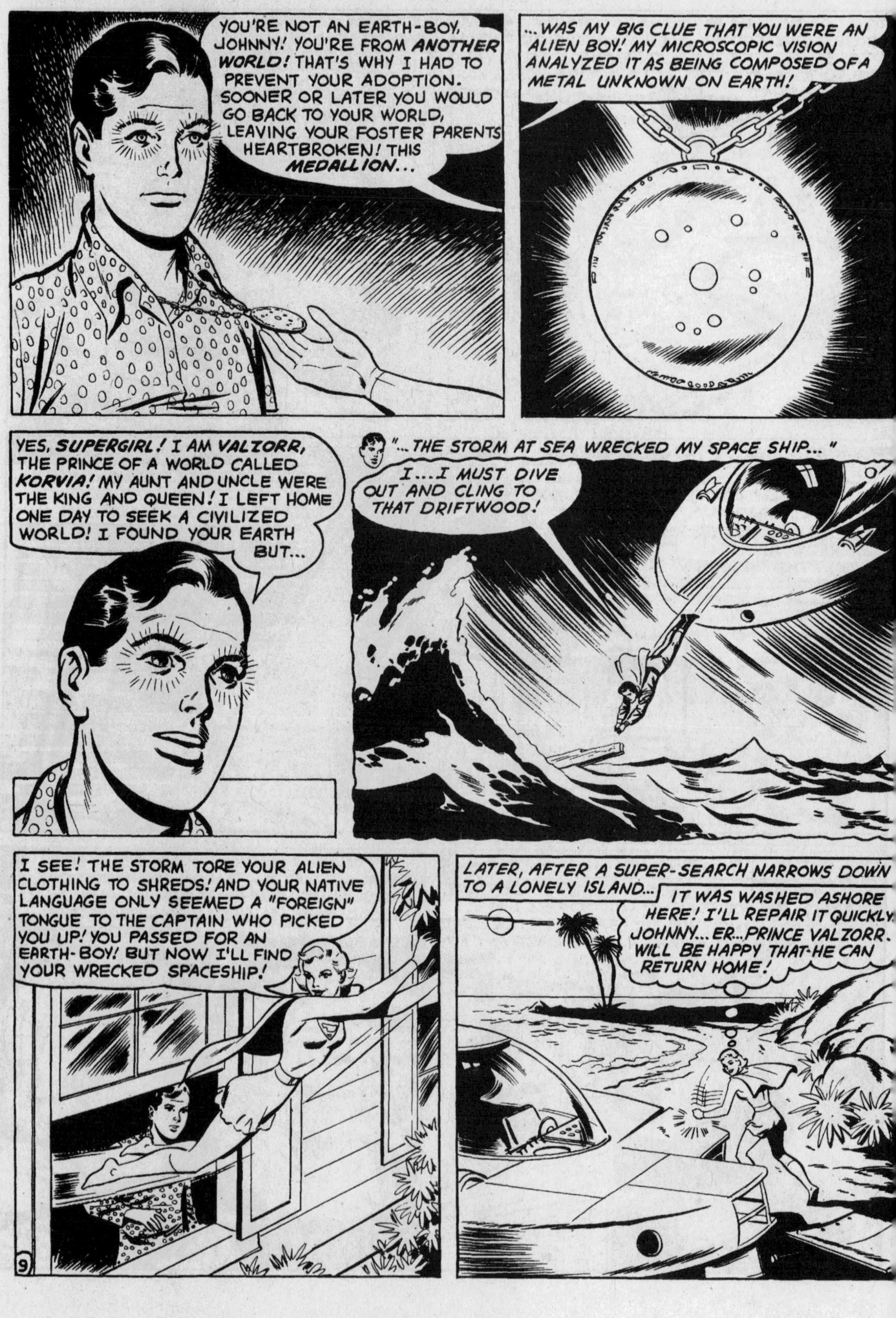
YOU'RE NOT AN EARTH-BOY, JOHNNY! YOU'RE FROM ANOTHER WORLD! THAT'S WHY I HAD TO PREVENT YOUR ADOPTION. SOONER OR LATER YOU WOULD GO BACK TO YOUR WORLD, LEAVING YOUR FOSTER PARENTS HEARTBROKEN! THIS MEDALLION...
...WAS MY BIG CLUE THAT YOU WERE AN ALIEN BOY! MY MICROSCOPIC VISION ANALYZED IT AS BEING COMPOSED OF A METAL UNKNOWN ON EARTH!
YES, SUPERGIRL! I AM VALZORR, THE PRINCE OF A WORLD CALLED KORVIA! MY AUNT AND UNCLE WERE THE KING AND QUEEN! I LEFT HOME ONE DAY TO SEEK A CIVILIZED WORLD! I FOUND YOUR EARTH BUT...
"...THE STORM AT SEA WRECKED MY SPACE SHIP..."
I...I MUST DIVE OUT AND CLING TO THAT DRIFTWOOD!
I SEE! THE STORM TORE YOUR ALIEN CLOTHING TO SHREDS! AND YOUR NATIVE LANGUAGE ONLY SEEMED A "FOREIGN" TONGUE TO THE CAPTAIN WHO PICKED YOU UP! YOU PASSED FOR AN EARTH-BOY! BUT NOW I'LL FIND YOUR WRECKED SPACESHIP!
9
LATER, AFTER A SUPER-SEARCH NARROWS DOWN TO A LONELY ISLAND...
IT WAS WASHED ASHORE HERE! I'LL REPAIR IT QUICKLY. JOHNNY... ER...PRINCE VALZORR... WILL BE HAPPY THAT HE CAN RETURN HOME!

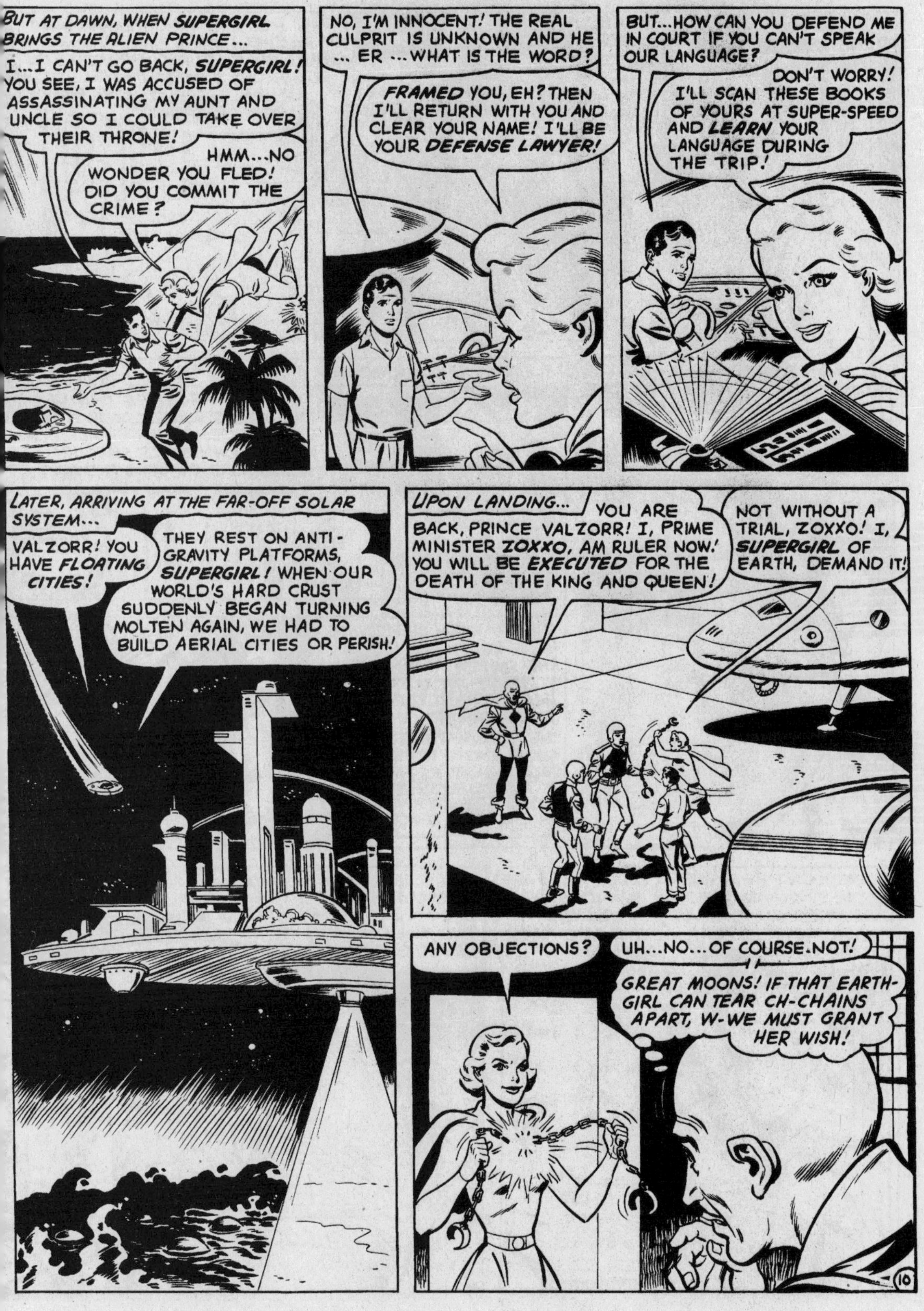
BUT AT DAWN, WHEN SUPERGIRL BRINGS THE ALIEN PRINCE...
I...I CAN'T GO BACK, SUPERGIRL! YOU SEE, I WAS ACCUSED OF ASSASSINATING MY AUNT AND UNCLE SO I COULD TAKE OVER THEIR THRONE!
HMM...NO WONDER YOU FLED! DID YOU COMMIT THE CRIME?
NO, I'M INNOCENT! THE REAL CULPRIT IS UNKNOWN AND HE ... ER ... WHAT IS THE WORD?
FRAMED YOU, EH? THEN I'LL RETURN WITH YOU AND CLEAR YOUR NAME! I'LL BE YOUR DEFENSE LAWYER!
BUT...HOW CAN YOU DEFEND ME IN COURT IF YOU CAN'T SPEAK OUR LANGUAGE?
DON'T WORRY! I'LL SCAN THESE BOOKS OF YOURS AT SUPER-SPEED AND LEARN YOUR LANGUAGE DURING THE TRIP!
LATER, ARRIVING AT THE FAR-OFF SOLAR SYSTEM...
VALZORR! YOU HAVE FLOATING CITIES!
THEY REST ON ANTI-GRAVITY PLATFORMS, SUPERGIRL! WHEN OUR WORLD'S HARD CRUST SUDDENLY BEGAN TURNING MOLTEN AGAIN, WE HAD TO BUILD AERIAL CITIES OR PERISH!
UPON LANDING...
YOU ARE BACK, PRINCE VALZORR! I, PRIME MINISTER ZOXXO, AM RULER NOW! YOU WILL BE EXECUTED FOR THE DEATH OF THE KING AND QUEEN!
NOT WITHOUT A TRIAL, ZOXXO! I, SUPERGIRL OF EARTH, DEMAND IT!
ANY OBJECTIONS?
UH...NO...OF COURSE NOT!
GREAT MOONS! IF THAT EARTH-GIRL CAN TEAR CH-CHAINS APART, W-WE MUST GRANT HER WISH!
10

AS THE TRIAL BEGINS... PROCEED, PROSECUTOR *ZOXXO!*

FIRST, I WILL MAKE THE CRIME CLEAR TO THE EARTH-GIRL! THAT DANGEROUS BEAST WE CAPTURED BREATHES OUT POISONOUS FUMES! WE WILL GET RID OF HIM IN THE *ATOM TRANSPORTER* CABINET!

THE *ATOM TRANSPORTER* WILL NOW BROADCAST HIS SCATTERED ATOMS INTO THIN AIR, MAKING HIM DISAPPEAR! EACH CREATURE OR PERSON HAS HIS OWN WAVELENGTH! WE USE IT TO TRAVEL FROM PLACE TO PLACE!

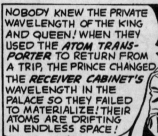

ACROSS THE COURTROOM A MOMENT LATER...

NOW AS I TUNE THIS *RECEIVER CABINET* TO THE *WRONG* WAVELENGTH, THE BEAST DOESN'T MATERIALIZE! AND THAT IS HOW PRINCE VALZORR MURDERED THE KING AND QUEEN!

NOBODY KNEW THE PRIVATE WAVELENGTH OF THE KING AND QUEEN! WHEN THEY USED THE *ATOM TRANSPORTER* TO RETURN FROM A TRIP, THE PRINCE CHANGED THE *RECEIVER CABINET'S* WAVELENGTH IN THE PALACE SO THEY FAILED TO MATERIALIZE! THEIR ATOMS ARE DRIFTING IN ENDLESS SPACE!

HMMM!

IT WOULDN'T BE MURDER IF THE KING AND QUEEN RETURNED *ALIVE*, WOULD IT? I'LL TRY THE PUSH-BUTTONS...

FOOL! THERE ARE *MILLIONS* OF WAVELENGTHS! YOU CAN NEVER FIND THE RIGHT COMBINATION OF BUTTONS!

I WILL IF I WORK AT *SUPER-SPEED!* THERE, I'VE TRIED ONE MILLION COMBINATIONS... TWO MILLION...AH, I HIT THE RIGHT ONE!

THE KING AND QUEEN ARE M-MATERIALIZING.

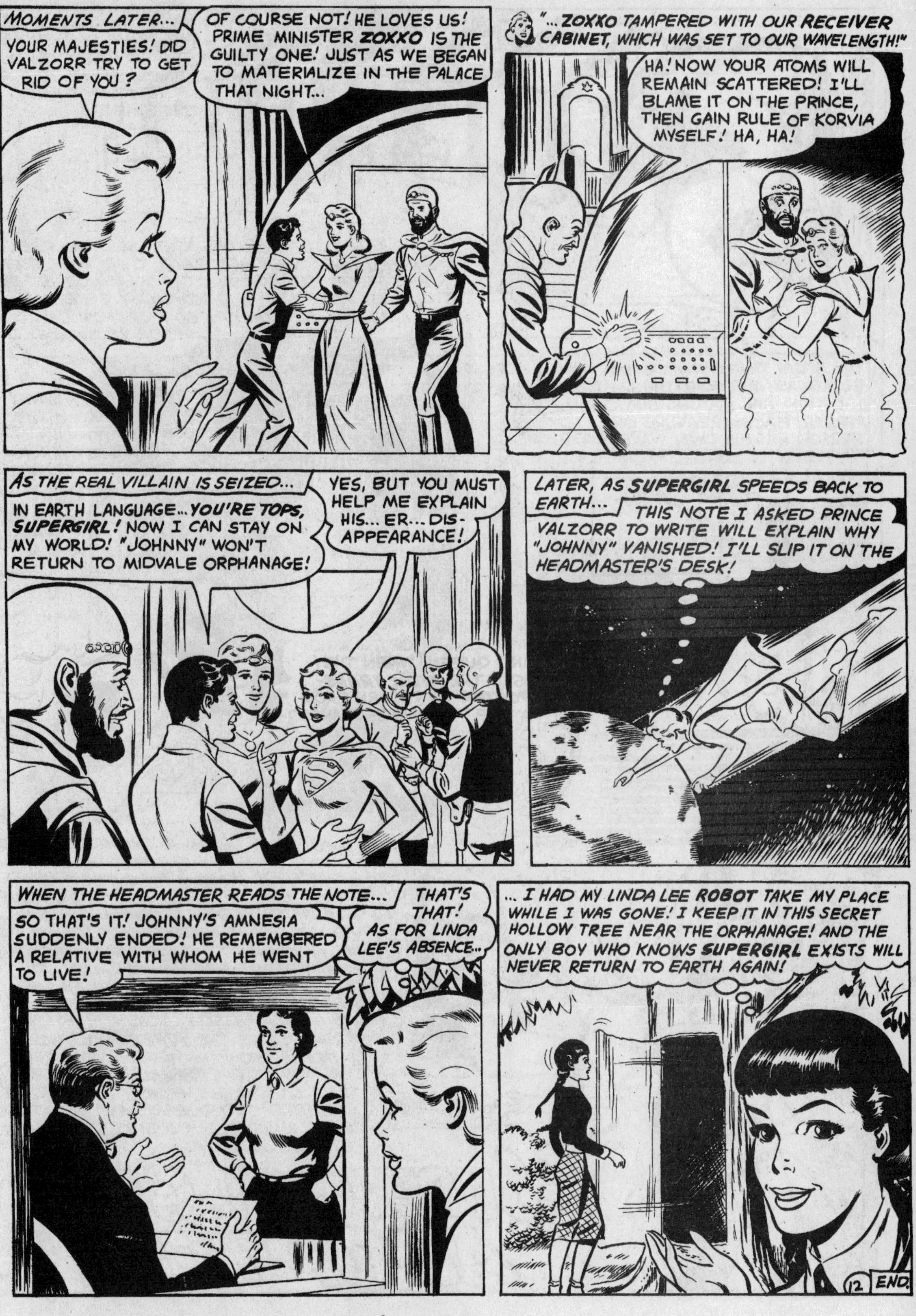
MOMENTS LATER...
YOUR MAJESTIES! DID VALZORR TRY TO GET RID OF YOU?
OF COURSE NOT! HE LOVES US! PRIME MINISTER ZOXXO IS THE GUILTY ONE! JUST AS WE BEGAN TO MATERIALIZE IN THE PALACE THAT NIGHT...
"...ZOXXO TAMPERED WITH OUR RECEIVER CABINET, WHICH WAS SET TO OUR WAVELENGTH!"
HA! NOW YOUR ATOMS WILL REMAIN SCATTERED! I'LL BLAME IT ON THE PRINCE, THEN GAIN RULE OF KORVIA MYSELF! HA, HA!
AS THE REAL VILLAIN IS SEIZED...
IN EARTH LANGUAGE...YOU'RE TOPS, SUPERGIRL! NOW I CAN STAY ON MY WORLD! "JOHNNY" WON'T RETURN TO MIDVALE ORPHANAGE!
YES, BUT YOU MUST HELP ME EXPLAIN HIS... ER... DIS-APPEARANCE!
LATER, AS SUPERGIRL SPEEDS BACK TO EARTH...
THIS NOTE I ASKED PRINCE VALZORR TO WRITE WILL EXPLAIN WHY "JOHNNY" VANISHED! I'LL SLIP IT ON THE HEADMASTER'S DESK!
WHEN THE HEADMASTER READS THE NOTE...
SO THAT'S IT! JOHNNY'S AMNESIA SUDDENLY ENDED! HE REMEMBERED A RELATIVE WITH WHOM HE WENT TO LIVE!
THAT'S THAT! AS FOR LINDA LEE'S ABSENCE...
...I HAD MY LINDA LEE ROBOT TAKE MY PLACE WHILE I WAS GONE! I KEEP IT IN THIS SECRET HOLLOW TREE NEAR THE ORPHANAGE! AND THE ONLY BOY WHO KNOWS SUPERGIRL EXISTS WILL NEVER RETURN TO EARTH AGAIN!
12
END.

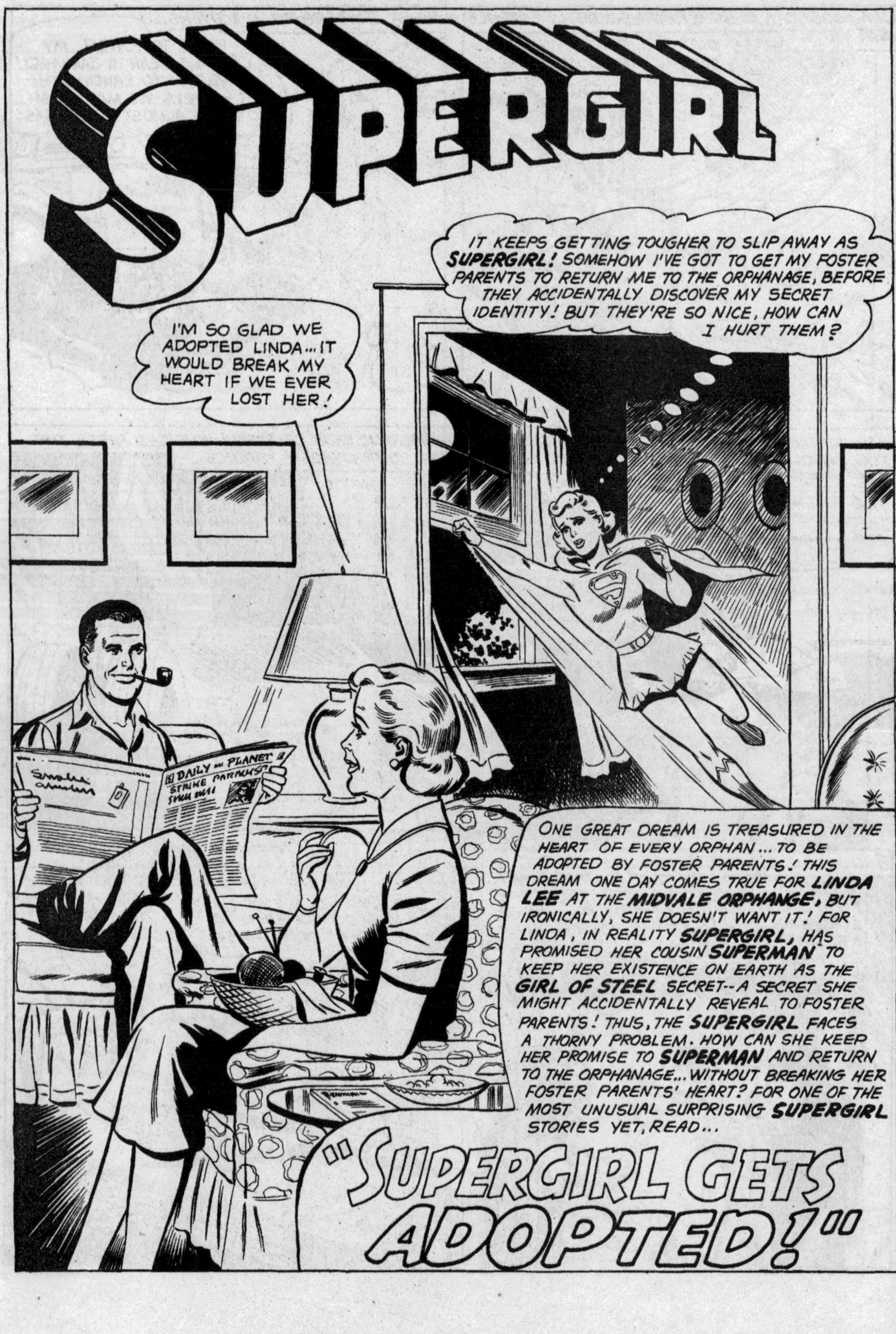
SUPERGIRL
I'M SO GLAD WE ADOPTED LINDA... IT WOULD BREAK MY HEART IF WE EVER LOST HER!
IT KEEPS GETTING TOUGHER TO SLIP AWAY AS SUPERGIRL! SOMEHOW I'VE GOT TO GET MY FOSTER PARENTS TO RETURN ME TO THE ORPHANAGE, BEFORE THEY ACCIDENTALLY DISCOVER MY SECRET IDENTITY! BUT THEY'RE SO NICE, HOW CAN I HURT THEM?
DAILY PLANET
ONE GREAT DREAM IS TREASURED IN THE HEART OF EVERY ORPHAN... TO BE ADOPTED BY FOSTER PARENTS! THIS DREAM ONE DAY COMES TRUE FOR LINDA LEE AT THE MIDVALE ORPHANGE, BUT IRONICALLY, SHE DOESN'T WANT IT! FOR LINDA, IN REALITY SUPERGIRL, HAS PROMISED HER COUSIN SUPERMAN TO KEEP HER EXISTENCE ON EARTH AS THE GIRL OF STEEL SECRET--A SECRET SHE MIGHT ACCIDENTALLY REVEAL TO FOSTER PARENTS! THUS, THE SUPERGIRL FACES A THORNY PROBLEM. HOW CAN SHE KEEP HER PROMISE TO SUPERMAN AND RETURN TO THE ORPHANAGE... WITHOUT BREAKING HER FOSTER PARENTS' HEART? FOR ONE OF THE MOST UNUSUAL SURPRISING SUPERGIRL STORIES YET, READ...
"SUPERGIRL GETS ADOPTED!"

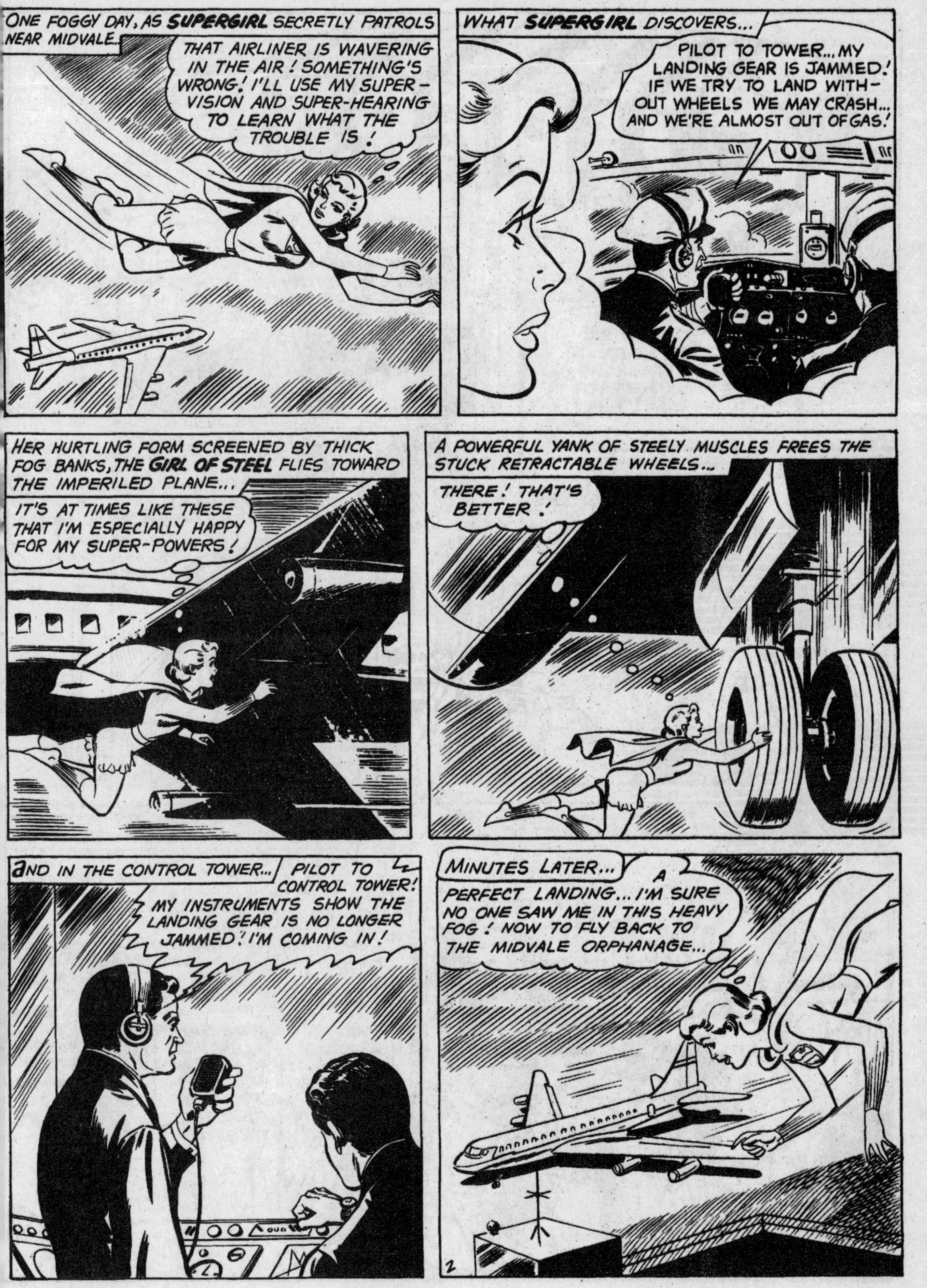
ONE FOGGY DAY, AS SUPERGIRL SECRETLY PATROLS NEAR MIDVALE...
THAT AIRLINER IS WAVERING IN THE AIR! SOMETHING'S WRONG! I'LL USE MY SUPER-VISION AND SUPER-HEARING TO LEARN WHAT THE TROUBLE IS!
WHAT SUPERGIRL DISCOVERS...
PILOT TO TOWER... MY LANDING GEAR IS JAMMED! IF WE TRY TO LAND WITHOUT WHEELS WE MAY CRASH... AND WE'RE ALMOST OUT OF GAS!
HER HURTLING FORM SCREENED BY THICK FOG BANKS, THE GIRL OF STEEL FLIES TOWARD THE IMPERILED PLANE...
IT'S AT TIMES LIKE THESE THAT I'M ESPECIALLY HAPPY FOR MY SUPER-POWERS!
A POWERFUL YANK OF STEELY MUSCLES FREES THE STUCK RETRACTABLE WHEELS...
THERE! THAT'S BETTER!
AND IN THE CONTROL TOWER...
PILOT TO CONTROL TOWER! MY INSTRUMENTS SHOW THE LANDING GEAR IS NO LONGER JAMMED! I'M COMING IN!
MINUTES LATER...
A PERFECT LANDING... I'M SURE NO ONE SAW ME IN THIS HEAVY FOG! NOW TO FLY BACK TO THE MIDVALE ORPHANAGE...
2

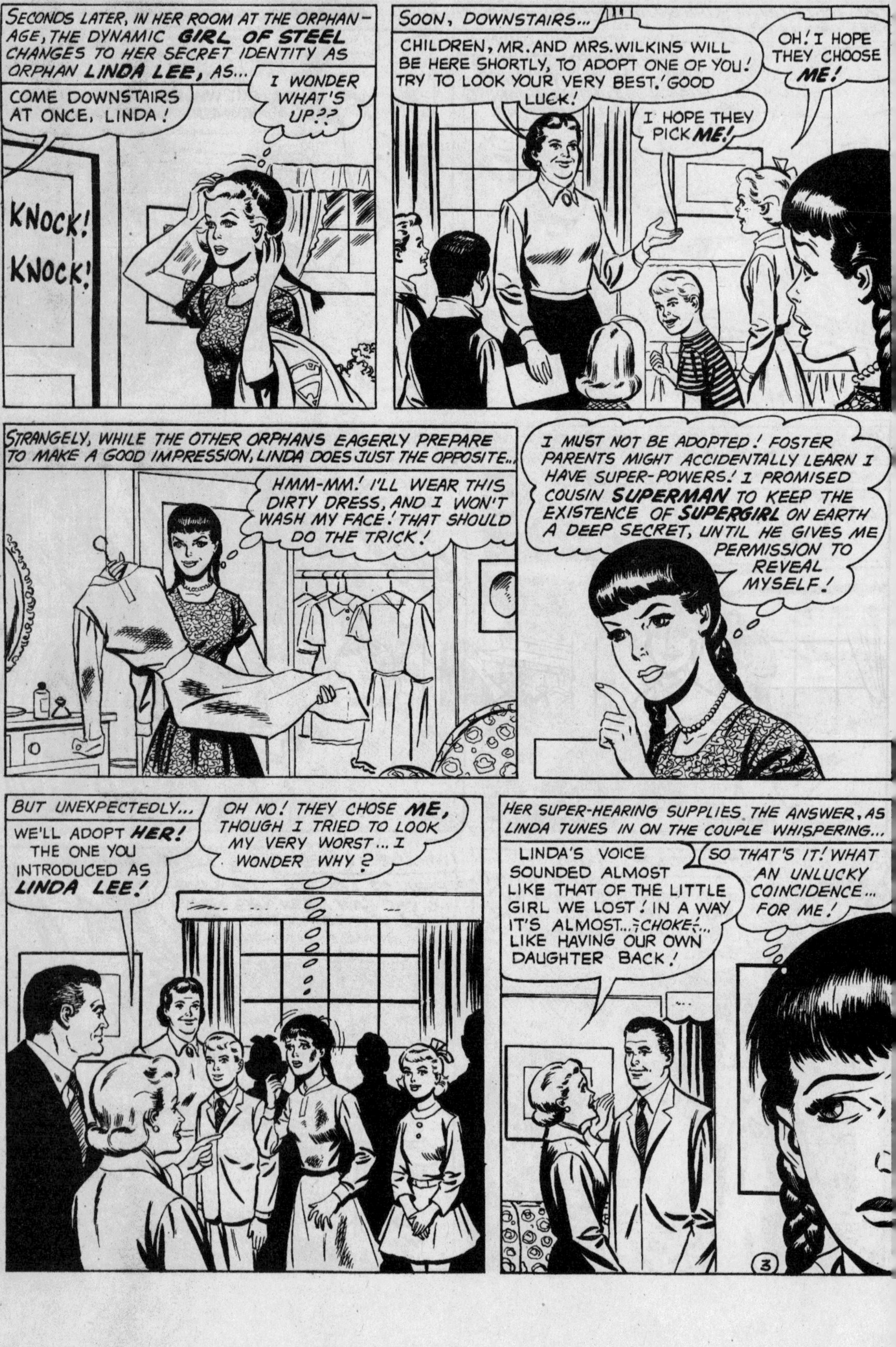
SECONDS LATER, IN HER ROOM AT THE ORPHANAGE, THE DYNAMIC GIRL OF STEEL CHANGES TO HER SECRET IDENTITY AS ORPHAN LINDA LEE, AS...
COME DOWNSTAIRS AT ONCE, LINDA!
I WONDER WHAT'S UP??
KNOCK! KNOCK!
SOON, DOWNSTAIRS...
CHILDREN, MR. AND MRS. WILKINS WILL BE HERE SHORTLY, TO ADOPT ONE OF YOU! TRY TO LOOK YOUR VERY BEST! GOOD LUCK!
I HOPE THEY PICK ME!
OH! I HOPE THEY CHOOSE ME!
STRANGELY, WHILE THE OTHER ORPHANS EAGERLY PREPARE TO MAKE A GOOD IMPRESSION, LINDA DOES JUST THE OPPOSITE...
HMM-MM! I'LL WEAR THIS DIRTY DRESS, AND I WON'T WASH MY FACE! THAT SHOULD DO THE TRICK!
I MUST NOT BE ADOPTED! FOSTER PARENTS MIGHT ACCIDENTALLY LEARN I HAVE SUPER-POWERS! I PROMISED COUSIN SUPERMAN TO KEEP THE EXISTENCE OF SUPERGIRL ON EARTH A DEEP SECRET, UNTIL HE GIVES ME PERMISSION TO REVEAL MYSELF!
BUT UNEXPECTEDLY...
WE'LL ADOPT HER! THE ONE YOU INTRODUCED AS LINDA LEE!
OH NO! THEY CHOSE ME, THOUGH I TRIED TO LOOK MY VERY WORST... I WONDER WHY?
HER SUPER-HEARING SUPPLIES THE ANSWER, AS LINDA TUNES IN ON THE COUPLE WHISPERING...
LINDA'S VOICE SOUNDED ALMOST LIKE THAT OF THE LITTLE GIRL WE LOST! IN A WAY IT'S ALMOST...CHOKE...LIKE HAVING OUR OWN DAUGHTER BACK!
SO THAT'S IT! WHAT AN UNLUCKY COINCIDENCE... FOR ME!
3

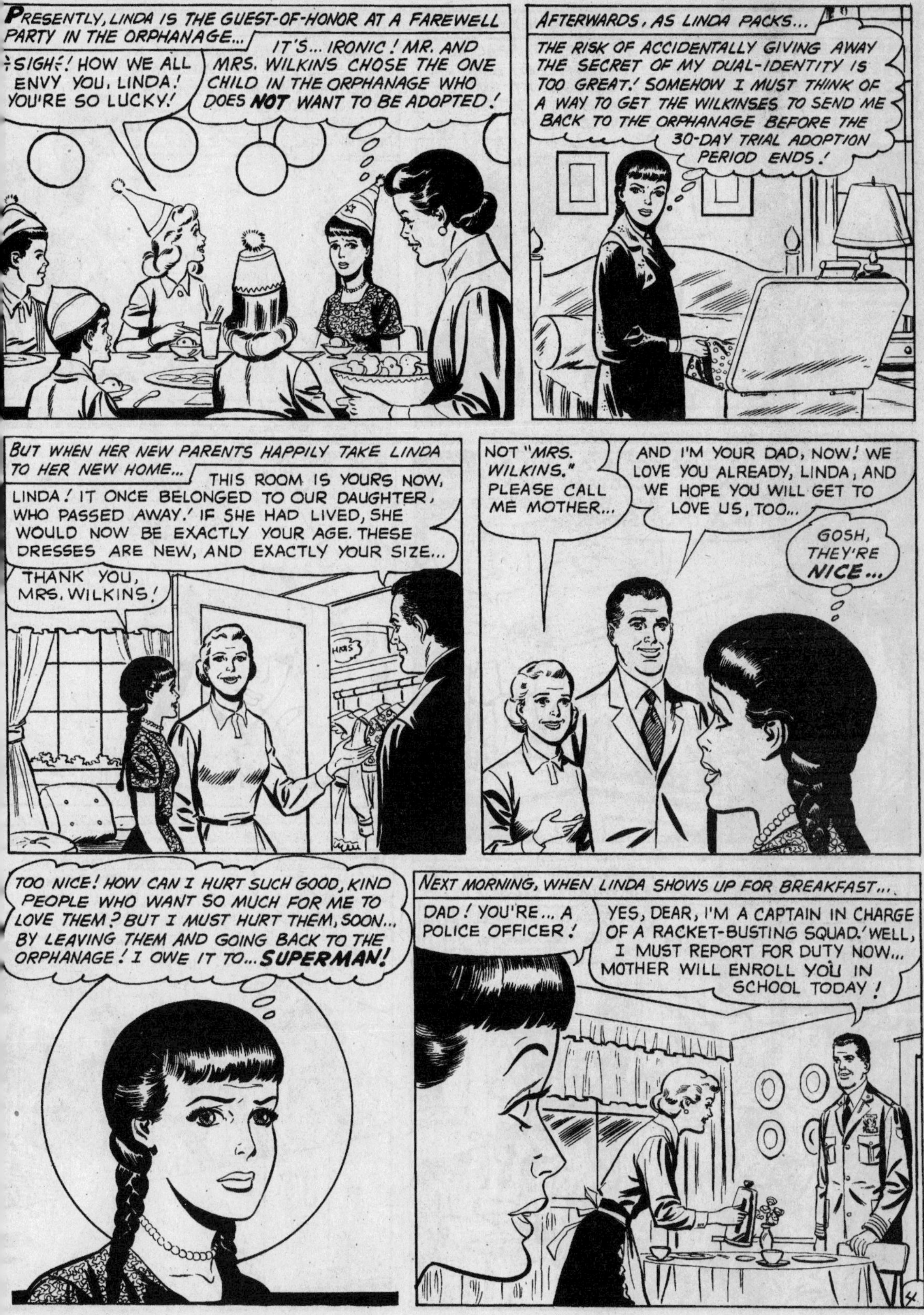
PRESENTLY, LINDA IS THE GUEST-OF-HONOR AT A FAREWELL PARTY IN THE ORPHANAGE...
-SIGH-! HOW WE ALL ENVY YOU, LINDA! YOU'RE SO LUCKY!
IT'S... IRONIC! MR. AND MRS. WILKINS CHOSE THE ONE CHILD IN THE ORPHANAGE WHO DOES NOT WANT TO BE ADOPTED!
AFTERWARDS, AS LINDA PACKS...
THE RISK OF ACCIDENTALLY GIVING AWAY THE SECRET OF MY DUAL-IDENTITY IS TOO GREAT! SOMEHOW I MUST THINK OF A WAY TO GET THE WILKINSES TO SEND ME BACK TO THE ORPHANAGE BEFORE THE 30-DAY TRIAL ADOPTION PERIOD ENDS!
BUT WHEN HER NEW PARENTS HAPPILY TAKE LINDA TO HER NEW HOME...
THIS ROOM IS YOURS NOW, LINDA! IT ONCE BELONGED TO OUR DAUGHTER, WHO PASSED AWAY! IF SHE HAD LIVED, SHE WOULD NOW BE EXACTLY YOUR AGE. THESE DRESSES ARE NEW, AND EXACTLY YOUR SIZE...
THANK YOU, MRS. WILKINS!
NOT "MRS. WILKINS." PLEASE CALL ME MOTHER...
AND I'M YOUR DAD, NOW! WE LOVE YOU ALREADY, LINDA, AND WE HOPE YOU WILL GET TO LOVE US, TOO...
GOSH, THEY'RE NICE...
TOO NICE! HOW CAN I HURT SUCH GOOD, KIND PEOPLE WHO WANT SO MUCH FOR ME TO LOVE THEM? BUT I MUST HURT THEM, SOON... BY LEAVING THEM AND GOING BACK TO THE ORPHANAGE! I OWE IT TO... SUPERMAN!
NEXT MORNING, WHEN LINDA SHOWS UP FOR BREAKFAST...
DAD! YOU'RE... A POLICE OFFICER!
YES, DEAR, I'M A CAPTAIN IN CHARGE OF A RACKET-BUSTING SQUAD! WELL, I MUST REPORT FOR DUTY NOW... MOTHER WILL ENROLL YOU IN SCHOOL TODAY!
4

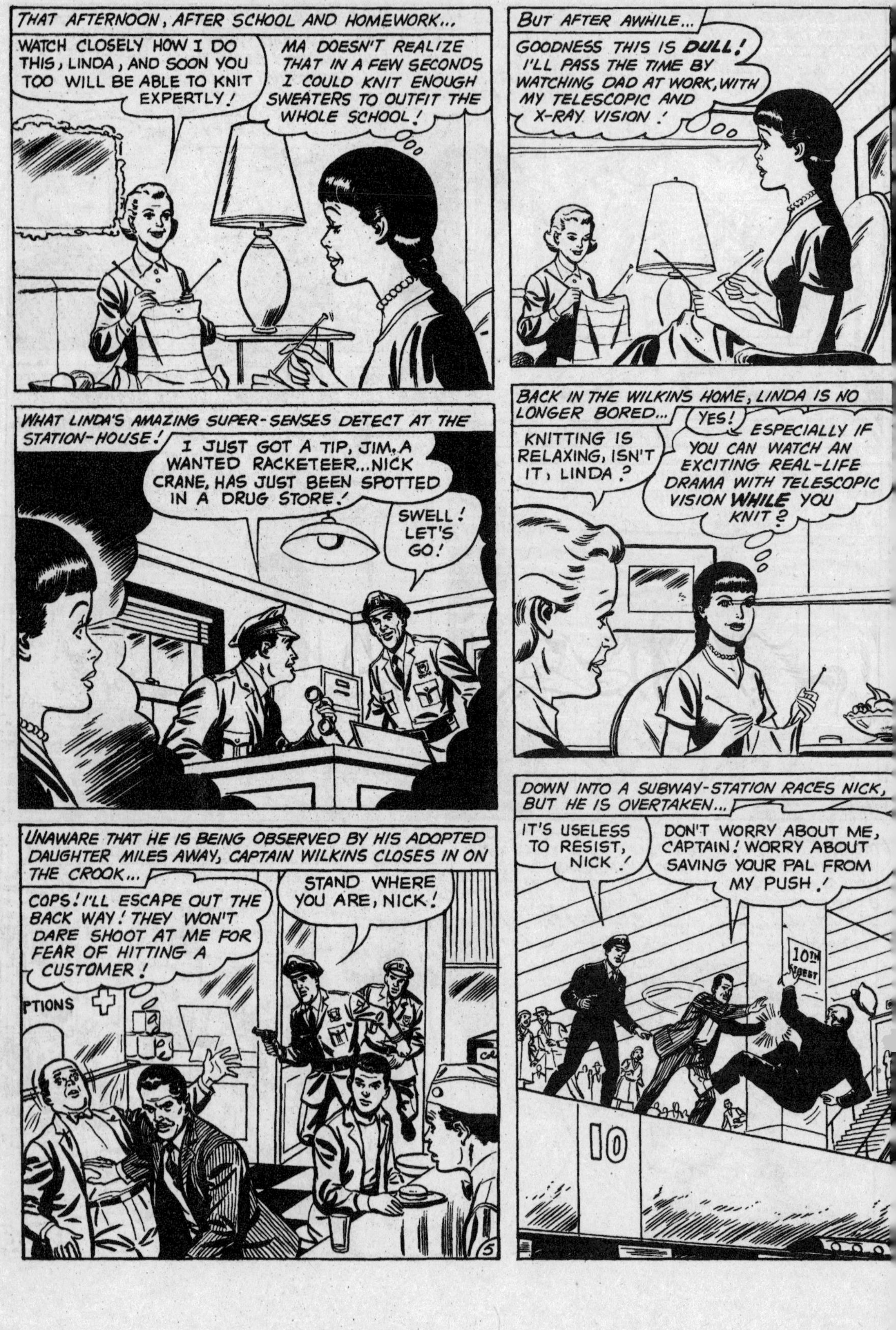
THAT AFTERNOON, AFTER SCHOOL AND HOMEWORK...
WATCH CLOSELY HOW I DO THIS, LINDA, AND SOON YOU TOO WILL BE ABLE TO KNIT EXPERTLY!
MA DOESN'T REALIZE THAT IN A FEW SECONDS I COULD KNIT ENOUGH SWEATERS TO OUTFIT THE WHOLE SCHOOL!
BUT AFTER AWHILE...
GOODNESS THIS IS DULL! I'LL PASS THE TIME BY WATCHING DAD AT WORK, WITH MY TELESCOPIC AND X-RAY VISION!
WHAT LINDA'S AMAZING SUPER-SENSES DETECT AT THE STATION-HOUSE!
I JUST GOT A TIP, JIM. A WANTED RACKETEER...NICK CRANE, HAS JUST BEEN SPOTTED IN A DRUG STORE!
SWELL! LET'S GO!
BACK IN THE WILKINS HOME, LINDA IS NO LONGER BORED...
KNITTING IS RELAXING, ISN'T IT, LINDA?
YES!
ESPECIALLY IF YOU CAN WATCH AN EXCITING REAL-LIFE DRAMA WITH TELESCOPIC VISION WHILE YOU KNIT?
UNAWARE THAT HE IS BEING OBSERVED BY HIS ADOPTED DAUGHTER MILES AWAY, CAPTAIN WILKINS CLOSES IN ON THE CROOK...
COPS! I'LL ESCAPE OUT THE BACK WAY! THEY WON'T DARE SHOOT AT ME FOR FEAR OF HITTING A CUSTOMER!
STAND WHERE YOU ARE, NICK!
PTIONS
5
DOWN INTO A SUBWAY-STATION RACES NICK, BUT HE IS OVERTAKEN...
IT'S USELESS TO RESIST, NICK!
DON'T WORRY ABOUT ME, CAPTAIN! WORRY ABOUT SAVING YOUR PAL FROM MY PUSH!
10TH STREET
10

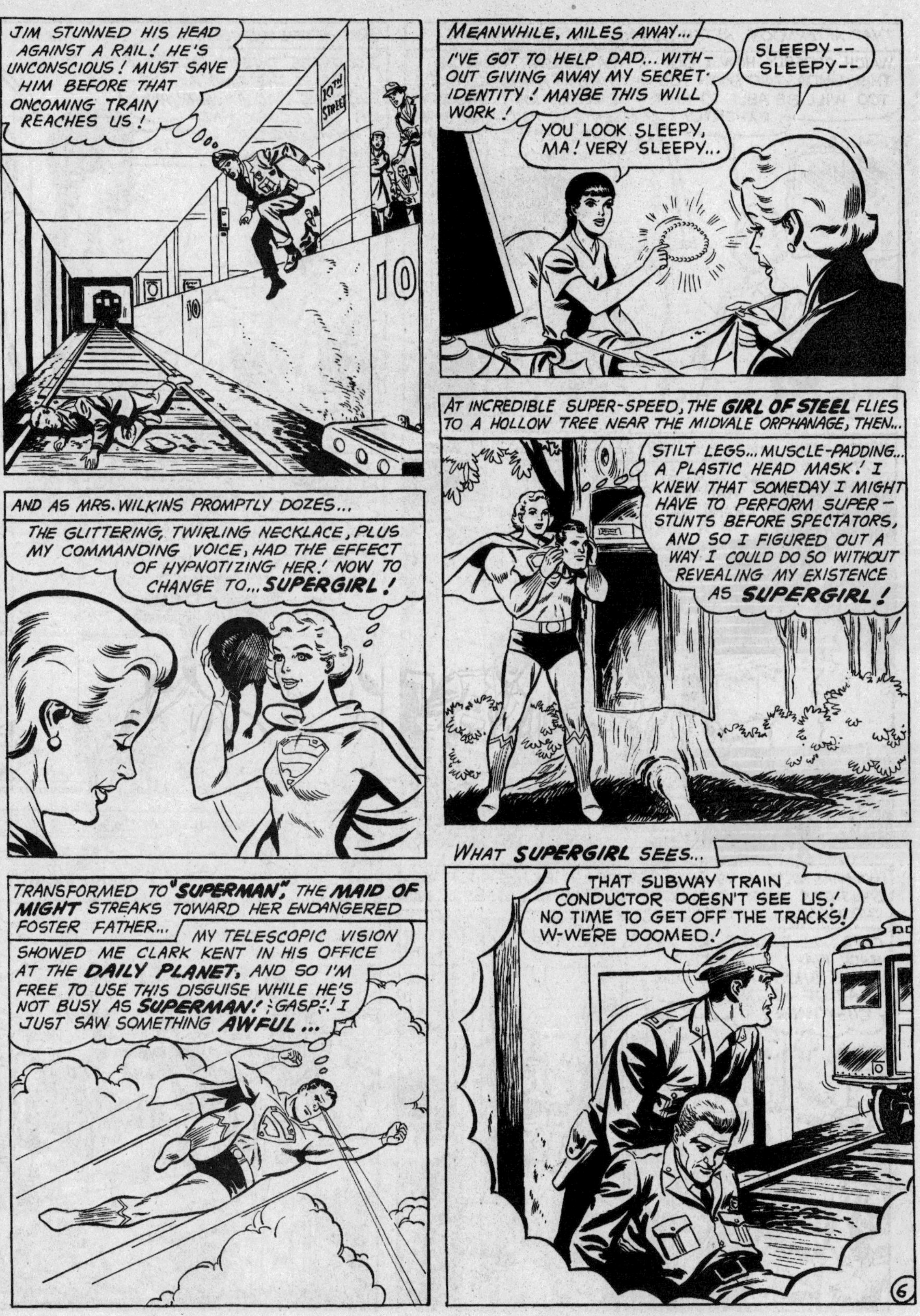
JIM STUNNED HIS HEAD AGAINST A RAIL! HE'S UNCONSCIOUS! MUST SAVE HIM BEFORE THAT ONCOMING TRAIN REACHES US!
10TH STREET
10
10
MEANWHILE, MILES AWAY...
I'VE GOT TO HELP DAD... WITHOUT GIVING AWAY MY SECRET IDENTITY! MAYBE THIS WILL WORK!
YOU LOOK SLEEPY, MA! VERY SLEEPY...
SLEEPY-- SLEEPY--
AND AS MRS. WILKINS PROMPTLY DOZES...
THE GLITTERING, TWIRLING NECKLACE, PLUS MY COMMANDING VOICE, HAD THE EFFECT OF HYPNOTIZING HER! NOW TO CHANGE TO... SUPERGIRL!
AT INCREDIBLE SUPER-SPEED, THE GIRL OF STEEL FLIES TO A HOLLOW TREE NEAR THE MIDVALE ORPHANAGE, THEN...
STILT LEGS... MUSCLE-PADDING... A PLASTIC HEAD MASK! I KNEW THAT SOMEDAY I MIGHT HAVE TO PERFORM SUPER-STUNTS BEFORE SPECTATORS, AND SO I FIGURED OUT A WAY I COULD DO SO WITHOUT REVEALING MY EXISTENCE AS SUPERGIRL!
TRANSFORMED TO "SUPERMAN", THE MAID OF MIGHT STREAKS TOWARD HER ENDANGERED FOSTER FATHER...
MY TELESCOPIC VISION SHOWED ME CLARK KENT IN HIS OFFICE AT THE DAILY PLANET, AND SO I'M FREE TO USE THIS DISGUISE WHILE HE'S NOT BUSY AS SUPERMAN! -GASP-! I JUST SAW SOMETHING AWFUL...
WHAT SUPERGIRL SEES...
THAT SUBWAY TRAIN CONDUCTOR DOESN'T SEE US! NO TIME TO GET OFF THE TRACKS! W-WE'RE DOOMED!
6

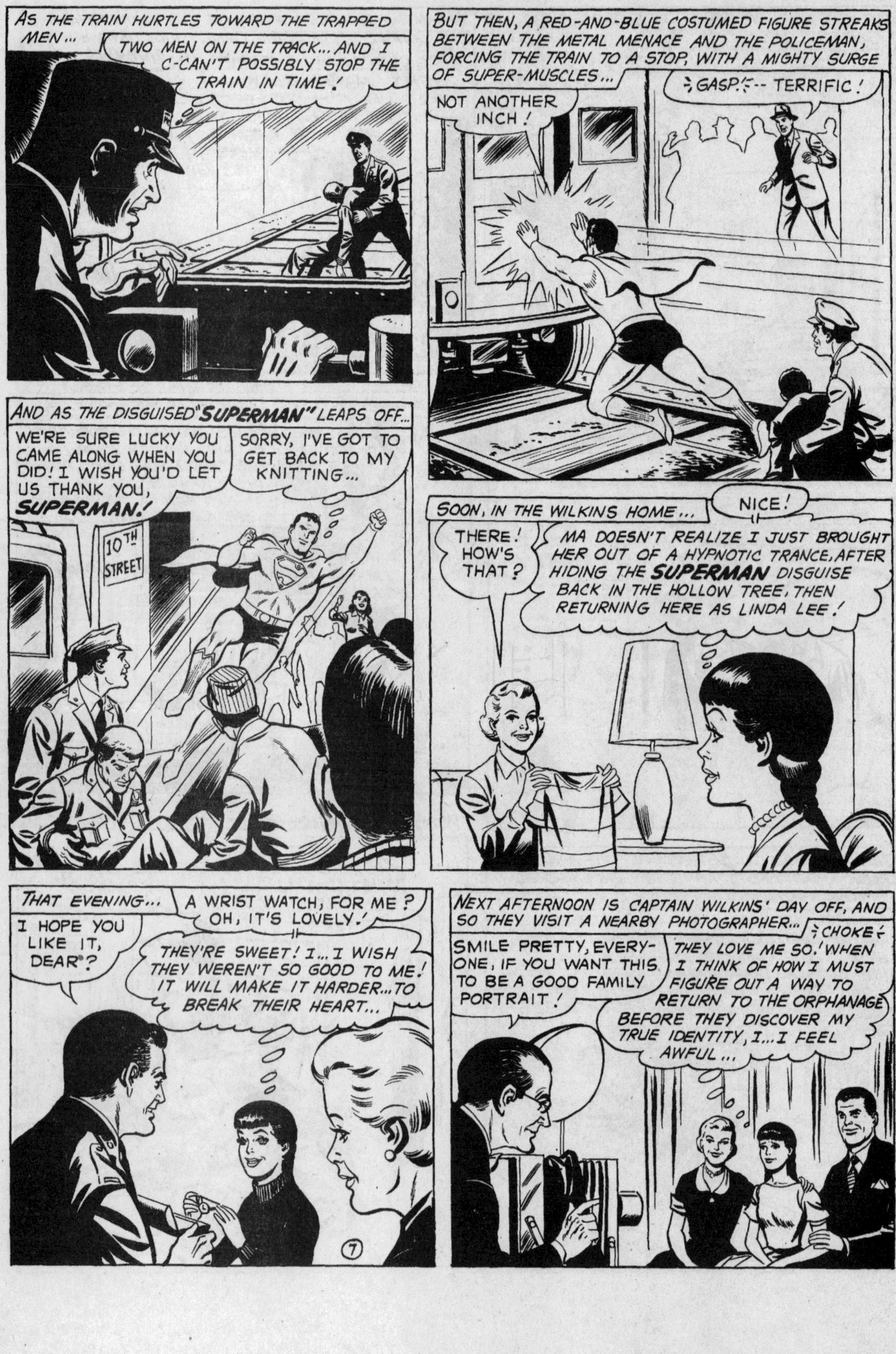
AS THE TRAIN HURTLES TOWARD THE TRAPPED MEN...
TWO MEN ON THE TRACK... AND I C-CAN'T POSSIBLY STOP THE TRAIN IN TIME!
BUT THEN, A RED-AND-BLUE COSTUMED FIGURE STREAKS BETWEEN THE METAL MENACE AND THE POLICEMAN, FORCING THE TRAIN TO A STOP, WITH A MIGHTY SURGE OF SUPER-MUSCLES...
NOT ANOTHER INCH!
GASP! -- TERRIFIC!
AND AS THE DISGUISED "SUPERMAN" LEAPS OFF...
WE'RE SURE LUCKY YOU CAME ALONG WHEN YOU DID! I WISH YOU'D LET US THANK YOU, SUPERMAN!
SORRY, I'VE GOT TO GET BACK TO MY KNITTING...
10TH STREET
SOON, IN THE WILKINS HOME...
THERE! HOW'S THAT?
NICE!
MA DOESN'T REALIZE I JUST BROUGHT HER OUT OF A HYPNOTIC TRANCE, AFTER HIDING THE SUPERMAN DISGUISE BACK IN THE HOLLOW TREE, THEN RETURNING HERE AS LINDA LEE!
THAT EVENING...
I HOPE YOU LIKE IT, DEAR?
A WRIST WATCH, FOR ME? OH, IT'S LOVELY!
THEY'RE SWEET! I... I WISH THEY WEREN'T SO GOOD TO ME! IT WILL MAKE IT HARDER...TO BREAK THEIR HEART...
7
NEXT AFTERNOON IS CAPTAIN WILKINS' DAY OFF, AND SO THEY VISIT A NEARBY PHOTOGRAPHER...
SMILE PRETTY, EVERY-ONE, IF YOU WANT THIS TO BE A GOOD FAMILY PORTRAIT!
CHOKE
THEY LOVE ME SO! WHEN I THINK OF HOW I MUST FIGURE OUT A WAY TO RETURN TO THE ORPHANAGE BEFORE THEY DISCOVER MY TRUE IDENTITY, I... I FEEL AWFUL...

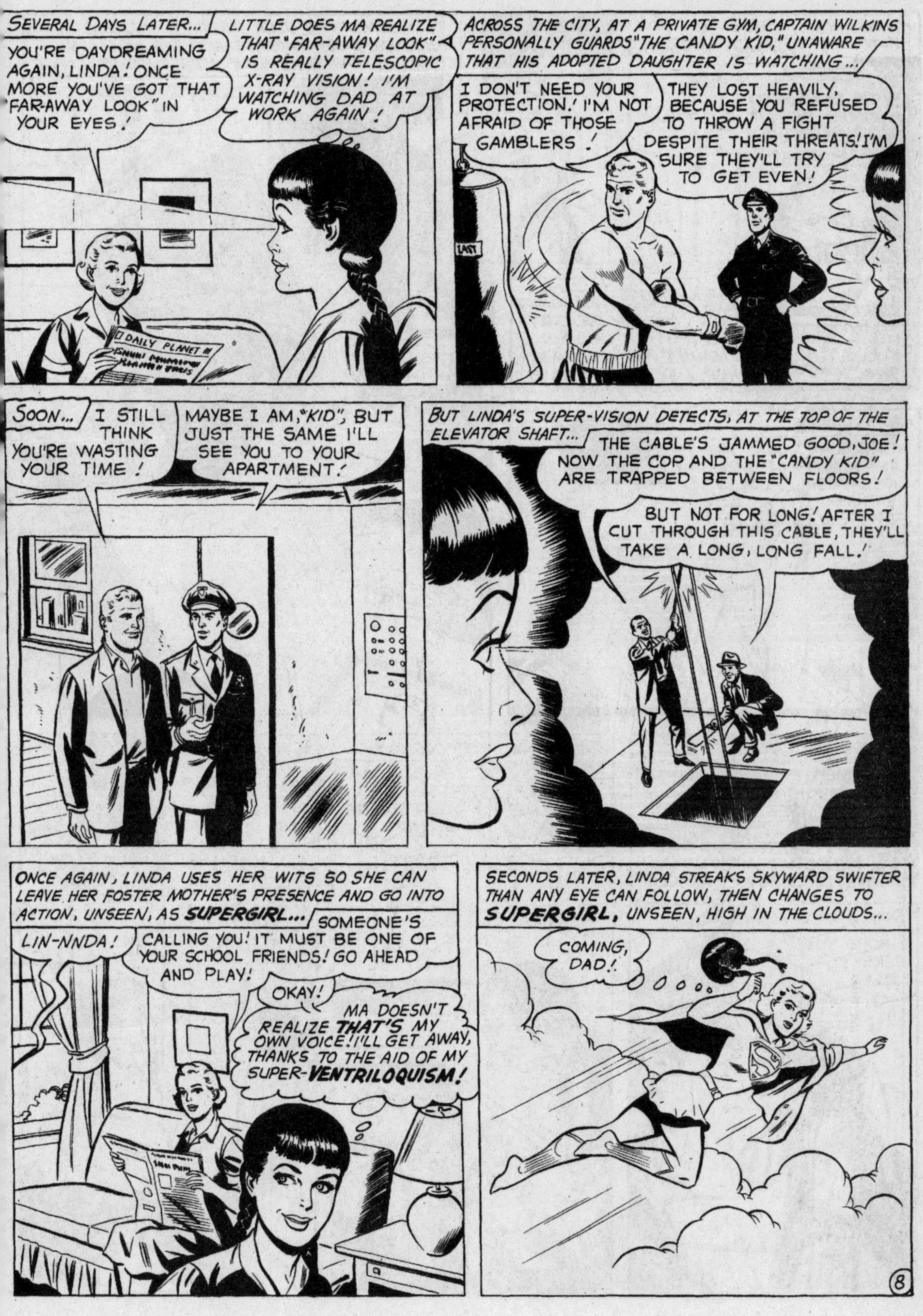
SEVERAL DAYS LATER...
YOU'RE DAYDREAMING AGAIN, LINDA! ONCE MORE YOU'VE GOT THAT "FAR-AWAY LOOK" IN YOUR EYES!
LITTLE DOES MA REALIZE THAT "FAR-AWAY LOOK" IS REALLY TELESCOPIC X-RAY VISION! I'M WATCHING DAD AT WORK AGAIN!
DAILY PLANET
ACROSS THE CITY, AT A PRIVATE GYM, CAPTAIN WILKINS PERSONALLY GUARDS "THE CANDY KID," UNAWARE THAT HIS ADOPTED DAUGHTER IS WATCHING...
I DON'T NEED YOUR PROTECTION! I'M NOT AFRAID OF THOSE GAMBLERS!
THEY LOST HEAVILY, BECAUSE YOU REFUSED TO THROW A FIGHT DESPITE THEIR THREATS! I'M SURE THEY'LL TRY TO GET EVEN!
SOON...
I STILL THINK YOU'RE WASTING YOUR TIME!
MAYBE I AM, "KID", BUT JUST THE SAME I'LL SEE YOU TO YOUR APARTMENT!
BUT LINDA'S SUPER-VISION DETECTS, AT THE TOP OF THE ELEVATOR SHAFT...
THE CABLE'S JAMMED GOOD, JOE! NOW THE COP AND THE "CANDY KID" ARE TRAPPED BETWEEN FLOORS!
BUT NOT FOR LONG! AFTER I CUT THROUGH THIS CABLE, THEY'LL TAKE A LONG, LONG FALL!
ONCE AGAIN, LINDA USES HER WITS SO SHE CAN LEAVE HER FOSTER MOTHER'S PRESENCE AND GO INTO ACTION, UNSEEN, AS SUPERGIRL...
LIN-NNDA!
SOMEONE'S CALLING YOU! IT MUST BE ONE OF YOUR SCHOOL FRIENDS! GO AHEAD AND PLAY!
OKAY!
MA DOESN'T REALIZE THAT'S MY OWN VOICE! I'LL GET AWAY, THANKS TO THE AID OF MY SUPER-VENTRILOQUISM!
SECONDS LATER, LINDA STREAKS SKYWARD SWIFTER THAN ANY EYE CAN FOLLOW, THEN CHANGES TO SUPERGIRL, UNSEEN, HIGH IN THE CLOUDS...
COMING, DAD!
8

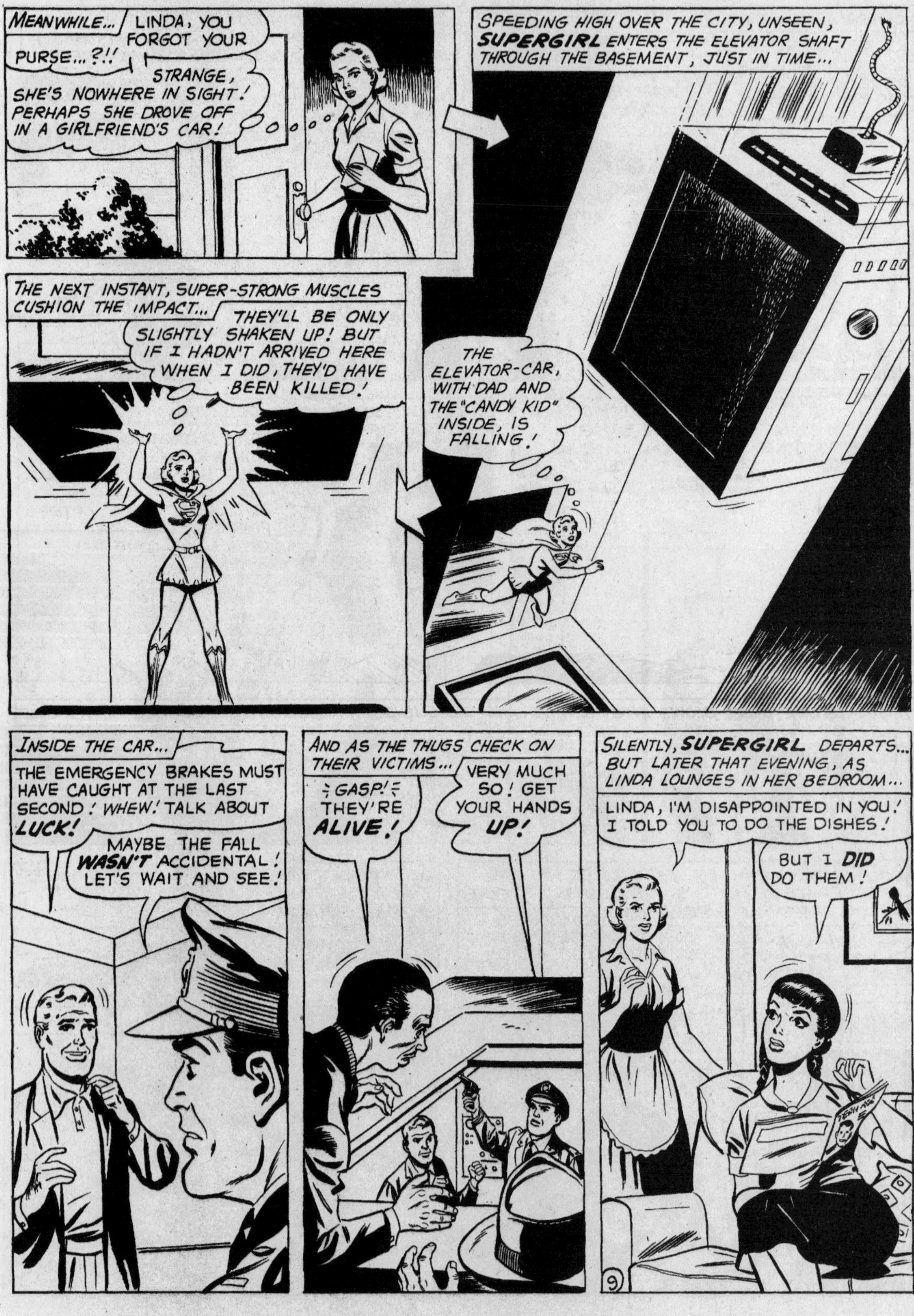
MEANWHILE...
LINDA, YOU FORGOT YOUR PURSE...?!!
STRANGE, SHE'S NOWHERE IN SIGHT! PERHAPS SHE DROVE OFF IN A GIRLFRIEND'S CAR!
SPEEDING HIGH OVER THE CITY, UNSEEN, SUPERGIRL ENTERS THE ELEVATOR SHAFT THROUGH THE BASEMENT, JUST IN TIME...
THE ELEVATOR-CAR, WITH DAD AND THE "CANDY KID" INSIDE, IS FALLING!
THE NEXT INSTANT, SUPER-STRONG MUSCLES CUSHION THE IMPACT...
THEY'LL BE ONLY SLIGHTLY SHAKEN UP! BUT IF I HADN'T ARRIVED HERE WHEN I DID, THEY'D HAVE BEEN KILLED!
INSIDE THE CAR...
THE EMERGENCY BRAKES MUST HAVE CAUGHT AT THE LAST SECOND! WHEW! TALK ABOUT LUCK!
MAYBE THE FALL WASN'T ACCIDENTAL! LET'S WAIT AND SEE!
AND AS THE THUGS CHECK ON THEIR VICTIMS...
GASP! THEY'RE ALIVE!
VERY MUCH SO! GET YOUR HANDS UP!
SILENTLY, SUPERGIRL DEPARTS... BUT LATER THAT EVENING, AS LINDA LOUNGES IN HER BEDROOM...
LINDA, I'M DISAPPOINTED IN YOU! I TOLD YOU TO DO THE DISHES!
BUT I DID DO THEM!
9

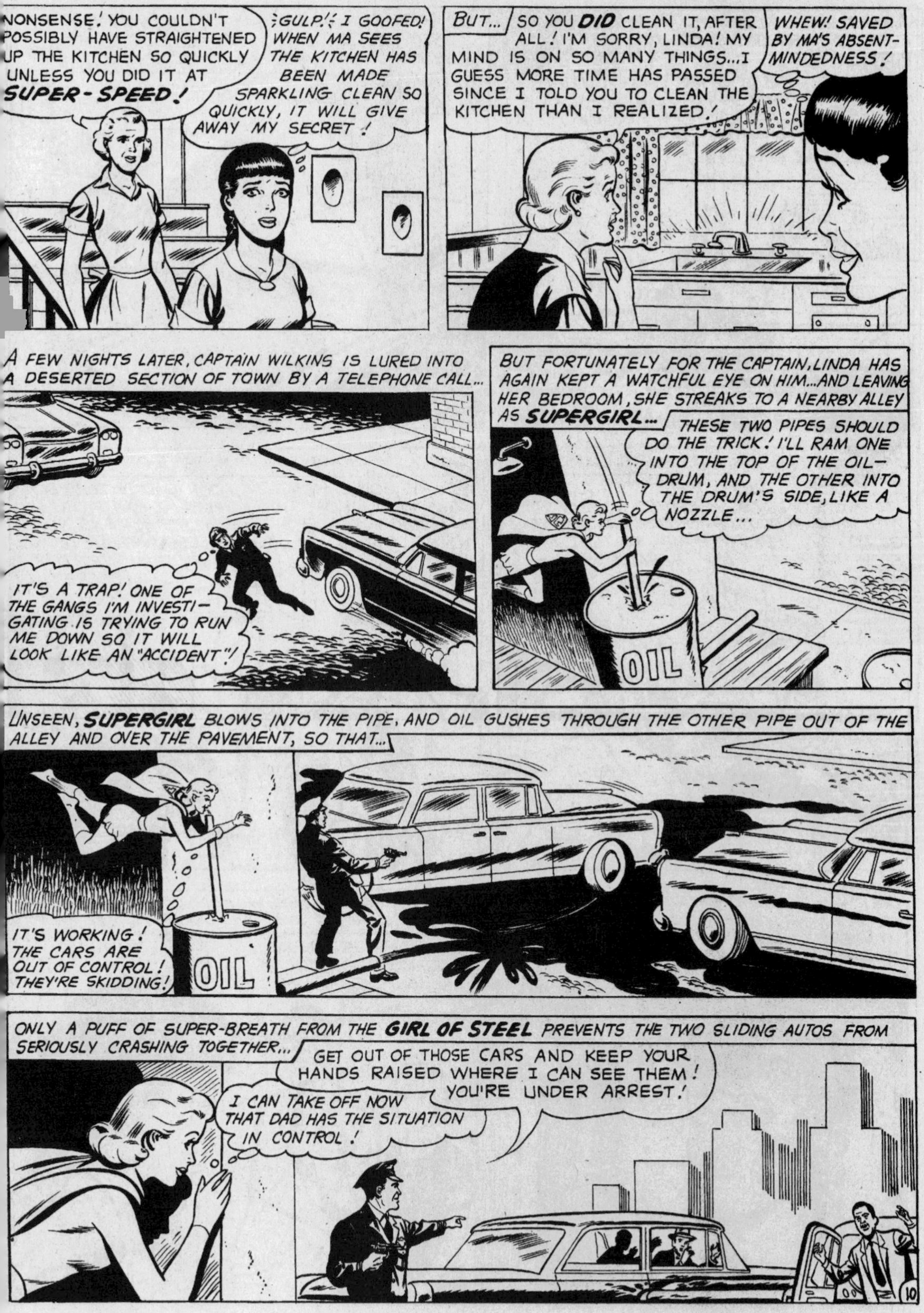
NONSENSE! YOU COULDN'T POSSIBLY HAVE STRAIGHTENED UP THE KITCHEN SO QUICKLY UNLESS YOU DID IT AT SUPER-SPEED!
GULP! I GOOFED! WHEN MA SEES THE KITCHEN HAS BEEN MADE SPARKLING CLEAN SO QUICKLY, IT WILL GIVE AWAY MY SECRET!
BUT...
SO YOU DID CLEAN IT, AFTER ALL! I'M SORRY, LINDA! MY MIND IS ON SO MANY THINGS...I GUESS MORE TIME HAS PASSED SINCE I TOLD YOU TO CLEAN THE KITCHEN THAN I REALIZED!
WHEW! SAVED BY MA'S ABSENT-MINDEDNESS!
A FEW NIGHTS LATER, CAPTAIN WILKINS IS LURED INTO A DESERTED SECTION OF TOWN BY A TELEPHONE CALL...
IT'S A TRAP! ONE OF THE GANGS I'M INVESTIGATING IS TRYING TO RUN ME DOWN SO IT WILL LOOK LIKE AN "ACCIDENT"!
BUT FORTUNATELY FOR THE CAPTAIN, LINDA HAS AGAIN KEPT A WATCHFUL EYE ON HIM...AND LEAVING HER BEDROOM, SHE STREAKS TO A NEARBY ALLEY AS SUPERGIRL...
THESE TWO PIPES SHOULD DO THE TRICK! I'LL RAM ONE INTO THE TOP OF THE OIL-DRUM, AND THE OTHER INTO THE DRUM'S SIDE, LIKE A NOZZLE...
OIL
UNSEEN, SUPERGIRL BLOWS INTO THE PIPE, AND OIL GUSHES THROUGH THE OTHER PIPE OUT OF THE ALLEY AND OVER THE PAVEMENT, SO THAT...
IT'S WORKING! THE CARS ARE OUT OF CONTROL! THEY'RE SKIDDING!
OIL
ONLY A PUFF OF SUPER-BREATH FROM THE GIRL OF STEEL PREVENTS THE TWO SLIDING AUTOS FROM SERIOUSLY CRASHING TOGETHER...
I CAN TAKE OFF NOW THAT DAD HAS THE SITUATION IN CONTROL!
GET OUT OF THOSE CARS AND KEEP YOUR HANDS RAISED WHERE I CAN SEE THEM! YOU'RE UNDER ARREST!
10

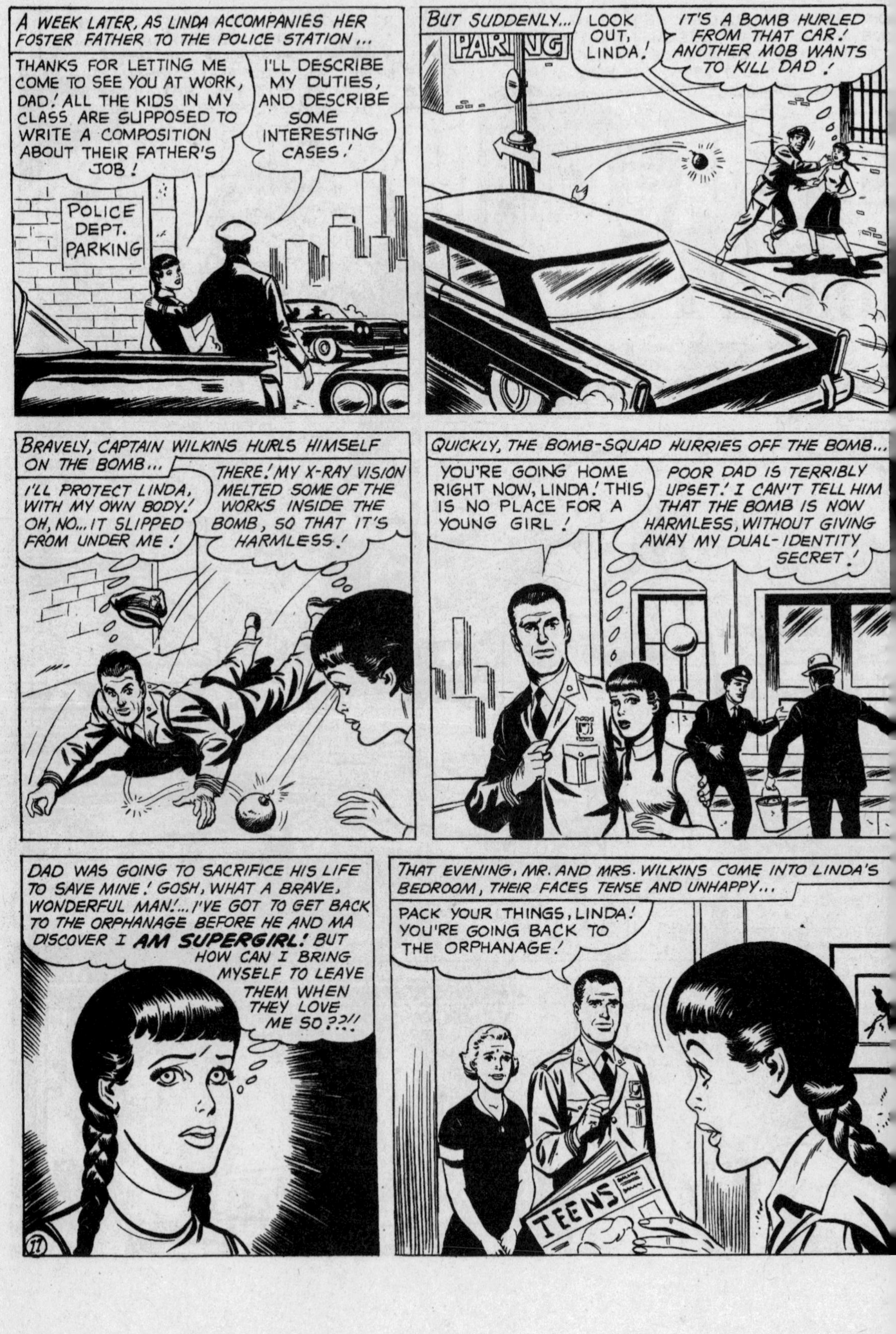
A WEEK LATER, AS LINDA ACCOMPANIES HER FOSTER FATHER TO THE POLICE STATION...
THANKS FOR LETTING ME COME TO SEE YOU AT WORK, DAD! ALL THE KIDS IN MY CLASS ARE SUPPOSED TO WRITE A COMPOSITION ABOUT THEIR FATHER'S JOB!
I'LL DESCRIBE MY DUTIES, AND DESCRIBE SOME INTERESTING CASES!
POLICE DEPT. PARKING
BUT SUDDENLY...
LOOK OUT, LINDA!
IT'S A BOMB HURLED FROM THAT CAR! ANOTHER MOB WANTS TO KILL DAD!
PARKING
BRAVELY, CAPTAIN WILKINS HURLS HIMSELF ON THE BOMB...
I'LL PROTECT LINDA, WITH MY OWN BODY! OH, NO...IT SLIPPED FROM UNDER ME!
THERE! MY X-RAY VISION MELTED SOME OF THE WORKS INSIDE THE BOMB, SO THAT IT'S HARMLESS!
QUICKLY, THE BOMB-SQUAD HURRIES OFF THE BOMB...
YOU'RE GOING HOME RIGHT NOW, LINDA! THIS IS NO PLACE FOR A YOUNG GIRL!
POOR DAD IS TERRIBLY UPSET! I CAN'T TELL HIM THAT THE BOMB IS NOW HARMLESS, WITHOUT GIVING AWAY MY DUAL-IDENTITY SECRET!
DAD WAS GOING TO SACRIFICE HIS LIFE TO SAVE MINE! GOSH, WHAT A BRAVE, WONDERFUL MAN!... I'VE GOT TO GET BACK TO THE ORPHANAGE BEFORE HE AND MA DISCOVER I **AM SUPERGIRL!** BUT HOW CAN I BRING MYSELF TO LEAVE THEM WHEN THEY LOVE ME SO??!!
11
THAT EVENING, MR. AND MRS. WILKINS COME INTO LINDA'S BEDROOM, THEIR FACES TENSE AND UNHAPPY...
PACK YOUR THINGS, LINDA! YOU'RE GOING BACK TO THE ORPHANAGE!
TEENS

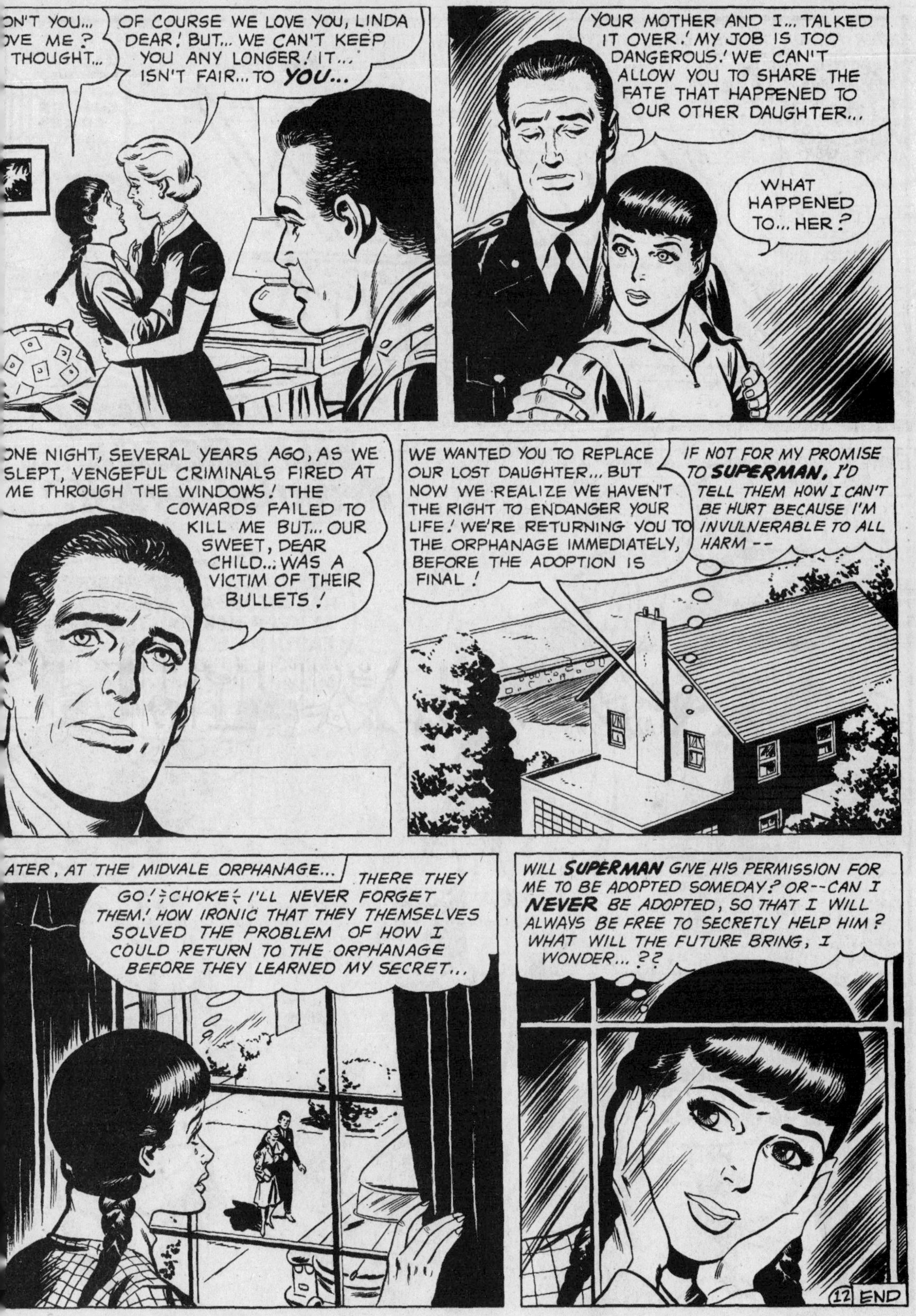
ON'T YOU... OVE ME? THOUGHT...
OF COURSE WE LOVE YOU, LINDA DEAR! BUT... WE CAN'T KEEP YOU ANY LONGER! IT... ISN'T FAIR... TO YOU...
YOUR MOTHER AND I... TALKED IT OVER! MY JOB IS TOO DANGEROUS! WE CAN'T ALLOW YOU TO SHARE THE FATE THAT HAPPENED TO OUR OTHER DAUGHTER...
WHAT HAPPENED TO... HER?
ONE NIGHT, SEVERAL YEARS AGO, AS WE SLEPT, VENGEFUL CRIMINALS FIRED AT ME THROUGH THE WINDOWS! THE COWARDS FAILED TO KILL ME BUT... OUR SWEET, DEAR CHILD... WAS A VICTIM OF THEIR BULLETS!
WE WANTED YOU TO REPLACE OUR LOST DAUGHTER... BUT NOW WE REALIZE WE HAVEN'T THE RIGHT TO ENDANGER YOUR LIFE! WE'RE RETURNING YOU TO THE ORPHANAGE IMMEDIATELY, BEFORE THE ADOPTION IS FINAL!
IF NOT FOR MY PROMISE TO SUPERMAN, I'D TELL THEM HOW I CAN'T BE HURT BECAUSE I'M INVULNERABLE TO ALL HARM --
ATER, AT THE MIDVALE ORPHANAGE...
THERE THEY GO! ÷CHOKE÷ I'LL NEVER FORGET THEM! HOW IRONIC THAT THEY THEMSELVES SOLVED THE PROBLEM OF HOW I COULD RETURN TO THE ORPHANAGE BEFORE THEY LEARNED MY SECRET...
WILL SUPERMAN GIVE HIS PERMISSION FOR ME TO BE ADOPTED SOMEDAY? OR--CAN I NEVER BE ADOPTED, SO THAT I WILL ALWAYS BE FREE TO SECRETLY HELP HIM? WHAT WILL THE FUTURE BRING, I WONDER...??
12 END

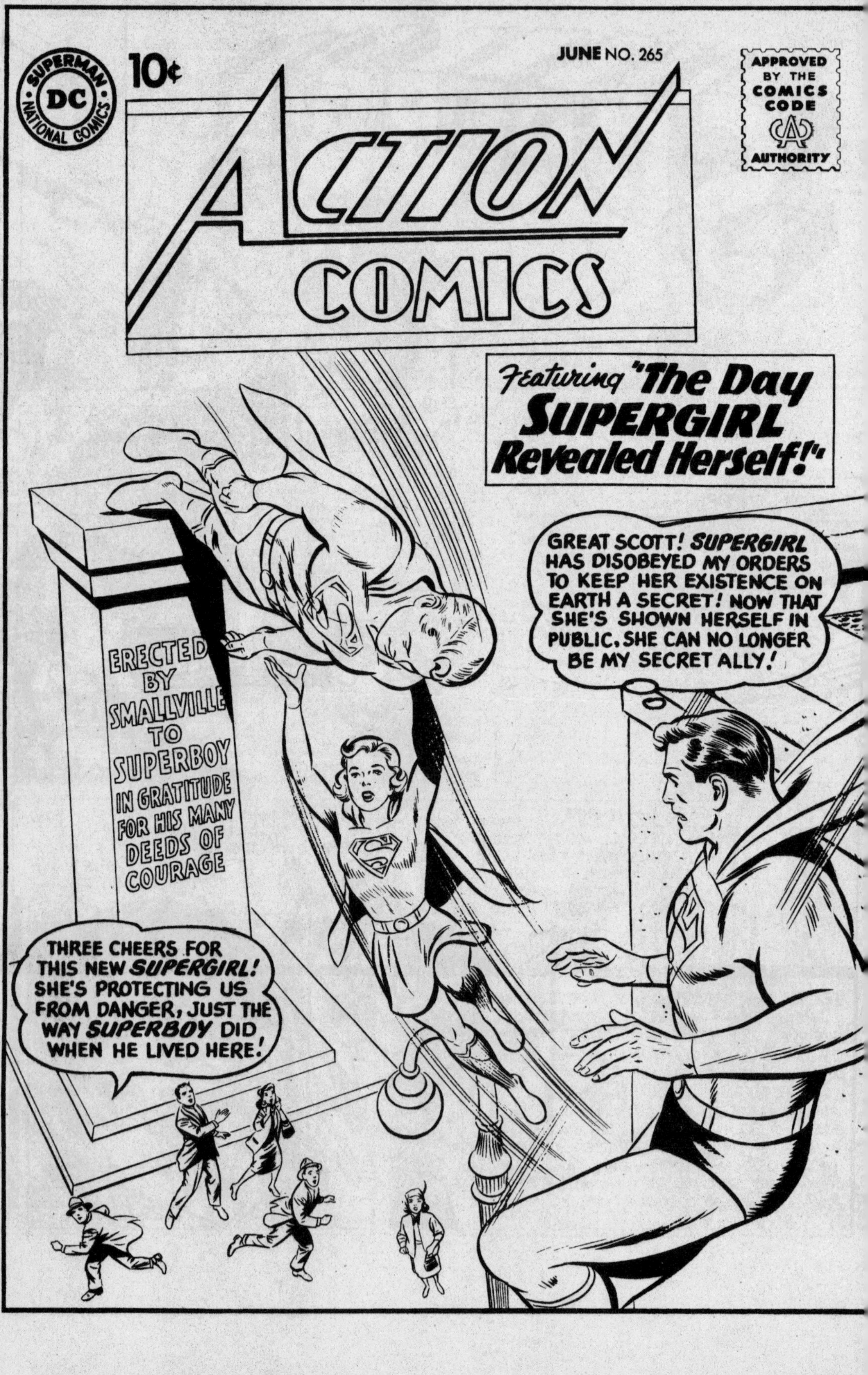
SUPERMAN DC NATIONAL COMICS
10¢
JUNE NO. 265
APPROVED BY THE COMICS CODE AUTHORITY
ACTION COMICS
Featuring "The Day SUPERGIRL Revealed Herself!"
GREAT SCOTT! SUPERGIRL HAS DISOBEYED MY ORDERS TO KEEP HER EXISTENCE ON EARTH A SECRET! NOW THAT SHE'S SHOWN HERSELF IN PUBLIC, SHE CAN NO LONGER BE MY SECRET ALLY!
ERECTED BY SMALLVILLE TO SUPERBOY IN GRATITUDE FOR HIS MANY DEEDS OF COURAGE
THREE CHEERS FOR THIS NEW SUPERGIRL! SHE'S PROTECTING US FROM DANGER, JUST THE WAY SUPERBOY DID WHEN HE LIVED HERE!

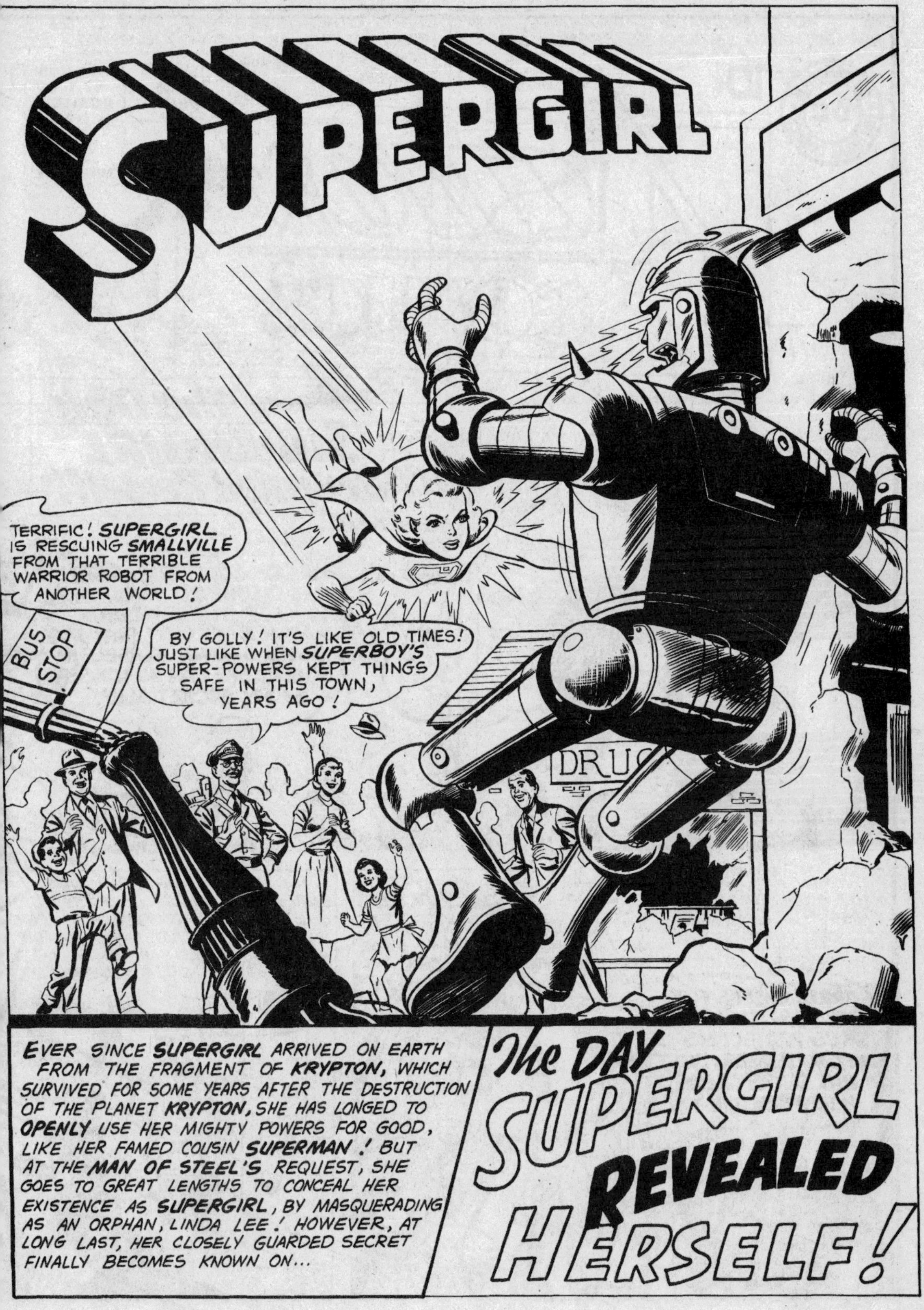
SUPERGIRL
TERRIFIC! SUPERGIRL IS RESCUING SMALLVILLE FROM THAT TERRIBLE WARRIOR ROBOT FROM ANOTHER WORLD!
BUS STOP
BY GOLLY! IT'S LIKE OLD TIMES! JUST LIKE WHEN SUPERBOY'S SUPER-POWERS KEPT THINGS SAFE IN THIS TOWN, YEARS AGO!
EVER SINCE SUPERGIRL ARRIVED ON EARTH FROM THE FRAGMENT OF KRYPTON, WHICH SURVIVED FOR SOME YEARS AFTER THE DESTRUCTION OF THE PLANET KRYPTON, SHE HAS LONGED TO OPENLY USE HER MIGHTY POWERS FOR GOOD, LIKE HER FAMED COUSIN SUPERMAN! BUT AT THE MAN OF STEEL'S REQUEST, SHE GOES TO GREAT LENGTHS TO CONCEAL HER EXISTENCE AS SUPERGIRL, BY MASQUERADING AS AN ORPHAN, LINDA LEE! HOWEVER, AT LONG LAST, HER CLOSELY GUARDED SECRET FINALLY BECOMES KNOWN ON...
The DAY SUPERGIRL REVEALED HERSELF!

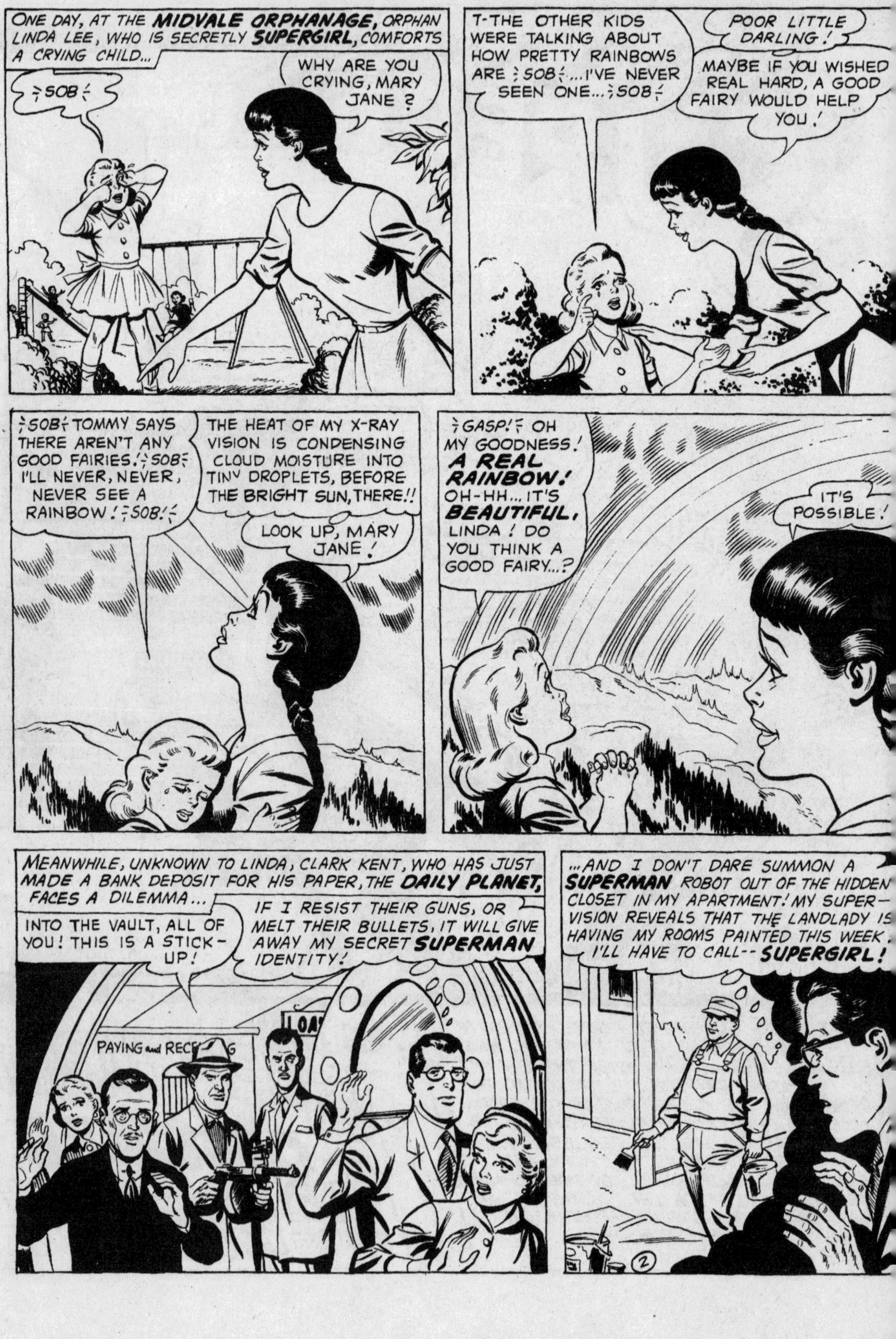
ONE DAY, AT THE MIDVALE ORPHANAGE, ORPHAN LINDA LEE, WHO IS SECRETLY SUPERGIRL, COMFORTS A CRYING CHILD...
WHY ARE YOU CRYING, MARY JANE ?
-SOB-
T-THE OTHER KIDS WERE TALKING ABOUT HOW PRETTY RAINBOWS ARE -SOB-...I'VE NEVER SEEN ONE...-SOB-
POOR LITTLE DARLING !
MAYBE IF YOU WISHED REAL HARD, A GOOD FAIRY WOULD HELP YOU !
-SOB- TOMMY SAYS THERE AREN'T ANY GOOD FAIRIES! -SOB- I'LL NEVER, NEVER, NEVER SEE A RAINBOW ! -SOB!-
THE HEAT OF MY X-RAY VISION IS CONDENSING CLOUD MOISTURE INTO TINY DROPLETS, BEFORE THE BRIGHT SUN, THERE!!
LOOK UP, MARY JANE !
-GASP!- OH MY GOODNESS! A REAL RAINBOW! OH-HH... IT'S BEAUTIFUL, LINDA ! DO YOU THINK A GOOD FAIRY...?
IT'S POSSIBLE !
MEANWHILE, UNKNOWN TO LINDA, CLARK KENT, WHO HAS JUST MADE A BANK DEPOSIT FOR HIS PAPER, THE DAILY PLANET, FACES A DILEMMA...
INTO THE VAULT, ALL OF YOU! THIS IS A STICK-UP!
IF I RESIST THEIR GUNS, OR MELT THEIR BULLETS, IT WILL GIVE AWAY MY SECRET SUPERMAN IDENTITY!
PAYING and REC
...AND I DON'T DARE SUMMON A SUPERMAN ROBOT OUT OF THE HIDDEN CLOSET IN MY APARTMENT! MY SUPER-VISION REVEALS THAT THE LANDLADY IS HAVING MY ROOMS PAINTED THIS WEEK. I'LL HAVE TO CALL-- SUPERGIRL!
2

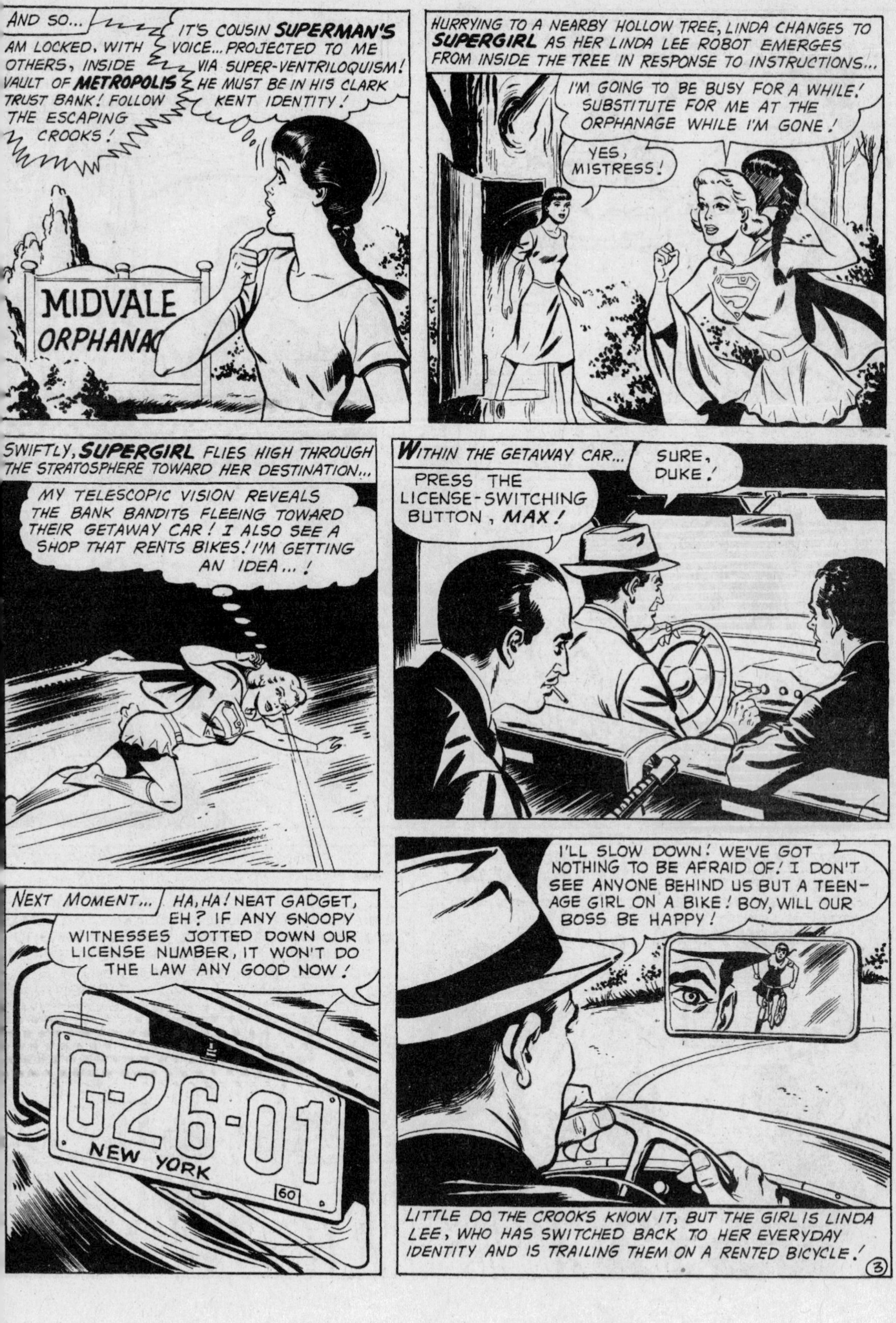
AND SO...
AM LOCKED, WITH OTHERS, INSIDE VAULT OF METROPOLIS TRUST BANK! FOLLOW THE ESCAPING CROOKS!
IT'S COUSIN SUPERMAN'S VOICE... PROJECTED TO ME VIA SUPER-VENTRILOQUISM! HE MUST BE IN HIS CLARK KENT IDENTITY!
MIDVALE ORPHANAG
HURRYING TO A NEARBY HOLLOW TREE, LINDA CHANGES TO SUPERGIRL AS HER LINDA LEE ROBOT EMERGES FROM INSIDE THE TREE IN RESPONSE TO INSTRUCTIONS...
I'M GOING TO BE BUSY FOR A WHILE! SUBSTITUTE FOR ME AT THE ORPHANAGE WHILE I'M GONE!
YES, MISTRESS!
SWIFTLY, SUPERGIRL FLIES HIGH THROUGH THE STRATOSPHERE TOWARD HER DESTINATION...
MY TELESCOPIC VISION REVEALS THE BANK BANDITS FLEEING TOWARD THEIR GETAWAY CAR! I ALSO SEE A SHOP THAT RENTS BIKES! I'M GETTING AN IDEA...!
WITHIN THE GETAWAY CAR...
PRESS THE LICENSE-SWITCHING BUTTON, MAX!
SURE, DUKE!
NEXT MOMENT...
HA, HA! NEAT GADGET, EH? IF ANY SNOOPY WITNESSES JOTTED DOWN OUR LICENSE NUMBER, IT WON'T DO THE LAW ANY GOOD NOW!
G-26-01
NEW YORK
60
I'LL SLOW DOWN! WE'VE GOT NOTHING TO BE AFRAID OF! I DON'T SEE ANYONE BEHIND US BUT A TEEN-AGE GIRL ON A BIKE! BOY, WILL OUR BOSS BE HAPPY!
LITTLE DO THE CROOKS KNOW IT, BUT THE GIRL IS LINDA LEE, WHO HAS SWITCHED BACK TO HER EVERYDAY IDENTITY AND IS TRAILING THEM ON A RENTED BICYCLE!
3

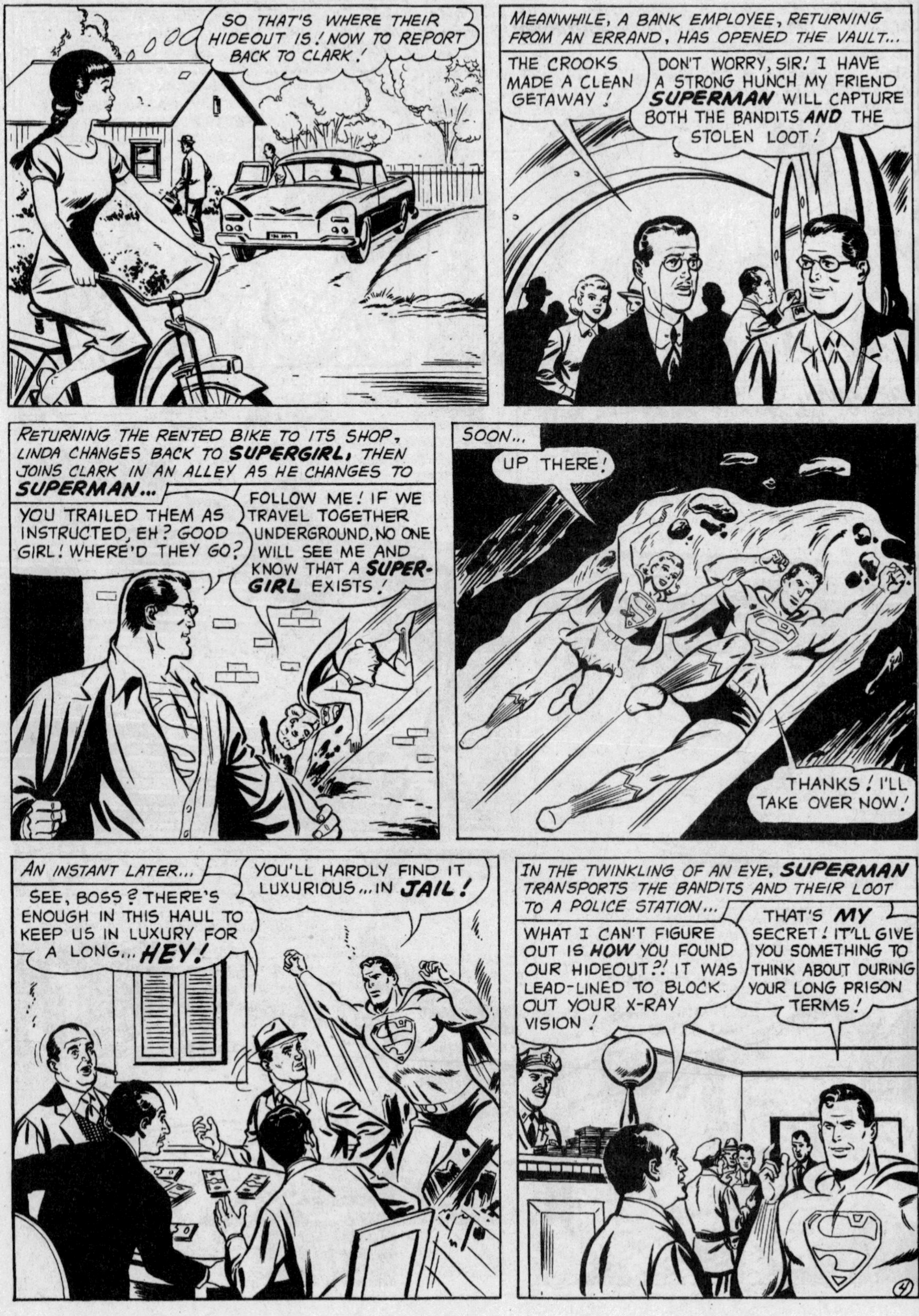
SO THAT'S WHERE THEIR HIDEOUT IS! NOW TO REPORT BACK TO CLARK!
MEANWHILE, A BANK EMPLOYEE, RETURNING FROM AN ERRAND, HAS OPENED THE VAULT...
THE CROOKS MADE A CLEAN GETAWAY!
DON'T WORRY, SIR! I HAVE A STRONG HUNCH MY FRIEND SUPERMAN WILL CAPTURE BOTH THE BANDITS AND THE STOLEN LOOT!
RETURNING THE RENTED BIKE TO ITS SHOP, LINDA CHANGES BACK TO SUPERGIRL, THEN JOINS CLARK IN AN ALLEY AS HE CHANGES TO SUPERMAN...
YOU TRAILED THEM AS INSTRUCTED, EH? GOOD GIRL! WHERE'D THEY GO?
FOLLOW ME! IF WE TRAVEL TOGETHER UNDERGROUND, NO ONE WILL SEE ME AND KNOW THAT A SUPER-GIRL EXISTS!
SOON...
UP THERE!
THANKS! I'LL TAKE OVER NOW!
AN INSTANT LATER...
SEE, BOSS? THERE'S ENOUGH IN THIS HAUL TO KEEP US IN LUXURY FOR A LONG... HEY!
YOU'LL HARDLY FIND IT LUXURIOUS... IN JAIL!
IN THE TWINKLING OF AN EYE, SUPERMAN TRANSPORTS THE BANDITS AND THEIR LOOT TO A POLICE STATION...
WHAT I CAN'T FIGURE OUT IS HOW YOU FOUND OUR HIDEOUT?! IT WAS LEAD-LINED TO BLOCK OUT YOUR X-RAY VISION!
THAT'S MY SECRET! IT'LL GIVE YOU SOMETHING TO THINK ABOUT DURING YOUR LONG PRISON TERMS!
4

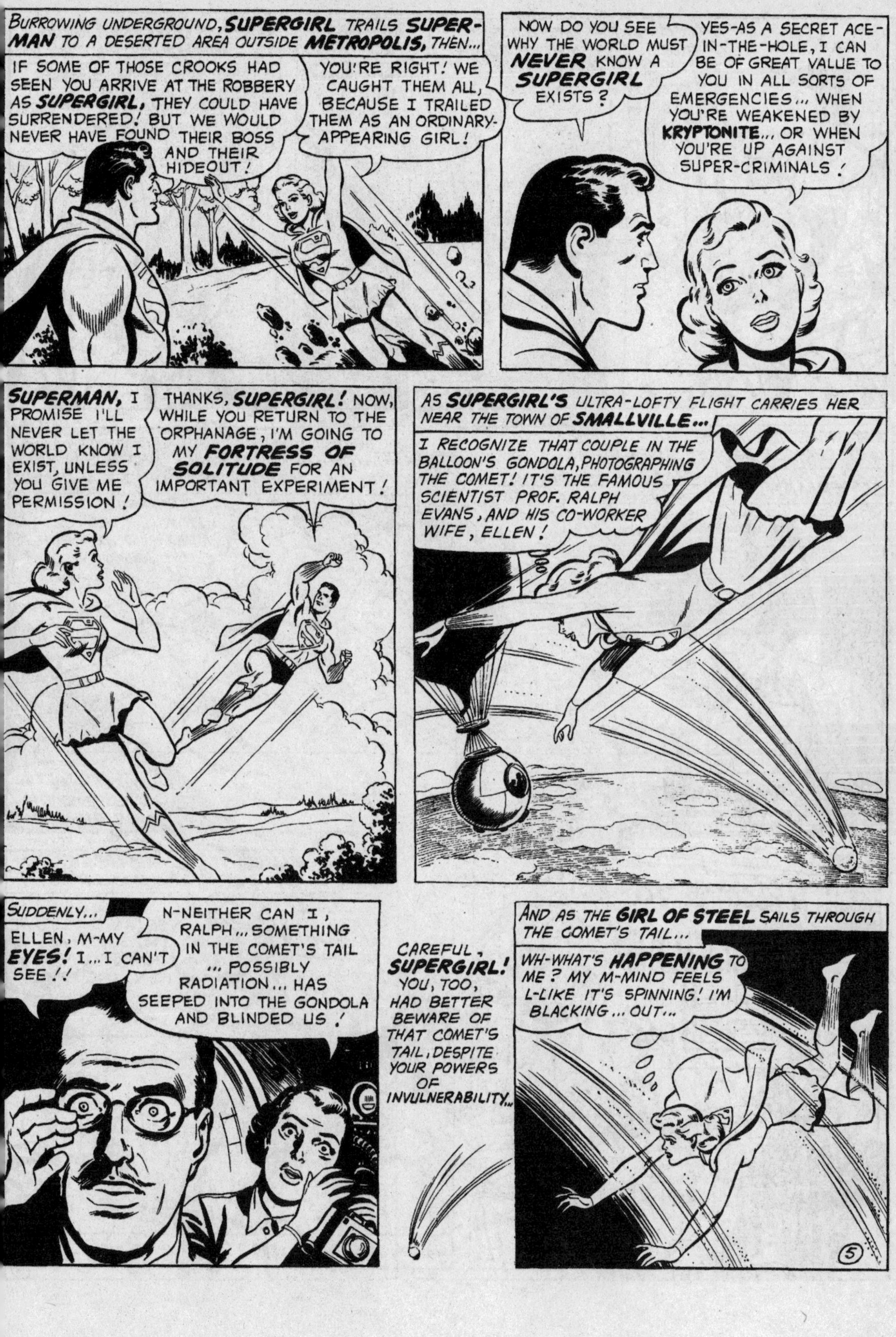
BURROWING UNDERGROUND, SUPERGIRL TRAILS SUPERMAN TO A DESERTED AREA OUTSIDE METROPOLIS, THEN...
IF SOME OF THOSE CROOKS HAD SEEN YOU ARRIVE AT THE ROBBERY AS SUPERGIRL, THEY COULD HAVE SURRENDERED! BUT WE WOULD NEVER HAVE FOUND THEIR BOSS AND THEIR HIDEOUT!
YOU'RE RIGHT! WE CAUGHT THEM ALL, BECAUSE I TRAILED THEM AS AN ORDINARY-APPEARING GIRL!
NOW DO YOU SEE WHY THE WORLD MUST NEVER KNOW A SUPERGIRL EXISTS?
YES-AS A SECRET ACE-IN-THE-HOLE, I CAN BE OF GREAT VALUE TO YOU IN ALL SORTS OF EMERGENCIES... WHEN YOU'RE WEAKENED BY KRYPTONITE... OR WHEN YOU'RE UP AGAINST SUPER-CRIMINALS!
SUPERMAN, I PROMISE I'LL NEVER LET THE WORLD KNOW I EXIST, UNLESS YOU GIVE ME PERMISSION!
THANKS, SUPERGIRL! NOW, WHILE YOU RETURN TO THE ORPHANAGE, I'M GOING TO MY FORTRESS OF SOLITUDE FOR AN IMPORTANT EXPERIMENT!
AS SUPERGIRL'S ULTRA-LOFTY FLIGHT CARRIES HER NEAR THE TOWN OF SMALLVILLE...
I RECOGNIZE THAT COUPLE IN THE BALLOON'S GONDOLA, PHOTOGRAPHING THE COMET! IT'S THE FAMOUS SCIENTIST PROF. RALPH EVANS, AND HIS CO-WORKER WIFE, ELLEN!
SUDDENLY...
ELLEN, M-MY EYES! I...I CAN'T SEE!!
N-NEITHER CAN I, RALPH... SOMETHING IN THE COMET'S TAIL ... POSSIBLY RADIATION... HAS SEEPED INTO THE GONDOLA AND BLINDED US!
CAREFUL, SUPERGIRL! YOU, TOO, HAD BETTER BEWARE OF THAT COMET'S TAIL, DESPITE YOUR POWERS OF INVULNERABILITY...
AND AS THE GIRL OF STEEL SAILS THROUGH THE COMET'S TAIL...
WH-WHAT'S HAPPENING TO ME? MY M-MIND FEELS L-LIKE IT'S SPINNING! I'M BLACKING... OUT...
5

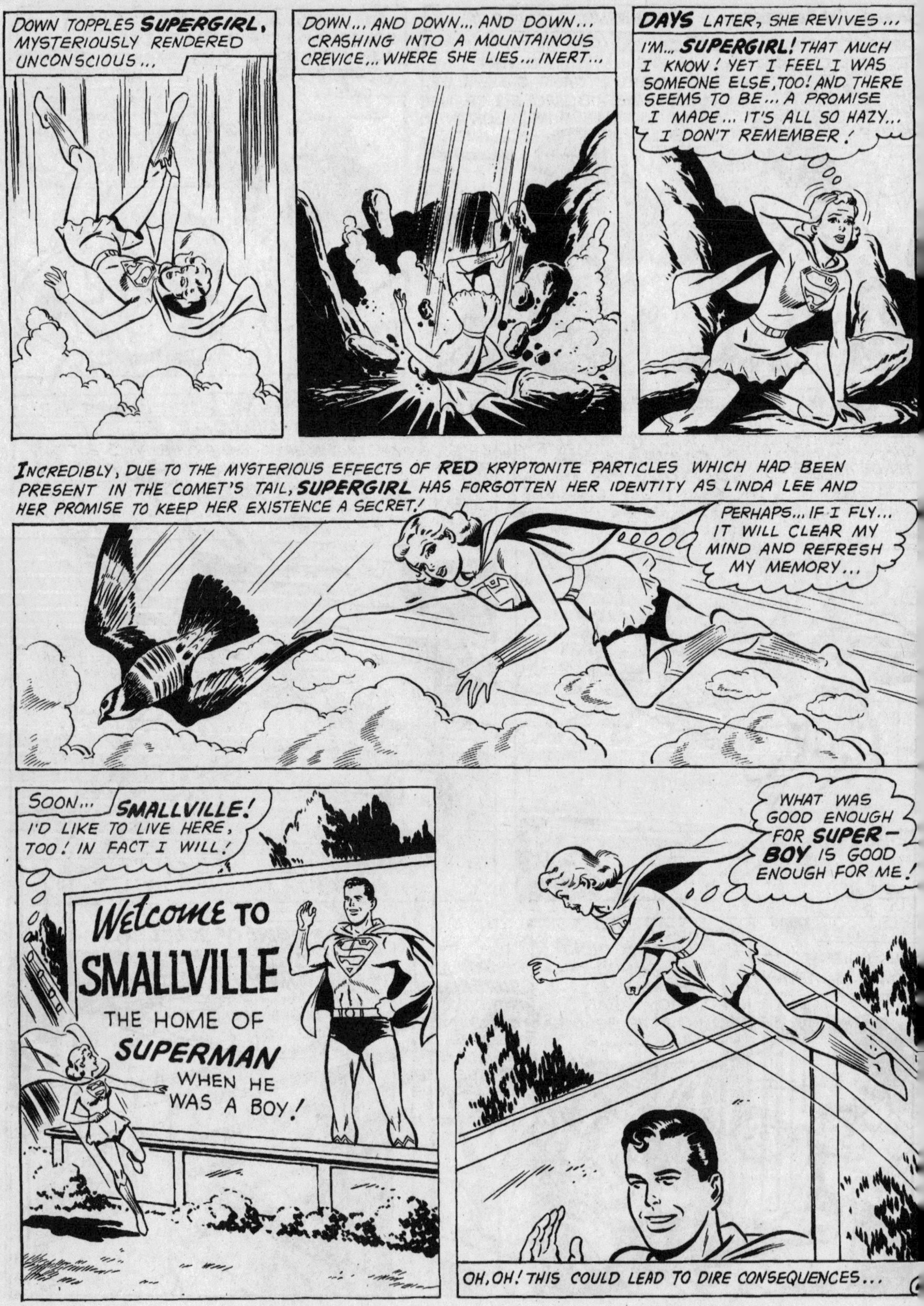
DOWN TOPPLES SUPERGIRL, MYSTERIOUSLY RENDERED UNCONSCIOUS...
DOWN... AND DOWN... AND DOWN... CRASHING INTO A MOUNTAINOUS CREVICE... WHERE SHE LIES... INERT...
DAYS LATER, SHE REVIVES...
I'M... SUPERGIRL! THAT MUCH I KNOW! YET I FEEL I WAS SOMEONE ELSE, TOO! AND THERE SEEMS TO BE... A PROMISE I MADE... IT'S ALL SO HAZY... I DON'T REMEMBER!
INCREDIBLY, DUE TO THE MYSTERIOUS EFFECTS OF RED KRYPTONITE PARTICLES WHICH HAD BEEN PRESENT IN THE COMET'S TAIL, SUPERGIRL HAS FORGOTTEN HER IDENTITY AS LINDA LEE AND HER PROMISE TO KEEP HER EXISTENCE A SECRET!
PERHAPS... IF I FLY... IT WILL CLEAR MY MIND AND REFRESH MY MEMORY...
SOON...
SMALLVILLE! I'D LIKE TO LIVE HERE, TOO! IN FACT I WILL!
WELCOME TO SMALLVILLE THE HOME OF SUPERMAN WHEN HE WAS A BOY!
WHAT WAS GOOD ENOUGH FOR SUPERBOY IS GOOD ENOUGH FOR ME!
OH, OH! THIS COULD LEAD TO DIRE CONSEQUENCES...

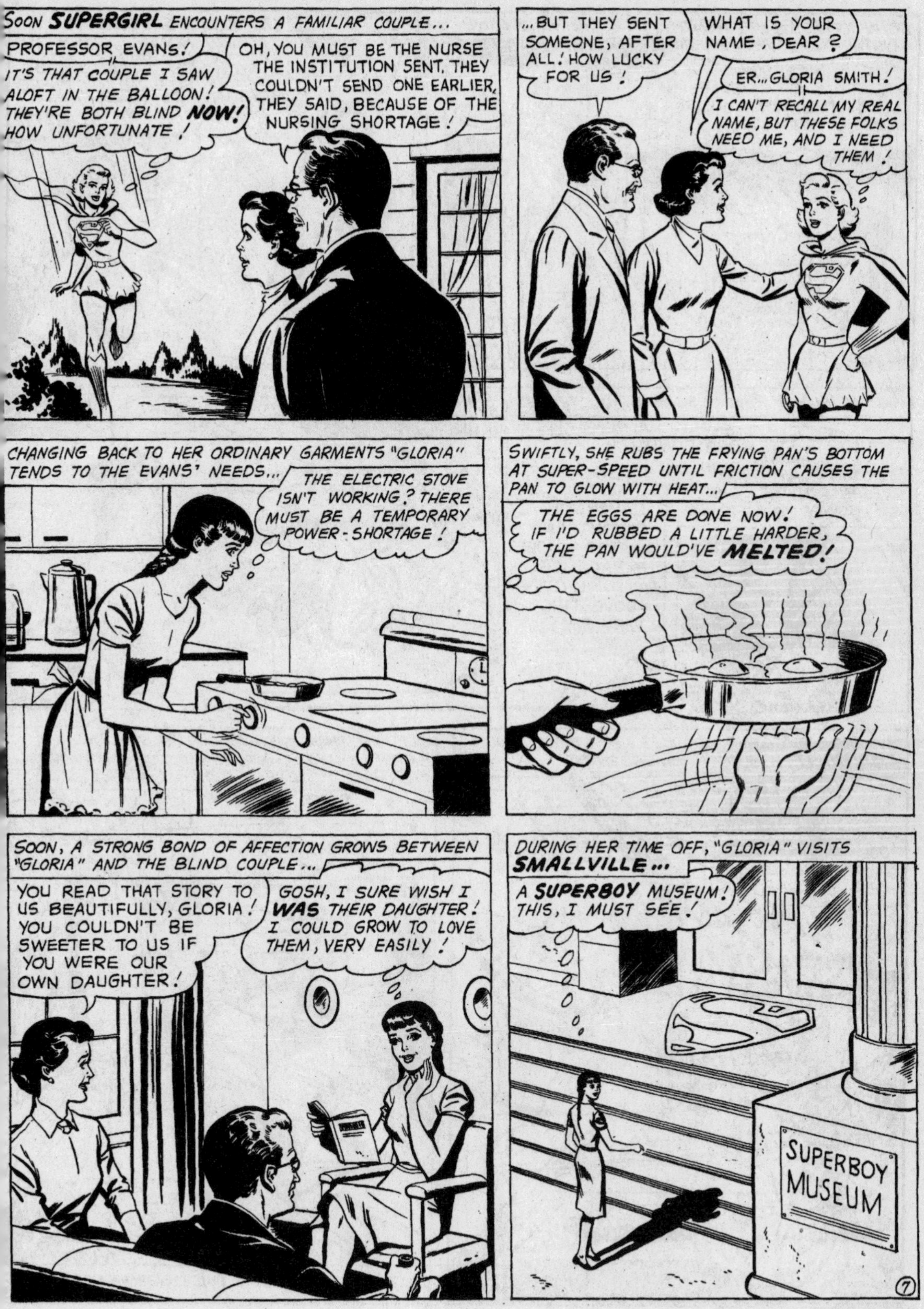
SOON SUPERGIRL ENCOUNTERS A FAMILIAR COUPLE...
PROFESSOR EVANS!
IT'S THAT COUPLE I SAW ALOFT IN THE BALLOON! THEY'RE BOTH BLIND NOW! HOW UNFORTUNATE!
OH, YOU MUST BE THE NURSE THE INSTITUTION SENT. THEY COULDN'T SEND ONE EARLIER, THEY SAID, BECAUSE OF THE NURSING SHORTAGE!
...BUT THEY SENT SOMEONE, AFTER ALL! HOW LUCKY FOR US!
WHAT IS YOUR NAME, DEAR?
ER...GLORIA SMITH!
I CAN'T RECALL MY REAL NAME, BUT THESE FOLKS NEED ME, AND I NEED THEM!
CHANGING BACK TO HER ORDINARY GARMENTS "GLORIA" TENDS TO THE EVANS' NEEDS...
THE ELECTRIC STOVE ISN'T WORKING? THERE MUST BE A TEMPORARY POWER-SHORTAGE!
SWIFTLY, SHE RUBS THE FRYING PAN'S BOTTOM AT SUPER-SPEED UNTIL FRICTION CAUSES THE PAN TO GLOW WITH HEAT...
THE EGGS ARE DONE NOW! IF I'D RUBBED A LITTLE HARDER, THE PAN WOULD'VE MELTED!
SOON, A STRONG BOND OF AFFECTION GROWS BETWEEN "GLORIA" AND THE BLIND COUPLE...
YOU READ THAT STORY TO US BEAUTIFULLY, GLORIA! YOU COULDN'T BE SWEETER TO US IF YOU WERE OUR OWN DAUGHTER!
GOSH, I SURE WISH I WAS THEIR DAUGHTER! I COULD GROW TO LOVE THEM, VERY EASILY!
DURING HER TIME OFF, "GLORIA" VISITS SMALLVILLE...
A SUPERBOY MUSEUM! THIS, I MUST SEE!
SUPERBOY MUSEUM
7

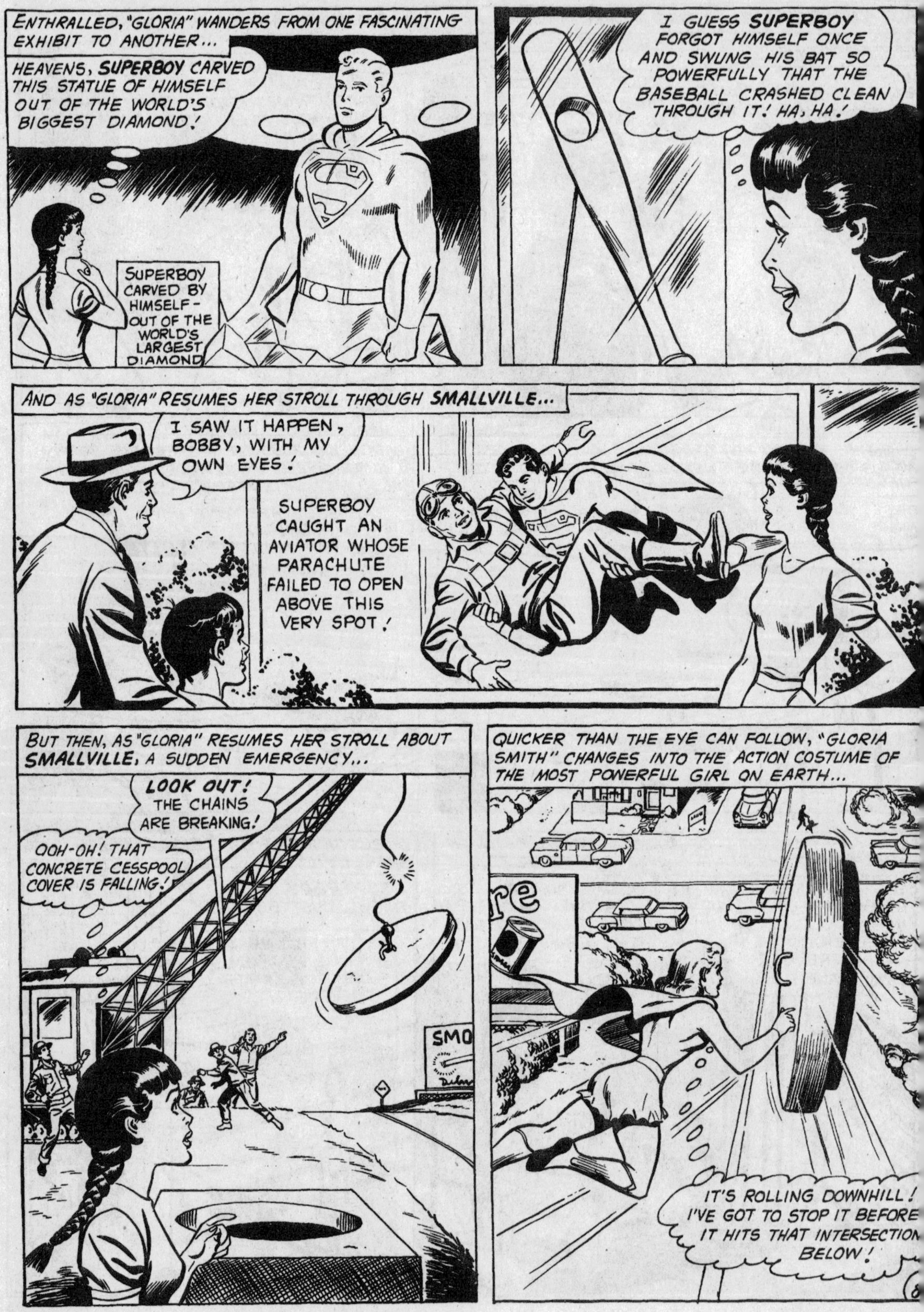
ENTHRALLED, "GLORIA" WANDERS FROM ONE FASCINATING EXHIBIT TO ANOTHER...
HEAVENS, SUPERBOY CARVED THIS STATUE OF HIMSELF OUT OF THE WORLD'S BIGGEST DIAMOND!
SUPERBOY CARVED BY HIMSELF-OUT OF THE WORLD'S LARGEST DIAMOND
I GUESS SUPERBOY FORGOT HIMSELF ONCE AND SWUNG HIS BAT SO POWERFULLY THAT THE BASEBALL CRASHED CLEAN THROUGH IT! HA, HA!
AND AS "GLORIA" RESUMES HER STROLL THROUGH SMALLVILLE...
I SAW IT HAPPEN, BOBBY, WITH MY OWN EYES!
SUPERBOY CAUGHT AN AVIATOR WHOSE PARACHUTE FAILED TO OPEN ABOVE THIS VERY SPOT!
BUT THEN, AS "GLORIA" RESUMES HER STROLL ABOUT SMALLVILLE, A SUDDEN EMERGENCY...
LOOK OUT! THE CHAINS ARE BREAKING!
OOH-OH! THAT CONCRETE CESSPOOL COVER IS FALLING!
SMO
QUICKER THAN THE EYE CAN FOLLOW, "GLORIA SMITH" CHANGES INTO THE ACTION COSTUME OF THE MOST POWERFUL GIRL ON EARTH...
IT'S ROLLING DOWNHILL! I'VE GOT TO STOP IT BEFORE IT HITS THAT INTERSECTION BELOW!

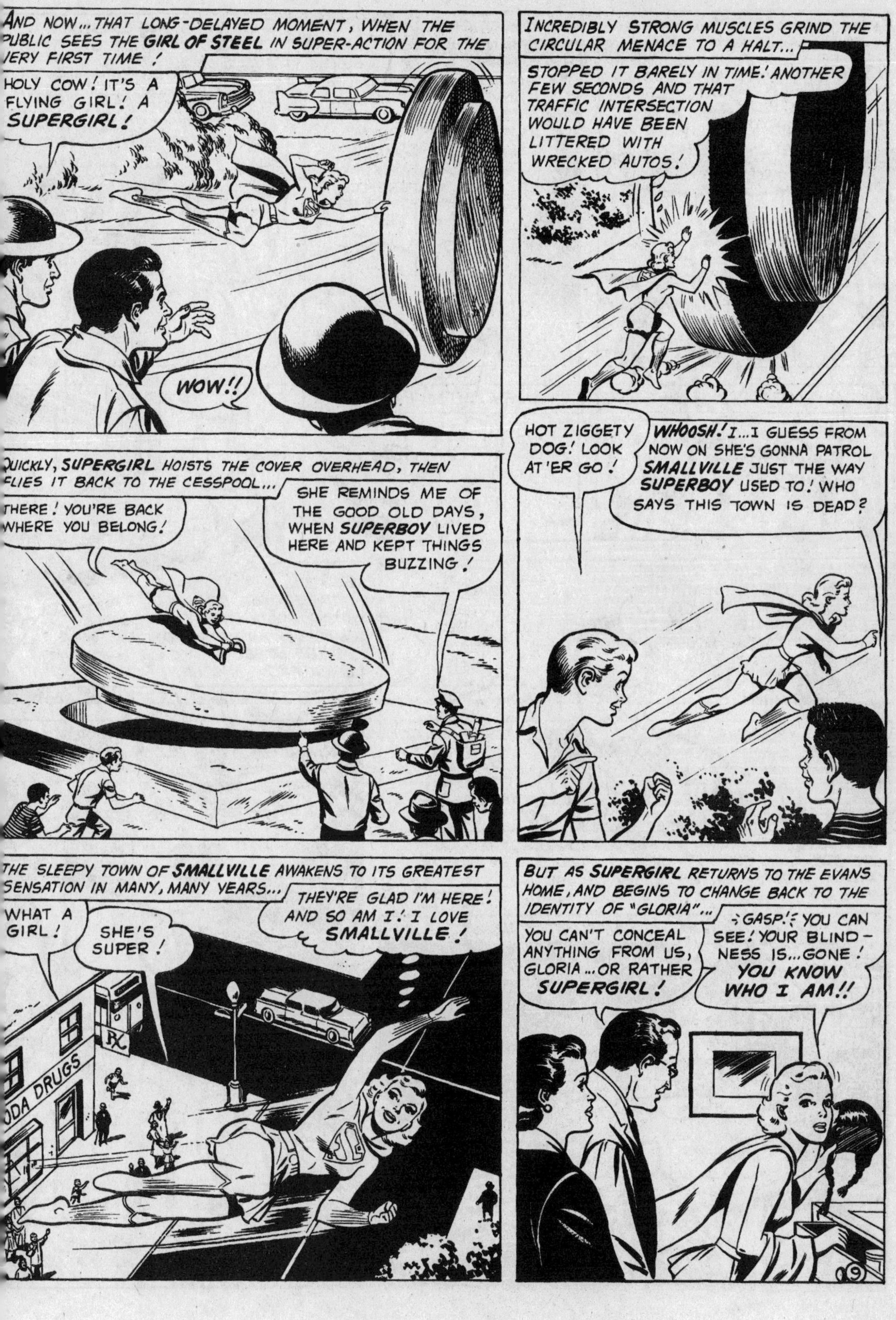
AND NOW...THAT LONG-DELAYED MOMENT, WHEN THE PUBLIC SEES THE GIRL OF STEEL IN SUPER-ACTION FOR THE VERY FIRST TIME!
HOLY COW! IT'S A FLYING GIRL! A SUPERGIRL!
WOW!!
INCREDIBLY STRONG MUSCLES GRIND THE CIRCULAR MENACE TO A HALT...
STOPPED IT BARELY IN TIME! ANOTHER FEW SECONDS AND THAT TRAFFIC INTERSECTION WOULD HAVE BEEN LITTERED WITH WRECKED AUTOS!
QUICKLY, SUPERGIRL HOISTS THE COVER OVERHEAD, THEN FLIES IT BACK TO THE CESSPOOL...
THERE! YOU'RE BACK WHERE YOU BELONG!
SHE REMINDS ME OF THE GOOD OLD DAYS, WHEN SUPERBOY LIVED HERE AND KEPT THINGS BUZZING!
HOT ZIGGETY DOG! LOOK AT'ER GO!
WHOOSH! I...I GUESS FROM NOW ON SHE'S GONNA PATROL SMALLVILLE JUST THE WAY SUPERBOY USED TO! WHO SAYS THIS TOWN IS DEAD?
THE SLEEPY TOWN OF SMALLVILLE AWAKENS TO ITS GREATEST SENSATION IN MANY, MANY YEARS...
WHAT A GIRL!
SHE'S SUPER!
THEY'RE GLAD I'M HERE! AND SO AM I! I LOVE SMALLVILLE!
Rx
ODA DRUGS
BUT AS SUPERGIRL RETURNS TO THE EVANS HOME, AND BEGINS TO CHANGE BACK TO THE IDENTITY OF "GLORIA"...
YOU CAN'T CONCEAL ANYTHING FROM US, GLORIA...OR RATHER SUPERGIRL!
GASP! YOU CAN SEE! YOUR BLINDNESS IS...GONE! YOU KNOW WHO I AM!!
9

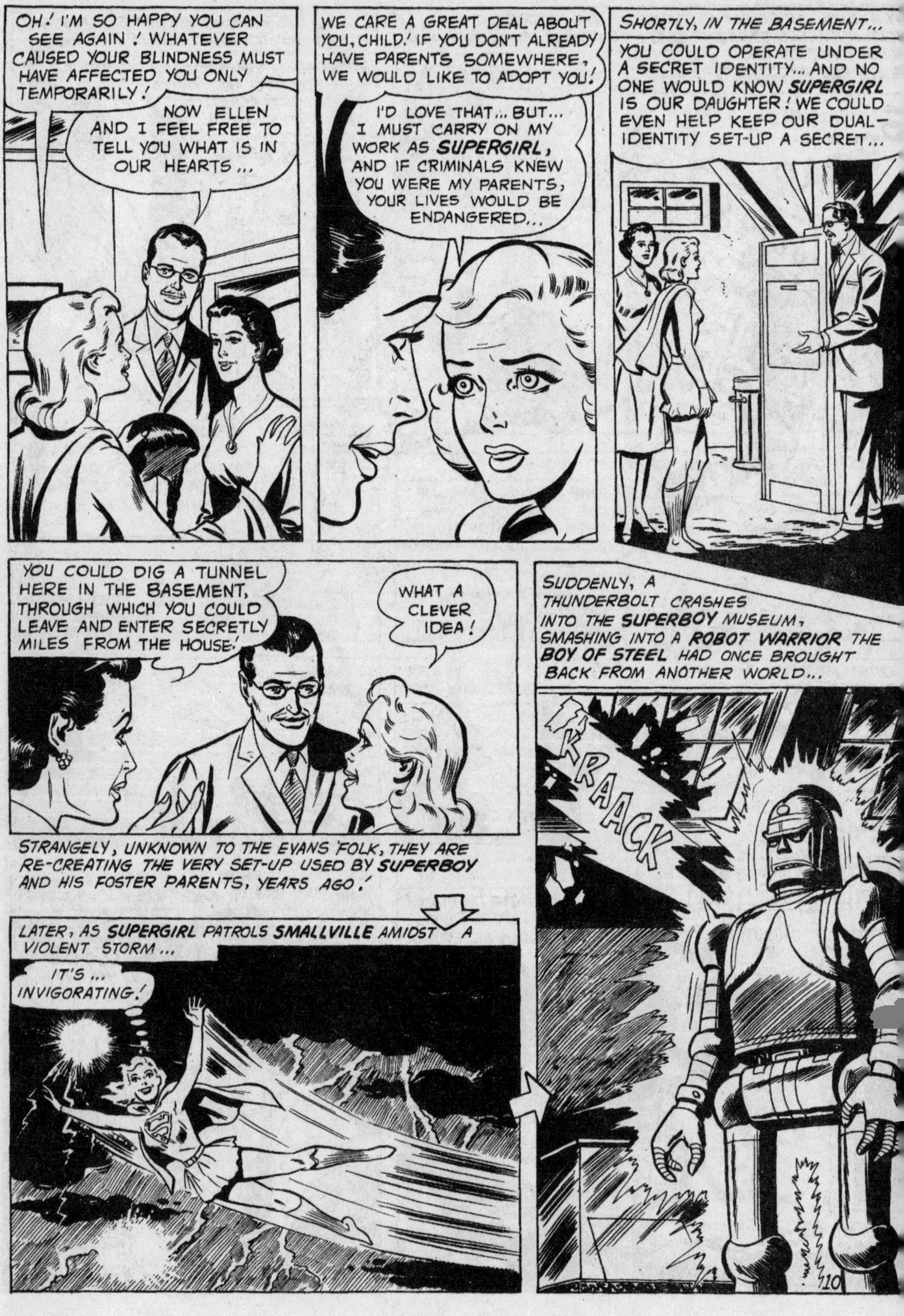
OH! I'M SO HAPPY YOU CAN SEE AGAIN! WHATEVER CAUSED YOUR BLINDNESS MUST HAVE AFFECTED YOU ONLY TEMPORARILY!
NOW ELLEN AND I FEEL FREE TO TELL YOU WHAT IS IN OUR HEARTS...
WE CARE A GREAT DEAL ABOUT YOU, CHILD! IF YOU DON'T ALREADY HAVE PARENTS SOMEWHERE, WE WOULD LIKE TO ADOPT YOU!
I'D LOVE THAT... BUT... I MUST CARRY ON MY WORK AS SUPERGIRL, AND IF CRIMINALS KNEW YOU WERE MY PARENTS, YOUR LIVES WOULD BE ENDANGERED...
SHORTLY, IN THE BASEMENT...
YOU COULD OPERATE UNDER A SECRET IDENTITY... AND NO ONE WOULD KNOW SUPERGIRL IS OUR DAUGHTER! WE COULD EVEN HELP KEEP OUR DUAL-IDENTITY SET-UP A SECRET...
YOU COULD DIG A TUNNEL HERE IN THE BASEMENT, THROUGH WHICH YOU COULD LEAVE AND ENTER SECRETLY MILES FROM THE HOUSE!
WHAT A CLEVER IDEA!
STRANGELY, UNKNOWN TO THE EVANS FOLK, THEY ARE RE-CREATING THE VERY SET-UP USED BY SUPERBOY AND HIS FOSTER PARENTS, YEARS AGO!
LATER, AS SUPERGIRL PATROLS SMALLVILLE AMIDST A VIOLENT STORM...
IT'S... INVIGORATING!
SUDDENLY, A THUNDERBOLT CRASHES INTO THE SUPERBOY MUSEUM, SMASHING INTO A ROBOT WARRIOR THE BOY OF STEEL HAD ONCE BROUGHT BACK FROM ANOTHER WORLD...
KRAACK
10

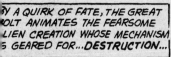

BY A QUIRK OF FATE, THE GREAT BOLT ANIMATES THE FEARSOME ALIEN CREATION WHOSE MECHANISM IS GEARED FOR...DESTRUCTION...

GROAR

SUPERBOY M

THE WARRIOR ROBOT IS LOOSE!

NOTHING CAN STOP IT! IF ONLY SUPERBOY WERE STILL HERE TO SAVE US!

PERHAPS SUPERBOY ISN'T PRESENT, BUT SUPERGIRL CERTAINLY IS...

A RAMPAGING ROBOT... WANTONLY DESTROYING! IF ITS ELECTRIC-BOLTS HIT THAT CHEMICAL PLANT, THE EXPLOSION WILL DESTROY SEVERAL CITY BLOCKS!

CHEMICAL WORKS INC.

JUST IN TIME! ONE SECOND SLOWER, AND THIS SECTION OF TOWN WOULD HAVE BEEN ONLY A MEMORY!

CHEMI

SEEKING TO FLEE, THE ROBOT LAUNCHES A FINAL, DESTRUCTIVE ELECTRIC-BOLT...

THE BOLT KNOCKED OVER THE SUPERBOY STATUE.!...BUT, LOOK! THE ROBOT'S COLLAPSING!

IT'S DONE FOR! MY X-RAY VISION HAS MELTED ITS INNER WORKS INTO MOLTEN METAL!

AWRRK!

11

SOON...

I SAW IT, BUT I STILL CAN'T BELIEVE IT.!

THAT LITTLE SLIP OF A GIRL OVERCAME THAT HORRIFY— ING CREATURE SINGLE-HANDED.!

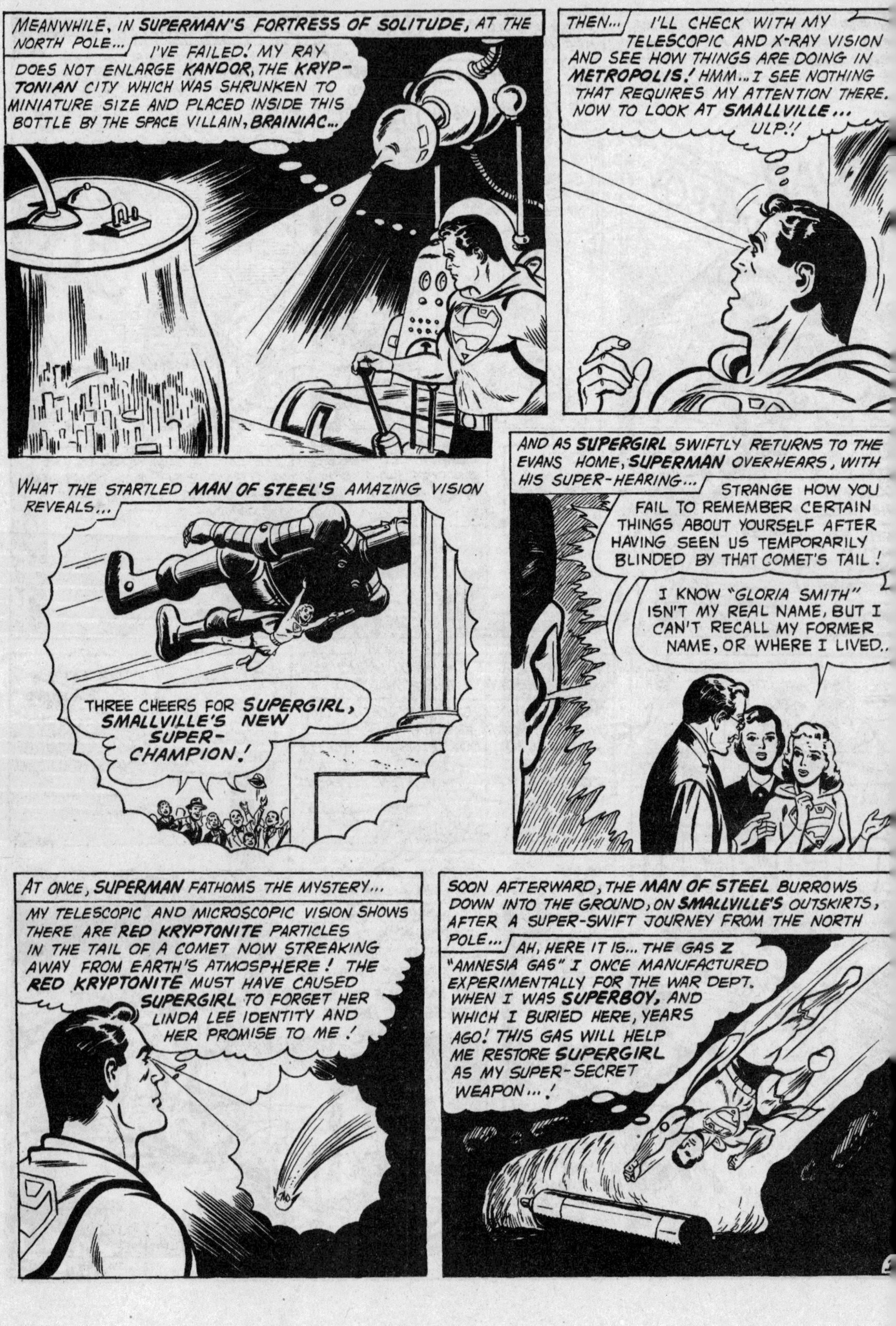
MEANWHILE, IN SUPERMAN'S FORTRESS OF SOLITUDE, AT THE NORTH POLE...
I'VE FAILED! MY RAY DOES NOT ENLARGE KANDOR, THE KRYPTONIAN CITY WHICH WAS SHRUNKEN TO MINIATURE SIZE AND PLACED INSIDE THIS BOTTLE BY THE SPACE VILLAIN, BRAINIAC...
THEN...
I'LL CHECK WITH MY TELESCOPIC AND X-RAY VISION AND SEE HOW THINGS ARE DOING IN METROPOLIS! HMM.. I SEE NOTHING THAT REQUIRES MY ATTENTION THERE. NOW TO LOOK AT SMALLVILLE... ULP!!
WHAT THE STARTLED MAN OF STEEL'S AMAZING VISION REVEALS...
THREE CHEERS FOR SUPERGIRL, SMALLVILLE'S NEW SUPER-CHAMPION!
AND AS SUPERGIRL SWIFTLY RETURNS TO THE EVANS HOME, SUPERMAN OVERHEARS, WITH HIS SUPER-HEARING...
STRANGE HOW YOU FAIL TO REMEMBER CERTAIN THINGS ABOUT YOURSELF AFTER HAVING SEEN US TEMPORARILY BLINDED BY THAT COMET'S TAIL!
I KNOW "GLORIA SMITH" ISN'T MY REAL NAME, BUT I CAN'T RECALL MY FORMER NAME, OR WHERE I LIVED..
AT ONCE, SUPERMAN FATHOMS THE MYSTERY...
MY TELESCOPIC AND MICROSCOPIC VISION SHOWS THERE ARE RED KRYPTONITE PARTICLES IN THE TAIL OF A COMET NOW STREAKING AWAY FROM EARTH'S ATMOSPHERE! THE RED KRYPTONITE MUST HAVE CAUSED SUPERGIRL TO FORGET HER LINDA LEE IDENTITY AND HER PROMISE TO ME!
SOON AFTERWARD, THE MAN OF STEEL BURROWS DOWN INTO THE GROUND, ON SMALLVILLE'S OUTSKIRTS, AFTER A SUPER-SWIFT JOURNEY FROM THE NORTH POLE...
AH, HERE IT IS... THE GAS Z "AMNESIA GAS" I ONCE MANUFACTURED EXPERIMENTALLY FOR THE WAR DEPT. WHEN I WAS SUPERBOY, AND WHICH I BURIED HERE, YEARS AGO! THIS GAS WILL HELP ME RESTORE SUPERGIRL AS MY SUPER-SECRET WEAPON...!

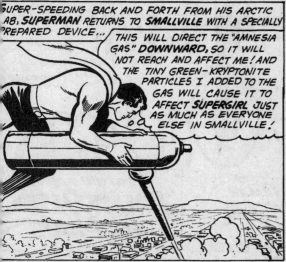

SUPER-SPEEDING BACK AND FORTH FROM HIS ARCTIC LAB, **SUPERMAN** RETURNS TO **SMALLVILLE** WITH A SPECIALLY PREPARED DEVICE...

THIS WILL DIRECT THE "AMNESIA GAS" **DOWNWARD**, SO IT WILL NOT REACH AND AFFECT ME! AND THE TINY GREEN-KRYPTONITE PARTICLES I ADDED TO THE GAS WILL CAUSE IT TO AFFECT **SUPERGIRL** JUST AS MUCH AS EVERYONE ELSE IN SMALLVILLE!

THEN, JUST AS SUPER-SWIFTLY...

I'M PRINTING NEW COPIES OF THE **SMALLVILLE GAZETTE'S** LAST SEVERAL DAYS' EDITIONS, OMITTING ALL MENTION OF **SUPERGIRL**! I'LL SUBSTITUTE THESE FOR THE REMAINING COPIES OF THE ORIGINAL EDITIONS, THROUGHOUT TOWN!

AMAZINGLY, THE GAS ERASES MEMORY OF SUPERGIRL'S APPEARANCE--AND ALL ELSE THAT OCCURRED DURING THE LAST SEVERAL DAYS--FROM THE MINDS OF EVERYONE, INCLUDING **SUPERGIRL!**

IT'S FANTASTIC, ELLEN... NO ONE CAN REMEMBER THE EVENTS OF THE LAST FEW DAYS!

NEITHER CAN WE... BUT MY INSTINCT TELLS ME THAT SOMETHING VERY WONDERFUL HAPPENED DURING THAT TIME...

MEANWHILE, PATROLLING THE EMPTY COUNTRYSIDE, THE EFFECTS OF **RED KRYPTONITE** WEAR OFF AND... **SUPERGIRL** FLIES BACK TO MIDVALE, HER MEMORY OF THE LAST FEW DAYS BRAINWASHED BY GAS Z...

YOU WERE GONE A LONG TIME, MISTRESS!

STRANGEST THING IS, I CAN'T REMEMBER WHAT HAPPENED! I'LL CHANGE BACK TO LINDA LEE NOW, ROBOT!

FROM A GREAT DISTANCE, **SUPERMAN** OBSERVES LINDA RETURN TO THE ORPHANAGE...

SUPERGIRL AND I ARE ALWAYS AFFECTED IN UNPREDICTABLE WAYS BY **RED KRYPTONITE!** I WONDER WHAT WILL HAPPEN THE NEXT TIME WE ENCOUNTER THE TRICKY STUFF??

AND IN HER ROOM, SOON AFTER, LINDA PONDERS AN ENIGMA... UNAWARE OF THE IRONY OF THE SITUATION...

I WONDER HOW PEOPLE ON EARTH WOULD REACT IF THEY LEARNED THERE IS A **SUPERGIRL** ON EARTH? ¿SIGH¿ BECAUSE OF MY PROMISE TO **SUPERMAN,** I GUESS I'LL NEVER KNOW!

BUT **WE** KNOW, SUPERGIRL!

⑬ END

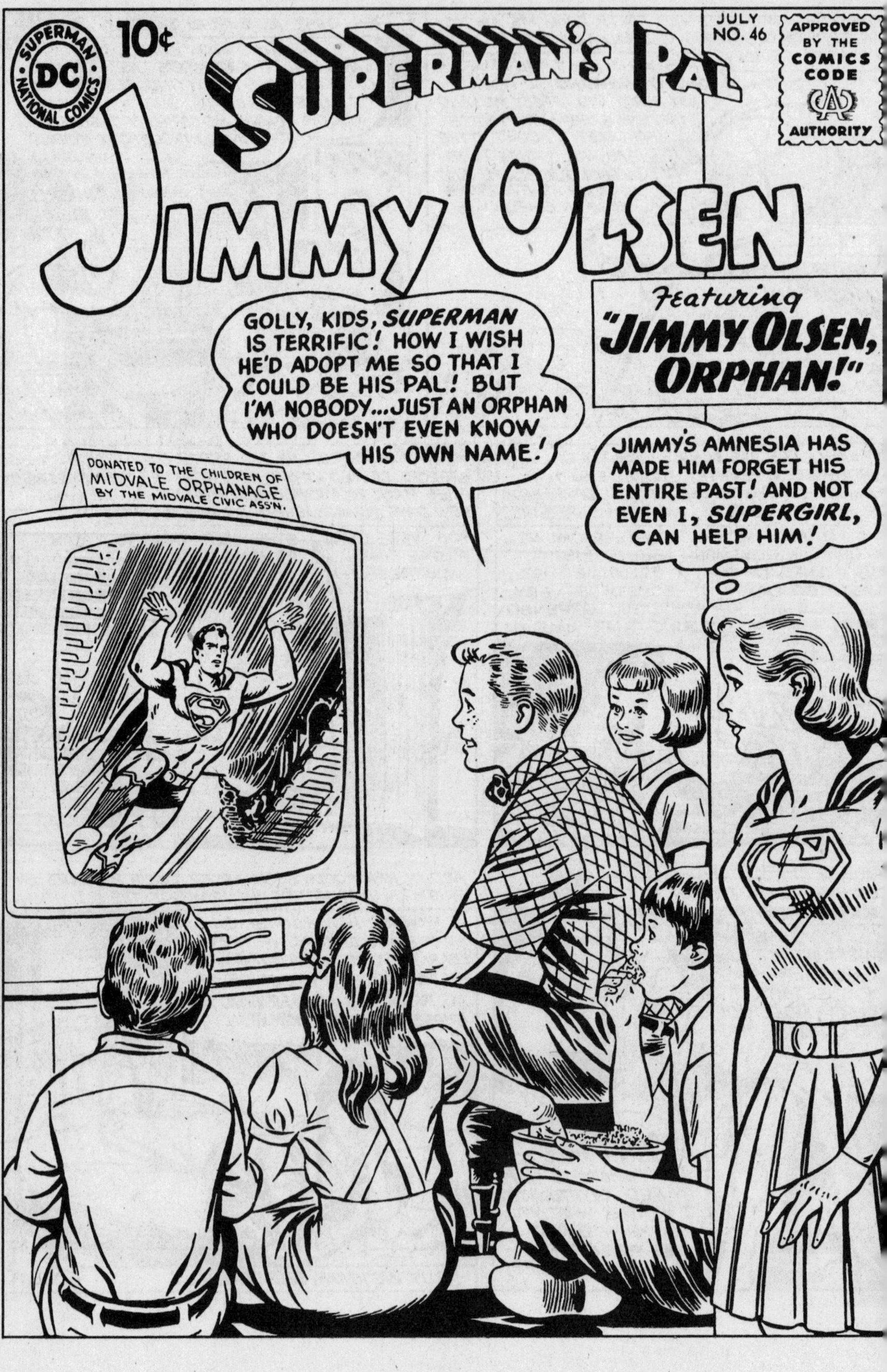
10¢
SUPERMAN NATIONAL COMICS DC
JULY NO. 46
APPROVED BY THE COMICS CODE AUTHORITY
SUPERMAN'S PAL JIMMY OLSEN
Featuring "JIMMY OLSEN, ORPHAN!"
GOLLY, KIDS, SUPERMAN IS TERRIFIC! HOW I WISH HE'D ADOPT ME SO THAT I COULD BE HIS PAL! BUT I'M NOBODY...JUST AN ORPHAN WHO DOESN'T EVEN KNOW HIS OWN NAME!
DONATED TO THE CHILDREN OF MIDVALE ORPHANAGE BY THE MIDVALE CIVIC ASS'N.
JIMMY'S AMNESIA HAS MADE HIM FORGET HIS ENTIRE PAST! AND NOT EVEN I, SUPERGIRL, CAN HELP HIM!

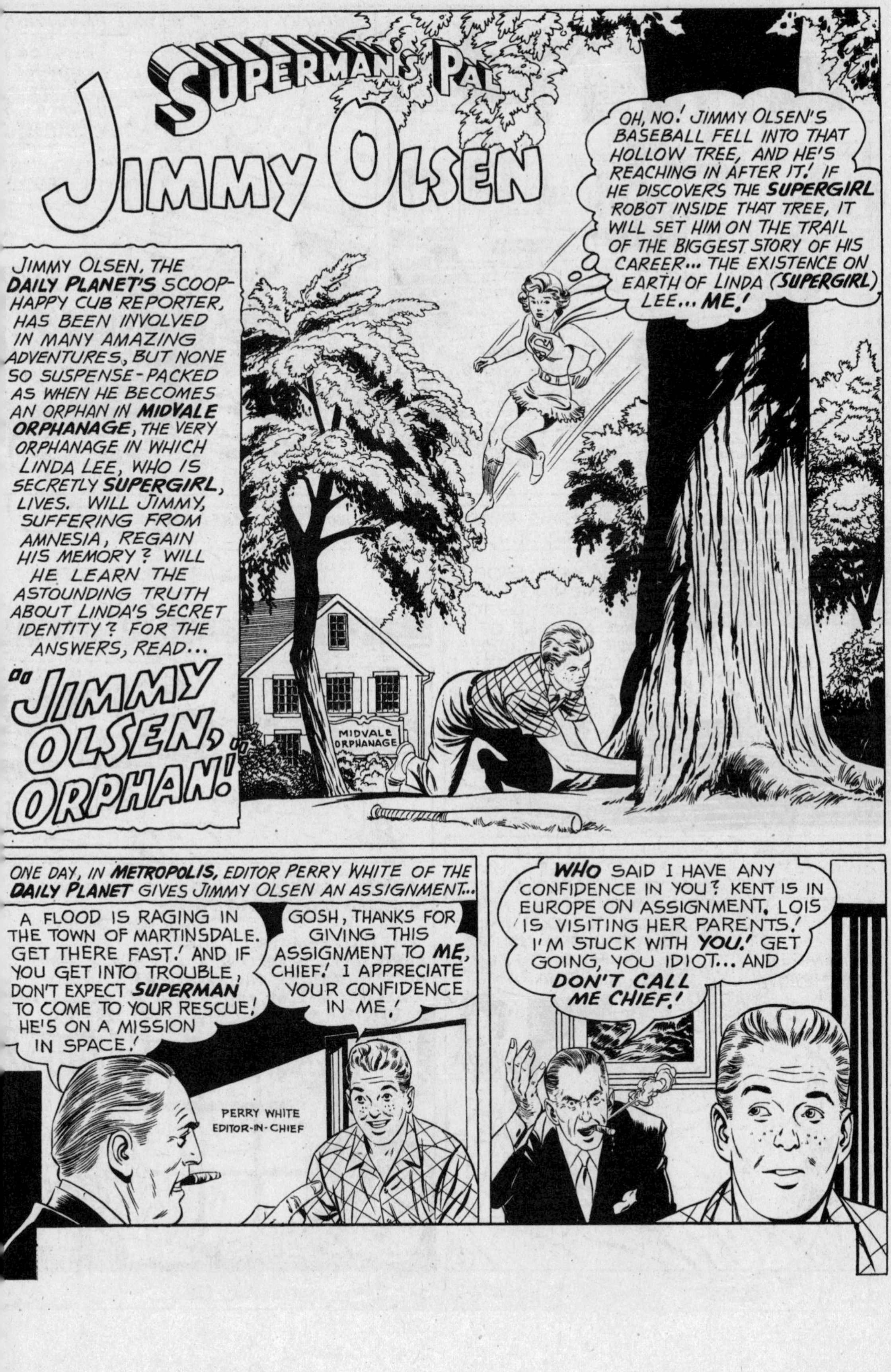
SUPERMAN'S PAL
JIMMY OLSEN
JIMMY OLSEN, THE DAILY PLANET'S SCOOP-HAPPY CUB REPORTER, HAS BEEN INVOLVED IN MANY AMAZING ADVENTURES, BUT NONE SO SUSPENSE-PACKED AS WHEN HE BECOMES AN ORPHAN IN MIDVALE ORPHANAGE, THE VERY ORPHANAGE IN WHICH LINDA LEE, WHO IS SECRETLY SUPERGIRL, LIVES. WILL JIMMY, SUFFERING FROM AMNESIA, REGAIN HIS MEMORY? WILL HE LEARN THE ASTOUNDING TRUTH ABOUT LINDA'S SECRET IDENTITY? FOR THE ANSWERS, READ...
"JIMMY OLSEN, ORPHAN!"
OH, NO! JIMMY OLSEN'S BASEBALL FELL INTO THAT HOLLOW TREE, AND HE'S REACHING IN AFTER IT! IF HE DISCOVERS THE SUPERGIRL ROBOT INSIDE THAT TREE, IT WILL SET HIM ON THE TRAIL OF THE BIGGEST STORY OF HIS CAREER... THE EXISTENCE ON EARTH OF LINDA (SUPERGIRL) LEE... ME!
MIDVALE ORPHANAGE
ONE DAY, IN METROPOLIS, EDITOR PERRY WHITE OF THE DAILY PLANET GIVES JIMMY OLSEN AN ASSIGNMENT...
A FLOOD IS RAGING IN THE TOWN OF MARTINSDALE. GET THERE FAST! AND IF YOU GET INTO TROUBLE, DON'T EXPECT SUPERMAN TO COME TO YOUR RESCUE! HE'S ON A MISSION IN SPACE!
GOSH, THANKS FOR GIVING THIS ASSIGNMENT TO ME, CHIEF! I APPRECIATE YOUR CONFIDENCE IN ME!
PERRY WHITE EDITOR-IN-CHIEF
WHO SAID I HAVE ANY CONFIDENCE IN YOU? KENT IS IN EUROPE ON ASSIGNMENT, LOIS IS VISITING HER PARENTS! I'M STUCK WITH YOU! GET GOING, YOU IDIOT... AND DON'T CALL ME CHIEF!

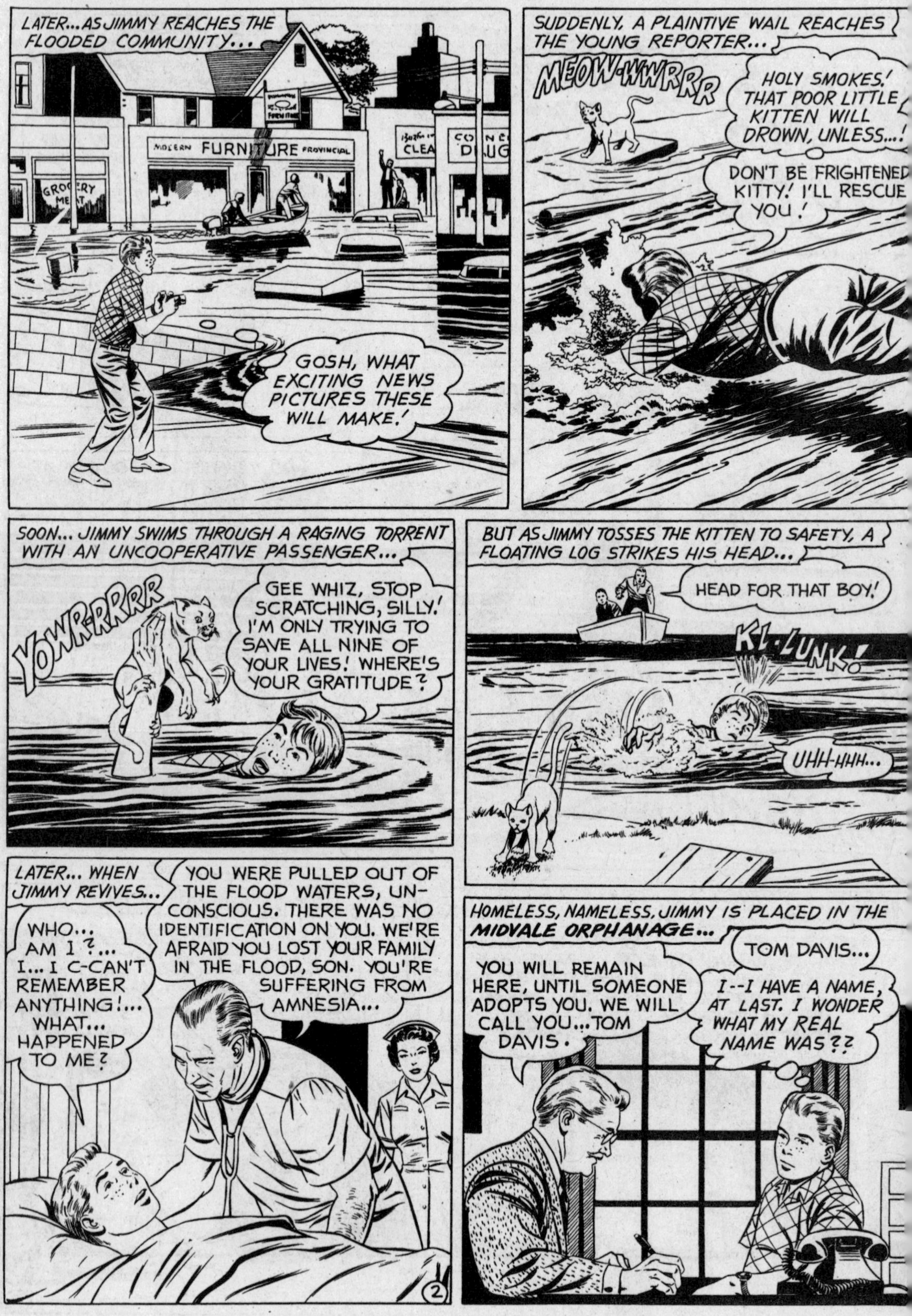
LATER...AS JIMMY REACHES THE FLOODED COMMUNITY...
MODERN FURNITURE PROVINCIAL
GOSH, WHAT EXCITING NEWS PICTURES THESE WILL MAKE!
SUDDENLY, A PLAINTIVE WAIL REACHES THE YOUNG REPORTER...
MEOW-WWRRR
HOLY SMOKES! THAT POOR LITTLE KITTEN WILL DROWN, UNLESS...!
DON'T BE FRIGHTENED KITTY! I'LL RESCUE YOU!
SOON... JIMMY SWIMS THROUGH A RAGING TORRENT WITH AN UNCOOPERATIVE PASSENGER...
YOWR-RRRR
GEE WHIZ, STOP SCRATCHING, SILLY! I'M ONLY TRYING TO SAVE ALL NINE OF YOUR LIVES! WHERE'S YOUR GRATITUDE?
BUT AS JIMMY TOSSES THE KITTEN TO SAFETY, A FLOATING LOG STRIKES HIS HEAD...
HEAD FOR THAT BOY!
KL-LUNK!
UHH-HHH...
LATER... WHEN JIMMY REVIVES...
YOU WERE PULLED OUT OF THE FLOOD WATERS, UN-CONSCIOUS. THERE WAS NO IDENTIFICATION ON YOU. WE'RE AFRAID YOU LOST YOUR FAMILY IN THE FLOOD, SON. YOU'RE SUFFERING FROM AMNESIA...
WHO... AM I?... I... I C-CAN'T REMEMBER ANYTHING!... WHAT... HAPPENED TO ME?
2
HOMELESS, NAMELESS, JIMMY IS PLACED IN THE MIDVALE ORPHANAGE...
YOU WILL REMAIN HERE, UNTIL SOMEONE ADOPTS YOU. WE WILL CALL YOU...TOM DAVIS.
TOM DAVIS...
I--I HAVE A NAME, AT LAST. I WONDER WHAT MY REAL NAME WAS??

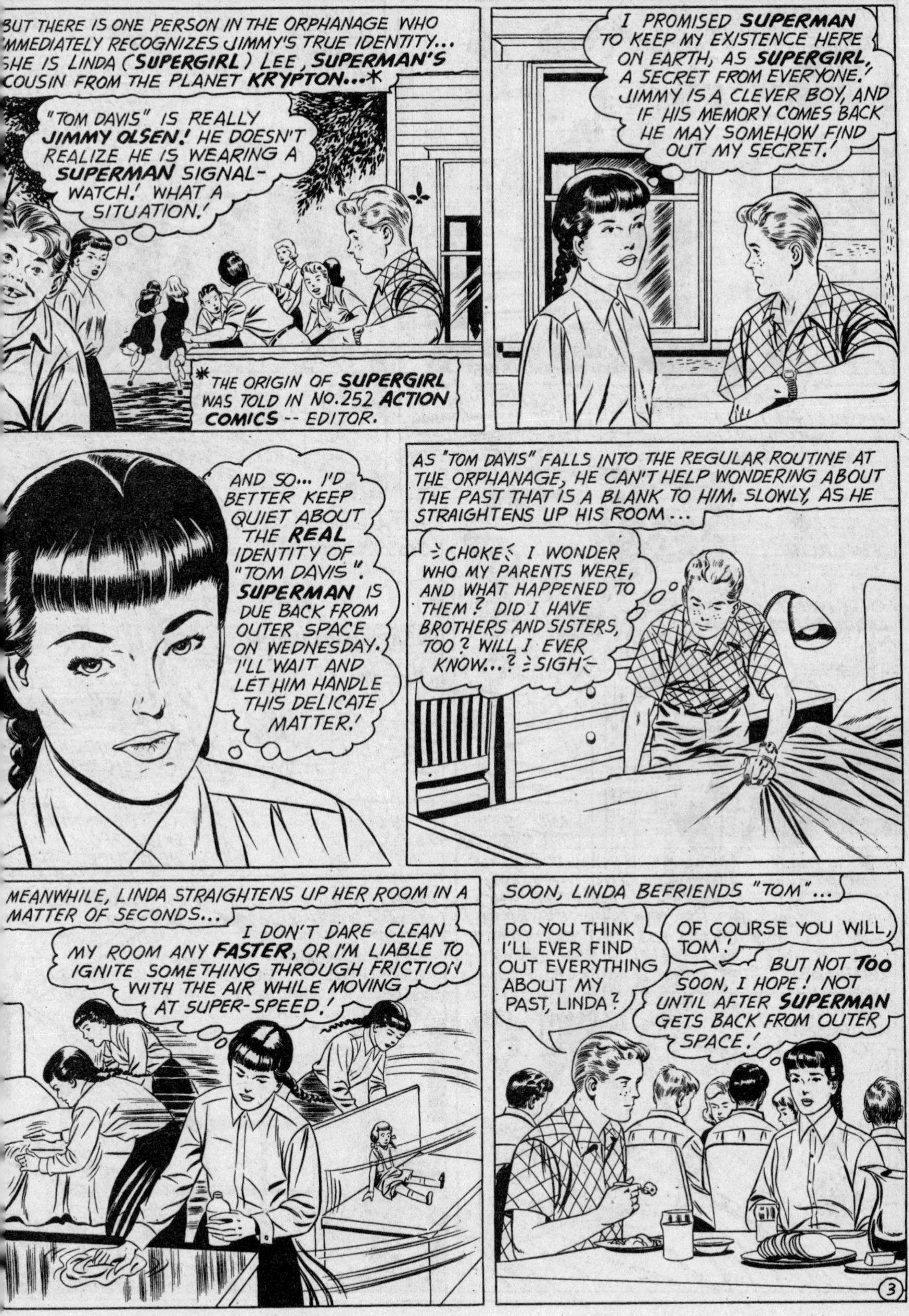
BUT THERE IS ONE PERSON IN THE ORPHANAGE WHO IMMEDIATELY RECOGNIZES JIMMY'S TRUE IDENTITY... SHE IS LINDA (SUPERGIRL) LEE, SUPERMAN'S COUSIN FROM THE PLANET KRYPTON...*
"TOM DAVIS" IS REALLY JIMMY OLSEN! HE DOESN'T REALIZE HE IS WEARING A SUPERMAN SIGNAL-WATCH! WHAT A SITUATION!
* THE ORIGIN OF SUPERGIRL WAS TOLD IN NO.252 ACTION COMICS -- EDITOR.
I PROMISED SUPERMAN TO KEEP MY EXISTENCE HERE ON EARTH, AS SUPERGIRL, A SECRET FROM EVERYONE! JIMMY IS A CLEVER BOY, AND IF HIS MEMORY COMES BACK HE MAY SOMEHOW FIND OUT MY SECRET!
AND SO... I'D BETTER KEEP QUIET ABOUT THE REAL IDENTITY OF "TOM DAVIS". SUPERMAN IS DUE BACK FROM OUTER SPACE ON WEDNESDAY. I'LL WAIT AND LET HIM HANDLE THIS DELICATE MATTER!
AS "TOM DAVIS" FALLS INTO THE REGULAR ROUTINE AT THE ORPHANAGE, HE CAN'T HELP WONDERING ABOUT THE PAST THAT IS A BLANK TO HIM. SLOWLY, AS HE STRAIGHTENS UP HIS ROOM...
CHOKE I WONDER WHO MY PARENTS WERE, AND WHAT HAPPENED TO THEM? DID I HAVE BROTHERS AND SISTERS, TOO? WILL I EVER KNOW...? SIGH
MEANWHILE, LINDA STRAIGHTENS UP HER ROOM IN A MATTER OF SECONDS...
I DON'T DARE CLEAN MY ROOM ANY FASTER, OR I'M LIABLE TO IGNITE SOMETHING THROUGH FRICTION WITH THE AIR WHILE MOVING AT SUPER-SPEED!
SOON, LINDA BEFRIENDS "TOM"...
DO YOU THINK I'LL EVER FIND OUT EVERYTHING ABOUT MY PAST, LINDA?
OF COURSE YOU WILL, TOM!
BUT NOT TOO SOON, I HOPE! NOT UNTIL AFTER SUPERMAN GETS BACK FROM OUTER SPACE!
3

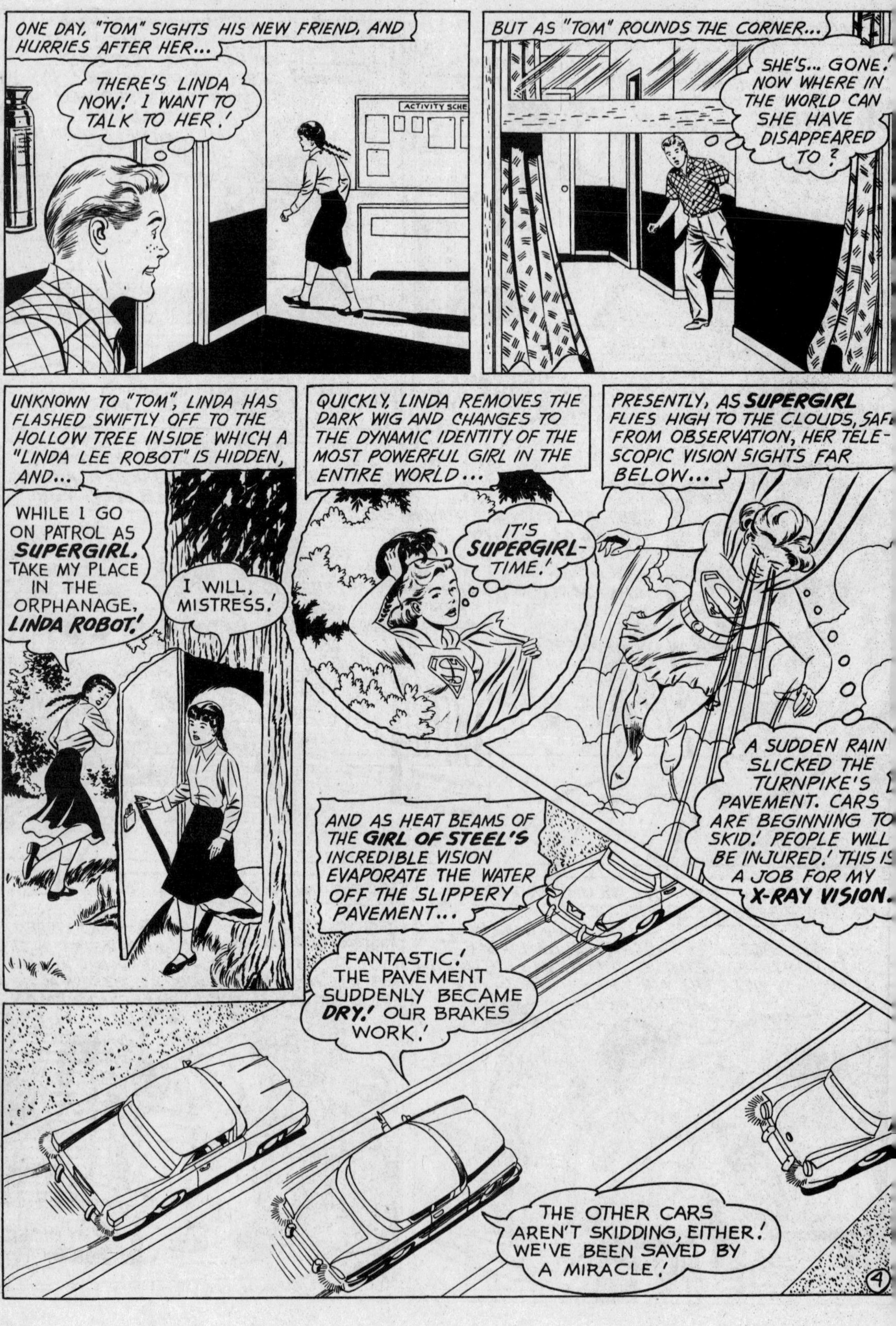
ONE DAY, "TOM" SIGHTS HIS NEW FRIEND, AND HURRIES AFTER HER...
THERE'S LINDA NOW! I WANT TO TALK TO HER!
ACTIVITY SCHE
BUT AS "TOM" ROUNDS THE CORNER...
SHE'S... GONE! NOW WHERE IN THE WORLD CAN SHE HAVE DISAPPEARED TO?
UNKNOWN TO "TOM", LINDA HAS FLASHED SWIFTLY OFF TO THE HOLLOW TREE INSIDE WHICH A "LINDA LEE ROBOT" IS HIDDEN, AND...
WHILE I GO ON PATROL AS **SUPERGIRL**, TAKE MY PLACE IN THE ORPHANAGE, **LINDA ROBOT!**
I WILL, MISTRESS!
QUICKLY, LINDA REMOVES THE DARK WIG AND CHANGES TO THE DYNAMIC IDENTITY OF THE MOST POWERFUL GIRL IN THE ENTIRE WORLD...
IT'S **SUPERGIRL**-TIME!
PRESENTLY, AS **SUPERGIRL** FLIES HIGH TO THE CLOUDS, SAF FROM OBSERVATION, HER TELESCOPIC VISION SIGHTS FAR BELOW...
A SUDDEN RAIN SLICKED THE TURNPIKE'S PAVEMENT. CARS ARE BEGINNING TO SKID! PEOPLE WILL BE INJURED! THIS IS A JOB FOR MY **X-RAY VISION**.
AND AS HEAT BEAMS OF THE **GIRL OF STEEL'S** INCREDIBLE VISION EVAPORATE THE WATER OFF THE SLIPPERY PAVEMENT...
FANTASTIC! THE PAVEMENT SUDDENLY BECAME **DRY!** OUR BRAKES WORK!
THE OTHER CARS AREN'T SKIDDING, EITHER! WE'VE BEEN SAVED BY A MIRACLE!
4

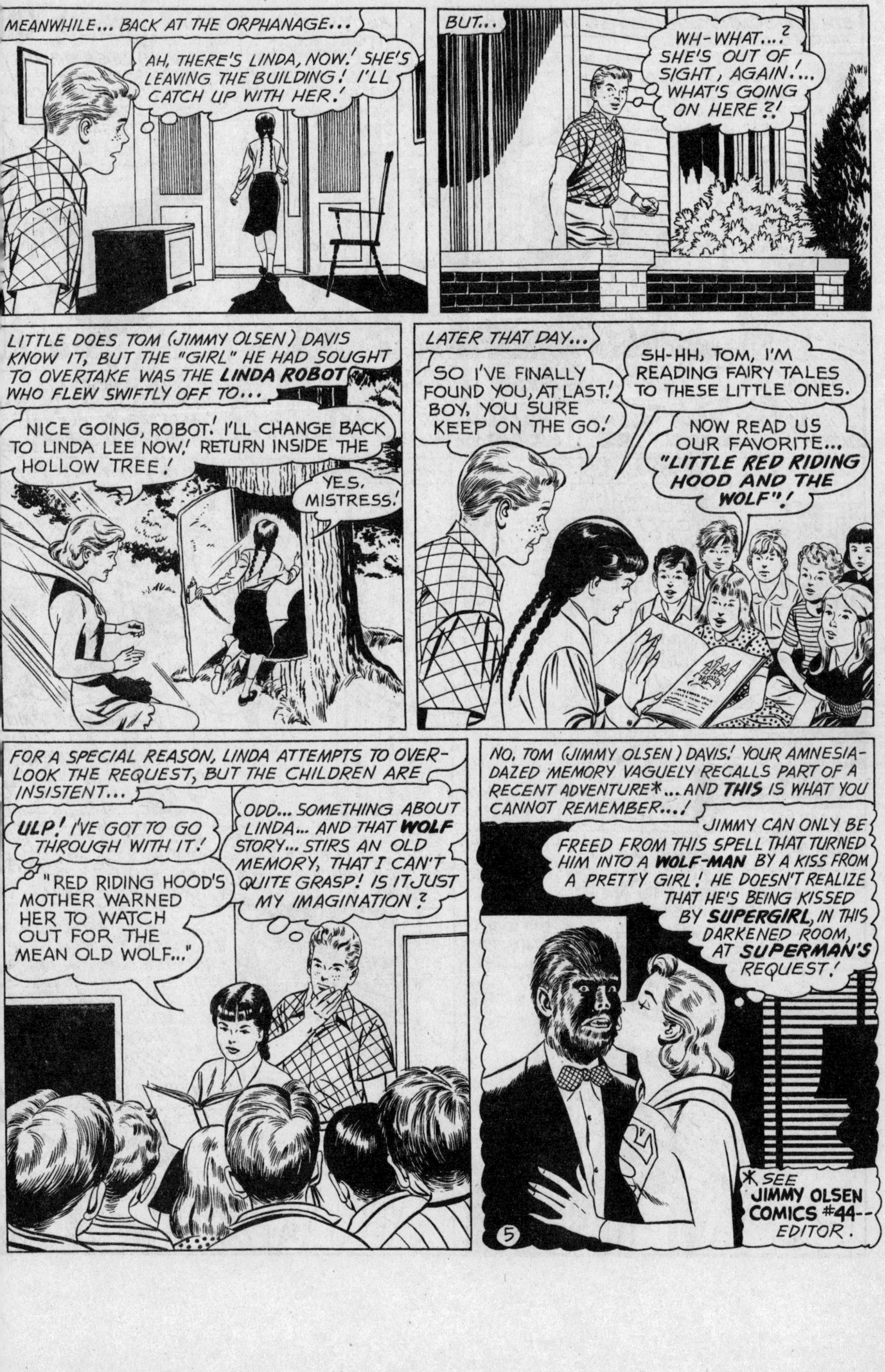
MEANWHILE... BACK AT THE ORPHANAGE...
AH, THERE'S LINDA, NOW! SHE'S LEAVING THE BUILDING! I'LL CATCH UP WITH HER!
BUT...
WH-WHAT...? SHE'S OUT OF SIGHT, AGAIN!... WHAT'S GOING ON HERE?!
LITTLE DOES TOM (JIMMY OLSEN) DAVIS KNOW IT, BUT THE "GIRL" HE HAD SOUGHT TO OVERTAKE WAS THE LINDA ROBOT WHO FLEW SWIFTLY OFF TO...
NICE GOING, ROBOT! I'LL CHANGE BACK TO LINDA LEE NOW! RETURN INSIDE THE HOLLOW TREE!
YES, MISTRESS!
LATER THAT DAY...
SO I'VE FINALLY FOUND YOU, AT LAST! BOY, YOU SURE KEEP ON THE GO!
SH-HH, TOM, I'M READING FAIRY TALES TO THESE LITTLE ONES.
NOW READ US OUR FAVORITE... "LITTLE RED RIDING HOOD AND THE WOLF"!
FOR A SPECIAL REASON, LINDA ATTEMPTS TO OVERLOOK THE REQUEST, BUT THE CHILDREN ARE INSISTENT...
ULP! I'VE GOT TO GO THROUGH WITH IT!
"RED RIDING HOOD'S MOTHER WARNED HER TO WATCH OUT FOR THE MEAN OLD WOLF..."
ODD... SOMETHING ABOUT LINDA... AND THAT WOLF STORY... STIRS AN OLD MEMORY, THAT I CAN'T QUITE GRASP! IS IT JUST MY IMAGINATION?
NO, TOM (JIMMY OLSEN) DAVIS! YOUR AMNESIA-DAZED MEMORY VAGUELY RECALLS PART OF A RECENT ADVENTURE*... AND THIS IS WHAT YOU CANNOT REMEMBER...!
JIMMY CAN ONLY BE FREED FROM THIS SPELL THAT TURNED HIM INTO A WOLF-MAN BY A KISS FROM A PRETTY GIRL! HE DOESN'T REALIZE THAT HE'S BEING KISSED BY SUPERGIRL, IN THIS DARKENED ROOM, AT SUPERMAN'S REQUEST!
*SEE JIMMY OLSEN COMICS #44-- EDITOR.
5

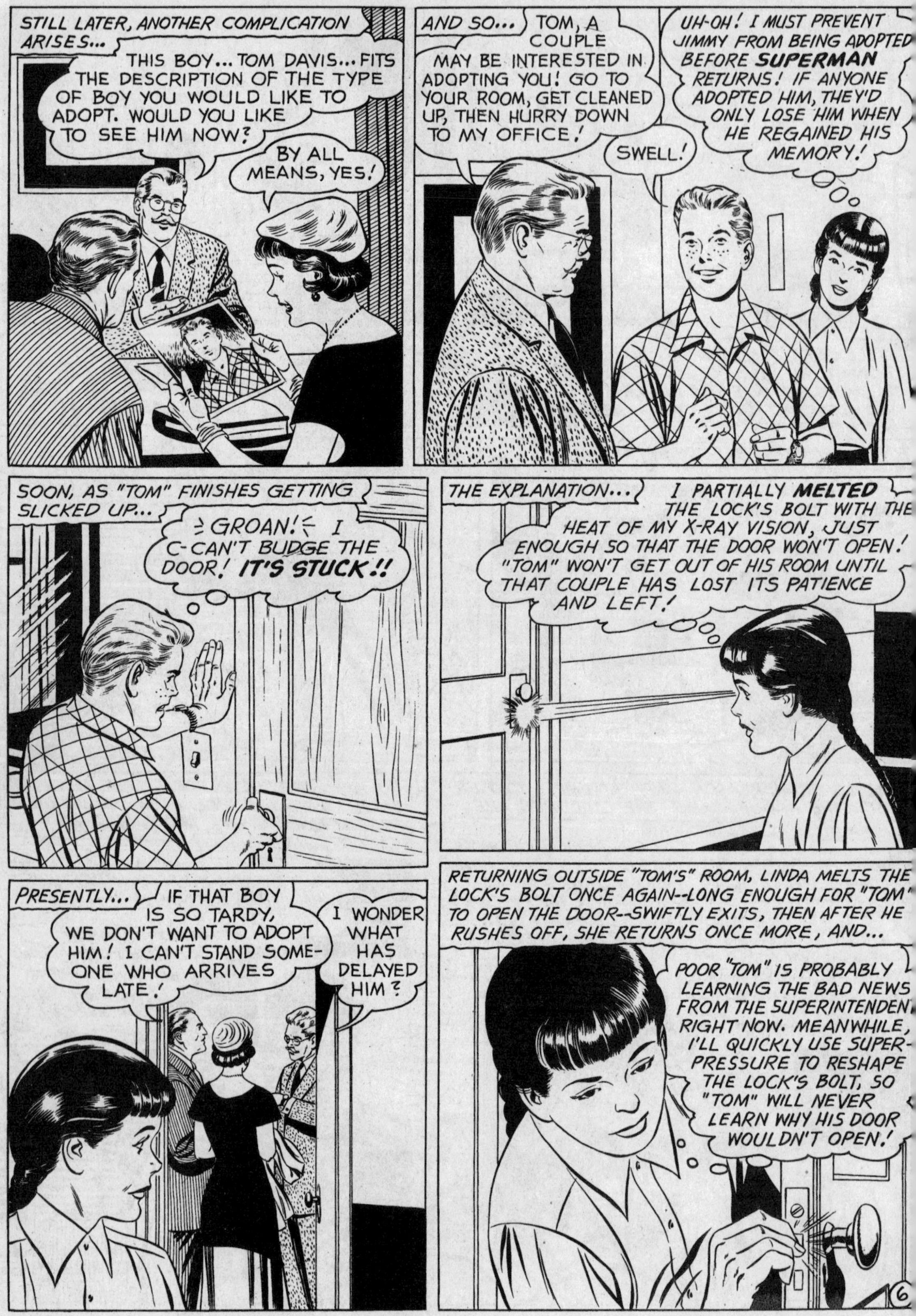
STILL LATER, ANOTHER COMPLICATION ARISES...
THIS BOY... TOM DAVIS... FITS THE DESCRIPTION OF THE TYPE OF BOY YOU WOULD LIKE TO ADOPT. WOULD YOU LIKE TO SEE HIM NOW?
BY ALL MEANS, YES!
AND SO...
TOM, A COUPLE MAY BE INTERESTED IN ADOPTING YOU! GO TO YOUR ROOM, GET CLEANED UP, THEN HURRY DOWN TO MY OFFICE!
SWELL!
UH-OH! I MUST PREVENT JIMMY FROM BEING ADOPTED BEFORE **SUPERMAN** RETURNS! IF ANYONE ADOPTED HIM, THEY'D ONLY LOSE HIM WHEN HE REGAINED HIS MEMORY!
SOON, AS "TOM" FINISHES GETTING SLICKED UP...
GROAN! I C-CAN'T BUDGE THE DOOR! **IT'S STUCK!!**
THE EXPLANATION...
I PARTIALLY **MELTED** THE LOCK'S BOLT WITH THE HEAT OF MY X-RAY VISION, JUST ENOUGH SO THAT THE DOOR WON'T OPEN! "TOM" WON'T GET OUT OF HIS ROOM UNTIL THAT COUPLE HAS LOST ITS PATIENCE AND LEFT!
PRESENTLY...
IF THAT BOY IS SO TARDY, WE DON'T WANT TO ADOPT HIM! I CAN'T STAND SOME-ONE WHO ARRIVES LATE!
I WONDER WHAT HAS DELAYED HIM?
RETURNING OUTSIDE "TOM'S" ROOM, LINDA MELTS THE LOCK'S BOLT ONCE AGAIN--LONG ENOUGH FOR "TOM" TO OPEN THE DOOR--SWIFTLY EXITS, THEN AFTER HE RUSHES OFF, SHE RETURNS ONCE MORE, AND...
POOR "TOM" IS PROBABLY LEARNING THE BAD NEWS FROM THE SUPERINTENDENT RIGHT NOW. MEANWHILE, I'LL QUICKLY USE SUPER-PRESSURE TO RESHAPE THE LOCK'S BOLT, SO "TOM" WILL NEVER LEARN WHY HIS DOOR WOULDN'T OPEN!
6

THOUGH DISAPPOINTED AT HIS LOST OPPORTUNITY, "TOM" RECOVERS HIS GOOD SPIRITS AND CONTRIBUTES A NEWSY COLUMN TO THE ORPHANAGE NEWSPAPER...

YOUR ARTICLE IS VERY WELL-WRITTEN, TOM.

HA, HA! MAYBE I WAS A PROFESSIONAL REPORTER, BEFORE I GOT AMNESIA!

≶ULP!≷ H-HE'S TELLING THE TRUTH, BUT DOESN'T REALIZE IT!

NEXT MORNING...AS "TOM" AWAKENS...

≶GASP!≷ MY MEMORY HAS RETURNED! I... I'M NOT REALLY "ORPHAN TOM DAVIS"! I'M JIMMY OLSEN, BOY REPORTER!...I MUST HAVE HURT MY HEAD DURING THE FLOOD, AND IT GAVE ME TEMPORARY AMNESIA!

FOXILY, JIMMY CONFIDES ONLY IN LINDA...

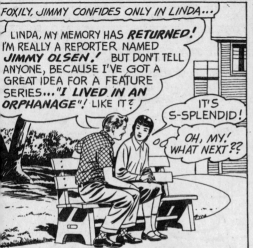

LINDA, MY MEMORY HAS RETURNED! I'M REALLY A REPORTER NAMED JIMMY OLSEN! BUT DON'T TELL ANYONE, BECAUSE I'VE GOT A GREAT IDEA FOR A FEATURE SERIES..."I LIVED IN AN ORPHANAGE"! LIKE IT?

IT'S S-SPLENDID!

OH, MY! WHAT NEXT??

I'LL STICK AROUND HERE AS "TOM DAVIS", SO I CAN SECRETLY DIG UP MORE BACKGROUND MATERIAL! I'LL PLAY YOU UP BIG... IT MIGHT GET SOMEONE TO ADOPT YOU! NICE, EH?

SWELL!

SWELL, MY EYE! THE LAST THING I WANT IS TO GET ADOPTED! FOSTER PARENTS MIGHT LEARN I HAVE SUPER-POWERS... AND MY PROMISE TO SUPERMAN WOULD BE BROKEN!

BUT LINDA ISN'T THE ONLY ONE IN THE ORPHAN-AGE WHO NOW DOES NOT WANT TO BE ADOPTED...

TOM, YOU'RE GOING TO HAVE ANOTHER CHANCE TO BE ADOPTED! A COUPLE WANT TO ADOPT A TEEN-AGE BOY... AND THE CHOICE IS BETWEEN YOU AND HAROLD! YOU ENTER THE NEXT ROOM FIRST, SO THEY CAN SEE YOU!

YIPES! HOW'LL I GET OUT OF THIS?

IT'S ANOTHER SUPER-JOB FOR YOURS TRULY!

⑦

THROUGH THE NEXT ROOM WHIZZES LINDA, USING SUPER-SPEED TO ALTER THE COUPLE'S GLASSES...

I'VE DISTORTED THEIR LENSES, LIKE A FUN-HOUSE MIRROR!

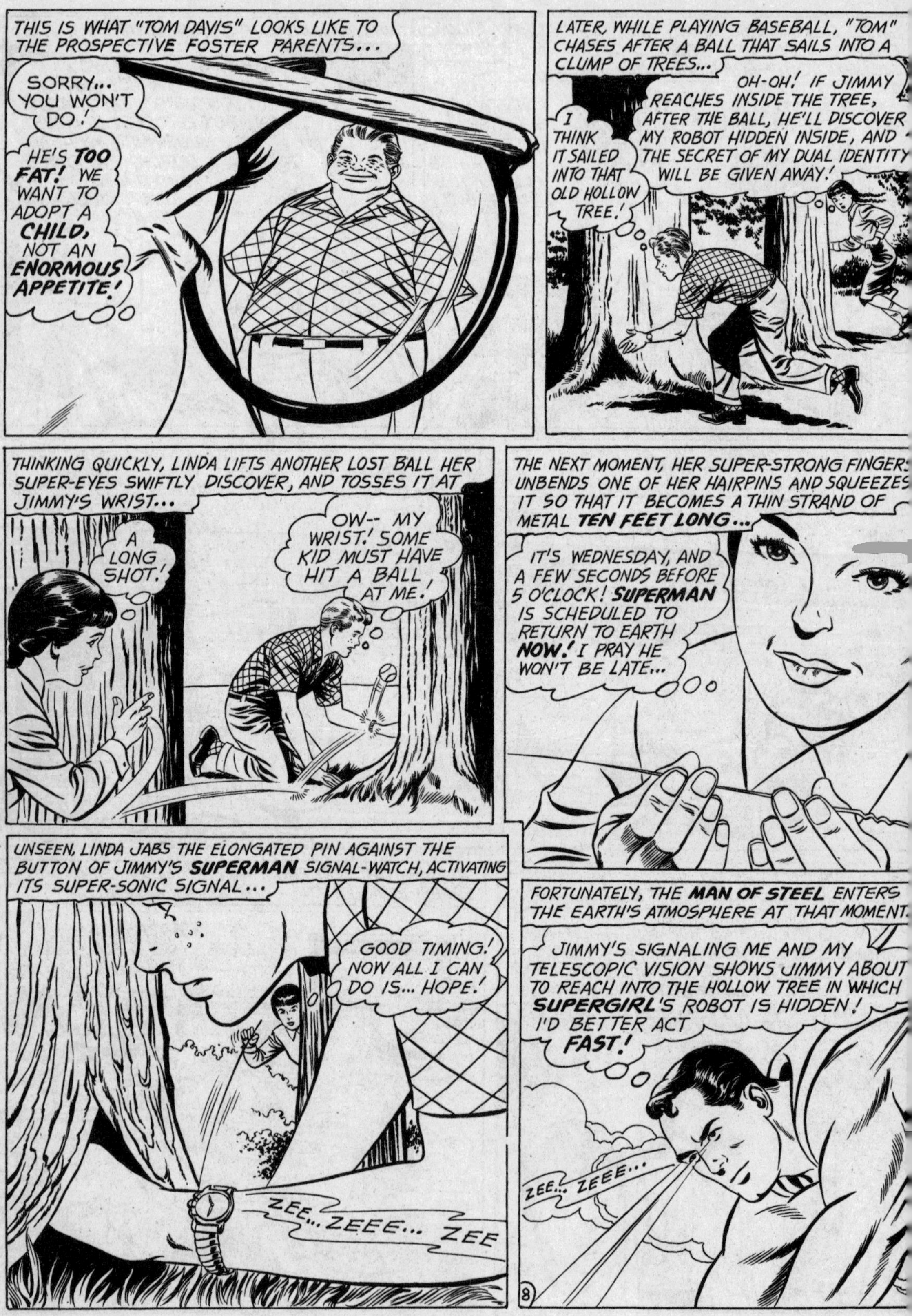
THIS IS WHAT "TOM DAVIS" LOOKS LIKE TO THE PROSPECTIVE FOSTER PARENTS...
SORRY... YOU WON'T DO!
HE'S TOO FAT! WE WANT TO ADOPT A CHILD, NOT AN ENORMOUS APPETITE!
LATER, WHILE PLAYING BASEBALL, "TOM" CHASES AFTER A BALL THAT SAILS INTO A CLUMP OF TREES...
I THINK IT SAILED INTO THAT OLD HOLLOW TREE!
OH-OH! IF JIMMY REACHES INSIDE THE TREE, AFTER THE BALL, HE'LL DISCOVER MY ROBOT HIDDEN INSIDE, AND THE SECRET OF MY DUAL IDENTITY WILL BE GIVEN AWAY!
THINKING QUICKLY, LINDA LIFTS ANOTHER LOST BALL HER SUPER-EYES SWIFTLY DISCOVER, AND TOSSES IT AT JIMMY'S WRIST...
A LONG SHOT!
OW-- MY WRIST! SOME KID MUST HAVE HIT A BALL AT ME!
THE NEXT MOMENT, HER SUPER-STRONG FINGERS UNBENDS ONE OF HER HAIRPINS AND SQUEEZES IT SO THAT IT BECOMES A THIN STRAND OF METAL TEN FEET LONG...
IT'S WEDNESDAY, AND A FEW SECONDS BEFORE 5 O'CLOCK! SUPERMAN IS SCHEDULED TO RETURN TO EARTH NOW! I PRAY HE WON'T BE LATE...
UNSEEN, LINDA JABS THE ELONGATED PIN AGAINST THE BUTTON OF JIMMY'S SUPERMAN SIGNAL-WATCH, ACTIVATING ITS SUPER-SONIC SIGNAL...
GOOD TIMING! NOW ALL I CAN DO IS... HOPE!
ZEE... ZEEE... ZEE
FORTUNATELY, THE MAN OF STEEL ENTERS THE EARTH'S ATMOSPHERE AT THAT MOMENT.
JIMMY'S SIGNALING ME AND MY TELESCOPIC VISION SHOWS JIMMY ABOUT TO REACH INTO THE HOLLOW TREE IN WHICH SUPERGIRL'S ROBOT IS HIDDEN! I'D BETTER ACT FAST!
ZEE... ZEEE...
8

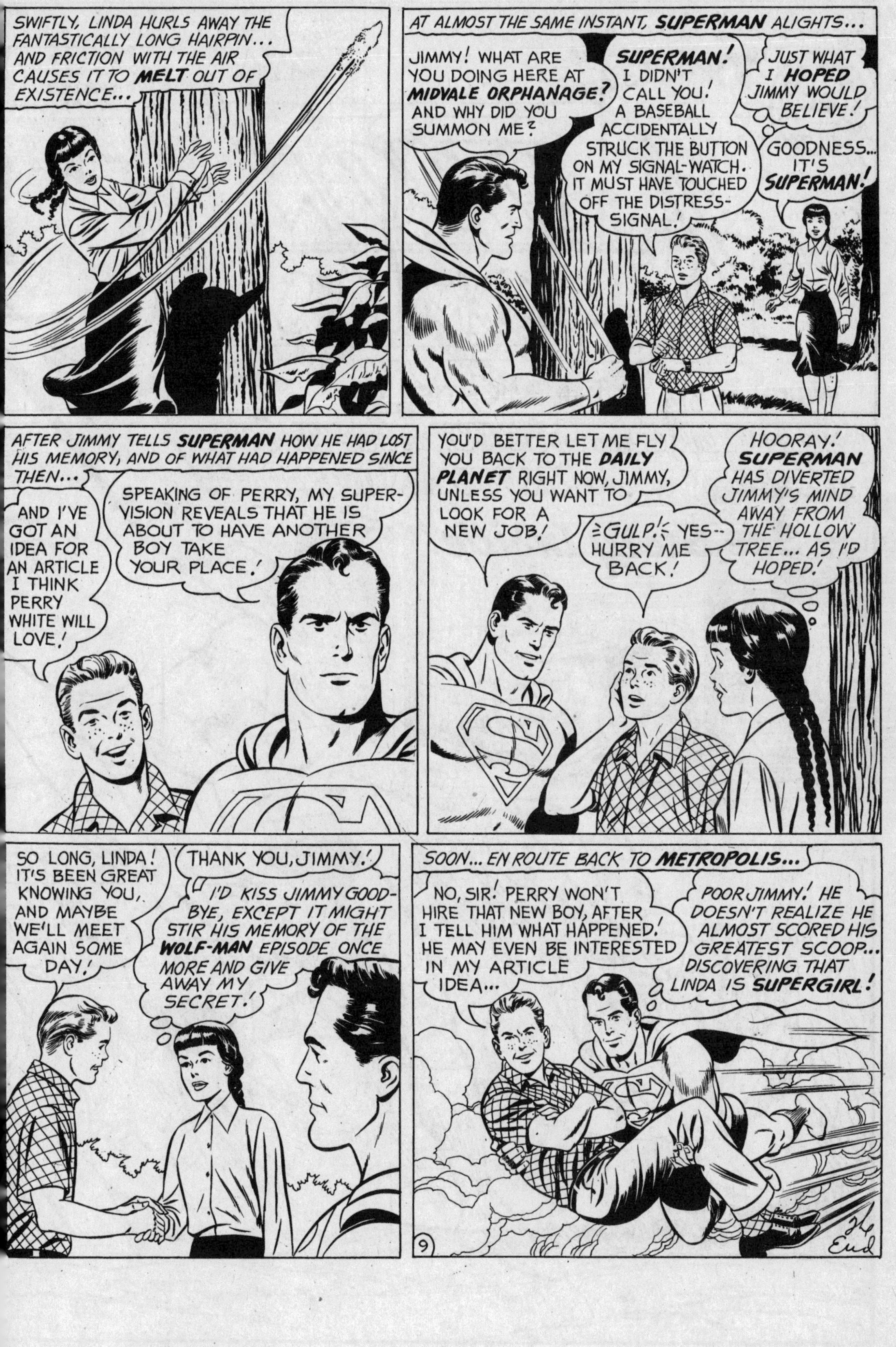
SWIFTLY, LINDA HURLS AWAY THE FANTASTICALLY LONG HAIRPIN... AND FRICTION WITH THE AIR CAUSES IT TO MELT OUT OF EXISTENCE...
AT ALMOST THE SAME INSTANT, SUPERMAN ALIGHTS...
JIMMY! WHAT ARE YOU DOING HERE AT MIDVALE ORPHANAGE? AND WHY DID YOU SUMMON ME?
SUPERMAN! I DIDN'T CALL YOU! A BASEBALL ACCIDENTALLY STRUCK THE BUTTON ON MY SIGNAL-WATCH. IT MUST HAVE TOUCHED OFF THE DISTRESS-SIGNAL!
JUST WHAT I HOPED JIMMY WOULD BELIEVE!
GOODNESS... IT'S SUPERMAN!
AFTER JIMMY TELLS SUPERMAN HOW HE HAD LOST HIS MEMORY, AND OF WHAT HAD HAPPENED SINCE THEN...
AND I'VE GOT AN IDEA FOR AN ARTICLE I THINK PERRY WHITE WILL LOVE!
SPEAKING OF PERRY, MY SUPER-VISION REVEALS THAT HE IS ABOUT TO HAVE ANOTHER BOY TAKE YOUR PLACE!
YOU'D BETTER LET ME FLY YOU BACK TO THE DAILY PLANET RIGHT NOW, JIMMY, UNLESS YOU WANT TO LOOK FOR A NEW JOB!
GULP! YES-- HURRY ME BACK!
HOORAY! SUPERMAN HAS DIVERTED JIMMY'S MIND AWAY FROM THE HOLLOW TREE... AS I'D HOPED!
SO LONG, LINDA! IT'S BEEN GREAT KNOWING YOU, AND MAYBE WE'LL MEET AGAIN SOME DAY!
THANK YOU, JIMMY!
I'D KISS JIMMY GOOD-BYE, EXCEPT IT MIGHT STIR HIS MEMORY OF THE WOLF-MAN EPISODE ONCE MORE AND GIVE AWAY MY SECRET!
9
SOON... EN ROUTE BACK TO METROPOLIS...
NO, SIR! PERRY WON'T HIRE THAT NEW BOY, AFTER I TELL HIM WHAT HAPPENED! HE MAY EVEN BE INTERESTED IN MY ARTICLE IDEA...
POOR JIMMY! HE DOESN'T REALIZE HE ALMOST SCORED HIS GREATEST SCOOP... DISCOVERING THAT LINDA IS SUPERGIRL!
The End

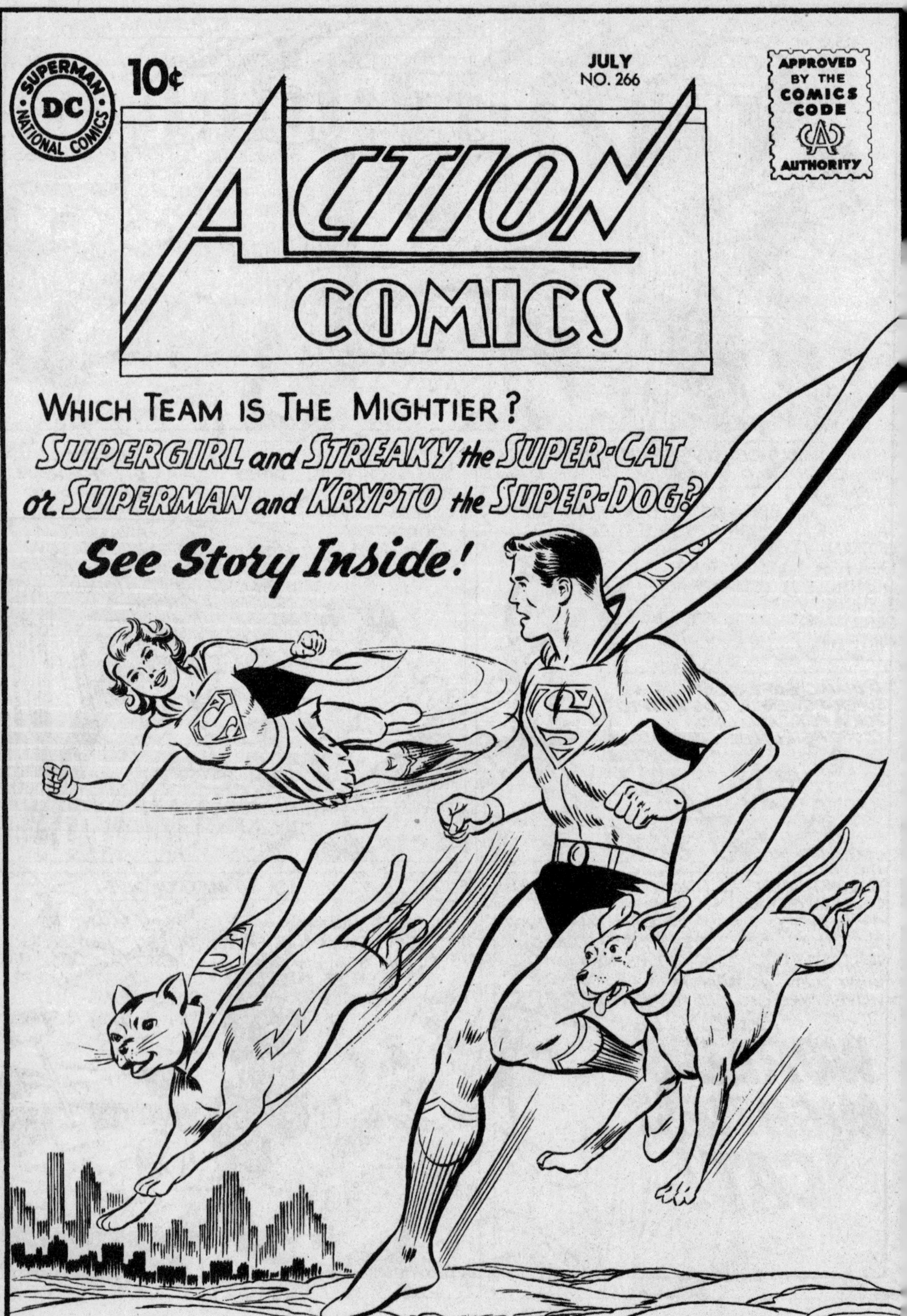
SUPERMAN DC NATIONAL COMICS
10¢
JULY
NO. 266
APPROVED BY THE COMICS CODE AUTHORITY
ACTION COMICS
WHICH TEAM IS THE MIGHTIER?
SUPERGIRL and STREAKY the SUPER-CAT
or SUPERMAN and KRYPTO the SUPER-DOG?
See Story Inside!

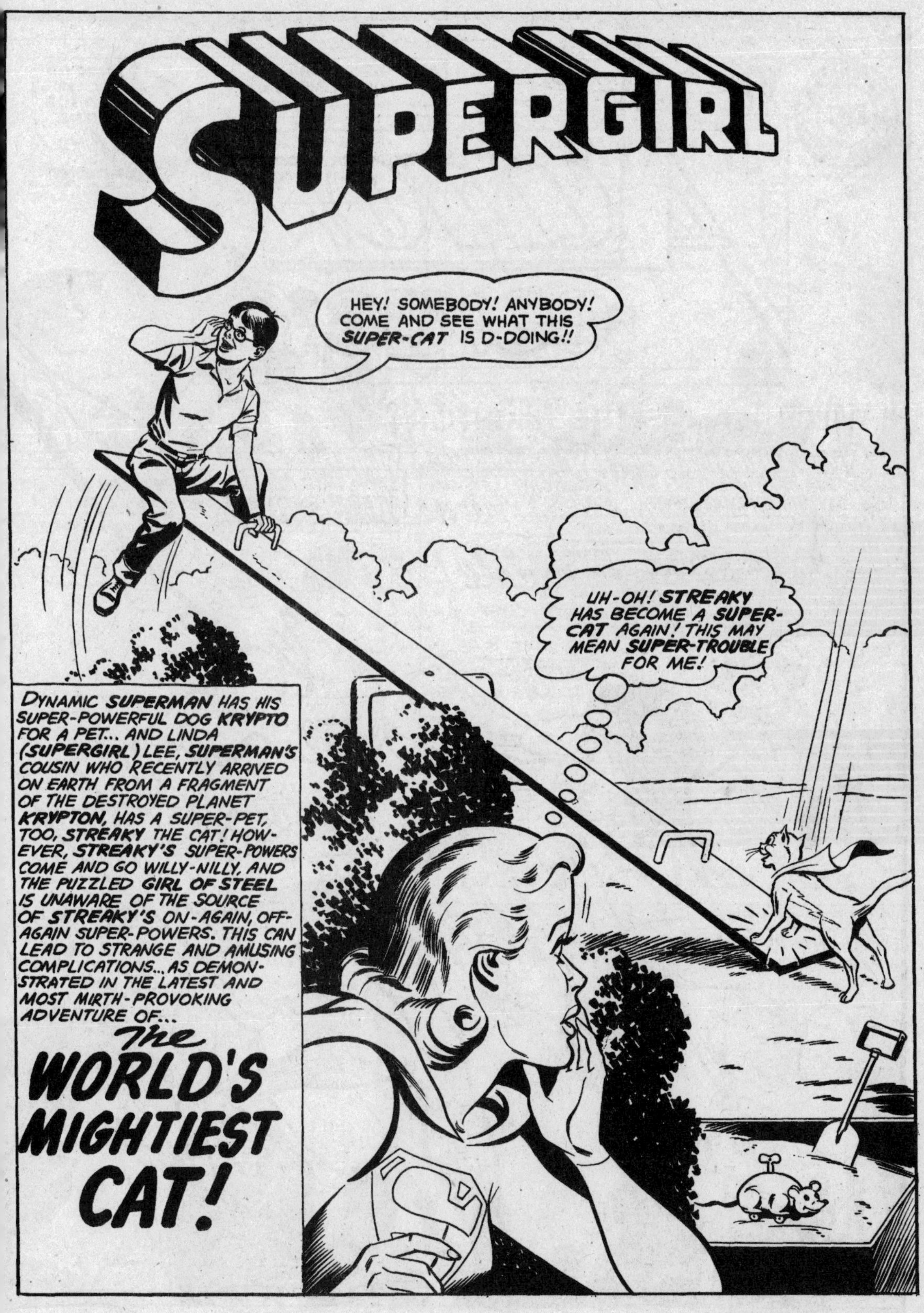
SUPERGIRL
HEY! SOMEBODY! ANYBODY! COME AND SEE WHAT THIS SUPER-CAT IS D-DOING!!
DYNAMIC SUPERMAN HAS HIS SUPER-POWERFUL DOG KRYPTO FOR A PET... AND LINDA (SUPERGIRL) LEE, SUPERMAN'S COUSIN WHO RECENTLY ARRIVED ON EARTH FROM A FRAGMENT OF THE DESTROYED PLANET KRYPTON, HAS A SUPER-PET, TOO, STREAKY THE CAT! HOW-EVER, STREAKY'S SUPER-POWERS COME AND GO WILLY-NILLY, AND THE PUZZLED GIRL OF STEEL IS UNAWARE OF THE SOURCE OF STREAKY'S ON-AGAIN, OFF-AGAIN SUPER-POWERS. THIS CAN LEAD TO STRANGE AND AMUSING COMPLICATIONS... AS DEMON-STRATED IN THE LATEST AND MOST MIRTH-PROVOKING ADVENTURE OF...
The WORLD'S MIGHTIEST CAT!
UH-OH! STREAKY HAS BECOME A SUPER-CAT AGAIN! THIS MAY MEAN SUPER-TROUBLE FOR ME!

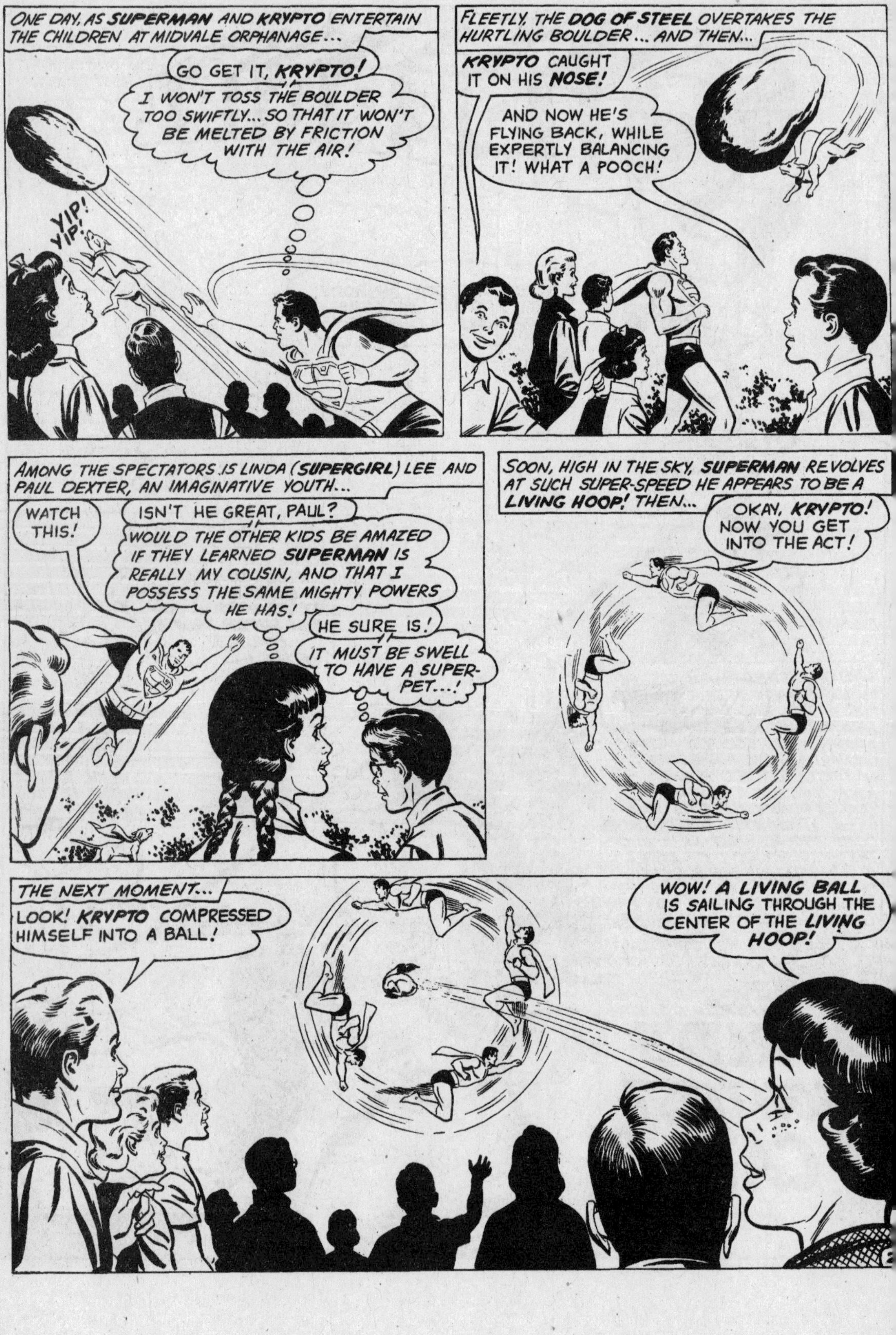
ONE DAY, AS SUPERMAN AND KRYPTO ENTERTAIN THE CHILDREN AT MIDVALE ORPHANAGE...
GO GET IT, KRYPTO!
I WON'T TOSS THE BOULDER TOO SWIFTLY... SO THAT IT WON'T BE MELTED BY FRICTION WITH THE AIR!
YIP! YIP!
FLEETLY, THE DOG OF STEEL OVERTAKES THE HURTLING BOULDER... AND THEN...
KRYPTO CAUGHT IT ON HIS NOSE!
AND NOW HE'S FLYING BACK, WHILE EXPERTLY BALANCING IT! WHAT A POOCH!
AMONG THE SPECTATORS IS LINDA (SUPERGIRL) LEE AND PAUL DEXTER, AN IMAGINATIVE YOUTH...
WATCH THIS!
ISN'T HE GREAT, PAUL?
WOULD THE OTHER KIDS BE AMAZED IF THEY LEARNED SUPERMAN IS REALLY MY COUSIN, AND THAT I POSSESS THE SAME MIGHTY POWERS HE HAS!
HE SURE IS!
IT MUST BE SWELL TO HAVE A SUPER-PET...!
SOON, HIGH IN THE SKY, SUPERMAN REVOLVES AT SUCH SUPER-SPEED HE APPEARS TO BE A LIVING HOOP! THEN...
OKAY, KRYPTO! NOW YOU GET INTO THE ACT!
THE NEXT MOMENT...
LOOK! KRYPTO COMPRESSED HIMSELF INTO A BALL!
WOW! A LIVING BALL IS SAILING THROUGH THE CENTER OF THE LIVING HOOP!

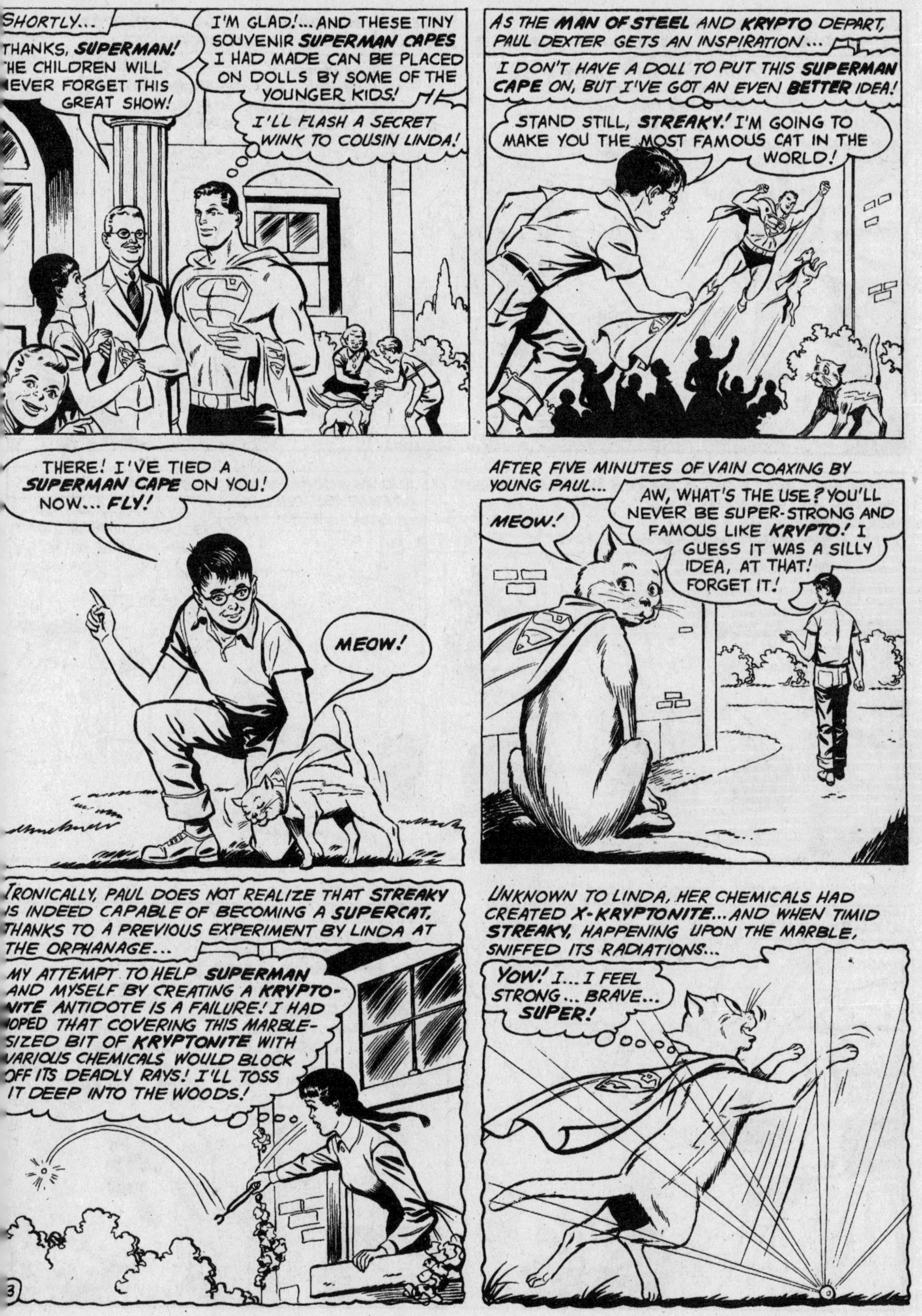
SHORTLY...
THANKS, SUPERMAN! THE CHILDREN WILL NEVER FORGET THIS GREAT SHOW!
I'M GLAD!... AND THESE TINY SOUVENIR SUPERMAN CAPES I HAD MADE CAN BE PLACED ON DOLLS BY SOME OF THE YOUNGER KIDS!
I'LL FLASH A SECRET WINK TO COUSIN LINDA!
AS THE MAN OF STEEL AND KRYPTO DEPART, PAUL DEXTER GETS AN INSPIRATION...
I DON'T HAVE A DOLL TO PUT THIS SUPERMAN CAPE ON, BUT I'VE GOT AN EVEN BETTER IDEA!
STAND STILL, STREAKY! I'M GOING TO MAKE YOU THE MOST FAMOUS CAT IN THE WORLD!
THERE! I'VE TIED A SUPERMAN CAPE ON YOU! NOW... FLY!
MEOW!
AFTER FIVE MINUTES OF VAIN COAXING BY YOUNG PAUL...
MEOW!
AW, WHAT'S THE USE? YOU'LL NEVER BE SUPER-STRONG AND FAMOUS LIKE KRYPTO! I GUESS IT WAS A SILLY IDEA, AT THAT! FORGET IT!
IRONICALLY, PAUL DOES NOT REALIZE THAT STREAKY IS INDEED CAPABLE OF BECOMING A SUPERCAT, THANKS TO A PREVIOUS EXPERIMENT BY LINDA AT THE ORPHANAGE...
MY ATTEMPT TO HELP SUPERMAN AND MYSELF BY CREATING A KRYPTONITE ANTIDOTE IS A FAILURE! I HAD HOPED THAT COVERING THIS MARBLE-SIZED BIT OF KRYPTONITE WITH VARIOUS CHEMICALS WOULD BLOCK OFF ITS DEADLY RAYS! I'LL TOSS IT DEEP INTO THE WOODS!
3
UNKNOWN TO LINDA, HER CHEMICALS HAD CREATED X-KRYPTONITE... AND WHEN TIMID STREAKY, HAPPENING UPON THE MARBLE, SNIFFED ITS RADIATIONS...
YOW! I... I FEEL STRONG... BRAVE... SUPER!

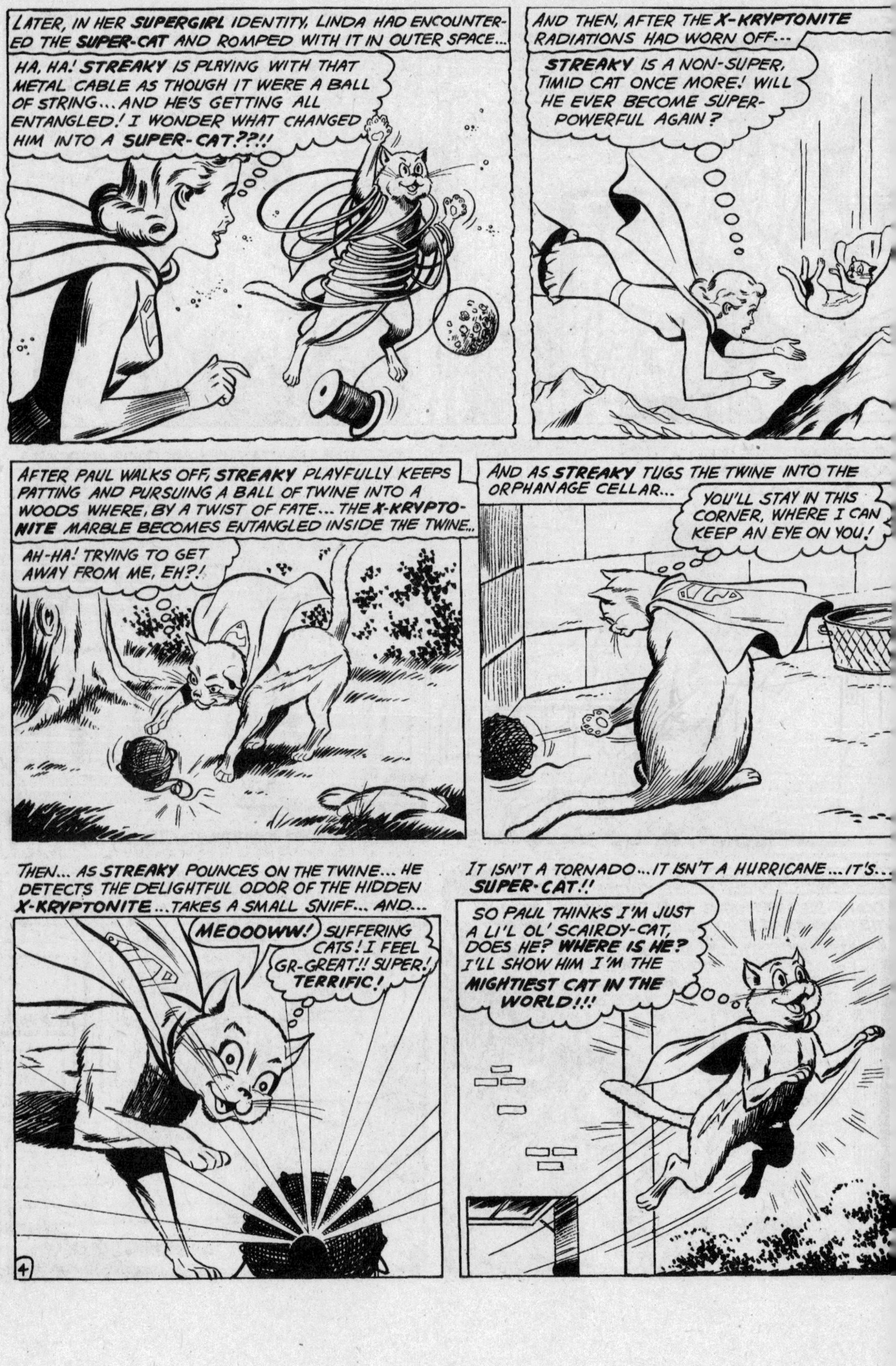
LATER, IN HER SUPERGIRL IDENTITY, LINDA HAD ENCOUNTERED THE SUPER-CAT AND ROMPED WITH IT IN OUTER SPACE...
HA, HA! STREAKY IS PLAYING WITH THAT METAL CABLE AS THOUGH IT WERE A BALL OF STRING... AND HE'S GETTING ALL ENTANGLED! I WONDER WHAT CHANGED HIM INTO A SUPER-CAT??!!
AND THEN, AFTER THE X-KRYPTONITE RADIATIONS HAD WORN OFF...
STREAKY IS A NON-SUPER, TIMID CAT ONCE MORE! WILL HE EVER BECOME SUPER-POWERFUL AGAIN?
AFTER PAUL WALKS OFF, STREAKY PLAYFULLY KEEPS PATTING AND PURSUING A BALL OF TWINE INTO A WOODS WHERE, BY A TWIST OF FATE... THE X-KRYPTONITE MARBLE BECOMES ENTANGLED INSIDE THE TWINE...
AH-HA! TRYING TO GET AWAY FROM ME, EH?!
AND AS STREAKY TUGS THE TWINE INTO THE ORPHANAGE CELLAR...
YOU'LL STAY IN THIS CORNER, WHERE I CAN KEEP AN EYE ON YOU!
THEN... AS STREAKY POUNCES ON THE TWINE... HE DETECTS THE DELIGHTFUL ODOR OF THE HIDDEN X-KRYPTONITE... TAKES A SMALL SNIFF... AND...
MEOOOWW!
SUFFERING CATS! I FEEL GR-GREAT!! SUPER! TERRIFIC!
4
IT ISN'T A TORNADO... IT ISN'T A HURRICANE... IT'S... SUPER-CAT!!
SO PAUL THINKS I'M JUST A LI'L OL' SCAIRDY-CAT, DOES HE? WHERE IS HE? I'LL SHOW HIM I'M THE MIGHTIEST CAT IN THE WORLD!!!

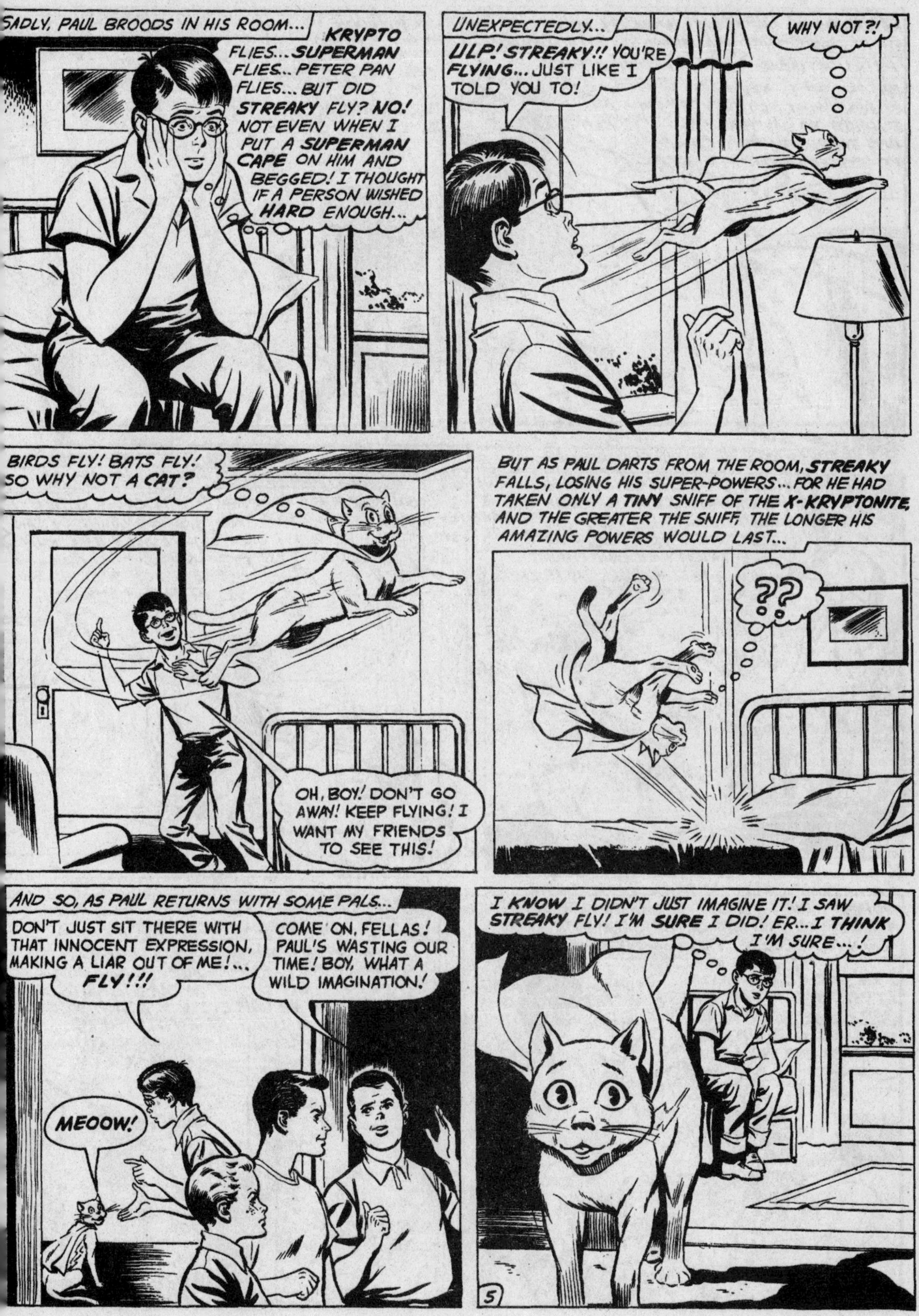
SADLY, PAUL BROODS IN HIS ROOM...
KRYPTO FLIES... SUPERMAN FLIES.. PETER PAN FLIES... BUT DID STREAKY FLY? NO! NOT EVEN WHEN I PUT A SUPERMAN CAPE ON HIM AND BEGGED! I THOUGHT IF A PERSON WISHED HARD ENOUGH...
UNEXPECTEDLY...
ULP! STREAKY!! YOU'RE FLYING... JUST LIKE I TOLD YOU TO!
WHY NOT?!
BIRDS FLY! BATS FLY! SO WHY NOT A CAT?
OH, BOY! DON'T GO AWAY! KEEP FLYING! I WANT MY FRIENDS TO SEE THIS!
BUT AS PAUL DARTS FROM THE ROOM, STREAKY FALLS, LOSING HIS SUPER-POWERS... FOR HE HAD TAKEN ONLY A TINY SNIFF OF THE X-KRYPTONITE, AND THE GREATER THE SNIFF, THE LONGER HIS AMAZING POWERS WOULD LAST...
??
AND SO, AS PAUL RETURNS WITH SOME PALS...
DON'T JUST SIT THERE WITH THAT INNOCENT EXPRESSION, MAKING A LIAR OUT OF ME!... FLY!!!
COME ON, FELLAS! PAUL'S WASTING OUR TIME! BOY, WHAT A WILD IMAGINATION!
MEOOW!
I KNOW I DIDN'T JUST IMAGINE IT! I SAW STREAKY FLY! I'M SURE I DID! ER... I THINK I'M SURE...!
5

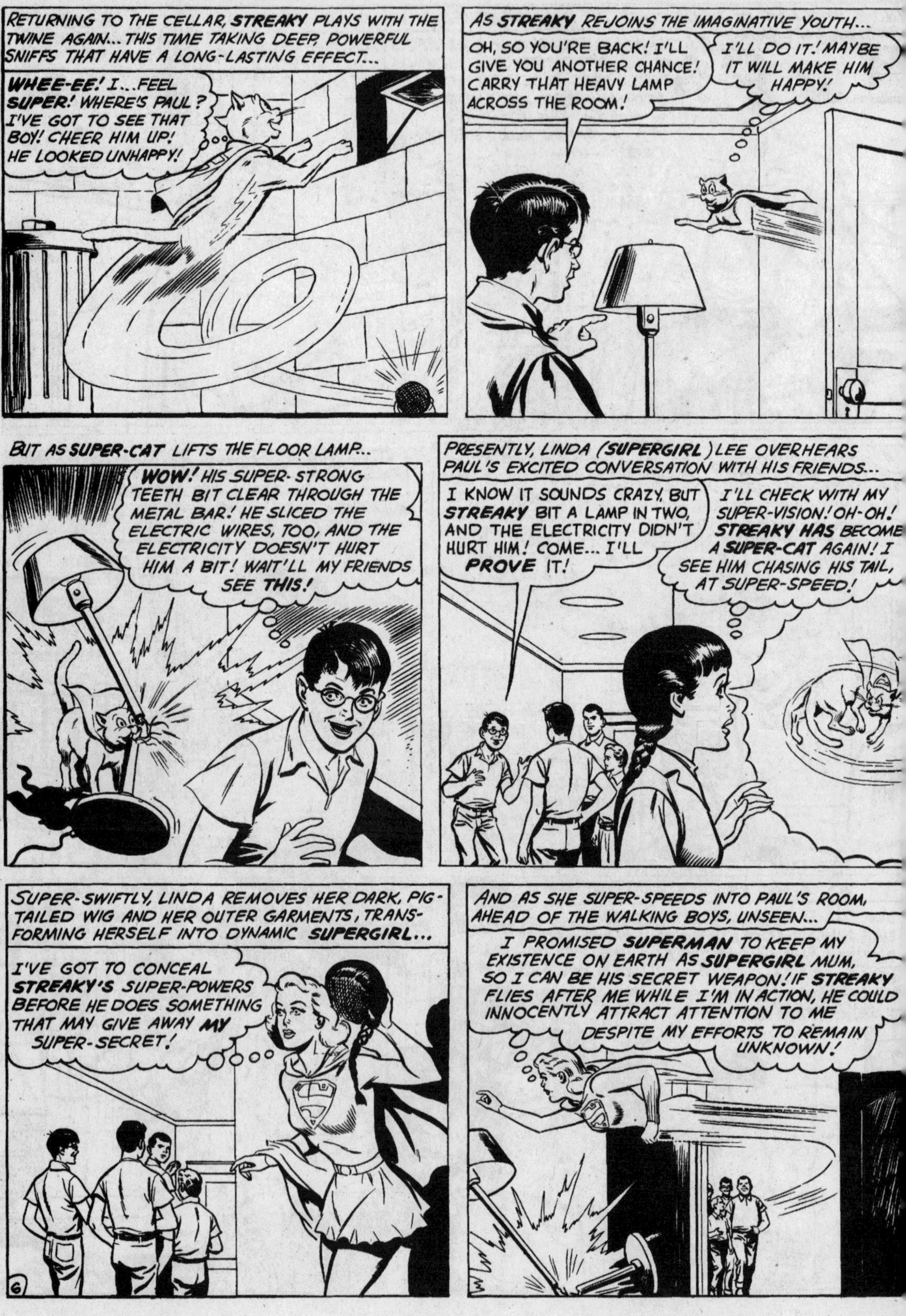
RETURNING TO THE CELLAR, STREAKY PLAYS WITH THE TWINE AGAIN... THIS TIME TAKING DEEP, POWERFUL SNIFFS THAT HAVE A LONG-LASTING EFFECT...
WHEE-EE! I...FEEL SUPER! WHERE'S PAUL? I'VE GOT TO SEE THAT BOY! CHEER HIM UP! HE LOOKED UNHAPPY!
AS STREAKY REJOINS THE IMAGINATIVE YOUTH...
OH, SO YOU'RE BACK! I'LL GIVE YOU ANOTHER CHANCE! CARRY THAT HEAVY LAMP ACROSS THE ROOM!
I'LL DO IT! MAYBE IT WILL MAKE HIM HAPPY!
BUT AS SUPER-CAT LIFTS THE FLOOR LAMP...
WOW! HIS SUPER-STRONG TEETH BIT CLEAR THROUGH THE METAL BAR! HE SLICED THE ELECTRIC WIRES, TOO, AND THE ELECTRICITY DOESN'T HURT HIM A BIT! WAIT'LL MY FRIENDS SEE THIS!
PRESENTLY, LINDA (SUPERGIRL) LEE OVERHEARS PAUL'S EXCITED CONVERSATION WITH HIS FRIENDS...
I KNOW IT SOUNDS CRAZY, BUT STREAKY BIT A LAMP IN TWO, AND THE ELECTRICITY DIDN'T HURT HIM! COME... I'LL PROVE IT!
I'LL CHECK WITH MY SUPER-VISION! OH-OH! STREAKY HAS BECOME A SUPER-CAT AGAIN! I SEE HIM CHASING HIS TAIL, AT SUPER-SPEED!
SUPER-SWIFTLY, LINDA REMOVES HER DARK, PIG-TAILED WIG AND HER OUTER GARMENTS, TRANSFORMING HERSELF INTO DYNAMIC SUPERGIRL...
I'VE GOT TO CONCEAL STREAKY'S SUPER-POWERS BEFORE HE DOES SOMETHING THAT MAY GIVE AWAY MY SUPER-SECRET!
6
AND AS SHE SUPER-SPEEDS INTO PAUL'S ROOM, AHEAD OF THE WALKING BOYS, UNSEEN...
I PROMISED SUPERMAN TO KEEP MY EXISTENCE ON EARTH AS SUPERGIRL MUM, SO I CAN BE HIS SECRET WEAPON! IF STREAKY FLIES AFTER ME WHILE I'M IN ACTION, HE COULD INNOCENTLY ATTRACT ATTENTION TO ME DESPITE MY EFFORTS TO REMAIN UNKNOWN!

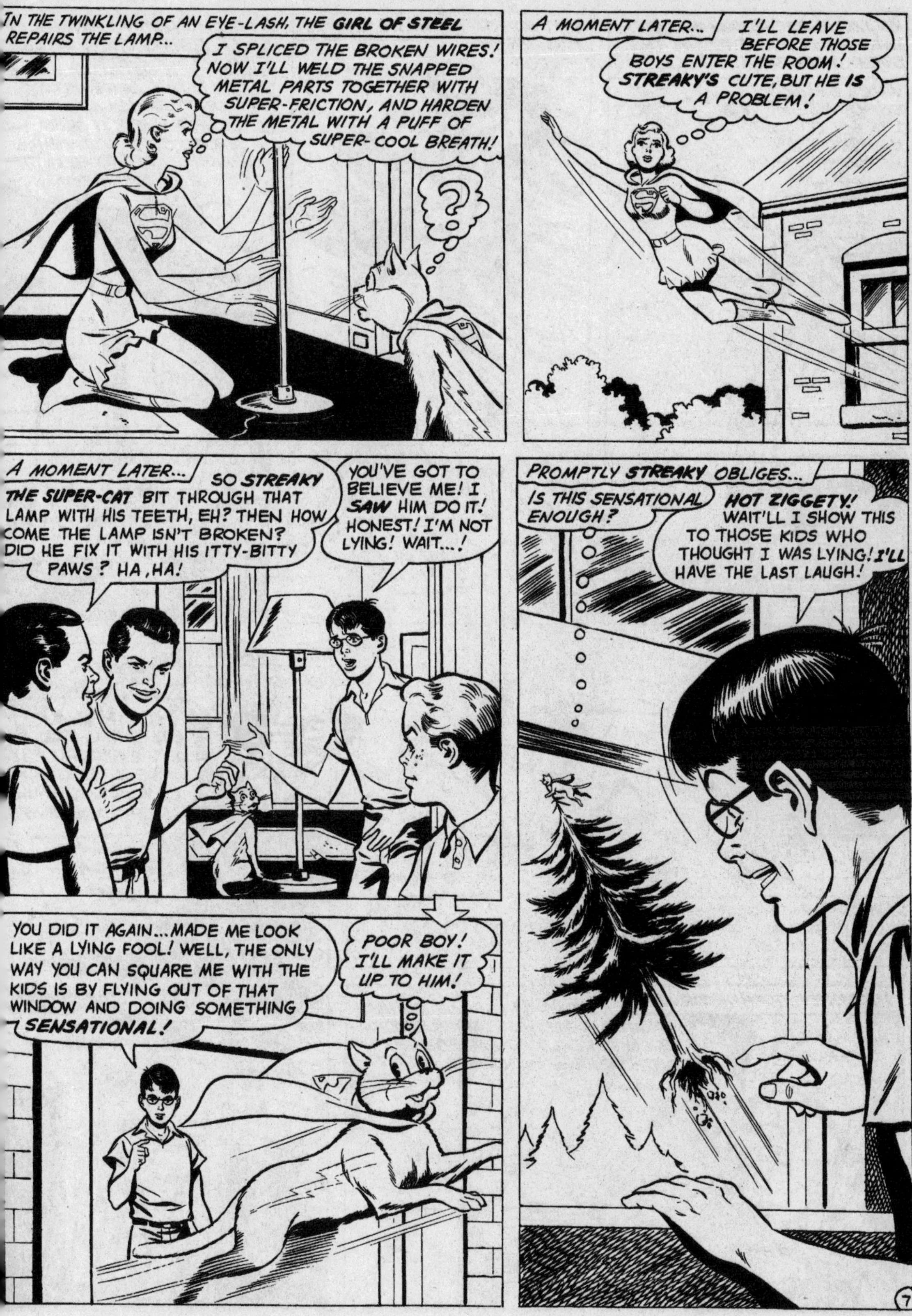
IN THE TWINKLING OF AN EYE-LASH, THE GIRL OF STEEL REPAIRS THE LAMP...
I SPLICED THE BROKEN WIRES! NOW I'LL WELD THE SNAPPED METAL PARTS TOGETHER WITH SUPER-FRICTION, AND HARDEN THE METAL WITH A PUFF OF SUPER-COOL BREATH!
?
A MOMENT LATER...
I'LL LEAVE BEFORE THOSE BOYS ENTER THE ROOM! STREAKY'S CUTE, BUT HE IS A PROBLEM!
A MOMENT LATER...
SO STREAKY THE SUPER-CAT BIT THROUGH THAT LAMP WITH HIS TEETH, EH? THEN HOW COME THE LAMP ISN'T BROKEN? DID HE FIX IT WITH HIS ITTY-BITTY PAWS? HA, HA!
YOU'VE GOT TO BELIEVE ME! I SAW HIM DO IT! HONEST! I'M NOT LYING! WAIT...!
YOU DID IT AGAIN...MADE ME LOOK LIKE A LYING FOOL! WELL, THE ONLY WAY YOU CAN SQUARE ME WITH THE KIDS IS BY FLYING OUT OF THAT WINDOW AND DOING SOMETHING SENSATIONAL!
POOR BOY! I'LL MAKE IT UP TO HIM!
PROMPTLY STREAKY OBLIGES...
IS THIS SENSATIONAL ENOUGH?
HOT ZIGGETY! WAIT'LL I SHOW THIS TO THOSE KIDS WHO THOUGHT I WAS LYING! I'LL HAVE THE LAST LAUGH!
7

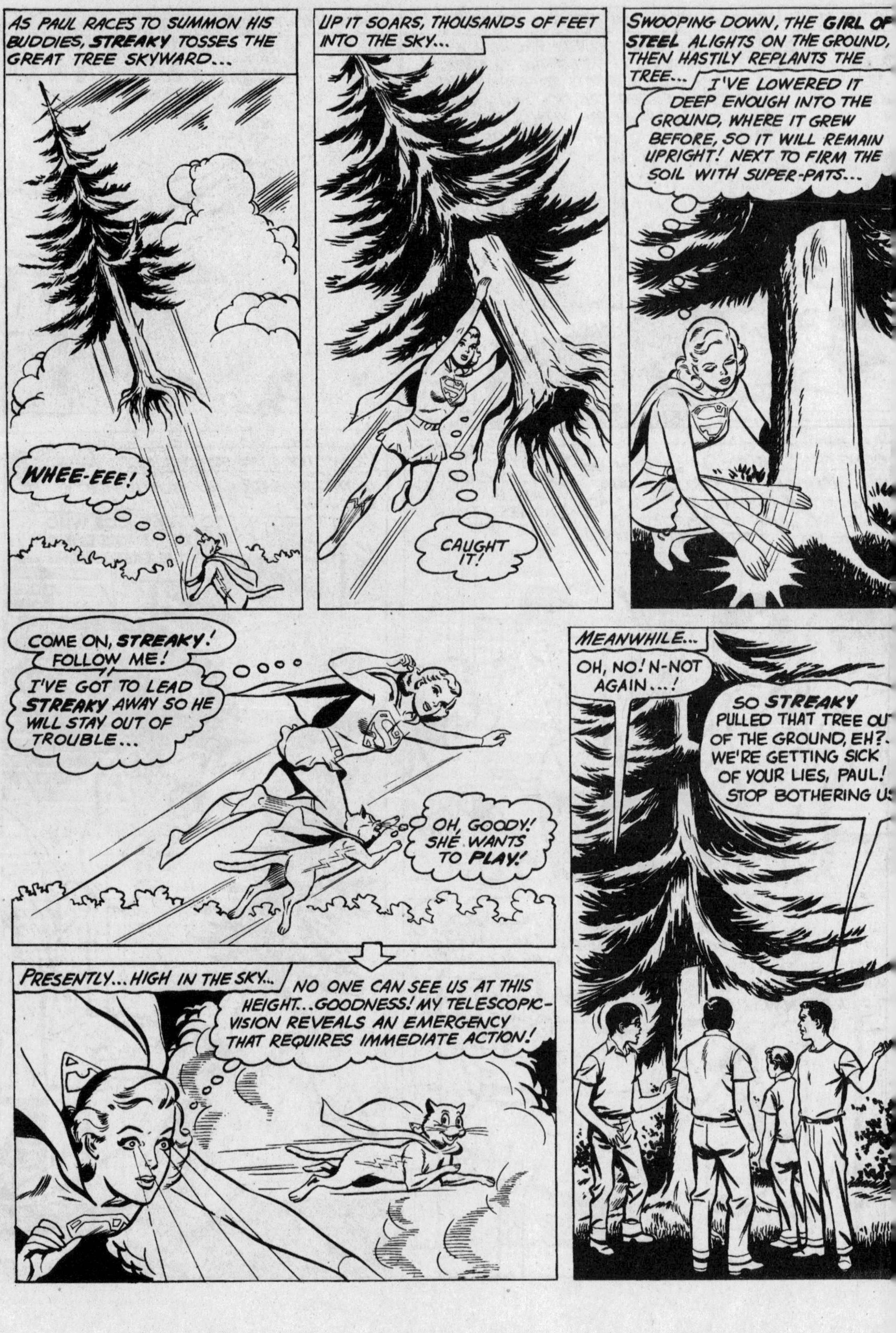
AS PAUL RACES TO SUMMON HIS BUDDIES, STREAKY TOSSES THE GREAT TREE SKYWARD...
WHEE-EEE!
UP IT SOARS, THOUSANDS OF FEET INTO THE SKY...
CAUGHT IT!
SWOOPING DOWN, THE GIRL OF STEEL ALIGHTS ON THE GROUND, THEN HASTILY REPLANTS THE TREE...
I'VE LOWERED IT DEEP ENOUGH INTO THE GROUND, WHERE IT GREW BEFORE, SO IT WILL REMAIN UPRIGHT! NEXT TO FIRM THE SOIL WITH SUPER-PATS...
COME ON, STREAKY! FOLLOW ME!
I'VE GOT TO LEAD STREAKY AWAY SO HE WILL STAY OUT OF TROUBLE...
OH, GOODY! SHE WANTS TO PLAY!
PRESENTLY...HIGH IN THE SKY...
NO ONE CAN SEE US AT THIS HEIGHT...GOODNESS! MY TELESCOPIC-VISION REVEALS AN EMERGENCY THAT REQUIRES IMMEDIATE ACTION!
MEANWHILE...
OH, NO! N-NOT AGAIN...!
SO STREAKY PULLED THAT TREE OU OF THE GROUND, EH?.. WE'RE GETTING SICK OF YOUR LIES, PAUL! STOP BOTHERING U

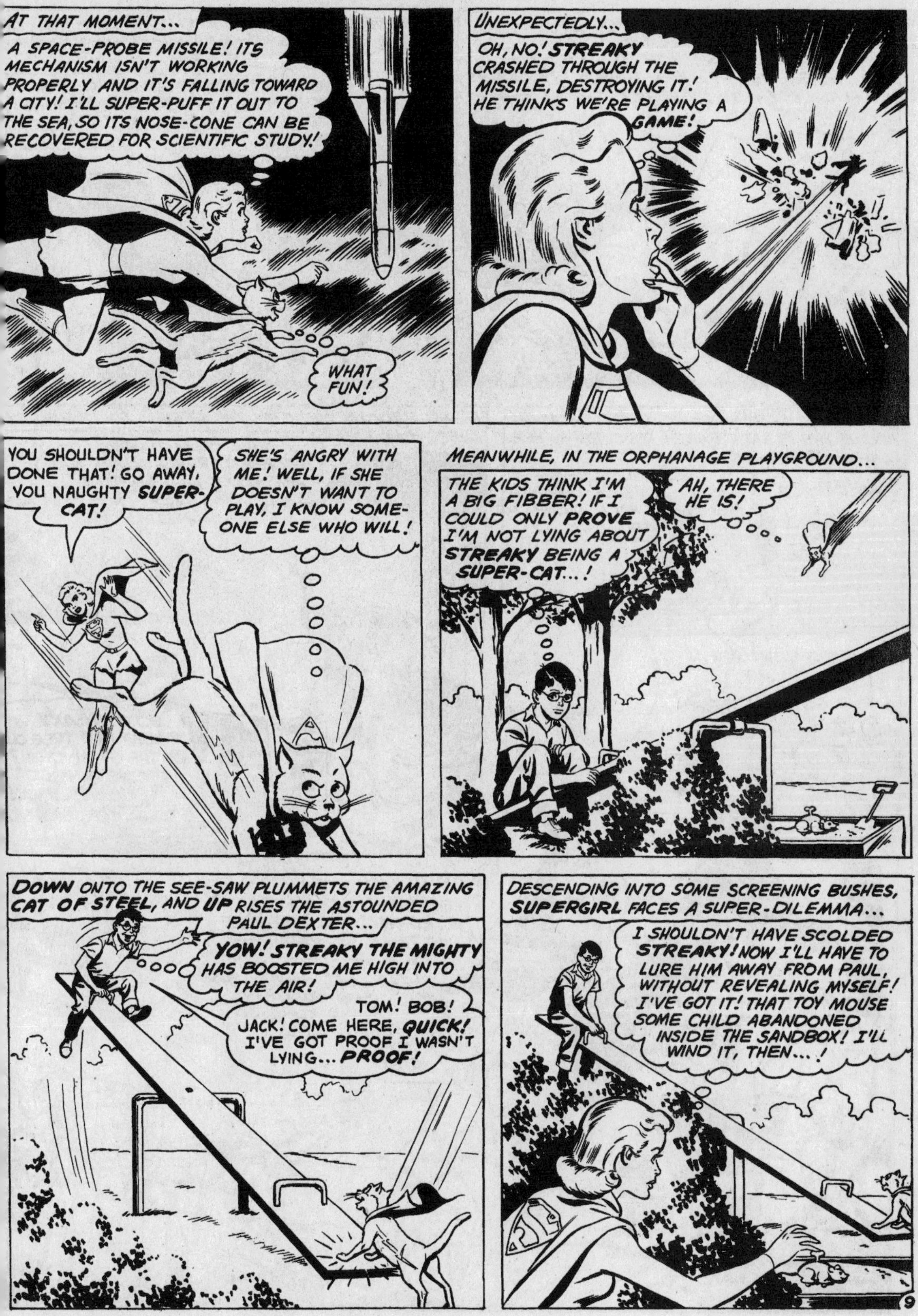
AT THAT MOMENT...
A SPACE-PROBE MISSILE! ITS MECHANISM ISN'T WORKING PROPERLY AND IT'S FALLING TOWARD A CITY! I'LL SUPER-PUFF IT OUT TO THE SEA, SO ITS NOSE-CONE CAN BE RECOVERED FOR SCIENTIFIC STUDY!
WHAT FUN!
UNEXPECTEDLY...
OH, NO! STREAKY CRASHED THROUGH THE MISSILE, DESTROYING IT! HE THINKS WE'RE PLAYING A GAME!
YOU SHOULDN'T HAVE DONE THAT! GO AWAY, YOU NAUGHTY SUPER-CAT!
SHE'S ANGRY WITH ME! WELL, IF SHE DOESN'T WANT TO PLAY, I KNOW SOME-ONE ELSE WHO WILL!
MEANWHILE, IN THE ORPHANAGE PLAYGROUND...
THE KIDS THINK I'M A BIG FIBBER! IF I COULD ONLY PROVE I'M NOT LYING ABOUT STREAKY BEING A SUPER-CAT...!
AH, THERE HE IS!
DOWN ONTO THE SEE-SAW PLUMMETS THE AMAZING CAT OF STEEL, AND UP RISES THE ASTOUNDED PAUL DEXTER...
YOW! STREAKY THE MIGHTY HAS BOOSTED ME HIGH INTO THE AIR!
TOM! BOB! JACK! COME HERE, QUICK! I'VE GOT PROOF I WASN'T LYING... PROOF!
DESCENDING INTO SOME SCREENING BUSHES, SUPERGIRL FACES A SUPER-DILEMMA...
I SHOULDN'T HAVE SCOLDED STREAKY! NOW I'LL HAVE TO LURE HIM AWAY FROM PAUL, WITHOUT REVEALING MYSELF! I'VE GOT IT! THAT TOY MOUSE SOME CHILD ABANDONED INSIDE THE SANDBOX! I'LL WIND IT, THEN...!
9

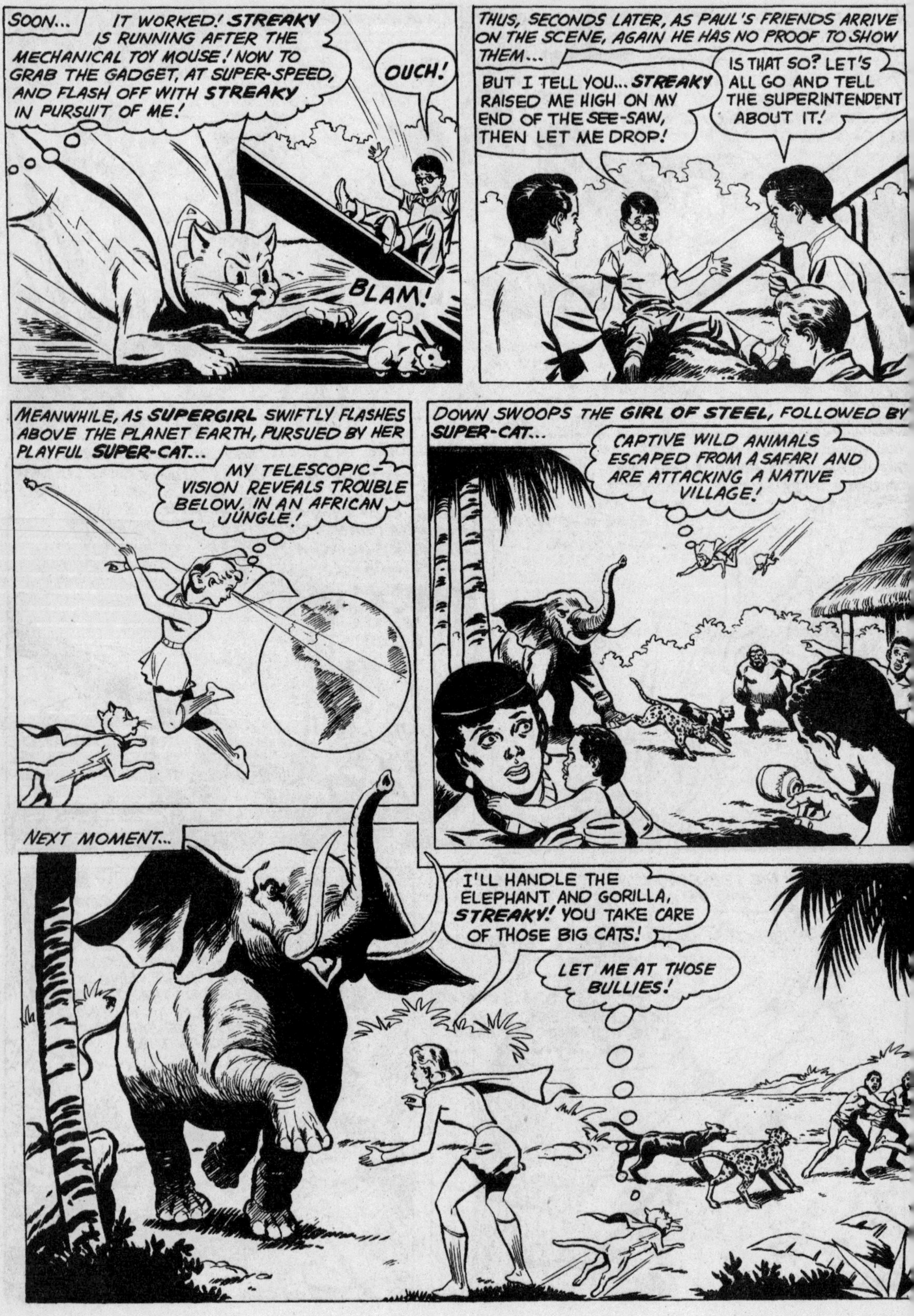
SOON...
IT WORKED! STREAKY IS RUNNING AFTER THE MECHANICAL TOY MOUSE! NOW TO GRAB THE GADGET, AT SUPER-SPEED, AND FLASH OFF WITH STREAKY IN PURSUIT OF ME!
OUCH!
BLAM!
THUS, SECONDS LATER, AS PAUL'S FRIENDS ARRIVE ON THE SCENE, AGAIN HE HAS NO PROOF TO SHOW THEM...
BUT I TELL YOU... STREAKY RAISED ME HIGH ON MY END OF THE SEE-SAW, THEN LET ME DROP!
IS THAT SO? LET'S ALL GO AND TELL THE SUPERINTENDENT ABOUT IT!
MEANWHILE, AS SUPERGIRL SWIFTLY FLASHES ABOVE THE PLANET EARTH, PURSUED BY HER PLAYFUL SUPER-CAT...
MY TELESCOPIC-VISION REVEALS TROUBLE BELOW, IN AN AFRICAN JUNGLE!
DOWN SWOOPS THE GIRL OF STEEL, FOLLOWED BY SUPER-CAT...
CAPTIVE WILD ANIMALS ESCAPED FROM A SAFARI AND ARE ATTACKING A NATIVE VILLAGE!
NEXT MOMENT...
I'LL HANDLE THE ELEPHANT AND GORILLA, STREAKY! YOU TAKE CARE OF THOSE BIG CATS!
LET ME AT THOSE BULLIES!

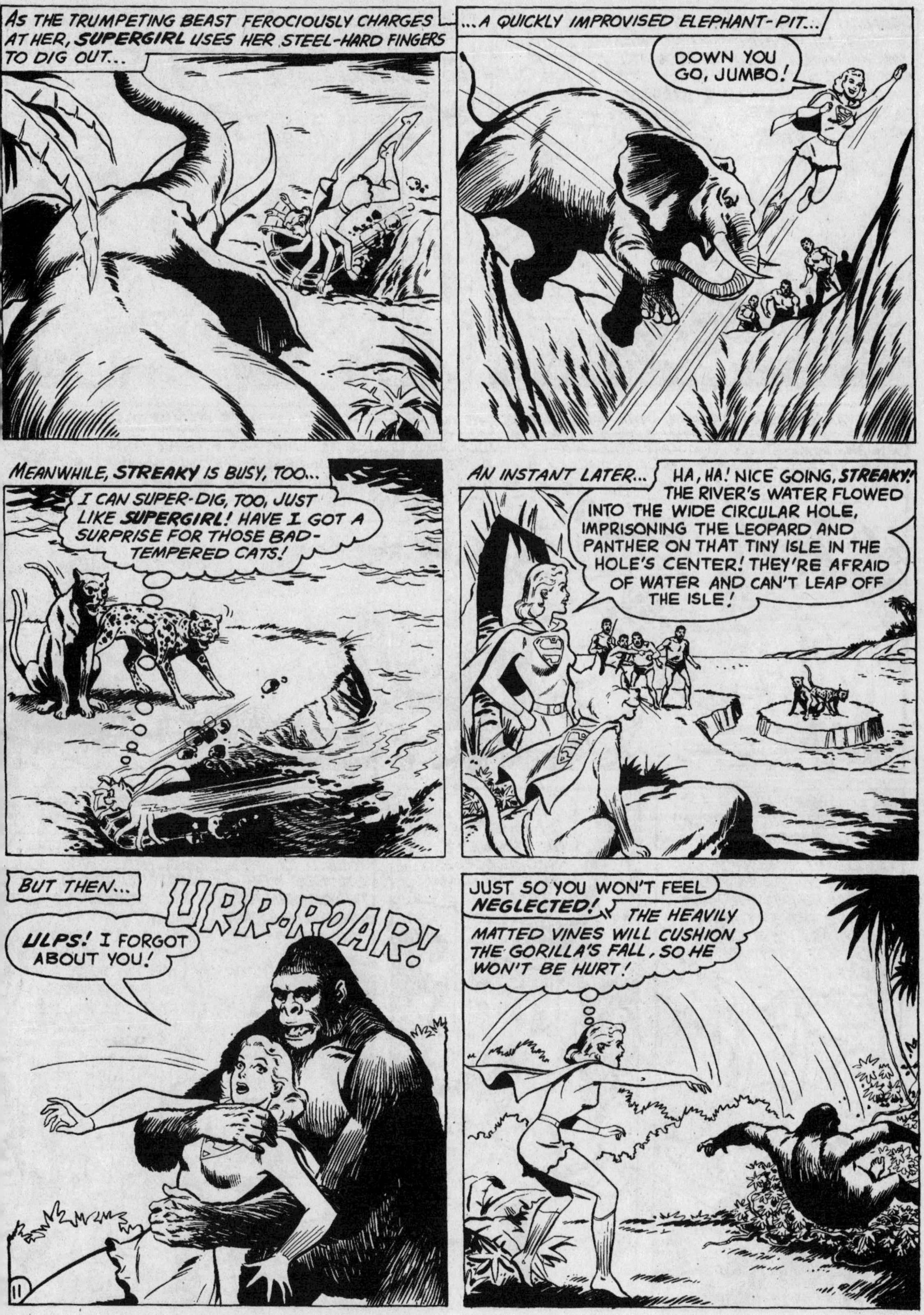
AS THE TRUMPETING BEAST FEROCIOUSLY CHARGES AT HER, SUPERGIRL USES HER STEEL-HARD FINGERS TO DIG OUT...
...A QUICKLY IMPROVISED ELEPHANT-PIT...
DOWN YOU GO, JUMBO!
MEANWHILE, STREAKY IS BUSY, TOO...
I CAN SUPER-DIG, TOO, JUST LIKE SUPERGIRL! HAVE I GOT A SURPRISE FOR THOSE BAD-TEMPERED CATS!
AN INSTANT LATER...
HA, HA! NICE GOING, STREAKY! THE RIVER'S WATER FLOWED INTO THE WIDE CIRCULAR HOLE, IMPRISONING THE LEOPARD AND PANTHER ON THAT TINY ISLE IN THE HOLE'S CENTER! THEY'RE AFRAID OF WATER AND CAN'T LEAP OFF THE ISLE!
BUT THEN...
URR-ROAR!
ULPS! I FORGOT ABOUT YOU!
11
JUST SO YOU WON'T FEEL NEGLECTED!
THE HEAVILY MATTED VINES WILL CUSHION THE GORILLA'S FALL, SO HE WON'T BE HURT!

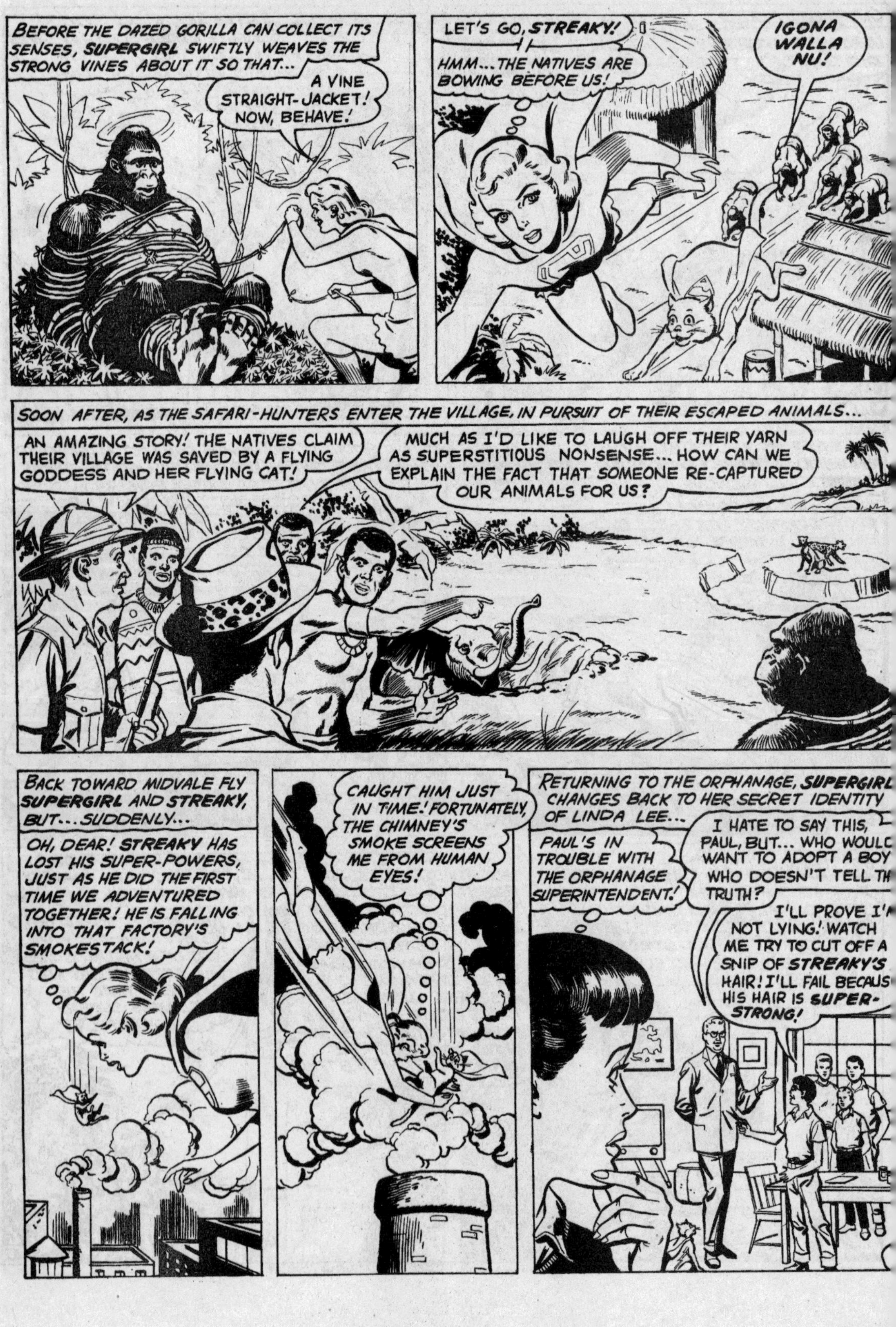
BEFORE THE DAZED GORILLA CAN COLLECT ITS SENSES, SUPERGIRL SWIFTLY WEAVES THE STRONG VINES ABOUT IT SO THAT...
A VINE STRAIGHT-JACKET! NOW, BEHAVE!
LET'S GO, STREAKY!
HMM... THE NATIVES ARE BOWING BEFORE US!
IGONA WALLA NU!
SOON AFTER, AS THE SAFARI-HUNTERS ENTER THE VILLAGE, IN PURSUIT OF THEIR ESCAPED ANIMALS...
AN AMAZING STORY! THE NATIVES CLAIM THEIR VILLAGE WAS SAVED BY A FLYING GODDESS AND HER FLYING CAT!
MUCH AS I'D LIKE TO LAUGH OFF THEIR YARN AS SUPERSTITIOUS NONSENSE... HOW CAN WE EXPLAIN THE FACT THAT SOMEONE RE-CAPTURED OUR ANIMALS FOR US?
BACK TOWARD MIDVALE FLY SUPERGIRL AND STREAKY, BUT... SUDDENLY...
OH, DEAR! STREAKY HAS LOST HIS SUPER-POWERS, JUST AS HE DID THE FIRST TIME WE ADVENTURED TOGETHER! HE IS FALLING INTO THAT FACTORY'S SMOKESTACK!
CAUGHT HIM JUST IN TIME! FORTUNATELY, THE CHIMNEY'S SMOKE SCREENS ME FROM HUMAN EYES!
RETURNING TO THE ORPHANAGE, SUPERGIRL CHANGES BACK TO HER SECRET IDENTITY OF LINDA LEE...
PAUL'S IN TROUBLE WITH THE ORPHANAGE SUPERINTENDENT!
I HATE TO SAY THIS, PAUL, BUT... WHO WOULD WANT TO ADOPT A BOY WHO DOESN'T TELL TH TRUTH?
I'LL PROVE I' NOT LYING! WATCH ME TRY TO CUT OFF A SNIP OF STREAKY'S HAIR! I'LL FAIL BECAUS HIS HAIR IS SUPER-STRONG!

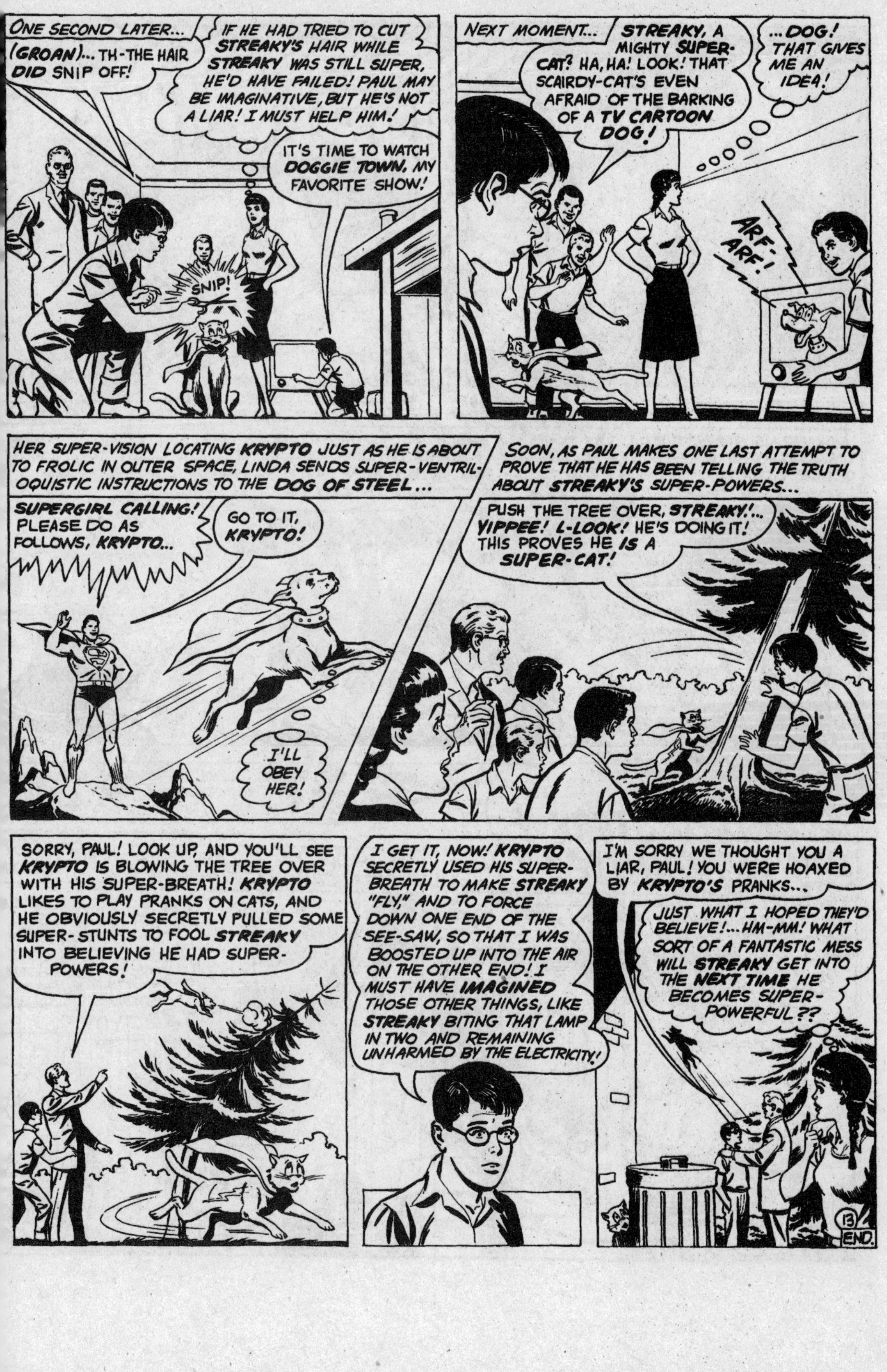
ONE SECOND LATER...
(GROAN)... TH-THE HAIR DID SNIP OFF!
IF HE HAD TRIED TO CUT STREAKY'S HAIR WHILE STREAKY WAS STILL SUPER, HE'D HAVE FAILED! PAUL MAY BE IMAGINATIVE, BUT HE'S NOT A LIAR! I MUST HELP HIM!
IT'S TIME TO WATCH DOGGIE TOWN, MY FAVORITE SHOW!
SNIP!
NEXT MOMENT...
STREAKY, A MIGHTY SUPER-CAT? HA, HA! LOOK! THAT SCAIRDY-CAT'S EVEN AFRAID OF THE BARKING OF A TV CARTOON DOG!
...DOG! THAT GIVES ME AN IDEA!
ARF-ARF!
HER SUPER-VISION LOCATING KRYPTO JUST AS HE IS ABOUT TO FROLIC IN OUTER SPACE, LINDA SENDS SUPER-VENTRILOQUISTIC INSTRUCTIONS TO THE DOG OF STEEL...
SUPERGIRL CALLING! PLEASE DO AS FOLLOWS, KRYPTO...
GO TO IT, KRYPTO!
I'LL OBEY HER!
SOON, AS PAUL MAKES ONE LAST ATTEMPT TO PROVE THAT HE HAS BEEN TELLING THE TRUTH ABOUT STREAKY'S SUPER-POWERS...
PUSH THE TREE OVER, STREAKY!... YIPPEE! L-LOOK! HE'S DOING IT! THIS PROVES HE IS A SUPER-CAT!
SORRY, PAUL! LOOK UP, AND YOU'LL SEE KRYPTO IS BLOWING THE TREE OVER WITH HIS SUPER-BREATH! KRYPTO LIKES TO PLAY PRANKS ON CATS, AND HE OBVIOUSLY SECRETLY PULLED SOME SUPER-STUNTS TO FOOL STREAKY INTO BELIEVING HE HAD SUPER-POWERS!
I GET IT, NOW! KRYPTO SECRETLY USED HIS SUPER-BREATH TO MAKE STREAKY "FLY," AND TO FORCE DOWN ONE END OF THE SEE-SAW, SO THAT I WAS BOOSTED UP INTO THE AIR ON THE OTHER END! I MUST HAVE IMAGINED THOSE OTHER THINGS, LIKE STREAKY BITING THAT LAMP IN TWO AND REMAINING UNHARMED BY THE ELECTRICITY!
I'M SORRY WE THOUGHT YOU A LIAR, PAUL! YOU WERE HOAXED BY KRYPTO'S PRANKS...
JUST WHAT I HOPED THEY'D BELIEVE!... HM-MM! WHAT SORT OF A FANTASTIC MESS WILL STREAKY GET INTO THE NEXT TIME HE BECOMES SUPER-POWERFUL??
13
END.

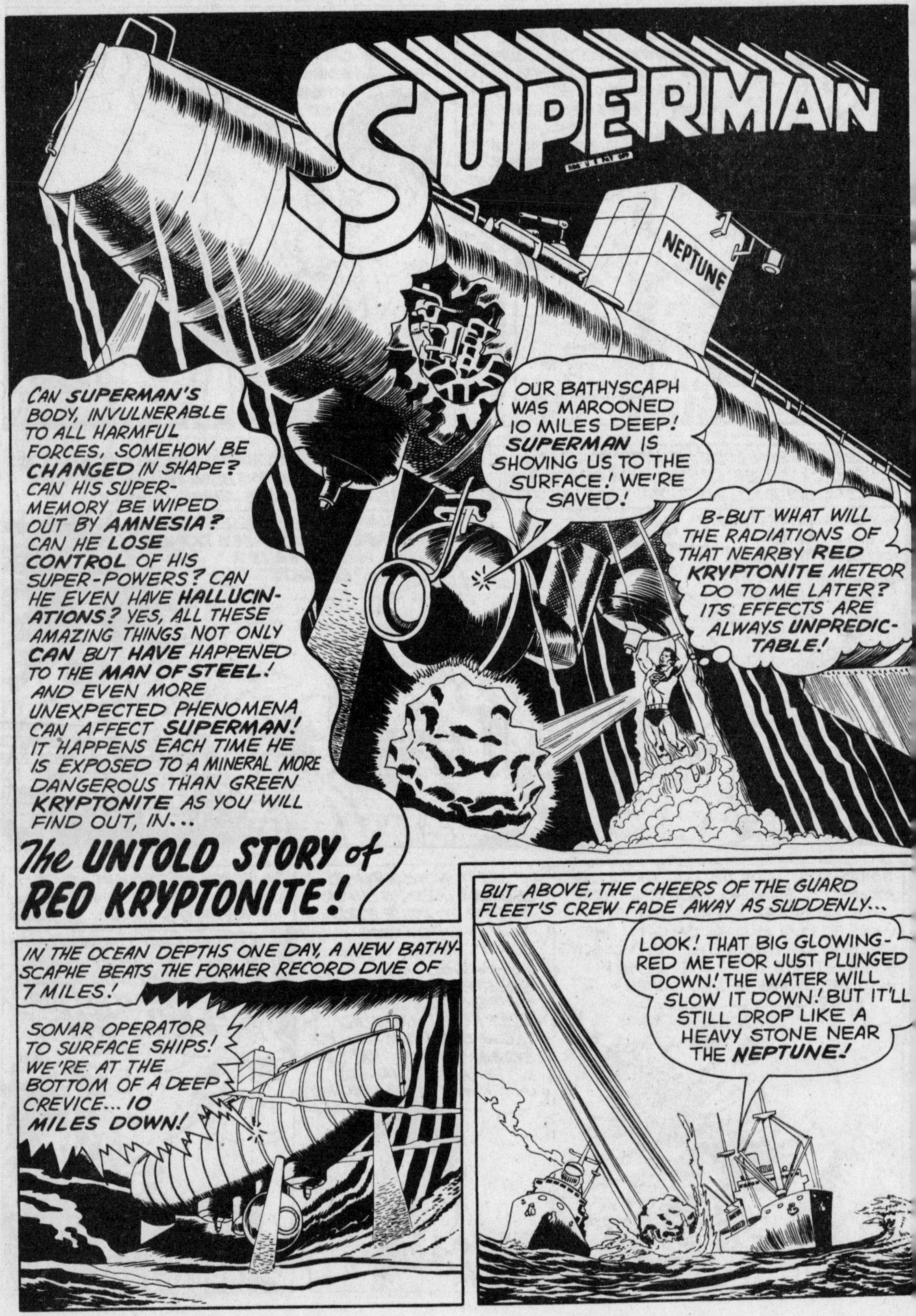
SUPERMAN
NEPTUNE
CAN SUPERMAN'S BODY, INVULNERABLE TO ALL HARMFUL FORCES, SOMEHOW BE CHANGED IN SHAPE? CAN HIS SUPER-MEMORY BE WIPED OUT BY AMNESIA? CAN HE LOSE CONTROL OF HIS SUPER-POWERS? CAN HE EVEN HAVE HALLUCIN-ATIONS? YES, ALL THESE AMAZING THINGS NOT ONLY CAN BUT HAVE HAPPENED TO THE MAN OF STEEL! AND EVEN MORE UNEXPECTED PHENOMENA CAN AFFECT SUPERMAN! IT HAPPENS EACH TIME HE IS EXPOSED TO A MINERAL MORE DANGEROUS THAN GREEN KRYPTONITE AS YOU WILL FIND OUT, IN...
OUR BATHYSCAPH WAS MAROONED 10 MILES DEEP! SUPERMAN IS SHOVING US TO THE SURFACE! WE'RE SAVED!
B-BUT WHAT WILL THE RADIATIONS OF THAT NEARBY RED KRYPTONITE METEOR DO TO ME LATER? ITS EFFECTS ARE ALWAYS UNPREDIC-TABLE!
The UNTOLD STORY of RED KRYPTONITE!
IN THE OCEAN DEPTHS ONE DAY, A NEW BATHY-SCAPHE BEATS THE FORMER RECORD DIVE OF 7 MILES!
SONAR OPERATOR TO SURFACE SHIPS! WE'RE AT THE BOTTOM OF A DEEP CREVICE... 10 MILES DOWN!
BUT ABOVE, THE CHEERS OF THE GUARD FLEET'S CREW FADE AWAY AS SUDDENLY...
LOOK! THAT BIG GLOWING-RED METEOR JUST PLUNGED DOWN! THE WATER WILL SLOW IT DOWN! BUT IT'LL STILL DROP LIKE A HEAVY STONE NEAR THE NEPTUNE!

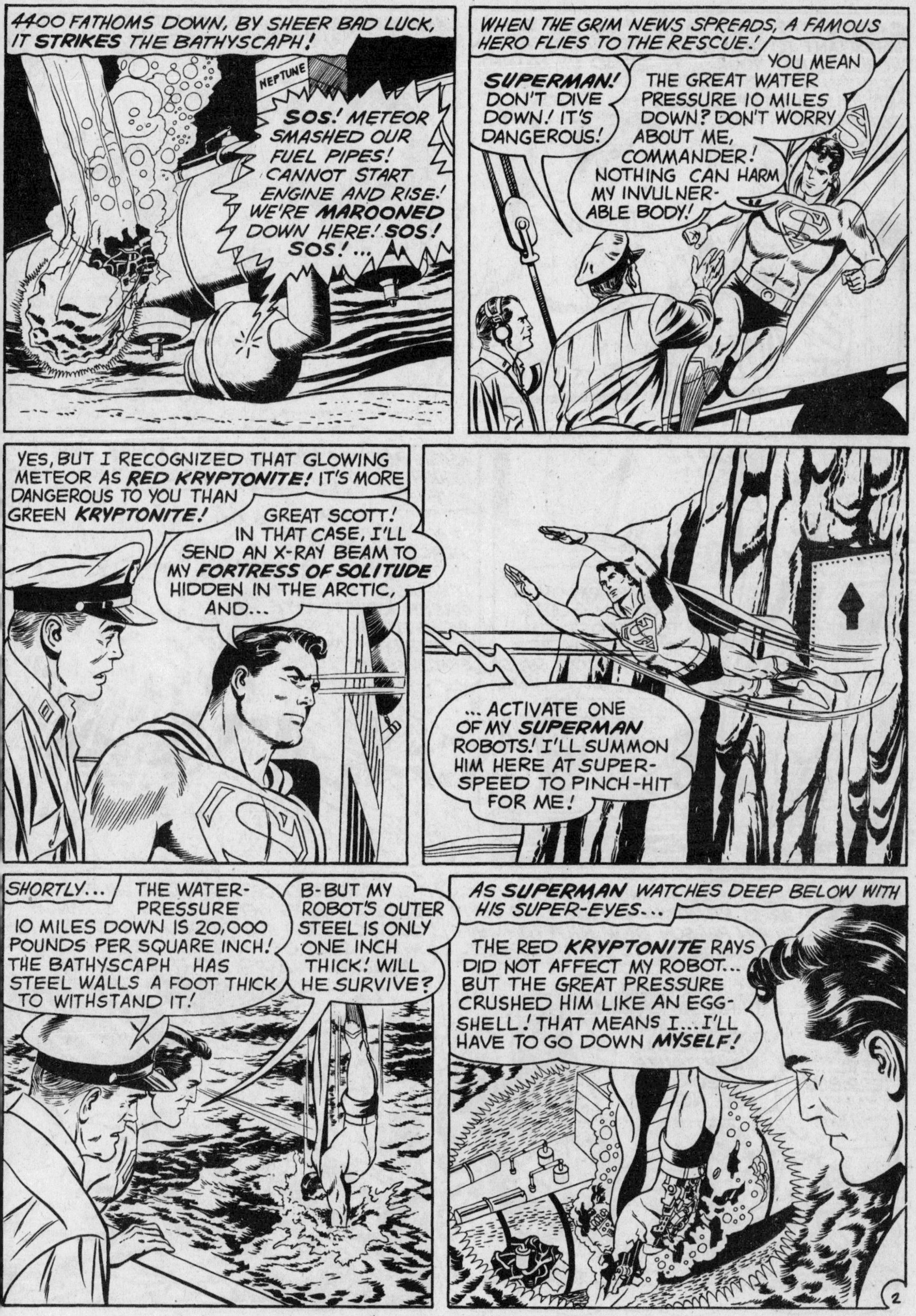
4400 FATHOMS DOWN, BY SHEER BAD LUCK, IT STRIKES THE BATHYSCAPH!
NEPTUNE
SOS! METEOR SMASHED OUR FUEL PIPES! CANNOT START ENGINE AND RISE! WE'RE MAROONED DOWN HERE! SOS! SOS! ...
WHEN THE GRIM NEWS SPREADS, A FAMOUS HERO FLIES TO THE RESCUE!
SUPERMAN! DON'T DIVE DOWN! IT'S DANGEROUS!
YOU MEAN THE GREAT WATER PRESSURE 10 MILES DOWN? DON'T WORRY ABOUT ME, COMMANDER! NOTHING CAN HARM MY INVULNERABLE BODY!
YES, BUT I RECOGNIZED THAT GLOWING METEOR AS RED KRYPTONITE! IT'S MORE DANGEROUS TO YOU THAN GREEN KRYPTONITE!
GREAT SCOTT! IN THAT CASE, I'LL SEND AN X-RAY BEAM TO MY FORTRESS OF SOLITUDE HIDDEN IN THE ARCTIC, AND...
... ACTIVATE ONE OF MY SUPERMAN ROBOTS! I'LL SUMMON HIM HERE AT SUPER-SPEED TO PINCH-HIT FOR ME!
SHORTLY...
THE WATER-PRESSURE 10 MILES DOWN IS 20,000 POUNDS PER SQUARE INCH! THE BATHYSCAPH HAS STEEL WALLS A FOOT THICK TO WITHSTAND IT!
B-BUT MY ROBOT'S OUTER STEEL IS ONLY ONE INCH THICK! WILL HE SURVIVE?
AS SUPERMAN WATCHES DEEP BELOW WITH HIS SUPER-EYES...
THE RED KRYPTONITE RAYS DID NOT AFFECT MY ROBOT... BUT THE GREAT PRESSURE CRUSHED HIM LIKE AN EGG-SHELL! THAT MEANS I... I'LL HAVE TO GO DOWN MYSELF!
2

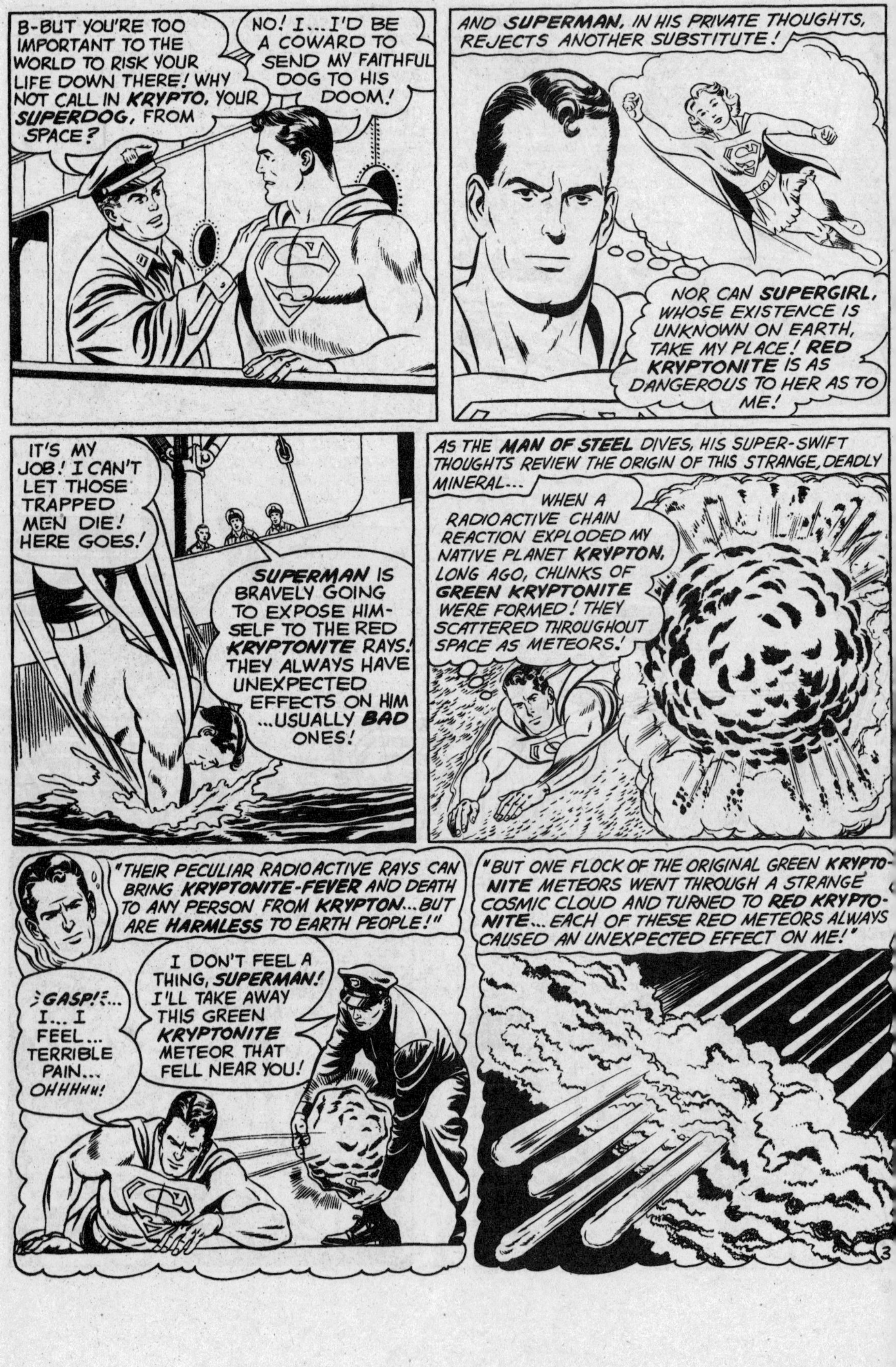
B-BUT YOU'RE TOO IMPORTANT TO THE WORLD TO RISK YOUR LIFE DOWN THERE! WHY NOT CALL IN KRYPTO, YOUR SUPERDOG, FROM SPACE?
NO! I...I'D BE A COWARD TO SEND MY FAITHFUL DOG TO HIS DOOM!
AND SUPERMAN, IN HIS PRIVATE THOUGHTS, REJECTS ANOTHER SUBSTITUTE!
NOR CAN SUPERGIRL, WHOSE EXISTENCE IS UNKNOWN ON EARTH, TAKE MY PLACE! RED KRYPTONITE IS AS DANGEROUS TO HER AS TO ME!
IT'S MY JOB! I CAN'T LET THOSE TRAPPED MEN DIE! HERE GOES!
SUPERMAN IS BRAVELY GOING TO EXPOSE HIMSELF TO THE RED KRYPTONITE RAYS! THEY ALWAYS HAVE UNEXPECTED EFFECTS ON HIM ...USUALLY BAD ONES!
AS THE MAN OF STEEL DIVES, HIS SUPER-SWIFT THOUGHTS REVIEW THE ORIGIN OF THIS STRANGE, DEADLY MINERAL...
WHEN A RADIOACTIVE CHAIN REACTION EXPLODED MY NATIVE PLANET KRYPTON, LONG AGO, CHUNKS OF GREEN KRYPTONITE WERE FORMED! THEY SCATTERED THROUGHOUT SPACE AS METEORS!
"THEIR PECULIAR RADIOACTIVE RAYS CAN BRING KRYPTONITE-FEVER AND DEATH TO ANY PERSON FROM KRYPTON...BUT ARE HARMLESS TO EARTH PEOPLE!"
GASP!... I... I FEEL... TERRIBLE PAIN... OHHHHH!
I DON'T FEEL A THING, SUPERMAN! I'LL TAKE AWAY THIS GREEN KRYPTONITE METEOR THAT FELL NEAR YOU!
"BUT ONE FLOCK OF THE ORIGINAL GREEN KRYPTONITE METEORS WENT THROUGH A STRANGE COSMIC CLOUD AND TURNED TO RED KRYPTONITE... EACH OF THESE RED METEORS ALWAYS CAUSED AN UNEXPECTED EFFECT ON ME!"
3

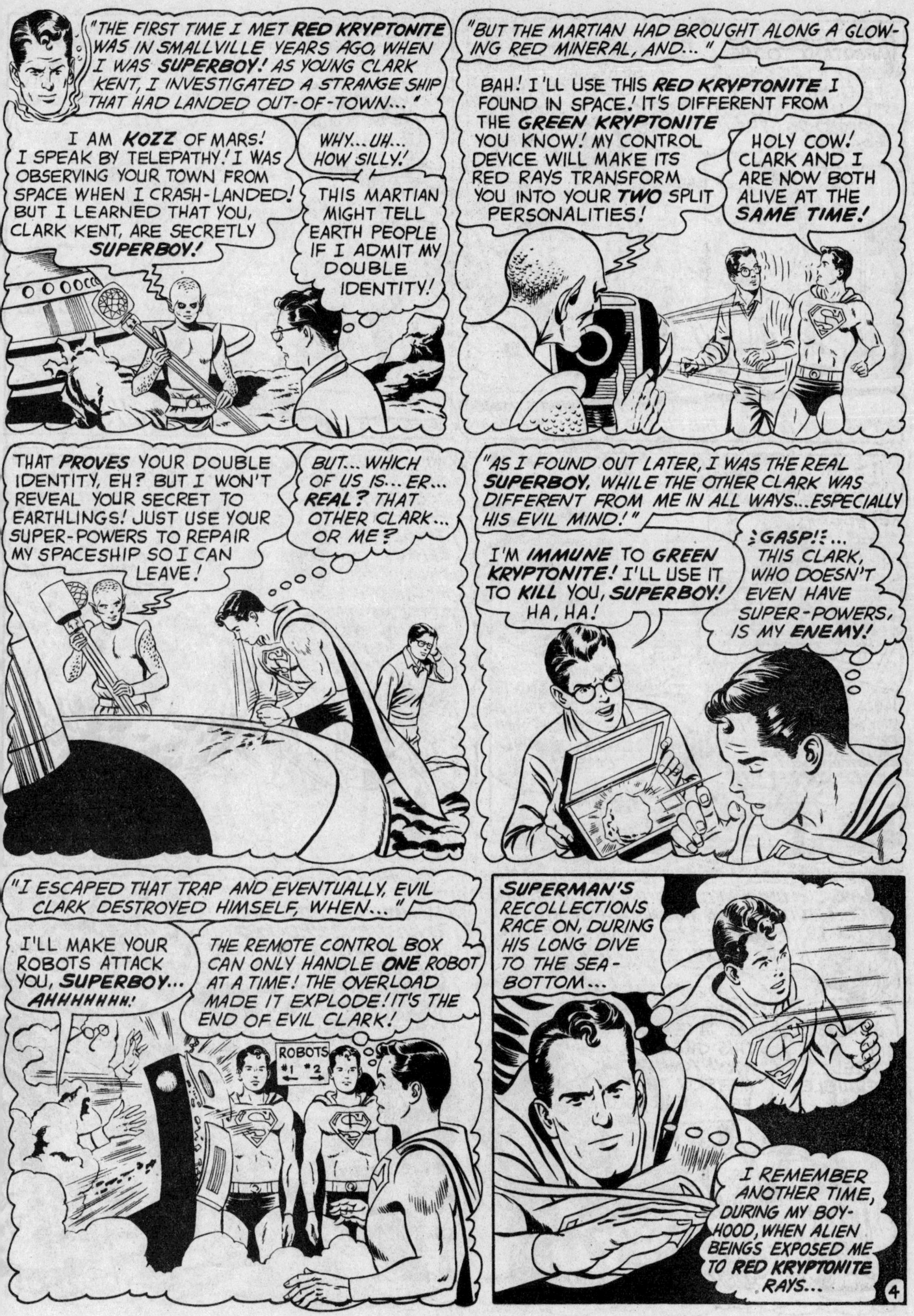
"THE FIRST TIME I MET RED KRYPTONITE WAS IN SMALLVILLE YEARS AGO, WHEN I WAS SUPERBOY! AS YOUNG CLARK KENT, I INVESTIGATED A STRANGE SHIP THAT HAD LANDED OUT-OF-TOWN..."
I AM KOZZ OF MARS! I SPEAK BY TELEPATHY! I WAS OBSERVING YOUR TOWN FROM SPACE WHEN I CRASH-LANDED! BUT I LEARNED THAT YOU, CLARK KENT, ARE SECRETLY SUPERBOY!
WHY...UH... HOW SILLY!
THIS MARTIAN MIGHT TELL EARTH PEOPLE IF I ADMIT MY DOUBLE IDENTITY!
"BUT THE MARTIAN HAD BROUGHT ALONG A GLOWING RED MINERAL, AND..."
BAH! I'LL USE THIS RED KRYPTONITE I FOUND IN SPACE! IT'S DIFFERENT FROM THE GREEN KRYPTONITE YOU KNOW! MY CONTROL DEVICE WILL MAKE ITS RED RAYS TRANSFORM YOU INTO YOUR TWO SPLIT PERSONALITIES!
HOLY COW! CLARK AND I ARE NOW BOTH ALIVE AT THE SAME TIME!
THAT PROVES YOUR DOUBLE IDENTITY, EH? BUT I WON'T REVEAL YOUR SECRET TO EARTHLINGS! JUST USE YOUR SUPER-POWERS TO REPAIR MY SPACESHIP SO I CAN LEAVE!
BUT... WHICH OF US IS... ER... REAL? THAT OTHER CLARK... OR ME?
"AS I FOUND OUT LATER, I WAS THE REAL SUPERBOY, WHILE THE OTHER CLARK WAS DIFFERENT FROM ME IN ALL WAYS...ESPECIALLY HIS EVIL MIND!"
I'M IMMUNE TO GREEN KRYPTONITE! I'LL USE IT TO KILL YOU, SUPERBOY! HA, HA!
GASP!... THIS CLARK, WHO DOESN'T EVEN HAVE SUPER-POWERS, IS MY ENEMY!
"I ESCAPED THAT TRAP AND EVENTUALLY, EVIL CLARK DESTROYED HIMSELF, WHEN..."
I'LL MAKE YOUR ROBOTS ATTACK YOU, SUPERBOY... AHHHHHHH!
THE REMOTE CONTROL BOX CAN ONLY HANDLE ONE ROBOT AT A TIME! THE OVERLOAD MADE IT EXPLODE! IT'S THE END OF EVIL CLARK!
ROBOTS #1 #2
SUPERMAN'S RECOLLECTIONS RACE ON, DURING HIS LONG DIVE TO THE SEA-BOTTOM...
I REMEMBER ANOTHER TIME, DURING MY BOYHOOD, WHEN ALIEN BEINGS EXPOSED ME TO RED KRYPTONITE RAYS...
4

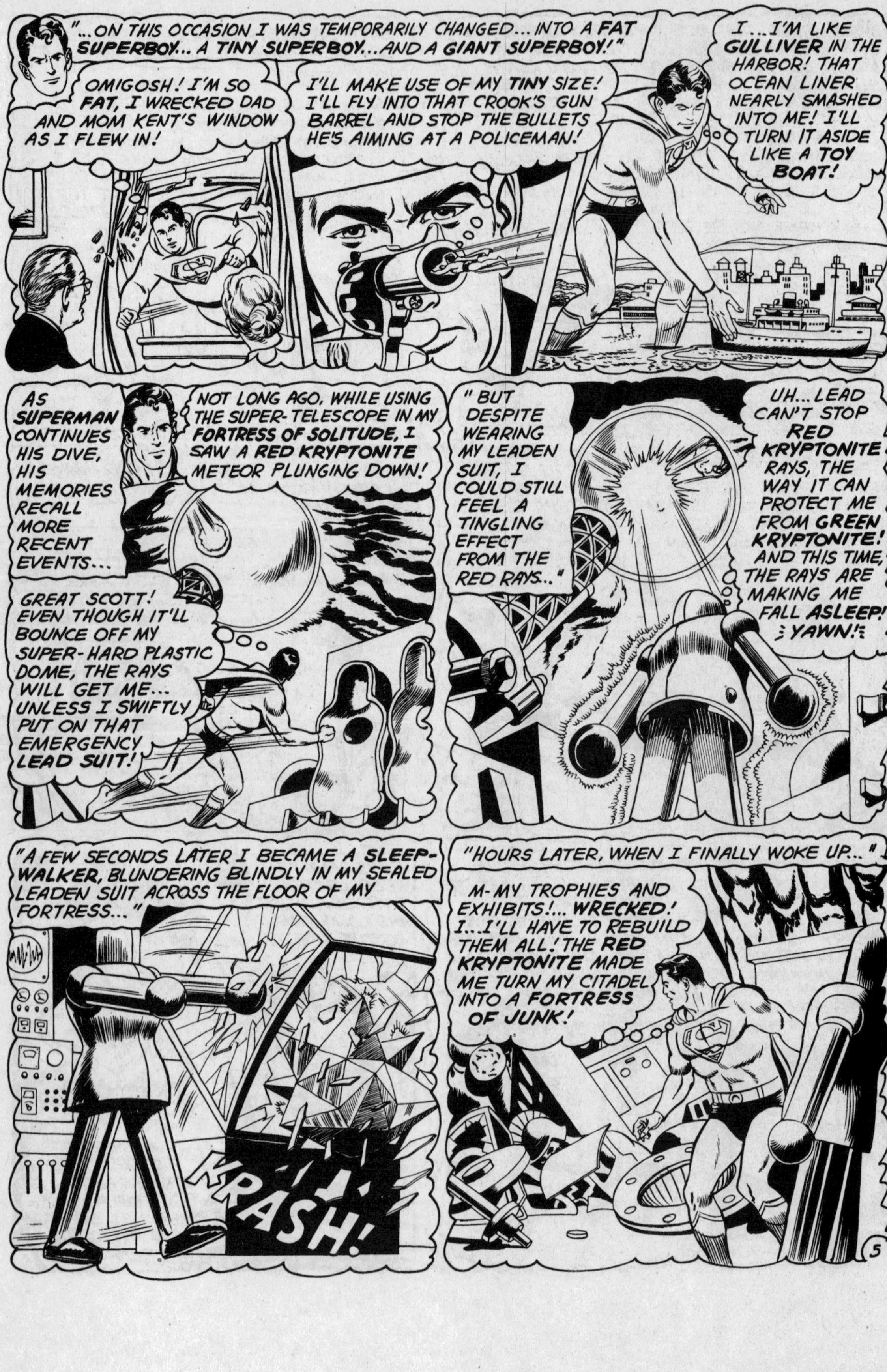
"...ON THIS OCCASION I WAS TEMPORARILY CHANGED... INTO A FAT SUPERBOY... A TINY SUPERBOY... AND A GIANT SUPERBOY!"
OMIGOSH! I'M SO FAT, I WRECKED DAD AND MOM KENT'S WINDOW AS I FLEW IN!
I'LL MAKE USE OF MY TINY SIZE! I'LL FLY INTO THAT CROOK'S GUN BARREL AND STOP THE BULLETS HE'S AIMING AT A POLICEMAN!
I...I'M LIKE GULLIVER IN THE HARBOR! THAT OCEAN LINER NEARLY SMASHED INTO ME! I'LL TURN IT ASIDE LIKE A TOY BOAT!
AS SUPERMAN CONTINUES HIS DIVE, HIS MEMORIES RECALL MORE RECENT EVENTS...
NOT LONG AGO, WHILE USING THE SUPER-TELESCOPE IN MY FORTRESS OF SOLITUDE, I SAW A RED KRYPTONITE METEOR PLUNGING DOWN!
GREAT SCOTT! EVEN THOUGH IT'LL BOUNCE OFF MY SUPER-HARD PLASTIC DOME, THE RAYS WILL GET ME... UNLESS I SWIFTLY PUT ON THAT EMERGENCY LEAD SUIT!
" BUT DESPITE WEARING MY LEADEN SUIT, I COULD STILL FEEL A TINGLING EFFECT FROM THE RED RAYS..."
UH... LEAD CAN'T STOP RED KRYPTONITE RAYS, THE WAY IT CAN PROTECT ME FROM GREEN KRYPTONITE! AND THIS TIME, THE RAYS ARE MAKING ME FALL ASLEEP! ;YAWN!;
"A FEW SECONDS LATER I BECAME A SLEEP-WALKER, BLUNDERING BLINDLY IN MY SEALED LEADEN SUIT ACROSS THE FLOOR OF MY FORTRESS..."
KRASH!
"HOURS LATER, WHEN I FINALLY WOKE UP..."
M-MY TROPHIES AND EXHIBITS!... WRECKED! I...I'LL HAVE TO REBUILD THEM ALL! THE RED KRYPTONITE MADE ME TURN MY CITADEL INTO A FORTRESS OF JUNK!
5

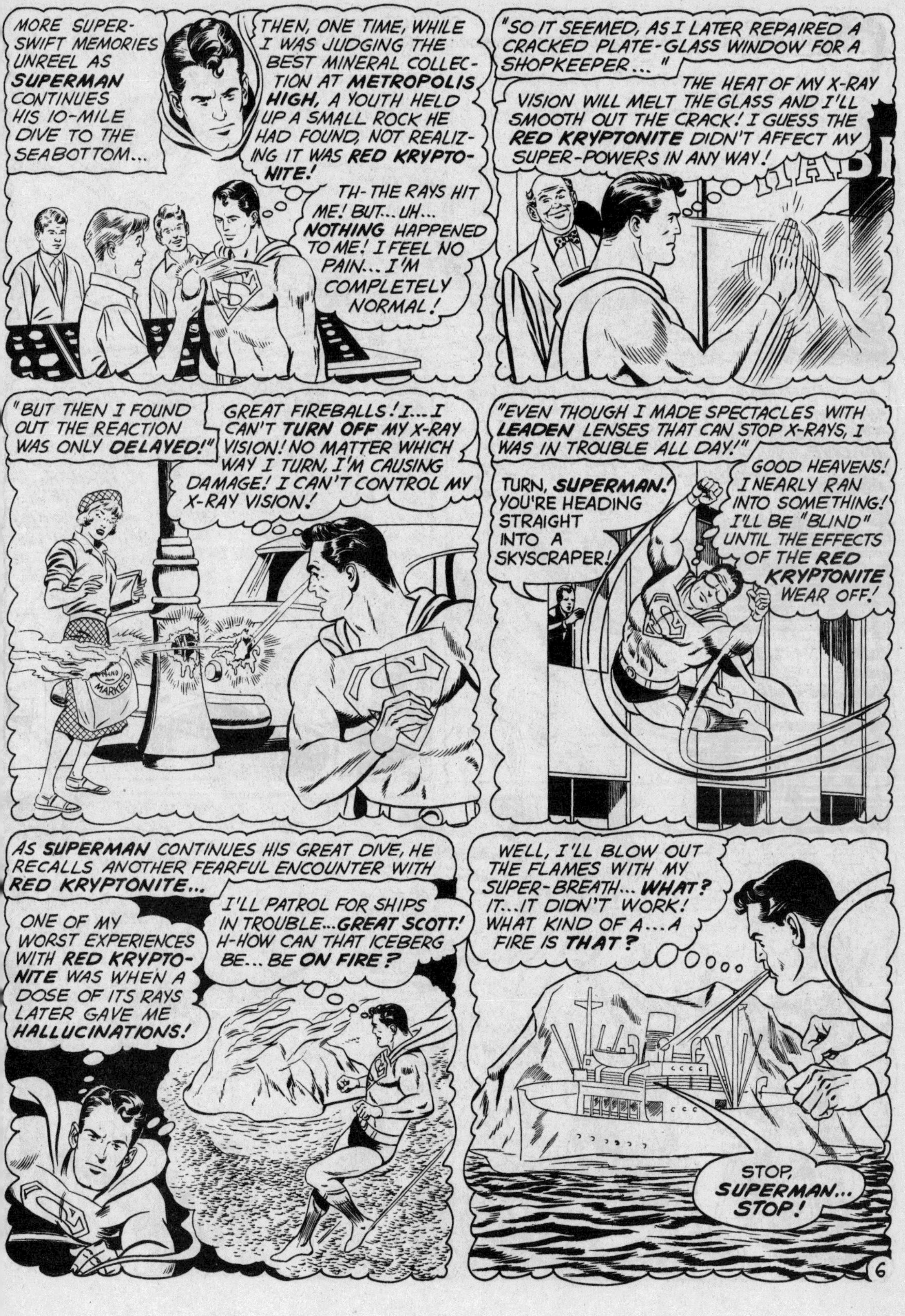
MORE SUPER-SWIFT MEMORIES UNREEL AS SUPERMAN CONTINUES HIS 10-MILE DIVE TO THE SEABOTTOM...
THEN, ONE TIME, WHILE I WAS JUDGING THE BEST MINERAL COLLECTION AT METROPOLIS HIGH, A YOUTH HELD UP A SMALL ROCK HE HAD FOUND, NOT REALIZING IT WAS RED KRYPTONITE!
TH-THE RAYS HIT ME! BUT...UH... NOTHING HAPPENED TO ME! I FEEL NO PAIN... I'M COMPLETELY NORMAL!
"SO IT SEEMED, AS I LATER REPAIRED A CRACKED PLATE-GLASS WINDOW FOR A SHOPKEEPER..."
THE HEAT OF MY X-RAY VISION WILL MELT THE GLASS AND I'LL SMOOTH OUT THE CRACK! I GUESS THE RED KRYPTONITE DIDN'T AFFECT MY SUPER-POWERS IN ANY WAY!
"BUT THEN I FOUND OUT THE REACTION WAS ONLY DELAYED!"
GREAT FIREBALLS! I... I CAN'T TURN OFF MY X-RAY VISION! NO MATTER WHICH WAY I TURN, I'M CAUSING DAMAGE! I CAN'T CONTROL MY X-RAY VISION!
MARKETS
"EVEN THOUGH I MADE SPECTACLES WITH LEADEN LENSES THAT CAN STOP X-RAYS, I WAS IN TROUBLE ALL DAY!"
TURN, SUPERMAN! YOU'RE HEADING STRAIGHT INTO A SKYSCRAPER!
GOOD HEAVENS! I NEARLY RAN INTO SOMETHING! I'LL BE "BLIND" UNTIL THE EFFECTS OF THE RED KRYPTONITE WEAR OFF!
AS SUPERMAN CONTINUES HIS GREAT DIVE, HE RECALLS ANOTHER FEARFUL ENCOUNTER WITH RED KRYPTONITE...
ONE OF MY WORST EXPERIENCES WITH RED KRYPTONITE WAS WHEN A DOSE OF ITS RAYS LATER GAVE ME HALLUCINATIONS!
I'LL PATROL FOR SHIPS IN TROUBLE...GREAT SCOTT! H-HOW CAN THAT ICEBERG BE... BE ON FIRE?
WELL, I'LL BLOW OUT THE FLAMES WITH MY SUPER-BREATH... WHAT? IT...IT DIDN'T WORK! WHAT KIND OF A... A FIRE IS THAT?
STOP, SUPERMAN... STOP!
6

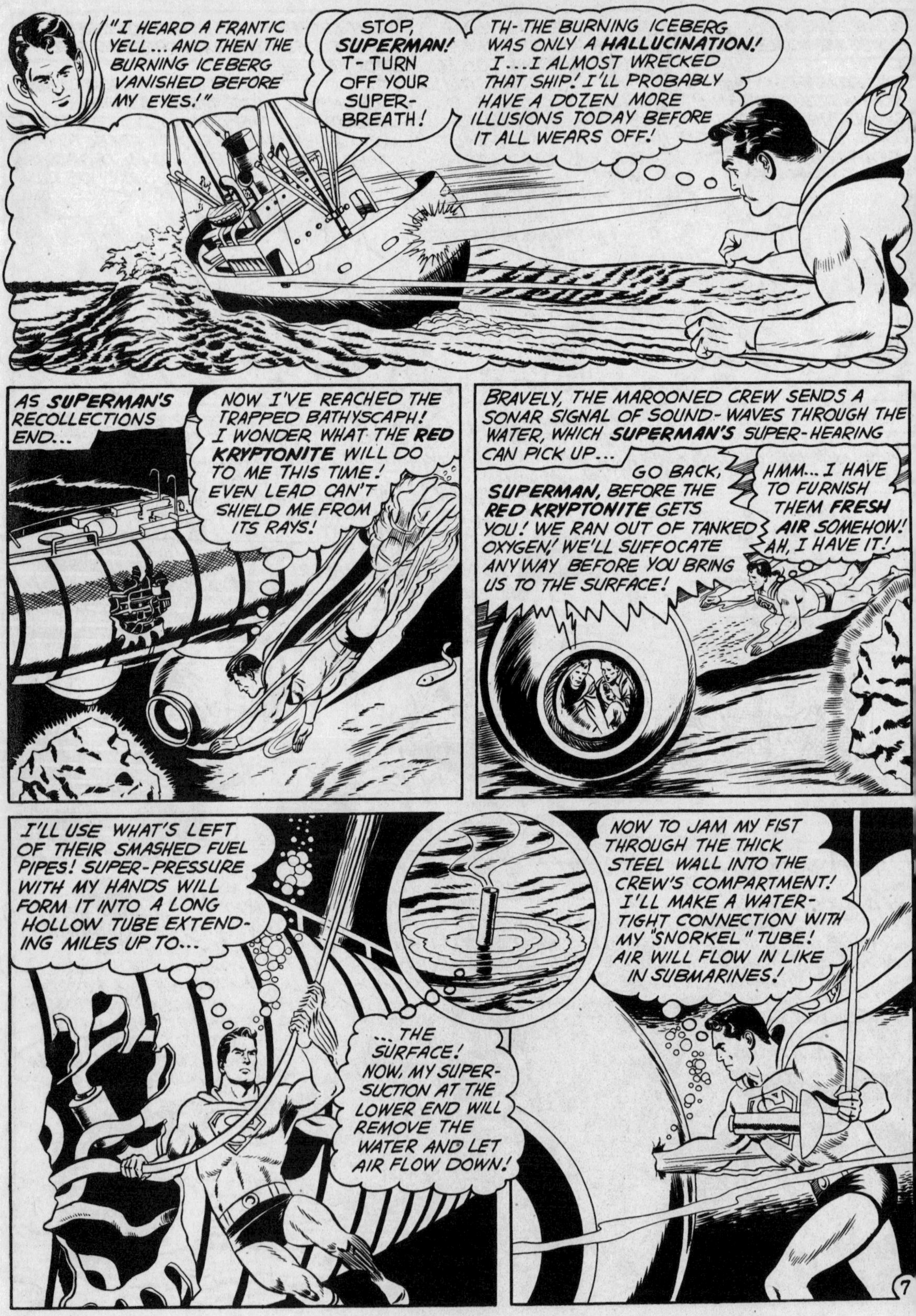
"I HEARD A FRANTIC YELL... AND THEN THE BURNING ICEBERG VANISHED BEFORE MY EYES!"
STOP, SUPERMAN! T-TURN OFF YOUR SUPER-BREATH!
TH-THE BURNING ICEBERG WAS ONLY A HALLUCINATION! I...I ALMOST WRECKED THAT SHIP! I'LL PROBABLY HAVE A DOZEN MORE ILLUSIONS TODAY BEFORE IT ALL WEARS OFF!
AS SUPERMAN'S RECOLLECTIONS END...
NOW I'VE REACHED THE TRAPPED BATHYSCAPH! I WONDER WHAT THE RED KRYPTONITE WILL DO TO ME THIS TIME! EVEN LEAD CAN'T SHIELD ME FROM ITS RAYS!
BRAVELY, THE MAROONED CREW SENDS A SONAR SIGNAL OF SOUND-WAVES THROUGH THE WATER, WHICH SUPERMAN'S SUPER-HEARING CAN PICK UP...
GO BACK, SUPERMAN, BEFORE THE RED KRYPTONITE GETS YOU! WE RAN OUT OF TANKED OXYGEN! WE'LL SUFFOCATE ANYWAY BEFORE YOU BRING US TO THE SURFACE!
HMM... I HAVE TO FURNISH THEM FRESH AIR SOMEHOW! AH, I HAVE IT!
I'LL USE WHAT'S LEFT OF THEIR SMASHED FUEL PIPES! SUPER-PRESSURE WITH MY HANDS WILL FORM IT INTO A LONG HOLLOW TUBE EXTENDING MILES UP TO...
...THE SURFACE! NOW, MY SUPER-SUCTION AT THE LOWER END WILL REMOVE THE WATER AND LET AIR FLOW DOWN!
NOW TO JAM MY FIST THROUGH THE THICK STEEL WALL INTO THE CREW'S COMPARTMENT! I'LL MAKE A WATER-TIGHT CONNECTION WITH MY "SNORKEL" TUBE! AIR WILL FLOW IN LIKE IN SUBMARINES!
7

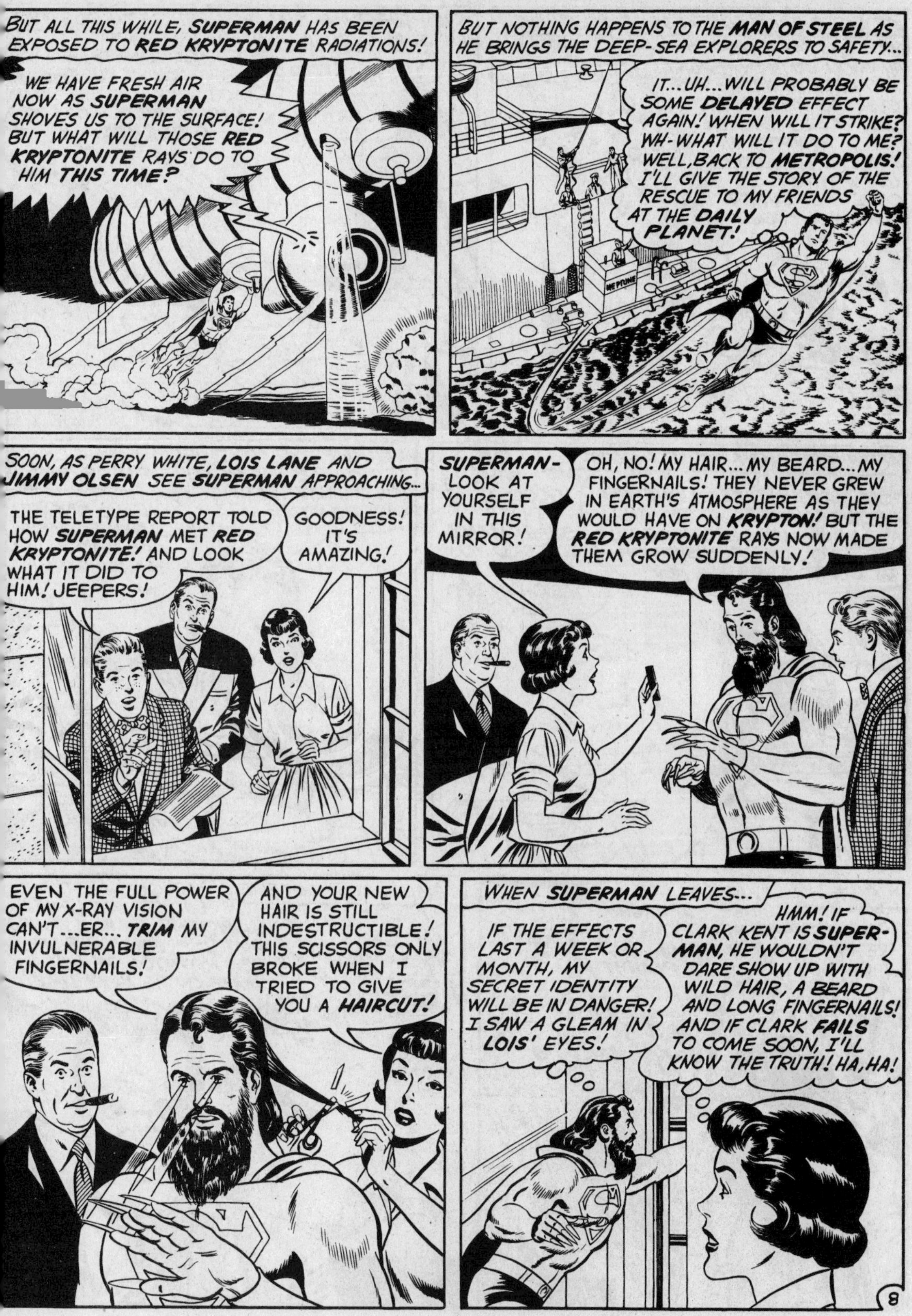
BUT ALL THIS WHILE, SUPERMAN HAS BEEN EXPOSED TO RED KRYPTONITE RADIATIONS!
WE HAVE FRESH AIR NOW AS SUPERMAN SHOVES US TO THE SURFACE! BUT WHAT WILL THOSE RED KRYPTONITE RAYS DO TO HIM THIS TIME?
BUT NOTHING HAPPENS TO THE MAN OF STEEL AS HE BRINGS THE DEEP-SEA EXPLORERS TO SAFETY...
IT...UH...WILL PROBABLY BE SOME DELAYED EFFECT AGAIN! WHEN WILL IT STRIKE? WH-WHAT WILL IT DO TO ME? WELL, BACK TO METROPOLIS! I'LL GIVE THE STORY OF THE RESCUE TO MY FRIENDS AT THE DAILY PLANET!
NEPTUNE
SOON, AS PERRY WHITE, LOIS LANE AND JIMMY OLSEN SEE SUPERMAN APPROACHING...
THE TELETYPE REPORT TOLD HOW SUPERMAN MET RED KRYPTONITE! AND LOOK WHAT IT DID TO HIM! JEEPERS!
GOODNESS! IT'S AMAZING!
SUPERMAN-LOOK AT YOURSELF IN THIS MIRROR!
OH, NO! MY HAIR... MY BEARD... MY FINGERNAILS! THEY NEVER GREW IN EARTH'S ATMOSPHERE AS THEY WOULD HAVE ON KRYPTON! BUT THE RED KRYPTONITE RAYS NOW MADE THEM GROW SUDDENLY!
EVEN THE FULL POWER OF MY X-RAY VISION CAN'T...ER...TRIM MY INVULNERABLE FINGERNAILS!
AND YOUR NEW HAIR IS STILL INDESTRUCTIBLE! THIS SCISSORS ONLY BROKE WHEN I TRIED TO GIVE YOU A HAIRCUT!
WHEN SUPERMAN LEAVES...
IF THE EFFECTS LAST A WEEK OR MONTH, MY SECRET IDENTITY WILL BE IN DANGER! I SAW A GLEAM IN LOIS' EYES!
HMM! IF CLARK KENT IS SUPER-MAN, HE WOULDN'T DARE SHOW UP WITH WILD HAIR, A BEARD AND LONG FINGERNAILS! AND IF CLARK FAILS TO COME SOON, I'LL KNOW THE TRUTH! HA, HA!
8

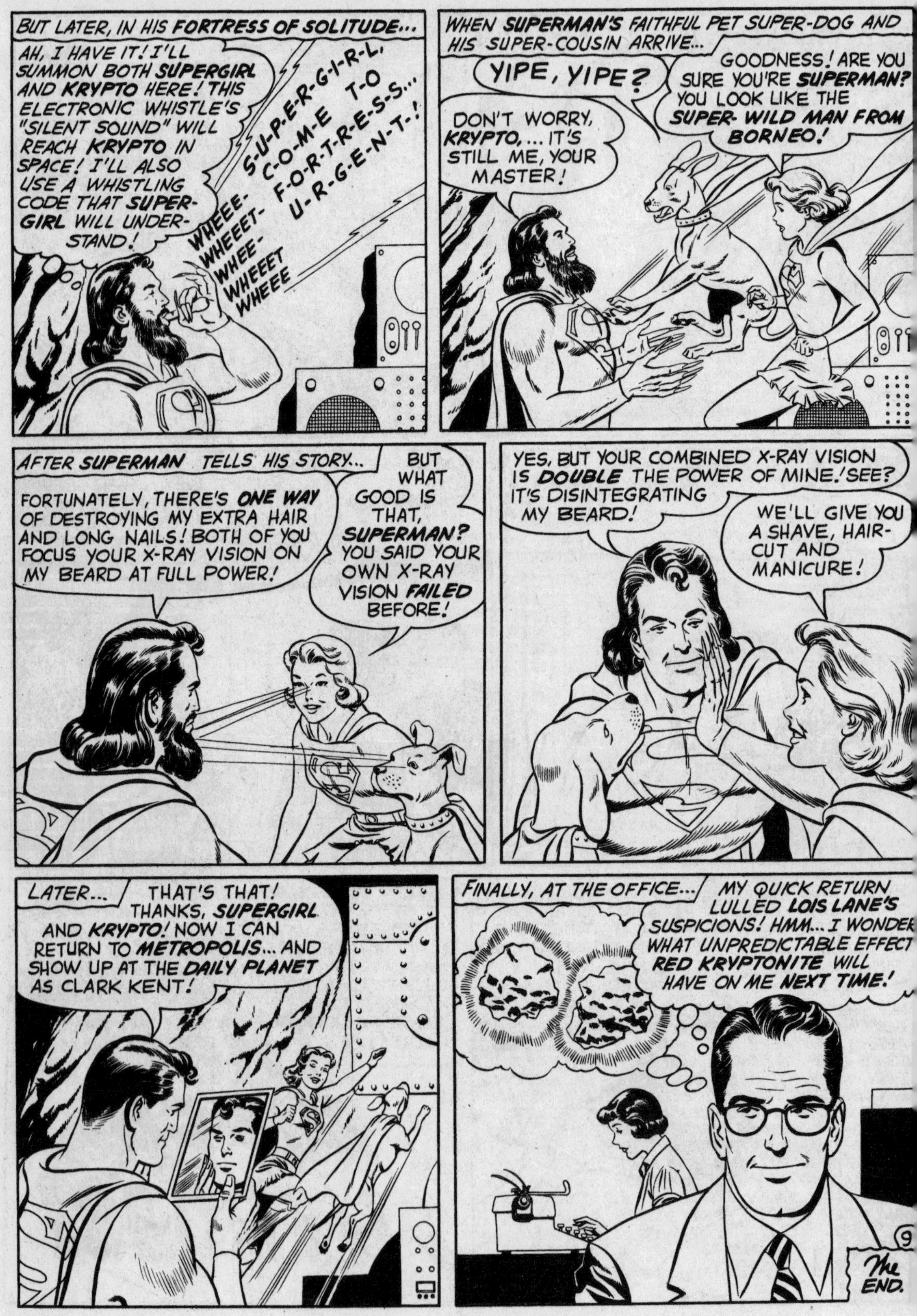
BUT LATER, IN HIS FORTRESS OF SOLITUDE...
AH, I HAVE IT! I'LL SUMMON BOTH SUPERGIRL AND KRYPTO HERE! THIS ELECTRONIC WHISTLE'S "SILENT SOUND" WILL REACH KRYPTO IN SPACE! I'LL ALSO USE A WHISTLING CODE THAT SUPERGIRL WILL UNDERSTAND!
S-U-P-E-R-G-I-R-L, C-O-M-E T-O F-O-R-T-R-E-S-S... U-R-G-E-N-T-!
WHEEE- WHEEET- WHEE- WHEEET WHEEE
WHEN SUPERMAN'S FAITHFUL PET SUPER-DOG AND HIS SUPER-COUSIN ARRIVE...
YIPE, YIPE?
GOODNESS! ARE YOU SURE YOU'RE SUPERMAN? YOU LOOK LIKE THE SUPER-WILD MAN FROM BORNEO!
DON'T WORRY, KRYPTO, ... IT'S STILL ME, YOUR MASTER!
AFTER SUPERMAN TELLS HIS STORY...
FORTUNATELY, THERE'S ONE WAY OF DESTROYING MY EXTRA HAIR AND LONG NAILS! BOTH OF YOU FOCUS YOUR X-RAY VISION ON MY BEARD AT FULL POWER!
BUT WHAT GOOD IS THAT, SUPERMAN? YOU SAID YOUR OWN X-RAY VISION FAILED BEFORE!
YES, BUT YOUR COMBINED X-RAY VISION IS DOUBLE THE POWER OF MINE! SEE? IT'S DISINTEGRATING MY BEARD!
WE'LL GIVE YOU A SHAVE, HAIR-CUT AND MANICURE!
LATER...
THAT'S THAT! THANKS, SUPERGIRL AND KRYPTO! NOW I CAN RETURN TO METROPOLIS... AND SHOW UP AT THE DAILY PLANET AS CLARK KENT!
FINALLY, AT THE OFFICE...
MY QUICK RETURN LULLED LOIS LANE'S SUSPICIONS! HMM... I WONDER WHAT UNPREDICTABLE EFFECT RED KRYPTONITE WILL HAVE ON ME NEXT TIME!
9
The END.

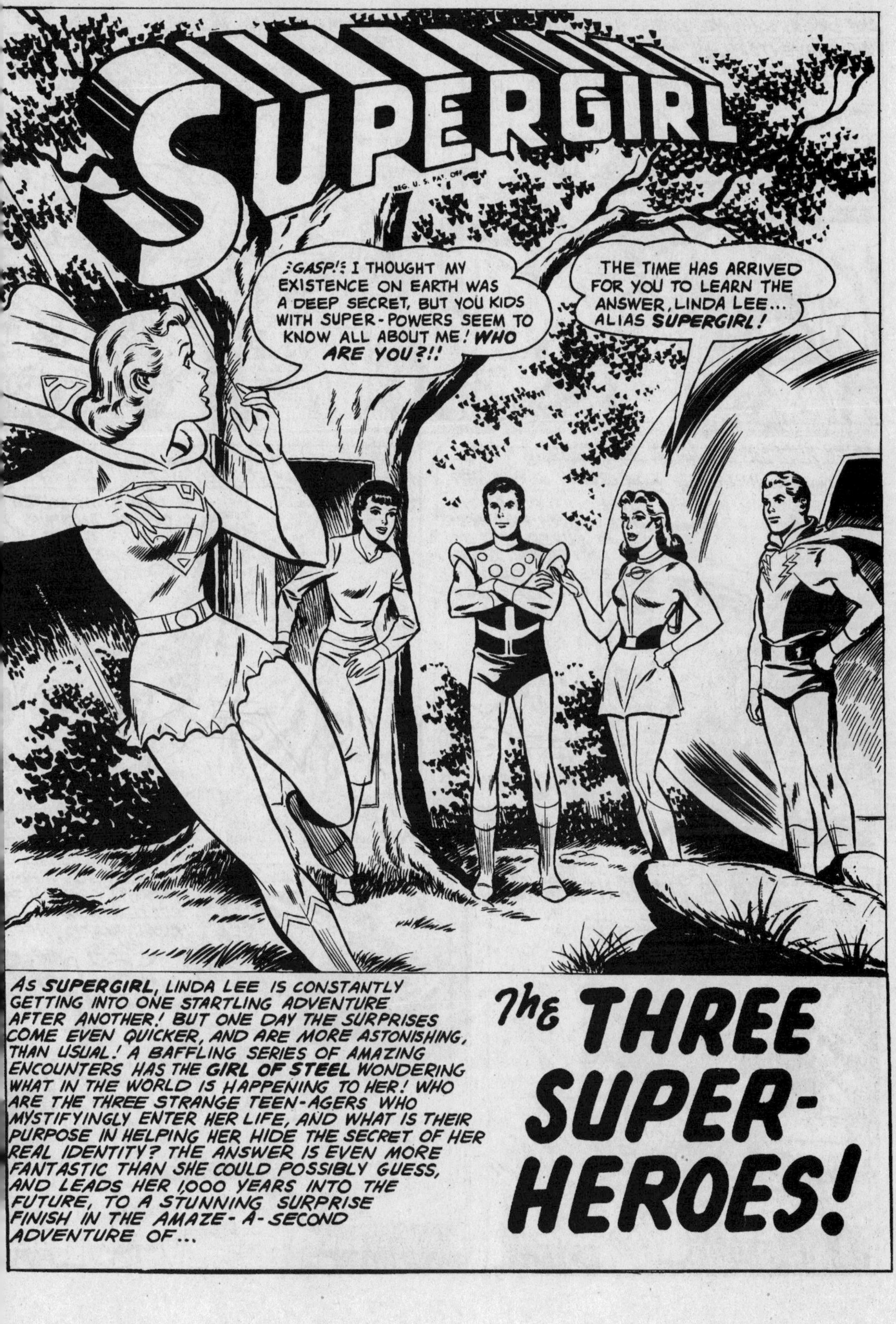
SUPERGIRL
REG. U.S. PAT. OFF.
GASP! I THOUGHT MY EXISTENCE ON EARTH WAS A DEEP SECRET, BUT YOU KIDS WITH SUPER-POWERS SEEM TO KNOW ALL ABOUT ME! WHO ARE YOU?!!
THE TIME HAS ARRIVED FOR YOU TO LEARN THE ANSWER, LINDA LEE... ALIAS SUPERGIRL!
AS SUPERGIRL, LINDA LEE IS CONSTANTLY GETTING INTO ONE STARTLING ADVENTURE AFTER ANOTHER! BUT ONE DAY THE SURPRISES COME EVEN QUICKER, AND ARE MORE ASTONISHING, THAN USUAL! A BAFFLING SERIES OF AMAZING ENCOUNTERS HAS THE GIRL OF STEEL WONDERING WHAT IN THE WORLD IS HAPPENING TO HER! WHO ARE THE THREE STRANGE TEEN-AGERS WHO MYSTIFYINGLY ENTER HER LIFE, AND WHAT IS THEIR PURPOSE IN HELPING HER HIDE THE SECRET OF HER REAL IDENTITY? THE ANSWER IS EVEN MORE FANTASTIC THAN SHE COULD POSSIBLY GUESS, AND LEADS HER 1,000 YEARS INTO THE FUTURE, TO A STUNNING SURPRISE FINISH IN THE AMAZE-A-SECOND ADVENTURE OF...
The THREE SUPER-HEROES!

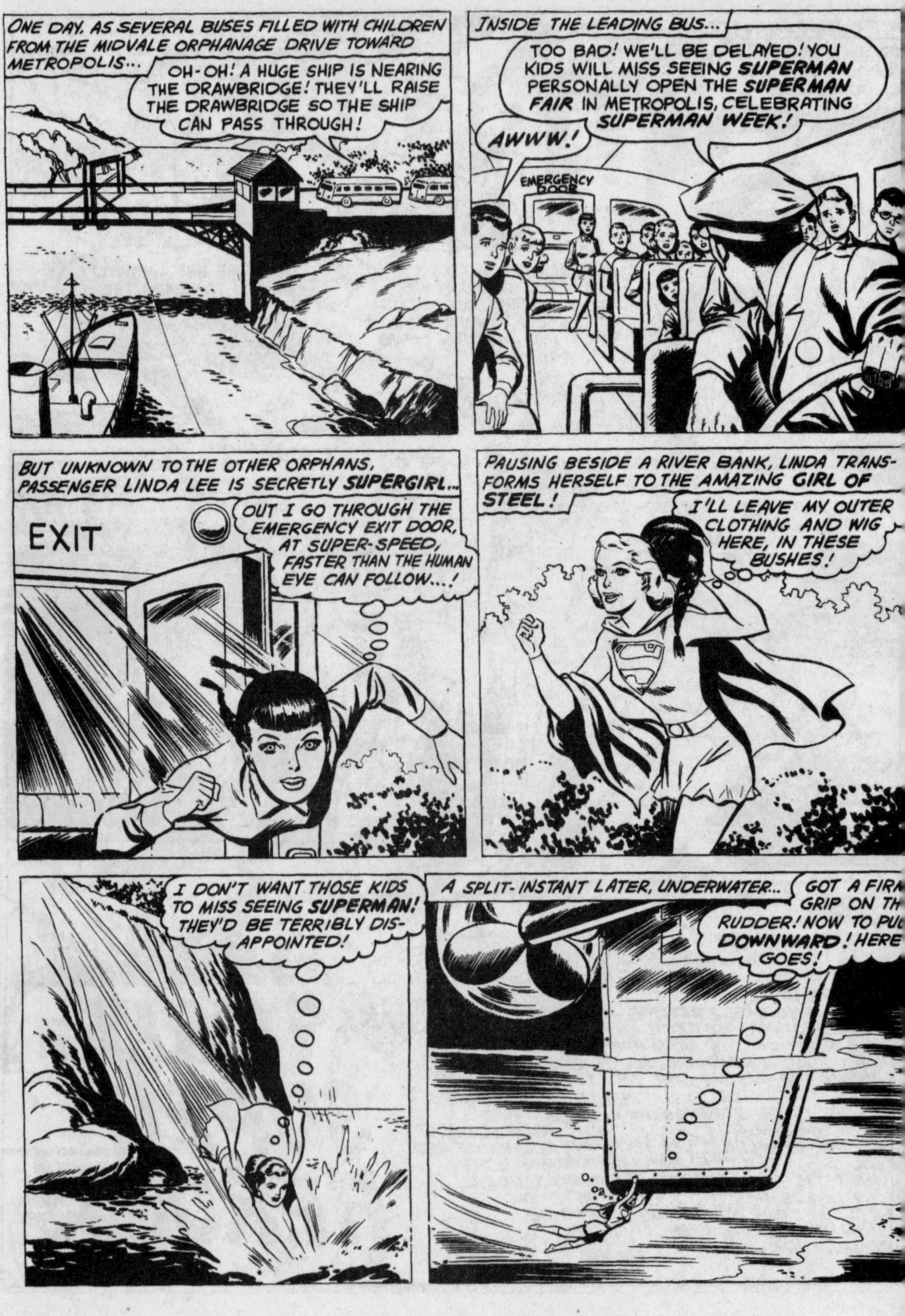
ONE DAY, AS SEVERAL BUSES FILLED WITH CHILDREN FROM THE MIDVALE ORPHANAGE DRIVE TOWARD METROPOLIS...
OH-OH! A HUGE SHIP IS NEARING THE DRAWBRIDGE! THEY'LL RAISE THE DRAWBRIDGE SO THE SHIP CAN PASS THROUGH!
INSIDE THE LEADING BUS...
TOO BAD! WE'LL BE DELAYED! YOU KIDS WILL MISS SEEING SUPERMAN PERSONALLY OPEN THE SUPERMAN FAIR IN METROPOLIS, CELEBRATING SUPERMAN WEEK!
AWWW!
EMERGENCY DOOR
BUT UNKNOWN TO THE OTHER ORPHANS, PASSENGER LINDA LEE IS SECRETLY SUPERGIRL...
EXIT
OUT I GO THROUGH THE EMERGENCY EXIT DOOR, AT SUPER-SPEED, FASTER THAN THE HUMAN EYE CAN FOLLOW...!
PAUSING BESIDE A RIVER BANK, LINDA TRANSFORMS HERSELF TO THE AMAZING GIRL OF STEEL!
I'LL LEAVE MY OUTER CLOTHING AND WIG HERE, IN THESE BUSHES!
I DON'T WANT THOSE KIDS TO MISS SEEING SUPERMAN! THEY'D BE TERRIBLY DISAPPOINTED!
A SPLIT-INSTANT LATER, UNDERWATER...

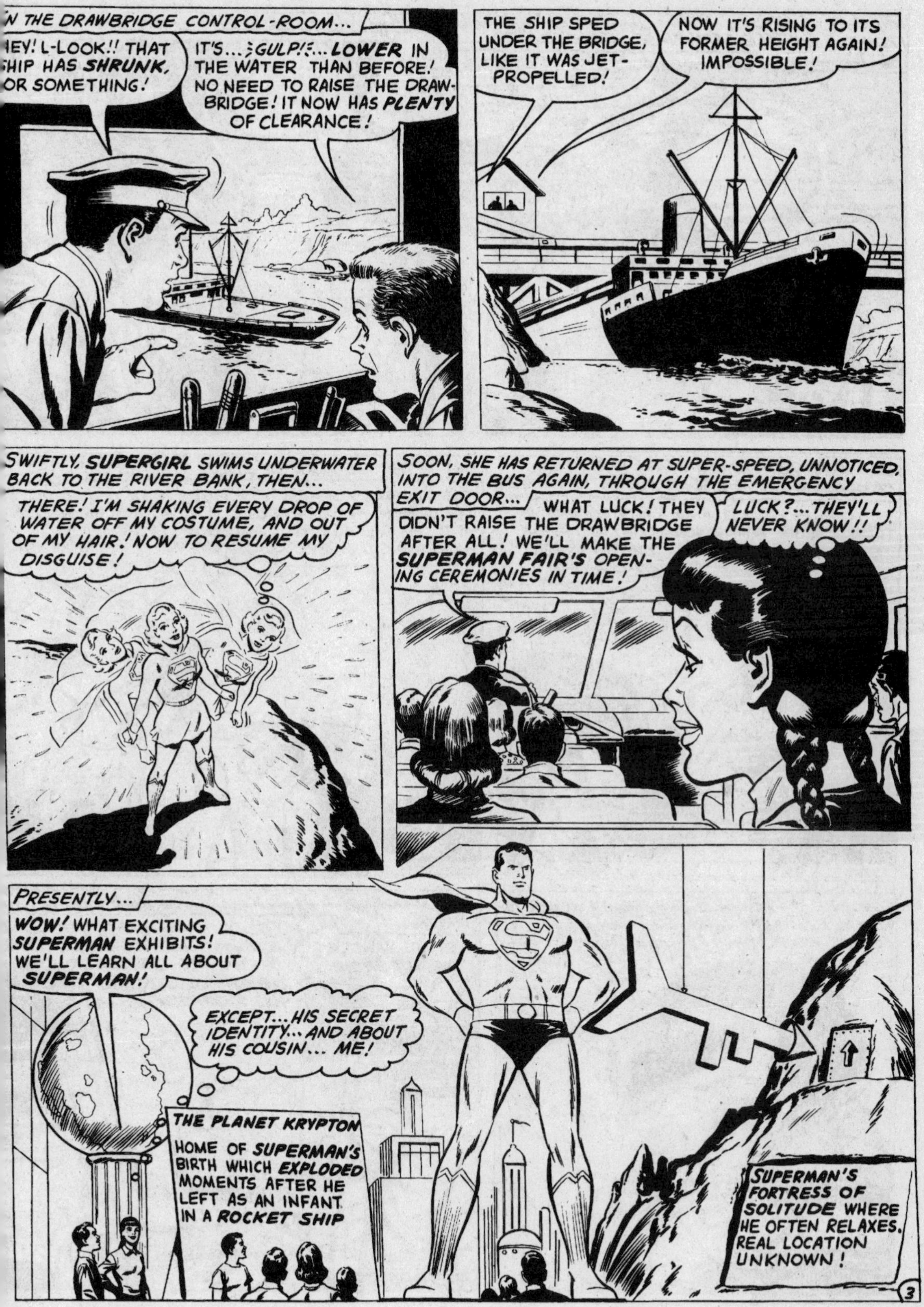

N THE DRAWBRIDGE CONTROL-ROOM...
HEY! L-LOOK!! THAT SHIP HAS SHRUNK, OR SOMETHING!
IT'S...GULP!...LOWER IN THE WATER THAN BEFORE! NO NEED TO RAISE THE DRAW-BRIDGE! IT NOW HAS PLENTY OF CLEARANCE!
THE SHIP SPED UNDER THE BRIDGE, LIKE IT WAS JET-PROPELLED!
NOW IT'S RISING TO ITS FORMER HEIGHT AGAIN! IMPOSSIBLE!
SWIFTLY, SUPERGIRL SWIMS UNDERWATER BACK TO THE RIVER BANK, THEN...
THERE! I'M SHAKING EVERY DROP OF WATER OFF MY COSTUME, AND OUT OF MY HAIR! NOW TO RESUME MY DISGUISE!
SOON, SHE HAS RETURNED AT SUPER-SPEED, UNNOTICED, INTO THE BUS AGAIN, THROUGH THE EMERGENCY EXIT DOOR...
WHAT LUCK! THEY DIDN'T RAISE THE DRAWBRIDGE AFTER ALL! WE'LL MAKE THE SUPERMAN FAIR'S OPEN-ING CEREMONIES IN TIME!
LUCK?...THEY'LL NEVER KNOW!!
PRESENTLY...
WOW! WHAT EXCITING SUPERMAN EXHIBITS! WE'LL LEARN ALL ABOUT SUPERMAN!
EXCEPT...HIS SECRET IDENTITY...AND ABOUT HIS COUSIN... ME!
THE PLANET KRYPTON
HOME OF SUPERMAN'S BIRTH WHICH EXPLODED MOMENTS AFTER HE LEFT AS AN INFANT IN A ROCKET SHIP
SUPERMAN'S FORTRESS OF SOLITUDE WHERE HE OFTEN RELAXES. REAL LOCATION UNKNOWN!
3

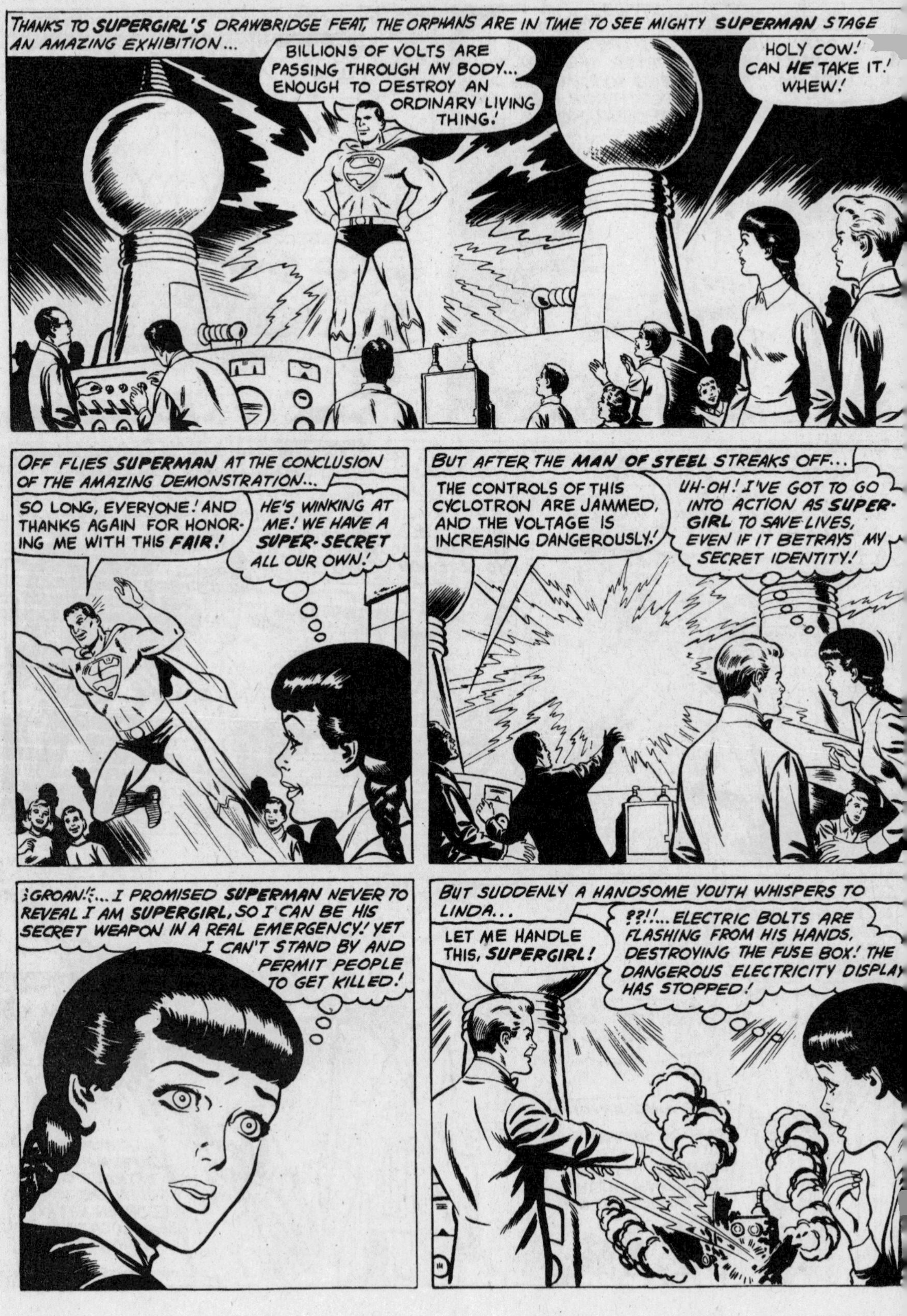
THANKS TO SUPERGIRL'S DRAWBRIDGE FEAT, THE ORPHANS ARE IN TIME TO SEE MIGHTY SUPERMAN STAGE AN AMAZING EXHIBITION...
BILLIONS OF VOLTS ARE PASSING THROUGH MY BODY... ENOUGH TO DESTROY AN ORDINARY LIVING THING!
HOLY COW! CAN HE TAKE IT! WHEW!
OFF FLIES SUPERMAN AT THE CONCLUSION OF THE AMAZING DEMONSTRATION...
SO LONG, EVERYONE! AND THANKS AGAIN FOR HONORING ME WITH THIS FAIR!
HE'S WINKING AT ME! WE HAVE A SUPER-SECRET ALL OUR OWN!
BUT AFTER THE MAN OF STEEL STREAKS OFF...
THE CONTROLS OF THIS CYCLOTRON ARE JAMMED, AND THE VOLTAGE IS INCREASING DANGEROUSLY!
UH-OH! I'VE GOT TO GO INTO ACTION AS SUPERGIRL TO SAVE LIVES, EVEN IF IT BETRAYS MY SECRET IDENTITY!
GROAN!... I PROMISED SUPERMAN NEVER TO REVEAL I AM SUPERGIRL, SO I CAN BE HIS SECRET WEAPON IN A REAL EMERGENCY! YET I CAN'T STAND BY AND PERMIT PEOPLE TO GET KILLED!
BUT SUDDENLY A HANDSOME YOUTH WHISPERS TO LINDA...
LET ME HANDLE THIS, SUPERGIRL!
??!... ELECTRIC BOLTS ARE FLASHING FROM HIS HANDS, DESTROYING THE FUSE BOX! THE DANGEROUS ELECTRICITY DISPLA HAS STOPPED!

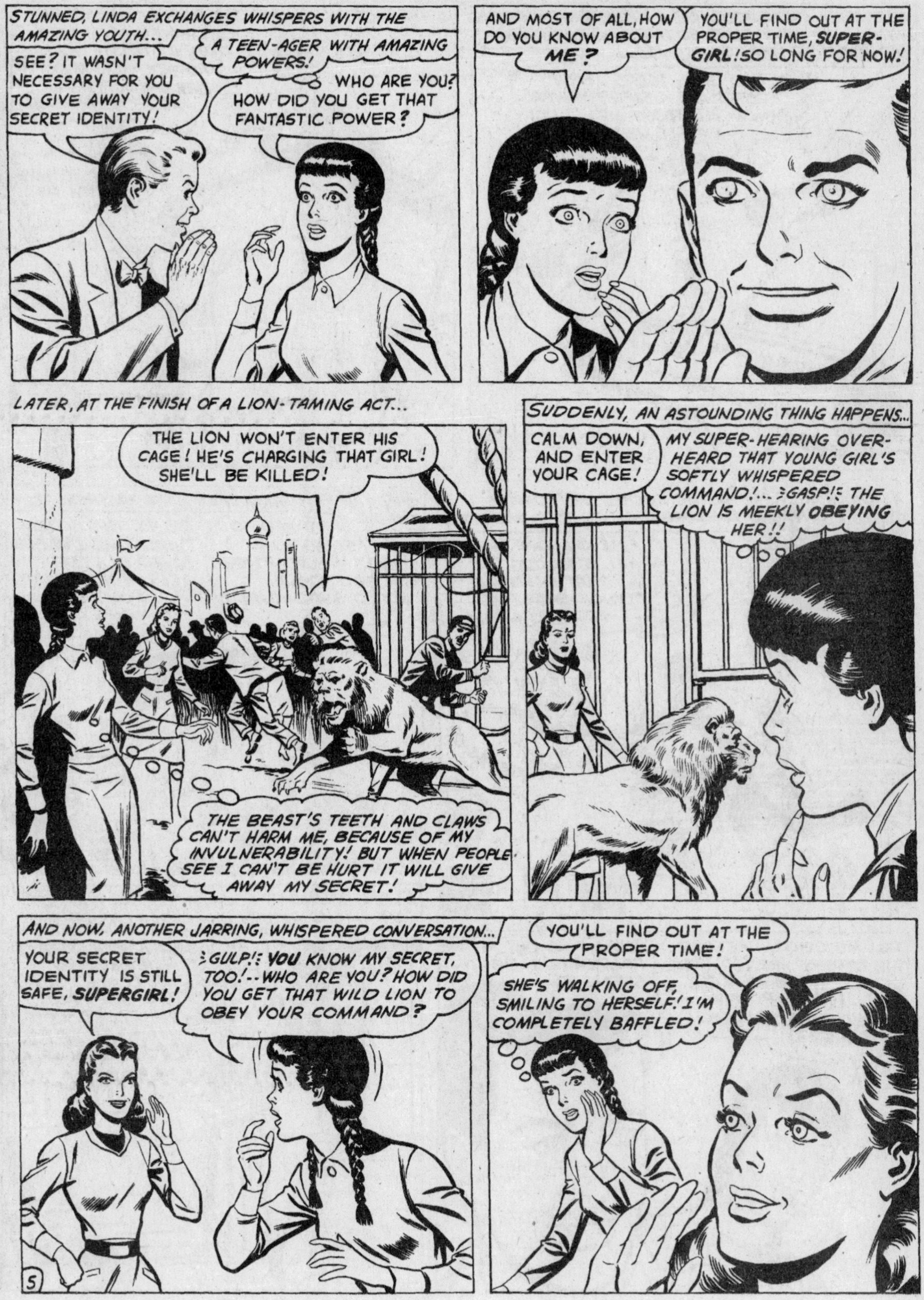
STUNNED, LINDA EXCHANGES WHISPERS WITH THE AMAZING YOUTH...
SEE? IT WASN'T NECESSARY FOR YOU TO GIVE AWAY YOUR SECRET IDENTITY!
A TEEN-AGER WITH AMAZING POWERS!
WHO ARE YOU? HOW DID YOU GET THAT FANTASTIC POWER?
AND MOST OF ALL, HOW DO YOU KNOW ABOUT ME?
YOU'LL FIND OUT AT THE PROPER TIME, SUPERGIRL! SO LONG FOR NOW!
LATER, AT THE FINISH OF A LION-TAMING ACT...
THE LION WON'T ENTER HIS CAGE! HE'S CHARGING THAT GIRL! SHE'LL BE KILLED!
THE BEAST'S TEETH AND CLAWS CAN'T HARM ME, BECAUSE OF MY INVULNERABILITY! BUT WHEN PEOPLE SEE I CAN'T BE HURT IT WILL GIVE AWAY MY SECRET!
SUDDENLY, AN ASTOUNDING THING HAPPENS...
CALM DOWN, AND ENTER YOUR CAGE!
MY SUPER-HEARING OVERHEARD THAT YOUNG GIRL'S SOFTLY WHISPERED COMMAND!... GASP! THE LION IS MEEKLY OBEYING HER!!
AND NOW, ANOTHER JARRING, WHISPERED CONVERSATION...
YOUR SECRET IDENTITY IS STILL SAFE, SUPERGIRL!
GULP! YOU KNOW MY SECRET, TOO!-- WHO ARE YOU? HOW DID YOU GET THAT WILD LION TO OBEY YOUR COMMAND?
5
YOU'LL FIND OUT AT THE PROPER TIME!
SHE'S WALKING OFF, SMILING TO HERSELF! I'M COMPLETELY BAFFLED!

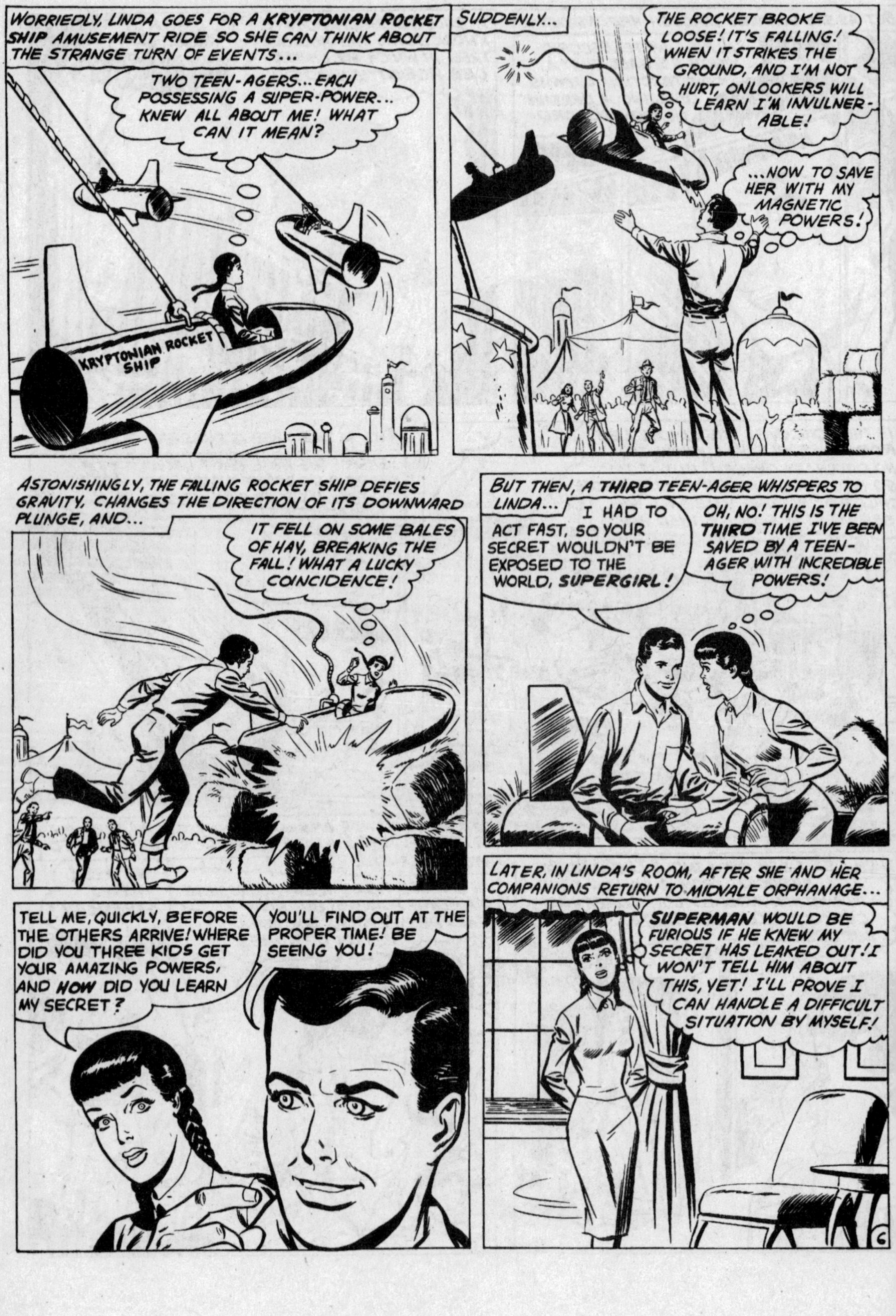
WORRIEDLY, LINDA GOES FOR A KRYPTONIAN ROCKET SHIP AMUSEMENT RIDE SO SHE CAN THINK ABOUT THE STRANGE TURN OF EVENTS...
TWO TEEN-AGERS... EACH POSSESSING A SUPER-POWER... KNEW ALL ABOUT ME! WHAT CAN IT MEAN?
KRYPTONIAN ROCKET SHIP
SUDDENLY...
THE ROCKET BROKE LOOSE! IT'S FALLING! WHEN IT STRIKES THE GROUND, AND I'M NOT HURT, ONLOOKERS WILL LEARN I'M INVULNERABLE!
...NOW TO SAVE HER WITH MY MAGNETIC POWERS!
ASTONISHINGLY, THE FALLING ROCKET SHIP DEFIES GRAVITY, CHANGES THE DIRECTION OF ITS DOWNWARD PLUNGE, AND...
IT FELL ON SOME BALES OF HAY, BREAKING THE FALL! WHAT A LUCKY COINCIDENCE!
BUT THEN, A THIRD TEEN-AGER WHISPERS TO LINDA...
I HAD TO ACT FAST, SO YOUR SECRET WOULDN'T BE EXPOSED TO THE WORLD, SUPERGIRL!
OH, NO! THIS IS THE THIRD TIME I'VE BEEN SAVED BY A TEEN-AGER WITH INCREDIBLE POWERS!
TELL ME, QUICKLY, BEFORE THE OTHERS ARRIVE! WHERE DID YOU THREE KIDS GET YOUR AMAZING POWERS, AND HOW DID YOU LEARN MY SECRET?
YOU'LL FIND OUT AT THE PROPER TIME! BE SEEING YOU!
LATER, IN LINDA'S ROOM, AFTER SHE AND HER COMPANIONS RETURN TO MIDVALE ORPHANAGE...
SUPERMAN WOULD BE FURIOUS IF HE KNEW MY SECRET HAS LEAKED OUT! I WON'T TELL HIM ABOUT THIS, YET! I'LL PROVE I CAN HANDLE A DIFFICULT SITUATION BY MYSELF!
6

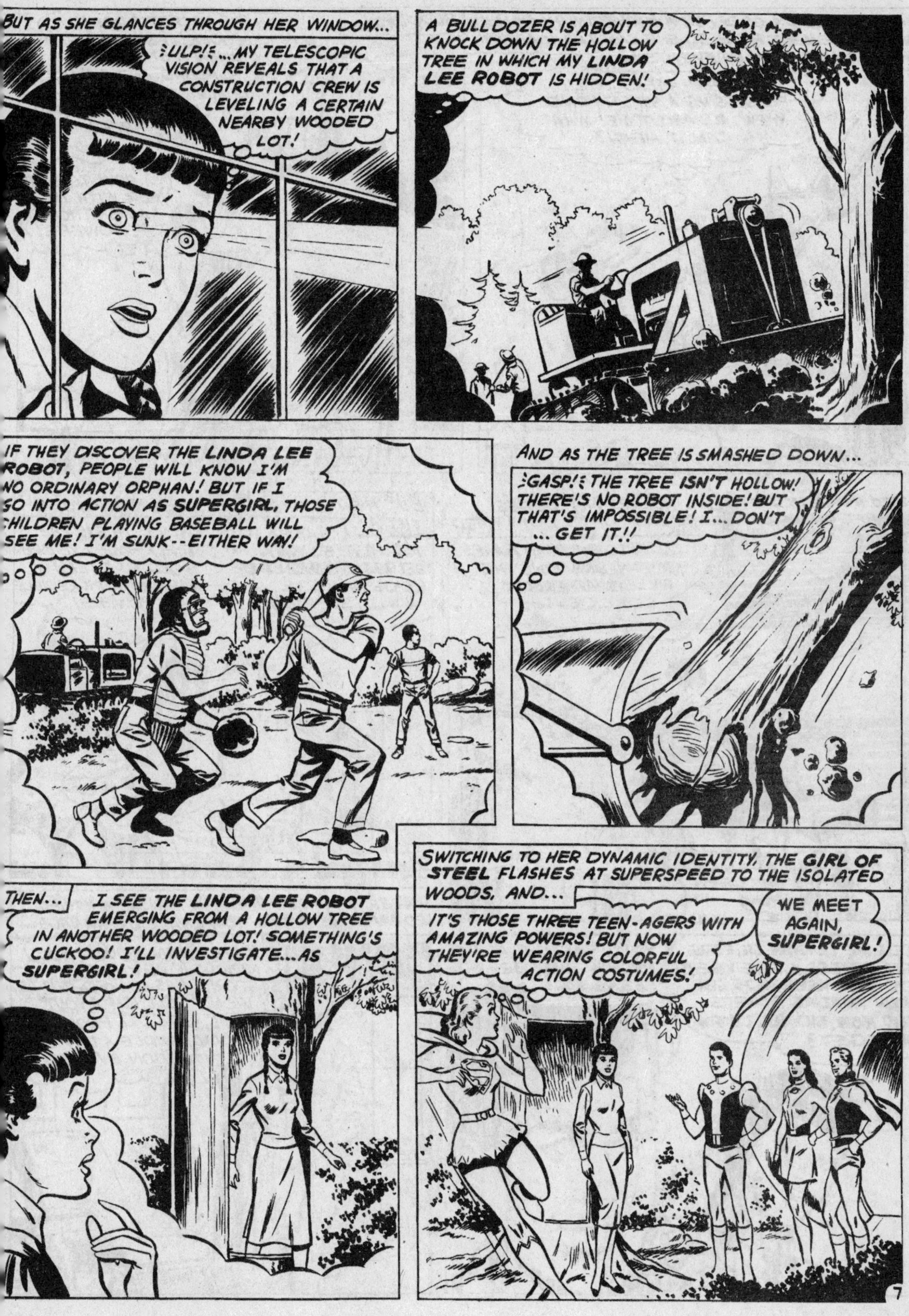
BUT AS SHE GLANCES THROUGH HER WINDOW...
ULP! ...MY TELESCOPIC VISION REVEALS THAT A CONSTRUCTION CREW IS LEVELING A CERTAIN NEARBY WOODED LOT!
A BULLDOZER IS ABOUT TO KNOCK DOWN THE HOLLOW TREE IN WHICH MY LINDA LEE ROBOT IS HIDDEN!
IF THEY DISCOVER THE LINDA LEE ROBOT, PEOPLE WILL KNOW I'M NO ORDINARY ORPHAN! BUT IF I GO INTO ACTION AS SUPERGIRL, THOSE CHILDREN PLAYING BASEBALL WILL SEE ME! I'M SUNK--EITHER WAY!
AND AS THE TREE IS SMASHED DOWN...
GASP! THE TREE ISN'T HOLLOW! THERE'S NO ROBOT INSIDE! BUT THAT'S IMPOSSIBLE! I... DON'T ... GET IT!!
THEN...
I SEE THE LINDA LEE ROBOT EMERGING FROM A HOLLOW TREE IN ANOTHER WOODED LOT! SOMETHING'S CUCKOO! I'LL INVESTIGATE...AS SUPERGIRL!
SWITCHING TO HER DYNAMIC IDENTITY, THE GIRL OF STEEL FLASHES AT SUPERSPEED TO THE ISOLATED WOODS, AND...
IT'S THOSE THREE TEEN-AGERS WITH AMAZING POWERS! BUT NOW THEY'RE WEARING COLORFUL ACTION COSTUMES!
WE MEET AGAIN, SUPERGIRL!
7

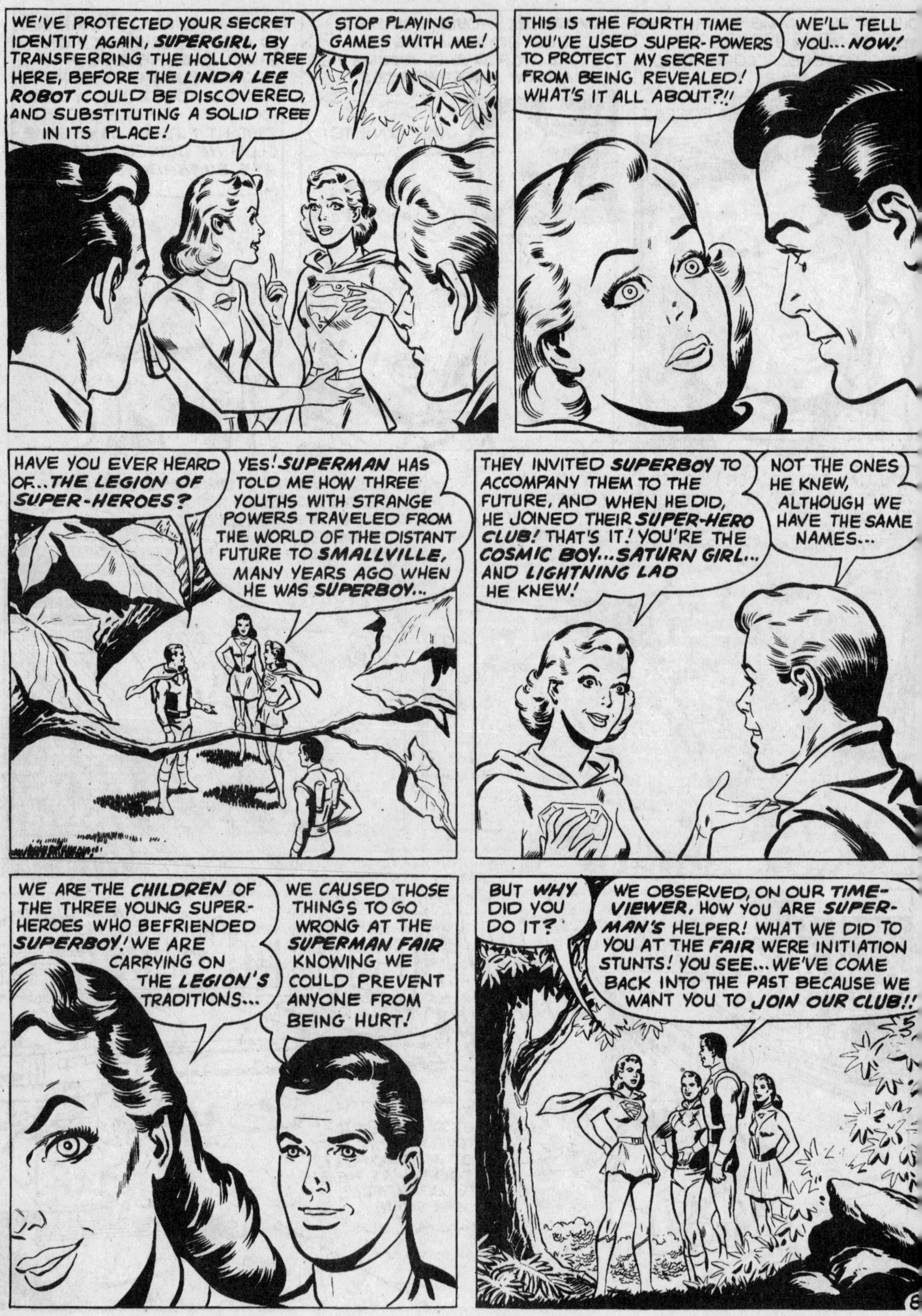
WE'VE PROTECTED YOUR SECRET IDENTITY AGAIN, SUPERGIRL, BY TRANSFERRING THE HOLLOW TREE HERE, BEFORE THE LINDA LEE ROBOT COULD BE DISCOVERED, AND SUBSTITUTING A SOLID TREE IN ITS PLACE!
STOP PLAYING GAMES WITH ME!
THIS IS THE FOURTH TIME YOU'VE USED SUPER-POWERS TO PROTECT MY SECRET FROM BEING REVEALED! WHAT'S IT ALL ABOUT?!!
WE'LL TELL YOU... NOW!
HAVE YOU EVER HEARD OF... THE LEGION OF SUPER-HEROES?
YES! SUPERMAN HAS TOLD ME HOW THREE YOUTHS WITH STRANGE POWERS TRAVELED FROM THE WORLD OF THE DISTANT FUTURE TO SMALLVILLE, MANY YEARS AGO WHEN HE WAS SUPERBOY...
THEY INVITED SUPERBOY TO ACCOMPANY THEM TO THE FUTURE, AND WHEN HE DID, HE JOINED THEIR SUPER-HERO CLUB! THAT'S IT! YOU'RE THE COSMIC BOY... SATURN GIRL... AND LIGHTNING LAD HE KNEW!
NOT THE ONES HE KNEW, ALTHOUGH WE HAVE THE SAME NAMES...
WE ARE THE CHILDREN OF THE THREE YOUNG SUPER-HEROES WHO BEFRIENDED SUPERBOY! WE ARE CARRYING ON THE LEGION'S TRADITIONS...
WE CAUSED THOSE THINGS TO GO WRONG AT THE SUPERMAN FAIR KNOWING WE COULD PREVENT ANYONE FROM BEING HURT!
BUT WHY DID YOU DO IT?
WE OBSERVED, ON OUR TIME-VIEWER, HOW YOU ARE SUPERMAN'S HELPER! WHAT WE DID TO YOU AT THE FAIR WERE INITIATION STUNTS! YOU SEE... WE'VE COME BACK INTO THE PAST BECAUSE WE WANT YOU TO JOIN OUR CLUB!!
8

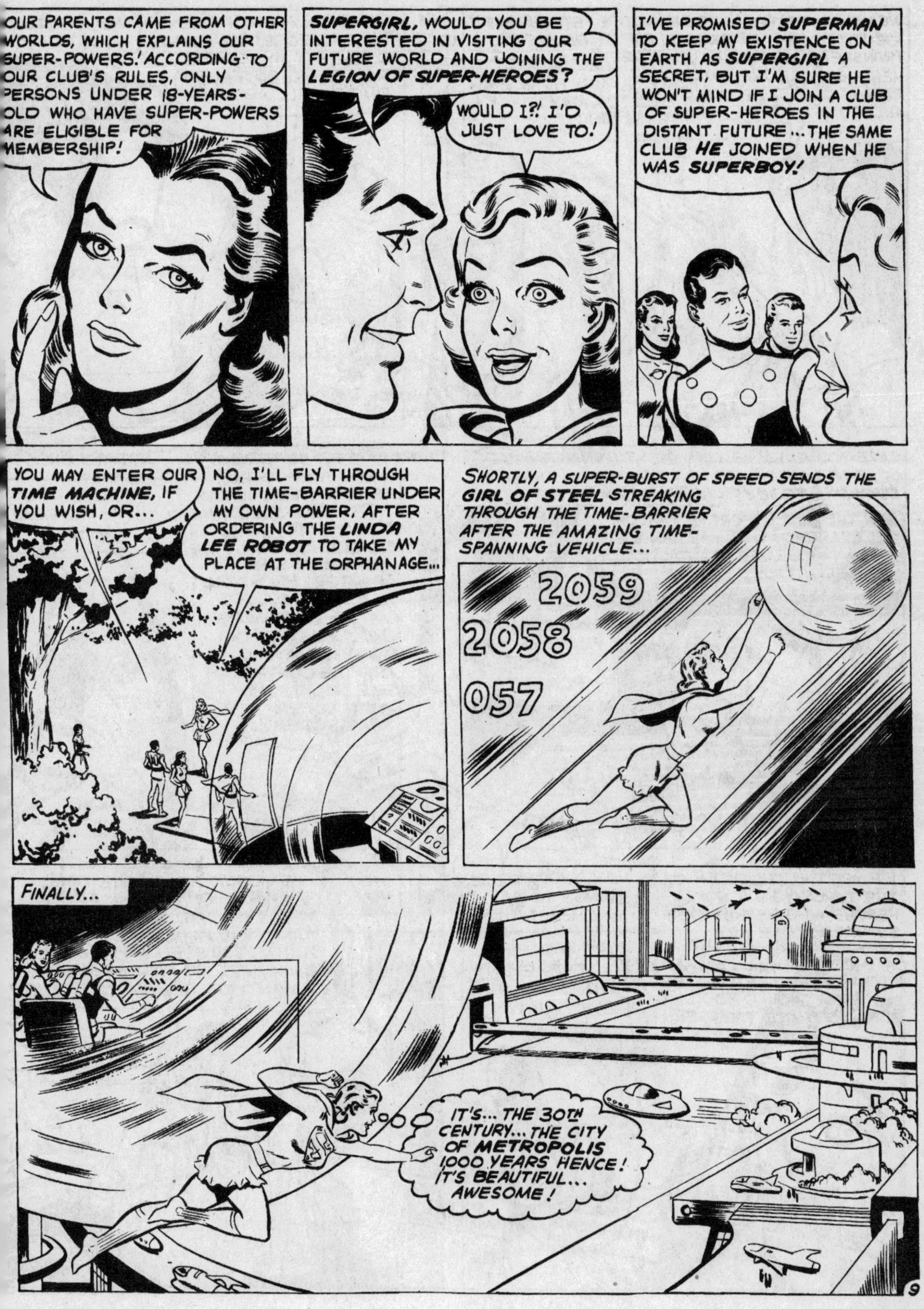
OUR PARENTS CAME FROM OTHER WORLDS, WHICH EXPLAINS OUR SUPER-POWERS! ACCORDING TO OUR CLUB'S RULES, ONLY PERSONS UNDER 18-YEARS-OLD WHO HAVE SUPER-POWERS ARE ELIGIBLE FOR MEMBERSHIP!
SUPERGIRL, WOULD YOU BE INTERESTED IN VISITING OUR FUTURE WORLD AND JOINING THE LEGION OF SUPER-HEROES?
WOULD I?! I'D JUST LOVE TO!
I'VE PROMISED SUPERMAN TO KEEP MY EXISTENCE ON EARTH AS SUPERGIRL A SECRET, BUT I'M SURE HE WON'T MIND IF I JOIN A CLUB OF SUPER-HEROES IN THE DISTANT FUTURE... THE SAME CLUB HE JOINED WHEN HE WAS SUPERBOY!
YOU MAY ENTER OUR TIME MACHINE, IF YOU WISH, OR...
NO, I'LL FLY THROUGH THE TIME-BARRIER UNDER MY OWN POWER, AFTER ORDERING THE LINDA LEE ROBOT TO TAKE MY PLACE AT THE ORPHANAGE...
SHORTLY, A SUPER-BURST OF SPEED SENDS THE GIRL OF STEEL STREAKING THROUGH THE TIME-BARRIER AFTER THE AMAZING TIME-SPANNING VEHICLE...
2059
2058
057
FINALLY...
IT'S... THE 30TH CENTURY... THE CITY OF METROPOLIS 1000 YEARS HENCE! IT'S BEAUTIFUL... AWESOME!
9

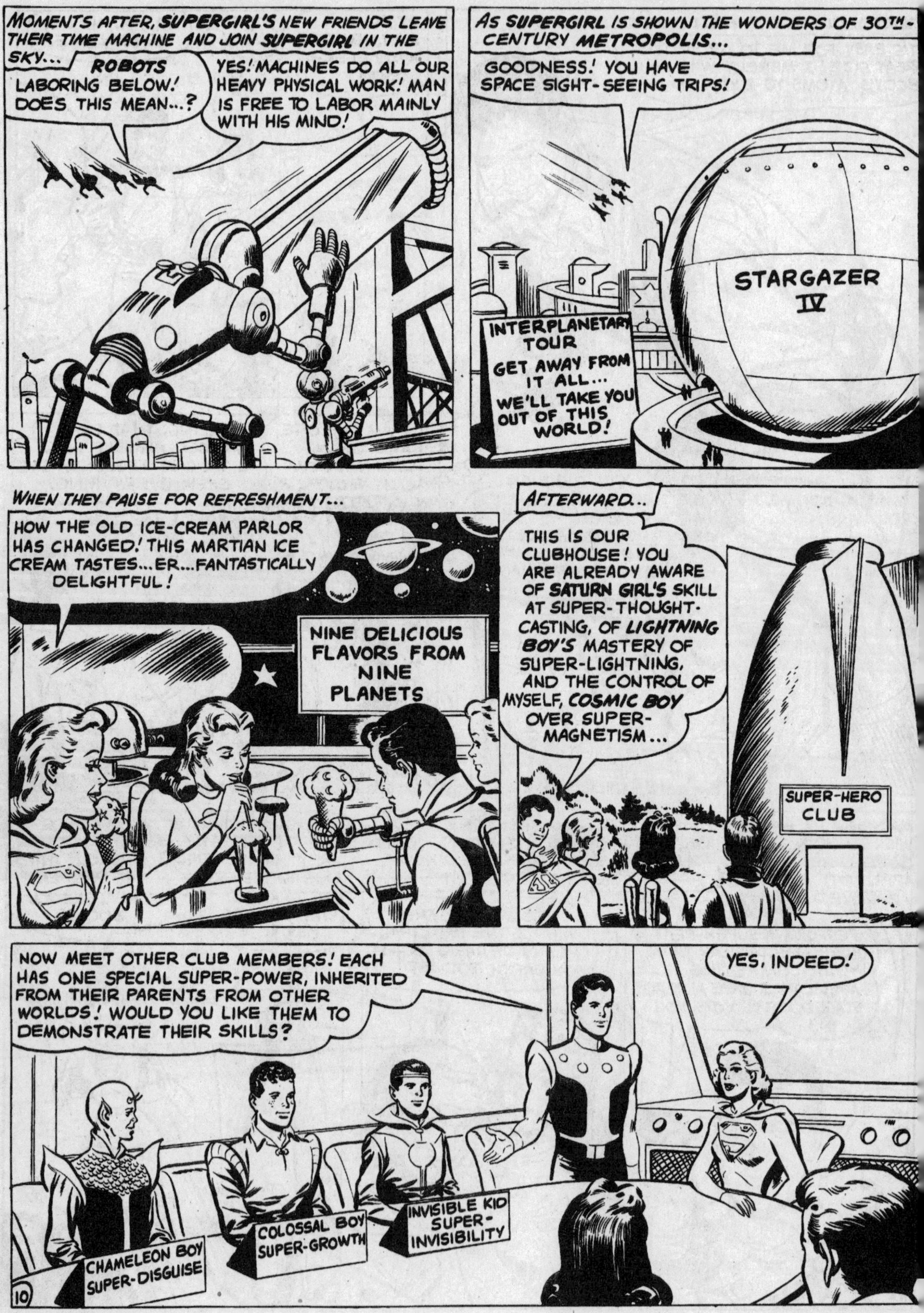
MOMENTS AFTER, SUPERGIRL'S NEW FRIENDS LEAVE THEIR TIME MACHINE AND JOIN SUPERGIRL IN THE SKY...
ROBOTS LABORING BELOW! DOES THIS MEAN...?
YES! MACHINES DO ALL OUR HEAVY PHYSICAL WORK! MAN IS FREE TO LABOR MAINLY WITH HIS MIND!
AS SUPERGIRL IS SHOWN THE WONDERS OF 30TH-CENTURY METROPOLIS...
GOODNESS! YOU HAVE SPACE SIGHT-SEEING TRIPS!
INTERPLANETARY TOUR GET AWAY FROM IT ALL... WE'LL TAKE YOU OUT OF THIS WORLD!
STARGAZER IV
WHEN THEY PAUSE FOR REFRESHMENT...
HOW THE OLD ICE-CREAM PARLOR HAS CHANGED! THIS MARTIAN ICE CREAM TASTES...ER...FANTASTICALLY DELIGHTFUL!
NINE DELICIOUS FLAVORS FROM NINE PLANETS
AFTERWARD...
THIS IS OUR CLUBHOUSE! YOU ARE ALREADY AWARE OF SATURN GIRL'S SKILL AT SUPER-THOUGHT-CASTING, OF LIGHTNING BOY'S MASTERY OF SUPER-LIGHTNING, AND THE CONTROL OF MYSELF, COSMIC BOY OVER SUPER-MAGNETISM...
SUPER-HERO CLUB
NOW MEET OTHER CLUB MEMBERS! EACH HAS ONE SPECIAL SUPER-POWER, INHERITED FROM THEIR PARENTS FROM OTHER WORLDS! WOULD YOU LIKE THEM TO DEMONSTRATE THEIR SKILLS?
YES, INDEED!
CHAMELEON BOY SUPER-DISGUISE
COLOSSAL BOY SUPER-GROWTH
INVISIBLE KID SUPER-INVISIBILITY
10

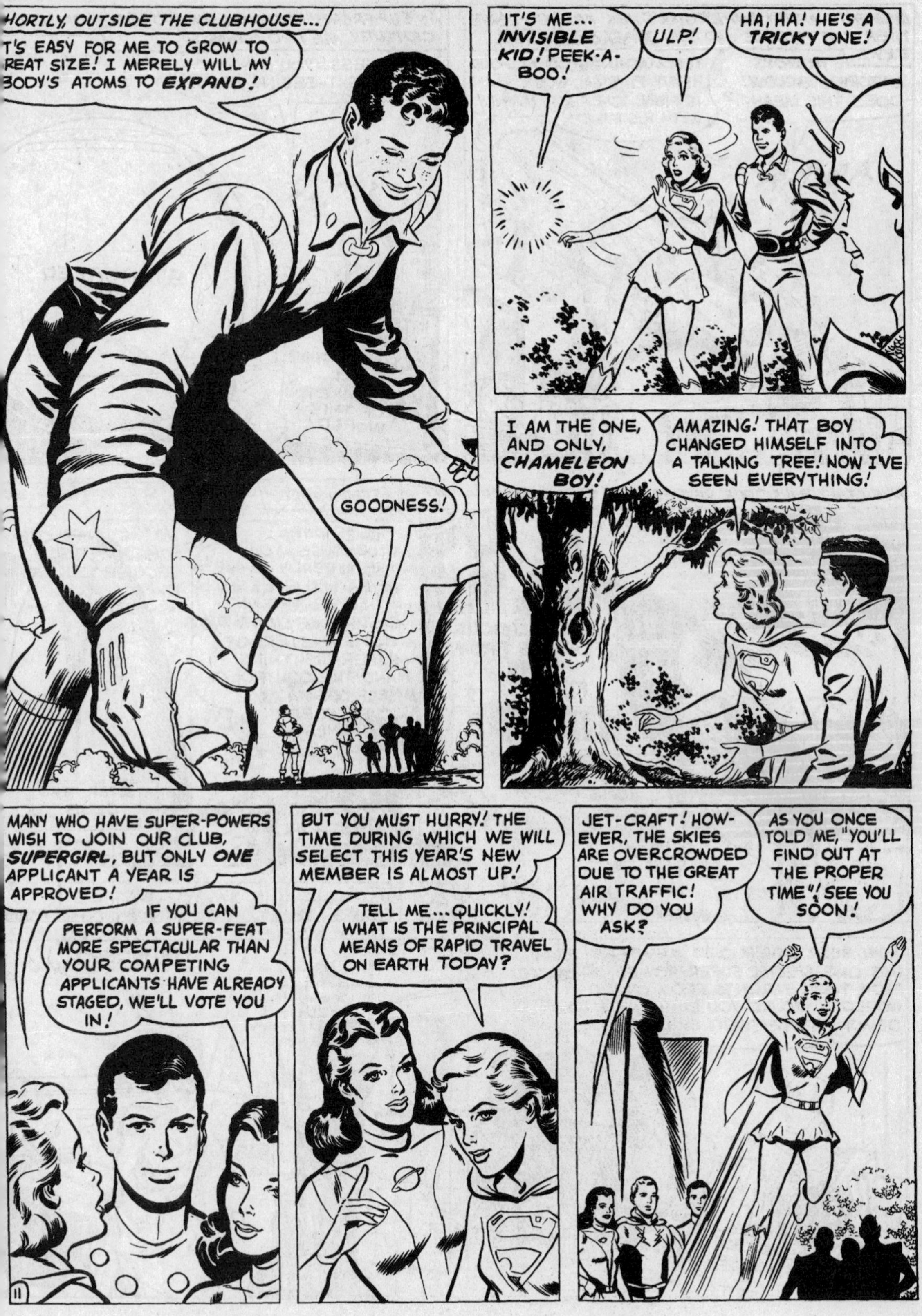
HORTLY, OUTSIDE THE CLUBHOUSE...
T'S EASY FOR ME TO GROW TO REAT SIZE! I MERELY WILL MY BODY'S ATOMS TO EXPAND!
GOODNESS!
IT'S ME... INVISIBLE KID! PEEK-A-BOO!
ULP!
HA, HA! HE'S A TRICKY ONE!
I AM THE ONE, AND ONLY, CHAMELEON BOY!
AMAZING! THAT BOY CHANGED HIMSELF INTO A TALKING TREE! NOW I'VE SEEN EVERYTHING!
MANY WHO HAVE SUPER-POWERS WISH TO JOIN OUR CLUB, SUPERGIRL, BUT ONLY ONE APPLICANT A YEAR IS APPROVED!
IF YOU CAN PERFORM A SUPER-FEAT MORE SPECTACULAR THAN YOUR COMPETING APPLICANTS HAVE ALREADY STAGED, WE'LL VOTE YOU IN!
11
BUT YOU MUST HURRY! THE TIME DURING WHICH WE WILL SELECT THIS YEAR'S NEW MEMBER IS ALMOST UP!
TELL ME... QUICKLY! WHAT IS THE PRINCIPAL MEANS OF RAPID TRAVEL ON EARTH TODAY?
JET-CRAFT! HOWEVER, THE SKIES ARE OVERCROWDED DUE TO THE GREAT AIR TRAFFIC! WHY DO YOU ASK?
AS YOU ONCE TOLD ME, "YOU'LL FIND OUT AT THE PROPER TIME"! SEE YOU SOON!

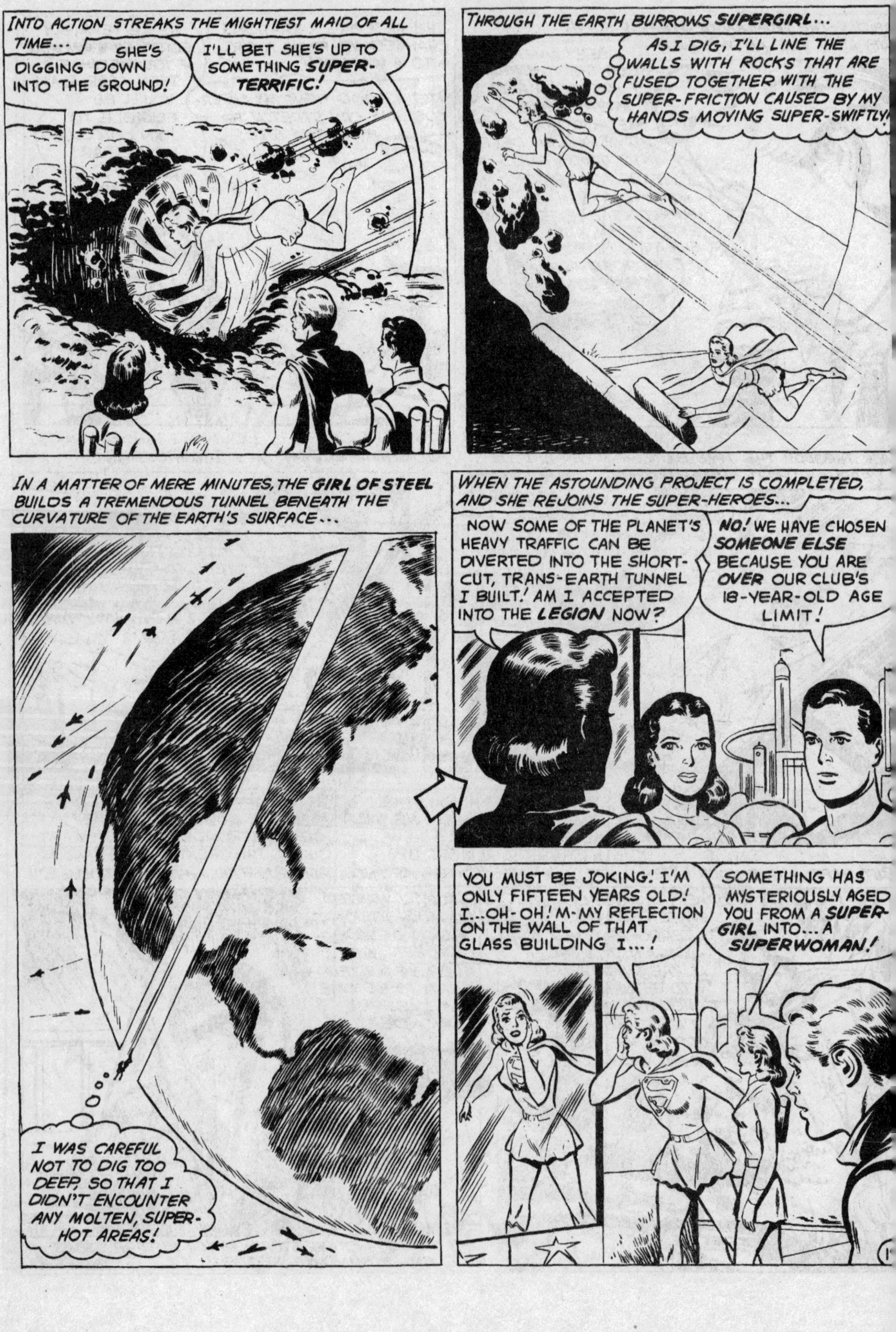
INTO ACTION STREAKS THE MIGHTIEST MAID OF ALL TIME...
SHE'S DIGGING DOWN INTO THE GROUND!
I'LL BET SHE'S UP TO SOMETHING SUPER-TERRIFIC!
THROUGH THE EARTH BURROWS SUPERGIRL...
AS I DIG, I'LL LINE THE WALLS WITH ROCKS THAT ARE FUSED TOGETHER WITH THE SUPER-FRICTION CAUSED BY MY HANDS MOVING SUPER-SWIFTLY!
IN A MATTER OF MERE MINUTES, THE GIRL OF STEEL BUILDS A TREMENDOUS TUNNEL BENEATH THE CURVATURE OF THE EARTH'S SURFACE...
I WAS CAREFUL NOT TO DIG TOO DEEP, SO THAT I DIDN'T ENCOUNTER ANY MOLTEN, SUPER-HOT AREAS!
WHEN THE ASTOUNDING PROJECT IS COMPLETED, AND SHE REJOINS THE SUPER-HEROES...
NOW SOME OF THE PLANET'S HEAVY TRAFFIC CAN BE DIVERTED INTO THE SHORT-CUT, TRANS-EARTH TUNNEL I BUILT! AM I ACCEPTED INTO THE LEGION NOW?
NO! WE HAVE CHOSEN SOMEONE ELSE BECAUSE YOU ARE OVER OUR CLUB'S 18-YEAR-OLD AGE LIMIT!
YOU MUST BE JOKING! I'M ONLY FIFTEEN YEARS OLD! I...OH-OH! M-MY REFLECTION ON THE WALL OF THAT GLASS BUILDING I...!
SOMETHING HAS MYSTERIOUSLY AGED YOU FROM A SUPER-GIRL INTO... A SUPERWOMAN!

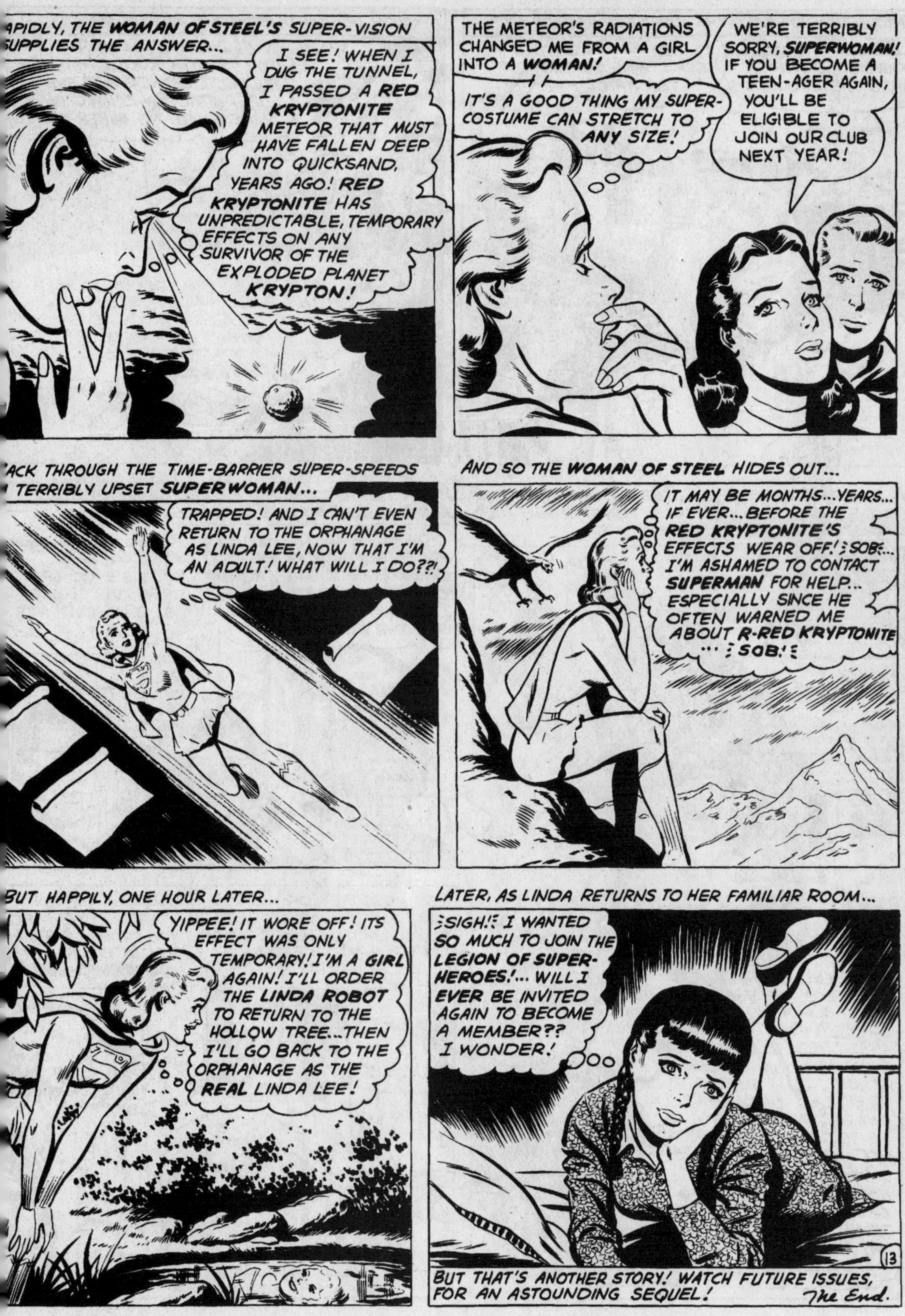
APIDLY, THE WOMAN OF STEEL'S SUPER-VISION SUPPLIES THE ANSWER...
I SEE! WHEN I DUG THE TUNNEL, I PASSED A RED KRYPTONITE METEOR THAT MUST HAVE FALLEN DEEP INTO QUICKSAND, YEARS AGO! RED KRYPTONITE HAS UNPREDICTABLE, TEMPORARY EFFECTS ON ANY SURVIVOR OF THE EXPLODED PLANET KRYPTON!
THE METEOR'S RADIATIONS CHANGED ME FROM A GIRL INTO A WOMAN!
IT'S A GOOD THING MY SUPER-COSTUME CAN STRETCH TO ANY SIZE!
WE'RE TERRIBLY SORRY, SUPERWOMAN! IF YOU BECOME A TEEN-AGER AGAIN, YOU'LL BE ELIGIBLE TO JOIN OUR CLUB NEXT YEAR!
ACK THROUGH THE TIME-BARRIER SUPER-SPEEDS TERRIBLY UPSET SUPERWOMAN...
TRAPPED! AND I CAN'T EVEN RETURN TO THE ORPHANAGE AS LINDA LEE, NOW THAT I'M AN ADULT! WHAT WILL I DO??!
AND SO THE WOMAN OF STEEL HIDES OUT...
IT MAY BE MONTHS...YEARS... IF EVER...BEFORE THE RED KRYPTONITE'S EFFECTS WEAR OFF! SOB... I'M ASHAMED TO CONTACT SUPERMAN FOR HELP... ESPECIALLY SINCE HE OFTEN WARNED ME ABOUT R-RED KRYPTONITE ... SOB!
BUT HAPPILY, ONE HOUR LATER...
YIPPEE! IT WORE OFF! ITS EFFECT WAS ONLY TEMPORARY! I'M A GIRL AGAIN! I'LL ORDER THE LINDA ROBOT TO RETURN TO THE HOLLOW TREE...THEN I'LL GO BACK TO THE ORPHANAGE AS THE REAL LINDA LEE!
LATER, AS LINDA RETURNS TO HER FAMILIAR ROOM...
SIGH! I WANTED SO MUCH TO JOIN THE LEGION OF SUPER-HEROES!... WILL I EVER BE INVITED AGAIN TO BECOME A MEMBER?? I WONDER!
13
BUT THAT'S ANOTHER STORY! WATCH FUTURE ISSUES, FOR AN ASTOUNDING SEQUEL! The End.

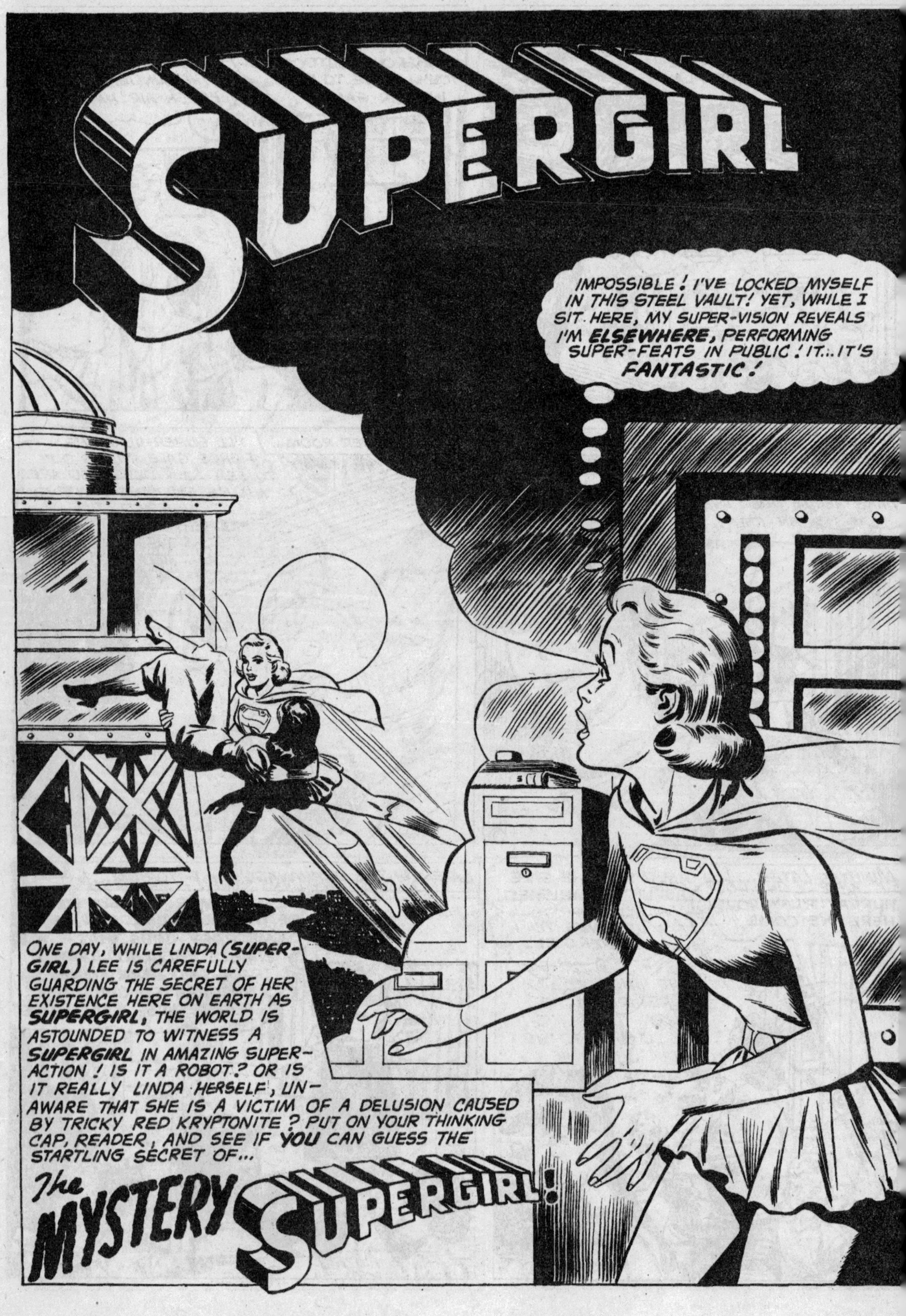
SUPERGIRL
IMPOSSIBLE! I'VE LOCKED MYSELF IN THIS STEEL VAULT! YET, WHILE I SIT HERE, MY SUPER-VISION REVEALS I'M ELSEWHERE, PERFORMING SUPER-FEATS IN PUBLIC! IT...IT'S FANTASTIC!
ONE DAY, WHILE LINDA (SUPERGIRL) LEE IS CAREFULLY GUARDING THE SECRET OF HER EXISTENCE HERE ON EARTH AS SUPERGIRL, THE WORLD IS ASTOUNDED TO WITNESS A SUPERGIRL IN AMAZING SUPER-ACTION! IS IT A ROBOT? OR IS IT REALLY LINDA HERSELF, UNAWARE THAT SHE IS A VICTIM OF A DELUSION CAUSED BY TRICKY RED KRYPTONITE? PUT ON YOUR THINKING CAP, READER, AND SEE IF YOU CAN GUESS THE STARTLING SECRET OF...
The MYSTERY SUPERGIRL!

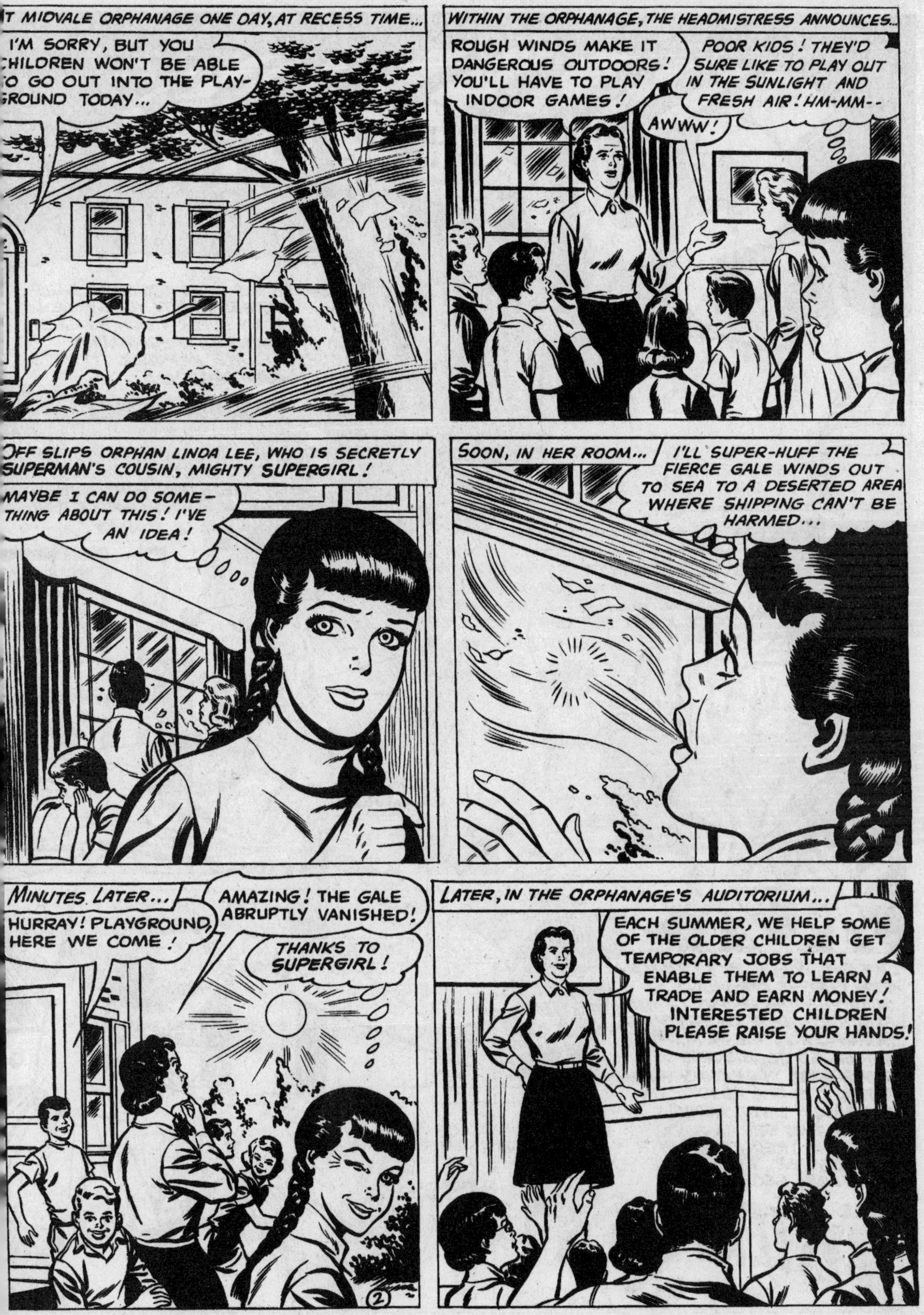
T MIDVALE ORPHANAGE ONE DAY, AT RECESS TIME...
I'M SORRY, BUT YOU HILDREN WON'T BE ABLE O GO OUT INTO THE PLAY-ROUND TODAY...
WITHIN THE ORPHANAGE, THE HEADMISTRESS ANNOUNCES...
ROUGH WINDS MAKE IT DANGEROUS OUTDOORS! YOU'LL HAVE TO PLAY INDOOR GAMES!
POOR KIDS! THEY'D SURE LIKE TO PLAY OUT IN THE SUNLIGHT AND FRESH AIR! HM-MM--
AWWW!
OFF SLIPS ORPHAN LINDA LEE, WHO IS SECRETLY SUPERMAN'S COUSIN, MIGHTY SUPERGIRL!
MAYBE I CAN DO SOME-THING ABOUT THIS! I'VE AN IDEA!
SOON, IN HER ROOM...
I'LL SUPER-HUFF THE FIERCE GALE WINDS OUT TO SEA TO A DESERTED AREA WHERE SHIPPING CAN'T BE HARMED...
MINUTES LATER...
HURRAY! PLAYGROUND, HERE WE COME!
AMAZING! THE GALE ABRUPTLY VANISHED!
THANKS TO SUPERGIRL!
2
LATER, IN THE ORPHANAGE'S AUDITORIUM...
EACH SUMMER, WE HELP SOME OF THE OLDER CHILDREN GET TEMPORARY JOBS THAT ENABLE THEM TO LEARN A TRADE AND EARN MONEY! INTERESTED CHILDREN PLEASE RAISE YOUR HANDS!

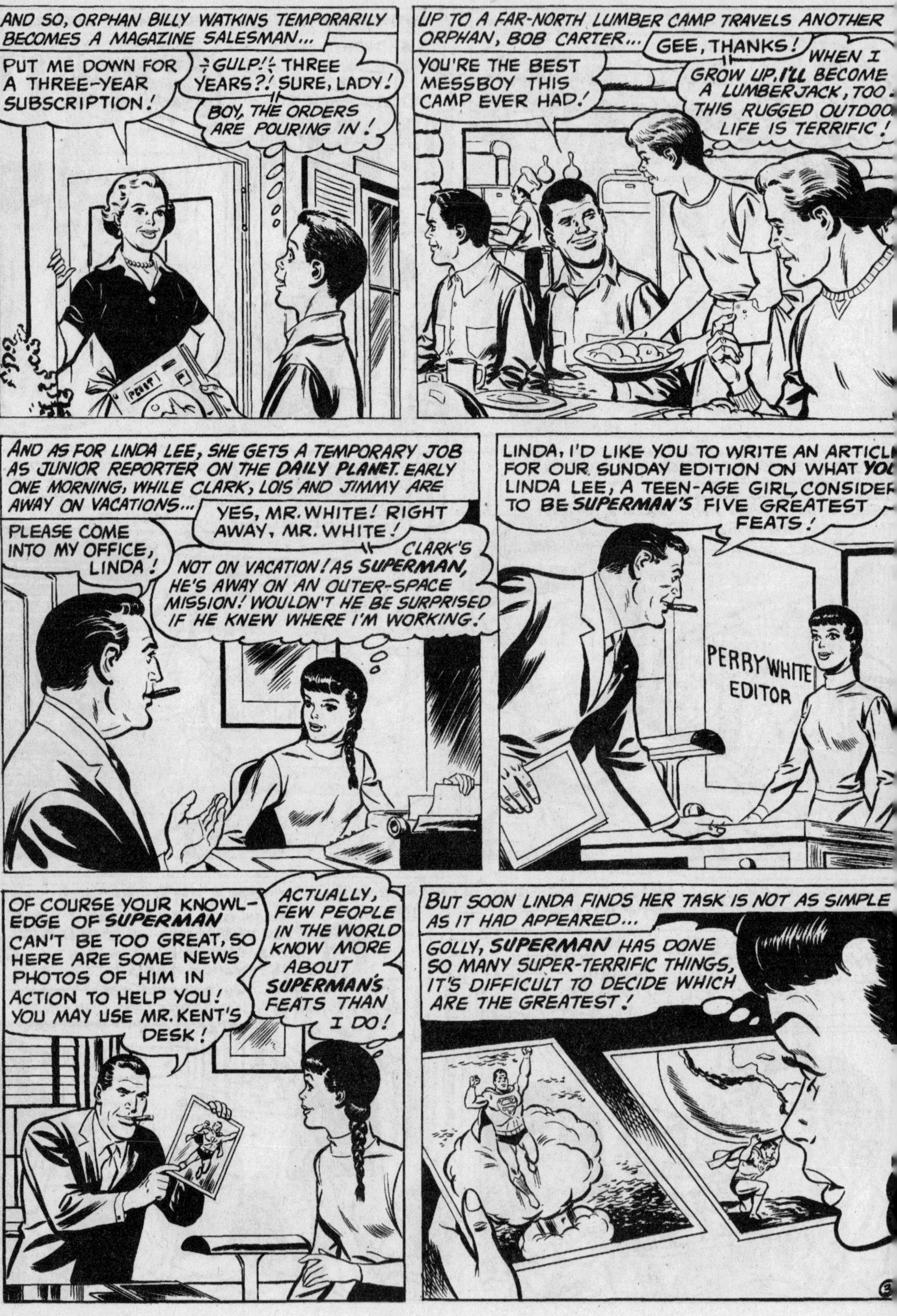
AND SO, ORPHAN BILLY WATKINS TEMPORARILY BECOMES A MAGAZINE SALESMAN...
PUT ME DOWN FOR A THREE-YEAR SUBSCRIPTION!
GULP! THREE YEARS?! SURE, LADY!
BOY, THE ORDERS ARE POURING IN!
UP TO A FAR-NORTH LUMBER CAMP TRAVELS ANOTHER ORPHAN, BOB CARTER...
YOU'RE THE BEST MESSBOY THIS CAMP EVER HAD!
GEE, THANKS!
WHEN I GROW UP, I'LL BECOME A LUMBERJACK, TOO. THIS RUGGED OUTDOO LIFE IS TERRIFIC!
AND AS FOR LINDA LEE, SHE GETS A TEMPORARY JOB AS JUNIOR REPORTER ON THE DAILY PLANET. EARLY ONE MORNING, WHILE CLARK, LOIS AND JIMMY ARE AWAY ON VACATIONS...
PLEASE COME INTO MY OFFICE, LINDA!
YES, MR. WHITE! RIGHT AWAY, MR. WHITE!
CLARK'S NOT ON VACATION! AS SUPERMAN, HE'S AWAY ON AN OUTER-SPACE MISSION! WOULDN'T HE BE SURPRISED IF HE KNEW WHERE I'M WORKING!
LINDA, I'D LIKE YOU TO WRITE AN ARTICL FOR OUR SUNDAY EDITION ON WHAT YO LINDA LEE, A TEEN-AGE GIRL, CONSIDE TO BE SUPERMAN'S FIVE GREATEST FEATS!
PERRY WHITE EDITOR
OF COURSE YOUR KNOWLEDGE OF SUPERMAN CAN'T BE TOO GREAT, SO HERE ARE SOME NEWS PHOTOS OF HIM IN ACTION TO HELP YOU! YOU MAY USE MR. KENT'S DESK!
ACTUALLY, FEW PEOPLE IN THE WORLD KNOW MORE ABOUT SUPERMAN'S FEATS THAN I DO!
BUT SOON LINDA FINDS HER TASK IS NOT AS SIMPLE AS IT HAD APPEARED...
GOLLY, SUPERMAN HAS DONE SO MANY SUPER-TERRIFIC THINGS, IT'S DIFFICULT TO DECIDE WHICH ARE THE GREATEST!

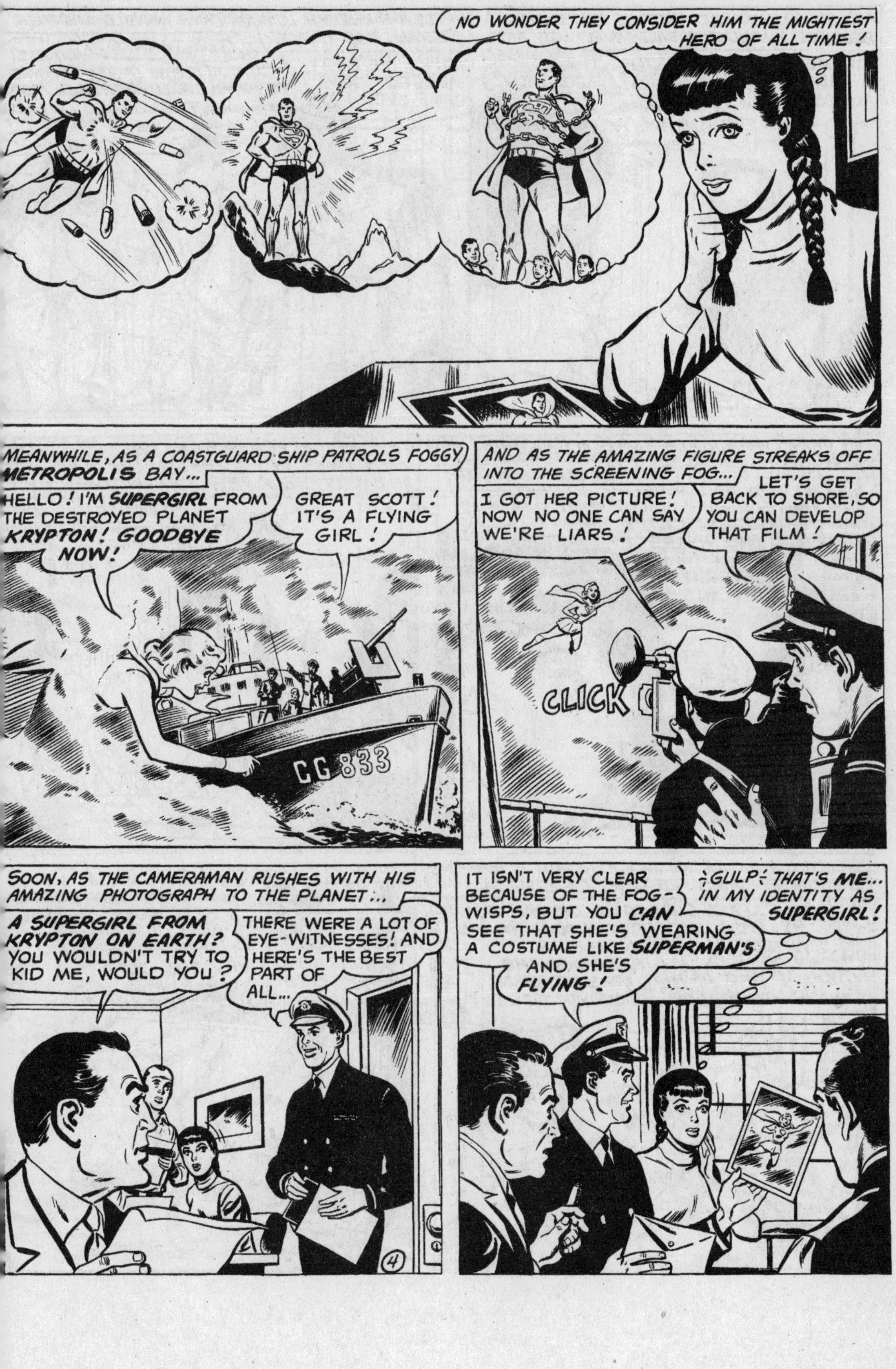
NO WONDER THEY CONSIDER HIM THE MIGHTIEST HERO OF ALL TIME!
MEANWHILE, AS A COASTGUARD SHIP PATROLS FOGGY METROPOLIS BAY...
HELLO! I'M SUPERGIRL FROM THE DESTROYED PLANET KRYPTON! GOODBYE NOW!
GREAT SCOTT! IT'S A FLYING GIRL!
CG 833
AND AS THE AMAZING FIGURE STREAKS OFF INTO THE SCREENING FOG...
I GOT HER PICTURE! NOW NO ONE CAN SAY WE'RE LIARS!
LET'S GET BACK TO SHORE, SO YOU CAN DEVELOP THAT FILM!
CLICK
SOON, AS THE CAMERAMAN RUSHES WITH HIS AMAZING PHOTOGRAPH TO THE PLANET...
A SUPERGIRL FROM KRYPTON ON EARTH? YOU WOULDN'T TRY TO KID ME, WOULD YOU?
THERE WERE A LOT OF EYE-WITNESSES! AND HERE'S THE BEST PART OF ALL...
4
IT ISN'T VERY CLEAR BECAUSE OF THE FOG-WISPS, BUT YOU CAN SEE THAT SHE'S WEARING A COSTUME LIKE SUPERMAN'S AND SHE'S FLYING!
÷GULP÷ THAT'S ME... IN MY IDENTITY AS SUPERGIRL!

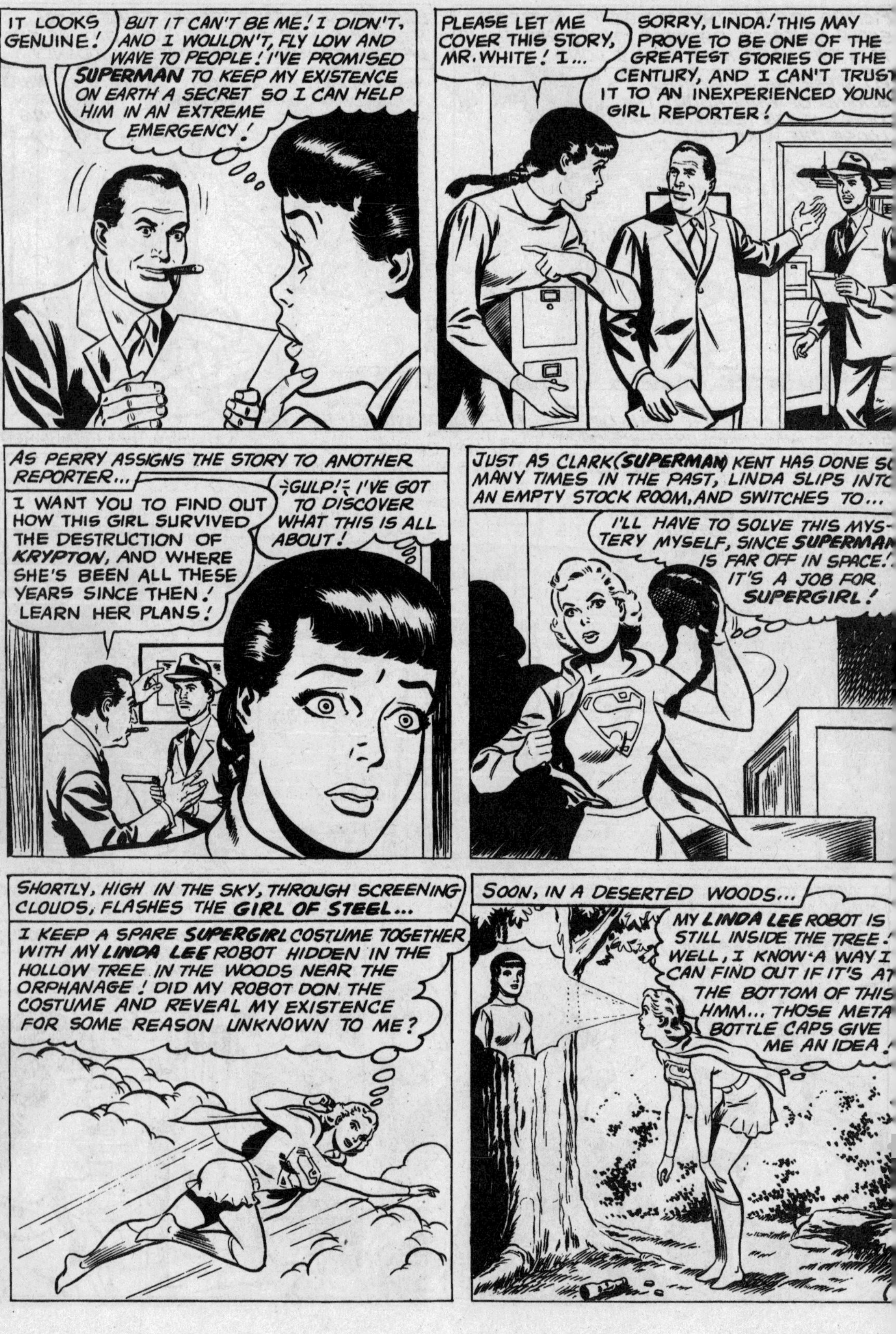
IT LOOKS GENUINE!
BUT IT CAN'T BE ME! I DIDN'T, AND I WOULDN'T, FLY LOW AND WAVE TO PEOPLE! I'VE PROMISED SUPERMAN TO KEEP MY EXISTENCE ON EARTH A SECRET SO I CAN HELP HIM IN AN EXTREME EMERGENCY!
PLEASE LET ME COVER THIS STORY, MR. WHITE! I...
SORRY, LINDA! THIS MAY PROVE TO BE ONE OF THE GREATEST STORIES OF THE CENTURY, AND I CAN'T TRUS IT TO AN INEXPERIENCED YOUN GIRL REPORTER!
AS PERRY ASSIGNS THE STORY TO ANOTHER REPORTER...
I WANT YOU TO FIND OUT HOW THIS GIRL SURVIVED THE DESTRUCTION OF KRYPTON, AND WHERE SHE'S BEEN ALL THESE YEARS SINCE THEN! LEARN HER PLANS!
GULP! I'VE GOT TO DISCOVER WHAT THIS IS ALL ABOUT!
JUST AS CLARK (SUPERMAN) KENT HAS DONE S MANY TIMES IN THE PAST, LINDA SLIPS INT AN EMPTY STOCK ROOM, AND SWITCHES TO...
I'LL HAVE TO SOLVE THIS MYSTERY MYSELF, SINCE SUPERMA IS FAR OFF IN SPACE! IT'S A JOB FOR SUPERGIRL!
SHORTLY, HIGH IN THE SKY, THROUGH SCREENING CLOUDS, FLASHES THE GIRL OF STEEL...
I KEEP A SPARE SUPERGIRL COSTUME TOGETHER WITH MY LINDA LEE ROBOT HIDDEN IN THE HOLLOW TREE IN THE WOODS NEAR THE ORPHANAGE! DID MY ROBOT DON THE COSTUME AND REVEAL MY EXISTENCE FOR SOME REASON UNKNOWN TO ME?
SOON, IN A DESERTED WOODS...
MY LINDA LEE ROBOT IS STILL INSIDE THE TREE! WELL, I KNOW A WAY I CAN FIND OUT IF IT'S A THE BOTTOM OF THIS HMM... THOSE META BOTTLE CAPS GIVE ME AN IDEA!

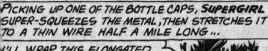

PICKING UP ONE OF THE BOTTLE CAPS, **SUPERGIRL** SUPER-SQUEEZES THE METAL, THEN STRETCHES IT TO A THIN WIRE HALF A MILE LONG...

I'LL WRAP THIS ELONGATED STRAND OF WIRE ABOUT THE TREE-- IF THE ROBOT BREAKS LOOSE, THE WIRE WILL SNAP!

BACK TO THE **PLANET** SPEEDS **SUPERGIRL** RESUMING HER GUISE AS LINDA, BUT AS SHE LISTENS TO RADIO BROADCASTS, SUDDENLY...

NEWS FLASH! A GIRL WITH ASTOUNDING SUPER-POWERS HAS RACED INTO A CIRCUS IN LONDON'S PICCADILLY SECTION AND IS AMAZING THE SPECTATORS!

THIS IS WHAT I'VE BEEN WAITING FOR!

SPANNING AN OCEAN, THE **GIRL OF STEEL'S** AMAZING SUPER-VISION UNERRINGLY LOCATES ITS DISTANT TARGET...

⸘GASP!⸘ IT IS A **SUPERGIRL**, AND SHE'S LEAPING AT SOME ESCAPING CIRCUS ANIMALS TO PROTECT THE AUDIENCE!

WHAT LINDA WITNESSES...

YOU MAY BE THE KING OF THE JUNGLE WHERE YOU COME FROM, BUT TO ME, YOU'RE JUST AN OVERGROWN PUSSYCAT!

BLIMEY, THAT RED-HAIRED GIRL IS A BLOODY TERROR!

I WARN YOU, DON'T ANNOY ME TOO MUCH! YOU'D MAKE A BEAUTIFUL LEOPARD-SKIN RUG!

BY JOVE, THAT **SUPERGIRL** IS JOLLY WELL FANTASTIC!

PRESENTLY, WHEN LINDA CHECKS ON THE HOLLOW TREE WITH HER SUPER-SIGHT...

THE WIRE ISN'T BROKEN, AND THE ROBOT IS STILL INSIDE THE TREE! WHOEVER-- OR **WHATEVER**...THAT **SUPERGIRL** IS, SHE DEFINITELY **ISN'T** MY ROBOT!

6

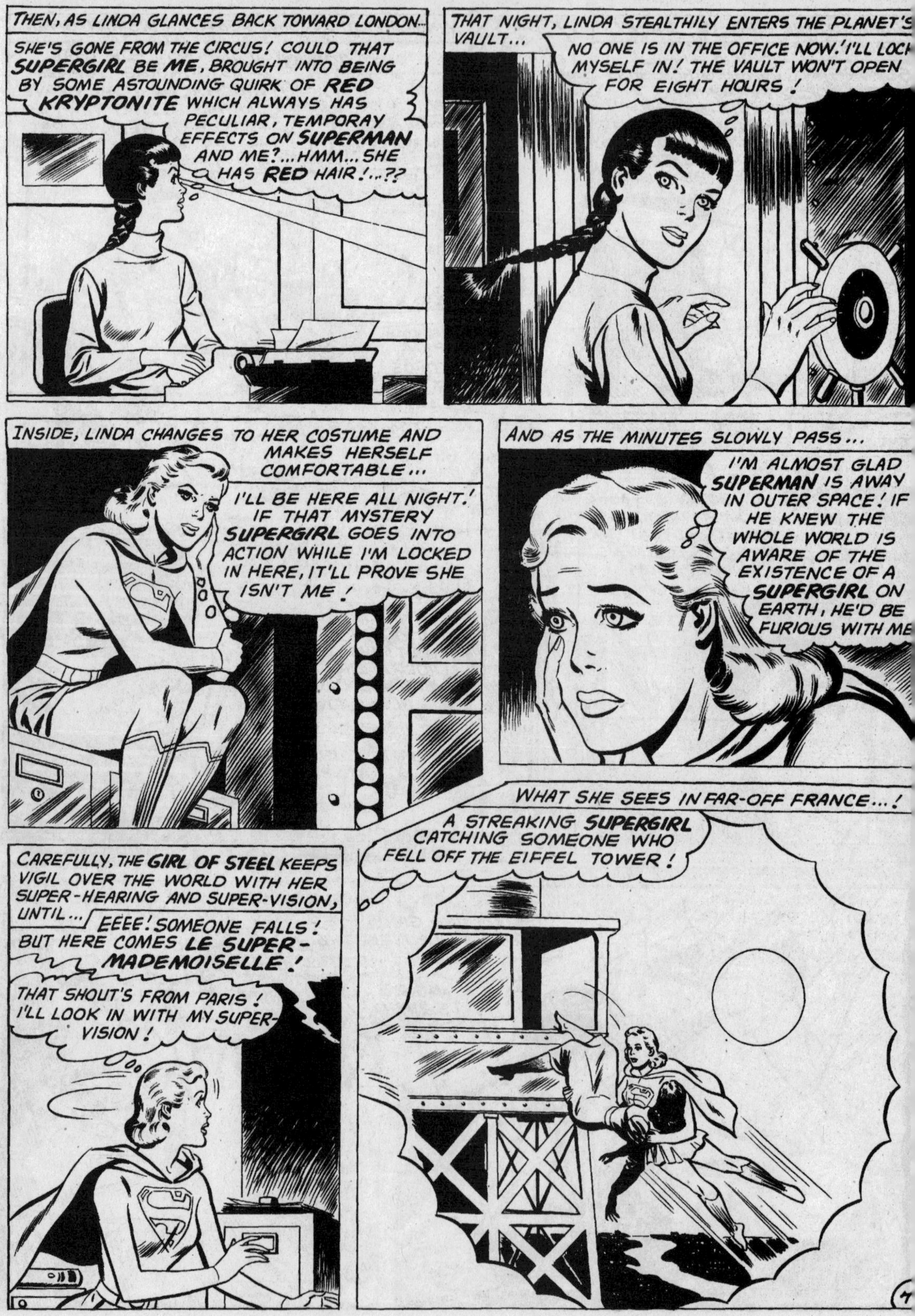
THEN, AS LINDA GLANCES BACK TOWARD LONDON...
SHE'S GONE FROM THE CIRCUS! COULD THAT SUPERGIRL BE ME, BROUGHT INTO BEING BY SOME ASTOUNDING QUIRK OF RED KRYPTONITE WHICH ALWAYS HAS PECULIAR, TEMPORAY EFFECTS ON SUPERMAN AND ME?...HMM...SHE HAS RED HAIR!...??
THAT NIGHT, LINDA STEALTHILY ENTERS THE PLANET'S VAULT...
NO ONE IS IN THE OFFICE NOW! I'LL LOCK MYSELF IN! THE VAULT WON'T OPEN FOR EIGHT HOURS!
INSIDE, LINDA CHANGES TO HER COSTUME AND MAKES HERSELF COMFORTABLE...
I'LL BE HERE ALL NIGHT! IF THAT MYSTERY SUPERGIRL GOES INTO ACTION WHILE I'M LOCKED IN HERE, IT'LL PROVE SHE ISN'T ME!
AND AS THE MINUTES SLOWLY PASS...
I'M ALMOST GLAD SUPERMAN IS AWAY IN OUTER SPACE! IF HE KNEW THE WHOLE WORLD IS AWARE OF THE EXISTENCE OF A SUPERGIRL ON EARTH, HE'D BE FURIOUS WITH ME
CAREFULLY, THE GIRL OF STEEL KEEPS VIGIL OVER THE WORLD WITH HER SUPER-HEARING AND SUPER-VISION, UNTIL...
EEEE! SOMEONE FALLS! BUT HERE COMES LE SUPER-MADEMOISELLE!
THAT SHOUT'S FROM PARIS! I'LL LOOK IN WITH MY SUPER-VISION!
WHAT SHE SEES IN FAR-OFF FRANCE...!
A STREAKING SUPERGIRL CATCHING SOMEONE WHO FELL OFF THE EIFFEL TOWER!

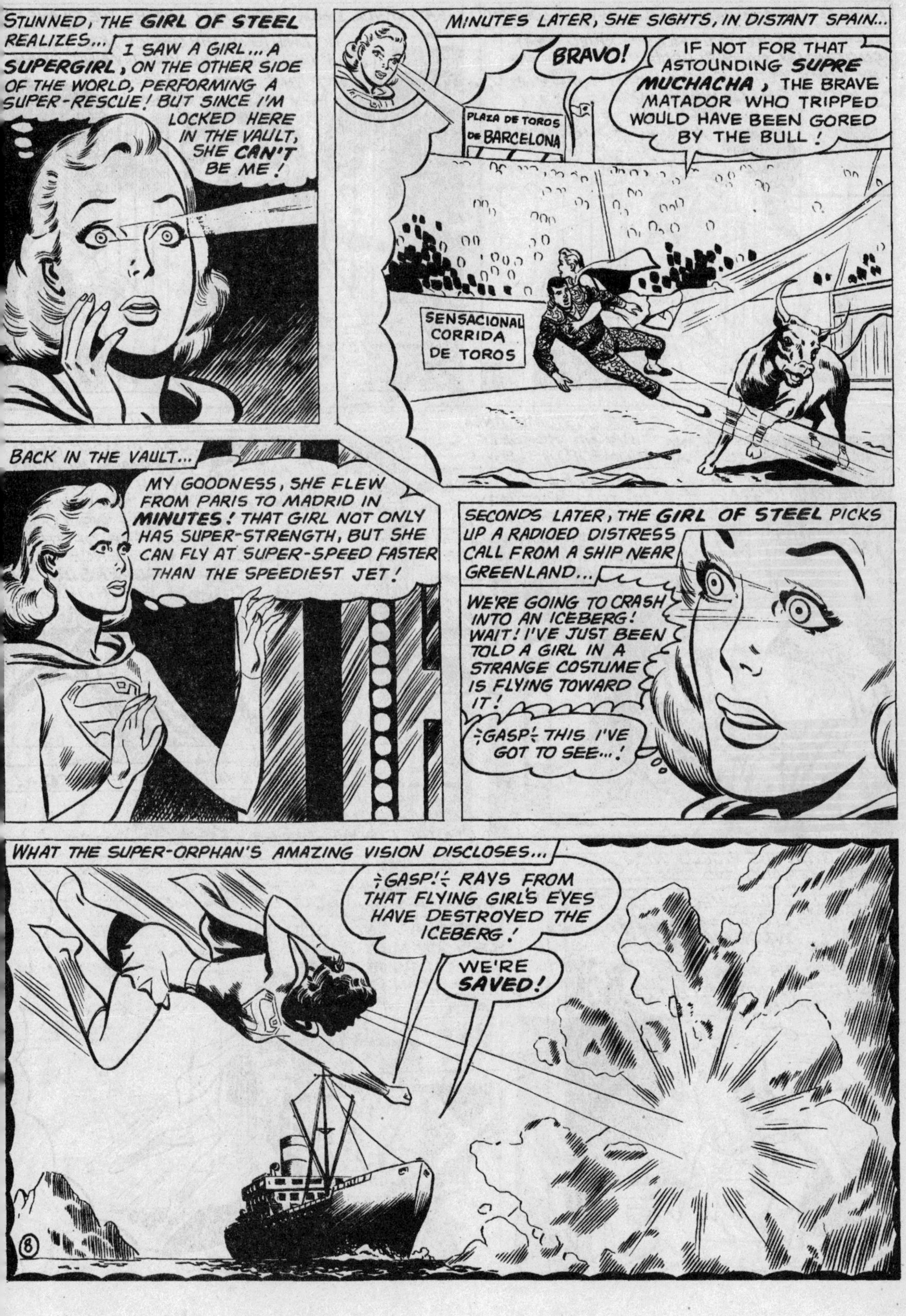
STUNNED, THE GIRL OF STEEL REALIZES...
I SAW A GIRL... A SUPERGIRL, ON THE OTHER SIDE OF THE WORLD, PERFORMING A SUPER-RESCUE! BUT SINCE I'M LOCKED HERE IN THE VAULT, SHE CAN'T BE ME!
MINUTES LATER, SHE SIGHTS, IN DISTANT SPAIN...
BRAVO!
IF NOT FOR THAT ASTOUNDING SUPRE MUCHACHA, THE BRAVE MATADOR WHO TRIPPED WOULD HAVE BEEN GORED BY THE BULL!
PLAZA DE TOROS DE BARCELONA
SENSACIONAL CORRIDA DE TOROS
BACK IN THE VAULT...
MY GOODNESS, SHE FLEW FROM PARIS TO MADRID IN MINUTES! THAT GIRL NOT ONLY HAS SUPER-STRENGTH, BUT SHE CAN FLY AT SUPER-SPEED FASTER THAN THE SPEEDIEST JET!
SECONDS LATER, THE GIRL OF STEEL PICKS UP A RADIOED DISTRESS CALL FROM A SHIP NEAR GREENLAND...
WE'RE GOING TO CRASH INTO AN ICEBERG! WAIT! I'VE JUST BEEN TOLD A GIRL IN A STRANGE COSTUME IS FLYING TOWARD IT!
÷GASP!÷ THIS I'VE GOT TO SEE...!
WHAT THE SUPER-ORPHAN'S AMAZING VISION DISCLOSES...
÷GASP!÷ RAYS FROM THAT FLYING GIRL'S EYES HAVE DESTROYED THE ICEBERG!
WE'RE SAVED!
8

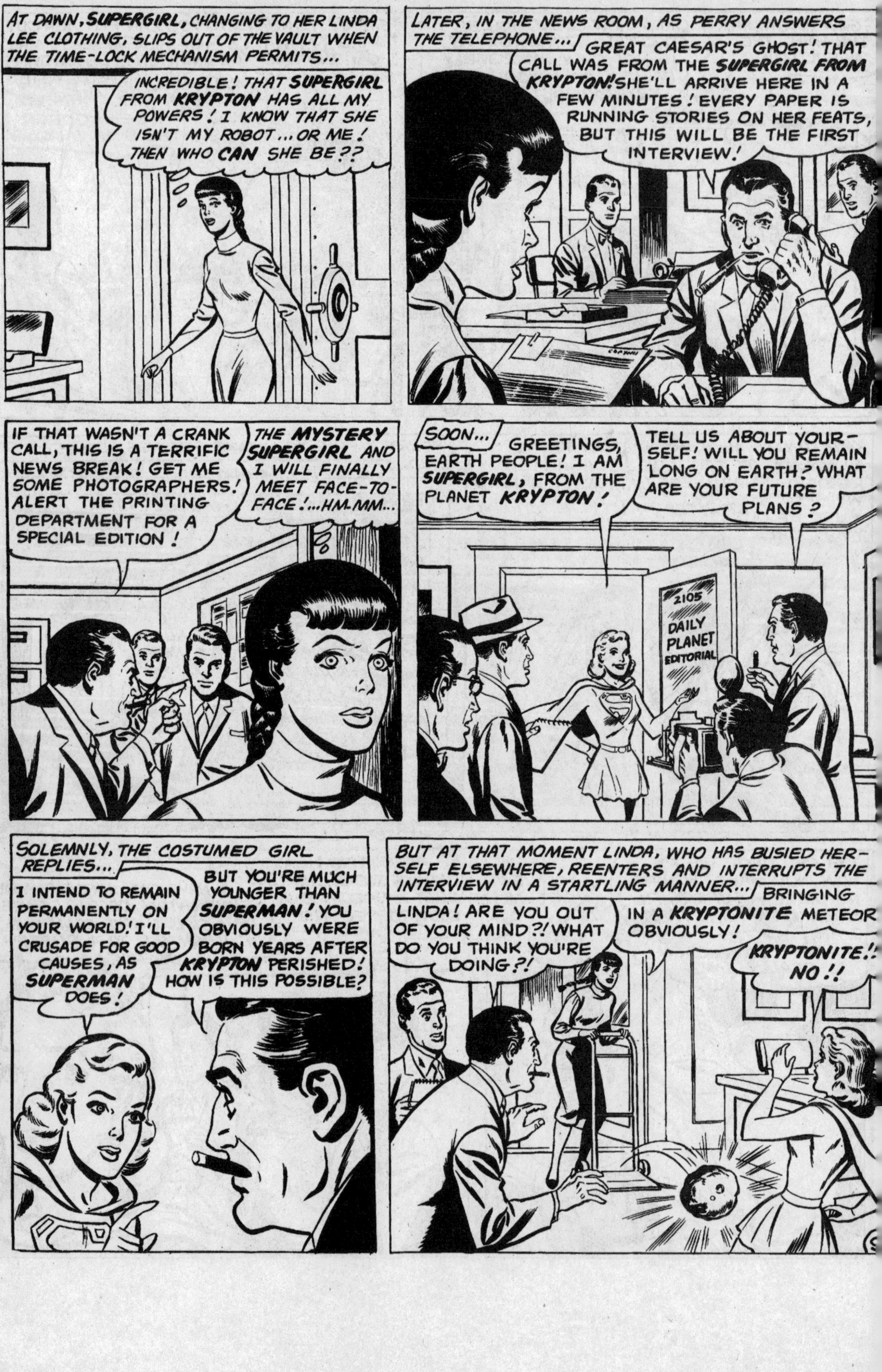
AT DAWN, SUPERGIRL, CHANGING TO HER LINDA LEE CLOTHING, SLIPS OUT OF THE VAULT WHEN THE TIME-LOCK MECHANISM PERMITS...
INCREDIBLE! THAT SUPERGIRL FROM KRYPTON HAS ALL MY POWERS! I KNOW THAT SHE ISN'T MY ROBOT... OR ME! THEN WHO CAN SHE BE??
LATER, IN THE NEWS ROOM, AS PERRY ANSWERS THE TELEPHONE...
GREAT CAESAR'S GHOST! THAT CALL WAS FROM THE SUPERGIRL FROM KRYPTON! SHE'LL ARRIVE HERE IN A FEW MINUTES! EVERY PAPER IS RUNNING STORIES ON HER FEATS, BUT THIS WILL BE THE FIRST INTERVIEW!
IF THAT WASN'T A CRANK CALL, THIS IS A TERRIFIC NEWS BREAK! GET ME SOME PHOTOGRAPHERS! ALERT THE PRINTING DEPARTMENT FOR A SPECIAL EDITION!
THE MYSTERY SUPERGIRL AND I WILL FINALLY MEET FACE-TO-FACE!...HM-MM...
SOON...
GREETINGS, EARTH PEOPLE! I AM SUPERGIRL, FROM THE PLANET KRYPTON!
TELL US ABOUT YOURSELF! WILL YOU REMAIN LONG ON EARTH? WHAT ARE YOUR FUTURE PLANS?
2105
DAILY PLANET EDITORIAL
SOLEMNLY, THE COSTUMED GIRL REPLIES...
I INTEND TO REMAIN PERMANENTLY ON YOUR WORLD! I'LL CRUSADE FOR GOOD CAUSES, AS SUPERMAN DOES!
BUT YOU'RE MUCH YOUNGER THAN SUPERMAN! YOU OBVIOUSLY WERE BORN YEARS AFTER KRYPTON PERISHED! HOW IS THIS POSSIBLE?
BUT AT THAT MOMENT LINDA, WHO HAS BUSIED HERSELF ELSEWHERE, REENTERS AND INTERRUPTS THE INTERVIEW IN A STARTLING MANNER...
BRINGING IN A KRYPTONITE METEOR OBVIOUSLY!
LINDA! ARE YOU OUT OF YOUR MIND?! WHAT DO YOU THINK YOU'RE DOING?!
KRYPTONITE!! NO!!

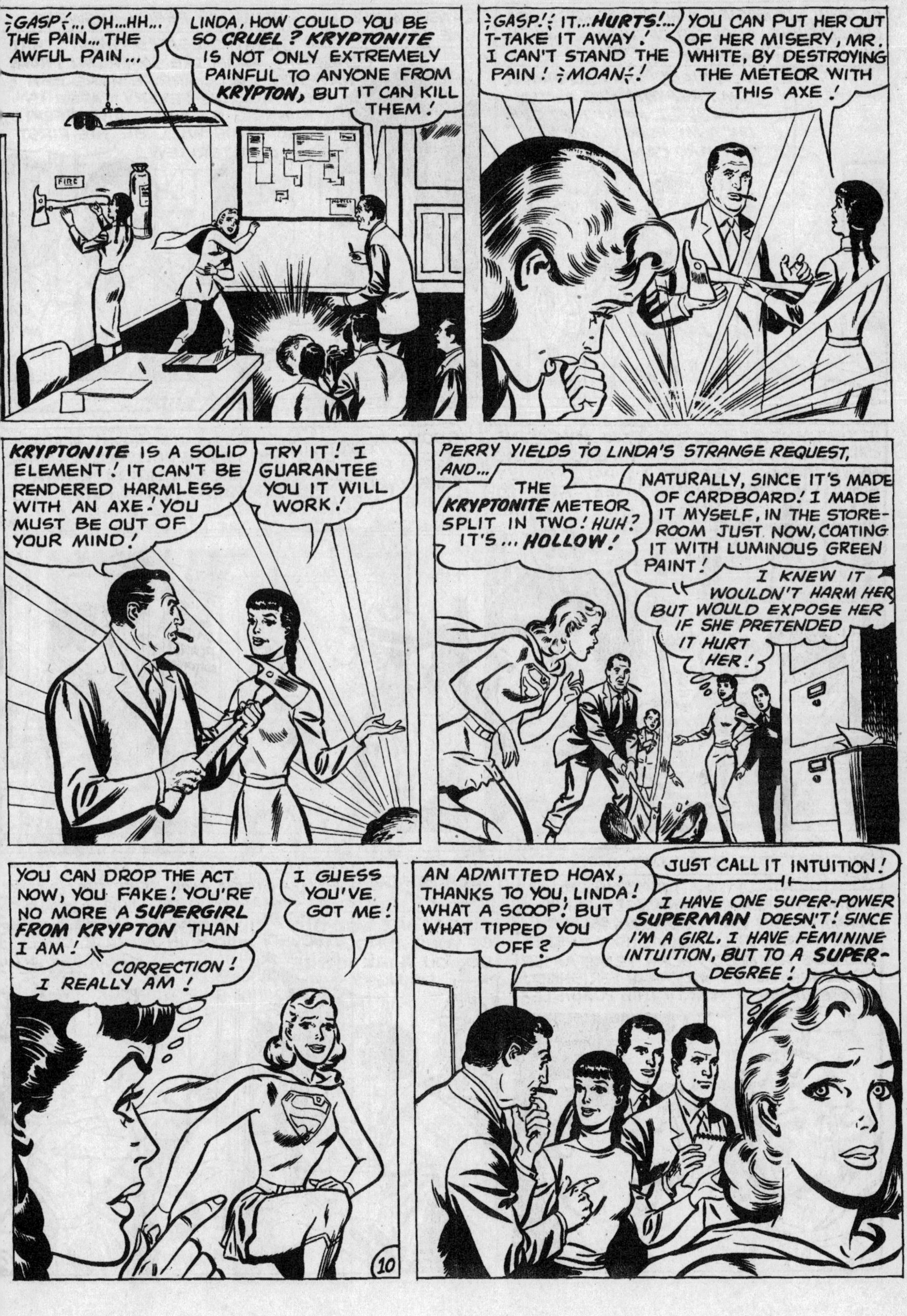
-GASP-... OH...HH... THE PAIN... THE AWFUL PAIN...
LINDA, HOW COULD YOU BE SO CRUEL? KRYPTONITE IS NOT ONLY EXTREMELY PAINFUL TO ANYONE FROM KRYPTON, BUT IT CAN KILL THEM!
FIRE
-GASP!- IT... HURTS!... T-TAKE IT AWAY! I CAN'T STAND THE PAIN! -MOAN-!
YOU CAN PUT HER OUT OF HER MISERY, MR. WHITE, BY DESTROYING THE METEOR WITH THIS AXE!
KRYPTONITE IS A SOLID ELEMENT! IT CAN'T BE RENDERED HARMLESS WITH AN AXE! YOU MUST BE OUT OF YOUR MIND!
TRY IT! I GUARANTEE YOU IT WILL WORK!
PERRY YIELDS TO LINDA'S STRANGE REQUEST, AND...
THE KRYPTONITE METEOR SPLIT IN TWO! HUH? IT'S... HOLLOW!
NATURALLY, SINCE IT'S MADE OF CARDBOARD! I MADE IT MYSELF, IN THE STORE-ROOM JUST NOW, COATING IT WITH LUMINOUS GREEN PAINT!
I KNEW IT WOULDN'T HARM HER, BUT WOULD EXPOSE HER IF SHE PRETENDED IT HURT HER!
YOU CAN DROP THE ACT NOW, YOU FAKE! YOU'RE NO MORE A SUPERGIRL FROM KRYPTON THAN I AM!
CORRECTION! I REALLY AM!
I GUESS YOU'VE GOT ME!
10
AN ADMITTED HOAX, THANKS TO YOU, LINDA! WHAT A SCOOP! BUT WHAT TIPPED YOU OFF?
JUST CALL IT INTUITION!
I HAVE ONE SUPER-POWER SUPERMAN DOESN'T! SINCE I'M A GIRL, I HAVE FEMININE INTUITION, BUT TO A SUPER-DEGREE!

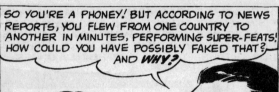

SO YOU'RE A PHONEY! BUT ACCORDING TO NEWS REPORTS, YOU FLEW FROM ONE COUNTRY TO ANOTHER IN MINUTES, PERFORMING SUPER-FEATS! HOW COULD YOU HAVE POSSIBLY FAKED THAT? AND *WHY?*

I HAD HOPED THE HOAX COULD BE PROLONGED FOR AT LEAST SEVERAL MORE HOURS. COME WITH ME, AND YOU'LL LEARN ALL YOU WANT TO KNOW!

SOON... IT'S ALL RIGHT, JOE! THEY'RE WITH ME!

A MOVIE STUDIO! IT FIGURES!

IT WAS ALL A PUBLICITY STUNT FOR A NEW MOVIE!

ACE STUDIO

MINUTES LATER, AS THE STUDIO'S PUBLICITY CHIEF CONDUCTS A TOUR OF SEVERAL BIZARRE SETS...

FOLKS, THIS IS WHERE INDOOR SHOOTING OF OUR SENSATIONAL NEW FILM, "*THE SUPERGIRL FROM KRYPTON*" WAS FILMED! TO YOUR RIGHT IS A MODEL OF THE PLANET *KRYPTON*...

THIS BACKDROP IS A PAINTING OF THE KRYPTONIAN CITY *TOZ*, THE CITY FROM WHICH OUR FICTIONAL *SUPERGIRL* WAS SHOT INTO SPACE. IMAGINATIVE, EH? YOU'VE GOT TO ADMIT IT'LL BE A SENSATIONAL MOVIE!

PUBLICITY! AND I FELL FOR IT!

IN OUR STORY, THIS TEST SPACE SHIP WAS DAMAGED IN ITS BLAST-OFF FROM *KRYPTON!* INSIDE IT, "*SUPERGIRL*" CIRCLED EARTH IN A STATE OF SUSPENDED ANIMATION FOR YEARS UNTIL A GLANCING BLOW FROM A METEOR CAUSED THE SHIP TO WORK AGAIN... "

11

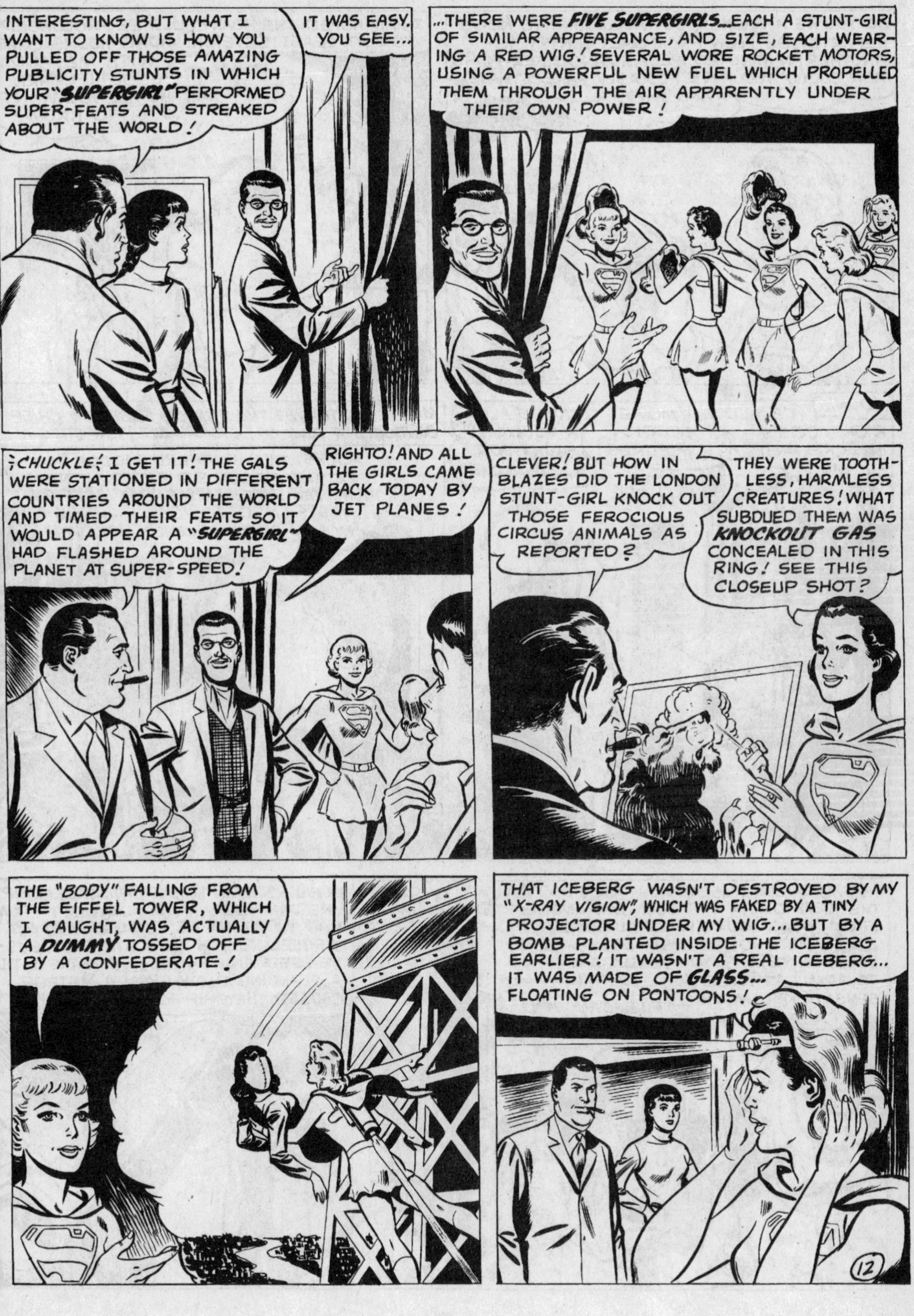
INTERESTING, BUT WHAT I WANT TO KNOW IS HOW YOU PULLED OFF THOSE AMAZING PUBLICITY STUNTS IN WHICH YOUR "SUPERGIRL" PERFORMED SUPER-FEATS AND STREAKED ABOUT THE WORLD!
IT WAS EASY. YOU SEE...
...THERE WERE FIVE SUPERGIRLS...EACH A STUNT-GIRL OF SIMILAR APPEARANCE, AND SIZE, EACH WEARING A RED WIG! SEVERAL WORE ROCKET MOTORS, USING A POWERFUL NEW FUEL WHICH PROPELLED THEM THROUGH THE AIR APPARENTLY UNDER THEIR OWN POWER!
¡CHUCKLE¡ I GET IT! THE GALS WERE STATIONED IN DIFFERENT COUNTRIES AROUND THE WORLD AND TIMED THEIR FEATS SO IT WOULD APPEAR A "SUPERGIRL" HAD FLASHED AROUND THE PLANET AT SUPER-SPEED!
RIGHTO! AND ALL THE GIRLS CAME BACK TODAY BY JET PLANES!
CLEVER! BUT HOW IN BLAZES DID THE LONDON STUNT-GIRL KNOCK OUT THOSE FEROCIOUS CIRCUS ANIMALS AS REPORTED?
THEY WERE TOOTHLESS, HARMLESS CREATURES! WHAT SUBDUED THEM WAS KNOCKOUT GAS CONCEALED IN THIS RING! SEE THIS CLOSEUP SHOT?
THE "BODY" FALLING FROM THE EIFFEL TOWER, WHICH I CAUGHT, WAS ACTUALLY A DUMMY TOSSED OFF BY A CONFEDERATE!
THAT ICEBERG WASN'T DESTROYED BY MY "X-RAY VISION", WHICH WAS FAKED BY A TINY PROJECTOR UNDER MY WIG... BUT BY A BOMB PLANTED INSIDE THE ICEBERG EARLIER! IT WASN'T A REAL ICEBERG... IT WAS MADE OF GLASS... FLOATING ON PONTOONS!
12

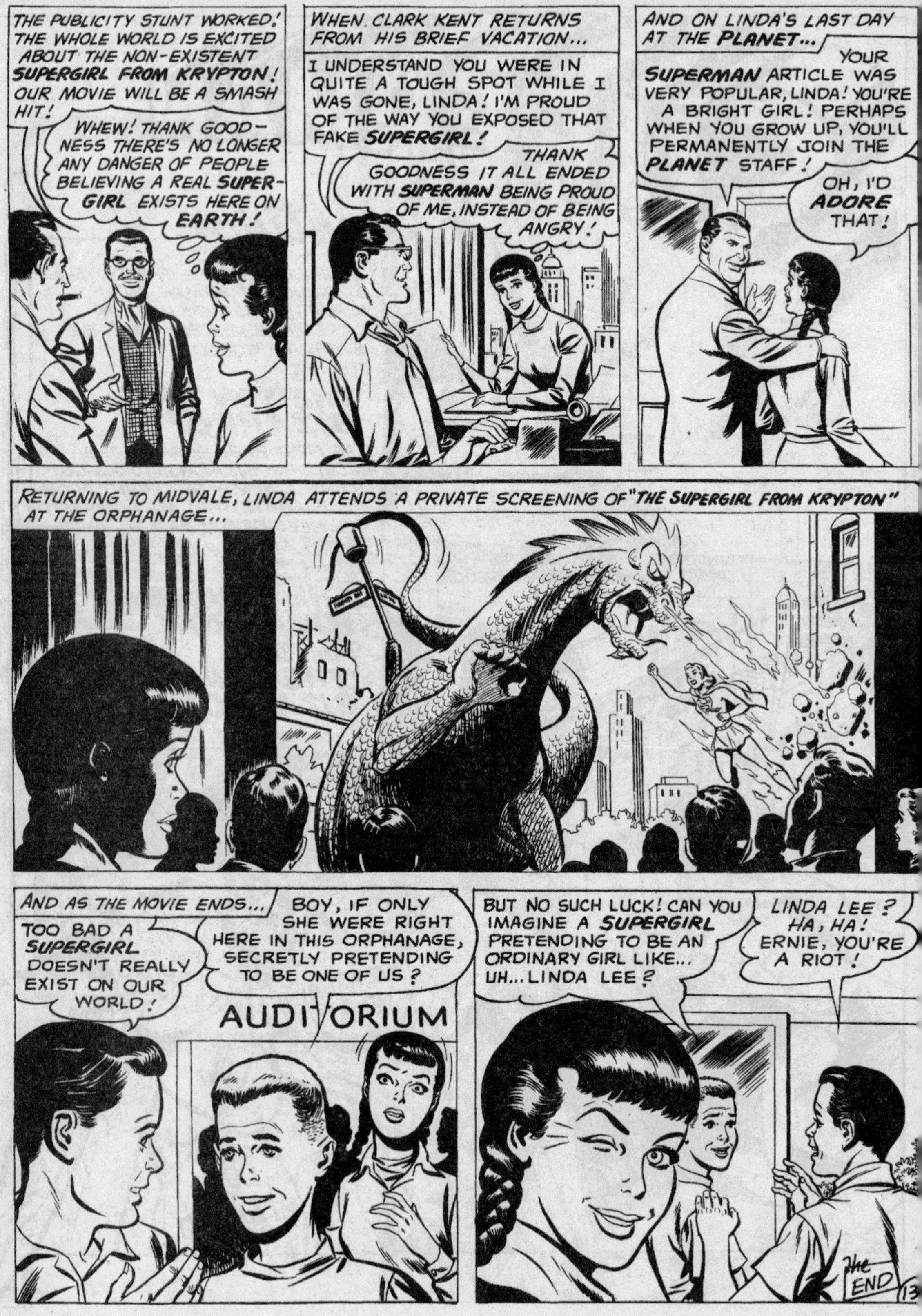
THE PUBLICITY STUNT WORKED! THE WHOLE WORLD IS EXCITED ABOUT THE NON-EXISTENT SUPERGIRL FROM KRYPTON! OUR MOVIE WILL BE A SMASH HIT!
WHEW! THANK GOODNESS THERE'S NO LONGER ANY DANGER OF PEOPLE BELIEVING A REAL SUPERGIRL EXISTS HERE ON EARTH!
WHEN CLARK KENT RETURNS FROM HIS BRIEF VACATION...
I UNDERSTAND YOU WERE IN QUITE A TOUGH SPOT WHILE I WAS GONE, LINDA! I'M PROUD OF THE WAY YOU EXPOSED THAT FAKE SUPERGIRL!
THANK GOODNESS IT ALL ENDED WITH SUPERMAN BEING PROUD OF ME, INSTEAD OF BEING ANGRY!
AND ON LINDA'S LAST DAY AT THE PLANET...
YOUR SUPERMAN ARTICLE WAS VERY POPULAR, LINDA! YOU'RE A BRIGHT GIRL! PERHAPS WHEN YOU GROW UP, YOU'LL PERMANENTLY JOIN THE PLANET STAFF!
OH, I'D ADORE THAT!
RETURNING TO MIDVALE, LINDA ATTENDS A PRIVATE SCREENING OF "THE SUPERGIRL FROM KRYPTON" AT THE ORPHANAGE...
AND AS THE MOVIE ENDS...
TOO BAD A SUPERGIRL DOESN'T REALLY EXIST ON OUR WORLD!
BOY, IF ONLY SHE WERE RIGHT HERE IN THIS ORPHANAGE, SECRETLY PRETENDING TO BE ONE OF US?
AUDITORIUM
BUT NO SUCH LUCK! CAN YOU IMAGINE A SUPERGIRL PRETENDING TO BE AN ORDINARY GIRL LIKE... UH... LINDA LEE?
LINDA LEE? HA, HA! ERNIE, YOU'RE A RIOT!
THE END
13

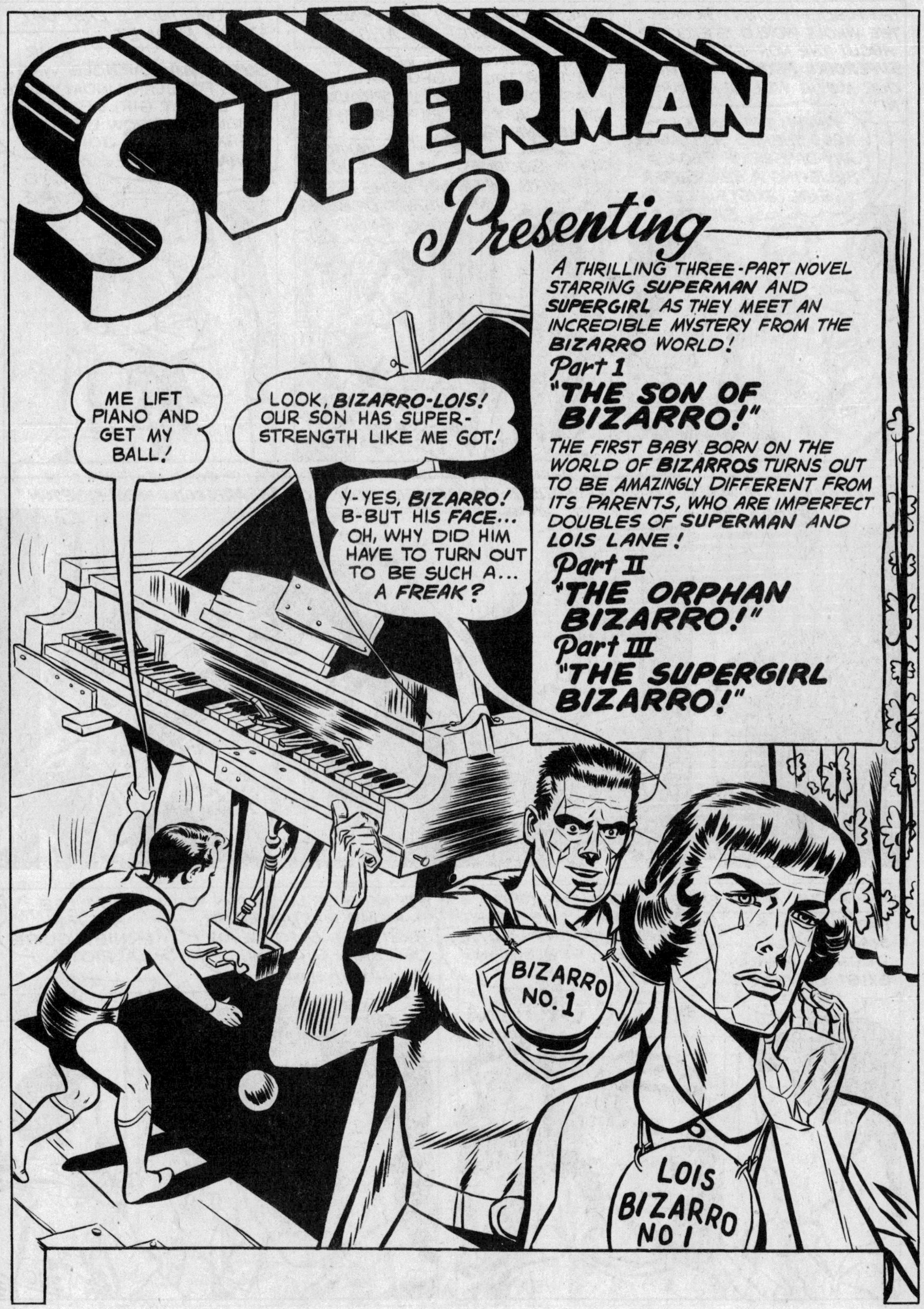
SUPERMAN
Presenting
A THRILLING THREE-PART NOVEL STARRING SUPERMAN AND SUPERGIRL AS THEY MEET AN INCREDIBLE MYSTERY FROM THE BIZARRO WORLD!
Part 1
"THE SON OF BIZARRO!"
THE FIRST BABY BORN ON THE WORLD OF BIZARROS TURNS OUT TO BE AMAZINGLY DIFFERENT FROM ITS PARENTS, WHO ARE IMPERFECT DOUBLES OF SUPERMAN AND LOIS LANE!
Part II
"THE ORPHAN BIZARRO!"
Part III
"THE SUPERGIRL BIZARRO!"
ME LIFT PIANO AND GET MY BALL!
LOOK, BIZARRO-LOIS! OUR SON HAS SUPER-STRENGTH LIKE ME GOT!
Y-YES, BIZARRO! B-BUT HIS FACE... OH, WHY DID HIM HAVE TO TURN OUT TO BE SUCH A... A FREAK?
BIZARRO NO. 1
LOIS BIZARRO NO I

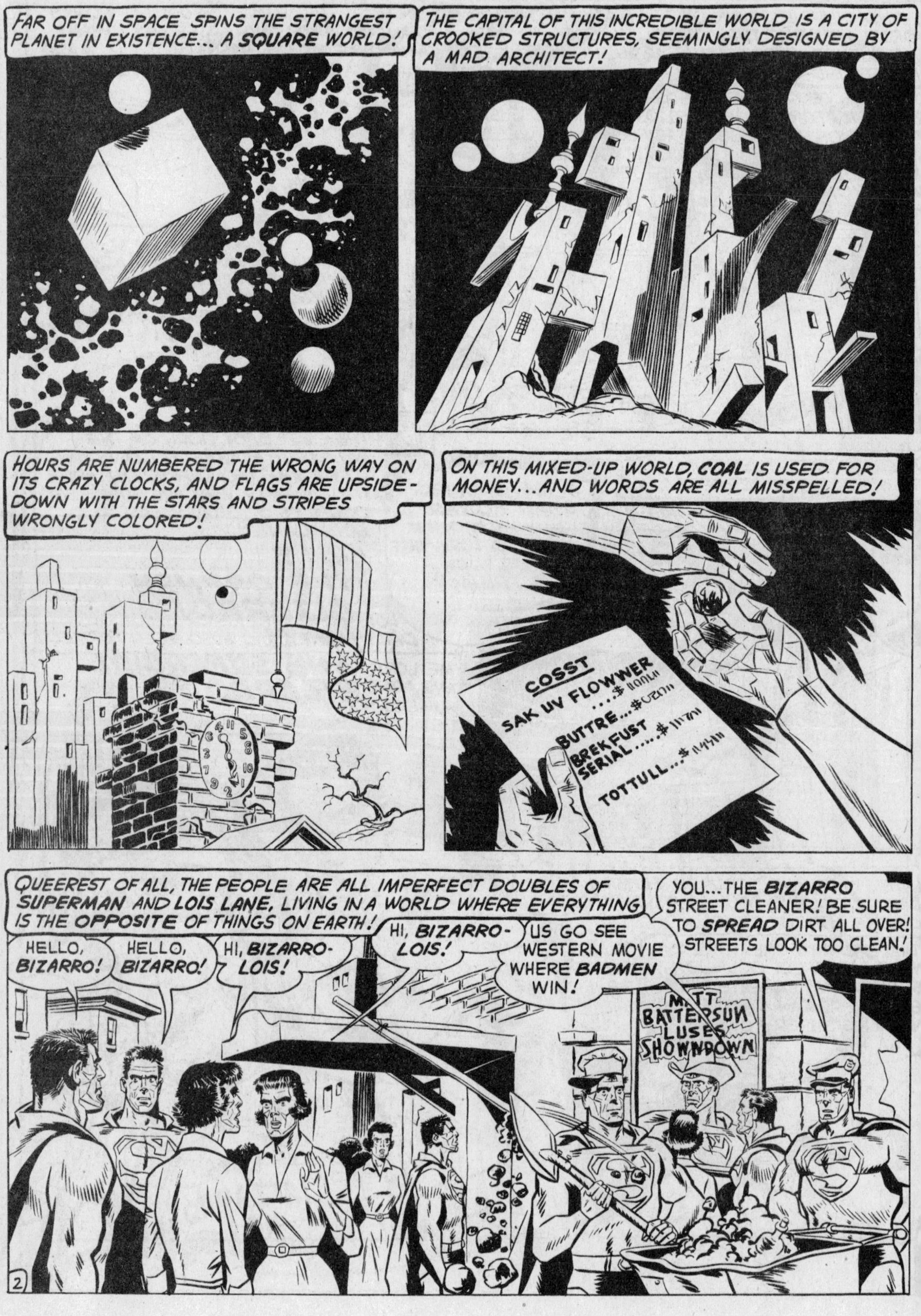
FAR OFF IN SPACE SPINS THE STRANGEST PLANET IN EXISTENCE... A **SQUARE** WORLD!
THE CAPITAL OF THIS INCREDIBLE WORLD IS A CITY OF CROOKED STRUCTURES, SEEMINGLY DESIGNED BY A MAD ARCHITECT!
HOURS ARE NUMBERED THE WRONG WAY ON ITS CRAZY CLOCKS, AND FLAGS ARE UPSIDE-DOWN WITH THE STARS AND STRIPES WRONGLY COLORED!
ON THIS MIXED-UP WORLD, **COAL** IS USED FOR MONEY... AND WORDS ARE ALL MISSPELLED!
COSST
SAK UV FLOWWER
BUTTRE
BREKFUST SERIAL
TOTTULL
QUEEREST OF ALL, THE PEOPLE ARE ALL IMPERFECT DOUBLES OF **SUPERMAN** AND **LOIS LANE**, LIVING IN A WORLD WHERE EVERYTHING IS THE **OPPOSITE** OF THINGS ON EARTH!
HELLO, BIZARRO!
HELLO, BIZARRO!
HI, **BIZARRO-LOIS!**
HI, **BIZARRO-LOIS!**
US GO SEE WESTERN MOVIE WHERE **BADMEN** WIN!
YOU... THE **BIZARRO** STREET CLEANER! BE SURE TO **SPREAD** DIRT ALL OVER! STREETS LOOK TOO CLEAN!
BATTERSUN LUSES SHOWNDOWN
2

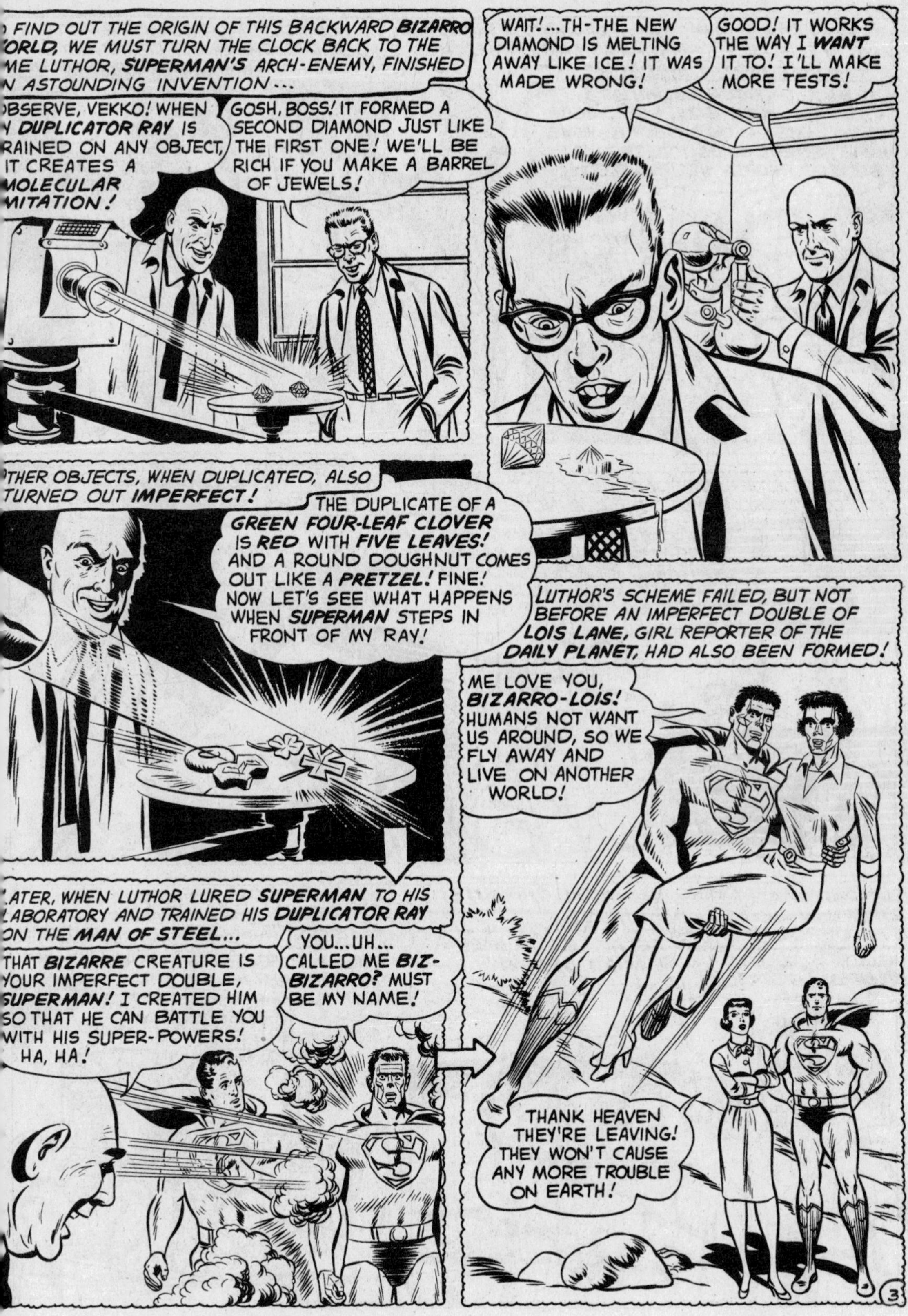
FIND OUT THE ORIGIN OF THIS BACKWARD BIZARRO ORLD, WE MUST TURN THE CLOCK BACK TO THE ME LUTHOR, SUPERMAN'S ARCH-ENEMY, FINISHED N ASTOUNDING INVENTION...
BSERVE, VEKKO! WHEN DUPLICATOR RAY IS RAINED ON ANY OBJECT, IT CREATES A MOLECULAR MITATION!
GOSH, BOSS! IT FORMED A SECOND DIAMOND JUST LIKE THE FIRST ONE! WE'LL BE RICH IF YOU MAKE A BARREL OF JEWELS!
WAIT! ...TH-THE NEW DIAMOND IS MELTING AWAY LIKE ICE! IT WAS MADE WRONG!
GOOD! IT WORKS THE WAY I WANT IT TO! I'LL MAKE MORE TESTS!
THER OBJECTS, WHEN DUPLICATED, ALSO TURNED OUT IMPERFECT!
THE DUPLICATE OF A GREEN FOUR-LEAF CLOVER IS RED WITH FIVE LEAVES! AND A ROUND DOUGHNUT COMES OUT LIKE A PRETZEL! FINE! NOW LET'S SEE WHAT HAPPENS WHEN SUPERMAN STEPS IN FRONT OF MY RAY!
ATER, WHEN LUTHOR LURED SUPERMAN TO HIS ABORATORY AND TRAINED HIS DUPLICATOR RAY ON THE MAN OF STEEL...
THAT BIZARRE CREATURE IS YOUR IMPERFECT DOUBLE, SUPERMAN! I CREATED HIM SO THAT HE CAN BATTLE YOU WITH HIS SUPER-POWERS! HA, HA!
YOU...UH... CALLED ME BIZ-BIZARRO? MUST BE MY NAME!
LUTHOR'S SCHEME FAILED, BUT NOT BEFORE AN IMPERFECT DOUBLE OF LOIS LANE, GIRL REPORTER OF THE DAILY PLANET, HAD ALSO BEEN FORMED!
ME LOVE YOU, BIZARRO-LOIS! HUMANS NOT WANT US AROUND, SO WE FLY AWAY AND LIVE ON ANOTHER WORLD!
THANK HEAVEN THEY'RE LEAVING! THEY WON'T CAUSE ANY MORE TROUBLE ON EARTH!
3

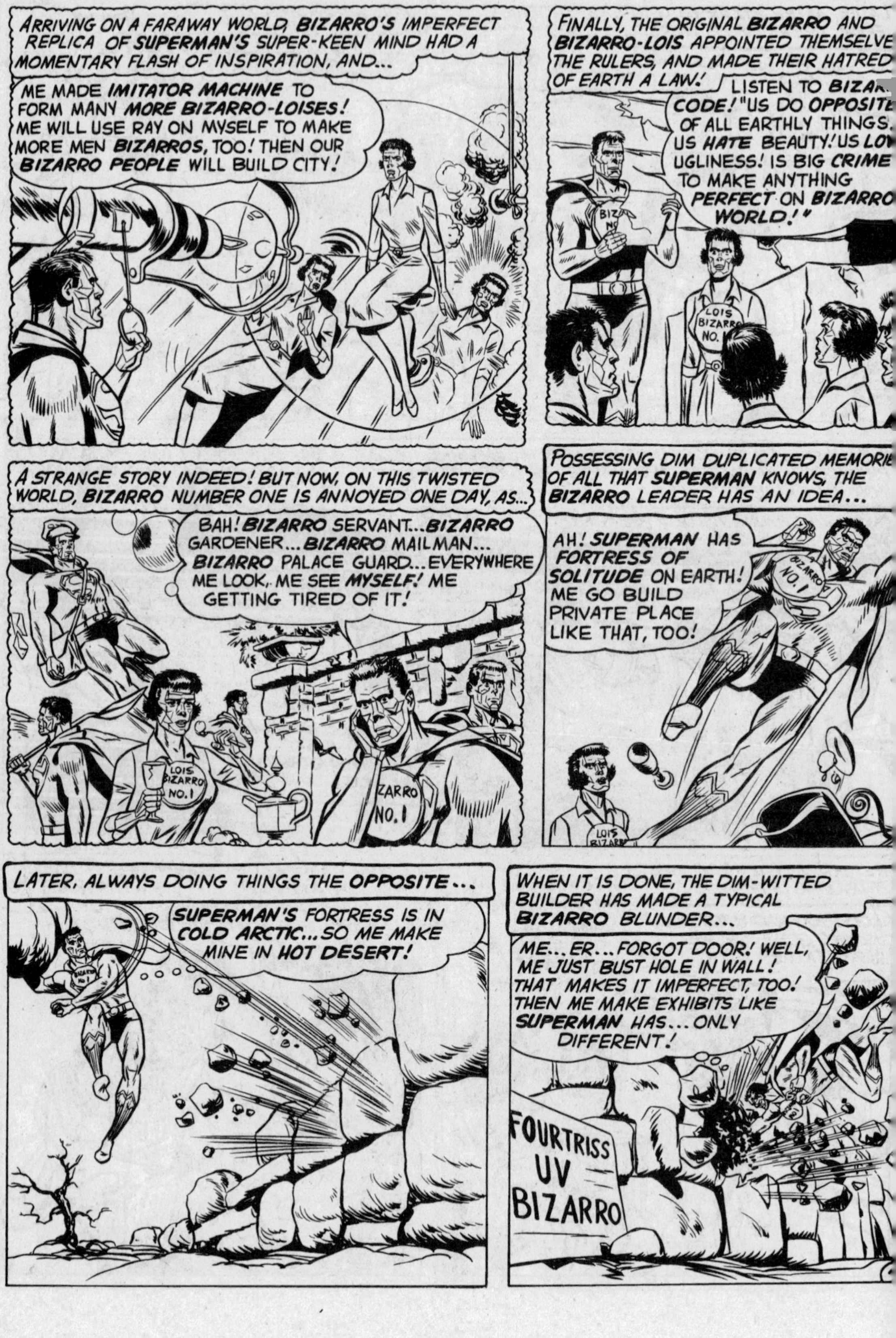
ARRIVING ON A FARAWAY WORLD, BIZARRO'S IMPERFECT REPLICA OF SUPERMAN'S SUPER-KEEN MIND HAD A MOMENTARY FLASH OF INSPIRATION, AND...
ME MADE IMITATOR MACHINE TO FORM MANY MORE BIZARRO-LOISES! ME WILL USE RAY ON MYSELF TO MAKE MORE MEN BIZARROS, TOO! THEN OUR BIZARRO PEOPLE WILL BUILD CITY!
FINALLY, THE ORIGINAL BIZARRO AND BIZARRO-LOIS APPOINTED THEMSELVE THE RULERS, AND MADE THEIR HATRED OF EARTH A LAW!
LISTEN TO BIZAR CODE! "US DO OPPOSITE OF ALL EARTHLY THINGS. US HATE BEAUTY! US LOV UGLINESS! IS BIG CRIME TO MAKE ANYTHING PERFECT ON BIZARRO WORLD!"
LOIS BIZARRO NO. 1
A STRANGE STORY INDEED! BUT NOW, ON THIS TWISTED WORLD, BIZARRO NUMBER ONE IS ANNOYED ONE DAY, AS...
BAH! BIZARRO SERVANT...BIZARRO GARDENER...BIZARRO MAILMAN... BIZARRO PALACE GUARD...EVERYWHERE ME LOOK, ME SEE MYSELF! ME GETTING TIRED OF IT!
LOIS BIZARRO NO. 1
ZARRO NO. 1
POSSESSING DIM DUPLICATED MEMORIE OF ALL THAT SUPERMAN KNOWS, THE BIZARRO LEADER HAS AN IDEA...
AH! SUPERMAN HAS FORTRESS OF SOLITUDE ON EARTH! ME GO BUILD PRIVATE PLACE LIKE THAT, TOO!
BIZARRO NO. 1
LATER, ALWAYS DOING THINGS THE OPPOSITE...
SUPERMAN'S FORTRESS IS IN COLD ARCTIC...SO ME MAKE MINE IN HOT DESERT!
WHEN IT IS DONE, THE DIM-WITTED BUILDER HAS MADE A TYPICAL BIZARRO BLUNDER...
ME...ER...FORGOT DOOR! WELL, ME JUST BUST HOLE IN WALL! THAT MAKES IT IMPERFECT, TOO! THEN ME MAKE EXHIBITS LIKE SUPERMAN HAS...ONLY DIFFERENT!
FOURTRISS UV BIZARRO

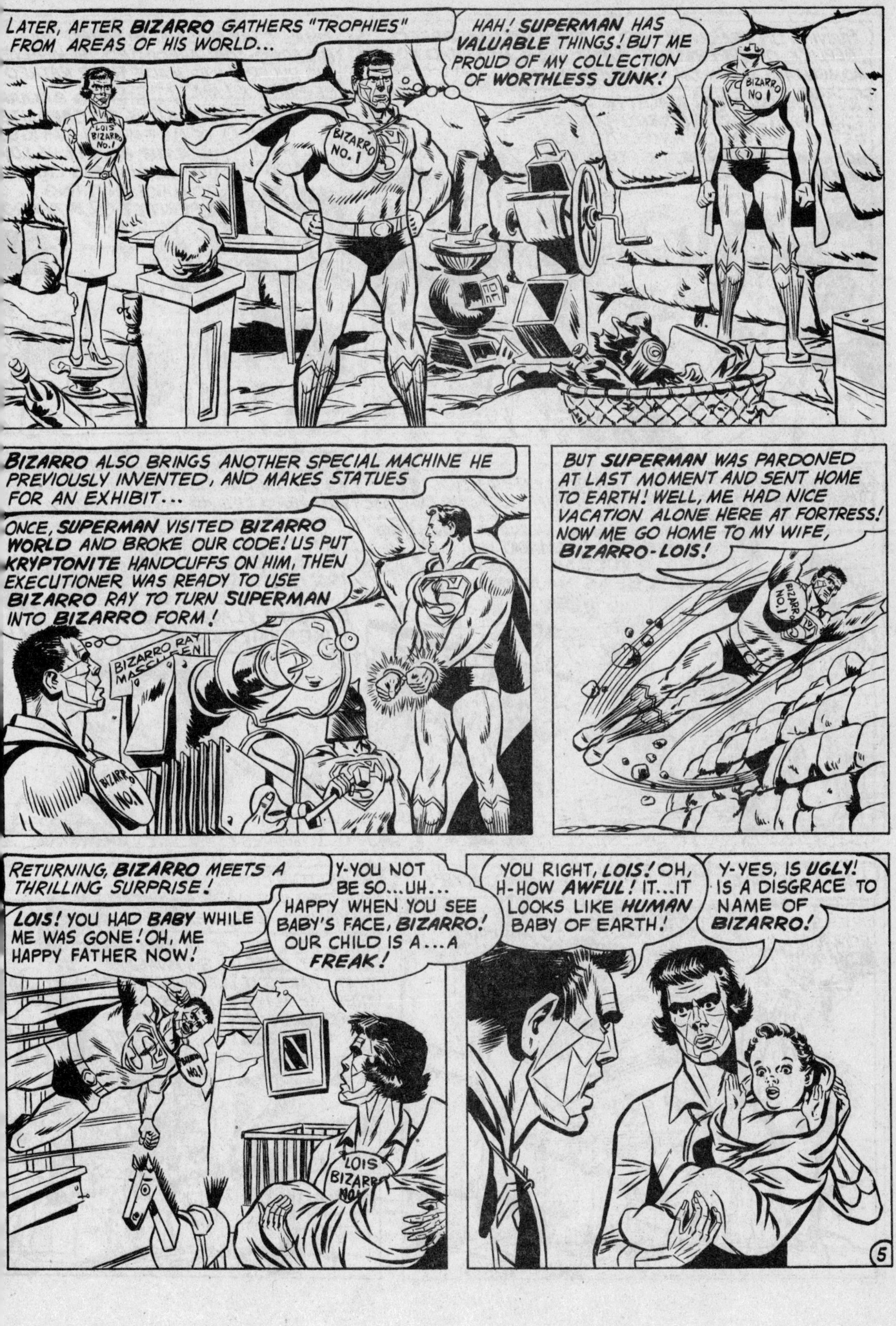
LATER, AFTER BIZARRO GATHERS "TROPHIES" FROM AREAS OF HIS WORLD...
HAH! SUPERMAN HAS VALUABLE THINGS! BUT ME PROUD OF MY COLLECTION OF WORTHLESS JUNK!
LOIS BIZARRO NO. 1
BIZARRO NO. 1
BIZARRO NO 1
BIZARRO ALSO BRINGS ANOTHER SPECIAL MACHINE HE PREVIOUSLY INVENTED, AND MAKES STATUES FOR AN EXHIBIT...
ONCE, SUPERMAN VISITED BIZARRO WORLD AND BROKE OUR CODE! US PUT KRYPTONITE HANDCUFFS ON HIM, THEN EXECUTIONER WAS READY TO USE BIZARRO RAY TO TURN SUPERMAN INTO BIZARRO FORM!
BIZARRO RAY
BIZARRO NO. 1
BUT SUPERMAN WAS PARDONED AT LAST MOMENT AND SENT HOME TO EARTH! WELL, ME HAD NICE VACATION ALONE HERE AT FORTRESS! NOW ME GO HOME TO MY WIFE, BIZARRO-LOIS!
BIZARRO NO. 1
RETURNING, BIZARRO MEETS A THRILLING SURPRISE!
LOIS! YOU HAD BABY WHILE ME WAS GONE! OH, ME HAPPY FATHER NOW!
Y-YOU NOT BE SO...UH... HAPPY WHEN YOU SEE BABY'S FACE, BIZARRO! OUR CHILD IS A...A FREAK!
BIZARRO NO. 1
LOIS BIZARRO
YOU RIGHT, LOIS! OH, H-HOW AWFUL! IT...IT LOOKS LIKE HUMAN BABY OF EARTH!
Y-YES, IS UGLY! IS A DISGRACE TO NAME OF BIZARRO!
5

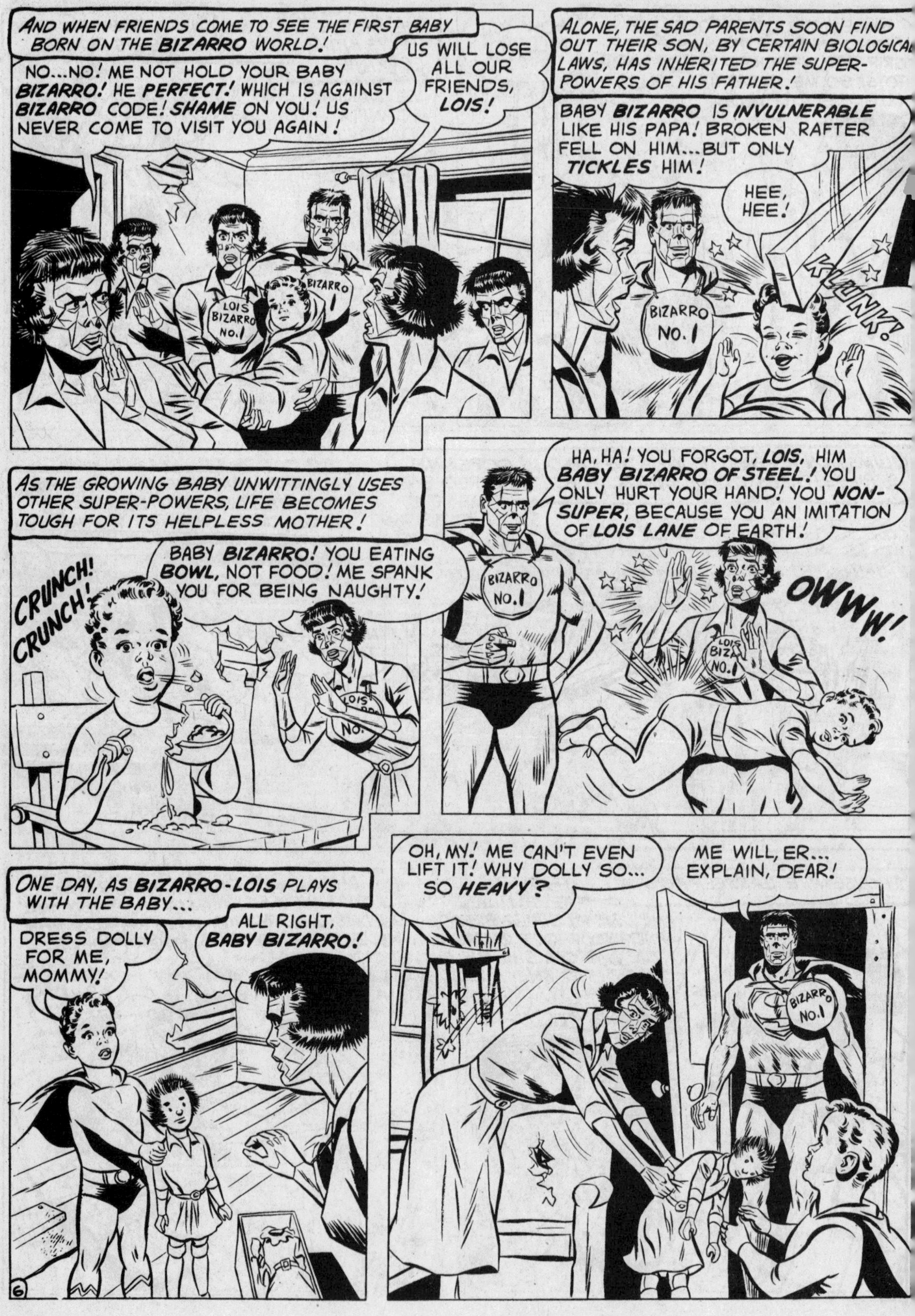
AND WHEN FRIENDS COME TO SEE THE FIRST BABY BORN ON THE BIZARRO WORLD!
NO...NO! ME NOT HOLD YOUR BABY BIZARRO! HE PERFECT! WHICH IS AGAINST BIZARRO CODE! SHAME ON YOU! US NEVER COME TO VISIT YOU AGAIN!
US WILL LOSE ALL OUR FRIENDS, LOIS!
BIZARRO
LOIS BIZARRO NO. 1
ALONE, THE SAD PARENTS SOON FIND OUT THEIR SON, BY CERTAIN BIOLOGICAL LAWS, HAS INHERITED THE SUPER-POWERS OF HIS FATHER!
BABY BIZARRO IS INVULNERABLE LIKE HIS PAPA! BROKEN RAFTER FELL ON HIM...BUT ONLY TICKLES HIM!
HEE, HEE!
KLUNK!
BIZARRO NO. 1
AS THE GROWING BABY UNWITTINGLY USES OTHER SUPER-POWERS, LIFE BECOMES TOUGH FOR ITS HELPLESS MOTHER!
BABY BIZARRO! YOU EATING BOWL, NOT FOOD! ME SPANK YOU FOR BEING NAUGHTY!
CRUNCH! CRUNCH!
HA, HA! YOU FORGOT, LOIS, HIM BABY BIZARRO OF STEEL! YOU ONLY HURT YOUR HAND! YOU NON-SUPER, BECAUSE YOU AN IMITATION OF LOIS LANE OF EARTH!
OWWW!
BIZARRO NO. 1
ONE DAY, AS BIZARRO-LOIS PLAYS WITH THE BABY...
DRESS DOLLY FOR ME, MOMMY!
ALL RIGHT, BABY BIZARRO!
6
OH, MY! ME CAN'T EVEN LIFT IT! WHY DOLLY SO... SO HEAVY?
ME WILL, ER... EXPLAIN, DEAR!
BIZARRO NO. 1

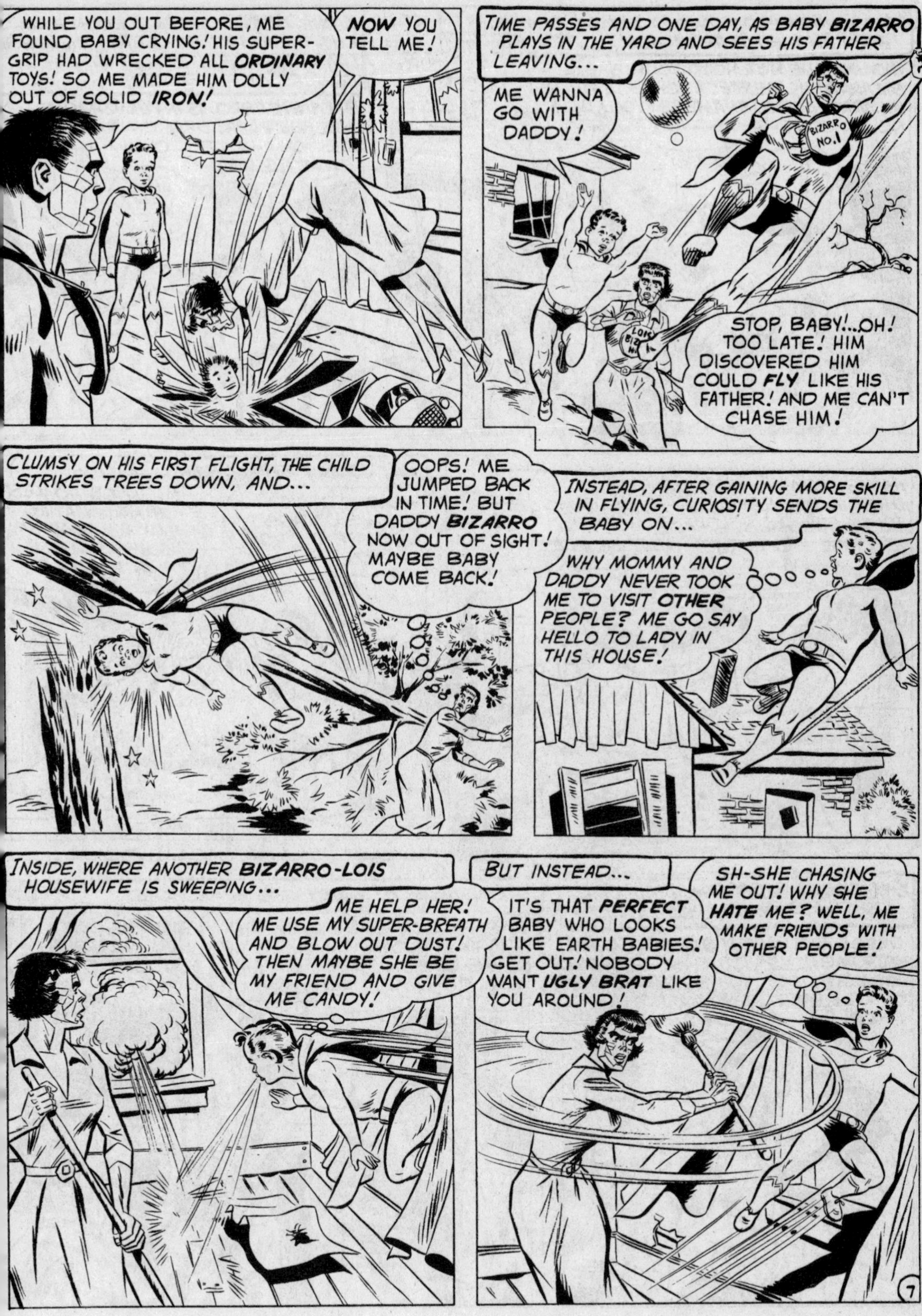
WHILE YOU OUT BEFORE, ME FOUND BABY CRYING! HIS SUPER-GRIP HAD WRECKED ALL ORDINARY TOYS! SO ME MADE HIM DOLLY OUT OF SOLID IRON!
NOW YOU TELL ME!
TIME PASSES AND ONE DAY, AS BABY BIZARRO PLAYS IN THE YARD AND SEES HIS FATHER LEAVING...
ME WANNA GO WITH DADDY!
BIZARRO NO. 1
STOP, BABY!...OH! TOO LATE! HIM DISCOVERED HIM COULD FLY LIKE HIS FATHER! AND ME CAN'T CHASE HIM!
CLUMSY ON HIS FIRST FLIGHT, THE CHILD STRIKES TREES DOWN, AND...
OOPS! ME JUMPED BACK IN TIME! BUT DADDY BIZARRO NOW OUT OF SIGHT! MAYBE BABY COME BACK!
INSTEAD, AFTER GAINING MORE SKILL IN FLYING, CURIOSITY SENDS THE BABY ON...
WHY MOMMY AND DADDY NEVER TOOK ME TO VISIT OTHER PEOPLE? ME GO SAY HELLO TO LADY IN THIS HOUSE!
INSIDE, WHERE ANOTHER BIZARRO-LOIS HOUSEWIFE IS SWEEPING...
ME HELP HER! ME USE MY SUPER-BREATH AND BLOW OUT DUST! THEN MAYBE SHE BE MY FRIEND AND GIVE ME CANDY!
BUT INSTEAD...
IT'S THAT PERFECT BABY WHO LOOKS LIKE EARTH BABIES! GET OUT! NOBODY WANT UGLY BRAT LIKE YOU AROUND!
SH-SHE CHASING ME OUT! WHY SHE HATE ME? WELL, ME MAKE FRIENDS WITH OTHER PEOPLE!
7

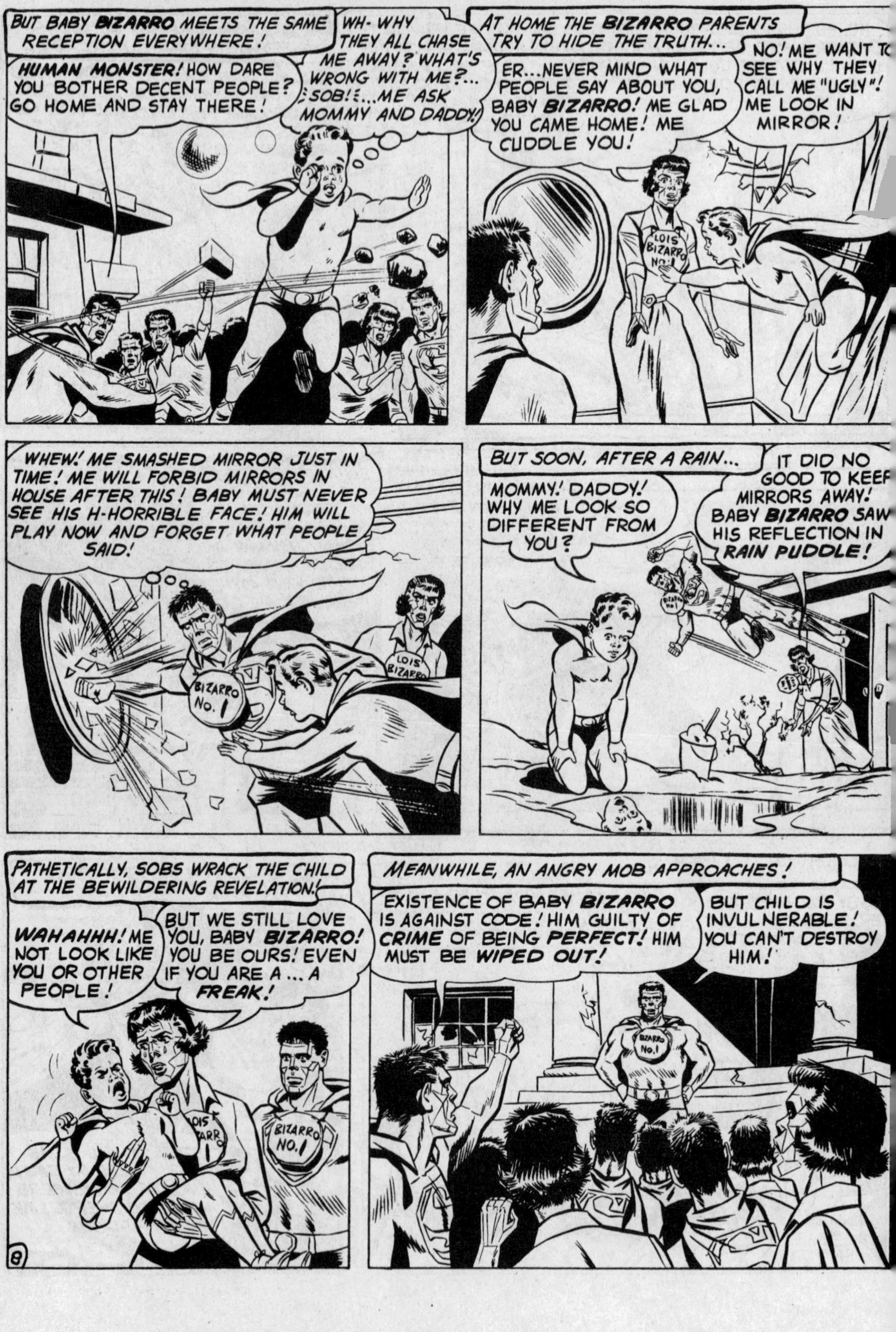
BUT BABY BIZARRO MEETS THE SAME RECEPTION EVERYWHERE!
HUMAN MONSTER! HOW DARE YOU BOTHER DECENT PEOPLE? GO HOME AND STAY THERE!
WH- WHY THEY ALL CHASE ME AWAY? WHAT'S WRONG WITH ME?... SOB!... ME ASK MOMMY AND DADDY!
AT HOME THE BIZARRO PARENTS TRY TO HIDE THE TRUTH...
ER...NEVER MIND WHAT PEOPLE SAY ABOUT YOU, BABY BIZARRO! ME GLAD YOU CAME HOME! ME CUDDLE YOU!
NO! ME WANT TO SEE WHY THEY CALL ME "UGLY"! ME LOOK IN MIRROR!
LOIS BIZARRO NO. 1
WHEW! ME SMASHED MIRROR JUST IN TIME! ME WILL FORBID MIRRORS IN HOUSE AFTER THIS! BABY MUST NEVER SEE HIS H-HORRIBLE FACE! HIM WILL PLAY NOW AND FORGET WHAT PEOPLE SAID!
BIZARRO NO. 1
LOIS BIZARRO
BUT SOON, AFTER A RAIN...
MOMMY! DADDY! WHY ME LOOK SO DIFFERENT FROM YOU?
IT DID NO GOOD TO KEEP MIRRORS AWAY! BABY BIZARRO SAW HIS REFLECTION IN RAIN PUDDLE!
PATHETICALLY, SOBS WRACK THE CHILD AT THE BEWILDERING REVELATION!
WAHAHHH! ME NOT LOOK LIKE YOU OR OTHER PEOPLE!
BUT WE STILL LOVE YOU, BABY BIZARRO! YOU BE OURS! EVEN IF YOU ARE A ... A FREAK!
LOIS BIZARRO 1
BIZARRO NO. 1
8
MEANWHILE, AN ANGRY MOB APPROACHES!
EXISTENCE OF BABY BIZARRO IS AGAINST CODE! HIM GUILTY OF CRIME OF BEING PERFECT! HIM MUST BE WIPED OUT!
BUT CHILD IS INVULNERABLE! YOU CAN'T DESTROY HIM!
BIZARRO NO. 1

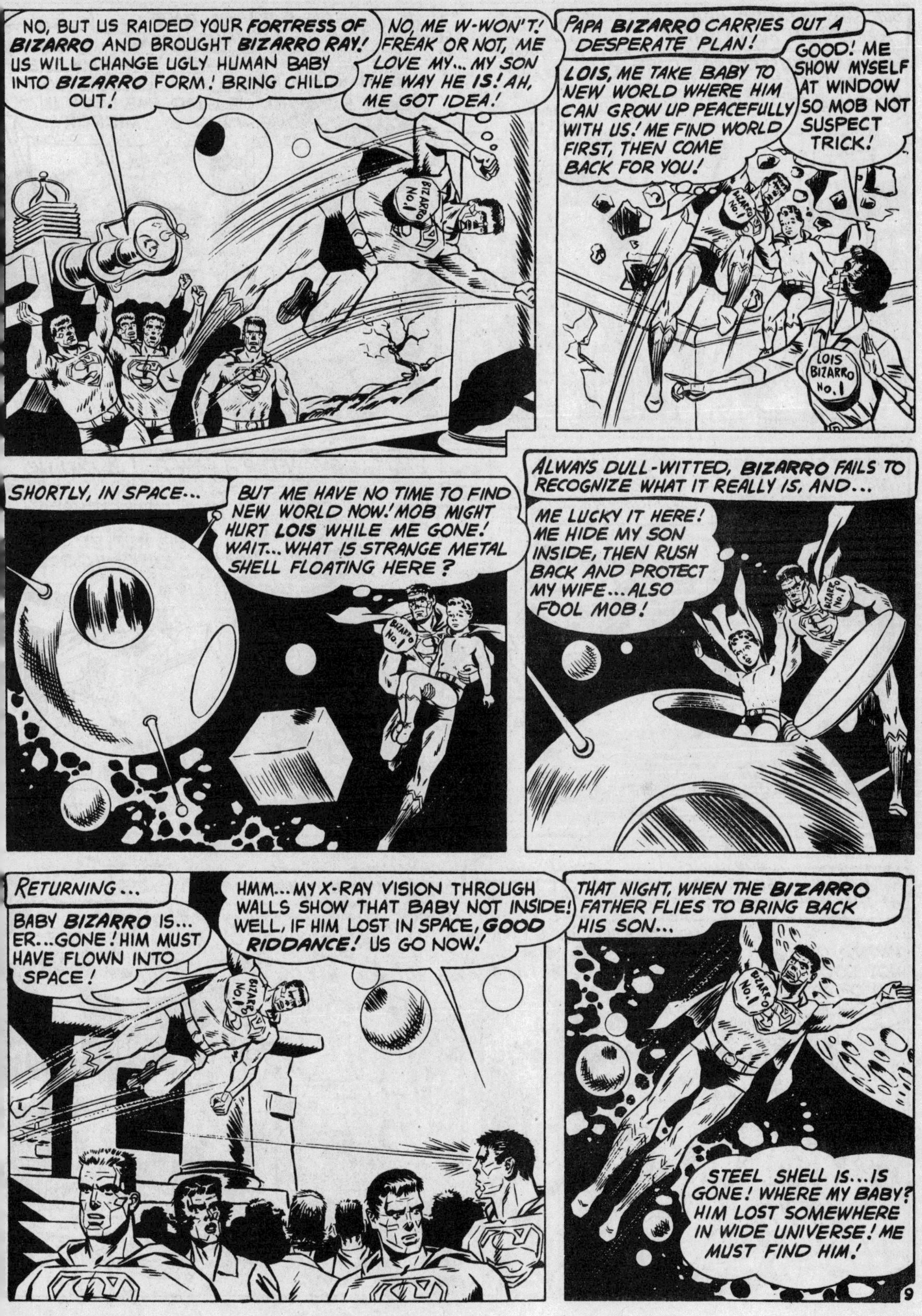
NO, BUT US RAIDED YOUR FORTRESS OF BIZARRO AND BROUGHT BIZARRO RAY! US WILL CHANGE UGLY HUMAN BABY INTO BIZARRO FORM! BRING CHILD OUT!
NO, ME W-WON'T! FREAK OR NOT, ME LOVE MY... MY SON THE WAY HE IS! AH, ME GOT IDEA!
BIZARRO No. 1
PAPA BIZARRO CARRIES OUT A DESPERATE PLAN!
LOIS, ME TAKE BABY TO NEW WORLD WHERE HIM CAN GROW UP PEACEFULLY WITH US! ME FIND WORLD FIRST, THEN COME BACK FOR YOU!
GOOD! ME SHOW MYSELF AT WINDOW SO MOB NOT SUSPECT TRICK!
BIZARRO No. 1
LOIS BIZARRO No. 1
SHORTLY, IN SPACE...
BUT ME HAVE NO TIME TO FIND NEW WORLD NOW! MOB MIGHT HURT LOIS WHILE ME GONE! WAIT... WHAT IS STRANGE METAL SHELL FLOATING HERE?
BIZARRO No. 1
ALWAYS DULL-WITTED, BIZARRO FAILS TO RECOGNIZE WHAT IT REALLY IS, AND...
ME LUCKY IT HERE! ME HIDE MY SON INSIDE, THEN RUSH BACK AND PROTECT MY WIFE... ALSO FOOL MOB!
BIZARRO No. 1
RETURNING...
BABY BIZARRO IS... ER... GONE! HIM MUST HAVE FLOWN INTO SPACE!
HMM... MY X-RAY VISION THROUGH WALLS SHOW THAT BABY NOT INSIDE! WELL, IF HIM LOST IN SPACE, GOOD RIDDANCE! US GO NOW!
BIZARRO No. 1
THAT NIGHT, WHEN THE BIZARRO FATHER FLIES TO BRING BACK HIS SON...
BIZARRO No. 1
STEEL SHELL IS... IS GONE! WHERE MY BABY? HIM LOST SOMEWHERE IN WIDE UNIVERSE! ME MUST FIND HIM!
9

BUT HOURS LATER, *BIZARRO* RETURNS WITH HEART-BREAKING NEWS!

ME SEARCHED A MILLION MILES B-BUT BABY *BIZARRO* LOST FOREVER!

OH, US NEVER SEE OUR SON AGAIN... ¿SOB.¡ MAYBE POOR CHILD WILL LAND ON LONELY WORLD WHERE NO PEOPLE LIVE!

BIZARRO No. 1

LOIS BIZARRO

BUT UNKNOWN TO THE *BIZARRO* PARENTS, THE STEEL SHELL WAS A *SPACE ROCKET* THAT IS NOW ORBITING BACK TO *EARTH* UNDER AUTOMATIC CONTROLS!

ATTENTION! SPACE PROBE RETURNING! WILL FALL IN AREA Z-13! RUSH THERE TO RESCUE SPACE PHOTO-GRAPHS FROM WRECKAGE!

STRANGELY, IT IS ALMOST LIKE WHEN THE *KRYPTON* ROCKET OF *JOR-EL* LANDED HIS INFANT SON ON EARTH, WHO BECAME *SUPER-BABY* AND GREW UP INTO *SUPERBOY* AND *SUPERMAN!*

ZZZZZ

CRASH!

UNHARMED BY THE CRASH, AND NOT EVEN WAKENING, THE SON OF *BIZARRO* SLEEPS ON, HIDDEN FROM THE SCIENTIFIC CREW THAT ARRIVES SOON...

WE'LL HAUL THE WRECKAGE TO OUR LAB, THEN EXAMINE THE FILM! GOOD THING NO PILOT WAS IN THIS SPACE PROBE! *NOBODY* COULD HAVE COME OUT OF THIS WRECK *ALIVE!*

ZZZZ-ZZ

LATER, JUST LIKE AFTER *SUPERBABY* CRASHED ON EARTH, THE *BIZARRO* BABY IS FOUND WHEN IT AWAKENS AND CRIES...

LOOK, DEAR... THAT BABY MUST HAVE BEEN ABANDONED HERE! WE'LL TAKE IT TO THE NEAREST ORPHANAGE, POOR THING!

WAH-H-HH!

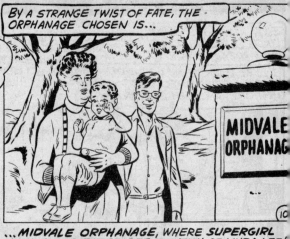

BY A STRANGE TWIST OF FATE, THE ORPHANAGE CHOSEN IS...

MIDVALE ORPHANAGE

10

...*MIDVALE ORPHANAGE*, WHERE *SUPERGIRL* LIVES UNDER THE SECRET IDENTITY OF LINDA LEE! WHAT WILL HAPPEN AS THIS SUPER-BABY LIVES ON EARTH, WITH NO ONE AWARE IT CAME FROM THE *BIZARRO WORLD?* SEE THE NEXT THRILLING CHAPTER IN THIS ISSUE!   END-PART I.

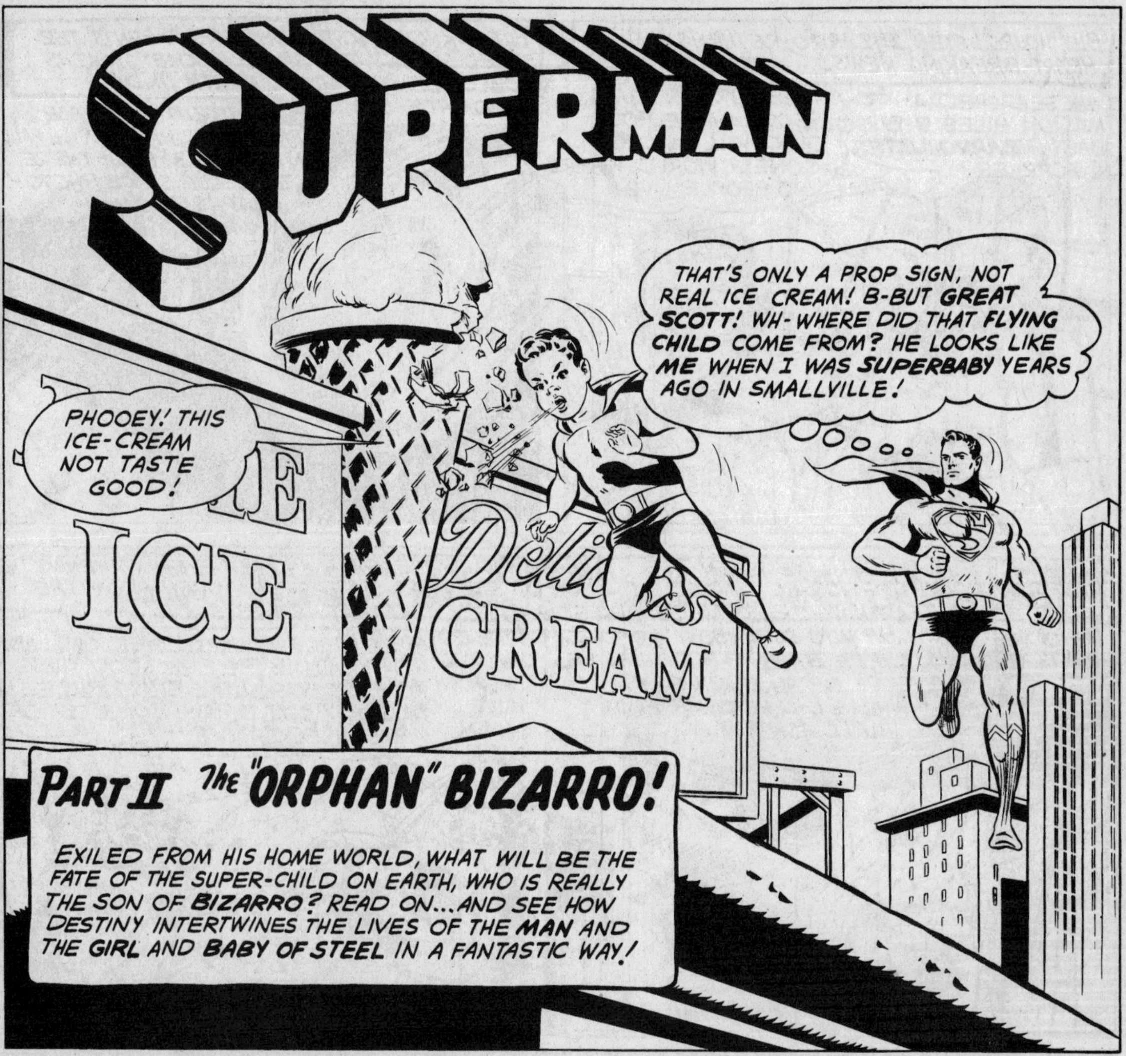
SUPERMAN
ICE
Delicious
CREAM
PHOOEY! THIS ICE-CREAM NOT TASTE GOOD!
THAT'S ONLY A PROP SIGN, NOT REAL ICE CREAM! B-BUT GREAT SCOTT! WH-WHERE DID THAT FLYING CHILD COME FROM? HE LOOKS LIKE ME WHEN I WAS SUPERBABY YEARS AGO IN SMALLVILLE!
PART II The "ORPHAN" BIZARRO!
EXILED FROM HIS HOME WORLD, WHAT WILL BE THE FATE OF THE SUPER-CHILD ON EARTH, WHO IS REALLY THE SON OF BIZARRO? READ ON...AND SEE HOW DESTINY INTERTWINES THE LIVES OF THE MAN AND THE GIRL AND BABY OF STEEL IN A FANTASTIC WAY!

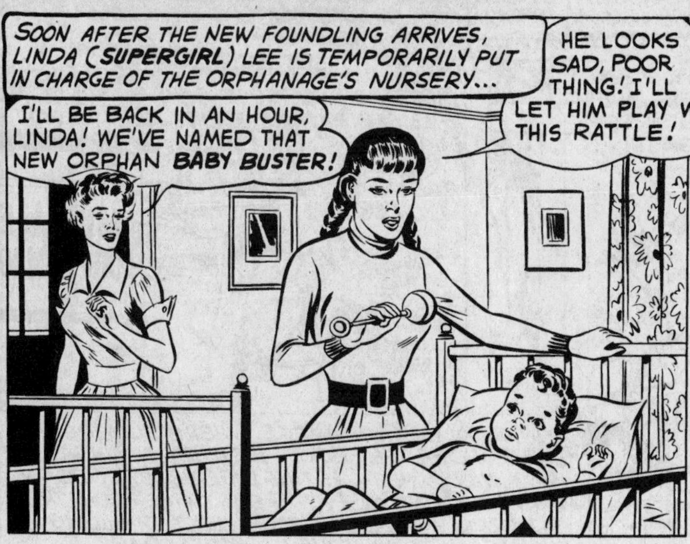
SOON AFTER THE NEW FOUNDLING ARRIVES, LINDA (SUPERGIRL) LEE IS TEMPORARILY PUT IN CHARGE OF THE ORPHANAGE'S NURSERY...
I'LL BE BACK IN AN HOUR, LINDA! WE'VE NAMED THAT NEW ORPHAN BABY BUSTER!
HE LOOKS SAD, POOR THING! I'LL LET HIM PLAY WITH THIS RATTLE!

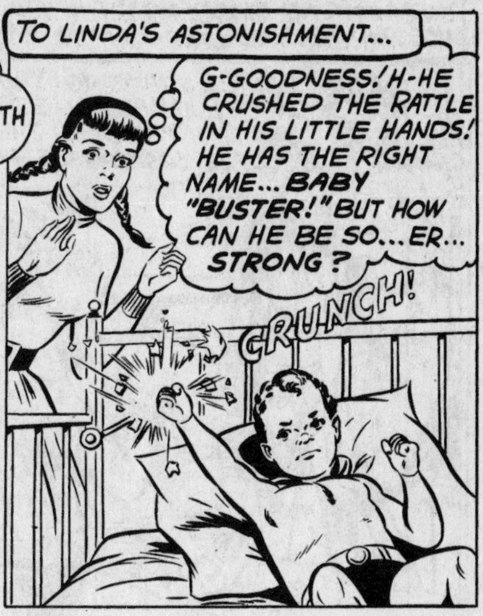
TO LINDA'S ASTONISHMENT...
G-GOODNESS! H-HE CRUSHED THE RATTLE IN HIS LITTLE HANDS! HE HAS THE RIGHT NAME... BABY "BUSTER!" BUT HOW CAN HE BE SO...ER... STRONG?
CRUNCH!

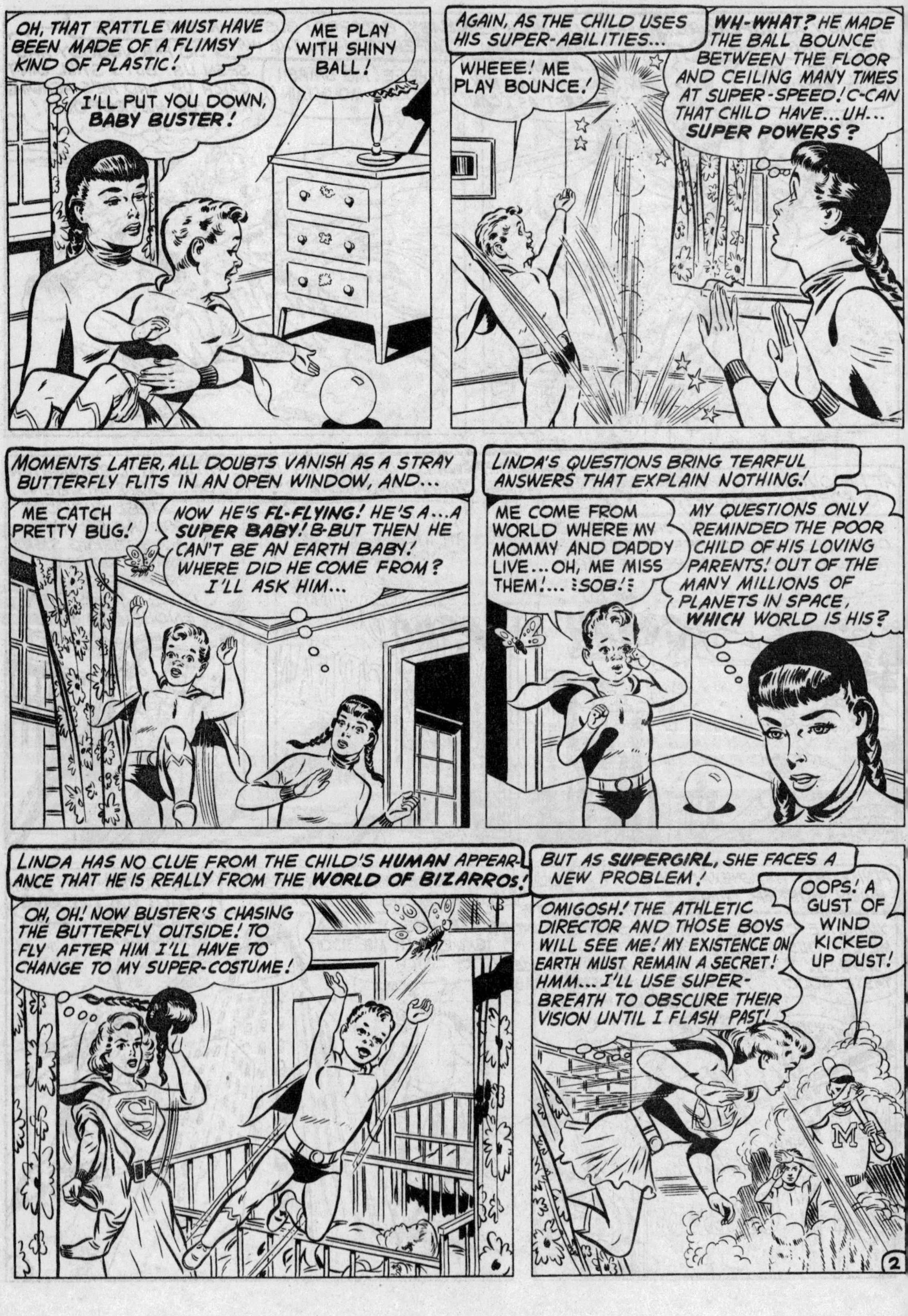
OH, THAT RATTLE MUST HAVE BEEN MADE OF A FLIMSY KIND OF PLASTIC!
I'LL PUT YOU DOWN, BABY BUSTER!
ME PLAY WITH SHINY BALL!
AGAIN, AS THE CHILD USES HIS SUPER-ABILITIES...
WHEEE! ME PLAY BOUNCE!
WH-WHAT? HE MADE THE BALL BOUNCE BETWEEN THE FLOOR AND CEILING MANY TIMES AT SUPER-SPEED! C-CAN THAT CHILD HAVE...UH... SUPER POWERS?
MOMENTS LATER, ALL DOUBTS VANISH AS A STRAY BUTTERFLY FLITS IN AN OPEN WINDOW, AND...
ME CATCH PRETTY BUG!
NOW HE'S FL-FLYING! HE'S A...A SUPER BABY! B-BUT THEN HE CAN'T BE AN EARTH BABY! WHERE DID HE COME FROM? I'LL ASK HIM...
LINDA'S QUESTIONS BRING TEARFUL ANSWERS THAT EXPLAIN NOTHING!
ME COME FROM WORLD WHERE MY MOMMY AND DADDY LIVE...OH, ME MISS THEM!... SOB!
MY QUESTIONS ONLY REMINDED THE POOR CHILD OF HIS LOVING PARENTS! OUT OF THE MANY MILLIONS OF PLANETS IN SPACE, WHICH WORLD IS HIS?
LINDA HAS NO CLUE FROM THE CHILD'S HUMAN APPEARANCE THAT HE IS REALLY FROM THE WORLD OF BIZARROS!
OH, OH! NOW BUSTER'S CHASING THE BUTTERFLY OUTSIDE! TO FLY AFTER HIM I'LL HAVE TO CHANGE TO MY SUPER-COSTUME!
BUT AS SUPERGIRL, SHE FACES A NEW PROBLEM!
OMIGOSH! THE ATHLETIC DIRECTOR AND THOSE BOYS WILL SEE ME! MY EXISTENCE ON EARTH MUST REMAIN A SECRET! HMM... I'LL USE SUPER-BREATH TO OBSCURE THEIR VISION UNTIL I FLASH PAST!
OOPS! A GUST OF WIND KICKED UP DUST!
M
2

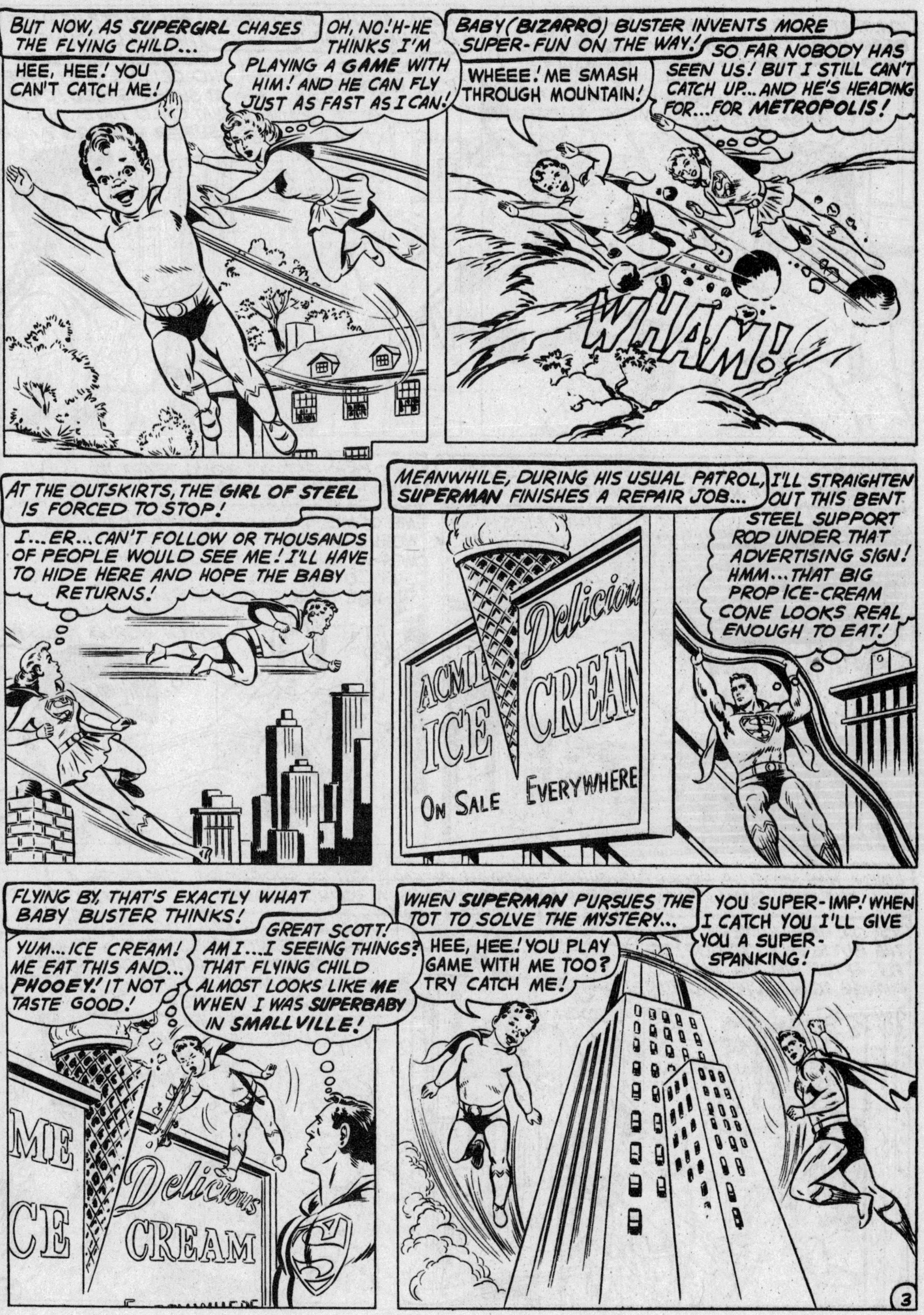
BUT NOW, AS SUPERGIRL CHASES THE FLYING CHILD...
HEE, HEE! YOU CAN'T CATCH ME!
OH, NO! H-HE THINKS I'M PLAYING A GAME WITH HIM! AND HE CAN FLY JUST AS FAST AS I CAN!
BABY (BIZARRO) BUSTER INVENTS MORE SUPER-FUN ON THE WAY!
WHEEE! ME SMASH THROUGH MOUNTAIN!
SO FAR NOBODY HAS SEEN US! BUT I STILL CAN'T CATCH UP... AND HE'S HEADING FOR... FOR METROPOLIS!
WHAM!
AT THE OUTSKIRTS, THE GIRL OF STEEL IS FORCED TO STOP!
I... ER... CAN'T FOLLOW OR THOUSANDS OF PEOPLE WOULD SEE ME! I'LL HAVE TO HIDE HERE AND HOPE THE BABY RETURNS!
MEANWHILE, DURING HIS USUAL PATROL, SUPERMAN FINISHES A REPAIR JOB...
ICE
ON SALE EVERYWHERE
I'LL STRAIGHTEN OUT THIS BENT STEEL SUPPORT ROD UNDER THAT ADVERTISING SIGN! HMM... THAT BIG PROP ICE-CREAM CONE LOOKS REAL ENOUGH TO EAT!
FLYING BY, THAT'S EXACTLY WHAT BABY BUSTER THINKS!
YUM... ICE CREAM! ME EAT THIS AND... PHOOEY! IT NOT TASTE GOOD!
GREAT SCOTT! AM I... I SEEING THINGS? THAT FLYING CHILD ALMOST LOOKS LIKE ME WHEN I WAS SUPERBABY IN SMALLVILLE!
Delicious
CREAM
WHEN SUPERMAN PURSUES THE TOT TO SOLVE THE MYSTERY...
HEE, HEE! YOU PLAY GAME WITH ME TOO? TRY CATCH ME!
YOU SUPER-IMP! WHEN I CATCH YOU I'LL GIVE YOU A SUPER-SPANKING!
3

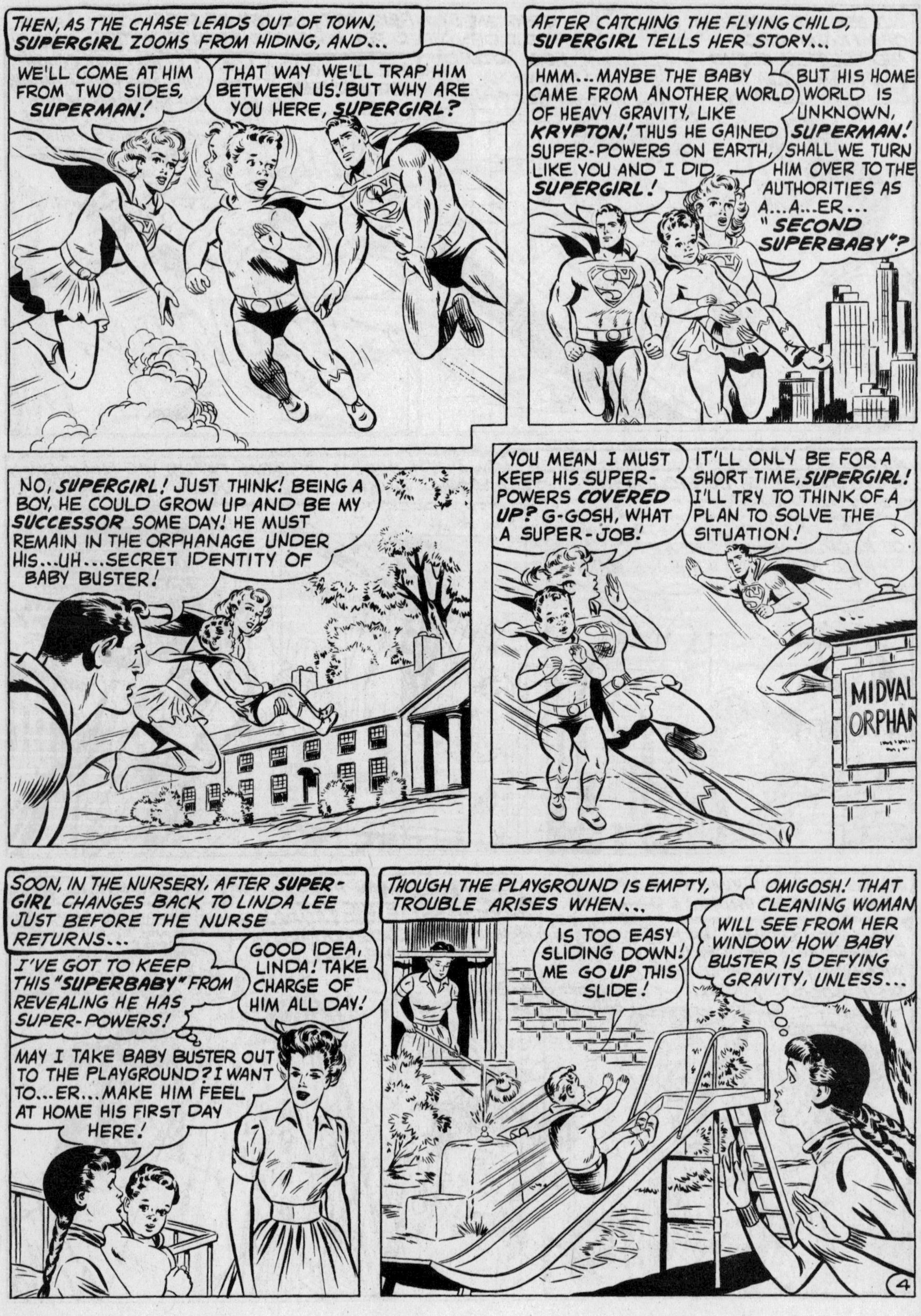
THEN, AS THE CHASE LEADS OUT OF TOWN, SUPERGIRL ZOOMS FROM HIDING, AND...
WE'LL COME AT HIM FROM TWO SIDES, SUPERMAN!
THAT WAY WE'LL TRAP HIM BETWEEN US! BUT WHY ARE YOU HERE, SUPERGIRL?
AFTER CATCHING THE FLYING CHILD, SUPERGIRL TELLS HER STORY...
HMM...MAYBE THE BABY CAME FROM ANOTHER WORLD OF HEAVY GRAVITY, LIKE KRYPTON! THUS HE GAINED SUPER-POWERS ON EARTH, LIKE YOU AND I DID, SUPERGIRL!
BUT HIS HOME WORLD IS UNKNOWN, SUPERMAN! SHALL WE TURN HIM OVER TO THE AUTHORITIES AS A...A...ER... "SECOND SUPERBABY"?
NO, SUPERGIRL! JUST THINK! BEING A BOY, HE COULD GROW UP AND BE MY SUCCESSOR SOME DAY! HE MUST REMAIN IN THE ORPHANAGE UNDER HIS...UH...SECRET IDENTITY OF BABY BUSTER!
YOU MEAN I MUST KEEP HIS SUPER-POWERS COVERED UP? G-GOSH, WHAT A SUPER-JOB!
IT'LL ONLY BE FOR A SHORT TIME, SUPERGIRL! I'LL TRY TO THINK OF A PLAN TO SOLVE THE SITUATION!
MIDVAL
ORPHAN
SOON, IN THE NURSERY, AFTER SUPERGIRL CHANGES BACK TO LINDA LEE JUST BEFORE THE NURSE RETURNS...
I'VE GOT TO KEEP THIS "SUPERBABY" FROM REVEALING HE HAS SUPER-POWERS!
GOOD IDEA, LINDA! TAKE CHARGE OF HIM ALL DAY!
MAY I TAKE BABY BUSTER OUT TO THE PLAYGROUND? I WANT TO...ER...MAKE HIM FEEL AT HOME HIS FIRST DAY HERE!
THOUGH THE PLAYGROUND IS EMPTY, TROUBLE ARISES WHEN...
IS TOO EASY SLIDING DOWN! ME GO UP THIS SLIDE!
OMIGOSH! THAT CLEANING WOMAN WILL SEE FROM HER WINDOW HOW BABY BUSTER IS DEFYING GRAVITY, UNLESS...
4

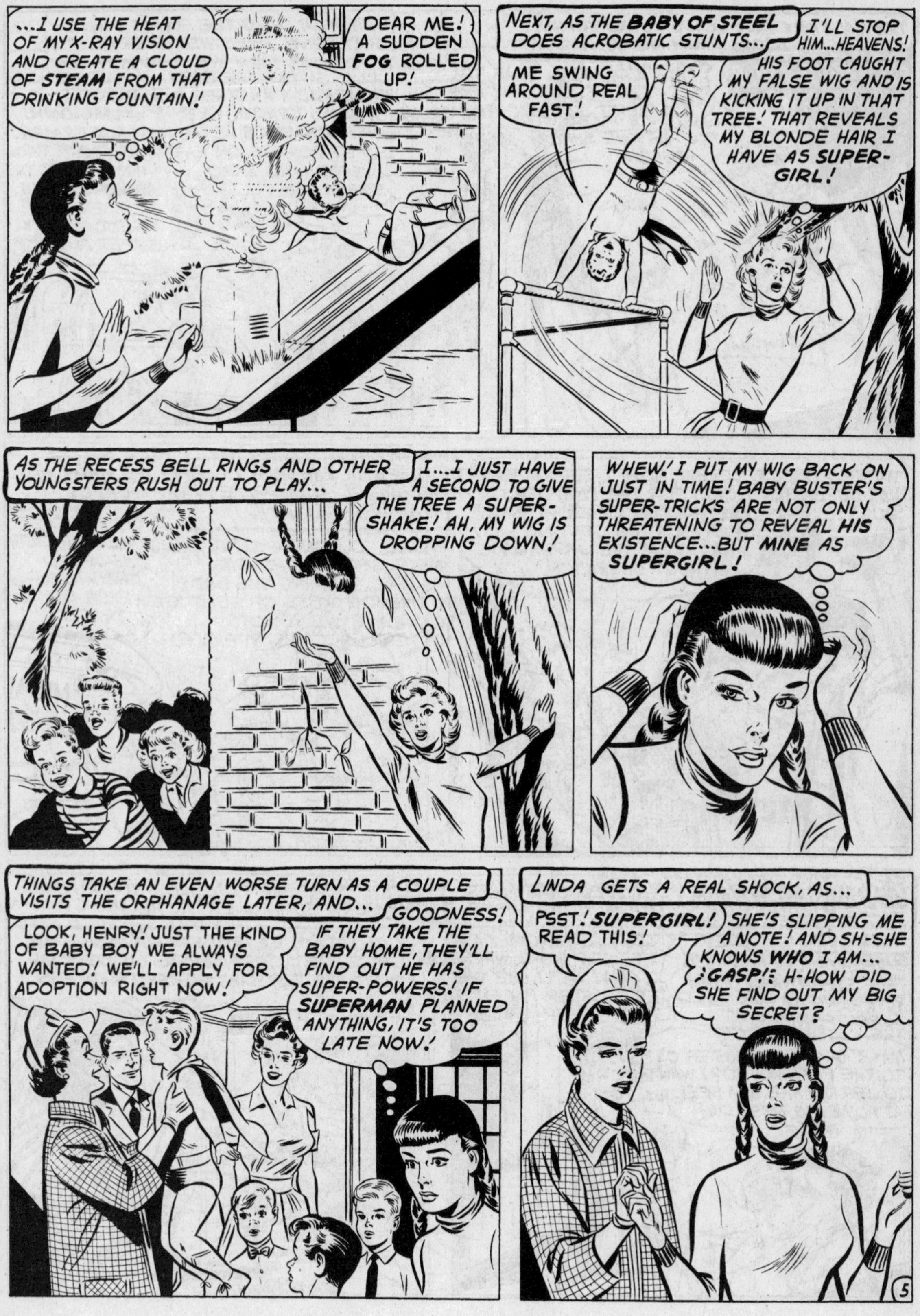
...I USE THE HEAT OF MY X-RAY VISION AND CREATE A CLOUD OF STEAM FROM THAT DRINKING FOUNTAIN!
DEAR ME! A SUDDEN FOG ROLLED UP!
NEXT, AS THE BABY OF STEEL DOES ACROBATIC STUNTS...
ME SWING AROUND REAL FAST!
I'LL STOP HIM...HEAVENS! HIS FOOT CAUGHT MY FALSE WIG AND IS KICKING IT UP IN THAT TREE! THAT REVEALS MY BLONDE HAIR I HAVE AS SUPER-GIRL!
AS THE RECESS BELL RINGS AND OTHER YOUNGSTERS RUSH OUT TO PLAY...
I...I JUST HAVE A SECOND TO GIVE THE TREE A SUPER-SHAKE! AH, MY WIG IS DROPPING DOWN!
WHEW! I PUT MY WIG BACK ON JUST IN TIME! BABY BUSTER'S SUPER-TRICKS ARE NOT ONLY THREATENING TO REVEAL HIS EXISTENCE...BUT MINE AS SUPERGIRL!
THINGS TAKE AN EVEN WORSE TURN AS A COUPLE VISITS THE ORPHANAGE LATER, AND...
LOOK, HENRY! JUST THE KIND OF BABY BOY WE ALWAYS WANTED! WE'LL APPLY FOR ADOPTION RIGHT NOW!
GOODNESS! IF THEY TAKE THE BABY HOME, THEY'LL FIND OUT HE HAS SUPER-POWERS! IF SUPERMAN PLANNED ANYTHING, IT'S TOO LATE NOW!
LINDA GETS A REAL SHOCK, AS...
PSST! SUPERGIRL! READ THIS!
SHE'S SLIPPING ME A NOTE! AND SH-SHE KNOWS WHO I AM... ¡GASP!¡ H-HOW DID SHE FIND OUT MY BIG SECRET?
5

THE MYSTERY GROWS...

IT'S *SUPERMAN'S* GENUINE HANDWRITING! B-BUT WHY WOULD MY OWN COUSIN GIVE AWAY *MY* SECRET EXISTENCE ALONG WITH THAT OF THE SUPER-CHILD?

Supergirl! Let Mr. and Mrs. Crandall adopt Baby Buster! They know all about him... and you!

Superman

LATER, AFTER TRIAL ADOPTION PAPERS ALLOW THE CRANDALLS TO DRIVE AWAY WITH BABY BUSTER, *SUPERGIRL* FOLLOWS THEM INTO A SWAMPY REGION...

STOP, MR. CRANDALL! WHY DID *SUPERMAN* REVEAL TO YOU THE SECRET OF MY EXISTENCE?

THE ANSWER IS SIMPLE, MY DEAR!

WE'RE *ROBOTS* THAT *SUPERMAN* BUILT!

GOSH, NOW I SEE! IT WAS ONLY FOR THE PURPOSE OF *PRETENDING* TO ADOPT BABY BUSTER, THUS GETTING HIM AWAY FROM THE ORPHANAGE WITHOUT SUSPICION!

PRESENTLY, THE ROBOTS LEAVE THE BABY WITH *SUPERGIRL* AND DRIVE INTO A NEARBY BED OF QUICKSAND!

WE'RE FOLLOWING *SUPERMAN'S* INSTRUCTIONS, *SUPERGIRL!* YOU ARE TO BRING THE BABY TO THE FORTRESS OF SOLITUDE NOW, WHILE WE ROBOTS MYSTERIOUSLY "DISAPPEAR" FOREVER!

THEN NEITHER THEY, NOR THEIR "ADOPTED CHILD" CAN EVER BE TRACED!

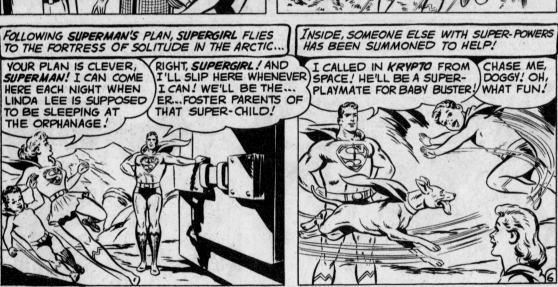

FOLLOWING *SUPERMAN'S* PLAN, *SUPERGIRL* FLIES TO THE FORTRESS OF SOLITUDE IN THE ARCTIC...

YOUR PLAN IS CLEVER, *SUPERMAN!* I CAN COME HERE EACH NIGHT WHEN LINDA LEE IS SUPPOSED TO BE SLEEPING AT THE ORPHANAGE!

RIGHT, *SUPERGIRL!* AND I'LL SLIP HERE WHENEVER I CAN! WE'LL BE THE... ER...FOSTER PARENTS OF THAT SUPER-CHILD!

INSIDE, SOMEONE ELSE WITH SUPER-POWERS HAS BEEN SUMMONED TO HELP!

I CALLED IN *KRYPTO* FROM SPACE! HE'LL BE A SUPER-PLAYMATE FOR BABY BUSTER!

CHASE ME, DOGGY! OH, WHAT FUN!

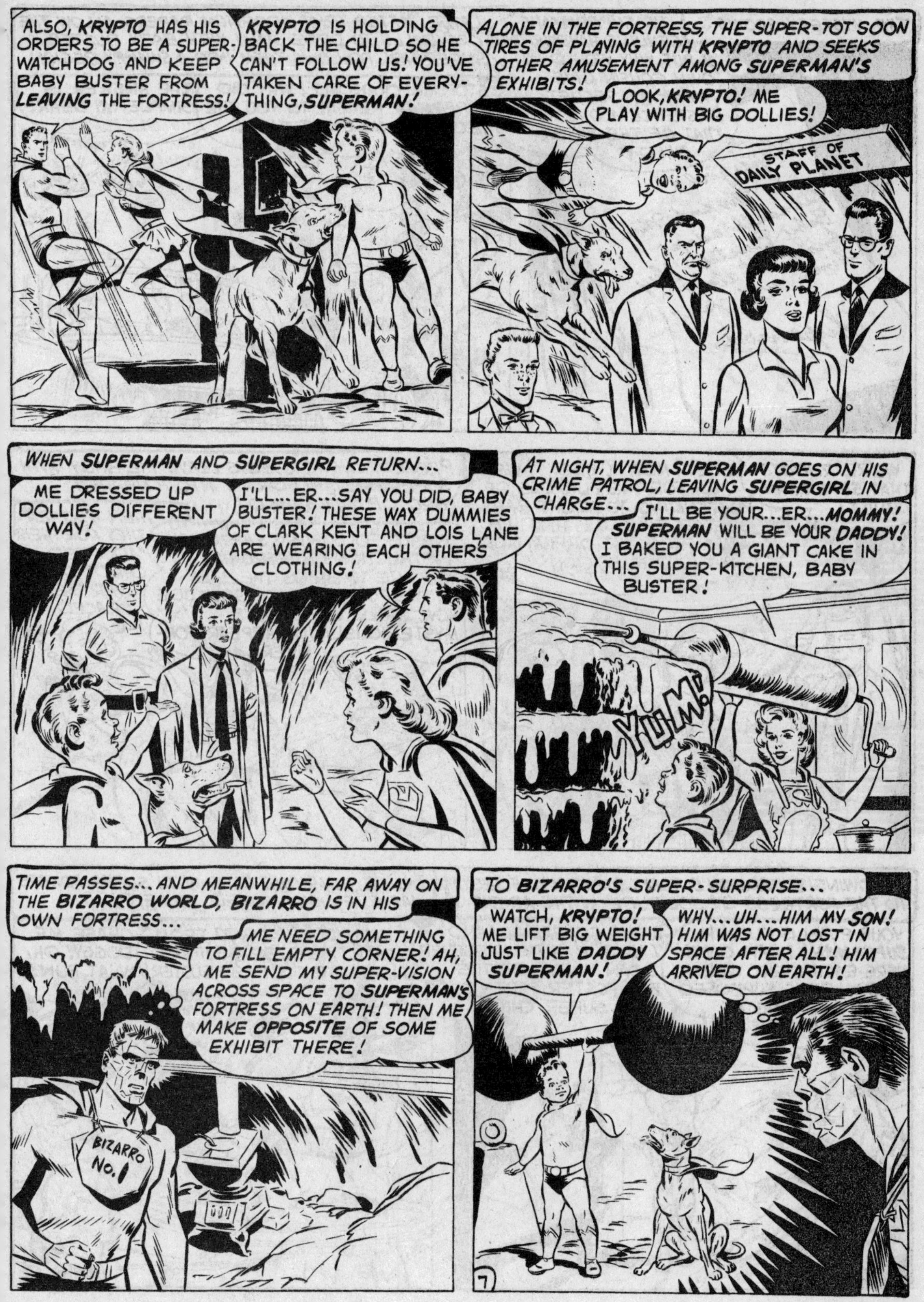
ALSO, KRYPTO HAS HIS ORDERS TO BE A SUPER-WATCHDOG AND KEEP BABY BUSTER FROM LEAVING THE FORTRESS!
KRYPTO IS HOLDING BACK THE CHILD SO HE CAN'T FOLLOW US! YOU'VE TAKEN CARE OF EVERY-THING, SUPERMAN!
ALONE IN THE FORTRESS, THE SUPER-TOT SOON TIRES OF PLAYING WITH KRYPTO AND SEEKS OTHER AMUSEMENT AMONG SUPERMAN'S EXHIBITS!
LOOK, KRYPTO! ME PLAY WITH BIG DOLLIES!
STAFF OF DAILY PLANET
WHEN SUPERMAN AND SUPERGIRL RETURN...
ME DRESSED UP DOLLIES DIFFERENT WAY!
I'LL...ER...SAY YOU DID, BABY BUSTER! THESE WAX DUMMIES OF CLARK KENT AND LOIS LANE ARE WEARING EACH OTHERS CLOTHING!
AT NIGHT, WHEN SUPERMAN GOES ON HIS CRIME PATROL, LEAVING SUPERGIRL IN CHARGE...
I'LL BE YOUR...ER...MOMMY! SUPERMAN WILL BE YOUR DADDY! I BAKED YOU A GIANT CAKE IN THIS SUPER-KITCHEN, BABY BUSTER!
YUM!
TIME PASSES...AND MEANWHILE, FAR AWAY ON THE BIZARRO WORLD, BIZARRO IS IN HIS OWN FORTRESS...
ME NEED SOMETHING TO FILL EMPTY CORNER! AH, ME SEND MY SUPER-VISION ACROSS SPACE TO SUPERMAN'S FORTRESS ON EARTH! THEN ME MAKE OPPOSITE OF SOME EXHIBIT THERE!
BIZARRO No. 1
TO BIZARRO'S SUPER-SURPRISE...
WATCH, KRYPTO! ME LIFT BIG WEIGHT JUST LIKE DADDY SUPERMAN!
WHY...UH...HIM MY SON! HIM WAS NOT LOST IN SPACE AFTER ALL! HIM ARRIVED ON EARTH!
7

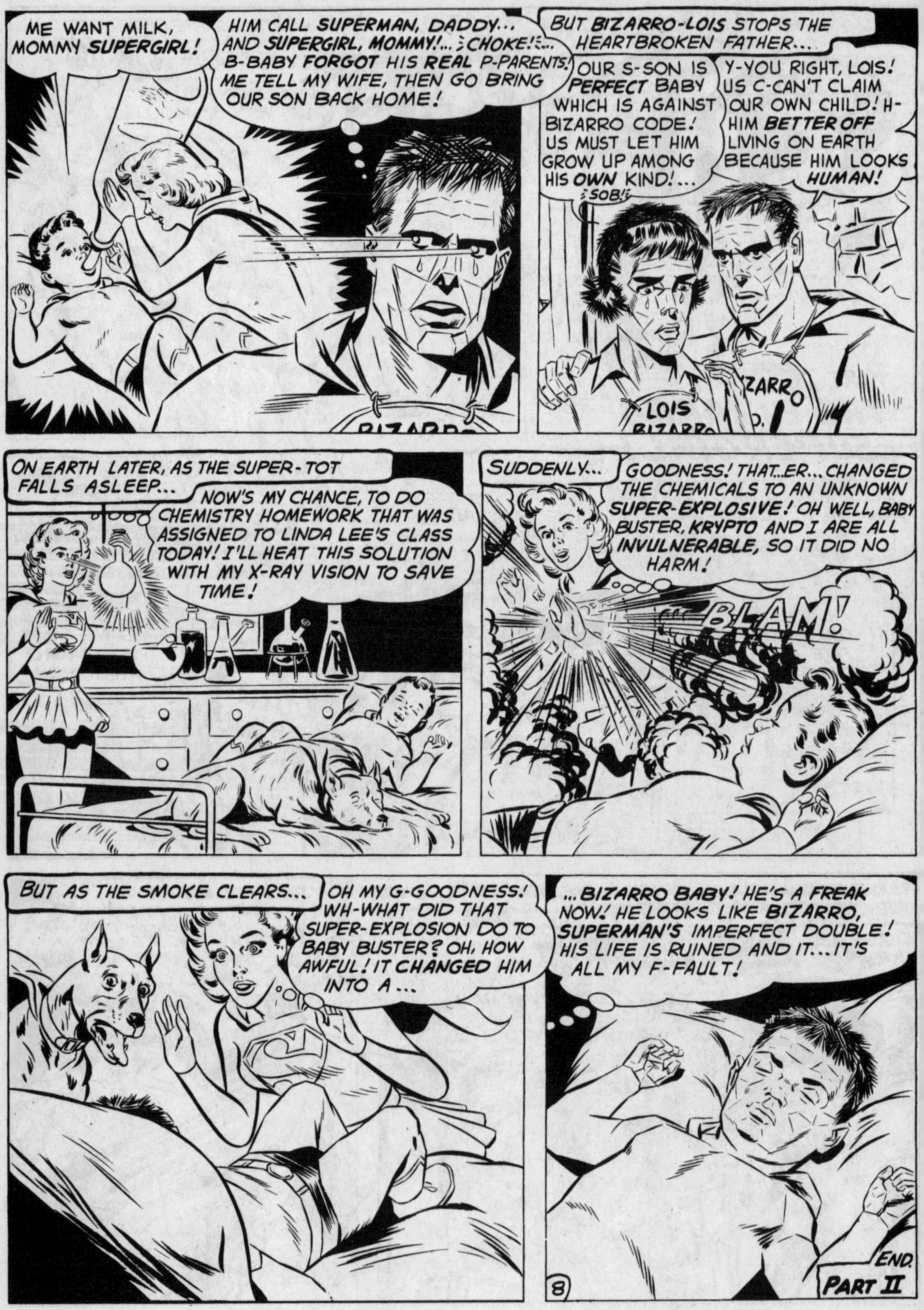
ME WANT MILK, MOMMY SUPERGIRL!
HIM CALL SUPERMAN, DADDY... AND SUPERGIRL, MOMMY!... CHOKE! B-BABY FORGOT HIS REAL P-PARENTS! ME TELL MY WIFE, THEN GO BRING OUR SON BACK HOME!
BIZARRO
BUT BIZARRO-LOIS STOPS THE HEARTBROKEN FATHER...
OUR S-SON IS PERFECT BABY WHICH IS AGAINST BIZARRO CODE! US MUST LET HIM GROW UP AMONG HIS OWN KIND!... SOB!
Y-YOU RIGHT, LOIS! US C-CAN'T CLAIM OUR OWN CHILD! H-HIM BETTER OFF LIVING ON EARTH BECAUSE HIM LOOKS HUMAN!
LOIS BIZARRO
BIZARRO
ON EARTH LATER, AS THE SUPER-TOT FALLS ASLEEP...
NOW'S MY CHANCE, TO DO CHEMISTRY HOMEWORK THAT WAS ASSIGNED TO LINDA LEE'S CLASS TODAY! I'LL HEAT THIS SOLUTION WITH MY X-RAY VISION TO SAVE TIME!
SUDDENLY...
GOODNESS! THAT...ER...CHANGED THE CHEMICALS TO AN UNKNOWN SUPER-EXPLOSIVE! OH WELL, BABY BUSTER, KRYPTO AND I ARE ALL INVULNERABLE, SO IT DID NO HARM!
BLAM!
BUT AS THE SMOKE CLEARS...
OH MY G-GOODNESS! WH-WHAT DID THAT SUPER-EXPLOSION DO TO BABY BUSTER? OH, HOW AWFUL! IT CHANGED HIM INTO A...
...BIZARRO BABY! HE'S A FREAK NOW! HE LOOKS LIKE BIZARRO, SUPERMAN'S IMPERFECT DOUBLE! HIS LIFE IS RUINED AND IT...IT'S ALL MY F-FAULT!
8
END PART II

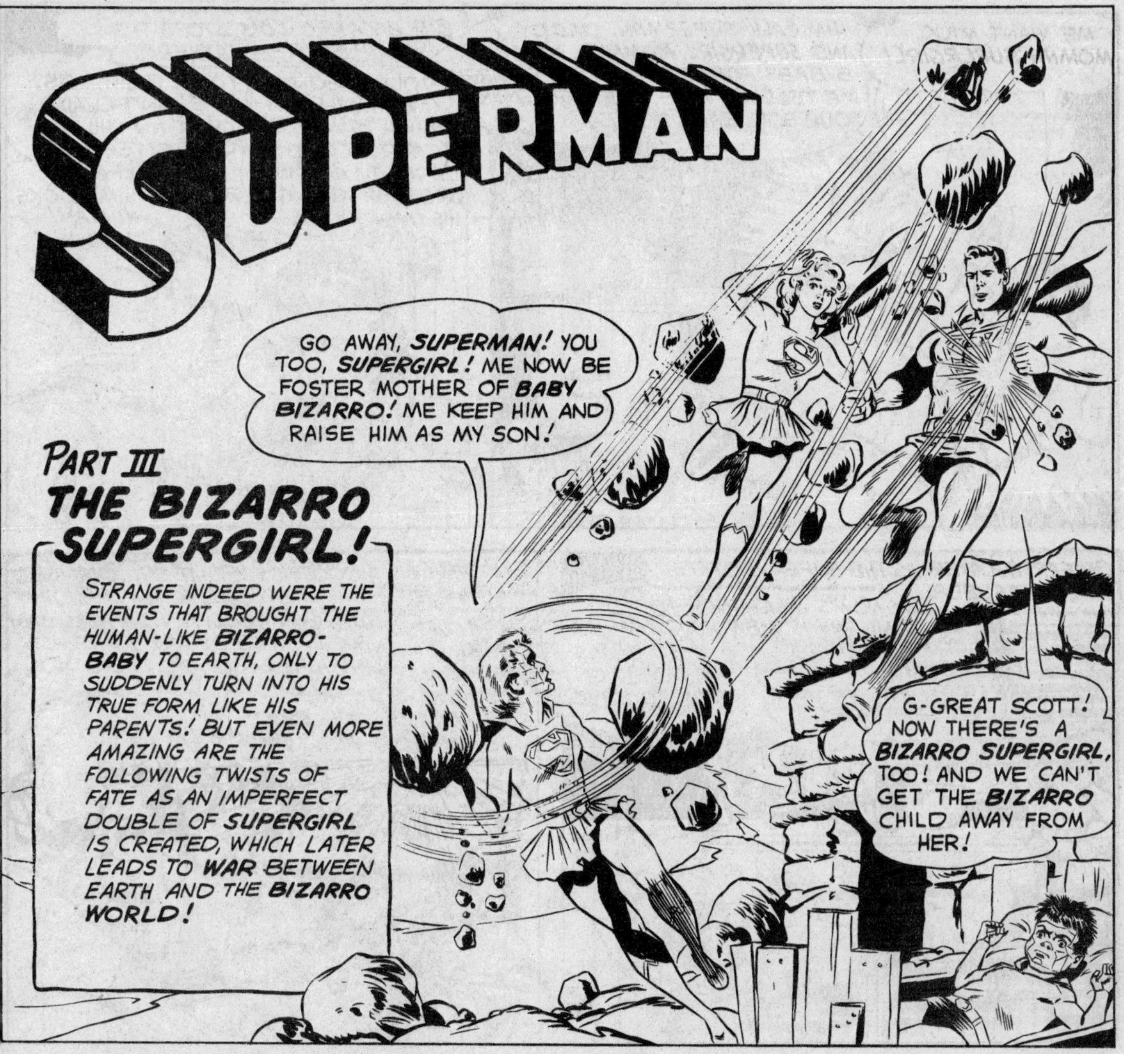
SUPERMAN
GO AWAY, SUPERMAN! YOU TOO, SUPERGIRL! ME NOW BE FOSTER MOTHER OF BABY BIZARRO! ME KEEP HIM AND RAISE HIM AS MY SON!
PART III
THE BIZARRO SUPERGIRL!
STRANGE INDEED WERE THE EVENTS THAT BROUGHT THE HUMAN-LIKE BIZARRO-BABY TO EARTH, ONLY TO SUDDENLY TURN INTO HIS TRUE FORM LIKE HIS PARENTS! BUT EVEN MORE AMAZING ARE THE FOLLOWING TWISTS OF FATE AS AN IMPERFECT DOUBLE OF SUPERGIRL IS CREATED, WHICH LATER LEADS TO WAR BETWEEN EARTH AND THE BIZARRO WORLD!
G-GREAT SCOTT! NOW THERE'S A BIZARRO SUPERGIRL, TOO! AND WE CAN'T GET THE BIZARRO CHILD AWAY FROM HER!

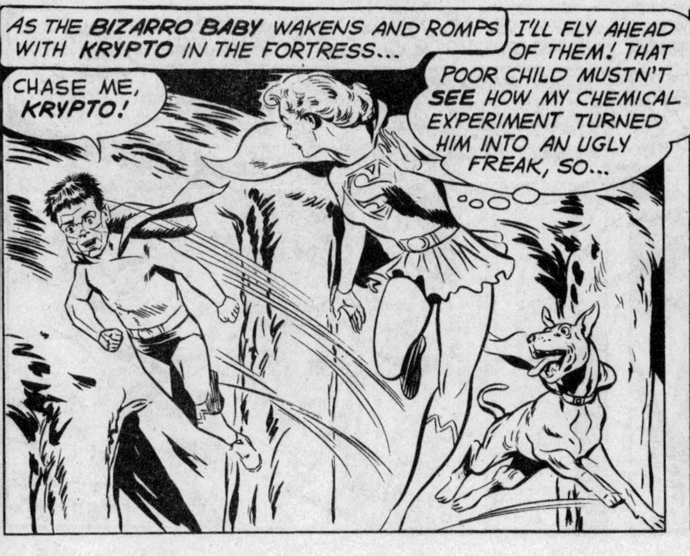
AS THE BIZARRO BABY WAKENS AND ROMPS WITH KRYPTO IN THE FORTRESS...
CHASE ME, KRYPTO!
I'LL FLY AHEAD OF THEM! THAT POOR CHILD MUSTN'T SEE HOW MY CHEMICAL EXPERIMENT TURNED HIM INTO AN UGLY FREAK, SO...

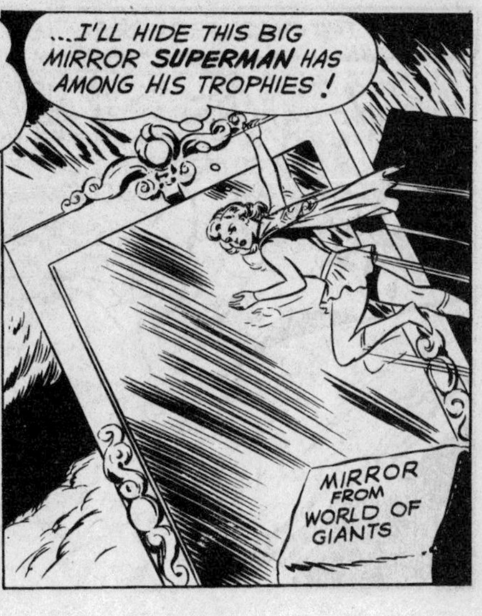
...I'LL HIDE THIS BIG MIRROR SUPERMAN HAS AMONG HIS TROPHIES!
MIRROR FROM WORLD OF GIANTS

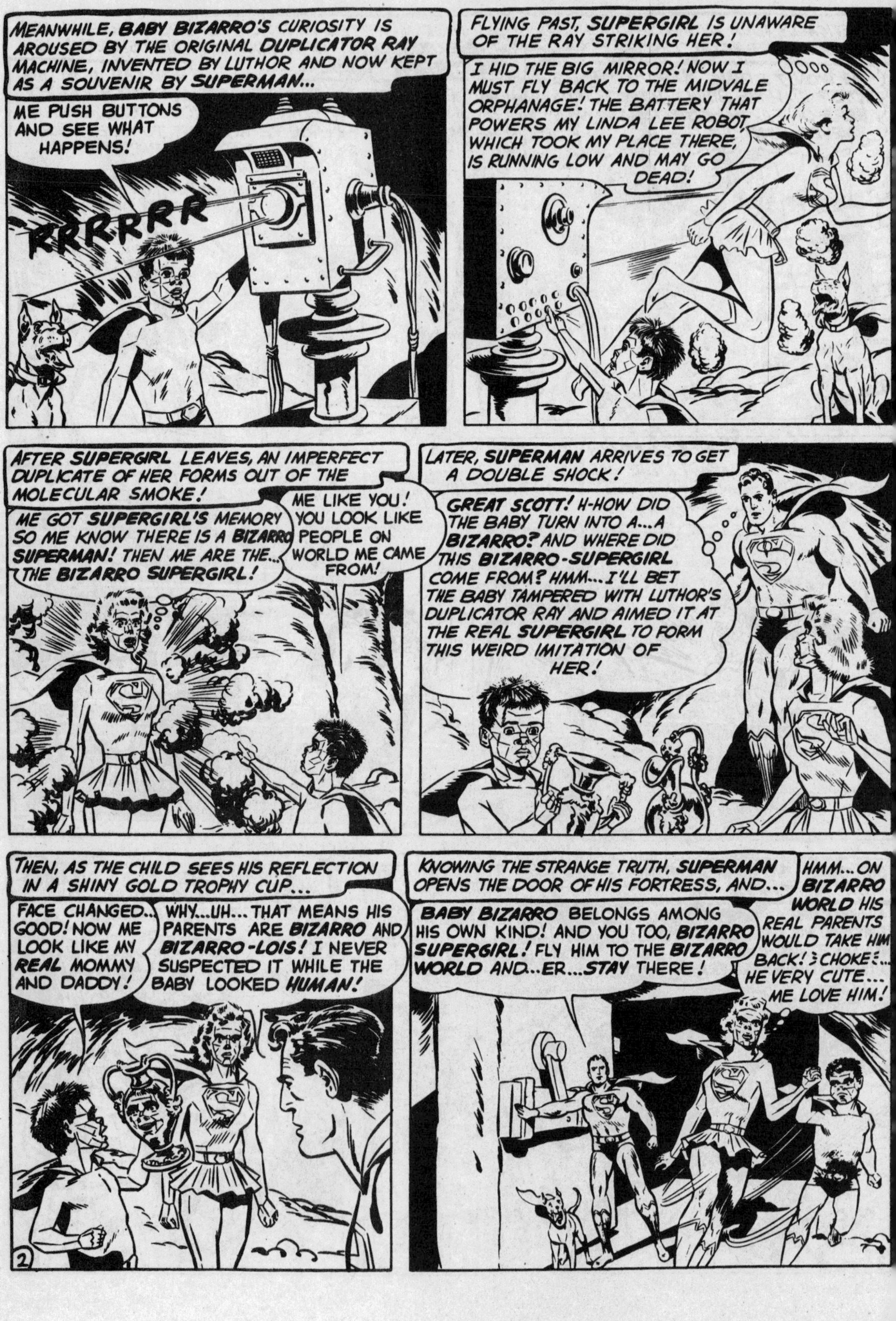
MEANWHILE, BABY BIZARRO'S CURIOSITY IS AROUSED BY THE ORIGINAL DUPLICATOR RAY MACHINE, INVENTED BY LUTHOR AND NOW KEPT AS A SOUVENIR BY SUPERMAN...
ME PUSH BUTTONS AND SEE WHAT HAPPENS!
RRRRRR
FLYING PAST, SUPERGIRL IS UNAWARE OF THE RAY STRIKING HER!
I HID THE BIG MIRROR! NOW I MUST FLY BACK TO THE MIDVALE ORPHANAGE! THE BATTERY THAT POWERS MY LINDA LEE ROBOT, WHICH TOOK MY PLACE THERE, IS RUNNING LOW AND MAY GO DEAD!
AFTER SUPERGIRL LEAVES, AN IMPERFECT DUPLICATE OF HER FORMS OUT OF THE MOLECULAR SMOKE!
ME GOT SUPERGIRL'S MEMORY SO ME KNOW THERE IS A BIZARRO SUPERMAN! THEN ME ARE THE... THE BIZARRO SUPERGIRL!
ME LIKE YOU! YOU LOOK LIKE PEOPLE ON WORLD ME CAME FROM!
LATER, SUPERMAN ARRIVES TO GET A DOUBLE SHOCK!
GREAT SCOTT! H-HOW DID THE BABY TURN INTO A...A BIZARRO? AND WHERE DID THIS BIZARRO-SUPERGIRL COME FROM? HMM...I'LL BET THE BABY TAMPERED WITH LUTHOR'S DUPLICATOR RAY AND AIMED IT AT THE REAL SUPERGIRL TO FORM THIS WEIRD IMITATION OF HER!
THEN, AS THE CHILD SEES HIS REFLECTION IN A SHINY GOLD TROPHY CUP...
FACE CHANGED... GOOD! NOW ME LOOK LIKE MY REAL MOMMY AND DADDY!
WHY...UH... THAT MEANS HIS PARENTS ARE BIZARRO AND BIZARRO-LOIS! I NEVER SUSPECTED IT WHILE THE BABY LOOKED HUMAN!
2
KNOWING THE STRANGE TRUTH, SUPERMAN OPENS THE DOOR OF HIS FORTRESS, AND...
BABY BIZARRO BELONGS AMONG HIS OWN KIND! AND YOU TOO, BIZARRO SUPERGIRL! FLY HIM TO THE BIZARRO WORLD AND...ER...STAY THERE!
HMM...ON BIZARRO WORLD HIS REAL PARENTS WOULD TAKE HIM BACK! ;CHOKE;... HE VERY CUTE... ME LOVE HIM!

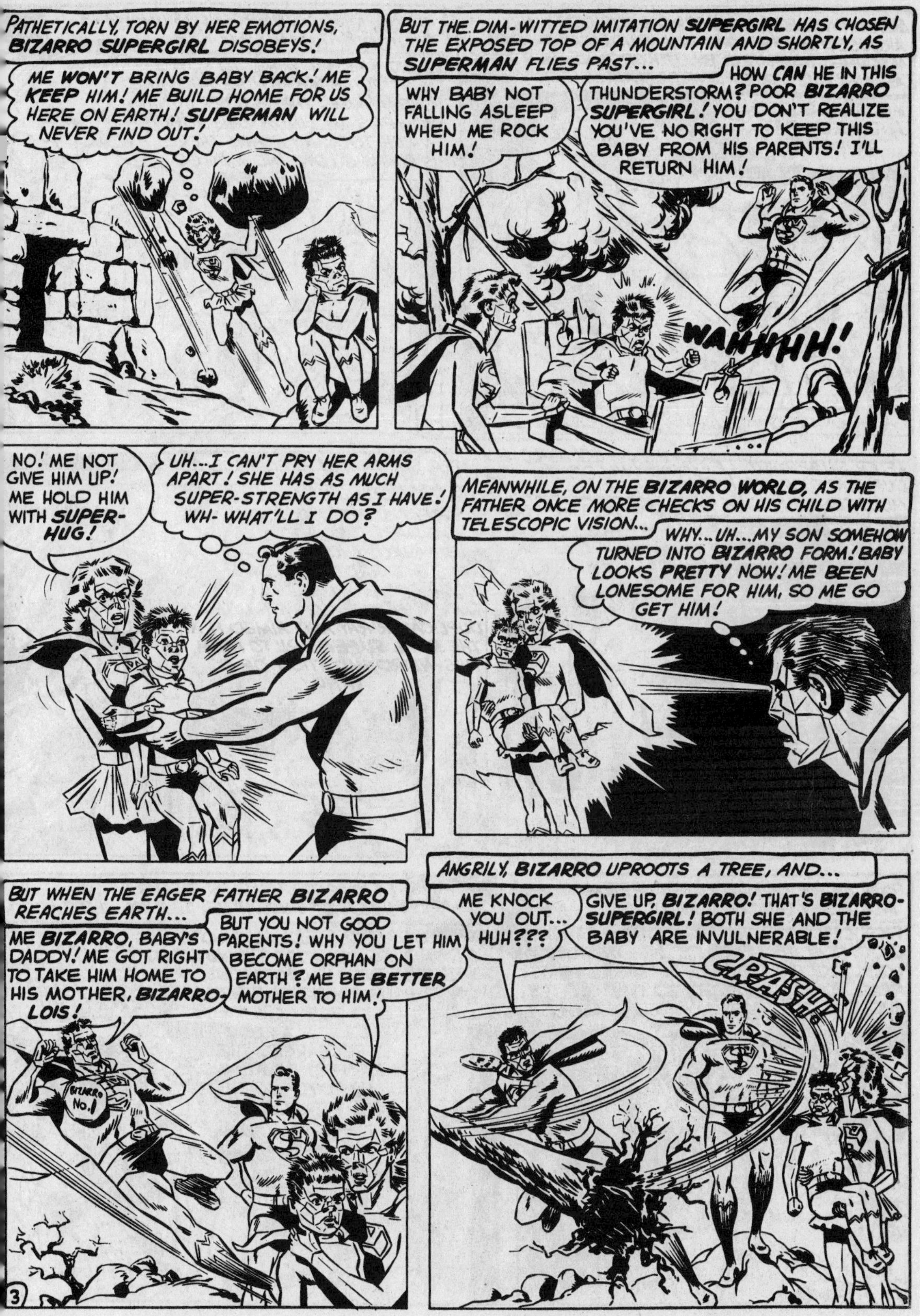
PATHETICALLY, TORN BY HER EMOTIONS, BIZARRO SUPERGIRL DISOBEYS!
ME WON'T BRING BABY BACK! ME KEEP HIM! ME BUILD HOME FOR US HERE ON EARTH! SUPERMAN WILL NEVER FIND OUT!
BUT THE DIM-WITTED IMITATION SUPERGIRL HAS CHOSEN THE EXPOSED TOP OF A MOUNTAIN AND SHORTLY, AS SUPERMAN FLIES PAST...
WHY BABY NOT FALLING ASLEEP WHEN ME ROCK HIM!
HOW CAN HE IN THIS THUNDERSTORM? POOR BIZARRO SUPERGIRL! YOU DON'T REALIZE YOU'VE NO RIGHT TO KEEP THIS BABY FROM HIS PARENTS! I'LL RETURN HIM!
WAHWHH!
NO! ME NOT GIVE HIM UP! ME HOLD HIM WITH SUPER-HUG!
UH...I CAN'T PRY HER ARMS APART! SHE HAS AS MUCH SUPER-STRENGTH AS I HAVE! WH- WHAT'LL I DO?
MEANWHILE, ON THE BIZARRO WORLD, AS THE FATHER ONCE MORE CHECKS ON HIS CHILD WITH TELESCOPIC VISION...
WHY...UH...MY SON SOMEHOW TURNED INTO BIZARRO FORM! BABY LOOKS PRETTY NOW! ME BEEN LONESOME FOR HIM, SO ME GO GET HIM!
BUT WHEN THE EAGER FATHER BIZARRO REACHES EARTH...
ME BIZARRO, BABY'S DADDY! ME GOT RIGHT TO TAKE HIM HOME TO HIS MOTHER, BIZARRO-LOIS!
BUT YOU NOT GOOD PARENTS! WHY YOU LET HIM BECOME ORPHAN ON EARTH? ME BE BETTER MOTHER TO HIM!
BIZARRO No. 1
3
ANGRILY, BIZARRO UPROOTS A TREE, AND...
ME KNOCK YOU OUT... HUH???
GIVE UP, BIZARRO! THAT'S BIZARRO-SUPERGIRL! BOTH SHE AND THE BABY ARE INVULNERABLE!
CRASH!

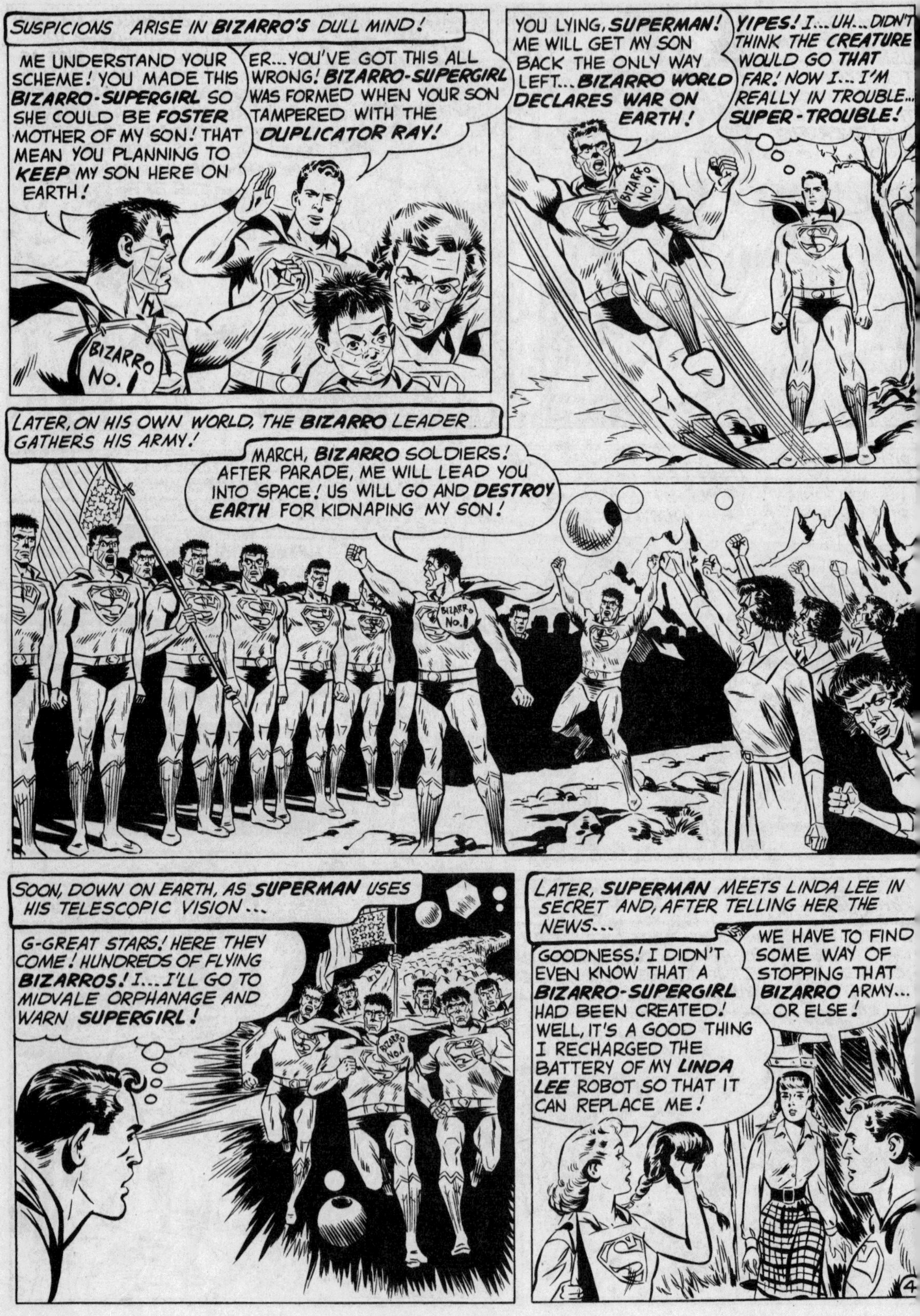
SUSPICIONS ARISE IN BIZARRO'S DULL MIND!
ME UNDERSTAND YOUR SCHEME! YOU MADE THIS BIZARRO-SUPERGIRL SO SHE COULD BE FOSTER MOTHER OF MY SON! THAT MEAN YOU PLANNING TO KEEP MY SON HERE ON EARTH!
ER...YOU'VE GOT THIS ALL WRONG! BIZARRO-SUPERGIRL WAS FORMED WHEN YOUR SON TAMPERED WITH THE DUPLICATOR RAY!
BIZARRO No. 1
YOU LYING, SUPERMAN! ME WILL GET MY SON BACK THE ONLY WAY LEFT...BIZARRO WORLD DECLARES WAR ON EARTH!
YIPES! I...UH...DIDN'T THINK THE CREATURE WOULD GO THAT FAR! NOW I... I'M REALLY IN TROUBLE... SUPER-TROUBLE!
BIZARRO No. 1
LATER, ON HIS OWN WORLD, THE BIZARRO LEADER GATHERS HIS ARMY!
MARCH, BIZARRO SOLDIERS! AFTER PARADE, ME WILL LEAD YOU INTO SPACE! US WILL GO AND DESTROY EARTH FOR KIDNAPING MY SON!
BIZARRO No. 1
SOON, DOWN ON EARTH, AS SUPERMAN USES HIS TELESCOPIC VISION...
G-GREAT STARS! HERE THEY COME! HUNDREDS OF FLYING BIZARROS! I...I'LL GO TO MIDVALE ORPHANAGE AND WARN SUPERGIRL!
BIZARRO No. 1
LATER, SUPERMAN MEETS LINDA LEE IN SECRET AND, AFTER TELLING HER THE NEWS...
GOODNESS! I DIDN'T EVEN KNOW THAT A BIZARRO-SUPERGIRL HAD BEEN CREATED! WELL, IT'S A GOOD THING I RECHARGED THE BATTERY OF MY LINDA LEE ROBOT SO THAT IT CAN REPLACE ME!
WE HAVE TO FIND SOME WAY OF STOPPING THAT BIZARRO ARMY... OR ELSE!
4

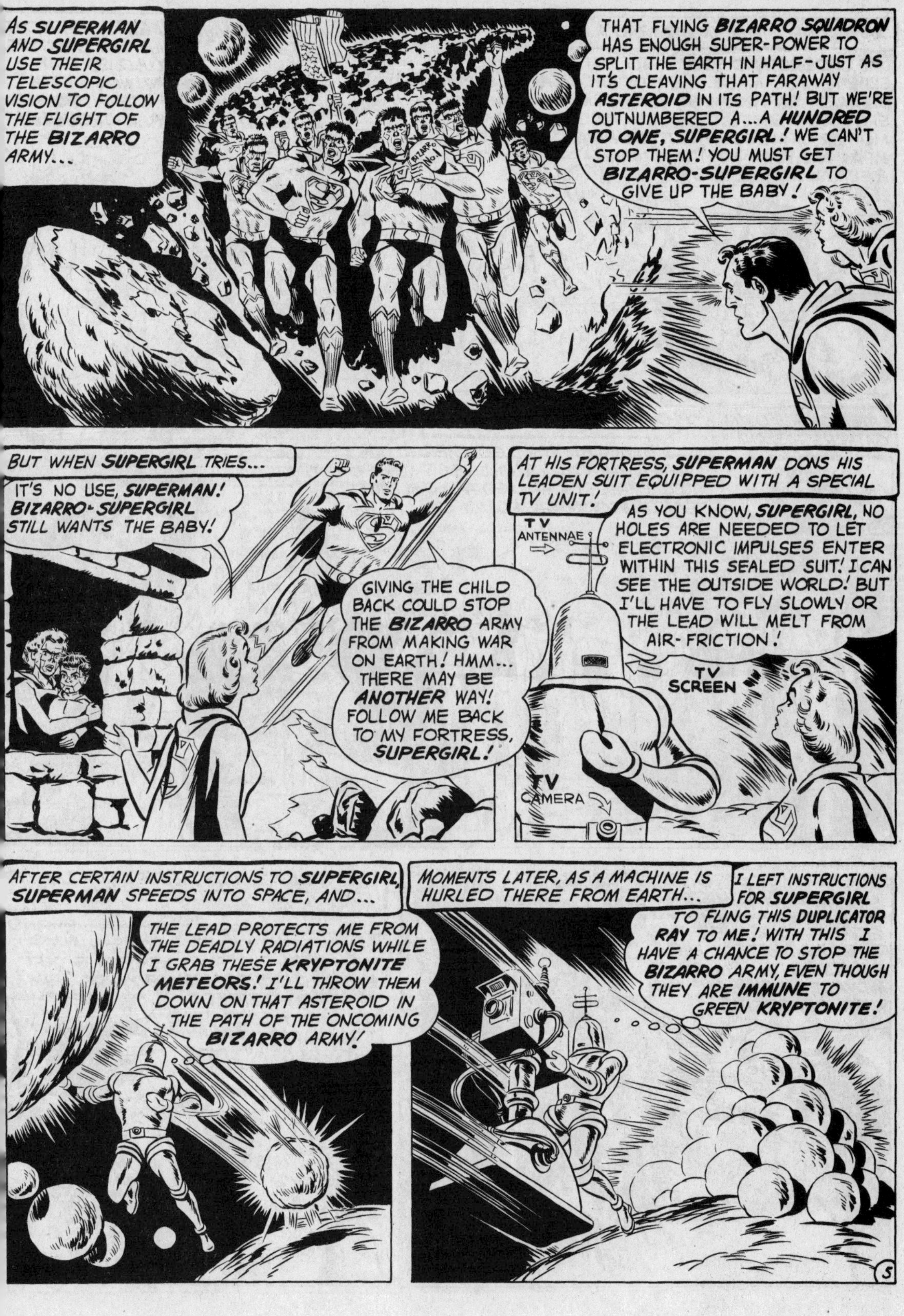
AS SUPERMAN AND SUPERGIRL USE THEIR TELESCOPIC VISION TO FOLLOW THE FLIGHT OF THE BIZARRO ARMY...
BIZARRO No. 1
THAT FLYING BIZARRO SQUADRON HAS ENOUGH SUPER-POWER TO SPLIT THE EARTH IN HALF-JUST AS IT'S CLEAVING THAT FARAWAY ASTEROID IN ITS PATH! BUT WE'RE OUTNUMBERED A...A HUNDRED TO ONE, SUPERGIRL! WE CAN'T STOP THEM! YOU MUST GET BIZARRO-SUPERGIRL TO GIVE UP THE BABY!
BUT WHEN SUPERGIRL TRIES...
IT'S NO USE, SUPERMAN! BIZARRO-SUPERGIRL STILL WANTS THE BABY!
GIVING THE CHILD BACK COULD STOP THE BIZARRO ARMY FROM MAKING WAR ON EARTH! HMM... THERE MAY BE ANOTHER WAY! FOLLOW ME BACK TO MY FORTRESS, SUPERGIRL!
AT HIS FORTRESS, SUPERMAN DONS HIS LEADEN SUIT EQUIPPED WITH A SPECIAL TV UNIT!
TV ANTENNAE
AS YOU KNOW, SUPERGIRL, NO HOLES ARE NEEDED TO LET ELECTRONIC IMPULSES ENTER WITHIN THIS SEALED SUIT! I CAN SEE THE OUTSIDE WORLD! BUT I'LL HAVE TO FLY SLOWLY OR THE LEAD WILL MELT FROM AIR-FRICTION!
TV SCREEN
TV CAMERA
AFTER CERTAIN INSTRUCTIONS TO SUPERGIRL, SUPERMAN SPEEDS INTO SPACE, AND...
THE LEAD PROTECTS ME FROM THE DEADLY RADIATIONS WHILE I GRAB THESE KRYPTONITE METEORS! I'LL THROW THEM DOWN ON THAT ASTEROID IN THE PATH OF THE ONCOMING BIZARRO ARMY!
MOMENTS LATER, AS A MACHINE IS HURLED THERE FROM EARTH...
I LEFT INSTRUCTIONS FOR SUPERGIRL TO FLING THIS DUPLICATOR RAY TO ME! WITH THIS I HAVE A CHANCE TO STOP THE BIZARRO ARMY, EVEN THOUGH THEY ARE IMMUNE TO GREEN KRYPTONITE!
5

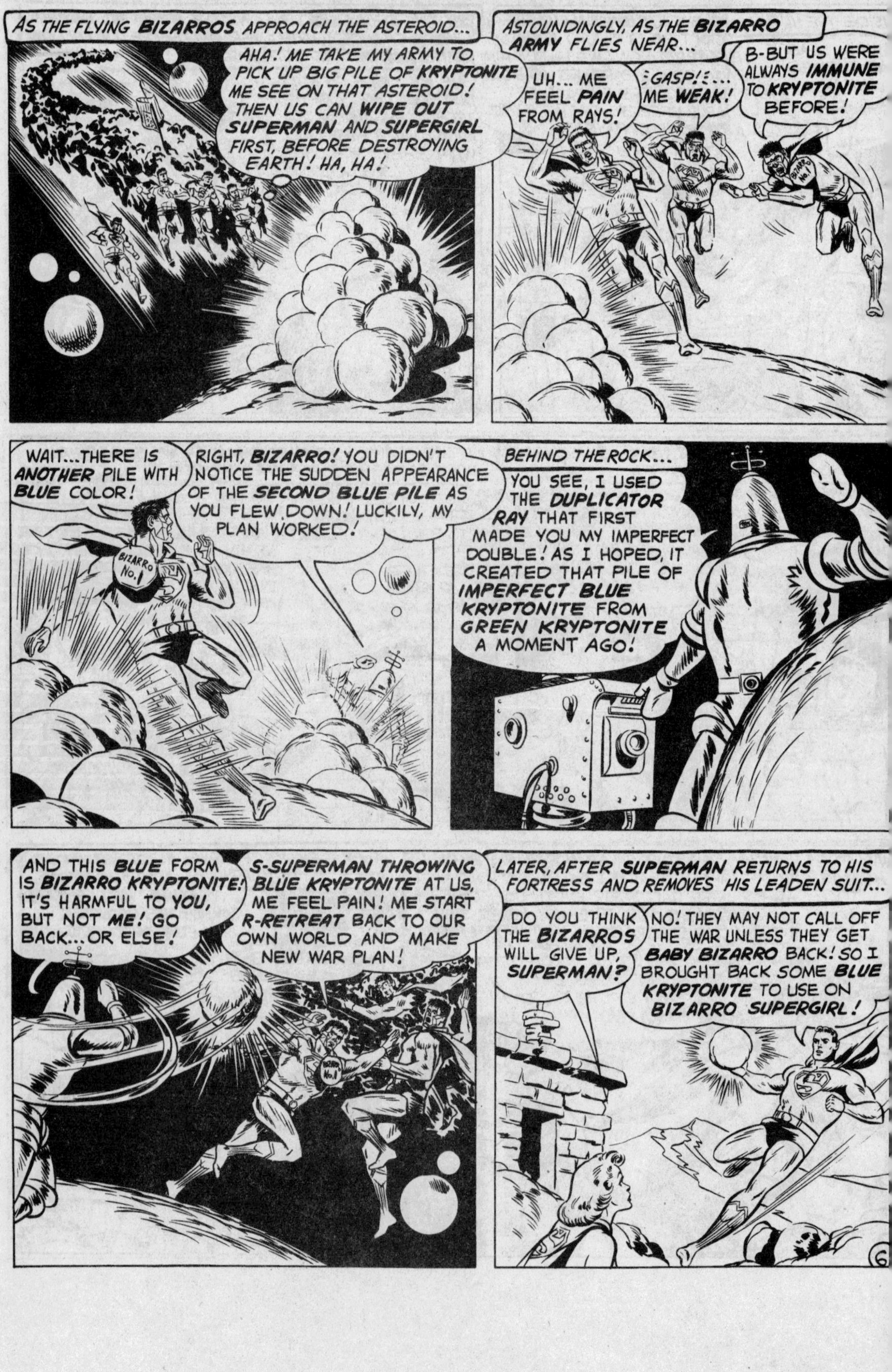
AS THE FLYING BIZARROS APPROACH THE ASTEROID...
AHA! ME TAKE MY ARMY TO PICK UP BIG PILE OF KRYPTONITE ME SEE ON THAT ASTEROID! THEN US CAN WIPE OUT SUPERMAN AND SUPERGIRL FIRST, BEFORE DESTROYING EARTH! HA, HA!
ASTOUNDINGLY, AS THE BIZARRO ARMY FLIES NEAR...
UH... ME FEEL PAIN FROM RAYS!
GASP!... ME WEAK!
B-BUT US WERE ALWAYS IMMUNE TO KRYPTONITE BEFORE!
BIZARRO No. 1
WAIT...THERE IS ANOTHER PILE WITH BLUE COLOR!
RIGHT, BIZARRO! YOU DIDN'T NOTICE THE SUDDEN APPEARANCE OF THE SECOND BLUE PILE AS YOU FLEW DOWN! LUCKILY, MY PLAN WORKED!
BEHIND THE ROCK...
YOU SEE, I USED THE DUPLICATOR RAY THAT FIRST MADE YOU MY IMPERFECT DOUBLE! AS I HOPED, IT CREATED THAT PILE OF IMPERFECT BLUE KRYPTONITE FROM GREEN KRYPTONITE A MOMENT AGO!
AND THIS BLUE FORM IS BIZARRO KRYPTONITE! IT'S HARMFUL TO YOU, BUT NOT ME! GO BACK...OR ELSE!
S-SUPERMAN THROWING BLUE KRYPTONITE AT US, ME FEEL PAIN! ME START R-RETREAT BACK TO OUR OWN WORLD AND MAKE NEW WAR PLAN!
BIZARRO No. 1
LATER, AFTER SUPERMAN RETURNS TO HIS FORTRESS AND REMOVES HIS LEADEN SUIT...
DO YOU THINK THE BIZARROS WILL GIVE UP, SUPERMAN?
NO! THEY MAY NOT CALL OFF THE WAR UNLESS THEY GET BABY BIZARRO BACK! SO I BROUGHT BACK SOME BLUE KRYPTONITE TO USE ON BIZARRO SUPERGIRL!
6

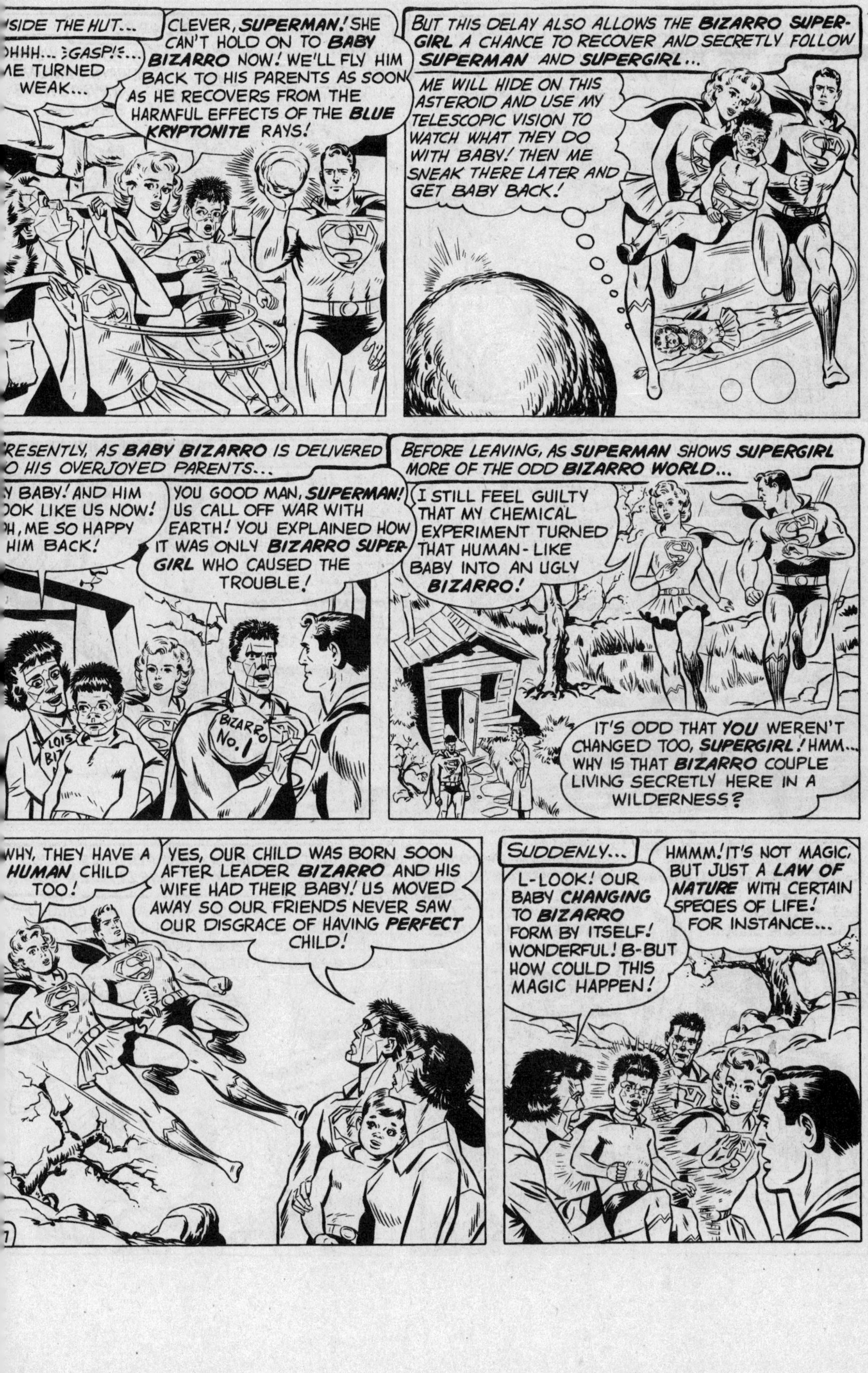
SIDE THE HUT...
OHHH... GASP!... ME TURNED WEAK...
CLEVER, SUPERMAN! SHE CAN'T HOLD ON TO BABY BIZARRO NOW! WE'LL FLY HIM BACK TO HIS PARENTS AS SOON AS HE RECOVERS FROM THE HARMFUL EFFECTS OF THE BLUE KRYPTONITE RAYS!
BUT THIS DELAY ALSO ALLOWS THE BIZARRO SUPERGIRL A CHANCE TO RECOVER AND SECRETLY FOLLOW SUPERMAN AND SUPERGIRL...
ME WILL HIDE ON THIS ASTEROID AND USE MY TELESCOPIC VISION TO WATCH WHAT THEY DO WITH BABY! THEN ME SNEAK THERE LATER AND GET BABY BACK!
RESENTLY, AS BABY BIZARRO IS DELIVERED O HIS OVERJOYED PARENTS...
Y BABY! AND HIM OOK LIKE US NOW! H, ME SO HAPPY HIM BACK!
YOU GOOD MAN, SUPERMAN! US CALL OFF WAR WITH EARTH! YOU EXPLAINED HOW IT WAS ONLY BIZARRO SUPERGIRL WHO CAUSED THE TROUBLE!
BIZARRO No. 1
BEFORE LEAVING, AS SUPERMAN SHOWS SUPERGIRL MORE OF THE ODD BIZARRO WORLD...
I STILL FEEL GUILTY THAT MY CHEMICAL EXPERIMENT TURNED THAT HUMAN-LIKE BABY INTO AN UGLY BIZARRO!
IT'S ODD THAT YOU WEREN'T CHANGED TOO, SUPERGIRL! HMM... WHY IS THAT BIZARRO COUPLE LIVING SECRETLY HERE IN A WILDERNESS?
WHY, THEY HAVE A HUMAN CHILD TOO!
YES, OUR CHILD WAS BORN SOON AFTER LEADER BIZARRO AND HIS WIFE HAD THEIR BABY! US MOVED AWAY SO OUR FRIENDS NEVER SAW OUR DISGRACE OF HAVING PERFECT CHILD!
SUDDENLY...
L-LOOK! OUR BABY CHANGING TO BIZARRO FORM BY ITSELF! WONDERFUL! B-BUT HOW COULD THIS MAGIC HAPPEN!
HMMM! IT'S NOT MAGIC, BUT JUST A LAW OF NATURE WITH CERTAIN SPECIES OF LIFE! FOR INSTANCE...

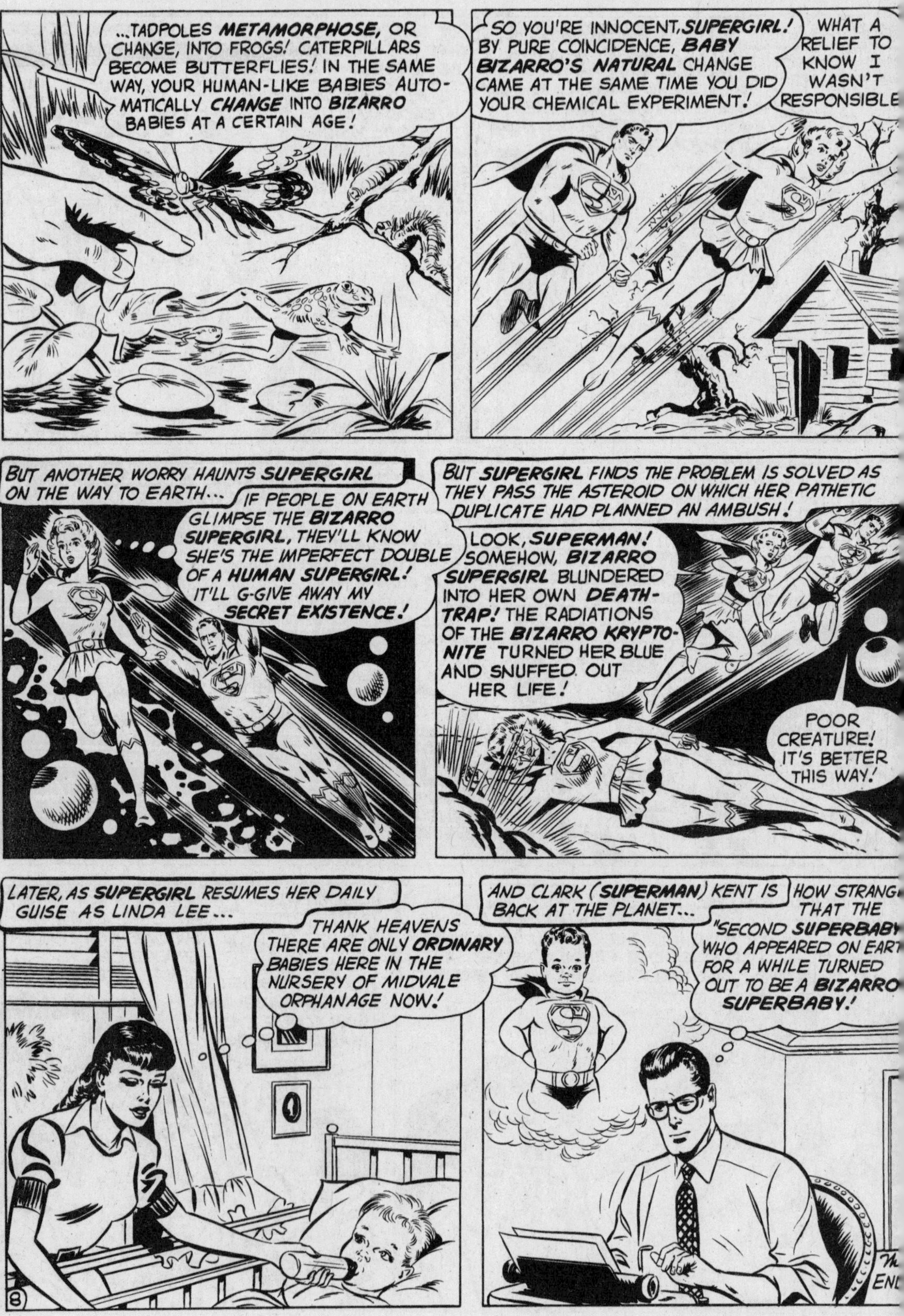
...TADPOLES METAMORPHOSE, OR CHANGE, INTO FROGS! CATERPILLARS BECOME BUTTERFLIES! IN THE SAME WAY, YOUR HUMAN-LIKE BABIES AUTOMATICALLY CHANGE INTO BIZARRO BABIES AT A CERTAIN AGE!
SO YOU'RE INNOCENT, SUPERGIRL! BY PURE COINCIDENCE, BABY BIZARRO'S NATURAL CHANGE CAME AT THE SAME TIME YOU DID YOUR CHEMICAL EXPERIMENT!
WHAT A RELIEF TO KNOW I WASN'T RESPONSIBLE
BUT ANOTHER WORRY HAUNTS SUPERGIRL ON THE WAY TO EARTH...
IF PEOPLE ON EARTH GLIMPSE THE BIZARRO SUPERGIRL, THEY'LL KNOW SHE'S THE IMPERFECT DOUBLE OF A HUMAN SUPERGIRL! IT'LL G-GIVE AWAY MY SECRET EXISTENCE!
BUT SUPERGIRL FINDS THE PROBLEM IS SOLVED AS THEY PASS THE ASTEROID ON WHICH HER PATHETIC DUPLICATE HAD PLANNED AN AMBUSH!
LOOK, SUPERMAN! SOMEHOW, BIZARRO SUPERGIRL BLUNDERED INTO HER OWN DEATH-TRAP! THE RADIATIONS OF THE BIZARRO KRYPTONITE TURNED HER BLUE AND SNUFFED OUT HER LIFE!
POOR CREATURE! IT'S BETTER THIS WAY!
LATER, AS SUPERGIRL RESUMES HER DAILY GUISE AS LINDA LEE...
THANK HEAVENS THERE ARE ONLY ORDINARY BABIES HERE IN THE NURSERY OF MIDVALE ORPHANAGE NOW!
8
AND CLARK (SUPERMAN) KENT IS BACK AT THE PLANET...
HOW STRANG THAT THE "SECOND SUPERBABY WHO APPEARED ON EART FOR A WHILE TURNED OUT TO BE A BIZARRO SUPERBABY!

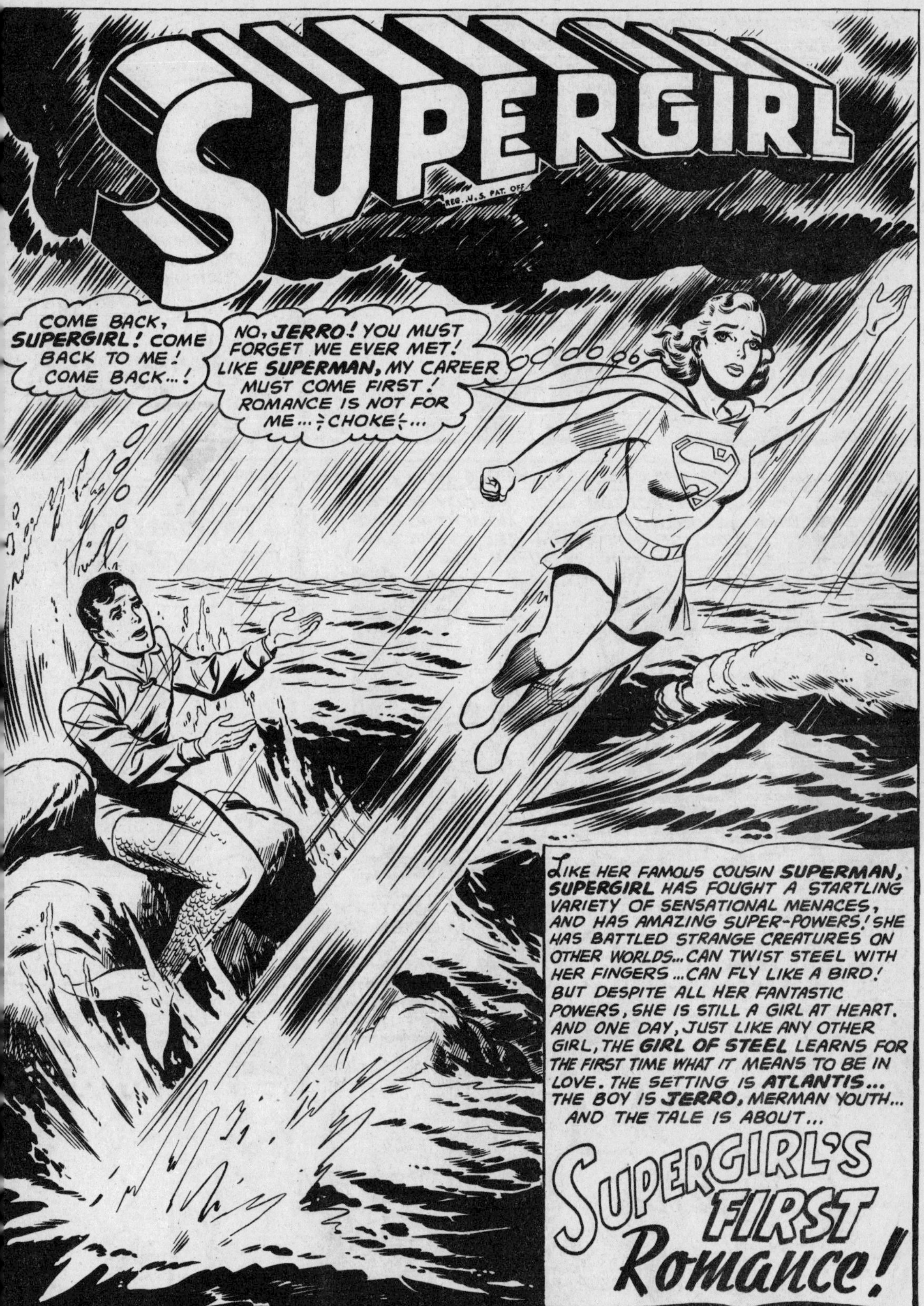
SUPERGIRL
REG. U.S. PAT. OFF.
COME BACK, SUPERGIRL! COME BACK TO ME! COME BACK...!
NO, JERRO! YOU MUST FORGET WE EVER MET! LIKE SUPERMAN, MY CAREER MUST COME FIRST! ROMANCE IS NOT FOR ME... -CHOKE-...
LIKE HER FAMOUS COUSIN SUPERMAN, SUPERGIRL HAS FOUGHT A STARTLING VARIETY OF SENSATIONAL MENACES, AND HAS AMAZING SUPER-POWERS! SHE HAS BATTLED STRANGE CREATURES ON OTHER WORLDS... CAN TWIST STEEL WITH HER FINGERS ... CAN FLY LIKE A BIRD! BUT DESPITE ALL HER FANTASTIC POWERS, SHE IS STILL A GIRL AT HEART. AND ONE DAY, JUST LIKE ANY OTHER GIRL, THE GIRL OF STEEL LEARNS FOR THE FIRST TIME WHAT IT MEANS TO BE IN LOVE. THE SETTING IS ATLANTIS... THE BOY IS JERRO, MERMAN YOUTH... AND THE TALE IS ABOUT...
SUPERGIRL'S FIRST Romance!

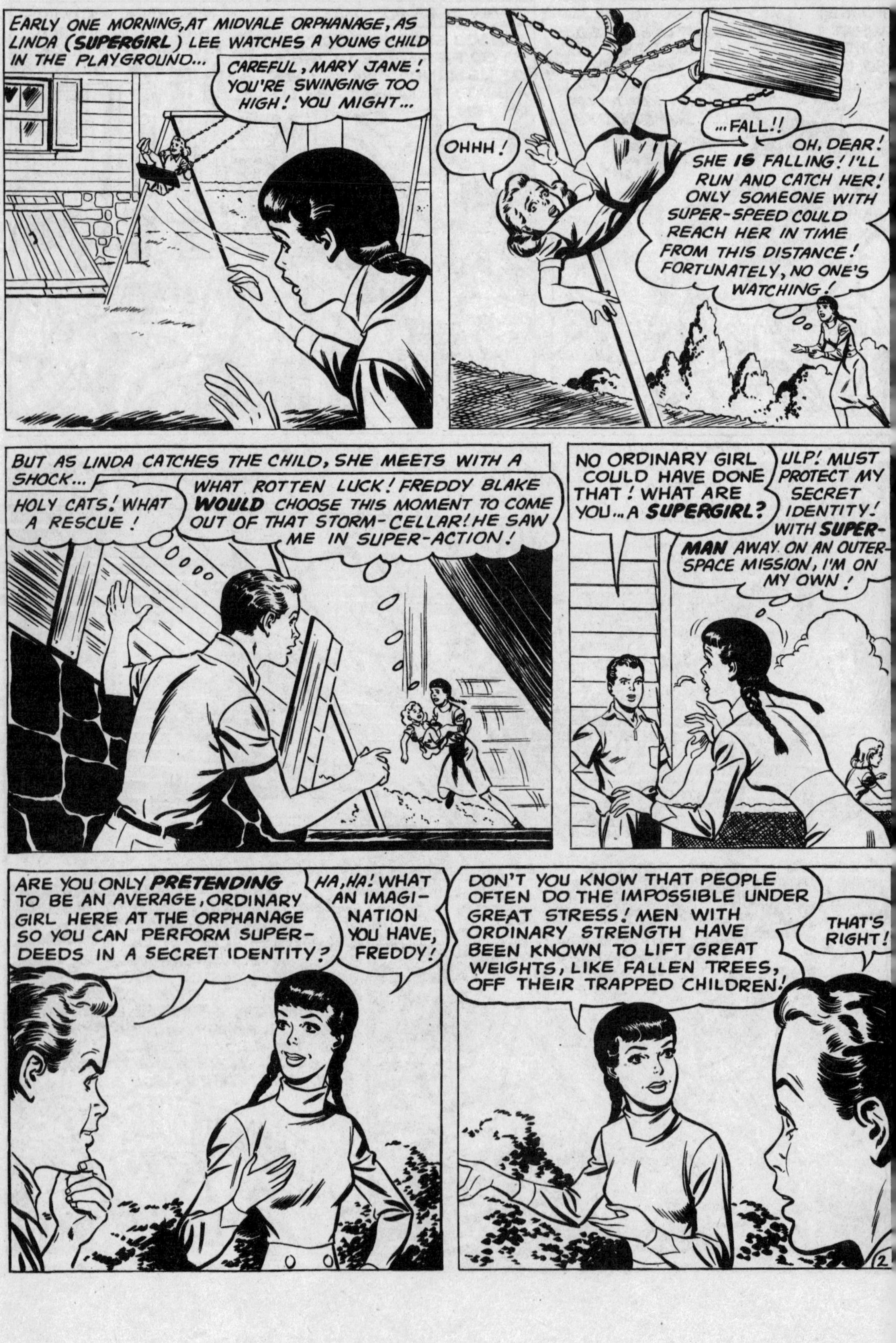
EARLY ONE MORNING, AT MIDVALE ORPHANAGE, AS LINDA (SUPERGIRL) LEE WATCHES A YOUNG CHILD IN THE PLAYGROUND...
CAREFUL, MARY JANE! YOU'RE SWINGING TOO HIGH! YOU MIGHT...
OHHH!
...FALL!!
OH, DEAR! SHE IS FALLING! I'LL RUN AND CATCH HER! ONLY SOMEONE WITH SUPER-SPEED COULD REACH HER IN TIME FROM THIS DISTANCE! FORTUNATELY, NO ONE'S WATCHING!
BUT AS LINDA CATCHES THE CHILD, SHE MEETS WITH A SHOCK...
HOLY CATS! WHAT A RESCUE!
WHAT ROTTEN LUCK! FREDDY BLAKE WOULD CHOOSE THIS MOMENT TO COME OUT OF THAT STORM-CELLAR! HE SAW ME IN SUPER-ACTION!
NO ORDINARY GIRL COULD HAVE DONE THAT! WHAT ARE YOU...A SUPERGIRL?
ULP! MUST PROTECT MY SECRET IDENTITY! WITH SUPERMAN AWAY ON AN OUTER-SPACE MISSION, I'M ON MY OWN!
ARE YOU ONLY PRETENDING TO BE AN AVERAGE, ORDINARY GIRL HERE AT THE ORPHANAGE SO YOU CAN PERFORM SUPER-DEEDS IN A SECRET IDENTITY?
HA, HA! WHAT AN IMAGINATION YOU HAVE, FREDDY!
DON'T YOU KNOW THAT PEOPLE OFTEN DO THE IMPOSSIBLE UNDER GREAT STRESS! MEN WITH ORDINARY STRENGTH HAVE BEEN KNOWN TO LIFT GREAT WEIGHTS, LIKE FALLEN TREES, OFF THEIR TRAPPED CHILDREN!
THAT'S RIGHT!
2

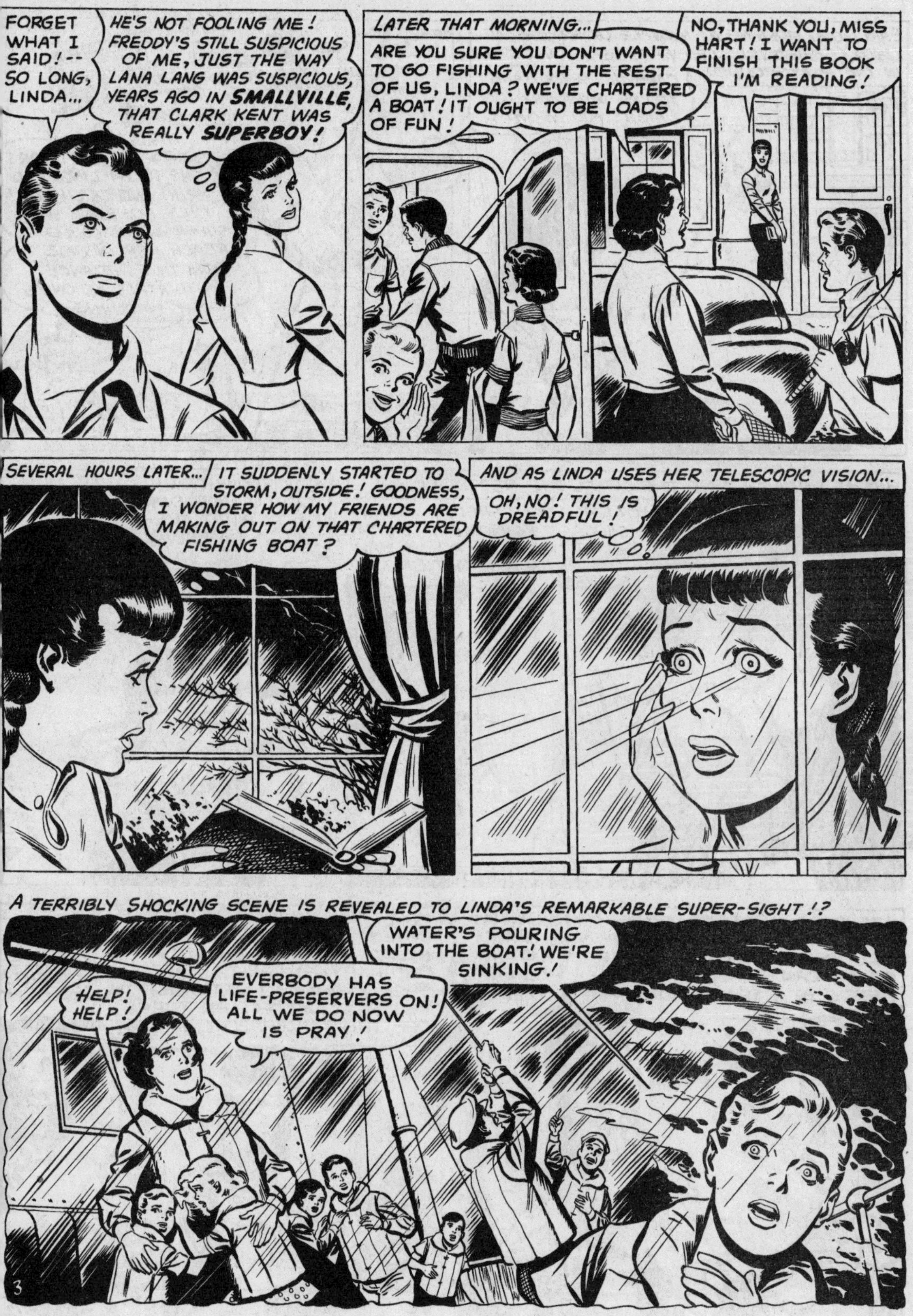
FORGET WHAT I SAID! -- SO LONG, LINDA...
HE'S NOT FOOLING ME! FREDDY'S STILL SUSPICIOUS OF ME, JUST THE WAY LANA LANG WAS SUSPICIOUS, YEARS AGO IN SMALLVILLE, THAT CLARK KENT WAS REALLY SUPERBOY!
LATER THAT MORNING...
ARE YOU SURE YOU DON'T WANT TO GO FISHING WITH THE REST OF US, LINDA? WE'VE CHARTERED A BOAT! IT OUGHT TO BE LOADS OF FUN!
NO, THANK YOU, MISS HART! I WANT TO FINISH THIS BOOK I'M READING!
SEVERAL HOURS LATER...
IT SUDDENLY STARTED TO STORM, OUTSIDE! GOODNESS, I WONDER HOW MY FRIENDS ARE MAKING OUT ON THAT CHARTERED FISHING BOAT?
AND AS LINDA USES HER TELESCOPIC VISION...
OH, NO! THIS IS DREADFUL!
A TERRIBLY SHOCKING SCENE IS REVEALED TO LINDA'S REMARKABLE SUPER-SIGHT!?
HELP! HELP!
EVERBODY HAS LIFE-PRESERVERS ON! ALL WE DO NOW IS PRAY!
WATER'S POURING INTO THE BOAT! WE'RE SINKING!
3

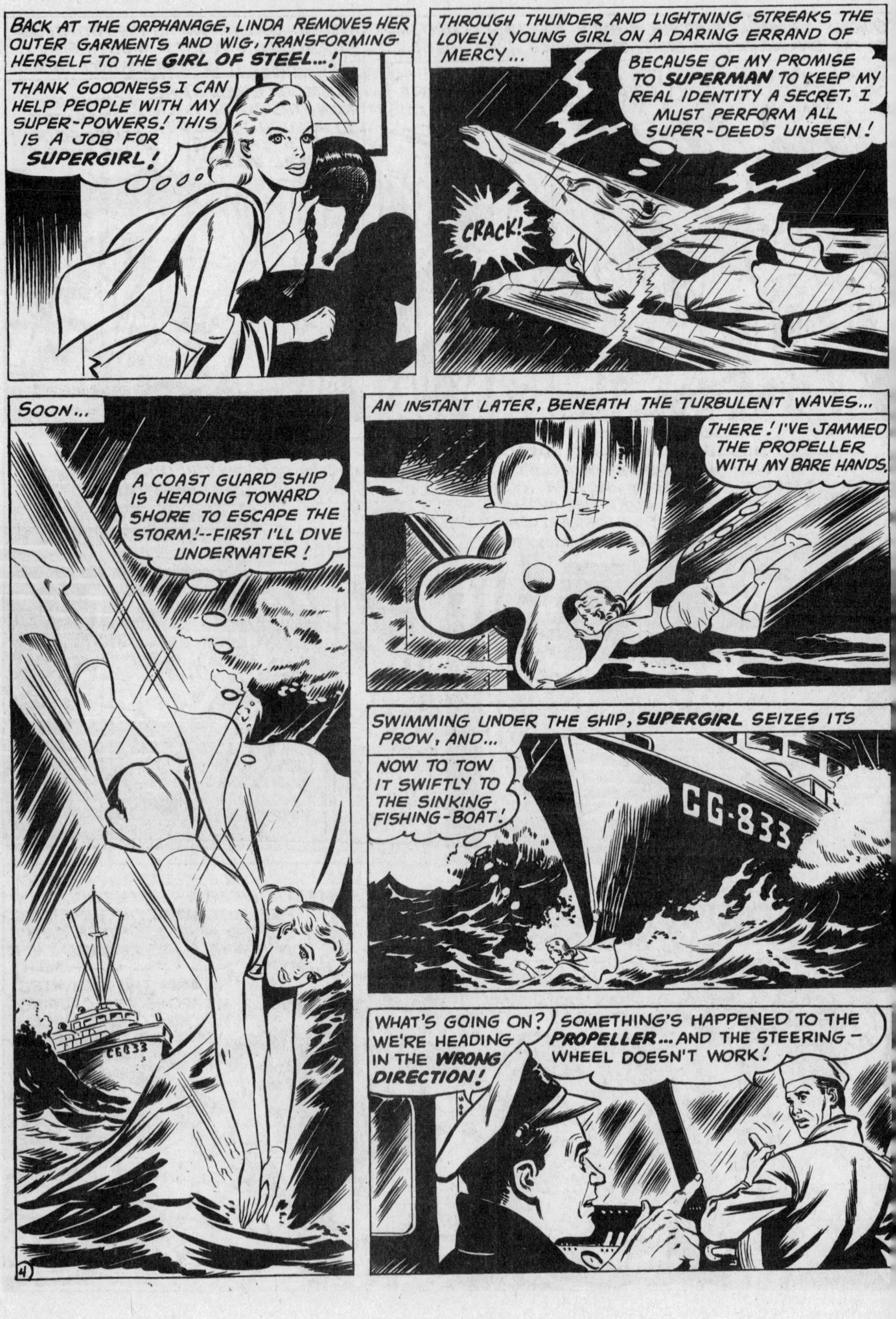
BACK AT THE ORPHANAGE, LINDA REMOVES HER OUTER GARMENTS AND WIG, TRANSFORMING HERSELF TO THE **GIRL OF STEEL**...!
THANK GOODNESS I CAN HELP PEOPLE WITH MY SUPER-POWERS! THIS IS A JOB FOR **SUPERGIRL**!
THROUGH THUNDER AND LIGHTNING STREAKS THE LOVELY YOUNG GIRL ON A DARING ERRAND OF MERCY...
BECAUSE OF MY PROMISE TO **SUPERMAN** TO KEEP MY REAL IDENTITY A SECRET, I MUST PERFORM ALL SUPER-DEEDS UNSEEN!
CRACK!
SOON...
A COAST GUARD SHIP IS HEADING TOWARD SHORE TO ESCAPE THE STORM!--FIRST I'LL DIVE UNDERWATER!
CG833
4
AN INSTANT LATER, BENEATH THE TURBULENT WAVES...
THERE! I'VE JAMMED THE PROPELLER WITH MY BARE HANDS!
SWIMMING UNDER THE SHIP, **SUPERGIRL** SEIZES ITS PROW, AND...
NOW TO TOW IT SWIFTLY TO THE SINKING FISHING-BOAT!
CG-833
WHAT'S GOING ON? WE'RE HEADING IN THE **WRONG DIRECTION**!
SOMETHING'S HAPPENED TO THE **PROPELLER**... AND THE STEERING-WHEEL DOESN'T WORK!

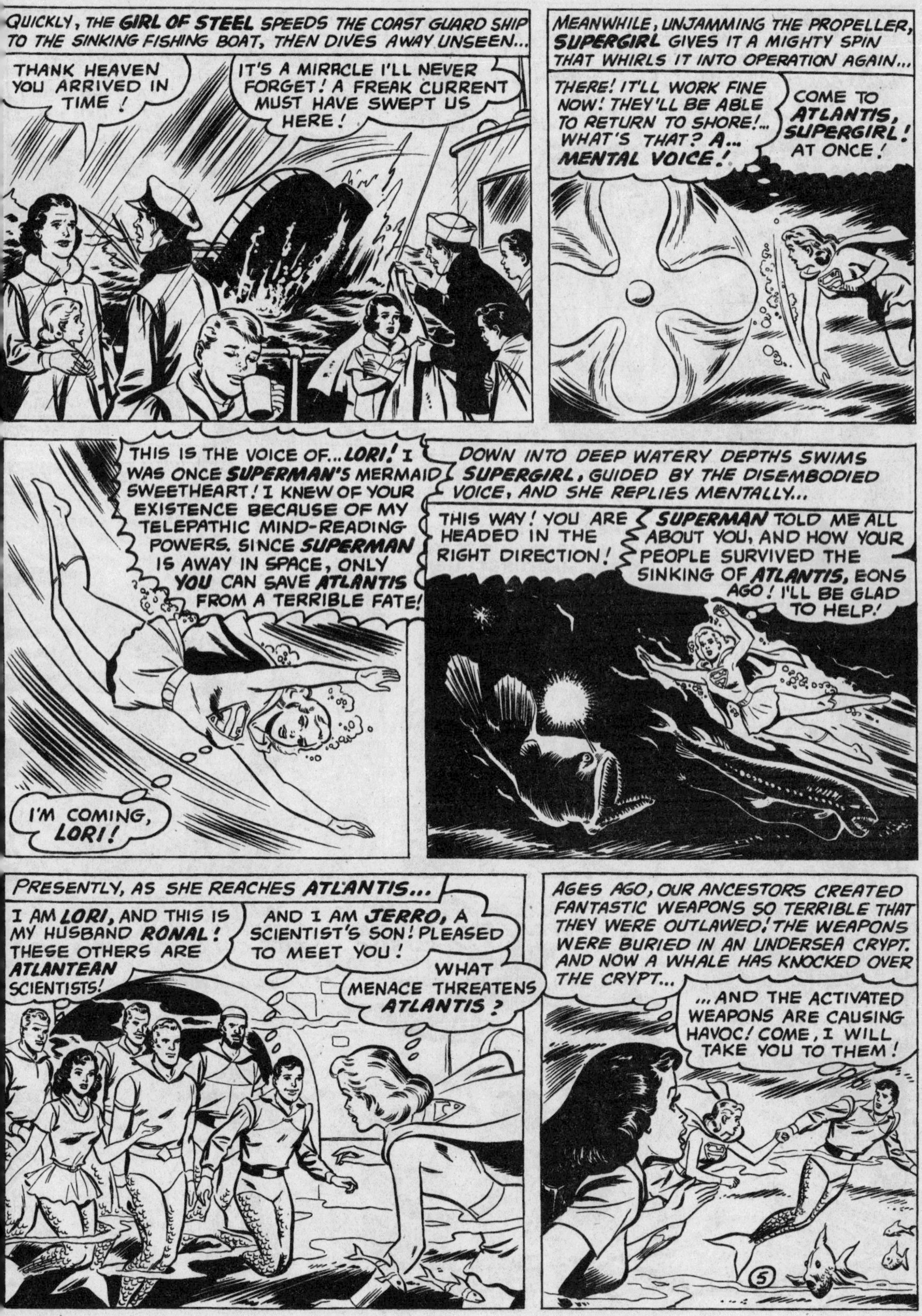
QUICKLY, THE GIRL OF STEEL SPEEDS THE COAST GUARD SHIP TO THE SINKING FISHING BOAT, THEN DIVES AWAY UNSEEN...
THANK HEAVEN YOU ARRIVED IN TIME!
IT'S A MIRACLE I'LL NEVER FORGET! A FREAK CURRENT MUST HAVE SWEPT US HERE!
MEANWHILE, UNJAMMING THE PROPELLER, SUPERGIRL GIVES IT A MIGHTY SPIN THAT WHIRLS IT INTO OPERATION AGAIN...
THERE! IT'LL WORK FINE NOW! THEY'LL BE ABLE TO RETURN TO SHORE!... WHAT'S THAT? A... MENTAL VOICE!
COME TO ATLANTIS, SUPERGIRL! AT ONCE!
THIS IS THE VOICE OF... LORI! I WAS ONCE SUPERMAN'S MERMAID SWEETHEART! I KNEW OF YOUR EXISTENCE BECAUSE OF MY TELEPATHIC MIND-READING POWERS. SINCE SUPERMAN IS AWAY IN SPACE, ONLY YOU CAN SAVE ATLANTIS FROM A TERRIBLE FATE!
I'M COMING, LORI!
DOWN INTO DEEP WATERY DEPTHS SWIMS SUPERGIRL, GUIDED BY THE DISEMBODIED VOICE, AND SHE REPLIES MENTALLY...
THIS WAY! YOU ARE HEADED IN THE RIGHT DIRECTION!
SUPERMAN TOLD ME ALL ABOUT YOU, AND HOW YOUR PEOPLE SURVIVED THE SINKING OF ATLANTIS, EONS AGO! I'LL BE GLAD TO HELP!
PRESENTLY, AS SHE REACHES ATLANTIS...
I AM LORI, AND THIS IS MY HUSBAND RONAL! THESE OTHERS ARE ATLANTEAN SCIENTISTS!
AND I AM JERRO, A SCIENTIST'S SON! PLEASED TO MEET YOU!
WHAT MENACE THREATENS ATLANTIS?
AGES AGO, OUR ANCESTORS CREATED FANTASTIC WEAPONS SO TERRIBLE THAT THEY WERE OUTLAWED! THE WEAPONS WERE BURIED IN AN UNDERSEA CRYPT. AND NOW A WHALE HAS KNOCKED OVER THE CRYPT...
...AND THE ACTIVATED WEAPONS ARE CAUSING HAVOC! COME, I WILL TAKE YOU TO THEM!
5

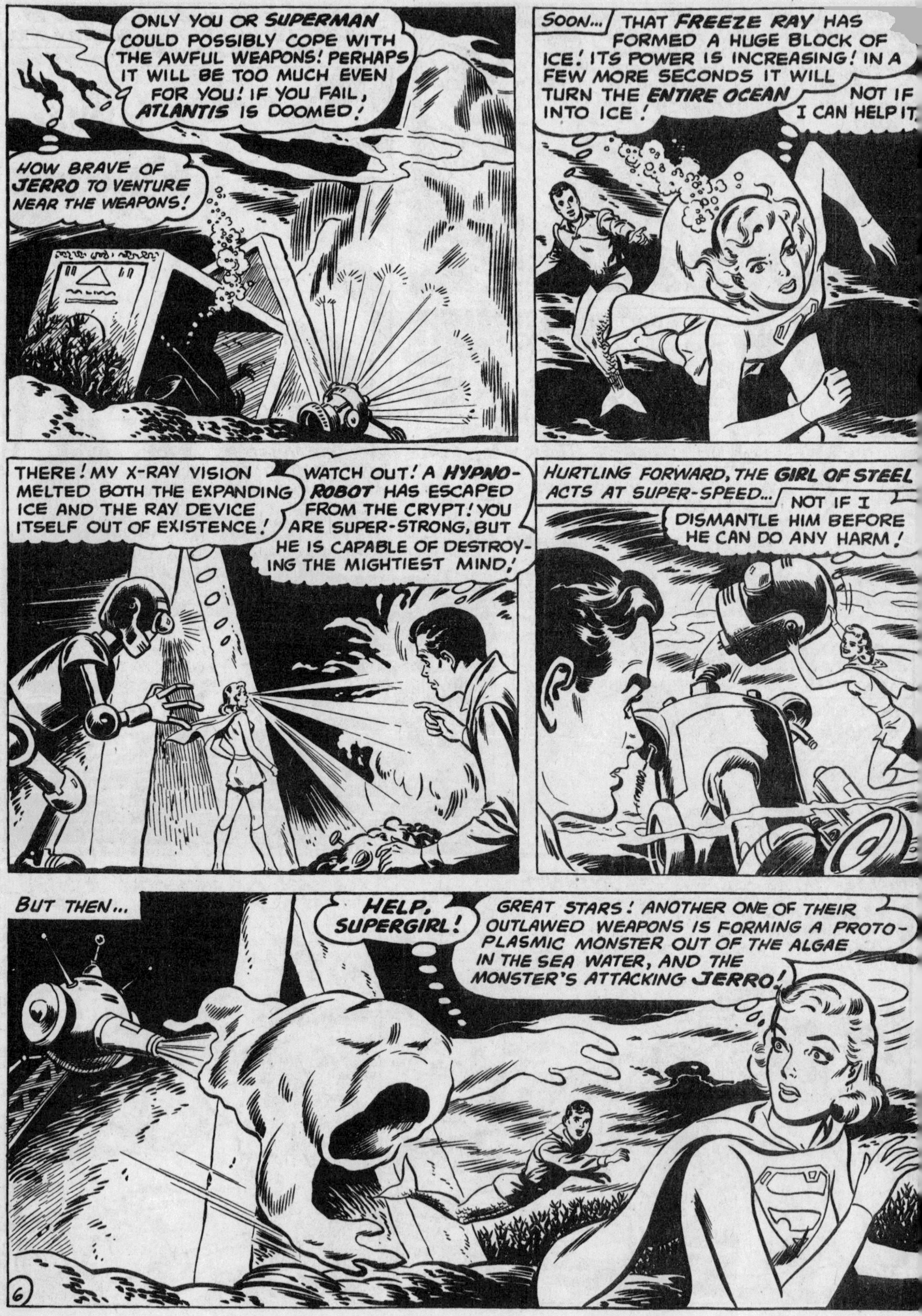
ONLY YOU OR SUPERMAN COULD POSSIBLY COPE WITH THE AWFUL WEAPONS! PERHAPS IT WILL BE TOO MUCH EVEN FOR YOU! IF YOU FAIL, ATLANTIS IS DOOMED!
HOW BRAVE OF JERRO TO VENTURE NEAR THE WEAPONS!
SOON... THAT FREEZE RAY HAS FORMED A HUGE BLOCK OF ICE! ITS POWER IS INCREASING! IN A FEW MORE SECONDS IT WILL TURN THE ENTIRE OCEAN INTO ICE!
NOT IF I CAN HELP IT.
THERE! MY X-RAY VISION MELTED BOTH THE EXPANDING ICE AND THE RAY DEVICE ITSELF OUT OF EXISTENCE!
WATCH OUT! A HYPNO-ROBOT HAS ESCAPED FROM THE CRYPT! YOU ARE SUPER-STRONG, BUT HE IS CAPABLE OF DESTROYING THE MIGHTIEST MIND!
HURTLING FORWARD, THE GIRL OF STEEL ACTS AT SUPER-SPEED...
NOT IF I DISMANTLE HIM BEFORE HE CAN DO ANY HARM!
BUT THEN...
HELP, SUPERGIRL!
GREAT STARS! ANOTHER ONE OF THEIR OUTLAWED WEAPONS IS FORMING A PROTO-PLASMIC MONSTER OUT OF THE ALGAE IN THE SEA WATER, AND THE MONSTER'S ATTACKING JERRO!
6

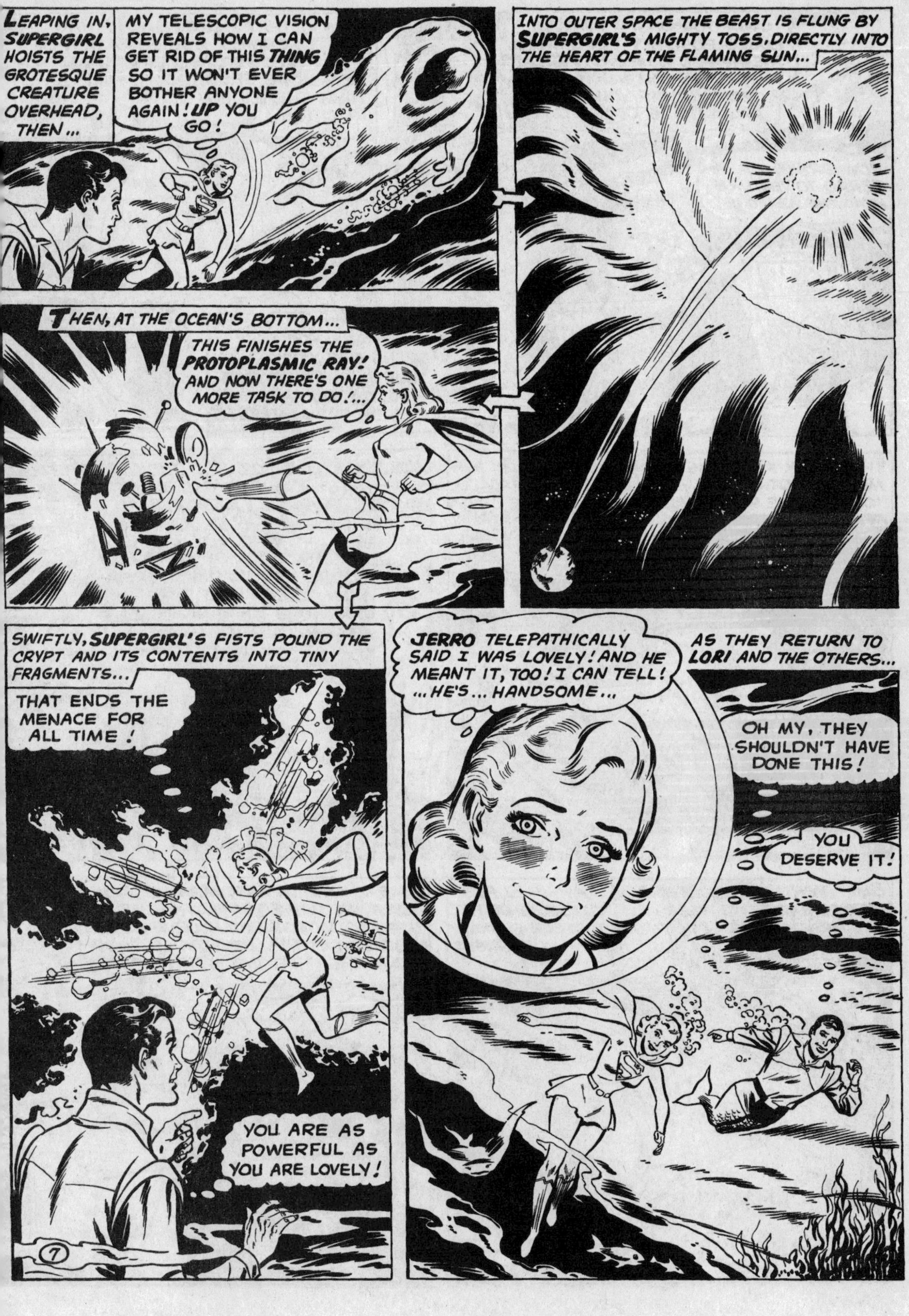
LEAPING IN, SUPERGIRL HOISTS THE GROTESQUE CREATURE OVERHEAD, THEN...
MY TELESCOPIC VISION REVEALS HOW I CAN GET RID OF THIS THING SO IT WON'T EVER BOTHER ANYONE AGAIN! UP YOU GO!
INTO OUTER SPACE THE BEAST IS FLUNG BY SUPERGIRL'S MIGHTY TOSS, DIRECTLY INTO THE HEART OF THE FLAMING SUN...
THEN, AT THE OCEAN'S BOTTOM...
THIS FINISHES THE PROTOPLASMIC RAY! AND NOW THERE'S ONE MORE TASK TO DO!...
SWIFTLY, SUPERGIRL'S FISTS POUND THE CRYPT AND ITS CONTENTS INTO TINY FRAGMENTS...
THAT ENDS THE MENACE FOR ALL TIME!
YOU ARE AS POWERFUL AS YOU ARE LOVELY!
7
JERRO TELEPATHICALLY SAID I WAS LOVELY! AND HE MEANT IT, TOO! I CAN TELL! ...HE'S... HANDSOME...
AS THEY RETURN TO LORI AND THE OTHERS...
OH MY, THEY SHOULDN'T HAVE DONE THIS!
YOU DESERVE IT!

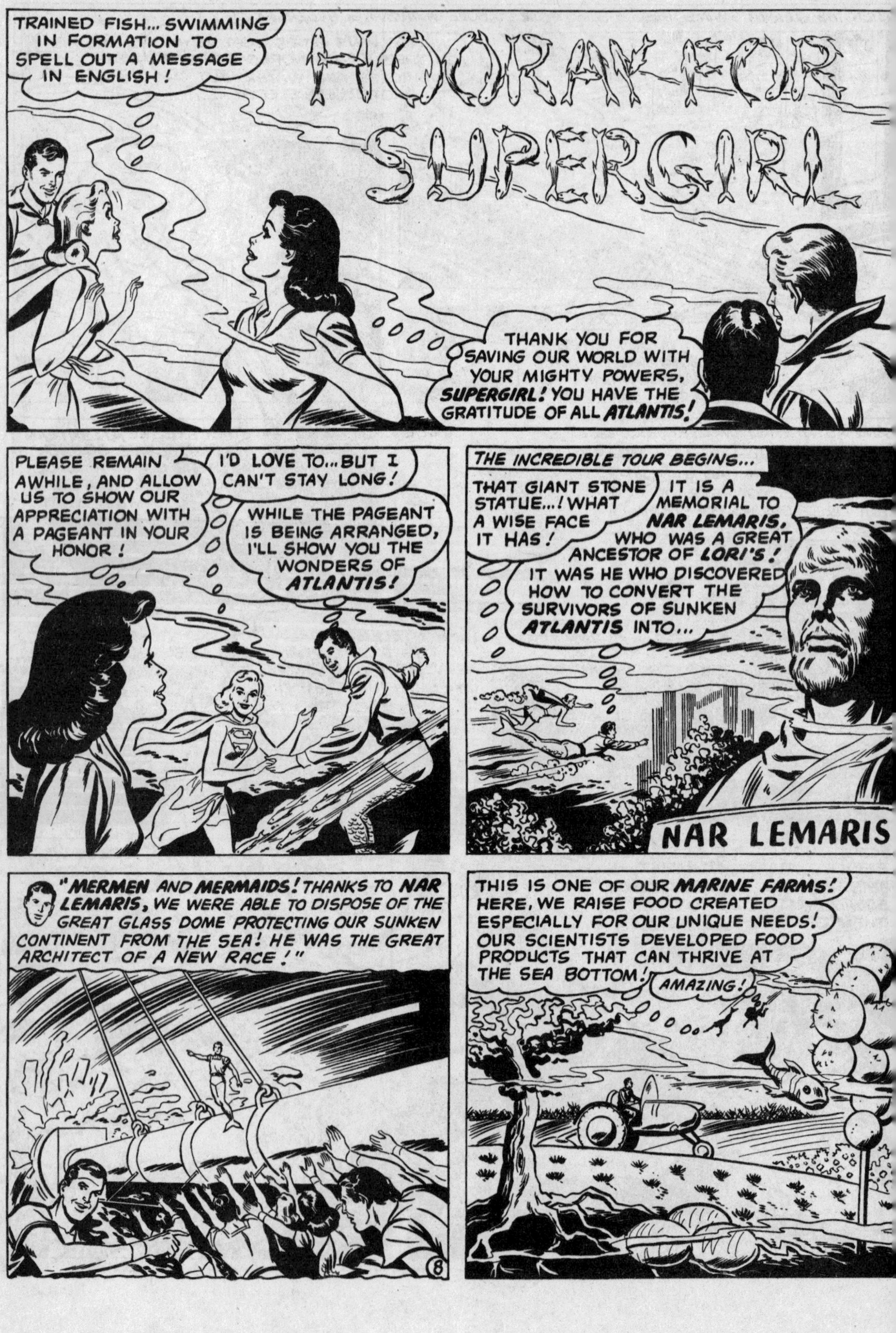
TRAINED FISH... SWIMMING IN FORMATION TO SPELL OUT A MESSAGE IN ENGLISH!
HOORAY FOR SUPERGIRL
THANK YOU FOR SAVING OUR WORLD WITH YOUR MIGHTY POWERS, SUPERGIRL! YOU HAVE THE GRATITUDE OF ALL ATLANTIS!
PLEASE REMAIN AWHILE, AND ALLOW US TO SHOW OUR APPRECIATION WITH A PAGEANT IN YOUR HONOR!
I'D LOVE TO...BUT I CAN'T STAY LONG!
WHILE THE PAGEANT IS BEING ARRANGED, I'LL SHOW YOU THE WONDERS OF ATLANTIS!
THE INCREDIBLE TOUR BEGINS...
THAT GIANT STONE STATUE...! WHAT A WISE FACE IT HAS!
IT IS A MEMORIAL TO NAR LEMARIS, WHO WAS A GREAT ANCESTOR OF LORI'S!
IT WAS HE WHO DISCOVERED HOW TO CONVERT THE SURVIVORS OF SUNKEN ATLANTIS INTO...
NAR LEMARIS
"MERMEN AND MERMAIDS! THANKS TO NAR LEMARIS, WE WERE ABLE TO DISPOSE OF THE GREAT GLASS DOME PROTECTING OUR SUNKEN CONTINENT FROM THE SEA! HE WAS THE GREAT ARCHITECT OF A NEW RACE!"
8
THIS IS ONE OF OUR MARINE FARMS! HERE, WE RAISE FOOD CREATED ESPECIALLY FOR OUR UNIQUE NEEDS! OUR SCIENTISTS DEVELOPED FOOD PRODUCTS THAT CAN THRIVE AT THE SEA BOTTOM!
AMAZING!

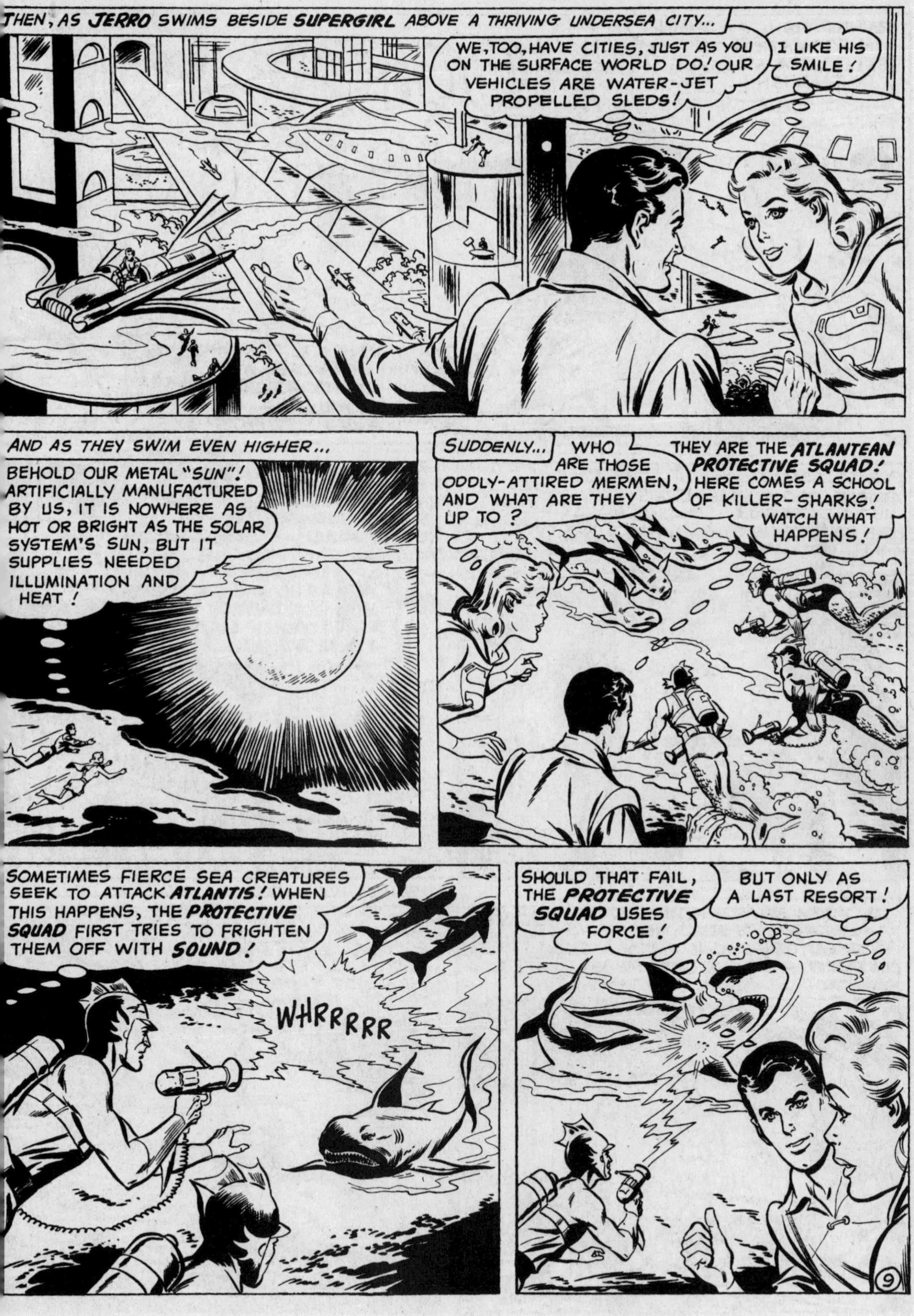
THEN, AS JERRO SWIMS BESIDE SUPERGIRL ABOVE A THRIVING UNDERSEA CITY...
WE, TOO, HAVE CITIES, JUST AS YOU ON THE SURFACE WORLD DO! OUR VEHICLES ARE WATER-JET PROPELLED SLEDS!
I LIKE HIS SMILE!
AND AS THEY SWIM EVEN HIGHER...
BEHOLD OUR METAL "SUN"! ARTIFICIALLY MANUFACTURED BY US, IT IS NOWHERE AS HOT OR BRIGHT AS THE SOLAR SYSTEM'S SUN, BUT IT SUPPLIES NEEDED ILLUMINATION AND HEAT!
SUDDENLY...
WHO ARE THOSE ODDLY-ATTIRED MERMEN, AND WHAT ARE THEY UP TO?
THEY ARE THE ATLANTEAN PROTECTIVE SQUAD! HERE COMES A SCHOOL OF KILLER-SHARKS! WATCH WHAT HAPPENS!
SOMETIMES FIERCE SEA CREATURES SEEK TO ATTACK ATLANTIS! WHEN THIS HAPPENS, THE PROTECTIVE SQUAD FIRST TRIES TO FRIGHTEN THEM OFF WITH SOUND!
WHRRRRR
SHOULD THAT FAIL, THE PROTECTIVE SQUAD USES FORCE!
BUT ONLY AS A LAST RESORT!
9

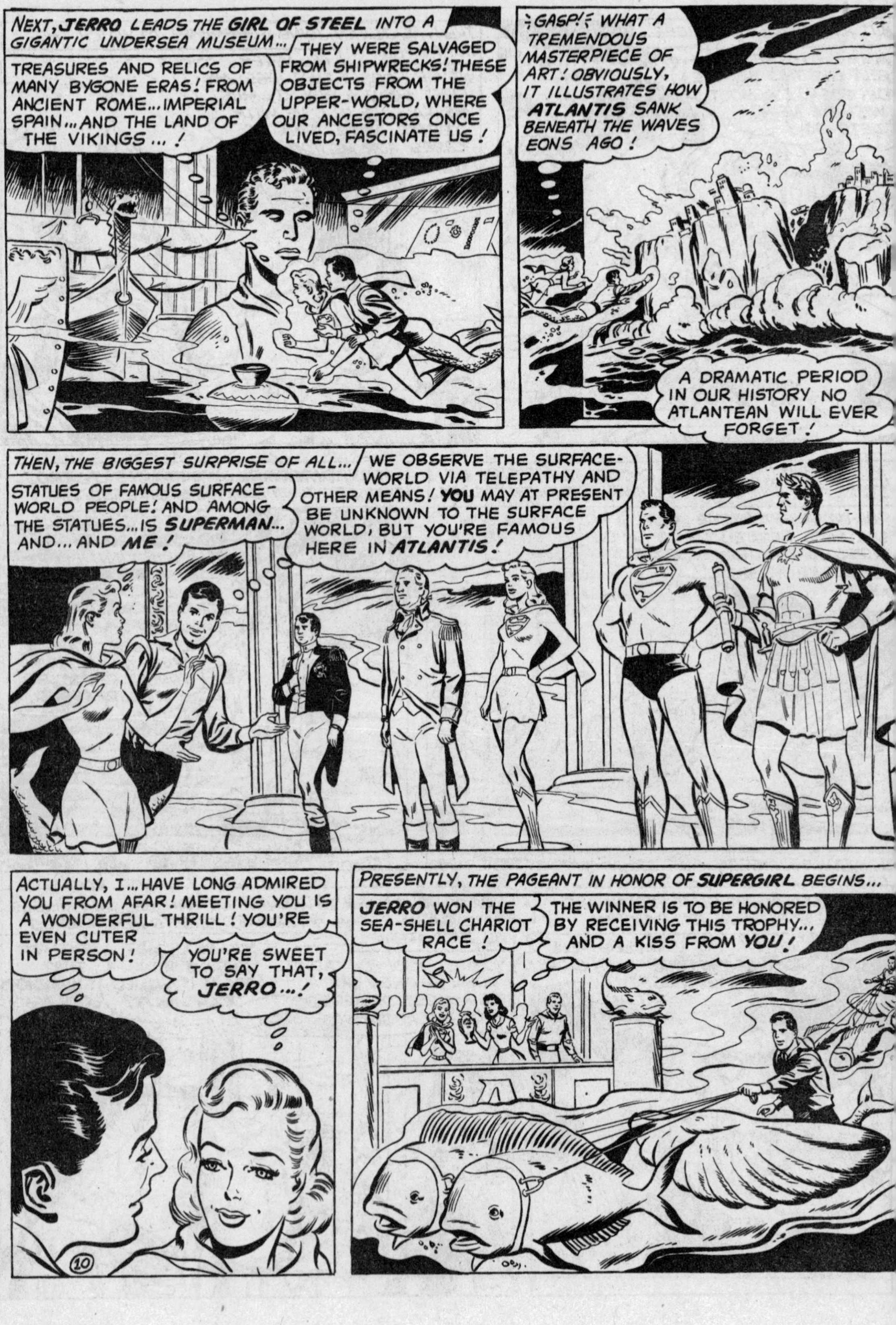
NEXT, JERRO LEADS THE GIRL OF STEEL INTO A GIGANTIC UNDERSEA MUSEUM...
TREASURES AND RELICS OF MANY BYGONE ERAS! FROM ANCIENT ROME... IMPERIAL SPAIN... AND THE LAND OF THE VIKINGS...!
THEY WERE SALVAGED FROM SHIPWRECKS! THESE OBJECTS FROM THE UPPER-WORLD, WHERE OUR ANCESTORS ONCE LIVED, FASCINATE US!
GASP! WHAT A TREMENDOUS MASTERPIECE OF ART! OBVIOUSLY, IT ILLUSTRATES HOW ATLANTIS SANK BENEATH THE WAVES EONS AGO!
A DRAMATIC PERIOD IN OUR HISTORY NO ATLANTEAN WILL EVER FORGET!
THEN, THE BIGGEST SURPRISE OF ALL...
STATUES OF FAMOUS SURFACE-WORLD PEOPLE! AND AMONG THE STATUES... IS SUPERMAN... AND... AND ME!
WE OBSERVE THE SURFACE-WORLD VIA TELEPATHY AND OTHER MEANS! YOU MAY AT PRESENT BE UNKNOWN TO THE SURFACE WORLD, BUT YOU'RE FAMOUS HERE IN ATLANTIS!
ACTUALLY, I... HAVE LONG ADMIRED YOU FROM AFAR! MEETING YOU IS A WONDERFUL THRILL! YOU'RE EVEN CUTER IN PERSON!
YOU'RE SWEET TO SAY THAT, JERRO...!
10
PRESENTLY, THE PAGEANT IN HONOR OF SUPERGIRL BEGINS...
JERRO WON THE SEA-SHELL CHARIOT RACE!
THE WINNER IS TO BE HONORED BY RECEIVING THIS TROPHY... AND A KISS FROM YOU!

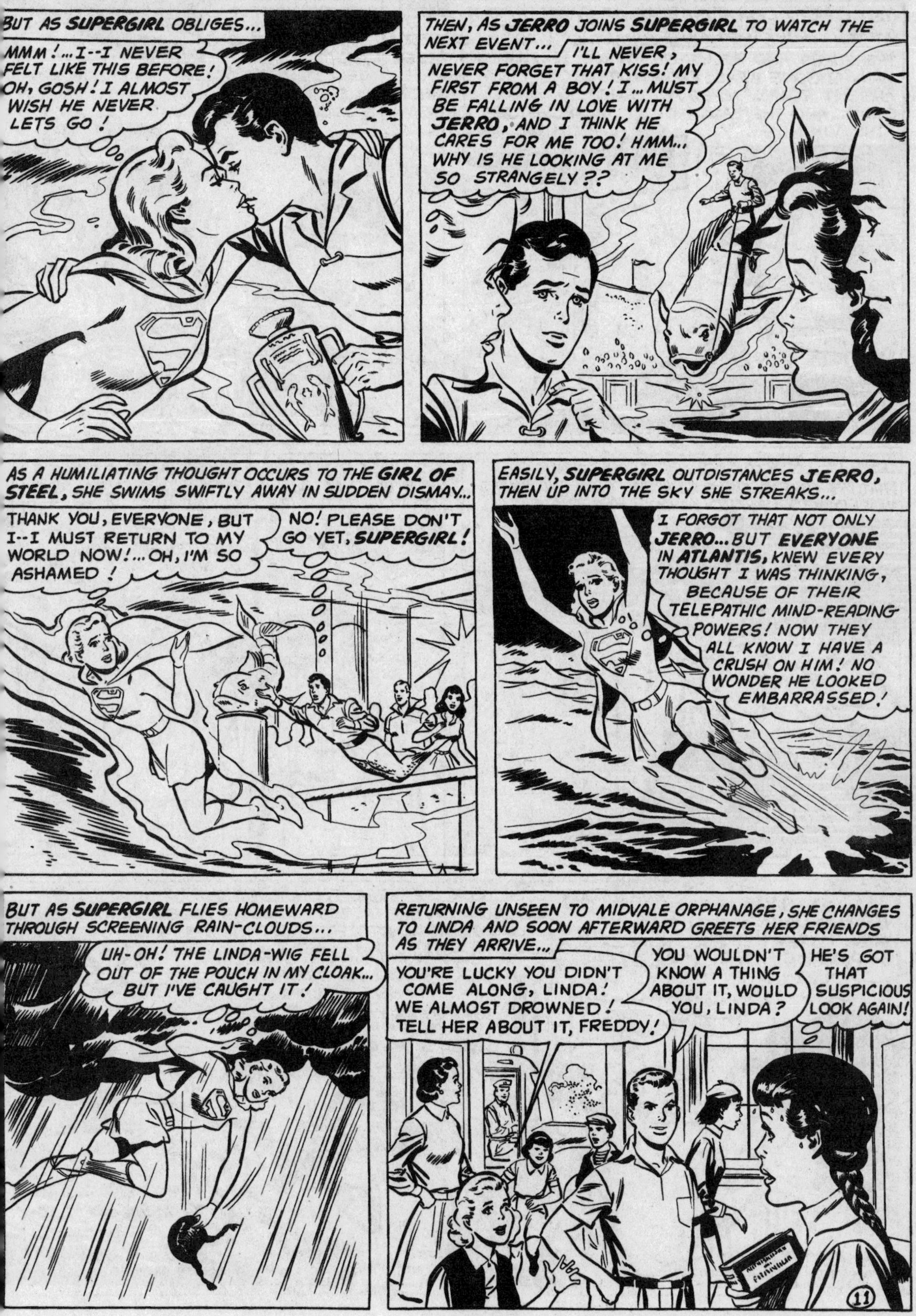
BUT AS SUPERGIRL OBLIGES...
MMM!...I--I NEVER FELT LIKE THIS BEFORE! OH, GOSH! I ALMOST WISH HE NEVER LETS GO!
THEN, AS JERRO JOINS SUPERGIRL TO WATCH THE NEXT EVENT...
I'LL NEVER, NEVER FORGET THAT KISS! MY FIRST FROM A BOY! I...MUST BE FALLING IN LOVE WITH JERRO, AND I THINK HE CARES FOR ME TOO! HMM... WHY IS HE LOOKING AT ME SO STRANGELY??
AS A HUMILIATING THOUGHT OCCURS TO THE GIRL OF STEEL, SHE SWIMS SWIFTLY AWAY IN SUDDEN DISMAY...
THANK YOU, EVERYONE, BUT I--I MUST RETURN TO MY WORLD NOW!...OH, I'M SO ASHAMED!
NO! PLEASE DON'T GO YET, SUPERGIRL!
EASILY, SUPERGIRL OUTDISTANCES JERRO, THEN UP INTO THE SKY SHE STREAKS...
I FORGOT THAT NOT ONLY JERRO...BUT EVERYONE IN ATLANTIS, KNEW EVERY THOUGHT I WAS THINKING, BECAUSE OF THEIR TELEPATHIC MIND-READING POWERS! NOW THEY ALL KNOW I HAVE A CRUSH ON HIM! NO WONDER HE LOOKED EMBARRASSED!
BUT AS SUPERGIRL FLIES HOMEWARD THROUGH SCREENING RAIN-CLOUDS...
UH-OH! THE LINDA-WIG FELL OUT OF THE POUCH IN MY CLOAK... BUT I'VE CAUGHT IT!
RETURNING UNSEEN TO MIDVALE ORPHANAGE, SHE CHANGES TO LINDA AND SOON AFTERWARD GREETS HER FRIENDS AS THEY ARRIVE...
YOU'RE LUCKY YOU DIDN'T COME ALONG, LINDA! WE ALMOST DROWNED! TELL HER ABOUT IT, FREDDY!
YOU WOULDN'T KNOW A THING ABOUT IT, WOULD YOU, LINDA?
HE'S GOT THAT SUSPICIOUS LOOK AGAIN!
11

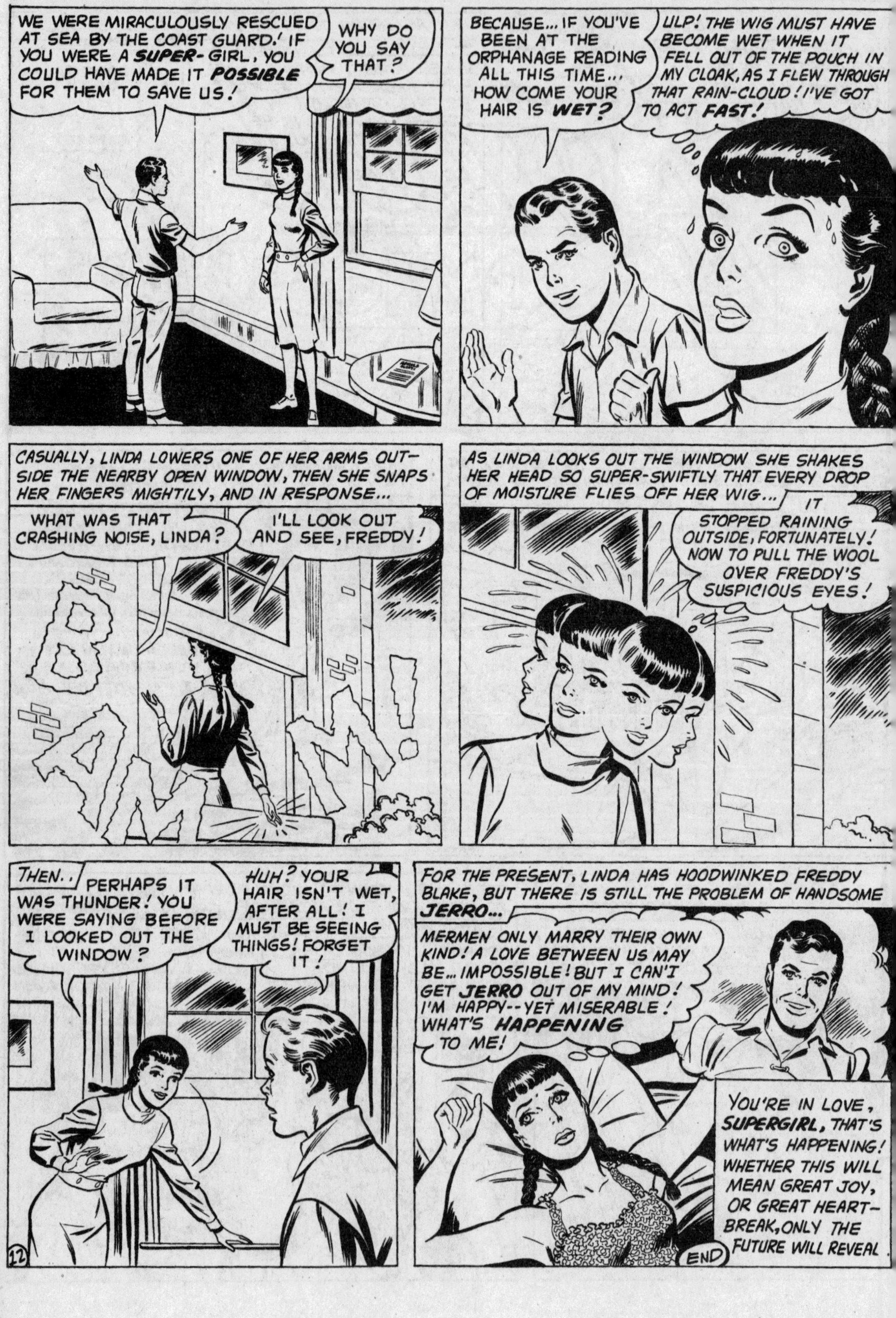
WE WERE MIRACULOUSLY RESCUED AT SEA BY THE COAST GUARD! IF YOU WERE A SUPER-GIRL, YOU COULD HAVE MADE IT POSSIBLE FOR THEM TO SAVE US!
WHY DO YOU SAY THAT?
BECAUSE... IF YOU'VE BEEN AT THE ORPHANAGE READING ALL THIS TIME... HOW COME YOUR HAIR IS WET?
ULP! THE WIG MUST HAVE BECOME WET WHEN IT FELL OUT OF THE POUCH IN MY CLOAK, AS I FLEW THROUGH THAT RAIN-CLOUD! I'VE GOT TO ACT FAST!
CASUALLY, LINDA LOWERS ONE OF HER ARMS OUTSIDE THE NEARBY OPEN WINDOW, THEN SHE SNAPS HER FINGERS MIGHTILY, AND IN RESPONSE...
WHAT WAS THAT CRASHING NOISE, LINDA?
I'LL LOOK OUT AND SEE, FREDDY!
BAM!
AS LINDA LOOKS OUT THE WINDOW SHE SHAKES HER HEAD SO SUPER-SWIFTLY THAT EVERY DROP OF MOISTURE FLIES OFF HER WIG...
IT STOPPED RAINING OUTSIDE, FORTUNATELY! NOW TO PULL THE WOOL OVER FREDDY'S SUSPICIOUS EYES!
THEN..
PERHAPS IT WAS THUNDER! YOU WERE SAYING BEFORE I LOOKED OUT THE WINDOW?
HUH? YOUR HAIR ISN'T WET, AFTER ALL! I MUST BE SEEING THINGS! FORGET IT!
12
FOR THE PRESENT, LINDA HAS HOODWINKED FREDDY BLAKE, BUT THERE IS STILL THE PROBLEM OF HANDSOME JERRO...
MERMEN ONLY MARRY THEIR OWN KIND! A LOVE BETWEEN US MAY BE... IMPOSSIBLE! BUT I CAN'T GET JERRO OUT OF MY MIND! I'M HAPPY--YET MISERABLE! WHAT'S HAPPENING TO ME!
YOU'RE IN LOVE, SUPERGIRL, THAT'S WHAT'S HAPPENING! WHETHER THIS WILL MEAN GREAT JOY, OR GREAT HEART-BREAK, ONLY THE FUTURE WILL REVEAL
END

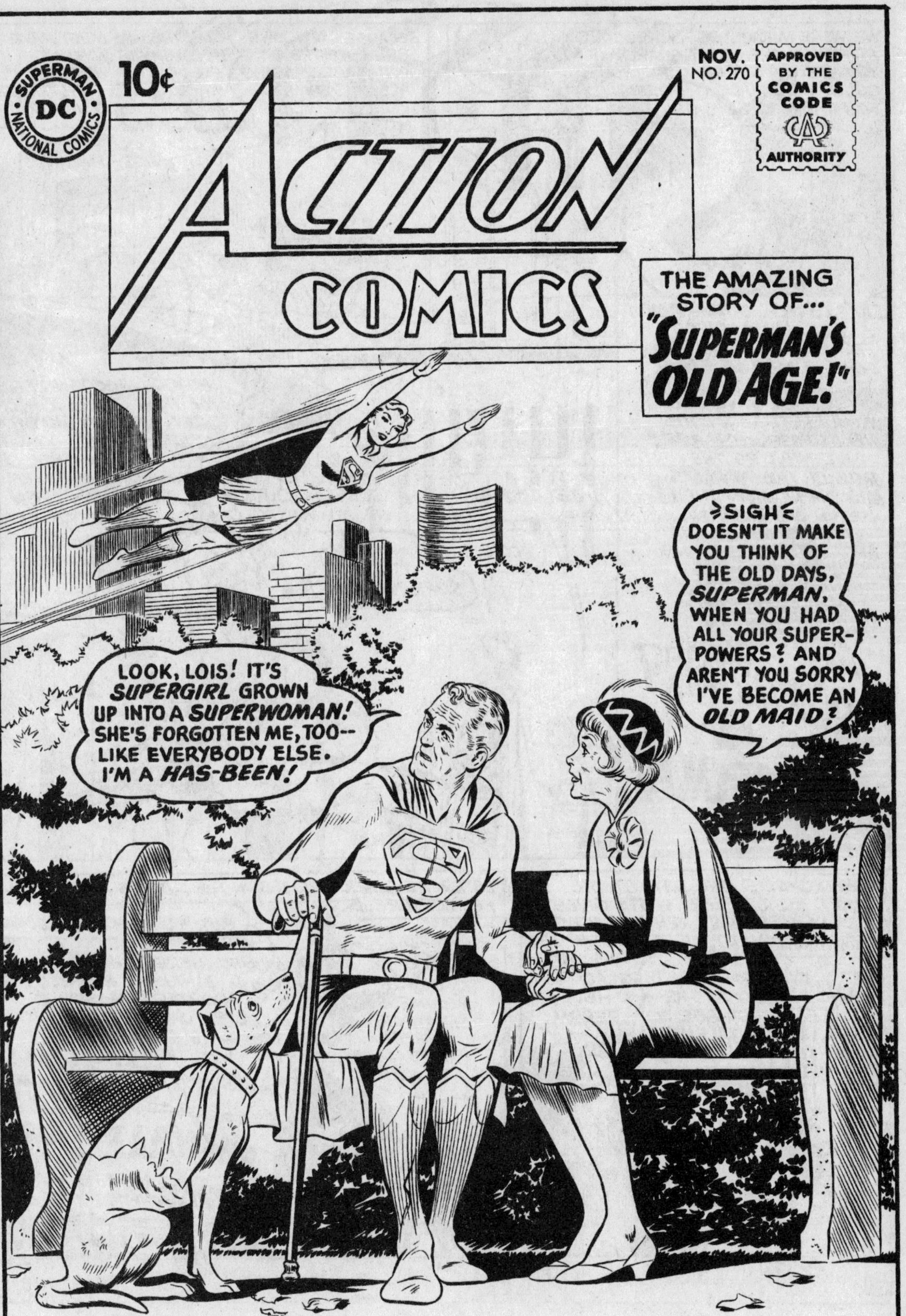
SUPERMAN DC NATIONAL COMICS
10¢
NOV. NO. 270
APPROVED BY THE COMICS CODE AUTHORITY
ACTION COMICS
THE AMAZING STORY OF... "SUPERMAN'S OLD AGE!"
LOOK, LOIS! IT'S SUPERGIRL GROWN UP INTO A SUPERWOMAN! SHE'S FORGOTTEN ME, TOO-- LIKE EVERYBODY ELSE. I'M A HAS-BEEN!
SIGH DOESN'T IT MAKE YOU THINK OF THE OLD DAYS, SUPERMAN, WHEN YOU HAD ALL YOUR SUPER-POWERS? AND AREN'T YOU SORRY I'VE BECOME AN OLD MAID?

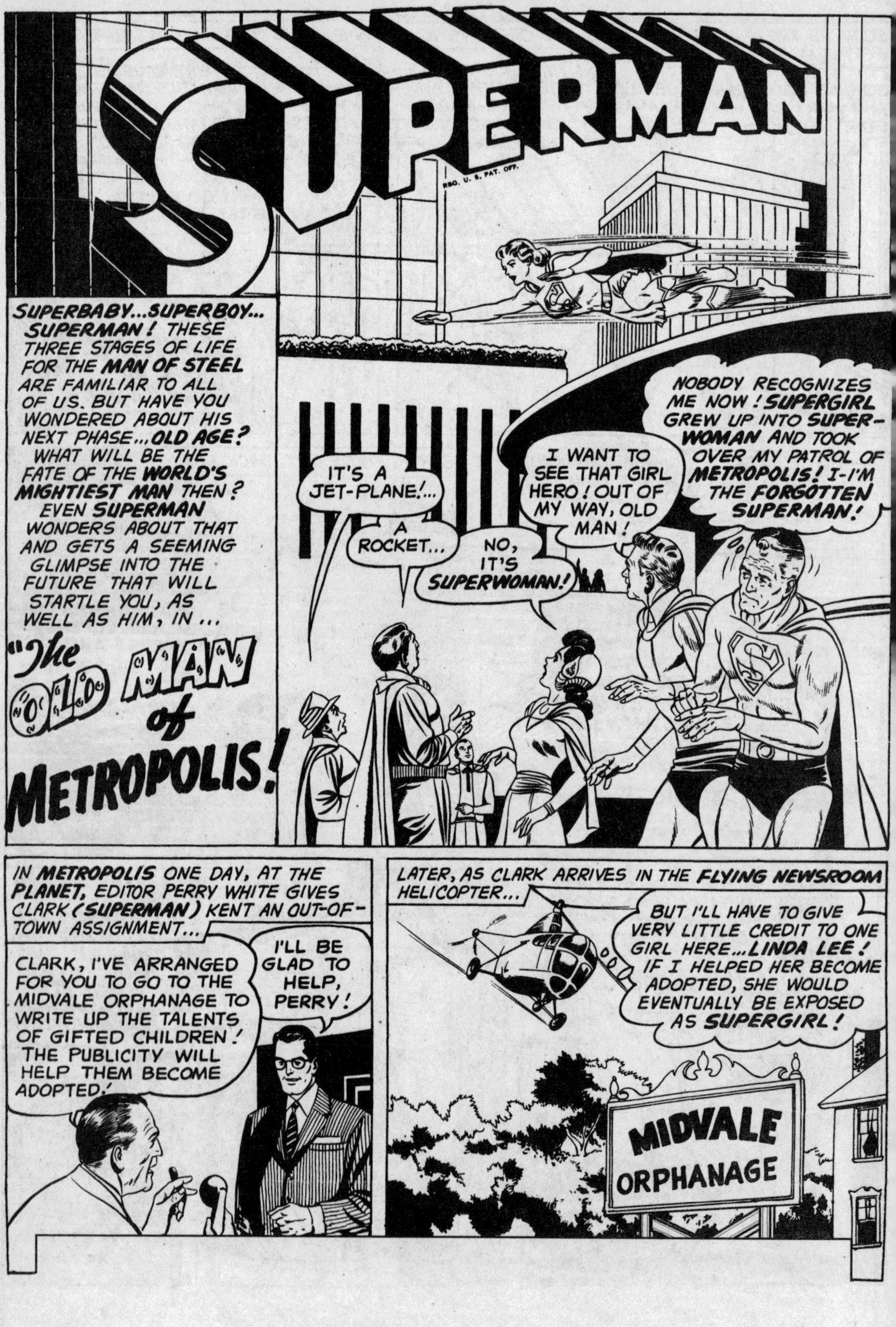
SUPERMAN
REG. U. S. PAT. OFF.
SUPERBABY...SUPERBOY... SUPERMAN! THESE THREE STAGES OF LIFE FOR THE MAN OF STEEL ARE FAMILIAR TO ALL OF US. BUT HAVE YOU WONDERED ABOUT HIS NEXT PHASE...OLD AGE? WHAT WILL BE THE FATE OF THE WORLD'S MIGHTIEST MAN THEN? EVEN SUPERMAN WONDERS ABOUT THAT AND GETS A SEEMING GLIMPSE INTO THE FUTURE THAT WILL STARTLE YOU, AS WELL AS HIM, IN ...
"The OLD MAN of METROPOLIS!
IT'S A JET-PLANE!...
A ROCKET...
NO, IT'S SUPERWOMAN!
I WANT TO SEE THAT GIRL HERO! OUT OF MY WAY, OLD MAN!
NOBODY RECOGNIZES ME NOW! SUPERGIRL GREW UP INTO SUPER-WOMAN AND TOOK OVER MY PATROL OF METROPOLIS! I-I'M THE FORGOTTEN SUPERMAN!
IN METROPOLIS ONE DAY, AT THE PLANET, EDITOR PERRY WHITE GIVES CLARK (SUPERMAN) KENT AN OUT-OF-TOWN ASSIGNMENT...
CLARK, I'VE ARRANGED FOR YOU TO GO TO THE MIDVALE ORPHANAGE TO WRITE UP THE TALENTS OF GIFTED CHILDREN! THE PUBLICITY WILL HELP THEM BECOME ADOPTED!
I'LL BE GLAD TO HELP, PERRY!
LATER, AS CLARK ARRIVES IN THE FLYING NEWSROOM HELICOPTER...
BUT I'LL HAVE TO GIVE VERY LITTLE CREDIT TO ONE GIRL HERE...LINDA LEE! IF I HELPED HER BECOME ADOPTED, SHE WOULD EVENTUALLY BE EXPOSED AS SUPERGIRL!
MIDVALE ORPHANAGE

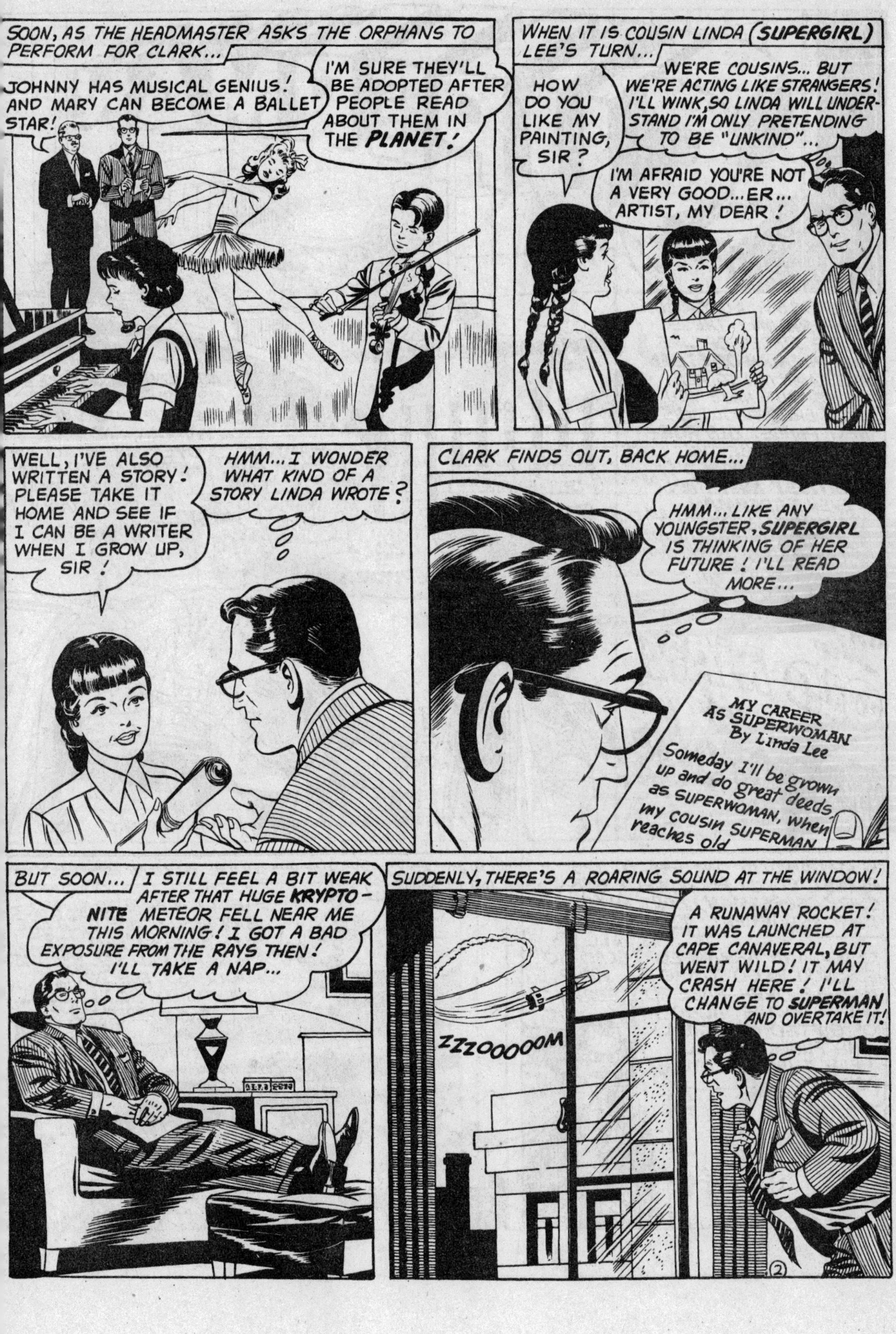
SOON, AS THE HEADMASTER ASKS THE ORPHANS TO PERFORM FOR CLARK...
JOHNNY HAS MUSICAL GENIUS! AND MARY CAN BECOME A BALLET STAR!
I'M SURE THEY'LL BE ADOPTED AFTER PEOPLE READ ABOUT THEM IN THE PLANET!
WHEN IT IS COUSIN LINDA (SUPERGIRL) LEE'S TURN...
HOW DO YOU LIKE MY PAINTING, SIR?
WE'RE COUSINS... BUT WE'RE ACTING LIKE STRANGERS! I'LL WINK, SO LINDA WILL UNDERSTAND I'M ONLY PRETENDING TO BE "UNKIND"...
I'M AFRAID YOU'RE NOT A VERY GOOD...ER... ARTIST, MY DEAR!
WELL, I'VE ALSO WRITTEN A STORY! PLEASE TAKE IT HOME AND SEE IF I CAN BE A WRITER WHEN I GROW UP, SIR!
HMM...I WONDER WHAT KIND OF A STORY LINDA WROTE?
CLARK FINDS OUT, BACK HOME...
HMM... LIKE ANY YOUNGSTER, SUPERGIRL IS THINKING OF HER FUTURE! I'LL READ MORE...
MY CAREER AS SUPERWOMAN
By Linda Lee
Someday I'll be grown up and do great deeds, as SUPERWOMAN, when my cousin SUPERMAN reaches old
BUT SOON...
I STILL FEEL A BIT WEAK AFTER THAT HUGE KRYPTONITE METEOR FELL NEAR ME THIS MORNING! I GOT A BAD EXPOSURE FROM THE RAYS THEN! I'LL TAKE A NAP...
SUDDENLY, THERE'S A ROARING SOUND AT THE WINDOW!
A RUNAWAY ROCKET! IT WAS LAUNCHED AT CAPE CANAVERAL, BUT WENT WILD! IT MAY CRASH HERE! I'LL CHANGE TO SUPERMAN AND OVERTAKE IT!
ZZZOOOOOM
2

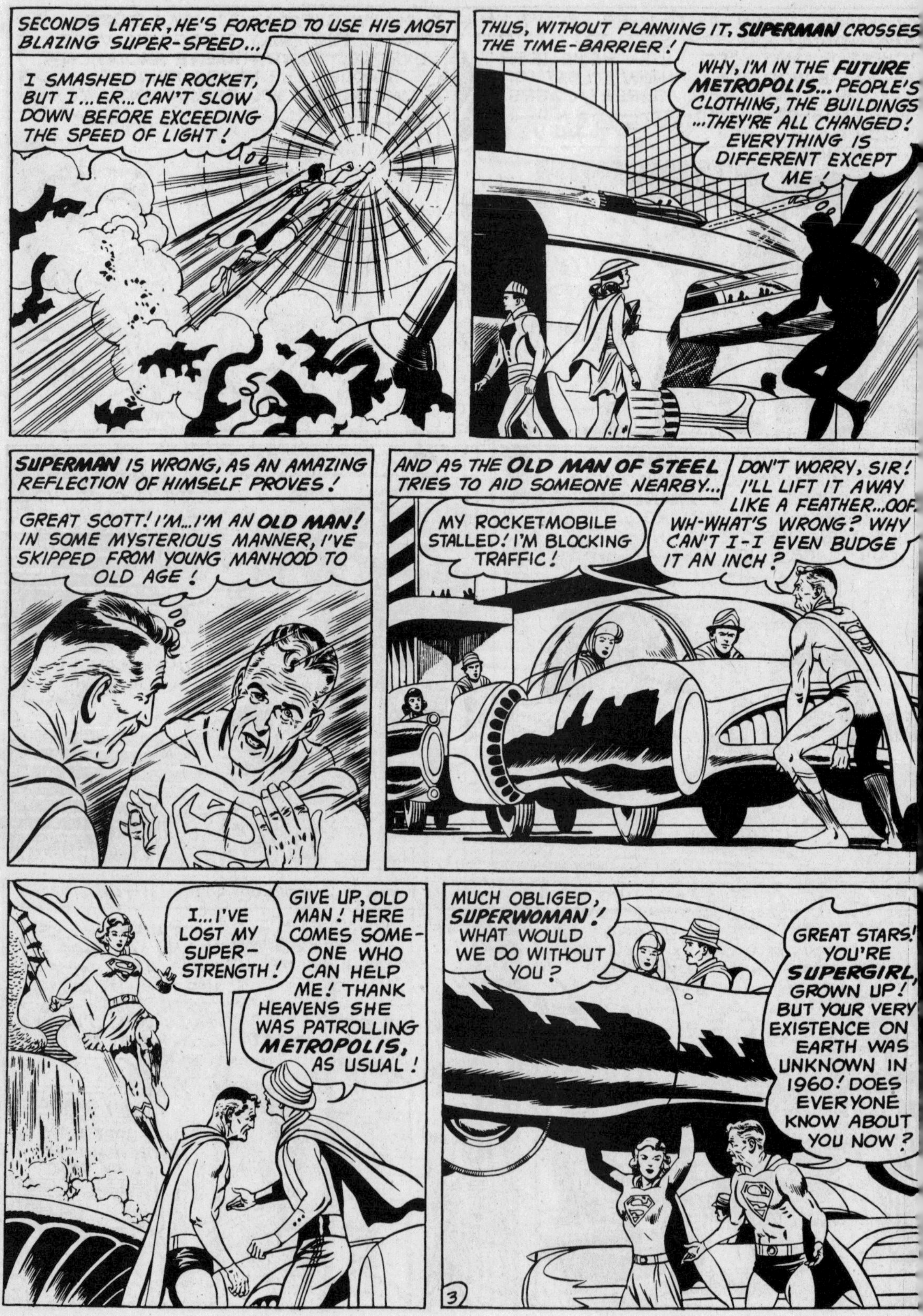
SECONDS LATER, HE'S FORCED TO USE HIS MOST BLAZING SUPER-SPEED...
I SMASHED THE ROCKET, BUT I...ER...CAN'T SLOW DOWN BEFORE EXCEEDING THE SPEED OF LIGHT!
THUS, WITHOUT PLANNING IT, SUPERMAN CROSSES THE TIME-BARRIER!
WHY, I'M IN THE FUTURE METROPOLIS... PEOPLE'S CLOTHING, THE BUILDINGS ...THEY'RE ALL CHANGED! EVERYTHING IS DIFFERENT EXCEPT ME!
SUPERMAN IS WRONG, AS AN AMAZING REFLECTION OF HIMSELF PROVES!
GREAT SCOTT! I'M...I'M AN OLD MAN! IN SOME MYSTERIOUS MANNER, I'VE SKIPPED FROM YOUNG MANHOOD TO OLD AGE!
AND AS THE OLD MAN OF STEEL TRIES TO AID SOMEONE NEARBY...
MY ROCKETMOBILE STALLED! I'M BLOCKING TRAFFIC!
DON'T WORRY, SIR! I'LL LIFT IT AWAY LIKE A FEATHER...OOF! WH-WHAT'S WRONG? WHY CAN'T I-I EVEN BUDGE IT AN INCH?
I...I'VE LOST MY SUPER-STRENGTH!
GIVE UP, OLD MAN! HERE COMES SOME-ONE WHO CAN HELP ME! THANK HEAVENS SHE WAS PATROLLING METROPOLIS, AS USUAL!
MUCH OBLIGED, SUPERWOMAN! WHAT WOULD WE DO WITHOUT YOU?
GREAT STARS! YOU'RE SUPERGIRL, GROWN UP! BUT YOUR VERY EXISTENCE ON EARTH WAS UNKNOWN IN 1960! DOES EVERYONE KNOW ABOUT YOU NOW?
3

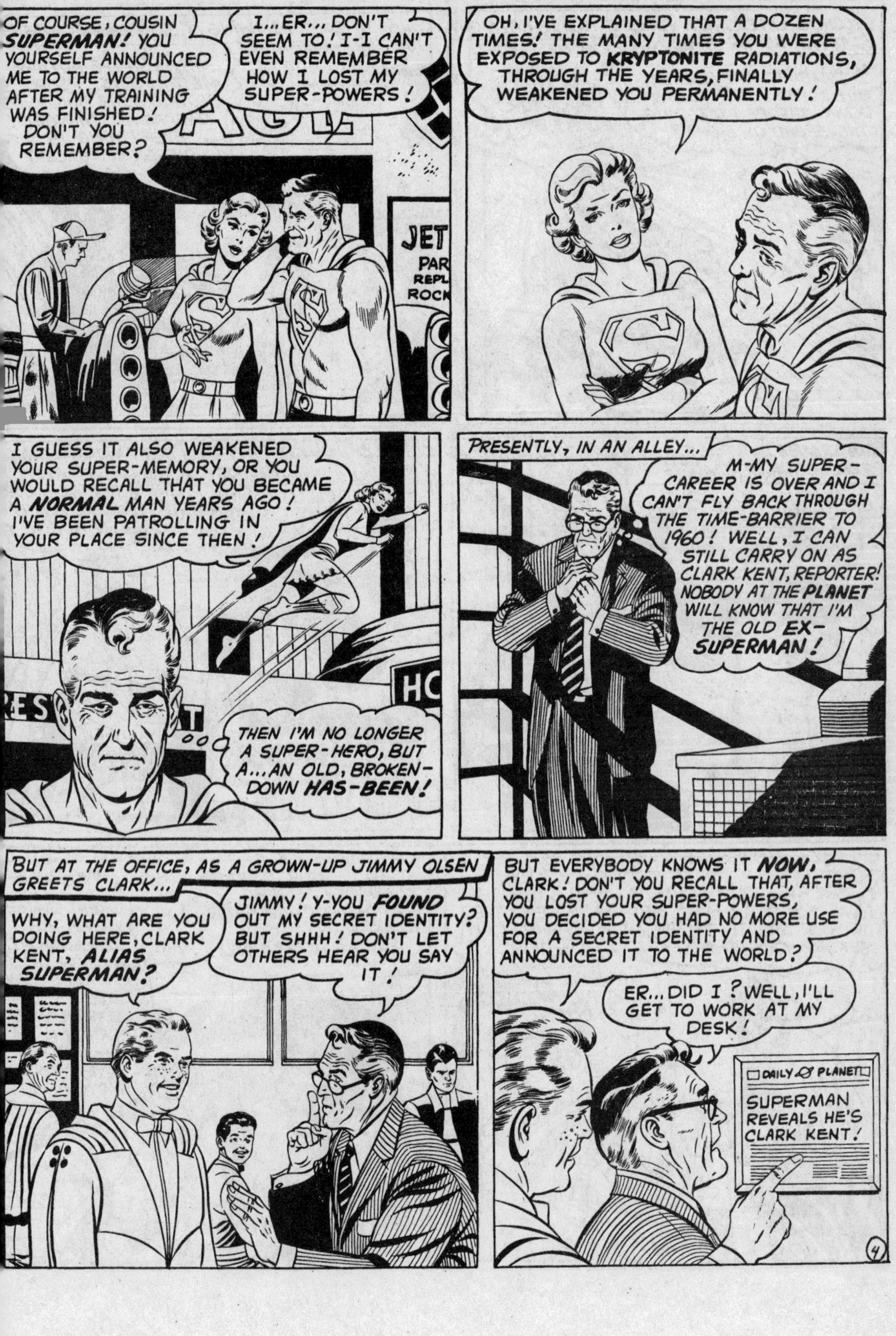
OF COURSE, COUSIN SUPERMAN! YOU YOURSELF ANNOUNCED ME TO THE WORLD AFTER MY TRAINING WAS FINISHED! DON'T YOU REMEMBER?
I...ER... DON'T SEEM TO! I-I CAN'T EVEN REMEMBER HOW I LOST MY SUPER-POWERS!
JET PAR REPL ROCK
OH, I'VE EXPLAINED THAT A DOZEN TIMES! THE MANY TIMES YOU WERE EXPOSED TO KRYPTONITE RADIATIONS, THROUGH THE YEARS, FINALLY WEAKENED YOU PERMANENTLY!
I GUESS IT ALSO WEAKENED YOUR SUPER-MEMORY, OR YOU WOULD RECALL THAT YOU BECAME A NORMAL MAN YEARS AGO! I'VE BEEN PATROLLING IN YOUR PLACE SINCE THEN!
THEN I'M NO LONGER A SUPER-HERO, BUT A...AN OLD, BROKEN-DOWN HAS-BEEN!
PRESENTLY, IN AN ALLEY...
M-MY SUPER-CAREER IS OVER AND I CAN'T FLY BACK THROUGH THE TIME-BARRIER TO 1960! WELL, I CAN STILL CARRY ON AS CLARK KENT, REPORTER! NOBODY AT THE PLANET WILL KNOW THAT I'M THE OLD EX-SUPERMAN!
BUT AT THE OFFICE, AS A GROWN-UP JIMMY OLSEN GREETS CLARK...
WHY, WHAT ARE YOU DOING HERE, CLARK KENT, ALIAS SUPERMAN?
JIMMY! Y-YOU FOUND OUT MY SECRET IDENTITY? BUT SHHH! DON'T LET OTHERS HEAR YOU SAY IT!
BUT EVERYBODY KNOWS IT NOW, CLARK! DON'T YOU RECALL THAT, AFTER YOU LOST YOUR SUPER-POWERS, YOU DECIDED YOU HAD NO MORE USE FOR A SECRET IDENTITY AND ANNOUNCED IT TO THE WORLD?
ER... DID I? WELL, I'LL GET TO WORK AT MY DESK!
DAILY PLANET
SUPERMAN REVEALS HE'S CLARK KENT!
4

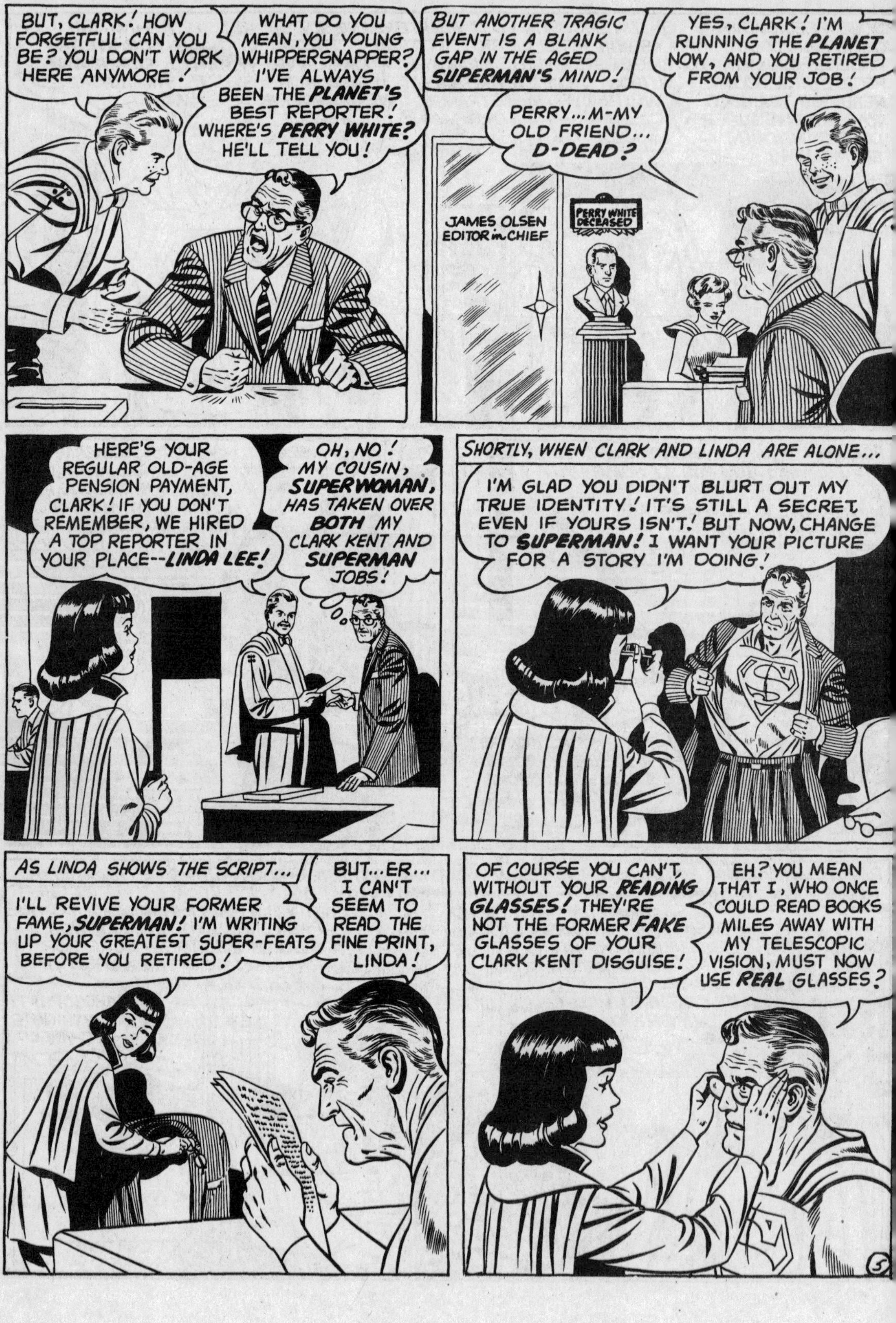
BUT, CLARK! HOW FORGETFUL CAN YOU BE? YOU DON'T WORK HERE ANYMORE!
WHAT DO YOU MEAN, YOU YOUNG WHIPPERSNAPPER? I'VE ALWAYS BEEN THE PLANET'S BEST REPORTER! WHERE'S PERRY WHITE? HE'LL TELL YOU!
BUT ANOTHER TRAGIC EVENT IS A BLANK GAP IN THE AGED SUPERMAN'S MIND!
YES, CLARK! I'M RUNNING THE PLANET NOW, AND YOU RETIRED FROM YOUR JOB!
PERRY... M-MY OLD FRIEND... D-DEAD?
JAMES OLSEN EDITOR in CHIEF
PERRY WHITE DECEASED
HERE'S YOUR REGULAR OLD-AGE PENSION PAYMENT, CLARK! IF YOU DON'T REMEMBER, WE HIRED A TOP REPORTER IN YOUR PLACE--LINDA LEE!
OH, NO! MY COUSIN, SUPERWOMAN, HAS TAKEN OVER BOTH MY CLARK KENT AND SUPERMAN JOBS!
SHORTLY, WHEN CLARK AND LINDA ARE ALONE...
I'M GLAD YOU DIDN'T BLURT OUT MY TRUE IDENTITY! IT'S STILL A SECRET, EVEN IF YOURS ISN'T! BUT NOW, CHANGE TO SUPERMAN! I WANT YOUR PICTURE FOR A STORY I'M DOING!
AS LINDA SHOWS THE SCRIPT...
I'LL REVIVE YOUR FORMER FAME, SUPERMAN! I'M WRITING UP YOUR GREATEST SUPER-FEATS BEFORE YOU RETIRED!
BUT...ER... I CAN'T SEEM TO READ THE FINE PRINT, LINDA!
OF COURSE YOU CAN'T, WITHOUT YOUR READING GLASSES! THEY'RE NOT THE FORMER FAKE GLASSES OF YOUR CLARK KENT DISGUISE!
EH? YOU MEAN THAT I, WHO ONCE COULD READ BOOKS MILES AWAY WITH MY TELESCOPIC VISION, MUST NOW USE REAL GLASSES?
5

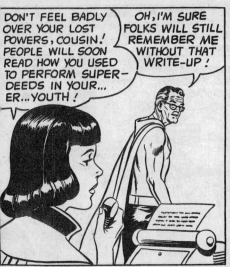

DON'T FEEL BADLY OVER YOUR LOST POWERS, COUSIN! PEOPLE WILL SOON READ HOW YOU USED TO PERFORM SUPER-DEEDS IN YOUR...ER...YOUTH!

OH, I'M SURE FOLKS WILL STILL REMEMBER ME WITHOUT THAT WRITE-UP!

BUT HEARTBREAKINGLY...

GRANNY! WHO'S THAT STRANGE OLD MAN?

HMM...I'VE SEEN HIM SOMEWHERE BEFORE, YEARS AGO...

I-I'M THE FORGOTTEN SUPERMAN! ...CHOKE!

FORLORN, THAT EVENING SUPERMAN LOOKS UP HIS FORMER BOY PAL AT HOME, BUT...

LUCY LANE, LOIS LANE'S SISTER! WHAT ARE YOU DOING HERE?

OH, YOU'RE JOKING, OLD SUPERMAN! YOU KNOW JIMMY AND I GOT MARRIED! WHY, YOU WERE THE BEST MAN AT THE WEDDING!

I...UH...SEE YOU'RE A BUSY FATHER, JIMMY! I'LL GO...

HERE, SUPERMAN! TAKE MY SIGNAL-WATCH, WHICH YOU GAVE ME LONG AGO! YOU MIGHT NEED IT TO CALL SUPERWOMAN, JUST AS I USED TO CALL YOU!

LATER, SUPERMAN FINDS USE FOR THE ULTRASONIC SIGNAL!

CITY HA[LL]

LUTHOR, MY OLD ENEMY! THAT RENEGADE SCIENTIST MAY BE CARRYING A BOMB IN HIS BRIEFCASE, TO BLOW UP CITY HALL! I'LL CALL SUPERWOMAN!

AFTER THE WOMAN OF STEEL ARRIVES AND HEARS THE WARNING...

THE LUTHOR SERUM

TSK-TSK! LUTHOR REFORMED AND WAS PARDONED, WHEN HIS LUTHOR SERUM BECAME A CURE FOR CANCER! HE'S THE MAYOR OF METROPOLIS NOW!

JEHOSOPHAT! EVERYTHING'S CHANGED!

LUTHOR MAYOR

6

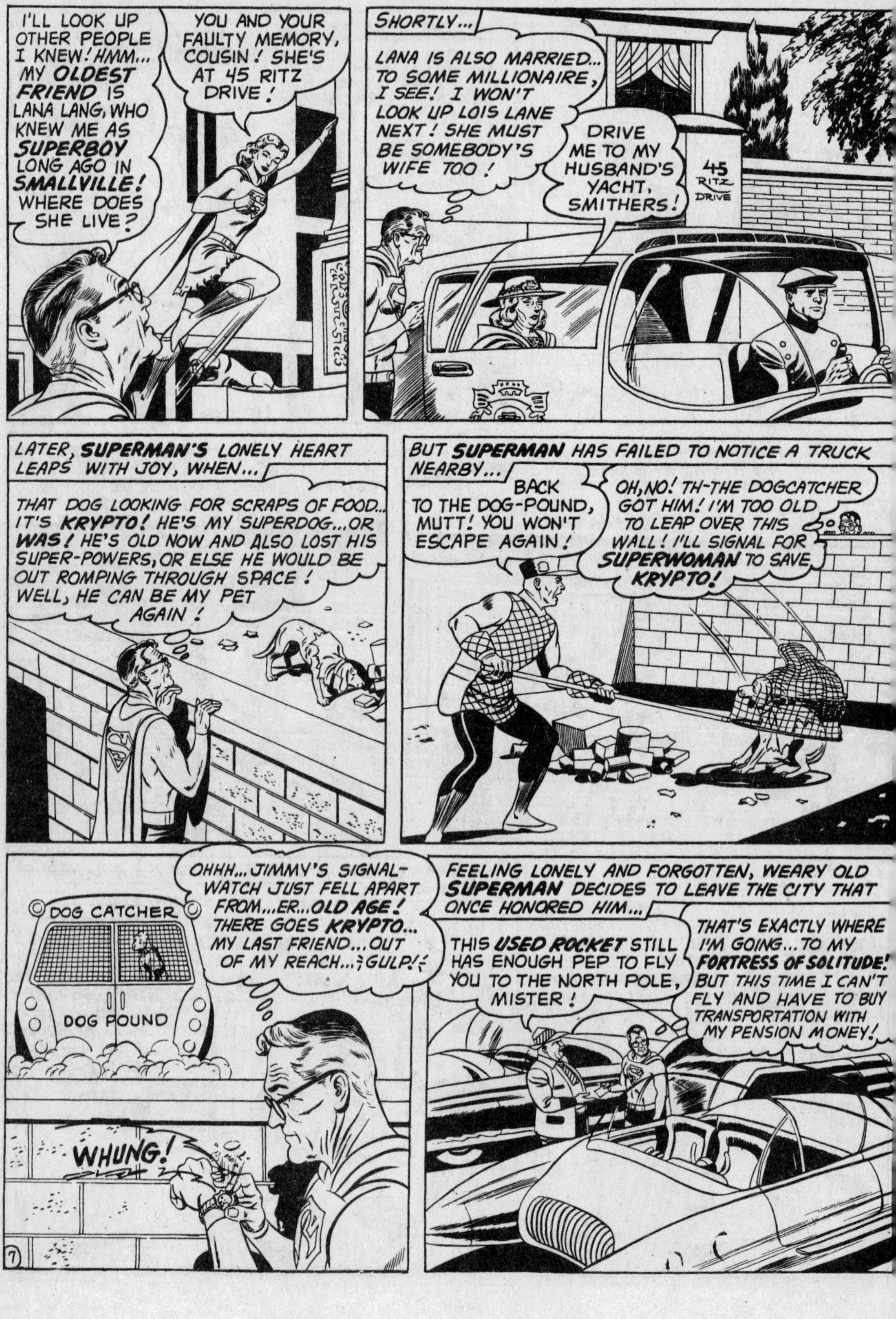
I'LL LOOK UP OTHER PEOPLE I KNEW! HMM... MY OLDEST FRIEND IS LANA LANG, WHO KNEW ME AS SUPERBOY LONG AGO IN SMALLVILLE! WHERE DOES SHE LIVE?
YOU AND YOUR FAULTY MEMORY, COUSIN! SHE'S AT 45 RITZ DRIVE!
SHORTLY...
LANA IS ALSO MARRIED... TO SOME MILLIONAIRE, I SEE! I WON'T LOOK UP LOIS LANE NEXT! SHE MUST BE SOMEBODY'S WIFE TOO!
DRIVE ME TO MY HUSBAND'S YACHT, SMITHERS!
45 RITZ DRIVE
LATER, SUPERMAN'S LONELY HEART LEAPS WITH JOY, WHEN...
THAT DOG LOOKING FOR SCRAPS OF FOOD... IT'S KRYPTO! HE'S MY SUPERDOG... OR WAS! HE'S OLD NOW AND ALSO LOST HIS SUPER-POWERS, OR ELSE HE WOULD BE OUT ROMPING THROUGH SPACE! WELL, HE CAN BE MY PET AGAIN!
BUT SUPERMAN HAS FAILED TO NOTICE A TRUCK NEARBY...
BACK TO THE DOG-POUND, MUTT! YOU WON'T ESCAPE AGAIN!
OH, NO! TH-THE DOGCATCHER GOT HIM! I'M TOO OLD TO LEAP OVER THIS WALL! I'LL SIGNAL FOR SUPERWOMAN TO SAVE KRYPTO!
DOG CATCHER
DOG POUND
OHHH... JIMMY'S SIGNAL-WATCH JUST FELL APART FROM... ER... OLD AGE! THERE GOES KRYPTO... MY LAST FRIEND... OUT OF MY REACH... ¿GULP!¿
WHUNG!
7
FEELING LONELY AND FORGOTTEN, WEARY OLD SUPERMAN DECIDES TO LEAVE THE CITY THAT ONCE HONORED HIM...
THIS USED ROCKET STILL HAS ENOUGH PEP TO FLY YOU TO THE NORTH POLE, MISTER!
THAT'S EXACTLY WHERE I'M GOING... TO MY FORTRESS OF SOLITUDE! BUT THIS TIME I CAN'T FLY AND HAVE TO BUY TRANSPORTATION WITH MY PENSION MONEY!

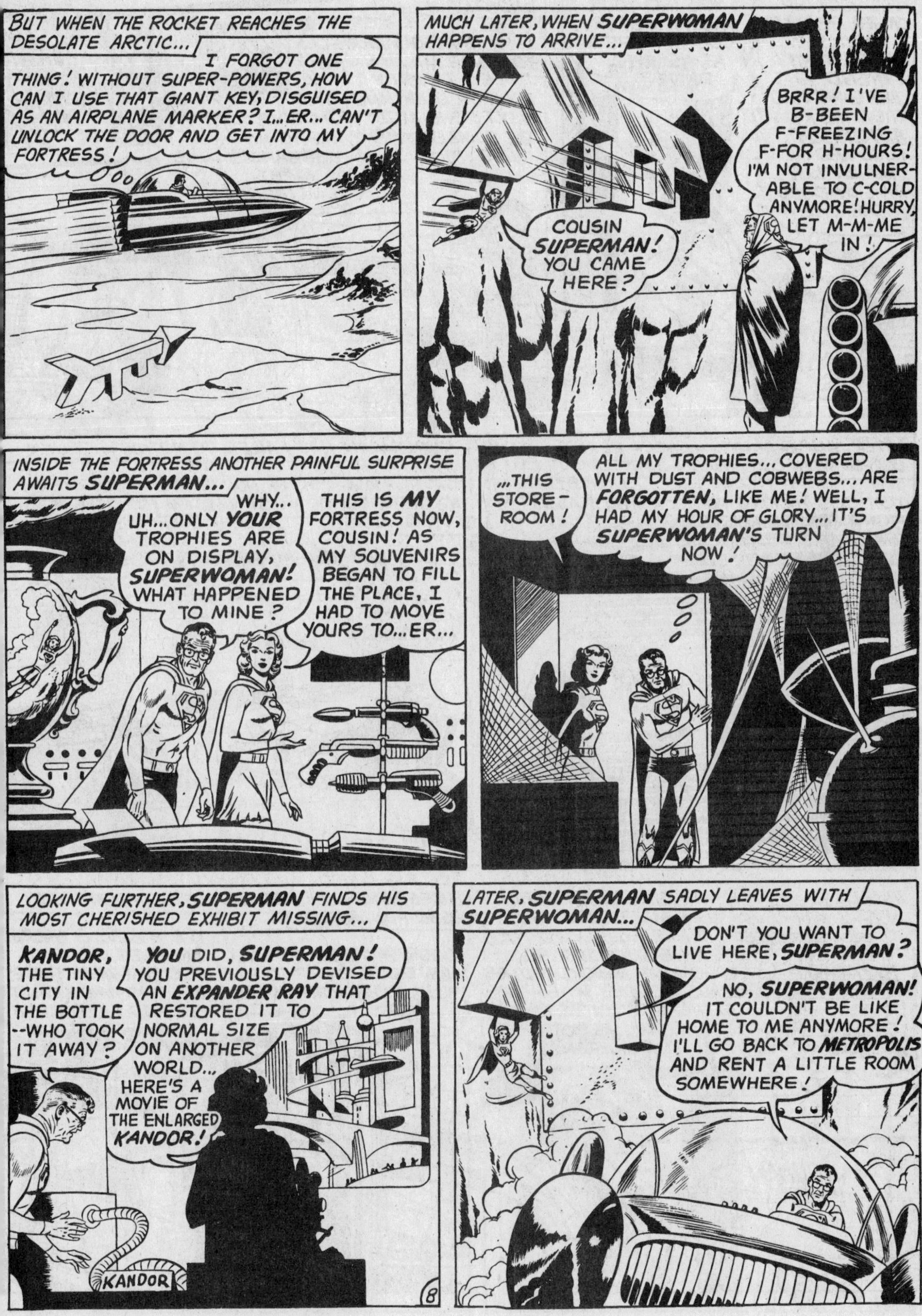
BUT WHEN THE ROCKET REACHES THE DESOLATE ARCTIC...
I FORGOT ONE THING! WITHOUT SUPER-POWERS, HOW CAN I USE THAT GIANT KEY, DISGUISED AS AN AIRPLANE MARKER? I...ER... CAN'T UNLOCK THE DOOR AND GET INTO MY FORTRESS!
MUCH LATER, WHEN SUPERWOMAN HAPPENS TO ARRIVE...
BRRR! I'VE B-BEEN F-FREEZING F-FOR H-HOURS! I'M NOT INVULNERABLE TO C-COLD ANYMORE! HURRY, LET M-M-ME IN!
COUSIN SUPERMAN! YOU CAME HERE?
INSIDE THE FORTRESS ANOTHER PAINFUL SURPRISE AWAITS SUPERMAN...
WHY... UH...ONLY YOUR TROPHIES ARE ON DISPLAY, SUPERWOMAN! WHAT HAPPENED TO MINE?
THIS IS MY FORTRESS NOW, COUSIN! AS MY SOUVENIRS BEGAN TO FILL THE PLACE, I HAD TO MOVE YOURS TO...ER...
...THIS STORE-ROOM!
ALL MY TROPHIES..., COVERED WITH DUST AND COBWEBS... ARE FORGOTTEN, LIKE ME! WELL, I HAD MY HOUR OF GLORY... IT'S SUPERWOMAN'S TURN NOW!
LOOKING FURTHER, SUPERMAN FINDS HIS MOST CHERISHED EXHIBIT MISSING...
KANDOR, THE TINY CITY IN THE BOTTLE --WHO TOOK IT AWAY?
YOU DID, SUPERMAN! YOU PREVIOUSLY DEVISED AN EXPANDER RAY THAT RESTORED IT TO NORMAL SIZE ON ANOTHER WORLD... HERE'S A MOVIE OF THE ENLARGED KANDOR!
KANDOR
8
LATER, SUPERMAN SADLY LEAVES WITH SUPERWOMAN...
DON'T YOU WANT TO LIVE HERE, SUPERMAN?
NO, SUPERWOMAN! IT COULDN'T BE LIKE HOME TO ME ANYMORE! I'LL GO BACK TO METROPOLIS AND RENT A LITTLE ROOM SOMEWHERE!

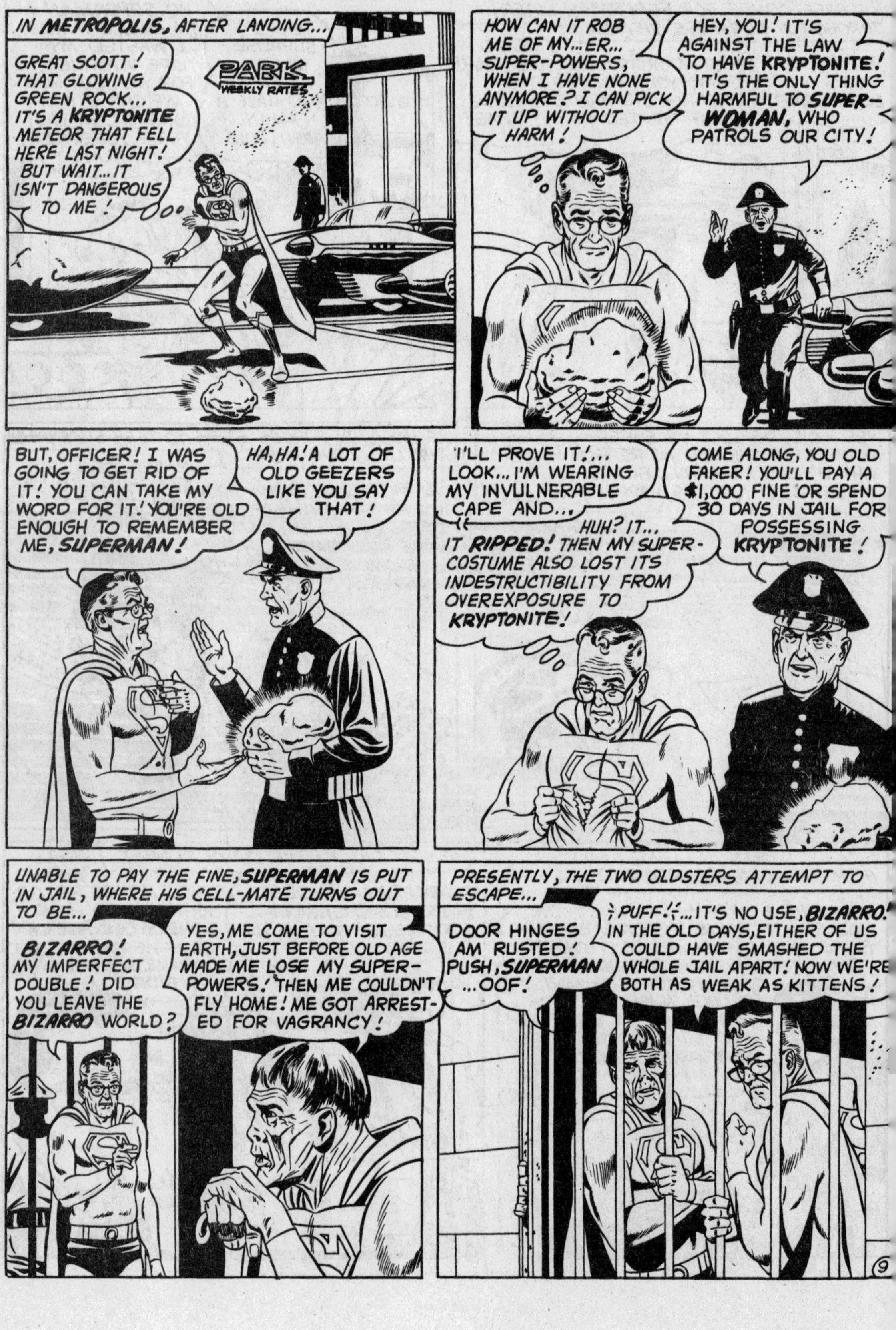
IN METROPOLIS, AFTER LANDING...
GREAT SCOTT! THAT GLOWING GREEN ROCK... IT'S A KRYPTONITE METEOR THAT FELL HERE LAST NIGHT! BUT WAIT... IT ISN'T DANGEROUS TO ME!
PARK WEEKLY RATES
HOW CAN IT ROB ME OF MY... ER... SUPER-POWERS, WHEN I HAVE NONE ANYMORE? I CAN PICK IT UP WITHOUT HARM!
HEY, YOU! IT'S AGAINST THE LAW TO HAVE KRYPTONITE! IT'S THE ONLY THING HARMFUL TO SUPER-WOMAN, WHO PATROLS OUR CITY!
BUT, OFFICER! I WAS GOING TO GET RID OF IT! YOU CAN TAKE MY WORD FOR IT! YOU'RE OLD ENOUGH TO REMEMBER ME, SUPERMAN!
HA, HA! A LOT OF OLD GEEZERS LIKE YOU SAY THAT!
I'LL PROVE IT!... LOOK... I'M WEARING MY INVULNERABLE CAPE AND...
HUH? IT... IT RIPPED! THEN MY SUPER-COSTUME ALSO LOST ITS INDESTRUCTIBILITY FROM OVEREXPOSURE TO KRYPTONITE!
COME ALONG, YOU OLD FAKER! YOU'LL PAY A $1,000 FINE OR SPEND 30 DAYS IN JAIL FOR POSSESSING KRYPTONITE!
UNABLE TO PAY THE FINE, SUPERMAN IS PUT IN JAIL, WHERE HIS CELL-MATE TURNS OUT TO BE...
BIZARRO! MY IMPERFECT DOUBLE! DID YOU LEAVE THE BIZARRO WORLD?
YES, ME COME TO VISIT EARTH, JUST BEFORE OLD AGE MADE ME LOSE MY SUPER-POWERS! THEN ME COULDN'T FLY HOME! ME GOT ARREST-ED FOR VAGRANCY!
PRESENTLY, THE TWO OLDSTERS ATTEMPT TO ESCAPE...
DOOR HINGES AM RUSTED! PUSH, SUPERMAN ...OOF!
PUFF! ...IT'S NO USE, BIZARRO! IN THE OLD DAYS, EITHER OF US COULD HAVE SMASHED THE WHOLE JAIL APART! NOW WE'RE BOTH AS WEAK AS KITTENS!
9

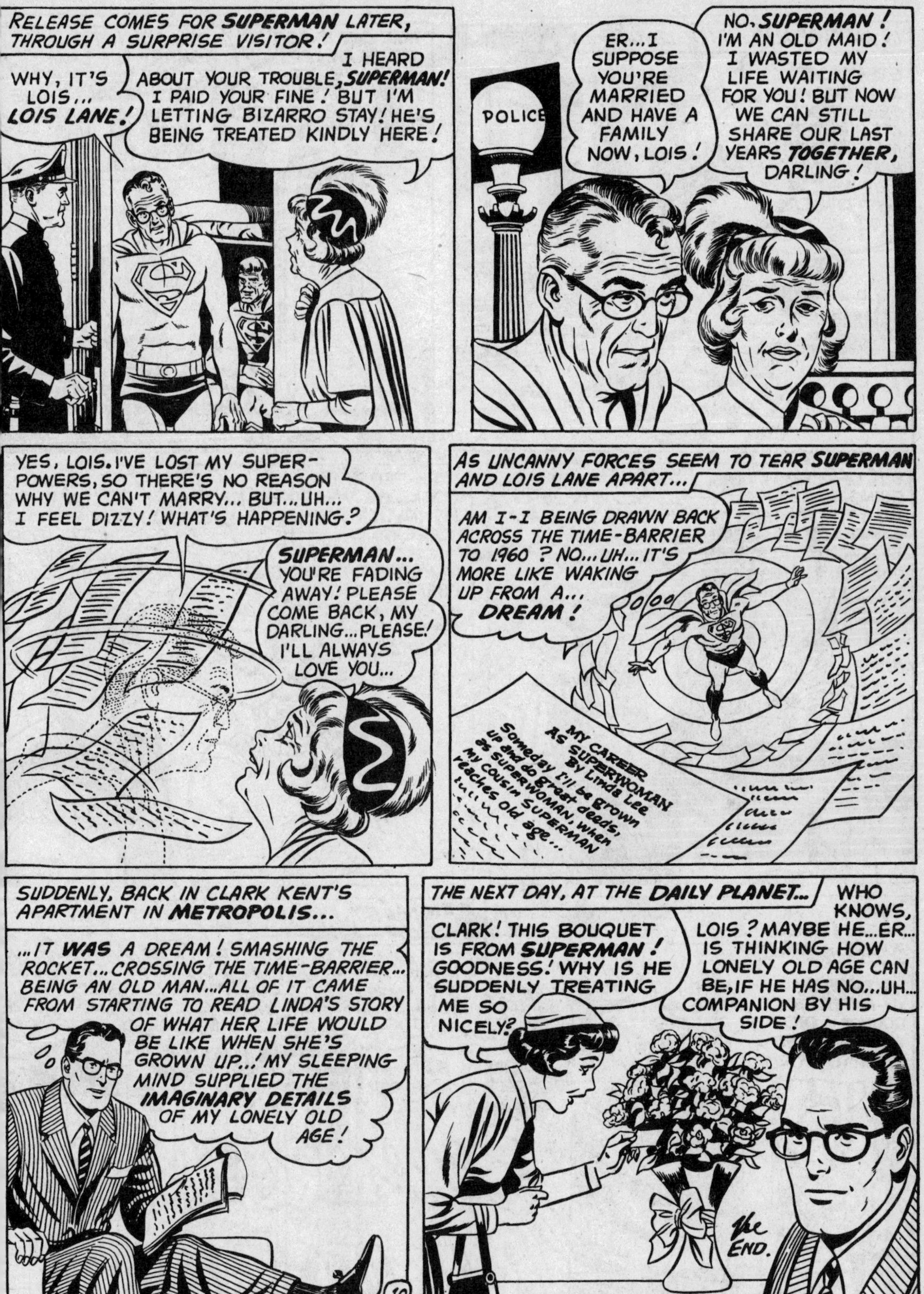
RELEASE COMES FOR SUPERMAN LATER, THROUGH A SURPRISE VISITOR!
WHY, IT'S LOIS... LOIS LANE!
I HEARD ABOUT YOUR TROUBLE, SUPERMAN! I PAID YOUR FINE! BUT I'M LETTING BIZARRO STAY! HE'S BEING TREATED KINDLY HERE!
POLICE
ER...I SUPPOSE YOU'RE MARRIED AND HAVE A FAMILY NOW, LOIS!
NO, SUPERMAN! I'M AN OLD MAID! I WASTED MY LIFE WAITING FOR YOU! BUT NOW WE CAN STILL SHARE OUR LAST YEARS TOGETHER, DARLING!
YES, LOIS. I'VE LOST MY SUPER-POWERS, SO THERE'S NO REASON WHY WE CAN'T MARRY... BUT... UH... I FEEL DIZZY! WHAT'S HAPPENING?
SUPERMAN... YOU'RE FADING AWAY! PLEASE COME BACK, MY DARLING... PLEASE! I'LL ALWAYS LOVE YOU...
AS UNCANNY FORCES SEEM TO TEAR SUPERMAN AND LOIS LANE APART...
AM I-I BEING DRAWN BACK ACROSS THE TIME-BARRIER TO 1960? NO... UH... IT'S MORE LIKE WAKING UP FROM A... DREAM!
MY CAREER AS SUPERWOMAN By Linda Lee
Someday I'll be grown up and do great deeds, as SUPERWOMAN, when my cousin SUPERMAN reaches old age...
SUDDENLY, BACK IN CLARK KENT'S APARTMENT IN METROPOLIS...
...IT WAS A DREAM! SMASHING THE ROCKET... CROSSING THE TIME-BARRIER... BEING AN OLD MAN... ALL OF IT CAME FROM STARTING TO READ LINDA'S STORY OF WHAT HER LIFE WOULD BE LIKE WHEN SHE'S GROWN UP...! MY SLEEPING MIND SUPPLIED THE IMAGINARY DETAILS OF MY LONELY OLD AGE!
10
THE NEXT DAY, AT THE DAILY PLANET...
CLARK! THIS BOUQUET IS FROM SUPERMAN! GOODNESS! WHY IS HE SUDDENLY TREATING ME SO NICELY?
WHO KNOWS, LOIS? MAYBE HE...ER... IS THINKING HOW LONELY OLD AGE CAN BE, IF HE HAS NO...UH... COMPANION BY HIS SIDE!
The END.

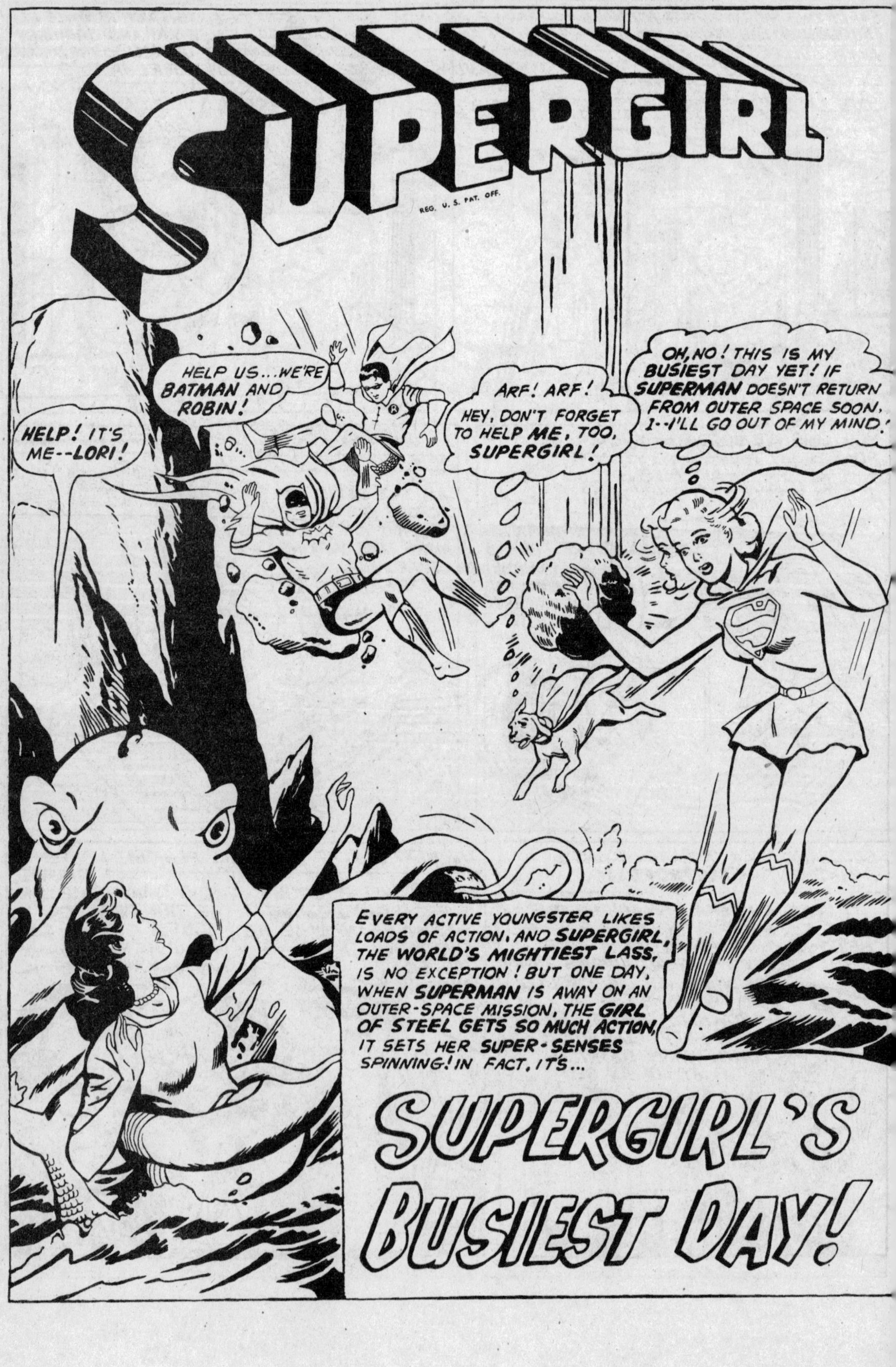
SUPERGIRL
REG. U.S. PAT. OFF.
HELP! IT'S ME--LORI!
HELP US...WE'RE BATMAN AND ROBIN!
ARF! ARF! HEY, DON'T FORGET TO HELP ME, TOO, SUPERGIRL!
OH, NO! THIS IS MY BUSIEST DAY YET! IF SUPERMAN DOESN'T RETURN FROM OUTER SPACE SOON, I--I'LL GO OUT OF MY MIND!
EVERY ACTIVE YOUNGSTER LIKES LOADS OF ACTION, AND SUPERGIRL, THE WORLD'S MIGHTIEST LASS, IS NO EXCEPTION! BUT ONE DAY, WHEN SUPERMAN IS AWAY ON AN OUTER-SPACE MISSION, THE GIRL OF STEEL GETS SO MUCH ACTION, IT SETS HER SUPER-SENSES SPINNING! IN FACT, IT'S...
SUPERGIRL'S BUSIEST DAY!

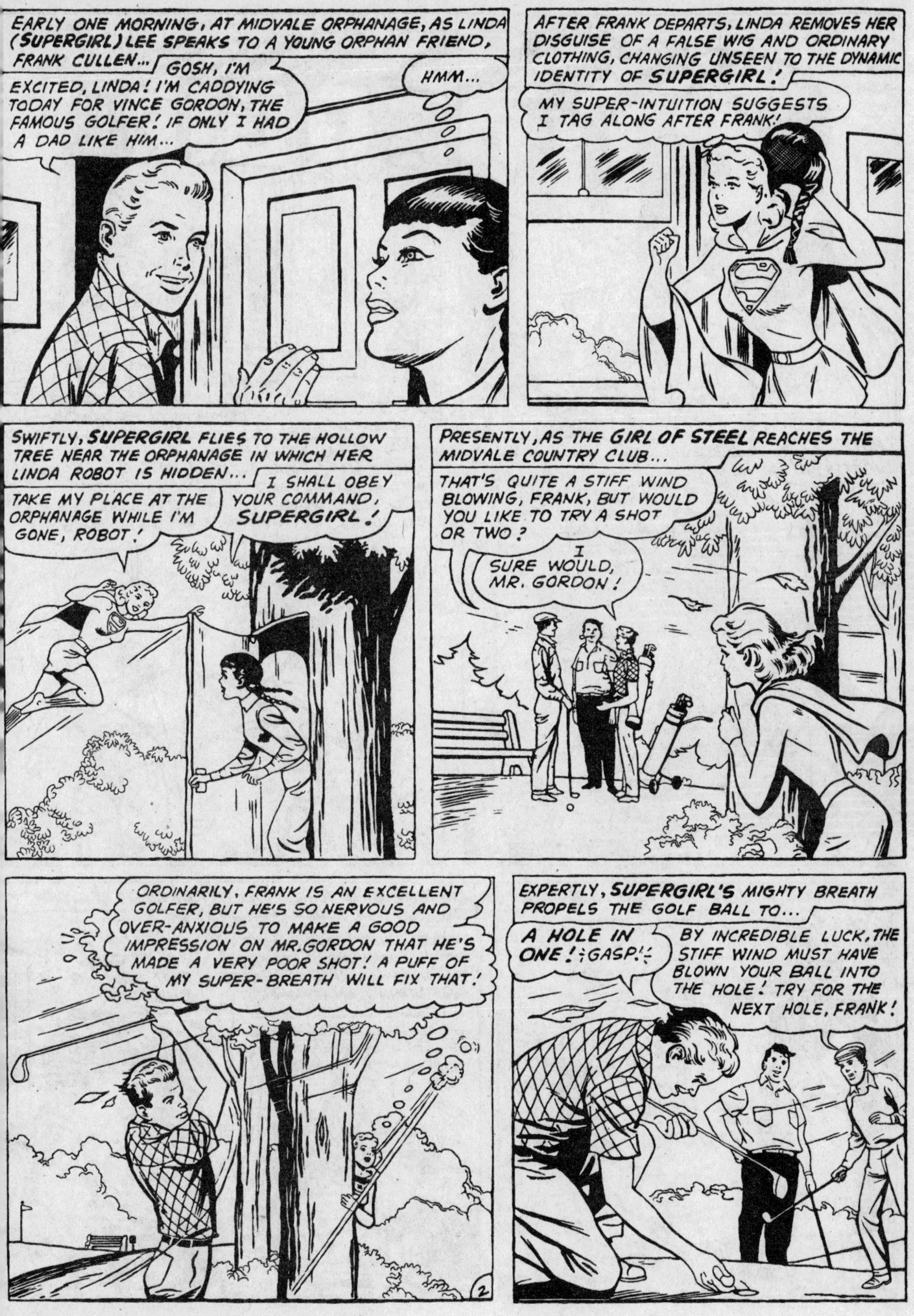
EARLY ONE MORNING, AT MIDVALE ORPHANAGE, AS LINDA (SUPERGIRL) LEE SPEAKS TO A YOUNG ORPHAN FRIEND, FRANK CULLEN...
GOSH, I'M EXCITED, LINDA! I'M CADDYING TODAY FOR VINCE GORDON, THE FAMOUS GOLFER! IF ONLY I HAD A DAD LIKE HIM...
HMM...
AFTER FRANK DEPARTS, LINDA REMOVES HER DISGUISE OF A FALSE WIG AND ORDINARY CLOTHING, CHANGING UNSEEN TO THE DYNAMIC IDENTITY OF SUPERGIRL!
MY SUPER-INTUITION SUGGESTS I TAG ALONG AFTER FRANK!
SWIFTLY, SUPERGIRL FLIES TO THE HOLLOW TREE NEAR THE ORPHANAGE IN WHICH HER LINDA ROBOT IS HIDDEN...
TAKE MY PLACE AT THE ORPHANAGE WHILE I'M GONE, ROBOT!
I SHALL OBEY YOUR COMMAND, SUPERGIRL!
PRESENTLY, AS THE GIRL OF STEEL REACHES THE MIDVALE COUNTRY CLUB...
THAT'S QUITE A STIFF WIND BLOWING, FRANK, BUT WOULD YOU LIKE TO TRY A SHOT OR TWO?
I SURE WOULD, MR. GORDON!
ORDINARILY, FRANK IS AN EXCELLENT GOLFER, BUT HE'S SO NERVOUS AND OVER-ANXIOUS TO MAKE A GOOD IMPRESSION ON MR. GORDON THAT HE'S MADE A VERY POOR SHOT! A PUFF OF MY SUPER-BREATH WILL FIX THAT!
2
EXPERTLY, SUPERGIRL'S MIGHTY BREATH PROPELS THE GOLF BALL TO...
A HOLE IN ONE! -GASP!-
BY INCREDIBLE LUCK, THE STIFF WIND MUST HAVE BLOWN YOUR BALL INTO THE HOLE! TRY FOR THE NEXT HOLE, FRANK!

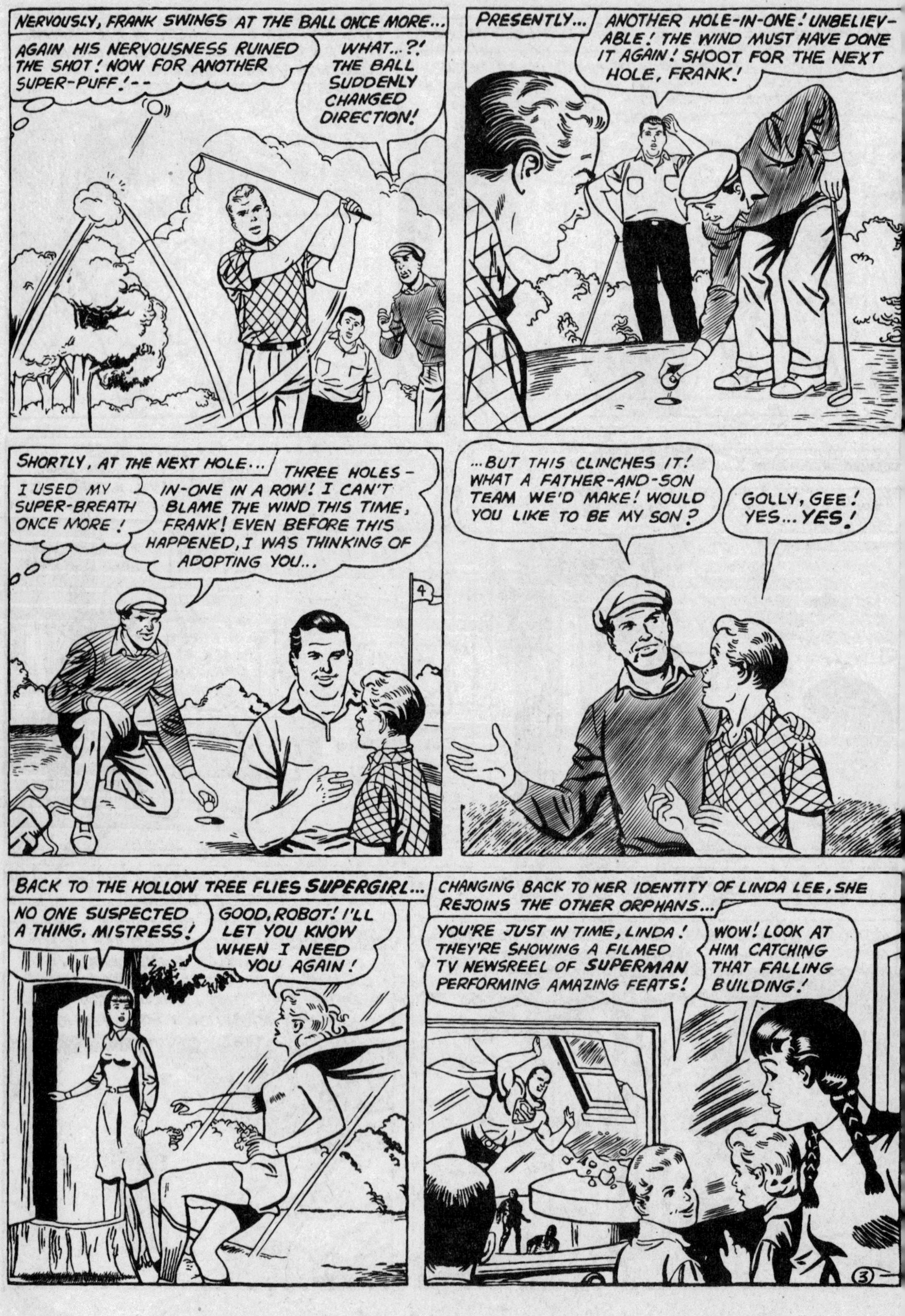
NERVOUSLY, FRANK SWINGS AT THE BALL ONCE MORE...
AGAIN HIS NERVOUSNESS RUINED THE SHOT! NOW FOR ANOTHER SUPER-PUFF!--
WHAT...?! THE BALL SUDDENLY CHANGED DIRECTION!
PRESENTLY...
ANOTHER HOLE-IN-ONE! UNBELIEV-ABLE! THE WIND MUST HAVE DONE IT AGAIN! SHOOT FOR THE NEXT HOLE, FRANK!
SHORTLY, AT THE NEXT HOLE...
I USED MY SUPER-BREATH ONCE MORE!
THREE HOLES-IN-ONE IN A ROW! I CAN'T BLAME THE WIND THIS TIME, FRANK! EVEN BEFORE THIS HAPPENED, I WAS THINKING OF ADOPTING YOU...
4
...BUT THIS CLINCHES IT! WHAT A FATHER-AND-SON TEAM WE'D MAKE! WOULD YOU LIKE TO BE MY SON?
GOLLY, GEE! YES... YES!
BACK TO THE HOLLOW TREE FLIES SUPERGIRL...
NO ONE SUSPECTED A THING, MISTRESS!
GOOD, ROBOT! I'LL LET YOU KNOW WHEN I NEED YOU AGAIN!
CHANGING BACK TO HER IDENTITY OF LINDA LEE, SHE REJOINS THE OTHER ORPHANS...
YOU'RE JUST IN TIME, LINDA! THEY'RE SHOWING A FILMED TV NEWSREEL OF SUPERMAN PERFORMING AMAZING FEATS!
WOW! LOOK AT HIM CATCHING THAT FALLING BUILDING!
3

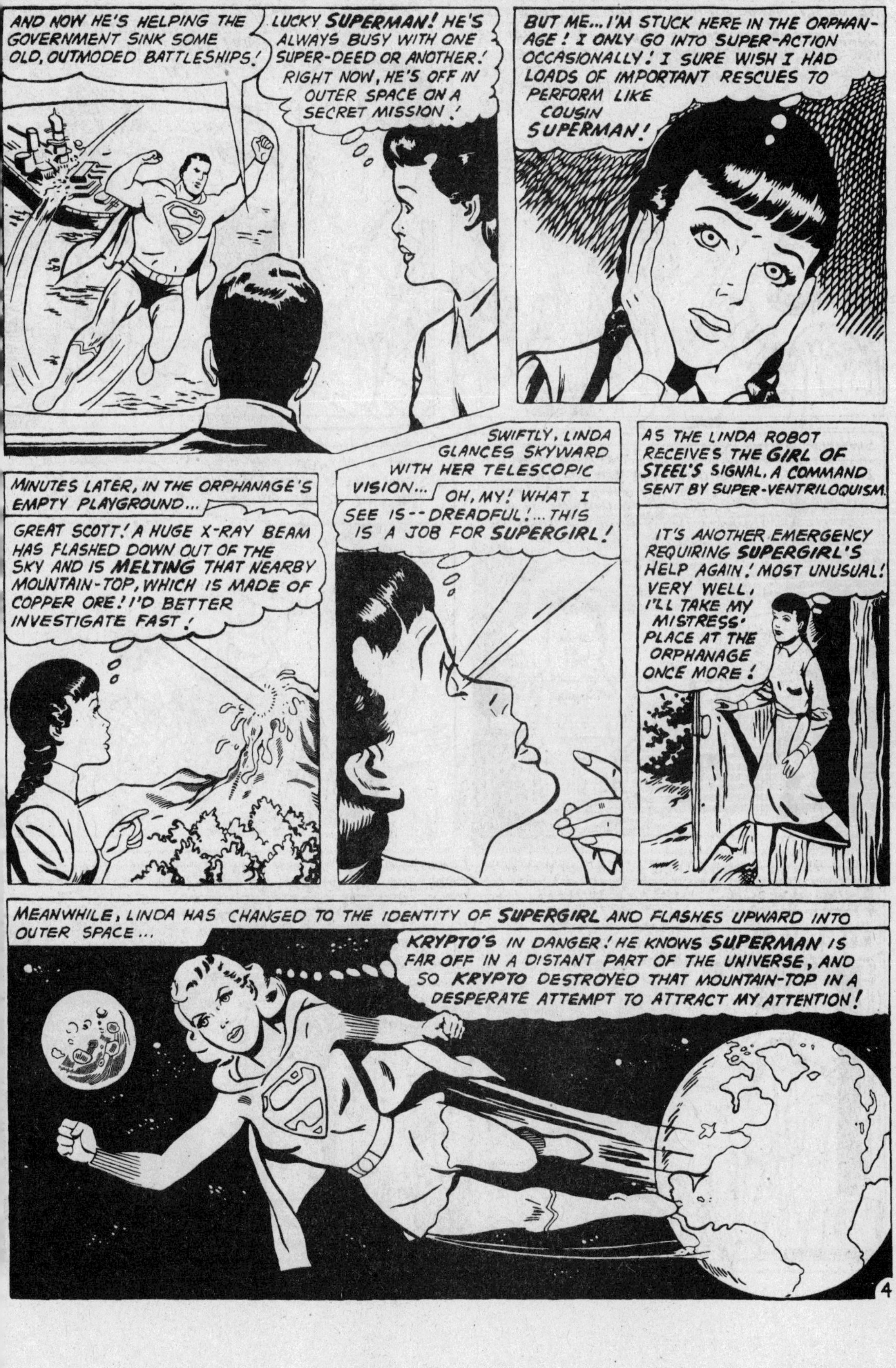
AND NOW HE'S HELPING THE GOVERNMENT SINK SOME OLD, OUTMODED BATTLESHIPS!
LUCKY SUPERMAN! HE'S ALWAYS BUSY WITH ONE SUPER-DEED OR ANOTHER! RIGHT NOW, HE'S OFF IN OUTER SPACE ON A SECRET MISSION!
BUT ME...I'M STUCK HERE IN THE ORPHANAGE! I ONLY GO INTO SUPER-ACTION OCCASIONALLY! I SURE WISH I HAD LOADS OF IMPORTANT RESCUES TO PERFORM LIKE COUSIN SUPERMAN!
MINUTES LATER, IN THE ORPHANAGE'S EMPTY PLAYGROUND...
GREAT SCOTT! A HUGE X-RAY BEAM HAS FLASHED DOWN OUT OF THE SKY AND IS MELTING THAT NEARBY MOUNTAIN-TOP, WHICH IS MADE OF COPPER ORE! I'D BETTER INVESTIGATE FAST!
SWIFTLY, LINDA GLANCES SKYWARD WITH HER TELESCOPIC VISION...
OH, MY! WHAT I SEE IS--DREADFUL!...THIS IS A JOB FOR SUPERGIRL!
AS THE LINDA ROBOT RECEIVES THE GIRL OF STEEL'S SIGNAL, A COMMAND SENT BY SUPER-VENTRILOQUISM.
IT'S ANOTHER EMERGENCY REQUIRING SUPERGIRL'S HELP AGAIN! MOST UNUSUAL! VERY WELL, I'LL TAKE MY MISTRESS' PLACE AT THE ORPHANAGE ONCE MORE!
MEANWHILE, LINDA HAS CHANGED TO THE IDENTITY OF SUPERGIRL AND FLASHES UPWARD INTO OUTER SPACE...
KRYPTO'S IN DANGER! HE KNOWS SUPERMAN IS FAR OFF IN A DISTANT PART OF THE UNIVERSE, AND SO KRYPTO DESTROYED THAT MOUNTAIN-TOP IN A DESPERATE ATTEMPT TO ATTRACT MY ATTENTION!
4

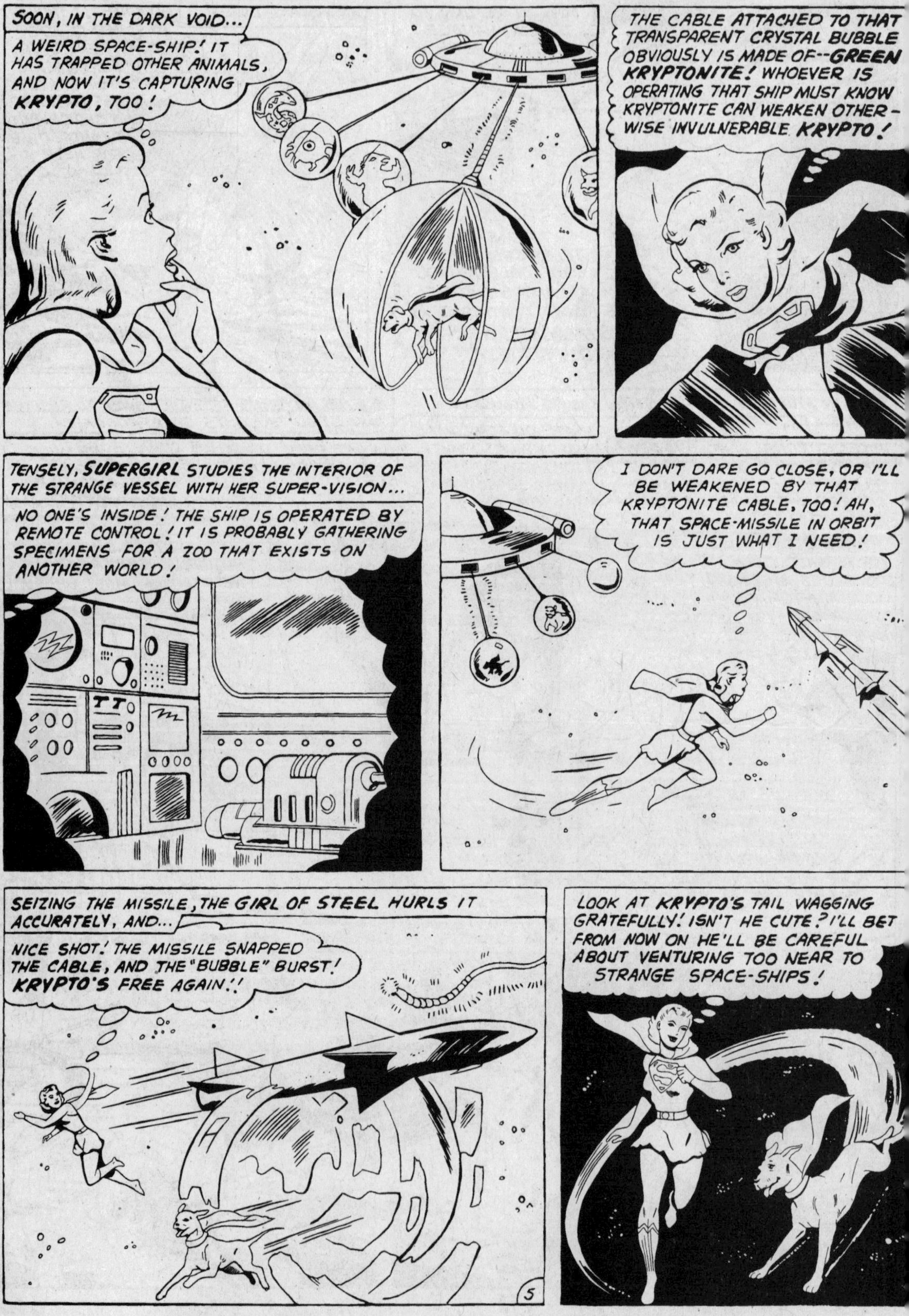
SOON, IN THE DARK VOID...
A WEIRD SPACE-SHIP! IT HAS TRAPPED OTHER ANIMALS, AND NOW IT'S CAPTURING KRYPTO, TOO!
THE CABLE ATTACHED TO THAT TRANSPARENT CRYSTAL BUBBLE OBVIOUSLY IS MADE OF--GREEN KRYPTONITE! WHOEVER IS OPERATING THAT SHIP MUST KNOW KRYPTONITE CAN WEAKEN OTHER-WISE INVULNERABLE KRYPTO!
TENSELY, SUPERGIRL STUDIES THE INTERIOR OF THE STRANGE VESSEL WITH HER SUPER-VISION...
NO ONE'S INSIDE! THE SHIP IS OPERATED BY REMOTE CONTROL! IT IS PROBABLY GATHERING SPECIMENS FOR A ZOO THAT EXISTS ON ANOTHER WORLD!
I DON'T DARE GO CLOSE, OR I'LL BE WEAKENED BY THAT KRYPTONITE CABLE, TOO! AH, THAT SPACE-MISSILE IN ORBIT IS JUST WHAT I NEED!
SEIZING THE MISSILE, THE GIRL OF STEEL HURLS IT ACCURATELY, AND...
NICE SHOT! THE MISSILE SNAPPED THE CABLE, AND THE "BUBBLE" BURST! KRYPTO'S FREE AGAIN!!
5
LOOK AT KRYPTO'S TAIL WAGGING GRATEFULLY! ISN'T HE CUTE? I'LL BET FROM NOW ON HE'LL BE CAREFUL ABOUT VENTURING TOO NEAR TO STRANGE SPACE-SHIPS!

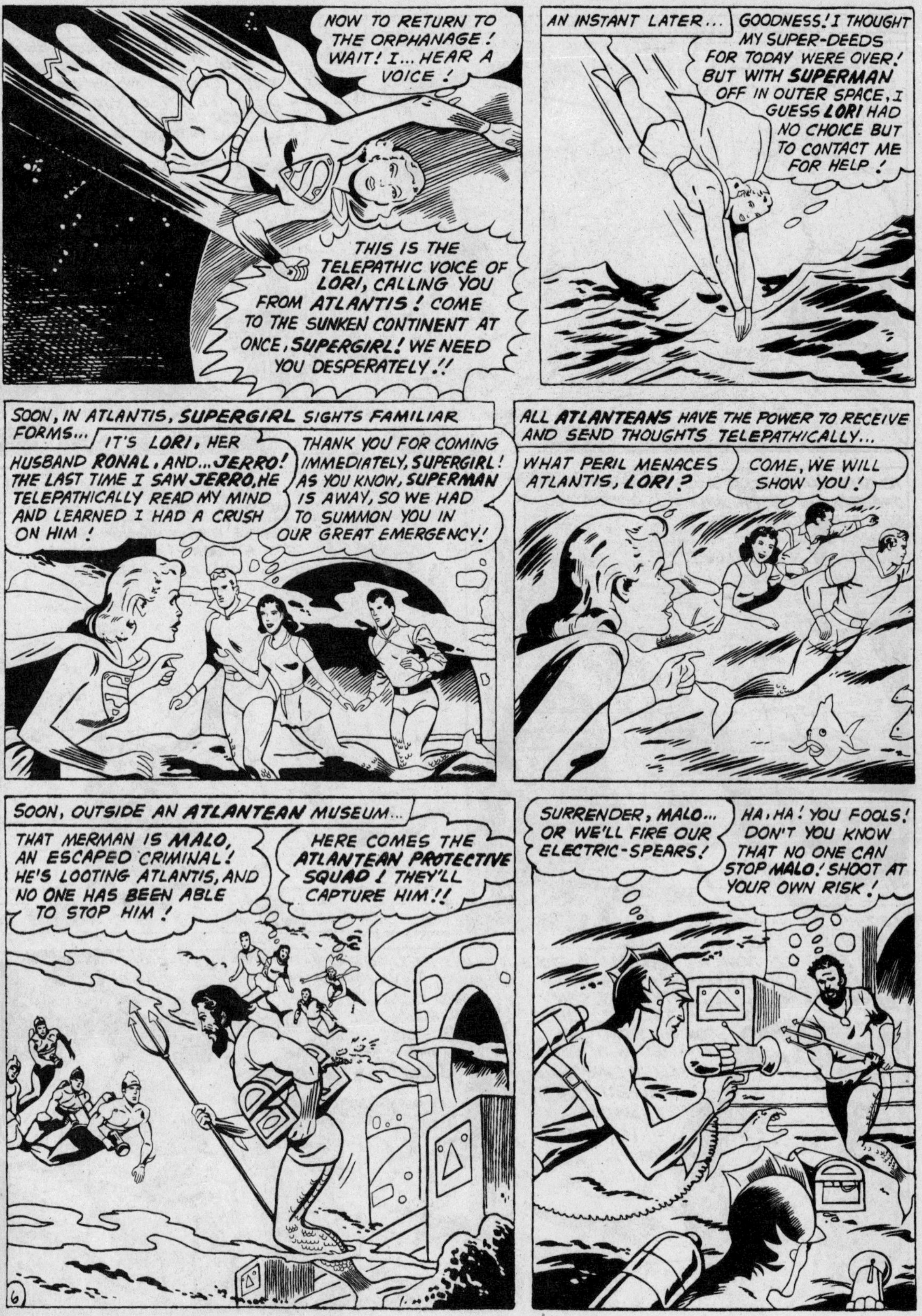
NOW TO RETURN TO THE ORPHANAGE! WAIT! I... HEAR A VOICE!
THIS IS THE TELEPATHIC VOICE OF LORI, CALLING YOU FROM ATLANTIS! COME TO THE SUNKEN CONTINENT AT ONCE, SUPERGIRL! WE NEED YOU DESPERATELY!!
AN INSTANT LATER...
GOODNESS! I THOUGHT MY SUPER-DEEDS FOR TODAY WERE OVER! BUT WITH SUPERMAN OFF IN OUTER SPACE, I GUESS LORI HAD NO CHOICE BUT TO CONTACT ME FOR HELP!
SOON, IN ATLANTIS, SUPERGIRL SIGHTS FAMILIAR FORMS...
IT'S LORI, HER HUSBAND RONAL, AND... JERRO! THE LAST TIME I SAW JERRO, HE TELEPATHICALLY READ MY MIND AND LEARNED I HAD A CRUSH ON HIM!
THANK YOU FOR COMING IMMEDIATELY, SUPERGIRL! AS YOU KNOW, SUPERMAN IS AWAY, SO WE HAD TO SUMMON YOU IN OUR GREAT EMERGENCY!
ALL ATLANTEANS HAVE THE POWER TO RECEIVE AND SEND THOUGHTS TELEPATHICALLY...
WHAT PERIL MENACES ATLANTIS, LORI?
COME, WE WILL SHOW YOU!
SOON, OUTSIDE AN ATLANTEAN MUSEUM...
THAT MERMAN IS MALO, AN ESCAPED CRIMINAL! HE'S LOOTING ATLANTIS, AND NO ONE HAS BEEN ABLE TO STOP HIM!
HERE COMES THE ATLANTEAN PROTECTIVE SQUAD! THEY'LL CAPTURE HIM!!
6
SURRENDER, MALO... OR WE'LL FIRE OUR ELECTRIC-SPEARS!
HA, HA! YOU FOOLS! DON'T YOU KNOW THAT NO ONE CAN STOP MALO! SHOOT AT YOUR OWN RISK!

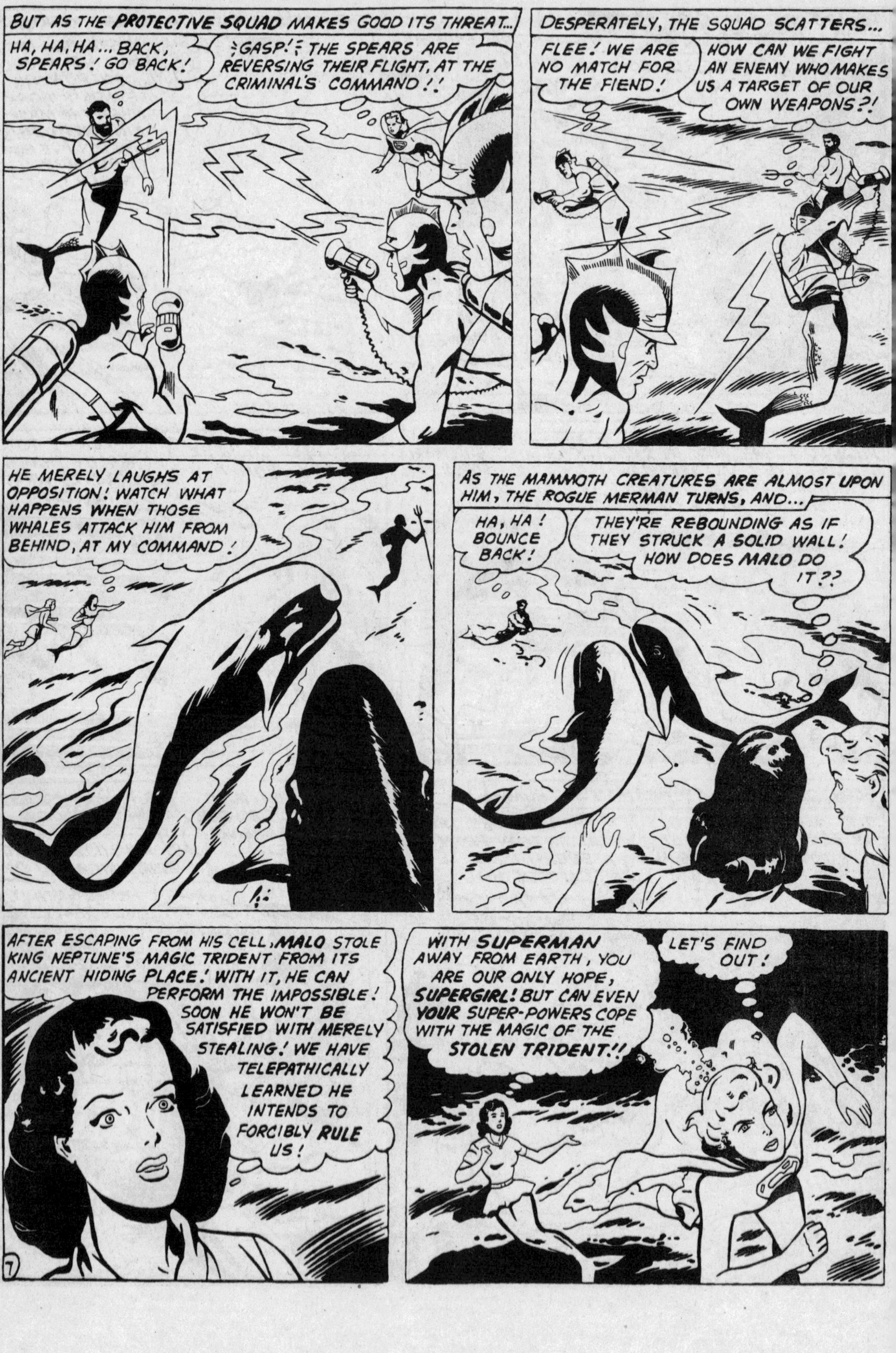
BUT AS THE PROTECTIVE SQUAD MAKES GOOD ITS THREAT...
HA, HA, HA... BACK, SPEARS! GO BACK!
GASP! THE SPEARS ARE REVERSING THEIR FLIGHT, AT THE CRIMINAL'S COMMAND!!
DESPERATELY, THE SQUAD SCATTERS...
FLEE! WE ARE NO MATCH FOR THE FIEND!
HOW CAN WE FIGHT AN ENEMY WHO MAKES US A TARGET OF OUR OWN WEAPONS?!
HE MERELY LAUGHS AT OPPOSITION! WATCH WHAT HAPPENS WHEN THOSE WHALES ATTACK HIM FROM BEHIND, AT MY COMMAND!
AS THE MAMMOTH CREATURES ARE ALMOST UPON HIM, THE ROGUE MERMAN TURNS, AND...
HA, HA! BOUNCE BACK!
THEY'RE REBOUNDING AS IF THEY STRUCK A SOLID WALL! HOW DOES MALO DO IT??
AFTER ESCAPING FROM HIS CELL, MALO STOLE KING NEPTUNE'S MAGIC TRIDENT FROM ITS ANCIENT HIDING PLACE! WITH IT, HE CAN PERFORM THE IMPOSSIBLE! SOON HE WON'T BE SATISFIED WITH MERELY STEALING! WE HAVE TELEPATHICALLY LEARNED HE INTENDS TO FORCIBLY RULE US!
7
WITH SUPERMAN AWAY FROM EARTH, YOU ARE OUR ONLY HOPE, SUPERGIRL! BUT CAN EVEN YOUR SUPER-POWERS COPE WITH THE MAGIC OF THE STOLEN TRIDENT!!
LET'S FIND OUT!

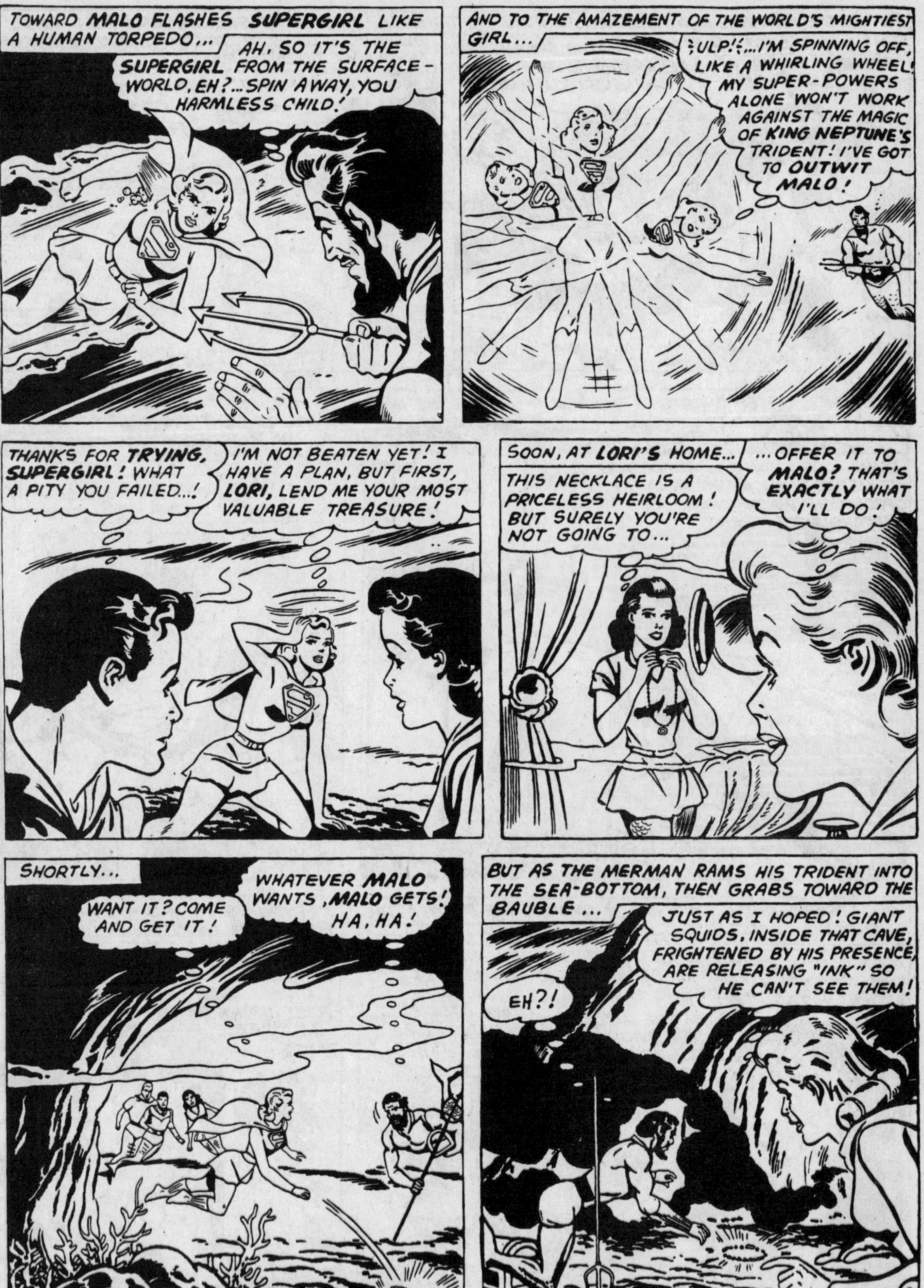
TOWARD MALO FLASHES SUPERGIRL LIKE A HUMAN TORPEDO...
AH, SO IT'S THE SUPERGIRL FROM THE SURFACE-WORLD, EH?...SPIN AWAY, YOU HARMLESS CHILD!
AND TO THE AMAZEMENT OF THE WORLD'S MIGHTIEST GIRL...
ULP!...I'M SPINNING OFF, LIKE A WHIRLING WHEEL! MY SUPER-POWERS ALONE WON'T WORK AGAINST THE MAGIC OF KING NEPTUNE'S TRIDENT! I'VE GOT TO OUTWIT MALO!
THANKS FOR TRYING, SUPERGIRL! WHAT A PITY YOU FAILED...!
I'M NOT BEATEN YET! I HAVE A PLAN, BUT FIRST, LORI, LEND ME YOUR MOST VALUABLE TREASURE!
SOON, AT LORI'S HOME...
THIS NECKLACE IS A PRICELESS HEIRLOOM! BUT SURELY YOU'RE NOT GOING TO...
...OFFER IT TO MALO? THAT'S EXACTLY WHAT I'LL DO!
SHORTLY...
WANT IT? COME AND GET IT!
WHATEVER MALO WANTS, MALO GETS! HA, HA!
BUT AS THE MERMAN RAMS HIS TRIDENT INTO THE SEA-BOTTOM, THEN GRABS TOWARD THE BAUBLE...
JUST AS I HOPED! GIANT SQUIDS, INSIDE THAT CAVE, FRIGHTENED BY HIS PRESENCE, ARE RELEASING "INK" SO HE CAN'T SEE THEM!
EH?!
8

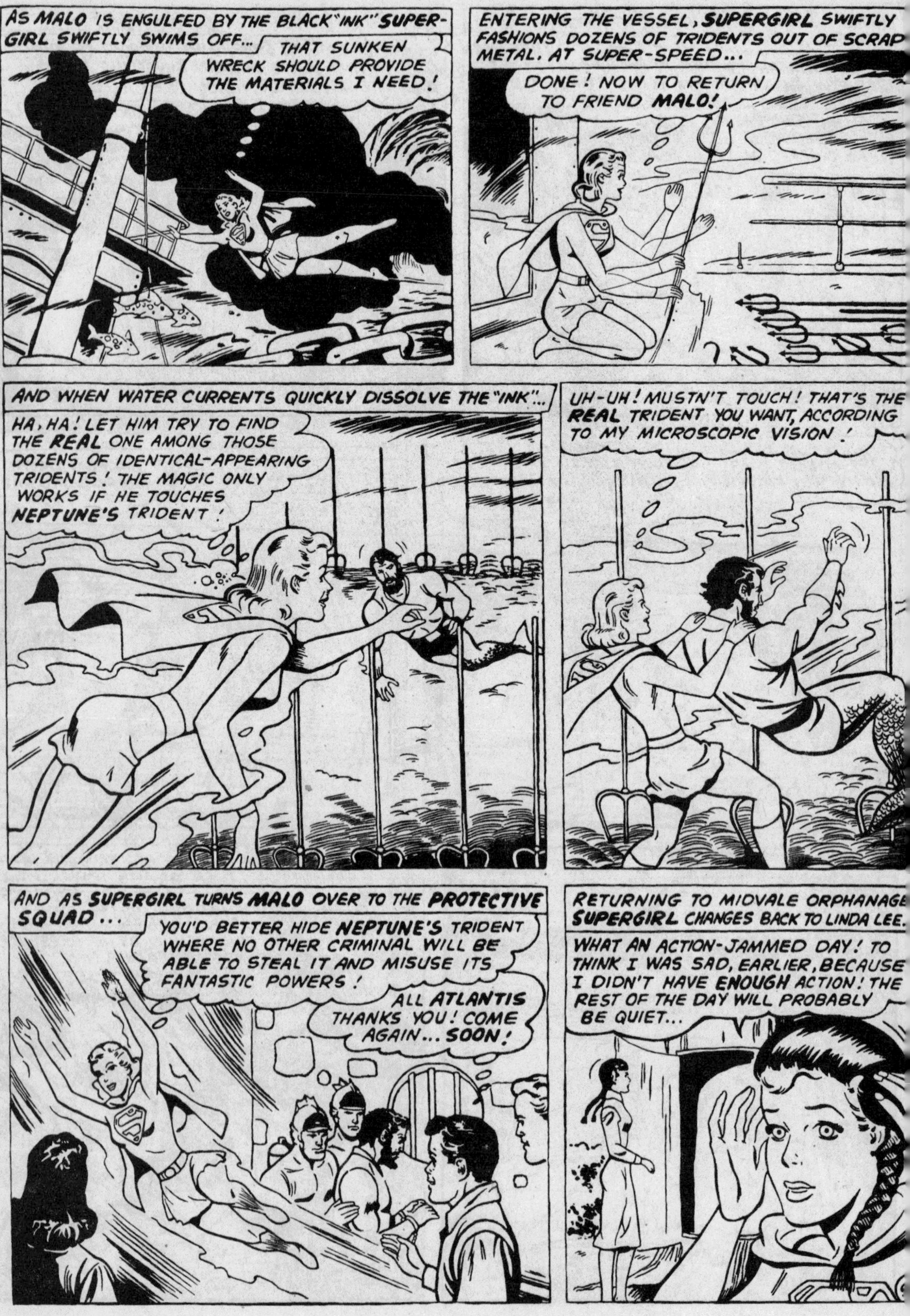
AS MALO IS ENGULFED BY THE BLACK "INK" SUPERGIRL SWIFTLY SWIMS OFF...
THAT SUNKEN WRECK SHOULD PROVIDE THE MATERIALS I NEED!
ENTERING THE VESSEL, SUPERGIRL SWIFTLY FASHIONS DOZENS OF TRIDENTS OUT OF SCRAP METAL, AT SUPER-SPEED...
DONE! NOW TO RETURN TO FRIEND MALO!
AND WHEN WATER CURRENTS QUICKLY DISSOLVE THE "INK"...
HA, HA! LET HIM TRY TO FIND THE REAL ONE AMONG THOSE DOZENS OF IDENTICAL-APPEARING TRIDENTS! THE MAGIC ONLY WORKS IF HE TOUCHES NEPTUNE'S TRIDENT!
UH-UH! MUSTN'T TOUCH! THAT'S THE REAL TRIDENT YOU WANT, ACCORDING TO MY MICROSCOPIC VISION!
AND AS SUPERGIRL TURNS MALO OVER TO THE PROTECTIVE SQUAD...
YOU'D BETTER HIDE NEPTUNE'S TRIDENT WHERE NO OTHER CRIMINAL WILL BE ABLE TO STEAL IT AND MISUSE ITS FANTASTIC POWERS!
ALL ATLANTIS THANKS YOU! COME AGAIN... SOON!
RETURNING TO MIDVALE ORPHANAGE SUPERGIRL CHANGES BACK TO LINDA LEE.
WHAT AN ACTION-JAMMED DAY! TO THINK I WAS SAD, EARLIER, BECAUSE I DIDN'T HAVE ENOUGH ACTION! THE REST OF THE DAY WILL PROBABLY BE QUIET...

BUT LATER, AS LINDA HELPS STRAIGHTEN UP A STORAGE ROOM...

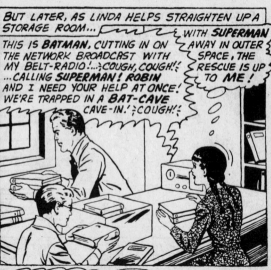

THIS IS BATMAN, CUTTING IN ON THE NETWORK BROADCAST WITH MY BELT-RADIO!...;COUGH, COUGH!;...CALLING SUPERMAN! ROBIN AND I NEED YOUR HELP AT ONCE! WE'RE TRAPPED IN A BAT-CAVE CAVE-IN.! ;COUGH!;

WITH SUPERMAN AWAY IN OUTER SPACE, THE RESCUE IS UP TO ME!

BUT AS SHE USES HER SUPER-VISION...

I CAN'T CHANGE TO SUPERGIRL IN FRONT OF THE OTHERS AND LEAVE WITHOUT REVEALING MY TRUE IDENTITY...MY SUPER-VISION, SEES A HUNTER NEAR THE HOLLOW TREE! I CAN'T SEND MY ROBOT OR IT WOULD BE SEEN!

YET I CAN'T STAY HERE, AND ALLOW BATMAN AND ROBIN TO SUFFOCATE FROM LACK OF OXYGEN! WAIT, THAT GIVES ME AN IDEA!

QUICKLY, LINDA INHALES MOST OF THE OXYGEN IN THE ROOM...WITH HER SUPER-POWERFUL LUNGS...

THE OTHERS HAVE BEEN RENDERED TEMPORARILY UNCONSCIOUS, BUT I'VE LEFT ENOUGH OXYGEN IN THE ROOM SO THEY CAN'T POSSIBLY BE HARMED! NOW TO CHANGE TO SUPERGIRL!

THEN SHE EXITS AT SUPER-SPEED...

I OPENED AND SHUT THE DOOR SO QUICKLY, MORE OXYGEN DIDN'T HAVE TIME TO ENTER THE ROOM! I'LL BE BACK IN A FLASH!

STORE ROOM

THROUGH THE SKY TO GOTHAM CITY STREAKS SUPERGIRL, FASTER THAN THE HUMAN EYE CAN FOLLOW...

THERE'S THE HOME OF WEALTHY SOCIALITE BRUCE WAYNE AND HIS YOUNG WARD DICK GRAYSON, BELOW! SECRETLY, THEY'RE BATMAN AND ROBIN!

10

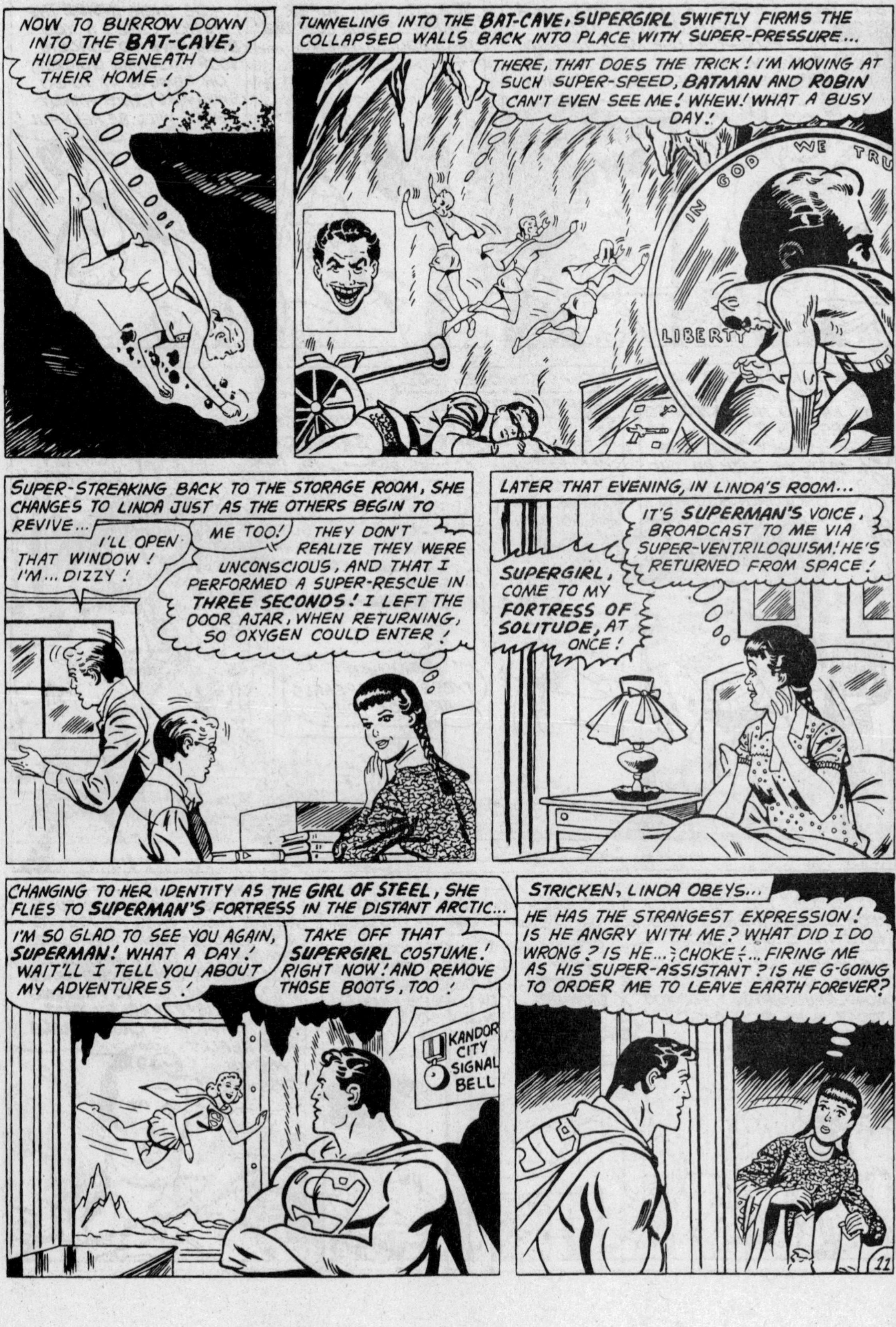
NOW TO BURROW DOWN INTO THE **BAT-CAVE**, HIDDEN BENEATH THEIR HOME!
TUNNELING INTO THE **BAT-CAVE**, **SUPERGIRL** SWIFTLY FIRMS THE COLLAPSED WALLS BACK INTO PLACE WITH SUPER-PRESSURE...
THERE, THAT DOES THE TRICK! I'M MOVING AT SUCH SUPER-SPEED, **BATMAN AND ROBIN** CAN'T EVEN SEE ME! WHEW! WHAT A BUSY DAY!
IN GOD WE TRU
LIBERTY
SUPER-STREAKING BACK TO THE STORAGE ROOM, SHE CHANGES TO LINDA JUST AS THE OTHERS BEGIN TO REVIVE...
I'LL OPEN THAT WINDOW! I'M... DIZZY!
ME TOO!
THEY DON'T REALIZE THEY WERE UNCONSCIOUS, AND THAT I PERFORMED A SUPER-RESCUE IN **THREE SECONDS**! I LEFT THE DOOR AJAR, WHEN RETURNING, SO OXYGEN COULD ENTER!
LATER THAT EVENING, IN LINDA'S ROOM...
SUPERGIRL, COME TO MY **FORTRESS OF SOLITUDE**, AT ONCE!
IT'S **SUPERMAN'S** VOICE, BROADCAST TO ME VIA SUPER-VENTRILOQUISM! HE'S RETURNED FROM SPACE!
CHANGING TO HER IDENTITY AS THE **GIRL OF STEEL**, SHE FLIES TO **SUPERMAN'S** FORTRESS IN THE DISTANT ARCTIC...
I'M SO GLAD TO SEE YOU AGAIN, **SUPERMAN**! WHAT A DAY! WAIT'LL I TELL YOU ABOUT MY ADVENTURES!
TAKE OFF THAT **SUPERGIRL** COSTUME! RIGHT NOW! AND REMOVE THOSE BOOTS, TOO!
KANDOR CITY SIGNAL BELL
STRICKEN, LINDA OBEYS...
HE HAS THE STRANGEST EXPRESSION! IS HE ANGRY WITH ME? WHAT DID I DO WRONG? IS HE...*CHOKE*... FIRING ME AS HIS SUPER-ASSISTANT? IS HE G-GOING TO ORDER ME TO LEAVE EARTH FOREVER?
11

BUT THEN... HERE'S A LITTLE GIFT, LINDA! A MAKE-UP KIT! YOU'RE OLD ENOUGH TO USE MAKE-UP NOW! THIS FINE LIPSTICK CASE MAY BE VERY HELPFUL TO YOU! WATCH...

SEE, YOU CAN SUPER-COMPRESS YOUR COSTUME AND BOOTS, THEN...

...HIDE THEM *INSIDE* THE LIPSTICK CASE! IF YOU EVER HAVE TO CONCEAL YOUR COSTUME QUICKLY, OR REMOVE IT TO GO SWIMMING, THIS HANDY DEVICE WILL BE HELPFUL!

HE ISN'T ANGRY WITH ME! WHAT A RELIEF! I WONDER WHY HE HAD THAT STRANGE EXPRESSION?

PUT YOUR COSTUME BACK ON AND WAIT HERE! I'LL BE BACK IN A SECOND!

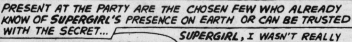

AND AS SHE DOES SO...

HAPPY BIRTHDAY SUPERGIRL! HOW DOES IT FEEL TO BE *SWEET SIXTEEN*?!

SURPRISE! THIS *BATGIRL* COSTUME IS FOR YOU, TOO!

ARF! ARF!

OH, MY GOODNESS!!

SURPRISE! THESE *GIANT PEARLS* ARE FOR YOU!

Happy Birthday SUPERGIRL

PRESENT AT THE PARTY ARE THE CHOSEN FEW WHO ALREADY KNOW OF *SUPERGIRL'S* PRESENCE ON EARTH OR CAN BE TRUSTED WITH THE SECRET...

A SURPRISE BIRTHDAY PARTY... FOR ME! OH, THANK YOU FOR THE WONDERFUL GIFTS! I FORGOT TODAY IS MY *SIXTEENTH* BIRTHDAY!

SUPERGIRL, I WASN'T REALLY AWAY ON A SECRET SPACE MISSION! ALL THOSE SUPER-DANGERS, TODAY, WERE FAKED! SINCE YOU ENJOY SOLVING DIFFICULT PROBLEMS WITH YOUR SUPER-WITS...

...WE THOUGHT WE'D TOSS SOME REALLY TOUGH ONES AT YOU AS A SPECIAL BIRTHDAY TREAT! YOU DID GREAT! IT WAS *I* WHO BUILT THAT REMOTE-CONTROLLED SPACE SHIP, AND HAD *KRYPTO* PRETEND HE WAS WEAKENED BY THAT FAKE KRYPTONITE CABLE! *MALO* WAS REALLY *ME* IN DISGUISE!!

12

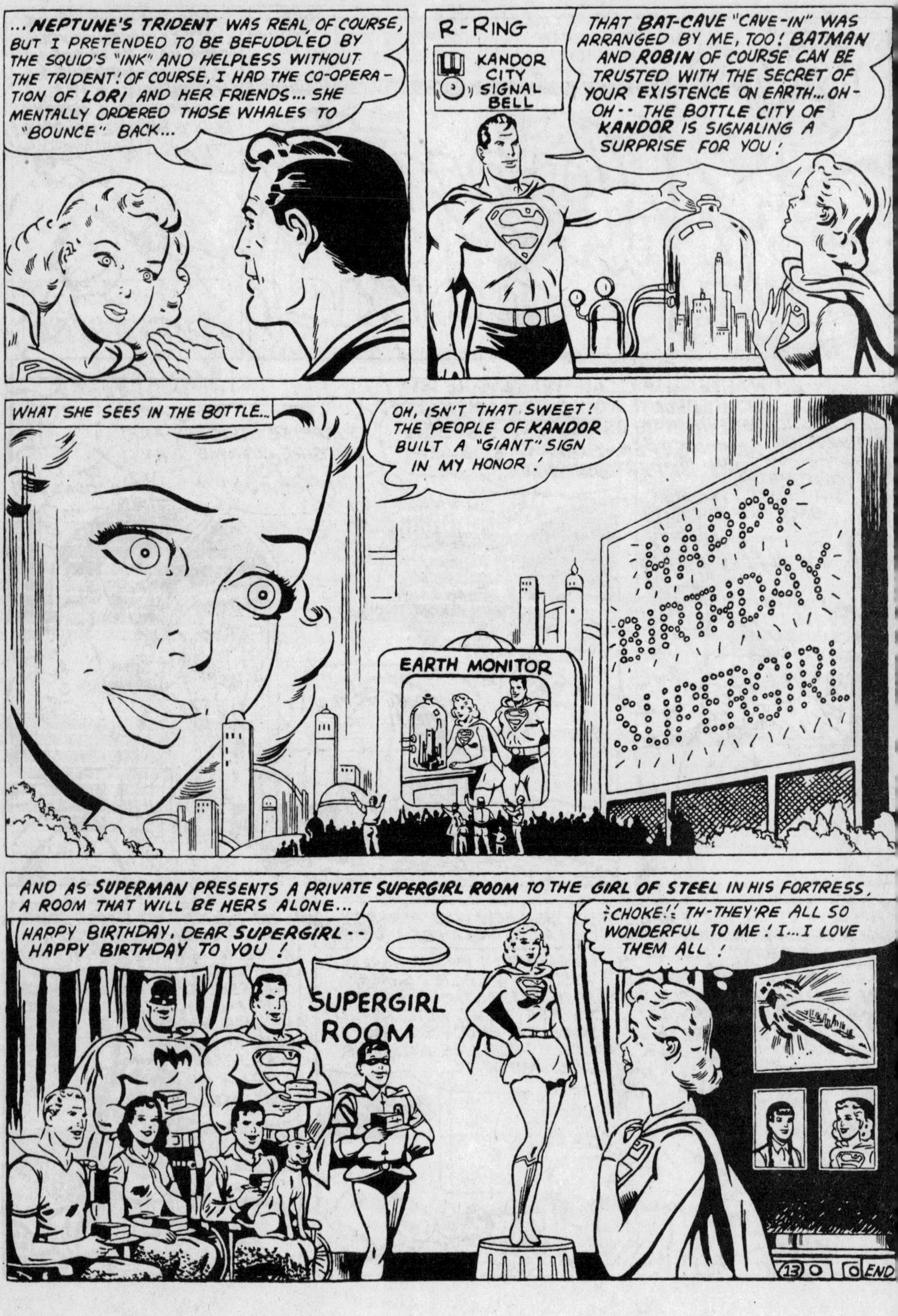
...NEPTUNE'S TRIDENT WAS REAL, OF COURSE, BUT I PRETENDED TO BE BEFUDDLED BY THE SQUID'S "INK" AND HELPLESS WITHOUT THE TRIDENT! OF COURSE, I HAD THE CO-OPERATION OF LORI AND HER FRIENDS... SHE MENTALLY ORDERED THOSE WHALES TO "BOUNCE" BACK...
R-RING
KANDOR CITY SIGNAL BELL
THAT BAT-CAVE "CAVE-IN" WAS ARRANGED BY ME, TOO! BATMAN AND ROBIN OF COURSE CAN BE TRUSTED WITH THE SECRET OF YOUR EXISTENCE ON EARTH... OH-OH-- THE BOTTLE CITY OF KANDOR IS SIGNALING A SURPRISE FOR YOU!
WHAT SHE SEES IN THE BOTTLE...
OH, ISN'T THAT SWEET! THE PEOPLE OF KANDOR BUILT A "GIANT" SIGN IN MY HONOR!
EARTH MONITOR
HAPPY BIRTHDAY SUPERGIRL...
AND AS SUPERMAN PRESENTS A PRIVATE SUPERGIRL ROOM TO THE GIRL OF STEEL IN HIS FORTRESS, A ROOM THAT WILL BE HERS ALONE...
HAPPY BIRTHDAY, DEAR SUPERGIRL-- HAPPY BIRTHDAY TO YOU!
SUPERGIRL ROOM
¡CHOKE!¡ TH-THEY'RE ALL SO WONDERFUL TO ME! I...I LOVE THEM ALL!
13
END

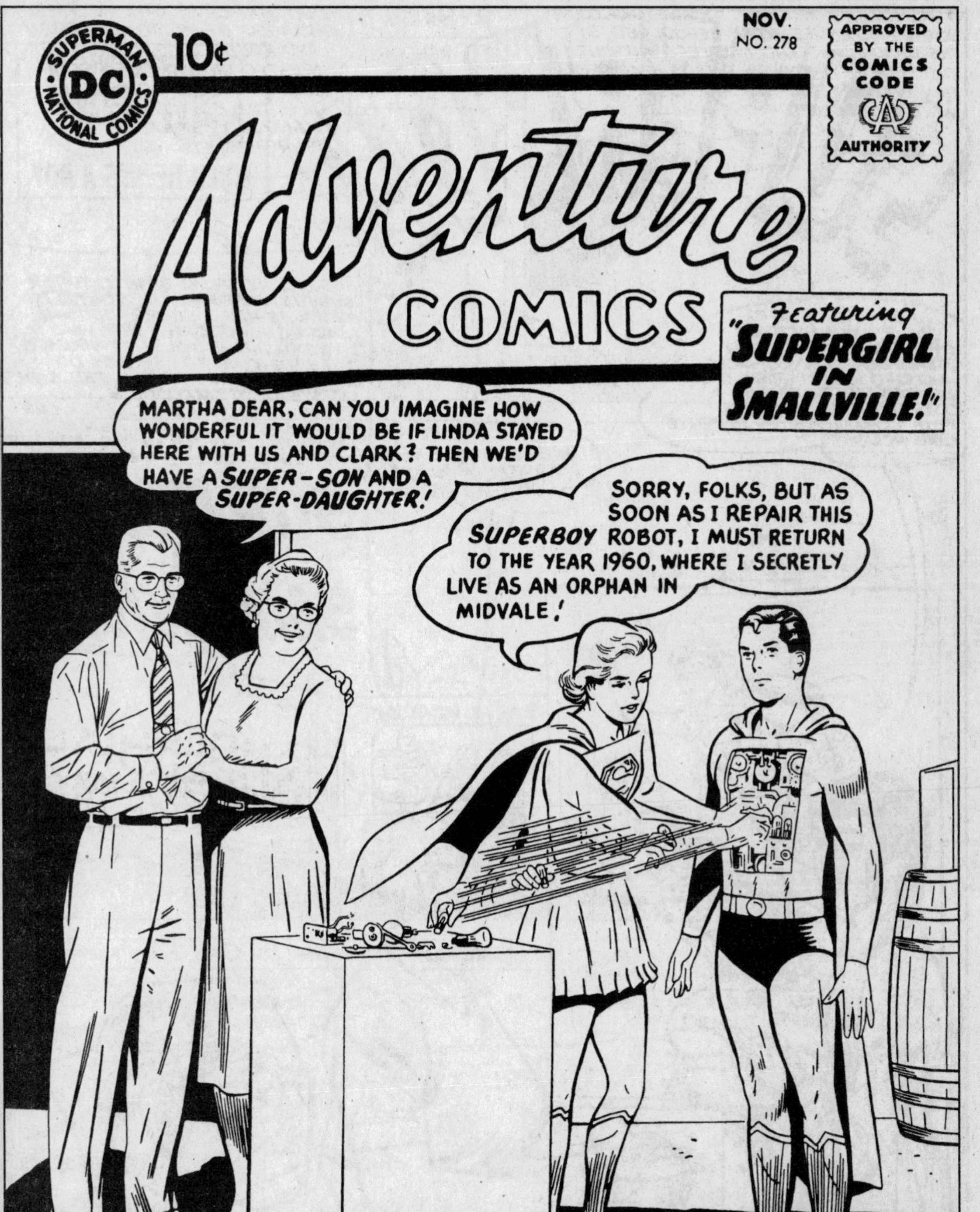
SUPERMAN DC NATIONAL COMICS
10¢
NOV.
NO. 278
APPROVED BY THE COMICS CODE AUTHORITY
Adventure COMICS
Featuring "SUPERGIRL IN SMALLVILLE!"
MARTHA DEAR, CAN YOU IMAGINE HOW WONDERFUL IT WOULD BE IF LINDA STAYED HERE WITH US AND CLARK? THEN WE'D HAVE A SUPER-SON AND A SUPER-DAUGHTER!
SORRY, FOLKS, BUT AS SOON AS I REPAIR THIS SUPERBOY ROBOT, I MUST RETURN TO THE YEAR 1960, WHERE I SECRETLY LIVE AS AN ORPHAN IN MIDVALE!

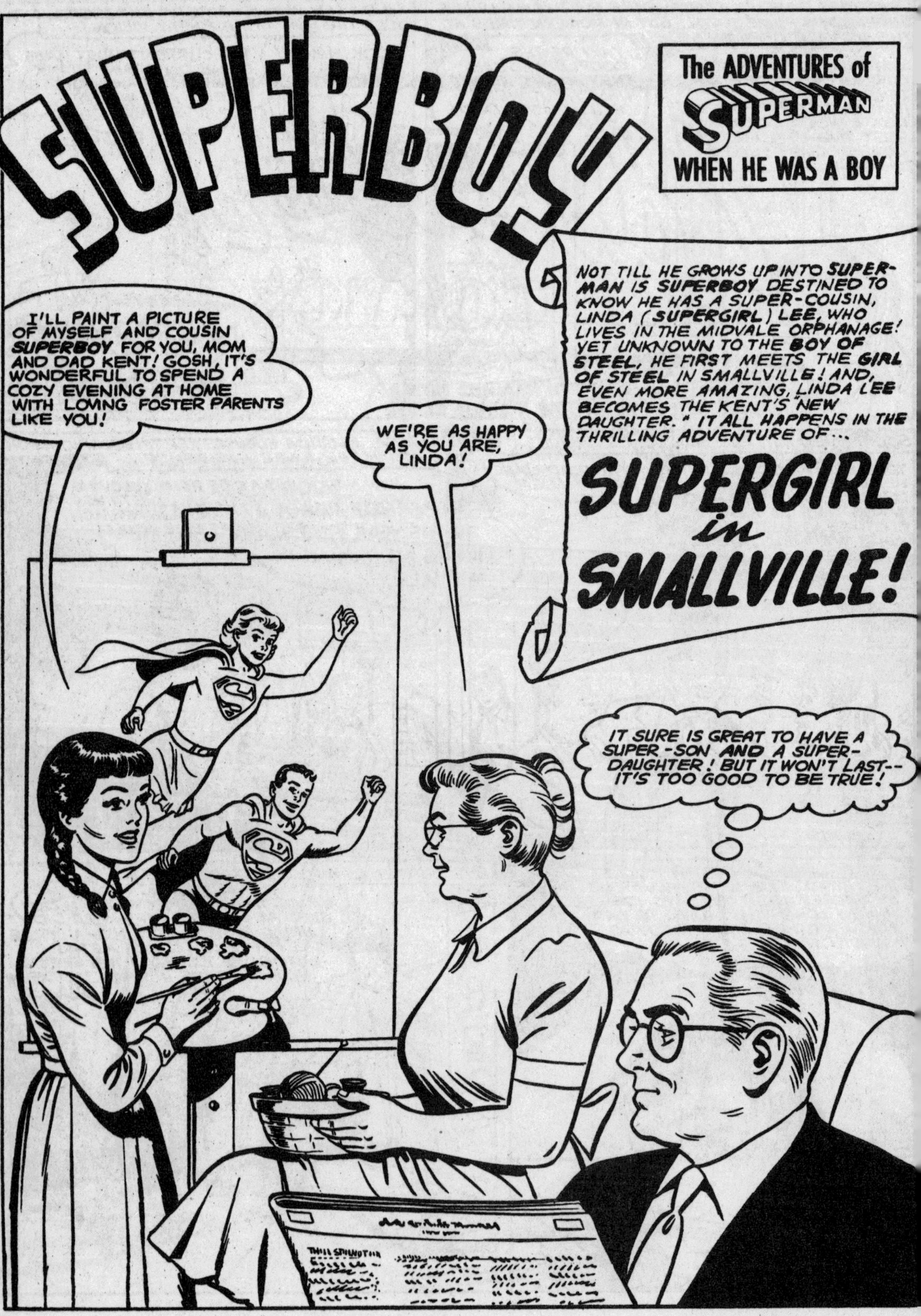
SUPERBOY
The ADVENTURES of SUPERMAN WHEN HE WAS A BOY
NOT TILL HE GROWS UP INTO SUPERMAN IS SUPERBOY DESTINED TO KNOW HE HAS A SUPER-COUSIN, LINDA (SUPERGIRL) LEE, WHO LIVES IN THE MIDVALE ORPHANAGE! YET UNKNOWN TO THE BOY OF STEEL, HE FIRST MEETS THE GIRL OF STEEL IN SMALLVILLE! AND, EVEN MORE AMAZING, LINDA LEE BECOMES THE KENT'S "NEW DAUGHTER." IT ALL HAPPENS IN THE THRILLING ADVENTURE OF...
SUPERGIRL in SMALLVILLE!
I'LL PAINT A PICTURE OF MYSELF AND COUSIN SUPERBOY FOR YOU, MOM AND DAD KENT! GOSH, IT'S WONDERFUL TO SPEND A COZY EVENING AT HOME WITH LOVING FOSTER PARENTS LIKE YOU!
WE'RE AS HAPPY AS YOU ARE, LINDA!
IT SURE IS GREAT TO HAVE A SUPER-SON AND A SUPER-DAUGHTER! BUT IT WON'T LAST--IT'S TOO GOOD TO BE TRUE!

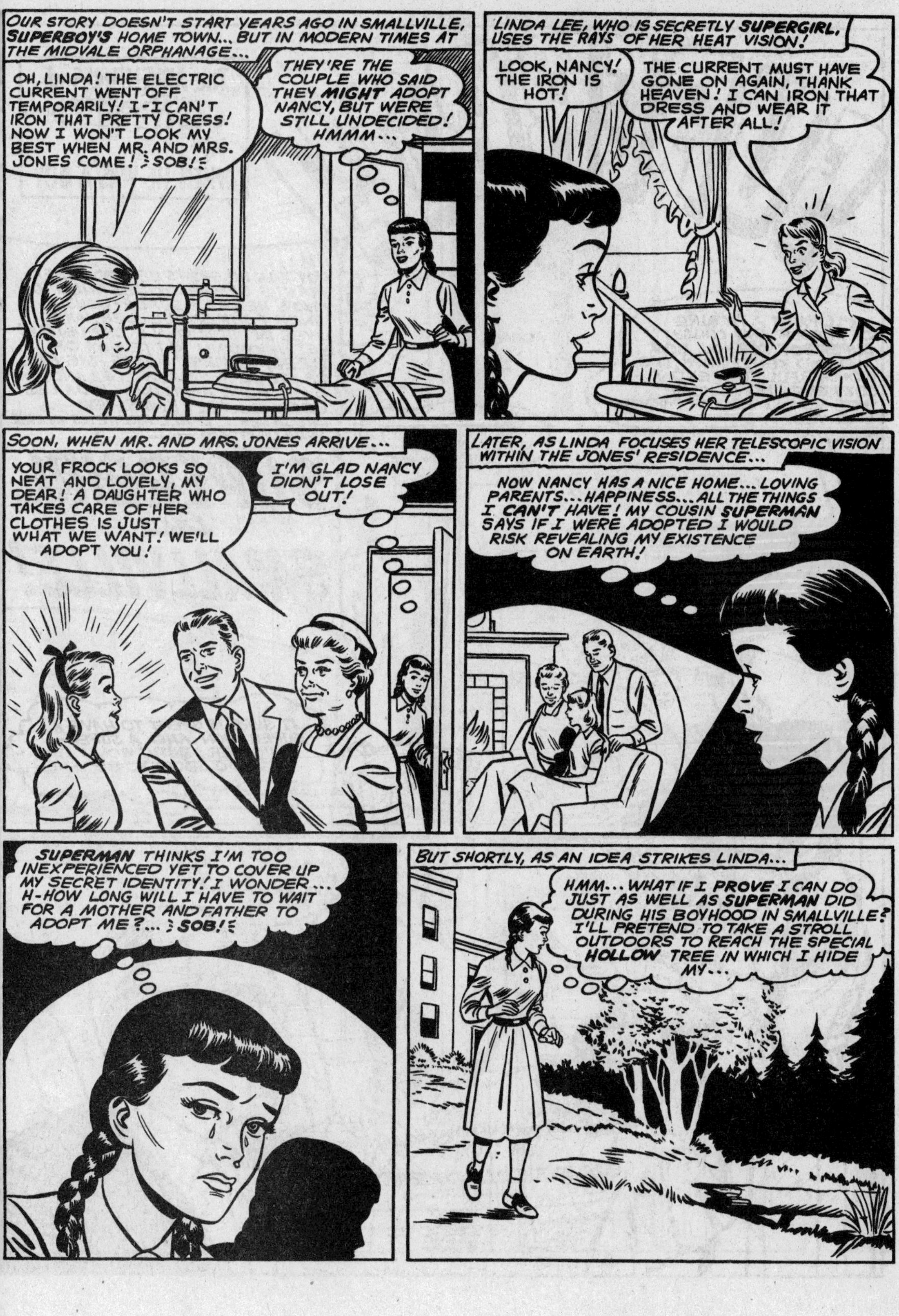
OUR STORY DOESN'T START YEARS AGO IN SMALLVILLE, SUPERBOY'S HOME TOWN... BUT IN MODERN TIMES AT THE MIDVALE ORPHANAGE...
OH, LINDA! THE ELECTRIC CURRENT WENT OFF TEMPORARILY! I-I CAN'T IRON THAT PRETTY DRESS! NOW I WON'T LOOK MY BEST WHEN MR. AND MRS. JONES COME! SOB!
THEY'RE THE COUPLE WHO SAID THEY MIGHT ADOPT NANCY, BUT WERE STILL UNDECIDED! HMMM...
LINDA LEE, WHO IS SECRETLY SUPERGIRL, USES THE RAYS OF HER HEAT VISION!
LOOK, NANCY! THE IRON IS HOT!
THE CURRENT MUST HAVE GONE ON AGAIN, THANK HEAVEN! I CAN IRON THAT DRESS AND WEAR IT AFTER ALL!
SOON, WHEN MR. AND MRS. JONES ARRIVE...
YOUR FROCK LOOKS SO NEAT AND LOVELY, MY DEAR! A DAUGHTER WHO TAKES CARE OF HER CLOTHES IS JUST WHAT WE WANT! WE'LL ADOPT YOU!
I'M GLAD NANCY DIDN'T LOSE OUT!
LATER, AS LINDA FOCUSES HER TELESCOPIC VISION WITHIN THE JONES' RESIDENCE...
NOW NANCY HAS A NICE HOME... LOVING PARENTS... HAPPINESS... ALL THE THINGS I CAN'T HAVE! MY COUSIN SUPERMAN SAYS IF I WERE ADOPTED I WOULD RISK REVEALING MY EXISTENCE ON EARTH!
SUPERMAN THINKS I'M TOO INEXPERIENCED YET TO COVER UP MY SECRET IDENTITY! I WONDER... H-HOW LONG WILL I HAVE TO WAIT FOR A MOTHER AND FATHER TO ADOPT ME?... SOB!
BUT SHORTLY, AS AN IDEA STRIKES LINDA...
HMM... WHAT IF I PROVE I CAN DO JUST AS WELL AS SUPERMAN DID DURING HIS BOYHOOD IN SMALLVILLE? I'LL PRETEND TO TAKE A STROLL OUTDOORS TO REACH THE SPECIAL HOLLOW TREE IN WHICH I HIDE MY...

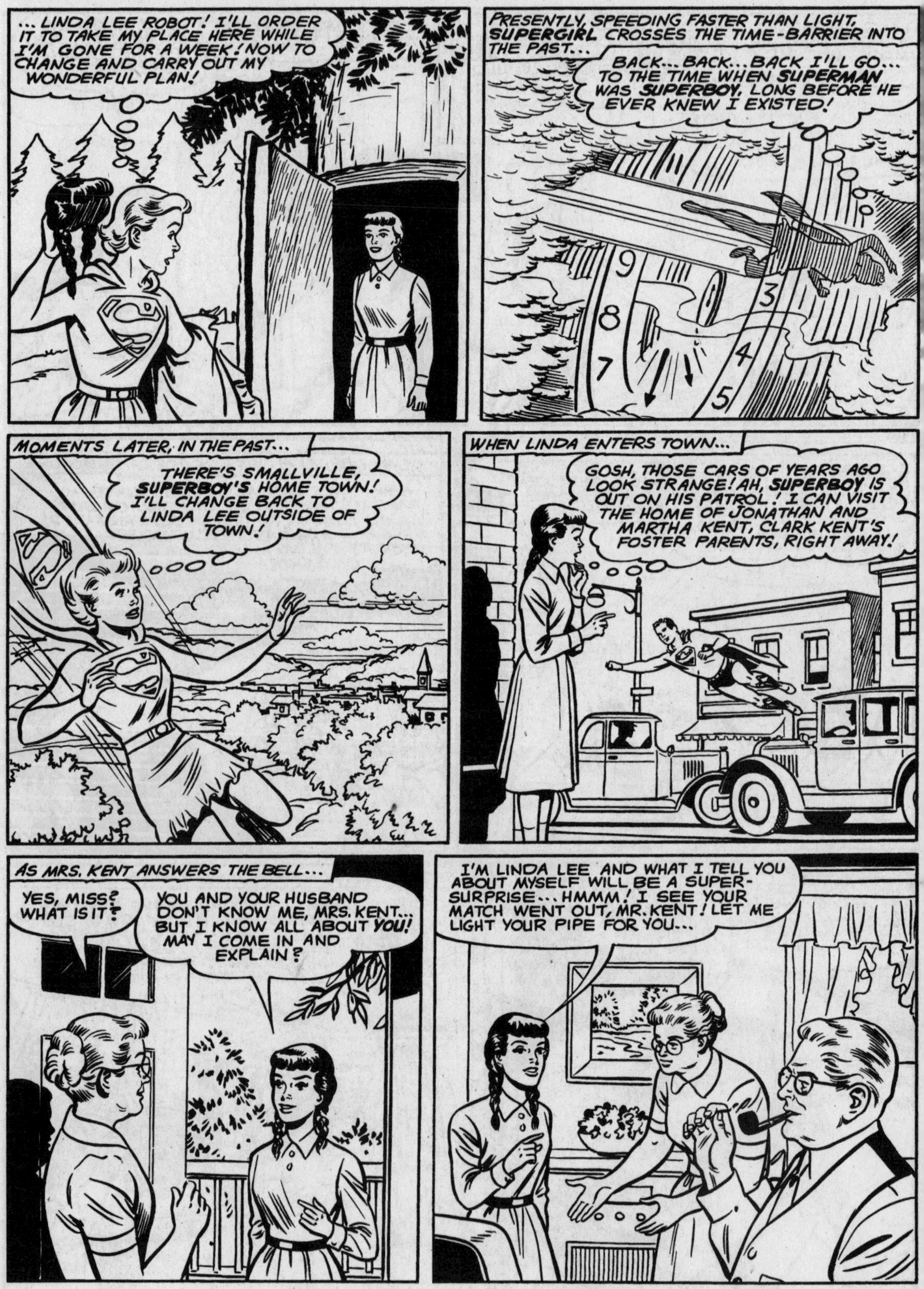
... LINDA LEE ROBOT! I'LL ORDER IT TO TAKE MY PLACE HERE WHILE I'M GONE FOR A WEEK! NOW TO CHANGE AND CARRY OUT MY WONDERFUL PLAN!
PRESENTLY, SPEEDING FASTER THAN LIGHT, SUPERGIRL CROSSES THE TIME-BARRIER INTO THE PAST...
BACK... BACK... BACK I'LL GO... TO THE TIME WHEN SUPERMAN WAS SUPERBOY, LONG BEFORE HE EVER KNEW I EXISTED!
9
8
7
3
4
5
MOMENTS LATER, IN THE PAST...
THERE'S SMALLVILLE, SUPERBOY'S HOME TOWN! I'LL CHANGE BACK TO LINDA LEE OUTSIDE OF TOWN!
WHEN LINDA ENTERS TOWN...
GOSH, THOSE CARS OF YEARS AGO LOOK STRANGE! AH, SUPERBOY IS OUT ON HIS PATROL! I CAN VISIT THE HOME OF JONATHAN AND MARTHA KENT, CLARK KENT'S FOSTER PARENTS, RIGHT AWAY!
AS MRS. KENT ANSWERS THE BELL...
YES, MISS? WHAT IS IT?
YOU AND YOUR HUSBAND DON'T KNOW ME, MRS. KENT... BUT I KNOW ALL ABOUT YOU! MAY I COME IN AND EXPLAIN?
I'M LINDA LEE AND WHAT I TELL YOU ABOUT MYSELF WILL BE A SUPER-SURPRISE... HMMM! I SEE YOUR MATCH WENT OUT, MR. KENT! LET ME LIGHT YOUR PIPE FOR YOU...

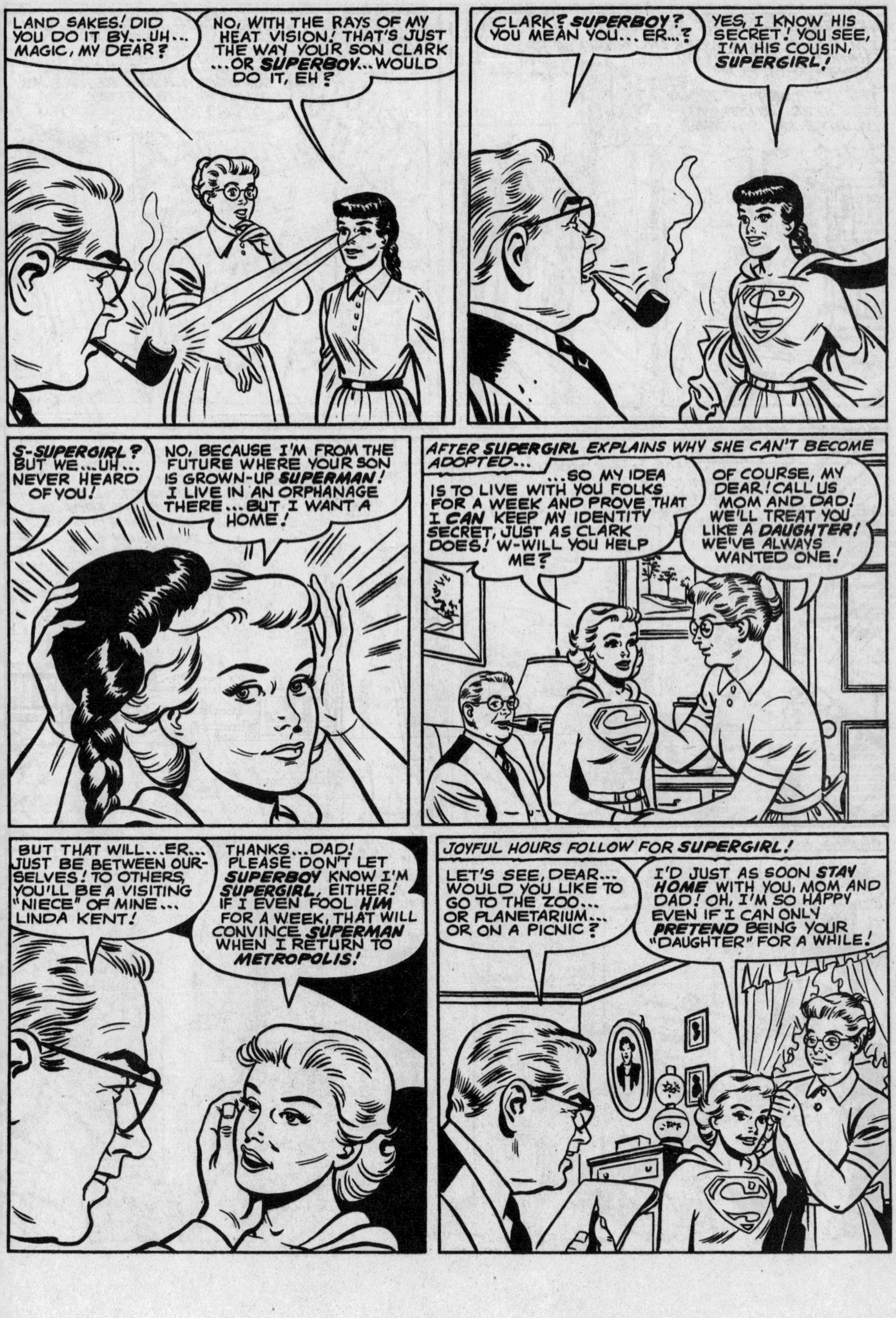
LAND SAKES! DID YOU DO IT BY...UH... MAGIC, MY DEAR?
NO, WITH THE RAYS OF MY HEAT VISION! THAT'S JUST THE WAY YOUR SON CLARK ...OR SUPERBOY...WOULD DO IT, EH?
CLARK? SUPERBOY? YOU MEAN YOU... ER...?
YES, I KNOW HIS SECRET! YOU SEE, I'M HIS COUSIN, SUPERGIRL!
S-SUPERGIRL? BUT WE...UH... NEVER HEARD OF YOU!
NO, BECAUSE I'M FROM THE FUTURE WHERE YOUR SON IS GROWN-UP SUPERMAN! I LIVE IN AN ORPHANAGE THERE... BUT I WANT A HOME!
AFTER SUPERGIRL EXPLAINS WHY SHE CAN'T BECOME ADOPTED...
...SO MY IDEA IS TO LIVE WITH YOU FOLKS FOR A WEEK AND PROVE THAT I CAN KEEP MY IDENTITY SECRET, JUST AS CLARK DOES! W-WILL YOU HELP ME?
OF COURSE, MY DEAR! CALL US MOM AND DAD! WE'LL TREAT YOU LIKE A DAUGHTER! WE'VE ALWAYS WANTED ONE!
BUT THAT WILL...ER... JUST BE BETWEEN OURSELVES! TO OTHERS, YOU'LL BE A VISITING "NIECE" OF MINE... LINDA KENT!
THANKS...DAD! PLEASE DON'T LET SUPERBOY KNOW I'M SUPERGIRL, EITHER! IF I EVEN FOOL HIM FOR A WEEK, THAT WILL CONVINCE SUPERMAN WHEN I RETURN TO METROPOLIS!
JOYFUL HOURS FOLLOW FOR SUPERGIRL!
LET'S SEE, DEAR... WOULD YOU LIKE TO GO TO THE ZOO... OR PLANETARIUM... OR ON A PICNIC?
I'D JUST AS SOON STAY HOME WITH YOU, MOM AND DAD! OH, I'M SO HAPPY EVEN IF I CAN ONLY PRETEND BEING YOUR "DAUGHTER" FOR A WHILE!

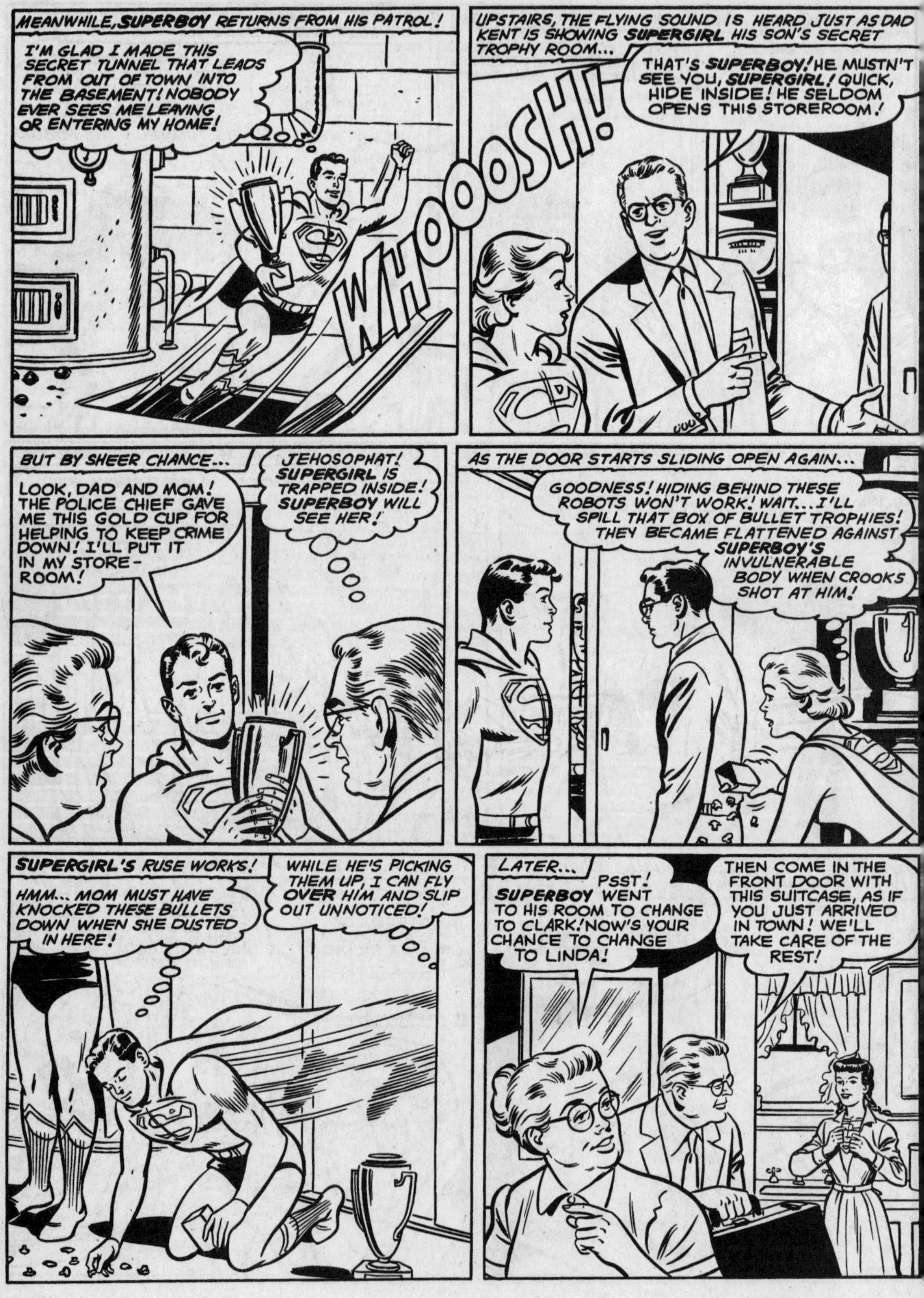
MEANWHILE, SUPERBOY RETURNS FROM HIS PATROL!
I'M GLAD I MADE THIS SECRET TUNNEL THAT LEADS FROM OUT OF TOWN INTO THE BASEMENT! NOBODY EVER SEES ME LEAVING OR ENTERING MY HOME!
WHOOOSH!
UPSTAIRS, THE FLYING SOUND IS HEARD JUST AS DAD KENT IS SHOWING SUPERGIRL HIS SON'S SECRET TROPHY ROOM...
THAT'S SUPERBOY! HE MUSTN'T SEE YOU, SUPERGIRL! QUICK, HIDE INSIDE! HE SELDOM OPENS THIS STOREROOM!
BUT BY SHEER CHANCE...
LOOK, DAD AND MOM! THE POLICE CHIEF GAVE ME THIS GOLD CUP FOR HELPING TO KEEP CRIME DOWN! I'LL PUT IT IN MY STORE-ROOM!
JEHOSOPHAT! SUPERGIRL IS TRAPPED INSIDE! SUPERBOY WILL SEE HER!
AS THE DOOR STARTS SLIDING OPEN AGAIN...
GOODNESS! HIDING BEHIND THESE ROBOTS WON'T WORK! WAIT... I'LL SPILL THAT BOX OF BULLET TROPHIES! THEY BECAME FLATTENED AGAINST SUPERBOY'S INVULNERABLE BODY WHEN CROOKS SHOT AT HIM!
SUPERGIRL'S RUSE WORKS!
HMM... MOM MUST HAVE KNOCKED THESE BULLETS DOWN WHEN SHE DUSTED IN HERE!
WHILE HE'S PICKING THEM UP, I CAN FLY OVER HIM AND SLIP OUT UNNOTICED!
LATER...
PSST! SUPERBOY WENT TO HIS ROOM TO CHANGE TO CLARK! NOW'S YOUR CHANCE TO CHANGE TO LINDA!
THEN COME IN THE FRONT DOOR WITH THIS SUITCASE, AS IF YOU JUST ARRIVED IN TOWN! WE'LL TAKE CARE OF THE REST!

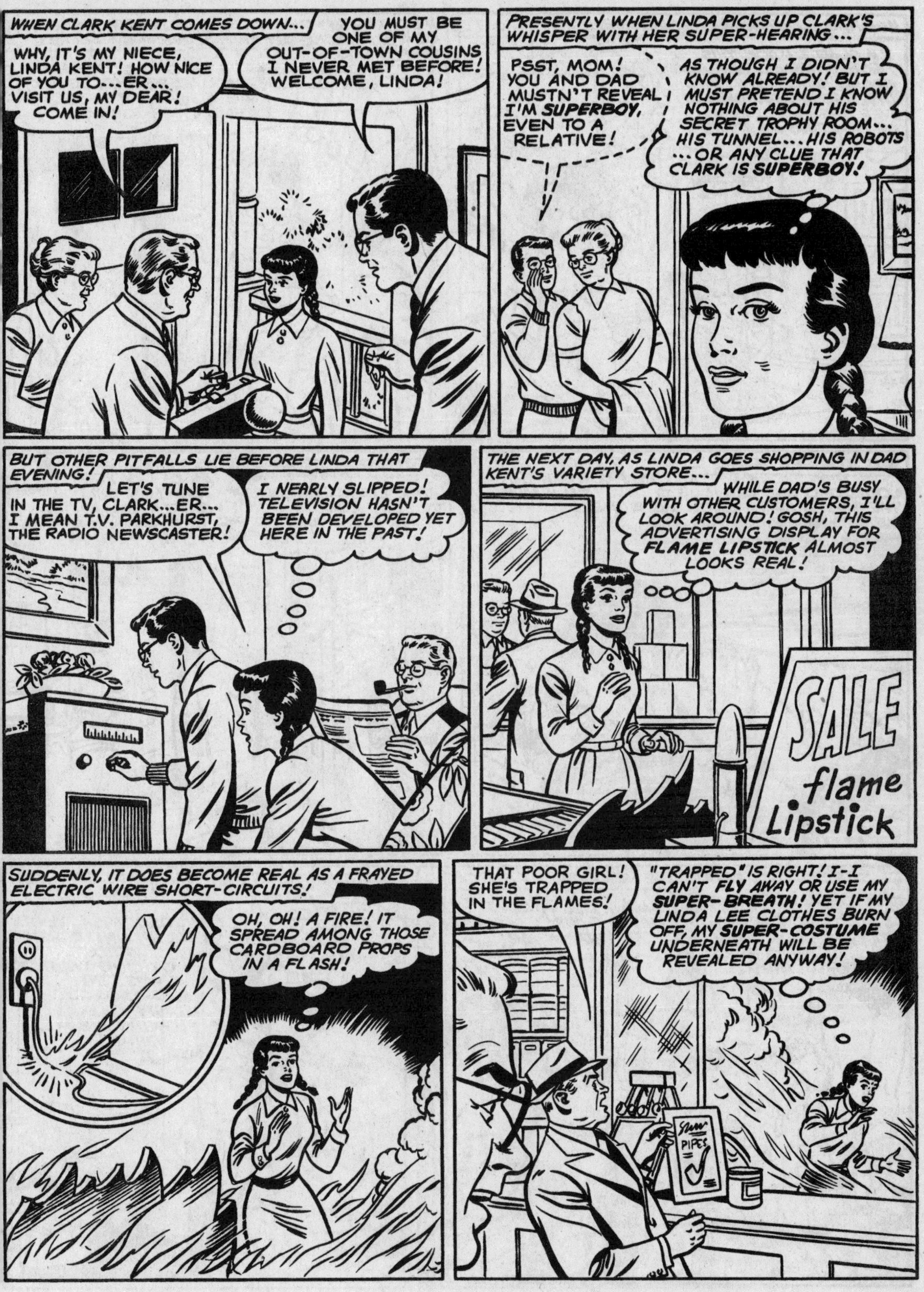
WHEN CLARK KENT COMES DOWN...
WHY, IT'S MY NIECE, LINDA KENT! HOW NICE OF YOU TO...ER... VISIT US, MY DEAR! COME IN!
YOU MUST BE ONE OF MY OUT-OF-TOWN COUSINS I NEVER MET BEFORE! WELCOME, LINDA!
PRESENTLY WHEN LINDA PICKS UP CLARK'S WHISPER WITH HER SUPER-HEARING...
PSST, MOM! YOU AND DAD MUSTN'T REVEAL I'M SUPERBOY, EVEN TO A RELATIVE!
AS THOUGH I DIDN'T KNOW ALREADY! BUT I MUST PRETEND I KNOW NOTHING ABOUT HIS SECRET TROPHY ROOM... HIS TUNNEL... HIS ROBOTS ...OR ANY CLUE THAT CLARK IS SUPERBOY!
BUT OTHER PITFALLS LIE BEFORE LINDA THAT EVENING!
LET'S TUNE IN THE TV, CLARK...ER... I MEAN T.V. PARKHURST, THE RADIO NEWSCASTER!
I NEARLY SLIPPED! TELEVISION HASN'T BEEN DEVELOPED YET HERE IN THE PAST!
THE NEXT DAY, AS LINDA GOES SHOPPING IN DAD KENT'S VARIETY STORE...
WHILE DAD'S BUSY WITH OTHER CUSTOMERS, I'LL LOOK AROUND! GOSH, THIS ADVERTISING DISPLAY FOR FLAME LIPSTICK ALMOST LOOKS REAL!
SALE flame Lipstick
SUDDENLY, IT DOES BECOME REAL AS A FRAYED ELECTRIC WIRE SHORT-CIRCUITS!
OH, OH! A FIRE! IT SPREAD AMONG THOSE CARDBOARD PROPS IN A FLASH!
THAT POOR GIRL! SHE'S TRAPPED IN THE FLAMES!
"TRAPPED" IS RIGHT! I-I CAN'T FLY AWAY OR USE MY SUPER-BREATH! YET IF MY LINDA LEE CLOTHES BURN OFF, MY SUPER-COSTUME UNDERNEATH WILL BE REVEALED ANYWAY!
PIPES

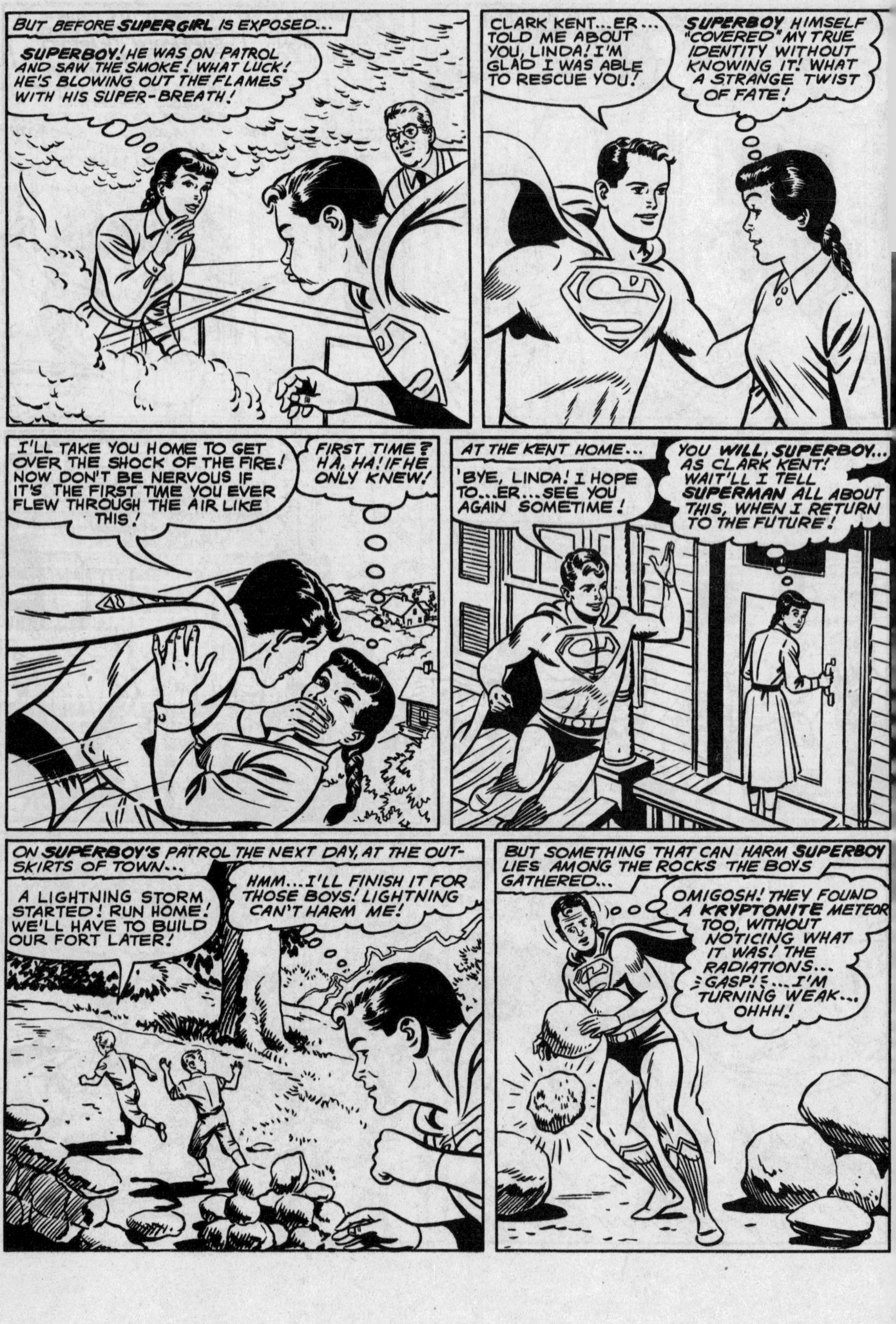
BUT BEFORE SUPERGIRL IS EXPOSED...
SUPERBOY! HE WAS ON PATROL AND SAW THE SMOKE! WHAT LUCK! HE'S BLOWING OUT THE FLAMES WITH HIS SUPER-BREATH!
CLARK KENT...ER... TOLD ME ABOUT YOU, LINDA! I'M GLAD I WAS ABLE TO RESCUE YOU!
SUPERBOY HIMSELF "COVERED" MY TRUE IDENTITY WITHOUT KNOWING IT! WHAT A STRANGE TWIST OF FATE!
I'LL TAKE YOU HOME TO GET OVER THE SHOCK OF THE FIRE! NOW DON'T BE NERVOUS IF IT'S THE FIRST TIME YOU EVER FLEW THROUGH THE AIR LIKE THIS!
FIRST TIME? HA, HA! IF HE ONLY KNEW!
AT THE KENT HOME...
'BYE, LINDA! I HOPE TO...ER...SEE YOU AGAIN SOMETIME!
YOU WILL, SUPERBOY... AS CLARK KENT! WAIT'LL I TELL SUPERMAN ALL ABOUT THIS, WHEN I RETURN TO THE FUTURE!
ON SUPERBOY'S PATROL THE NEXT DAY, AT THE OUTSKIRTS OF TOWN...
A LIGHTNING STORM STARTED! RUN HOME! WE'LL HAVE TO BUILD OUR FORT LATER!
HMM...I'LL FINISH IT FOR THOSE BOYS! LIGHTNING CAN'T HARM ME!
BUT SOMETHING THAT CAN HARM SUPERBOY LIES AMONG THE ROCKS THE BOYS GATHERED...
OMIGOSH! THEY FOUND A KRYPTONITE METEOR TOO, WITHOUT NOTICING WHAT IT WAS! THE RADIATIONS... GASP!...I'M TURNING WEAK... OHHH!

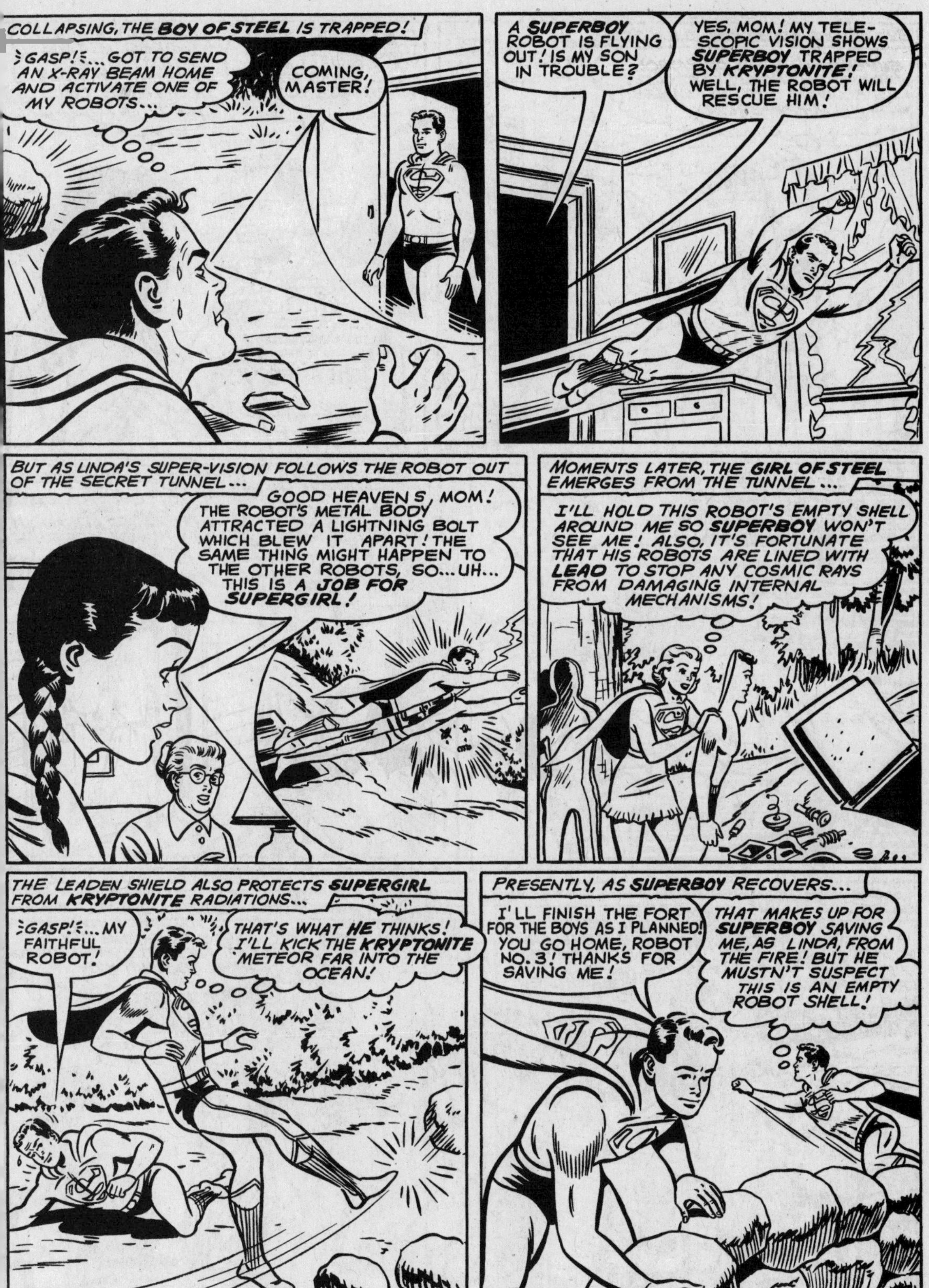
COLLAPSING, THE BOY OF STEEL IS TRAPPED!
GASP! ... GOT TO SEND AN X-RAY BEAM HOME AND ACTIVATE ONE OF MY ROBOTS...
COMING, MASTER!
A SUPERBOY ROBOT IS FLYING OUT! IS MY SON IN TROUBLE?
YES, MOM! MY TELE-SCOPIC VISION SHOWS SUPERBOY TRAPPED BY KRYPTONITE! WELL, THE ROBOT WILL RESCUE HIM!
BUT AS LINDA'S SUPER-VISION FOLLOWS THE ROBOT OUT OF THE SECRET TUNNEL...
GOOD HEAVENS, MOM! THE ROBOT'S METAL BODY ATTRACTED A LIGHTNING BOLT WHICH BLEW IT APART! THE SAME THING MIGHT HAPPEN TO THE OTHER ROBOTS, SO... UH... THIS IS A JOB FOR SUPERGIRL!
MOMENTS LATER, THE GIRL OF STEEL EMERGES FROM THE TUNNEL...
I'LL HOLD THIS ROBOT'S EMPTY SHELL AROUND ME SO SUPERBOY WON'T SEE ME! ALSO, IT'S FORTUNATE THAT HIS ROBOTS ARE LINED WITH LEAD TO STOP ANY COSMIC RAYS FROM DAMAGING INTERNAL MECHANISMS!
THE LEADEN SHIELD ALSO PROTECTS SUPERGIRL FROM KRYPTONITE RADIATIONS...
GASP! ... MY FAITHFUL ROBOT!
THAT'S WHAT HE THINKS! I'LL KICK THE KRYPTONITE METEOR FAR INTO THE OCEAN!
PRESENTLY, AS SUPERBOY RECOVERS...
I'LL FINISH THE FORT FOR THE BOYS AS I PLANNED! YOU GO HOME, ROBOT NO. 3! THANKS FOR SAVING ME!
THAT MAKES UP FOR SUPERBOY SAVING ME, AS LINDA, FROM THE FIRE! BUT HE MUSTN'T SUSPECT THIS IS AN EMPTY ROBOT SHELL!

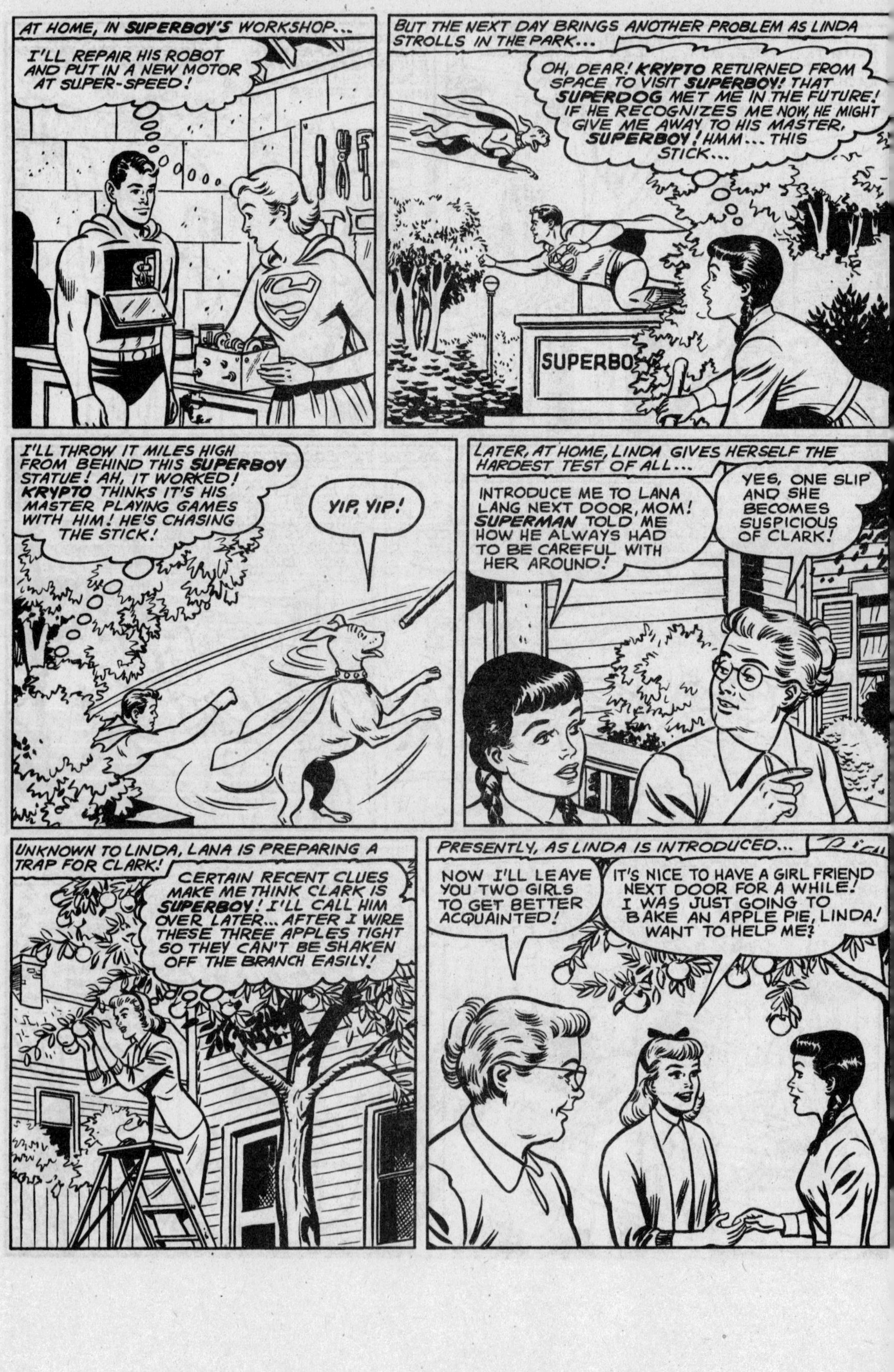
AT HOME, IN SUPERBOY'S WORKSHOP...
I'LL REPAIR HIS ROBOT AND PUT IN A NEW MOTOR AT SUPER-SPEED!
BUT THE NEXT DAY BRINGS ANOTHER PROBLEM AS LINDA STROLLS IN THE PARK...
OH, DEAR! KRYPTO RETURNED FROM SPACE TO VISIT SUPERBOY! THAT SUPERDOG MET ME IN THE FUTURE! IF HE RECOGNIZES ME NOW, HE MIGHT GIVE ME AWAY TO HIS MASTER, SUPERBOY! HMM... THIS STICK...
SUPERBO
I'LL THROW IT MILES HIGH FROM BEHIND THIS SUPERBOY STATUE! AH, IT WORKED! KRYPTO THINKS IT'S HIS MASTER PLAYING GAMES WITH HIM! HE'S CHASING THE STICK!
YIP, YIP!
LATER, AT HOME, LINDA GIVES HERSELF THE HARDEST TEST OF ALL...
INTRODUCE ME TO LANA LANG NEXT DOOR, MOM! SUPERMAN TOLD ME HOW HE ALWAYS HAD TO BE CAREFUL WITH HER AROUND!
YES, ONE SLIP AND SHE BECOMES SUSPICIOUS OF CLARK!
UNKNOWN TO LINDA, LANA IS PREPARING A TRAP FOR CLARK!
CERTAIN RECENT CLUES MAKE ME THINK CLARK IS SUPERBOY! I'LL CALL HIM OVER LATER... AFTER I WIRE THESE THREE APPLES TIGHT SO THEY CAN'T BE SHAKEN OFF THE BRANCH EASILY!
PRESENTLY, AS LINDA IS INTRODUCED...
NOW I'LL LEAVE YOU TWO GIRLS TO GET BETTER ACQUAINTED!
IT'S NICE TO HAVE A GIRL FRIEND NEXT DOOR FOR A WHILE! I WAS JUST GOING TO BAKE AN APPLE PIE, LINDA! WANT TO HELP ME?

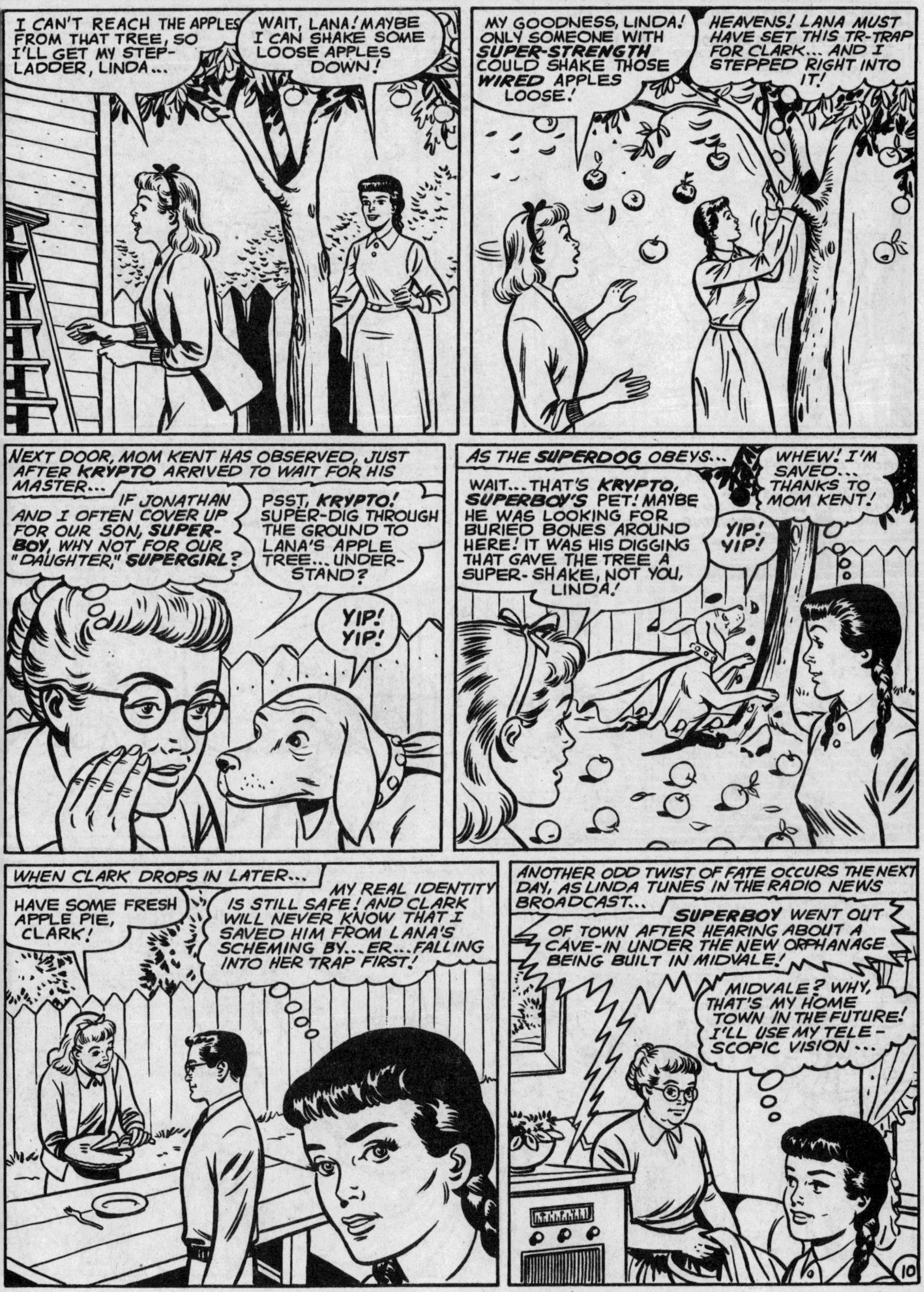
I CAN'T REACH THE APPLES FROM THAT TREE, SO I'LL GET MY STEP-LADDER, LINDA...
WAIT, LANA! MAYBE I CAN SHAKE SOME LOOSE APPLES DOWN!
MY GOODNESS, LINDA! ONLY SOMEONE WITH SUPER-STRENGTH COULD SHAKE THOSE WIRED APPLES LOOSE!
HEAVENS! LANA MUST HAVE SET THIS TR-TRAP FOR CLARK... AND I STEPPED RIGHT INTO IT!
NEXT DOOR, MOM KENT HAS OBSERVED, JUST AFTER KRYPTO ARRIVED TO WAIT FOR HIS MASTER...
IF JONATHAN AND I OFTEN COVER UP FOR OUR SON, SUPERBOY, WHY NOT FOR OUR "DAUGHTER," SUPERGIRL?
PSST, KRYPTO! SUPER-DIG THROUGH THE GROUND TO LANA'S APPLE TREE... UNDERSTAND?
YIP! YIP!
AS THE SUPERDOG OBEYS...
WAIT... THAT'S KRYPTO, SUPERBOY'S PET! MAYBE HE WAS LOOKING FOR BURIED BONES AROUND HERE! IT WAS HIS DIGGING THAT GAVE THE TREE A SUPER-SHAKE, NOT YOU, LINDA!
YIP! YIP!
WHEW! I'M SAVED... THANKS TO MOM KENT!
WHEN CLARK DROPS IN LATER...
HAVE SOME FRESH APPLE PIE, CLARK!
MY REAL IDENTITY IS STILL SAFE! AND CLARK WILL NEVER KNOW THAT I SAVED HIM FROM LANA'S SCHEMING BY... ER... FALLING INTO HER TRAP FIRST!
ANOTHER ODD TWIST OF FATE OCCURS THE NEXT DAY, AS LINDA TUNES IN THE RADIO NEWS BROADCAST...
SUPERBOY WENT OUT OF TOWN AFTER HEARING ABOUT A CAVE-IN UNDER THE NEW ORPHANAGE BEING BUILT IN MIDVALE!
MIDVALE? WHY, THAT'S MY HOME TOWN IN THE FUTURE! I'LL USE MY TELE-SCOPIC VISION...
10

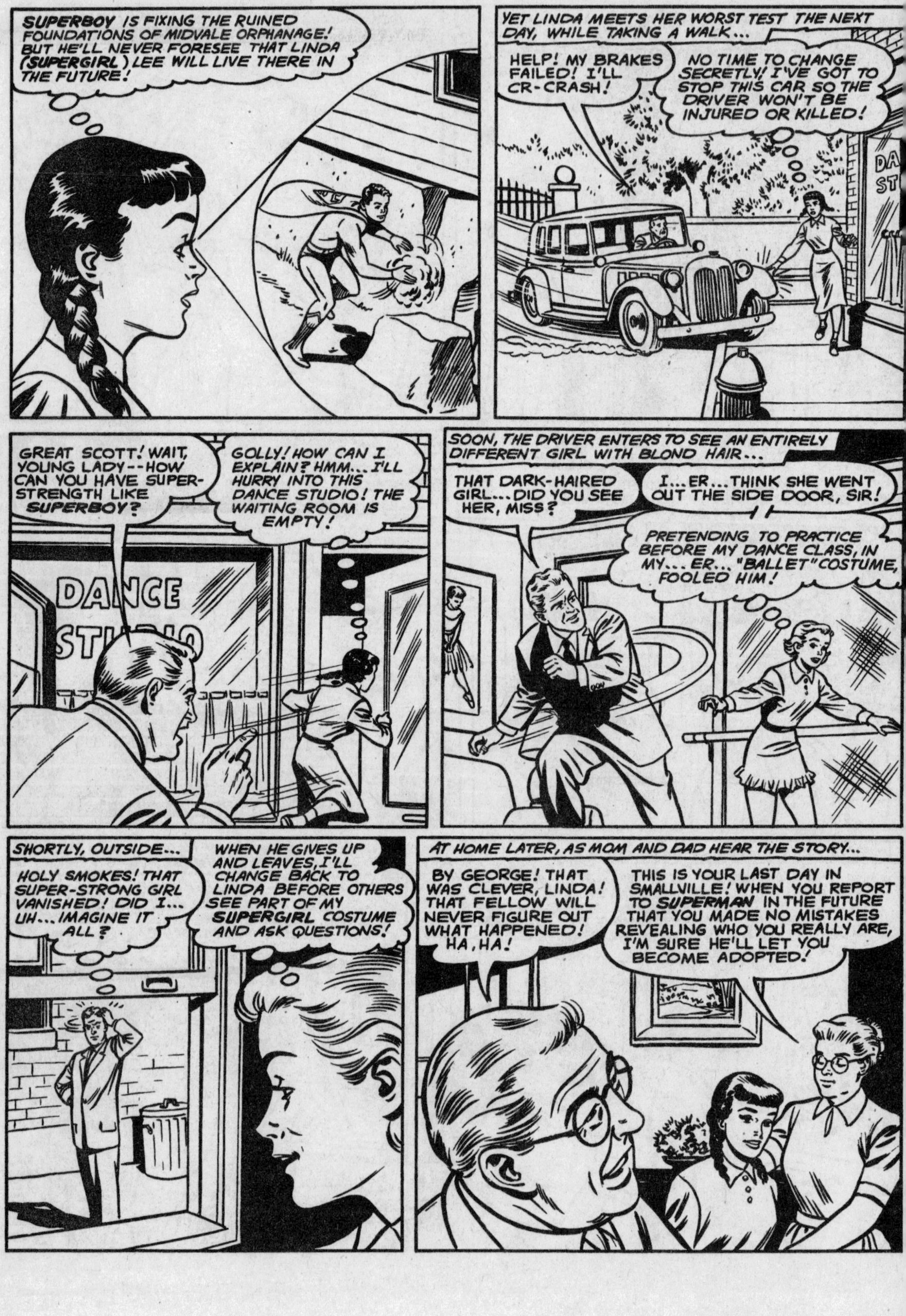
SUPERBOY IS FIXING THE RUINED FOUNDATIONS OF MIDVALE ORPHANAGE! BUT HE'LL NEVER FORESEE THAT LINDA (SUPERGIRL) LEE WILL LIVE THERE IN THE FUTURE!
YET LINDA MEETS HER WORST TEST THE NEXT DAY, WHILE TAKING A WALK...
HELP! MY BRAKES FAILED! I'LL CR-CRASH!
NO TIME TO CHANGE SECRETLY! I'VE GOT TO STOP THIS CAR SO THE DRIVER WON'T BE INJURED OR KILLED!
GREAT SCOTT! WAIT, YOUNG LADY--HOW CAN YOU HAVE SUPER-STRENGTH LIKE SUPERBOY?
GOLLY! HOW CAN I EXPLAIN? HMM... I'LL HURRY INTO THIS DANCE STUDIO! THE WAITING ROOM IS EMPTY!
DANCE STUDIO
SOON, THE DRIVER ENTERS TO SEE AN ENTIRELY DIFFERENT GIRL WITH BLOND HAIR...
THAT DARK-HAIRED GIRL... DID YOU SEE HER, MISS?
I... ER... THINK SHE WENT OUT THE SIDE DOOR, SIR!
PRETENDING TO PRACTICE BEFORE MY DANCE CLASS, IN MY... ER... "BALLET" COSTUME, FOOLED HIM!
SHORTLY, OUTSIDE...
HOLY SMOKES! THAT SUPER-STRONG GIRL VANISHED! DID I... UH... IMAGINE IT ALL?
WHEN HE GIVES UP AND LEAVES, I'LL CHANGE BACK TO LINDA BEFORE OTHERS SEE PART OF MY SUPERGIRL COSTUME AND ASK QUESTIONS!
AT HOME LATER, AS MOM AND DAD HEAR THE STORY...
BY GEORGE! THAT WAS CLEVER, LINDA! THAT FELLOW WILL NEVER FIGURE OUT WHAT HAPPENED! HA, HA!
THIS IS YOUR LAST DAY IN SMALLVILLE! WHEN YOU REPORT TO SUPERMAN IN THE FUTURE THAT YOU MADE NO MISTAKES REVEALING WHO YOU REALLY ARE, I'M SURE HE'LL LET YOU BECOME ADOPTED!

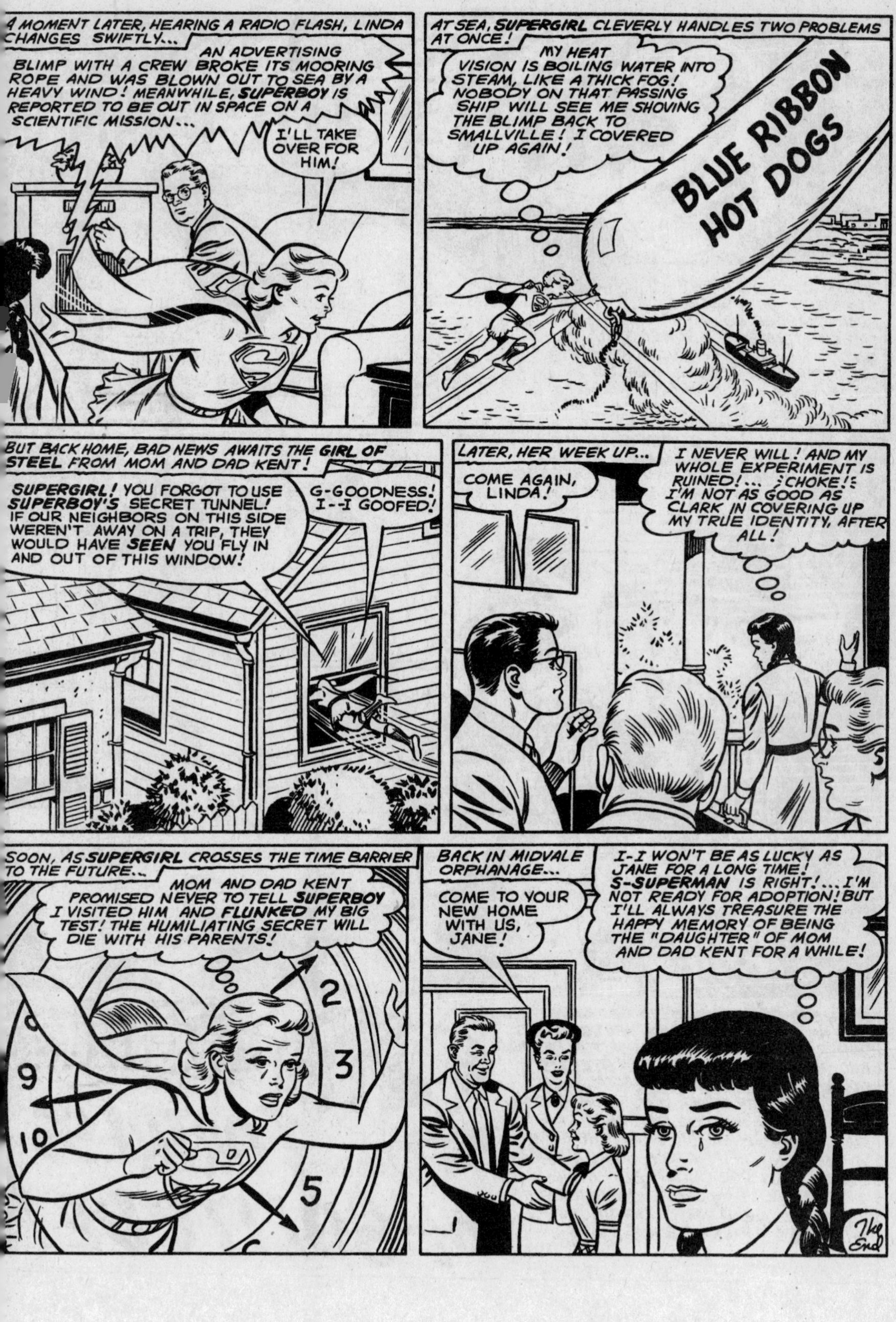
A MOMENT LATER, HEARING A RADIO FLASH, LINDA CHANGES SWIFTLY...
AN ADVERTISING BLIMP WITH A CREW BROKE ITS MOORING ROPE AND WAS BLOWN OUT TO SEA BY A HEAVY WIND! MEANWHILE, SUPERBOY IS REPORTED TO BE OUT IN SPACE ON A SCIENTIFIC MISSION...
I'LL TAKE OVER FOR HIM!
AT SEA, SUPERGIRL CLEVERLY HANDLES TWO PROBLEMS AT ONCE!
MY HEAT VISION IS BOILING WATER INTO STEAM, LIKE A THICK FOG! NOBODY ON THAT PASSING SHIP WILL SEE ME SHOVING THE BLIMP BACK TO SMALLVILLE! I COVERED UP AGAIN!
BLUE RIBBON HOT DOGS
BUT BACK HOME, BAD NEWS AWAITS THE GIRL OF STEEL FROM MOM AND DAD KENT!
SUPERGIRL! YOU FORGOT TO USE SUPERBOY'S SECRET TUNNEL! IF OUR NEIGHBORS ON THIS SIDE WEREN'T AWAY ON A TRIP, THEY WOULD HAVE SEEN YOU FLY IN AND OUT OF THIS WINDOW!
G-GOODNESS! I--I GOOFED!
LATER, HER WEEK UP...
COME AGAIN, LINDA!
I NEVER WILL! AND MY WHOLE EXPERIMENT IS RUINED!... ;CHOKE!; I'M NOT AS GOOD AS CLARK IN COVERING UP MY TRUE IDENTITY, AFTER ALL!
SOON, AS SUPERGIRL CROSSES THE TIME BARRIER TO THE FUTURE...
MOM AND DAD KENT PROMISED NEVER TO TELL SUPERBOY I VISITED HIM AND FLUNKED MY BIG TEST! THE HUMILIATING SECRET WILL DIE WITH HIS PARENTS!
BACK IN MIDVALE ORPHANAGE...
COME TO YOUR NEW HOME WITH US, JANE!
I-I WON'T BE AS LUCKY AS JANE FOR A LONG TIME! S-SUPERMAN IS RIGHT!... I'M NOT READY FOR ADOPTION! BUT I'LL ALWAYS TREASURE THE HAPPY MEMORY OF BEING THE "DAUGHTER" OF MOM AND DAD KENT FOR A WHILE!
The End

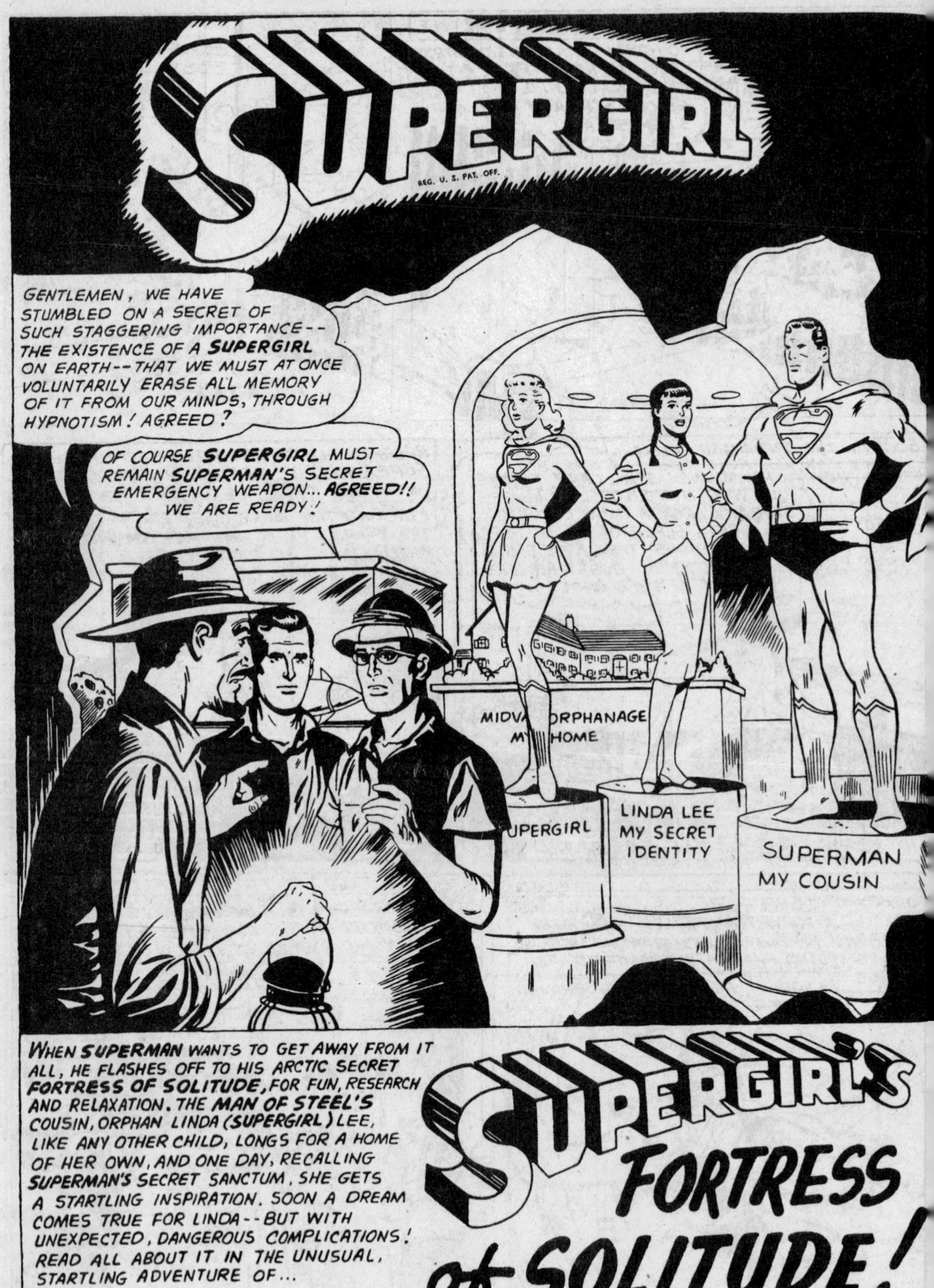
SUPERGIRL
REG. U. S. PAT. OFF.
GENTLEMEN, WE HAVE STUMBLED ON A SECRET OF SUCH STAGGERING IMPORTANCE-- THE EXISTENCE OF A SUPERGIRL ON EARTH--THAT WE MUST AT ONCE VOLUNTARILY ERASE ALL MEMORY OF IT FROM OUR MINDS, THROUGH HYPNOTISM! AGREED?
OF COURSE SUPERGIRL MUST REMAIN SUPERMAN'S SECRET EMERGENCY WEAPON... AGREED!! WE ARE READY!
MIDVA ORPHANAGE MY HOME
UPERGIRL
LINDA LEE MY SECRET IDENTITY
SUPERMAN MY COUSIN
WHEN SUPERMAN WANTS TO GET AWAY FROM IT ALL, HE FLASHES OFF TO HIS ARCTIC SECRET FORTRESS OF SOLITUDE, FOR FUN, RESEARCH AND RELAXATION. THE MAN OF STEEL'S COUSIN, ORPHAN LINDA (SUPERGIRL) LEE, LIKE ANY OTHER CHILD, LONGS FOR A HOME OF HER OWN, AND ONE DAY, RECALLING SUPERMAN'S SECRET SANCTUM, SHE GETS A STARTLING INSPIRATION. SOON A DREAM COMES TRUE FOR LINDA--BUT WITH UNEXPECTED, DANGEROUS COMPLICATIONS! READ ALL ABOUT IT IN THE UNUSUAL, STARTLING ADVENTURE OF...
SUPERGIRL'S FORTRESS of SOLITUDE!

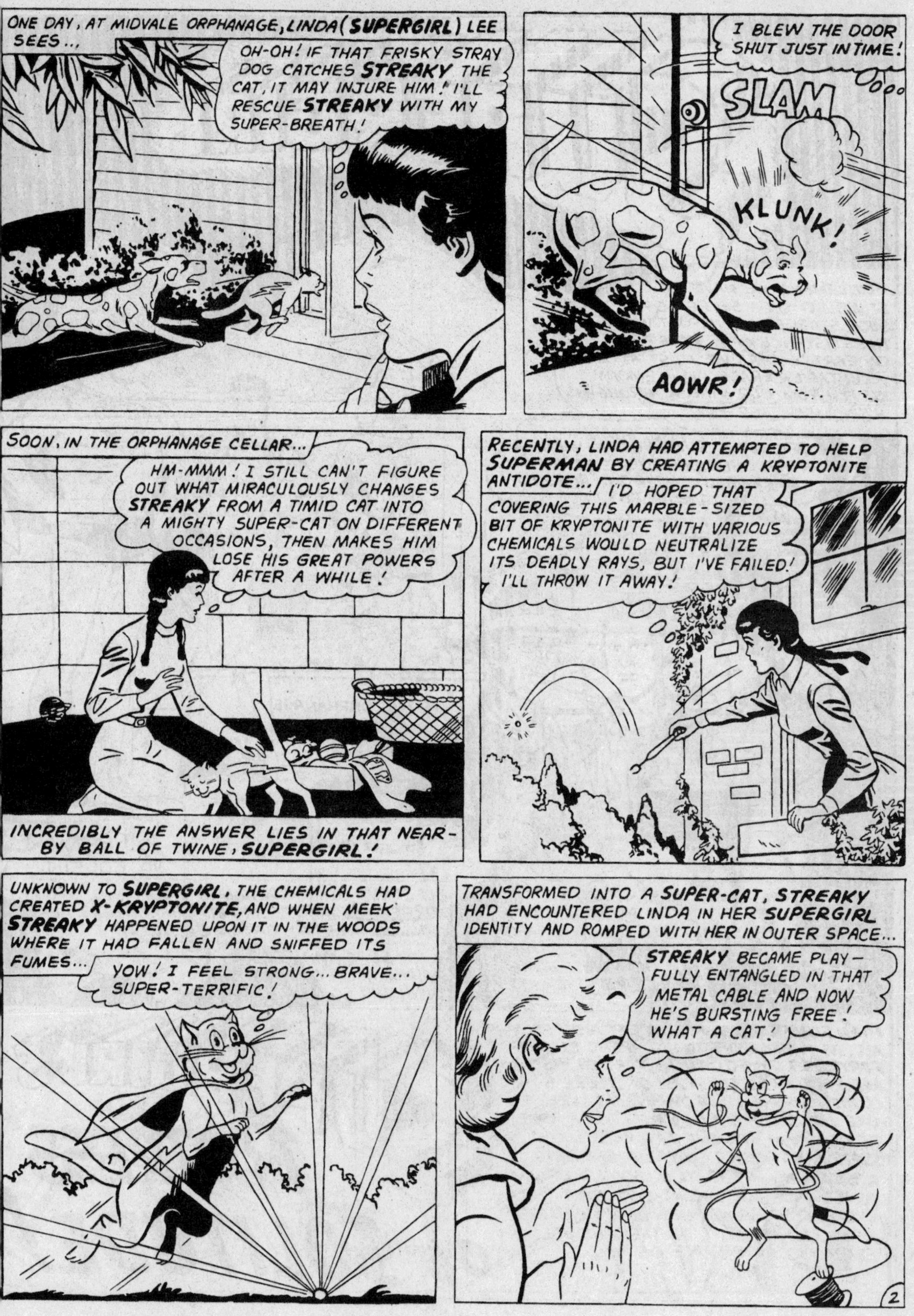
ONE DAY, AT MIDVALE ORPHANAGE, LINDA (SUPERGIRL) LEE SEES...
OH-OH! IF THAT FRISKY STRAY DOG CATCHES STREAKY THE CAT, IT MAY INJURE HIM! I'LL RESCUE STREAKY WITH MY SUPER-BREATH!
I BLEW THE DOOR SHUT JUST IN TIME!
SLAM
KLUNK!
AOWR!
SOON, IN THE ORPHANAGE CELLAR...
HM-MMM! I STILL CAN'T FIGURE OUT WHAT MIRACULOUSLY CHANGES STREAKY FROM A TIMID CAT INTO A MIGHTY SUPER-CAT ON DIFFERENT OCCASIONS, THEN MAKES HIM LOSE HIS GREAT POWERS AFTER A WHILE!
INCREDIBLY THE ANSWER LIES IN THAT NEAR-BY BALL OF TWINE, SUPERGIRL!
RECENTLY, LINDA HAD ATTEMPTED TO HELP SUPERMAN BY CREATING A KRYPTONITE ANTIDOTE...
I'D HOPED THAT COVERING THIS MARBLE-SIZED BIT OF KRYPTONITE WITH VARIOUS CHEMICALS WOULD NEUTRALIZE ITS DEADLY RAYS, BUT I'VE FAILED! I'LL THROW IT AWAY!
UNKNOWN TO SUPERGIRL, THE CHEMICALS HAD CREATED X-KRYPTONITE, AND WHEN MEEK STREAKY HAPPENED UPON IT IN THE WOODS WHERE IT HAD FALLEN AND SNIFFED ITS FUMES...
YOW! I FEEL STRONG... BRAVE... SUPER-TERRIFIC!
TRANSFORMED INTO A SUPER-CAT, STREAKY HAD ENCOUNTERED LINDA IN HER SUPERGIRL IDENTITY AND ROMPED WITH HER IN OUTER SPACE...
STREAKY BECAME PLAY-FULLY ENTANGLED IN THAT METAL CABLE AND NOW HE'S BURSTING FREE! WHAT A CAT!
2

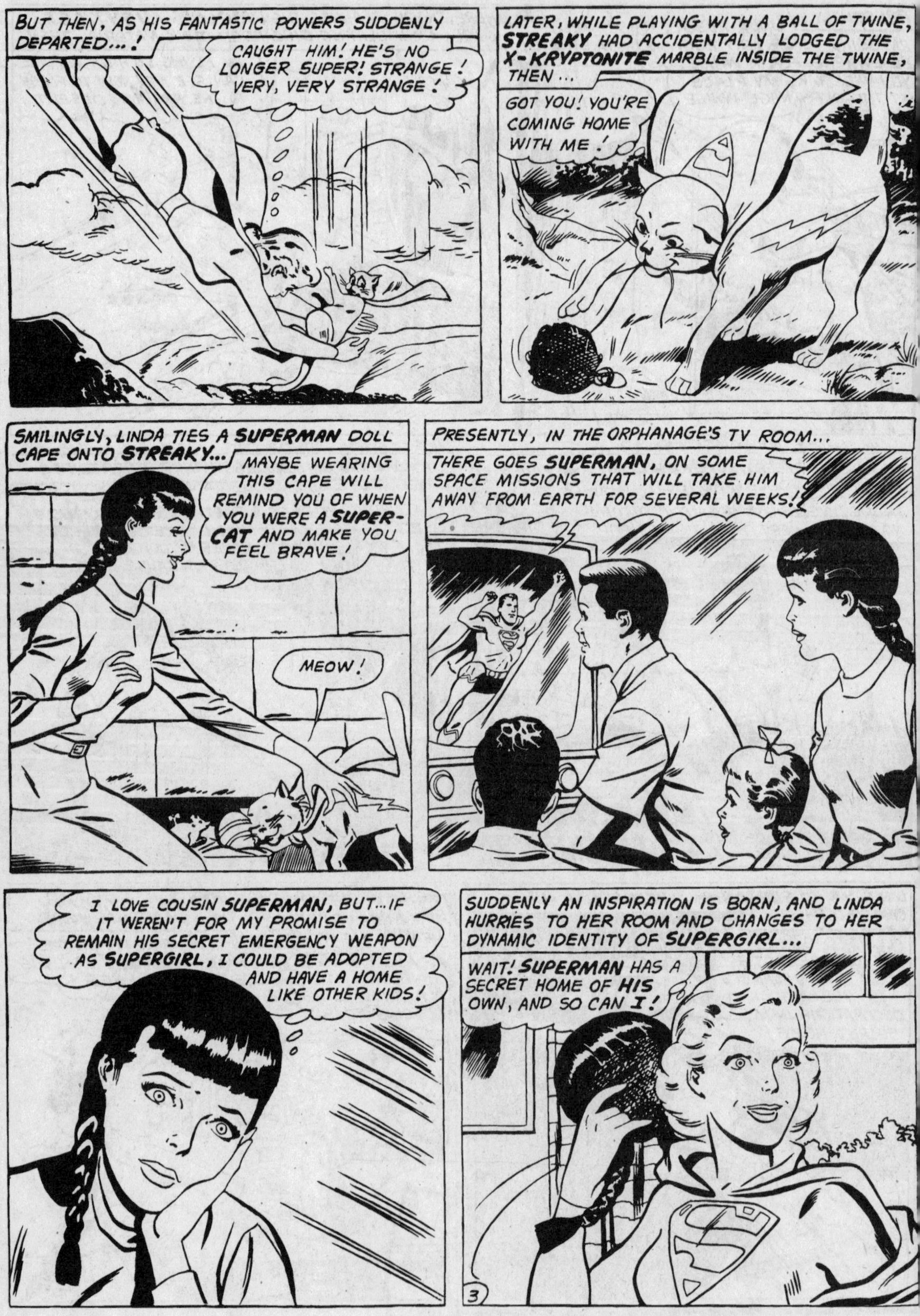
BUT THEN, AS HIS FANTASTIC POWERS SUDDENLY DEPARTED...!
CAUGHT HIM! HE'S NO LONGER SUPER! STRANGE! VERY, VERY STRANGE!
LATER, WHILE PLAYING WITH A BALL OF TWINE, STREAKY HAD ACCIDENTALLY LODGED THE X-KRYPTONITE MARBLE INSIDE THE TWINE, THEN...
GOT YOU! YOU'RE COMING HOME WITH ME!
SMILINGLY, LINDA TIES A SUPERMAN DOLL CAPE ONTO STREAKY...
MAYBE WEARING THIS CAPE WILL REMIND YOU OF WHEN YOU WERE A SUPER-CAT AND MAKE YOU FEEL BRAVE!
MEOW!
PRESENTLY, IN THE ORPHANAGE'S TV ROOM...
THERE GOES SUPERMAN, ON SOME SPACE MISSIONS THAT WILL TAKE HIM AWAY FROM EARTH FOR SEVERAL WEEKS!
I LOVE COUSIN SUPERMAN, BUT...IF IT WEREN'T FOR MY PROMISE TO REMAIN HIS SECRET EMERGENCY WEAPON AS SUPERGIRL, I COULD BE ADOPTED AND HAVE A HOME LIKE OTHER KIDS!
SUDDENLY AN INSPIRATION IS BORN, AND LINDA HURRIES TO HER ROOM AND CHANGES TO HER DYNAMIC IDENTITY OF SUPERGIRL...
WAIT! SUPERMAN HAS A SECRET HOME OF HIS OWN, AND SO CAN I!
3

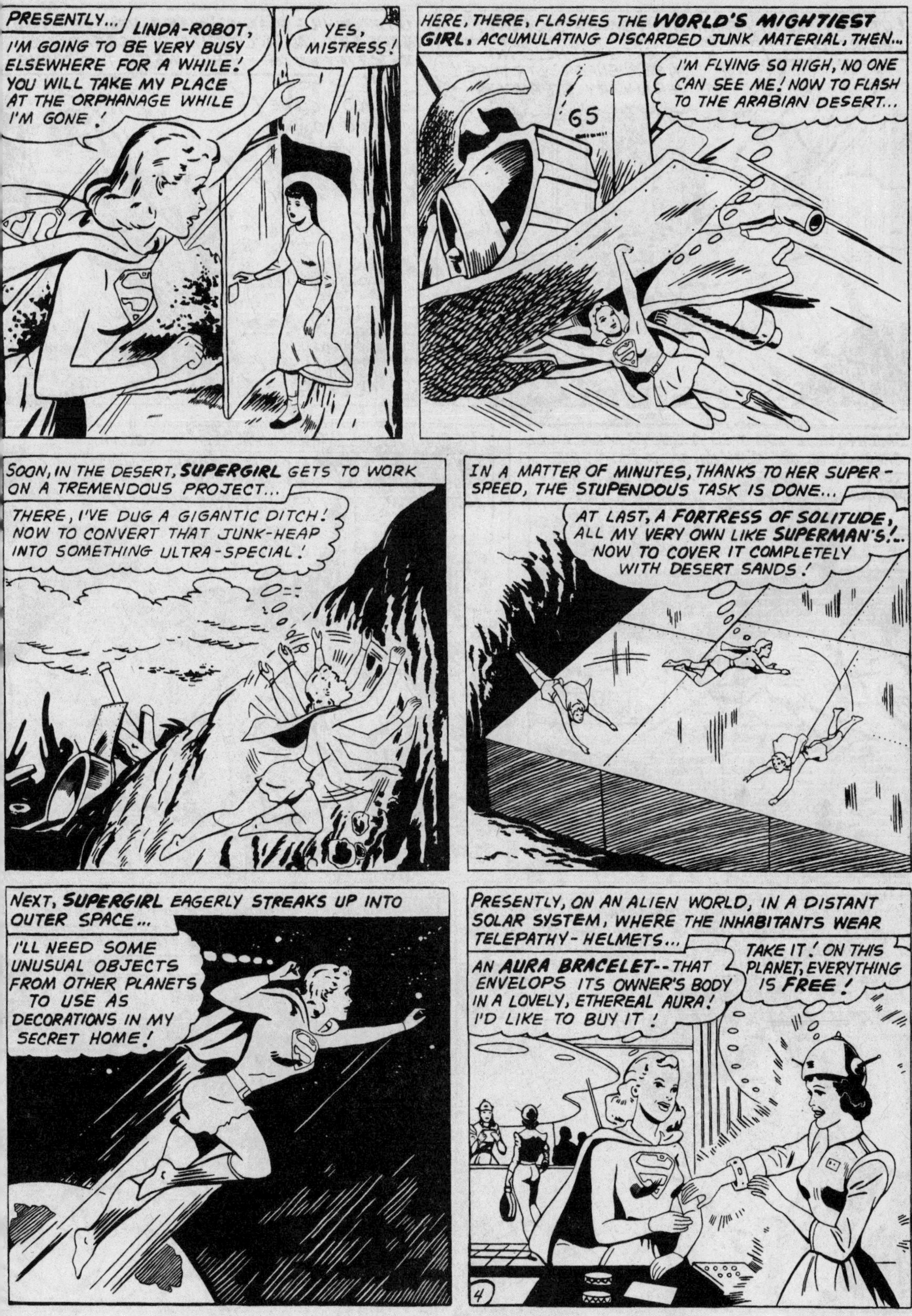
PRESENTLY...
LINDA-ROBOT, I'M GOING TO BE VERY BUSY ELSEWHERE FOR A WHILE! YOU WILL TAKE MY PLACE AT THE ORPHANAGE WHILE I'M GONE!
YES, MISTRESS!
HERE, THERE, FLASHES THE WORLD'S MIGHTIEST GIRL, ACCUMULATING DISCARDED JUNK MATERIAL, THEN...
I'M FLYING SO HIGH, NO ONE CAN SEE ME! NOW TO FLASH TO THE ARABIAN DESERT...
65
SOON, IN THE DESERT, SUPERGIRL GETS TO WORK ON A TREMENDOUS PROJECT...
THERE, I'VE DUG A GIGANTIC DITCH! NOW TO CONVERT THAT JUNK-HEAP INTO SOMETHING ULTRA-SPECIAL!
IN A MATTER OF MINUTES, THANKS TO HER SUPER-SPEED, THE STUPENDOUS TASK IS DONE...
AT LAST, A FORTRESS OF SOLITUDE, ALL MY VERY OWN LIKE SUPERMAN'S!... NOW TO COVER IT COMPLETELY WITH DESERT SANDS!
NEXT, SUPERGIRL EAGERLY STREAKS UP INTO OUTER SPACE...
I'LL NEED SOME UNUSUAL OBJECTS FROM OTHER PLANETS TO USE AS DECORATIONS IN MY SECRET HOME!
PRESENTLY, ON AN ALIEN WORLD, IN A DISTANT SOLAR SYSTEM, WHERE THE INHABITANTS WEAR TELEPATHY-HELMETS...
AN AURA BRACELET--THAT ENVELOPS ITS OWNER'S BODY IN A LOVELY, ETHEREAL AURA! I'D LIKE TO BUY IT!
TAKE IT! ON THIS PLANET, EVERYTHING IS FREE!
4

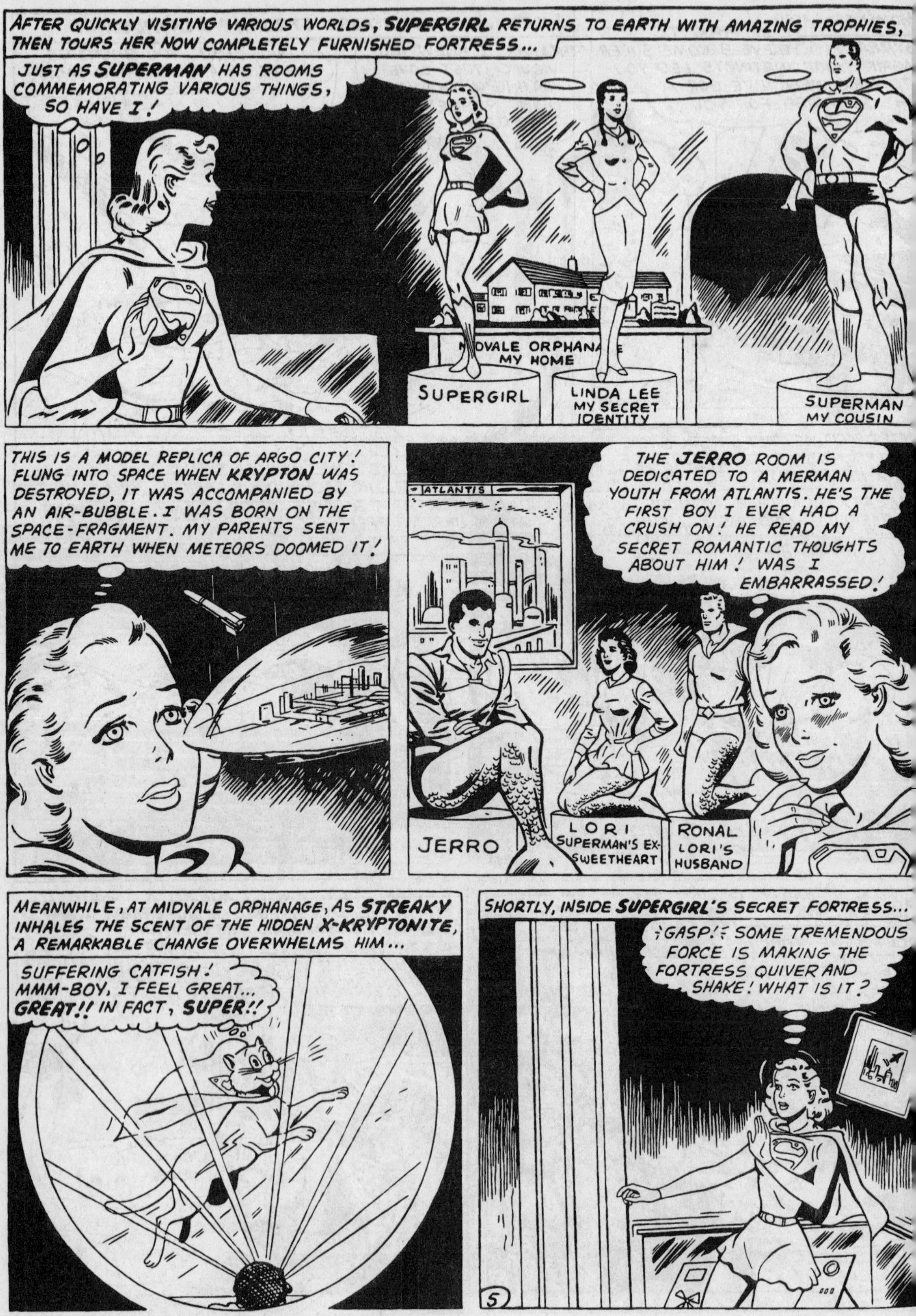
AFTER QUICKLY VISITING VARIOUS WORLDS, SUPERGIRL RETURNS TO EARTH WITH AMAZING TROPHIES, THEN TOURS HER NOW COMPLETELY FURNISHED FORTRESS...
JUST AS SUPERMAN HAS ROOMS COMMEMORATING VARIOUS THINGS, SO HAVE I!
MIDVALE ORPHANAGE MY HOME
SUPERGIRL
LINDA LEE MY SECRET IDENTITY
SUPERMAN MY COUSIN
THIS IS A MODEL REPLICA OF ARGO CITY! FLUNG INTO SPACE WHEN KRYPTON WAS DESTROYED, IT WAS ACCOMPANIED BY AN AIR-BUBBLE. I WAS BORN ON THE SPACE-FRAGMENT. MY PARENTS SENT ME TO EARTH WHEN METEORS DOOMED IT!
ATLANTIS
THE JERRO ROOM IS DEDICATED TO A MERMAN YOUTH FROM ATLANTIS. HE'S THE FIRST BOY I EVER HAD A CRUSH ON! HE READ MY SECRET ROMANTIC THOUGHTS ABOUT HIM! WAS I EMBARRASSED!
JERRO
LORI SUPERMAN'S EX-SWEETHEART
RONAL LORI'S HUSBAND
MEANWHILE, AT MIDVALE ORPHANAGE, AS STREAKY INHALES THE SCENT OF THE HIDDEN X-KRYPTONITE, A REMARKABLE CHANGE OVERWHELMS HIM...
SUFFERING CATFISH! MMM-BOY, I FEEL GREAT... GREAT!! IN FACT, SUPER!!
SHORTLY, INSIDE SUPERGIRL'S SECRET FORTRESS...
¡GASP!¡ SOME TREMENDOUS FORCE IS MAKING THE FORTRESS QUIVER AND SHAKE! WHAT IS IT?
5

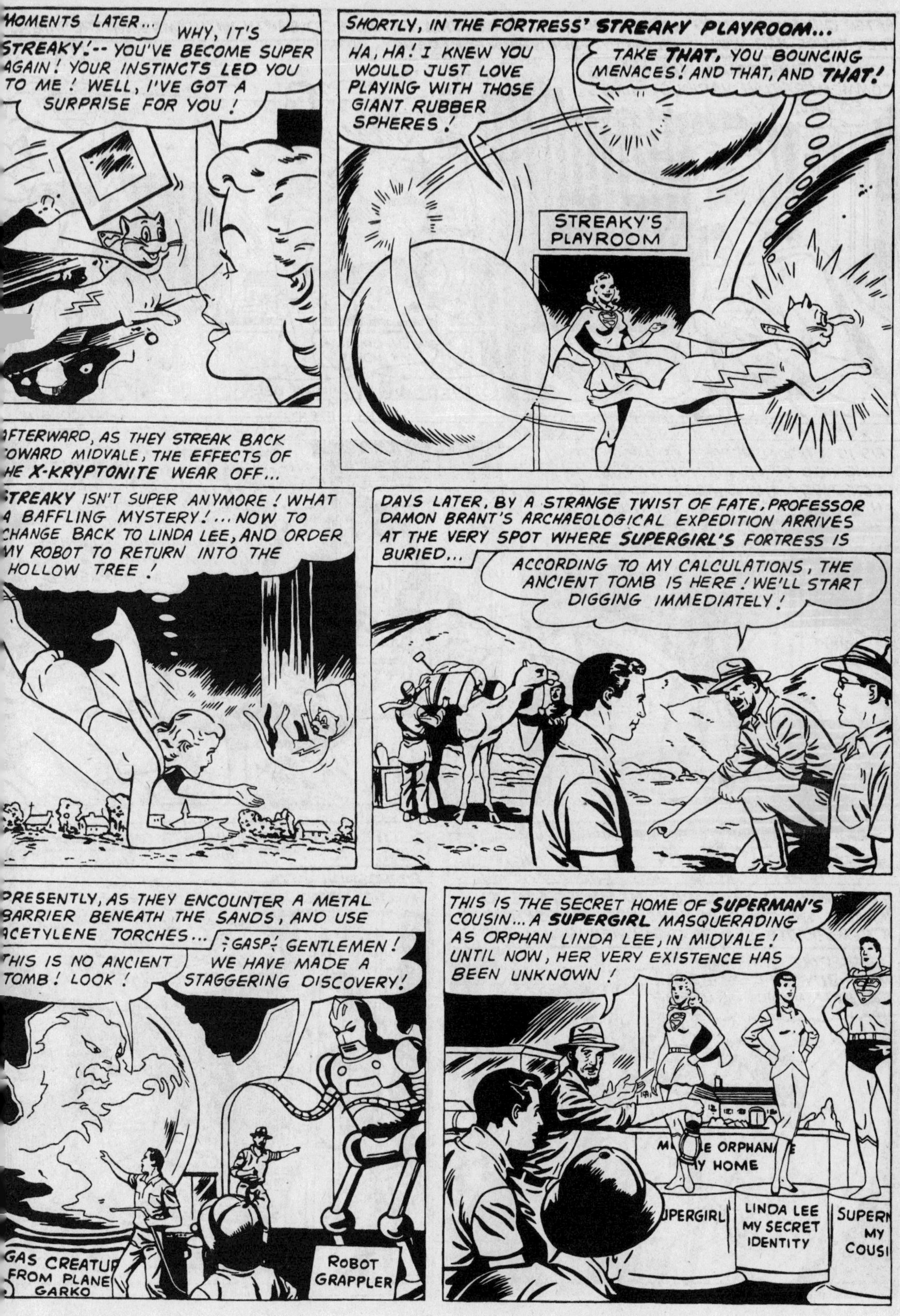
MOMENTS LATER...
WHY, IT'S STREAKY!-- YOU'VE BECOME SUPER AGAIN! YOUR INSTINCTS LED YOU TO ME! WELL, I'VE GOT A SURPRISE FOR YOU!
SHORTLY, IN THE FORTRESS' STREAKY PLAYROOM...
HA, HA! I KNEW YOU WOULD JUST LOVE PLAYING WITH THOSE GIANT RUBBER SPHERES!
TAKE THAT, YOU BOUNCING MENACES! AND THAT, AND THAT!
STREAKY'S PLAYROOM
AFTERWARD, AS THEY STREAK BACK TOWARD MIDVALE, THE EFFECTS OF THE X-KRYPTONITE WEAR OFF...
STREAKY ISN'T SUPER ANYMORE! WHAT A BAFFLING MYSTERY!... NOW TO CHANGE BACK TO LINDA LEE, AND ORDER MY ROBOT TO RETURN INTO THE HOLLOW TREE!
DAYS LATER, BY A STRANGE TWIST OF FATE, PROFESSOR DAMON BRANT'S ARCHAEOLOGICAL EXPEDITION ARRIVES AT THE VERY SPOT WHERE SUPERGIRL'S FORTRESS IS BURIED...
ACCORDING TO MY CALCULATIONS, THE ANCIENT TOMB IS HERE! WE'LL START DIGGING IMMEDIATELY!
PRESENTLY, AS THEY ENCOUNTER A METAL BARRIER BENEATH THE SANDS, AND USE ACETYLENE TORCHES...
THIS IS NO ANCIENT TOMB! LOOK!
¿GASP¿ GENTLEMEN! WE HAVE MADE A STAGGERING DISCOVERY!
GAS CREATUR FROM PLANE GARKO
ROBOT GRAPPLER
THIS IS THE SECRET HOME OF SUPERMAN'S COUSIN... A SUPERGIRL MASQUERADING AS ORPHAN LINDA LEE, IN MIDVALE! UNTIL NOW, HER VERY EXISTENCE HAS BEEN UNKNOWN!
ORPHANA
Y HOME
PERGIRL
LINDA LEE MY SECRET IDENTITY
SUPER MY COUSI

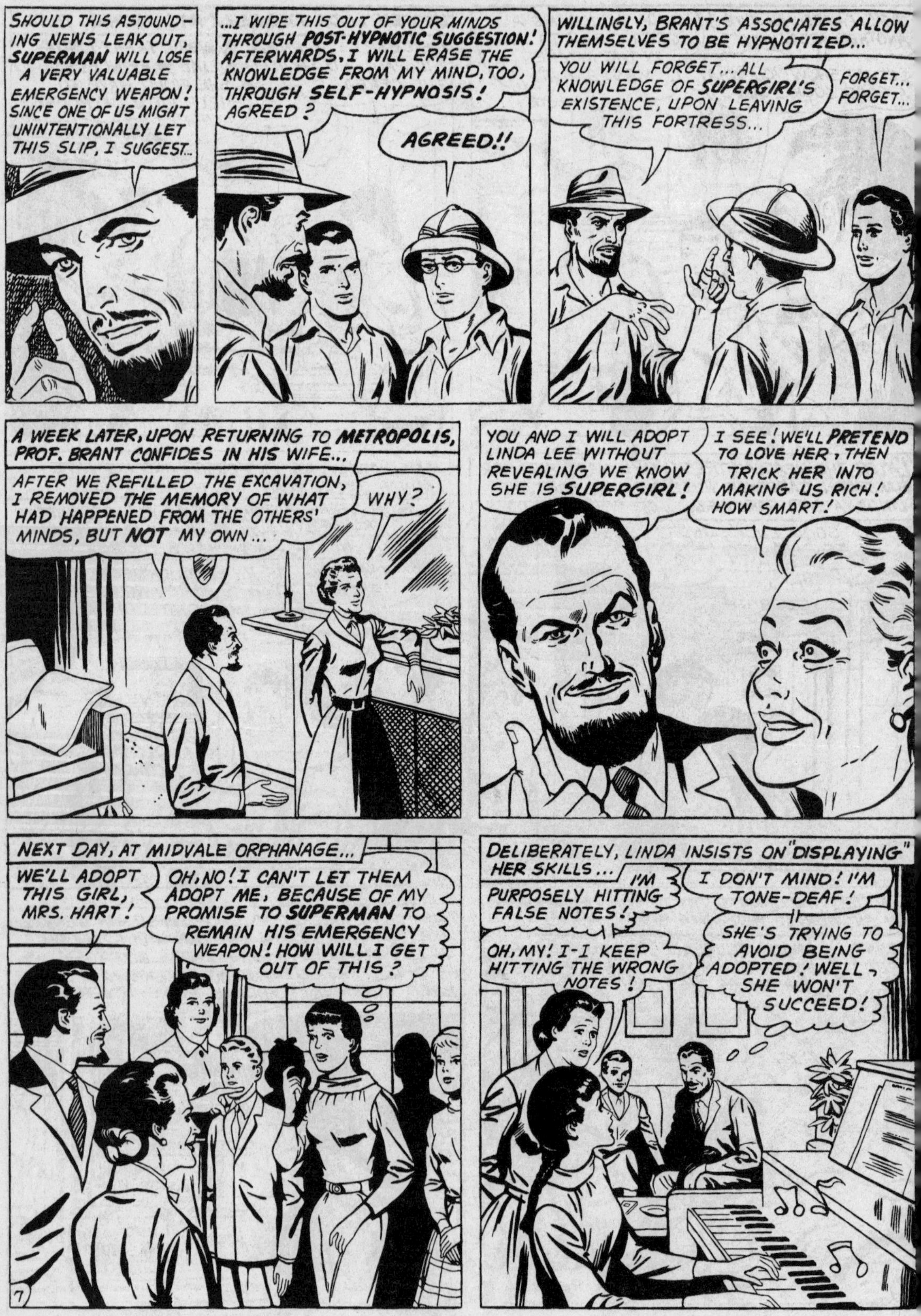
SHOULD THIS ASTOUNDING NEWS LEAK OUT, SUPERMAN WILL LOSE A VERY VALUABLE EMERGENCY WEAPON! SINCE ONE OF US MIGHT UNINTENTIONALLY LET THIS SLIP, I SUGGEST...
...I WIPE THIS OUT OF YOUR MINDS THROUGH POST-HYPNOTIC SUGGESTION! AFTERWARDS, I WILL ERASE THE KNOWLEDGE FROM MY MIND, TOO, THROUGH SELF-HYPNOSIS! AGREED?
AGREED!!
WILLINGLY, BRANT'S ASSOCIATES ALLOW THEMSELVES TO BE HYPNOTIZED...
YOU WILL FORGET... ALL KNOWLEDGE OF SUPERGIRL'S EXISTENCE, UPON LEAVING THIS FORTRESS...
FORGET... FORGET...
A WEEK LATER, UPON RETURNING TO METROPOLIS, PROF. BRANT CONFIDES IN HIS WIFE...
AFTER WE REFILLED THE EXCAVATION, I REMOVED THE MEMORY OF WHAT HAD HAPPENED FROM THE OTHERS' MINDS, BUT NOT MY OWN...
WHY?
YOU AND I WILL ADOPT LINDA LEE WITHOUT REVEALING WE KNOW SHE IS SUPERGIRL!
I SEE! WE'LL PRETEND TO LOVE HER, THEN TRICK HER INTO MAKING US RICH! HOW SMART!
NEXT DAY, AT MIDVALE ORPHANAGE...
WE'LL ADOPT THIS GIRL, MRS. HART!
OH, NO! I CAN'T LET THEM ADOPT ME, BECAUSE OF MY PROMISE TO SUPERMAN TO REMAIN HIS EMERGENCY WEAPON! HOW WILL I GET OUT OF THIS?
7
DELIBERATELY, LINDA INSISTS ON "DISPLAYING" HER SKILLS...
I'M PURPOSELY HITTING FALSE NOTES!
OH, MY! I-I KEEP HITTING THE WRONG NOTES!
I DON'T MIND! I'M TONE-DEAF!
SHE'S TRYING TO AVOID BEING ADOPTED! WELL, SHE WON'T SUCCEED!

ULP! ...FAILED! AH, I'VE ANOTHER IDEA!

LET ME SHOW YOU WHAT A GOOD COOK I AM!

LINDA WOULD BE A GREAT HELP TO YOU IN THE KITCHEN, MRS. BRANT!

UNSEEN, LINDA USES HER X-RAY VISION SO THAT...

OH, DEAR! I BURNED THE PAN, AND SPOILED THE CEREAL!

WE'LL TREAT LINDA LIKE A PRINCESS! SHE WON'T HAVE TO HELP WITH THE HOUSEWORK!

OUTSMARTED HER AGAIN!

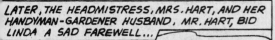

LATER, THE HEADMISTRESS, MRS. HART, AND HER HANDYMAN-GARDENER HUSBAND, MR. HART, BID LINDA A SAD FAREWELL...

GOOD LUCK, LINDA! ⁞SOB⁞ I HATE TO SEE YOU GO! HENRY AND I WILL MISS YOU! ⁞SOB!⁞

I'LL MISS YOU BOTH, TOO!

MRS. HART

IMMEDIATELY, THE PROFESSOR AND HIS WIFE LAUNCH THEIR PLAN TO WIN OVER LINDA...

⁞GASP!⁞ YOU SHOULDN'T HAVE BOUGHT ALL THOSE NEW CLOTHES FOR ME! YOU SPENT TOO MUCH!

HA, HA! WE'LL GET IT BACK A MILLION-FOLD FROM YOU, SUPERGIRL!

DRESS SHOP MODE DE

CRAFTILY, THE BRANTS TRY TO WIN LINDA'S TRUST BY SHOWERING HER WITH GOOD TIMES...

WHAT FUN!

ENJOY YOURSELF, DEAREST! OUR GOAL IN LIFE IS TO MAKE YOU AS HAPPY AS WE CAN!

BUT ONE NIGHT...

DAD, WHY ARE YOU UNHAPPY?

EXPEDITIONS COST FORTUNES, MY DEAR! NO ONE WILL SPONSOR MY NEW SCIENTIFIC PROJECT TO EXCAVATE SOME ANCIENT RUINS IN AFRICA!

8

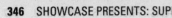

*THAT EVENING, LINDA CHANGES TO **SUPERGIRL**, THEN FLIES OFF TO A COAL MINE...*

MY SUPER-PRESSURE IS CONVERTING THESE LUMPS OF COAL INTO *ROUGH DIAMONDS!*

NEXT MORNING...

:GASP!: THIS PACKAGE, MYSTERIOUSLY LEFT BEFORE OUR DOOR, CONTAINS A FORTUNE IN UNFACETED DIAMONDS! THERE'S NO RETURN ADDRESS!

THIS CARD FROM THE PACKAGE READS, "GOOD LUCK ON YOUR PROJECTS!"

BUT WHEN THE PROFESSOR AND HIS WIFE ARE ALONE...

WE'RE RICH!

BAH, THAT'S JUST PEANUTS! WITH A SUPERGIRL FOR A DAUGHTER, WE DESERVE MUCH BETTER!

AND SO, LATER...

YOU'RE STILL... UNHAPPY...

MY FONDEST DESIRE IS TO SET UP A FUND TO FINANCE WORTHY EXPEDITIONS FOR FELLOW SCIENTISTS FOR MANY YEARS TO COME! I HAVEN'T ENOUGH MONEY FOR THAT...

*THAT EVENING, **SUPERGIRL** ONCE AGAIN GOES INTO ACTION...*

MY X-RAY VISION REVEALS WHICH OYSTERS CONTAIN PEARLS! THOSE ARE THE ONES I'LL GATHER!

NEXT DAY...

ANOTHER PACKAGE FROM AN ANONYMOUS DONOR! THIS ONE CRAMMED WITH PEARLS! HOW LUCKY YOU ARE!

LUCKY? I DON'T AGREE...

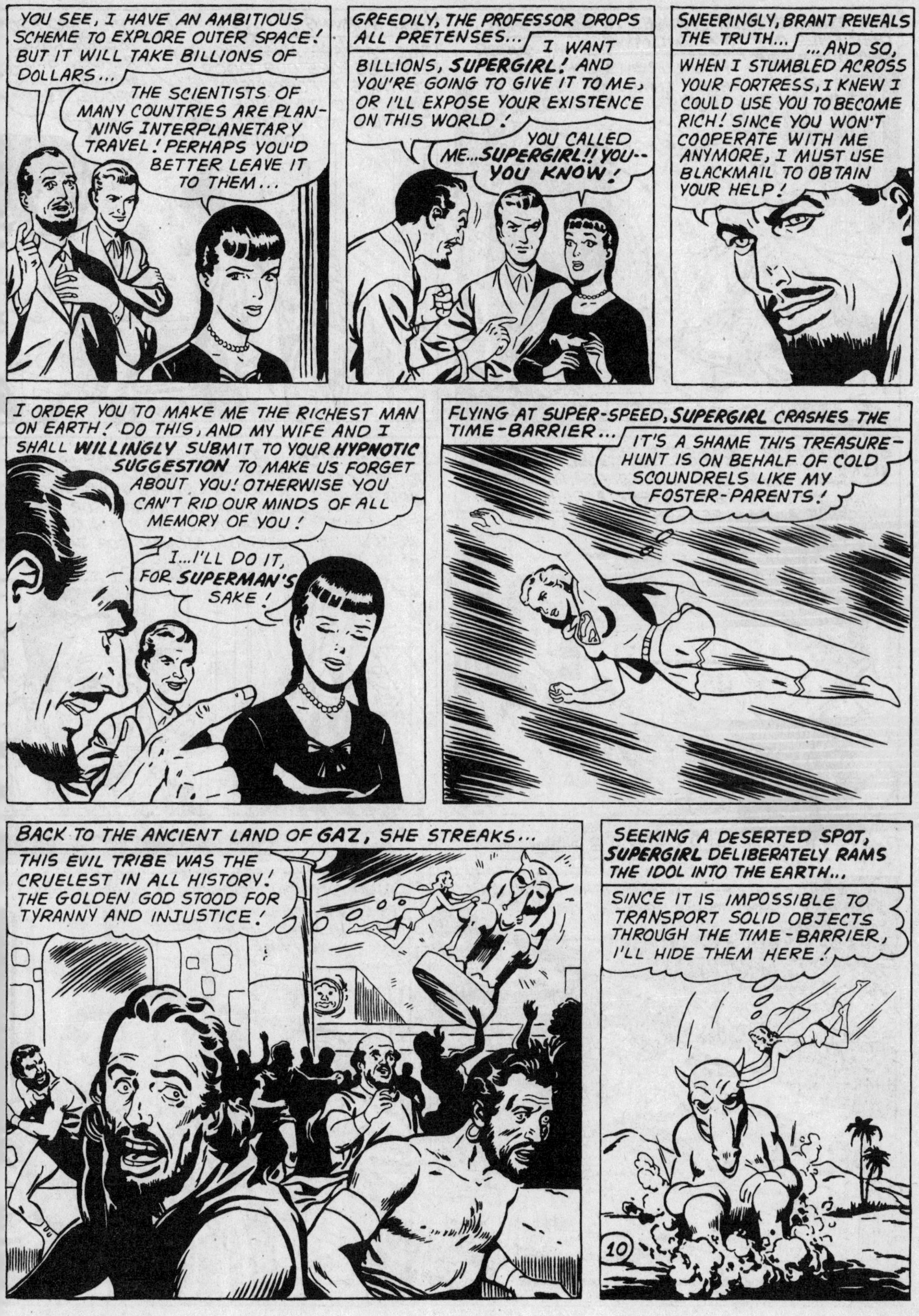
YOU SEE, I HAVE AN AMBITIOUS SCHEME TO EXPLORE OUTER SPACE! BUT IT WILL TAKE BILLIONS OF DOLLARS...
THE SCIENTISTS OF MANY COUNTRIES ARE PLANNING INTERPLANETARY TRAVEL! PERHAPS YOU'D BETTER LEAVE IT TO THEM...
GREEDILY, THE PROFESSOR DROPS ALL PRETENSES...
I WANT BILLIONS, SUPERGIRL! AND YOU'RE GOING TO GIVE IT TO ME, OR I'LL EXPOSE YOUR EXISTENCE ON THIS WORLD!
YOU CALLED ME...SUPERGIRL!! YOU--YOU KNOW!
SNEERINGLY, BRANT REVEALS THE TRUTH...
...AND SO, WHEN I STUMBLED ACROSS YOUR FORTRESS, I KNEW I COULD USE YOU TO BECOME RICH! SINCE YOU WON'T COOPERATE WITH ME ANYMORE, I MUST USE BLACKMAIL TO OBTAIN YOUR HELP!
I ORDER YOU TO MAKE ME THE RICHEST MAN ON EARTH! DO THIS, AND MY WIFE AND I SHALL WILLINGLY SUBMIT TO YOUR HYPNOTIC SUGGESTION TO MAKE US FORGET ABOUT YOU! OTHERWISE YOU CAN'T RID OUR MINDS OF ALL MEMORY OF YOU!
I...I'LL DO IT, FOR SUPERMAN'S SAKE!
FLYING AT SUPER-SPEED, SUPERGIRL CRASHES THE TIME-BARRIER...
IT'S A SHAME THIS TREASURE-HUNT IS ON BEHALF OF COLD SCOUNDRELS LIKE MY FOSTER-PARENTS!
BACK TO THE ANCIENT LAND OF GAZ, SHE STREAKS...
THIS EVIL TRIBE WAS THE CRUELEST IN ALL HISTORY! THE GOLDEN GOD STOOD FOR TYRANNY AND INJUSTICE!
SEEKING A DESERTED SPOT, SUPERGIRL DELIBERATELY RAMS THE IDOL INTO THE EARTH...
SINCE IT IS IMPOSSIBLE TO TRANSPORT SOLID OBJECTS THROUGH THE TIME-BARRIER, I'LL HIDE THEM HERE!
10

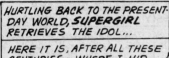

HURTLING BACK TO THE PRESENT-DAY WORLD, **SUPERGIRL** RETRIEVES THE IDOL...

HERE IT IS, AFTER ALL THESE CENTURIES...WHERE I HID IT! I'LL STORE IT IN THE ARABIAN DESERT, AND CONTINUE MY SEARCH FOR GREAT TREASURES!

THEN, ONCE AGAIN, SHE FLASHES THROUGH TIME, TO THE YEAR 1223 A.D., AND THE STOLEN LOOT OF **GENGHIS KHAN**'S RUTHLESS MONGOL PLUNDERERS...

THEIR WEAPONS ARE USELESS AGAINST ME! I'LL TAKE THEIR LOOT AND HIDE IT WHERE I CAN DIG IT UP IN THE YEAR 1960!

RETURNING TO THE PRESENT, **SUPERGIRL** DIGS UP THE TREASURE, THEN FLIES HER FOSTER PARENTS TO A PART OF THE ARABIAN DESERT, FAR FROM HER HIDDEN FORTRESS...

THIS EMERALD PALACE IS YOURS! I BUILT IT AND FILLED IT WITH TREASURES THAT STAGGER THE IMAGINATION!

SOON, IN THE PALACE...

SEE--I HAVE GIVEN YOU THE RICHES YOU DESIRE! NOW LET ME HYPNOTICALLY REMOVE MY SECRET FROM YOUR MINDS!...

WE'LL NEVER LET YOU OUT FROM UNDER OUR THUMBS, YOU TRUSTING FOOL! YOU'LL CONTINUE TO DO AS WE SAY...OR WE'LL EXPOSE YOU!

MEANWHILE, AT THE MIDVALE ORPHANAGE, **STREAKY** ONCE AGAIN SMELLS THE **X-KRYPTONITE** CONCEALED IN THE BALL OF TWINE, AND...

YAHOO! I'M MIGHTY AGAIN! WHEEE...

SECONDS LATER, AT THE PALACE...

OH, NO! **STREAKY** HAS BECOME SUPER-POWERFUL ONCE MORE! HIS INSTINCT LED HIM HERE! HE WANTS TO PLAY!

AWK! A S-SUPERCAT!

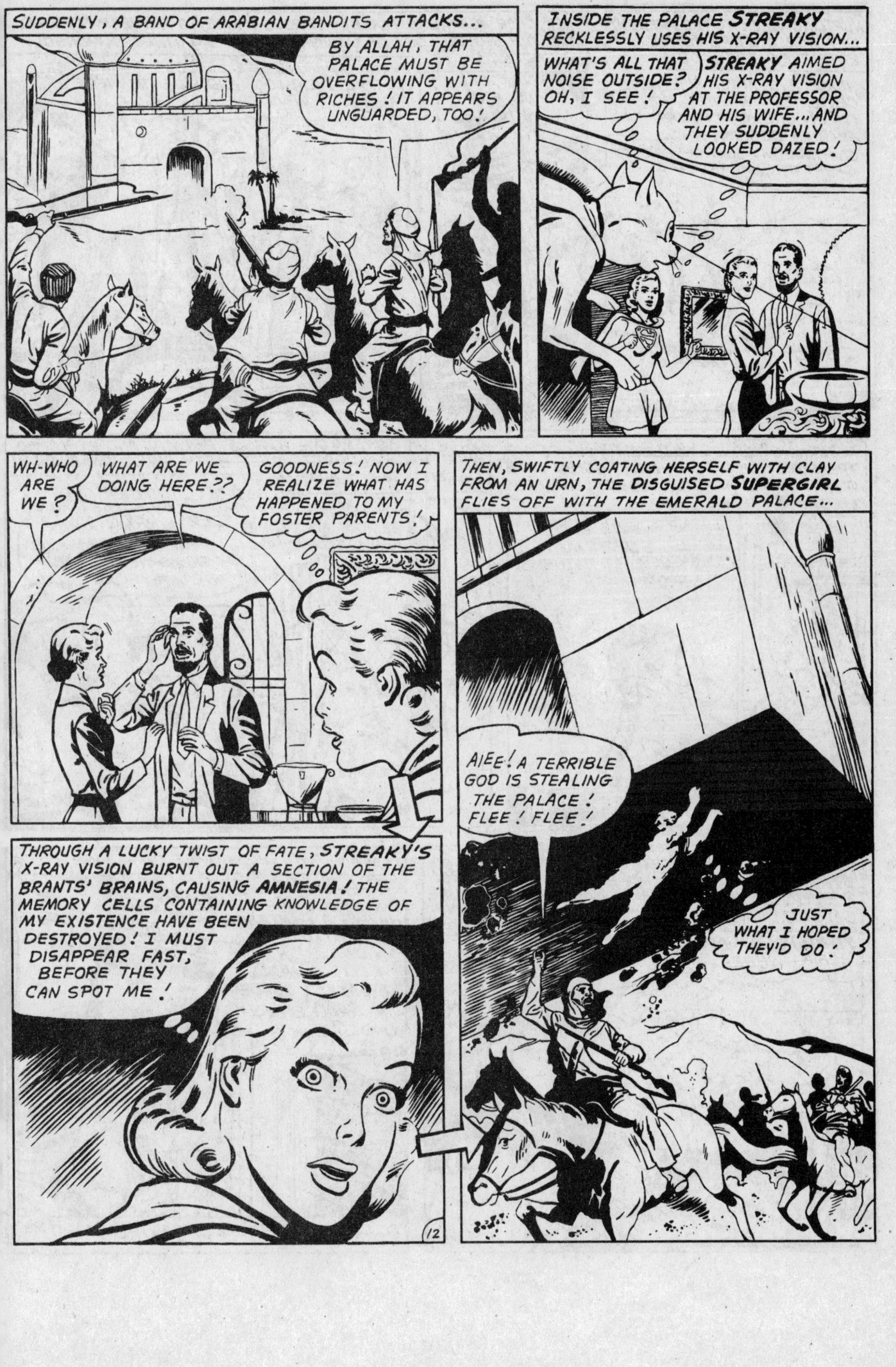
SUDDENLY, A BAND OF ARABIAN BANDITS ATTACKS...
BY ALLAH, THAT PALACE MUST BE OVERFLOWING WITH RICHES! IT APPEARS UNGUARDED, TOO!
INSIDE THE PALACE STREAKY RECKLESSLY USES HIS X-RAY VISION...
WHAT'S ALL THAT NOISE OUTSIDE? OH, I SEE!
STREAKY AIMED HIS X-RAY VISION AT THE PROFESSOR AND HIS WIFE...AND THEY SUDDENLY LOOKED DAZED!
WH-WHO ARE WE?
WHAT ARE WE DOING HERE??
GOODNESS! NOW I REALIZE WHAT HAS HAPPENED TO MY FOSTER PARENTS!
THROUGH A LUCKY TWIST OF FATE, STREAKY'S X-RAY VISION BURNT OUT A SECTION OF THE BRANTS' BRAINS, CAUSING AMNESIA! THE MEMORY CELLS CONTAINING KNOWLEDGE OF MY EXISTENCE HAVE BEEN DESTROYED! I MUST DISAPPEAR FAST, BEFORE THEY CAN SPOT ME!
12
THEN, SWIFTLY COATING HERSELF WITH CLAY FROM AN URN, THE DISGUISED SUPERGIRL FLIES OFF WITH THE EMERALD PALACE...
AIEE! A TERRIBLE GOD IS STEALING THE PALACE! FLEE! FLEE!
JUST WHAT I HOPED THEY'D DO!

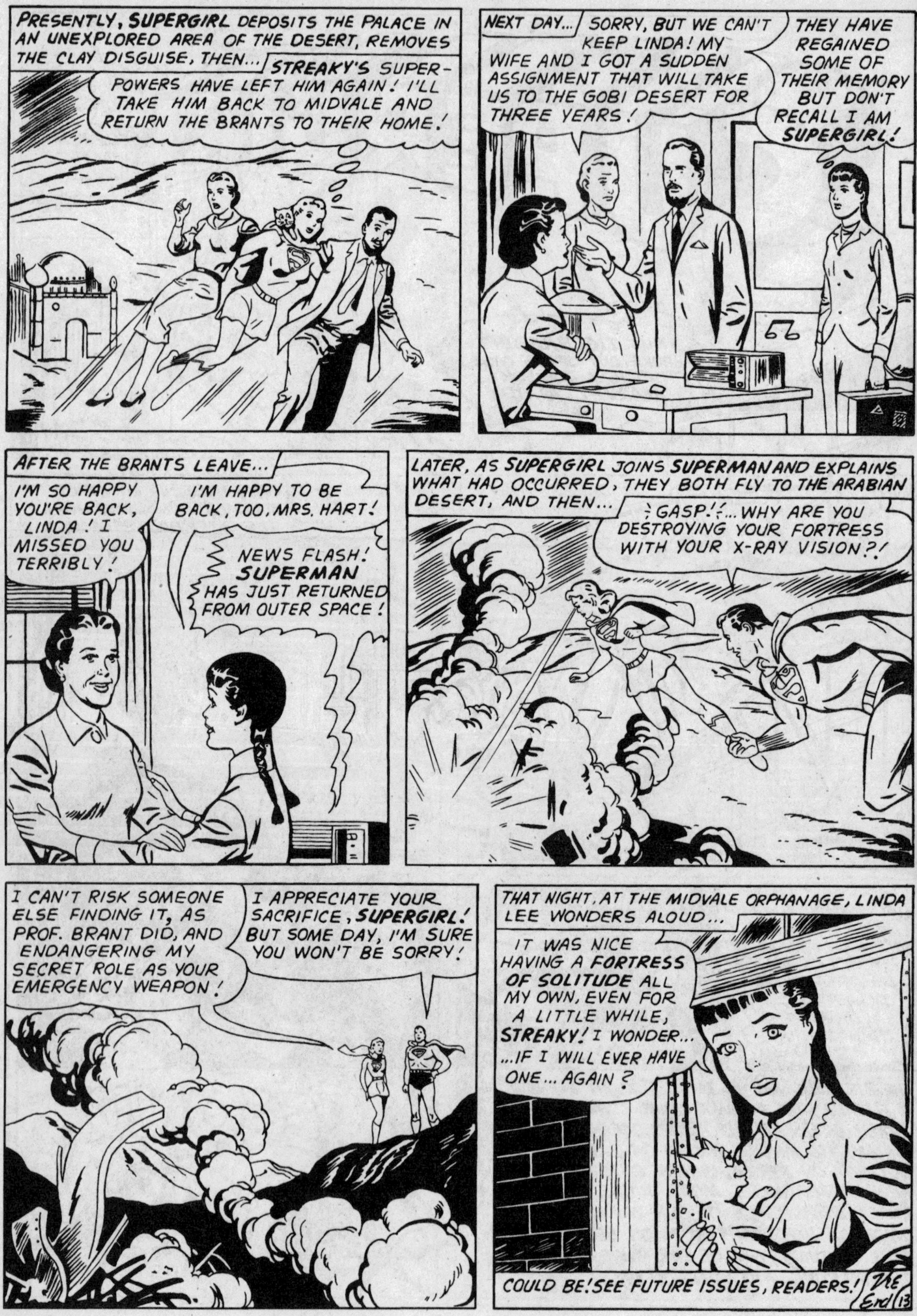
PRESENTLY, SUPERGIRL DEPOSITS THE PALACE IN AN UNEXPLORED AREA OF THE DESERT, REMOVES THE CLAY DISGUISE, THEN...
STREAKY'S SUPER-POWERS HAVE LEFT HIM AGAIN! I'LL TAKE HIM BACK TO MIDVALE AND RETURN THE BRANTS TO THEIR HOME!
NEXT DAY...
SORRY, BUT WE CAN'T KEEP LINDA! MY WIFE AND I GOT A SUDDEN ASSIGNMENT THAT WILL TAKE US TO THE GOBI DESERT FOR THREE YEARS!
THEY HAVE REGAINED SOME OF THEIR MEMORY BUT DON'T RECALL I AM SUPERGIRL!
AFTER THE BRANTS LEAVE...
I'M SO HAPPY YOU'RE BACK, LINDA! I MISSED YOU TERRIBLY!
I'M HAPPY TO BE BACK, TOO, MRS. HART!
NEWS FLASH! SUPERMAN HAS JUST RETURNED FROM OUTER SPACE!
LATER, AS SUPERGIRL JOINS SUPERMAN AND EXPLAINS WHAT HAD OCCURRED, THEY BOTH FLY TO THE ARABIAN DESERT, AND THEN...
¡GASP!¡... WHY ARE YOU DESTROYING YOUR FORTRESS WITH YOUR X-RAY VISION?!
I CAN'T RISK SOMEONE ELSE FINDING IT, AS PROF. BRANT DID, AND ENDANGERING MY SECRET ROLE AS YOUR EMERGENCY WEAPON!
I APPRECIATE YOUR SACRIFICE, SUPERGIRL! BUT SOME DAY, I'M SURE YOU WON'T BE SORRY!
THAT NIGHT, AT THE MIDVALE ORPHANAGE, LINDA LEE WONDERS ALOUD...
IT WAS NICE HAVING A FORTRESS OF SOLITUDE ALL MY OWN, EVEN FOR A LITTLE WHILE, STREAKY! I WONDER... ...IF I WILL EVER HAVE ONE... AGAIN?
COULD BE! SEE FUTURE ISSUES, READERS!
The End
13

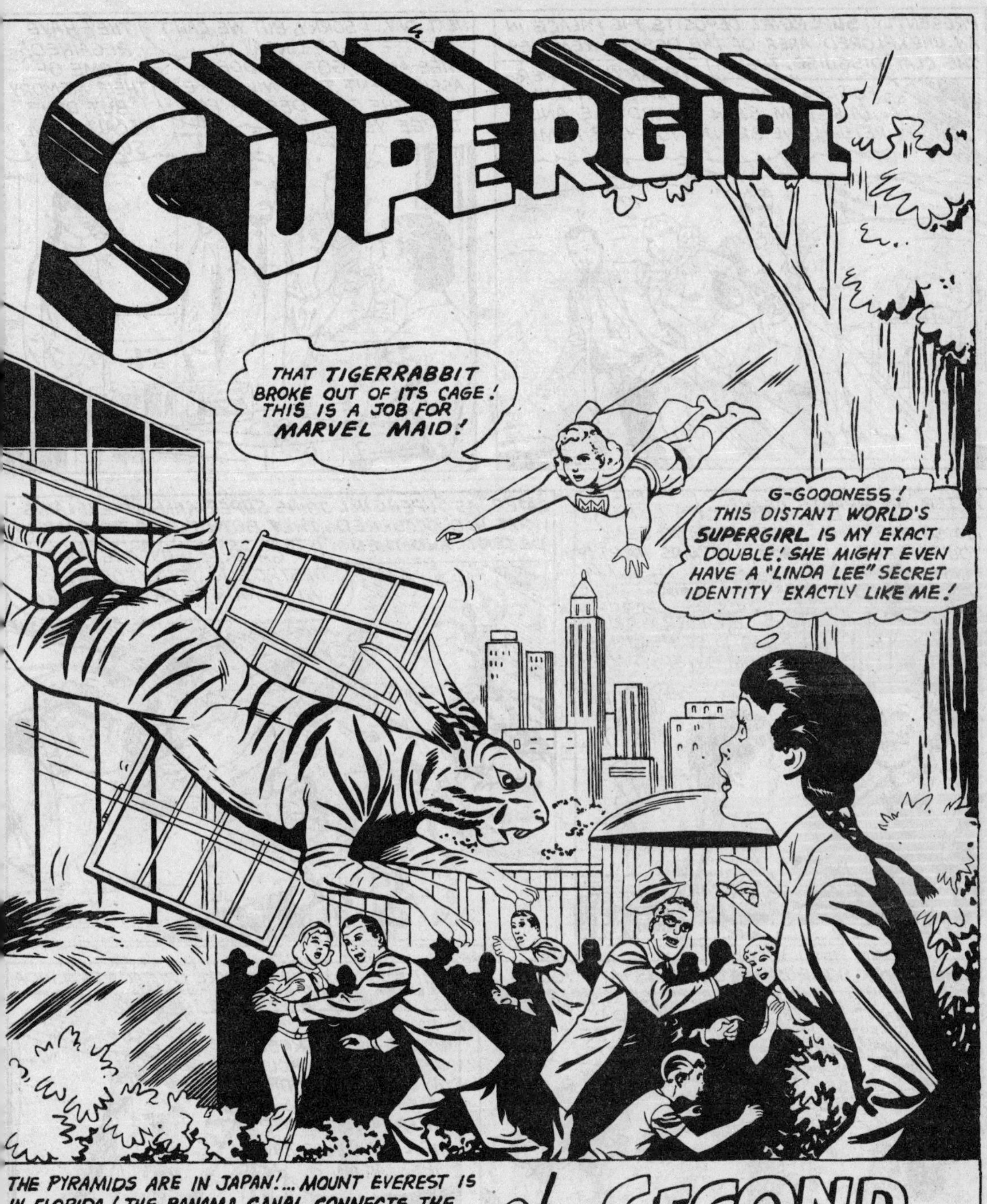
SUPERGIRL
THAT TIGERRABBIT BROKE OUT OF ITS CAGE! THIS IS A JOB FOR MARVEL MAID!
G-GOODNESS! THIS DISTANT WORLD'S SUPERGIRL IS MY EXACT DOUBLE! SHE MIGHT EVEN HAVE A "LINDA LEE" SECRET IDENTITY EXACTLY LIKE ME!
THE PYRAMIDS ARE IN JAPAN!... MOUNT EVEREST IS IN FLORIDA! THE PANAMA CANAL CONNECTS THE INDIAN OCEAN TO THE ARCTIC OCEAN! THESE STATEMENTS MAY BE WRONG ON EARTH... BUT NOT ON TERRA, WHERE, OUTSIDE OF A FEW DIFFERENCES, MOST THINGS ARE AN EXACT DUPLICATE OF OUR WORLD! AND WHEN AN IMPORTANT MISSION SENDS SUPERGIRL TO THAT "TWIN" OF EARTH, WE ENCOUNTER THE AMAZING PHENOMENON OF...
The SECOND SUPERGIRL!

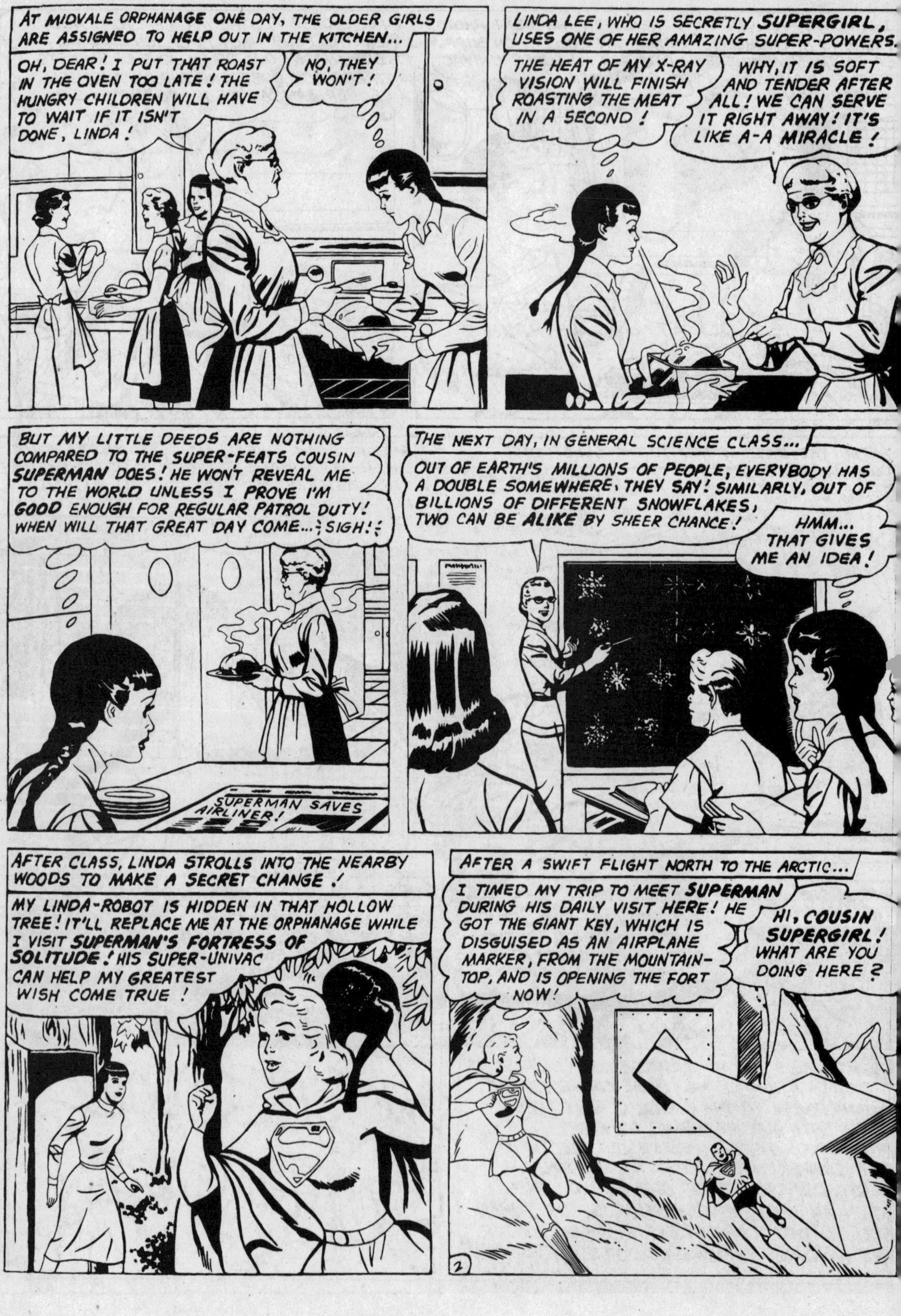
AT MIDVALE ORPHANAGE ONE DAY, THE OLDER GIRLS ARE ASSIGNED TO HELP OUT IN THE KITCHEN...
OH, DEAR! I PUT THAT ROAST IN THE OVEN TOO LATE! THE HUNGRY CHILDREN WILL HAVE TO WAIT IF IT ISN'T DONE, LINDA!
NO, THEY WON'T!
LINDA LEE, WHO IS SECRETLY SUPERGIRL, USES ONE OF HER AMAZING SUPER-POWERS.
THE HEAT OF MY X-RAY VISION WILL FINISH ROASTING THE MEAT IN A SECOND!
WHY, IT IS SOFT AND TENDER AFTER ALL! WE CAN SERVE IT RIGHT AWAY! IT'S LIKE A-A MIRACLE!
BUT MY LITTLE DEEDS ARE NOTHING COMPARED TO THE SUPER-FEATS COUSIN SUPERMAN DOES! HE WON'T REVEAL ME TO THE WORLD UNLESS I PROVE I'M GOOD ENOUGH FOR REGULAR PATROL DUTY! WHEN WILL THAT GREAT DAY COME... SIGH!
SUPERMAN SAVES AIRLINER!
THE NEXT DAY, IN GENERAL SCIENCE CLASS...
OUT OF EARTH'S MILLIONS OF PEOPLE, EVERYBODY HAS A DOUBLE SOMEWHERE, THEY SAY! SIMILARLY, OUT OF BILLIONS OF DIFFERENT SNOWFLAKES, TWO CAN BE ALIKE BY SHEER CHANCE!
HMM... THAT GIVES ME AN IDEA!
AFTER CLASS, LINDA STROLLS INTO THE NEARBY WOODS TO MAKE A SECRET CHANGE!
MY LINDA-ROBOT IS HIDDEN IN THAT HOLLOW TREE! IT'LL REPLACE ME AT THE ORPHANAGE WHILE I VISIT SUPERMAN'S FORTRESS OF SOLITUDE! HIS SUPER-UNIVAC CAN HELP MY GREATEST WISH COME TRUE!
AFTER A SWIFT FLIGHT NORTH TO THE ARCTIC...
I TIMED MY TRIP TO MEET SUPERMAN DURING HIS DAILY VISIT HERE! HE GOT THE GIANT KEY, WHICH IS DISGUISED AS AN AIRPLANE MARKER, FROM THE MOUNTAIN-TOP, AND IS OPENING THE FORT NOW!
HI, COUSIN SUPERGIRL! WHAT ARE YOU DOING HERE?
2

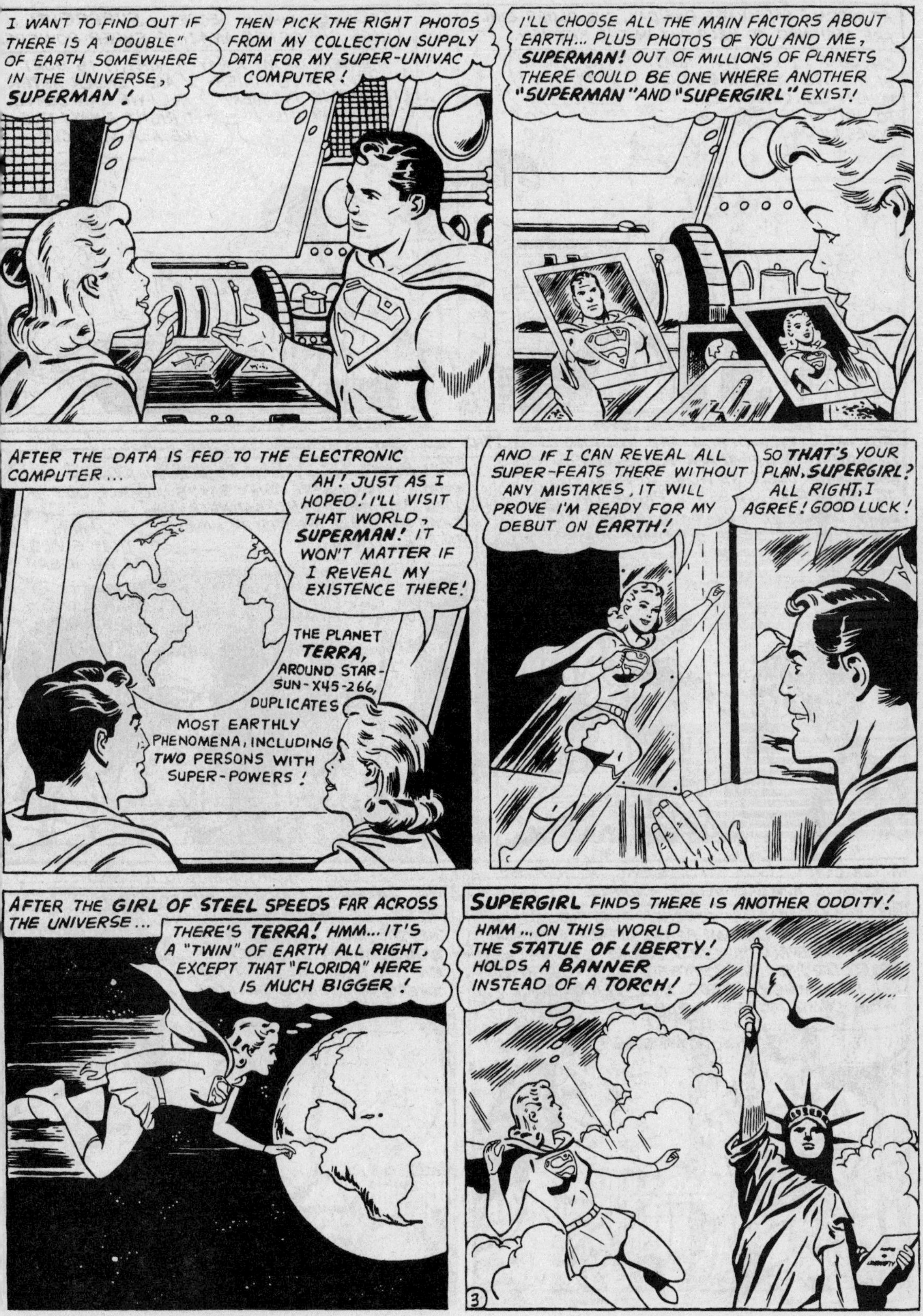
I WANT TO FIND OUT IF THERE IS A "DOUBLE" OF EARTH SOMEWHERE IN THE UNIVERSE, SUPERMAN!
THEN PICK THE RIGHT PHOTOS FROM MY COLLECTION SUPPLY DATA FOR MY SUPER-UNIVAC COMPUTER!
I'LL CHOOSE ALL THE MAIN FACTORS ABOUT EARTH... PLUS PHOTOS OF YOU AND ME, SUPERMAN! OUT OF MILLIONS OF PLANETS THERE COULD BE ONE WHERE ANOTHER "SUPERMAN" AND "SUPERGIRL" EXIST!
AFTER THE DATA IS FED TO THE ELECTRONIC COMPUTER...
AH! JUST AS I HOPED! I'LL VISIT THAT WORLD, SUPERMAN! IT WON'T MATTER IF I REVEAL MY EXISTENCE THERE!
THE PLANET TERRA, AROUND STAR-SUN-X45-266, DUPLICATES MOST EARTHLY PHENOMENA, INCLUDING TWO PERSONS WITH SUPER-POWERS!
AND IF I CAN REVEAL ALL SUPER-FEATS THERE WITHOUT ANY MISTAKES, IT WILL PROVE I'M READY FOR MY DEBUT ON EARTH!
SO THAT'S YOUR PLAN, SUPERGIRL? ALL RIGHT, I AGREE! GOOD LUCK!
AFTER THE GIRL OF STEEL SPEEDS FAR ACROSS THE UNIVERSE...
THERE'S TERRA! HMM... IT'S A "TWIN" OF EARTH ALL RIGHT, EXCEPT THAT "FLORIDA" HERE IS MUCH BIGGER!
SUPERGIRL FINDS THERE IS ANOTHER ODDITY!
HMM... ON THIS WORLD THE STATUE OF LIBERTY! HOLDS A BANNER INSTEAD OF A TORCH!
3

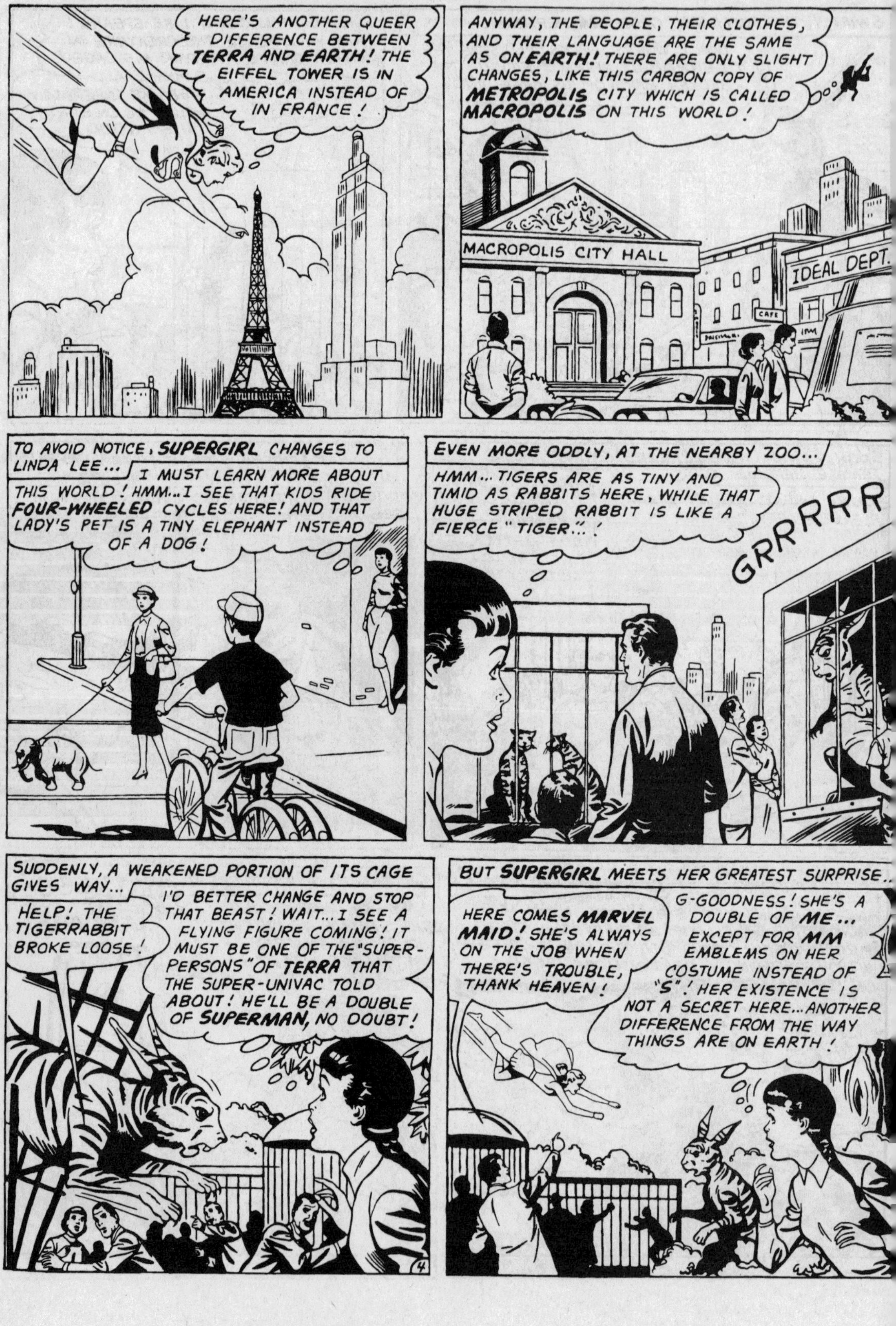
HERE'S ANOTHER QUEER DIFFERENCE BETWEEN TERRA AND EARTH! THE EIFFEL TOWER IS IN AMERICA INSTEAD OF IN FRANCE!
ANYWAY, THE PEOPLE, THEIR CLOTHES, AND THEIR LANGUAGE ARE THE SAME AS ON EARTH! THERE ARE ONLY SLIGHT CHANGES, LIKE THIS CARBON COPY OF METROPOLIS CITY WHICH IS CALLED MACROPOLIS ON THIS WORLD!
MACROPOLIS CITY HALL
IDEAL DEPT.
CAFE
TO AVOID NOTICE, SUPERGIRL CHANGES TO LINDA LEE...
I MUST LEARN MORE ABOUT THIS WORLD! HMM...I SEE THAT KIDS RIDE FOUR-WHEELED CYCLES HERE! AND THAT LADY'S PET IS A TINY ELEPHANT INSTEAD OF A DOG!
EVEN MORE ODDLY, AT THE NEARBY ZOO...
HMM... TIGERS ARE AS TINY AND TIMID AS RABBITS HERE, WHILE THAT HUGE STRIPED RABBIT IS LIKE A FIERCE "TIGER"...!
GRRRRR
SUDDENLY, A WEAKENED PORTION OF ITS CAGE GIVES WAY...
HELP! THE TIGERRABBIT BROKE LOOSE!
I'D BETTER CHANGE AND STOP THAT BEAST! WAIT...I SEE A FLYING FIGURE COMING! IT MUST BE ONE OF THE "SUPER-PERSONS" OF TERRA THAT THE SUPER-UNIVAC TOLD ABOUT! HE'LL BE A DOUBLE OF SUPERMAN, NO DOUBT!
4
BUT SUPERGIRL MEETS HER GREATEST SURPRISE...
HERE COMES MARVEL MAID! SHE'S ALWAYS ON THE JOB WHEN THERE'S TROUBLE, THANK HEAVEN!
G-GOODNESS! SHE'S A DOUBLE OF ME... EXCEPT FOR MM EMBLEMS ON HER COSTUME INSTEAD OF "S"! HER EXISTENCE IS NOT A SECRET HERE...ANOTHER DIFFERENCE FROM THE WAY THINGS ARE ON EARTH!

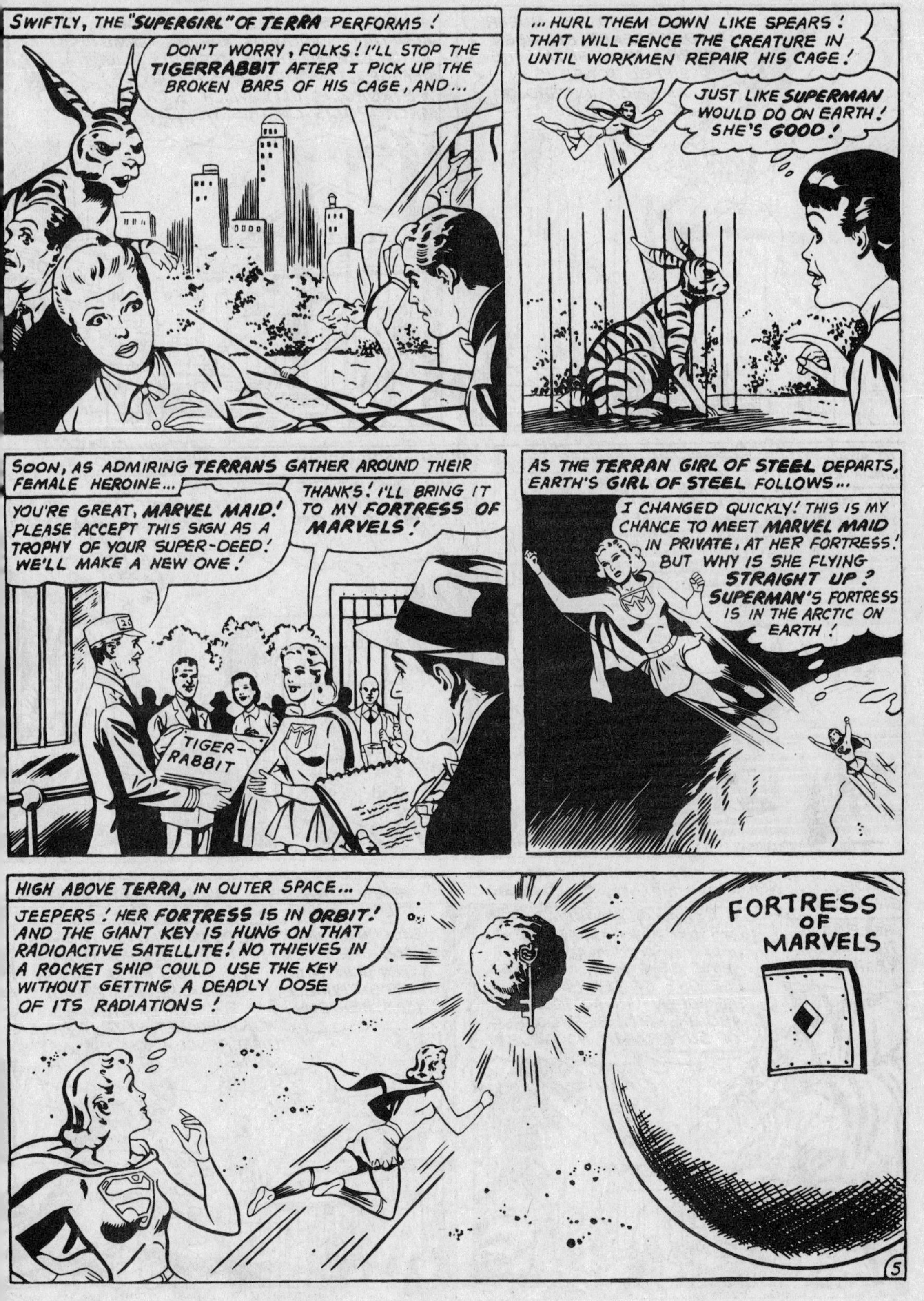
SWIFTLY, THE "SUPERGIRL" OF TERRA PERFORMS!
DON'T WORRY, FOLKS! I'LL STOP THE TIGERRABBIT AFTER I PICK UP THE BROKEN BARS OF HIS CAGE, AND...
...HURL THEM DOWN LIKE SPEARS! THAT WILL FENCE THE CREATURE IN UNTIL WORKMEN REPAIR HIS CAGE!
JUST LIKE SUPERMAN WOULD DO ON EARTH! SHE'S GOOD!
SOON, AS ADMIRING TERRANS GATHER AROUND THEIR FEMALE HEROINE...
YOU'RE GREAT, MARVEL MAID! PLEASE ACCEPT THIS SIGN AS A TROPHY OF YOUR SUPER-DEED! WE'LL MAKE A NEW ONE!
THANKS! I'LL BRING IT TO MY FORTRESS OF MARVELS!
TIGER-RABBIT
AS THE TERRAN GIRL OF STEEL DEPARTS, EARTH'S GIRL OF STEEL FOLLOWS...
I CHANGED QUICKLY! THIS IS MY CHANCE TO MEET MARVEL MAID IN PRIVATE, AT HER FORTRESS! BUT WHY IS SHE FLYING STRAIGHT UP? SUPERMAN'S FORTRESS IS IN THE ARCTIC ON EARTH!
HIGH ABOVE TERRA, IN OUTER SPACE...
JEEPERS! HER FORTRESS IS IN ORBIT! AND THE GIANT KEY IS HUNG ON THAT RADIOACTIVE SATELLITE! NO THIEVES IN A ROCKET SHIP COULD USE THE KEY WITHOUT GETTING A DEADLY DOSE OF ITS RADIATIONS!
FORTRESS OF MARVELS
5

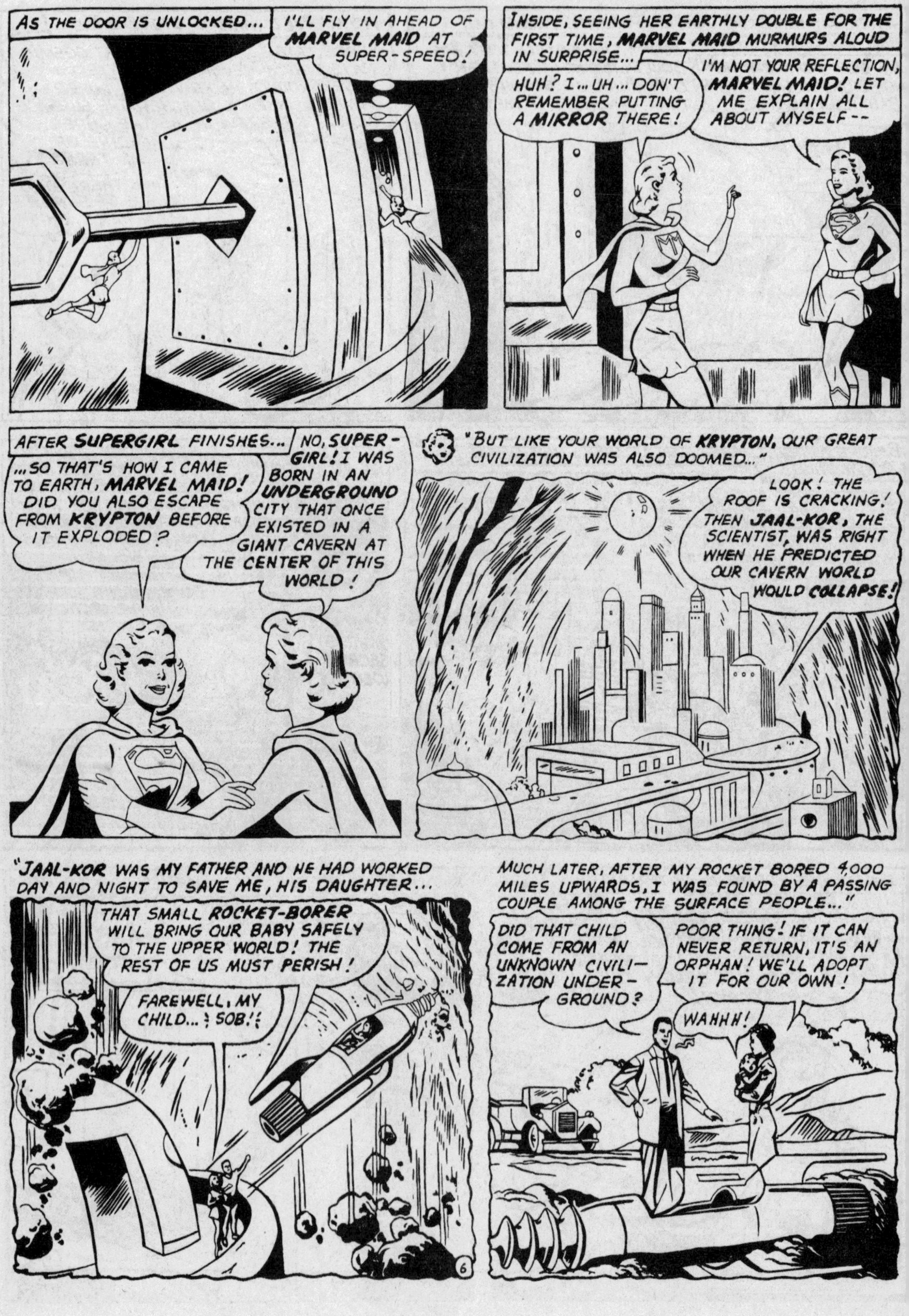
AS THE DOOR IS UNLOCKED...
I'LL FLY IN AHEAD OF MARVEL MAID AT SUPER-SPEED!
INSIDE, SEEING HER EARTHLY DOUBLE FOR THE FIRST TIME, MARVEL MAID MURMURS ALOUD IN SURPRISE...
HUH? I...UH...DON'T REMEMBER PUTTING A MIRROR THERE!
I'M NOT YOUR REFLECTION, MARVEL MAID! LET ME EXPLAIN ALL ABOUT MYSELF--
AFTER SUPERGIRL FINISHES...
...SO THAT'S HOW I CAME TO EARTH, MARVEL MAID! DID YOU ALSO ESCAPE FROM KRYPTON BEFORE IT EXPLODED?
NO, SUPERGIRL! I WAS BORN IN AN UNDERGROUND CITY THAT ONCE EXISTED IN A GIANT CAVERN AT THE CENTER OF THIS WORLD!
"BUT LIKE YOUR WORLD OF KRYPTON, OUR GREAT CIVILIZATION WAS ALSO DOOMED..."
LOOK! THE ROOF IS CRACKING! THEN JAAL-KOR, THE SCIENTIST, WAS RIGHT WHEN HE PREDICTED OUR CAVERN WORLD WOULD COLLAPSE!
"JAAL-KOR WAS MY FATHER AND HE HAD WORKED DAY AND NIGHT TO SAVE ME, HIS DAUGHTER...
THAT SMALL ROCKET-BORER WILL BRING OUR BABY SAFELY TO THE UPPER WORLD! THE REST OF US MUST PERISH!
FAREWELL, MY CHILD...{SOB!}
6
MUCH LATER, AFTER MY ROCKET BORED 4,000 MILES UPWARDS, I WAS FOUND BY A PASSING COUPLE AMONG THE SURFACE PEOPLE..."
DID THAT CHILD COME FROM AN UNKNOWN CIVILIZATION UNDERGROUND?
POOR THING! IF IT CAN NEVER RETURN, IT'S AN ORPHAN! WE'LL ADOPT IT FOR OUR OWN!
WAHHH!

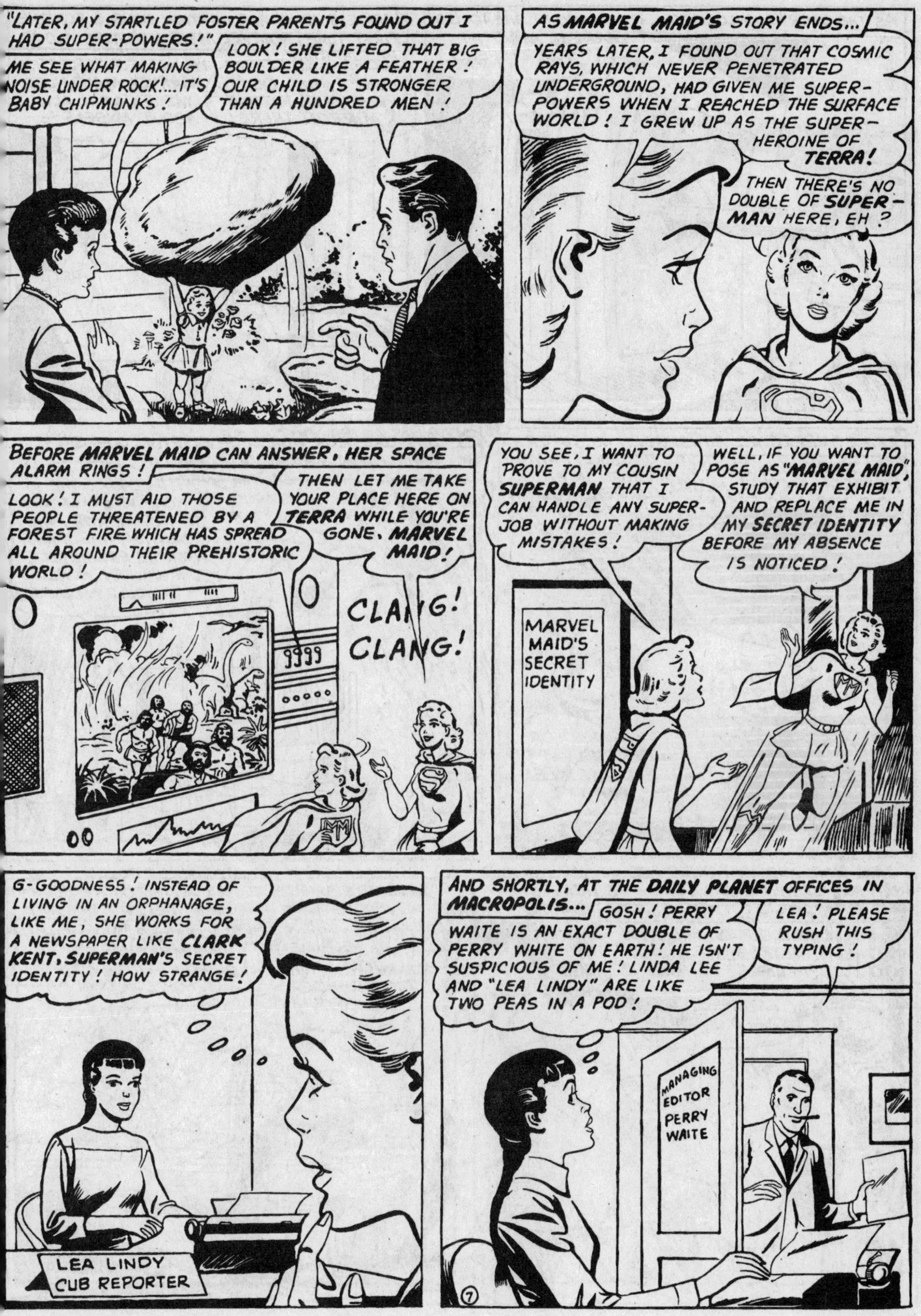
"LATER, MY STARTLED FOSTER PARENTS FOUND OUT I HAD SUPER-POWERS!"
ME SEE WHAT MAKING NOISE UNDER ROCK!...IT'S BABY CHIPMUNKS!
LOOK! SHE LIFTED THAT BIG BOULDER LIKE A FEATHER! OUR CHILD IS STRONGER THAN A HUNDRED MEN!
AS MARVEL MAID'S STORY ENDS...
YEARS LATER, I FOUND OUT THAT COSMIC RAYS, WHICH NEVER PENETRATED UNDERGROUND, HAD GIVEN ME SUPER-POWERS WHEN I REACHED THE SURFACE WORLD! I GREW UP AS THE SUPER-HEROINE OF TERRA!
THEN THERE'S NO DOUBLE OF SUPERMAN HERE, EH?
BEFORE MARVEL MAID CAN ANSWER, HER SPACE ALARM RINGS!
LOOK! I MUST AID THOSE PEOPLE THREATENED BY A FOREST FIRE WHICH HAS SPREAD ALL AROUND THEIR PREHISTORIC WORLD!
THEN LET ME TAKE YOUR PLACE HERE ON TERRA WHILE YOU'RE GONE, MARVEL MAID!
CLANG! CLANG!
YOU SEE, I WANT TO PROVE TO MY COUSIN SUPERMAN THAT I CAN HANDLE ANY SUPER-JOB WITHOUT MAKING MISTAKES!
WELL, IF YOU WANT TO POSE AS "MARVEL MAID", STUDY THAT EXHIBIT AND REPLACE ME IN MY SECRET IDENTITY BEFORE MY ABSENCE IS NOTICED!
MARVEL MAID'S SECRET IDENTITY
G-GOODNESS! INSTEAD OF LIVING IN AN ORPHANAGE, LIKE ME, SHE WORKS FOR A NEWSPAPER LIKE CLARK KENT, SUPERMAN'S SECRET IDENTITY! HOW STRANGE!
LEA LINDY CUB REPORTER
AND SHORTLY, AT THE DAILY PLANET OFFICES IN MACROPOLIS...
GOSH! PERRY WAITE IS AN EXACT DOUBLE OF PERRY WHITE ON EARTH! HE ISN'T SUSPICIOUS OF ME! LINDA LEE AND "LEA LINDY" ARE LIKE TWO PEAS IN A POD!
LEA! PLEASE RUSH THIS TYPING!
MANAGING EDITOR PERRY WAITE
7

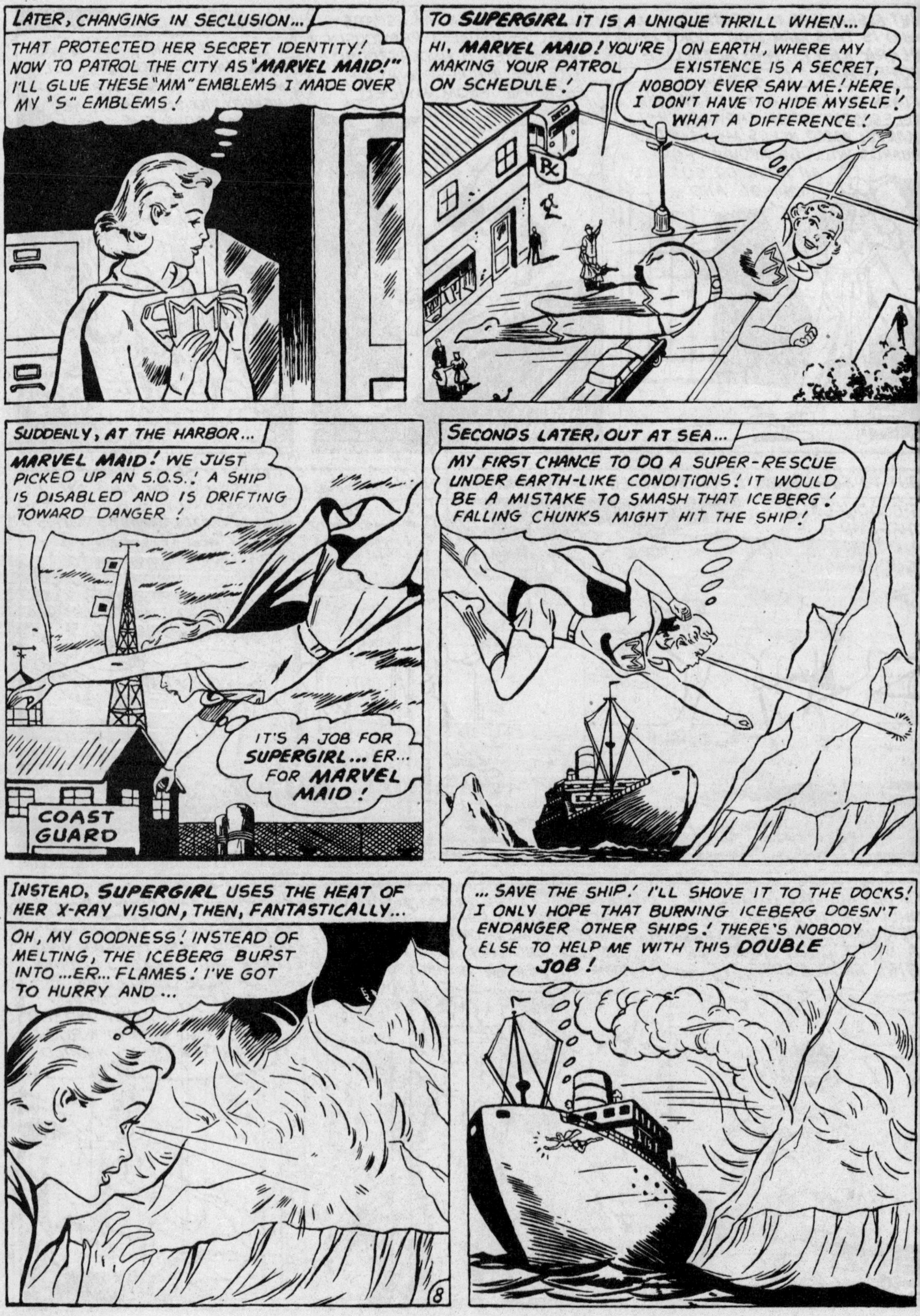
LATER, CHANGING IN SECLUSION...
THAT PROTECTED HER SECRET IDENTITY! NOW TO PATROL THE CITY AS "MARVEL MAID!" I'LL GLUE THESE "MM" EMBLEMS I MADE OVER MY "S" EMBLEMS!
TO SUPERGIRL IT IS A UNIQUE THRILL WHEN...
HI, MARVEL MAID! YOU'RE MAKING YOUR PATROL ON SCHEDULE!
ON EARTH, WHERE MY EXISTENCE IS A SECRET, NOBODY EVER SAW ME! HERE, I DON'T HAVE TO HIDE MYSELF! WHAT A DIFFERENCE!
Rx
SUDDENLY, AT THE HARBOR...
MARVEL MAID! WE JUST PICKED UP AN S.O.S.! A SHIP IS DISABLED AND IS DRIFTING TOWARD DANGER!
IT'S A JOB FOR SUPERGIRL... ER... FOR MARVEL MAID!
COAST GUARD
SECONDS LATER, OUT AT SEA...
MY FIRST CHANCE TO DO A SUPER-RESCUE UNDER EARTH-LIKE CONDITIONS! IT WOULD BE A MISTAKE TO SMASH THAT ICEBERG! FALLING CHUNKS MIGHT HIT THE SHIP!
INSTEAD, SUPERGIRL USES THE HEAT OF HER X-RAY VISION, THEN, FANTASTICALLY...
OH, MY GOODNESS! INSTEAD OF MELTING, THE ICEBERG BURST INTO ...ER... FLAMES! I'VE GOT TO HURRY AND ...
8
... SAVE THE SHIP! I'LL SHOVE IT TO THE DOCKS! I ONLY HOPE THAT BURNING ICEBERG DOESN'T ENDANGER OTHER SHIPS! THERE'S NOBODY ELSE TO HELP ME WITH THIS DOUBLE JOB!

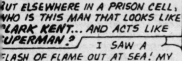

BUT ELSEWHERE IN A PRISON CELL, WHO IS THIS MAN THAT LOOKS LIKE CLARK KENT... AND ACTS LIKE SUPERMAN?

I SAW A FLASH OF FLAME OUT AT SEA! MY TELESCOPIC VISION SHOWED THAT MARVEL MAID NEEDS MY HELP! NO GUARDS WILL BE AROUND FOR AN HOUR OR SO! I'LL CHANGE AND...

...LEAVE THROUGH MY ESCAPE TUNNEL AS USUAL! I PREVIOUSLY SUPER-BORED IT UNDERGROUND! IT'S THE HANDIEST WAY OF "ESCAPING" FROM MY CELL!

MOMENTS LATER...

I LEFT MY TUNNEL AND BORED UP AT THE SEA BOTTOM! I'LL MAKE SURE NO SHIPS ARE NEARBY TO SEE ME IN ACTION ABOVE THE WATER'S SURFACE!

BUT TO **SUPERGIRL'S** ASTONISHMENT, RETURNING TO FINISH HER JOB...

G-GOODNESS! THAT MAN IS A-- A **DOUBLE** OF **SUPERMAN**!

SHOVING THE ICEBERG UNDERWATER WILL QUENCH THE FLAMES, **MARVEL MAID**! BUT YOU'RE SLIPPING, COUSIN! COULDN'T YOU TELL THIS WAS A **FALSE** ICEBERG MADE OF FLAMMABLE SALTS THAT CRYSTALLIZED OUT OF THE SEA WATER?

I'M NOT **MARVEL MAID**! I'M ONLY SUBSTITUTING FOR HER WHILE SHE'S AWAY ON A SPACE JOB! I'M **SUPERGIRL** FROM **EARTH**!

GREAT SCOTT! YOU'RE AN EXACT DOUBLE OF MY COUSIN! TELL ME ALL ABOUT YOURSELF AND WHY YOU CAME TO **TERRA**?

⑨

AFTER **SUPERGIRL** EXPLAINS...

BUT **MARVEL MAID** DIDN'T TELL ME ABOUT **YOU**! HOW DID YOU ESCAPE THE DESTRUCTION OF YOUR UNDERGROUND CIVILI- ZATION LONG AGO?

MY FATHER, WHO WAS **JAAL KOR'S** BROTHER, ALSO KNEW OF THE COMING DISASTER AND SENT ME AWAY IN A **ROCK PENETRATOR** AS A CHILD!

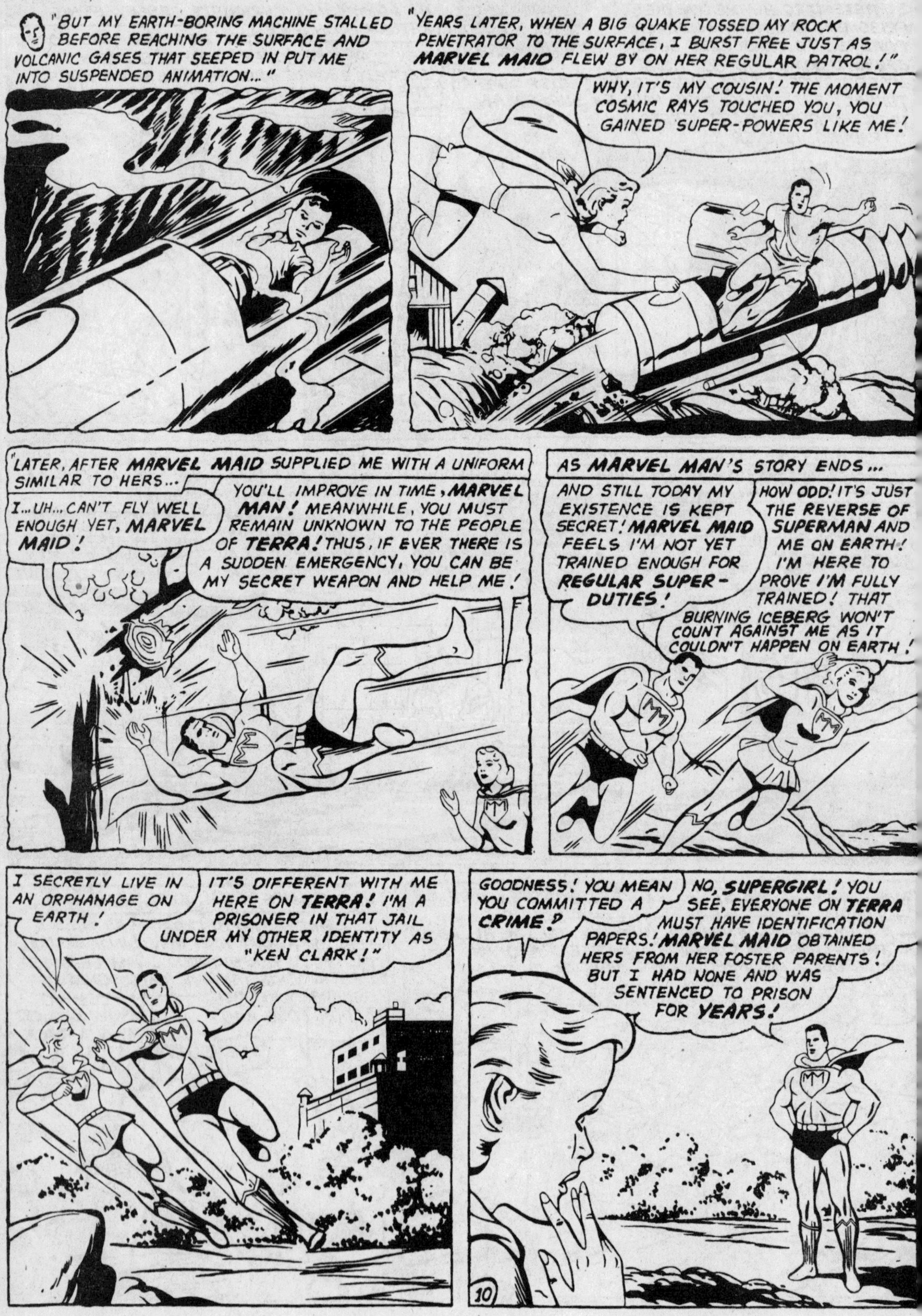
"BUT MY EARTH-BORING MACHINE STALLED BEFORE REACHING THE SURFACE AND VOLCANIC GASES THAT SEEPED IN PUT ME INTO SUSPENDED ANIMATION..."
"YEARS LATER, WHEN A BIG QUAKE TOSSED MY ROCK PENETRATOR TO THE SURFACE, I BURST FREE JUST AS MARVEL MAID FLEW BY ON HER REGULAR PATROL!"
WHY, IT'S MY COUSIN! THE MOMENT COSMIC RAYS TOUCHED YOU, YOU GAINED SUPER-POWERS LIKE ME!
"LATER, AFTER MARVEL MAID SUPPLIED ME WITH A UNIFORM SIMILAR TO HERS...
I...UH...CAN'T FLY WELL ENOUGH YET, MARVEL MAID!
YOU'LL IMPROVE IN TIME, MARVEL MAN! MEANWHILE, YOU MUST REMAIN UNKNOWN TO THE PEOPLE OF TERRA! THUS, IF EVER THERE IS A SUDDEN EMERGENCY, YOU CAN BE MY SECRET WEAPON AND HELP ME!
AS MARVEL MAN'S STORY ENDS...
AND STILL TODAY MY EXISTENCE IS KEPT SECRET! MARVEL MAID FEELS I'M NOT YET TRAINED ENOUGH FOR REGULAR SUPER-DUTIES!
HOW ODD! IT'S JUST THE REVERSE OF SUPERMAN AND ME ON EARTH! I'M HERE TO PROVE I'M FULLY TRAINED! THAT BURNING ICEBERG WON'T COUNT AGAINST ME AS IT COULDN'T HAPPEN ON EARTH!
I SECRETLY LIVE IN AN ORPHANAGE ON EARTH!
IT'S DIFFERENT WITH ME HERE ON TERRA! I'M A PRISONER IN THAT JAIL UNDER MY OTHER IDENTITY AS "KEN CLARK!"
GOODNESS! YOU MEAN YOU COMMITTED A CRIME?
NO, SUPERGIRL! YOU SEE, EVERYONE ON TERRA MUST HAVE IDENTIFICATION PAPERS! MARVEL MAID OBTAINED HERS FROM HER FOSTER PARENTS! BUT I HAD NONE AND WAS SENTENCED TO PRISON FOR YEARS!
10

I PRETEND TO BE THE "WEAKEST" PRISONER, TO COVER MY SUPER-POWERS! TO DO SECRET SUPER-JOBS, I COME AND GO FROM MY CELL THROUGH MY UNDERGROUND TUNNEL! BUT I MUST AVOID PAROLE UNTIL *MARVEL MAID* AGREES MY TRAINING IS OVER!

JUST LIKE *SUPERMAN* HAS ME AVOID ADOPTION ON EARTH!

AS *SUPERGIRL* CURIOUSLY OBSERVES HIS RETURN TO HIS CELL... HE'S CHANGING TO KEN CLARK, PRISONER, AND COVERING HIS SECRET ESCAPE TUNNEL! I'LL MAKE SURE THE WARDEN ISN'T SUSPICIOUS OF HIM...

IN THE WARDEN'S OFFICE, SUPER-HEARING TIPS OFF *SUPERGIRL* THAT TROUBLE IS BREWING FOR KEN CLARK!

I'M NOT SURE IF MY NEW *MUSCLE SERUM* WILL WORK AND DOUBLE A MAN'S STRENGTH! I WANT TO CONDUCT EXPERIMENTS AT MY LAB WITH YOUR WEAKEST PRISONER, WARDEN!

HMM...THAT WOULD BE KEN CLARK, PROFESSOR!

OH, OH!

PSST! THERE'S KEN CLARK WORKING ON THE ROCK PILE! HE CAN HARDLY LIFT HIS SLEDGEHAMMER!

IF HE'S THE WEAKEST MAN, SET HIM FREE ON PAROLE! HE CAN STAY AT MY LABORATORY DURING THE INJECTIONS OF MY *MUSCLE SERUM!*

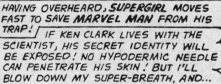

HAVING OVERHEARD, *SUPERGIRL* MOVES FAST TO SAVE *MARVEL MAN* FROM HIS TRAP!

IF KEN CLARK LIVES WITH THE SCIENTIST, HIS SECRET IDENTITY WILL BE EXPOSED! NO HYPODERMIC NEEDLE CAN PENETRATE HIS SKIN! BUT I'LL BLOW DOWN MY SUPER-BREATH, AND...

11

...MAKE KEN CLARK'S SLEDGEHAMMER BREAK A ROCK TO BITS!

WHY...ER...CLARK ISN'T AS WEAK AS I THOUGHT, PROFESSOR! PERHAPS HE'S BEEN EXERCISING DAILY, IN HIS CELL! WE'LL CHOOSE ANOTHER PRISONER!

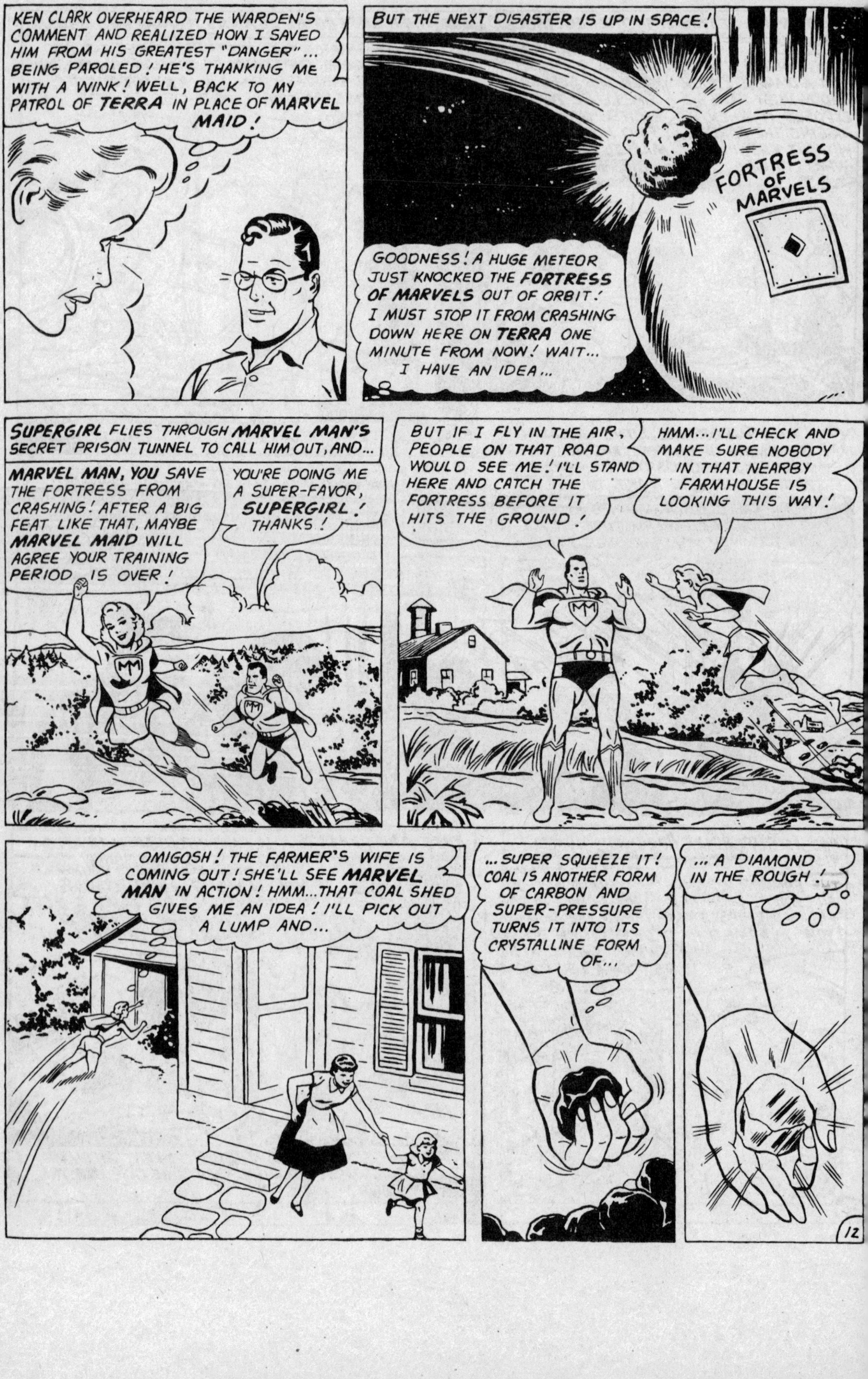
KEN CLARK OVERHEARD THE WARDEN'S COMMENT AND REALIZED HOW I SAVED HIM FROM HIS GREATEST "DANGER"... BEING PAROLED! HE'S THANKING ME WITH A WINK! WELL, BACK TO MY PATROL OF TERRA IN PLACE OF MARVEL MAID!
BUT THE NEXT DISASTER IS UP IN SPACE!
FORTRESS OF MARVELS
GOODNESS! A HUGE METEOR JUST KNOCKED THE FORTRESS OF MARVELS OUT OF ORBIT! I MUST STOP IT FROM CRASHING DOWN HERE ON TERRA ONE MINUTE FROM NOW! WAIT... I HAVE AN IDEA...
SUPERGIRL FLIES THROUGH MARVEL MAN'S SECRET PRISON TUNNEL TO CALL HIM OUT, AND...
MARVEL MAN, YOU SAVE THE FORTRESS FROM CRASHING! AFTER A BIG FEAT LIKE THAT, MAYBE MARVEL MAID WILL AGREE YOUR TRAINING PERIOD IS OVER!
YOU'RE DOING ME A SUPER-FAVOR, SUPERGIRL! THANKS!
BUT IF I FLY IN THE AIR, PEOPLE ON THAT ROAD WOULD SEE ME! I'LL STAND HERE AND CATCH THE FORTRESS BEFORE IT HITS THE GROUND!
HMM... I'LL CHECK AND MAKE SURE NOBODY IN THAT NEARBY FARMHOUSE IS LOOKING THIS WAY!
OMIGOSH! THE FARMER'S WIFE IS COMING OUT! SHE'LL SEE MARVEL MAN IN ACTION! HMM... THAT COAL SHED GIVES ME AN IDEA! I'LL PICK OUT A LUMP AND...
...SUPER SQUEEZE IT! COAL IS ANOTHER FORM OF CARBON AND SUPER-PRESSURE TURNS IT INTO ITS CRYSTALLINE FORM OF...
...A DIAMOND IN THE ROUGH!
12

AS *SUPERGIRL* LEAVES IT IN THE VEGETABLE GARDEN...

LOOK, CYNTHIA! IS THAT A DIAMOND? YOUR DADDY MUST HAVE EXPOSED IT WHEN DIGGING THE GARDEN, WITHOUT KNOWING WHAT IT WAS!

TRUST A *WOMAN* TO KNOW A DIAMOND WHEN SHE SEES ONE! SHE'LL BE TOO EXCITED OVER HER FIND NOW TO SEE *MARVEL MAN* ACROSS THE FIELD!

BUT WHEN *SUPERGIRL* RETURNS TO *MARVEL MAN*...

I...I COULDN'T CATCH THE FALLING FORTRESS, *SUPERGIRL*! I FEEL PAIN...¡GASP!...FROM THE REFLECTIONS OF THAT DIAMOND...WHICH WEAKENS ME!

HEAVENS! T-THEN DIAMONDS ARE YOUR *KRYPTONITE*!

"YES, *SUPERGIRL*... THE GREAT PRESSURE OF OUR COLLAPSING CAVERN FORMED DIAMONDS OUT OF CARBON, WHICH EXISTS IN MANY THINGS!"

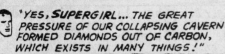

"THE CONCUSSION HURLED MANY SUPER-HARD DIAMONDS FROM THE CENTER OF *TERRA* TO THE SURFACE... BUT NEVER TO BE USED!"

SORRY, M'AM! YOU KNOW ALL DIAMOND JEWELRY IS *BANNED*! IT CAN BRING *DEATH* TO MARVEL MAID! WE WILL HAVE TO DESTROY YOUR NECKLACE!

AND AS *SUPERGIRL* USES HER SUPER-VISION...

THE FARMER WOMAN ISN'T *HAPPY* OVER HER FIND AS I FIRST THOUGHT, BUT, ALARMED!

POLICE? I FOUND A DIAMOND ON MY FARM! PLEASE SEND THE DIAMOND DEMOLITION SQUAD OVER! AND I ALSO HEARD A LOUD CRASH BEFORE!

YES...THE CRASH OF THE FORTRESS OF MARVELS!

I DIDN'T HELP YOU PROVE YOURSELF TO *MARVEL MAID*... NOR MYSELF TO *SUPERMAN*! OH, WHAT A MESS I'VE MADE OF THINGS HERE ON *TERRA*!

FOR THE OUTCOME OF *SUPERGIRL'S* GREAT DILEMMA, INCLUDING MORE AMAZING TWISTS OF *FATE*, SEE THE NEXT PAGE!

13

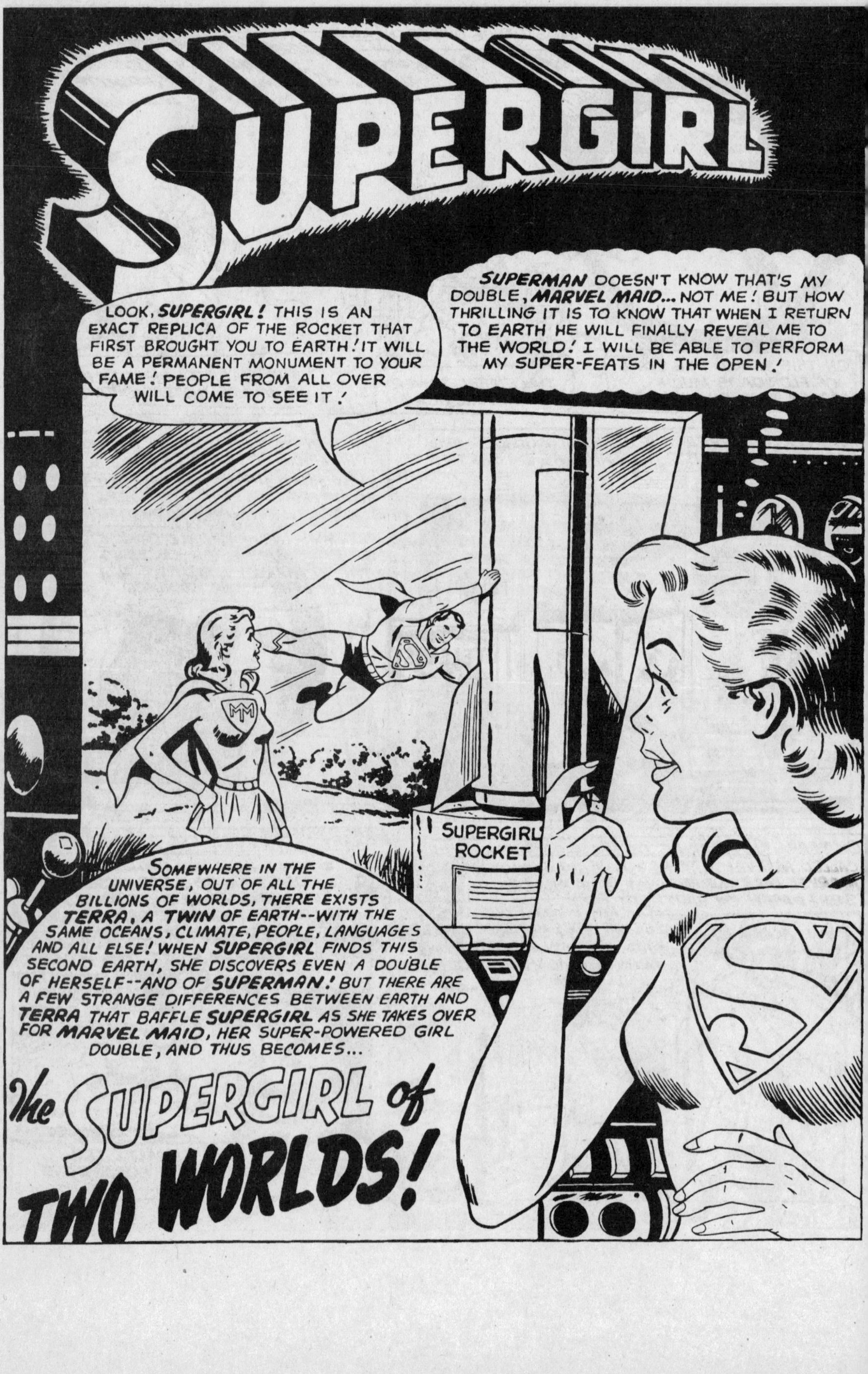
SUPERGIRL
LOOK, SUPERGIRL! THIS IS AN EXACT REPLICA OF THE ROCKET THAT FIRST BROUGHT YOU TO EARTH! IT WILL BE A PERMANENT MONUMENT TO YOUR FAME! PEOPLE FROM ALL OVER WILL COME TO SEE IT!
SUPERMAN DOESN'T KNOW THAT'S MY DOUBLE, MARVEL MAID... NOT ME! BUT HOW THRILLING IT IS TO KNOW THAT WHEN I RETURN TO EARTH HE WILL FINALLY REVEAL ME TO THE WORLD! I WILL BE ABLE TO PERFORM MY SUPER-FEATS IN THE OPEN!
SUPERGIRL ROCKET
SOMEWHERE IN THE UNIVERSE, OUT OF ALL THE BILLIONS OF WORLDS, THERE EXISTS TERRA, A TWIN OF EARTH--WITH THE SAME OCEANS, CLIMATE, PEOPLE, LANGUAGES AND ALL ELSE! WHEN SUPERGIRL FINDS THIS SECOND EARTH, SHE DISCOVERS EVEN A DOUBLE OF HERSELF--AND OF SUPERMAN! BUT THERE ARE A FEW STRANGE DIFFERENCES BETWEEN EARTH AND TERRA THAT BAFFLE SUPERGIRL AS SHE TAKES OVER FOR MARVEL MAID, HER SUPER-POWERED GIRL DOUBLE, AND THUS BECOMES...
The SUPERGIRL of TWO WORLDS!

FARAWAY IN ANOTHER SOLAR SYSTEM THERE SPINS A WORLD CALLED *TERRA* WHICH IS ALMOST AN EXACT TWIN OF EARTH, EXCEPT FOR A FEW STRANGE DIFFERENCES!

ON THIS WORLD THE STATE OF FLORIDA IS MUCH LARGER THAN ON EARTH!

THE EIFFEL TOWER IS IN AMERICA!

THE STATUE OF LIBERTY HOLDS A BANNER INSTEAD OF A TORCH!

HOWEVER, ON *TERRA*, THE CITIES, LANGUAGES AND PEOPLE ARE EXACTLY THE SAME AS ON EARTH!

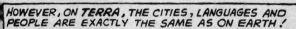

AND, BY ANOTHER STRANGE TWIST, THE CHAMPION OF *TERRA'S* PEOPLE IS A DOUBLE OF *SUPERGIRL* INSTEAD OF *SUPERMAN!*

SHE IS KNOWN AS *MARVEL MAID*...AND HER OTHER IDENTITY IS...*LEA LINDY!*

On *TERRA, SUPERMAN'S* DOUBLE ALSO EXISTS, BUT HE IS CALLED *MARVEL MAN!* HE IS THE *SECRET WEAPON* OF *MARVEL MAID*... THE REVERSE OF *SUPERGIRL* AND *SUPERMAN* ON EARTH!

THAT FARMER KID MUSTN'T SEE ME! MY EXISTENCE ON *TERRA* MUST REMAIN A SECRET UNTIL *MARVEL MAID* DECIDES I'M FULLY TRAINED!

THIS ODDITY IS THE MOST AMAZING OF ALL TO *SUPERGIRL,* WHO HAS COME FROM EARTH TO VISIT *TERRA* FOR A SPECIAL PURPOSE!

POOR *MARVEL MAN!* I KNOW HOW HE FEELS BUT IF I PERFORM SUPER-JOBS HERE WITHOUT MAKING ANY MISTAKE I KNOW THAT WHEN I RETURN TO EARTH, *SUPERMAN* WILL AGREE I'VE PROVEN I DON'T NEED ANY MORE TRAINING AND LET ME REVEAL MY EXISTENCE!

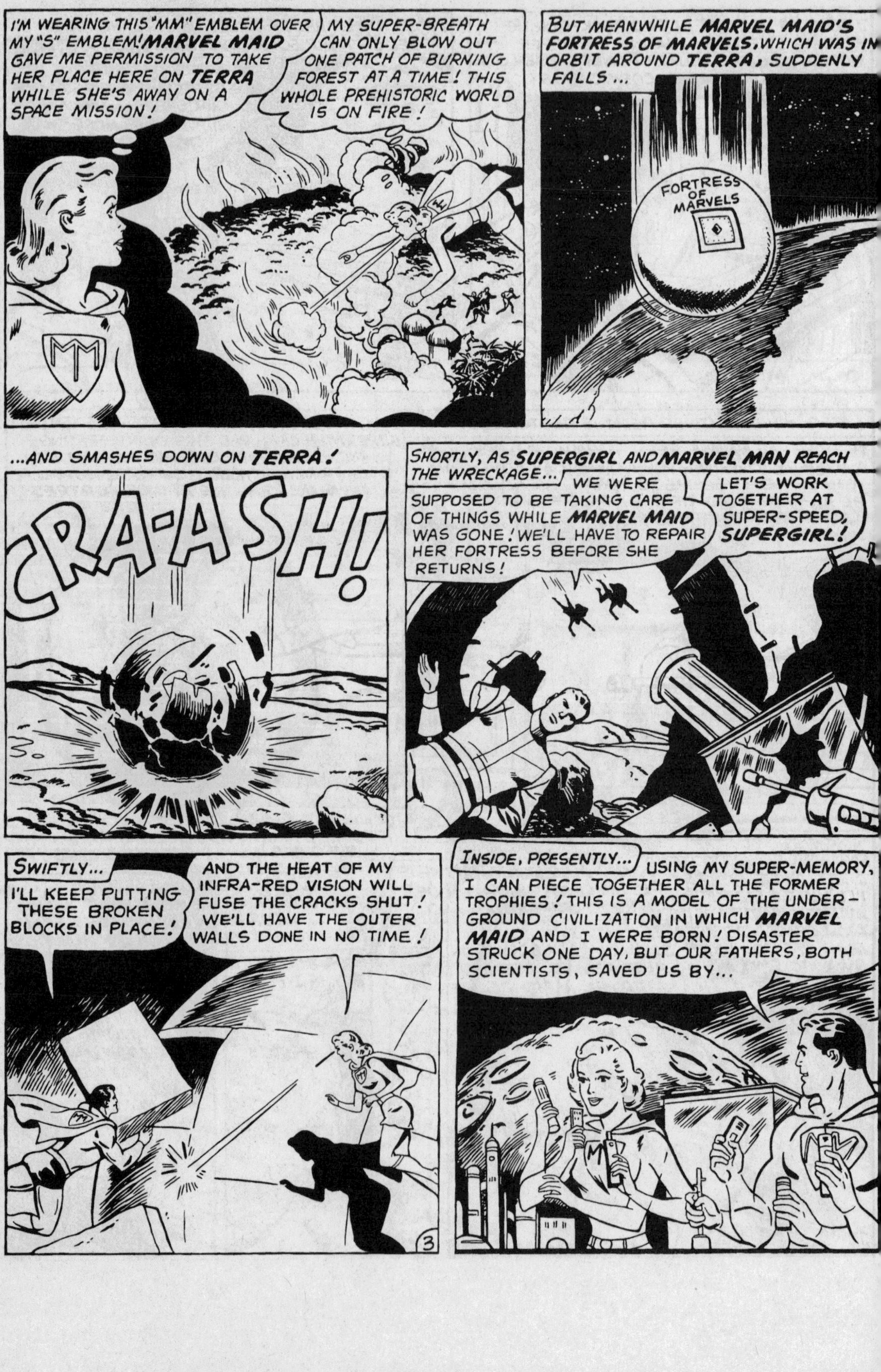
I'M WEARING THIS "MM" EMBLEM OVER MY "S" EMBLEM! MARVEL MAID GAVE ME PERMISSION TO TAKE HER PLACE HERE ON TERRA WHILE SHE'S AWAY ON A SPACE MISSION!
MY SUPER-BREATH CAN ONLY BLOW OUT ONE PATCH OF BURNING FOREST AT A TIME! THIS WHOLE PREHISTORIC WORLD IS ON FIRE!
BUT MEANWHILE MARVEL MAID'S FORTRESS OF MARVELS, WHICH WAS IN ORBIT AROUND TERRA, SUDDENLY FALLS...
FORTRESS OF MARVELS
...AND SMASHES DOWN ON TERRA!
CRA-ASH!
SHORTLY, AS SUPERGIRL AND MARVEL MAN REACH THE WRECKAGE...
WE WERE SUPPOSED TO BE TAKING CARE OF THINGS WHILE MARVEL MAID WAS GONE! WE'LL HAVE TO REPAIR HER FORTRESS BEFORE SHE RETURNS!
LET'S WORK TOGETHER AT SUPER-SPEED, SUPERGIRL!
SWIFTLY...
I'LL KEEP PUTTING THESE BROKEN BLOCKS IN PLACE!
AND THE HEAT OF MY INFRA-RED VISION WILL FUSE THE CRACKS SHUT! WE'LL HAVE THE OUTER WALLS DONE IN NO TIME!
3
INSIDE, PRESENTLY...
USING MY SUPER-MEMORY, I CAN PIECE TOGETHER ALL THE FORMER TROPHIES! THIS IS A MODEL OF THE UNDER-GROUND CIVILIZATION IN WHICH MARVEL MAID AND I WERE BORN! DISASTER STRUCK ONE DAY, BUT OUR FATHERS, BOTH SCIENTISTS, SAVED US BY...

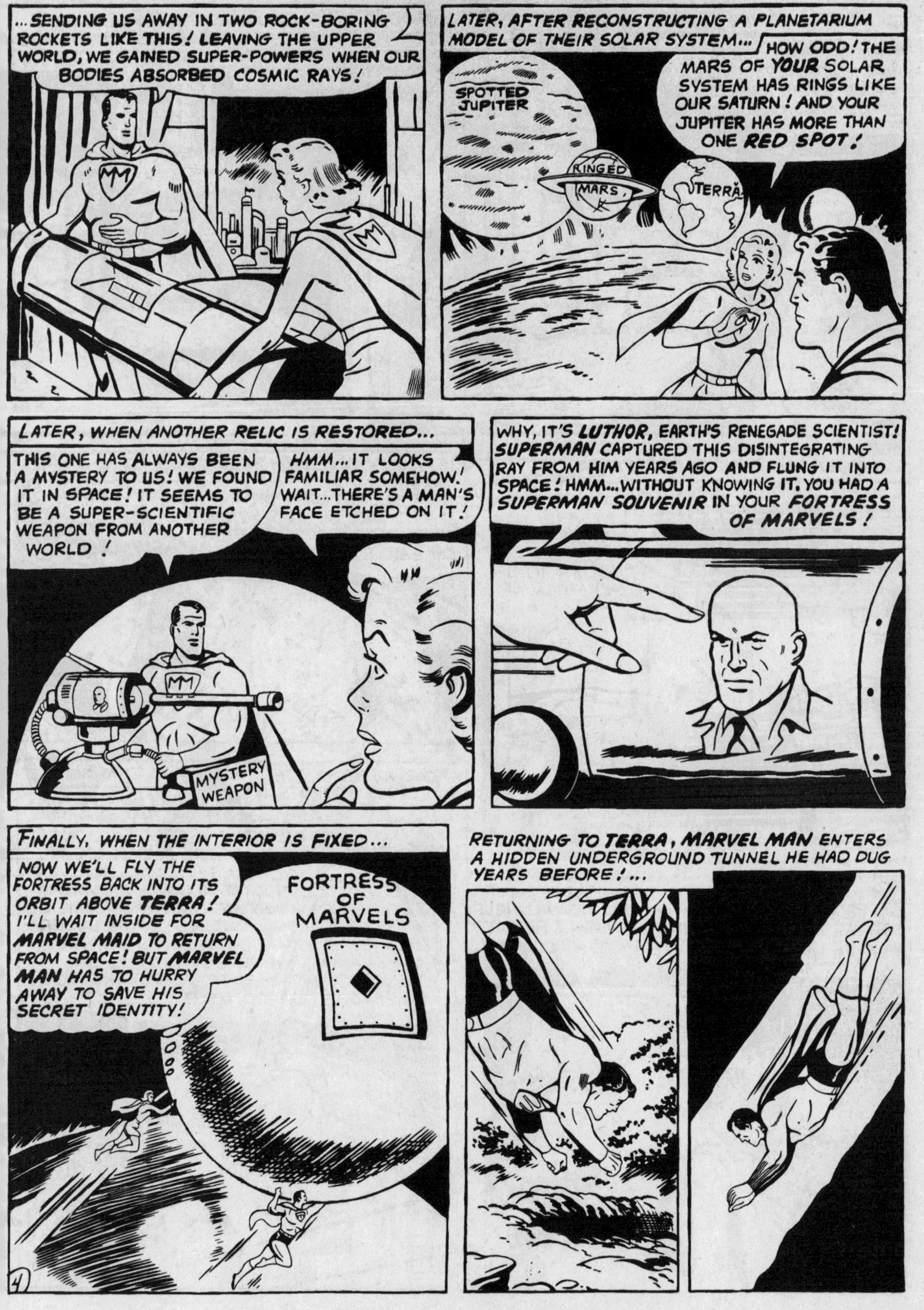
...SENDING US AWAY IN TWO ROCK-BORING ROCKETS LIKE THIS! LEAVING THE UPPER WORLD, WE GAINED SUPER-POWERS WHEN OUR BODIES ABSORBED COSMIC RAYS!
LATER, AFTER RECONSTRUCTING A PLANETARIUM MODEL OF THEIR SOLAR SYSTEM...
HOW ODD! THE MARS OF YOUR SOLAR SYSTEM HAS RINGS LIKE OUR SATURN! AND YOUR JUPITER HAS MORE THAN ONE RED SPOT!
SPOTTED JUPITER
RINGED MARS
TERRA
LATER, WHEN ANOTHER RELIC IS RESTORED...
THIS ONE HAS ALWAYS BEEN A MYSTERY TO US! WE FOUND IT IN SPACE! IT SEEMS TO BE A SUPER-SCIENTIFIC WEAPON FROM ANOTHER WORLD!
HMM... IT LOOKS FAMILIAR SOMEHOW! WAIT...THERE'S A MAN'S FACE ETCHED ON IT!
MYSTERY WEAPON
WHY, IT'S LUTHOR, EARTH'S RENEGADE SCIENTIST! SUPERMAN CAPTURED THIS DISINTEGRATING RAY FROM HIM YEARS AGO AND FLUNG IT INTO SPACE! HMM...WITHOUT KNOWING IT, YOU HAD A SUPERMAN SOUVENIR IN YOUR FORTRESS OF MARVELS!
FINALLY, WHEN THE INTERIOR IS FIXED...
NOW WE'LL FLY THE FORTRESS BACK INTO ITS ORBIT ABOVE TERRA! I'LL WAIT INSIDE FOR MARVEL MAID TO RETURN FROM SPACE! BUT MARVEL MAN HAS TO HURRY AWAY TO SAVE HIS SECRET IDENTITY!
FORTRESS OF MARVELS
4
RETURNING TO TERRA, MARVEL MAN ENTERS A HIDDEN UNDERGROUND TUNNEL HE HAD DUG YEARS BEFORE!...

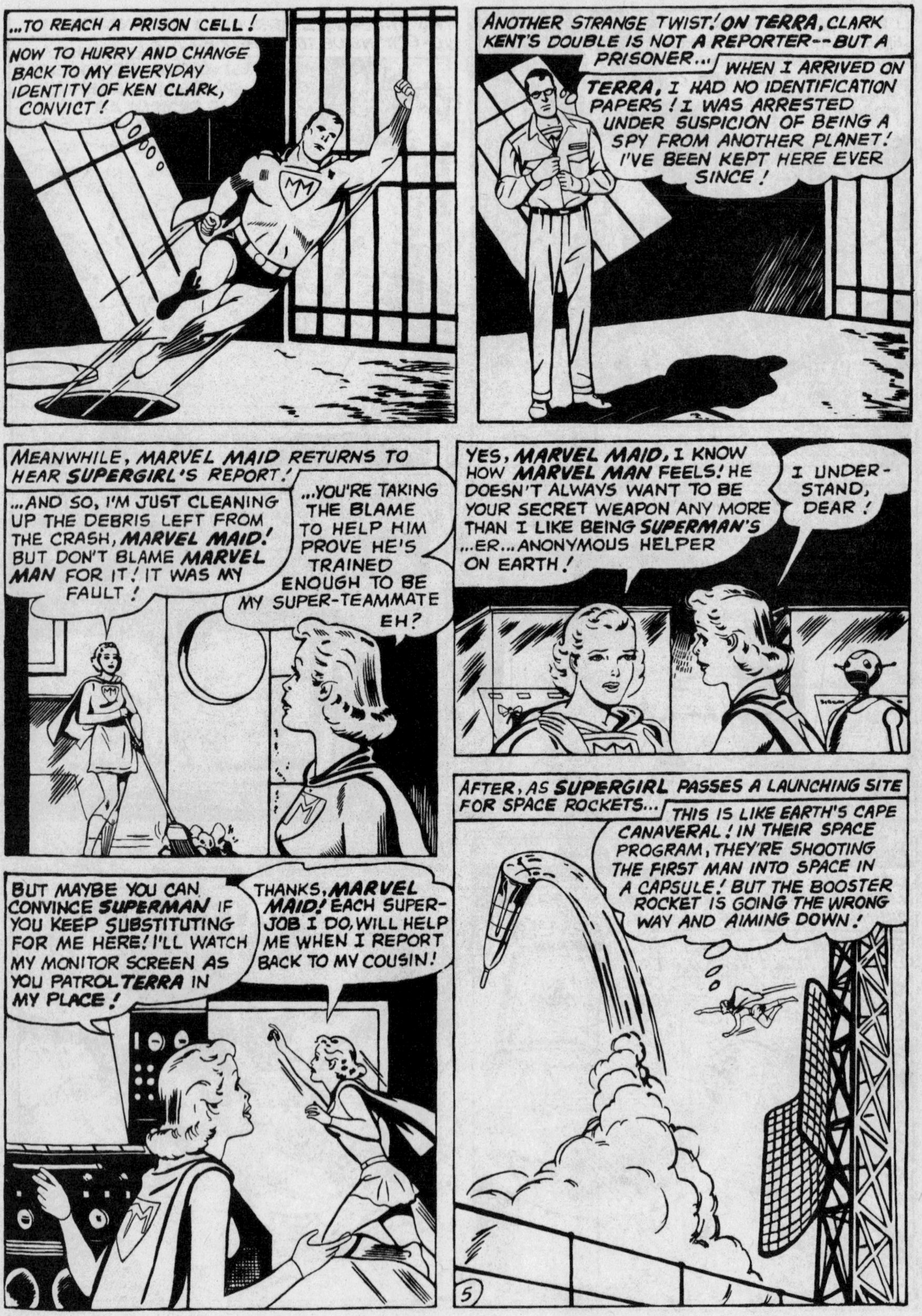
...TO REACH A PRISON CELL!
NOW TO HURRY AND CHANGE BACK TO MY EVERYDAY IDENTITY OF KEN CLARK, CONVICT!
ANOTHER STRANGE TWIST! ON TERRA, CLARK KENT'S DOUBLE IS NOT A REPORTER--BUT A PRISONER...
WHEN I ARRIVED ON TERRA, I HAD NO IDENTIFICATION PAPERS! I WAS ARRESTED UNDER SUSPICION OF BEING A SPY FROM ANOTHER PLANET! I'VE BEEN KEPT HERE EVER SINCE!
MEANWHILE, MARVEL MAID RETURNS TO HEAR SUPERGIRL'S REPORT!
...AND SO, I'M JUST CLEANING UP THE DEBRIS LEFT FROM THE CRASH, MARVEL MAID! BUT DON'T BLAME MARVEL MAN FOR IT! IT WAS MY FAULT!
...YOU'RE TAKING THE BLAME TO HELP HIM PROVE HE'S TRAINED ENOUGH TO BE MY SUPER-TEAMMATE EH?
YES, MARVEL MAID, I KNOW HOW MARVEL MAN FEELS! HE DOESN'T ALWAYS WANT TO BE YOUR SECRET WEAPON ANY MORE THAN I LIKE BEING SUPERMAN'S ...ER...ANONYMOUS HELPER ON EARTH!
I UNDERSTAND, DEAR!
BUT MAYBE YOU CAN CONVINCE SUPERMAN IF YOU KEEP SUBSTITUTING FOR ME HERE! I'LL WATCH MY MONITOR SCREEN AS YOU PATROL TERRA IN MY PLACE!
THANKS, MARVEL MAID! EACH SUPER-JOB I DO, WILL HELP ME WHEN I REPORT BACK TO MY COUSIN!
AFTER, AS SUPERGIRL PASSES A LAUNCHING SITE FOR SPACE ROCKETS...
THIS IS LIKE EARTH'S CAPE CANAVERAL! IN THEIR SPACE PROGRAM, THEY'RE SHOOTING THE FIRST MAN INTO SPACE IN A CAPSULE! BUT THE BOOSTER ROCKET IS GOING THE WRONG WAY AND AIMING DOWN!
5

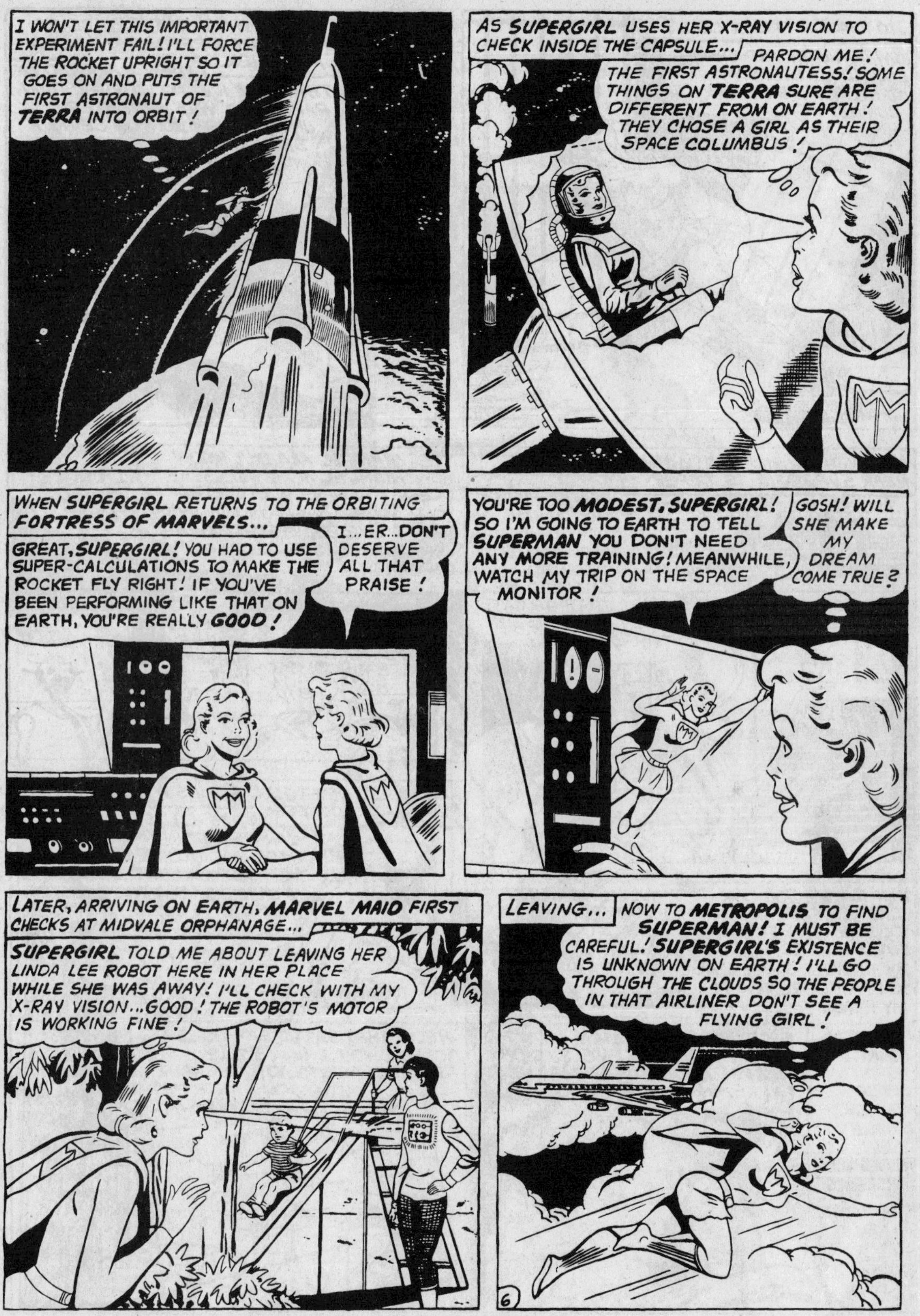
I WON'T LET THIS IMPORTANT EXPERIMENT FAIL! I'LL FORCE THE ROCKET UPRIGHT SO IT GOES ON AND PUTS THE FIRST ASTRONAUT OF TERRA INTO ORBIT!
AS SUPERGIRL USES HER X-RAY VISION TO CHECK INSIDE THE CAPSULE...
PARDON ME! THE FIRST ASTRONAUTESS! SOME THINGS ON TERRA SURE ARE DIFFERENT FROM ON EARTH! THEY CHOSE A GIRL AS THEIR SPACE COLUMBUS!
WHEN SUPERGIRL RETURNS TO THE ORBITING FORTRESS OF MARVELS...
GREAT, SUPERGIRL! YOU HAD TO USE SUPER-CALCULATIONS TO MAKE THE ROCKET FLY RIGHT! IF YOU'VE BEEN PERFORMING LIKE THAT ON EARTH, YOU'RE REALLY GOOD!
I...ER...DON'T DESERVE ALL THAT PRAISE!
YOU'RE TOO MODEST, SUPERGIRL! SO I'M GOING TO EARTH TO TELL SUPERMAN YOU DON'T NEED ANY MORE TRAINING! MEANWHILE, WATCH MY TRIP ON THE SPACE MONITOR!
GOSH! WILL SHE MAKE MY DREAM COME TRUE?
LATER, ARRIVING ON EARTH, MARVEL MAID FIRST CHECKS AT MIDVALE ORPHANAGE...
SUPERGIRL TOLD ME ABOUT LEAVING HER LINDA LEE ROBOT HERE IN HER PLACE WHILE SHE WAS AWAY! I'LL CHECK WITH MY X-RAY VISION...GOOD! THE ROBOT'S MOTOR IS WORKING FINE!
LEAVING...
NOW TO METROPOLIS TO FIND SUPERMAN! I MUST BE CAREFUL! SUPERGIRL'S EXISTENCE IS UNKNOWN ON EARTH! I'LL GO THROUGH THE CLOUDS SO THE PEOPLE IN THAT AIRLINER DON'T SEE A FLYING GIRL!
6

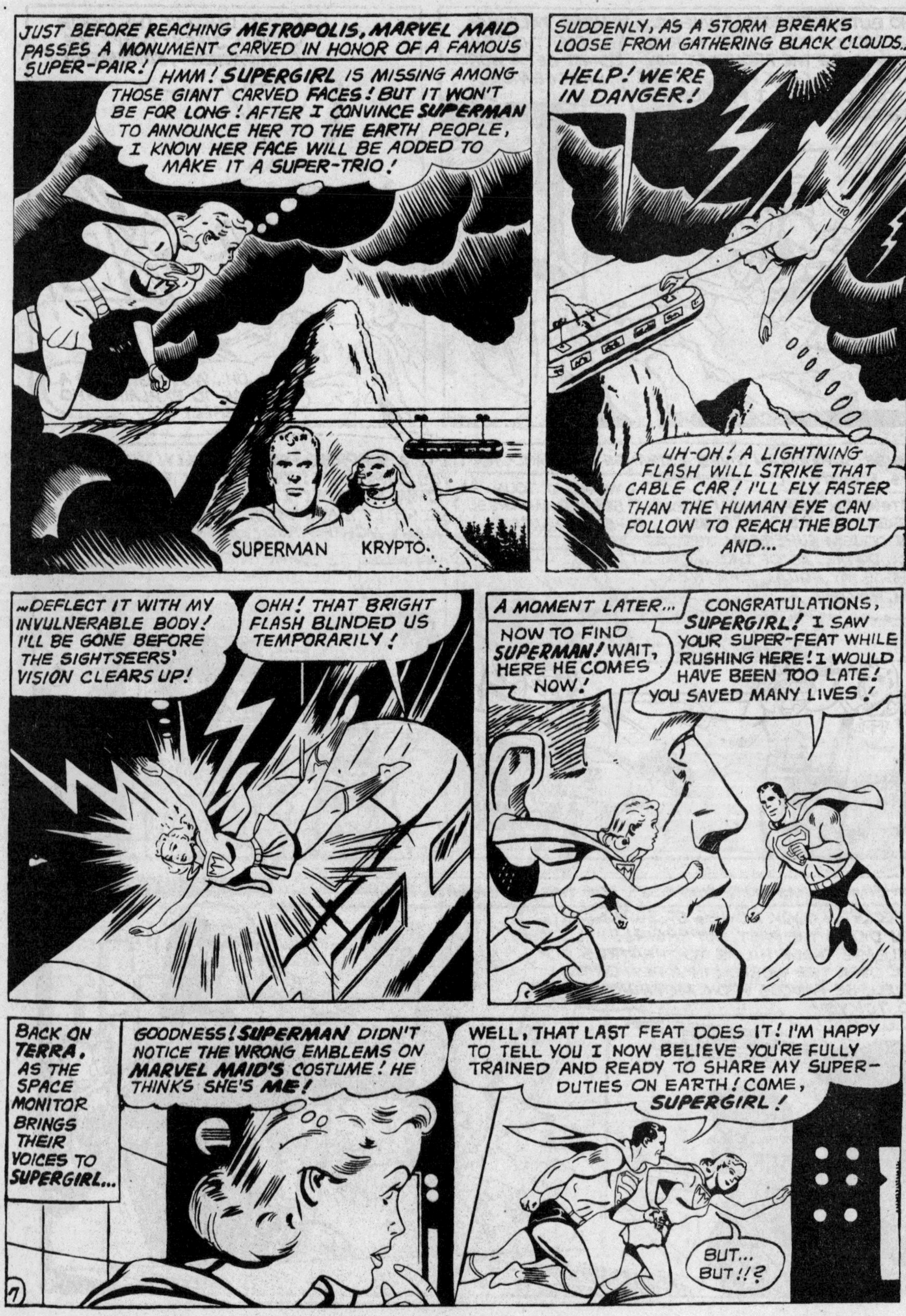
JUST BEFORE REACHING METROPOLIS, MARVEL MAID PASSES A MONUMENT CARVED IN HONOR OF A FAMOUS SUPER-PAIR!
HMM! SUPERGIRL IS MISSING AMONG THOSE GIANT CARVED FACES! BUT IT WON'T BE FOR LONG! AFTER I CONVINCE SUPERMAN TO ANNOUNCE HER TO THE EARTH PEOPLE, I KNOW HER FACE WILL BE ADDED TO MAKE IT A SUPER-TRIO!
SUPERMAN
KRYPTO
SUDDENLY, AS A STORM BREAKS LOOSE FROM GATHERING BLACK CLOUDS...
HELP! WE'RE IN DANGER!
UH-OH! A LIGHTNING FLASH WILL STRIKE THAT CABLE CAR! I'LL FLY FASTER THAN THE HUMAN EYE CAN FOLLOW TO REACH THE BOLT AND...
...DEFLECT IT WITH MY INVULNERABLE BODY! I'LL BE GONE BEFORE THE SIGHTSEERS' VISION CLEARS UP!
OHH! THAT BRIGHT FLASH BLINDED US TEMPORARILY!
A MOMENT LATER...
NOW TO FIND SUPERMAN! WAIT, HERE HE COMES NOW!
CONGRATULATIONS, SUPERGIRL! I SAW YOUR SUPER-FEAT WHILE RUSHING HERE! I WOULD HAVE BEEN TOO LATE! YOU SAVED MANY LIVES!
BACK ON TERRA, AS THE SPACE MONITOR BRINGS THEIR VOICES TO SUPERGIRL...
GOODNESS! SUPERMAN DIDN'T NOTICE THE WRONG EMBLEMS ON MARVEL MAID'S COSTUME! HE THINKS SHE'S ME!
7
WELL, THAT LAST FEAT DOES IT! I'M HAPPY TO TELL YOU I NOW BELIEVE YOU'RE FULLY TRAINED AND READY TO SHARE MY SUPER-DUTIES ON EARTH! COME, SUPERGIRL!
BUT... BUT!!?

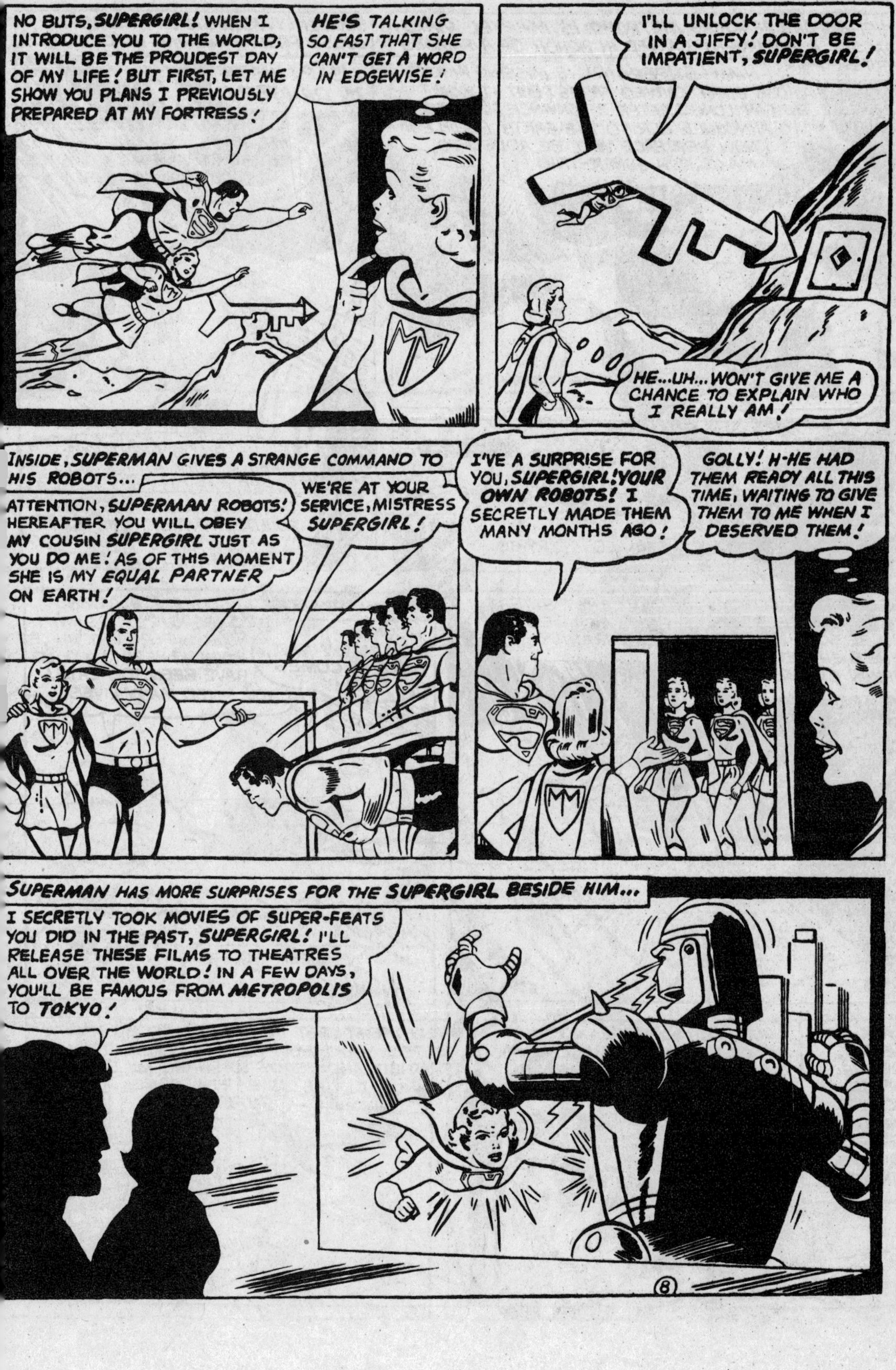
NO BUTS, SUPERGIRL! WHEN I INTRODUCE YOU TO THE WORLD, IT WILL BE THE PROUDEST DAY OF MY LIFE! BUT FIRST, LET ME SHOW YOU PLANS I PREVIOUSLY PREPARED AT MY FORTRESS!
HE'S TALKING SO FAST THAT SHE CAN'T GET A WORD IN EDGEWISE!
I'LL UNLOCK THE DOOR IN A JIFFY! DON'T BE IMPATIENT, SUPERGIRL!
HE...UH...WON'T GIVE ME A CHANCE TO EXPLAIN WHO I REALLY AM!
INSIDE, SUPERMAN GIVES A STRANGE COMMAND TO HIS ROBOTS...
ATTENTION, SUPERMAN ROBOTS! HEREAFTER YOU WILL OBEY MY COUSIN SUPERGIRL JUST AS YOU DO ME! AS OF THIS MOMENT SHE IS MY EQUAL PARTNER ON EARTH!
WE'RE AT YOUR SERVICE, MISTRESS SUPERGIRL!
I'VE A SURPRISE FOR YOU, SUPERGIRL! YOUR OWN ROBOTS! I SECRETLY MADE THEM MANY MONTHS AGO!
GOLLY! H-HE HAD THEM READY ALL THIS TIME, WAITING TO GIVE THEM TO ME WHEN I DESERVED THEM!
SUPERMAN HAS MORE SURPRISES FOR THE SUPERGIRL BESIDE HIM...
I SECRETLY TOOK MOVIES OF SUPER-FEATS YOU DID IN THE PAST, SUPERGIRL! I'LL RELEASE THESE FILMS TO THEATRES ALL OVER THE WORLD! IN A FEW DAYS, YOU'LL BE FAMOUS FROM METROPOLIS TO TOKYO!
8

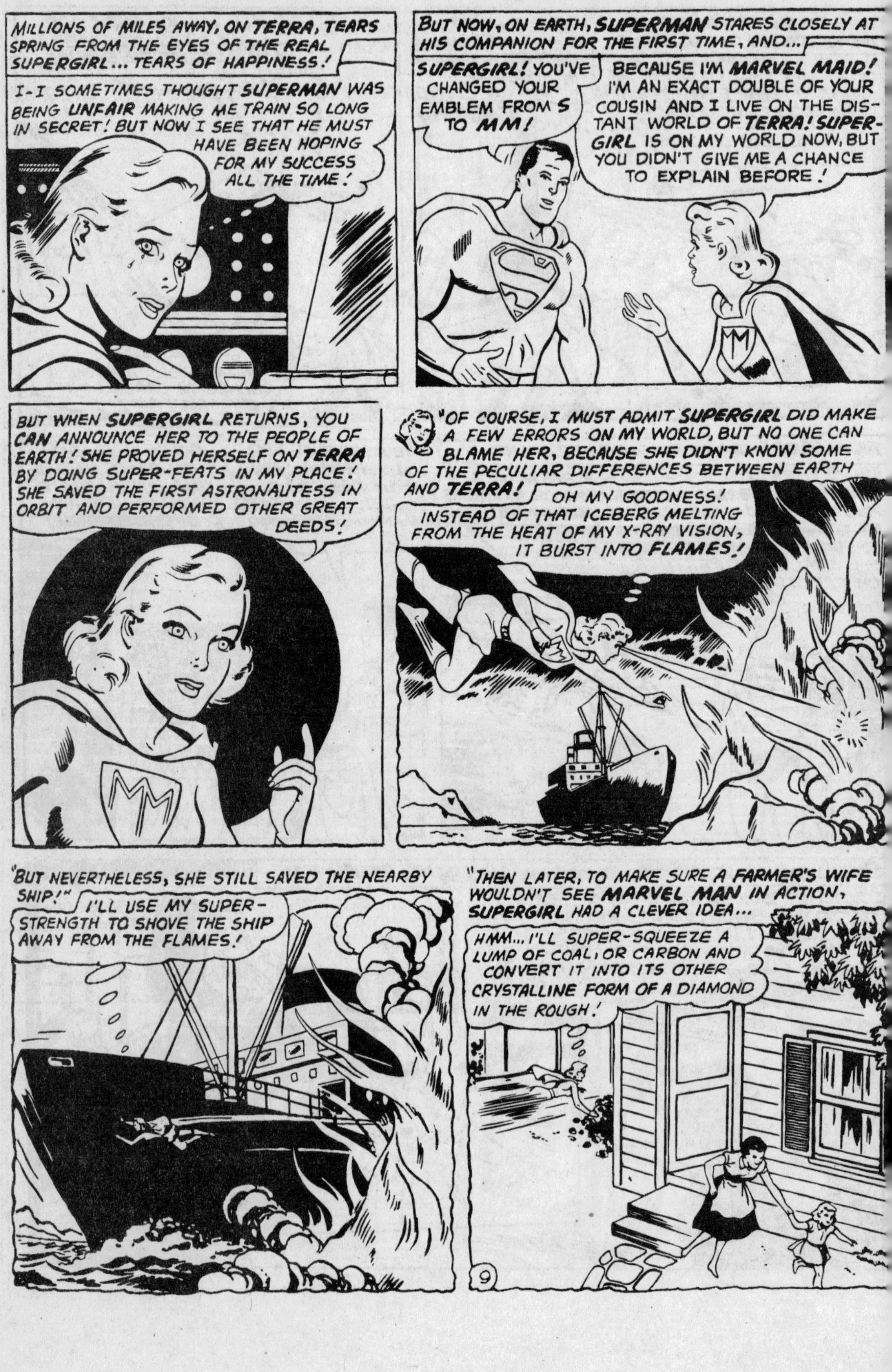
MILLIONS OF MILES AWAY, ON TERRA, TEARS SPRING FROM THE EYES OF THE REAL SUPERGIRL... TEARS OF HAPPINESS!
I-I SOMETIMES THOUGHT SUPERMAN WAS BEING UNFAIR MAKING ME TRAIN SO LONG IN SECRET! BUT NOW I SEE THAT HE MUST HAVE BEEN HOPING FOR MY SUCCESS ALL THE TIME!
BUT NOW, ON EARTH, SUPERMAN STARES CLOSELY AT HIS COMPANION FOR THE FIRST TIME, AND...
SUPERGIRL! YOU'VE CHANGED YOUR EMBLEM FROM S TO MM!
BECAUSE I'M MARVEL MAID! I'M AN EXACT DOUBLE OF YOUR COUSIN AND I LIVE ON THE DISTANT WORLD OF TERRA! SUPERGIRL IS ON MY WORLD NOW, BUT YOU DIDN'T GIVE ME A CHANCE TO EXPLAIN BEFORE!
BUT WHEN SUPERGIRL RETURNS, YOU CAN ANNOUNCE HER TO THE PEOPLE OF EARTH! SHE PROVED HERSELF ON TERRA BY DOING SUPER-FEATS IN MY PLACE! SHE SAVED THE FIRST ASTRONAUTESS IN ORBIT AND PERFORMED OTHER GREAT DEEDS!
"OF COURSE, I MUST ADMIT SUPERGIRL DID MAKE A FEW ERRORS ON MY WORLD, BUT NO ONE CAN BLAME HER, BECAUSE SHE DIDN'T KNOW SOME OF THE PECULIAR DIFFERENCES BETWEEN EARTH AND TERRA!
OH MY GOODNESS! INSTEAD OF THAT ICEBERG MELTING FROM THE HEAT OF MY X-RAY VISION, IT BURST INTO FLAMES!
"BUT NEVERTHELESS, SHE STILL SAVED THE NEARBY SHIP!"
I'LL USE MY SUPER-STRENGTH TO SHOVE THE SHIP AWAY FROM THE FLAMES!
"THEN LATER, TO MAKE SURE A FARMER'S WIFE WOULDN'T SEE MARVEL MAN IN ACTION, SUPERGIRL HAD A CLEVER IDEA...
HMM... I'LL SUPER-SQUEEZE A LUMP OF COAL, OR CARBON AND CONVERT IT INTO ITS OTHER CRYSTALLINE FORM OF A DIAMOND IN THE ROUGH!
9

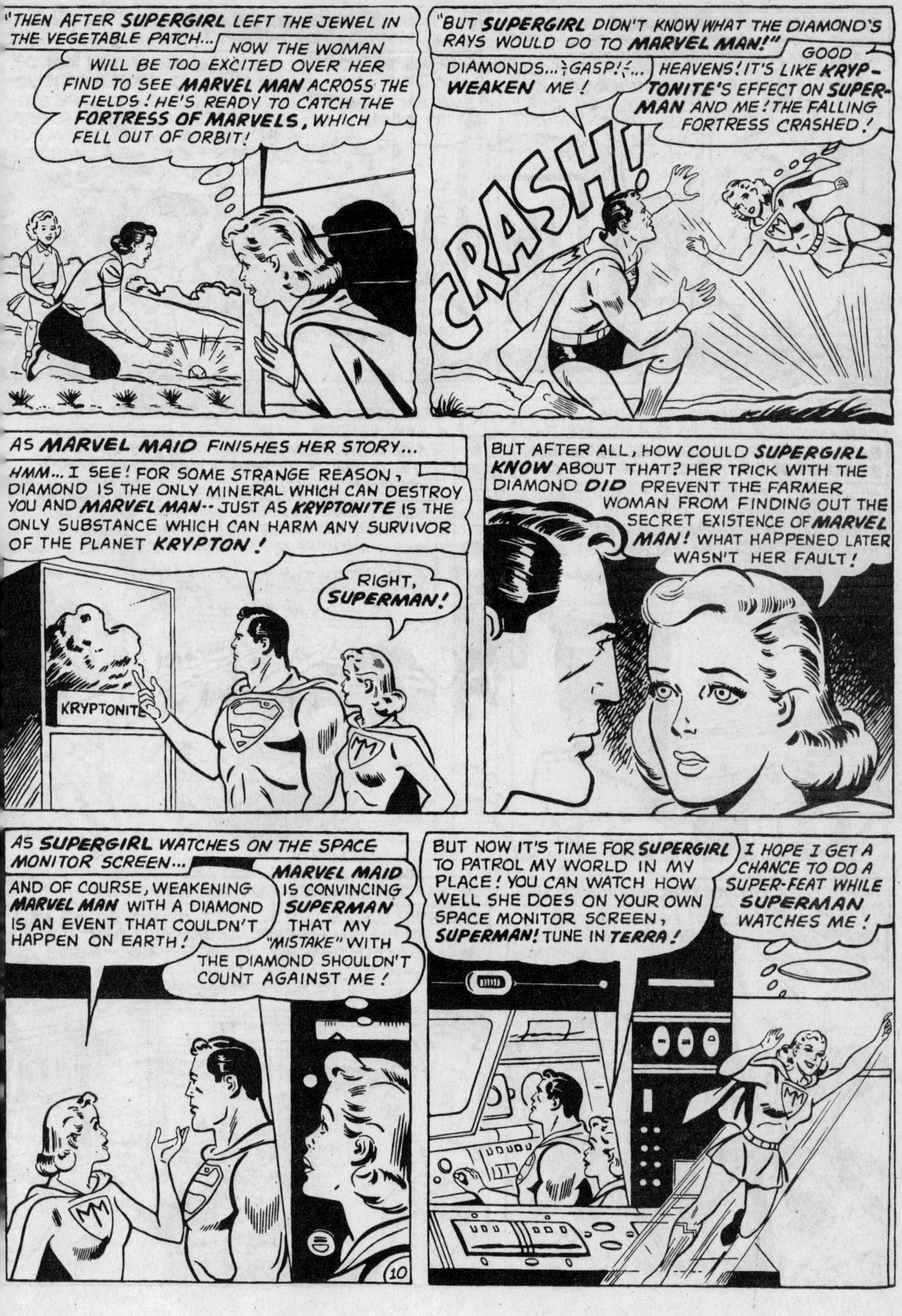
"THEN AFTER SUPERGIRL LEFT THE JEWEL IN THE VEGETABLE PATCH...
NOW THE WOMAN WILL BE TOO EXCITED OVER HER FIND TO SEE MARVEL MAN ACROSS THE FIELDS! HE'S READY TO CATCH THE FORTRESS OF MARVELS, WHICH FELL OUT OF ORBIT!
"BUT SUPERGIRL DIDN'T KNOW WHAT THE DIAMOND'S RAYS WOULD DO TO MARVEL MAN!"
DIAMONDS...GASP!...WEAKEN ME!
GOOD HEAVENS! IT'S LIKE KRYPTONITE'S EFFECT ON SUPERMAN AND ME! THE FALLING FORTRESS CRASHED!
CRASH!
AS MARVEL MAID FINISHES HER STORY...
HMM... I SEE! FOR SOME STRANGE REASON, DIAMOND IS THE ONLY MINERAL WHICH CAN DESTROY YOU AND MARVEL MAN-- JUST AS KRYPTONITE IS THE ONLY SUBSTANCE WHICH CAN HARM ANY SURVIVOR OF THE PLANET KRYPTON!
RIGHT, SUPERMAN!
KRYPTONITE
BUT AFTER ALL, HOW COULD SUPERGIRL KNOW ABOUT THAT? HER TRICK WITH THE DIAMOND DID PREVENT THE FARMER WOMAN FROM FINDING OUT THE SECRET EXISTENCE OF MARVEL MAN! WHAT HAPPENED LATER WASN'T HER FAULT!
AS SUPERGIRL WATCHES ON THE SPACE MONITOR SCREEN...
AND OF COURSE, WEAKENING MARVEL MAN WITH A DIAMOND IS AN EVENT THAT COULDN'T HAPPEN ON EARTH!
MARVEL MAID IS CONVINCING SUPERMAN THAT MY "MISTAKE" WITH THE DIAMOND SHOULDN'T COUNT AGAINST ME!
10
BUT NOW IT'S TIME FOR SUPERGIRL TO PATROL MY WORLD IN MY PLACE! YOU CAN WATCH HOW WELL SHE DOES ON YOUR OWN SPACE MONITOR SCREEN, SUPERMAN! TUNE IN TERRA!
I HOPE I GET A CHANCE TO DO A SUPER-FEAT WHILE SUPERMAN WATCHES ME!

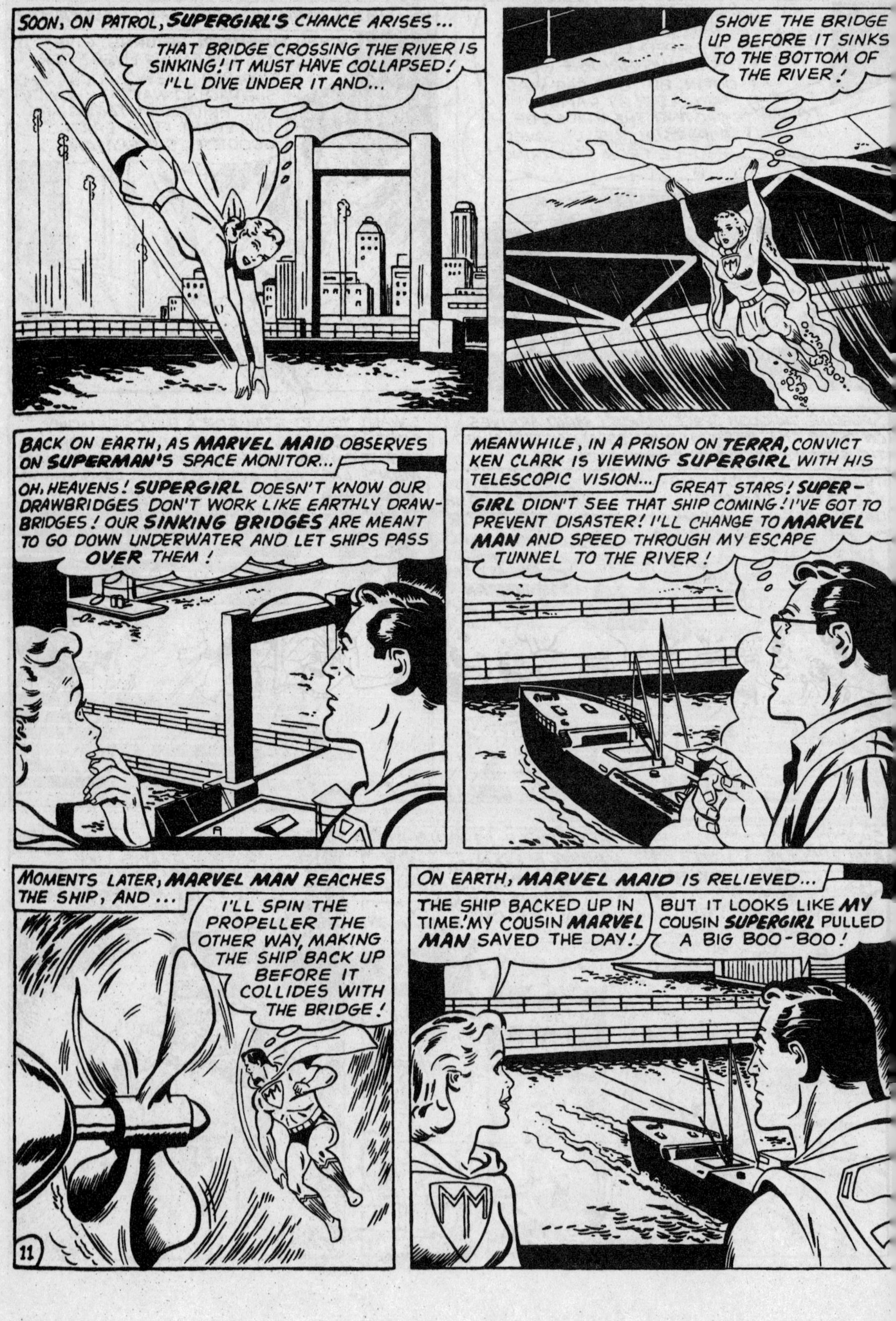
SOON, ON PATROL, SUPERGIRL'S CHANCE ARISES...
THAT BRIDGE CROSSING THE RIVER IS SINKING! IT MUST HAVE COLLAPSED! I'LL DIVE UNDER IT AND...
SHOVE THE BRIDGE UP BEFORE IT SINKS TO THE BOTTOM OF THE RIVER!
BACK ON EARTH, AS MARVEL MAID OBSERVES ON SUPERMAN'S SPACE MONITOR...
OH, HEAVENS! SUPERGIRL DOESN'T KNOW OUR DRAWBRIDGES DON'T WORK LIKE EARTHLY DRAWBRIDGES! OUR SINKING BRIDGES ARE MEANT TO GO DOWN UNDERWATER AND LET SHIPS PASS OVER THEM!
MEANWHILE, IN A PRISON ON TERRA, CONVICT KEN CLARK IS VIEWING SUPERGIRL WITH HIS TELESCOPIC VISION...
GREAT STARS! SUPERGIRL DIDN'T SEE THAT SHIP COMING! I'VE GOT TO PREVENT DISASTER! I'LL CHANGE TO MARVEL MAN AND SPEED THROUGH MY ESCAPE TUNNEL TO THE RIVER!
MOMENTS LATER, MARVEL MAN REACHES THE SHIP, AND...
I'LL SPIN THE PROPELLER THE OTHER WAY, MAKING THE SHIP BACK UP BEFORE IT COLLIDES WITH THE BRIDGE!
11
ON EARTH, MARVEL MAID IS RELIEVED...
THE SHIP BACKED UP IN TIME! MY COUSIN MARVEL MAN SAVED THE DAY!
BUT IT LOOKS LIKE MY COUSIN SUPERGIRL PULLED A BIG BOO-BOO!

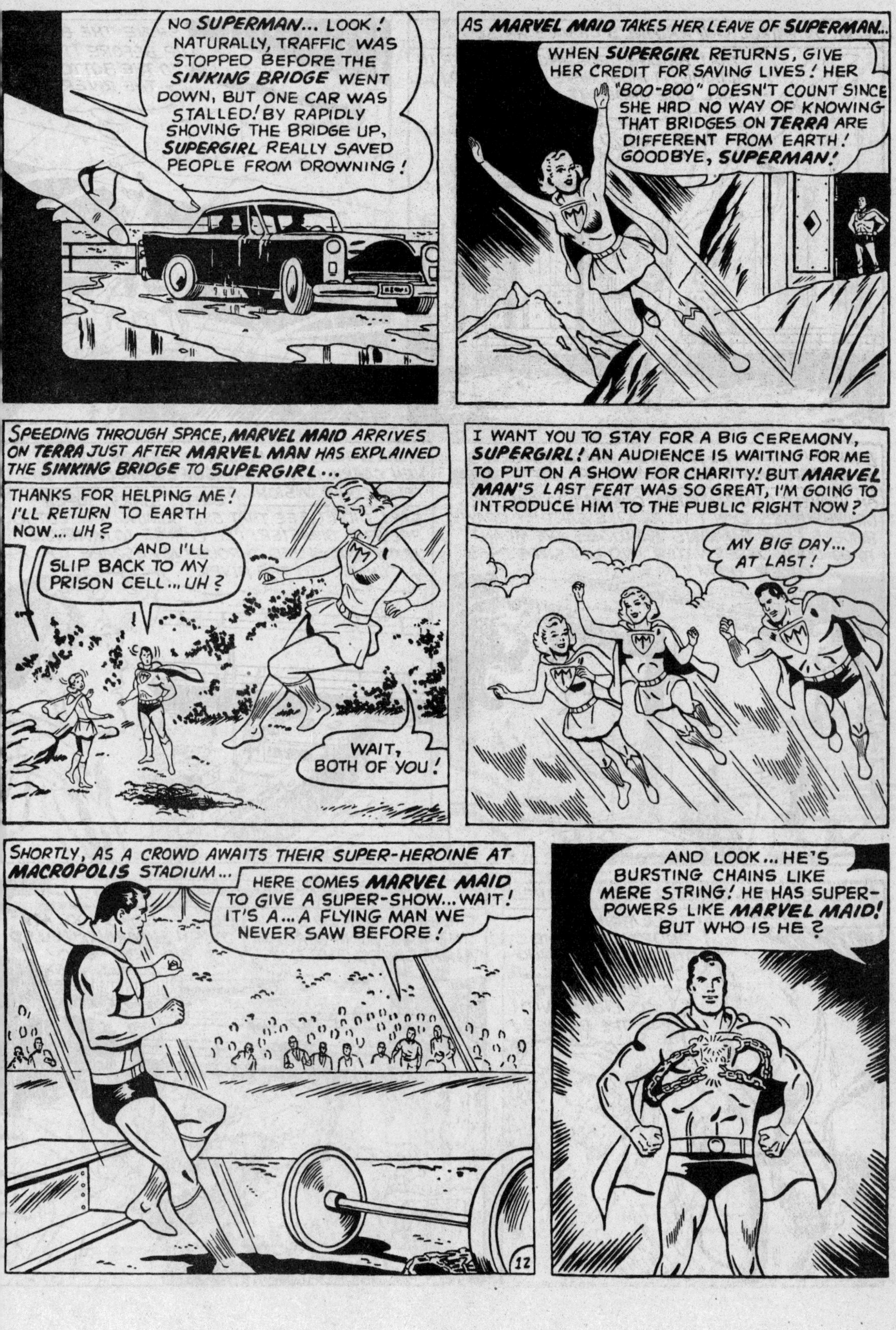
NO SUPERMAN... LOOK! NATURALLY, TRAFFIC WAS STOPPED BEFORE THE SINKING BRIDGE WENT DOWN, BUT ONE CAR WAS STALLED! BY RAPIDLY SHOVING THE BRIDGE UP, SUPERGIRL REALLY SAVED PEOPLE FROM DROWNING!
AS MARVEL MAID TAKES HER LEAVE OF SUPERMAN...
WHEN SUPERGIRL RETURNS, GIVE HER CREDIT FOR SAVING LIVES! HER "BOO-BOO" DOESN'T COUNT SINCE SHE HAD NO WAY OF KNOWING THAT BRIDGES ON TERRA ARE DIFFERENT FROM EARTH! GOODBYE, SUPERMAN!
SPEEDING THROUGH SPACE, MARVEL MAID ARRIVES ON TERRA JUST AFTER MARVEL MAN HAS EXPLAINED THE SINKING BRIDGE TO SUPERGIRL...
THANKS FOR HELPING ME! I'LL RETURN TO EARTH NOW... UH?
AND I'LL SLIP BACK TO MY PRISON CELL... UH?
WAIT, BOTH OF YOU!
I WANT YOU TO STAY FOR A BIG CEREMONY, SUPERGIRL! AN AUDIENCE IS WAITING FOR ME TO PUT ON A SHOW FOR CHARITY! BUT MARVEL MAN'S LAST FEAT WAS SO GREAT, I'M GOING TO INTRODUCE HIM TO THE PUBLIC RIGHT NOW?
MY BIG DAY... AT LAST!
SHORTLY, AS A CROWD AWAITS THEIR SUPER-HEROINE AT MACROPOLIS STADIUM...
HERE COMES MARVEL MAID TO GIVE A SUPER-SHOW... WAIT! IT'S A... A FLYING MAN WE NEVER SAW BEFORE!
12
AND LOOK... HE'S BURSTING CHAINS LIKE MERE STRING! HE HAS SUPER-POWERS LIKE MARVEL MAID! BUT WHO IS HE?

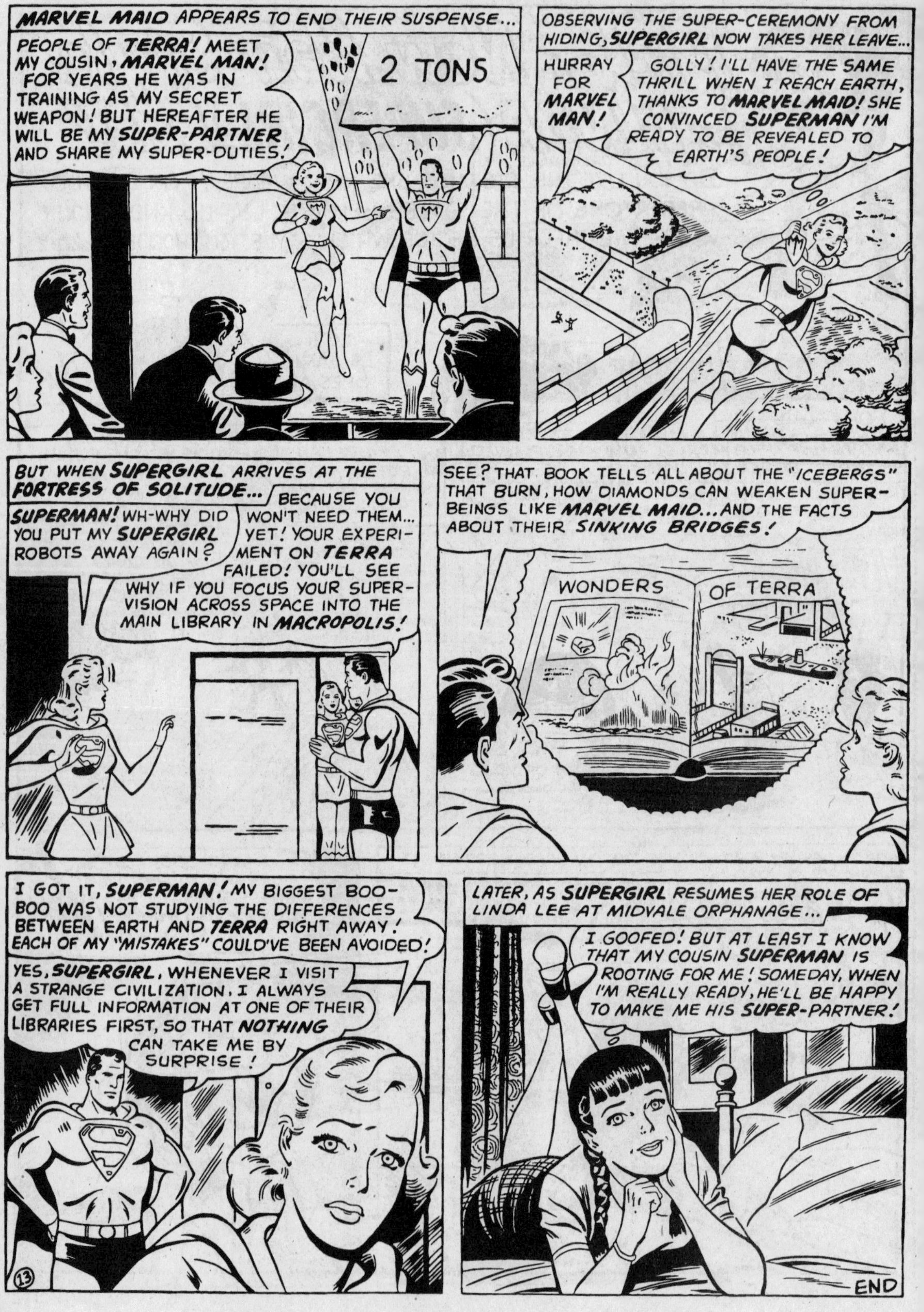
MARVEL MAID APPEARS TO END THEIR SUSPENSE...
PEOPLE OF TERRA! MEET MY COUSIN, MARVEL MAN! FOR YEARS HE WAS IN TRAINING AS MY SECRET WEAPON! BUT HEREAFTER HE WILL BE MY SUPER-PARTNER AND SHARE MY SUPER-DUTIES!
2 TONS
OBSERVING THE SUPER-CEREMONY FROM HIDING, SUPERGIRL NOW TAKES HER LEAVE...
HURRAY FOR MARVEL MAN!
GOLLY! I'LL HAVE THE SAME THRILL WHEN I REACH EARTH, THANKS TO MARVEL MAID! SHE CONVINCED SUPERMAN I'M READY TO BE REVEALED TO EARTH'S PEOPLE!
BUT WHEN SUPERGIRL ARRIVES AT THE FORTRESS OF SOLITUDE...
SUPERMAN! WH-WHY DID YOU PUT MY SUPERGIRL ROBOTS AWAY AGAIN?
BECAUSE YOU WON'T NEED THEM... YET! YOUR EXPERIMENT ON TERRA FAILED! YOU'LL SEE WHY IF YOU FOCUS YOUR SUPER-VISION ACROSS SPACE INTO THE MAIN LIBRARY IN MACROPOLIS!
SEE? THAT BOOK TELLS ALL ABOUT THE "ICEBERGS" THAT BURN, HOW DIAMONDS CAN WEAKEN SUPER-BEINGS LIKE MARVEL MAID... AND THE FACTS ABOUT THEIR SINKING BRIDGES!
WONDERS OF TERRA
I GOT IT, SUPERMAN! MY BIGGEST BOO-BOO WAS NOT STUDYING THE DIFFERENCES BETWEEN EARTH AND TERRA RIGHT AWAY! EACH OF MY "MISTAKES" COULD'VE BEEN AVOIDED!
YES, SUPERGIRL, WHENEVER I VISIT A STRANGE CIVILIZATION, I ALWAYS GET FULL INFORMATION AT ONE OF THEIR LIBRARIES FIRST, SO THAT NOTHING CAN TAKE ME BY SURPRISE!
13
LATER, AS SUPERGIRL RESUMES HER ROLE OF LINDA LEE AT MIDVALE ORPHANAGE...
I GOOFED! BUT AT LEAST I KNOW THAT MY COUSIN SUPERMAN IS ROOTING FOR ME! SOMEDAY, WHEN I'M REALLY READY, HE'LL BE HAPPY TO MAKE ME HIS SUPER-PARTNER!
END

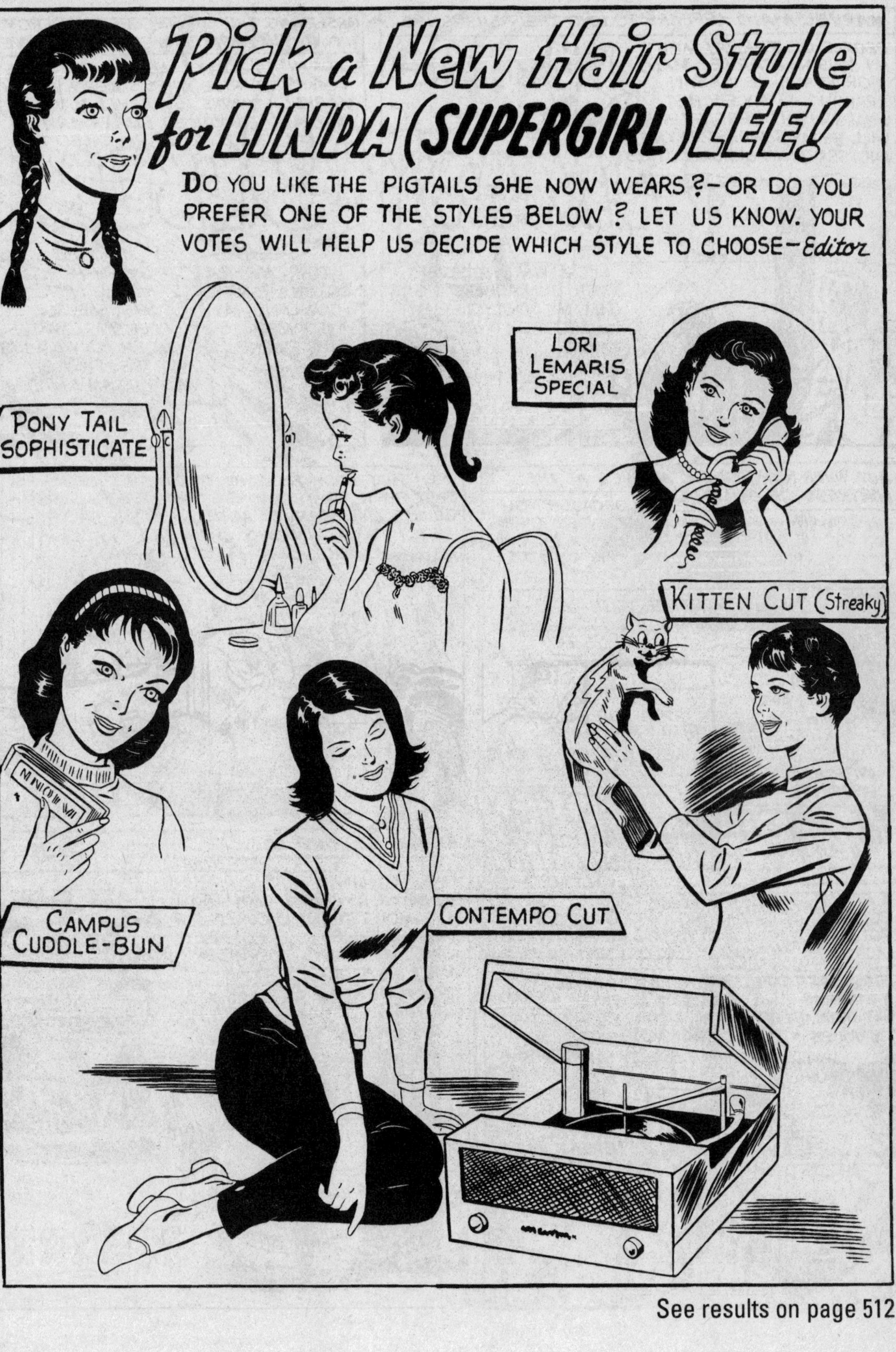
Pick a New Hair Style for LINDA (SUPERGIRL) LEE!
DO YOU LIKE THE PIGTAILS SHE NOW WEARS?—OR DO YOU PREFER ONE OF THE STYLES BELOW? LET US KNOW. YOUR VOTES WILL HELP US DECIDE WHICH STYLE TO CHOOSE—Editor
PONY TAIL SOPHISTICATE
LORI LEMARIS SPECIAL
KITTEN CUT (Streaky)
CAMPUS CUDDLE-BUN
CONTEMPO CUT

See results on page 512

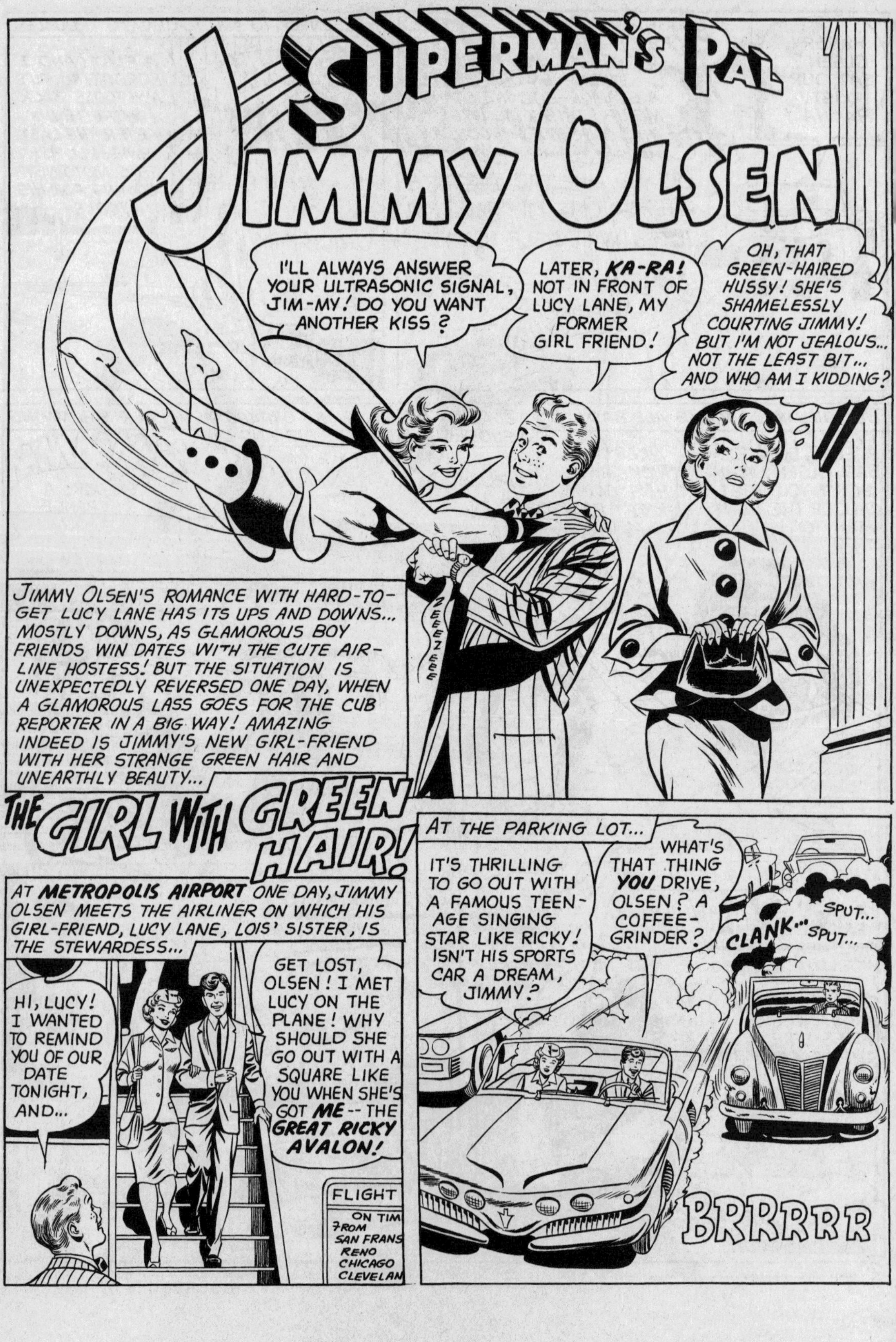
SUPERMAN'S PAL JIMMY OLSEN
I'LL ALWAYS ANSWER YOUR ULTRASONIC SIGNAL, JIM-MY! DO YOU WANT ANOTHER KISS?
LATER, KA-RA! NOT IN FRONT OF LUCY LANE, MY FORMER GIRL FRIEND!
OH, THAT GREEN-HAIRED HUSSY! SHE'S SHAMELESSLY COURTING JIMMY! BUT I'M NOT JEALOUS... NOT THE LEAST BIT... AND WHO AM I KIDDING?
ZEEEZEEE
JIMMY OLSEN'S ROMANCE WITH HARD-TO-GET LUCY LANE HAS ITS UPS AND DOWNS... MOSTLY DOWNS, AS GLAMOROUS BOY FRIENDS WIN DATES WITH THE CUTE AIR-LINE HOSTESS! BUT THE SITUATION IS UNEXPECTEDLY REVERSED ONE DAY, WHEN A GLAMOROUS LASS GOES FOR THE CUB REPORTER IN A BIG WAY! AMAZING INDEED IS JIMMY'S NEW GIRL-FRIEND WITH HER STRANGE GREEN HAIR AND UNEARTHLY BEAUTY...
THE GIRL WITH GREEN HAIR!
AT METROPOLIS AIRPORT ONE DAY, JIMMY OLSEN MEETS THE AIRLINER ON WHICH HIS GIRL-FRIEND, LUCY LANE, LOIS' SISTER, IS THE STEWARDESS...
HI, LUCY! I WANTED TO REMIND YOU OF OUR DATE TONIGHT, AND...
GET LOST, OLSEN! I MET LUCY ON THE PLANE! WHY SHOULD SHE GO OUT WITH A SQUARE LIKE YOU WHEN SHE'S GOT ME -- THE GREAT RICKY AVALON!
FLIGHT
ON TIM
FROM
SAN FRANS
RENO
CHICAGO
CLEVELAN
AT THE PARKING LOT...
IT'S THRILLING TO GO OUT WITH A FAMOUS TEEN-AGE SINGING STAR LIKE RICKY! ISN'T HIS SPORTS CAR A DREAM, JIMMY?
WHAT'S THAT THING YOU DRIVE, OLSEN? A COFFEE-GRINDER?
CLANK...
SPUT... SPUT...
BRRRRR

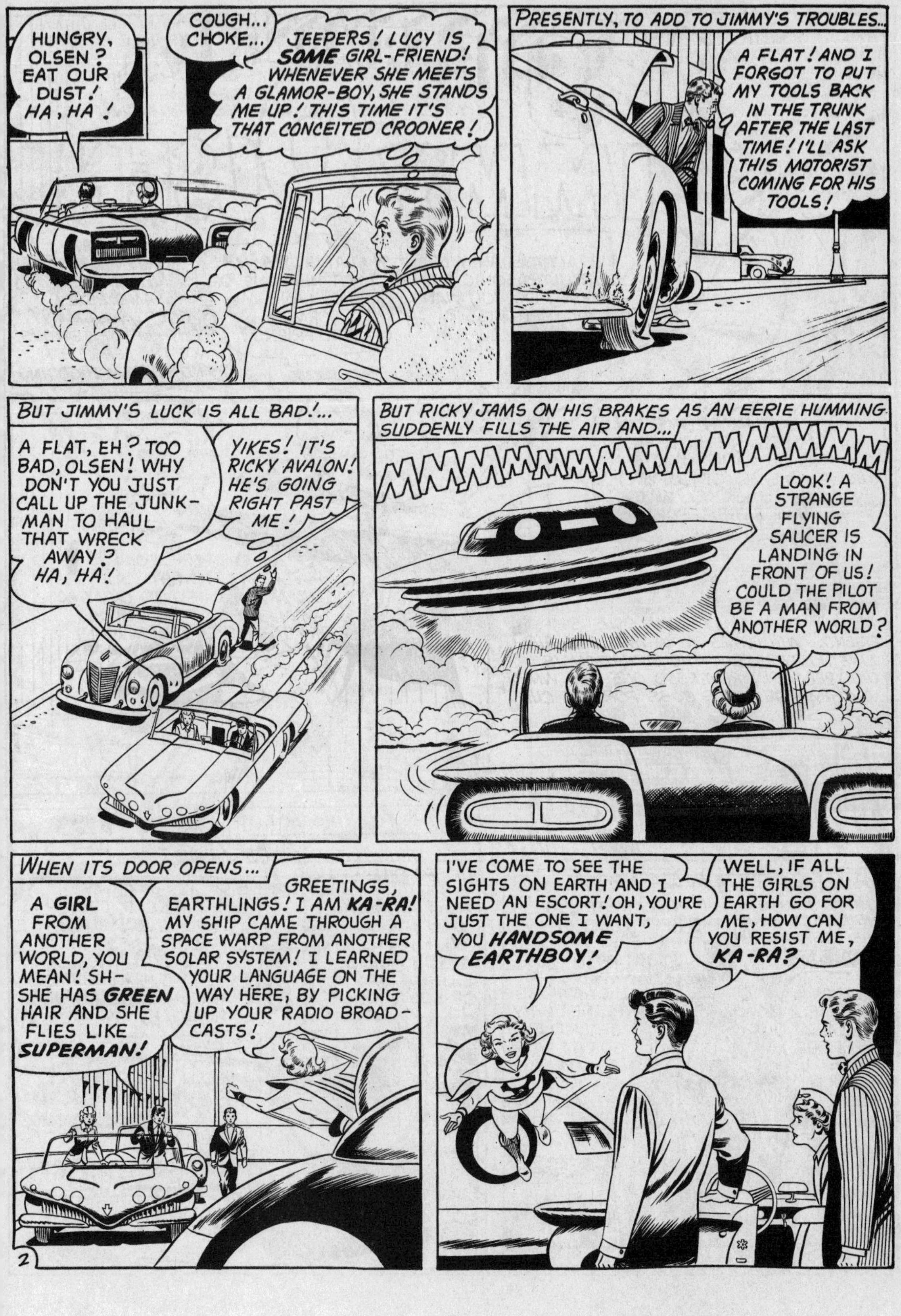
HUNGRY, OLSEN? EAT OUR DUST! HA, HA!
COUGH... CHOKE...
JEEPERS! LUCY IS SOME GIRL-FRIEND! WHENEVER SHE MEETS A GLAMOR-BOY, SHE STANDS ME UP! THIS TIME IT'S THAT CONCEITED CROONER!
PRESENTLY, TO ADD TO JIMMY'S TROUBLES...
A FLAT! AND I FORGOT TO PUT MY TOOLS BACK IN THE TRUNK AFTER THE LAST TIME! I'LL ASK THIS MOTORIST COMING FOR HIS TOOLS!
BUT JIMMY'S LUCK IS ALL BAD!...
A FLAT, EH? TOO BAD, OLSEN! WHY DON'T YOU JUST CALL UP THE JUNK-MAN TO HAUL THAT WRECK AWAY? HA, HA!
YIKES! IT'S RICKY AVALON! HE'S GOING RIGHT PAST ME!
BUT RICKY JAMS ON HIS BRAKES AS AN EERIE HUMMING SUDDENLY FILLS THE AIR AND...
MMMMMMMMMMMMMMMMMM
LOOK! A STRANGE FLYING SAUCER IS LANDING IN FRONT OF US! COULD THE PILOT BE A MAN FROM ANOTHER WORLD?
WHEN ITS DOOR OPENS...
A GIRL FROM ANOTHER WORLD, YOU MEAN! SH-SHE HAS GREEN HAIR AND SHE FLIES LIKE SUPERMAN!
GREETINGS, EARTHLINGS! I AM KA-RA! MY SHIP CAME THROUGH A SPACE WARP FROM ANOTHER SOLAR SYSTEM! I LEARNED YOUR LANGUAGE ON THE WAY HERE, BY PICKING UP YOUR RADIO BROAD-CASTS!
2
I'VE COME TO SEE THE SIGHTS ON EARTH AND I NEED AN ESCORT! OH, YOU'RE JUST THE ONE I WANT, YOU HANDSOME EARTHBOY!
WELL, IF ALL THE GIRLS ON EARTH GO FOR ME, HOW CAN YOU RESIST ME, KA-RA?

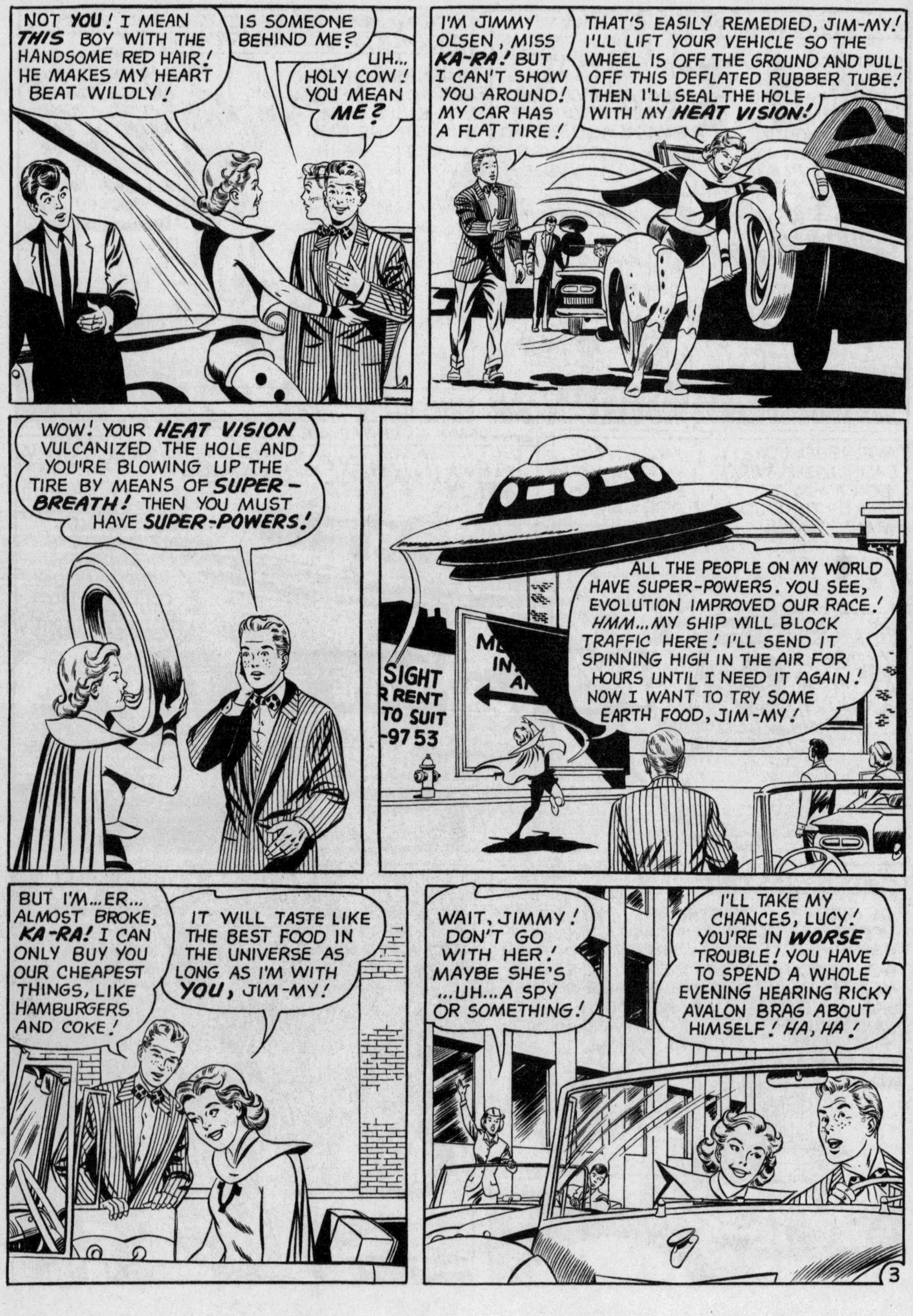
NOT YOU! I MEAN THIS BOY WITH THE HANDSOME RED HAIR! HE MAKES MY HEART BEAT WILDLY!
IS SOMEONE BEHIND ME?
UH... HOLY COW! YOU MEAN ME?
I'M JIMMY OLSEN, MISS KA-RA! BUT I CAN'T SHOW YOU AROUND! MY CAR HAS A FLAT TIRE!
THAT'S EASILY REMEDIED, JIM-MY! I'LL LIFT YOUR VEHICLE SO THE WHEEL IS OFF THE GROUND AND PULL OFF THIS DEFLATED RUBBER TUBE! THEN I'LL SEAL THE HOLE WITH MY HEAT VISION!
WOW! YOUR HEAT VISION VULCANIZED THE HOLE AND YOU'RE BLOWING UP THE TIRE BY MEANS OF SUPER-BREATH! THEN YOU MUST HAVE SUPER-POWERS!
ALL THE PEOPLE ON MY WORLD HAVE SUPER-POWERS. YOU SEE, EVOLUTION IMPROVED OUR RACE! HMM... MY SHIP WILL BLOCK TRAFFIC HERE! I'LL SEND IT SPINNING HIGH IN THE AIR FOR HOURS UNTIL I NEED IT AGAIN! NOW I WANT TO TRY SOME EARTH FOOD, JIM-MY!
SIGHT
R RENT
TO SUIT
-9753
BUT I'M...ER... ALMOST BROKE, KA-RA! I CAN ONLY BUY YOU OUR CHEAPEST THINGS, LIKE HAMBURGERS AND COKE!
IT WILL TASTE LIKE THE BEST FOOD IN THE UNIVERSE AS LONG AS I'M WITH YOU, JIM-MY!
WAIT, JIMMY! DON'T GO WITH HER! MAYBE SHE'S ...UH...A SPY OR SOMETHING!
I'LL TAKE MY CHANCES, LUCY! YOU'RE IN WORSE TROUBLE! YOU HAVE TO SPEND A WHOLE EVENING HEARING RICKY AVALON BRAG ABOUT HIMSELF! HA, HA!
3

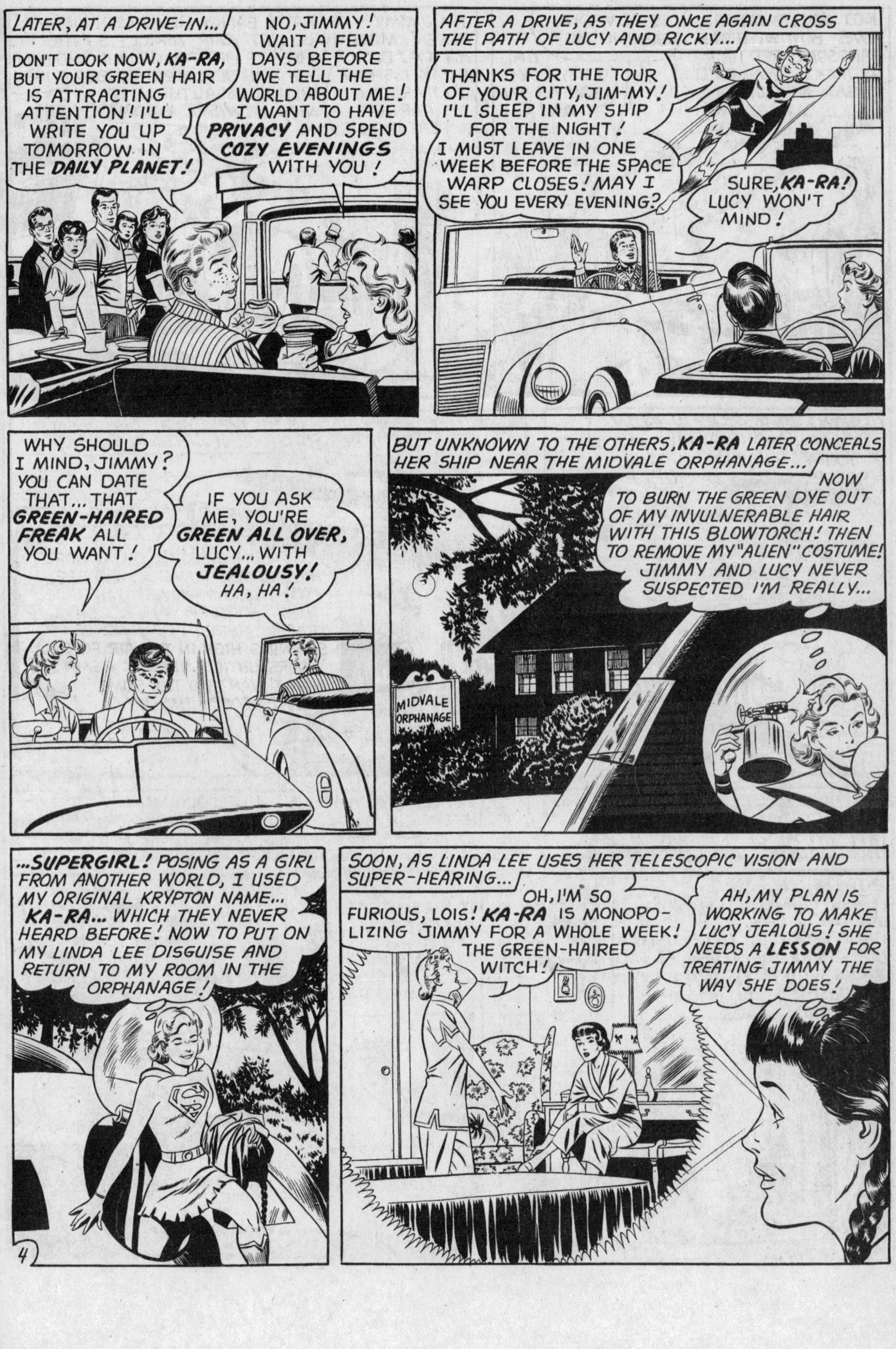
LATER, AT A DRIVE-IN...
DON'T LOOK NOW, KA-RA, BUT YOUR GREEN HAIR IS ATTRACTING ATTENTION! I'LL WRITE YOU UP TOMORROW IN THE DAILY PLANET!
NO, JIMMY! WAIT A FEW DAYS BEFORE WE TELL THE WORLD ABOUT ME! I WANT TO HAVE PRIVACY AND SPEND COZY EVENINGS WITH YOU!
AFTER A DRIVE, AS THEY ONCE AGAIN CROSS THE PATH OF LUCY AND RICKY...
THANKS FOR THE TOUR OF YOUR CITY, JIM-MY! I'LL SLEEP IN MY SHIP FOR THE NIGHT! I MUST LEAVE IN ONE WEEK BEFORE THE SPACE WARP CLOSES! MAY I SEE YOU EVERY EVENING?
SURE, KA-RA! LUCY WON'T MIND!
WHY SHOULD I MIND, JIMMY? YOU CAN DATE THAT... THAT GREEN-HAIRED FREAK ALL YOU WANT!
IF YOU ASK ME, YOU'RE GREEN ALL OVER, LUCY... WITH JEALOUSY! HA, HA!
BUT UNKNOWN TO THE OTHERS, KA-RA LATER CONCEALS HER SHIP NEAR THE MIDVALE ORPHANAGE...
NOW TO BURN THE GREEN DYE OUT OF MY INVULNERABLE HAIR WITH THIS BLOWTORCH! THEN TO REMOVE MY "ALIEN" COSTUME! JIMMY AND LUCY NEVER SUSPECTED I'M REALLY...
MIDVALE ORPHANAGE
...SUPERGIRL! POSING AS A GIRL FROM ANOTHER WORLD, I USED MY ORIGINAL KRYPTON NAME... KA-RA... WHICH THEY NEVER HEARD BEFORE! NOW TO PUT ON MY LINDA LEE DISGUISE AND RETURN TO MY ROOM IN THE ORPHANAGE!
4
SOON, AS LINDA LEE USES HER TELESCOPIC VISION AND SUPER-HEARING...
OH, I'M SO FURIOUS, LOIS! KA-RA IS MONOPO-LIZING JIMMY FOR A WHOLE WEEK! THE GREEN-HAIRED WITCH!
AH, MY PLAN IS WORKING TO MAKE LUCY JEALOUS! SHE NEEDS A LESSON FOR TREATING JIMMY THE WAY SHE DOES!

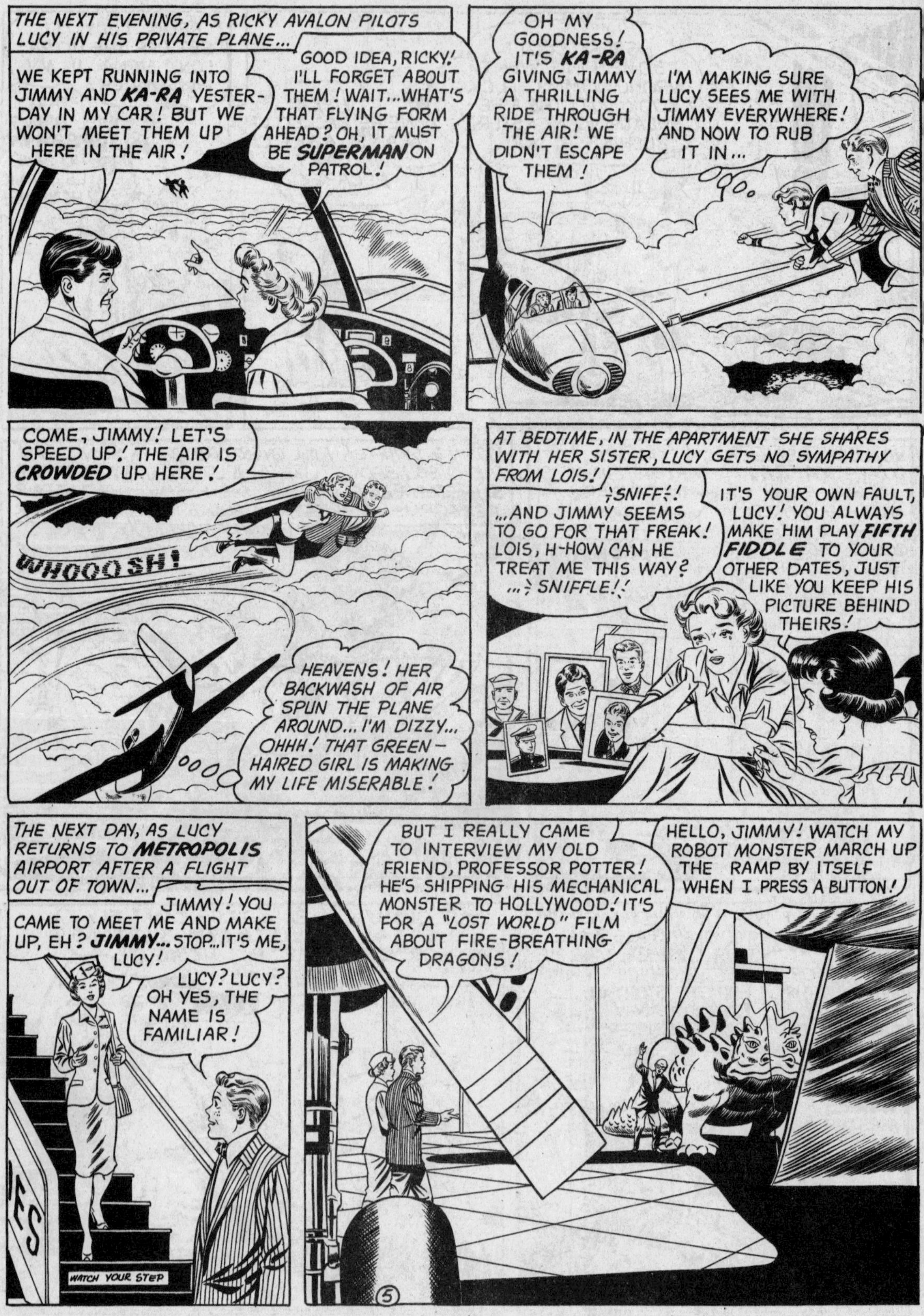
THE NEXT EVENING, AS RICKY AVALON PILOTS LUCY IN HIS PRIVATE PLANE...
WE KEPT RUNNING INTO JIMMY AND KA-RA YESTERDAY IN MY CAR! BUT WE WON'T MEET THEM UP HERE IN THE AIR!
GOOD IDEA, RICKY! I'LL FORGET ABOUT THEM! WAIT...WHAT'S THAT FLYING FORM AHEAD? OH, IT MUST BE SUPERMAN ON PATROL!
OH MY GOODNESS! IT'S KA-RA GIVING JIMMY A THRILLING RIDE THROUGH THE AIR! WE DIDN'T ESCAPE THEM!
I'M MAKING SURE LUCY SEES ME WITH JIMMY EVERYWHERE! AND NOW TO RUB IT IN...
COME, JIMMY! LET'S SPEED UP! THE AIR IS CROWDED UP HERE!
WHOOOOSH!
HEAVENS! HER BACKWASH OF AIR SPUN THE PLANE AROUND... I'M DIZZY... OHHH! THAT GREEN-HAIRED GIRL IS MAKING MY LIFE MISERABLE!
AT BEDTIME, IN THE APARTMENT SHE SHARES WITH HER SISTER, LUCY GETS NO SYMPATHY FROM LOIS!
¡SNIFF¡! ...AND JIMMY SEEMS TO GO FOR THAT FREAK! LOIS, H-HOW CAN HE TREAT ME THIS WAY? ...¡SNIFFLE!¡
IT'S YOUR OWN FAULT, LUCY! YOU ALWAYS MAKE HIM PLAY FIFTH FIDDLE TO YOUR OTHER DATES, JUST LIKE YOU KEEP HIS PICTURE BEHIND THEIRS!
THE NEXT DAY, AS LUCY RETURNS TO METROPOLIS AIRPORT AFTER A FLIGHT OUT OF TOWN...
JIMMY! YOU CAME TO MEET ME AND MAKE UP, EH? JIMMY... STOP...IT'S ME, LUCY!
LUCY? LUCY? OH YES, THE NAME IS FAMILIAR!
WATCH YOUR STEP
BUT I REALLY CAME TO INTERVIEW MY OLD FRIEND, PROFESSOR POTTER! HE'S SHIPPING HIS MECHANICAL MONSTER TO HOLLYWOOD! IT'S FOR A "LOST WORLD" FILM ABOUT FIRE-BREATHING DRAGONS!
HELLO, JIMMY! WATCH MY ROBOT MONSTER MARCH UP THE RAMP BY ITSELF WHEN I PRESS A BUTTON!
5

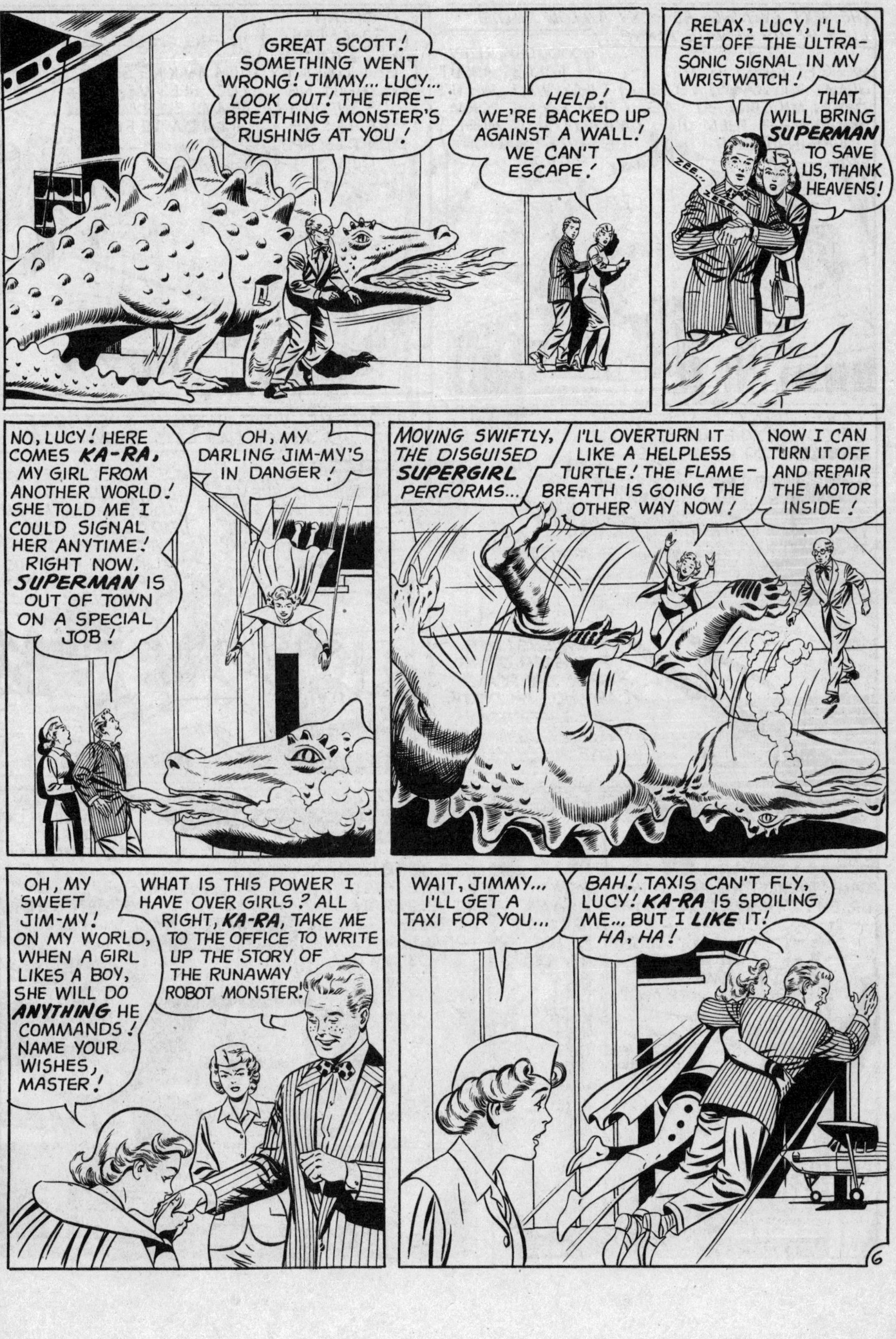
GREAT SCOTT! SOMETHING WENT WRONG! JIMMY... LUCY... LOOK OUT! THE FIRE-BREATHING MONSTER'S RUSHING AT YOU!
HELP! WE'RE BACKED UP AGAINST A WALL! WE CAN'T ESCAPE!
RELAX, LUCY, I'LL SET OFF THE ULTRA-SONIC SIGNAL IN MY WRISTWATCH!
THAT WILL BRING SUPERMAN TO SAVE US, THANK HEAVENS!
ZEE... ZEEE...
NO, LUCY! HERE COMES KA-RA, MY GIRL FROM ANOTHER WORLD! SHE TOLD ME I COULD SIGNAL HER ANYTIME! RIGHT NOW, SUPERMAN IS OUT OF TOWN ON A SPECIAL JOB!
OH, MY DARLING JIM-MY'S IN DANGER!
MOVING SWIFTLY, THE DISGUISED SUPERGIRL PERFORMS...
I'LL OVERTURN IT LIKE A HELPLESS TURTLE! THE FLAME-BREATH IS GOING THE OTHER WAY NOW!
NOW I CAN TURN IT OFF AND REPAIR THE MOTOR INSIDE!
OH, MY SWEET JIM-MY! ON MY WORLD, WHEN A GIRL LIKES A BOY, SHE WILL DO ANYTHING HE COMMANDS! NAME YOUR WISHES, MASTER!
WHAT IS THIS POWER I HAVE OVER GIRLS? ALL RIGHT, KA-RA, TAKE ME TO THE OFFICE TO WRITE UP THE STORY OF THE RUNAWAY ROBOT MONSTER!
WAIT, JIMMY... I'LL GET A TAXI FOR YOU...
BAH! TAXIS CAN'T FLY, LUCY! KA-RA IS SPOILING ME... BUT I LIKE IT! HA, HA!
6

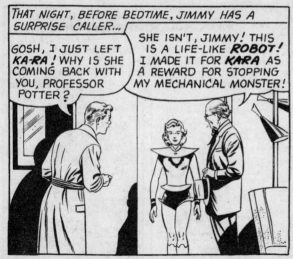

THAT NIGHT, BEFORE BEDTIME, JIMMY HAS A SURPRISE CALLER...

GOSH, I JUST LEFT KA-RA! WHY IS SHE COMING BACK WITH YOU, PROFESSOR POTTER?

SHE ISN'T, JIMMY! THIS IS A LIFE-LIKE ROBOT! I MADE IT FOR KARA AS A REWARD FOR STOPPING MY MECHANICAL MONSTER!

WILL YOU PRESENT IT TO KA-RA FOR ME, JIMMY?

SURE, PROFESSOR! I'LL KEEP IT IN THIS CLOSET! THIS LEVER CONTROLS THE ROBOT'S MOTORS, EH? KA-RA WILL BE TICKLED WITH YOUR GIFT!

THE NEXT DAY, AT THE APARTMENT OF THE LANE SISTERS...

WHAT IN THE WORLD ARE YOU UP TO, LUCY?

I'M COOKING A NICE MEAL FOR JIMMY! THE WAY TO A MAN'S HEART IS THROUGH HIS STOMACH, YOU KNOW! I'LL INVITE HIM HERE TONIGHT AND KEEP HIM OUT OF KA-RA'S CLUTCHES!

HAVING KEPT WATCH ON LUCY'S MOVES, SUPERGIRL PLANS TO THWART HER!

LUCY WON'T WIN BACK JIMMY THAT EASILY! I FLEW TO THE PLANET VENUS TO PICK UP SOME NON-EARTHLY KINDS OF FOOD HERE! JIMMY WILL HAVE DINNER WITH KA-RA!

AND THAT EVENING...

WHY DIDN'T JIMMY ANSWER HIS PHONE? I HAD TO TAXI TO HIS APARTMENT TO INVITE HIM TO DINNER AT MY PLACE...OH-OH! KARA'S SPACESHIP IS PARKED OUTSIDE HIS APARTMENT!

HUNGRY, JIMMY?

7

ENTERING, LUCY HEARS SHOCKING WORDS!

I HOPE YOU LIKE THAT VENUSIAN DRAGON-TAIL ROAST, JIM-MY! I WOULD LIKE TO COOK FOR YOU FOR LIFE!

KA-RA, ARE YOU PROPOSING TO JIMMY? BUT NICE GIRLS DON'T DO THAT, YOU... YOU SHAMELESS HUSSY!

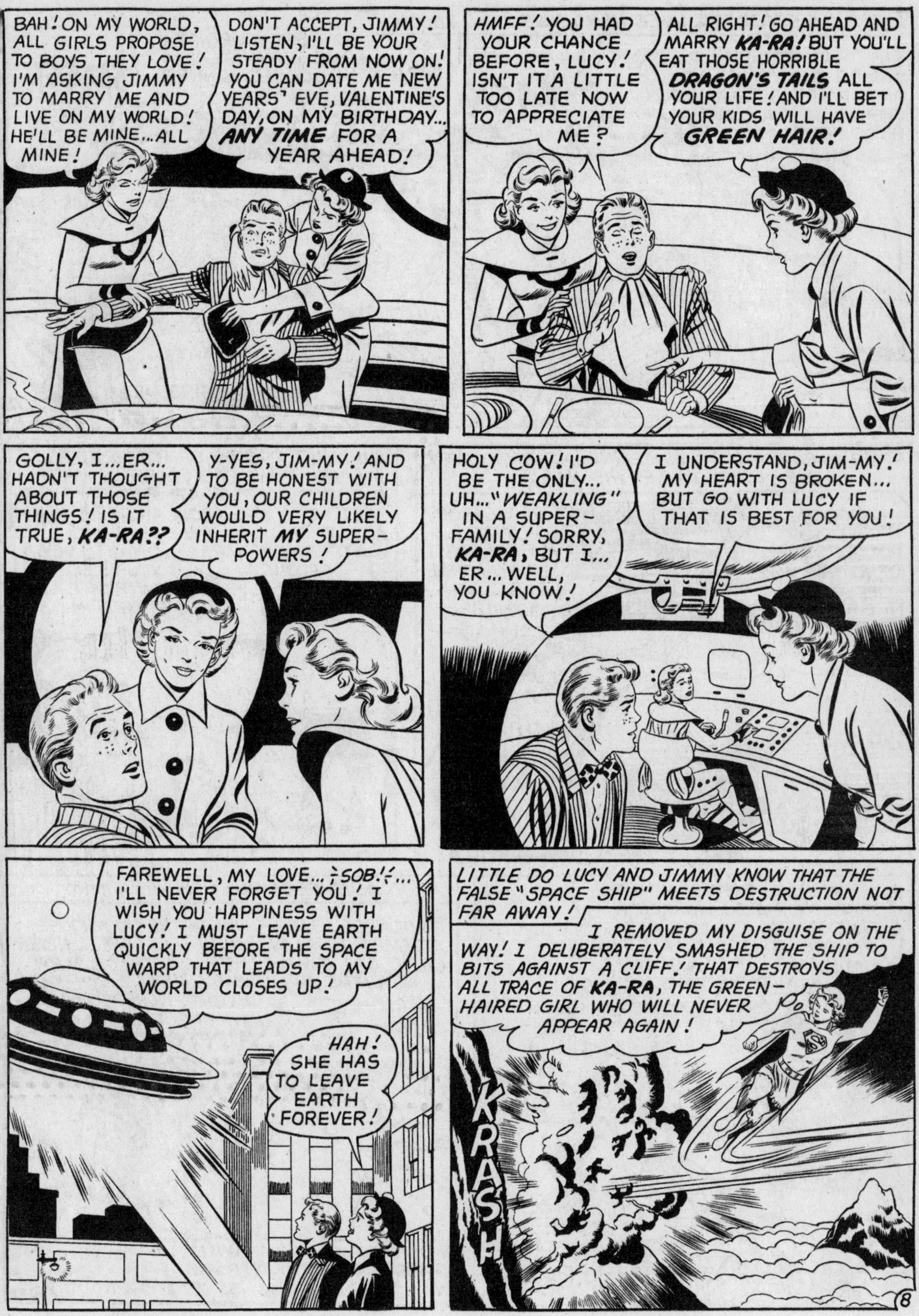
BAH! ON MY WORLD, ALL GIRLS PROPOSE TO BOYS THEY LOVE! I'M ASKING JIMMY TO MARRY ME AND LIVE ON MY WORLD! HE'LL BE MINE...ALL MINE!
DON'T ACCEPT, JIMMY! LISTEN, I'LL BE YOUR STEADY FROM NOW ON! YOU CAN DATE ME NEW YEARS' EVE, VALENTINE'S DAY, ON MY BIRTHDAY... ANY TIME FOR A YEAR AHEAD!
HMFF! YOU HAD YOUR CHANCE BEFORE, LUCY! ISN'T IT A LITTLE TOO LATE NOW TO APPRECIATE ME?
ALL RIGHT! GO AHEAD AND MARRY KA-RA! BUT YOU'LL EAT THOSE HORRIBLE DRAGON'S TAILS ALL YOUR LIFE! AND I'LL BET YOUR KIDS WILL HAVE GREEN HAIR!
GOLLY, I...ER... HADN'T THOUGHT ABOUT THOSE THINGS! IS IT TRUE, KA-RA??
Y-YES, JIM-MY! AND TO BE HONEST WITH YOU, OUR CHILDREN WOULD VERY LIKELY INHERIT MY SUPER-POWERS!
HOLY COW! I'D BE THE ONLY... UH..."WEAKLING" IN A SUPER-FAMILY! SORRY, KA-RA, BUT I... ER... WELL, YOU KNOW!
I UNDERSTAND, JIM-MY! MY HEART IS BROKEN... BUT GO WITH LUCY IF THAT IS BEST FOR YOU!
FAREWELL, MY LOVE... -SOB!-... I'LL NEVER FORGET YOU! I WISH YOU HAPPINESS WITH LUCY! I MUST LEAVE EARTH QUICKLY BEFORE THE SPACE WARP THAT LEADS TO MY WORLD CLOSES UP!
HAH! SHE HAS TO LEAVE EARTH FOREVER!
LITTLE DO LUCY AND JIMMY KNOW THAT THE FALSE "SPACE SHIP" MEETS DESTRUCTION NOT FAR AWAY!
I REMOVED MY DISGUISE ON THE WAY! I DELIBERATELY SMASHED THE SHIP TO BITS AGAINST A CLIFF! THAT DESTROYS ALL TRACE OF KA-RA, THE GREEN-HAIRED GIRL WHO WILL NEVER APPEAR AGAIN!
KRASH
8

LATER, AS **SUPERGIRL** USES HER TELESCOPIC VISION...

BUT THAT PATCHES UP THINGS BETWEEN LUCY AND JIMMY, AS I PLANNED! THEY'LL BE TWO LOVE-BIRDS FROM NOW ON!

SMACK

NOW GET YOUR HAT AND COME TO MY PLACE, JIMMY! I COOKED DINNER FOR YOU!

SMACK

WHO WANTS TO EAT? JUST KEEP KISSING ME!

AFTER MORE ROMANTIC LINGERING, AS JIMMY OPENS THE CLOSET TO GET HIS HAT...

OMIGOSH! PROFESSOR POTTER'S ROBOT OF **KA-RA** WAS DEFECTIVE, LIKE HIS MONSTER! IT FELL APART IN MY CLOSET!

PROFESSOR POTTER?... **KA-RA** ROBOT? OH, NOW I SEE IT ALL, YOU... YOU CHEAT!

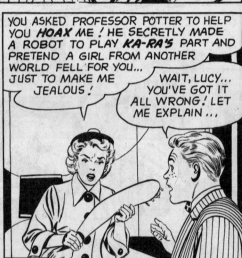

YOU ASKED PROFESSOR POTTER TO HELP YOU **HOAX** ME! HE SECRETLY MADE A ROBOT TO PLAY **KA-RA'S** PART AND PRETEND A GIRL FROM ANOTHER WORLD FELL FOR YOU... JUST TO MAKE ME JEALOUS!

WAIT, LUCY... YOU'VE GOT IT ALL WRONG! LET ME EXPLAIN...

YOU MEAN EXPLAIN HOW THE PROFESSOR ALSO WORKED A FAKE FLYING SAUCER WITH REMOTE-CONTROLS? ALL OUR DATES ARE OFF! I'M GOING OUT WITH RICKY AVALON AGAIN!

⑨

LATER, AS **SUPERGIRL** OBSERVES JIMMY...

GOODNESS! MY ATTEMPT TO PLAY CUPID GOT JIMMY NOWHERE!

I'M IN THE DOG-HOUSE WITH LUCY! SHE'LL NEVER BELIEVE THAT **KA-RA** WAS A **REAL** GIRL FROM ANOTHER WORLD! NOW I HAVEN'T GOT **KA-RA** AND I HAVEN'T GOT LUCY!

POOR JIMMY! WHAT WILL **SUPERGIRL** DO TO HELP HIM NOW? SEE A FUTURE ISSUE!

THE END

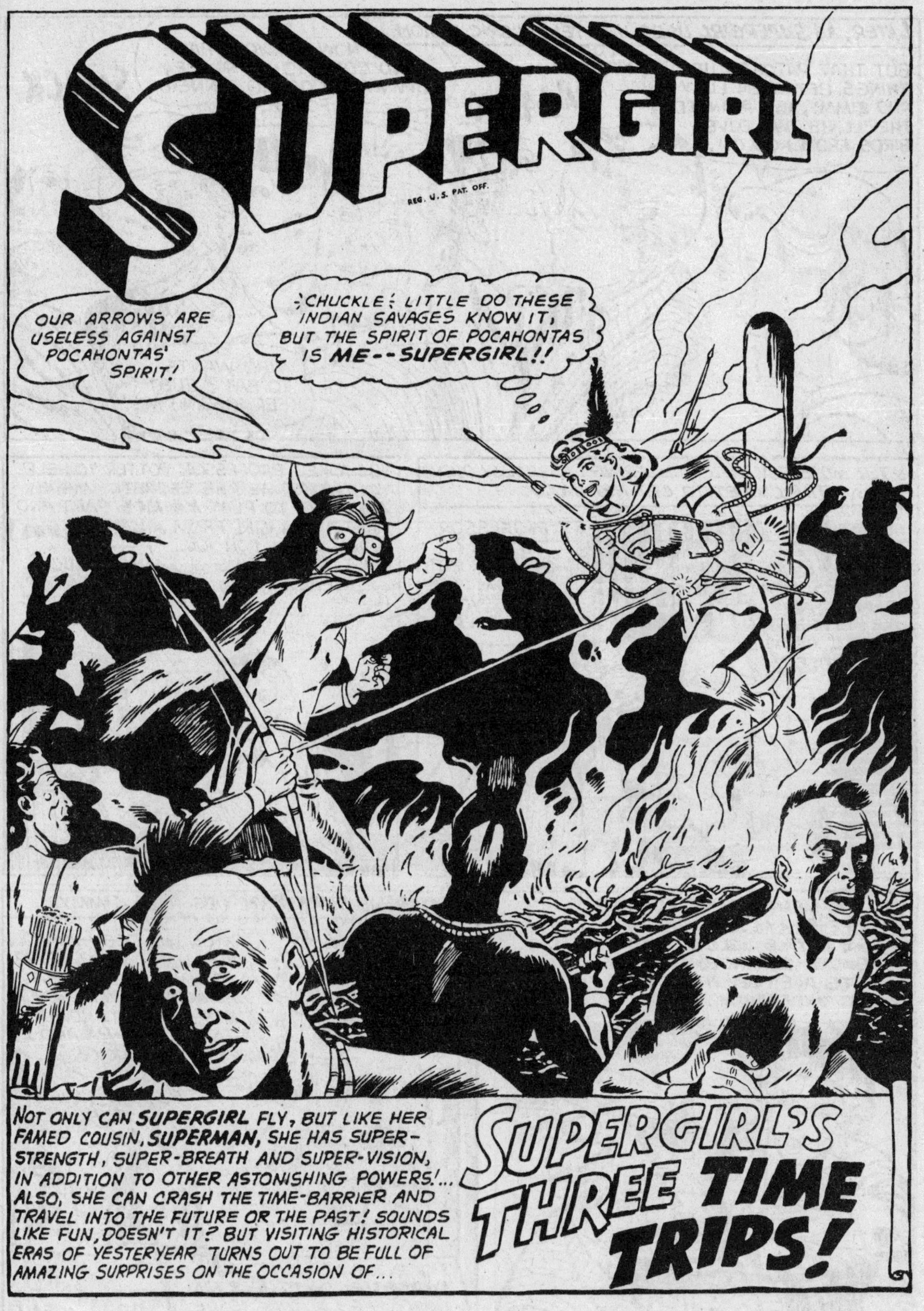
SUPERGIRL
REG. U.S. PAT. OFF.
OUR ARROWS ARE USELESS AGAINST POCAHONTAS' SPIRIT!
;CHUCKLE; LITTLE DO THESE INDIAN SAVAGES KNOW IT, BUT THE SPIRIT OF POCAHONTAS IS ME--SUPERGIRL!!
NOT ONLY CAN SUPERGIRL FLY, BUT LIKE HER FAMED COUSIN, SUPERMAN, SHE HAS SUPER-STRENGTH, SUPER-BREATH AND SUPER-VISION, IN ADDITION TO OTHER ASTONISHING POWERS!... ALSO, SHE CAN CRASH THE TIME-BARRIER AND TRAVEL INTO THE FUTURE OR THE PAST! SOUNDS LIKE FUN, DOESN'T IT? BUT VISITING HISTORICAL ERAS OF YESTERYEAR TURNS OUT TO BE FULL OF AMAZING SURPRISES ON THE OCCASION OF...
SUPERGIRL'S THREE TIME TRIPS!

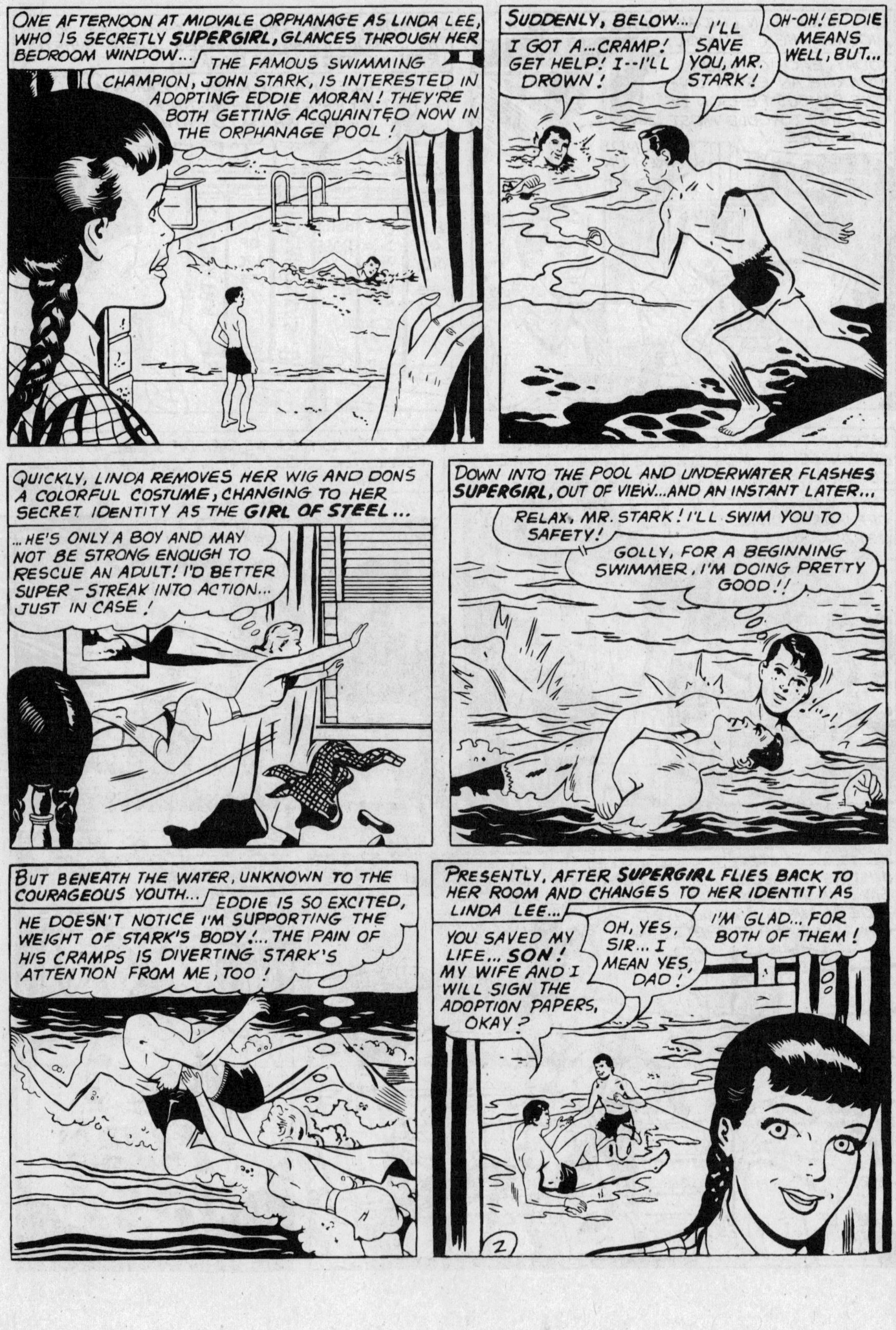
ONE AFTERNOON AT MIDVALE ORPHANAGE AS LINDA LEE, WHO IS SECRETLY **SUPERGIRL**, GLANCES THROUGH HER BEDROOM WINDOW...
THE FAMOUS SWIMMING CHAMPION, JOHN STARK, IS INTERESTED IN ADOPTING EDDIE MORAN! THEY'RE BOTH GETTING ACQUAINTED NOW IN THE ORPHANAGE POOL!
SUDDENLY, BELOW...
I GOT A...CRAMP! GET HELP! I--I'LL DROWN!
I'LL SAVE YOU, MR. STARK!
OH-OH! EDDIE MEANS WELL, BUT...
QUICKLY, LINDA REMOVES HER WIG AND DONS A COLORFUL **COSTUME**, CHANGING TO HER SECRET IDENTITY AS THE **GIRL OF STEEL**...
...HE'S ONLY A BOY AND MAY NOT BE STRONG ENOUGH TO RESCUE AN ADULT! I'D BETTER SUPER-STREAK INTO ACTION... JUST IN CASE!
DOWN INTO THE POOL AND UNDERWATER FLASHES **SUPERGIRL**, OUT OF VIEW...AND AN INSTANT LATER...
RELAX, MR. STARK! I'LL SWIM YOU TO SAFETY!
GOLLY, FOR A BEGINNING SWIMMER, I'M DOING PRETTY GOOD!!
BUT BENEATH THE WATER, UNKNOWN TO THE COURAGEOUS YOUTH...
EDDIE IS SO EXCITED, HE DOESN'T NOTICE I'M SUPPORTING THE WEIGHT OF STARK'S BODY!... THE PAIN OF HIS CRAMPS IS DIVERTING STARK'S ATTENTION FROM ME, TOO!
PRESENTLY, AFTER **SUPERGIRL** FLIES BACK TO HER ROOM AND CHANGES TO HER IDENTITY AS LINDA LEE...
YOU SAVED MY LIFE... **SON**! MY WIFE AND I WILL SIGN THE ADOPTION PAPERS, OKAY?
OH, YES, SIR... I MEAN YES, DAD!
I'M GLAD... FOR BOTH OF THEM!
2

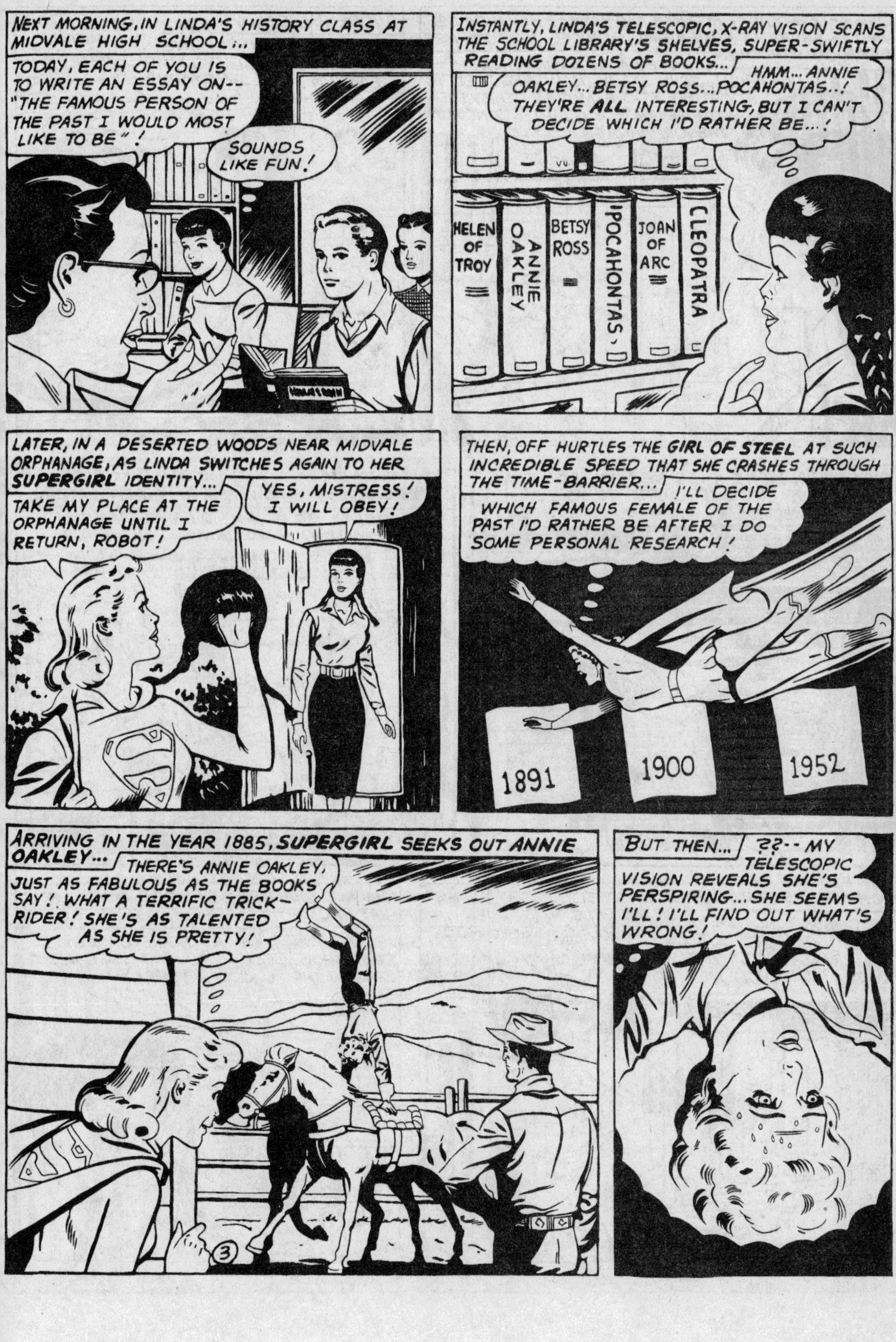
NEXT MORNING, IN LINDA'S HISTORY CLASS AT MIDVALE HIGH SCHOOL...
TODAY, EACH OF YOU IS TO WRITE AN ESSAY ON-- "THE FAMOUS PERSON OF THE PAST I WOULD MOST LIKE TO BE"!
SOUNDS LIKE FUN!
INSTANTLY, LINDA'S TELESCOPIC, X-RAY VISION SCANS THE SCHOOL LIBRARY'S SHELVES, SUPER-SWIFTLY READING DOZENS OF BOOKS...
HMM... ANNIE OAKLEY... BETSY ROSS... POCAHONTAS...! THEY'RE ALL INTERESTING, BUT I CAN'T DECIDE WHICH I'D RATHER BE...!
HELEN OF TROY
ANNIE OAKLEY
BETSY ROSS
POCAHONTAS
JOAN OF ARC
CLEOPATRA
LATER, IN A DESERTED WOODS NEAR MIDVALE ORPHANAGE, AS LINDA SWITCHES AGAIN TO HER SUPERGIRL IDENTITY...
TAKE MY PLACE AT THE ORPHANAGE UNTIL I RETURN, ROBOT!
YES, MISTRESS! I WILL OBEY!
THEN, OFF HURTLES THE GIRL OF STEEL AT SUCH INCREDIBLE SPEED THAT SHE CRASHES THROUGH THE TIME-BARRIER...
I'LL DECIDE WHICH FAMOUS FEMALE OF THE PAST I'D RATHER BE AFTER I DO SOME PERSONAL RESEARCH!
1891
1900
1952
ARRIVING IN THE YEAR 1885, SUPERGIRL SEEKS OUT ANNIE OAKLEY...
THERE'S ANNIE OAKLEY, JUST AS FABULOUS AS THE BOOKS SAY! WHAT A TERRIFIC TRICK-RIDER! SHE'S AS TALENTED AS SHE IS PRETTY!
3
BUT THEN...
??-- MY TELESCOPIC VISION REVEALS SHE'S PERSPIRING... SHE SEEMS I'LL! I'LL FIND OUT WHAT'S WRONG!

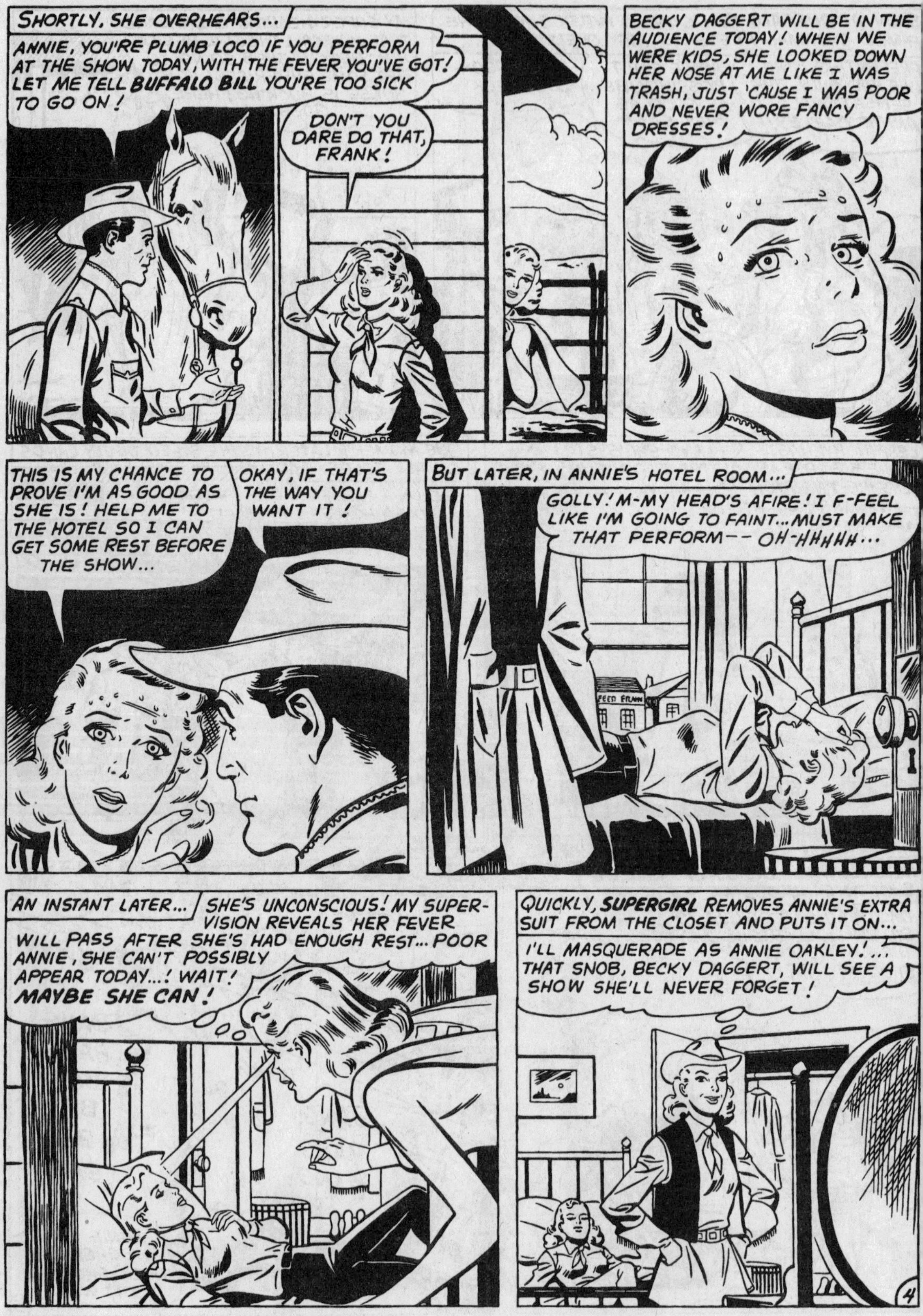
SHORTLY, SHE OVERHEARS...
ANNIE, YOU'RE PLUMB LOCO IF YOU PERFORM AT THE SHOW TODAY, WITH THE FEVER YOU'VE GOT! LET ME TELL BUFFALO BILL YOU'RE TOO SICK TO GO ON!
DON'T YOU DARE DO THAT, FRANK!
BECKY DAGGERT WILL BE IN THE AUDIENCE TODAY! WHEN WE WERE KIDS, SHE LOOKED DOWN HER NOSE AT ME LIKE I WAS TRASH, JUST 'CAUSE I WAS POOR AND NEVER WORE FANCY DRESSES!
THIS IS MY CHANCE TO PROVE I'M AS GOOD AS SHE IS! HELP ME TO THE HOTEL SO I CAN GET SOME REST BEFORE THE SHOW...
OKAY, IF THAT'S THE WAY YOU WANT IT!
BUT LATER, IN ANNIE'S HOTEL ROOM...
GOLLY! M-MY HEAD'S AFIRE! I F-FEEL LIKE I'M GOING TO FAINT... MUST MAKE THAT PERFORM-- OH-HHHHH...
FEED
AN INSTANT LATER...
SHE'S UNCONSCIOUS! MY SUPER-VISION REVEALS HER FEVER WILL PASS AFTER SHE'S HAD ENOUGH REST... POOR ANNIE, SHE CAN'T POSSIBLY APPEAR TODAY...! WAIT! MAYBE SHE CAN!
QUICKLY, SUPERGIRL REMOVES ANNIE'S EXTRA SUIT FROM THE CLOSET AND PUTS IT ON...
I'LL MASQUERADE AS ANNIE OAKLEY!... THAT SNOB, BECKY DAGGERT, WILL SEE A SHOW SHE'LL NEVER FORGET!
4

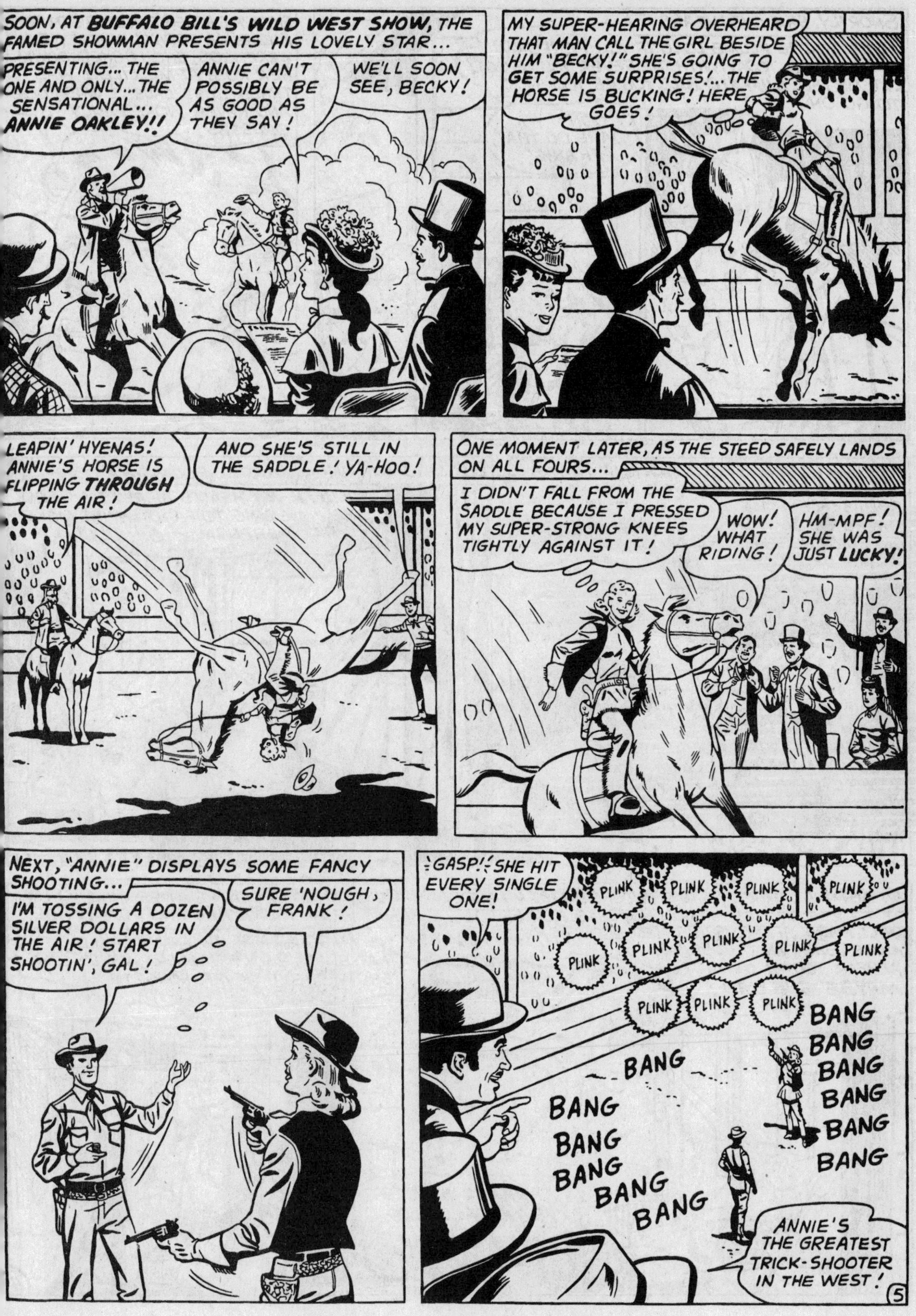
SOON, AT BUFFALO BILL'S WILD WEST SHOW, THE FAMED SHOWMAN PRESENTS HIS LOVELY STAR...
PRESENTING... THE ONE AND ONLY... THE SENSATIONAL... ANNIE OAKLEY!!
ANNIE CAN'T POSSIBLY BE AS GOOD AS THEY SAY!
WE'LL SOON SEE, BECKY!
MY SUPER-HEARING OVERHEARD THAT MAN CALL THE GIRL BESIDE HIM "BECKY!" SHE'S GOING TO GET SOME SURPRISES!... THE HORSE IS BUCKING! HERE GOES!
LEAPIN' HYENAS! ANNIE'S HORSE IS FLIPPING THROUGH THE AIR!
AND SHE'S STILL IN THE SADDLE! YA-HOO!
ONE MOMENT LATER, AS THE STEED SAFELY LANDS ON ALL FOURS...
I DIDN'T FALL FROM THE SADDLE BECAUSE I PRESSED MY SUPER-STRONG KNEES TIGHTLY AGAINST IT!
WOW! WHAT RIDING!
HM-MPF! SHE WAS JUST LUCKY!
NEXT, "ANNIE" DISPLAYS SOME FANCY SHOOTING...
I'M TOSSING A DOZEN SILVER DOLLARS IN THE AIR! START SHOOTIN', GAL!
SURE 'NOUGH, FRANK!
GASP! SHE HIT EVERY SINGLE ONE!
PLINK PLINK PLINK PLINK
PLINK PLINK PLINK PLINK PLINK
PLINK PLINK PLINK
BANG BANG BANG BANG BANG BANG
BANG
BANG BANG BANG BANG BANG
ANNIE'S THE GREATEST TRICK-SHOOTER IN THE WEST!
5

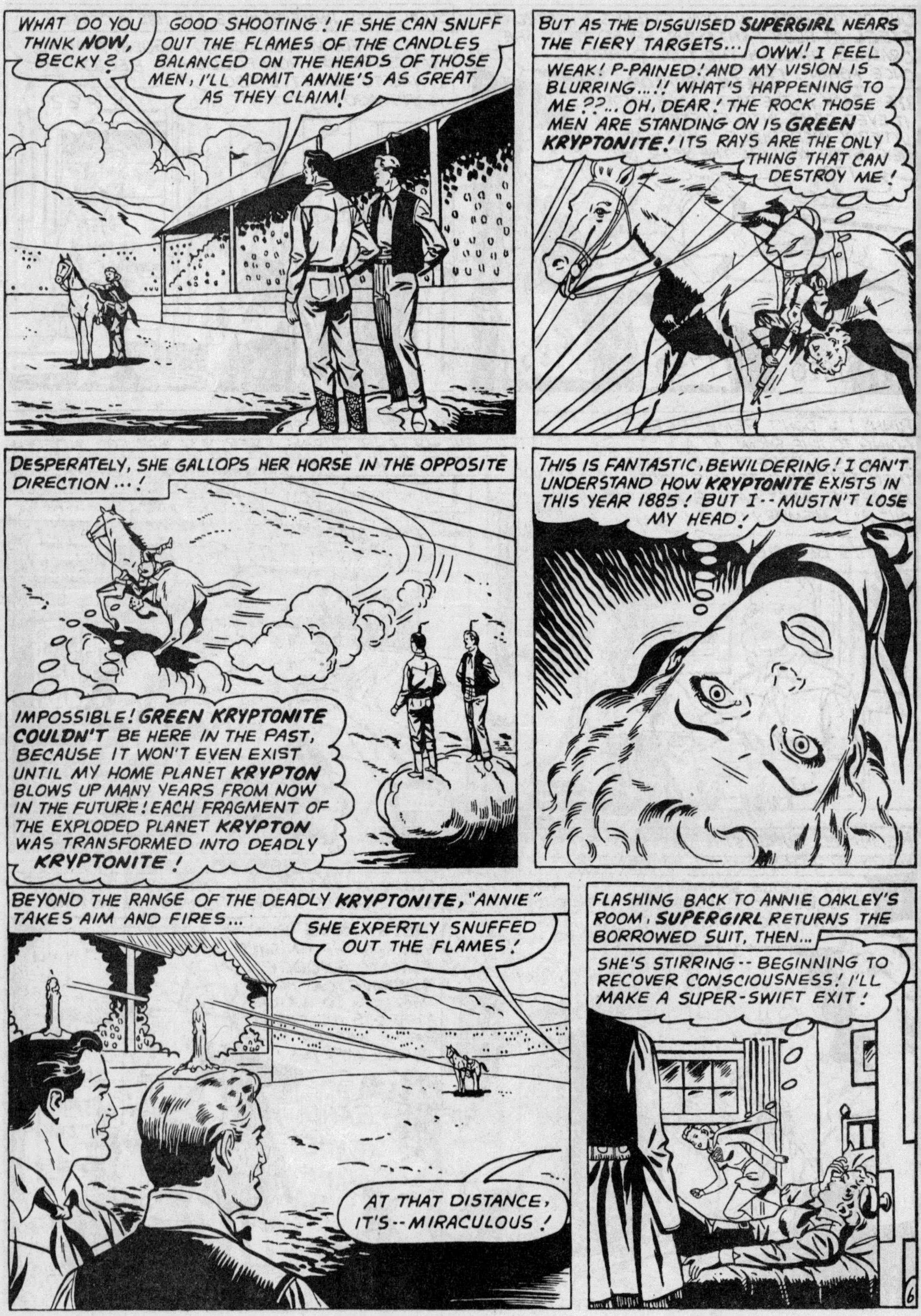
WHAT DO YOU THINK NOW, BECKY?
GOOD SHOOTING! IF SHE CAN SNUFF OUT THE FLAMES OF THE CANDLES BALANCED ON THE HEADS OF THOSE MEN, I'LL ADMIT ANNIE'S AS GREAT AS THEY CLAIM!
BUT AS THE DISGUISED SUPERGIRL NEARS THE FIERY TARGETS...
OWW! I FEEL WEAK! P-PAINED! AND MY VISION IS BLURRING...!! WHAT'S HAPPENING TO ME??... OH, DEAR! THE ROCK THOSE MEN ARE STANDING ON IS GREEN KRYPTONITE! ITS RAYS ARE THE ONLY THING THAT CAN DESTROY ME!
DESPERATELY, SHE GALLOPS HER HORSE IN THE OPPOSITE DIRECTION...!
IMPOSSIBLE! GREEN KRYPTONITE COULDN'T BE HERE IN THE PAST, BECAUSE IT WON'T EVEN EXIST UNTIL MY HOME PLANET KRYPTON BLOWS UP MANY YEARS FROM NOW IN THE FUTURE! EACH FRAGMENT OF THE EXPLODED PLANET KRYPTON WAS TRANSFORMED INTO DEADLY KRYPTONITE!
THIS IS FANTASTIC, BEWILDERING! I CAN'T UNDERSTAND HOW KRYPTONITE EXISTS IN THIS YEAR 1885! BUT I--MUSTN'T LOSE MY HEAD!
BEYOND THE RANGE OF THE DEADLY KRYPTONITE, "ANNIE" TAKES AIM AND FIRES...
SHE EXPERTLY SNUFFED OUT THE FLAMES!
AT THAT DISTANCE, IT'S--MIRACULOUS!
FLASHING BACK TO ANNIE OAKLEY'S ROOM, SUPERGIRL RETURNS THE BORROWED SUIT, THEN...
SHE'S STIRRING--BEGINNING TO RECOVER CONSCIOUSNESS! I'LL MAKE A SUPER-SWIFT EXIT!
6

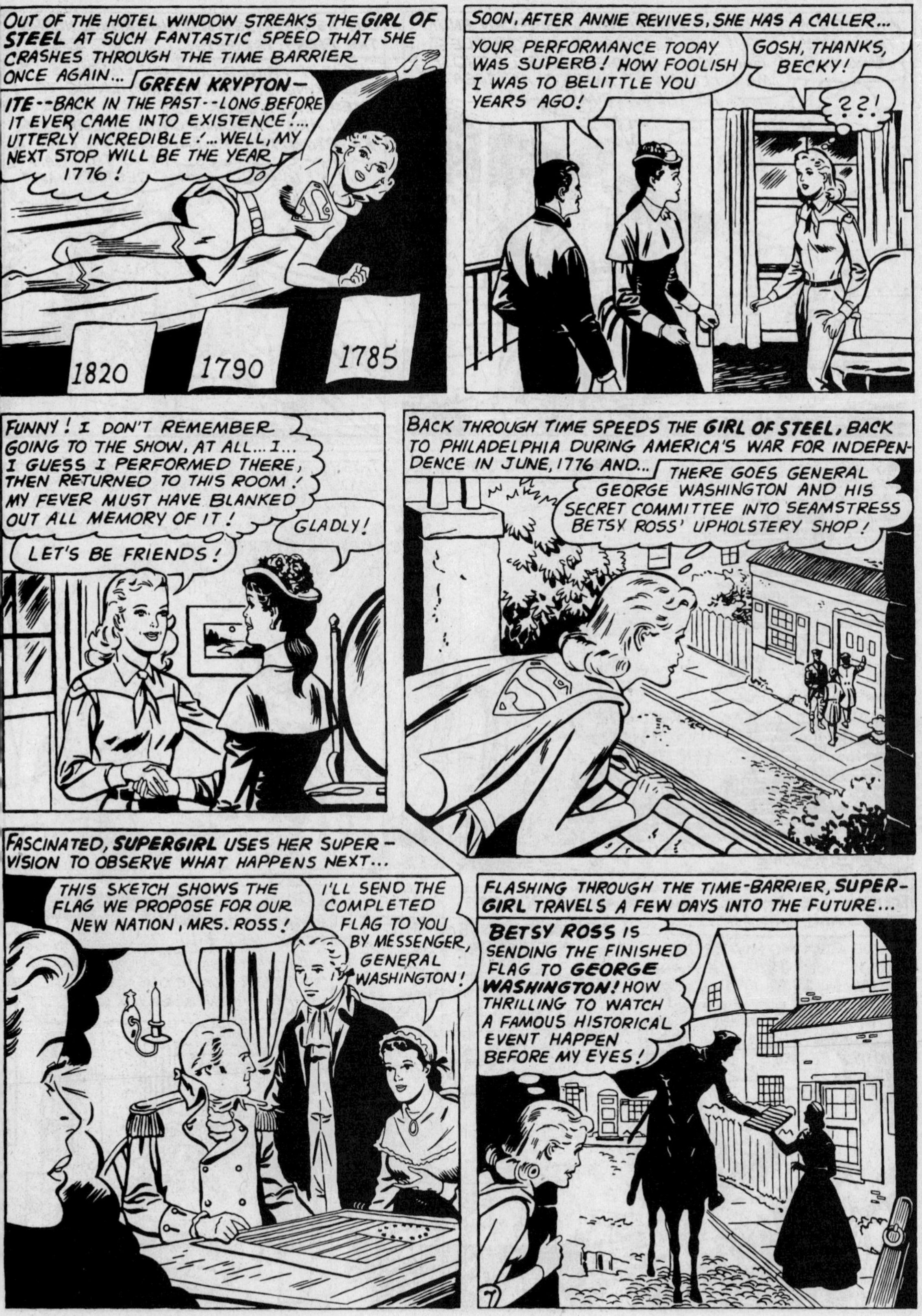
OUT OF THE HOTEL WINDOW STREAKS THE GIRL OF STEEL AT SUCH FANTASTIC SPEED THAT SHE CRASHES THROUGH THE TIME BARRIER ONCE AGAIN...
GREEN KRYPTONITE--BACK IN THE PAST--LONG BEFORE IT EVER CAME INTO EXISTENCE!... UTTERLY INCREDIBLE!...WELL, MY NEXT STOP WILL BE THE YEAR 1776!
1820
1790
1785
SOON, AFTER ANNIE REVIVES, SHE HAS A CALLER...
YOUR PERFORMANCE TODAY WAS SUPERB! HOW FOOLISH I WAS TO BELITTLE YOU YEARS AGO!
GOSH, THANKS, BECKY!
??!
FUNNY! I DON'T REMEMBER GOING TO THE SHOW, AT ALL... I... I GUESS I PERFORMED THERE, THEN RETURNED TO THIS ROOM! MY FEVER MUST HAVE BLANKED OUT ALL MEMORY OF IT!
LET'S BE FRIENDS!
GLADLY!
BACK THROUGH TIME SPEEDS THE GIRL OF STEEL, BACK TO PHILADELPHIA DURING AMERICA'S WAR FOR INDEPENDENCE IN JUNE, 1776 AND...
THERE GOES GENERAL GEORGE WASHINGTON AND HIS SECRET COMMITTEE INTO SEAMSTRESS BETSY ROSS' UPHOLSTERY SHOP!
FASCINATED, SUPERGIRL USES HER SUPER-VISION TO OBSERVE WHAT HAPPENS NEXT...
THIS SKETCH SHOWS THE FLAG WE PROPOSE FOR OUR NEW NATION, MRS. ROSS!
I'LL SEND THE COMPLETED FLAG TO YOU BY MESSENGER, GENERAL WASHINGTON!
FLASHING THROUGH THE TIME-BARRIER, SUPERGIRL TRAVELS A FEW DAYS INTO THE FUTURE...
BETSY ROSS IS SENDING THE FINISHED FLAG TO GEORGE WASHINGTON! HOW THRILLING TO WATCH A FAMOUS HISTORICAL EVENT HAPPEN BEFORE MY EYES!
7

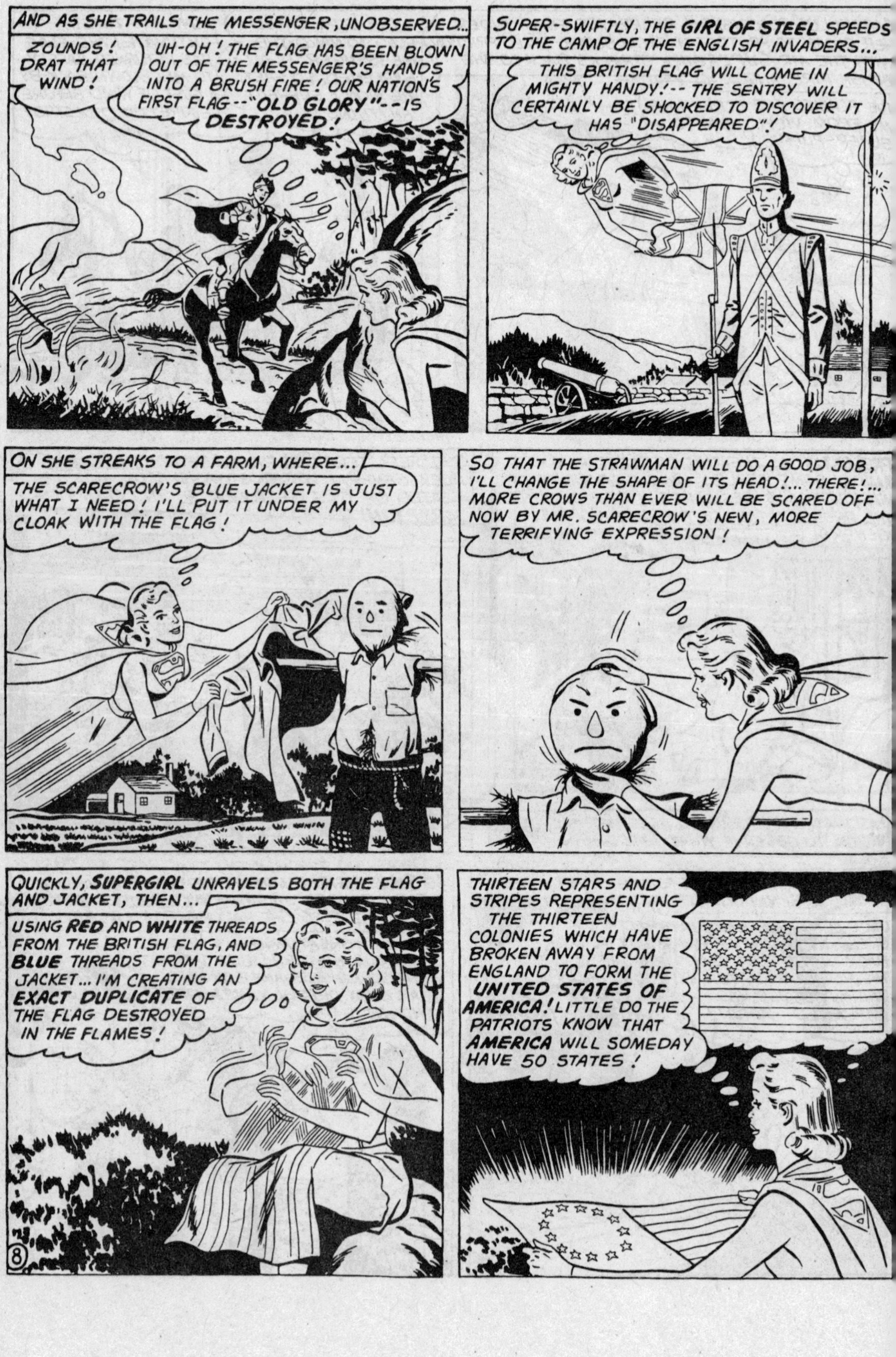
AND AS SHE TRAILS THE MESSENGER, UNOBSERVED...
ZOUNDS! DRAT THAT WIND!
UH-OH! THE FLAG HAS BEEN BLOWN OUT OF THE MESSENGER'S HANDS INTO A BRUSH FIRE! OUR NATION'S FIRST FLAG--"OLD GLORY"--IS DESTROYED!
SUPER-SWIFTLY, THE GIRL OF STEEL SPEEDS TO THE CAMP OF THE ENGLISH INVADERS...
THIS BRITISH FLAG WILL COME IN MIGHTY HANDY!--THE SENTRY WILL CERTAINLY BE SHOCKED TO DISCOVER IT HAS "DISAPPEARED"!
ON SHE STREAKS TO A FARM, WHERE...
THE SCARECROW'S BLUE JACKET IS JUST WHAT I NEED! I'LL PUT IT UNDER MY CLOAK WITH THE FLAG!
SO THAT THE STRAWMAN WILL DO A GOOD JOB, I'LL CHANGE THE SHAPE OF ITS HEAD!... THERE!... MORE CROWS THAN EVER WILL BE SCARED OFF NOW BY MR. SCARECROW'S NEW, MORE TERRIFYING EXPRESSION!
QUICKLY, SUPERGIRL UNRAVELS BOTH THE FLAG AND JACKET, THEN...
USING RED AND WHITE THREADS FROM THE BRITISH FLAG, AND BLUE THREADS FROM THE JACKET... I'M CREATING AN EXACT DUPLICATE OF THE FLAG DESTROYED IN THE FLAMES!
8
THIRTEEN STARS AND STRIPES REPRESENTING THE THIRTEEN COLONIES WHICH HAVE BROKEN AWAY FROM ENGLAND TO FORM THE UNITED STATES OF AMERICA! LITTLE DO THE PATRIOTS KNOW THAT AMERICA WILL SOMEDAY HAVE 50 STATES!

CAREFULLY PLACING THE RECREATED FLAG UNDER HER CLOAK TO PROTECT IT FROM SUPER-SPEED FRICTION WITH THE AIR, **SUPERGIRL** STREAKS BACK TO THE BRUSH FIRE, AND...

THE FLAMES ARE SCREENING ME FROM VIEW! NOW TO SUPER-PUFF...

...THE DUPLICATED FLAG TOWARD THE MESSENGER! IT ALL HAPPENED SO FAST, HE WON'T SUSPECT ANYTHING!

HOW AMAZINGLY FORTUNATE! THE FLAG HAS RETURNED SAFELY TO ME, BLOWN BACK BY A GUST OF WIND BEFORE THE FIRE COULD DESTROY IT!

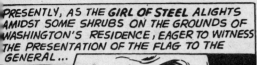

PRESENTLY, AS THE **GIRL OF STEEL** ALIGHTS AMIDST SOME SHRUBS ON THE GROUNDS OF WASHINGTON'S RESIDENCE, EAGER TO WITNESS THE PRESENTATION OF THE FLAG TO THE GENERAL...

ULP!

I-I FEEL TERRIBLE PAINS! THAT ROCK GENERAL WASHINGTON IS SEATED ON--IT'S G-GREEN **KRYPTONITE**!!

DESPERATELY, THE WORLD'S MIGHTIEST LASS ROCKETS SKYWARD...

!GASP!

ONCE AGAIN I'VE ENCOUNTERED A GREEN **KRYPTONITE** FRAGMENT BACK IN THE PAST, YEARS BEFORE THE PLANET **KRYPTON** EXPLODED! THE IMPOSSIBLE HAS HAPPENED--AGAIN!

AS **SUPERGIRL** GLANCES DOWNWARD, SHE SIGHTS GEORGE WASHINGTON PROUDLY EXAM-INING THE FLAG SHE HAD RECREATED, BUT...

THIS IS A GREAT MOMENT IN OUR COUNTRY'S HISTORY! BUT I DON'T WANT TO LINGER ANY LONGER NEAR THAT DEADLY **KRYPTONITE**, AND SO...!

9

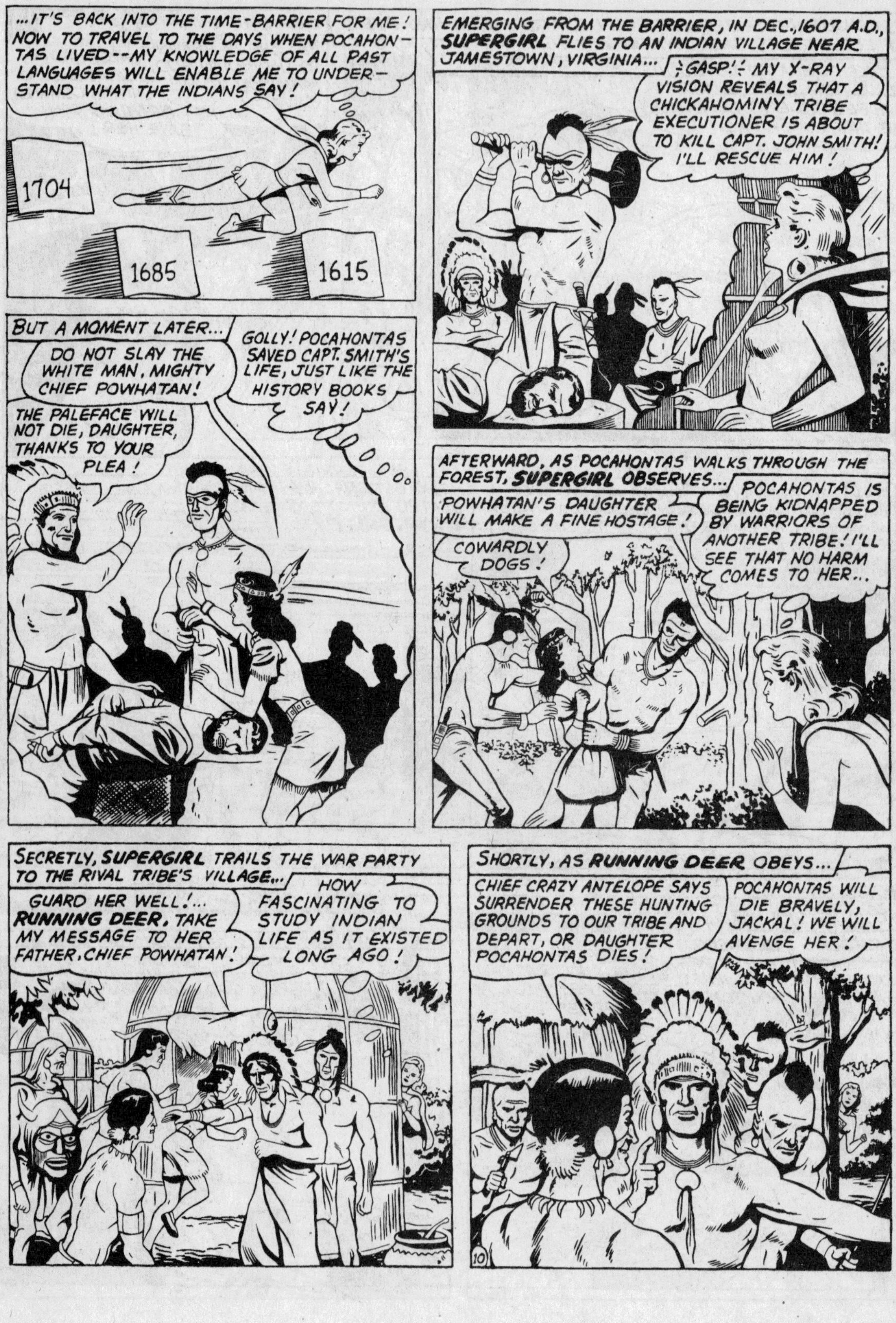
...IT'S BACK INTO THE TIME-BARRIER FOR ME! NOW TO TRAVEL TO THE DAYS WHEN POCAHONTAS LIVED--MY KNOWLEDGE OF ALL PAST LANGUAGES WILL ENABLE ME TO UNDERSTAND WHAT THE INDIANS SAY!
1704
1685
1615
EMERGING FROM THE BARRIER, IN DEC., 1607 A.D., SUPERGIRL FLIES TO AN INDIAN VILLAGE NEAR JAMESTOWN, VIRGINIA...
¿GASP!¿ MY X-RAY VISION REVEALS THAT A CHICKAHOMINY TRIBE EXECUTIONER IS ABOUT TO KILL CAPT. JOHN SMITH! I'LL RESCUE HIM!
BUT A MOMENT LATER...
DO NOT SLAY THE WHITE MAN, MIGHTY CHIEF POWHATAN!
GOLLY! POCAHONTAS SAVED CAPT. SMITH'S LIFE, JUST LIKE THE HISTORY BOOKS SAY!
THE PALEFACE WILL NOT DIE, DAUGHTER, THANKS TO YOUR PLEA!
AFTERWARD, AS POCAHONTAS WALKS THROUGH THE FOREST, SUPERGIRL OBSERVES...
POWHATAN'S DAUGHTER WILL MAKE A FINE HOSTAGE!
POCAHONTAS IS BEING KIDNAPPED BY WARRIORS OF ANOTHER TRIBE! I'LL SEE THAT NO HARM COMES TO HER...
COWARDLY DOGS!
SECRETLY, SUPERGIRL TRAILS THE WAR PARTY TO THE RIVAL TRIBE'S VILLAGE...
GUARD HER WELL!... RUNNING DEER, TAKE MY MESSAGE TO HER FATHER, CHIEF POWHATAN!
HOW FASCINATING TO STUDY INDIAN LIFE AS IT EXISTED LONG AGO!
SHORTLY, AS RUNNING DEER OBEYS...
CHIEF CRAZY ANTELOPE SAYS SURRENDER THESE HUNTING GROUNDS TO OUR TRIBE AND DEPART, OR DAUGHTER POCAHONTAS DIES!
POCAHONTAS WILL DIE BRAVELY, JACKAL! WE WILL AVENGE HER!
10

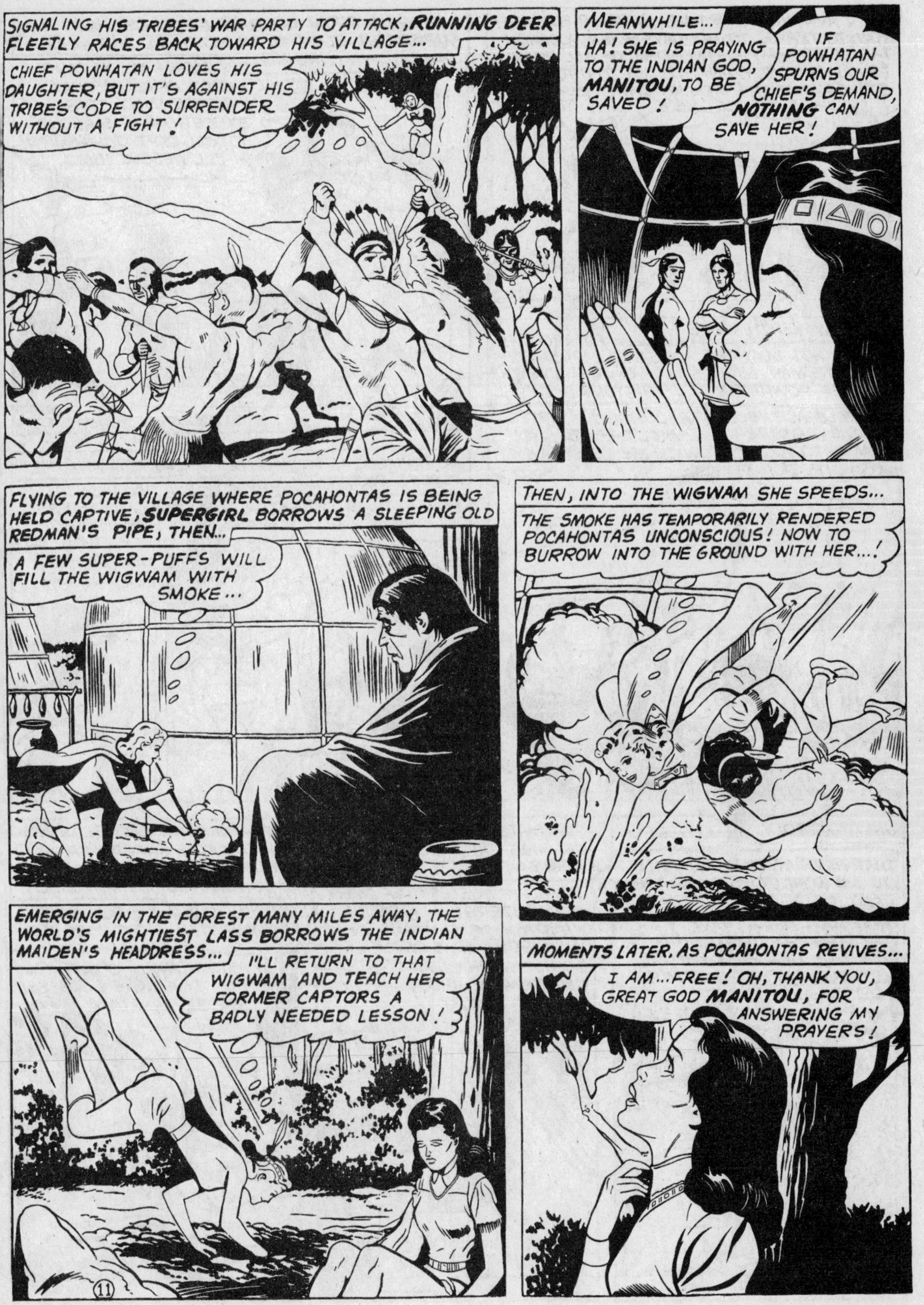
SIGNALING HIS TRIBES' WAR PARTY TO ATTACK, RUNNING DEER FLEETLY RACES BACK TOWARD HIS VILLAGE...
CHIEF POWHATAN LOVES HIS DAUGHTER, BUT IT'S AGAINST HIS TRIBE'S CODE TO SURRENDER WITHOUT A FIGHT!
MEANWHILE...
HA! SHE IS PRAYING TO THE INDIAN GOD, MANITOU, TO BE SAVED!
IF POWHATAN SPURNS OUR CHIEF'S DEMAND, NOTHING CAN SAVE HER!
FLYING TO THE VILLAGE WHERE POCAHONTAS IS BEING HELD CAPTIVE, SUPERGIRL BORROWS A SLEEPING OLD REDMAN'S PIPE, THEN...
A FEW SUPER-PUFFS WILL FILL THE WIGWAM WITH SMOKE...
THEN, INTO THE WIGWAM SHE SPEEDS...
THE SMOKE HAS TEMPORARILY RENDERED POCAHONTAS UNCONSCIOUS! NOW TO BURROW INTO THE GROUND WITH HER...!
EMERGING IN THE FOREST MANY MILES AWAY, THE WORLD'S MIGHTIEST LASS BORROWS THE INDIAN MAIDEN'S HEADDRESS...
I'LL RETURN TO THAT WIGWAM AND TEACH HER FORMER CAPTORS A BADLY NEEDED LESSON!
11
MOMENTS LATER, AS POCAHONTAS REVIVES...
I AM...FREE! OH, THANK YOU, GREAT GOD MANITOU, FOR ANSWERING MY PRAYERS!

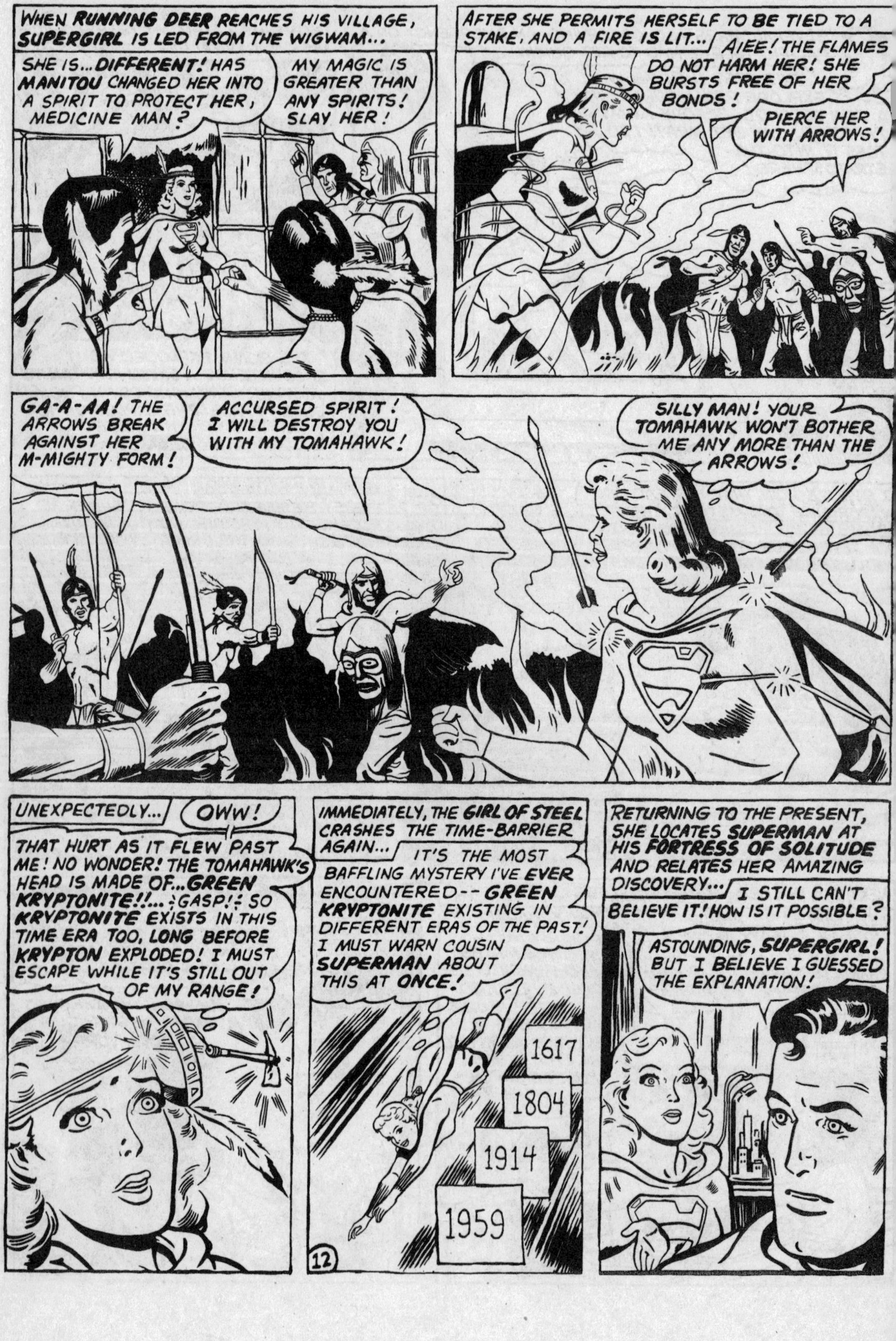
WHEN RUNNING DEER REACHES HIS VILLAGE, SUPERGIRL IS LED FROM THE WIGWAM...
SHE IS...DIFFERENT! HAS MANITOU CHANGED HER INTO A SPIRIT TO PROTECT HER, MEDICINE MAN?
MY MAGIC IS GREATER THAN ANY SPIRITS! SLAY HER!
AFTER SHE PERMITS HERSELF TO BE TIED TO A STAKE, AND A FIRE IS LIT...
AIEE! THE FLAMES DO NOT HARM HER! SHE BURSTS FREE OF HER BONDS!
PIERCE HER WITH ARROWS!
GA-A-AA! THE ARROWS BREAK AGAINST HER M-MIGHTY FORM!
ACCURSED SPIRIT! I WILL DESTROY YOU WITH MY TOMAHAWK!
SILLY MAN! YOUR TOMAHAWK WON'T BOTHER ME ANY MORE THAN THE ARROWS!
UNEXPECTEDLY...
OWW!
THAT HURT AS IT FLEW PAST ME! NO WONDER! THE TOMAHAWK'S HEAD IS MADE OF...GREEN KRYPTONITE!!... GASP! SO KRYPTONITE EXISTS IN THIS TIME ERA TOO, LONG BEFORE KRYPTON EXPLODED! I MUST ESCAPE WHILE IT'S STILL OUT OF MY RANGE!
IMMEDIATELY, THE GIRL OF STEEL CRASHES THE TIME-BARRIER AGAIN...
IT'S THE MOST BAFFLING MYSTERY I'VE EVER ENCOUNTERED-- GREEN KRYPTONITE EXISTING IN DIFFERENT ERAS OF THE PAST! I MUST WARN COUSIN SUPERMAN ABOUT THIS AT ONCE!
1617
1804
1914
1959
12
RETURNING TO THE PRESENT, SHE LOCATES SUPERMAN AT HIS FORTRESS OF SOLITUDE AND RELATES HER AMAZING DISCOVERY...
I STILL CAN'T BELIEVE IT! HOW IS IT POSSIBLE?
ASTOUNDING, SUPERGIRL! BUT I BELIEVE I GUESSED THE EXPLANATION!

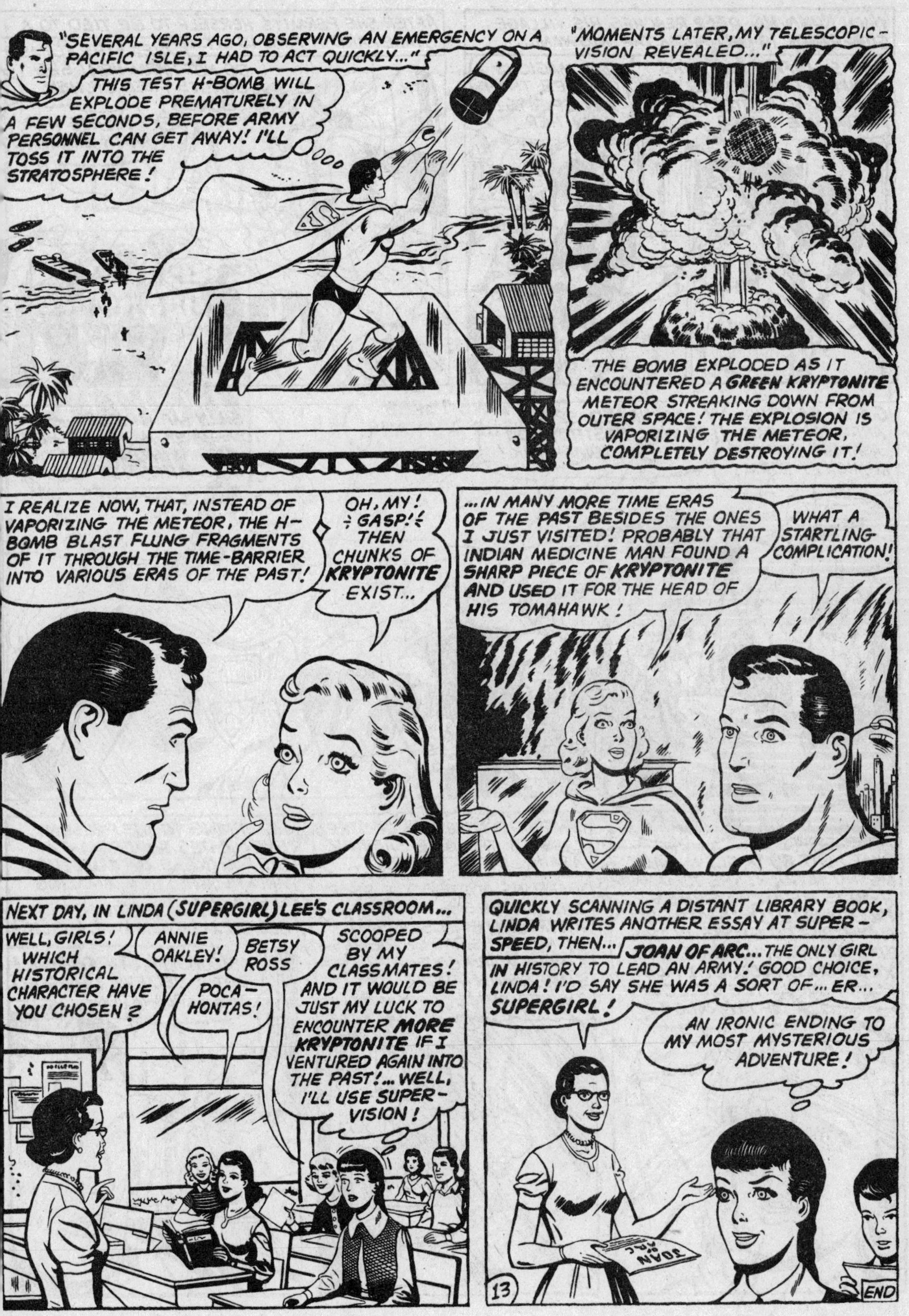
"SEVERAL YEARS AGO, OBSERVING AN EMERGENCY ON A PACIFIC ISLE, I HAD TO ACT QUICKLY..."
THIS TEST H-BOMB WILL EXPLODE PREMATURELY IN A FEW SECONDS, BEFORE ARMY PERSONNEL CAN GET AWAY! I'LL TOSS IT INTO THE STRATOSPHERE!
"MOMENTS LATER, MY TELESCOPIC-VISION REVEALED..."
THE BOMB EXPLODED AS IT ENCOUNTERED A GREEN KRYPTONITE METEOR STREAKING DOWN FROM OUTER SPACE! THE EXPLOSION IS VAPORIZING THE METEOR, COMPLETELY DESTROYING IT!
I REALIZE NOW, THAT, INSTEAD OF VAPORIZING THE METEOR, THE H-BOMB BLAST FLUNG FRAGMENTS OF IT THROUGH THE TIME-BARRIER INTO VARIOUS ERAS OF THE PAST!
OH, MY! GASP! THEN CHUNKS OF KRYPTONITE EXIST...
...IN MANY MORE TIME ERAS OF THE PAST BESIDES THE ONES I JUST VISITED! PROBABLY THAT INDIAN MEDICINE MAN FOUND A SHARP PIECE OF KRYPTONITE AND USED IT FOR THE HEAD OF HIS TOMAHAWK!
WHAT A STARTLING COMPLICATION!
NEXT DAY, IN LINDA (SUPERGIRL) LEE'S CLASSROOM...
WELL, GIRLS! WHICH HISTORICAL CHARACTER HAVE YOU CHOSEN?
ANNIE OAKLEY!
BETSY ROSS
POCA-HONTAS!
SCOOPED BY MY CLASSMATES! AND IT WOULD BE JUST MY LUCK TO ENCOUNTER MORE KRYPTONITE IF I VENTURED AGAIN INTO THE PAST!... WELL, I'LL USE SUPER-VISION!
QUICKLY SCANNING A DISTANT LIBRARY BOOK, LINDA WRITES ANOTHER ESSAY AT SUPER-SPEED, THEN...
JOAN OF ARC... THE ONLY GIRL IN HISTORY TO LEAD AN ARMY! GOOD CHOICE, LINDA! I'D SAY SHE WAS A SORT OF... ER... SUPERGIRL!
AN IRONIC ENDING TO MY MOST MYSTERIOUS ADVENTURE!
JOAN OF ARC
13
END

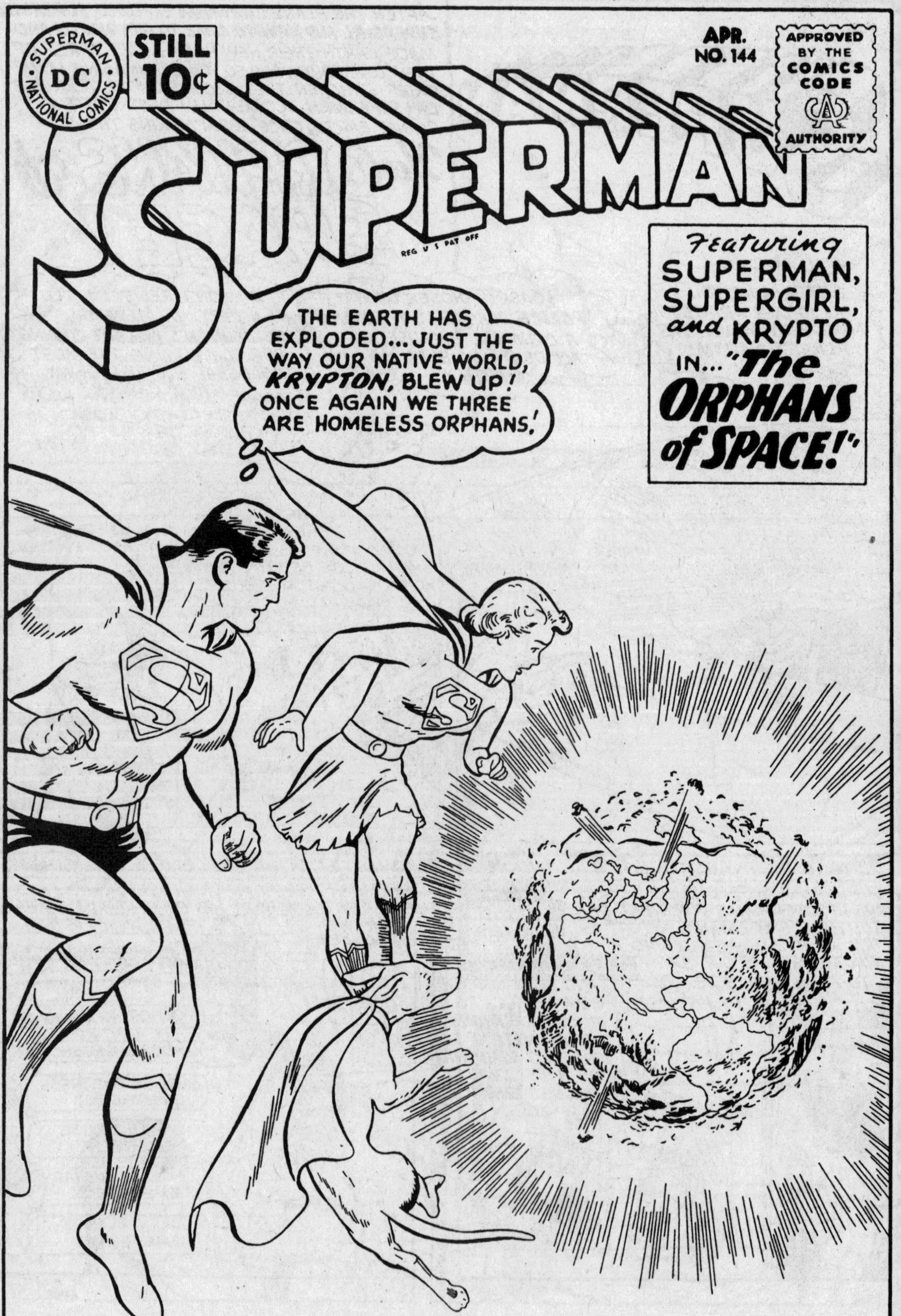
SUPERMAN DC NATIONAL COMICS
STILL 10¢
APR. NO. 144
APPROVED BY THE COMICS CODE AUTHORITY
SUPERMAN
REG U S PAT OFF
THE EARTH HAS EXPLODED... JUST THE WAY OUR NATIVE WORLD, KRYPTON, BLEW UP! ONCE AGAIN WE THREE ARE HOMELESS ORPHANS!
Featuring SUPERMAN, SUPERGIRL, and KRYPTO IN... "The ORPHANS of SPACE!"

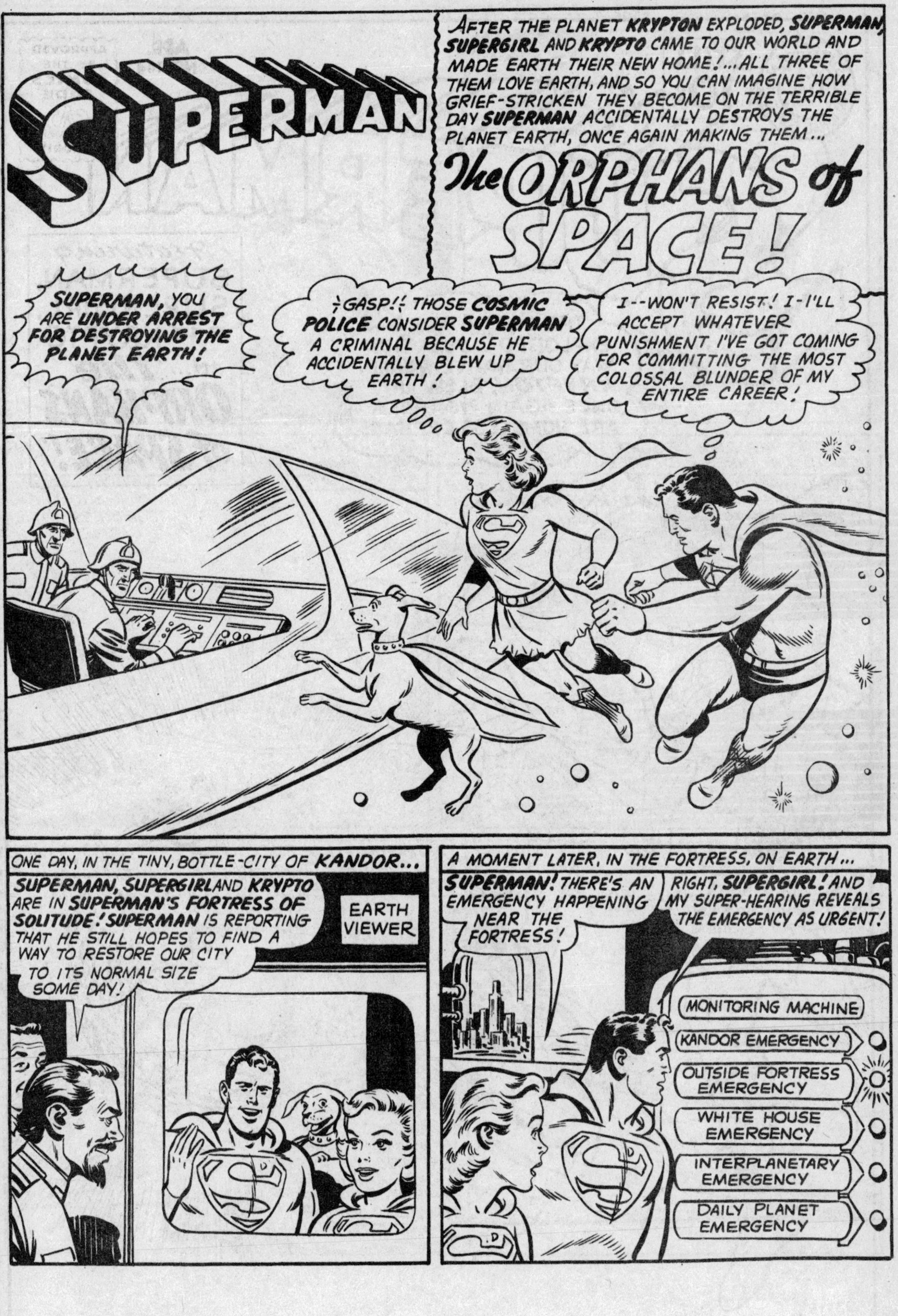
SUPERMAN
AFTER THE PLANET KRYPTON EXPLODED, SUPERMAN, SUPERGIRL AND KRYPTO CAME TO OUR WORLD AND MADE EARTH THEIR NEW HOME!... ALL THREE OF THEM LOVE EARTH, AND SO YOU CAN IMAGINE HOW GRIEF-STRICKEN THEY BECOME ON THE TERRIBLE DAY SUPERMAN ACCIDENTALLY DESTROYS THE PLANET EARTH, ONCE AGAIN MAKING THEM...
The ORPHANS of SPACE!
SUPERMAN, YOU ARE UNDER ARREST FOR DESTROYING THE PLANET EARTH!
GASP! THOSE COSMIC POLICE CONSIDER SUPERMAN A CRIMINAL BECAUSE HE ACCIDENTALLY BLEW UP EARTH!
I--WON'T RESIST! I-I'LL ACCEPT WHATEVER PUNISHMENT I'VE GOT COMING FOR COMMITTING THE MOST COLOSSAL BLUNDER OF MY ENTIRE CAREER!
ONE DAY, IN THE TINY, BOTTLE-CITY OF KANDOR...
SUPERMAN, SUPERGIRL AND KRYPTO ARE IN SUPERMAN'S FORTRESS OF SOLITUDE! SUPERMAN IS REPORTING THAT HE STILL HOPES TO FIND A WAY TO RESTORE OUR CITY TO ITS NORMAL SIZE SOME DAY!
EARTH VIEWER
A MOMENT LATER, IN THE FORTRESS, ON EARTH...
SUPERMAN! THERE'S AN EMERGENCY HAPPENING NEAR THE FORTRESS!
RIGHT, SUPERGIRL! AND MY SUPER-HEARING REVEALS THE EMERGENCY AS URGENT!
MONITORING MACHINE
KANDOR EMERGENCY
OUTSIDE FORTRESS EMERGENCY
WHITE HOUSE EMERGENCY
INTERPLANETARY EMERGENCY
DAILY PLANET EMERGENCY

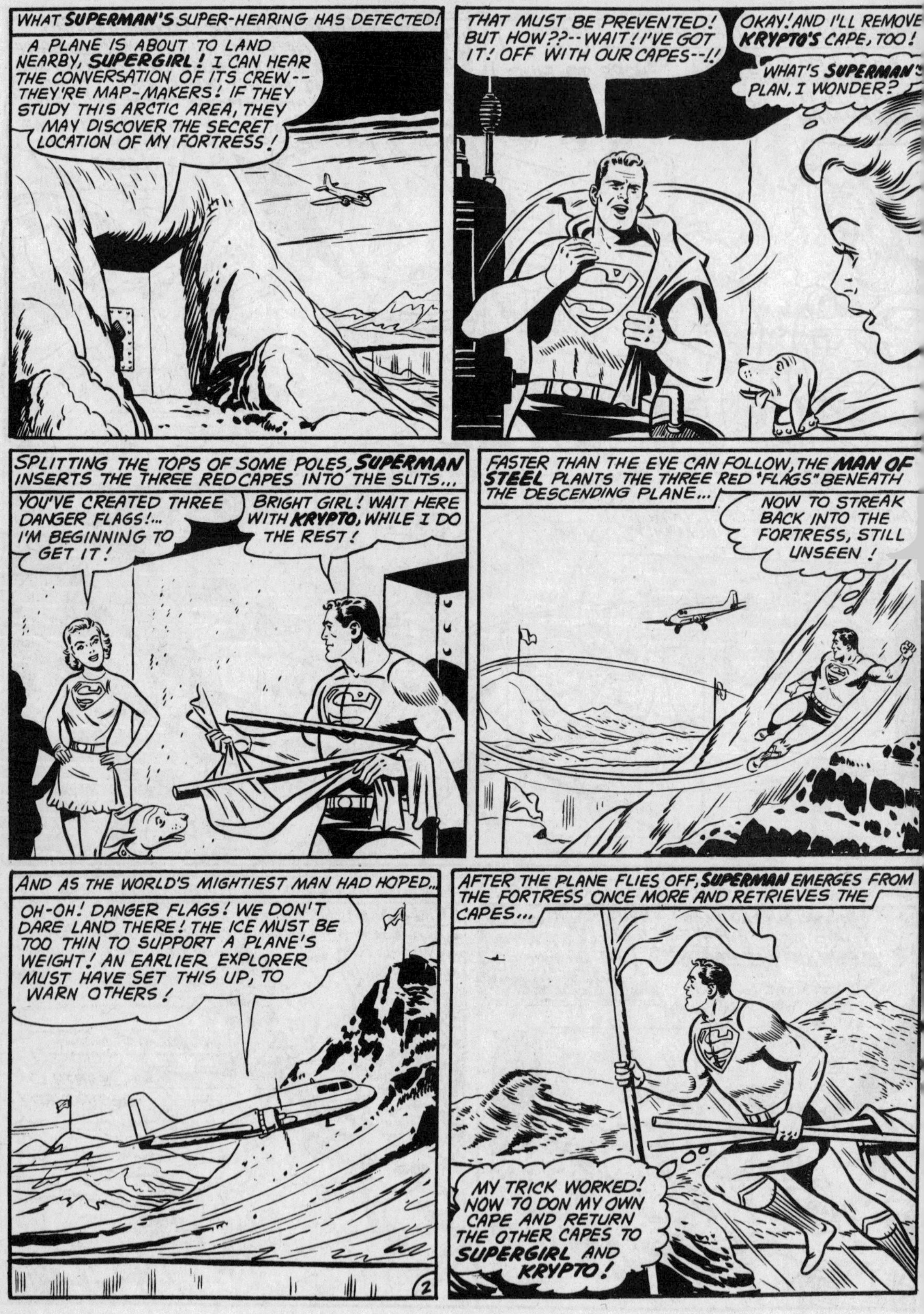
WHAT SUPERMAN'S SUPER-HEARING HAS DETECTED!
A PLANE IS ABOUT TO LAND NEARBY, SUPERGIRL! I CAN HEAR THE CONVERSATION OF ITS CREW--THEY'RE MAP-MAKERS! IF THEY STUDY THIS ARCTIC AREA, THEY MAY DISCOVER THE SECRET LOCATION OF MY FORTRESS!
THAT MUST BE PREVENTED! BUT HOW??--WAIT! I'VE GOT IT! OFF WITH OUR CAPES--!!
OKAY! AND I'LL REMOVE KRYPTO'S CAPE, TOO!
WHAT'S SUPERMAN'S PLAN, I WONDER?
SPLITTING THE TOPS OF SOME POLES, SUPERMAN INSERTS THE THREE RED CAPES INTO THE SLITS...
YOU'VE CREATED THREE DANGER FLAGS!... I'M BEGINNING TO GET IT!
BRIGHT GIRL! WAIT HERE WITH KRYPTO, WHILE I DO THE REST!
FASTER THAN THE EYE CAN FOLLOW, THE MAN OF STEEL PLANTS THE THREE RED "FLAGS" BENEATH THE DESCENDING PLANE...
NOW TO STREAK BACK INTO THE FORTRESS, STILL UNSEEN!
AND AS THE WORLD'S MIGHTIEST MAN HAD HOPED...
OH-OH! DANGER FLAGS! WE DON'T DARE LAND THERE! THE ICE MUST BE TOO THIN TO SUPPORT A PLANE'S WEIGHT! AN EARLIER EXPLORER MUST HAVE SET THIS UP, TO WARN OTHERS!
2
AFTER THE PLANE FLIES OFF, SUPERMAN EMERGES FROM THE FORTRESS ONCE MORE AND RETRIEVES THE CAPES...
MY TRICK WORKED! NOW TO DON MY OWN CAPE AND RETURN THE OTHER CAPES TO SUPERGIRL AND KRYPTO!

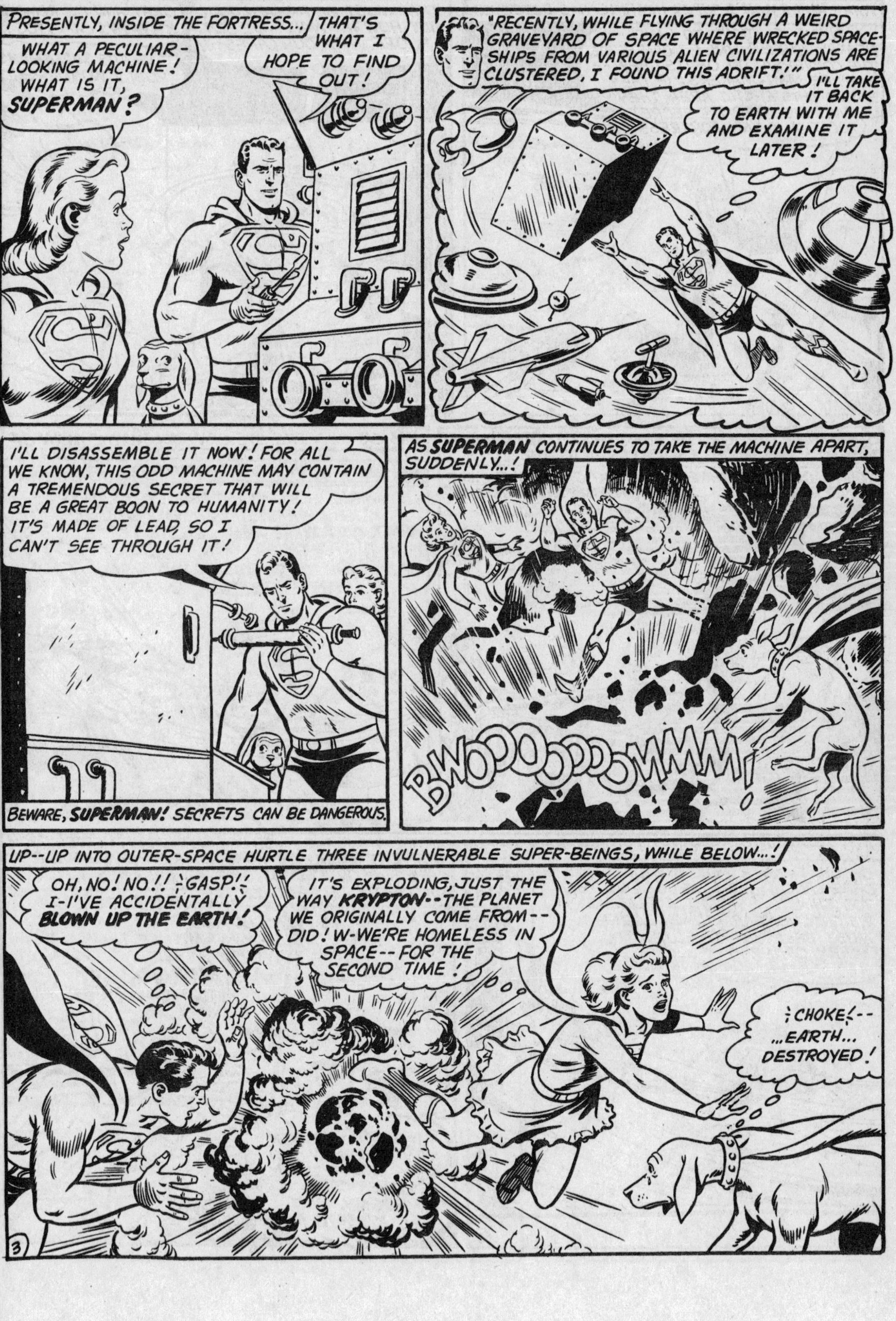
PRESENTLY, INSIDE THE FORTRESS...
WHAT A PECULIAR-LOOKING MACHINE! WHAT IS IT, SUPERMAN?
THAT'S WHAT I HOPE TO FIND OUT!
"RECENTLY, WHILE FLYING THROUGH A WEIRD GRAVEYARD OF SPACE WHERE WRECKED SPACE-SHIPS FROM VARIOUS ALIEN CIVILIZATIONS ARE CLUSTERED, I FOUND THIS ADRIFT!"
I'LL TAKE IT BACK TO EARTH WITH ME AND EXAMINE IT LATER!
I'LL DISASSEMBLE IT NOW! FOR ALL WE KNOW, THIS ODD MACHINE MAY CONTAIN A TREMENDOUS SECRET THAT WILL BE A GREAT BOON TO HUMANITY! IT'S MADE OF LEAD, SO I CAN'T SEE THROUGH IT!
BEWARE, SUPERMAN! SECRETS CAN BE DANGEROUS.
AS SUPERMAN CONTINUES TO TAKE THE MACHINE APART, SUDDENLY...!
BWOOOOOOOOMMM!
UP--UP INTO OUTER-SPACE HURTLE THREE INVULNERABLE SUPER-BEINGS, WHILE BELOW...!
OH, NO! NO!! -GASP!- I-I'VE ACCIDENTALLY BLOWN UP THE EARTH!
IT'S EXPLODING, JUST THE WAY KRYPTON--THE PLANET WE ORIGINALLY COME FROM--DID! W-WE'RE HOMELESS IN SPACE--FOR THE SECOND TIME!
-CHOKE!- ...EARTH... DESTROYED!
3

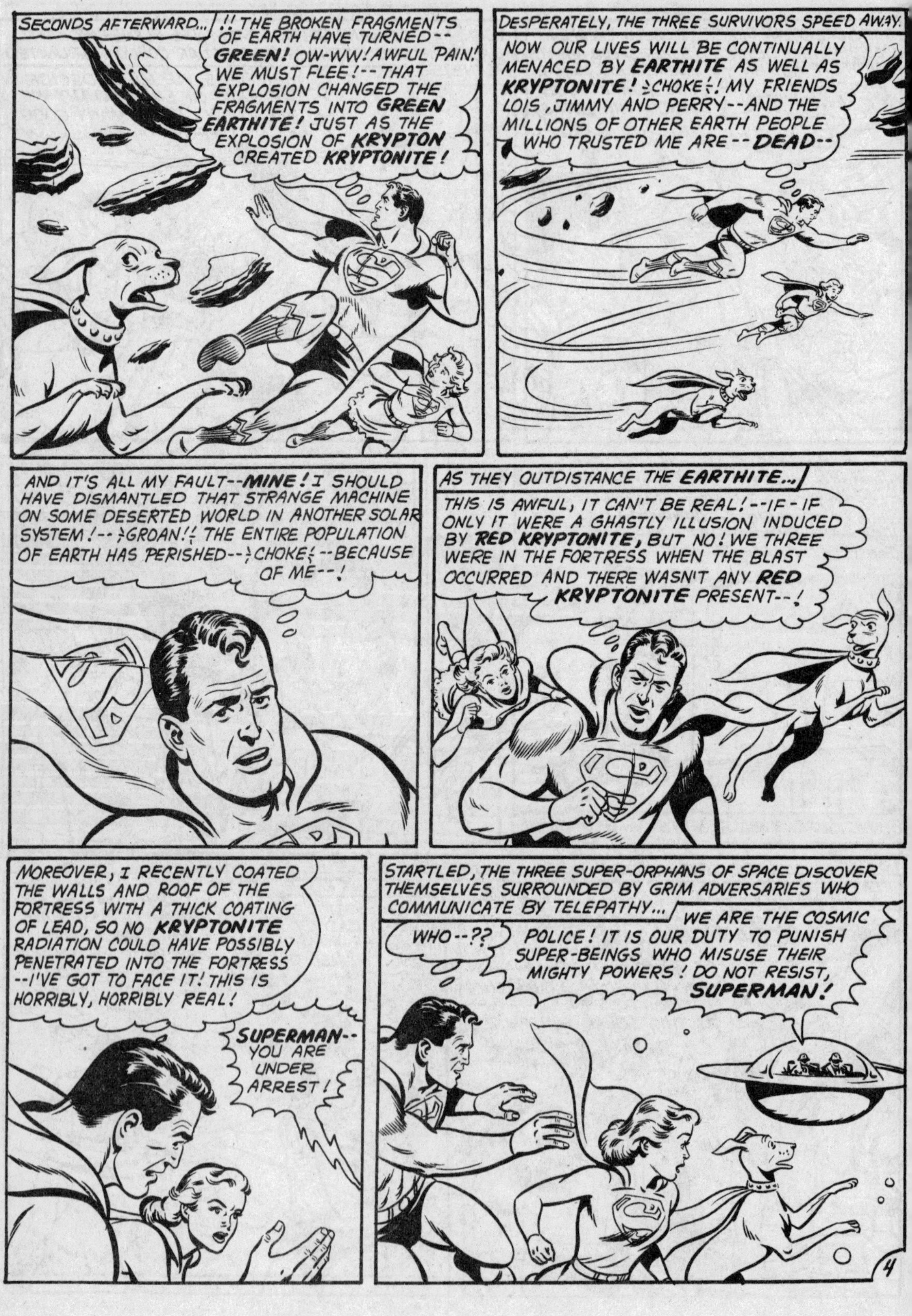
SECONDS AFTERWARD...
!! THE BROKEN FRAGMENTS OF EARTH HAVE TURNED-- GREEN! OW-WW! AWFUL PAIN! WE MUST FLEE! -- THAT EXPLOSION CHANGED THE FRAGMENTS INTO GREEN EARTHITE! JUST AS THE EXPLOSION OF KRYPTON CREATED KRYPTONITE!
DESPERATELY, THE THREE SURVIVORS SPEED AWAY.
NOW OUR LIVES WILL BE CONTINUALLY MENACED BY EARTHITE AS WELL AS KRYPTONITE! }CHOKE{! MY FRIENDS LOIS, JIMMY AND PERRY--AND THE MILLIONS OF OTHER EARTH PEOPLE WHO TRUSTED ME ARE -- DEAD--
AND IT'S ALL MY FAULT--MINE! I SHOULD HAVE DISMANTLED THAT STRANGE MACHINE ON SOME DESERTED WORLD IN ANOTHER SOLAR SYSTEM! -- }GROAN!{ THE ENTIRE POPULATION OF EARTH HAS PERISHED-- }CHOKE{ --BECAUSE OF ME--!
AS THEY OUTDISTANCE THE EARTHITE...
THIS IS AWFUL, IT CAN'T BE REAL! --IF - IF ONLY IT WERE A GHASTLY ILLUSION INDUCED BY RED KRYPTONITE, BUT NO! WE THREE WERE IN THE FORTRESS WHEN THE BLAST OCCURRED AND THERE WASN'T ANY RED KRYPTONITE PRESENT--!
MOREOVER, I RECENTLY COATED THE WALLS AND ROOF OF THE FORTRESS WITH A THICK COATING OF LEAD, SO NO KRYPTONITE RADIATION COULD HAVE POSSIBLY PENETRATED INTO THE FORTRESS --I'VE GOT TO FACE IT! THIS IS HORRIBLY, HORRIBLY REAL!
SUPERMAN-- YOU ARE UNDER ARREST!
STARTLED, THE THREE SUPER-ORPHANS OF SPACE DISCOVER THEMSELVES SURROUNDED BY GRIM ADVERSARIES WHO COMMUNICATE BY TELEPATHY...
WHO--??
WE ARE THE COSMIC POLICE! IT IS OUR DUTY TO PUNISH SUPER-BEINGS WHO MISUSE THEIR MIGHTY POWERS! DO NOT RESIST, SUPERMAN!
4

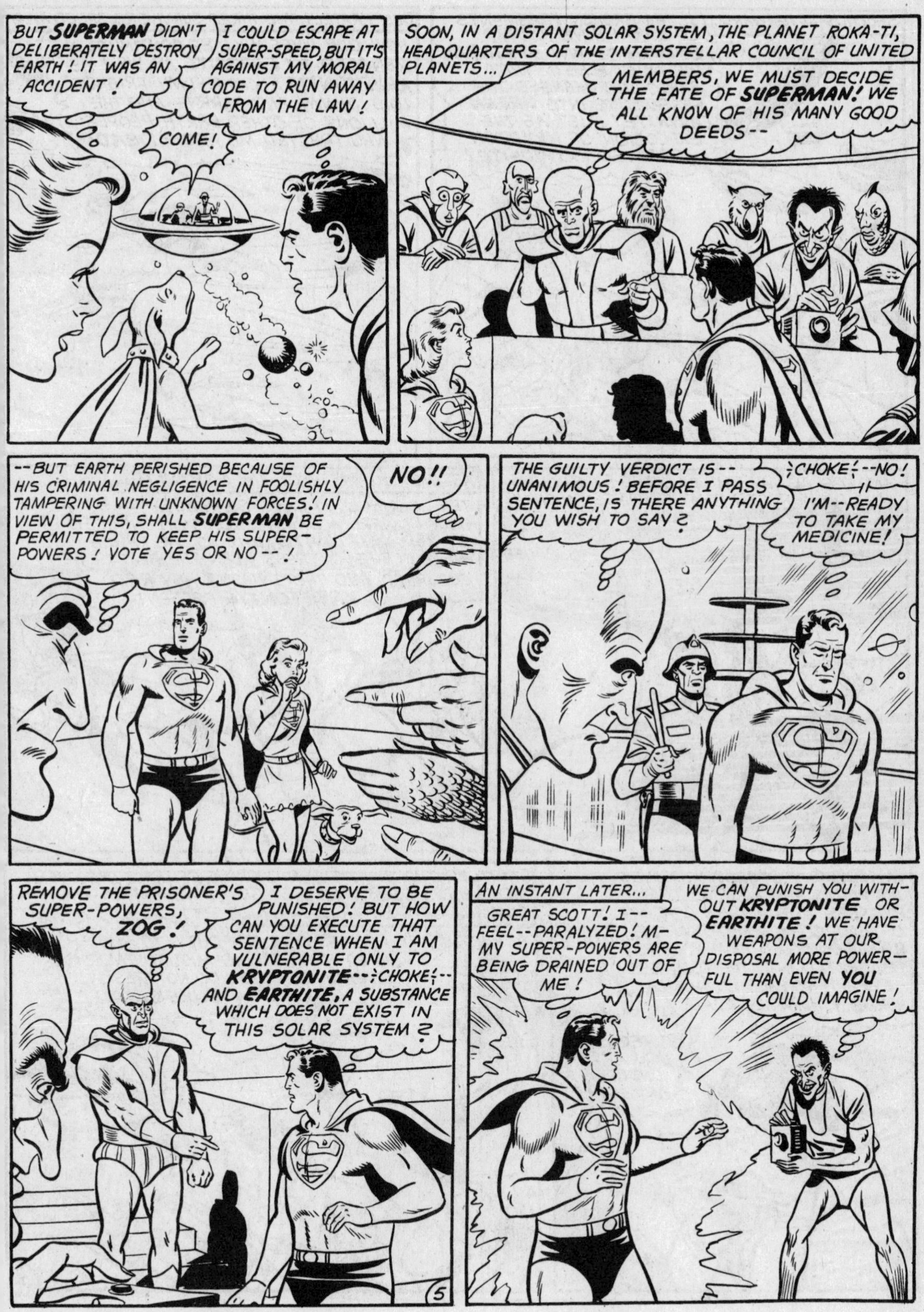
BUT SUPERMAN DIDN'T DELIBERATELY DESTROY EARTH! IT WAS AN ACCIDENT!
I COULD ESCAPE AT SUPER-SPEED, BUT IT'S AGAINST MY MORAL CODE TO RUN AWAY FROM THE LAW!
COME!
SOON, IN A DISTANT SOLAR SYSTEM, THE PLANET ROKA-TI, HEADQUARTERS OF THE INTERSTELLAR COUNCIL OF UNITED PLANETS...
MEMBERS, WE MUST DECIDE THE FATE OF SUPERMAN! WE ALL KNOW OF HIS MANY GOOD DEEDS--
--BUT EARTH PERISHED BECAUSE OF HIS CRIMINAL NEGLIGENCE IN FOOLISHLY TAMPERING WITH UNKNOWN FORCES! IN VIEW OF THIS, SHALL SUPERMAN BE PERMITTED TO KEEP HIS SUPER-POWERS! VOTE YES OR NO--!
NO!!
THE GUILTY VERDICT IS--UNANIMOUS! BEFORE I PASS SENTENCE, IS THERE ANYTHING YOU WISH TO SAY?
;CHOKE;--NO! I'M--READY TO TAKE MY MEDICINE!
REMOVE THE PRISONER'S SUPER-POWERS, ZOG!
I DESERVE TO BE PUNISHED! BUT HOW CAN YOU EXECUTE THAT SENTENCE WHEN I AM VULNERABLE ONLY TO KRYPTONITE--;CHOKE;--AND EARTHITE, A SUBSTANCE WHICH DOES NOT EXIST IN THIS SOLAR SYSTEM?
5
AN INSTANT LATER...
GREAT SCOTT! I--FEEL--PARALYZED! M-MY SUPER-POWERS ARE BEING DRAINED OUT OF ME!
WE CAN PUNISH YOU WITHOUT KRYPTONITE OR EARTHITE! WE HAVE WEAPONS AT OUR DISPOSAL MORE POWERFUL THAN EVEN YOU COULD IMAGINE!

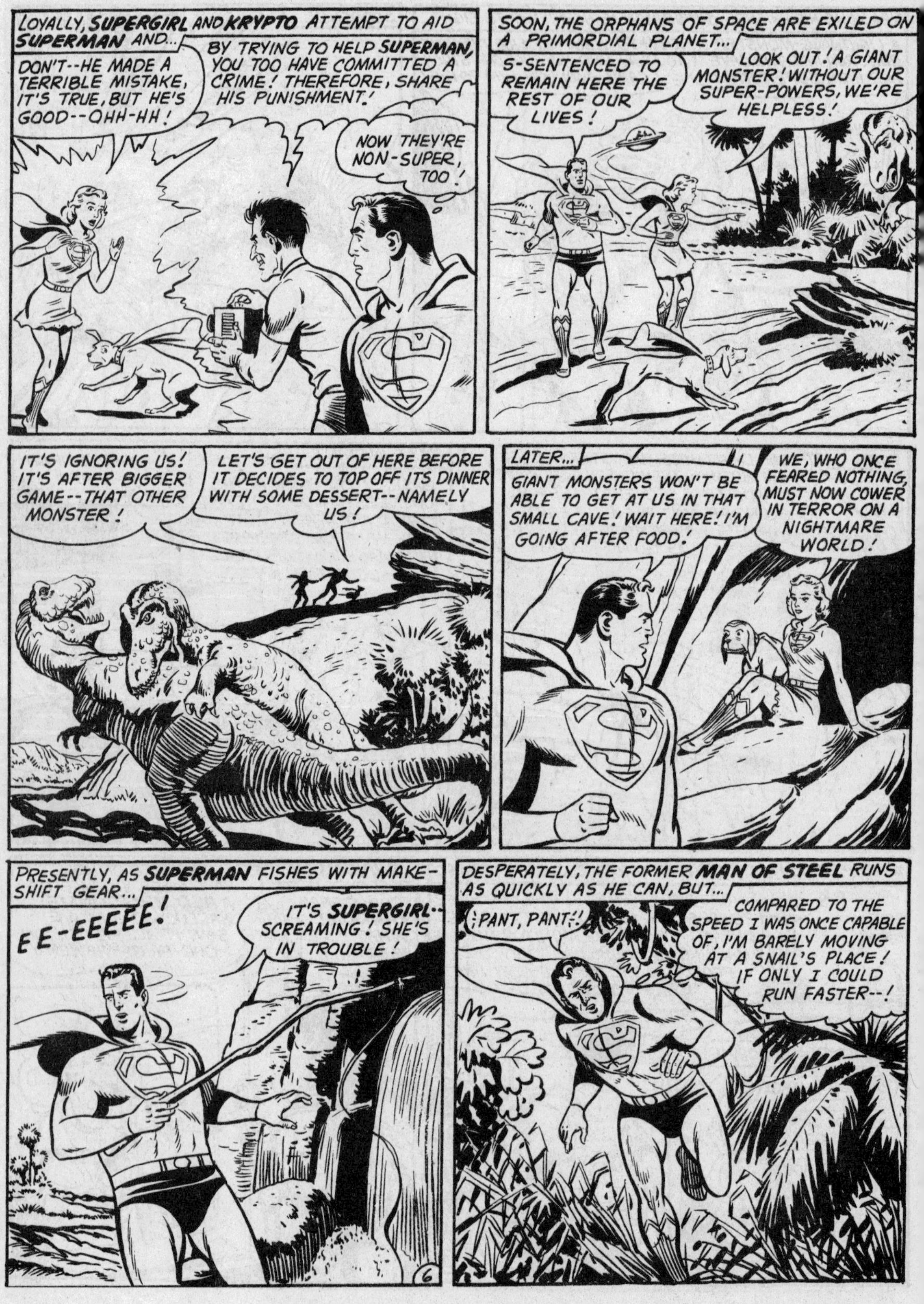
LOYALLY, SUPERGIRL AND KRYPTO ATTEMPT TO AID SUPERMAN AND...
DON'T--HE MADE A TERRIBLE MISTAKE, IT'S TRUE, BUT HE'S GOOD--OHH-HH!
BY TRYING TO HELP SUPERMAN, YOU TOO HAVE COMMITTED A CRIME! THEREFORE, SHARE HIS PUNISHMENT!
NOW THEY'RE NON-SUPER, TOO!
SOON, THE ORPHANS OF SPACE ARE EXILED ON A PRIMORDIAL PLANET...
S-SENTENCED TO REMAIN HERE THE REST OF OUR LIVES!
LOOK OUT! A GIANT MONSTER! WITHOUT OUR SUPER-POWERS, WE'RE HELPLESS!
IT'S IGNORING US! IT'S AFTER BIGGER GAME--THAT OTHER MONSTER!
LET'S GET OUT OF HERE BEFORE IT DECIDES TO TOP OFF ITS DINNER WITH SOME DESSERT--NAMELY US!
LATER...
GIANT MONSTERS WON'T BE ABLE TO GET AT US IN THAT SMALL CAVE! WAIT HERE! I'M GOING AFTER FOOD!
WE, WHO ONCE FEARED NOTHING, MUST NOW COWER IN TERROR ON A NIGHTMARE WORLD!
PRESENTLY, AS SUPERMAN FISHES WITH MAKE-SHIFT GEAR...
EE-EEEEE!
IT'S SUPERGIRL--SCREAMING! SHE'S IN TROUBLE!
6
DESPERATELY, THE FORMER MAN OF STEEL RUNS AS QUICKLY AS HE CAN, BUT...
PANT, PANT!
COMPARED TO THE SPEED I WAS ONCE CAPABLE OF, I'M BARELY MOVING AT A SNAIL'S PLACE! IF ONLY I COULD RUN FASTER--!

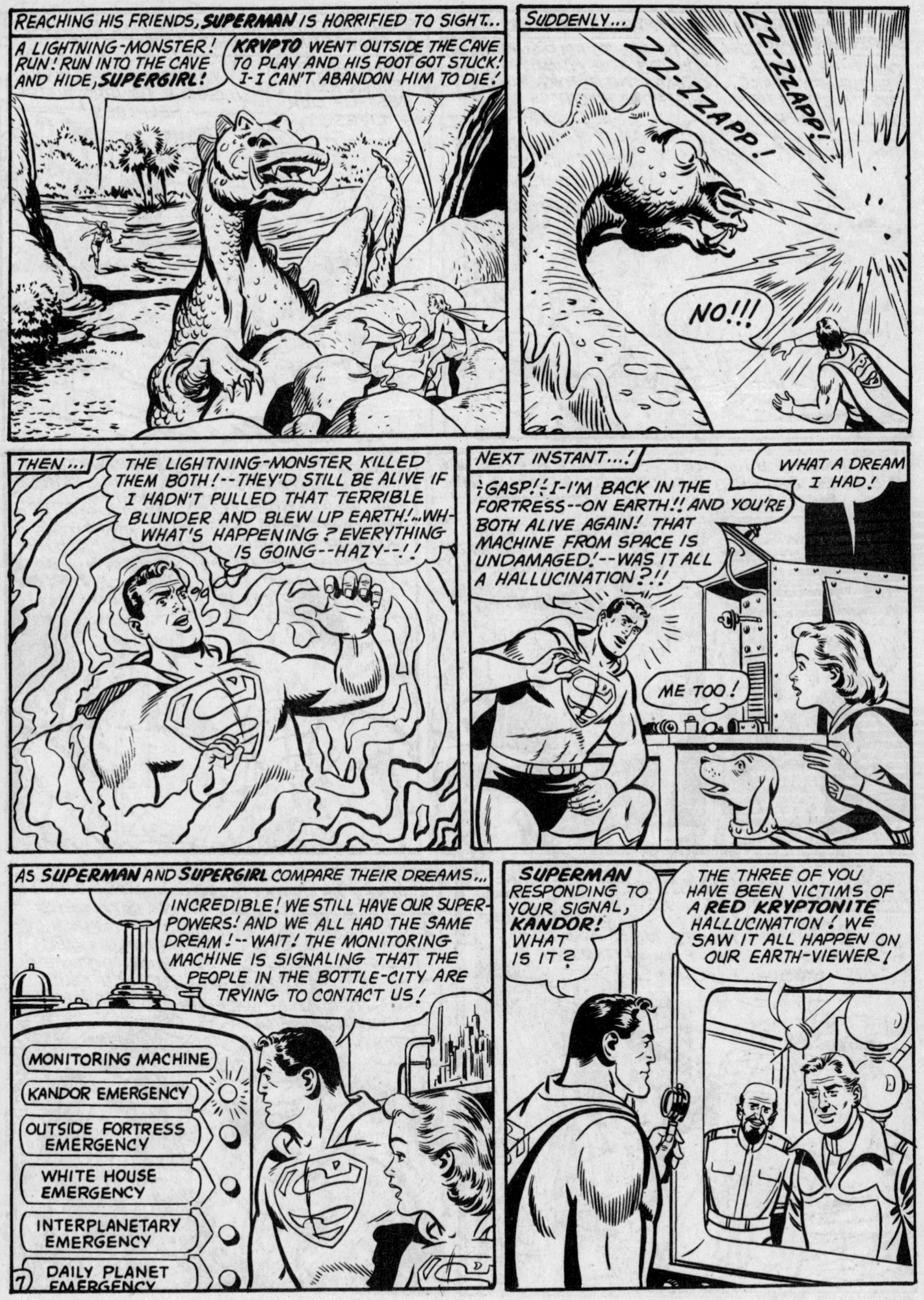
REACHING HIS FRIENDS, SUPERMAN IS HORRIFIED TO SIGHT...
A LIGHTNING-MONSTER! RUN! RUN INTO THE CAVE AND HIDE, SUPERGIRL!
KRYPTO WENT OUTSIDE THE CAVE TO PLAY AND HIS FOOT GOT STUCK! I-I CAN'T ABANDON HIM TO DIE!
SUDDENLY...
ZZ-ZZZAPP!
ZZ-ZZAPP!
NO!!!
THEN...
THE LIGHTNING-MONSTER KILLED THEM BOTH!--THEY'D STILL BE ALIVE IF I HADN'T PULLED THAT TERRIBLE BLUNDER AND BLEW UP EARTH!...WH-WHAT'S HAPPENING? EVERYTHING IS GOING--HAZY--!!
NEXT INSTANT...!
¿GASP!¿ I-I'M BACK IN THE FORTRESS--ON EARTH!! AND YOU'RE BOTH ALIVE AGAIN! THAT MACHINE FROM SPACE IS UNDAMAGED!--WAS IT ALL A HALLUCINATION?!!
WHAT A DREAM I HAD!
ME TOO!
AS SUPERMAN AND SUPERGIRL COMPARE THEIR DREAMS...
INCREDIBLE! WE STILL HAVE OUR SUPER-POWERS! AND WE ALL HAD THE SAME DREAM!--WAIT! THE MONITORING MACHINE IS SIGNALING THAT THE PEOPLE IN THE BOTTLE-CITY ARE TRYING TO CONTACT US!
MONITORING MACHINE
KANDOR EMERGENCY
OUTSIDE FORTRESS EMERGENCY
WHITE HOUSE EMERGENCY
INTERPLANETARY EMERGENCY
DAILY PLANET EMERGENCY
7
SUPERMAN RESPONDING TO YOUR SIGNAL, KANDOR! WHAT IS IT?
THE THREE OF YOU HAVE BEEN VICTIMS OF A RED KRYPTONITE HALLUCINATION! WE SAW IT ALL HAPPEN ON OUR EARTH-VIEWER!

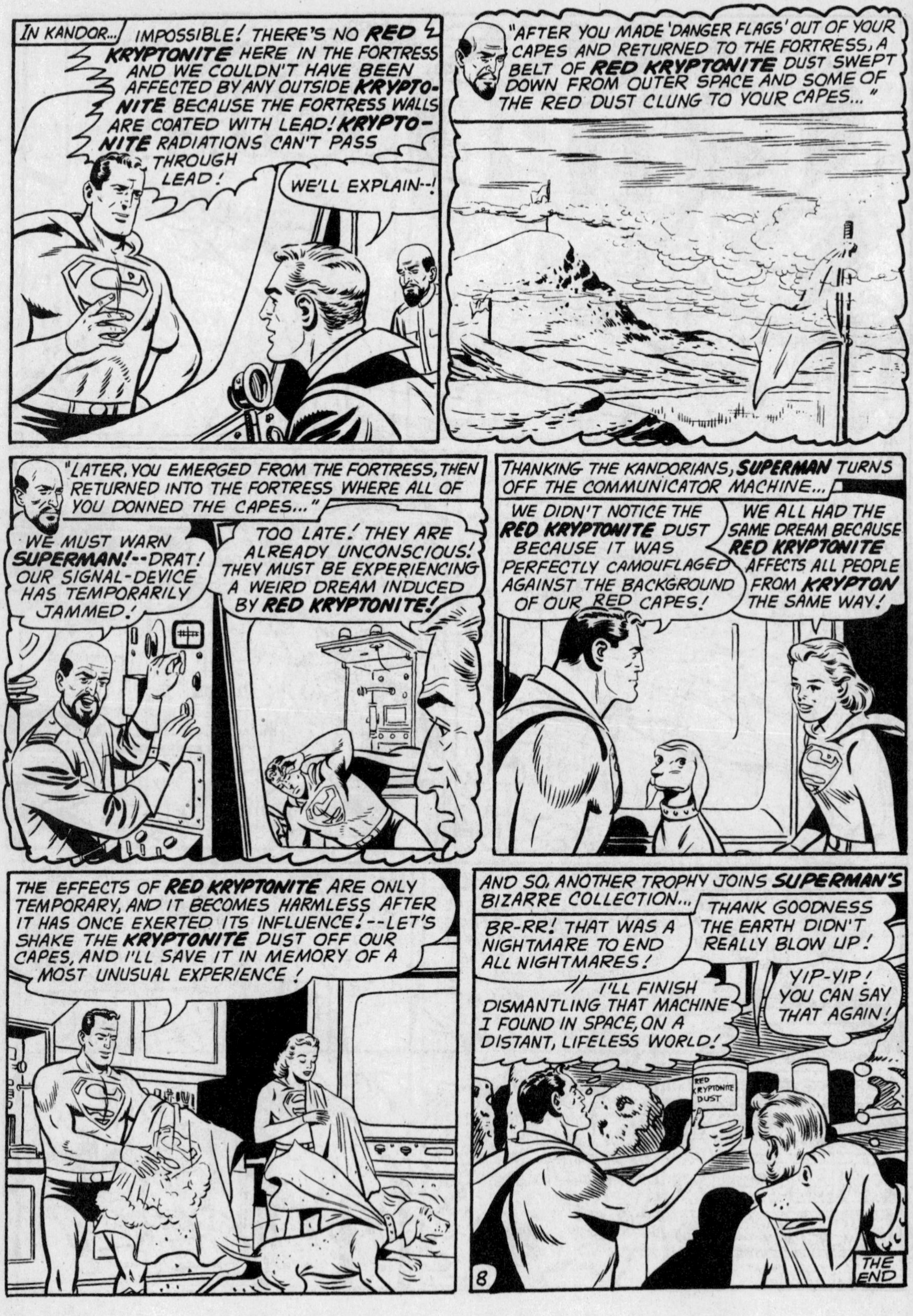
IN KANDOR...
IMPOSSIBLE! THERE'S NO RED KRYPTONITE HERE IN THE FORTRESS AND WE COULDN'T HAVE BEEN AFFECTED BY ANY OUTSIDE KRYPTONITE BECAUSE THE FORTRESS WALLS ARE COATED WITH LEAD! KRYPTONITE RADIATIONS CAN'T PASS THROUGH LEAD!
WE'LL EXPLAIN--!
"AFTER YOU MADE 'DANGER FLAGS' OUT OF YOUR CAPES AND RETURNED TO THE FORTRESS, A BELT OF RED KRYPTONITE DUST SWEPT DOWN FROM OUTER SPACE AND SOME OF THE RED DUST CLUNG TO YOUR CAPES..."
"LATER, YOU EMERGED FROM THE FORTRESS, THEN RETURNED INTO THE FORTRESS WHERE ALL OF YOU DONNED THE CAPES..."
WE MUST WARN SUPERMAN!--DRAT! OUR SIGNAL-DEVICE HAS TEMPORARILY JAMMED!
TOO LATE! THEY ARE ALREADY UNCONSCIOUS! THEY MUST BE EXPERIENCING A WEIRD DREAM INDUCED BY RED KRYPTONITE!
THANKING THE KANDORIANS, SUPERMAN TURNS OFF THE COMMUNICATOR MACHINE...
WE DIDN'T NOTICE THE RED KRYPTONITE DUST BECAUSE IT WAS PERFECTLY CAMOUFLAGED AGAINST THE BACKGROUND OF OUR RED CAPES!
WE ALL HAD THE SAME DREAM BECAUSE RED KRYPTONITE AFFECTS ALL PEOPLE FROM KRYPTON THE SAME WAY!
THE EFFECTS OF RED KRYPTONITE ARE ONLY TEMPORARY, AND IT BECOMES HARMLESS AFTER IT HAS ONCE EXERTED ITS INFLUENCE!--LET'S SHAKE THE KRYPTONITE DUST OFF OUR CAPES, AND I'LL SAVE IT IN MEMORY OF A MOST UNUSUAL EXPERIENCE!
8
AND SO, ANOTHER TROPHY JOINS SUPERMAN'S BIZARRE COLLECTION...
BR-RR! THAT WAS A NIGHTMARE TO END ALL NIGHTMARES!
THANK GOODNESS THE EARTH DIDN'T REALLY BLOW UP!
I'LL FINISH DISMANTLING THAT MACHINE I FOUND IN SPACE, ON A DISTANT, LIFELESS WORLD!
YIP-YIP! YOU CAN SAY THAT AGAIN!
RED KRYPTONITE DUST
THE END

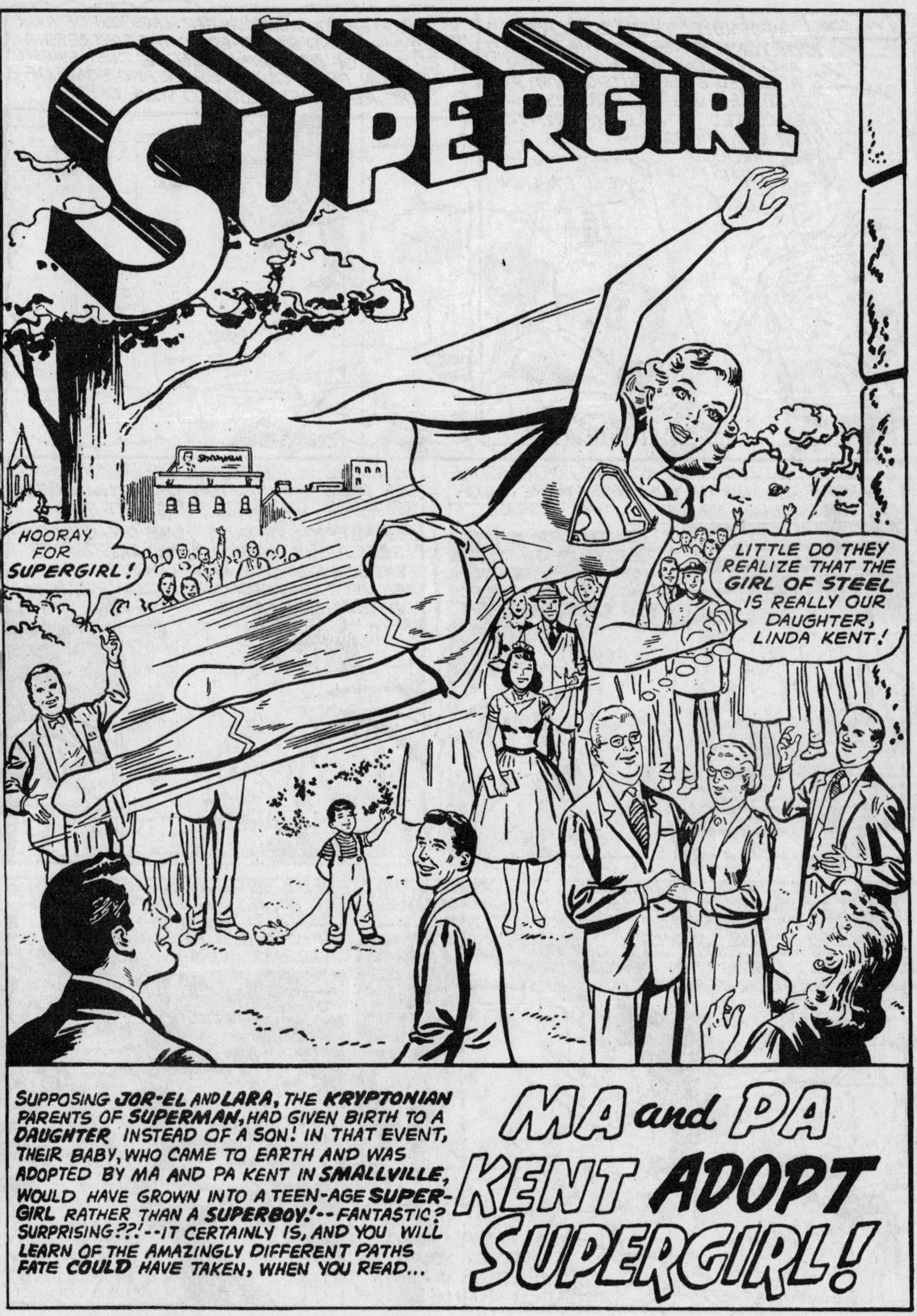
SUPERGIRL
HOORAY FOR SUPERGIRL!
LITTLE DO THEY REALIZE THAT THE GIRL OF STEEL IS REALLY OUR DAUGHTER, LINDA KENT!
SUPPOSING JOR-EL AND LARA, THE KRYPTONIAN PARENTS OF SUPERMAN, HAD GIVEN BIRTH TO A DAUGHTER INSTEAD OF A SON! IN THAT EVENT, THEIR BABY, WHO CAME TO EARTH AND WAS ADOPTED BY MA AND PA KENT IN SMALLVILLE, WOULD HAVE GROWN INTO A TEEN-AGE SUPER-GIRL RATHER THAN A SUPERBOY!--FANTASTIC? SURPRISING??!--IT CERTAINLY IS, AND YOU WILL LEARN OF THE AMAZINGLY DIFFERENT PATHS FATE COULD HAVE TAKEN, WHEN YOU READ...
MA and PA KENT ADOPT SUPERGIRL!

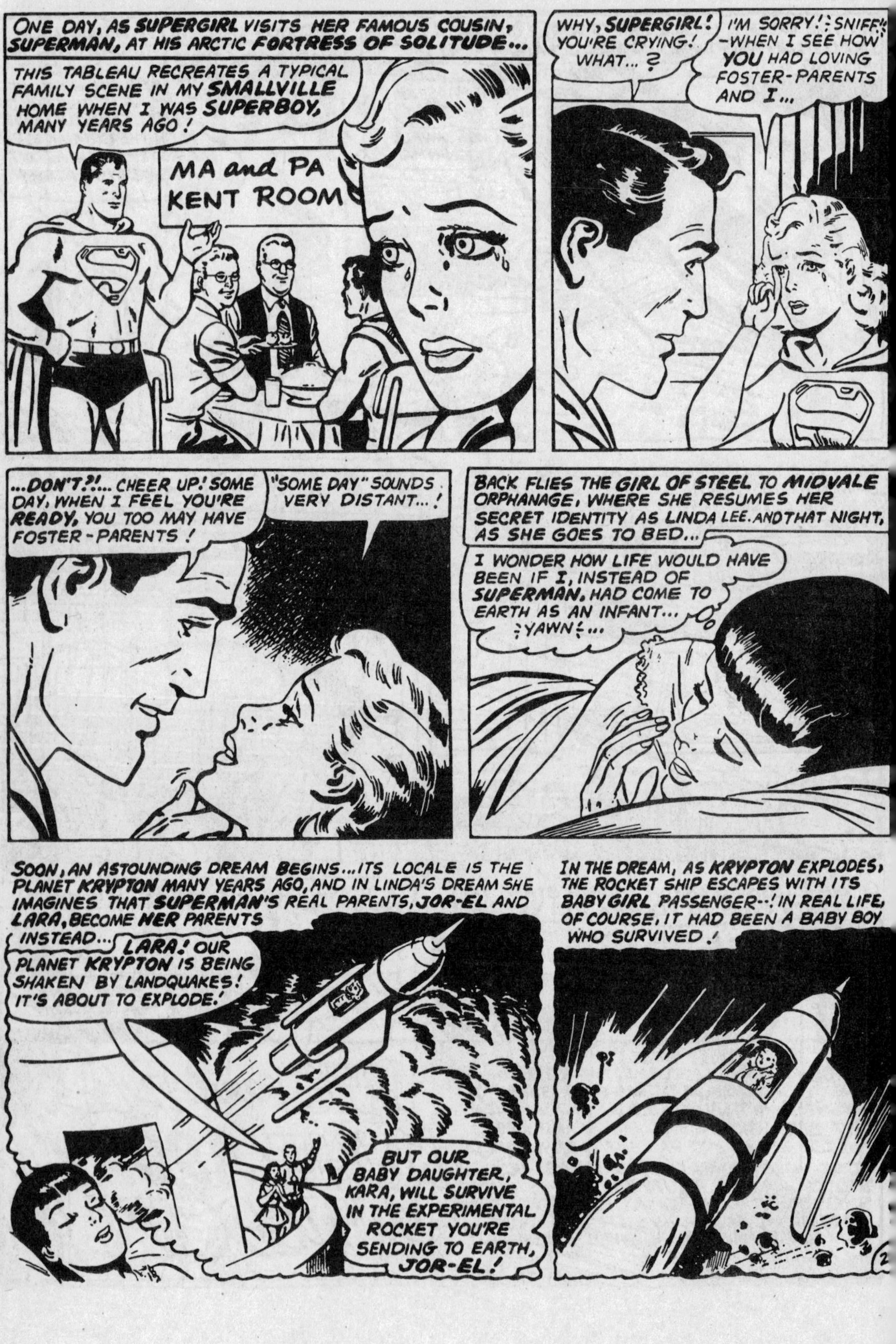
ONE DAY, AS SUPERGIRL VISITS HER FAMOUS COUSIN, SUPERMAN, AT HIS ARCTIC FORTRESS OF SOLITUDE...
THIS TABLEAU RECREATES A TYPICAL FAMILY SCENE IN MY SMALLVILLE HOME WHEN I WAS SUPERBOY, MANY YEARS AGO!
MA and PA KENT ROOM
WHY, SUPERGIRL! YOU'RE CRYING! WHAT... ?
I'M SORRY! SNIFF! -WHEN I SEE HOW YOU HAD LOVING FOSTER-PARENTS AND I...
...DON'T?!... CHEER UP! SOME DAY, WHEN I FEEL YOU'RE READY, YOU TOO MAY HAVE FOSTER-PARENTS!
"SOME DAY" SOUNDS VERY DISTANT...!
BACK FLIES THE GIRL OF STEEL TO MIDVALE ORPHANAGE, WHERE SHE RESUMES HER SECRET IDENTITY AS LINDA LEE. AND THAT NIGHT, AS SHE GOES TO BED...
I WONDER HOW LIFE WOULD HAVE BEEN IF I, INSTEAD OF SUPERMAN, HAD COME TO EARTH AS AN INFANT... YAWN...
SOON, AN ASTOUNDING DREAM BEGINS...ITS LOCALE IS THE PLANET KRYPTON MANY YEARS AGO, AND IN LINDA'S DREAM SHE IMAGINES THAT SUPERMAN'S REAL PARENTS, JOR-EL AND LARA, BECOME HER PARENTS INSTEAD...
LARA! OUR PLANET KRYPTON IS BEING SHAKEN BY LANDQUAKES! IT'S ABOUT TO EXPLODE!
BUT OUR BABY DAUGHTER, KARA, WILL SURVIVE IN THE EXPERIMENTAL ROCKET YOU'RE SENDING TO EARTH, JOR-EL!
IN THE DREAM, AS KRYPTON EXPLODES, THE ROCKET SHIP ESCAPES WITH ITS BABY GIRL PASSENGER--! IN REAL LIFE, OF COURSE, IT HAD BEEN A BABY BOY WHO SURVIVED!

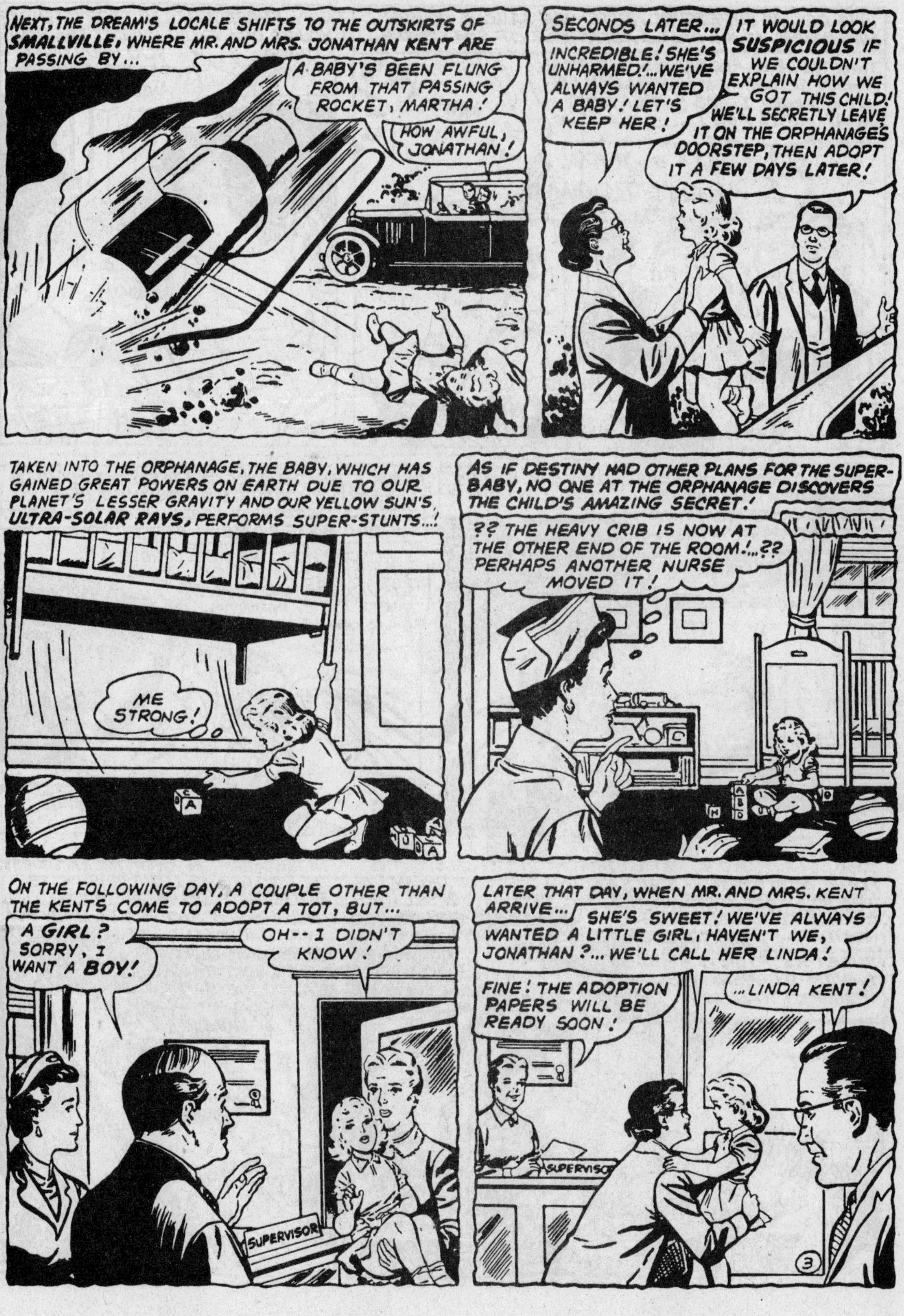
NEXT, THE DREAM'S LOCALE SHIFTS TO THE OUTSKIRTS OF SMALLVILLE, WHERE MR. AND MRS. JONATHAN KENT ARE PASSING BY...
A BABY'S BEEN FLUNG FROM THAT PASSING ROCKET, MARTHA!
HOW AWFUL, JONATHAN!
SECONDS LATER...
INCREDIBLE! SHE'S UNHARMED!...WE'VE ALWAYS WANTED A BABY! LET'S KEEP HER!
IT WOULD LOOK SUSPICIOUS IF WE COULDN'T EXPLAIN HOW WE GOT THIS CHILD! WE'LL SECRETLY LEAVE IT ON THE ORPHANAGE'S DOORSTEP, THEN ADOPT IT A FEW DAYS LATER!
TAKEN INTO THE ORPHANAGE, THE BABY, WHICH HAS GAINED GREAT POWERS ON EARTH DUE TO OUR PLANET'S LESSER GRAVITY AND OUR YELLOW SUN'S ULTRA-SOLAR RAYS, PERFORMS SUPER-STUNTS...!
ME STRONG!
AS IF DESTINY HAD OTHER PLANS FOR THE SUPER-BABY, NO ONE AT THE ORPHANAGE DISCOVERS THE CHILD'S AMAZING SECRET!
?? THE HEAVY CRIB IS NOW AT THE OTHER END OF THE ROOM!...?? PERHAPS ANOTHER NURSE MOVED IT!
ON THE FOLLOWING DAY, A COUPLE OTHER THAN THE KENTS COME TO ADOPT A TOT, BUT...
A GIRL? SORRY, I WANT A BOY!
OH--I DIDN'T KNOW!
SUPERVISOR
LATER THAT DAY, WHEN MR. AND MRS. KENT ARRIVE...
SHE'S SWEET! WE'VE ALWAYS WANTED A LITTLE GIRL, HAVEN'T WE, JONATHAN?... WE'LL CALL HER LINDA!
FINE! THE ADOPTION PAPERS WILL BE READY SOON!
...LINDA KENT!
SUPERVISOR
3

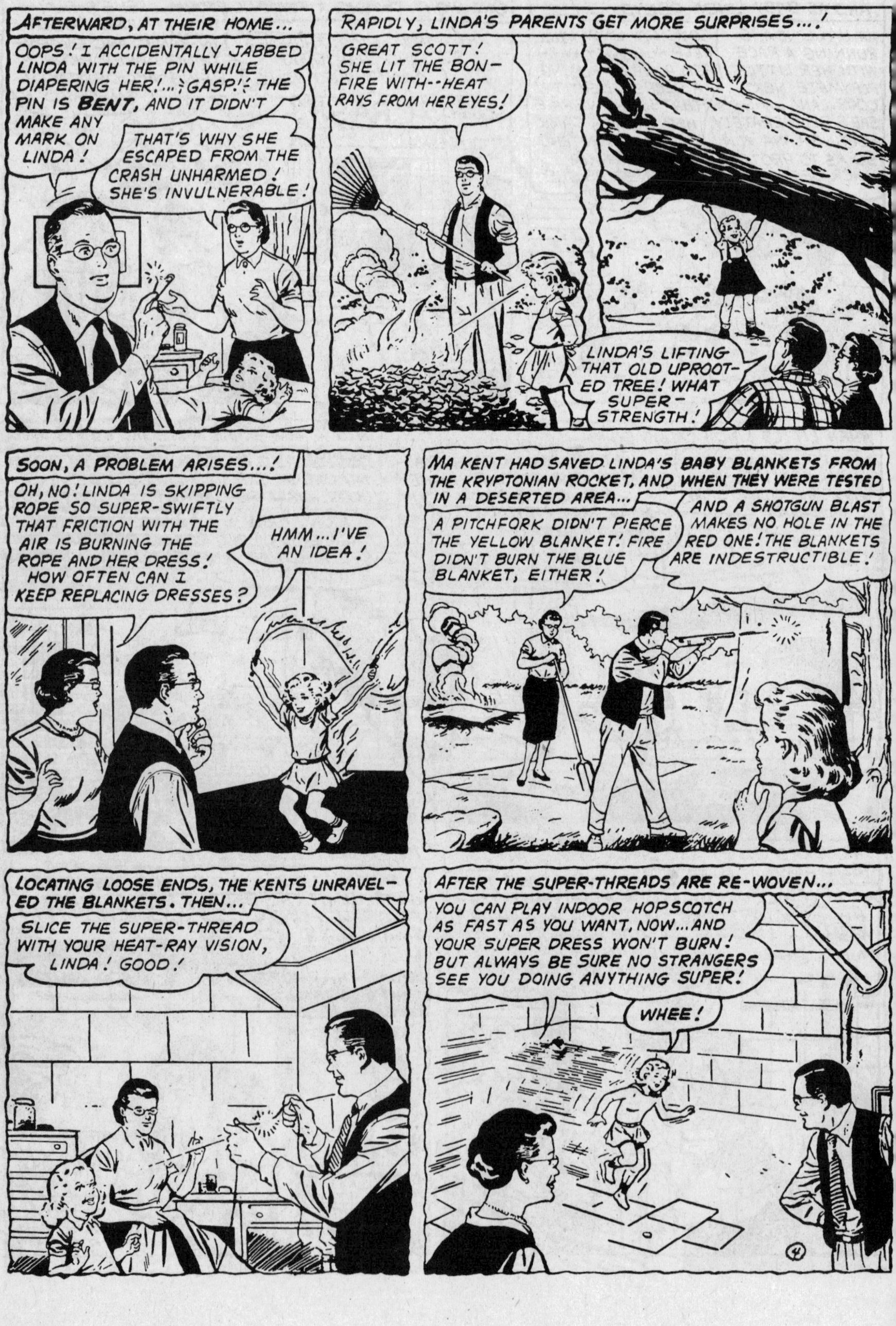
AFTERWARD, AT THEIR HOME...
OOPS! I ACCIDENTALLY JABBED LINDA WITH THE PIN WHILE DIAPERING HER!...GASP!-THE PIN IS BENT, AND IT DIDN'T MAKE ANY MARK ON LINDA!
THAT'S WHY SHE ESCAPED FROM THE CRASH UNHARMED! SHE'S INVULNERABLE!
RAPIDLY, LINDA'S PARENTS GET MORE SURPRISES...!
GREAT SCOTT! SHE LIT THE BON-FIRE WITH--HEAT RAYS FROM HER EYES!
LINDA'S LIFTING THAT OLD UPROOTED TREE! WHAT SUPER-STRENGTH!
SOON, A PROBLEM ARISES...!
OH, NO! LINDA IS SKIPPING ROPE SO SUPER-SWIFTLY THAT FRICTION WITH THE AIR IS BURNING THE ROPE AND HER DRESS! HOW OFTEN CAN I KEEP REPLACING DRESSES?
HMM...I'VE AN IDEA!
MA KENT HAD SAVED LINDA'S BABY BLANKETS FROM THE KRYPTONIAN ROCKET, AND WHEN THEY WERE TESTED IN A DESERTED AREA...
A PITCHFORK DIDN'T PIERCE THE YELLOW BLANKET! FIRE DIDN'T BURN THE BLUE BLANKET, EITHER!
AND A SHOTGUN BLAST MAKES NO HOLE IN THE RED ONE! THE BLANKETS ARE INDESTRUCTIBLE!
LOCATING LOOSE ENDS, THE KENTS UNRAVELED THE BLANKETS. THEN...
SLICE THE SUPER-THREAD WITH YOUR HEAT-RAY VISION, LINDA! GOOD!
AFTER THE SUPER-THREADS ARE RE-WOVEN...
YOU CAN PLAY INDOOR HOPSCOTCH AS FAST AS YOU WANT, NOW...AND YOUR SUPER DRESS WON'T BURN! BUT ALWAYS BE SURE NO STRANGERS SEE YOU DOING ANYTHING SUPER!
WHEE!
4

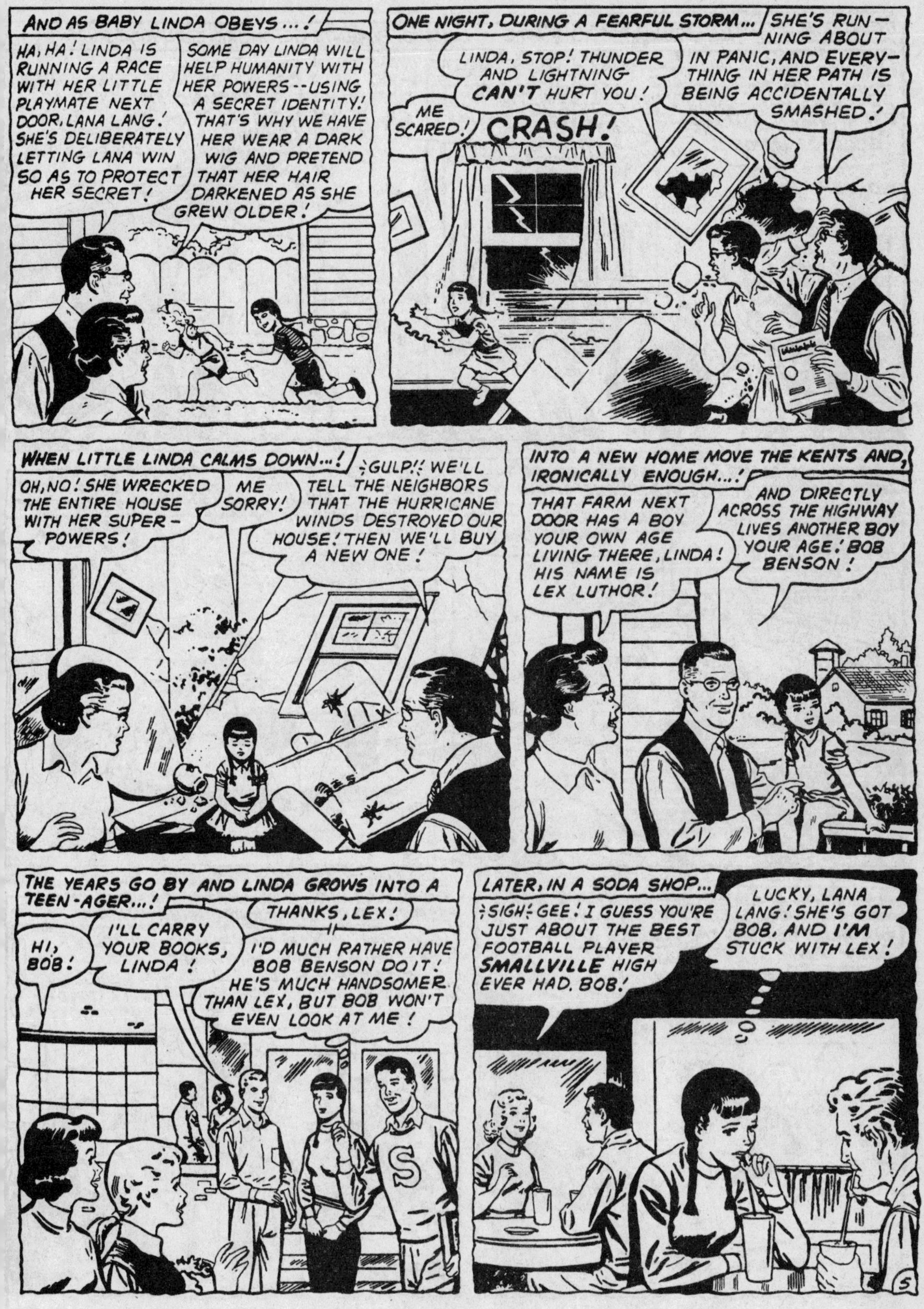
AND AS BABY LINDA OBEYS...!
HA, HA! LINDA IS RUNNING A RACE WITH HER LITTLE PLAYMATE NEXT DOOR, LANA LANG! SHE'S DELIBERATELY LETTING LANA WIN SO AS TO PROTECT HER SECRET!
SOME DAY LINDA WILL HELP HUMANITY WITH HER POWERS--USING A SECRET IDENTITY! THAT'S WHY WE HAVE HER WEAR A DARK WIG AND PRETEND THAT HER HAIR DARKENED AS SHE GREW OLDER!
ONE NIGHT, DURING A FEARFUL STORM...
SHE'S RUNNING ABOUT IN PANIC, AND EVERYTHING IN HER PATH IS BEING ACCIDENTALLY SMASHED!
LINDA, STOP! THUNDER AND LIGHTNING CAN'T HURT YOU!
ME SCARED!
CRASH!
WHEN LITTLE LINDA CALMS DOWN...!
OH, NO! SHE WRECKED THE ENTIRE HOUSE WITH HER SUPER-POWERS!
ME SORRY!
GULP! WE'LL TELL THE NEIGHBORS THAT THE HURRICANE WINDS DESTROYED OUR HOUSE! THEN WE'LL BUY A NEW ONE!
INTO A NEW HOME MOVE THE KENTS AND, IRONICALLY ENOUGH...!
THAT FARM NEXT DOOR HAS A BOY YOUR OWN AGE LIVING THERE, LINDA! HIS NAME IS LEX LUTHOR!
AND DIRECTLY ACROSS THE HIGHWAY LIVES ANOTHER BOY YOUR AGE! BOB BENSON!
THE YEARS GO BY AND LINDA GROWS INTO A TEEN-AGER...!
HI, BOB!
I'LL CARRY YOUR BOOKS, LINDA!
THANKS, LEX!
I'D MUCH RATHER HAVE BOB BENSON DO IT! HE'S MUCH HANDSOMER THAN LEX, BUT BOB WON'T EVEN LOOK AT ME!
S
LATER, IN A SODA SHOP...
SIGH! GEE! I GUESS YOU'RE JUST ABOUT THE BEST FOOTBALL PLAYER SMALLVILLE HIGH EVER HAD, BOB!
LUCKY, LANA LANG! SHE'S GOT BOB, AND I'M STUCK WITH LEX!
5

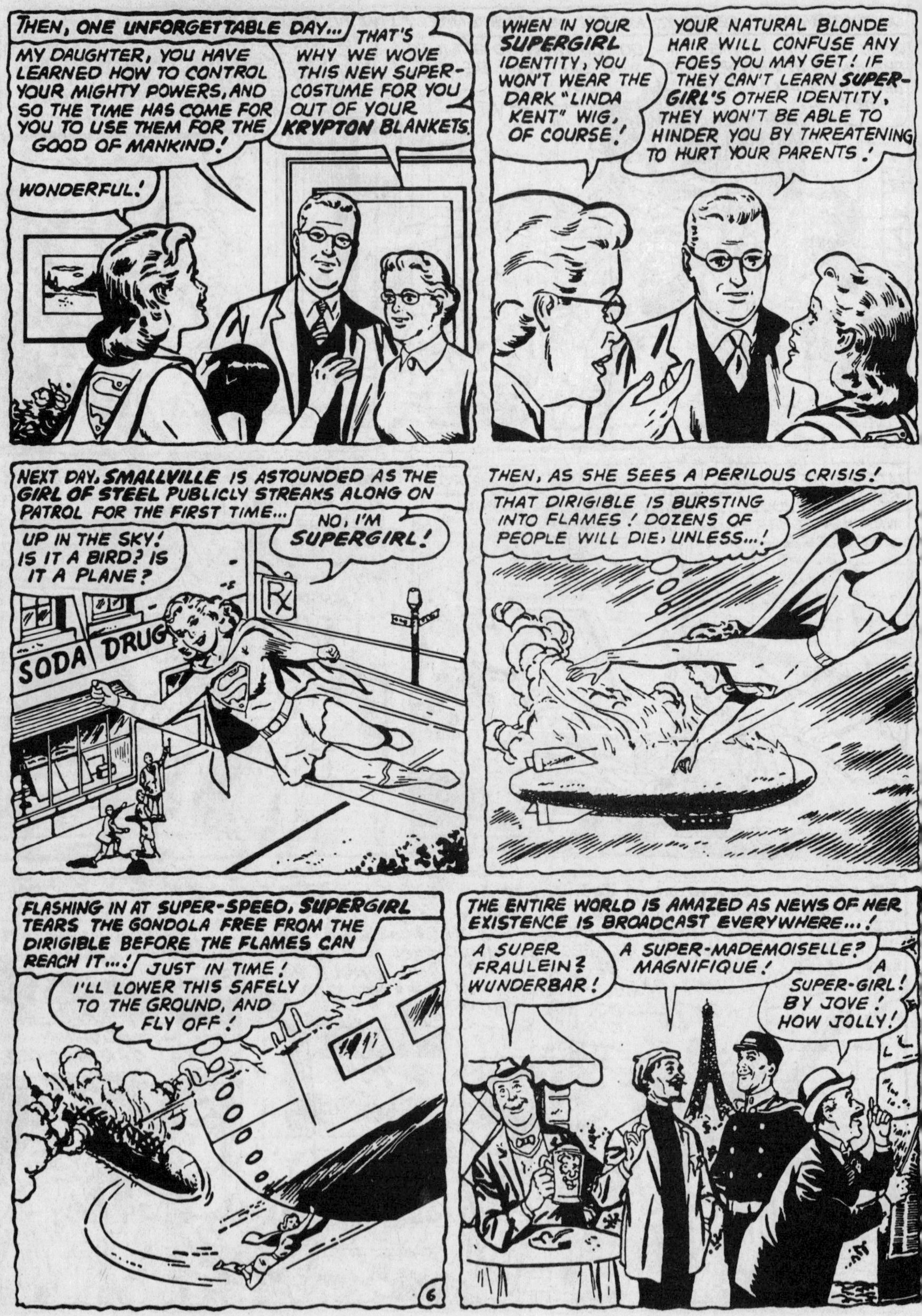
THEN, ONE UNFORGETTABLE DAY...
MY DAUGHTER, YOU HAVE LEARNED HOW TO CONTROL YOUR MIGHTY POWERS, AND SO THE TIME HAS COME FOR YOU TO USE THEM FOR THE GOOD OF MANKIND!
THAT'S WHY WE WOVE THIS NEW SUPER-COSTUME FOR YOU OUT OF YOUR KRYPTON BLANKETS.
WONDERFUL!
WHEN IN YOUR SUPERGIRL IDENTITY, YOU WON'T WEAR THE DARK "LINDA KENT" WIG, OF COURSE!
YOUR NATURAL BLONDE HAIR WILL CONFUSE ANY FOES YOU MAY GET! IF THEY CAN'T LEARN SUPER-GIRL'S OTHER IDENTITY, THEY WON'T BE ABLE TO HINDER YOU BY THREATENING TO HURT YOUR PARENTS!
NEXT DAY, SMALLVILLE IS ASTOUNDED AS THE GIRL OF STEEL PUBLICLY STREAKS ALONG ON PATROL FOR THE FIRST TIME...
UP IN THE SKY! IS IT A BIRD? IS IT A PLANE?
NO, I'M SUPERGIRL!
SODA
DRUG
Rx
THEN, AS SHE SEES A PERILOUS CRISIS!
THAT DIRIGIBLE IS BURSTING INTO FLAMES! DOZENS OF PEOPLE WILL DIE, UNLESS...!
FLASHING IN AT SUPER-SPEED, SUPERGIRL TEARS THE GONDOLA FREE FROM THE DIRIGIBLE BEFORE THE FLAMES CAN REACH IT...!
JUST IN TIME! I'LL LOWER THIS SAFELY TO THE GROUND, AND FLY OFF!
6
THE ENTIRE WORLD IS AMAZED AS NEWS OF HER EXISTENCE IS BROADCAST EVERYWHERE...!
A SUPER FRAULEIN? WUNDERBAR!
A SUPER-MADEMOISELLE? MAGNIFIQUE!
A SUPER-GIRL! BY JOVE! HOW JOLLY!

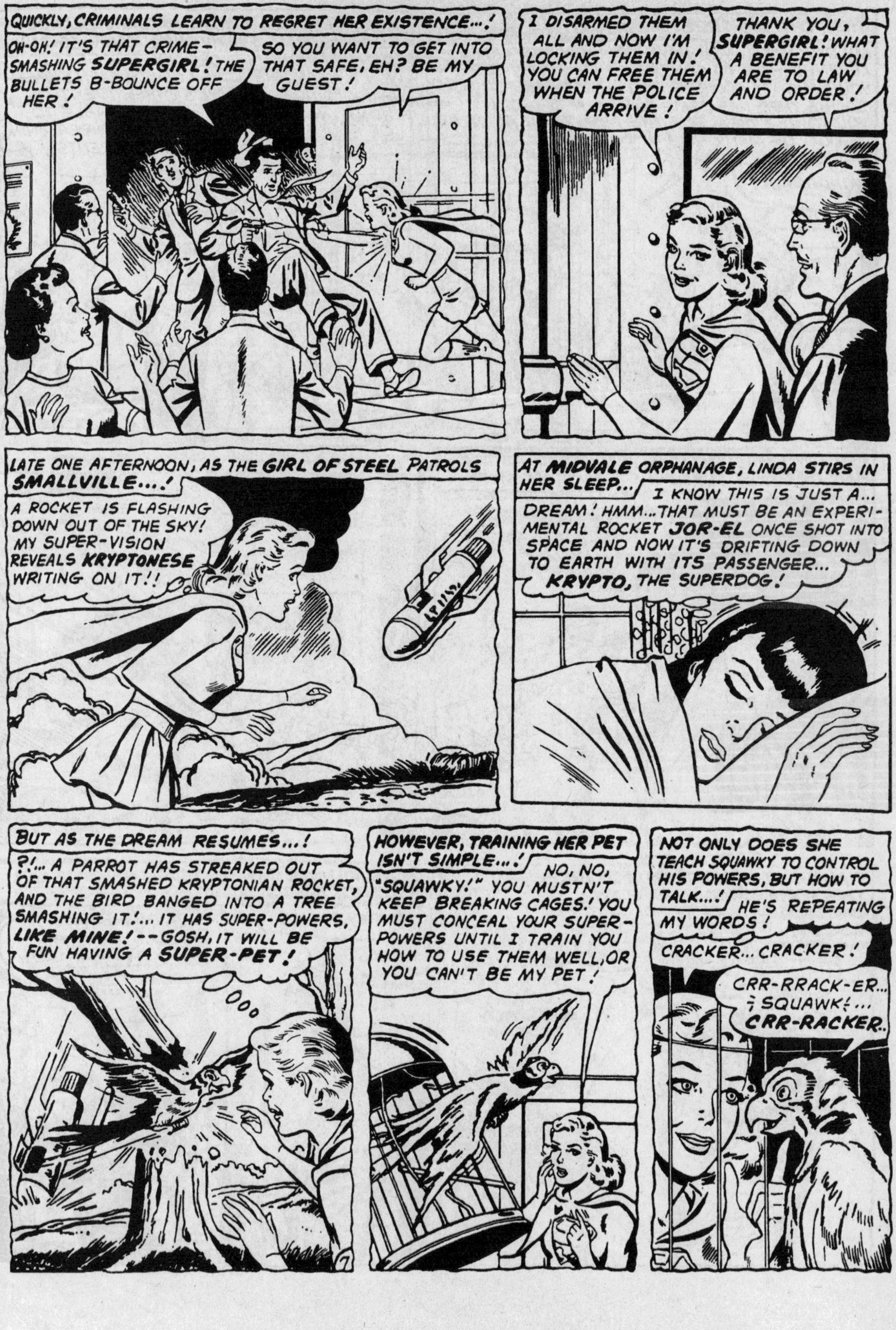
QUICKLY, CRIMINALS LEARN TO REGRET HER EXISTENCE...!
OH-OH! IT'S THAT CRIME-SMASHING SUPERGIRL! THE BULLETS B-BOUNCE OFF HER!
SO YOU WANT TO GET INTO THAT SAFE, EH? BE MY GUEST!
I DISARMED THEM ALL AND NOW I'M LOCKING THEM IN! YOU CAN FREE THEM WHEN THE POLICE ARRIVE!
THANK YOU, SUPERGIRL! WHAT A BENEFIT YOU ARE TO LAW AND ORDER!
LATE ONE AFTERNOON, AS THE GIRL OF STEEL PATROLS SMALLVILLE...!
A ROCKET IS FLASHING DOWN OUT OF THE SKY! MY SUPER-VISION REVEALS KRYPTONESE WRITING ON IT!!
AT MIDVALE ORPHANAGE, LINDA STIRS IN HER SLEEP...
I KNOW THIS IS JUST A... DREAM! HMM...THAT MUST BE AN EXPERIMENTAL ROCKET JOR-EL ONCE SHOT INTO SPACE AND NOW IT'S DRIFTING DOWN TO EARTH WITH ITS PASSENGER... KRYPTO, THE SUPERDOG!
BUT AS THE DREAM RESUMES...!
?!... A PARROT HAS STREAKED OUT OF THAT SMASHED KRYPTONIAN ROCKET, AND THE BIRD BANGED INTO A TREE SMASHING IT!... IT HAS SUPER-POWERS, LIKE MINE! --GOSH, IT WILL BE FUN HAVING A SUPER-PET!
HOWEVER, TRAINING HER PET ISN'T SIMPLE...!
NO, NO, "SQUAWKY!" YOU MUSTN'T KEEP BREAKING CAGES! YOU MUST CONCEAL YOUR SUPER-POWERS UNTIL I TRAIN YOU HOW TO USE THEM WELL, OR YOU CAN'T BE MY PET!
NOT ONLY DOES SHE TEACH SQUAWKY TO CONTROL HIS POWERS, BUT HOW TO TALK...!
HE'S REPEATING MY WORDS!
CRACKER... CRACKER!
CRR-RRACK-ER... ¿SQUAWK¿... CRR-RACKER..

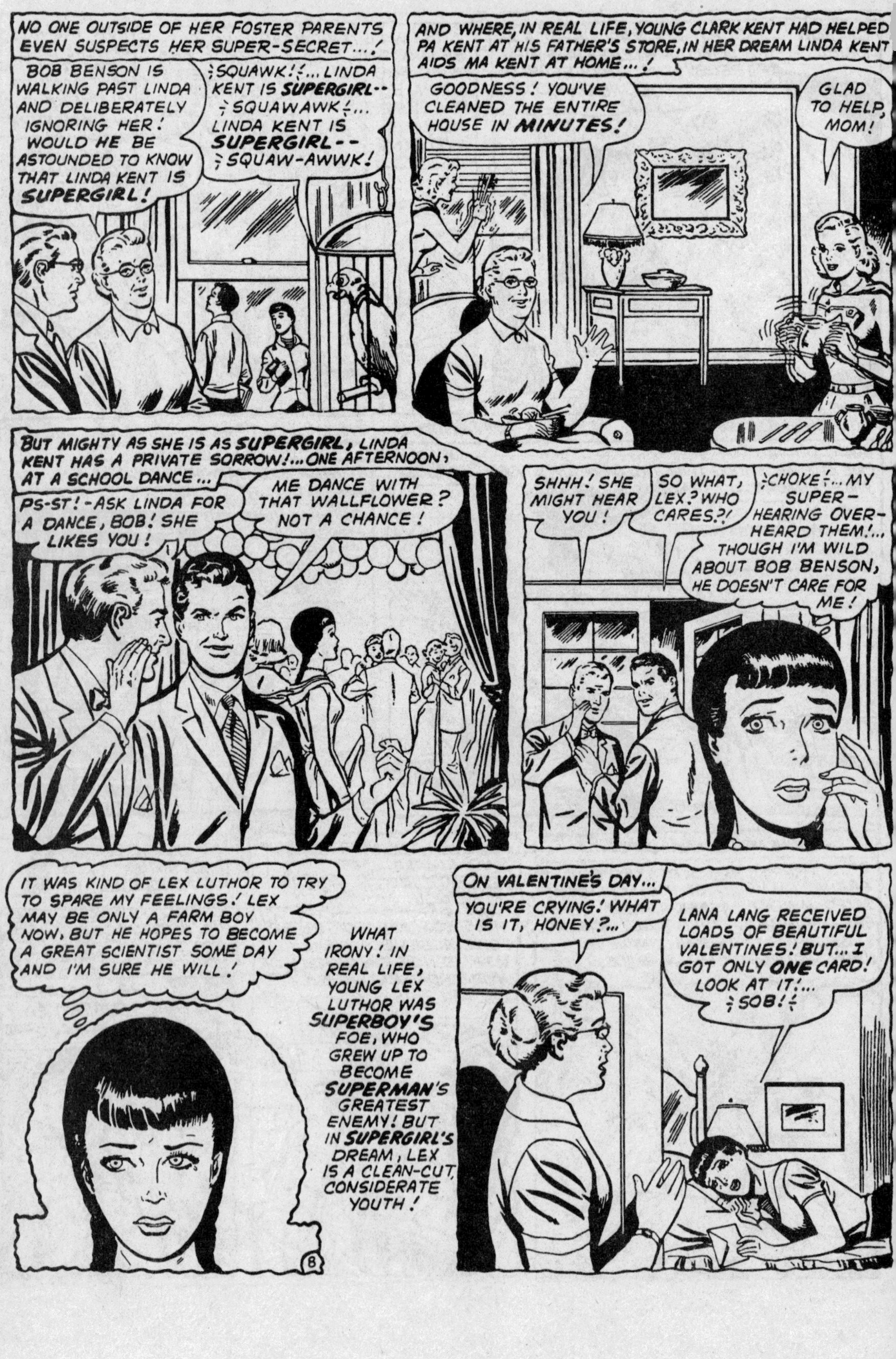
NO ONE OUTSIDE OF HER FOSTER PARENTS EVEN SUSPECTS HER SUPER-SECRET...!
BOB BENSON IS WALKING PAST LINDA AND DELIBERATELY IGNORING HER! WOULD HE BE ASTOUNDED TO KNOW THAT LINDA KENT IS SUPERGIRL!
-SQUAWK!-... LINDA KENT IS SUPERGIRL-- -SQUAWAWK-... LINDA KENT IS SUPERGIRL-- -SQUAW-AWWK!
AND WHERE, IN REAL LIFE, YOUNG CLARK KENT HAD HELPED PA KENT AT HIS FATHER'S STORE, IN HER DREAM LINDA KENT AIDS MA KENT AT HOME...!
GOODNESS! YOU'VE CLEANED THE ENTIRE HOUSE IN MINUTES!
GLAD TO HELP, MOM!
BUT MIGHTY AS SHE IS AS SUPERGIRL, LINDA KENT HAS A PRIVATE SORROW!...ONE AFTERNOON, AT A SCHOOL DANCE...
PS-ST! -ASK LINDA FOR A DANCE, BOB! SHE LIKES YOU!
ME DANCE WITH THAT WALLFLOWER? NOT A CHANCE!
SHHH! SHE MIGHT HEAR YOU!
SO WHAT, LEX? WHO CARES?!
-CHOKE-... MY SUPER-HEARING OVERHEARD THEM!... THOUGH I'M WILD ABOUT BOB BENSON, HE DOESN'T CARE FOR ME!
IT WAS KIND OF LEX LUTHOR TO TRY TO SPARE MY FEELINGS! LEX MAY BE ONLY A FARM BOY NOW, BUT HE HOPES TO BECOME A GREAT SCIENTIST SOME DAY AND I'M SURE HE WILL!
WHAT IRONY! IN REAL LIFE, YOUNG LEX LUTHOR WAS SUPERBOY'S FOE, WHO GREW UP TO BECOME SUPERMAN'S GREATEST ENEMY! BUT IN SUPERGIRL'S DREAM, LEX IS A CLEAN-CUT, CONSIDERATE YOUTH!
8
ON VALENTINE'S DAY...
YOU'RE CRYING! WHAT IS IT, HONEY?...
LANA LANG RECEIVED LOADS OF BEAUTIFUL VALENTINES! BUT... I GOT ONLY ONE CARD! LOOK AT IT!... -SOB!-

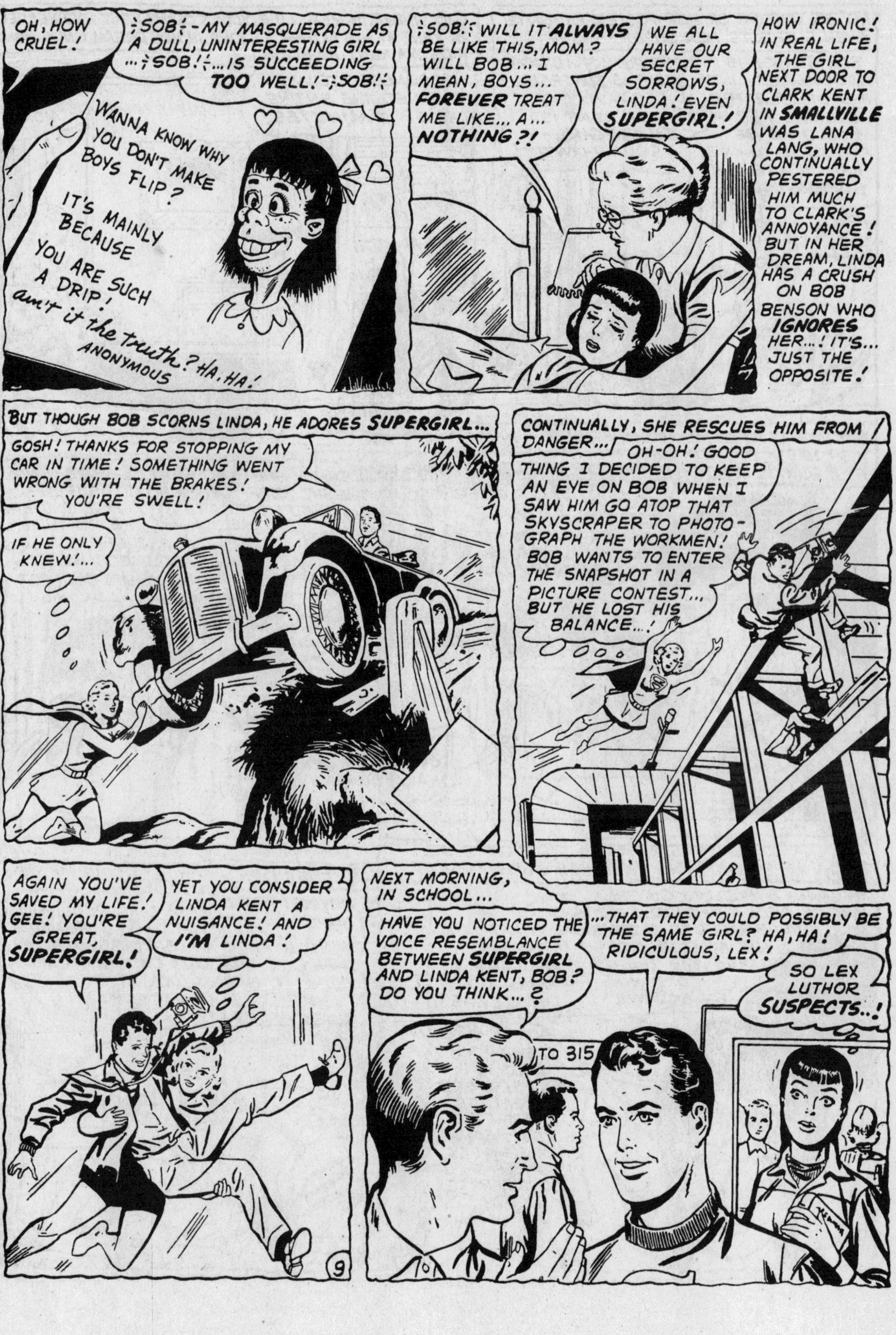
OH, HOW CRUEL!
-SOB!- MY MASQUERADE AS A DULL, UNINTERESTING GIRL ... -SOB!- ... IS SUCCEEDING TOO WELL! -SOB!-
WANNA KNOW WHY YOU DON'T MAKE BOYS FLIP? IT'S MAINLY BECAUSE YOU ARE SUCH A DRIP! ain't it the truth? HA, HA! ANONYMOUS
-SOB!- WILL IT ALWAYS BE LIKE THIS, MOM? WILL BOB ... I MEAN, BOYS ... FOREVER TREAT ME LIKE ... A ... NOTHING?!
WE ALL HAVE OUR SECRET SORROWS, LINDA! EVEN SUPERGIRL!
HOW IRONIC! IN REAL LIFE, THE GIRL NEXT DOOR TO CLARK KENT IN SMALLVILLE WAS LANA LANG, WHO CONTINUALLY PESTERED HIM MUCH TO CLARK'S ANNOYANCE! BUT IN HER DREAM, LINDA HAS A CRUSH ON BOB BENSON WHO IGNORES HER ...! IT'S ... JUST THE OPPOSITE!
BUT THOUGH BOB SCORNS LINDA, HE ADORES SUPERGIRL...
GOSH! THANKS FOR STOPPING MY CAR IN TIME! SOMETHING WENT WRONG WITH THE BRAKES! YOU'RE SWELL!
IF HE ONLY KNEW! ...
CONTINUALLY, SHE RESCUES HIM FROM DANGER...
OH-OH! GOOD THING I DECIDED TO KEEP AN EYE ON BOB WHEN I SAW HIM GO ATOP THAT SKYSCRAPER TO PHOTOGRAPH THE WORKMEN! BOB WANTS TO ENTER THE SNAPSHOT IN A PICTURE CONTEST... BUT HE LOST HIS BALANCE ...!
AGAIN YOU'VE SAVED MY LIFE! GEE! YOU'RE GREAT, SUPERGIRL!
YET YOU CONSIDER LINDA KENT A NUISANCE! AND I'M LINDA!
9
NEXT MORNING, IN SCHOOL...
HAVE YOU NOTICED THE VOICE RESEMBLANCE BETWEEN SUPERGIRL AND LINDA KENT, BOB? DO YOU THINK ... ?
... THAT THEY COULD POSSIBLY BE THE SAME GIRL? HA, HA! RIDICULOUS, LEX!
SO LEX LUTHOR SUSPECTS..!
TO 315
10

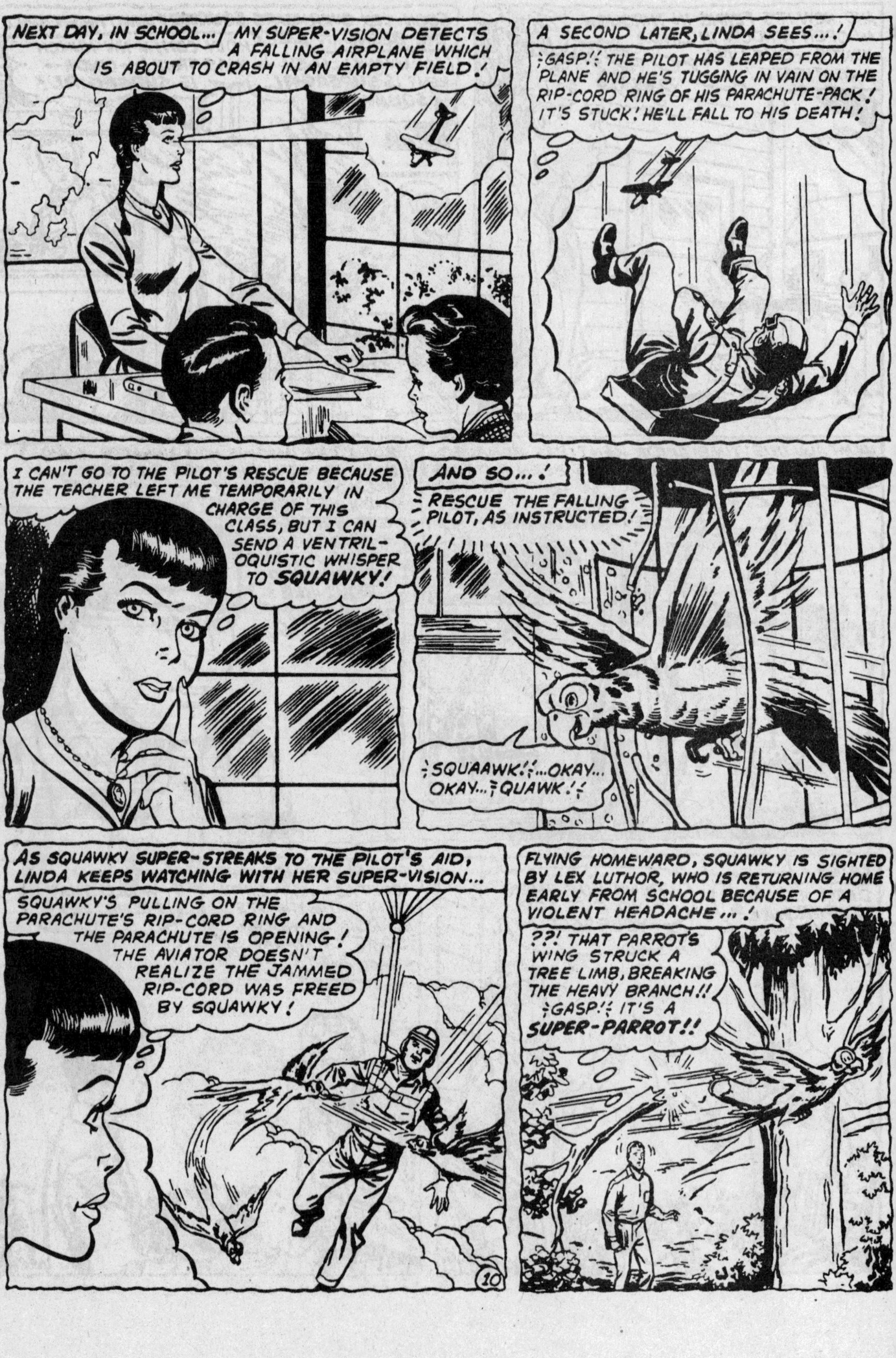
NEXT DAY, IN SCHOOL...
MY SUPER-VISION DETECTS A FALLING AIRPLANE WHICH IS ABOUT TO CRASH IN AN EMPTY FIELD!
A SECOND LATER, LINDA SEES...!
¡GASP!¡ THE PILOT HAS LEAPED FROM THE PLANE AND HE'S TUGGING IN VAIN ON THE RIP-CORD RING OF HIS PARACHUTE-PACK! IT'S STUCK! HE'LL FALL TO HIS DEATH!
I CAN'T GO TO THE PILOT'S RESCUE BECAUSE THE TEACHER LEFT ME TEMPORARILY IN CHARGE OF THIS CLASS, BUT I CAN SEND A VENTRILOQUISTIC WHISPER TO SQUAWKY!
AND SO...!
RESCUE THE FALLING PILOT, AS INSTRUCTED!
¡SQUAAWK!¡...OKAY... OKAY...¡QUAWK!¡
AS SQUAWKY SUPER-STREAKS TO THE PILOT'S AID, LINDA KEEPS WATCHING WITH HER SUPER-VISION...
SQUAWKY'S PULLING ON THE PARACHUTE'S RIP-CORD RING AND THE PARACHUTE IS OPENING! THE AVIATOR DOESN'T REALIZE THE JAMMED RIP-CORD WAS FREED BY SQUAWKY!
10
FLYING HOMEWARD, SQUAWKY IS SIGHTED BY LEX LUTHOR, WHO IS RETURNING HOME EARLY FROM SCHOOL BECAUSE OF A VIOLENT HEADACHE...!
??! THAT PARROT'S WING STRUCK A TREE LIMB, BREAKING THE HEAVY BRANCH!! ¡GASP!¡ IT'S A SUPER-PARROT!!

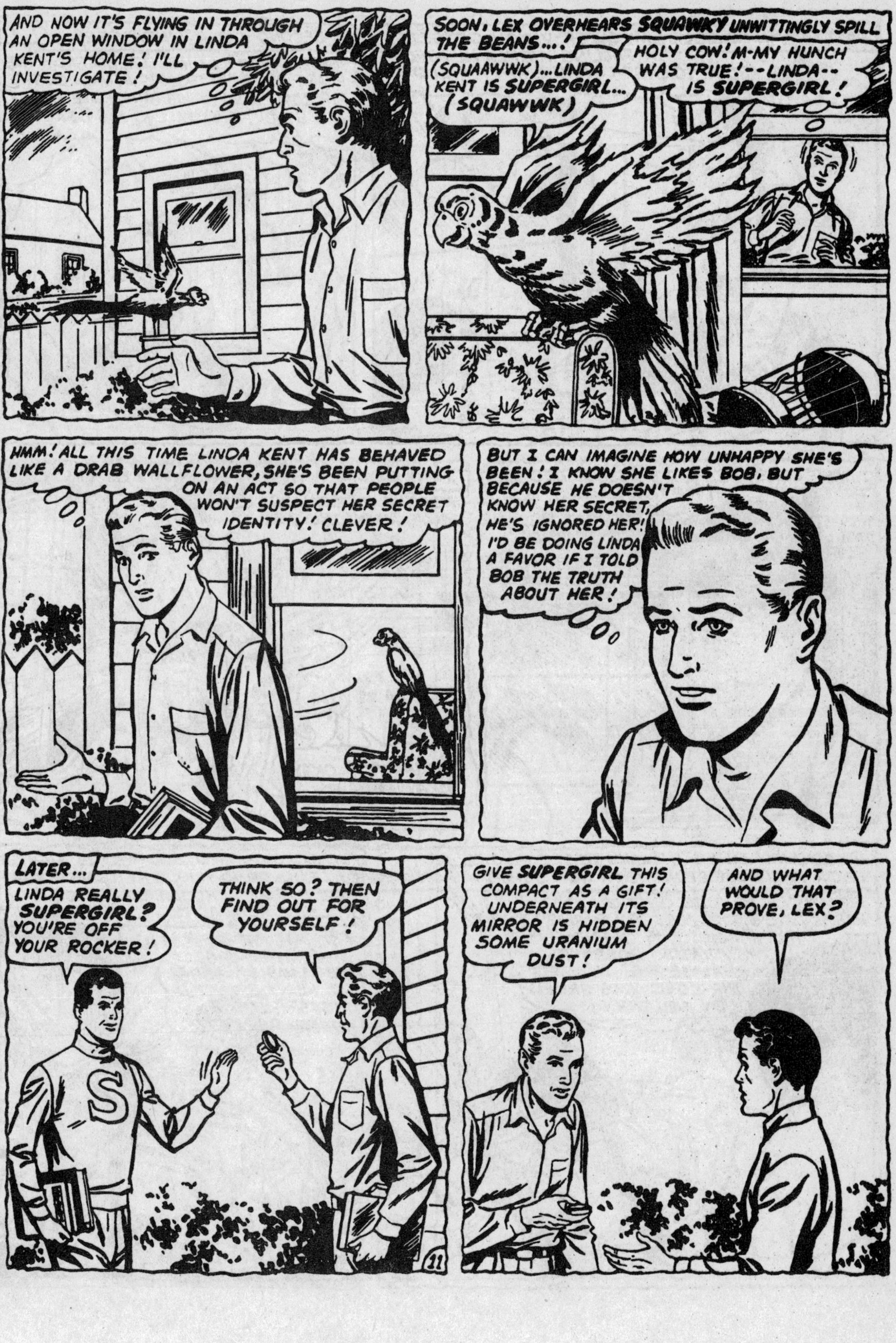
AND NOW IT'S FLYING IN THROUGH AN OPEN WINDOW IN LINDA KENT'S HOME! I'LL INVESTIGATE!
SOON, LEX OVERHEARS SQUAWKY UNWITTINGLY SPILL THE BEANS...!
(SQUAAWWK)...LINDA KENT IS SUPERGIRL... (SQUAWWK)
HOLY COW! M-MY HUNCH WAS TRUE! --LINDA-- IS SUPERGIRL!
HMM! ALL THIS TIME LINDA KENT HAS BEHAVED LIKE A DRAB WALLFLOWER, SHE'S BEEN PUTTING ON AN ACT SO THAT PEOPLE WON'T SUSPECT HER SECRET IDENTITY! CLEVER!
BUT I CAN IMAGINE HOW UNHAPPY SHE'S BEEN! I KNOW SHE LIKES BOB, BUT BECAUSE HE DOESN'T KNOW HER SECRET, HE'S IGNORED HER! I'D BE DOING LINDA A FAVOR IF I TOLD BOB THE TRUTH ABOUT HER!
LATER...
LINDA REALLY SUPERGIRL? YOU'RE OFF YOUR ROCKER!
THINK SO? THEN FIND OUT FOR YOURSELF!
11
GIVE SUPERGIRL THIS COMPACT AS A GIFT! UNDERNEATH ITS MIRROR IS HIDDEN SOME URANIUM DUST!
AND WHAT WOULD THAT PROVE, LEX?

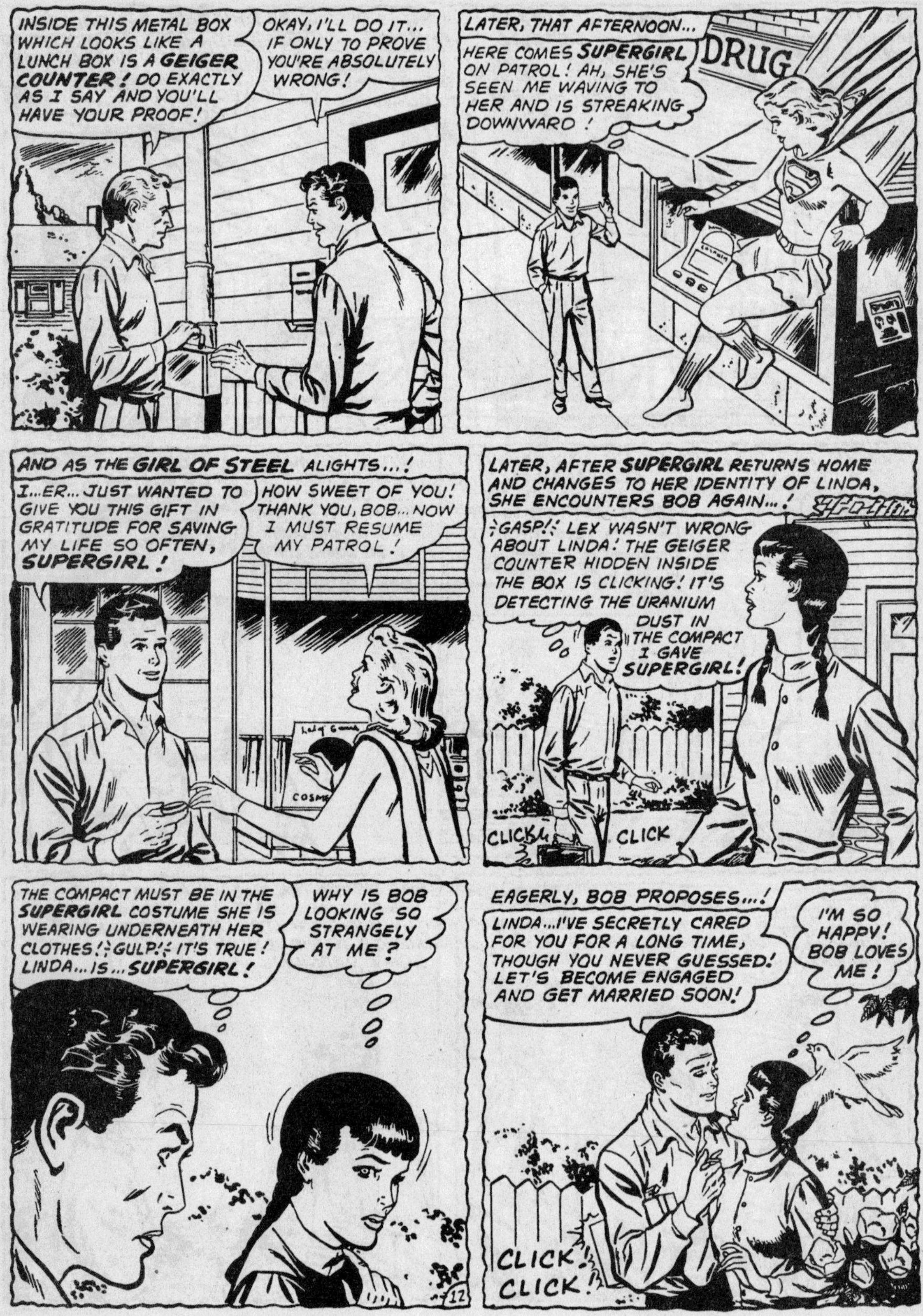
INSIDE THIS METAL BOX WHICH LOOKS LIKE A LUNCH BOX IS A GEIGER COUNTER! DO EXACTLY AS I SAY AND YOU'LL HAVE YOUR PROOF!
OKAY, I'LL DO IT... IF ONLY TO PROVE YOU'RE ABSOLUTELY WRONG!
LATER, THAT AFTERNOON...
HERE COMES SUPERGIRL ON PATROL! AH, SHE'S SEEN ME WAVING TO HER AND IS STREAKING DOWNWARD!
DRUG
AND AS THE GIRL OF STEEL ALIGHTS...!
I...ER... JUST WANTED TO GIVE YOU THIS GIFT IN GRATITUDE FOR SAVING MY LIFE SO OFTEN, SUPERGIRL!
HOW SWEET OF YOU! THANK YOU, BOB... NOW I MUST RESUME MY PATROL!
LATER, AFTER SUPERGIRL RETURNS HOME AND CHANGES TO HER IDENTITY OF LINDA, SHE ENCOUNTERS BOB AGAIN...!
GASP! LEX WASN'T WRONG ABOUT LINDA! THE GEIGER COUNTER HIDDEN INSIDE THE BOX IS CLICKING! IT'S DETECTING THE URANIUM DUST IN THE COMPACT I GAVE SUPERGIRL!
CLICK CLICK
THE COMPACT MUST BE IN THE SUPERGIRL COSTUME SHE IS WEARING UNDERNEATH HER CLOTHES! GULP! IT'S TRUE! LINDA... IS... SUPERGIRL!
WHY IS BOB LOOKING SO STRANGELY AT ME?
12
EAGERLY, BOB PROPOSES...!
LINDA...I'VE SECRETLY CARED FOR YOU FOR A LONG TIME, THOUGH YOU NEVER GUESSED! LET'S BECOME ENGAGED AND GET MARRIED SOON!
I'M SO HAPPY! BOB LOVES ME!
CLICK! CLICK!

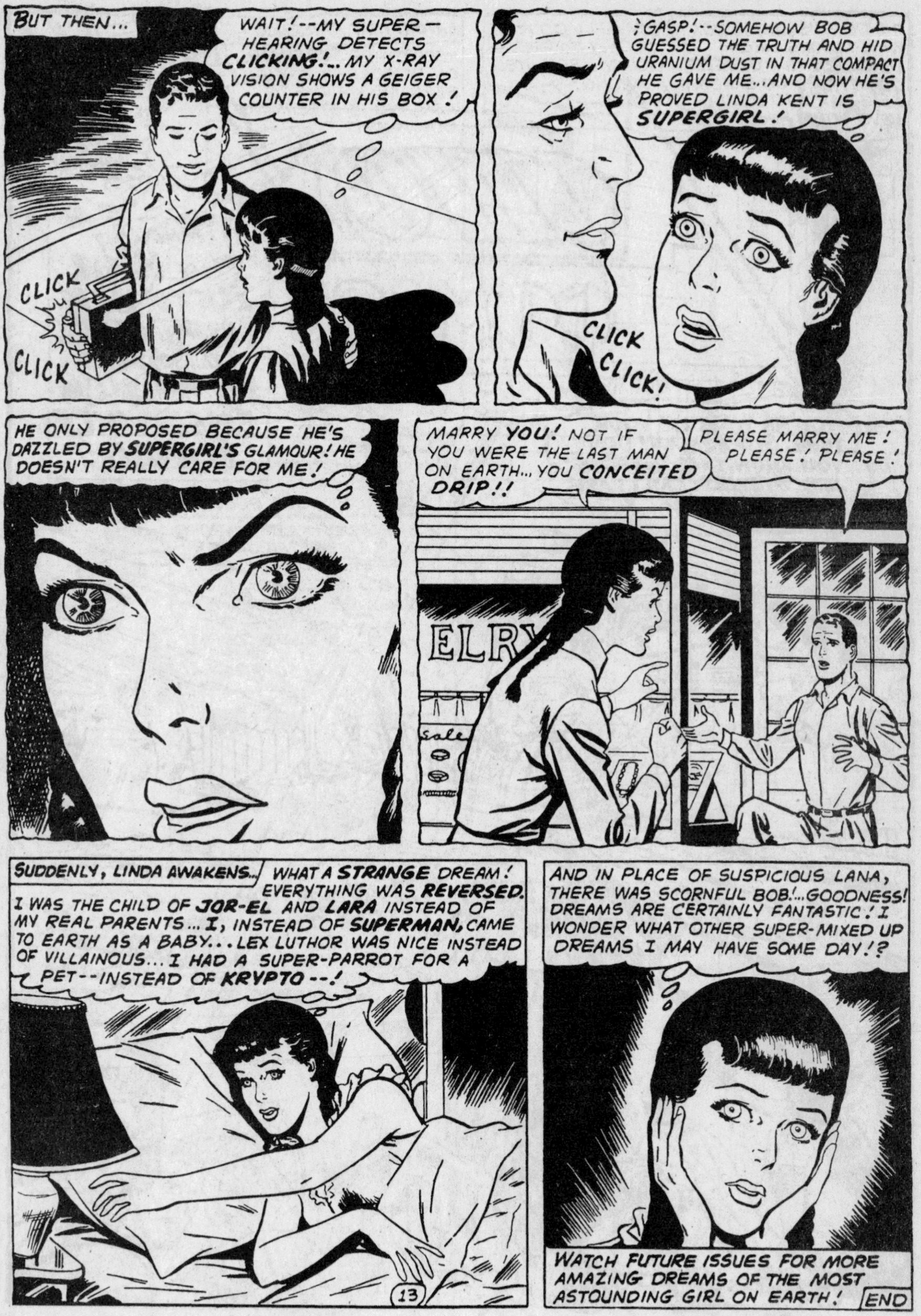
BUT THEN...
WAIT!--MY SUPER-HEARING DETECTS CLICKING!.. MY X-RAY VISION SHOWS A GEIGER COUNTER IN HIS BOX!
CLICK
CLICK
¡GASP!--SOMEHOW BOB GUESSED THE TRUTH AND HID URANIUM DUST IN THAT COMPACT HE GAVE ME...AND NOW HE'S PROVED LINDA KENT IS SUPERGIRL!
CLICK
CLICK!
HE ONLY PROPOSED BECAUSE HE'S DAZZLED BY SUPERGIRL'S GLAMOUR! HE DOESN'T REALLY CARE FOR ME!
MARRY YOU! NOT IF YOU WERE THE LAST MAN ON EARTH... YOU CONCEITED DRIP!!
PLEASE MARRY ME! PLEASE! PLEASE!
ELRY
sale
SUDDENLY, LINDA AWAKENS..
WHAT A STRANGE DREAM! EVERYTHING WAS REVERSED. I WAS THE CHILD OF JOR-EL AND LARA INSTEAD OF MY REAL PARENTS... I, INSTEAD OF SUPERMAN, CAME TO EARTH AS A BABY... LEX LUTHOR WAS NICE INSTEAD OF VILLAINOUS... I HAD A SUPER-PARROT FOR A PET--INSTEAD OF KRYPTO--!
13
AND IN PLACE OF SUSPICIOUS LANA, THERE WAS SCORNFUL BOB!...GOODNESS! DREAMS ARE CERTAINLY FANTASTIC! I WONDER WHAT OTHER SUPER-MIXED UP DREAMS I MAY HAVE SOME DAY!?
WATCH FUTURE ISSUES FOR MORE AMAZING DREAMS OF THE MOST ASTOUNDING GIRL ON EARTH!
END

SUPERMAN DC NATIONAL COMICS
STILL 10¢
MAY NO. 276
ACTION COMICS
APPROVED BY THE COMICS CODE AUTHORITY
Featuring "The WAR BETWEEN SUPERGIRL and the SUPERMAN EMERGENCY SQUAD!"
YOU'RE WASTING YOUR TIME, SUPERMAN! DON'T YOU KNOW THAT "STICKS" AND "STONES" CAN'T HARM A SUPERGIRL?

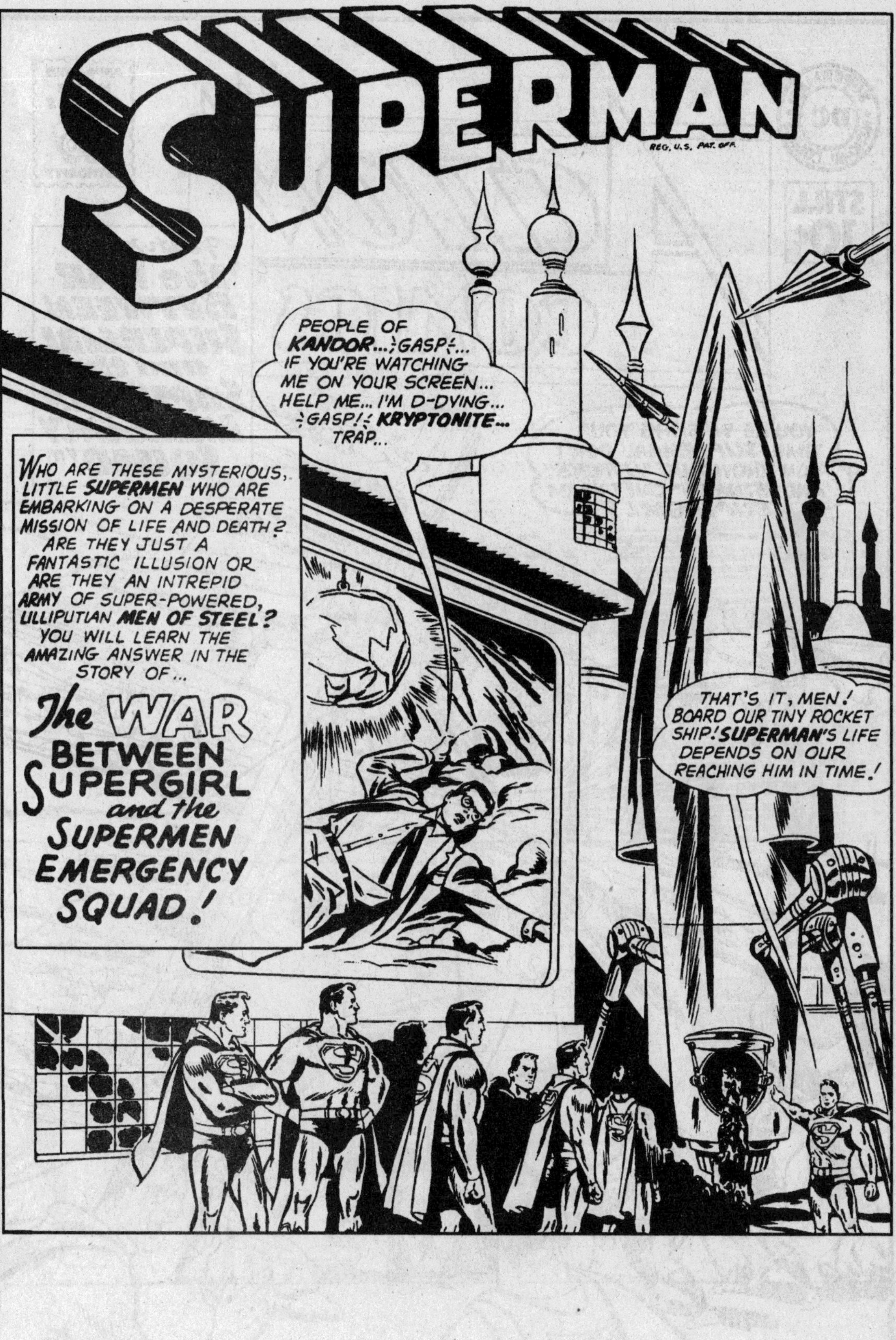
SUPERMAN
REG. U.S. PAT. OFF.
WHO ARE THESE MYSTERIOUS, LITTLE SUPERMEN WHO ARE EMBARKING ON A DESPERATE MISSION OF LIFE AND DEATH? ARE THEY JUST A FANTASTIC ILLUSION OR ARE THEY AN INTREPID ARMY OF SUPER-POWERED, LILLIPUTIAN MEN OF STEEL? YOU WILL LEARN THE AMAZING ANSWER IN THE STORY OF...
The WAR BETWEEN SUPERGIRL and the SUPERMEN EMERGENCY SQUAD!
PEOPLE OF KANDOR...-GASP-... IF YOU'RE WATCHING ME ON YOUR SCREEN... HELP ME... I'M D-DYING... -GASP!- KRYPTONITE... TRAP...
THAT'S IT, MEN! BOARD OUR TINY ROCKET SHIP! SUPERMAN'S LIFE DEPENDS ON OUR REACHING HIM IN TIME!

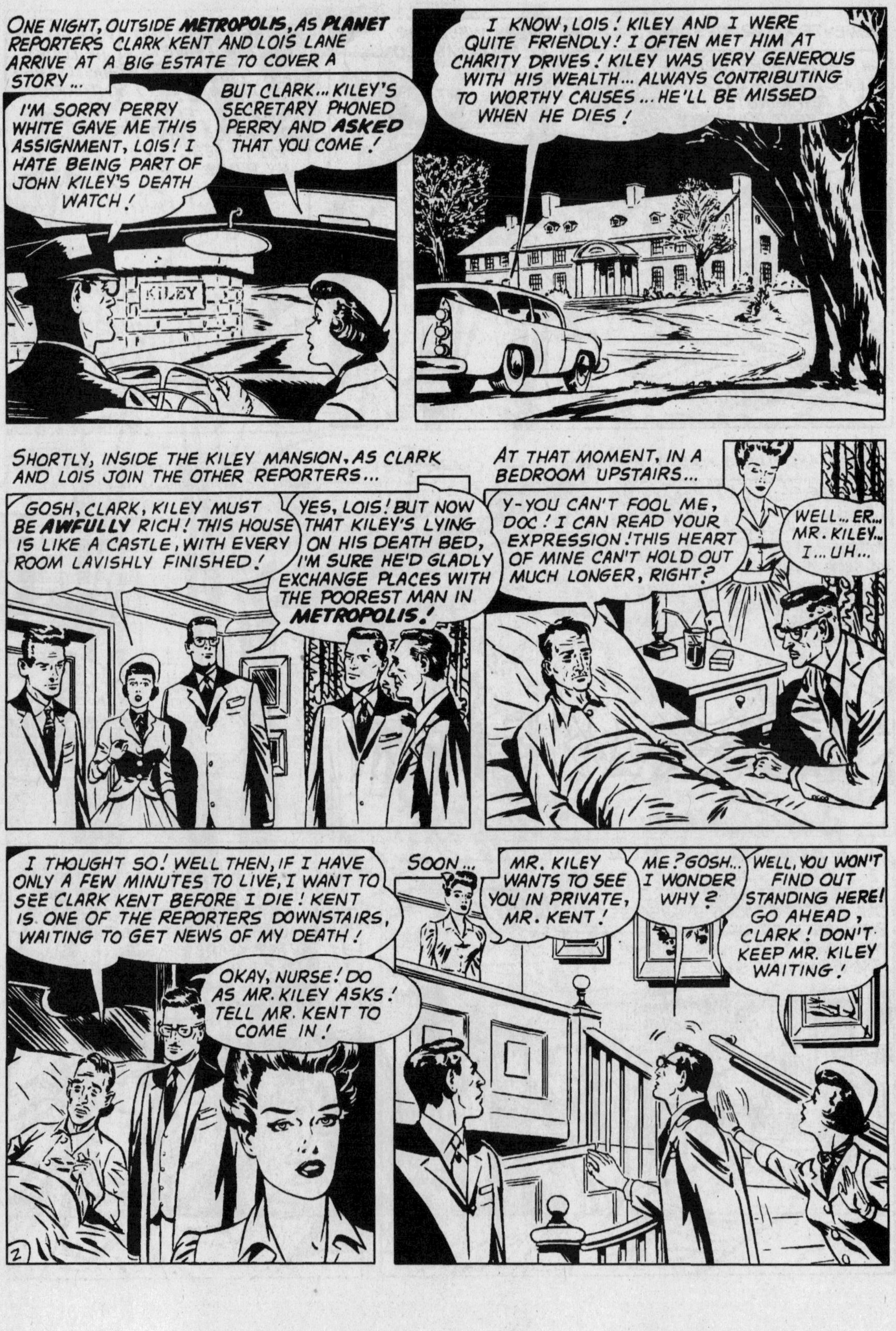
ONE NIGHT, OUTSIDE METROPOLIS, AS PLANET REPORTERS CLARK KENT AND LOIS LANE ARRIVE AT A BIG ESTATE TO COVER A STORY...
I'M SORRY PERRY WHITE GAVE ME THIS ASSIGNMENT, LOIS! I HATE BEING PART OF JOHN KILEY'S DEATH WATCH!
BUT CLARK... KILEY'S SECRETARY PHONED PERRY AND ASKED THAT YOU COME!
KILEY
I KNOW, LOIS! KILEY AND I WERE QUITE FRIENDLY! I OFTEN MET HIM AT CHARITY DRIVES! KILEY WAS VERY GENEROUS WITH HIS WEALTH... ALWAYS CONTRIBUTING TO WORTHY CAUSES... HE'LL BE MISSED WHEN HE DIES!
SHORTLY, INSIDE THE KILEY MANSION, AS CLARK AND LOIS JOIN THE OTHER REPORTERS...
GOSH, CLARK, KILEY MUST BE AWFULLY RICH! THIS HOUSE IS LIKE A CASTLE, WITH EVERY ROOM LAVISHLY FINISHED!
YES, LOIS! BUT NOW THAT KILEY'S LYING ON HIS DEATH BED, I'M SURE HE'D GLADLY EXCHANGE PLACES WITH THE POOREST MAN IN METROPOLIS!
AT THAT MOMENT, IN A BEDROOM UPSTAIRS...
Y-YOU CAN'T FOOL ME, DOC! I CAN READ YOUR EXPRESSION! THIS HEART OF MINE CAN'T HOLD OUT MUCH LONGER, RIGHT?
WELL... ER... MR. KILEY... I... UH...
I THOUGHT SO! WELL THEN, IF I HAVE ONLY A FEW MINUTES TO LIVE, I WANT TO SEE CLARK KENT BEFORE I DIE! KENT IS ONE OF THE REPORTERS DOWNSTAIRS, WAITING TO GET NEWS OF MY DEATH!
OKAY, NURSE! DO AS MR. KILEY ASKS! TELL MR. KENT TO COME IN!
SOON...
MR. KILEY WANTS TO SEE YOU IN PRIVATE, MR. KENT!
ME? GOSH... I WONDER WHY?
WELL, YOU WON'T FIND OUT STANDING HERE! GO AHEAD, CLARK! DON'T KEEP MR. KILEY WAITING!

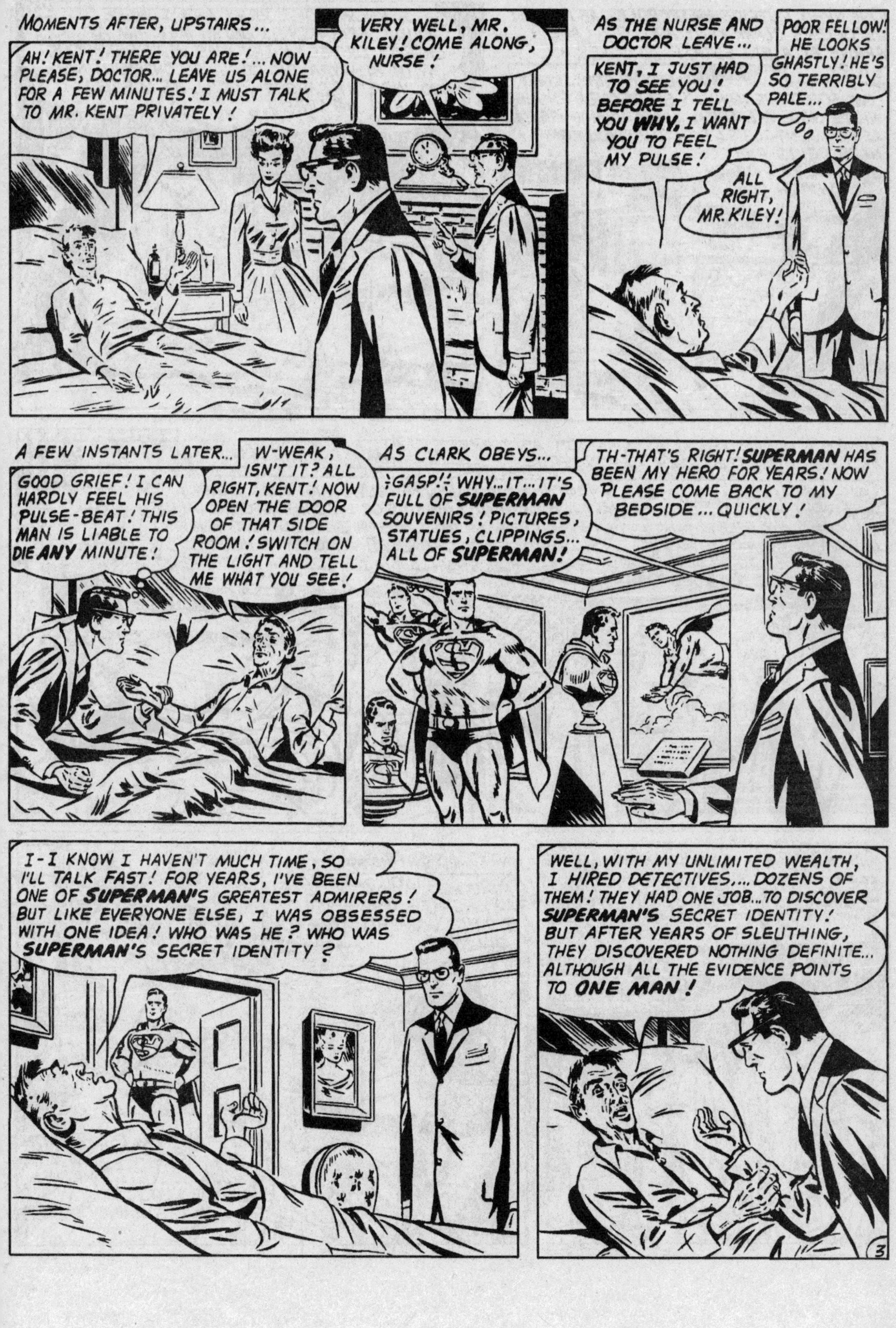
MOMENTS AFTER, UPSTAIRS...
AH! KENT! THERE YOU ARE!... NOW PLEASE, DOCTOR... LEAVE US ALONE FOR A FEW MINUTES! I MUST TALK TO MR. KENT PRIVATELY!
VERY WELL, MR. KILEY! COME ALONG, NURSE!
AS THE NURSE AND DOCTOR LEAVE...
POOR FELLOW! HE LOOKS GHASTLY! HE'S SO TERRIBLY PALE...
KENT, I JUST HAD TO SEE YOU! BEFORE I TELL YOU WHY, I WANT YOU TO FEEL MY PULSE!
ALL RIGHT, MR. KILEY!
A FEW INSTANTS LATER...
GOOD GRIEF! I CAN HARDLY FEEL HIS PULSE-BEAT! THIS MAN IS LIABLE TO DIE ANY MINUTE!
W-WEAK, ISN'T IT? ALL RIGHT, KENT! NOW OPEN THE DOOR OF THAT SIDE ROOM! SWITCH ON THE LIGHT AND TELL ME WHAT YOU SEE!
AS CLARK OBEYS...
¡GASP!¡ WHY... IT... IT'S FULL OF SUPERMAN SOUVENIRS! PICTURES, STATUES, CLIPPINGS... ALL OF SUPERMAN!
TH-THAT'S RIGHT! SUPERMAN HAS BEEN MY HERO FOR YEARS! NOW PLEASE COME BACK TO MY BEDSIDE... QUICKLY!
I-I KNOW I HAVEN'T MUCH TIME, SO I'LL TALK FAST! FOR YEARS, I'VE BEEN ONE OF SUPERMAN'S GREATEST ADMIRERS! BUT LIKE EVERYONE ELSE, I WAS OBSESSED WITH ONE IDEA! WHO WAS HE? WHO WAS SUPERMAN'S SECRET IDENTITY?
WELL, WITH MY UNLIMITED WEALTH, I HIRED DETECTIVES,... DOZENS OF THEM! THEY HAD ONE JOB... TO DISCOVER SUPERMAN'S SECRET IDENTITY! BUT AFTER YEARS OF SLEUTHING, THEY DISCOVERED NOTHING DEFINITE... ALTHOUGH ALL THE EVIDENCE POINTS TO ONE MAN!
3

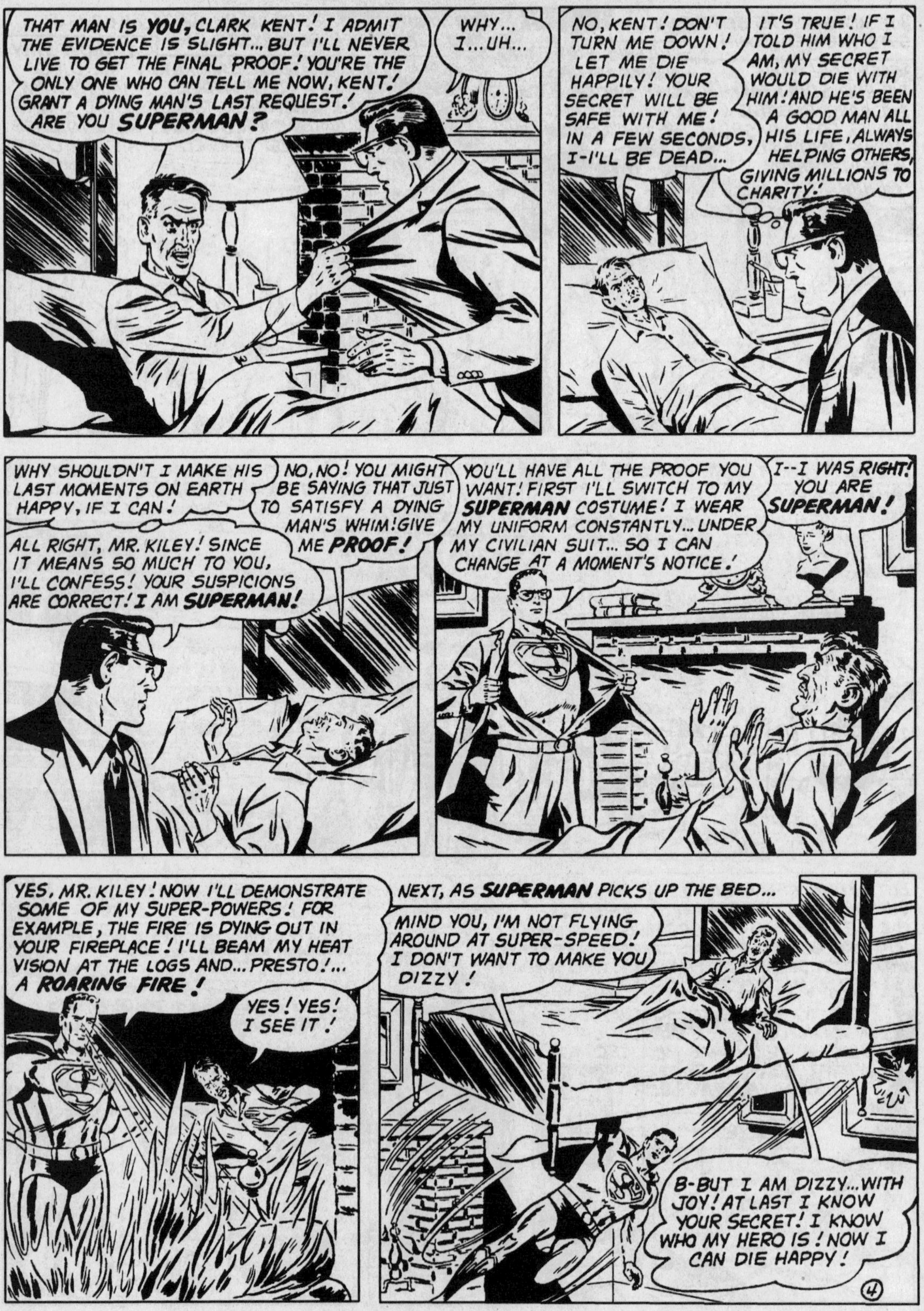
THAT MAN IS YOU, CLARK KENT! I ADMIT THE EVIDENCE IS SLIGHT... BUT I'LL NEVER LIVE TO GET THE FINAL PROOF! YOU'RE THE ONLY ONE WHO CAN TELL ME NOW, KENT! GRANT A DYING MAN'S LAST REQUEST! ARE YOU SUPERMAN?
WHY... I...UH...
NO, KENT! DON'T TURN ME DOWN! LET ME DIE HAPPILY! YOUR SECRET WILL BE SAFE WITH ME! IN A FEW SECONDS, I-I'LL BE DEAD...
IT'S TRUE! IF I TOLD HIM WHO I AM, MY SECRET WOULD DIE WITH HIM! AND HE'S BEEN A GOOD MAN ALL HIS LIFE, ALWAYS HELPING OTHERS, GIVING MILLIONS TO CHARITY!
WHY SHOULDN'T I MAKE HIS LAST MOMENTS ON EARTH HAPPY, IF I CAN!
ALL RIGHT, MR. KILEY! SINCE IT MEANS SO MUCH TO YOU, I'LL CONFESS! YOUR SUSPICIONS ARE CORRECT! I AM SUPERMAN!
NO, NO! YOU MIGHT BE SAYING THAT JUST TO SATISFY A DYING MAN'S WHIM! GIVE ME PROOF!
YOU'LL HAVE ALL THE PROOF YOU WANT! FIRST I'LL SWITCH TO MY SUPERMAN COSTUME! I WEAR MY UNIFORM CONSTANTLY... UNDER MY CIVILIAN SUIT... SO I CAN CHANGE AT A MOMENT'S NOTICE!
I--I WAS RIGHT! YOU ARE SUPERMAN!
YES, MR. KILEY! NOW I'LL DEMONSTRATE SOME OF MY SUPER-POWERS! FOR EXAMPLE, THE FIRE IS DYING OUT IN YOUR FIREPLACE! I'LL BEAM MY HEAT VISION AT THE LOGS AND... PRESTO!... A ROARING FIRE!
YES! YES! I SEE IT!
NEXT, AS SUPERMAN PICKS UP THE BED...
MIND YOU, I'M NOT FLYING AROUND AT SUPER-SPEED! I DON'T WANT TO MAKE YOU DIZZY!
B-BUT I AM DIZZY... WITH JOY! AT LAST I KNOW YOUR SECRET! I KNOW WHO MY HERO IS! NOW I CAN DIE HAPPY!
4

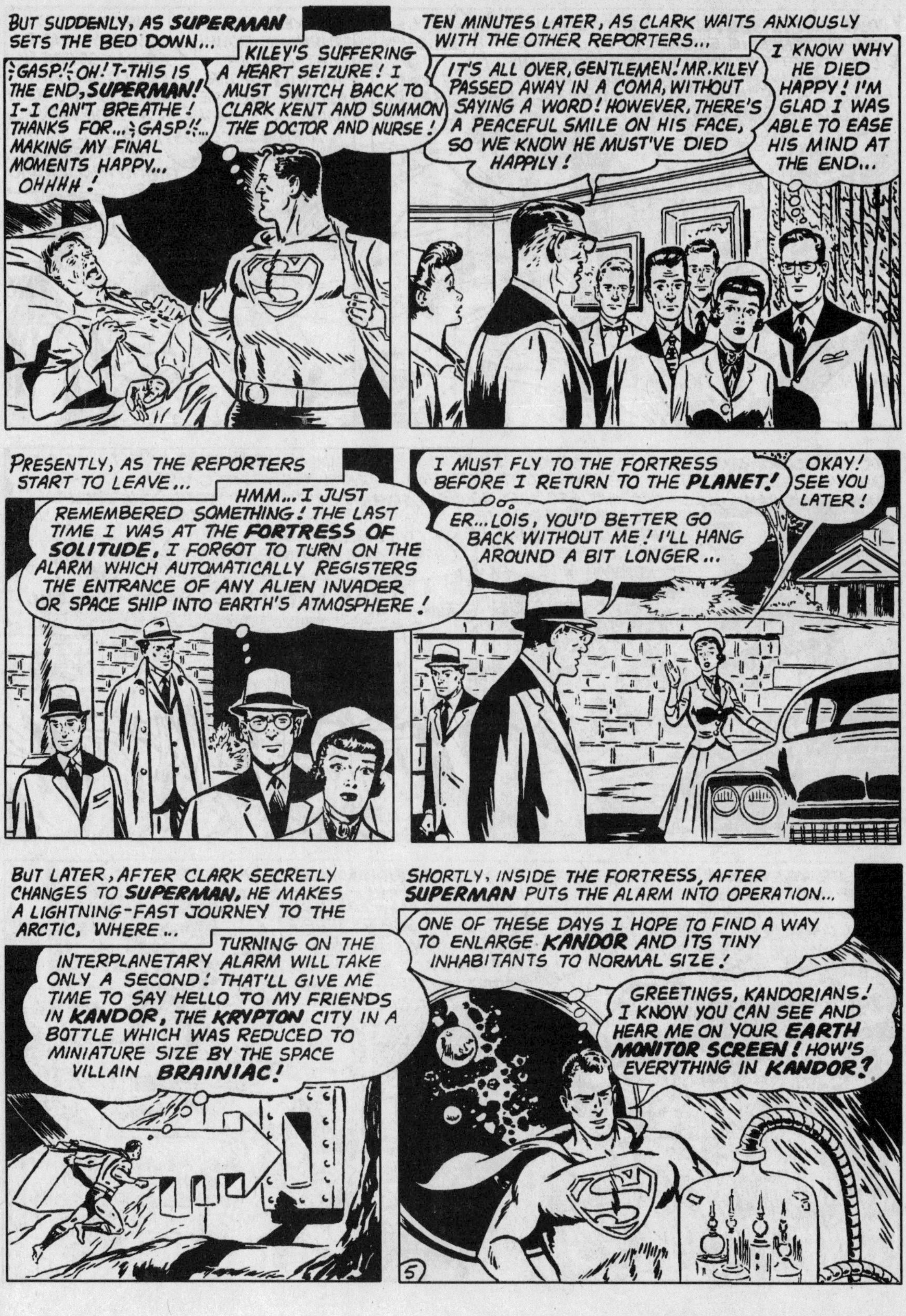
BUT SUDDENLY, AS SUPERMAN SETS THE BED DOWN...
;GASP!; OH! T-THIS IS THE END, SUPERMAN! I-I CAN'T BREATHE! THANKS FOR... ;GASP!;... MAKING MY FINAL MOMENTS HAPPY... OHHHH!
KILEY'S SUFFERING A HEART SEIZURE! I MUST SWITCH BACK TO CLARK KENT AND SUMMON THE DOCTOR AND NURSE!
TEN MINUTES LATER, AS CLARK WAITS ANXIOUSLY WITH THE OTHER REPORTERS...
IT'S ALL OVER, GENTLEMEN! MR. KILEY PASSED AWAY IN A COMA, WITHOUT SAYING A WORD! HOWEVER, THERE'S A PEACEFUL SMILE ON HIS FACE, SO WE KNOW HE MUST'VE DIED HAPPILY!
I KNOW WHY HE DIED HAPPY! I'M GLAD I WAS ABLE TO EASE HIS MIND AT THE END...
PRESENTLY, AS THE REPORTERS START TO LEAVE...
HMM... I JUST REMEMBERED SOMETHING! THE LAST TIME I WAS AT THE FORTRESS OF SOLITUDE, I FORGOT TO TURN ON THE ALARM WHICH AUTOMATICALLY REGISTERS THE ENTRANCE OF ANY ALIEN INVADER OR SPACE SHIP INTO EARTH'S ATMOSPHERE!
I MUST FLY TO THE FORTRESS BEFORE I RETURN TO THE PLANET!
ER... LOIS, YOU'D BETTER GO BACK WITHOUT ME! I'LL HANG AROUND A BIT LONGER...
OKAY! SEE YOU LATER!
BUT LATER, AFTER CLARK SECRETLY CHANGES TO SUPERMAN, HE MAKES A LIGHTNING-FAST JOURNEY TO THE ARCTIC, WHERE...
TURNING ON THE INTERPLANETARY ALARM WILL TAKE ONLY A SECOND! THAT'LL GIVE ME TIME TO SAY HELLO TO MY FRIENDS IN KANDOR, THE KRYPTON CITY IN A BOTTLE WHICH WAS REDUCED TO MINIATURE SIZE BY THE SPACE VILLAIN BRAINIAC!
SHORTLY, INSIDE THE FORTRESS, AFTER SUPERMAN PUTS THE ALARM INTO OPERATION...
ONE OF THESE DAYS I HOPE TO FIND A WAY TO ENLARGE KANDOR AND ITS TINY INHABITANTS TO NORMAL SIZE!
GREETINGS, KANDORIANS! I KNOW YOU CAN SEE AND HEAR ME ON YOUR EARTH MONITOR SCREEN! HOW'S EVERYTHING IN KANDOR?
5

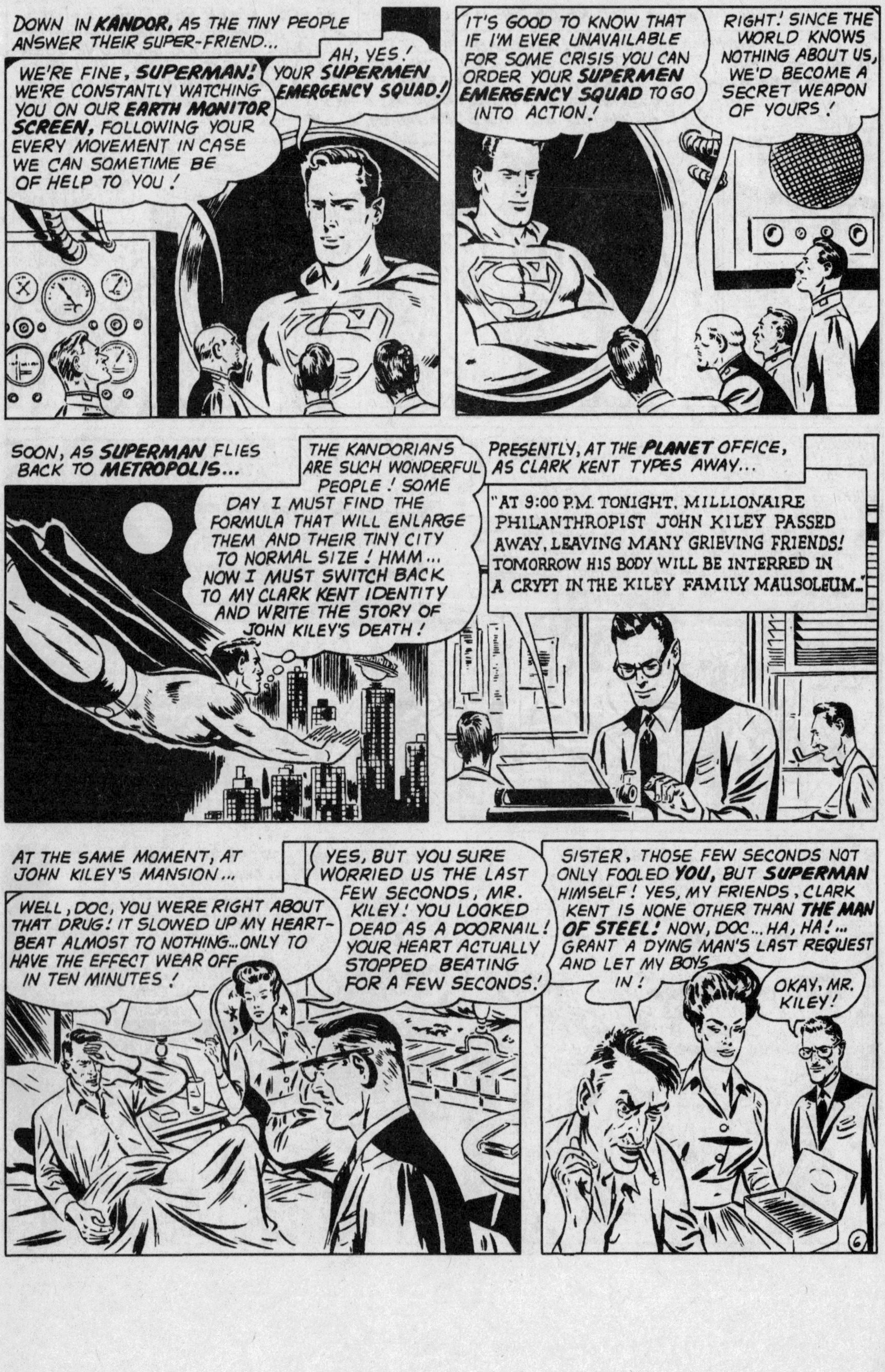
DOWN IN KANDOR, AS THE TINY PEOPLE ANSWER THEIR SUPER-FRIEND...
WE'RE FINE, SUPERMAN! WE'RE CONSTANTLY WATCHING YOU ON OUR EARTH MONITOR SCREEN, FOLLOWING YOUR EVERY MOVEMENT IN CASE WE CAN SOMETIME BE OF HELP TO YOU!
AH, YES! YOUR SUPERMEN EMERGENCY SQUAD!
IT'S GOOD TO KNOW THAT IF I'M EVER UNAVAILABLE FOR SOME CRISIS YOU CAN ORDER YOUR SUPERMEN EMERGENCY SQUAD TO GO INTO ACTION!
RIGHT! SINCE THE WORLD KNOWS NOTHING ABOUT US, WE'D BECOME A SECRET WEAPON OF YOURS!
SOON, AS SUPERMAN FLIES BACK TO METROPOLIS...
THE KANDORIANS ARE SUCH WONDERFUL PEOPLE! SOME DAY I MUST FIND THE FORMULA THAT WILL ENLARGE THEM AND THEIR TINY CITY TO NORMAL SIZE! HMM... NOW I MUST SWITCH BACK TO MY CLARK KENT IDENTITY AND WRITE THE STORY OF JOHN KILEY'S DEATH!
PRESENTLY, AT THE PLANET OFFICE, AS CLARK KENT TYPES AWAY...
"AT 9:00 P.M. TONIGHT, MILLIONAIRE PHILANTHROPIST JOHN KILEY PASSED AWAY, LEAVING MANY GRIEVING FRIENDS! TOMORROW HIS BODY WILL BE INTERRED IN A CRYPT IN THE KILEY FAMILY MAUSOLEUM..."
AT THE SAME MOMENT, AT JOHN KILEY'S MANSION...
WELL, DOC, YOU WERE RIGHT ABOUT THAT DRUG! IT SLOWED UP MY HEART-BEAT ALMOST TO NOTHING...ONLY TO HAVE THE EFFECT WEAR OFF IN TEN MINUTES!
YES, BUT YOU SURE WORRIED US THE LAST FEW SECONDS, MR. KILEY! YOU LOOKED DEAD AS A DOORNAIL! YOUR HEART ACTUALLY STOPPED BEATING FOR A FEW SECONDS!
SISTER, THOSE FEW SECONDS NOT ONLY FOOLED YOU, BUT SUPERMAN HIMSELF! YES, MY FRIENDS, CLARK KENT IS NONE OTHER THAN THE MAN OF STEEL! NOW, DOC... HA, HA!... GRANT A DYING MAN'S LAST REQUEST AND LET MY BOYS IN!
OKAY, MR. KILEY!
6

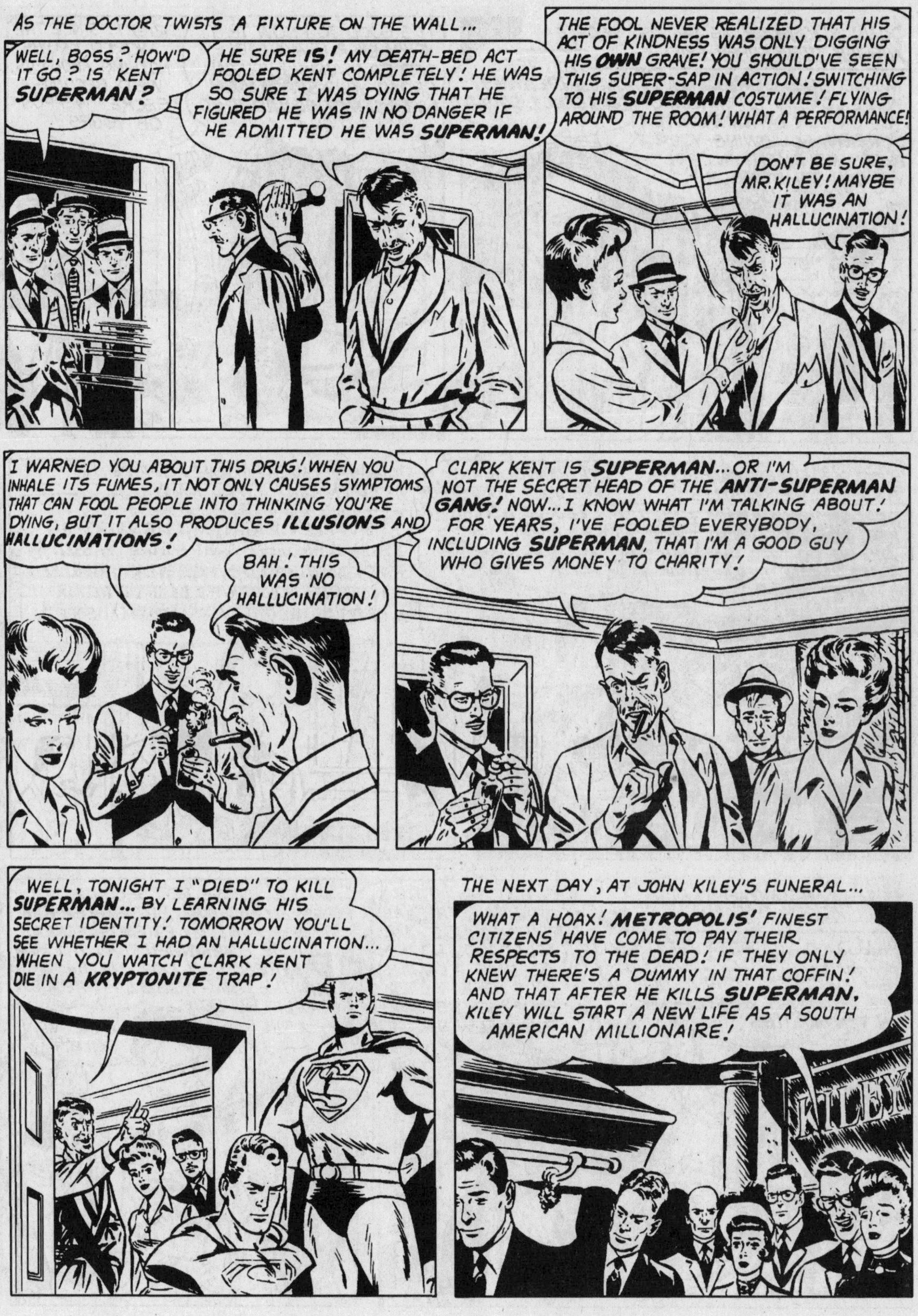
AS THE DOCTOR TWISTS A FIXTURE ON THE WALL...
WELL, BOSS? HOW'D IT GO? IS KENT SUPERMAN?
HE SURE IS! MY DEATH-BED ACT FOOLED KENT COMPLETELY! HE WAS SO SURE I WAS DYING THAT HE FIGURED HE WAS IN NO DANGER IF HE ADMITTED HE WAS SUPERMAN!
THE FOOL NEVER REALIZED THAT HIS ACT OF KINDNESS WAS ONLY DIGGING HIS OWN GRAVE! YOU SHOULD'VE SEEN THIS SUPER-SAP IN ACTION! SWITCHING TO HIS SUPERMAN COSTUME! FLYING AROUND THE ROOM! WHAT A PERFORMANCE!
DON'T BE SURE, MR. KILEY! MAYBE IT WAS AN HALLUCINATION!
I WARNED YOU ABOUT THIS DRUG! WHEN YOU INHALE ITS FUMES, IT NOT ONLY CAUSES SYMPTOMS THAT CAN FOOL PEOPLE INTO THINKING YOU'RE DYING, BUT IT ALSO PRODUCES ILLUSIONS AND HALLUCINATIONS!
BAH! THIS WAS NO HALLUCINATION!
CLARK KENT IS SUPERMAN...OR I'M NOT THE SECRET HEAD OF THE ANTI-SUPERMAN GANG! NOW...I KNOW WHAT I'M TALKING ABOUT! FOR YEARS, I'VE FOOLED EVERYBODY, INCLUDING SUPERMAN, THAT I'M A GOOD GUY WHO GIVES MONEY TO CHARITY!
WELL, TONIGHT I "DIED" TO KILL SUPERMAN... BY LEARNING HIS SECRET IDENTITY! TOMORROW YOU'LL SEE WHETHER I HAD AN HALLUCINATION... WHEN YOU WATCH CLARK KENT DIE IN A KRYPTONITE TRAP!
THE NEXT DAY, AT JOHN KILEY'S FUNERAL...
WHAT A HOAX! METROPOLIS' FINEST CITIZENS HAVE COME TO PAY THEIR RESPECTS TO THE DEAD! IF THEY ONLY KNEW THERE'S A DUMMY IN THAT COFFIN! AND THAT AFTER HE KILLS SUPERMAN, KILEY WILL START A NEW LIFE AS A SOUTH AMERICAN MILLIONAIRE!
KILEY

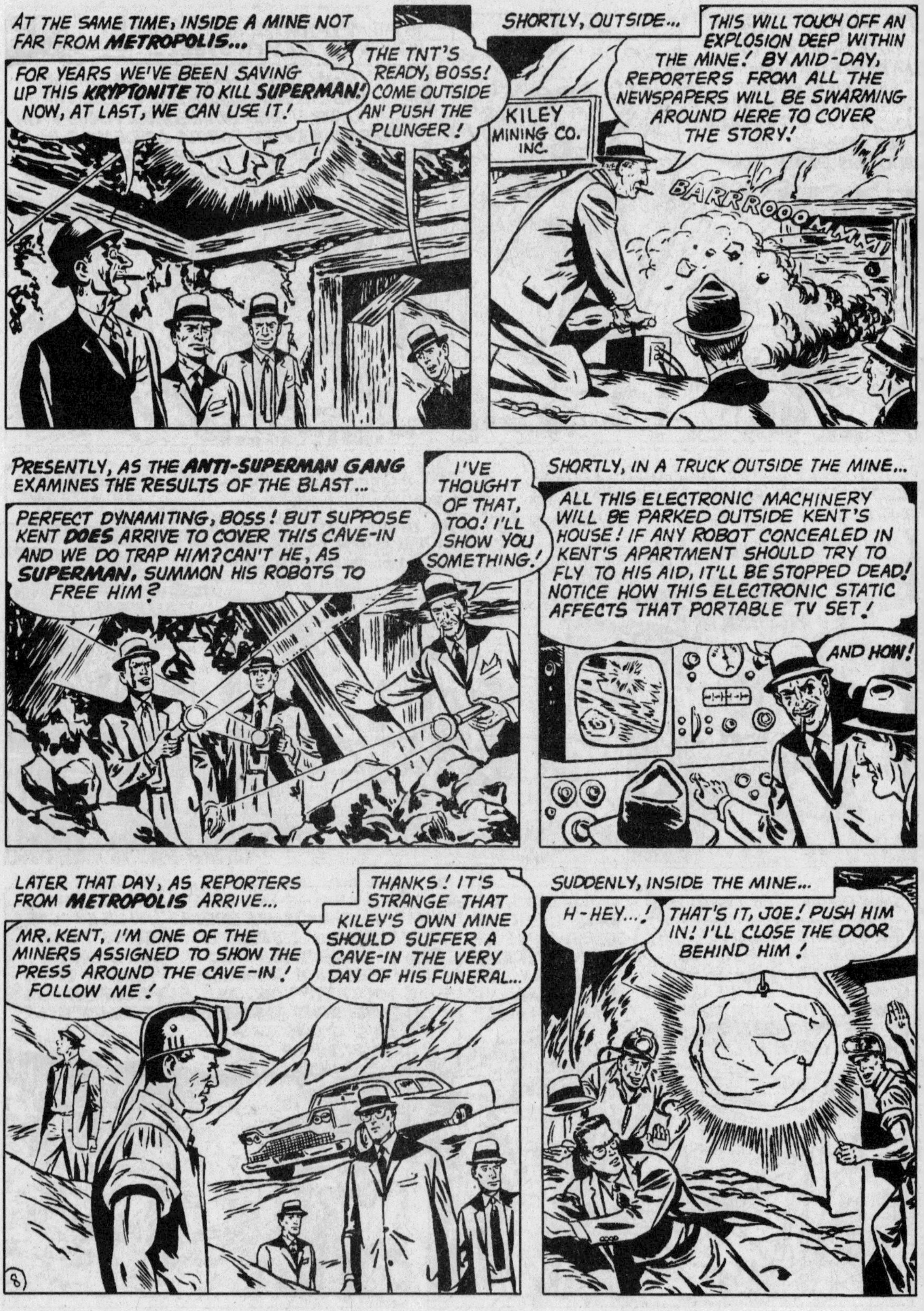
AT THE SAME TIME, INSIDE A MINE NOT FAR FROM METROPOLIS...
FOR YEARS WE'VE BEEN SAVING UP THIS KRYPTONITE TO KILL SUPERMAN! NOW, AT LAST, WE CAN USE IT!
THE TNT'S READY, BOSS! COME OUTSIDE AN' PUSH THE PLUNGER!
SHORTLY, OUTSIDE...
THIS WILL TOUCH OFF AN EXPLOSION DEEP WITHIN THE MINE! BY MID-DAY, REPORTERS FROM ALL THE NEWSPAPERS WILL BE SWARMING AROUND HERE TO COVER THE STORY!
KILEY MINING CO. INC.
BARRROOOMMM!
PRESENTLY, AS THE ANTI-SUPERMAN GANG EXAMINES THE RESULTS OF THE BLAST...
PERFECT DYNAMITING, BOSS! BUT SUPPOSE KENT DOES ARRIVE TO COVER THIS CAVE-IN AND WE DO TRAP HIM? CAN'T HE, AS SUPERMAN, SUMMON HIS ROBOTS TO FREE HIM?
I'VE THOUGHT OF THAT, TOO! I'LL SHOW YOU SOMETHING!
SHORTLY, IN A TRUCK OUTSIDE THE MINE...
ALL THIS ELECTRONIC MACHINERY WILL BE PARKED OUTSIDE KENT'S HOUSE! IF ANY ROBOT CONCEALED IN KENT'S APARTMENT SHOULD TRY TO FLY TO HIS AID, IT'LL BE STOPPED DEAD! NOTICE HOW THIS ELECTRONIC STATIC AFFECTS THAT PORTABLE TV SET!
AND HOW!
LATER THAT DAY, AS REPORTERS FROM METROPOLIS ARRIVE...
MR. KENT, I'M ONE OF THE MINERS ASSIGNED TO SHOW THE PRESS AROUND THE CAVE-IN! FOLLOW ME!
THANKS! IT'S STRANGE THAT KILEY'S OWN MINE SHOULD SUFFER A CAVE-IN THE VERY DAY OF HIS FUNERAL...
8
SUDDENLY, INSIDE THE MINE...
H-HEY...!
THAT'S IT, JOE! PUSH HIM IN! I'LL CLOSE THE DOOR BEHIND HIM!

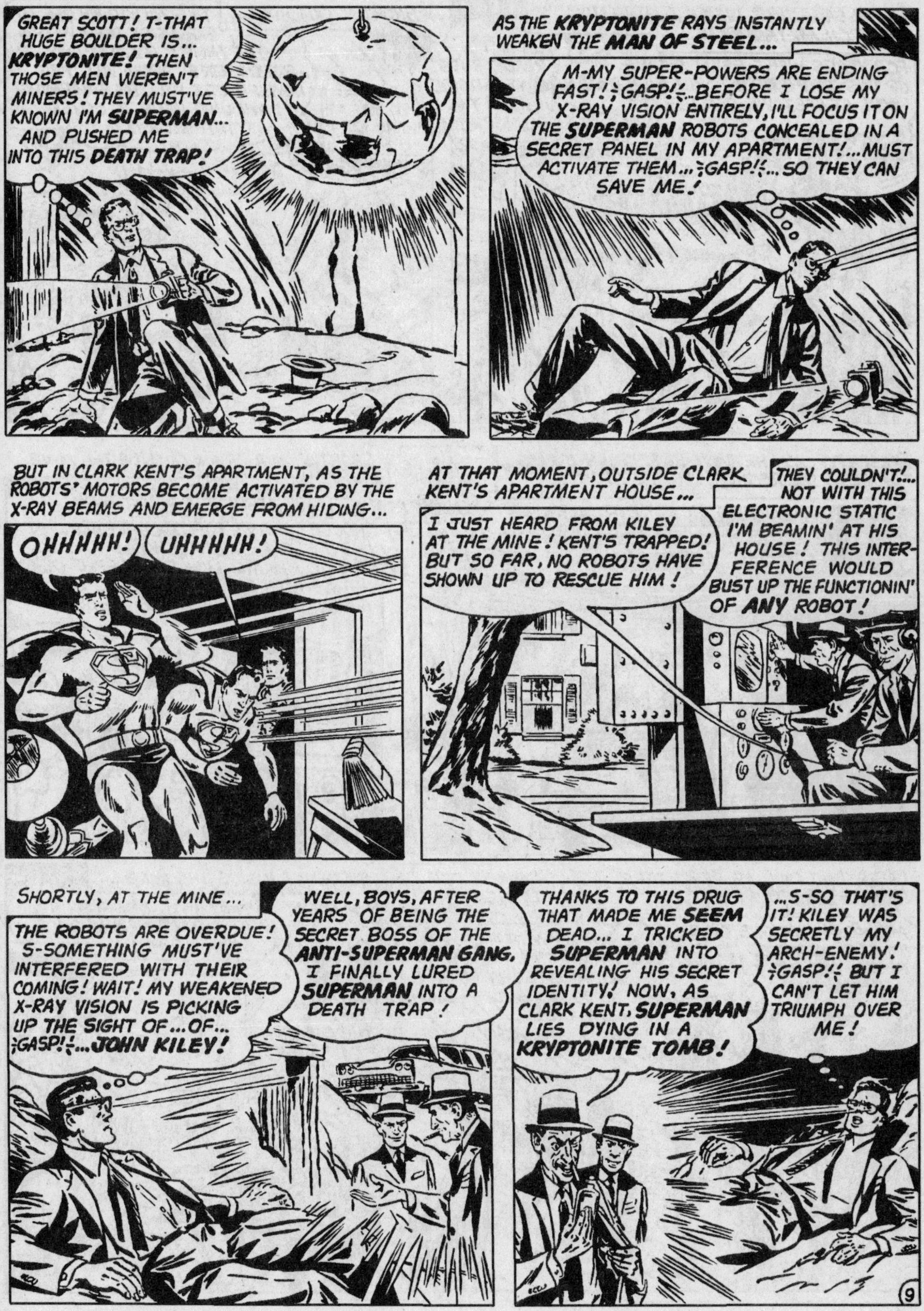
GREAT SCOTT! T-THAT HUGE BOULDER IS... KRYPTONITE! THEN THOSE MEN WEREN'T MINERS! THEY MUST'VE KNOWN I'M SUPERMAN... AND PUSHED ME INTO THIS DEATH TRAP!
AS THE KRYPTONITE RAYS INSTANTLY WEAKEN THE MAN OF STEEL...
M-MY SUPER-POWERS ARE ENDING FAST! ~GASP!~ ...BEFORE I LOSE MY X-RAY VISION ENTIRELY, I'LL FOCUS IT ON THE SUPERMAN ROBOTS CONCEALED IN A SECRET PANEL IN MY APARTMENT! ...MUST ACTIVATE THEM... ~GASP!~ ... SO THEY CAN SAVE ME!
BUT IN CLARK KENT'S APARTMENT, AS THE ROBOTS' MOTORS BECOME ACTIVATED BY THE X-RAY BEAMS AND EMERGE FROM HIDING...
OHHHHH!
UHHHHH!
AT THAT MOMENT, OUTSIDE CLARK KENT'S APARTMENT HOUSE...
I JUST HEARD FROM KILEY AT THE MINE! KENT'S TRAPPED! BUT SO FAR, NO ROBOTS HAVE SHOWN UP TO RESCUE HIM!
THEY COULDN'T!... NOT WITH THIS ELECTRONIC STATIC I'M BEAMIN' AT HIS HOUSE! THIS INTERFERENCE WOULD BUST UP THE FUNCTIONIN' OF ANY ROBOT!
SHORTLY, AT THE MINE...
THE ROBOTS ARE OVERDUE! S-SOMETHING MUST'VE INTERFERED WITH THEIR COMING! WAIT! MY WEAKENED X-RAY VISION IS PICKING UP THE SIGHT OF ... OF... ~GASP!~ ...JOHN KILEY!
WELL, BOYS, AFTER YEARS OF BEING THE SECRET BOSS OF THE ANTI-SUPERMAN GANG, I FINALLY LURED SUPERMAN INTO A DEATH TRAP!
THANKS TO THIS DRUG THAT MADE ME SEEM DEAD... I TRICKED SUPERMAN INTO REVEALING HIS SECRET IDENTITY! NOW, AS CLARK KENT, SUPERMAN LIES DYING IN A KRYPTONITE TOMB!
...S-SO THAT'S IT! KILEY WAS SECRETLY MY ARCH-ENEMY! ~GASP!~ BUT I CAN'T LET HIM TRIUMPH OVER ME!
9

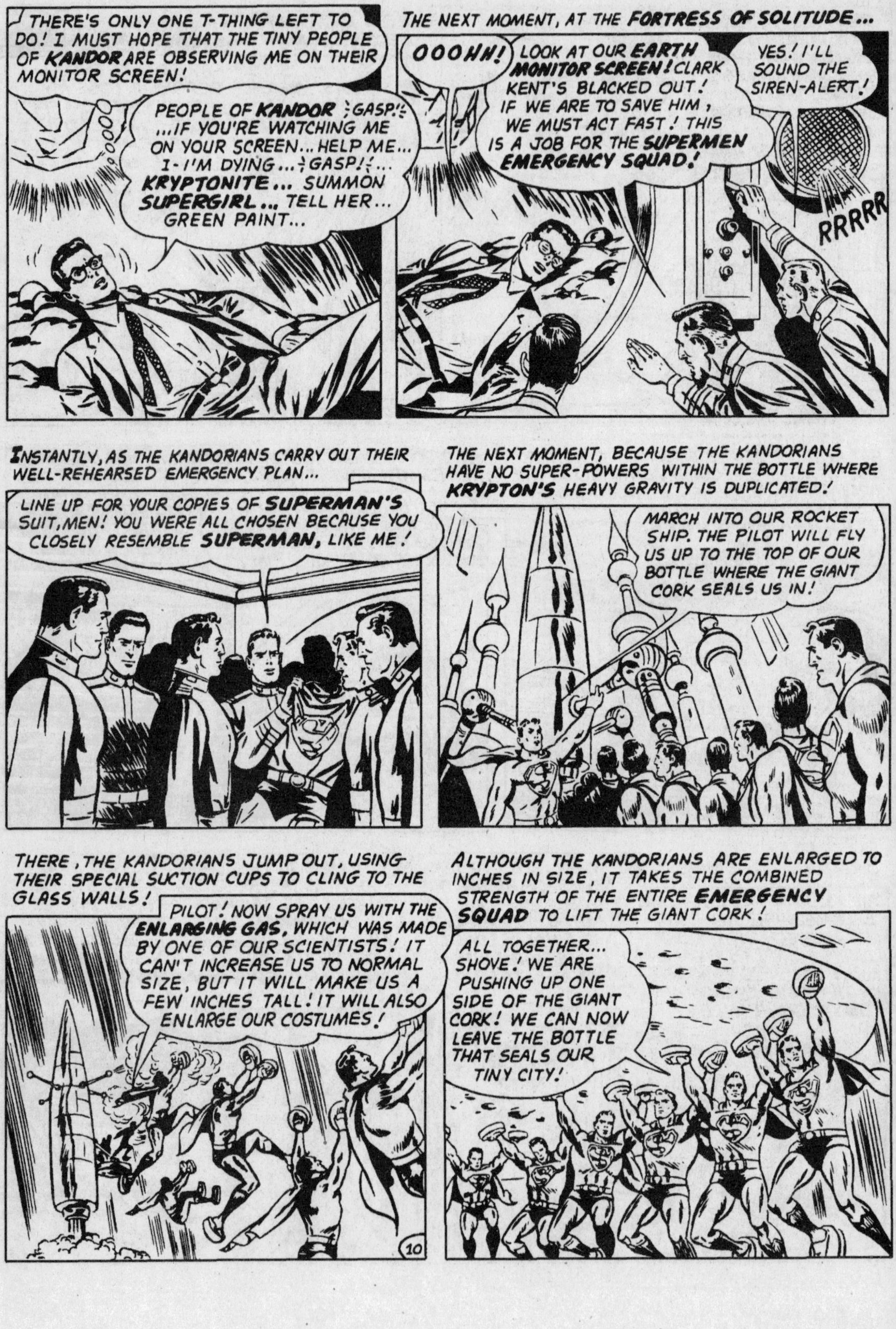
THERE'S ONLY ONE T-THING LEFT TO DO! I MUST HOPE THAT THE TINY PEOPLE OF KANDOR ARE OBSERVING ME ON THEIR MONITOR SCREEN!
PEOPLE OF KANDOR ;GASP!; ...IF YOU'RE WATCHING ME ON YOUR SCREEN... HELP ME... I-I'M DYING... ;GASP!;... KRYPTONITE... SUMMON SUPERGIRL... TELL HER... GREEN PAINT...
THE NEXT MOMENT, AT THE FORTRESS OF SOLITUDE...
OOOHN!
LOOK AT OUR EARTH MONITOR SCREEN! CLARK KENT'S BLACKED OUT! IF WE ARE TO SAVE HIM, WE MUST ACT FAST! THIS IS A JOB FOR THE SUPERMEN EMERGENCY SQUAD!
YES! I'LL SOUND THE SIREN-ALERT!
RRRRR
INSTANTLY, AS THE KANDORIANS CARRY OUT THEIR WELL-REHEARSED EMERGENCY PLAN...
LINE UP FOR YOUR COPIES OF SUPERMAN'S SUIT, MEN! YOU WERE ALL CHOSEN BECAUSE YOU CLOSELY RESEMBLE SUPERMAN, LIKE ME!
THE NEXT MOMENT, BECAUSE THE KANDORIANS HAVE NO SUPER-POWERS WITHIN THE BOTTLE WHERE KRYPTON'S HEAVY GRAVITY IS DUPLICATED!
MARCH INTO OUR ROCKET SHIP. THE PILOT WILL FLY US UP TO THE TOP OF OUR BOTTLE WHERE THE GIANT CORK SEALS US IN!
THERE, THE KANDORIANS JUMP OUT, USING THEIR SPECIAL SUCTION CUPS TO CLING TO THE GLASS WALLS!
PILOT! NOW SPRAY US WITH THE ENLARGING GAS, WHICH WAS MADE BY ONE OF OUR SCIENTISTS! IT CAN'T INCREASE US TO NORMAL SIZE, BUT IT WILL MAKE US A FEW INCHES TALL! IT WILL ALSO ENLARGE OUR COSTUMES!
10
ALTHOUGH THE KANDORIANS ARE ENLARGED TO INCHES IN SIZE, IT TAKES THE COMBINED STRENGTH OF THE ENTIRE EMERGENCY SQUAD TO LIFT THE GIANT CORK!
ALL TOGETHER... SHOVE! WE ARE PUSHING UP ONE SIDE OF THE GIANT CORK! WE CAN NOW LEAVE THE BOTTLE THAT SEALS OUR TINY CITY!

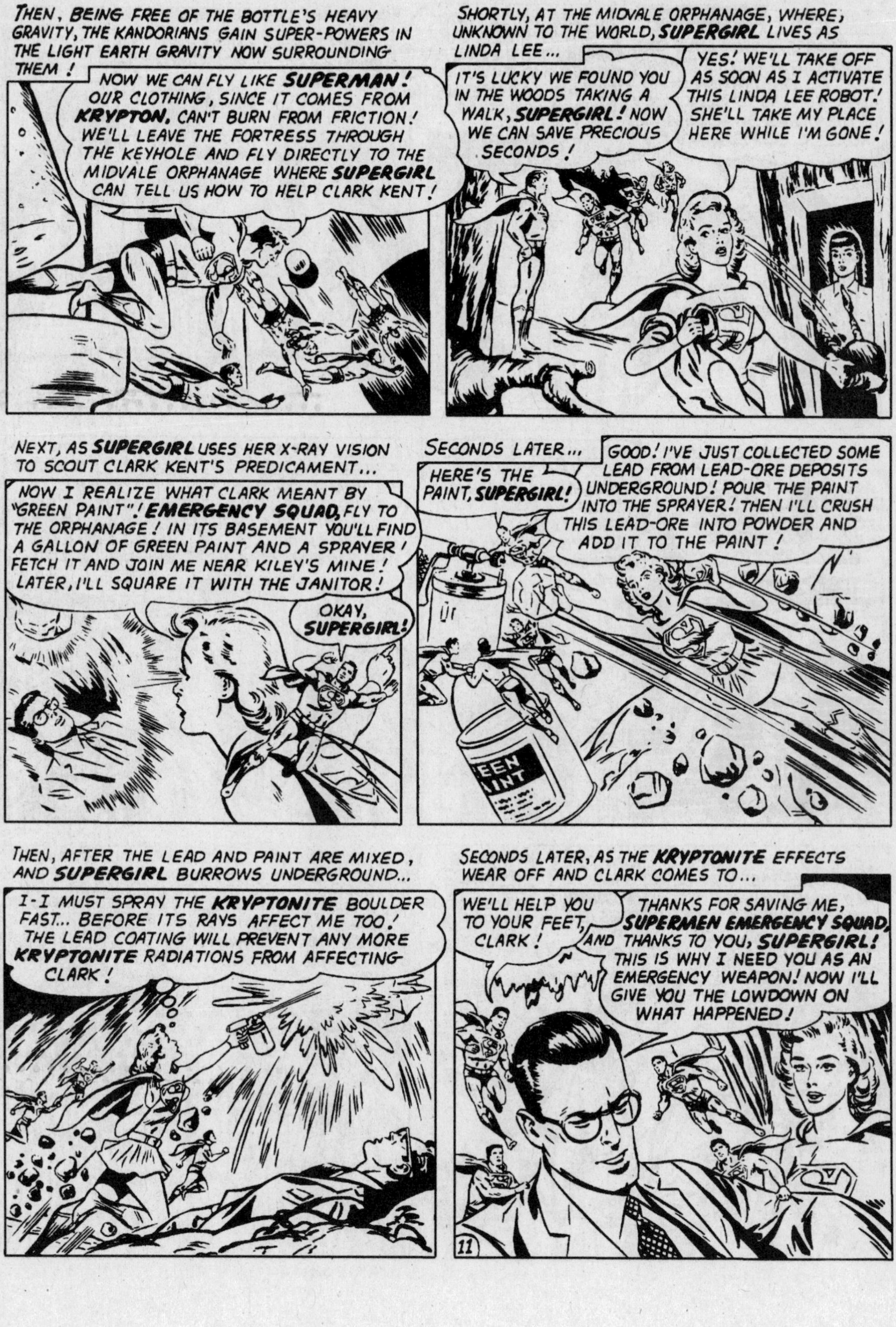
THEN, BEING FREE OF THE BOTTLE'S HEAVY GRAVITY, THE KANDORIANS GAIN SUPER-POWERS IN THE LIGHT EARTH GRAVITY NOW SURROUNDING THEM !
NOW WE CAN FLY LIKE SUPERMAN! OUR CLOTHING, SINCE IT COMES FROM KRYPTON, CAN'T BURN FROM FRICTION! WE'LL LEAVE THE FORTRESS THROUGH THE KEYHOLE AND FLY DIRECTLY TO THE MIDVALE ORPHANAGE WHERE SUPERGIRL CAN TELL US HOW TO HELP CLARK KENT!
SHORTLY, AT THE MIDVALE ORPHANAGE, WHERE, UNKNOWN TO THE WORLD, SUPERGIRL LIVES AS LINDA LEE...
IT'S LUCKY WE FOUND YOU IN THE WOODS TAKING A WALK, SUPERGIRL! NOW WE CAN SAVE PRECIOUS SECONDS!
YES! WE'LL TAKE OFF AS SOON AS I ACTIVATE THIS LINDA LEE ROBOT! SHE'LL TAKE MY PLACE HERE WHILE I'M GONE!
NEXT, AS SUPERGIRL USES HER X-RAY VISION TO SCOUT CLARK KENT'S PREDICAMENT...
NOW I REALIZE WHAT CLARK MEANT BY "GREEN PAINT"! EMERGENCY SQUAD, FLY TO THE ORPHANAGE! IN ITS BASEMENT YOU'LL FIND A GALLON OF GREEN PAINT AND A SPRAYER! FETCH IT AND JOIN ME NEAR KILEY'S MINE! LATER, I'LL SQUARE IT WITH THE JANITOR!
OKAY, SUPERGIRL!
SECONDS LATER...
HERE'S THE PAINT, SUPERGIRL!
GOOD! I'VE JUST COLLECTED SOME LEAD FROM LEAD-ORE DEPOSITS UNDERGROUND! POUR THE PAINT INTO THE SPRAYER! THEN I'LL CRUSH THIS LEAD-ORE INTO POWDER AND ADD IT TO THE PAINT!
THEN, AFTER THE LEAD AND PAINT ARE MIXED, AND SUPERGIRL BURROWS UNDERGROUND...
I-I MUST SPRAY THE KRYPTONITE BOULDER FAST... BEFORE ITS RAYS AFFECT ME TOO! THE LEAD COATING WILL PREVENT ANY MORE KRYPTONITE RADIATIONS FROM AFFECTING CLARK!
SECONDS LATER, AS THE KRYPTONITE EFFECTS WEAR OFF AND CLARK COMES TO...
WE'LL HELP YOU TO YOUR FEET, CLARK!
THANKS FOR SAVING ME, SUPERMEN EMERGENCY SQUAD, AND THANKS TO YOU, SUPERGIRL! THIS IS WHY I NEED YOU AS AN EMERGENCY WEAPON! NOW I'LL GIVE YOU THE LOWDOWN ON WHAT HAPPENED!
11

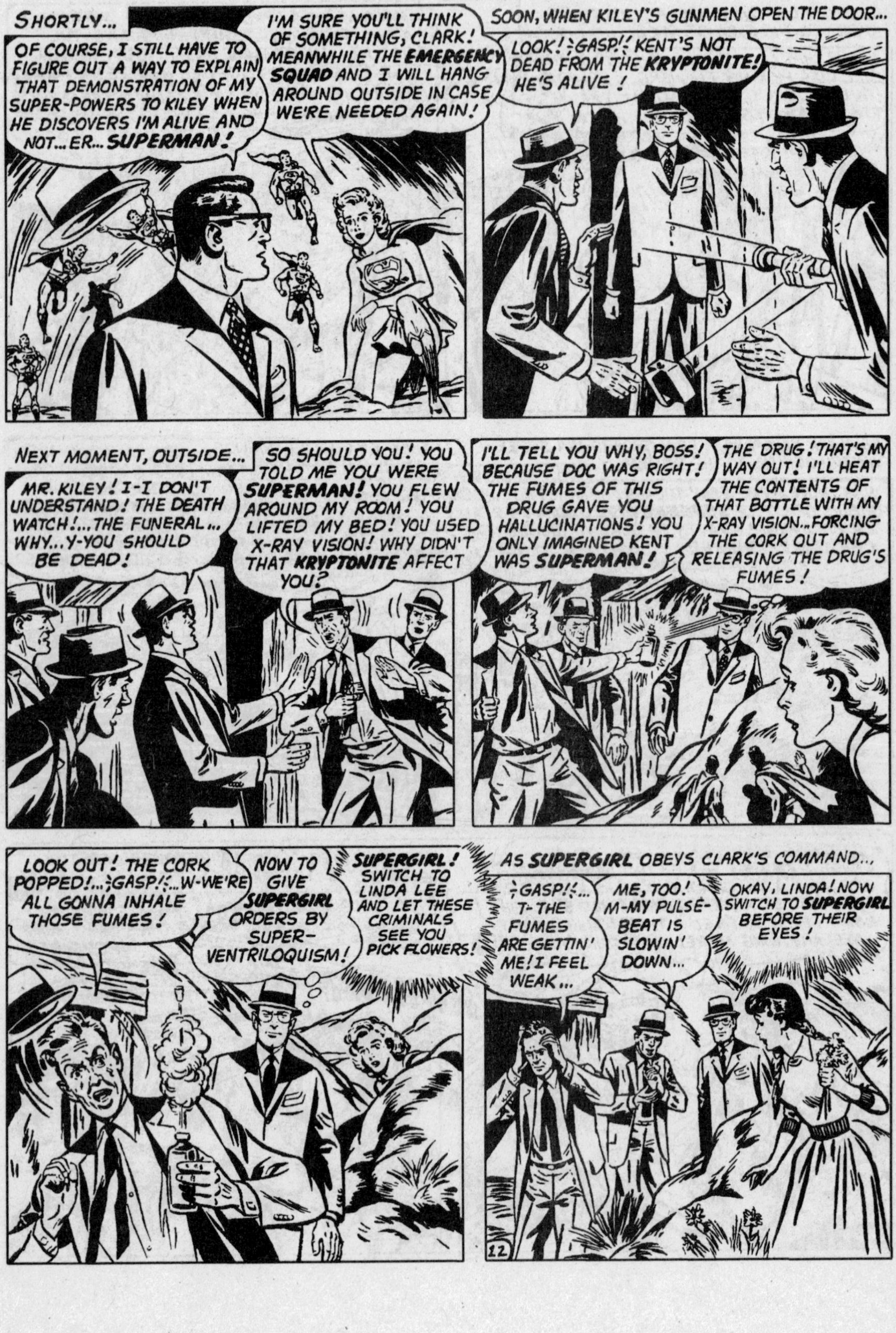
SHORTLY...
OF COURSE, I STILL HAVE TO FIGURE OUT A WAY TO EXPLAIN THAT DEMONSTRATION OF MY SUPER-POWERS TO KILEY WHEN HE DISCOVERS I'M ALIVE AND NOT... ER... SUPERMAN!
I'M SURE YOU'LL THINK OF SOMETHING, CLARK! MEANWHILE THE EMERGENCY SQUAD AND I WILL HANG AROUND OUTSIDE IN CASE WE'RE NEEDED AGAIN!
SOON, WHEN KILEY'S GUNMEN OPEN THE DOOR...
LOOK! -GASP!- KENT'S NOT DEAD FROM THE KRYPTONITE! HE'S ALIVE!
NEXT MOMENT, OUTSIDE...
MR. KILEY! I-I DON'T UNDERSTAND! THE DEATH WATCH!... THE FUNERAL... WHY... Y-YOU SHOULD BE DEAD!
SO SHOULD YOU! YOU TOLD ME YOU WERE SUPERMAN! YOU FLEW AROUND MY ROOM! YOU LIFTED MY BED! YOU USED X-RAY VISION! WHY DIDN'T THAT KRYPTONITE AFFECT YOU?
I'LL TELL YOU WHY, BOSS! BECAUSE DOC WAS RIGHT! THE FUMES OF THIS DRUG GAVE YOU HALLUCINATIONS! YOU ONLY IMAGINED KENT WAS SUPERMAN!
THE DRUG! THAT'S MY WAY OUT! I'LL HEAT THE CONTENTS OF THAT BOTTLE WITH MY X-RAY VISION... FORCING THE CORK OUT AND RELEASING THE DRUG'S FUMES!
LOOK OUT! THE CORK POPPED!... -GASP!-... W-WE'RE ALL GONNA INHALE THOSE FUMES!
NOW TO GIVE SUPERGIRL ORDERS BY SUPER-VENTRILOQUISM!
SUPERGIRL! SWITCH TO LINDA LEE AND LET THESE CRIMINALS SEE YOU PICK FLOWERS!
AS SUPERGIRL OBEYS CLARK'S COMMAND...
-GASP!-... T-THE FUMES ARE GETTIN' ME! I FEEL WEAK...
ME, TOO! M-MY PULSE-BEAT IS SLOWIN' DOWN...
OKAY, LINDA! NOW SWITCH TO SUPERGIRL BEFORE THEIR EYES!
12

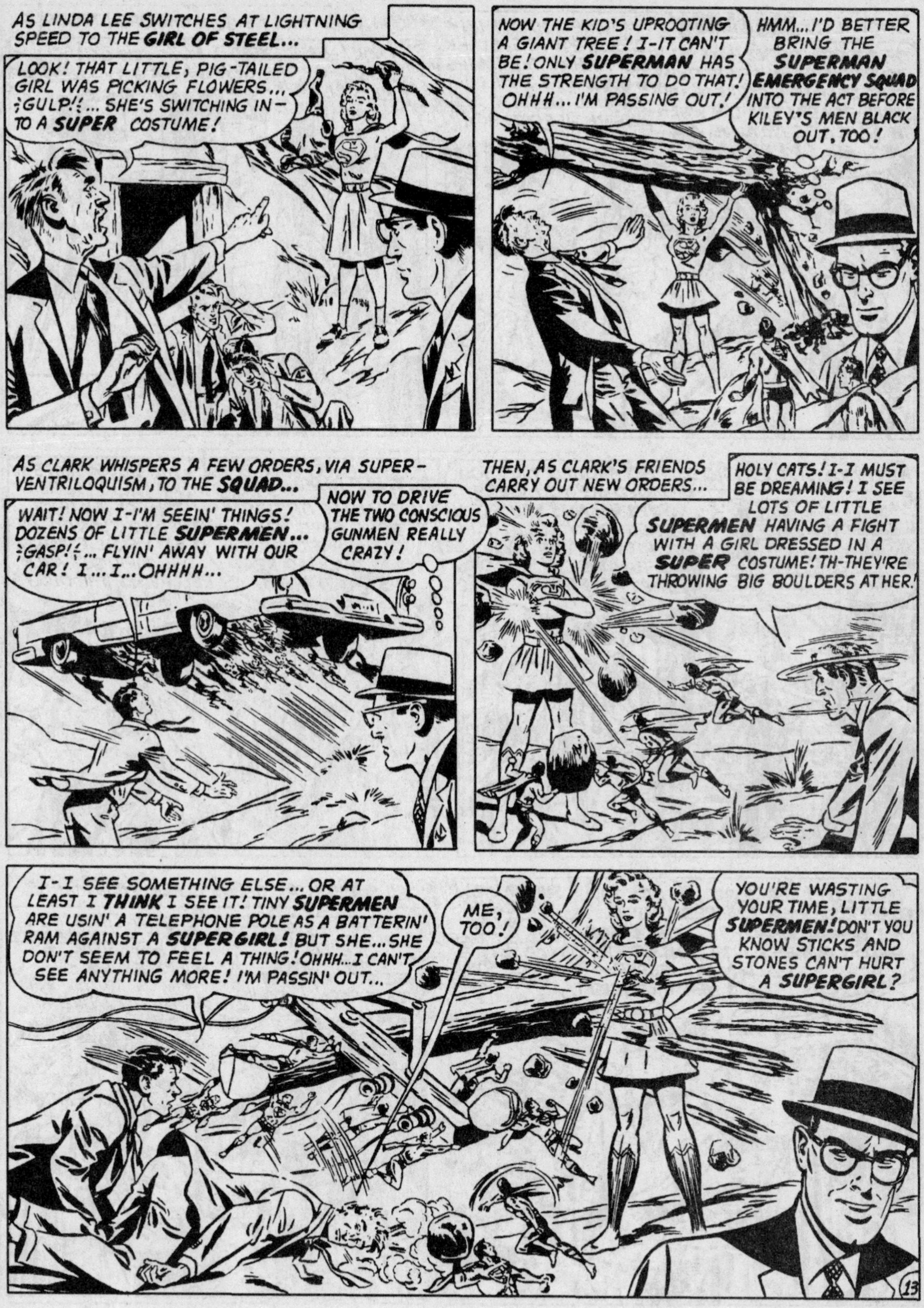
AS LINDA LEE SWITCHES AT LIGHTNING SPEED TO THE GIRL OF STEEL...
LOOK! THAT LITTLE, PIG-TAILED GIRL WAS PICKING FLOWERS... ¡GULP!¡... SHE'S SWITCHING INTO A SUPER COSTUME!
NOW THE KID'S UPROOTING A GIANT TREE! I-IT CAN'T BE! ONLY SUPERMAN HAS THE STRENGTH TO DO THAT! OHHH... I'M PASSING OUT!
HMM... I'D BETTER BRING THE SUPERMAN EMERGENCY SQUAD INTO THE ACT BEFORE KILEY'S MEN BLACK OUT, TOO!
AS CLARK WHISPERS A FEW ORDERS, VIA SUPER-VENTRILOQUISM, TO THE SQUAD...
WAIT! NOW I-I'M SEEIN' THINGS! DOZENS OF LITTLE SUPERMEN... ¡GASP!¡... FLYIN' AWAY WITH OUR CAR! I... I... OHHHH...
NOW TO DRIVE THE TWO CONSCIOUS GUNMEN REALLY CRAZY!
THEN, AS CLARK'S FRIENDS CARRY OUT NEW ORDERS...
HOLY CATS! I-I MUST BE DREAMING! I SEE LOTS OF LITTLE SUPERMEN HAVING A FIGHT WITH A GIRL DRESSED IN A SUPER COSTUME! TH-THEY'RE THROWING BIG BOULDERS AT HER!
I-I SEE SOMETHING ELSE... OR AT LEAST I THINK I SEE IT! TINY SUPERMEN ARE USIN' A TELEPHONE POLE AS A BATTERIN' RAM AGAINST A SUPERGIRL! BUT SHE... SHE DON'T SEEM TO FEEL A THING! OHHH... I CAN'T SEE ANYTHING MORE! I'M PASSIN' OUT...
ME, TOO!
YOU'RE WASTING YOUR TIME, LITTLE SUPERMEN! DON'T YOU KNOW STICKS AND STONES CAN'T HURT A SUPERGIRL?
13

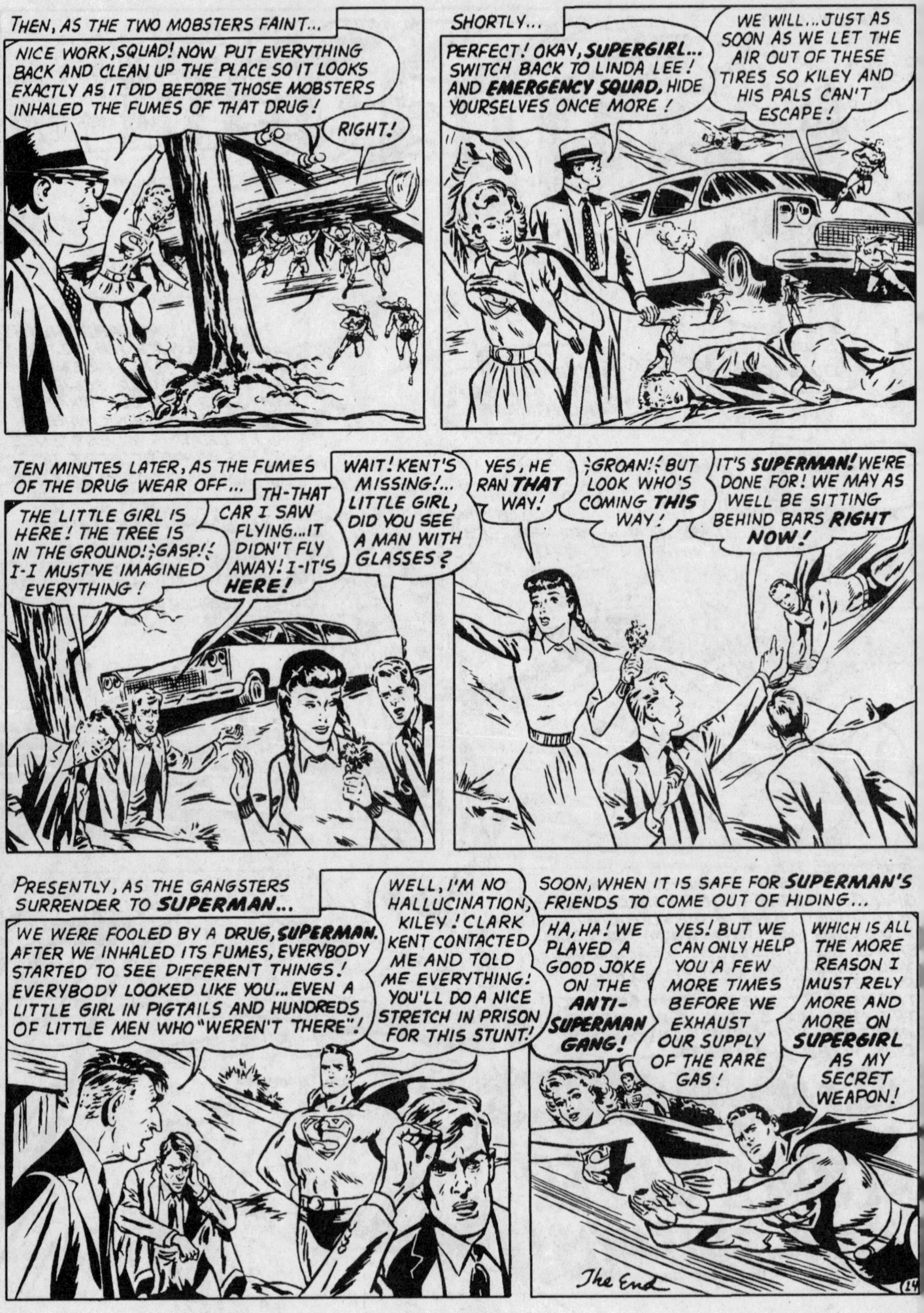
THEN, AS THE TWO MOBSTERS FAINT...
NICE WORK, SQUAD! NOW PUT EVERYTHING BACK AND CLEAN UP THE PLACE SO IT LOOKS EXACTLY AS IT DID BEFORE THOSE MOBSTERS INHALED THE FUMES OF THAT DRUG!
RIGHT!
SHORTLY...
PERFECT! OKAY, SUPERGIRL... SWITCH BACK TO LINDA LEE! AND EMERGENCY SQUAD, HIDE YOURSELVES ONCE MORE!
WE WILL... JUST AS SOON AS WE LET THE AIR OUT OF THESE TIRES SO KILEY AND HIS PALS CAN'T ESCAPE!
TEN MINUTES LATER, AS THE FUMES OF THE DRUG WEAR OFF...
THE LITTLE GIRL IS HERE! THE TREE IS IN THE GROUND! ;GASP!; I-I MUST'VE IMAGINED EVERYTHING!
TH-THAT CAR I SAW FLYING... IT DIDN'T FLY AWAY! I-IT'S HERE!
WAIT! KENT'S MISSING!... LITTLE GIRL, DID YOU SEE A MAN WITH GLASSES?
YES, HE RAN THAT WAY!
;GROAN!; BUT LOOK WHO'S COMING THIS WAY!
IT'S SUPERMAN! WE'RE DONE FOR! WE MAY AS WELL BE SITTING BEHIND BARS RIGHT NOW!
PRESENTLY, AS THE GANGSTERS SURRENDER TO SUPERMAN...
WE WERE FOOLED BY A DRUG, SUPERMAN. AFTER WE INHALED ITS FUMES, EVERYBODY STARTED TO SEE DIFFERENT THINGS! EVERYBODY LOOKED LIKE YOU... EVEN A LITTLE GIRL IN PIGTAILS AND HUNDREDS OF LITTLE MEN WHO "WEREN'T THERE"!
WELL, I'M NO HALLUCINATION, KILEY! CLARK KENT CONTACTED ME AND TOLD ME EVERYTHING! YOU'LL DO A NICE STRETCH IN PRISON FOR THIS STUNT!
SOON, WHEN IT IS SAFE FOR SUPERMAN'S FRIENDS TO COME OUT OF HIDING...
HA, HA! WE PLAYED A GOOD JOKE ON THE ANTI-SUPERMAN GANG!
YES! BUT WE CAN ONLY HELP YOU A FEW MORE TIMES BEFORE WE EXHAUST OUR SUPPLY OF THE RARE GAS!
WHICH IS ALL THE MORE REASON I MUST RELY MORE AND MORE ON SUPERGIRL AS MY SECRET WEAPON!
The End
14

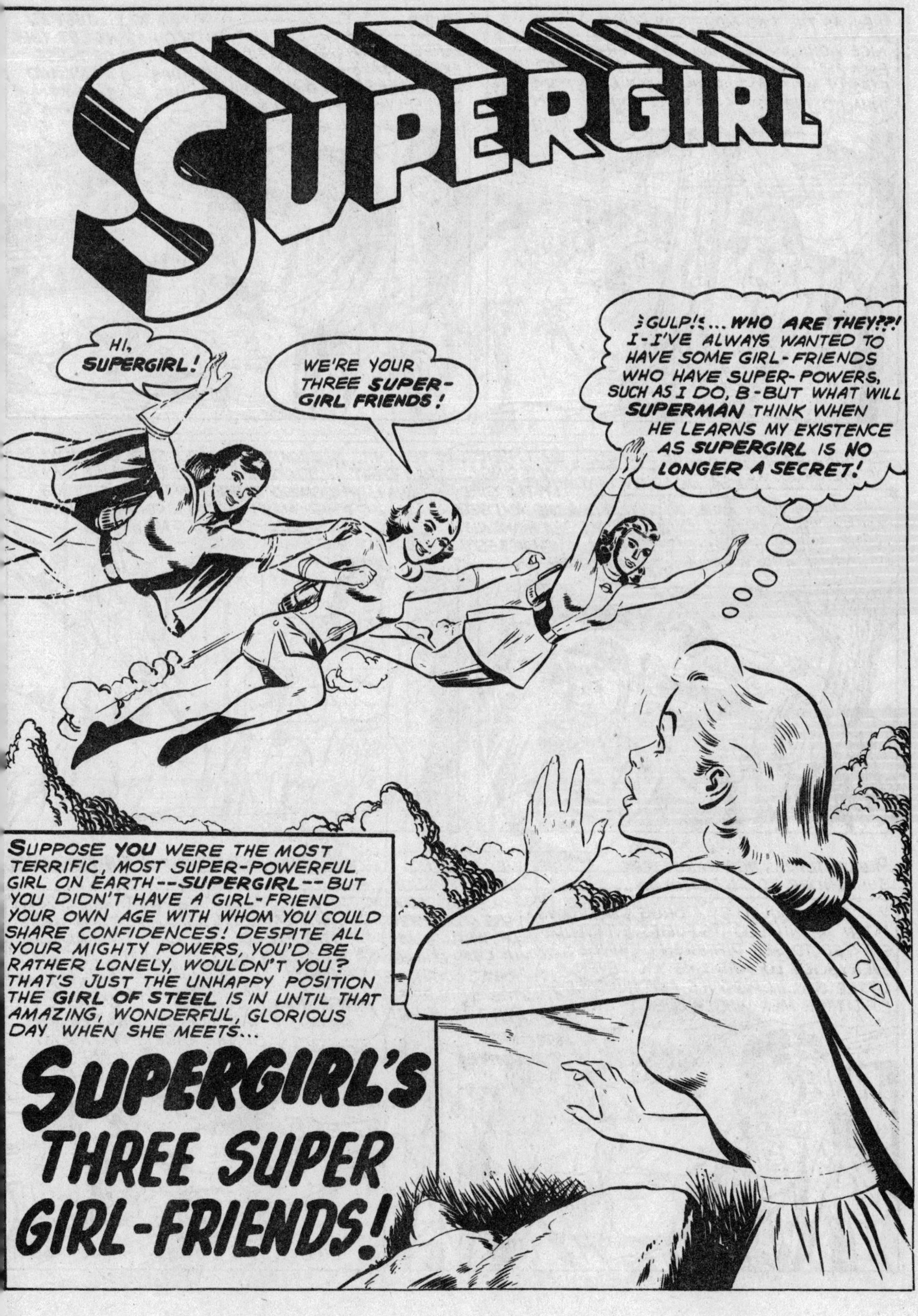
SUPERGIRL
HI, SUPERGIRL!
WE'RE YOUR THREE SUPER-GIRL FRIENDS!
GULP!... WHO ARE THEY??! I-I'VE ALWAYS WANTED TO HAVE SOME GIRL-FRIENDS WHO HAVE SUPER-POWERS, SUCH AS I DO, B-BUT WHAT WILL SUPERMAN THINK WHEN HE LEARNS MY EXISTENCE AS SUPERGIRL IS NO LONGER A SECRET!
SUPPOSE YOU WERE THE MOST TERRIFIC, MOST SUPER-POWERFUL GIRL ON EARTH--SUPERGIRL--BUT YOU DIDN'T HAVE A GIRL-FRIEND YOUR OWN AGE WITH WHOM YOU COULD SHARE CONFIDENCES! DESPITE ALL YOUR MIGHTY POWERS, YOU'D BE RATHER LONELY, WOULDN'T YOU? THAT'S JUST THE UNHAPPY POSITION THE GIRL OF STEEL IS IN UNTIL THAT AMAZING, WONDERFUL, GLORIOUS DAY WHEN SHE MEETS...
SUPERGIRL'S THREE SUPER GIRL-FRIENDS!

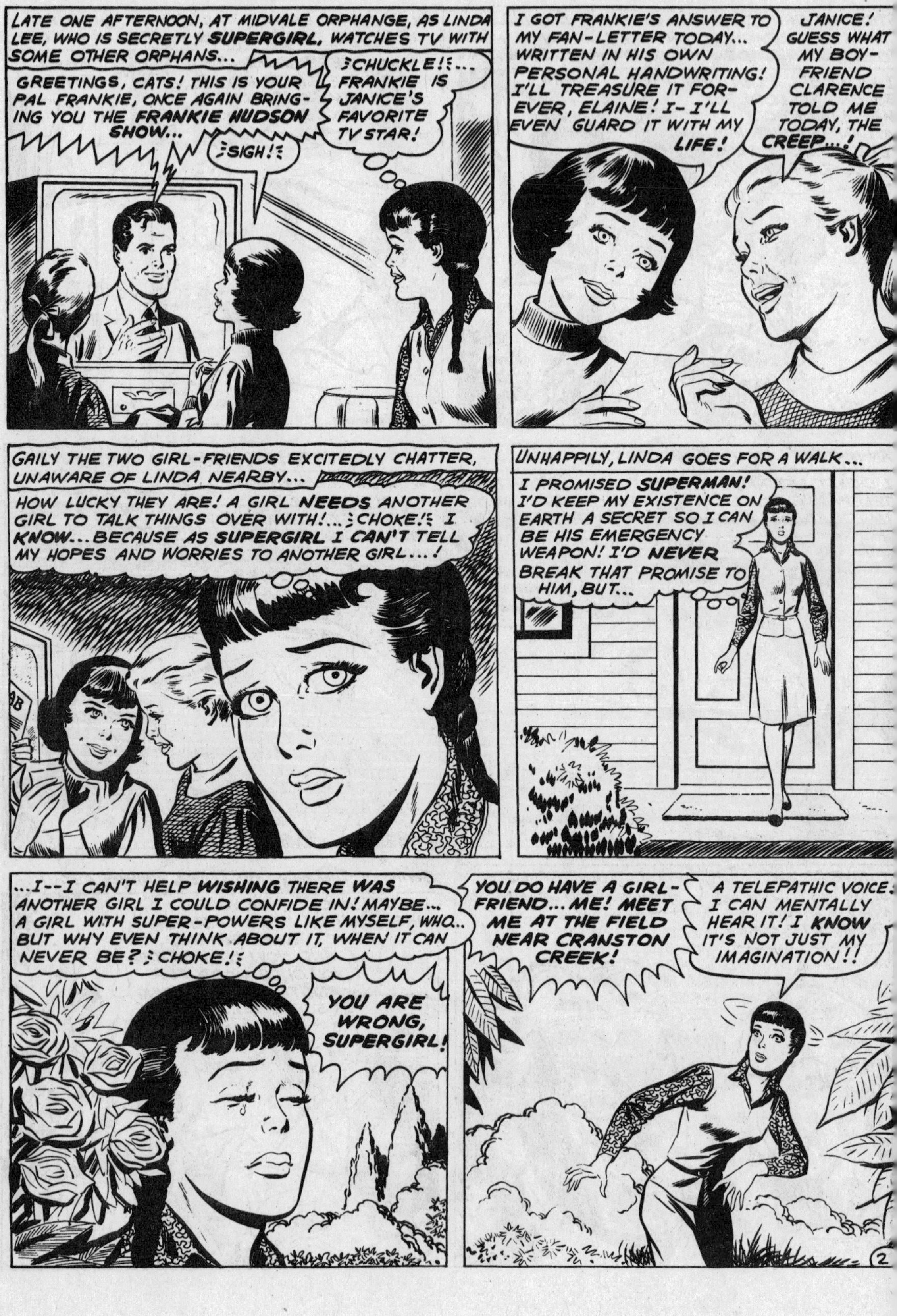
LATE ONE AFTERNOON, AT MIDVALE ORPHANGE, AS LINDA LEE, WHO IS SECRETLY SUPERGIRL, WATCHES TV WITH SOME OTHER ORPHANS...
GREETINGS, CATS! THIS IS YOUR PAL FRANKIE, ONCE AGAIN BRINGING YOU THE FRANKIE HUDSON SHOW...
SIGH!
CHUCKLE!... FRANKIE IS JANICE'S FAVORITE TV STAR!
I GOT FRANKIE'S ANSWER TO MY FAN-LETTER TODAY... WRITTEN IN HIS OWN PERSONAL HANDWRITING! I'LL TREASURE IT FOREVER, ELAINE! I- I'LL EVEN GUARD IT WITH MY LIFE!
JANICE! GUESS WHAT MY BOY-FRIEND CLARENCE TOLD ME TODAY, THE CREEP...!
GAILY THE TWO GIRL-FRIENDS EXCITEDLY CHATTER, UNAWARE OF LINDA NEARBY...
HOW LUCKY THEY ARE! A GIRL NEEDS ANOTHER GIRL TO TALK THINGS OVER WITH!... CHOKE! I KNOW... BECAUSE AS SUPERGIRL I CAN'T TELL MY HOPES AND WORRIES TO ANOTHER GIRL...!
UNHAPPILY, LINDA GOES FOR A WALK...
I PROMISED SUPERMAN! I'D KEEP MY EXISTENCE ON EARTH A SECRET SO I CAN BE HIS EMERGENCY WEAPON! I'D NEVER BREAK THAT PROMISE TO HIM, BUT...
...I--I CAN'T HELP WISHING THERE WAS ANOTHER GIRL I COULD CONFIDE IN! MAYBE... A GIRL WITH SUPER-POWERS LIKE MYSELF, WHO... BUT WHY EVEN THINK ABOUT IT, WHEN IT CAN NEVER BE? CHOKE!
YOU ARE WRONG, SUPERGIRL!
YOU DO HAVE A GIRL-FRIEND... ME! MEET ME AT THE FIELD NEAR CRANSTON CREEK!
A TELEPATHIC VOICE! I CAN MENTALLY HEAR IT! I KNOW IT'S NOT JUST MY IMAGINATION!!
2

STEPPING BEHIND SOME SCREENING BUSHES, LINDA LEE REMOVES HER WIG, SWIFTLY CHANGING TO HER SECRET IDENTITY OF DYNAMIC *SUPERGIRL!*

I WONDER...! CAN THAT VOICE BELONG TO *LORI,* THE MERMAID FROM ATLANTIS? SHE HAS TELEPATHIC POWERS! ...I'LL SOON KNOW!

EN ROUTE TO CRANSTON CREEK, AS THE *GIRL OF STEEL* PASSES A HOLLOW TREE IN A WOODS...

TAKE OVER FOR ME AT THE ORPHANAGE, LINDA ROBOT, WHILE I'M GONE! COVER MY ABSENCE!

I SHALL, MISTRESS!

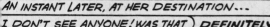

AN INSTANT LATER, AT HER DESTINATION...

I DON'T SEE ANYONE! WAS THAT TELEPATHIC VOICE ONLY IN MY IMAGINATION, AFTER ALL?

DEFINITELY NOT!... LOOK BEHIND YOU!

AND AS *SUPERGIRL* OBEYS...

A GIRL IN A *MASK!* MY X-RAY VISION CAN'T PENETRATE THE MASK! IT MUST BE MADE OF *LEAD!*

WHO ARE YOU?

I AM YOUR *SUPER GIRL-FRIEND!* WE HAVE MET BEFORE! CAN YOU GUESS MY IDENTITY, BEFORE I REMOVE THE SCREENING LEAD-MASK?

I HAVEN'T THE SLIGHTEST IDEA WHO YOU ARE! PLEASE TELL ME!

FIRST, TURN AND LOOK BEHIND YOU, AGAIN!

SWIFTLY, THE *GIRL OF STEEL* WHIRLS ABOUT...

≥GASP!≤ WHO ARE *YOU?!!*

I AM YOUR *SECOND SUPER GIRL-FRIEND!* AND NOW, LOOK BEHIND YOU ONCE MORE FOR *ANOTHER* ASTOUNDING SURPRISE!

③

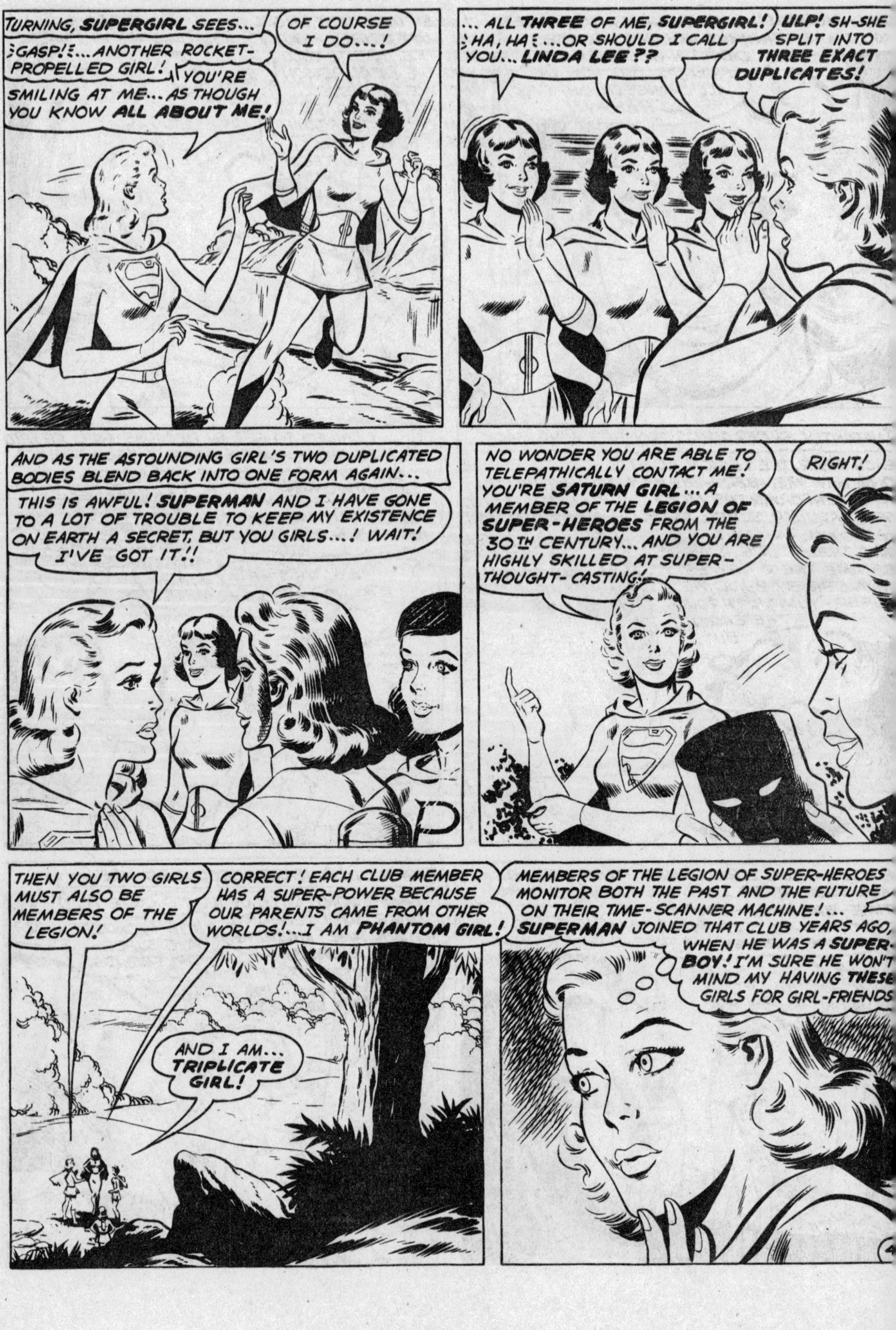
TURNING, SUPERGIRL SEES...
GASP! ...ANOTHER ROCKET-PROPELLED GIRL! YOU'RE SMILING AT ME... AS THOUGH YOU KNOW ALL ABOUT ME!
OF COURSE I DO...!
... ALL THREE OF ME, SUPERGIRL! HA, HA ...OR SHOULD I CALL YOU... LINDA LEE??
ULP! SH-SHE SPLIT INTO THREE EXACT DUPLICATES!
AND AS THE ASTOUNDING GIRL'S TWO DUPLICATED BODIES BLEND BACK INTO ONE FORM AGAIN...
THIS IS AWFUL! SUPERMAN AND I HAVE GONE TO A LOT OF TROUBLE TO KEEP MY EXISTENCE ON EARTH A SECRET, BUT YOU GIRLS...! WAIT! I'VE GOT IT!!
NO WONDER YOU ARE ABLE TO TELEPATHICALLY CONTACT ME! YOU'RE SATURN GIRL... A MEMBER OF THE LEGION OF SUPER-HEROES FROM THE 30TH CENTURY... AND YOU ARE HIGHLY SKILLED AT SUPER-THOUGHT-CASTING!
RIGHT!
THEN YOU TWO GIRLS MUST ALSO BE MEMBERS OF THE LEGION!
CORRECT! EACH CLUB MEMBER HAS A SUPER-POWER BECAUSE OUR PARENTS CAME FROM OTHER WORLDS!...I AM PHANTOM GIRL!
AND I AM... TRIPLICATE GIRL!
MEMBERS OF THE LEGION OF SUPER-HEROES MONITOR BOTH THE PAST AND THE FUTURE ON THEIR TIME-SCANNER MACHINE!... SUPERMAN JOINED THAT CLUB YEARS AGO, WHEN HE WAS A SUPER-BOY! I'M SURE HE WON'T MIND MY HAVING THESE GIRLS FOR GIRL-FRIENDS

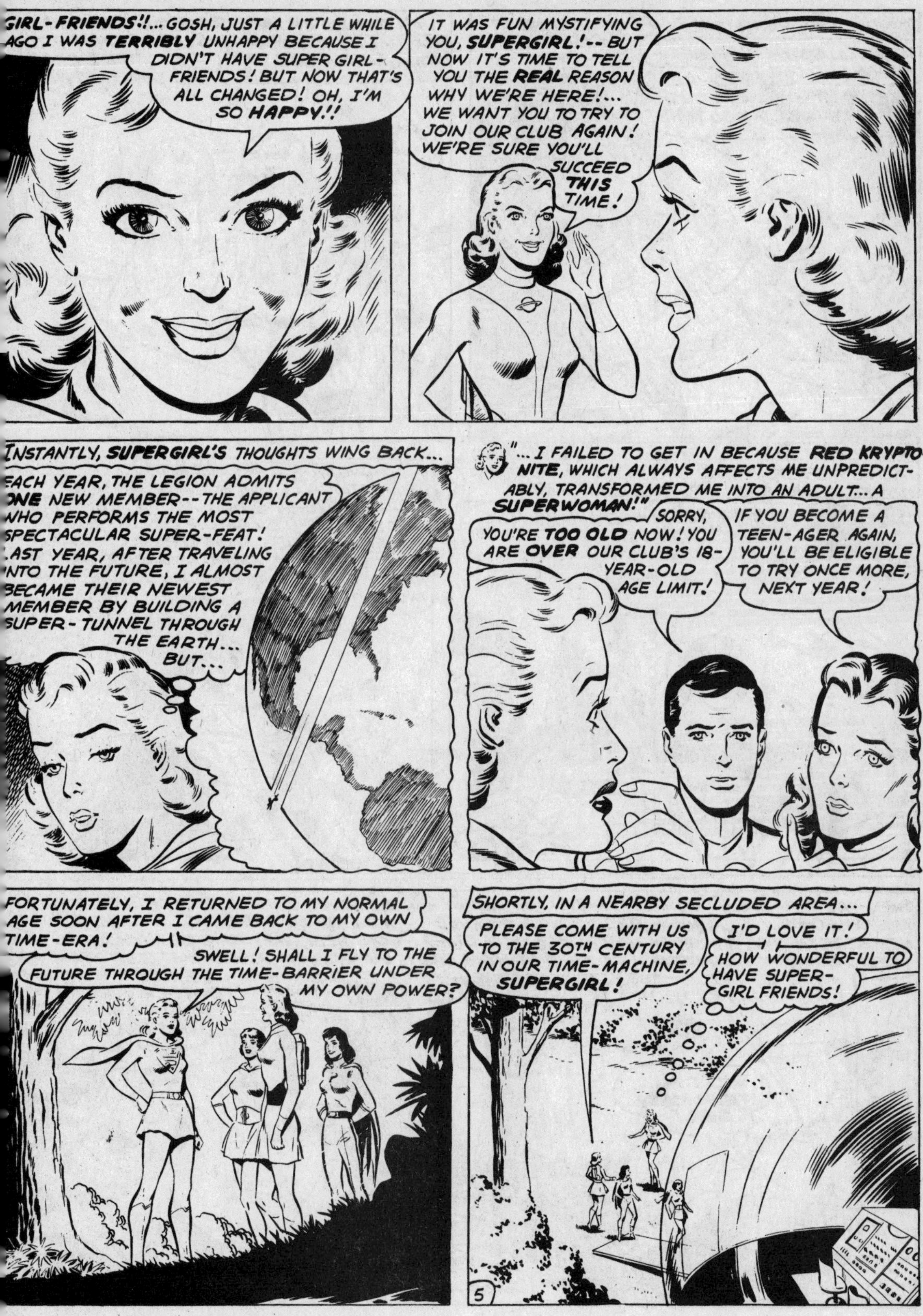
GIRL-FRIENDS!!... GOSH, JUST A LITTLE WHILE AGO I WAS TERRIBLY UNHAPPY BECAUSE I DIDN'T HAVE SUPER GIRL-FRIENDS! BUT NOW THAT'S ALL CHANGED! OH, I'M SO HAPPY!!
IT WAS FUN MYSTIFYING YOU, SUPERGIRL!-- BUT NOW IT'S TIME TO TELL YOU THE REAL REASON WHY WE'RE HERE!... WE WANT YOU TO TRY TO JOIN OUR CLUB AGAIN! WE'RE SURE YOU'LL SUCCEED THIS TIME!
INSTANTLY, SUPERGIRL'S THOUGHTS WING BACK...
EACH YEAR, THE LEGION ADMITS ONE NEW MEMBER--THE APPLICANT WHO PERFORMS THE MOST SPECTACULAR SUPER-FEAT! LAST YEAR, AFTER TRAVELING INTO THE FUTURE, I ALMOST BECAME THEIR NEWEST MEMBER BY BUILDING A SUPER-TUNNEL THROUGH THE EARTH... BUT...
"... I FAILED TO GET IN BECAUSE RED KRYPTONITE, WHICH ALWAYS AFFECTS ME UNPREDICTABLY, TRANSFORMED ME INTO AN ADULT... A SUPERWOMAN!"
SORRY, YOU'RE TOO OLD NOW! YOU ARE OVER OUR CLUB'S 18-YEAR-OLD AGE LIMIT!
IF YOU BECOME A TEEN-AGER AGAIN, YOU'LL BE ELIGIBLE TO TRY ONCE MORE, NEXT YEAR!
FORTUNATELY, I RETURNED TO MY NORMAL AGE SOON AFTER I CAME BACK TO MY OWN TIME-ERA!
SWELL! SHALL I FLY TO THE FUTURE THROUGH THE TIME-BARRIER UNDER MY OWN POWER?
SHORTLY, IN A NEARBY SECLUDED AREA...
PLEASE COME WITH US TO THE 30TH CENTURY IN OUR TIME-MACHINE, SUPERGIRL!
I'D LOVE IT!
HOW WONDERFUL TO HAVE SUPER-GIRL FRIENDS!
5

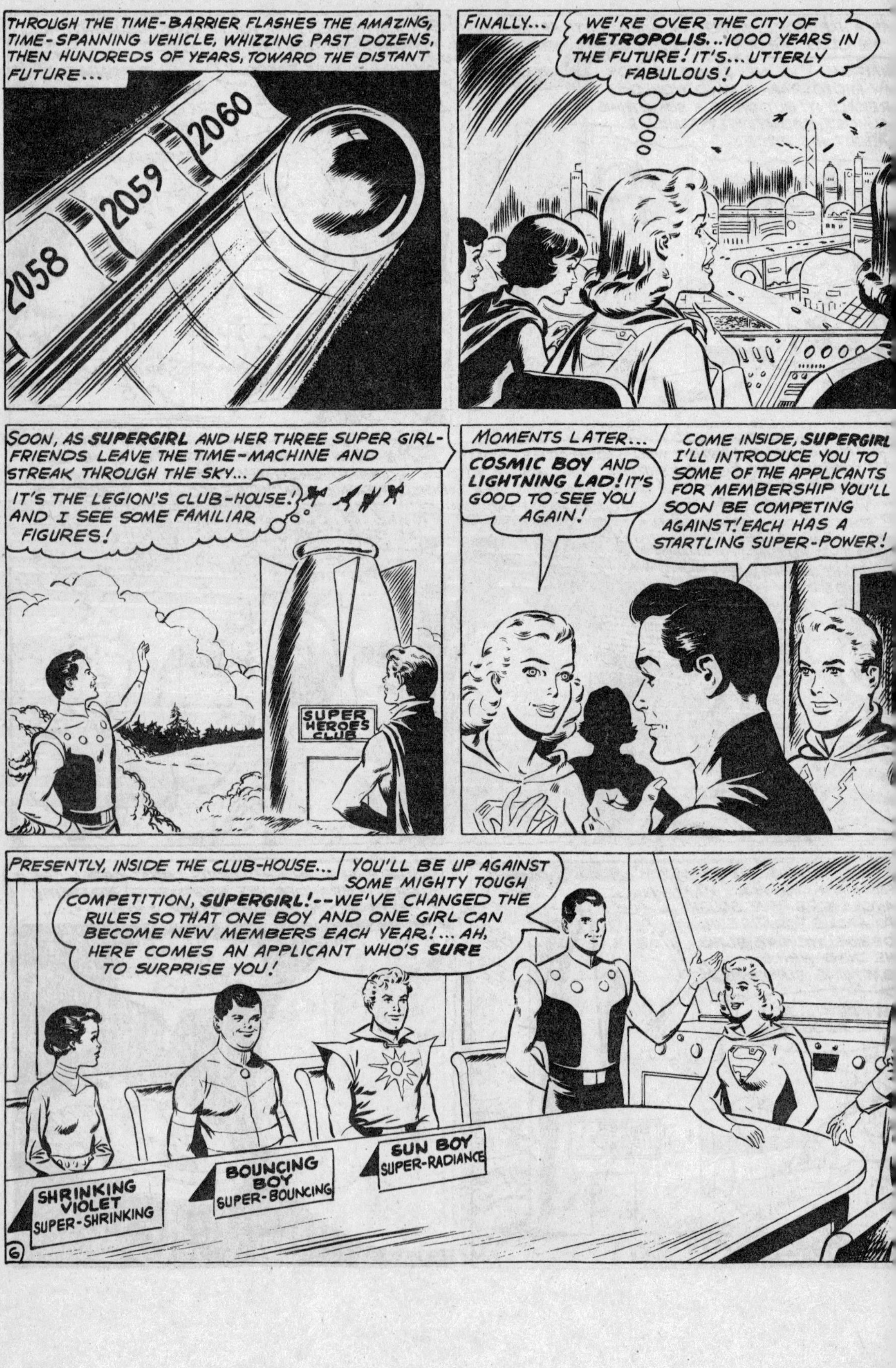
THROUGH THE TIME-BARRIER FLASHES THE AMAZING, TIME-SPANNING VEHICLE, WHIZZING PAST DOZENS, THEN HUNDREDS OF YEARS, TOWARD THE DISTANT FUTURE...
2060
2059
2058
FINALLY...
WE'RE OVER THE CITY OF METROPOLIS...1000 YEARS IN THE FUTURE! IT'S...UTTERLY FABULOUS!
SOON, AS SUPERGIRL AND HER THREE SUPER GIRL-FRIENDS LEAVE THE TIME-MACHINE AND STREAK THROUGH THE SKY...
IT'S THE LEGION'S CLUB-HOUSE! AND I SEE SOME FAMILIAR FIGURES!
SUPER HEROES CLUB
MOMENTS LATER...
COSMIC BOY AND LIGHTNING LAD! IT'S GOOD TO SEE YOU AGAIN!
COME INSIDE, SUPERGIRL I'LL INTRODUCE YOU TO SOME OF THE APPLICANTS FOR MEMBERSHIP YOU'LL SOON BE COMPETING AGAINST! EACH HAS A STARTLING SUPER-POWER!
PRESENTLY, INSIDE THE CLUB-HOUSE...
YOU'LL BE UP AGAINST SOME MIGHTY TOUGH COMPETITION, SUPERGIRL!--WE'VE CHANGED THE RULES SO THAT ONE BOY AND ONE GIRL CAN BECOME NEW MEMBERS EACH YEAR!... AH, HERE COMES AN APPLICANT WHO'S SURE TO SURPRISE YOU!
SHRINKING VIOLET SUPER-SHRINKING
BOUNCING BOY SUPER-BOUNCING
SUN BOY SUPER-RADIANCE
6

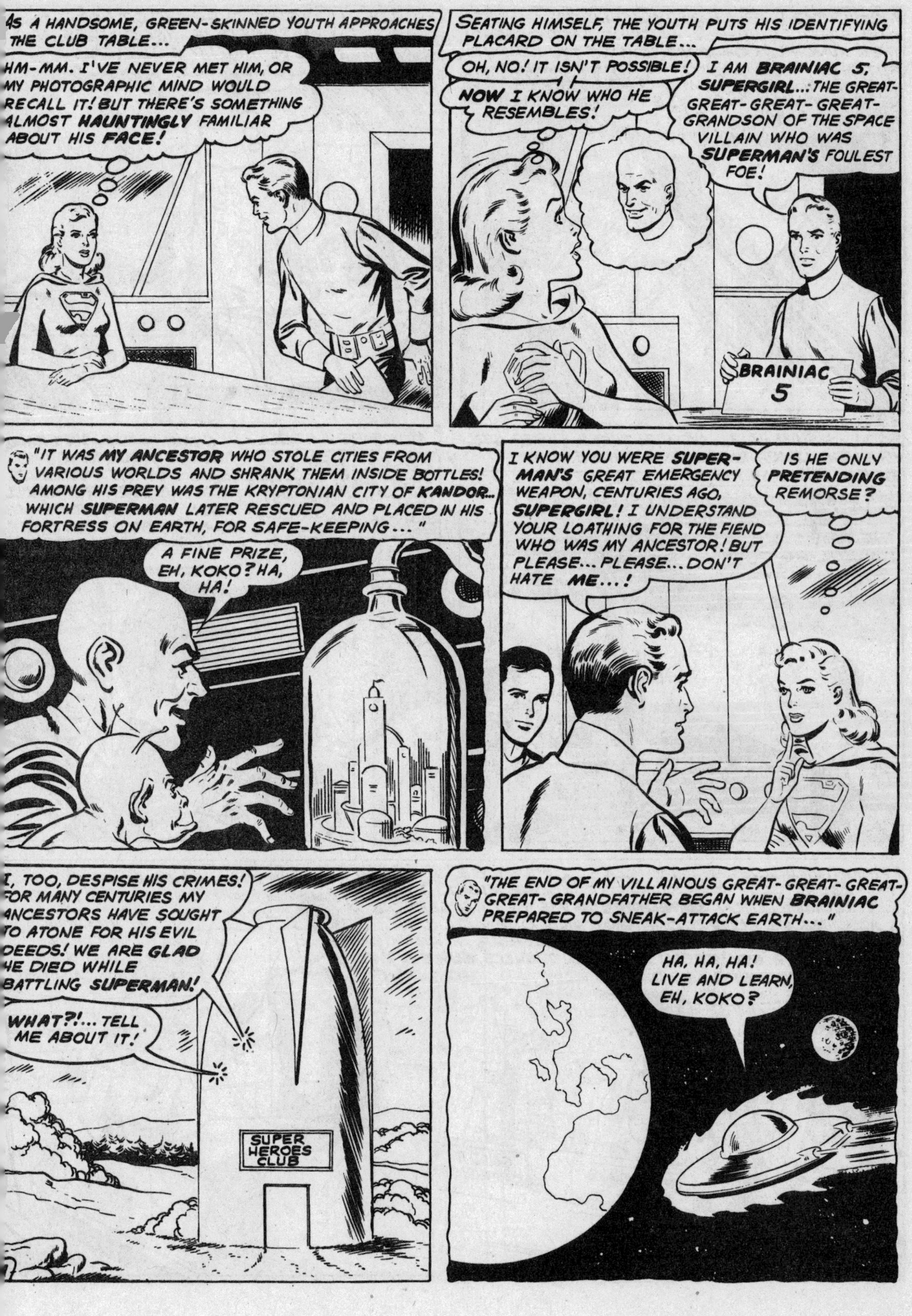
AS A HANDSOME, GREEN-SKINNED YOUTH APPROACHES THE CLUB TABLE...
HM-MM. I'VE NEVER MET HIM, OR MY PHOTOGRAPHIC MIND WOULD RECALL IT! BUT THERE'S SOMETHING ALMOST HAUNTINGLY FAMILIAR ABOUT HIS FACE!
SEATING HIMSELF, THE YOUTH PUTS HIS IDENTIFYING PLACARD ON THE TABLE...
OH, NO! IT ISN'T POSSIBLE!
NOW I KNOW WHO HE RESEMBLES!
I AM BRAINIAC 5, SUPERGIRL...THE GREAT-GREAT-GREAT-GREAT-GRANDSON OF THE SPACE VILLAIN WHO WAS SUPERMAN'S FOULEST FOE!
BRAINIAC 5
"IT WAS MY ANCESTOR WHO STOLE CITIES FROM VARIOUS WORLDS AND SHRANK THEM INSIDE BOTTLES! AMONG HIS PREY WAS THE KRYPTONIAN CITY OF KANDOR... WHICH SUPERMAN LATER RESCUED AND PLACED IN HIS FORTRESS ON EARTH, FOR SAFE-KEEPING..."
A FINE PRIZE, EH, KOKO? HA, HA!
I KNOW YOU WERE SUPERMAN'S GREAT EMERGENCY WEAPON, CENTURIES AGO, SUPERGIRL! I UNDERSTAND YOUR LOATHING FOR THE FIEND WHO WAS MY ANCESTOR! BUT PLEASE... PLEASE... DON'T HATE ME...!
IS HE ONLY PRETENDING REMORSE?
I, TOO, DESPISE HIS CRIMES! FOR MANY CENTURIES MY ANCESTORS HAVE SOUGHT TO ATONE FOR HIS EVIL DEEDS! WE ARE GLAD HE DIED WHILE BATTLING SUPERMAN!
WHAT?!... TELL ME ABOUT IT!
SUPER HEROES CLUB
"THE END OF MY VILLAINOUS GREAT-GREAT-GREAT-GREAT-GRANDFATHER BEGAN WHEN BRAINIAC PREPARED TO SNEAK-ATTACK EARTH..."
HA, HA, HA! LIVE AND LEARN, EH, KOKO?

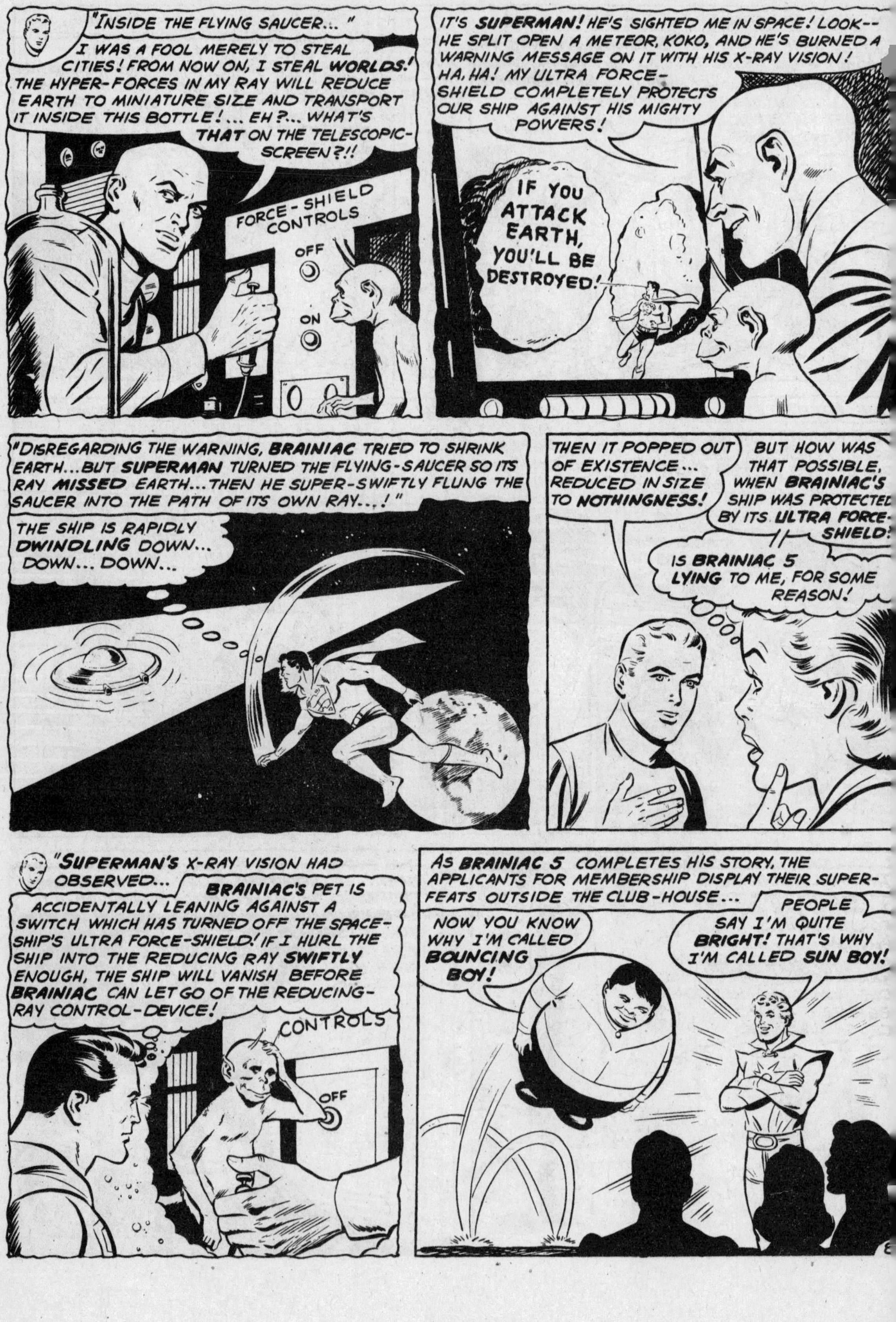
"INSIDE THE FLYING SAUCER..."
I WAS A FOOL MERELY TO STEAL CITIES! FROM NOW ON, I STEAL WORLDS! THE HYPER-FORCES IN MY RAY WILL REDUCE EARTH TO MINIATURE SIZE AND TRANSPORT IT INSIDE THIS BOTTLE!... EH?... WHAT'S THAT ON THE TELESCOPIC-SCREEN?!!
FORCE-SHIELD CONTROLS
OFF
ON
IT'S SUPERMAN! HE'S SIGHTED ME IN SPACE! LOOK-- HE SPLIT OPEN A METEOR, KOKO, AND HE'S BURNED A WARNING MESSAGE ON IT WITH HIS X-RAY VISION! HA, HA! MY ULTRA FORCE-SHIELD COMPLETELY PROTECTS OUR SHIP AGAINST HIS MIGHTY POWERS!
IF YOU ATTACK EARTH, YOU'LL BE DESTROYED!
"DISREGARDING THE WARNING, BRAINIAC TRIED TO SHRINK EARTH...BUT SUPERMAN TURNED THE FLYING-SAUCER SO ITS RAY MISSED EARTH...THEN HE SUPER-SWIFTLY FLUNG THE SAUCER INTO THE PATH OF ITS OWN RAY...!"
THE SHIP IS RAPIDLY DWINDLING DOWN... DOWN... DOWN...
THEN IT POPPED OUT OF EXISTENCE... REDUCED IN SIZE TO NOTHINGNESS!
BUT HOW WAS THAT POSSIBLE, WHEN BRAINIAC'S SHIP WAS PROTECTED BY ITS ULTRA FORCE-SHIELD?
IS BRAINIAC 5 LYING TO ME, FOR SOME REASON?
"SUPERMAN'S X-RAY VISION HAD OBSERVED...
BRAINIAC'S PET IS ACCIDENTALLY LEANING AGAINST A SWITCH WHICH HAS TURNED OFF THE SPACE-SHIP'S ULTRA FORCE-SHIELD! IF I HURL THE SHIP INTO THE REDUCING RAY SWIFTLY ENOUGH, THE SHIP WILL VANISH BEFORE BRAINIAC CAN LET GO OF THE REDUCING-RAY CONTROL-DEVICE!
CONTROLS
OFF
AS BRAINIAC 5 COMPLETES HIS STORY, THE APPLICANTS FOR MEMBERSHIP DISPLAY THEIR SUPER-FEATS OUTSIDE THE CLUB-HOUSE...
NOW YOU KNOW WHY I'M CALLED BOUNCING BOY!
PEOPLE SAY I'M QUITE BRIGHT! THAT'S WHY I'M CALLED SUN BOY!

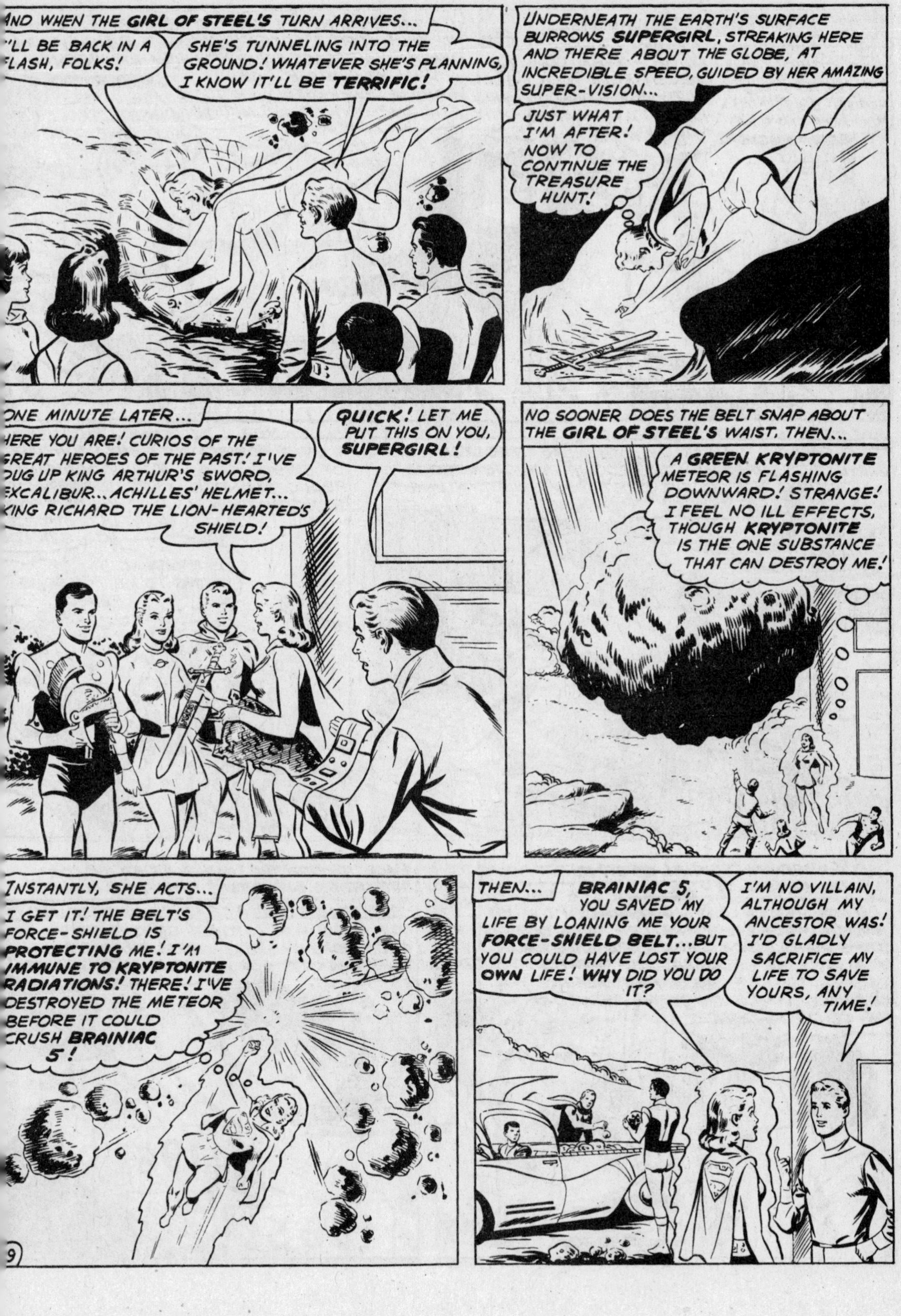
AND WHEN THE GIRL OF STEEL'S TURN ARRIVES...
I'LL BE BACK IN A FLASH, FOLKS!
SHE'S TUNNELING INTO THE GROUND! WHATEVER SHE'S PLANNING, I KNOW IT'LL BE TERRIFIC!
UNDERNEATH THE EARTH'S SURFACE BURROWS SUPERGIRL, STREAKING HERE AND THERE ABOUT THE GLOBE, AT INCREDIBLE SPEED, GUIDED BY HER AMAZING SUPER-VISION...
JUST WHAT I'M AFTER! NOW TO CONTINUE THE TREASURE HUNT!
ONE MINUTE LATER...
HERE YOU ARE! CURIOS OF THE GREAT HEROES OF THE PAST! I'VE DUG UP KING ARTHUR'S SWORD, EXCALIBUR... ACHILLES' HELMET... KING RICHARD THE LION-HEARTED'S SHIELD!
QUICK! LET ME PUT THIS ON YOU, SUPERGIRL!
NO SOONER DOES THE BELT SNAP ABOUT THE GIRL OF STEEL'S WAIST, THEN...
A GREEN KRYPTONITE METEOR IS FLASHING DOWNWARD! STRANGE! I FEEL NO ILL EFFECTS, THOUGH KRYPTONITE IS THE ONE SUBSTANCE THAT CAN DESTROY ME!
INSTANTLY, SHE ACTS...
I GET IT! THE BELT'S FORCE-SHIELD IS PROTECTING ME! I'M IMMUNE TO KRYPTONITE RADIATIONS! THERE! I'VE DESTROYED THE METEOR BEFORE IT COULD CRUSH BRAINIAC 5!
9
THEN...
BRAINIAC 5, YOU SAVED MY LIFE BY LOANING ME YOUR FORCE-SHIELD BELT...BUT YOU COULD HAVE LOST YOUR OWN LIFE! WHY DID YOU DO IT?
I'M NO VILLAIN, ALTHOUGH MY ANCESTOR WAS! I'D GLADLY SACRIFICE MY LIFE TO SAVE YOURS, ANY TIME!

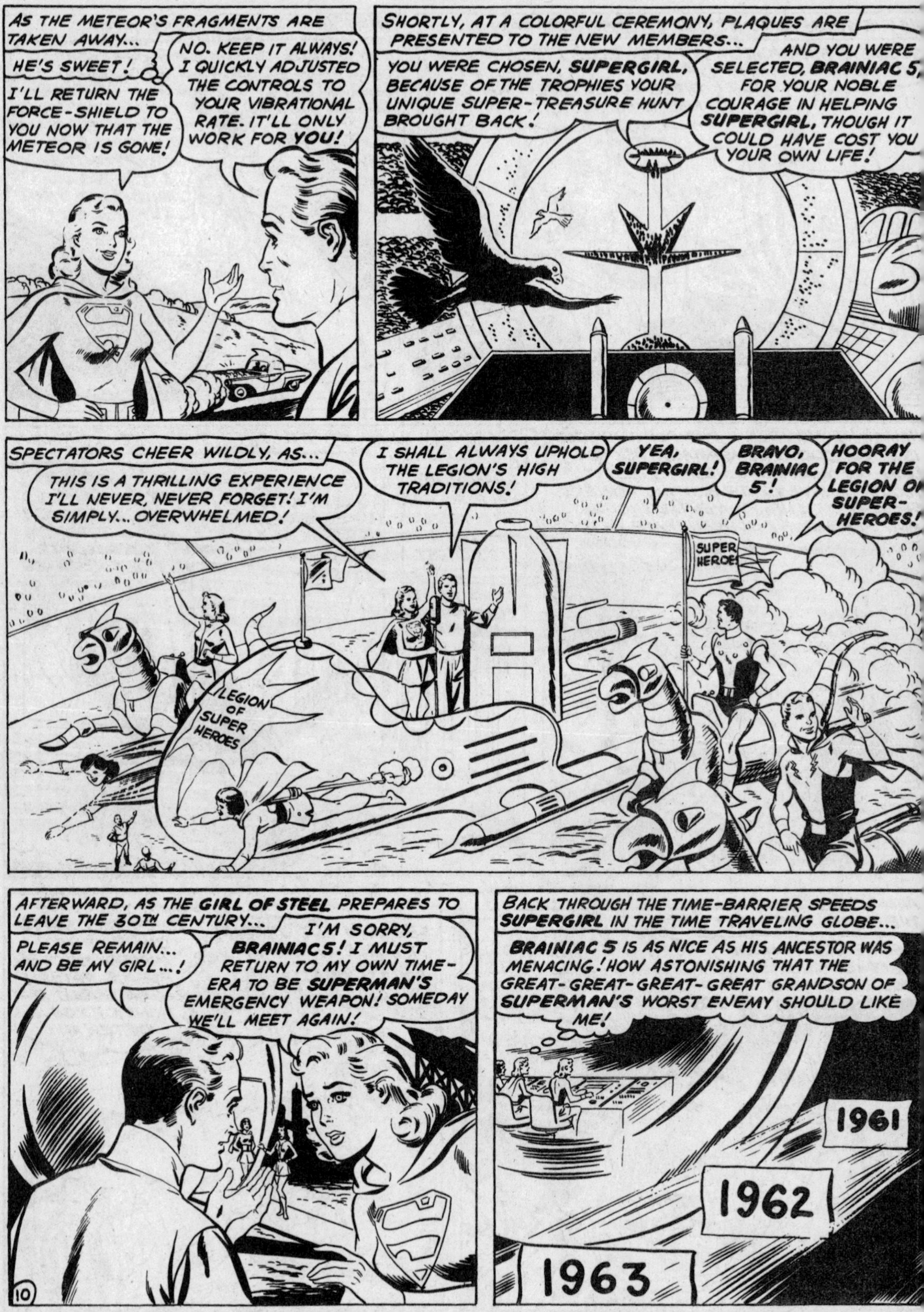
AS THE METEOR'S FRAGMENTS ARE TAKEN AWAY...
HE'S SWEET!
I'LL RETURN THE FORCE-SHIELD TO YOU NOW THAT THE METEOR IS GONE!
NO. KEEP IT ALWAYS! I QUICKLY ADJUSTED THE CONTROLS TO YOUR VIBRATIONAL RATE. IT'LL ONLY WORK FOR YOU!
SHORTLY, AT A COLORFUL CEREMONY, PLAQUES ARE PRESENTED TO THE NEW MEMBERS...
YOU WERE CHOSEN, SUPERGIRL, BECAUSE OF THE TROPHIES YOUR UNIQUE SUPER-TREASURE HUNT BROUGHT BACK!
AND YOU WERE SELECTED, BRAINIAC 5, FOR YOUR NOBLE COURAGE IN HELPING SUPERGIRL, THOUGH IT COULD HAVE COST YOU YOUR OWN LIFE!
SPECTATORS CHEER WILDLY, AS...
THIS IS A THRILLING EXPERIENCE I'LL NEVER, NEVER FORGET! I'M SIMPLY... OVERWHELMED!
I SHALL ALWAYS UPHOLD THE LEGION'S HIGH TRADITIONS!
YEA, SUPERGIRL!
BRAVO, BRAINIAC 5!
HOORAY FOR THE LEGION OF SUPER-HEROES!
SUPER HEROES
LEGION OF SUPER HEROES
AFTERWARD, AS THE GIRL OF STEEL PREPARES TO LEAVE THE 30TH CENTURY...
PLEASE REMAIN... AND BE MY GIRL...!
I'M SORRY, BRAINIAC 5! I MUST RETURN TO MY OWN TIME-ERA TO BE SUPERMAN'S EMERGENCY WEAPON! SOMEDAY WE'LL MEET AGAIN!
10
BACK THROUGH THE TIME-BARRIER SPEEDS SUPERGIRL IN THE TIME TRAVELING GLOBE...
BRAINIAC 5 IS AS NICE AS HIS ANCESTOR WAS MENACING! HOW ASTONISHING THAT THE GREAT-GREAT-GREAT-GREAT GRANDSON OF SUPERMAN'S WORST ENEMY SHOULD LIKE ME!
1961
1962
1963

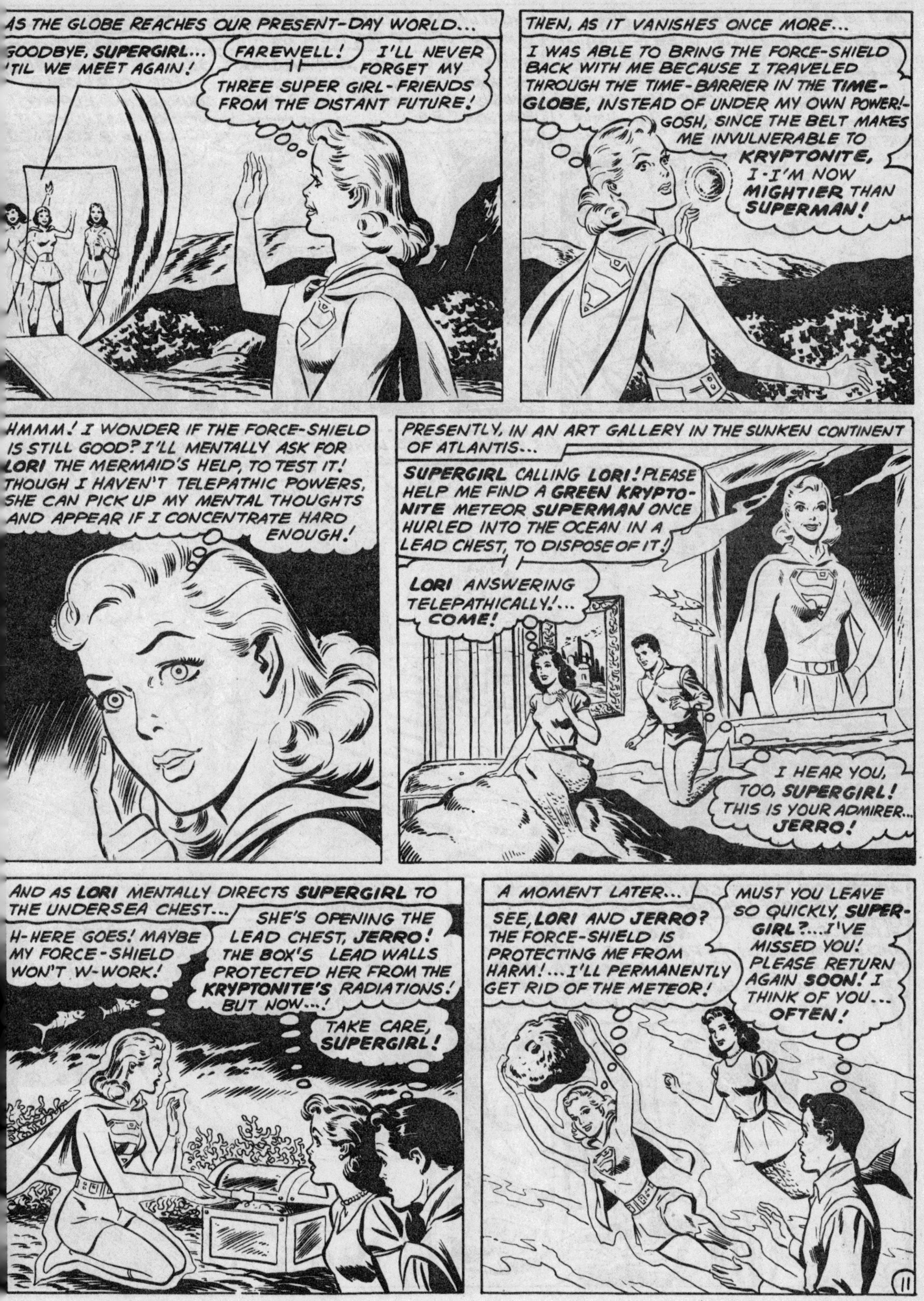
AS THE GLOBE REACHES OUR PRESENT-DAY WORLD...
GOODBYE, SUPERGIRL... 'TIL WE MEET AGAIN!
FAREWELL!
I'LL NEVER FORGET MY THREE SUPER GIRL-FRIENDS FROM THE DISTANT FUTURE!
THEN, AS IT VANISHES ONCE MORE...
I WAS ABLE TO BRING THE FORCE-SHIELD BACK WITH ME BECAUSE I TRAVELED THROUGH THE TIME-BARRIER IN THE TIME-GLOBE, INSTEAD OF UNDER MY OWN POWER!-GOSH, SINCE THE BELT MAKES ME INVULNERABLE TO KRYPTONITE, I-I'M NOW MIGHTIER THAN SUPERMAN!
HMMM! I WONDER IF THE FORCE-SHIELD IS STILL GOOD? I'LL MENTALLY ASK FOR LORI THE MERMAID'S HELP, TO TEST IT! THOUGH I HAVEN'T TELEPATHIC POWERS, SHE CAN PICK UP MY MENTAL THOUGHTS AND APPEAR IF I CONCENTRATE HARD ENOUGH!
PRESENTLY, IN AN ART GALLERY IN THE SUNKEN CONTINENT OF ATLANTIS...
SUPERGIRL CALLING LORI! PLEASE HELP ME FIND A GREEN KRYPTONITE METEOR SUPERMAN ONCE HURLED INTO THE OCEAN IN A LEAD CHEST, TO DISPOSE OF IT!
LORI ANSWERING TELEPATHICALLY!... COME!
I HEAR YOU, TOO, SUPERGIRL! THIS IS YOUR ADMIRER... JERRO!
AND AS LORI MENTALLY DIRECTS SUPERGIRL TO THE UNDERSEA CHEST...
H-HERE GOES! MAYBE MY FORCE-SHIELD WON'T W-WORK!
SHE'S OPENING THE LEAD CHEST, JERRO! THE BOX'S LEAD WALLS PROTECTED HER FROM THE KRYPTONITE'S RADIATIONS! BUT NOW...!
TAKE CARE, SUPERGIRL!
A MOMENT LATER...
SEE, LORI AND JERRO? THE FORCE-SHIELD IS PROTECTING ME FROM HARM!... I'LL PERMANENTLY GET RID OF THE METEOR!
MUST YOU LEAVE SO QUICKLY, SUPERGIRL?... I'VE MISSED YOU! PLEASE RETURN AGAIN SOON! I THINK OF YOU... OFTEN!
11

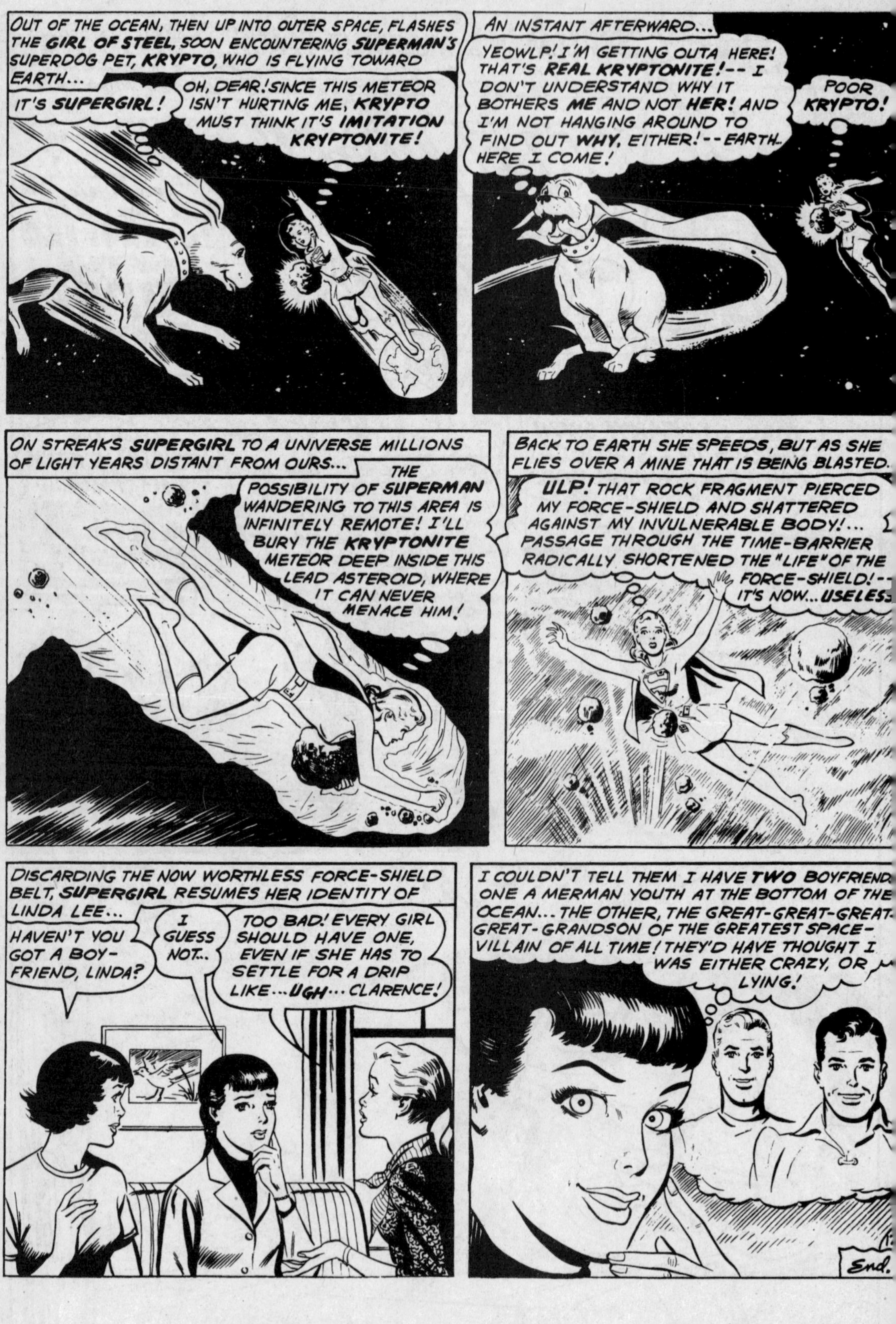
OUT OF THE OCEAN, THEN UP INTO OUTER SPACE, FLASHES THE GIRL OF STEEL, SOON ENCOUNTERING SUPERMAN'S SUPERDOG PET, KRYPTO, WHO IS FLYING TOWARD EARTH...
IT'S SUPERGIRL!
OH, DEAR! SINCE THIS METEOR ISN'T HURTING ME, KRYPTO MUST THINK IT'S IMITATION KRYPTONITE!
AN INSTANT AFTERWARD...
YEOWLP! I'M GETTING OUTA HERE! THAT'S REAL KRYPTONITE!-- I DON'T UNDERSTAND WHY IT BOTHERS ME AND NOT HER! AND I'M NOT HANGING AROUND TO FIND OUT WHY, EITHER!--EARTH, HERE I COME!
POOR KRYPTO!
ON STREAKS SUPERGIRL TO A UNIVERSE MILLIONS OF LIGHT YEARS DISTANT FROM OURS...
THE POSSIBILITY OF SUPERMAN WANDERING TO THIS AREA IS INFINITELY REMOTE! I'LL BURY THE KRYPTONITE METEOR DEEP INSIDE THIS LEAD ASTEROID, WHERE IT CAN NEVER MENACE HIM!
BACK TO EARTH SHE SPEEDS, BUT AS SHE FLIES OVER A MINE THAT IS BEING BLASTED.
ULP! THAT ROCK FRAGMENT PIERCED MY FORCE-SHIELD AND SHATTERED AGAINST MY INVULNERABLE BODY!... PASSAGE THROUGH THE TIME-BARRIER RADICALLY SHORTENED THE "LIFE" OF THE FORCE-SHIELD!-- IT'S NOW... USELESS
DISCARDING THE NOW WORTHLESS FORCE-SHIELD BELT, SUPERGIRL RESUMES HER IDENTITY OF LINDA LEE...
HAVEN'T YOU GOT A BOY-FRIEND, LINDA?
I GUESS NOT...
TOO BAD! EVERY GIRL SHOULD HAVE ONE, EVEN IF SHE HAS TO SETTLE FOR A DRIP LIKE...UGH...CLARENCE!
I COULDN'T TELL THEM I HAVE TWO BOYFRIENDS ONE A MERMAN YOUTH AT THE BOTTOM OF THE OCEAN... THE OTHER, THE GREAT-GREAT-GREAT-GREAT-GRANDSON OF THE GREATEST SPACE-VILLAIN OF ALL TIME! THEY'D HAVE THOUGHT I WAS EITHER CRAZY, OR LYING!
End.

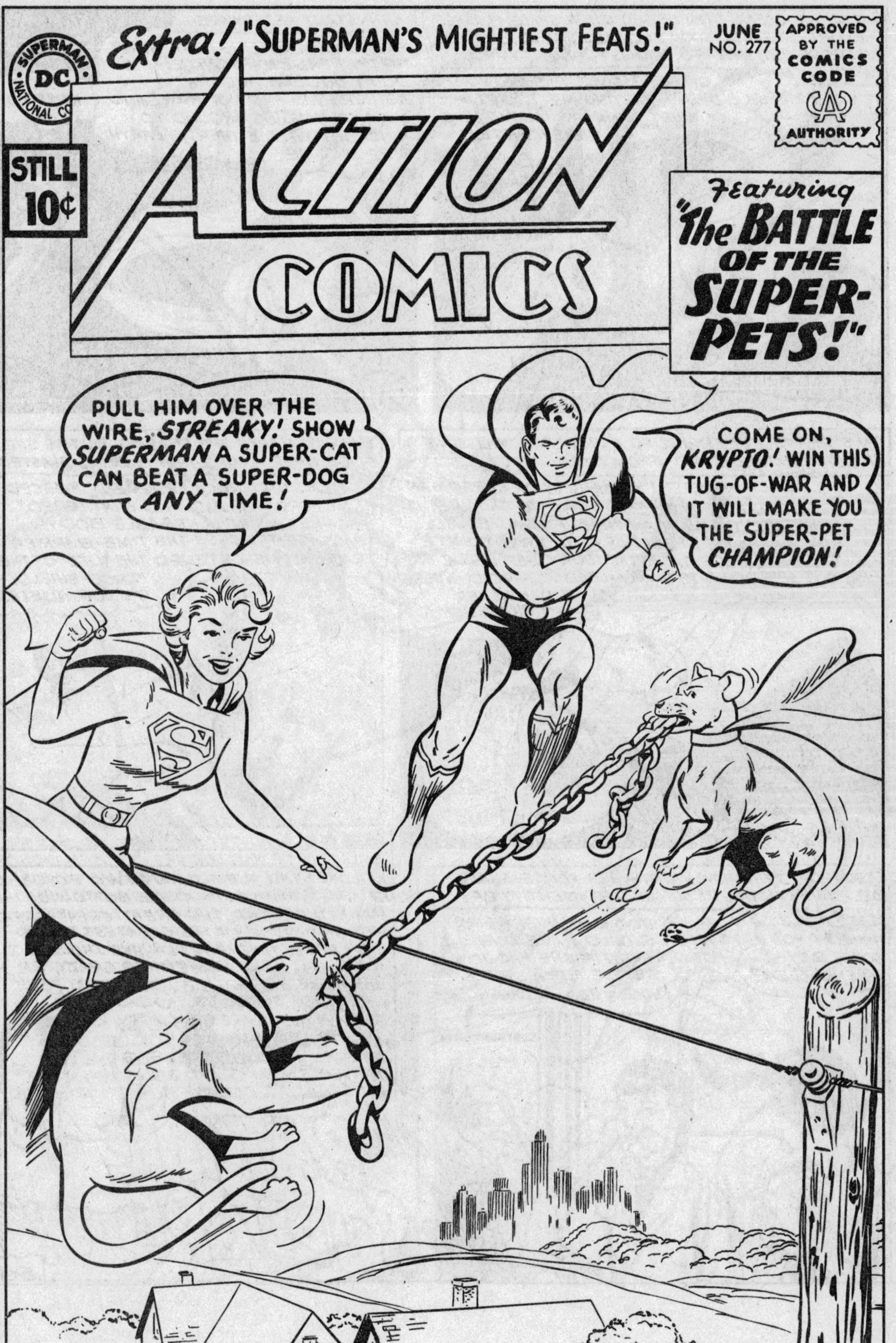
Extra! "SUPERMAN'S MIGHTIEST FEATS!"
SUPERMAN DC NATIONAL CO
JUNE NO. 277
APPROVED BY THE COMICS CODE AUTHORITY
STILL 10¢
ACTION COMICS
Featuring "The BATTLE OF THE SUPER-PETS!"
PULL HIM OVER THE WIRE, STREAKY! SHOW SUPERMAN A SUPER-CAT CAN BEAT A SUPER-DOG ANY TIME!
COME ON, KRYPTO! WIN THIS TUG-OF-WAR AND IT WILL MAKE YOU THE SUPER-PET CHAMPION!

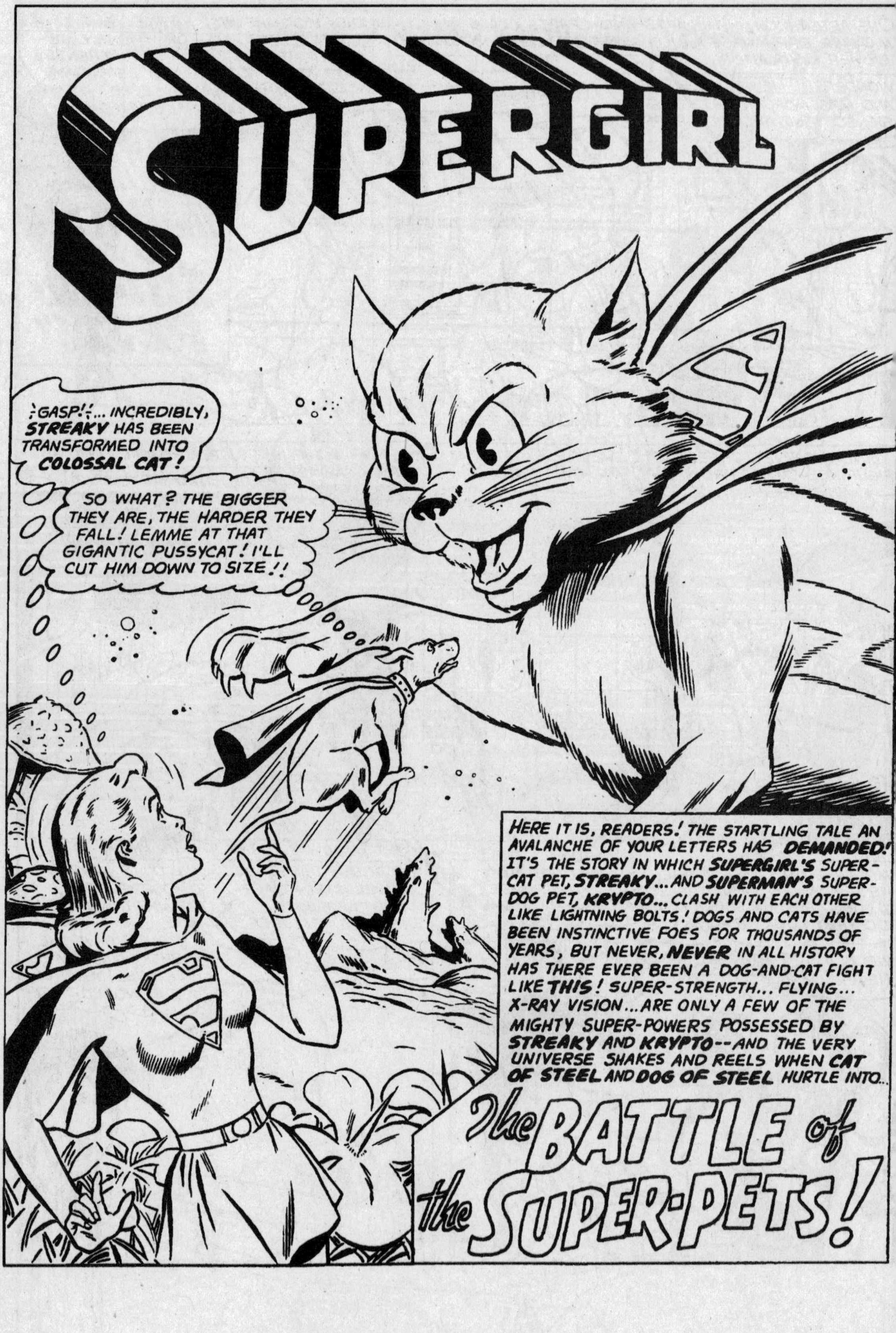
SUPERGIRL
¡GASP!¡... INCREDIBLY, STREAKY HAS BEEN TRANSFORMED INTO COLOSSAL CAT!
SO WHAT? THE BIGGER THEY ARE, THE HARDER THEY FALL! LEMME AT THAT GIGANTIC PUSSYCAT! I'LL CUT HIM DOWN TO SIZE!!
HERE IT IS, READERS! THE STARTLING TALE AN AVALANCHE OF YOUR LETTERS HAS DEMANDED! IT'S THE STORY IN WHICH SUPERGIRL'S SUPER-CAT PET, STREAKY... AND SUPERMAN'S SUPER-DOG PET, KRYPTO... CLASH WITH EACH OTHER LIKE LIGHTNING BOLTS! DOGS AND CATS HAVE BEEN INSTINCTIVE FOES FOR THOUSANDS OF YEARS, BUT NEVER, NEVER IN ALL HISTORY HAS THERE EVER BEEN A DOG-AND-CAT FIGHT LIKE THIS! SUPER-STRENGTH... FLYING... X-RAY VISION... ARE ONLY A FEW OF THE MIGHTY SUPER-POWERS POSSESSED BY STREAKY AND KRYPTO--AND THE VERY UNIVERSE SHAKES AND REELS WHEN CAT OF STEEL AND DOG OF STEEL HURTLE INTO...
The BATTLE of the SUPER-PETS!

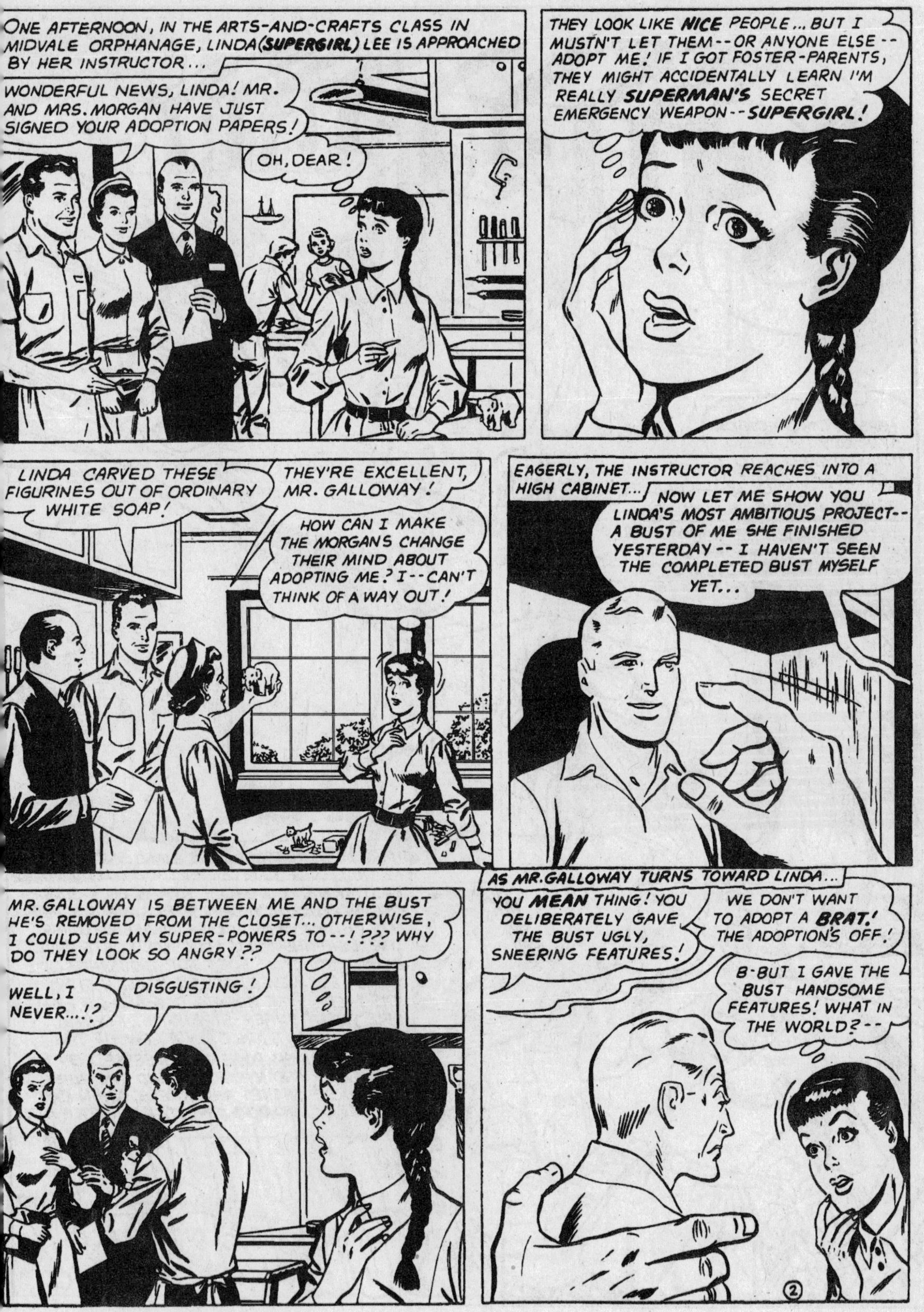
ONE AFTERNOON, IN THE ARTS-AND-CRAFTS CLASS IN MIDVALE ORPHANAGE, LINDA (SUPERGIRL) LEE IS APPROACHED BY HER INSTRUCTOR...
WONDERFUL NEWS, LINDA! MR. AND MRS. MORGAN HAVE JUST SIGNED YOUR ADOPTION PAPERS!
OH, DEAR!
THEY LOOK LIKE NICE PEOPLE ... BUT I MUSTN'T LET THEM--OR ANYONE ELSE--ADOPT ME! IF I GOT FOSTER-PARENTS, THEY MIGHT ACCIDENTALLY LEARN I'M REALLY SUPERMAN'S SECRET EMERGENCY WEAPON--SUPERGIRL!
LINDA CARVED THESE FIGURINES OUT OF ORDINARY WHITE SOAP!
THEY'RE EXCELLENT, MR. GALLOWAY!
HOW CAN I MAKE THE MORGANS CHANGE THEIR MIND ABOUT ADOPTING ME? I--CAN'T THINK OF A WAY OUT!
EAGERLY, THE INSTRUCTOR REACHES INTO A HIGH CABINET...
NOW LET ME SHOW YOU LINDA'S MOST AMBITIOUS PROJECT--A BUST OF ME SHE FINISHED YESTERDAY--I HAVEN'T SEEN THE COMPLETED BUST MYSELF YET...
MR. GALLOWAY IS BETWEEN ME AND THE BUST HE'S REMOVED FROM THE CLOSET... OTHERWISE, I COULD USE MY SUPER-POWERS TO--! ??? WHY DO THEY LOOK SO ANGRY??
WELL, I NEVER...!?
DISGUSTING!
AS MR. GALLOWAY TURNS TOWARD LINDA...
YOU MEAN THING! YOU DELIBERATELY GAVE THE BUST UGLY, SNEERING FEATURES!
WE DON'T WANT TO ADOPT A BRAT! THE ADOPTION'S OFF!
B-BUT I GAVE THE BUST HANDSOME FEATURES! WHAT IN THE WORLD?--
2

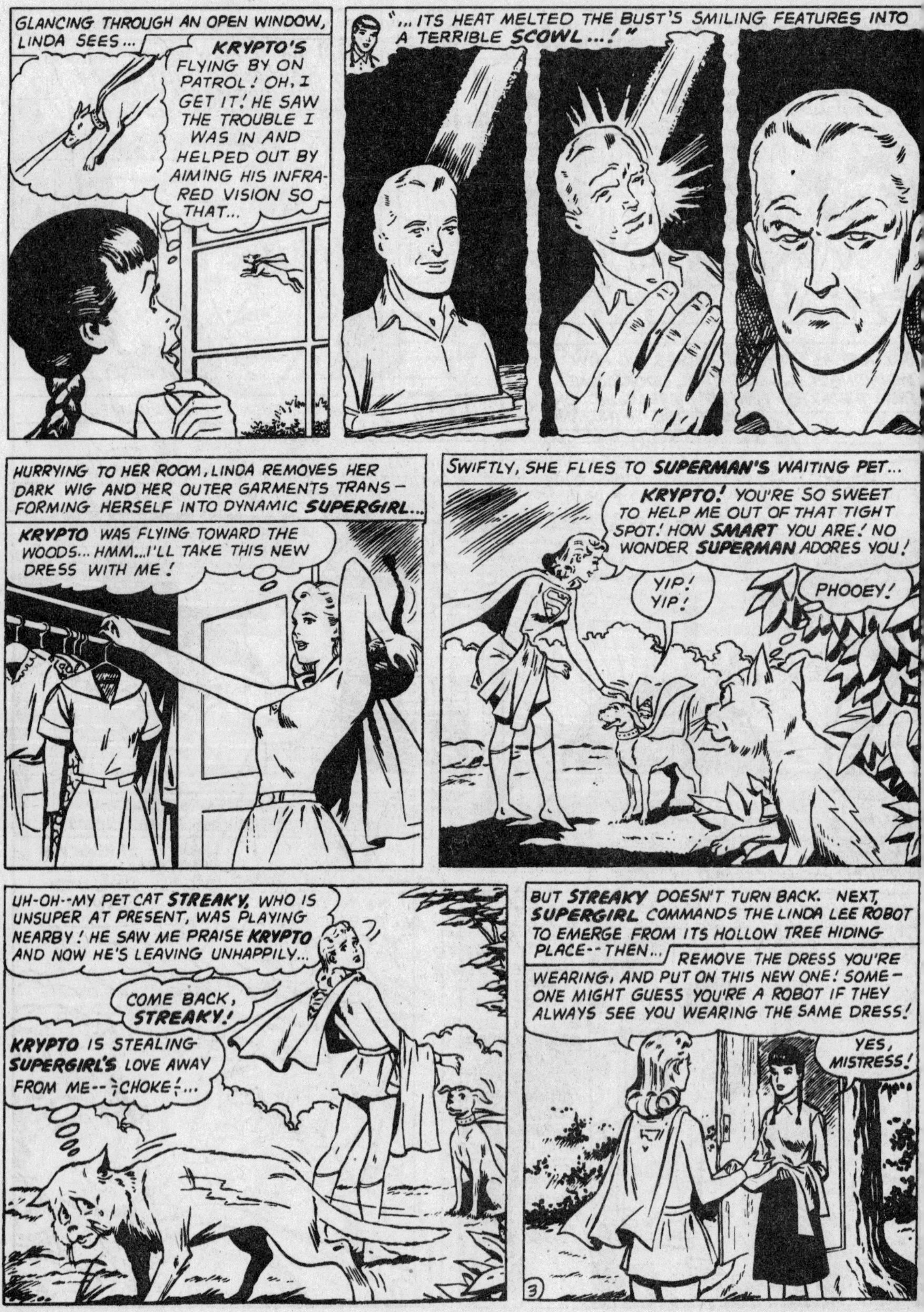
GLANCING THROUGH AN OPEN WINDOW, LINDA SEES...
KRYPTO'S FLYING BY ON PATROL! OH, I GET IT! HE SAW THE TROUBLE I WAS IN AND HELPED OUT BY AIMING HIS INFRA-RED VISION SO THAT...
"...ITS HEAT MELTED THE BUST'S SMILING FEATURES INTO A TERRIBLE SCOWL...!"
HURRYING TO HER ROOM, LINDA REMOVES HER DARK WIG AND HER OUTER GARMENTS TRANS-FORMING HERSELF INTO DYNAMIC SUPERGIRL...
KRYPTO WAS FLYING TOWARD THE WOODS... HMM...I'LL TAKE THIS NEW DRESS WITH ME!
SWIFTLY, SHE FLIES TO SUPERMAN'S WAITING PET...
KRYPTO! YOU'RE SO SWEET TO HELP ME OUT OF THAT TIGHT SPOT! HOW SMART YOU ARE! NO WONDER SUPERMAN ADORES YOU!
YIP! YIP!
PHOOEY!
UH-OH--MY PET CAT STREAKY, WHO IS UNSUPER AT PRESENT, WAS PLAYING NEARBY! HE SAW ME PRAISE KRYPTO AND NOW HE'S LEAVING UNHAPPILY...
COME BACK, STREAKY!
KRYPTO IS STEALING SUPERGIRL'S LOVE AWAY FROM ME-- CHOKE ...
BUT STREAKY DOESN'T TURN BACK. NEXT, SUPERGIRL COMMANDS THE LINDA LEE ROBOT TO EMERGE FROM ITS HOLLOW TREE HIDING PLACE--THEN...
REMOVE THE DRESS YOU'RE WEARING, AND PUT ON THIS NEW ONE! SOME-ONE MIGHT GUESS YOU'RE A ROBOT IF THEY ALWAYS SEE YOU WEARING THE SAME DRESS!
YES, MISTRESS!
3

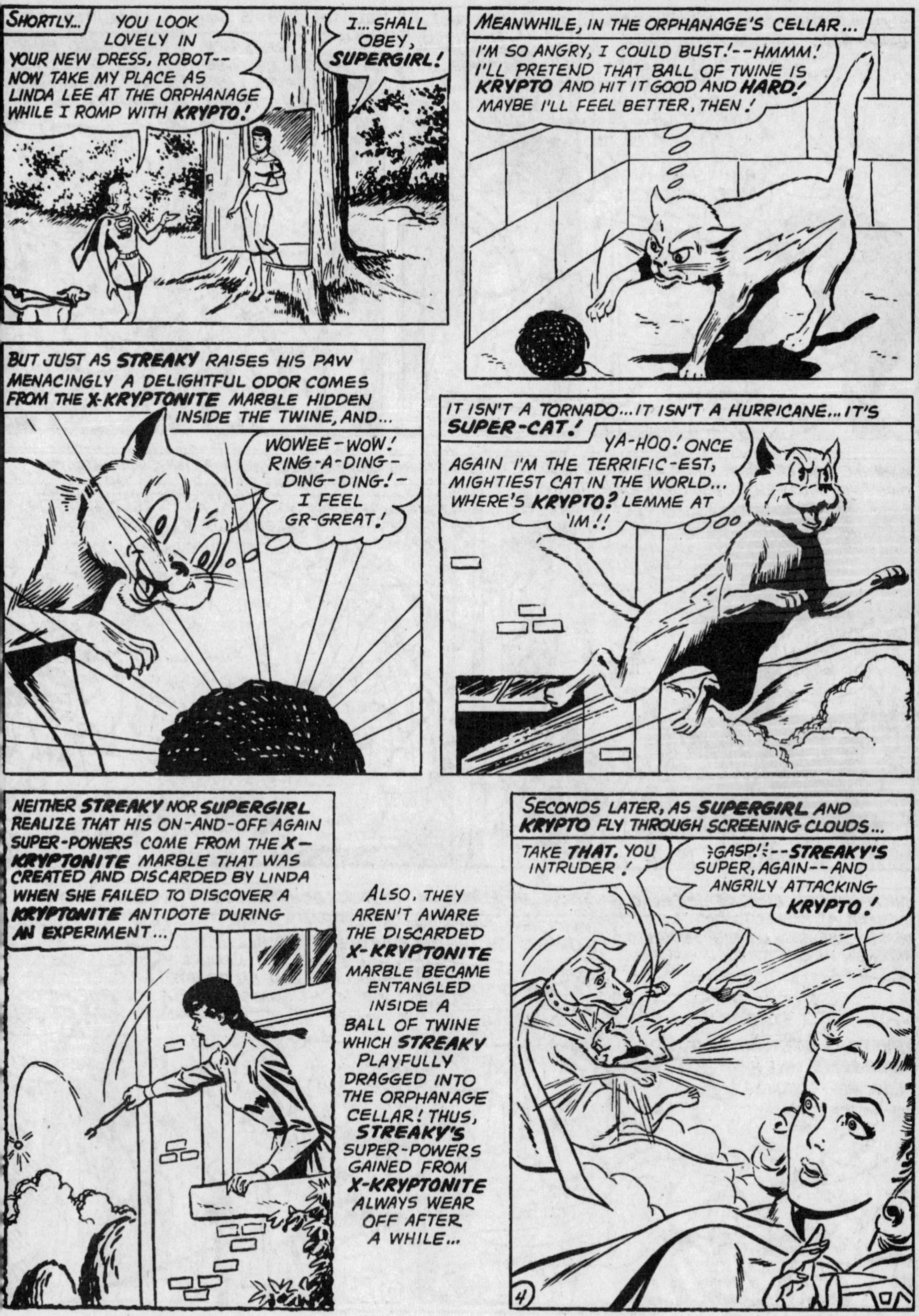
SHORTLY...
YOU LOOK LOVELY IN YOUR NEW DRESS, ROBOT--NOW TAKE MY PLACE AS LINDA LEE AT THE ORPHANAGE WHILE I ROMP WITH KRYPTO!
I... SHALL OBEY, SUPERGIRL!
MEANWHILE, IN THE ORPHANAGE'S CELLAR...
I'M SO ANGRY, I COULD BUST!--HMMM! I'LL PRETEND THAT BALL OF TWINE IS KRYPTO AND HIT IT GOOD AND HARD! MAYBE I'LL FEEL BETTER, THEN!
BUT JUST AS STREAKY RAISES HIS PAW MENACINGLY A DELIGHTFUL ODOR COMES FROM THE X-KRYPTONITE MARBLE HIDDEN INSIDE THE TWINE, AND...
WOWEE-WOW! RING-A-DING-DING-DING!- I FEEL GR-GREAT!
IT ISN'T A TORNADO...IT ISN'T A HURRICANE...IT'S SUPER-CAT!
YA-HOO! ONCE AGAIN I'M THE TERRIFIC-EST, MIGHTIEST CAT IN THE WORLD... WHERE'S KRYPTO? LEMME AT 'IM!!
NEITHER STREAKY NOR SUPERGIRL REALIZE THAT HIS ON-AND-OFF AGAIN SUPER-POWERS COME FROM THE X-KRYPTONITE MARBLE THAT WAS CREATED AND DISCARDED BY LINDA WHEN SHE FAILED TO DISCOVER A KRYPTONITE ANTIDOTE DURING AN EXPERIMENT...
ALSO, THEY AREN'T AWARE THE DISCARDED X-KRYPTONITE MARBLE BECAME ENTANGLED INSIDE A BALL OF TWINE WHICH STREAKY PLAYFULLY DRAGGED INTO THE ORPHANAGE CELLAR! THUS, STREAKY'S SUPER-POWERS GAINED FROM X-KRYPTONITE ALWAYS WEAR OFF AFTER A WHILE...
SECONDS LATER, AS SUPERGIRL AND KRYPTO FLY THROUGH SCREENING CLOUDS...
TAKE THAT, YOU INTRUDER!
GASP!--STREAKY'S SUPER, AGAIN--AND ANGRILY ATTACKING KRYPTO!
4

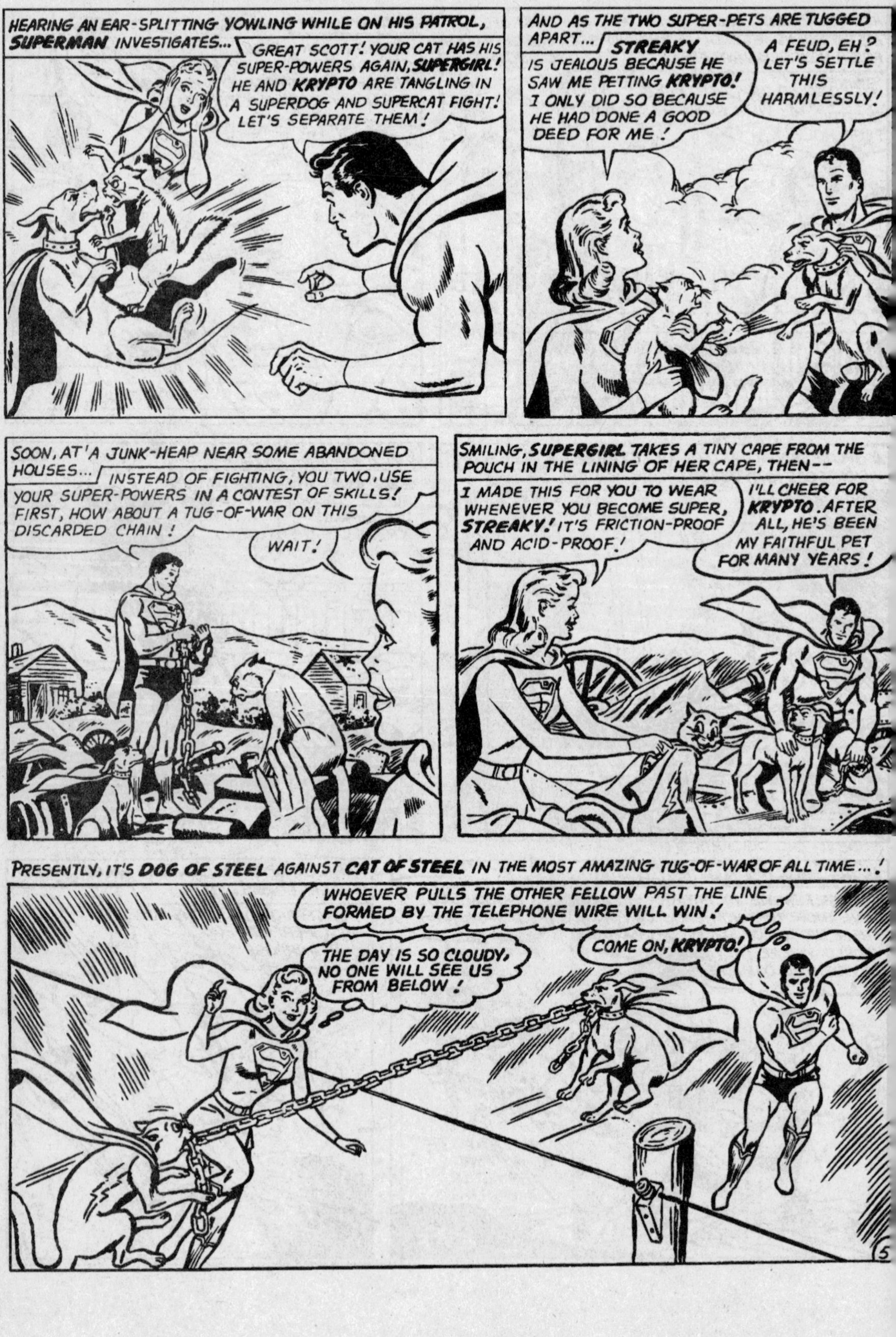
HEARING AN EAR-SPLITTING YOWLING WHILE ON HIS PATROL, SUPERMAN INVESTIGATES...
GREAT SCOTT! YOUR CAT HAS HIS SUPER-POWERS AGAIN, SUPERGIRL! HE AND KRYPTO ARE TANGLING IN A SUPERDOG AND SUPERCAT FIGHT! LET'S SEPARATE THEM!
AND AS THE TWO SUPER-PETS ARE TUGGED APART...
STREAKY IS JEALOUS BECAUSE HE SAW ME PETTING KRYPTO! I ONLY DID SO BECAUSE HE HAD DONE A GOOD DEED FOR ME!
A FEUD, EH? LET'S SETTLE THIS HARMLESSLY!
SOON, AT A JUNK-HEAP NEAR SOME ABANDONED HOUSES...
INSTEAD OF FIGHTING, YOU TWO USE YOUR SUPER-POWERS IN A CONTEST OF SKILLS! FIRST, HOW ABOUT A TUG-OF-WAR ON THIS DISCARDED CHAIN!
WAIT!
SMILING, SUPERGIRL TAKES A TINY CAPE FROM THE POUCH IN THE LINING OF HER CAPE, THEN--
I MADE THIS FOR YOU TO WEAR WHENEVER YOU BECOME SUPER, STREAKY! IT'S FRICTION-PROOF AND ACID-PROOF!
I'LL CHEER FOR KRYPTO. AFTER ALL, HE'S BEEN MY FAITHFUL PET FOR MANY YEARS!
PRESENTLY, IT'S DOG OF STEEL AGAINST CAT OF STEEL IN THE MOST AMAZING TUG-OF-WAR OF ALL TIME...!
THE DAY IS SO CLOUDY, NO ONE WILL SEE US FROM BELOW!
WHOEVER PULLS THE OTHER FELLOW PAST THE LINE FORMED BY THE TELEPHONE WIRE WILL WIN!
COME ON, KRYPTO!
5

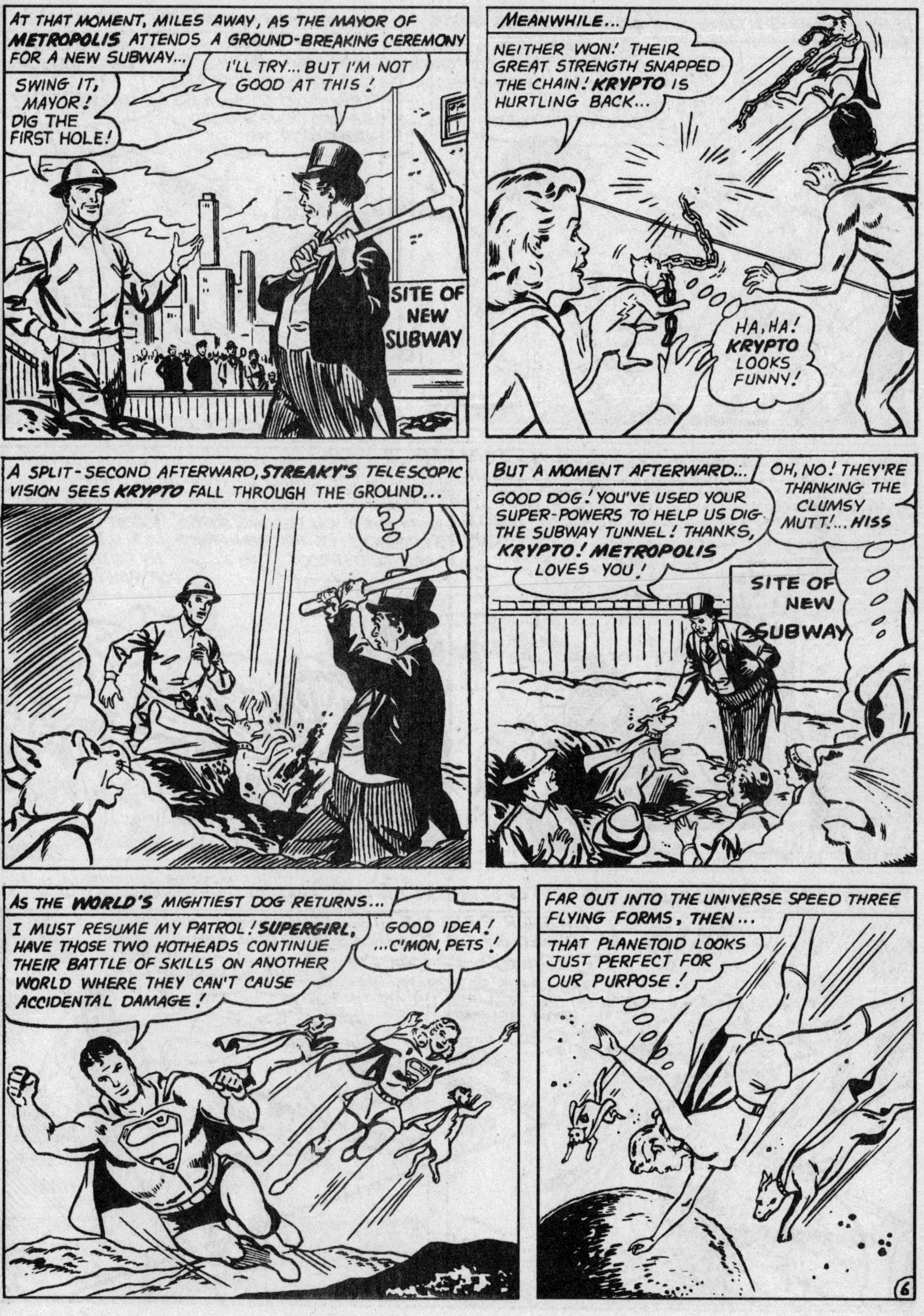
AT THAT MOMENT, MILES AWAY, AS THE MAYOR OF METROPOLIS ATTENDS A GROUND-BREAKING CEREMONY FOR A NEW SUBWAY...
SWING IT, MAYOR! DIG THE FIRST HOLE!
I'LL TRY... BUT I'M NOT GOOD AT THIS!
SITE OF NEW SUBWAY
MEANWHILE...
NEITHER WON! THEIR GREAT STRENGTH SNAPPED THE CHAIN! KRYPTO IS HURTLING BACK...
HA, HA! KRYPTO LOOKS FUNNY!
A SPLIT-SECOND AFTERWARD, STREAKY'S TELESCOPIC VISION SEES KRYPTO FALL THROUGH THE GROUND...
?
BUT A MOMENT AFTERWARD...
GOOD DOG! YOU'VE USED YOUR SUPER-POWERS TO HELP US DIG THE SUBWAY TUNNEL! THANKS, KRYPTO! METROPOLIS LOVES YOU!
OH, NO! THEY'RE THANKING THE CLUMSY MUTT!... HISS
SITE OF NEW SUBWAY
AS THE WORLD'S MIGHTIEST DOG RETURNS...
I MUST RESUME MY PATROL! SUPERGIRL, HAVE THOSE TWO HOTHEADS CONTINUE THEIR BATTLE OF SKILLS ON ANOTHER WORLD WHERE THEY CAN'T CAUSE ACCIDENTAL DAMAGE!
GOOD IDEA! ...C'MON, PETS!
FAR OUT INTO THE UNIVERSE SPEED THREE FLYING FORMS, THEN...
THAT PLANETOID LOOKS JUST PERFECT FOR OUR PURPOSE!
6

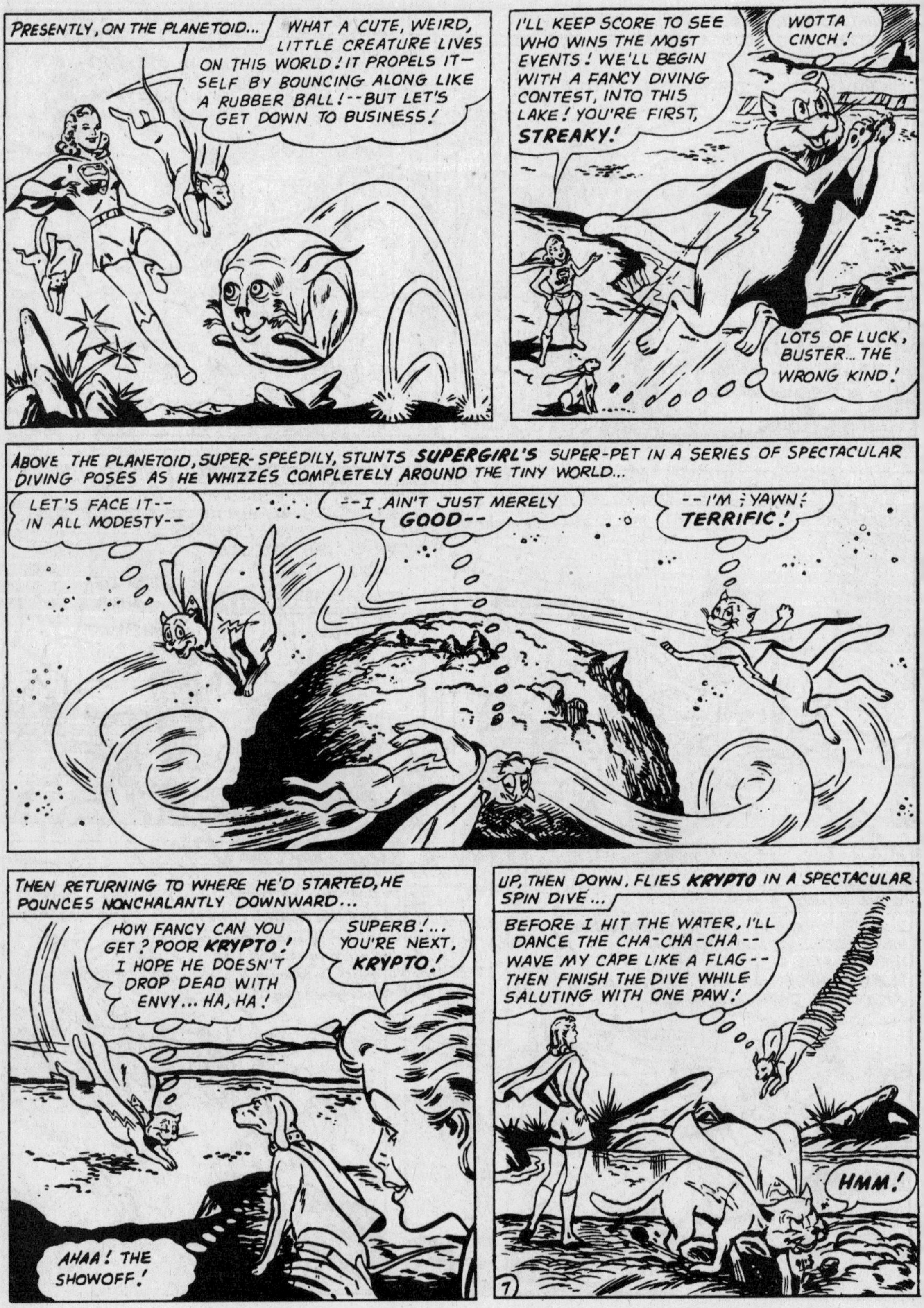
PRESENTLY, ON THE PLANETOID...
WHAT A CUTE, WEIRD, LITTLE CREATURE LIVES ON THIS WORLD! IT PROPELS IT-SELF BY BOUNCING ALONG LIKE A RUBBER BALL! --BUT LET'S GET DOWN TO BUSINESS!
I'LL KEEP SCORE TO SEE WHO WINS THE MOST EVENTS! WE'LL BEGIN WITH A FANCY DIVING CONTEST, INTO THIS LAKE! YOU'RE FIRST, STREAKY!
WOTTA CINCH!
LOTS OF LUCK, BUSTER... THE WRONG KIND!
ABOVE THE PLANETOID, SUPER-SPEEDILY, STUNTS SUPERGIRL'S SUPER-PET IN A SERIES OF SPECTACULAR DIVING POSES AS HE WHIZZES COMPLETELY AROUND THE TINY WORLD...
LET'S FACE IT-- IN ALL MODESTY--
--I AIN'T JUST MERELY GOOD--
--I'M ;YAWN; TERRIFIC!
THEN RETURNING TO WHERE HE'D STARTED, HE POUNCES NONCHALANTLY DOWNWARD...
HOW FANCY CAN YOU GET? POOR KRYPTO! I HOPE HE DOESN'T DROP DEAD WITH ENVY... HA, HA!
SUPERB!... YOU'RE NEXT, KRYPTO!
AHAA! THE SHOWOFF!
UP, THEN DOWN, FLIES KRYPTO IN A SPECTACULAR SPIN DIVE...
BEFORE I HIT THE WATER, I'LL DANCE THE CHA-CHA-CHA-- WAVE MY CAPE LIKE A FLAG-- THEN FINISH THE DIVE WHILE SALUTING WITH ONE PAW!
HMM!
7

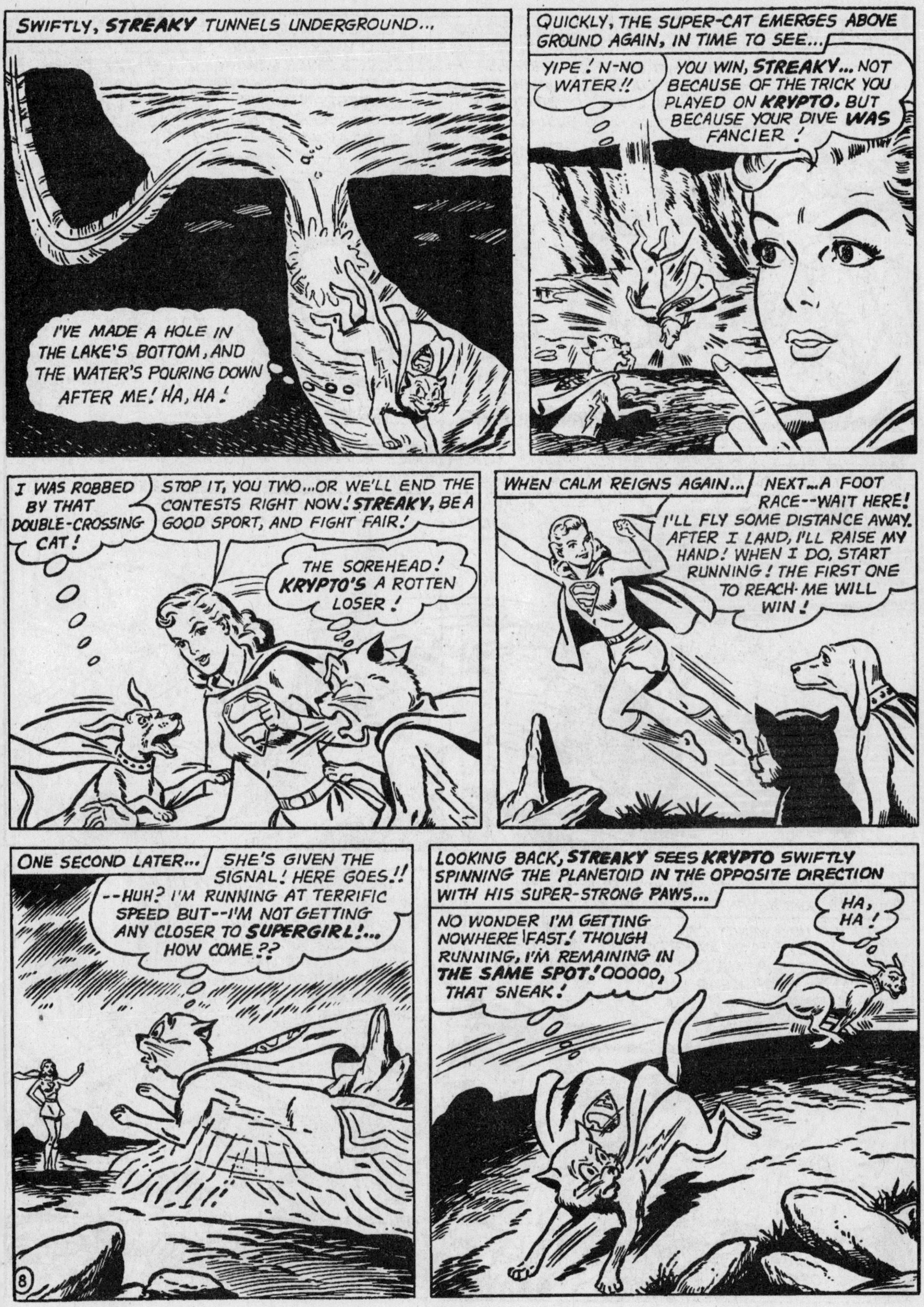
SWIFTLY, STREAKY TUNNELS UNDERGROUND...
I'VE MADE A HOLE IN THE LAKE'S BOTTOM, AND THE WATER'S POURING DOWN AFTER ME! HA, HA!
QUICKLY, THE SUPER-CAT EMERGES ABOVE GROUND AGAIN, IN TIME TO SEE...
YIPE! N-NO WATER!!
YOU WIN, STREAKY... NOT BECAUSE OF THE TRICK YOU PLAYED ON KRYPTO, BUT BECAUSE YOUR DIVE WAS FANCIER!
I WAS ROBBED BY THAT DOUBLE-CROSSING CAT!
STOP IT, YOU TWO...OR WE'LL END THE CONTESTS RIGHT NOW! STREAKY, BE A GOOD SPORT, AND FIGHT FAIR!
THE SOREHEAD! KRYPTO'S A ROTTEN LOSER!
WHEN CALM REIGNS AGAIN...
NEXT...A FOOT RACE--WAIT HERE! I'LL FLY SOME DISTANCE AWAY. AFTER I LAND, I'LL RAISE MY HAND! WHEN I DO, START RUNNING! THE FIRST ONE TO REACH ME WILL WIN!
ONE SECOND LATER...
SHE'S GIVEN THE SIGNAL! HERE GOES!! --HUH? I'M RUNNING AT TERRIFIC SPEED BUT--I'M NOT GETTING ANY CLOSER TO SUPERGIRL!... HOW COME??
8
LOOKING BACK, STREAKY SEES KRYPTO SWIFTLY SPINNING THE PLANETOID IN THE OPPOSITE DIRECTION WITH HIS SUPER-STRONG PAWS...
NO WONDER I'M GETTING NOWHERE FAST! THOUGH RUNNING, I'M REMAINING IN THE SAME SPOT! OOOOO, THAT SNEAK!
HA, HA!

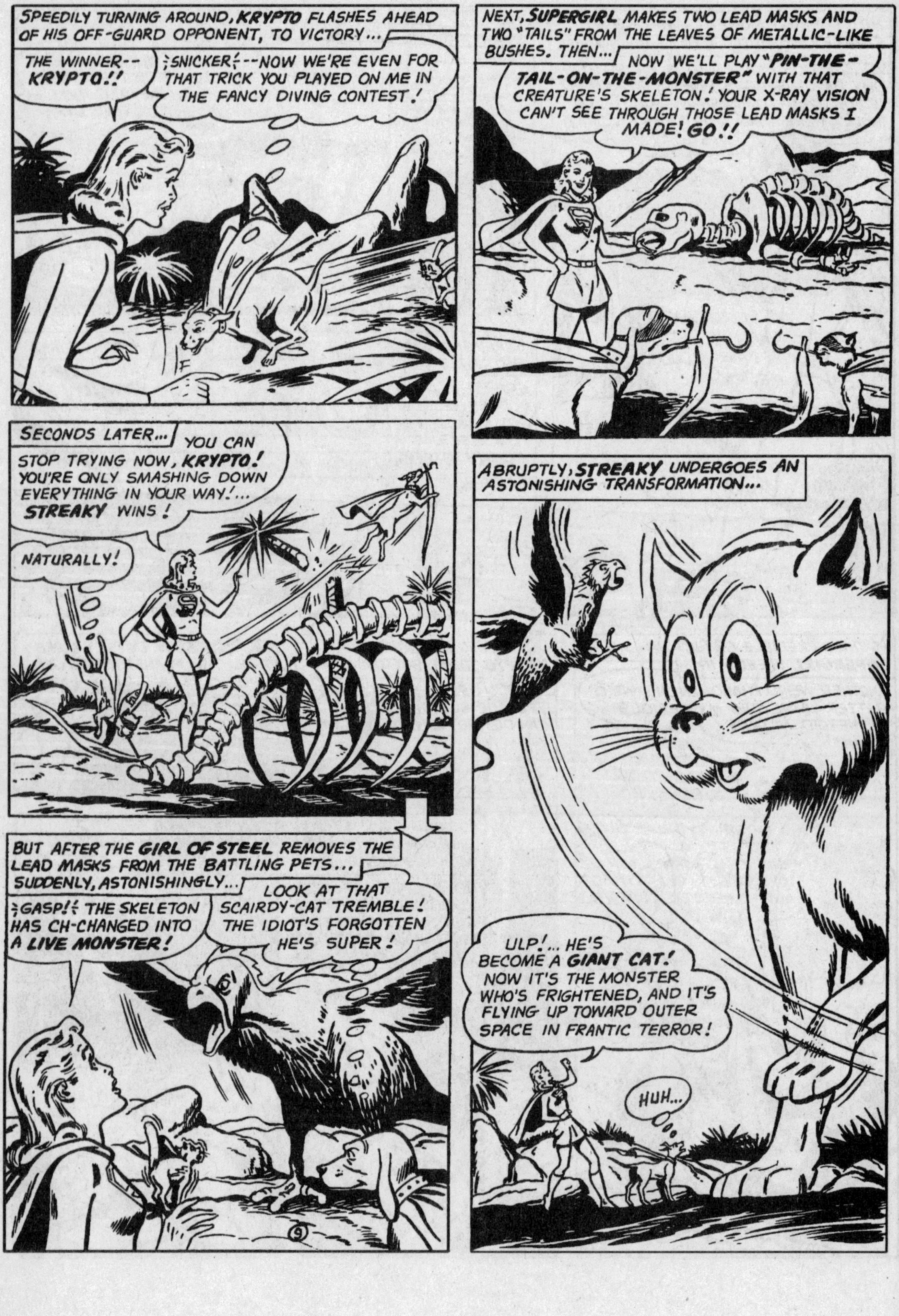
SPEEDILY TURNING AROUND, KRYPTO FLASHES AHEAD OF HIS OFF-GUARD OPPONENT, TO VICTORY...
THE WINNER-- KRYPTO!!
;SNICKER;--NOW WE'RE EVEN FOR THAT TRICK YOU PLAYED ON ME IN THE FANCY DIVING CONTEST!
NEXT, SUPERGIRL MAKES TWO LEAD MASKS AND TWO "TAILS" FROM THE LEAVES OF METALLIC-LIKE BUSHES. THEN...
NOW WE'LL PLAY "PIN-THE-TAIL-ON-THE-MONSTER" WITH THAT CREATURE'S SKELETON! YOUR X-RAY VISION CAN'T SEE THROUGH THOSE LEAD MASKS I MADE! GO!!
SECONDS LATER...
YOU CAN STOP TRYING NOW, KRYPTO! YOU'RE ONLY SMASHING DOWN EVERYTHING IN YOUR WAY!... STREAKY WINS!
NATURALLY!
BUT AFTER THE GIRL OF STEEL REMOVES THE LEAD MASKS FROM THE BATTLING PETS... SUDDENLY, ASTONISHINGLY...
;GASP!; THE SKELETON HAS CH-CHANGED INTO A LIVE MONSTER!
LOOK AT THAT SCAIRDY-CAT TREMBLE! THE IDIOT'S FORGOTTEN HE'S SUPER!
9
ABRUPTLY, STREAKY UNDERGOES AN ASTONISHING TRANSFORMATION...
ULP!... HE'S BECOME A GIANT CAT! NOW IT'S THE MONSTER WHO'S FRIGHTENED, AND IT'S FLYING UP TOWARD OUTER SPACE IN FRANTIC TERROR!
HUH...

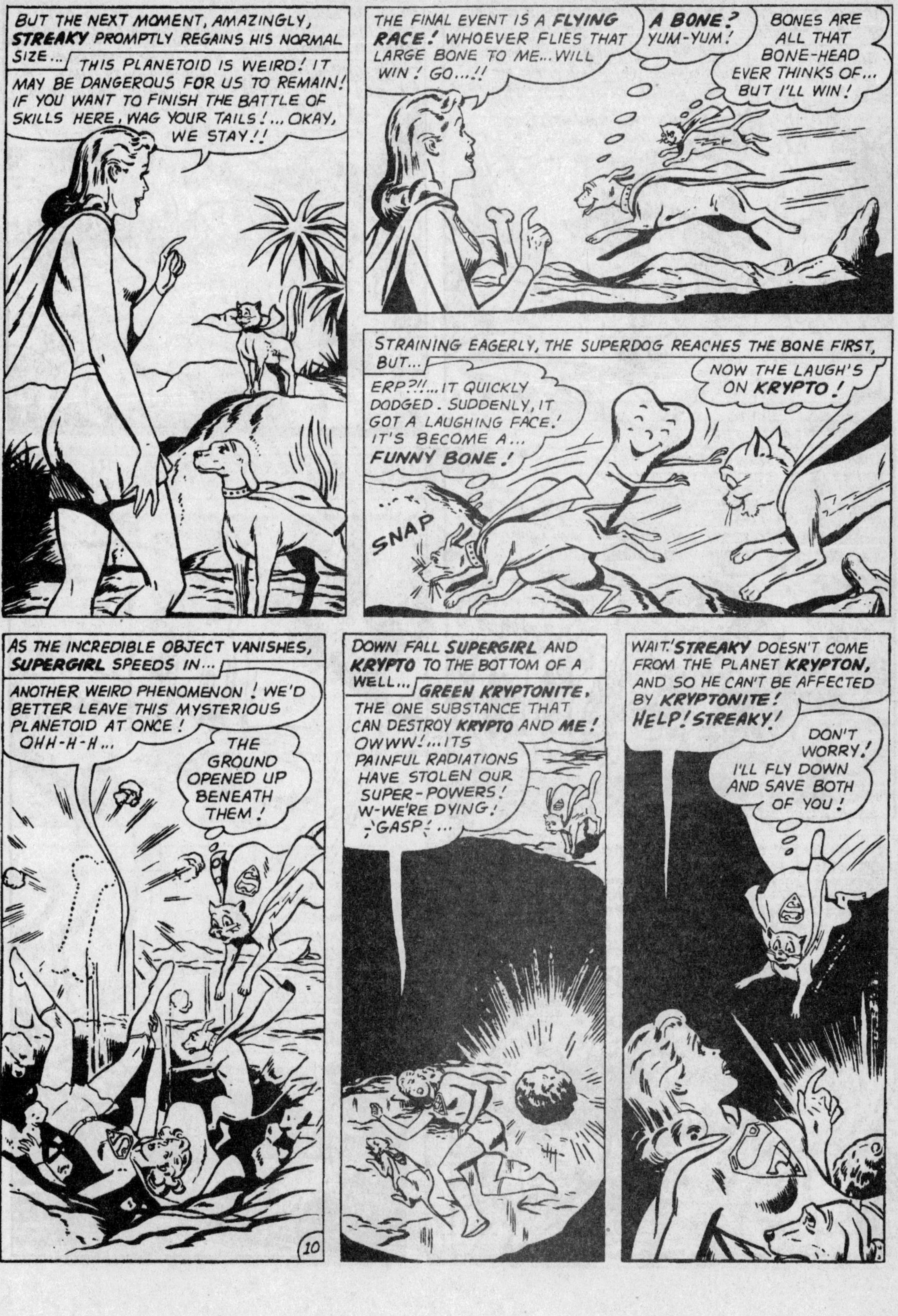
BUT THE NEXT MOMENT, AMAZINGLY, STREAKY PROMPTLY REGAINS HIS NORMAL SIZE...
THIS PLANETOID IS WEIRD! IT MAY BE DANGEROUS FOR US TO REMAIN! IF YOU WANT TO FINISH THE BATTLE OF SKILLS HERE, WAG YOUR TAILS!... OKAY, WE STAY!!
THE FINAL EVENT IS A FLYING RACE! WHOEVER FLIES THAT LARGE BONE TO ME... WILL WIN! GO...!!
A BONE? YUM-YUM!
BONES ARE ALL THAT BONE-HEAD EVER THINKS OF... BUT I'LL WIN!
STRAINING EAGERLY, THE SUPERDOG REACHES THE BONE FIRST, BUT...
ERP?!!... IT QUICKLY DODGED. SUDDENLY, IT GOT A LAUGHING FACE! IT'S BECOME A... FUNNY BONE!
NOW THE LAUGH'S ON KRYPTO!
SNAP
AS THE INCREDIBLE OBJECT VANISHES, SUPERGIRL SPEEDS IN...
ANOTHER WEIRD PHENOMENON! WE'D BETTER LEAVE THIS MYSTERIOUS PLANETOID AT ONCE! OHH-H-H...
THE GROUND OPENED UP BENEATH THEM!
10
DOWN FALL SUPERGIRL AND KRYPTO TO THE BOTTOM OF A WELL...
GREEN KRYPTONITE, THE ONE SUBSTANCE THAT CAN DESTROY KRYPTO AND ME! OWWW!... ITS PAINFUL RADIATIONS HAVE STOLEN OUR SUPER-POWERS! W-WE'RE DYING! GASP! ...
WAIT! STREAKY DOESN'T COME FROM THE PLANET KRYPTON, AND SO HE CAN'T BE AFFECTED BY KRYPTONITE! HELP! STREAKY!
DON'T WORRY! I'LL FLY DOWN AND SAVE BOTH OF YOU!

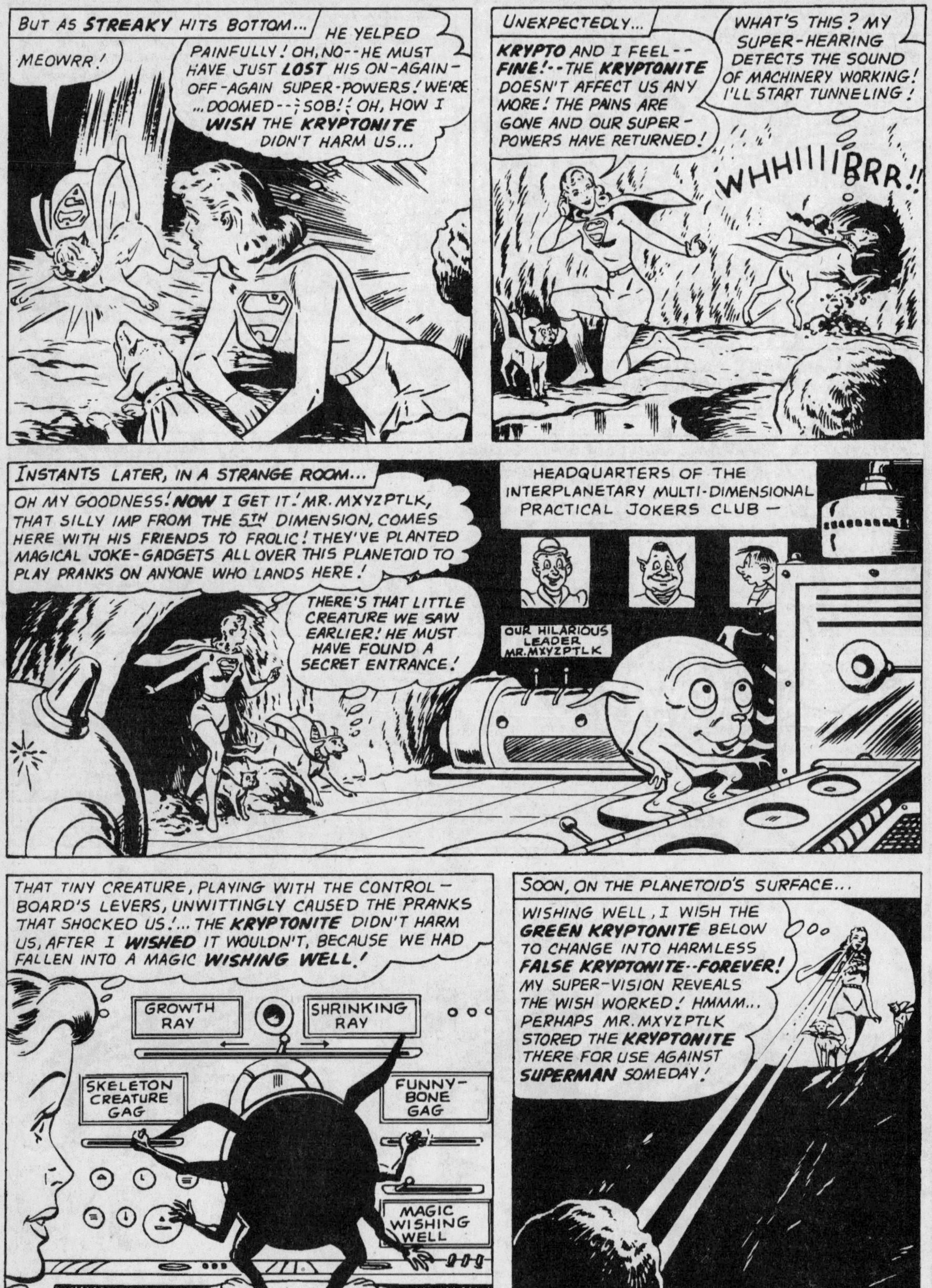
BUT AS STREAKY HITS BOTTOM...
MEOWRR!
HE YELPED PAINFULLY! OH, NO--HE MUST HAVE JUST LOST HIS ON-AGAIN-OFF-AGAIN SUPER-POWERS! WE'RE ...DOOMED-- SOB! OH, HOW I WISH THE KRYPTONITE DIDN'T HARM US...
UNEXPECTEDLY...
KRYPTO AND I FEEL--FINE!--THE KRYPTONITE DOESN'T AFFECT US ANY MORE! THE PAINS ARE GONE AND OUR SUPER-POWERS HAVE RETURNED!
WHAT'S THIS? MY SUPER-HEARING DETECTS THE SOUND OF MACHINERY WORKING! I'LL START TUNNELING!
WHHIIIIRRR!!
INSTANTS LATER, IN A STRANGE ROOM...
OH MY GOODNESS! NOW I GET IT! MR. MXYZPTLK, THAT SILLY IMP FROM THE 5TH DIMENSION, COMES HERE WITH HIS FRIENDS TO FROLIC! THEY'VE PLANTED MAGICAL JOKE-GADGETS ALL OVER THIS PLANETOID TO PLAY PRANKS ON ANYONE WHO LANDS HERE!
HEADQUARTERS OF THE INTERPLANETARY MULTI-DIMENSIONAL PRACTICAL JOKERS CLUB —
OUR HILARIOUS LEADER MR. MXYZPTLK
THERE'S THAT LITTLE CREATURE WE SAW EARLIER! HE MUST HAVE FOUND A SECRET ENTRANCE!
THAT TINY CREATURE, PLAYING WITH THE CONTROL-BOARD'S LEVERS, UNWITTINGLY CAUSED THE PRANKS THAT SHOCKED US!... THE KRYPTONITE DIDN'T HARM US, AFTER I WISHED IT WOULDN'T, BECAUSE WE HAD FALLEN INTO A MAGIC WISHING WELL!
GROWTH RAY
SHRINKING RAY
SKELETON CREATURE GAG
FUNNY-BONE GAG
MAGIC WISHING WELL
11
SOON, ON THE PLANETOID'S SURFACE...
WISHING WELL, I WISH THE GREEN KRYPTONITE BELOW TO CHANGE INTO HARMLESS FALSE KRYPTONITE--FOREVER! MY SUPER-VISION REVEALS THE WISH WORKED! HMMM... PERHAPS MR. MXYZPTLK STORED THE KRYPTONITE THERE FOR USE AGAINST SUPERMAN SOMEDAY!

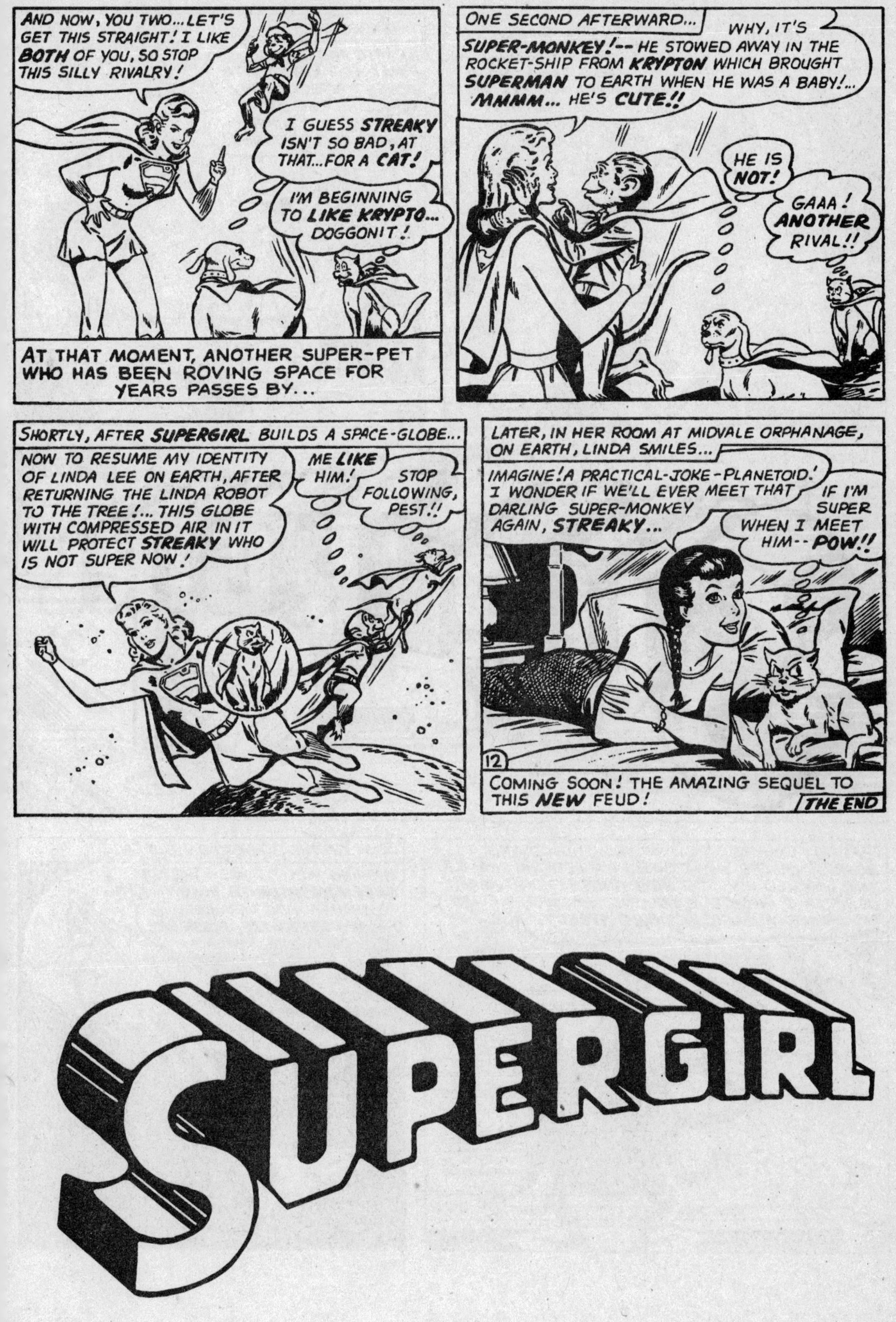
AND NOW, YOU TWO... LET'S GET THIS STRAIGHT! I LIKE BOTH OF YOU, SO STOP THIS SILLY RIVALRY!
I GUESS STREAKY ISN'T SO BAD, AT THAT...FOR A CAT!
I'M BEGINNING TO LIKE KRYPTO... DOGGONIT!
AT THAT MOMENT, ANOTHER SUPER-PET WHO HAS BEEN ROVING SPACE FOR YEARS PASSES BY...
ONE SECOND AFTERWARD...
WHY, IT'S SUPER-MONKEY!-- HE STOWED AWAY IN THE ROCKET-SHIP FROM KRYPTON WHICH BROUGHT SUPERMAN TO EARTH WHEN HE WAS A BABY!... MMMM... HE'S CUTE!!
HE IS NOT!
GAAA! ANOTHER RIVAL!!
SHORTLY, AFTER SUPERGIRL BUILDS A SPACE-GLOBE...
NOW TO RESUME MY IDENTITY OF LINDA LEE ON EARTH, AFTER RETURNING THE LINDA ROBOT TO THE TREE!... THIS GLOBE WITH COMPRESSED AIR IN IT WILL PROTECT STREAKY WHO IS NOT SUPER NOW!
ME LIKE HIM!
STOP FOLLOWING, PEST!!
LATER, IN HER ROOM AT MIDVALE ORPHANAGE, ON EARTH, LINDA SMILES...
IMAGINE! A PRACTICAL-JOKE-PLANETOID! I WONDER IF WE'LL EVER MEET THAT DARLING SUPER-MONKEY AGAIN, STREAKY...
IF I'M SUPER WHEN I MEET HIM-- POW!!
12
COMING SOON! THE AMAZING SEQUEL TO THIS NEW FEUD!
THE END

SUPERGIRL

SUPERGIRL

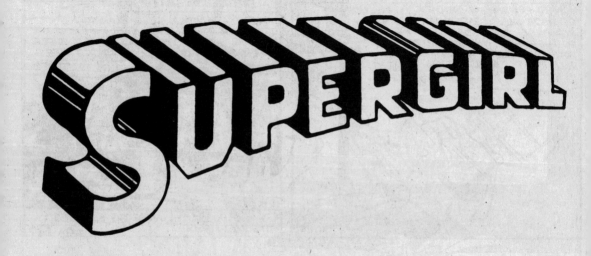

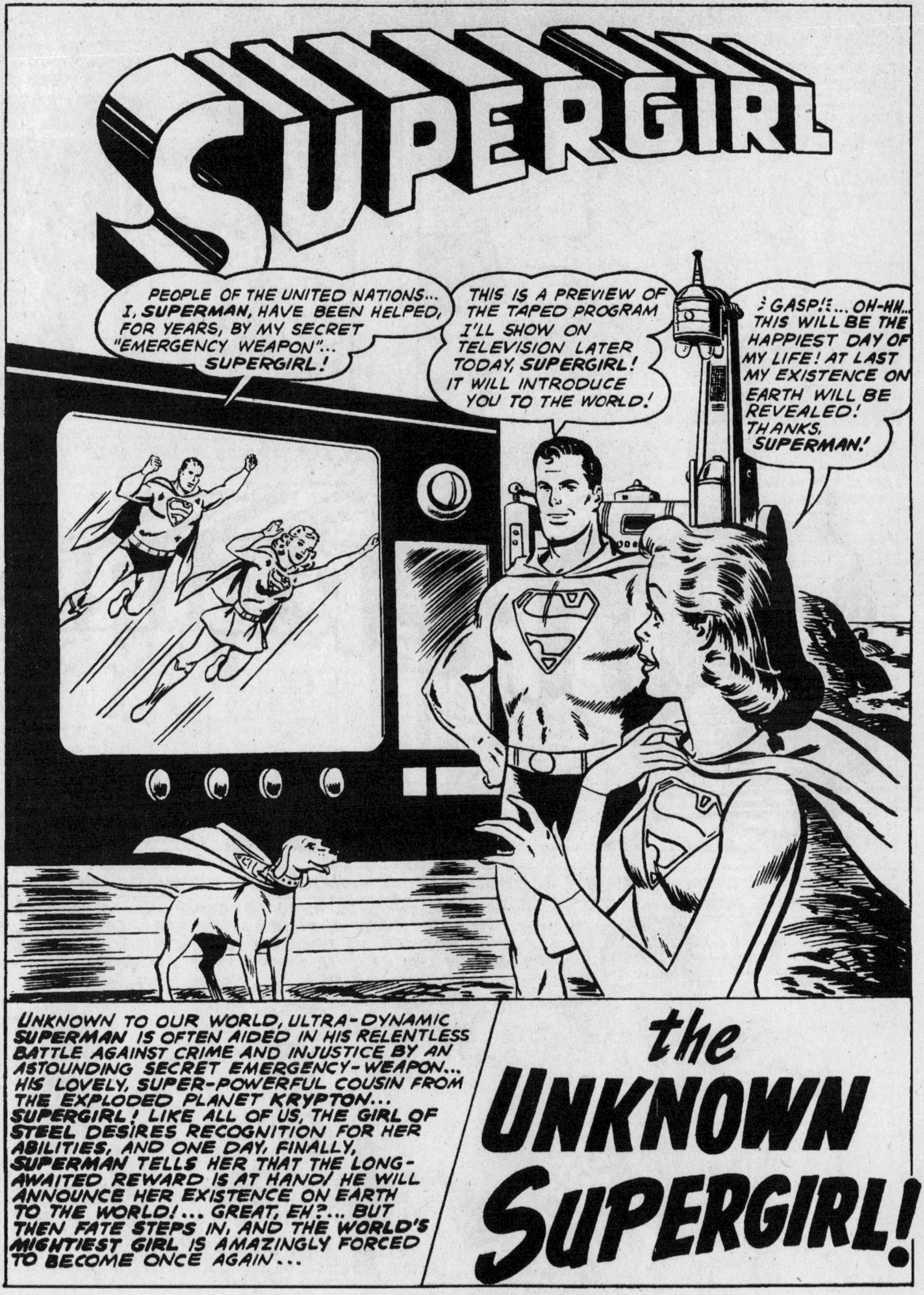
SUPERGIRL
PEOPLE OF THE UNITED NATIONS... I, SUPERMAN, HAVE BEEN HELPED, FOR YEARS, BY MY SECRET "EMERGENCY WEAPON"... SUPERGIRL!
THIS IS A PREVIEW OF THE TAPED PROGRAM I'LL SHOW ON TELEVISION LATER TODAY, SUPERGIRL! IT WILL INTRODUCE YOU TO THE WORLD!
GASP!... OH-HH... THIS WILL BE THE HAPPIEST DAY OF MY LIFE! AT LAST MY EXISTENCE ON EARTH WILL BE REVEALED! THANKS, SUPERMAN!
UNKNOWN TO OUR WORLD, ULTRA-DYNAMIC SUPERMAN IS OFTEN AIDED IN HIS RELENTLESS BATTLE AGAINST CRIME AND INJUSTICE BY AN ASTOUNDING SECRET EMERGENCY-WEAPON... HIS LOVELY, SUPER-POWERFUL COUSIN FROM THE EXPLODED PLANET KRYPTON... SUPERGIRL! LIKE ALL OF US, THE GIRL OF STEEL DESIRES RECOGNITION FOR HER ABILITIES, AND ONE DAY, FINALLY, SUPERMAN TELLS HER THAT THE LONG-AWAITED REWARD IS AT HAND! HE WILL ANNOUNCE HER EXISTENCE ON EARTH TO THE WORLD!... GREAT, EH?... BUT THEN FATE STEPS IN, AND THE WORLD'S MIGHTIEST GIRL IS AMAZINGLY FORCED TO BECOME ONCE AGAIN...
the UNKNOWN SUPERGIRL!

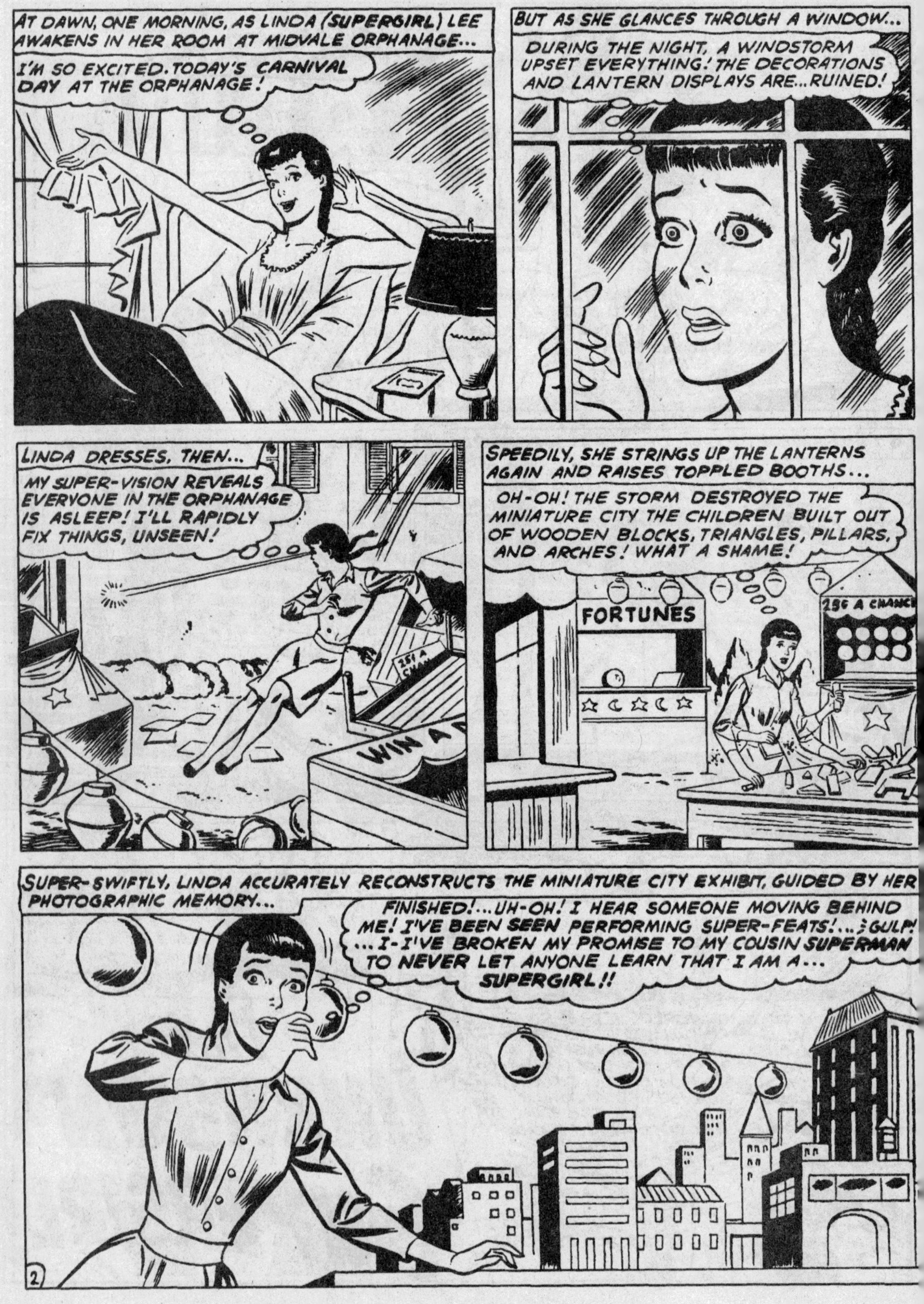
AT DAWN, ONE MORNING, AS LINDA (SUPERGIRL) LEE AWAKENS IN HER ROOM AT MIDVALE ORPHANAGE...
I'M SO EXCITED. TODAY'S CARNIVAL DAY AT THE ORPHANAGE!
BUT AS SHE GLANCES THROUGH A WINDOW...
DURING THE NIGHT, A WINDSTORM UPSET EVERYTHING! THE DECORATIONS AND LANTERN DISPLAYS ARE...RUINED!
LINDA DRESSES, THEN...
MY SUPER-VISION REVEALS EVERYONE IN THE ORPHANAGE IS ASLEEP! I'LL RAPIDLY FIX THINGS, UNSEEN!
WIN A
SPEEDILY, SHE STRINGS UP THE LANTERNS AGAIN AND RAISES TOPPLED BOOTHS...
OH-OH! THE STORM DESTROYED THE MINIATURE CITY THE CHILDREN BUILT OUT OF WOODEN BLOCKS, TRIANGLES, PILLARS, AND ARCHES! WHAT A SHAME!
FORTUNES
SUPER-SWIFTLY, LINDA ACCURATELY RECONSTRUCTS THE MINIATURE CITY EXHIBIT, GUIDED BY HER PHOTOGRAPHIC MEMORY...
FINISHED!...UH-OH! I HEAR SOMEONE MOVING BEHIND ME! I'VE BEEN SEEN PERFORMING SUPER-FEATS!...GULP! ...I-I'VE BROKEN MY PROMISE TO MY COUSIN SUPERMAN TO NEVER LET ANYONE LEARN THAT I AM A... SUPERGIRL!!

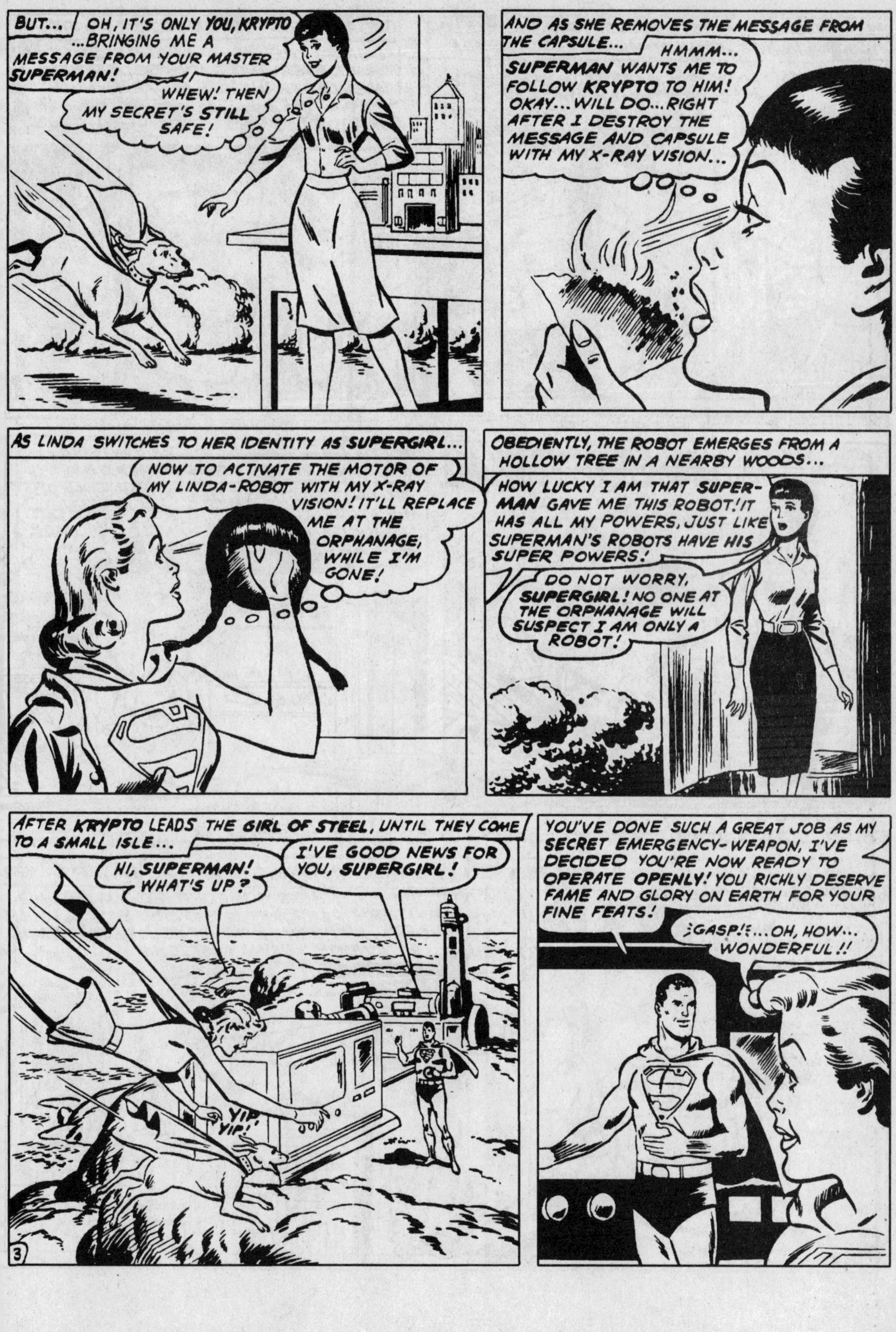
BUT...
OH, IT'S ONLY YOU, KRYPTO ...BRINGING ME A MESSAGE FROM YOUR MASTER SUPERMAN!
WHEW! THEN MY SECRET'S STILL SAFE!
AND AS SHE REMOVES THE MESSAGE FROM THE CAPSULE...
HMMM... SUPERMAN WANTS ME TO FOLLOW KRYPTO TO HIM! OKAY... WILL DO... RIGHT AFTER I DESTROY THE MESSAGE AND CAPSULE WITH MY X-RAY VISION...
AS LINDA SWITCHES TO HER IDENTITY AS SUPERGIRL...
NOW TO ACTIVATE THE MOTOR OF MY LINDA-ROBOT WITH MY X-RAY VISION! IT'LL REPLACE ME AT THE ORPHANAGE, WHILE I'M GONE!
OBEDIENTLY, THE ROBOT EMERGES FROM A HOLLOW TREE IN A NEARBY WOODS...
HOW LUCKY I AM THAT SUPERMAN GAVE ME THIS ROBOT! IT HAS ALL MY POWERS, JUST LIKE SUPERMAN'S ROBOTS HAVE HIS SUPER POWERS!
DO NOT WORRY, SUPERGIRL! NO ONE AT THE ORPHANAGE WILL SUSPECT I AM ONLY A ROBOT!
AFTER KRYPTO LEADS THE GIRL OF STEEL, UNTIL THEY COME TO A SMALL ISLE...
HI, SUPERMAN! WHAT'S UP?
I'VE GOOD NEWS FOR YOU, SUPERGIRL!
YIP, YIP!
3
YOU'VE DONE SUCH A GREAT JOB AS MY SECRET EMERGENCY-WEAPON, I'VE DECIDED YOU'RE NOW READY TO OPERATE OPENLY! YOU RICHLY DESERVE FAME AND GLORY ON EARTH FOR YOUR FINE FEATS!
GASP! ...OH, HOW... WONDERFUL!!

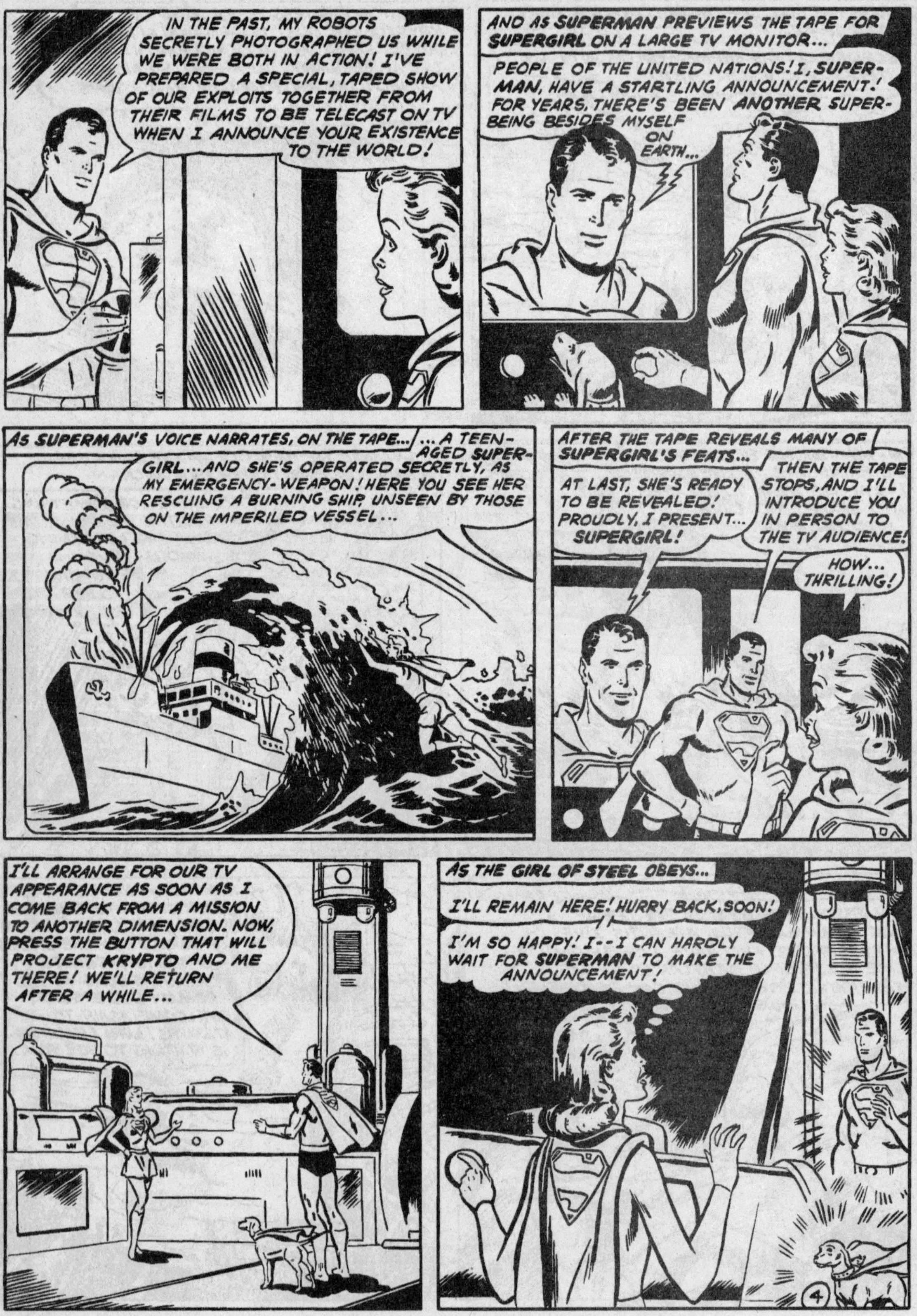
IN THE PAST, MY ROBOTS SECRETLY PHOTOGRAPHED US WHILE WE WERE BOTH IN ACTION! I'VE PREPARED A SPECIAL, TAPED SHOW OF OUR EXPLOITS TOGETHER FROM THEIR FILMS TO BE TELECAST ON TV WHEN I ANNOUNCE YOUR EXISTENCE TO THE WORLD!
AND AS SUPERMAN PREVIEWS THE TAPE FOR SUPERGIRL ON A LARGE TV MONITOR...
PEOPLE OF THE UNITED NATIONS! I, SUPERMAN, HAVE A STARTLING ANNOUNCEMENT! FOR YEARS, THERE'S BEEN ANOTHER SUPER-BEING BESIDES MYSELF ON EARTH...
AS SUPERMAN'S VOICE NARRATES, ON THE TAPE...
... A TEEN-AGED SUPER-GIRL... AND SHE'S OPERATED SECRETLY, AS MY EMERGENCY-WEAPON! HERE YOU SEE HER RESCUING A BURNING SHIP, UNSEEN BY THOSE ON THE IMPERILED VESSEL...
AFTER THE TAPE REVEALS MANY OF SUPERGIRL'S FEATS...
AT LAST, SHE'S READY TO BE REVEALED! PROUDLY, I PRESENT... SUPERGIRL!
THEN THE TAPE STOPS, AND I'LL INTRODUCE YOU IN PERSON TO THE TV AUDIENCE!
HOW... THRILLING!
I'LL ARRANGE FOR OUR TV APPEARANCE AS SOON AS I COME BACK FROM A MISSION TO ANOTHER DIMENSION. NOW, PRESS THE BUTTON THAT WILL PROJECT KRYPTO AND ME THERE! WE'LL RETURN AFTER A WHILE...
AS THE GIRL OF STEEL OBEYS...
I'LL REMAIN HERE! HURRY BACK, SOON!
I'M SO HAPPY! I--I CAN HARDLY WAIT FOR SUPERMAN TO MAKE THE ANNOUNCEMENT!
4

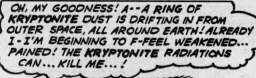

TO PASS THE TIME, SUPERGIRL LOOKS TOWARD OUTER SPACE...

I'LL WATCH SOME UNUSUAL SCENES ON THE OTHER WORLDS WITH MY TELESCOPIC VISION...ULP!!

OH, MY GOODNESS! A--A RING OF KRYPTONITE DUST IS DRIFTING IN FROM OUTER SPACE, ALL AROUND EARTH! ALREADY I-I'M BEGINNING TO F-FEEL WEAKENED... PAINED! THE KRYPTONITE RADIATIONS CAN...KILL ME...!

M-MY VISION'S BLURRING! THE PAINS ARE...INCREASING! I-I'M TOO WEAK TO ESCAPE INTO SPACE! I'LL DIVE INTO THE SEA...

DOWN INTO THE BRINY DEEP SHE SINKS, THEN ARMS SUDDENLY SEIZE HER AND...

SOMEONE...OR SOMETHING... IS PULLING ME DOWN! THE PAINS ARE LESSENING AND MY VISION IS B-BEGINNING TO... CLEAR...!

SHORTLY, SHE SEES...

MY RESCUER IS JERRO, THE TEEN-AGED MERMAN FROM ATLANTIS I'VE MET BEFORE, AND HAVE A CRUSH ON! LIKE ALL PEOPLE OF ATLANTIS, HE HAS TELEPATHIC POWERS AND CAN READ, AND TRANSMIT, THOUGHTS!

I LEARNED OF YOUR DANGER...

...WHILE MIND-READING YOUR THOUGHTS, SUPER-GIRL! YOU'LL BE OUT OF RANGE FROM THE EFFECTS OF THE KRYPTONITE RING, AS LONG AS YOU REMAIN UNDERSEAS! WELCOME AGAIN TO ATLANTIS! LORI LEMARIS IS WAITING TO SEE YOU...

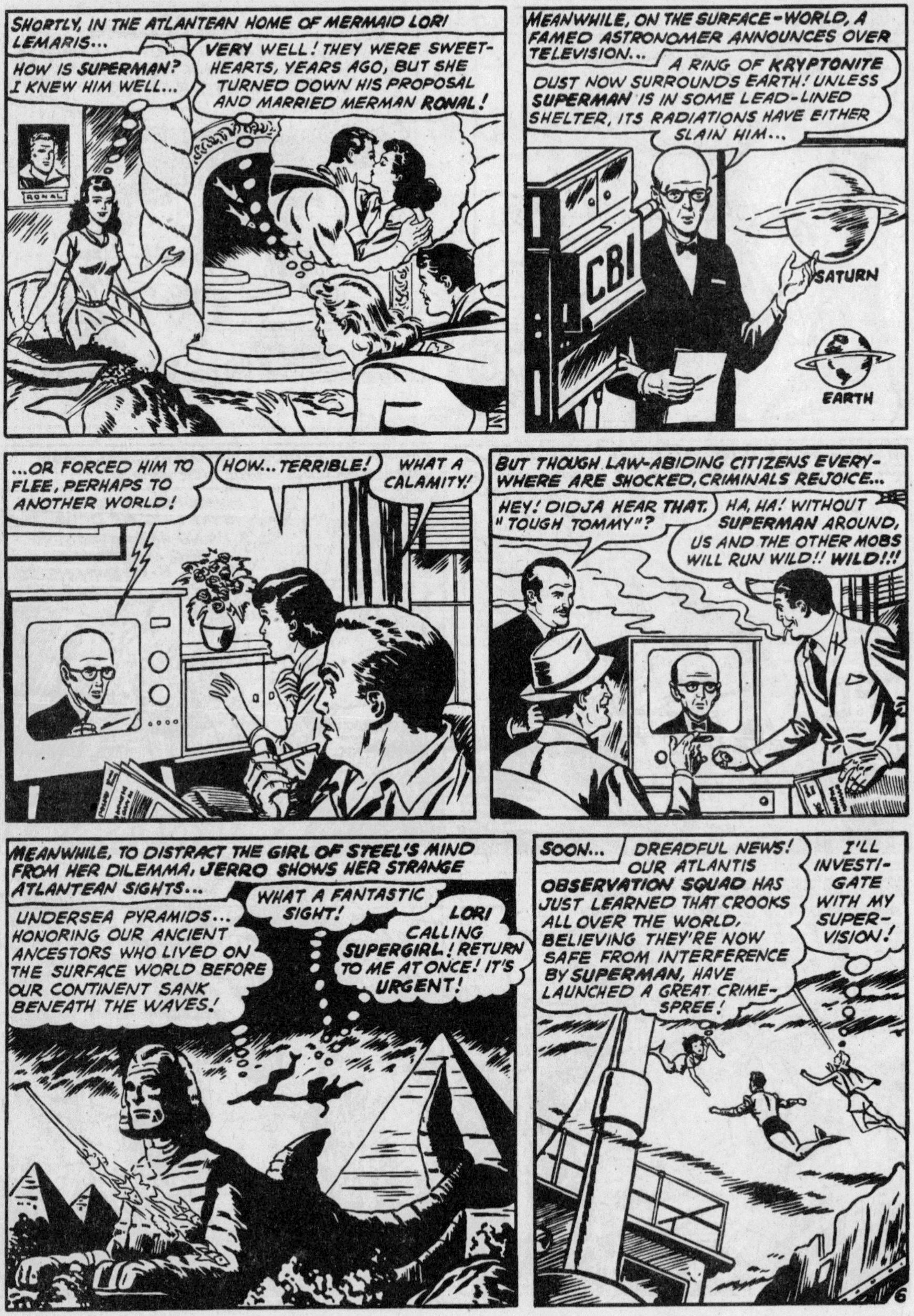
SHORTLY, IN THE ATLANTEAN HOME OF MERMAID LORI LEMARIS...
HOW IS SUPERMAN? I KNEW HIM WELL...
VERY WELL! THEY WERE SWEET-HEARTS, YEARS AGO, BUT SHE TURNED DOWN HIS PROPOSAL AND MARRIED MERMAN RONAL!
RONAL
MEANWHILE, ON THE SURFACE-WORLD, A FAMED ASTRONOMER ANNOUNCES OVER TELEVISION...
A RING OF KRYPTONITE DUST NOW SURROUNDS EARTH! UNLESS SUPERMAN IS IN SOME LEAD-LINED SHELTER, ITS RADIATIONS HAVE EITHER SLAIN HIM...
CBI
SATURN
EARTH
...OR FORCED HIM TO FLEE, PERHAPS TO ANOTHER WORLD!
HOW... TERRIBLE!
WHAT A CALAMITY!
BUT THOUGH LAW-ABIDING CITIZENS EVERY-WHERE ARE SHOCKED, CRIMINALS REJOICE...
HEY! DIDJA HEAR THAT, "TOUGH TOMMY"?
HA, HA! WITHOUT SUPERMAN AROUND, US AND THE OTHER MOBS WILL RUN WILD!! WILD!!!
MEANWHILE, TO DISTRACT THE GIRL OF STEEL'S MIND FROM HER DILEMMA, JERRO SHOWS HER STRANGE ATLANTEAN SIGHTS...
UNDERSEA PYRAMIDS... HONORING OUR ANCIENT ANCESTORS WHO LIVED ON THE SURFACE WORLD BEFORE OUR CONTINENT SANK BENEATH THE WAVES!
WHAT A FANTASTIC SIGHT!
LORI CALLING SUPERGIRL! RETURN TO ME AT ONCE! IT'S URGENT!
SOON...
DREADFUL NEWS! OUR ATLANTIS OBSERVATION SQUAD HAS JUST LEARNED THAT CROOKS ALL OVER THE WORLD, BELIEVING THEY'RE NOW SAFE FROM INTERFERENCE BY SUPERMAN, HAVE LAUNCHED A GREAT CRIME-SPREE!
I'LL INVESTI-GATE WITH MY SUPER-VISION!
6

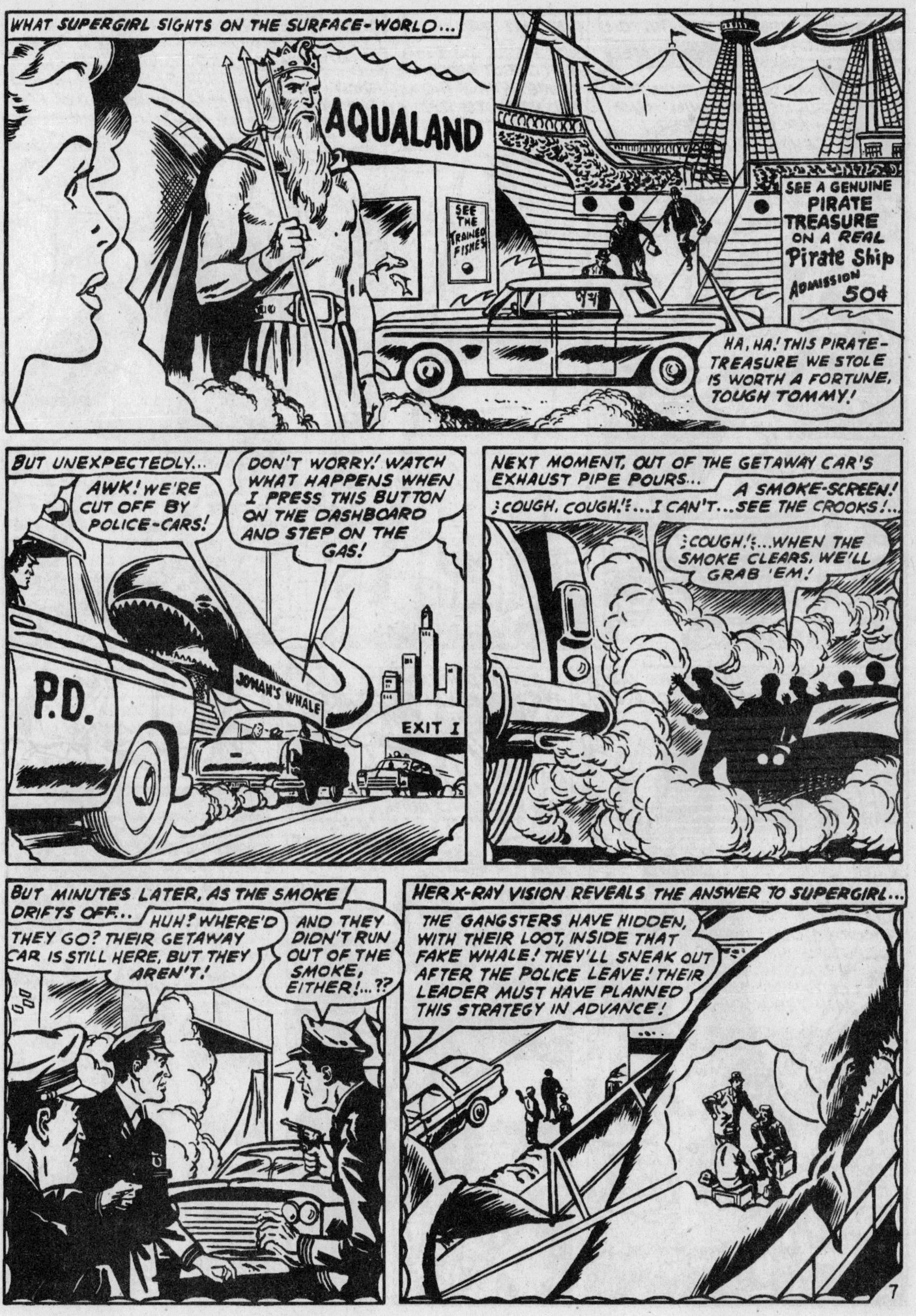
WHAT SUPERGIRL SIGHTS ON THE SURFACE-WORLD...
AQUALAND
SEE THE TRAINED FISHES
SEE A GENUINE PIRATE TREASURE ON A REAL Pirate Ship ADMISSION 50¢
HA, HA! THIS PIRATE-TREASURE WE STOLE IS WORTH A FORTUNE, TOUGH TOMMY!
BUT UNEXPECTEDLY...
AWK! WE'RE CUT OFF BY POLICE-CARS!
DON'T WORRY! WATCH WHAT HAPPENS WHEN I PRESS THIS BUTTON ON THE DASHBOARD AND STEP ON THE GAS!
P.D.
JONAH'S WHALE
EXIT 1
NEXT MOMENT, OUT OF THE GETAWAY CAR'S EXHAUST PIPE POURS...
A SMOKE-SCREEN!
¡COUGH, COUGH!!...I CAN'T...SEE THE CROOKS!...
¡COUGH!!...WHEN THE SMOKE CLEARS, WE'LL GRAB 'EM!
BUT MINUTES LATER, AS THE SMOKE DRIFTS OFF...
HUH! WHERE'D THEY GO? THEIR GETAWAY CAR IS STILL HERE, BUT THEY AREN'T!
AND THEY DIDN'T RUN OUT OF THE SMOKE, EITHER!...??
HER X-RAY VISION REVEALS THE ANSWER TO SUPERGIRL...
THE GANGSTERS HAVE HIDDEN, WITH THEIR LOOT, INSIDE THAT FAKE WHALE! THEY'LL SNEAK OUT AFTER THE POLICE LEAVE! THEIR LEADER MUST HAVE PLANNED THIS STRATEGY IN ADVANCE!
7

A MOMENT LATER, AT THE BOTTOM OF THE OCEAN...

THE LUMBER FROM THIS SUNKEN SHIP WILL MAKE A SPLENDID SUPER FISHING-POLE! THE ANCHOR, AND THESE ANCHOR-CHAINS, WILL COME IN HANDY, TOO!

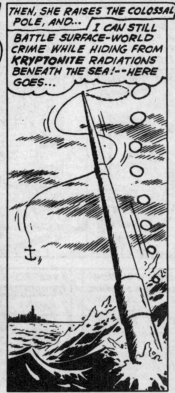

THEN, SHE RAISES THE COLOSSAL POLE, AND...

I CAN STILL BATTLE SURFACE-WORLD CRIME WHILE HIDING FROM KRYPTONITE RADIATIONS BENEATH THE SEA!--HERE GOES...

SHORTLY...

¡GASP!¿ THAT ANCHOR "HOOK," ATTACHED TO THE HUGE, CHAIN-LINK "FISHING-LINE," FLASHED DOWN AND SNAGGED THE FAKE WHALE'S MOUTH!

WHAT'S GOING ON HERE?!!

AS THE DISTANT SUPERGIRL YANKS ON THE TITANIC FISHING POLE...

YAA-AAA!

SO THAT'S WHERE YOU CROOKS HID!

HELP!

RAISE THOSE HANDS!

I GET IT! SUPERMAN'S ALIVE AND HIDING UNDER THE OCEAN TO ESCAPE THE KRYPTONITE RING'S RADIATIONS!

THOUGH TRAPPED UNDER THE SEA, HE'S USING HIS WITS AND SUPER-POWERS TO FIGHT CRIME! SWELL!

BAH!

MEANWHILE, IN ATLANTIS...

THEY'VE MISTAKEN ME FOR SUPERMAN! UH-OH! MY SUPER-VISION DISCLOSES ANOTHER JOB FOR... SUPERGIRL!

8

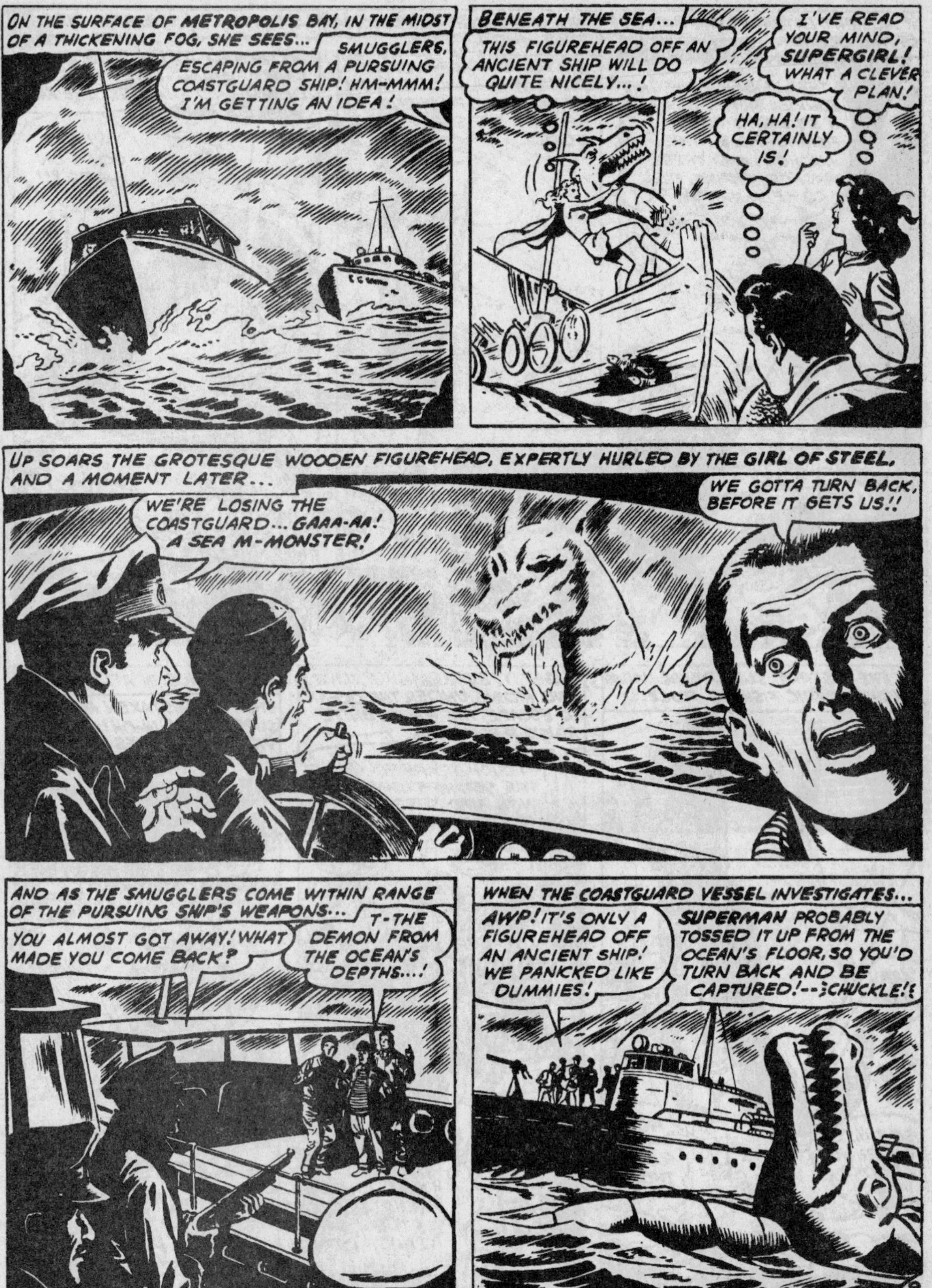
ON THE SURFACE OF METROPOLIS BAY, IN THE MIDST OF A THICKENING FOG, SHE SEES...
SMUGGLERS, ESCAPING FROM A PURSUING COASTGUARD SHIP! HM-MMM! I'M GETTING AN IDEA!
BENEATH THE SEA...
THIS FIGUREHEAD OFF AN ANCIENT SHIP WILL DO QUITE NICELY...!
I'VE READ YOUR MIND, SUPERGIRL! WHAT A CLEVER PLAN!
HA, HA! IT CERTAINLY IS!
UP SOARS THE GROTESQUE WOODEN FIGUREHEAD, EXPERTLY HURLED BY THE GIRL OF STEEL, AND A MOMENT LATER...
WE'RE LOSING THE COASTGUARD... GAAA-AA! A SEA M-MONSTER!
WE GOTTA TURN BACK, BEFORE IT GETS US!!
AND AS THE SMUGGLERS COME WITHIN RANGE OF THE PURSUING SHIP'S WEAPONS...
YOU ALMOST GOT AWAY! WHAT MADE YOU COME BACK?
T-THE DEMON FROM THE OCEAN'S DEPTHS...!
WHEN THE COASTGUARD VESSEL INVESTIGATES...
AWP! IT'S ONLY A FIGUREHEAD OFF AN ANCIENT SHIP! WE PANICKED LIKE DUMMIES!
SUPERMAN PROBABLY TOSSED IT UP FROM THE OCEAN'S FLOOR, SO YOU'D TURN BACK AND BE CAPTURED!--CHUCKLE!
9

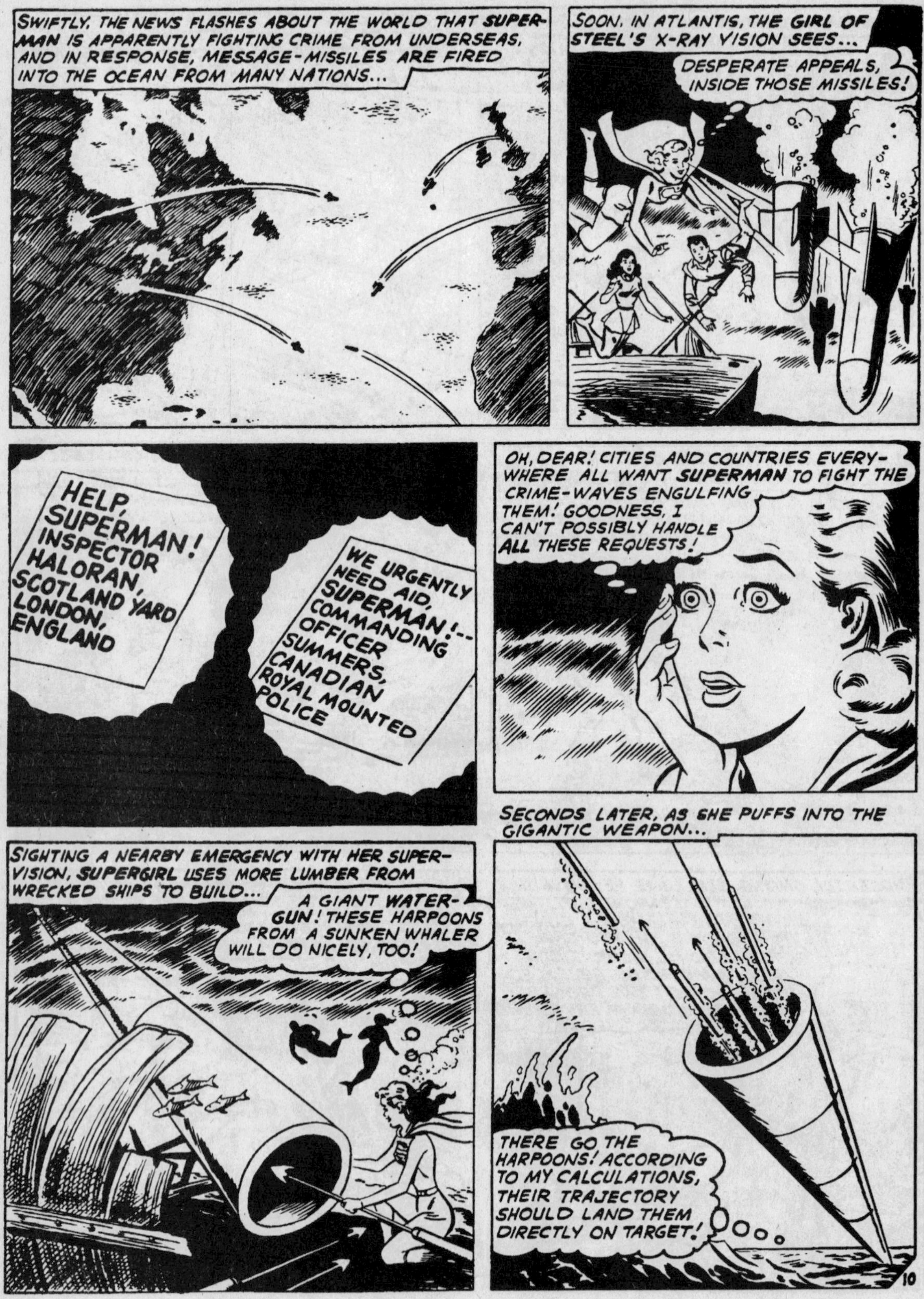
SWIFTLY, THE NEWS FLASHES ABOUT THE WORLD THAT SUPERMAN IS APPARENTLY FIGHTING CRIME FROM UNDERSEAS, AND IN RESPONSE, MESSAGE-MISSILES ARE FIRED INTO THE OCEAN FROM MANY NATIONS...
SOON, IN ATLANTIS, THE GIRL OF STEEL'S X-RAY VISION SEES...
DESPERATE APPEALS, INSIDE THOSE MISSILES!
HELP, SUPERMAN! INSPECTOR HALORAN, SCOTLAND YARD LONDON, ENGLAND
WE URGENTLY NEED AID, SUPERMAN!-- COMMANDING OFFICER SUMMERS, CANADIAN ROYAL MOUNTED POLICE
OH, DEAR! CITIES AND COUNTRIES EVERYWHERE ALL WANT SUPERMAN TO FIGHT THE CRIME-WAVES ENGULFING THEM! GOODNESS, I CAN'T POSSIBLY HANDLE ALL THESE REQUESTS!
SIGHTING A NEARBY EMERGENCY WITH HER SUPER-VISION, SUPERGIRL USES MORE LUMBER FROM WRECKED SHIPS TO BUILD...
A GIANT WATER-GUN! THESE HARPOONS FROM A SUNKEN WHALER WILL DO NICELY, TOO!
SECONDS LATER, AS SHE PUFFS INTO THE GIGANTIC WEAPON...
THERE GO THE HARPOONS! ACCORDING TO MY CALCULATIONS, THEIR TRAJECTORY SHOULD LAND THEM DIRECTLY ON TARGET!
10

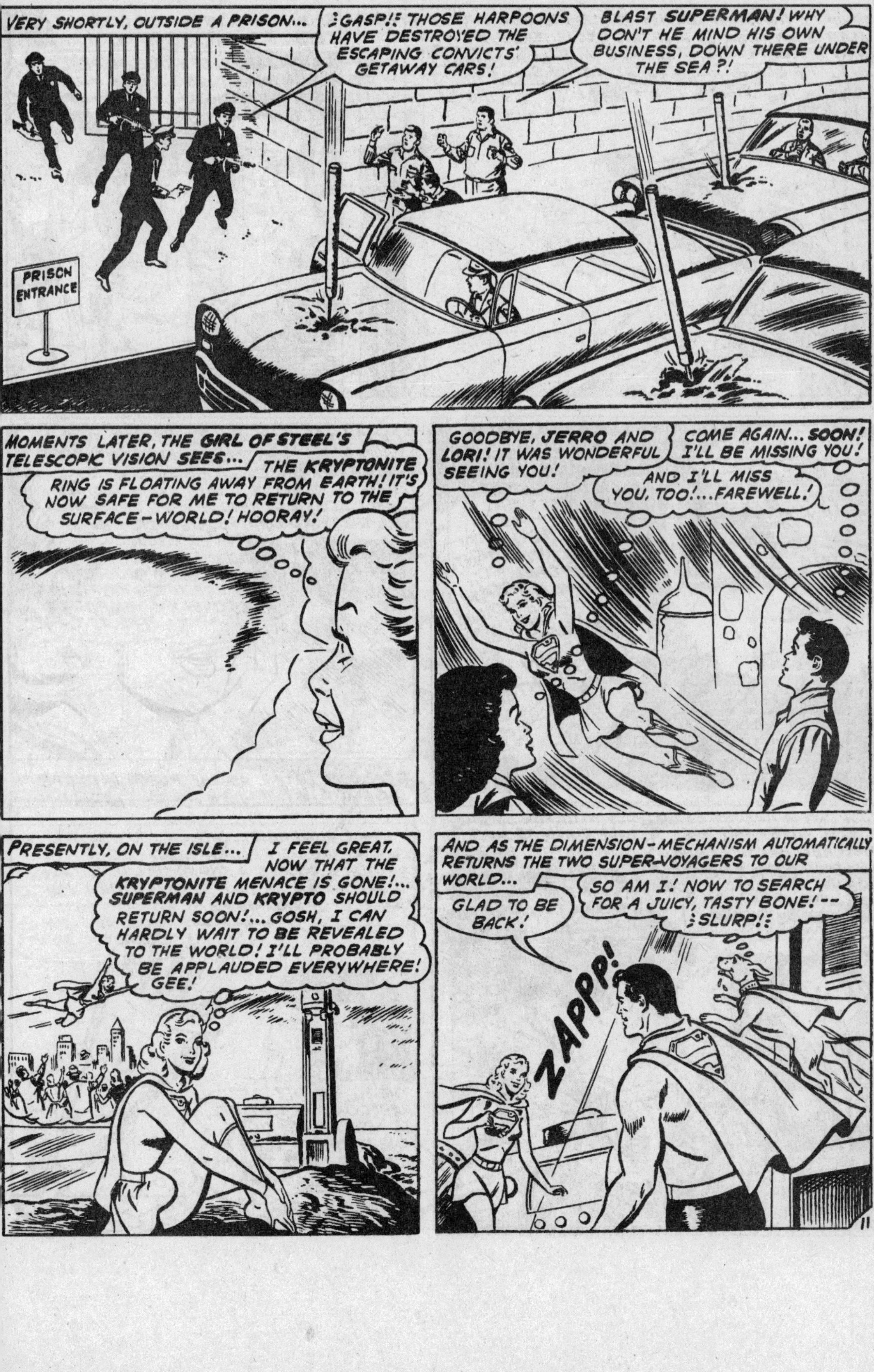
VERY SHORTLY, OUTSIDE A PRISON...
¡GASP!¡ THOSE HARPOONS HAVE DESTROYED THE ESCAPING CONVICTS' GETAWAY CARS!
BLAST SUPERMAN! WHY DON'T HE MIND HIS OWN BUSINESS, DOWN THERE UNDER THE SEA ?!
PRISON ENTRANCE
MOMENTS LATER, THE GIRL OF STEEL'S TELESCOPIC VISION SEES...
THE KRYPTONITE RING IS FLOATING AWAY FROM EARTH! IT'S NOW SAFE FOR ME TO RETURN TO THE SURFACE-WORLD! HOORAY!
GOODBYE, JERRO AND LORI! IT WAS WONDERFUL SEEING YOU!
COME AGAIN... SOON! I'LL BE MISSING YOU!
AND I'LL MISS YOU, TOO!... FAREWELL!
PRESENTLY, ON THE ISLE...
I FEEL GREAT, NOW THAT THE KRYPTONITE MENACE IS GONE!... SUPERMAN AND KRYPTO SHOULD RETURN SOON!... GOSH, I CAN HARDLY WAIT TO BE REVEALED TO THE WORLD! I'LL PROBABLY BE APPLAUDED EVERYWHERE! GEE!
AND AS THE DIMENSION-MECHANISM AUTOMATICALLY RETURNS THE TWO SUPER-VOYAGERS TO OUR WORLD...
GLAD TO BE BACK!
SO AM I! NOW TO SEARCH FOR A JUICY, TASTY BONE! -- ¡SLURP!¡
ZAPPP!
11

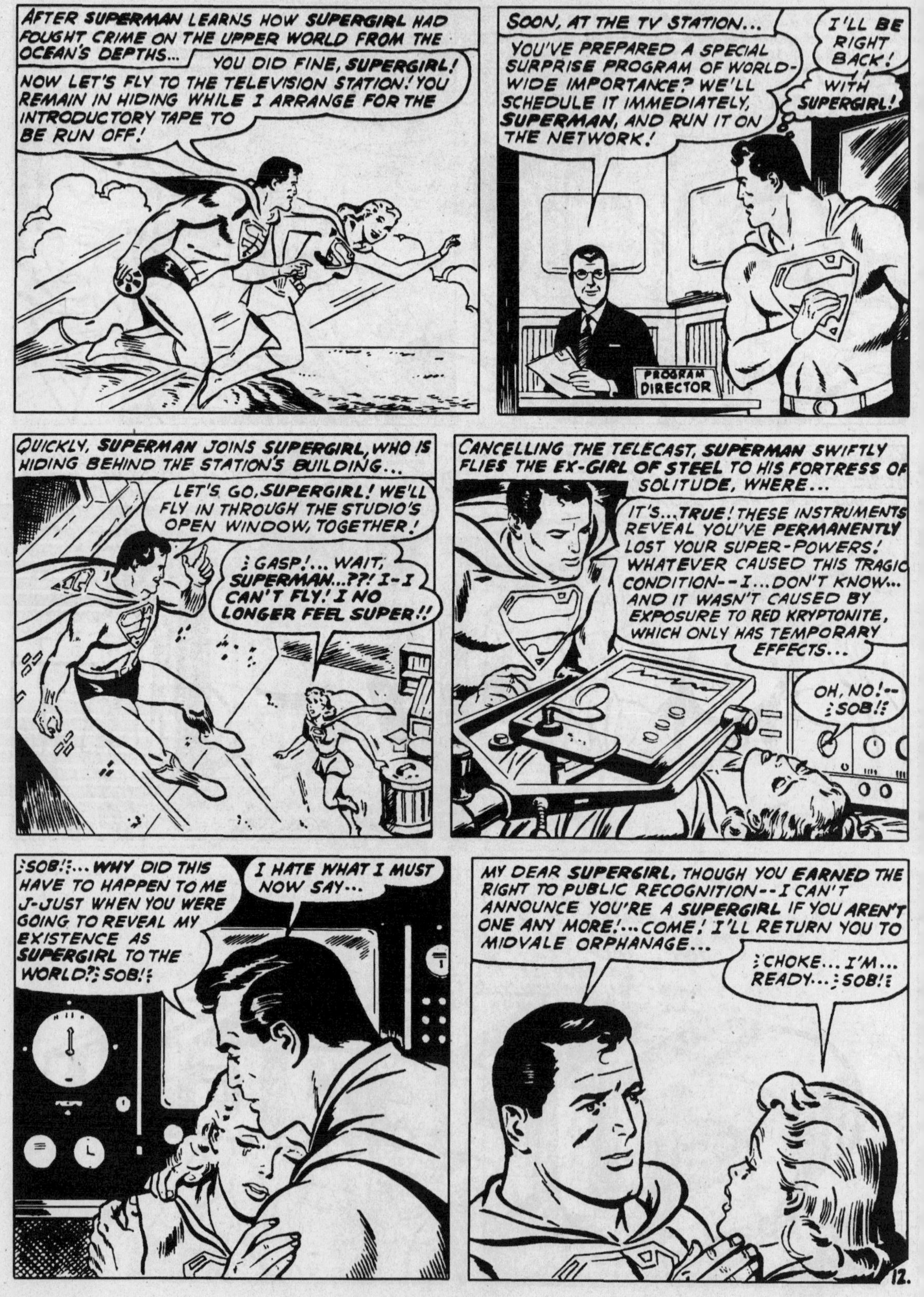
AFTER SUPERMAN LEARNS HOW SUPERGIRL HAD FOUGHT CRIME ON THE UPPER WORLD FROM THE OCEAN'S DEPTHS...
YOU DID FINE, SUPERGIRL! NOW LET'S FLY TO THE TELEVISION STATION! YOU REMAIN IN HIDING WHILE I ARRANGE FOR THE INTRODUCTORY TAPE TO BE RUN OFF!
SOON, AT THE TV STATION...
YOU'VE PREPARED A SPECIAL SURPRISE PROGRAM OF WORLD-WIDE IMPORTANCE? WE'LL SCHEDULE IT IMMEDIATELY, SUPERMAN, AND RUN IT ON THE NETWORK!
I'LL BE RIGHT BACK! WITH SUPERGIRL!
PROGRAM DIRECTOR
QUICKLY, SUPERMAN JOINS SUPERGIRL, WHO IS HIDING BEHIND THE STATION'S BUILDING...
LET'S GO, SUPERGIRL! WE'LL FLY IN THROUGH THE STUDIO'S OPEN WINDOW, TOGETHER!
:GASP!... WAIT, SUPERMAN...??! I-I CAN'T FLY! I NO LONGER FEEL SUPER!!
CANCELLING THE TELECAST, SUPERMAN SWIFTLY FLIES THE EX-GIRL OF STEEL TO HIS FORTRESS OF SOLITUDE, WHERE...
IT'S...TRUE! THESE INSTRUMENTS REVEAL YOU'VE PERMANENTLY LOST YOUR SUPER-POWERS! WHATEVER CAUSED THIS TRAGIC CONDITION--I...DON'T KNOW... AND IT WASN'T CAUSED BY EXPOSURE TO RED KRYPTONITE, WHICH ONLY HAS TEMPORARY EFFECTS...
OH, NO!-- :SOB!:
:SOB!:... WHY DID THIS HAVE TO HAPPEN TO ME J-JUST WHEN YOU WERE GOING TO REVEAL MY EXISTENCE AS SUPERGIRL TO THE WORLD?:SOB!:
I HATE WHAT I MUST NOW SAY...
MY DEAR SUPERGIRL, THOUGH YOU EARNED THE RIGHT TO PUBLIC RECOGNITION--I CAN'T ANNOUNCE YOU'RE A SUPERGIRL IF YOU AREN'T ONE ANY MORE!...COME! I'LL RETURN YOU TO MIDVALE ORPHANAGE...
:CHOKE... I'M... READY...:SOB!:
12.

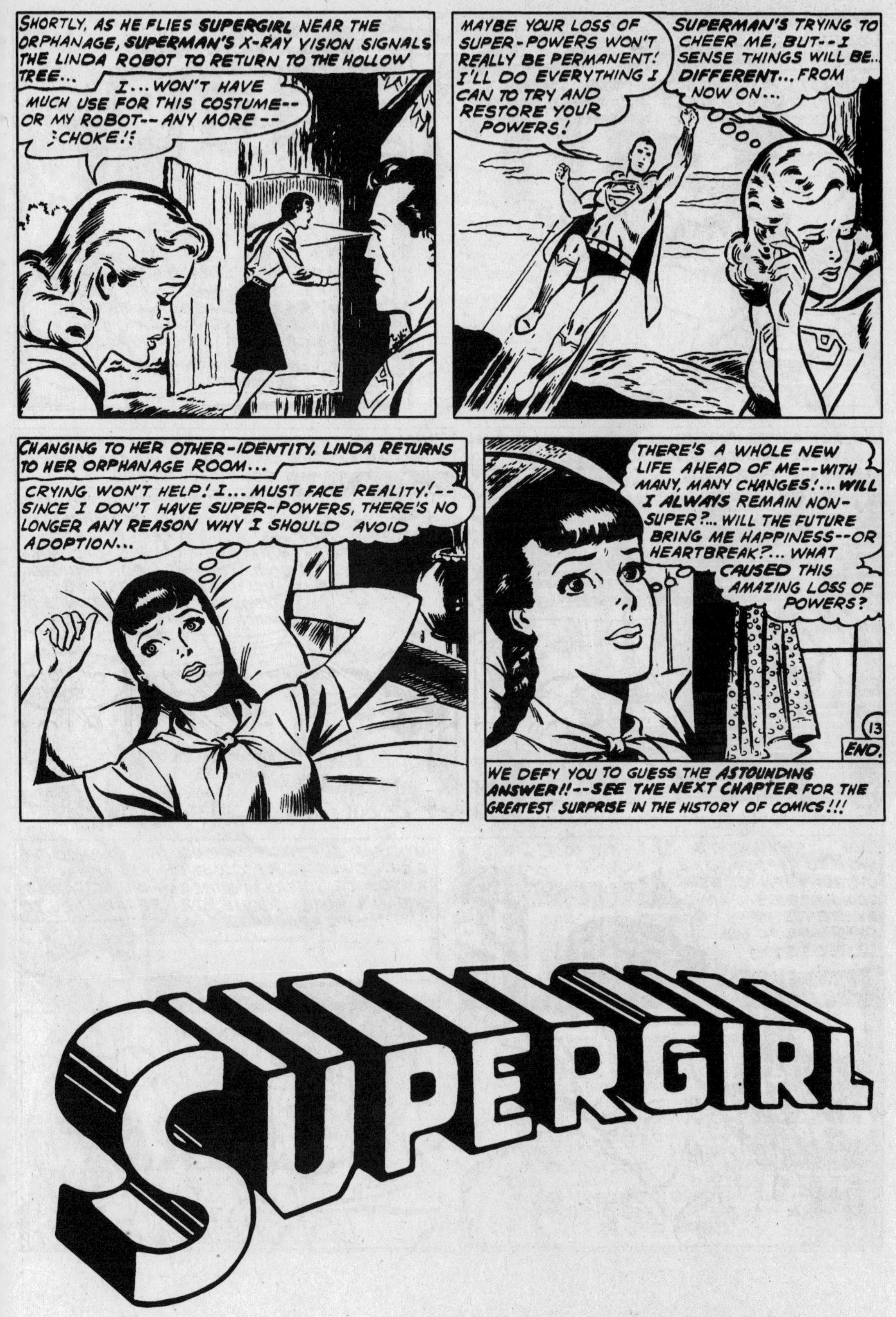
SHORTLY, AS HE FLIES SUPERGIRL NEAR THE ORPHANAGE, SUPERMAN'S X-RAY VISION SIGNALS THE LINDA ROBOT TO RETURN TO THE HOLLOW TREE...
I... WON'T HAVE MUCH USE FOR THIS COSTUME-- OR MY ROBOT-- ANY MORE -- ;CHOKE!;
MAYBE YOUR LOSS OF SUPER-POWERS WON'T REALLY BE PERMANENT! I'LL DO EVERYTHING I CAN TO TRY AND RESTORE YOUR POWERS!
SUPERMAN'S TRYING TO CHEER ME, BUT--I SENSE THINGS WILL BE... DIFFERENT... FROM NOW ON...
CHANGING TO HER OTHER-IDENTITY, LINDA RETURNS TO HER ORPHANAGE ROOM...
CRYING WON'T HELP! I... MUST FACE REALITY!-- SINCE I DON'T HAVE SUPER-POWERS, THERE'S NO LONGER ANY REASON WHY I SHOULD AVOID ADOPTION...
THERE'S A WHOLE NEW LIFE AHEAD OF ME--WITH MANY, MANY CHANGES!... WILL I ALWAYS REMAIN NON-SUPER?... WILL THE FUTURE BRING ME HAPPINESS--OR HEARTBREAK?... WHAT CAUSED THIS AMAZING LOSS OF POWERS?
13
END.
WE DEFY YOU TO GUESS THE ASTOUNDING ANSWER!!--SEE THE NEXT CHAPTER FOR THE GREATEST SURPRISE IN THE HISTORY OF COMICS!!!

SUPERGIRL

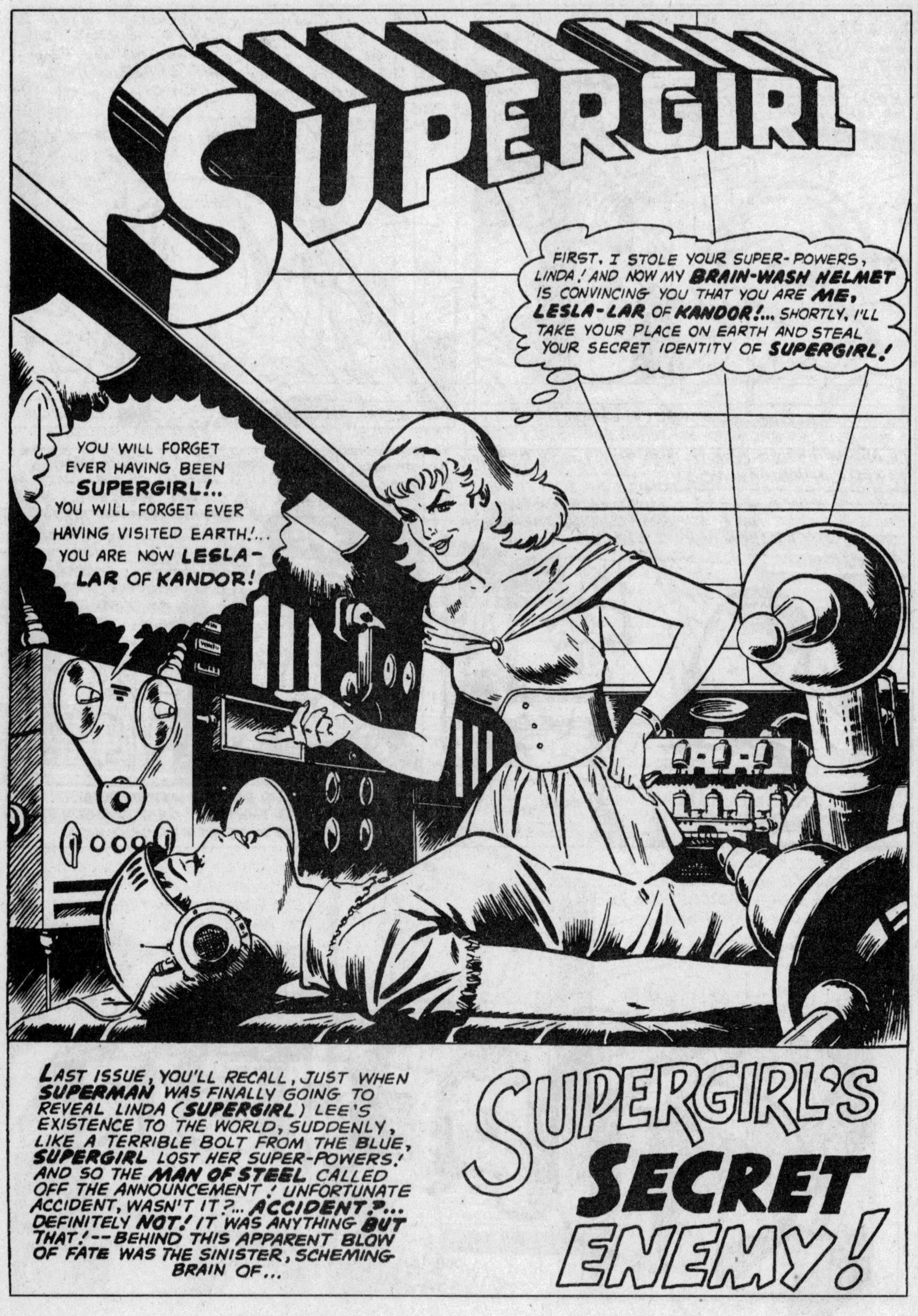
SUPERGIRL
FIRST, I STOLE YOUR SUPER-POWERS, LINDA! AND NOW MY BRAIN-WASH HELMET IS CONVINCING YOU THAT YOU ARE ME, LESLA-LAR OF KANDOR!... SHORTLY, I'LL TAKE YOUR PLACE ON EARTH AND STEAL YOUR SECRET IDENTITY OF SUPERGIRL!
YOU WILL FORGET EVER HAVING BEEN SUPERGIRL!.. YOU WILL FORGET EVER HAVING VISITED EARTH!... YOU ARE NOW LESLA-LAR OF KANDOR!
LAST ISSUE, YOU'LL RECALL, JUST WHEN SUPERMAN WAS FINALLY GOING TO REVEAL LINDA (SUPERGIRL) LEE'S EXISTENCE TO THE WORLD, SUDDENLY, LIKE A TERRIBLE BOLT FROM THE BLUE, SUPERGIRL LOST HER SUPER-POWERS! AND SO THE MAN OF STEEL CALLED OFF THE ANNOUNCEMENT! UNFORTUNATE ACCIDENT, WASN'T IT?... ACCIDENT?... DEFINITELY NOT! IT WAS ANYTHING BUT THAT!--BEHIND THIS APPARENT BLOW OF FATE WAS THE SINISTER, SCHEMING BRAIN OF...
SUPERGIRL'S SECRET ENEMY!

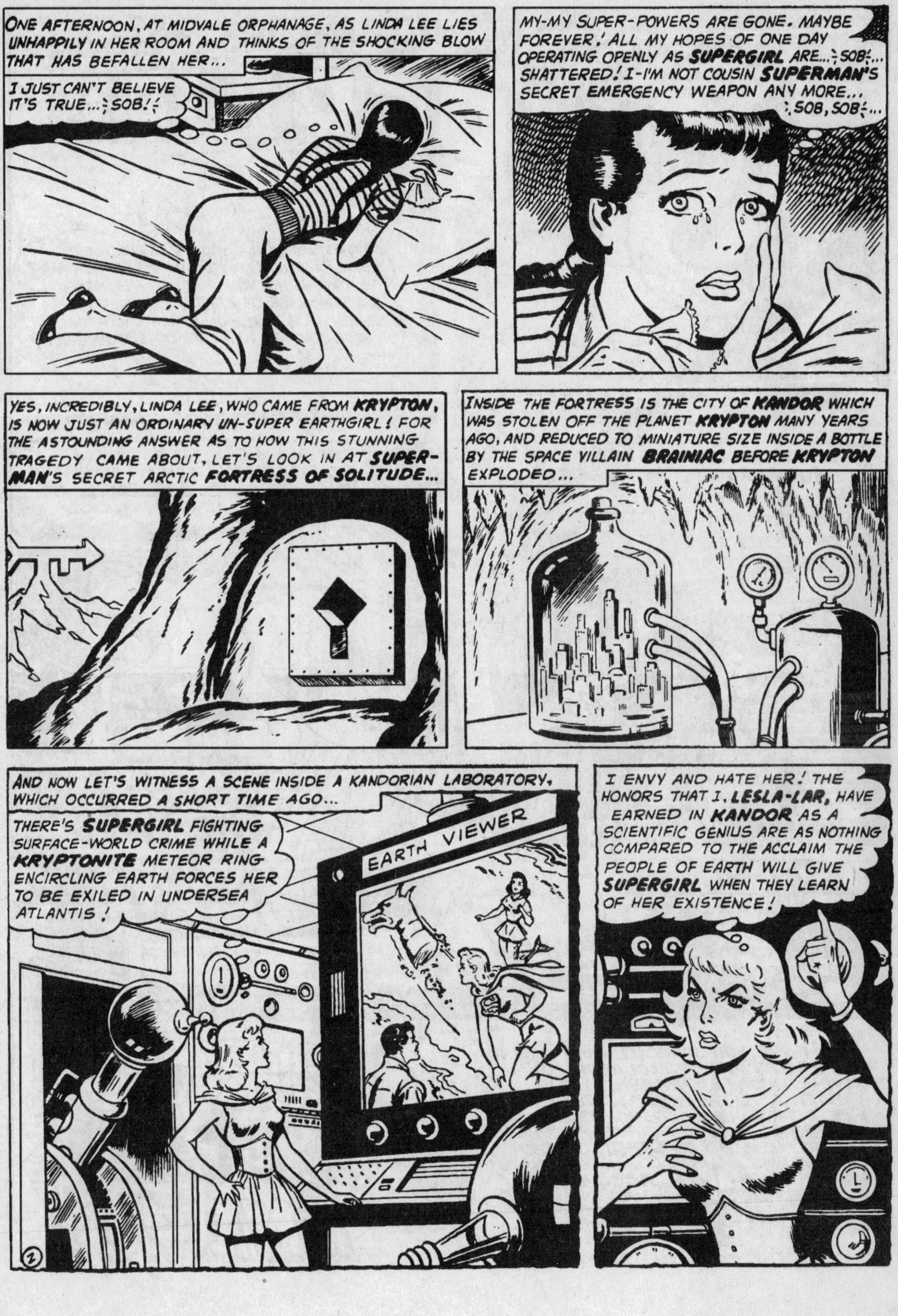
ONE AFTERNOON, AT MIDVALE ORPHANAGE, AS LINDA LEE LIES UNHAPPILY IN HER ROOM AND THINKS OF THE SHOCKING BLOW THAT HAS BEFALLEN HER...
I JUST CAN'T BELIEVE IT'S TRUE... SOB!
MY-MY SUPER-POWERS ARE GONE. MAYBE FOREVER! ALL MY HOPES OF ONE DAY OPERATING OPENLY AS SUPERGIRL ARE... SOB!... SHATTERED! I-I'M NOT COUSIN SUPERMAN'S SECRET EMERGENCY WEAPON ANY MORE... SOB, SOB...
YES, INCREDIBLY, LINDA LEE, WHO CAME FROM KRYPTON, IS NOW JUST AN ORDINARY UN-SUPER EARTHGIRL! FOR THE ASTOUNDING ANSWER AS TO HOW THIS STUNNING TRAGEDY CAME ABOUT, LET'S LOOK IN AT SUPERMAN'S SECRET ARCTIC FORTRESS OF SOLITUDE...
INSIDE THE FORTRESS IS THE CITY OF KANDOR WHICH WAS STOLEN OFF THE PLANET KRYPTON MANY YEARS AGO, AND REDUCED TO MINIATURE SIZE INSIDE A BOTTLE BY THE SPACE VILLAIN BRAINIAC BEFORE KRYPTON EXPLODED...
AND NOW LET'S WITNESS A SCENE INSIDE A KANDORIAN LABORATORY, WHICH OCCURRED A SHORT TIME AGO...
THERE'S SUPERGIRL FIGHTING SURFACE-WORLD CRIME WHILE A KRYPTONITE METEOR RING ENCIRCLING EARTH FORCES HER TO BE EXILED IN UNDERSEA ATLANTIS!
EARTH VIEWER
2
I ENVY AND HATE HER! THE HONORS THAT I, LESLA-LAR, HAVE EARNED IN KANDOR AS A SCIENTIFIC GENIUS ARE AS NOTHING COMPARED TO THE ACCLAIM THE PEOPLE OF EARTH WILL GIVE SUPERGIRL WHEN THEY LEARN OF HER EXISTENCE!

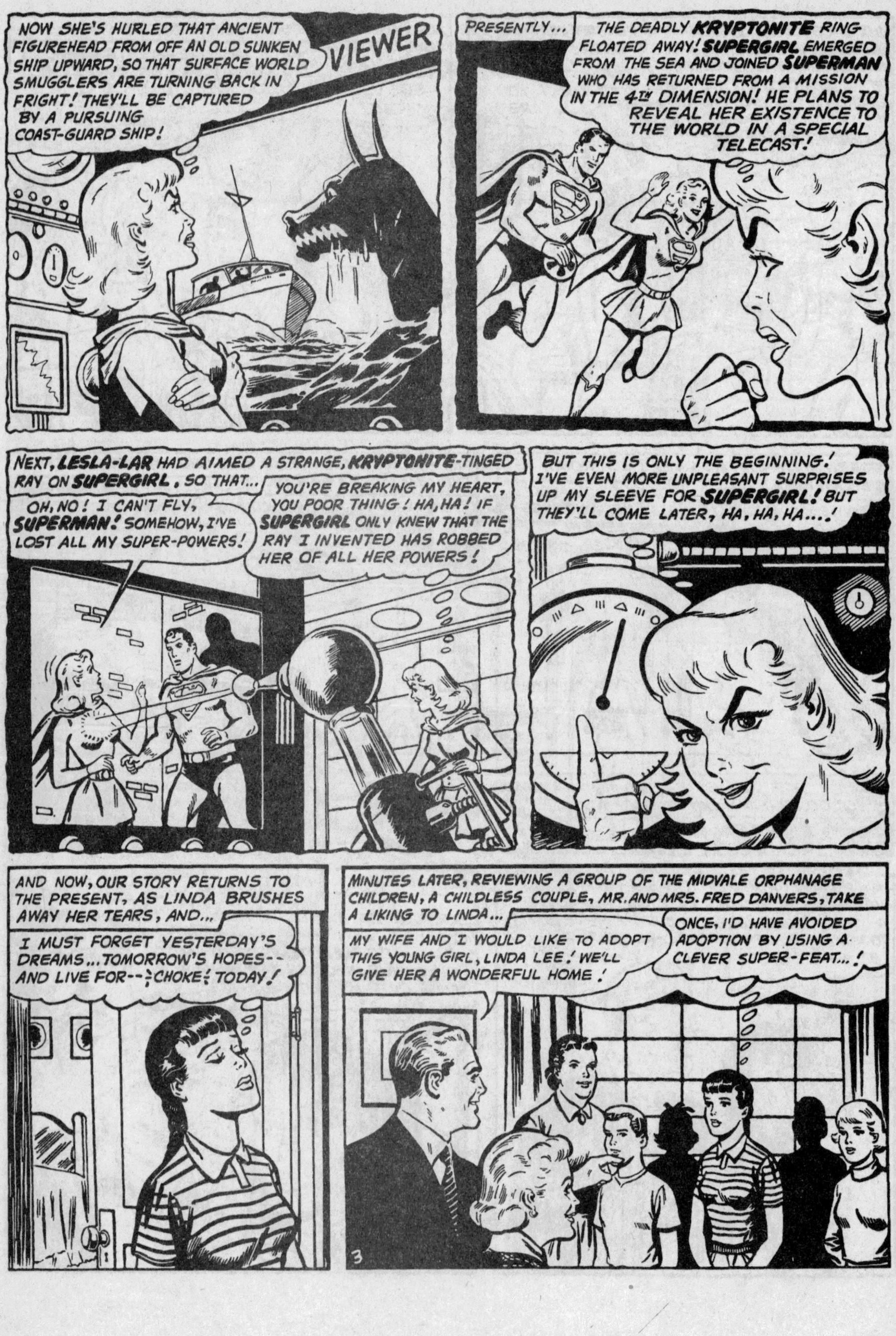
NOW SHE'S HURLED THAT ANCIENT FIGUREHEAD FROM OFF AN OLD SUNKEN SHIP UPWARD, SO THAT SURFACE WORLD SMUGGLERS ARE TURNING BACK IN FRIGHT! THEY'LL BE CAPTURED BY A PURSUING COAST-GUARD SHIP!
VIEWER
PRESENTLY...
THE DEADLY KRYPTONITE RING FLOATED AWAY! SUPERGIRL EMERGED FROM THE SEA AND JOINED SUPERMAN WHO HAS RETURNED FROM A MISSION IN THE 4TH DIMENSION! HE PLANS TO REVEAL HER EXISTENCE TO THE WORLD IN A SPECIAL TELECAST!
NEXT, LESLA-LAR HAD AIMED A STRANGE, KRYPTONITE-TINGED RAY ON SUPERGIRL, SO THAT...
OH, NO! I CAN'T FLY, SUPERMAN! SOMEHOW, I'VE LOST ALL MY SUPER-POWERS!
YOU'RE BREAKING MY HEART, YOU POOR THING! HA, HA! IF SUPERGIRL ONLY KNEW THAT THE RAY I INVENTED HAS ROBBED HER OF ALL HER POWERS!
BUT THIS IS ONLY THE BEGINNING! I'VE EVEN MORE UNPLEASANT SURPRISES UP MY SLEEVE FOR SUPERGIRL! BUT THEY'LL COME LATER, HA, HA, HA....!
AND NOW, OUR STORY RETURNS TO THE PRESENT, AS LINDA BRUSHES AWAY HER TEARS, AND...
I MUST FORGET YESTERDAY'S DREAMS... TOMORROW'S HOPES-- AND LIVE FOR-- ¦CHOKE¦ TODAY!
MINUTES LATER, REVIEWING A GROUP OF THE MIDVALE ORPHANAGE CHILDREN, A CHILDLESS COUPLE, MR. AND MRS. FRED DANVERS, TAKE A LIKING TO LINDA...
MY WIFE AND I WOULD LIKE TO ADOPT THIS YOUNG GIRL, LINDA LEE! WE'LL GIVE HER A WONDERFUL HOME!
ONCE, I'D HAVE AVOIDED ADOPTION BY USING A CLEVER SUPER-FEAT...!
3

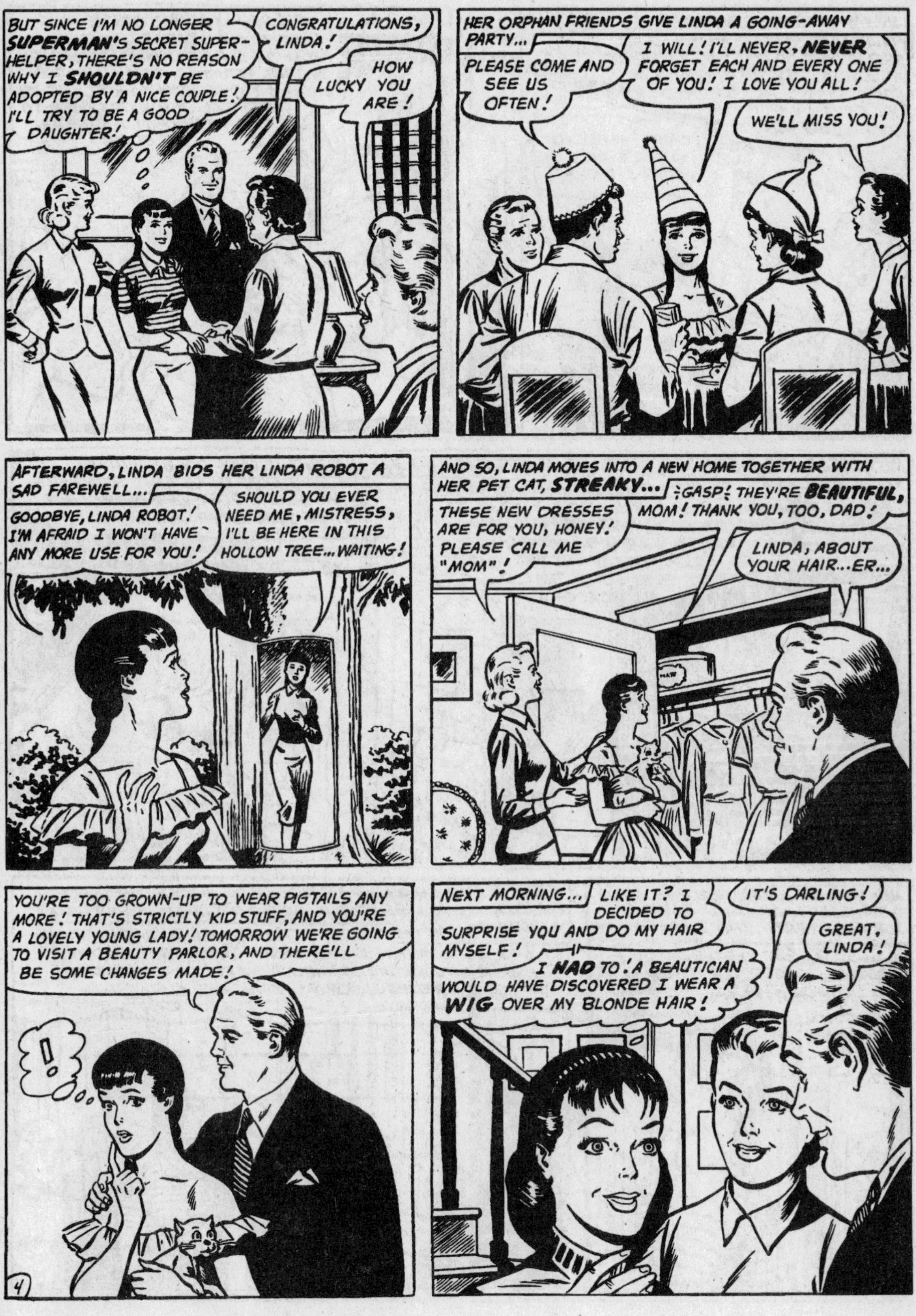
BUT SINCE I'M NO LONGER SUPERMAN'S SECRET SUPER-HELPER, THERE'S NO REASON WHY I SHOULDN'T BE ADOPTED BY A NICE COUPLE! I'LL TRY TO BE A GOOD DAUGHTER!
CONGRATULATIONS, LINDA!
HOW LUCKY YOU ARE!
HER ORPHAN FRIENDS GIVE LINDA A GOING-AWAY PARTY...
PLEASE COME AND SEE US OFTEN!
I WILL! I'LL NEVER, NEVER FORGET EACH AND EVERY ONE OF YOU! I LOVE YOU ALL!
WE'LL MISS YOU!
AFTERWARD, LINDA BIDS HER LINDA ROBOT A SAD FAREWELL...
GOODBYE, LINDA ROBOT! I'M AFRAID I WON'T HAVE ANY MORE USE FOR YOU!
SHOULD YOU EVER NEED ME, MISTRESS, I'LL BE HERE IN THIS HOLLOW TREE...WAITING!
AND SO, LINDA MOVES INTO A NEW HOME TOGETHER WITH HER PET CAT, STREAKY...
THESE NEW DRESSES ARE FOR YOU, HONEY! PLEASE CALL ME "MOM"!
GASP! THEY'RE BEAUTIFUL, MOM! THANK YOU, TOO, DAD!
LINDA, ABOUT YOUR HAIR...ER...
YOU'RE TOO GROWN-UP TO WEAR PIGTAILS ANY MORE! THAT'S STRICTLY KID STUFF, AND YOU'RE A LOVELY YOUNG LADY! TOMORROW WE'RE GOING TO VISIT A BEAUTY PARLOR, AND THERE'LL BE SOME CHANGES MADE!
!
4
NEXT MORNING...
LIKE IT? I DECIDED TO SURPRISE YOU AND DO MY HAIR MYSELF!
I HAD TO! A BEAUTICIAN WOULD HAVE DISCOVERED I WEAR A WIG OVER MY BLONDE HAIR!
IT'S DARLING!
GREAT, LINDA!

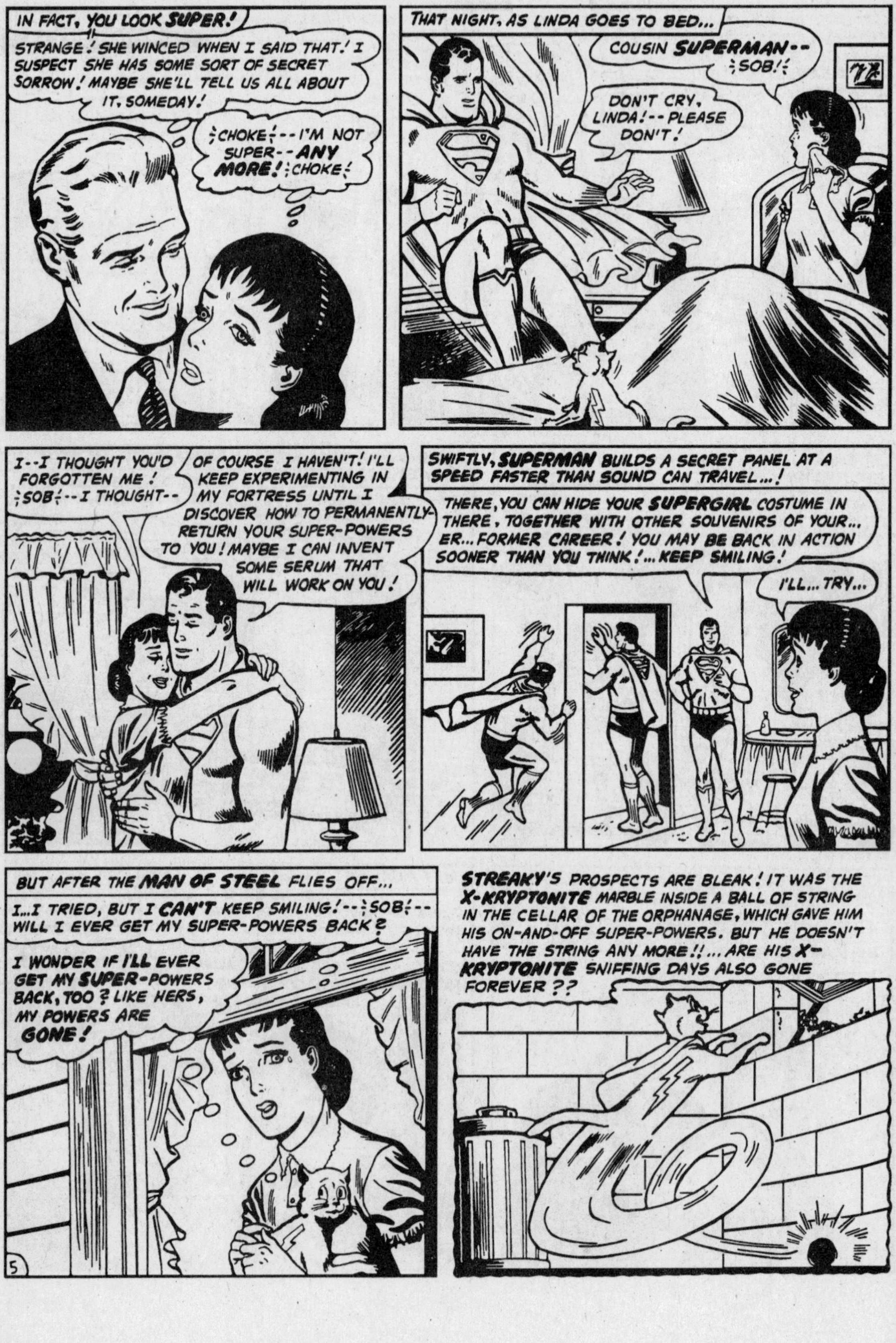
IN FACT, YOU LOOK SUPER!
STRANGE! SHE WINCED WHEN I SAID THAT! I SUSPECT SHE HAS SOME SORT OF SECRET SORROW! MAYBE SHE'LL TELL US ALL ABOUT IT, SOMEDAY!
CHOKE --I'M NOT SUPER--ANY MORE! CHOKE
THAT NIGHT, AS LINDA GOES TO BED...
COUSIN SUPERMAN-- SOB!
DON'T CRY, LINDA!--PLEASE DON'T!
I--I THOUGHT YOU'D FORGOTTEN ME! SOB--I THOUGHT--
OF COURSE I HAVEN'T! I'LL KEEP EXPERIMENTING IN MY FORTRESS UNTIL I DISCOVER HOW TO PERMANENTLY RETURN YOUR SUPER-POWERS TO YOU! MAYBE I CAN INVENT SOME SERUM THAT WILL WORK ON YOU!
SWIFTLY, SUPERMAN BUILDS A SECRET PANEL AT A SPEED FASTER THAN SOUND CAN TRAVEL...!
THERE, YOU CAN HIDE YOUR SUPERGIRL COSTUME IN THERE, TOGETHER WITH OTHER SOUVENIRS OF YOUR... ER...FORMER CAREER! YOU MAY BE BACK IN ACTION SOONER THAN YOU THINK!...KEEP SMILING!
I'LL...TRY...
BUT AFTER THE MAN OF STEEL FLIES OFF...
I...I TRIED, BUT I CAN'T KEEP SMILING!--SOB!--WILL I EVER GET MY SUPER-POWERS BACK?
I WONDER IF I'LL EVER GET MY SUPER-POWERS BACK, TOO? LIKE HERS, MY POWERS ARE GONE!
STREAKY'S PROSPECTS ARE BLEAK! IT WAS THE X-KRYPTONITE MARBLE INSIDE A BALL OF STRING IN THE CELLAR OF THE ORPHANAGE, WHICH GAVE HIM HIS ON-AND-OFF SUPER-POWERS. BUT HE DOESN'T HAVE THE STRING ANY MORE!!...ARE HIS X-KRYPTONITE SNIFFING DAYS ALSO GONE FOREVER??

SOON AFTERWARD, IN **LESLA-LAR'S** KANDORIAN LABORATORY...

SHE'S SLEEPING NOW! I'LL FOCUS THE **TELEPORT RAY** I INVENTED UPON HER!...AH, SHE'S SHRINKING AND...DISAPPEARING! -- IN ANOTHER MOMENT, SHE'LL MATERIALIZE...**HERE!**

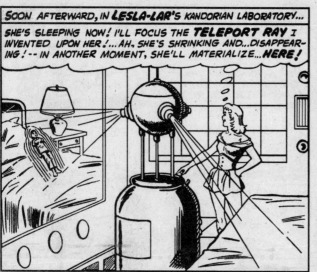

A SECOND LATER...

HERE SHE IS...AS I CALCULATED! SOUND ASLEEP, SHE'S UNAWARE OF WHAT'S HAPPENED! NOW TO PLACE THE **BRAIN-WASH HELMET** ON HER. IT WILL ERASE ALL HER FORMER MEMORIES AND ONLY PERMIT HER TO REMEMBER CERTAIN DETAILS ABOUT MY LIFE ON **KANDOR!**

DELIBERATELY, **LESLA-LAR** PLAYS A TAPE THAT SUPPLIES CERTAIN INFORMATION AND COMMANDS TO LINDA'S SLUMBERING MIND...

WHEN SHE AWAKENS HERE, AND AS LONG AS SHE REMAINS IN **KANDOR**, SHE WILL **BELIEVE** HERSELF TO BE **ME!**

YOU ARE NO LONGER **SUPERGIRL**...YOU ARE **LESLA-LAR**, A GIRL SCIENTIST... YOU NEVER MET **SUPERMAN** OF EARTH--

EXCHANGING GARMENTS WITH LINDA, **LESLA-LAR** STEPS BEFORE HER **TELEPORT RAY**...

AH...I'M BEING MAGNIFIED AND PROJECTED TO EARTH! THE "REVERSE" BUTTON ON MY **TELEPORT-BRACELET** WILL RETURN ME WHENEVER I DESIRE! SHOULD I PRESS THE BRACELET'S OTHER BUTTON, LINDA WILL INSTANTLY TELEPORT BACK TO EARTH!

A SPLIT INSTANT AFTERWARD, AS SHE MATERIALIZES IN LINDA'S ROOM ON EARTH...

;CHUCKLE;! GREAT KRYPTON! UNDER EARTH'S GRAVITY CONDITIONS, I NOW HAVE SUPER-POWERS... AS I **KNEW** I WOULD!

NEXT MORNING...

DID YOU HAVE A GOOD NIGHT'S REST, LINDA, DEAR?

YES, MOM!

HA, HA! MY DECEPTION IS WORKING! LITTLE DO THEY SUSPECT THAT THEIR "DAUGHTER" IS REALLY **LESLA-LAR** OF **KANDOR!**

6

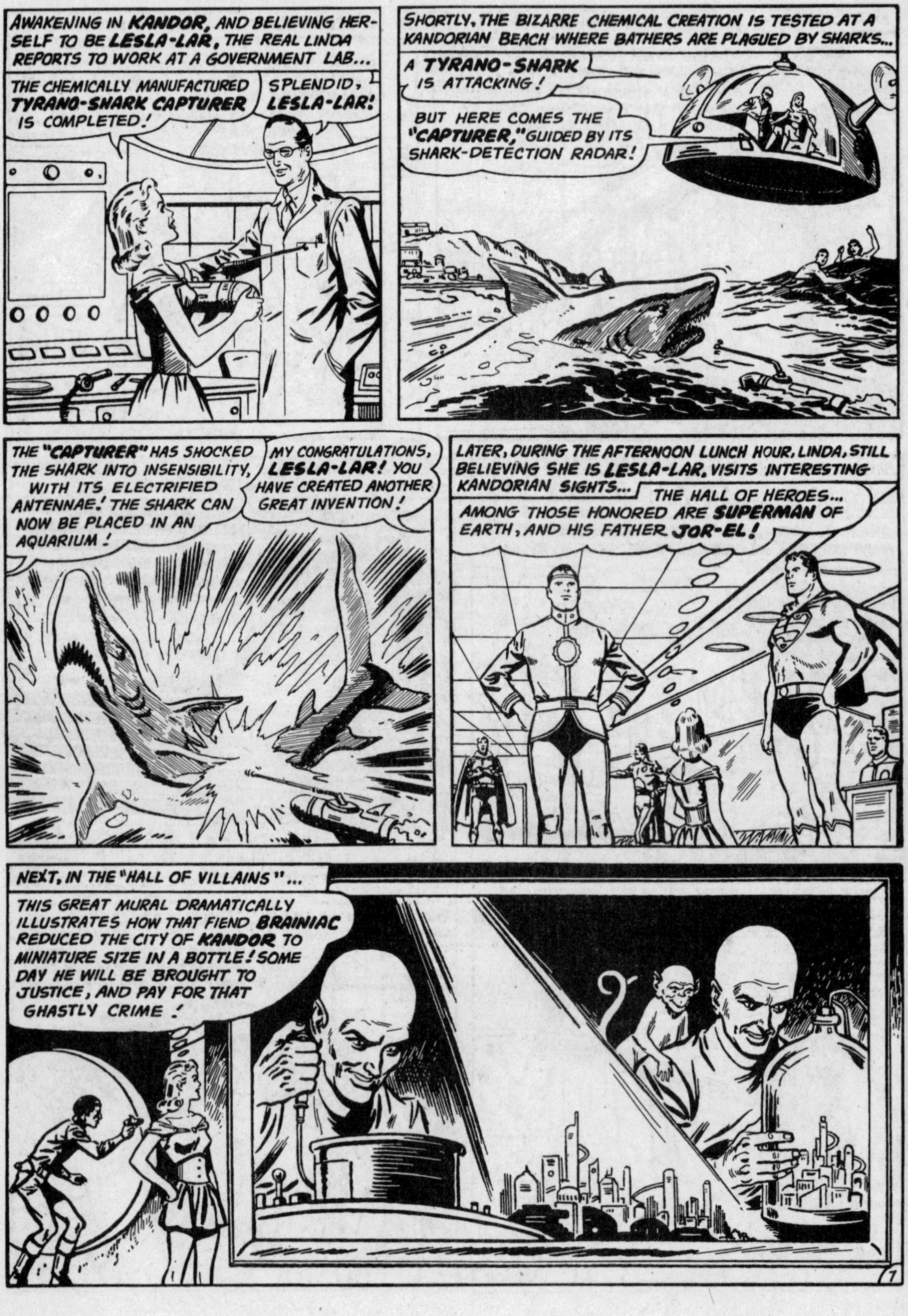
AWAKENING IN KANDOR, AND BELIEVING HERSELF TO BE LESLA-LAR, THE REAL LINDA REPORTS TO WORK AT A GOVERNMENT LAB...
THE CHEMICALLY MANUFACTURED TYRANO-SHARK CAPTURER IS COMPLETED!
SPLENDID, LESLA-LAR!
SHORTLY, THE BIZARRE CHEMICAL CREATION IS TESTED AT A KANDORIAN BEACH WHERE BATHERS ARE PLAGUED BY SHARKS...
A TYRANO-SHARK IS ATTACKING!
BUT HERE COMES THE "CAPTURER," GUIDED BY ITS SHARK-DETECTION RADAR!
THE "CAPTURER" HAS SHOCKED THE SHARK INTO INSENSIBILITY, WITH ITS ELECTRIFIED ANTENNAE! THE SHARK CAN NOW BE PLACED IN AN AQUARIUM!
MY CONGRATULATIONS, LESLA-LAR! YOU HAVE CREATED ANOTHER GREAT INVENTION!
LATER, DURING THE AFTERNOON LUNCH HOUR, LINDA, STILL BELIEVING SHE IS LESLA-LAR, VISITS INTERESTING KANDORIAN SIGHTS...
THE HALL OF HEROES... AMONG THOSE HONORED ARE SUPERMAN OF EARTH, AND HIS FATHER JOR-EL!
NEXT, IN THE "HALL OF VILLAINS"...
THIS GREAT MURAL DRAMATICALLY ILLUSTRATES HOW THAT FIEND BRAINIAC REDUCED THE CITY OF KANDOR TO MINIATURE SIZE IN A BOTTLE! SOME DAY HE WILL BE BROUGHT TO JUSTICE, AND PAY FOR THAT GHASTLY CRIME!
7

AFTERWARD... THIS IS "THE HALL OF SLEEPERS"... WHERE VOLUNTEERS ARE PLACED INTO A STATE OF SUSPENDED ANIMATION, TO BE AWAKENED 1000 YEARS FROM NOW! THEIR MISSION: TO PRESERVE PRESENT-DAY KANDORIAN IDEALS!... FORMERLY, SUSPENDED ANIMATION WAS ILLEGAL!

WHEN "LESLA-LAR" RETURNS TO WORK IN THE GOVERNMENT LAB, SUDDENLY...

WHAT'S GOING ON?

THE CRIME-DETECTOR APPARATUS REVEALS A FORBIDDEN EXPERIMENT IS OCCURRING HERE!

301 TO

CLANG CLANG!

SOON, SHE OBSERVES...

SO...YOU'VE PROCEEDED WITH THE Z-BOMB EXPERIMENT...EVEN THOUGH WARNED IT COULD ACCIDENTALLY BLOW UP *KANDOR!* THE PENALTY FOR THIS IS... *THE PHANTOM ZONE!*

THE PHANTOM ZONE?!! NO! *NO!!*

PRESENTLY, IN A *KANDORIAN* COURT-ROOM...

GUILTY!--THE SENTENCE...20 YEARS IN THE *PHANTOM ZONE!* PROCEED, EXECUTIONER!

HOW AWFUL! THE PUNISHMENT WEAPON IS MAKING THE PRISONER DISAPPEAR! HE'S DOOMED TO REMAIN A PHANTOM FOR 20 YEARS!

MEANWHILE, ON EARTH, THE REAL *LESLA-LAR,* MASQUERADING AS "LINDA", SPIES ON HER "FATHER" AS HE WORKS IN HIS HOME WORKSHOP!...

MY SUPER-VISION SECRETLY REVEALS "DAD" WORKING ON ROCKET EXPERIMENTS!

SOME DAY I'LL STEAL HIS IDEAS, AND USE THEM FOR MY OWN PURPOSES! MEANWHILE, I'VE SOME PLANS OF MY OWN...SINISTER PLANS, THAT WILL ASTOUND EARTH!--MY FIRST MOVE WILL TAKE PLACE *TONIGHT!*

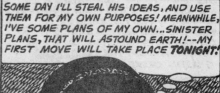

8

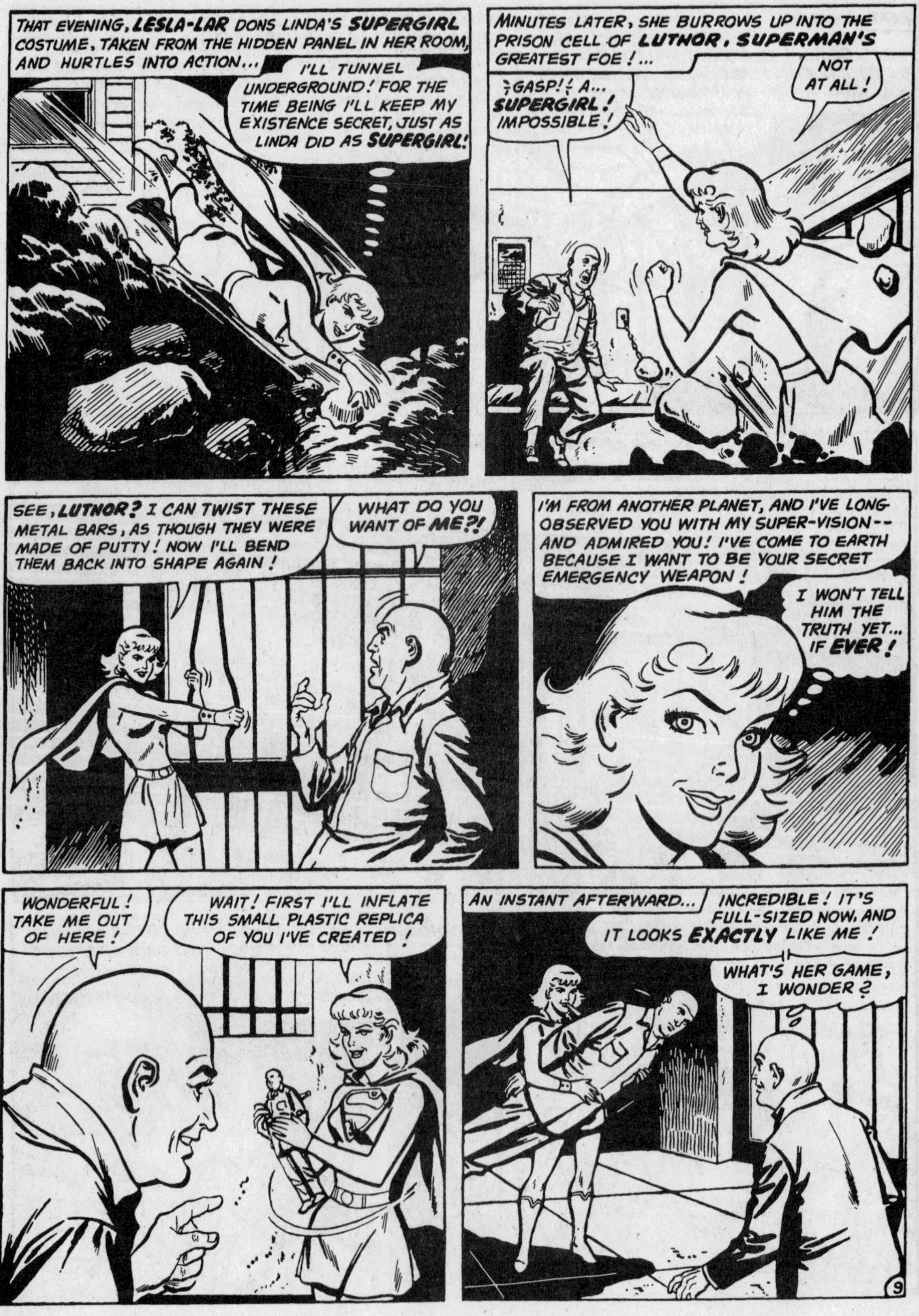
THAT EVENING, LESLA-LAR DONS LINDA'S SUPERGIRL COSTUME, TAKEN FROM THE HIDDEN PANEL IN HER ROOM, AND HURTLES INTO ACTION...
I'LL TUNNEL UNDERGROUND! FOR THE TIME BEING I'LL KEEP MY EXISTENCE SECRET, JUST AS LINDA DID AS SUPERGIRL!
MINUTES LATER, SHE BURROWS UP INTO THE PRISON CELL OF LUTHOR, SUPERMAN'S GREATEST FOE!...
GASP!! A... SUPERGIRL! IMPOSSIBLE!
NOT AT ALL!
SEE, LUTHOR? I CAN TWIST THESE METAL BARS, AS THOUGH THEY WERE MADE OF PUTTY! NOW I'LL BEND THEM BACK INTO SHAPE AGAIN!
WHAT DO YOU WANT OF ME?!
I'M FROM ANOTHER PLANET, AND I'VE LONG OBSERVED YOU WITH MY SUPER-VISION-- AND ADMIRED YOU! I'VE COME TO EARTH BECAUSE I WANT TO BE YOUR SECRET EMERGENCY WEAPON!
I WON'T TELL HIM THE TRUTH YET... IF EVER!
WONDERFUL! TAKE ME OUT OF HERE!
WAIT! FIRST I'LL INFLATE THIS SMALL PLASTIC REPLICA OF YOU I'VE CREATED!
AN INSTANT AFTERWARD...
INCREDIBLE! IT'S FULL-SIZED NOW, AND IT LOOKS EXACTLY LIKE ME!
WHAT'S HER GAME, I WONDER?
9

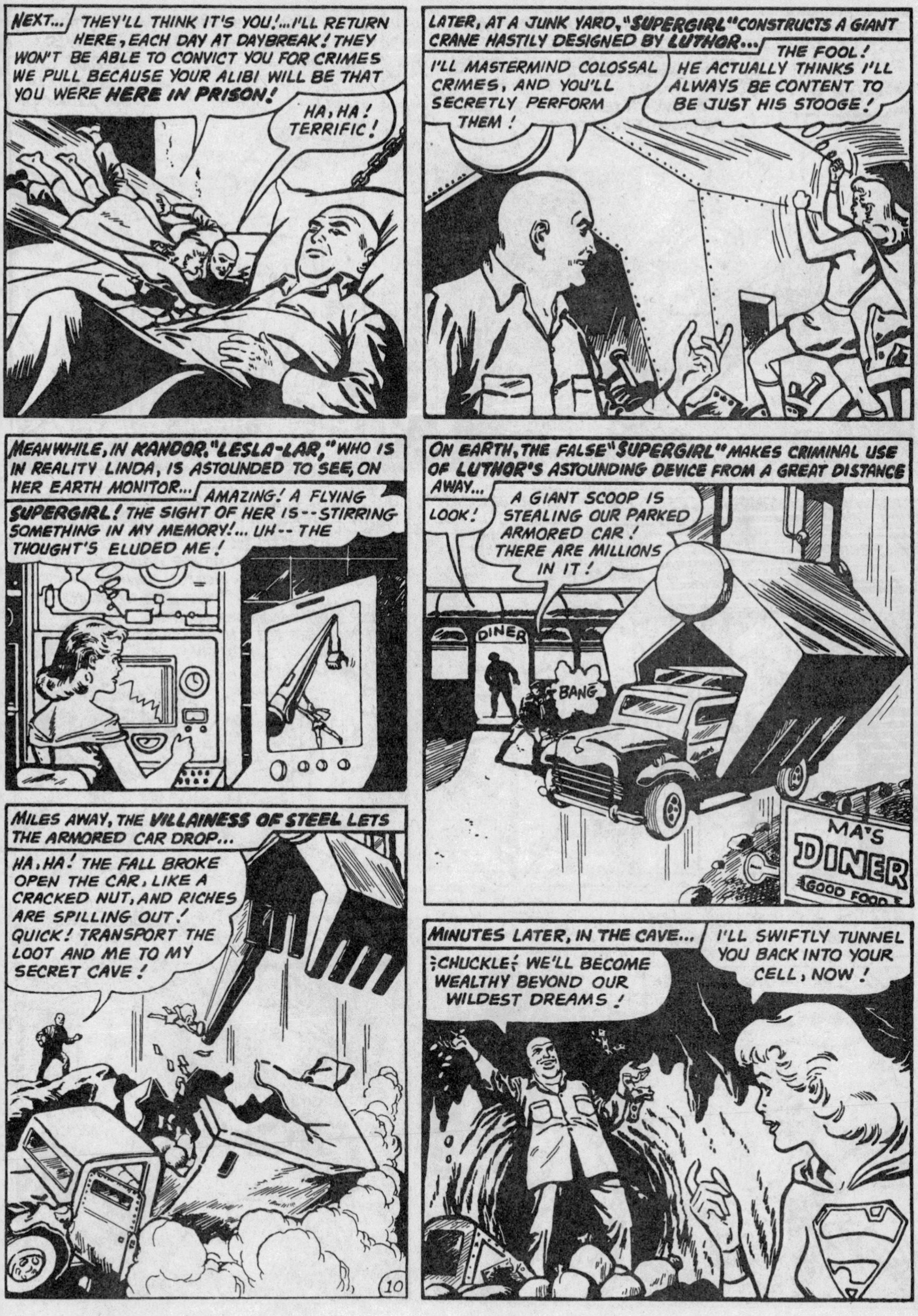
NEXT...
THEY'LL THINK IT'S YOU!...I'LL RETURN HERE, EACH DAY AT DAYBREAK! THEY WON'T BE ABLE TO CONVICT YOU FOR CRIMES WE PULL BECAUSE YOUR ALIBI WILL BE THAT YOU WERE HERE IN PRISON!
HA, HA! TERRIFIC!
LATER, AT A JUNK YARD, "SUPERGIRL" CONSTRUCTS A GIANT CRANE HASTILY DESIGNED BY LUTHOR...
I'LL MASTERMIND COLOSSAL CRIMES, AND YOU'LL SECRETLY PERFORM THEM!
THE FOOL! HE ACTUALLY THINKS I'LL ALWAYS BE CONTENT TO BE JUST HIS STOOGE!
MEANWHILE, IN KANDOR, "LESLA-LAR," WHO IS IN REALITY LINDA, IS ASTOUNDED TO SEE, ON HER EARTH MONITOR...
AMAZING! A FLYING SUPERGIRL! THE SIGHT OF HER IS--STIRRING SOMETHING IN MY MEMORY!... UH-- THE THOUGHT'S ELUDED ME!
ON EARTH, THE FALSE "SUPERGIRL" MAKES CRIMINAL USE OF LUTHOR'S ASTOUNDING DEVICE FROM A GREAT DISTANCE AWAY...
LOOK!
A GIANT SCOOP IS STEALING OUR PARKED ARMORED CAR! THERE ARE MILLIONS IN IT!
DINER
BANG
MA'S DINER GOOD FOOD
MILES AWAY, THE VILLAINESS OF STEEL LETS THE ARMORED CAR DROP...
HA, HA! THE FALL BROKE OPEN THE CAR, LIKE A CRACKED NUT, AND RICHES ARE SPILLING OUT! QUICK! TRANSPORT THE LOOT AND ME TO MY SECRET CAVE!
10
MINUTES LATER, IN THE CAVE...
CHUCKLE! WE'LL BECOME WEALTHY BEYOND OUR WILDEST DREAMS!
I'LL SWIFTLY TUNNEL YOU BACK INTO YOUR CELL, NOW!

SOON, AS POLICE LOCATE THE SMASHED ARMORED CAR...
IT'S BROKEN OPEN, AND ALL THE MONEY'S GONE!
THAT GIANT SCOOP SOUNDS LIKE ONE OF LUTHOR'S FANTASTIC CRIME-SCHEMES! WE'D BETTER CALL METROPOLIS PRISON IMMEDIATELY!
ALERTED, THE WARDEN HURRIES TO CHECK LUTHOR'S CELL...
HE HASN'T ESCAPED! THEN HE DIDN'T PULL THE CRIME!
¿CHUCKLE!¿ SUPERGIRL GOT ME BACK JUST IN TIME AND REMOVED THE PLASTIC FIGURE... WHAT A SENSATIONAL SECRET SUPER-HELPER SHE IS!
MEANWHILE, IN KANDOR, "LESLA-LAR," WHO HAS WITNESSED THE SUPER-CRIME BEING PERFORMED, HURRIES FOR HELP...
POLICE!...ALERT EARTH LAW-MEN THAT A CRIMINAL SUPERGIRL EXISTS THERE!!
EXIT
BUT THE REAL LESLA-LAR, WHO HAS RETURNED TO THE HOME OF HER "FOSTER-PARENTS" ON EARTH, OBSERVES WITH HER SUPER-MICROSCOPIC VISION...
¿GASP!¿ LINDA'S GOING TO BETRAY ME! I'LL PRESS THE BUTTON ON THE BRACE-LET THAT WILL TELEPORT HER BACK TO EARTH FROM KANDOR! SHE'LL RETURN HERE WITH NO MEMORY OF HER HAVING TAKEN MY PLACE ON KANDOR!
AS LINDA IS TELEPORTED BACK INTO HER BEDROOM, AT THE HOME OF HER FOSTER PARENTS, LESLA-LAR SUPER-SWIFTLY SWITCHES GARMENTS WITH HER, THEN...
NOW TO PRESS THE "REVERSE" BUTTON, AND SEND MYSELF BACK TO KANDOR, BEFORE SHE SIGHTS ME!
FINDING HERSELF IN THE DARKENED ROOM, LINDA SCREAMS...
YII...III! ...HELP! HELP!
WHAT'S WRONG, LINDA?
11

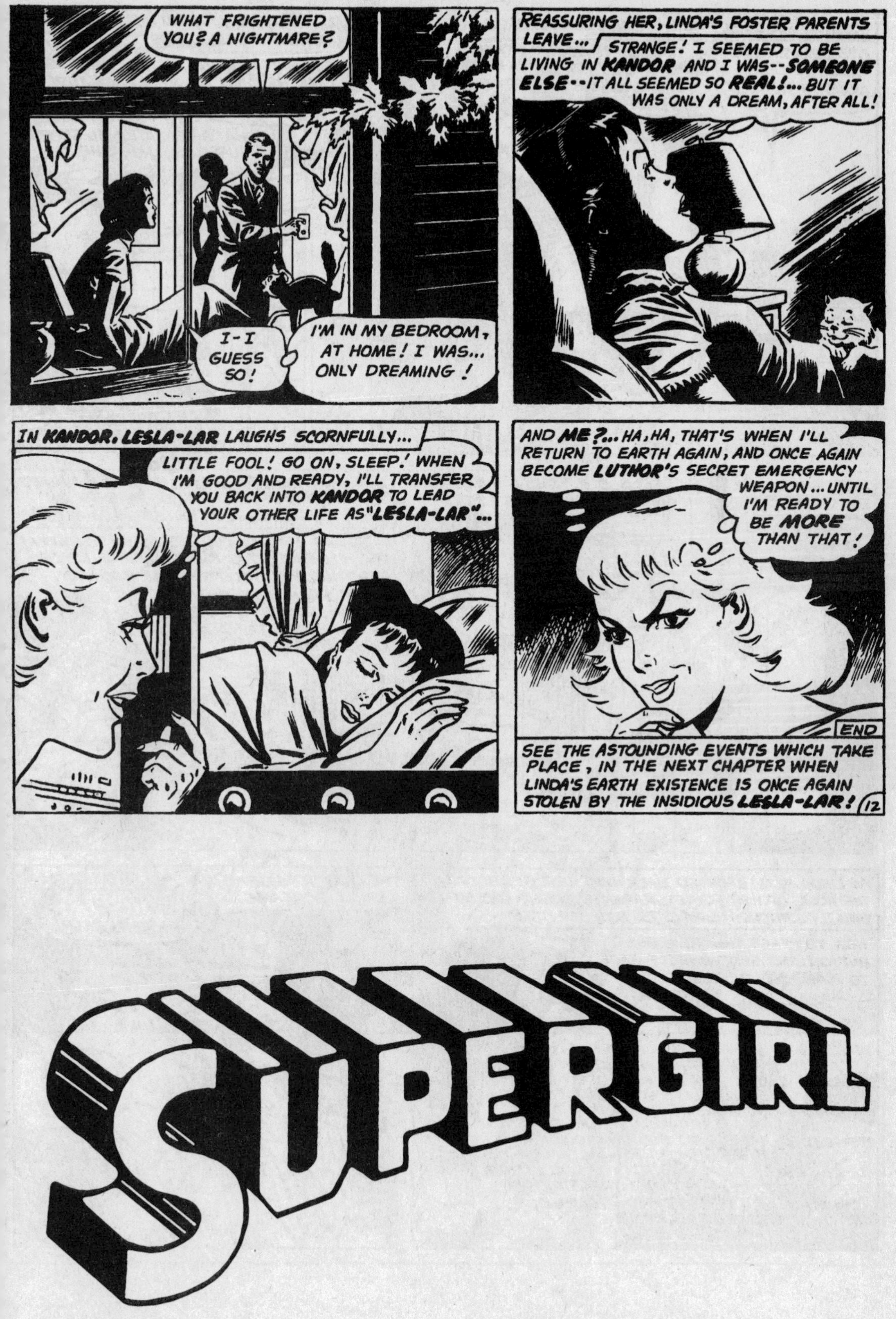
WHAT FRIGHTENED YOU? A NIGHTMARE?
I-I GUESS SO!
I'M IN MY BEDROOM, AT HOME! I WAS... ONLY DREAMING!
REASSURING HER, LINDA'S FOSTER PARENTS LEAVE...
STRANGE! I SEEMED TO BE LIVING IN KANDOR AND I WAS--SOMEONE ELSE--IT ALL SEEMED SO REAL!... BUT IT WAS ONLY A DREAM, AFTER ALL!
IN KANDOR, LESLA-LAR LAUGHS SCORNFULLY...
LITTLE FOOL! GO ON, SLEEP! WHEN I'M GOOD AND READY, I'LL TRANSFER YOU BACK INTO KANDOR TO LEAD YOUR OTHER LIFE AS "LESLA-LAR"...
AND ME?... HA, HA, THAT'S WHEN I'LL RETURN TO EARTH AGAIN, AND ONCE AGAIN BECOME LUTHOR'S SECRET EMERGENCY WEAPON... UNTIL I'M READY TO BE MORE THAN THAT!
END
SEE THE ASTOUNDING EVENTS WHICH TAKE PLACE, IN THE NEXT CHAPTER WHEN LINDA'S EARTH EXISTENCE IS ONCE AGAIN STOLEN BY THE INSIDIOUS LESLA-LAR!
12

SUPERGIRL

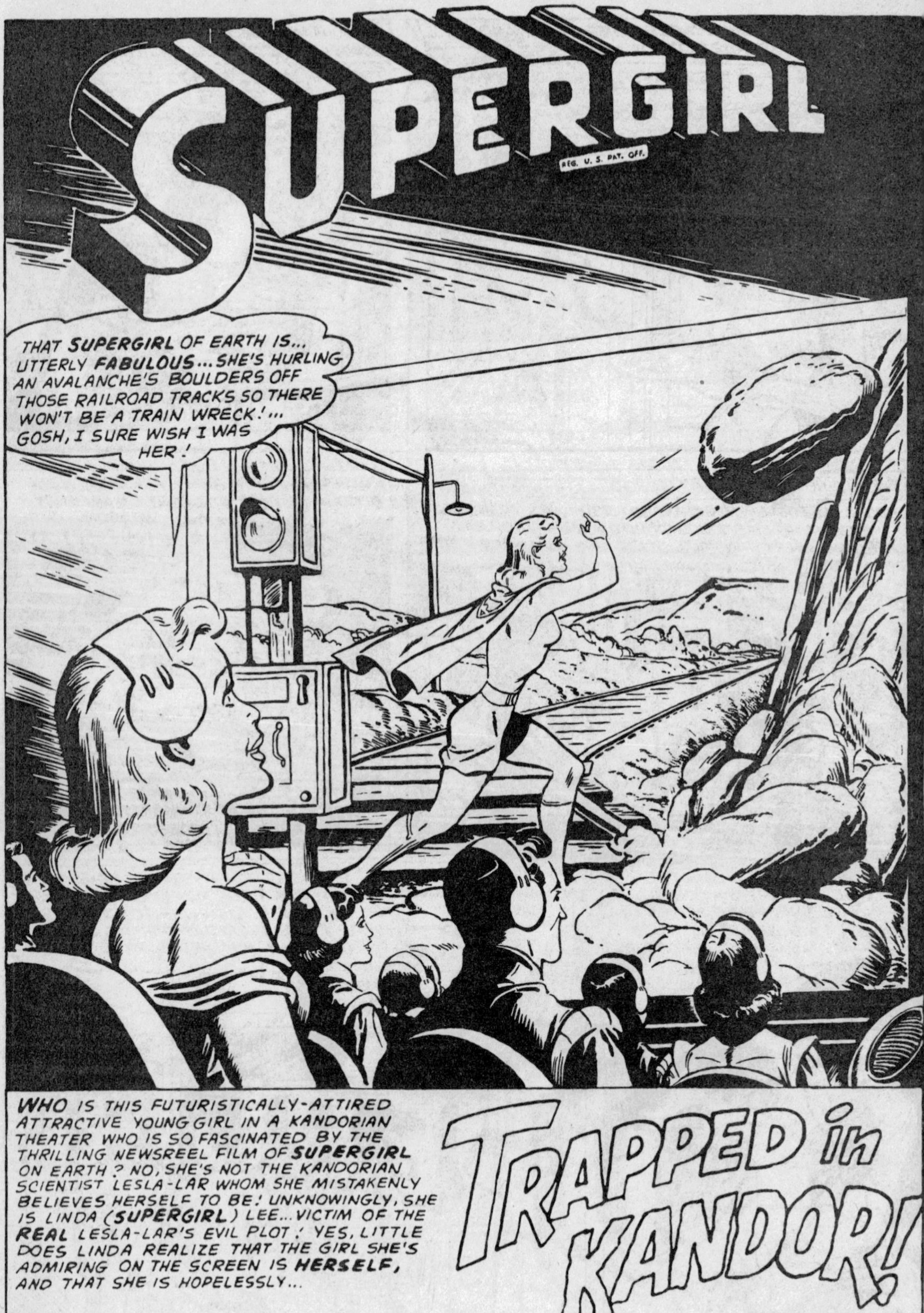
SUPERGIRL
REG. U.S. PAT. OFF.
THAT SUPERGIRL OF EARTH IS... UTTERLY FABULOUS... SHE'S HURLING AN AVALANCHE'S BOULDERS OFF THOSE RAILROAD TRACKS SO THERE WON'T BE A TRAIN WRECK!... GOSH, I SURE WISH I WAS HER!
WHO IS THIS FUTURISTICALLY-ATTIRED ATTRACTIVE YOUNG GIRL IN A KANDORIAN THEATER WHO IS SO FASCINATED BY THE THRILLING NEWSREEL FILM OF SUPERGIRL ON EARTH? NO, SHE'S NOT THE KANDORIAN SCIENTIST LESLA-LAR WHOM SHE MISTAKENLY BELIEVES HERSELF TO BE! UNKNOWINGLY, SHE IS LINDA (SUPERGIRL) LEE... VICTIM OF THE REAL LESLA-LAR'S EVIL PLOT! YES, LITTLE DOES LINDA REALIZE THAT THE GIRL SHE'S ADMIRING ON THE SCREEN IS HERSELF, AND THAT SHE IS HOPELESSLY...
TRAPPED in KANDOR!

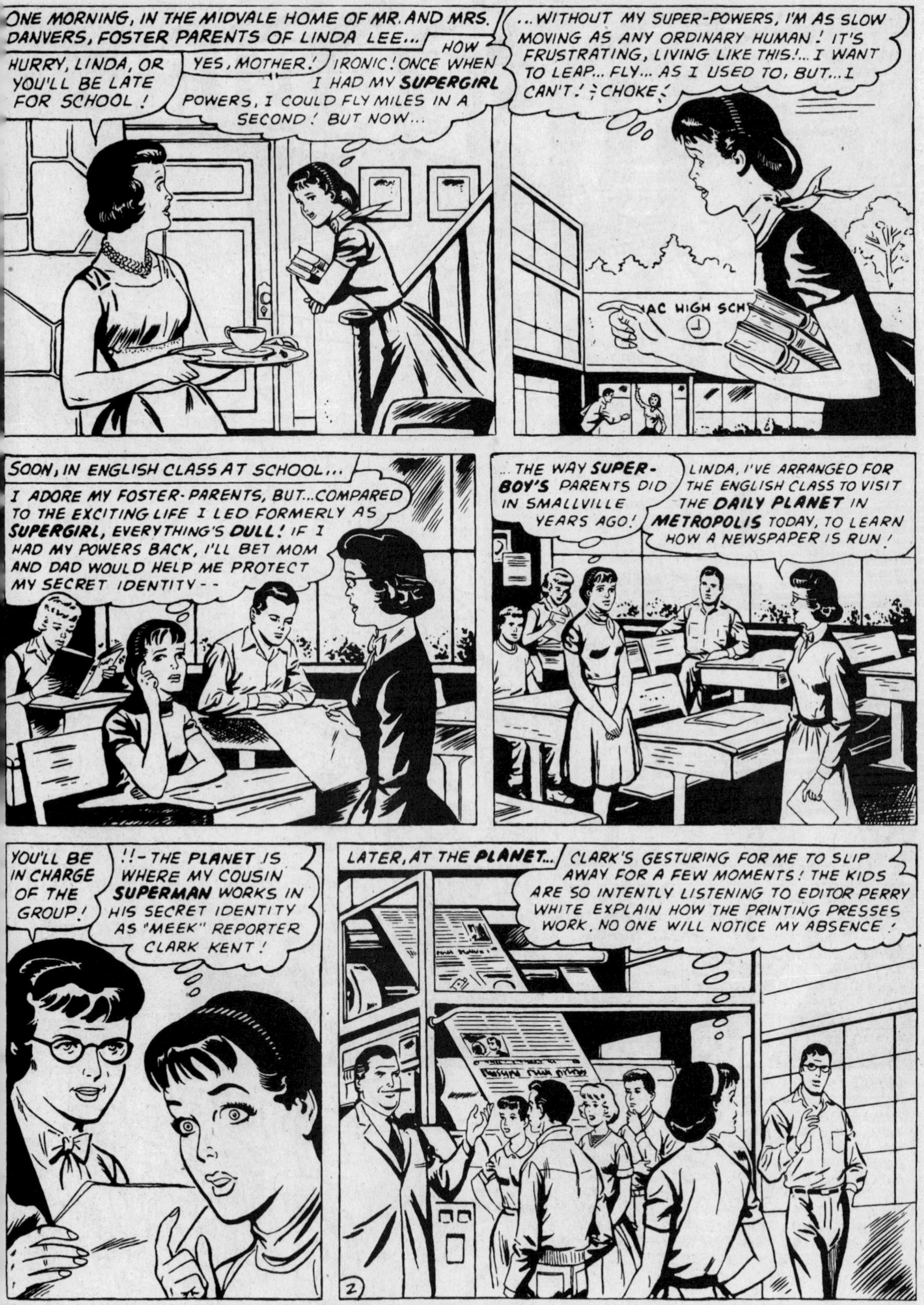
ONE MORNING, IN THE MIDVALE HOME OF MR. AND MRS. DANVERS, FOSTER PARENTS OF LINDA LEE...
HURRY, LINDA, OR YOU'LL BE LATE FOR SCHOOL!
YES, MOTHER!
HOW IRONIC! ONCE WHEN I HAD MY SUPERGIRL POWERS, I COULD FLY MILES IN A SECOND! BUT NOW...
...WITHOUT MY SUPER-POWERS, I'M AS SLOW MOVING AS ANY ORDINARY HUMAN! IT'S FRUSTRATING, LIVING LIKE THIS!... I WANT TO LEAP... FLY... AS I USED TO, BUT... I CAN'T! ;CHOKE;
AC HIGH SCH
SOON, IN ENGLISH CLASS AT SCHOOL...
I ADORE MY FOSTER-PARENTS, BUT... COMPARED TO THE EXCITING LIFE I LED FORMERLY AS SUPERGIRL, EVERYTHING'S DULL! IF I HAD MY POWERS BACK, I'LL BET MOM AND DAD WOULD HELP ME PROTECT MY SECRET IDENTITY--
...THE WAY SUPER-BOY'S PARENTS DID IN SMALLVILLE YEARS AGO!
LINDA, I'VE ARRANGED FOR THE ENGLISH CLASS TO VISIT THE DAILY PLANET IN METROPOLIS TODAY, TO LEARN HOW A NEWSPAPER IS RUN!
YOU'LL BE IN CHARGE OF THE GROUP!
!!-THE PLANET IS WHERE MY COUSIN SUPERMAN WORKS IN HIS SECRET IDENTITY AS "MEEK" REPORTER CLARK KENT!
LATER, AT THE PLANET...
CLARK'S GESTURING FOR ME TO SLIP AWAY FOR A FEW MOMENTS! THE KIDS ARE SO INTENTLY LISTENING TO EDITOR PERRY WHITE EXPLAIN HOW THE PRINTING PRESSES WORK, NO ONE WILL NOTICE MY ABSENCE!
2

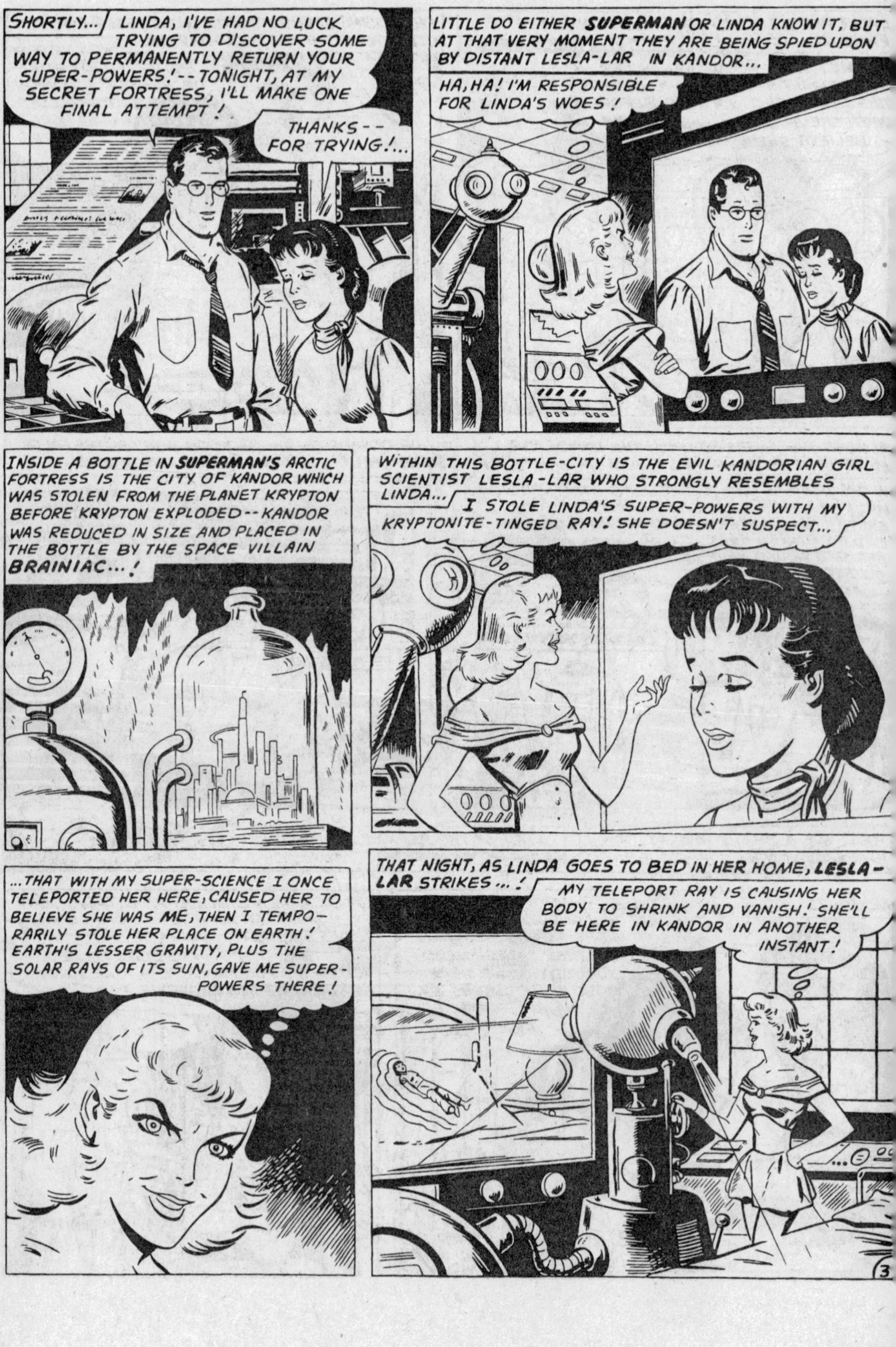
SHORTLY...
LINDA, I'VE HAD NO LUCK TRYING TO DISCOVER SOME WAY TO PERMANENTLY RETURN YOUR SUPER-POWERS!--TONIGHT, AT MY SECRET FORTRESS, I'LL MAKE ONE FINAL ATTEMPT!
THANKS--FOR TRYING!...
LITTLE DO EITHER SUPERMAN OR LINDA KNOW IT, BUT AT THAT VERY MOMENT THEY ARE BEING SPIED UPON BY DISTANT LESLA-LAR IN KANDOR...
HA, HA! I'M RESPONSIBLE FOR LINDA'S WOES!
INSIDE A BOTTLE IN SUPERMAN'S ARCTIC FORTRESS IS THE CITY OF KANDOR WHICH WAS STOLEN FROM THE PLANET KRYPTON BEFORE KRYPTON EXPLODED--KANDOR WAS REDUCED IN SIZE AND PLACED IN THE BOTTLE BY THE SPACE VILLAIN BRAINIAC...!
WITHIN THIS BOTTLE-CITY IS THE EVIL KANDORIAN GIRL SCIENTIST LESLA-LAR WHO STRONGLY RESEMBLES LINDA...
I STOLE LINDA'S SUPER-POWERS WITH MY KRYPTONITE-TINGED RAY! SHE DOESN'T SUSPECT...
...THAT WITH MY SUPER-SCIENCE I ONCE TELEPORTED HER HERE, CAUSED HER TO BELIEVE SHE WAS ME, THEN I TEMPORARILY STOLE HER PLACE ON EARTH! EARTH'S LESSER GRAVITY, PLUS THE SOLAR RAYS OF ITS SUN, GAVE ME SUPER-POWERS THERE!
THAT NIGHT, AS LINDA GOES TO BED IN HER HOME, LESLA-LAR STRIKES...!
MY TELEPORT RAY IS CAUSING HER BODY TO SHRINK AND VANISH! SHE'LL BE HERE IN KANDOR IN ANOTHER INSTANT!
3

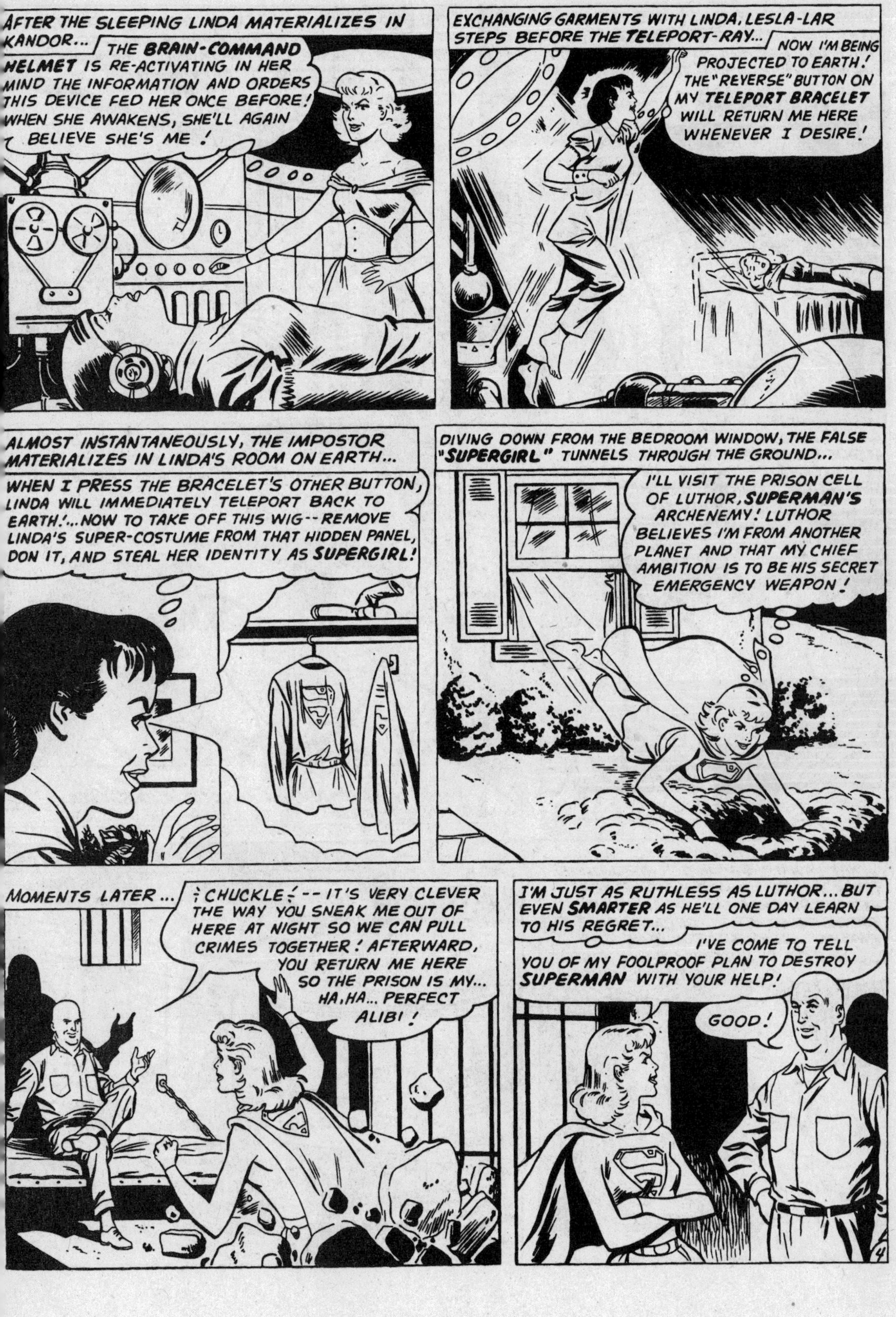
AFTER THE SLEEPING LINDA MATERIALIZES IN KANDOR...
THE BRAIN-COMMAND HELMET IS RE-ACTIVATING IN HER MIND THE INFORMATION AND ORDERS THIS DEVICE FED HER ONCE BEFORE! WHEN SHE AWAKENS, SHE'LL AGAIN BELIEVE SHE'S ME!
EXCHANGING GARMENTS WITH LINDA, LESLA-LAR STEPS BEFORE THE TELEPORT-RAY...
NOW I'M BEING PROJECTED TO EARTH! THE "REVERSE" BUTTON ON MY TELEPORT BRACELET WILL RETURN ME HERE WHENEVER I DESIRE!
ALMOST INSTANTANEOUSLY, THE IMPOSTOR MATERIALIZES IN LINDA'S ROOM ON EARTH...
WHEN I PRESS THE BRACELET'S OTHER BUTTON, LINDA WILL IMMEDIATELY TELEPORT BACK TO EARTH!...NOW TO TAKE OFF THIS WIG--REMOVE LINDA'S SUPER-COSTUME FROM THAT HIDDEN PANEL, DON IT, AND STEAL HER IDENTITY AS SUPERGIRL!
DIVING DOWN FROM THE BEDROOM WINDOW, THE FALSE "SUPERGIRL" TUNNELS THROUGH THE GROUND...
I'LL VISIT THE PRISON CELL OF LUTHOR, SUPERMAN'S ARCHENEMY! LUTHOR BELIEVES I'M FROM ANOTHER PLANET AND THAT MY CHIEF AMBITION IS TO BE HIS SECRET EMERGENCY WEAPON!
MOMENTS LATER...
CHUCKLE! -- IT'S VERY CLEVER THE WAY YOU SNEAK ME OUT OF HERE AT NIGHT SO WE CAN PULL CRIMES TOGETHER! AFTERWARD, YOU RETURN ME HERE SO THE PRISON IS MY... HA, HA... PERFECT ALIBI!
I'M JUST AS RUTHLESS AS LUTHOR... BUT EVEN SMARTER AS HE'LL ONE DAY LEARN TO HIS REGRET...
I'VE COME TO TELL YOU OF MY FOOLPROOF PLAN TO DESTROY SUPERMAN WITH YOUR HELP!
GOOD!
4

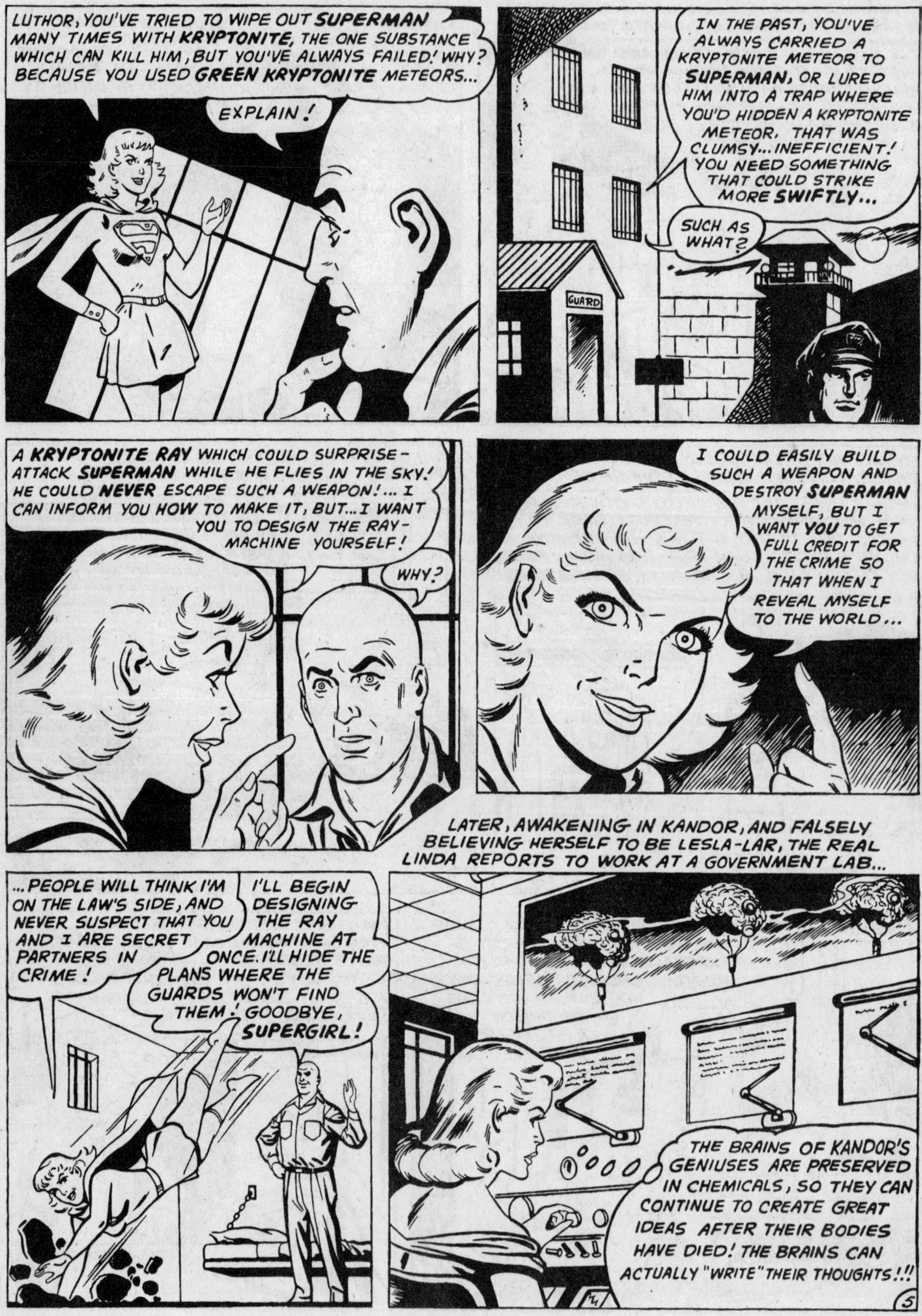
LUTHOR, YOU'VE TRIED TO WIPE OUT SUPERMAN MANY TIMES WITH KRYPTONITE, THE ONE SUBSTANCE WHICH CAN KILL HIM, BUT YOU'VE ALWAYS FAILED! WHY? BECAUSE YOU USED GREEN KRYPTONITE METEORS...
EXPLAIN!
IN THE PAST, YOU'VE ALWAYS CARRIED A KRYPTONITE METEOR TO SUPERMAN, OR LURED HIM INTO A TRAP WHERE YOU'D HIDDEN A KRYPTONITE METEOR. THAT WAS CLUMSY... INEFFICIENT! YOU NEED SOMETHING THAT COULD STRIKE MORE SWIFTLY...
SUCH AS WHAT?
GUARD
A KRYPTONITE RAY WHICH COULD SURPRISE-ATTACK SUPERMAN WHILE HE FLIES IN THE SKY! HE COULD NEVER ESCAPE SUCH A WEAPON! ... I CAN INFORM YOU HOW TO MAKE IT, BUT... I WANT YOU TO DESIGN THE RAY-MACHINE YOURSELF!
WHY?
I COULD EASILY BUILD SUCH A WEAPON AND DESTROY SUPERMAN MYSELF, BUT I WANT YOU TO GET FULL CREDIT FOR THE CRIME SO THAT WHEN I REVEAL MYSELF TO THE WORLD...
... PEOPLE WILL THINK I'M ON THE LAW'S SIDE, AND NEVER SUSPECT THAT YOU AND I ARE SECRET PARTNERS IN CRIME!
I'LL BEGIN DESIGNING THE RAY MACHINE AT ONCE. I'LL HIDE THE PLANS WHERE THE GUARDS WON'T FIND THEM! GOODBYE, SUPERGIRL!
LATER, AWAKENING IN KANDOR, AND FALSELY BELIEVING HERSELF TO BE LESLA-LAR, THE REAL LINDA REPORTS TO WORK AT A GOVERNMENT LAB...
THE BRAINS OF KANDOR'S GENIUSES ARE PRESERVED IN CHEMICALS, SO THEY CAN CONTINUE TO CREATE GREAT IDEAS AFTER THEIR BODIES HAVE DIED! THE BRAINS CAN ACTUALLY "WRITE" THEIR THOUGHTS!!!
5

WHEN HER FOUR-HOUR DAY IS FINISHED, SHE ENTERS A KANDORIAN THEATER...

"REALLY" MOVIES ARE FUN! THE AUDIENCE NOT ONLY SEES AND HEARS, BUT CAN *SMELL, TASTE* AND *FEEL* WHAT'S BEING SHOWN ON THE SCREEN!

SOON, AFTER READING DESCRIPTIVE MATTER, SHE WITNESSES...

THIS NEWSREEL OF LIFE ON LONG-AGO PERISHED KRYPTON WAS FILMED FROM INSIDE THE BOTTLE-CITY OF KANDOR AFTER KANDOR WAS CAPTURED BY *BRAINIAC* AND REDUCED BY HIS SHRINKING RAY!

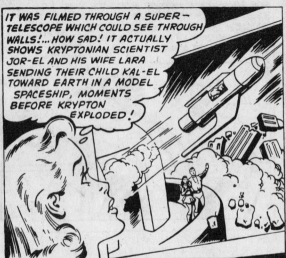

IT WAS FILMED THROUGH A SUPER-TELESCOPE WHICH COULD SEE THROUGH WALLS!... HOW SAD! IT ACTUALLY SHOWS KRYPTONIAN SCIENTIST JOR-EL AND HIS WIFE LARA SENDING THEIR CHILD KAL-EL TOWARD EARTH IN A MODEL SPACESHIP, MOMENTS BEFORE KRYPTON EXPLODED!

NOW *KRYPTON'S* BEING BLASTED APART BY AN ATOMIC CHAIN-REACTION! --IT'S... *AWESOME!*... OH, MY, A LARGE CHUNK OF THE PLANET IS BEING HURLED AWAY... WITH PEOPLE ON IT!

IT'S... *ARGO CITY* AND A BUBBLE OF AIR CAME ALONG WITH IT! GREAT SCOTT! *ARGO CITY* IS GLOWING... *GREEN!* THE NUCLEAR EXPLOSION WHICH DESTROYED KRYPTON IS CHANGING THE GROUND INTO *KRYPTONITE,* WHOSE RADIATIONS CAN KILL KRYPTONIANS!

HOORAY! SCIENTIST ZOR-EL, THE BROTHER OF JOR-EL, IS HAVING THE GROUND COVERED WITH *LEAD* SHEET METAL TAKEN FROM HIS LAB! KRYPTONITE RADIATIONS CAN'T PIERCE LEAD! THE PEOPLE WILL *LIVE!*

IRONICALLY, UNKNOWN TO "LINDA-LAR," ZOR-EL IS HER OWN FATHER!

6

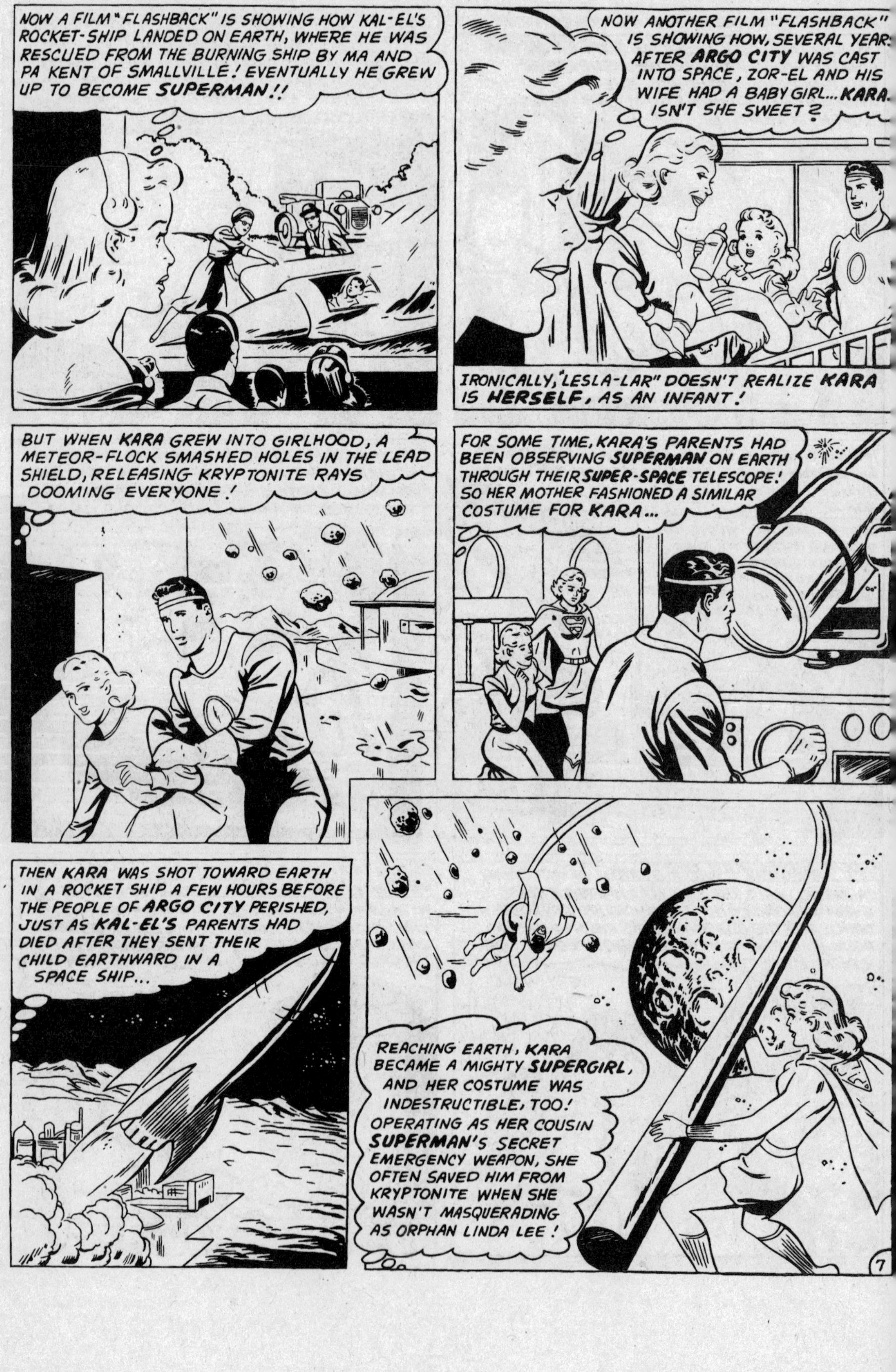
NOW A FILM "FLASHBACK" IS SHOWING HOW KAL-EL'S ROCKET-SHIP LANDED ON EARTH, WHERE HE WAS RESCUED FROM THE BURNING SHIP BY MA AND PA KENT OF SMALLVILLE! EVENTUALLY HE GREW UP TO BECOME SUPERMAN!!
NOW ANOTHER FILM "FLASHBACK" IS SHOWING HOW, SEVERAL YEARS AFTER ARGO CITY WAS CAST INTO SPACE, ZOR-EL AND HIS WIFE HAD A BABY GIRL... KARA. ISN'T SHE SWEET?
IRONICALLY, "LESLA-LAR" DOESN'T REALIZE KARA IS HERSELF, AS AN INFANT!
BUT WHEN KARA GREW INTO GIRLHOOD, A METEOR-FLOCK SMASHED HOLES IN THE LEAD SHIELD, RELEASING KRYPTONITE RAYS DOOMING EVERYONE!
FOR SOME TIME, KARA'S PARENTS HAD BEEN OBSERVING SUPERMAN ON EARTH THROUGH THEIR SUPER-SPACE TELESCOPE! SO HER MOTHER FASHIONED A SIMILAR COSTUME FOR KARA...
THEN KARA WAS SHOT TOWARD EARTH IN A ROCKET SHIP A FEW HOURS BEFORE THE PEOPLE OF ARGO CITY PERISHED, JUST AS KAL-EL'S PARENTS HAD DIED AFTER THEY SENT THEIR CHILD EARTHWARD IN A SPACE SHIP...
REACHING EARTH, KARA BECAME A MIGHTY SUPERGIRL, AND HER COSTUME WAS INDESTRUCTIBLE, TOO! OPERATING AS HER COUSIN SUPERMAN'S SECRET EMERGENCY WEAPON, SHE OFTEN SAVED HIM FROM KRYPTONITE WHEN SHE WASN'T MASQUERADING AS ORPHAN LINDA LEE!
7

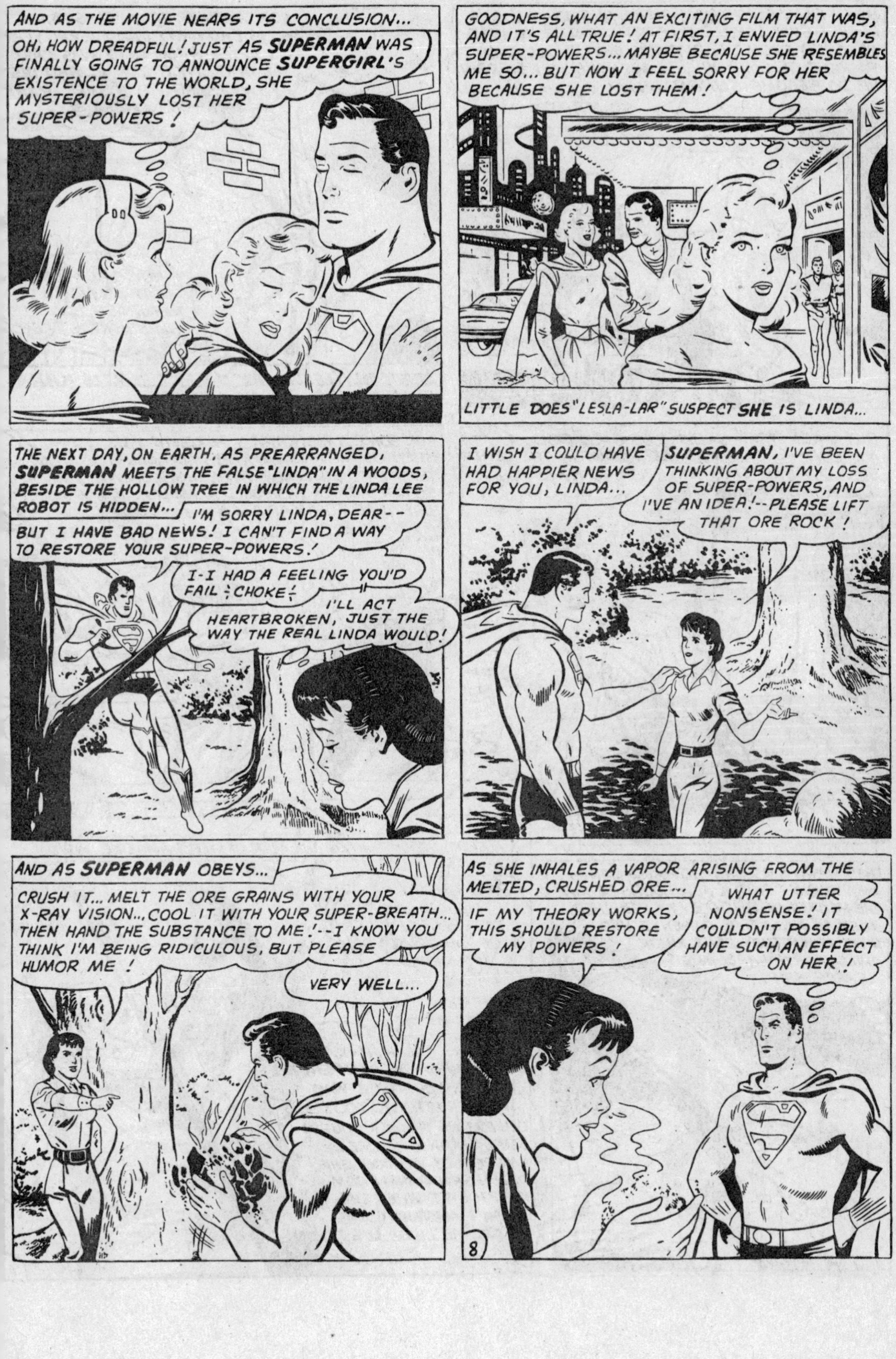
AND AS THE MOVIE NEARS ITS CONCLUSION...
OH, HOW DREADFUL! JUST AS SUPERMAN WAS FINALLY GOING TO ANNOUNCE SUPERGIRL'S EXISTENCE TO THE WORLD, SHE MYSTERIOUSLY LOST HER SUPER-POWERS!
GOODNESS, WHAT AN EXCITING FILM THAT WAS, AND IT'S ALL TRUE! AT FIRST, I ENVIED LINDA'S SUPER-POWERS... MAYBE BECAUSE SHE RESEMBLES ME SO... BUT NOW I FEEL SORRY FOR HER BECAUSE SHE LOST THEM!
LITTLE DOES "LESLA-LAR" SUSPECT SHE IS LINDA...
THE NEXT DAY, ON EARTH, AS PREARRANGED, SUPERMAN MEETS THE FALSE "LINDA" IN A WOODS, BESIDE THE HOLLOW TREE IN WHICH THE LINDA LEE ROBOT IS HIDDEN...
I'M SORRY LINDA, DEAR-- BUT I HAVE BAD NEWS! I CAN'T FIND A WAY TO RESTORE YOUR SUPER-POWERS!
I-I HAD A FEELING YOU'D FAIL ÷CHOKE÷!
I'LL ACT HEARTBROKEN, JUST THE WAY THE REAL LINDA WOULD!
I WISH I COULD HAVE HAD HAPPIER NEWS FOR YOU, LINDA...
SUPERMAN, I'VE BEEN THINKING ABOUT MY LOSS OF SUPER-POWERS, AND I'VE AN IDEA!--PLEASE LIFT THAT ORE ROCK!
AND AS SUPERMAN OBEYS...
CRUSH IT... MELT THE ORE GRAINS WITH YOUR X-RAY VISION... COOL IT WITH YOUR SUPER-BREATH... THEN HAND THE SUBSTANCE TO ME!--I KNOW YOU THINK I'M BEING RIDICULOUS, BUT PLEASE HUMOR ME!
VERY WELL...
AS SHE INHALES A VAPOR ARISING FROM THE MELTED, CRUSHED ORE...
IF MY THEORY WORKS, THIS SHOULD RESTORE MY POWERS!
WHAT UTTER NONSENSE! IT COULDN'T POSSIBLY HAVE SUCH AN EFFECT ON HER!
8

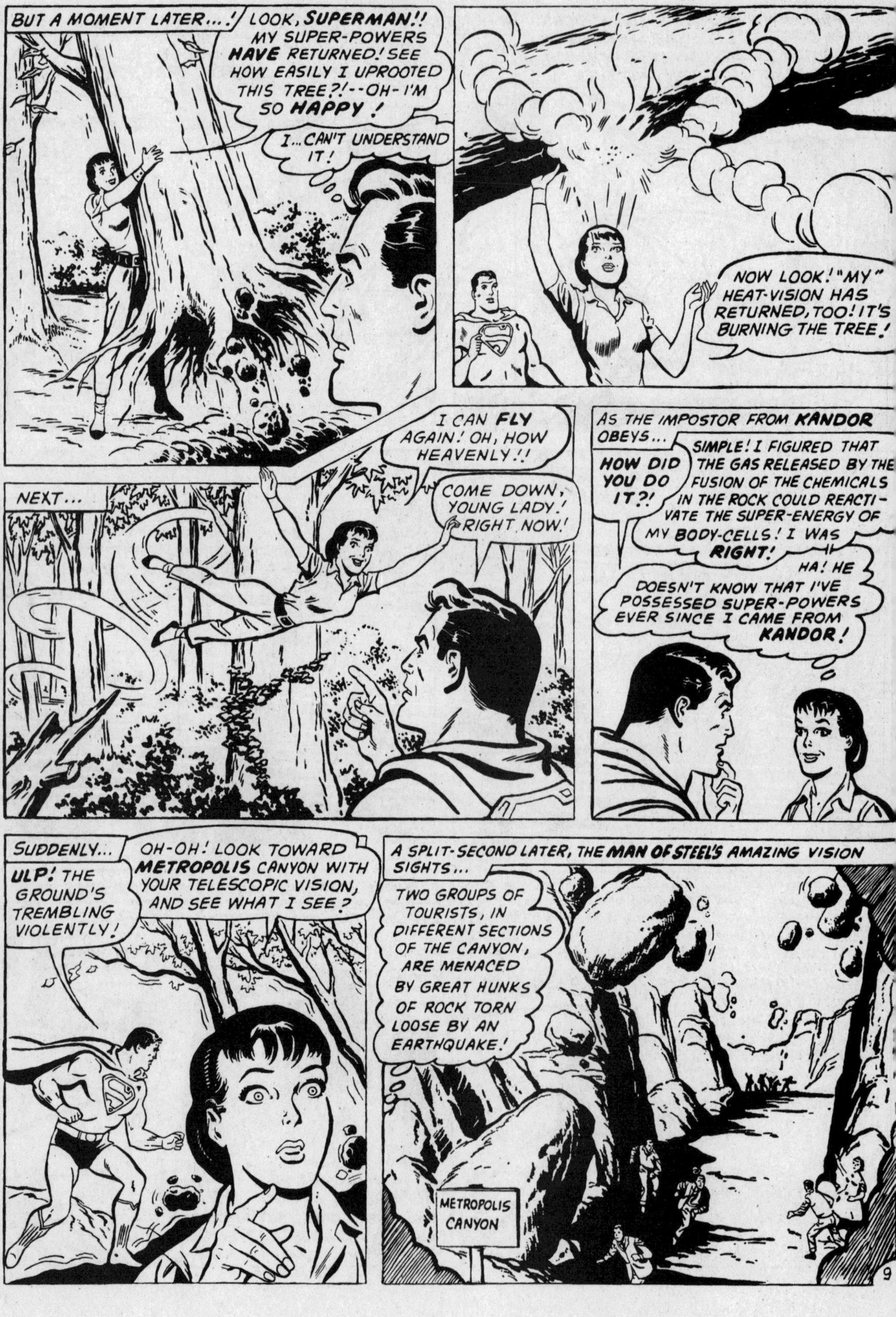
BUT A MOMENT LATER...!
LOOK, SUPERMAN!! MY SUPER-POWERS HAVE RETURNED! SEE HOW EASILY I UPROOTED THIS TREE?!--OH- I'M SO HAPPY!
I... CAN'T UNDERSTAND IT!
NOW LOOK! "MY" HEAT-VISION HAS RETURNED, TOO! IT'S BURNING THE TREE!
NEXT...
I CAN FLY AGAIN! OH, HOW HEAVENLY!!
COME DOWN, YOUNG LADY! RIGHT NOW!
AS THE IMPOSTOR FROM KANDOR OBEYS...
HOW DID YOU DO IT?!
SIMPLE! I FIGURED THAT THE GAS RELEASED BY THE FUSION OF THE CHEMICALS IN THE ROCK COULD REACTIVATE THE SUPER-ENERGY OF MY BODY-CELLS! I WAS RIGHT!
HA! HE DOESN'T KNOW THAT I'VE POSSESSED SUPER-POWERS EVER SINCE I CAME FROM KANDOR!
SUDDENLY...
ULP! THE GROUND'S TREMBLING VIOLENTLY!
OH-OH! LOOK TOWARD METROPOLIS CANYON WITH YOUR TELESCOPIC VISION, AND SEE WHAT I SEE?
A SPLIT-SECOND LATER, THE MAN OF STEEL'S AMAZING VISION SIGHTS...
TWO GROUPS OF TOURISTS, IN DIFFERENT SECTIONS OF THE CANYON, ARE MENACED BY GREAT HUNKS OF ROCK TORN LOOSE BY AN EARTHQUAKE!
METROPOLIS CANYON
9

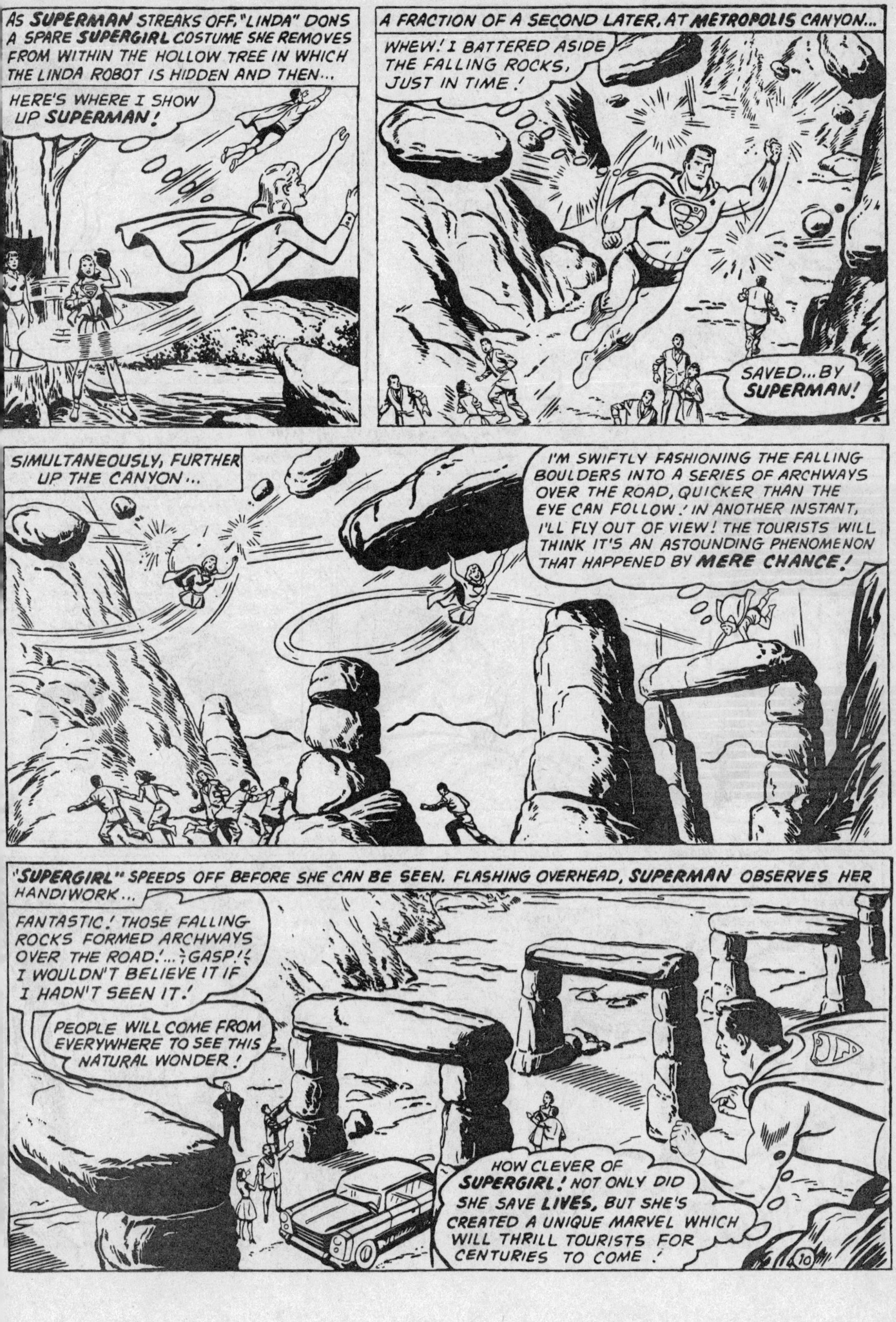
AS SUPERMAN STREAKS OFF, "LINDA" DONS A SPARE SUPERGIRL COSTUME SHE REMOVES FROM WITHIN THE HOLLOW TREE IN WHICH THE LINDA ROBOT IS HIDDEN AND THEN...
HERE'S WHERE I SHOW UP SUPERMAN!
A FRACTION OF A SECOND LATER, AT METROPOLIS CANYON...
WHEW! I BATTERED ASIDE THE FALLING ROCKS, JUST IN TIME!
SAVED...BY SUPERMAN!
SIMULTANEOUSLY, FURTHER UP THE CANYON...
I'M SWIFTLY FASHIONING THE FALLING BOULDERS INTO A SERIES OF ARCHWAYS OVER THE ROAD, QUICKER THAN THE EYE CAN FOLLOW! IN ANOTHER INSTANT, I'LL FLY OUT OF VIEW! THE TOURISTS WILL THINK IT'S AN ASTOUNDING PHENOMENON THAT HAPPENED BY MERE CHANCE!
"SUPERGIRL" SPEEDS OFF BEFORE SHE CAN BE SEEN. FLASHING OVERHEAD, SUPERMAN OBSERVES HER HANDIWORK...
FANTASTIC! THOSE FALLING ROCKS FORMED ARCHWAYS OVER THE ROAD!...GASP!! I WOULDN'T BELIEVE IT IF I HADN'T SEEN IT!
PEOPLE WILL COME FROM EVERYWHERE TO SEE THIS NATURAL WONDER!
HOW CLEVER OF SUPERGIRL! NOT ONLY DID SHE SAVE LIVES, BUT SHE'S CREATED A UNIQUE MARVEL WHICH WILL THRILL TOURISTS FOR CENTURIES TO COME!
10

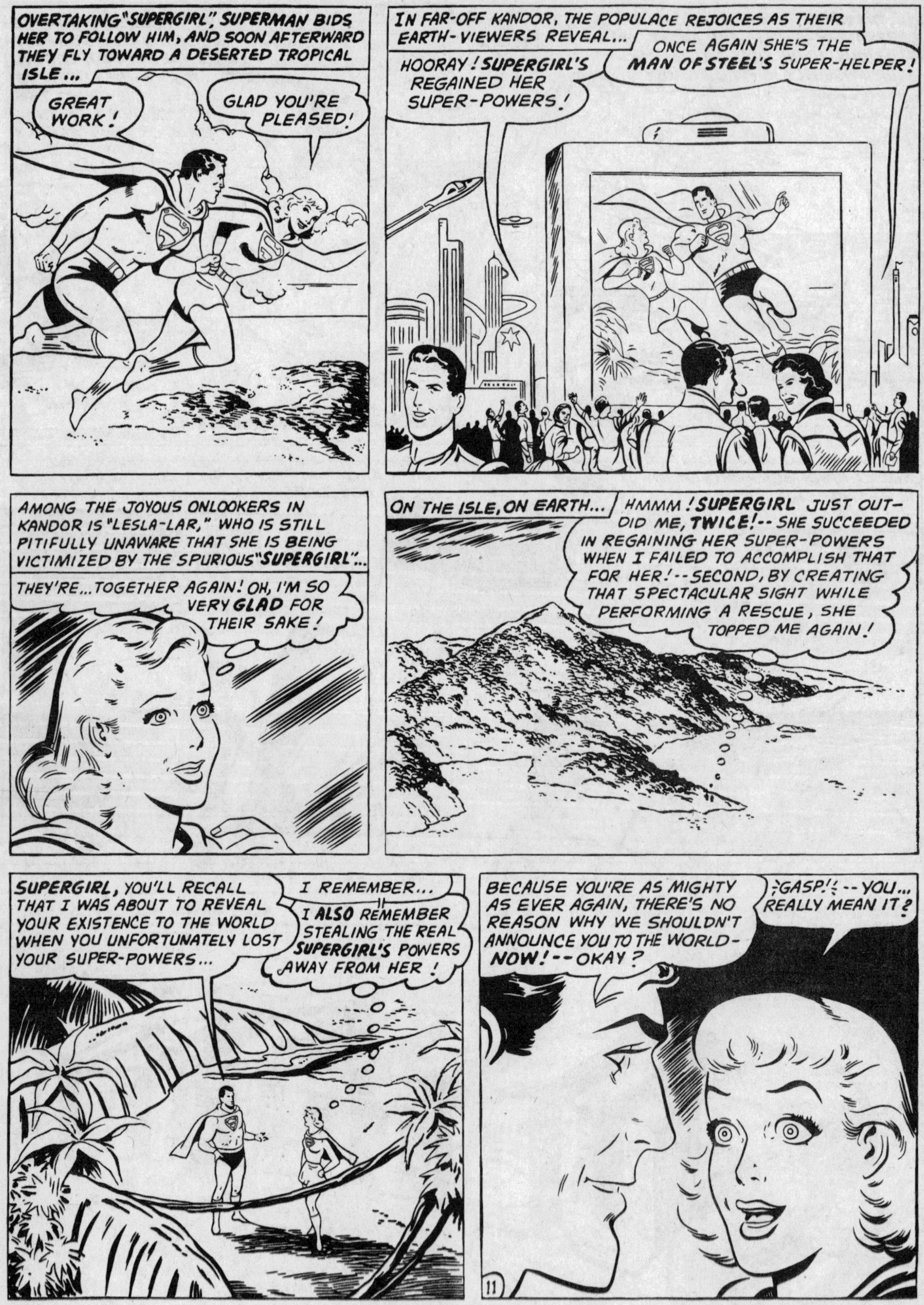
OVERTAKING "SUPERGIRL", SUPERMAN BIDS HER TO FOLLOW HIM, AND SOON AFTERWARD THEY FLY TOWARD A DESERTED TROPICAL ISLE...
GREAT WORK!
GLAD YOU'RE PLEASED!
IN FAR-OFF KANDOR, THE POPULACE REJOICES AS THEIR EARTH-VIEWERS REVEAL...
HOORAY! SUPERGIRL'S REGAINED HER SUPER-POWERS!
ONCE AGAIN SHE'S THE MAN OF STEEL'S SUPER-HELPER!
AMONG THE JOYOUS ONLOOKERS IN KANDOR IS "LESLA-LAR," WHO IS STILL PITIFULLY UNAWARE THAT SHE IS BEING VICTIMIZED BY THE SPURIOUS "SUPERGIRL"...
THEY'RE...TOGETHER AGAIN! OH, I'M SO VERY GLAD FOR THEIR SAKE!
ON THE ISLE, ON EARTH...
HMMM! SUPERGIRL JUST OUT-DID ME, TWICE!-- SHE SUCCEEDED IN REGAINING HER SUPER-POWERS WHEN I FAILED TO ACCOMPLISH THAT FOR HER!--SECOND, BY CREATING THAT SPECTACULAR SIGHT WHILE PERFORMING A RESCUE, SHE TOPPED ME AGAIN!
SUPERGIRL, YOU'LL RECALL THAT I WAS ABOUT TO REVEAL YOUR EXISTENCE TO THE WORLD WHEN YOU UNFORTUNATELY LOST YOUR SUPER-POWERS...
I REMEMBER...
I ALSO REMEMBER STEALING THE REAL SUPERGIRL'S POWERS AWAY FROM HER!
BECAUSE YOU'RE AS MIGHTY AS EVER AGAIN, THERE'S NO REASON WHY WE SHOULDN'T ANNOUNCE YOU TO THE WORLD-NOW!--OKAY?
¡GASP!¡--YOU... REALLY MEAN IT?
11

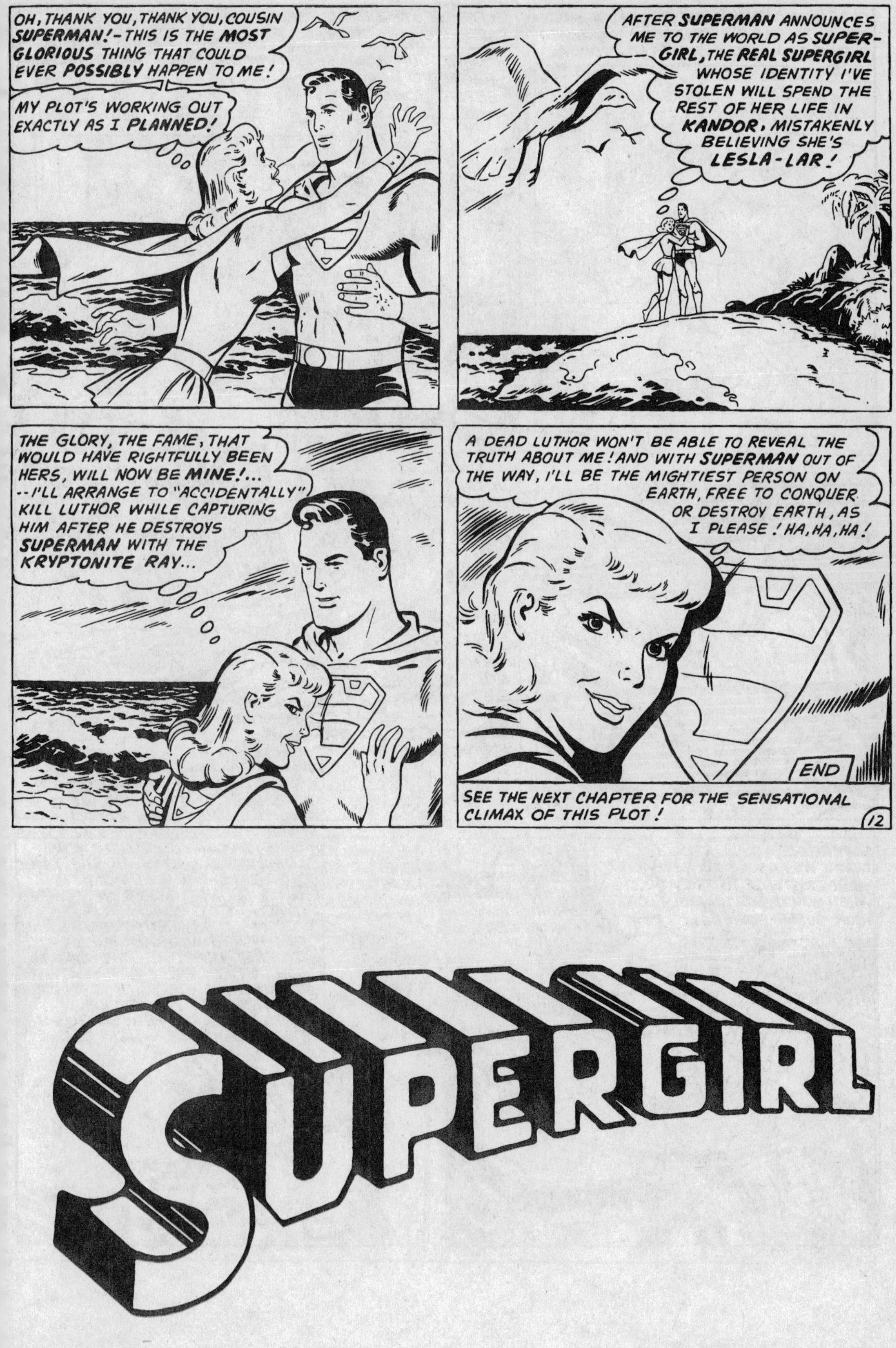
OH, THANK YOU, THANK YOU, COUSIN SUPERMAN! - THIS IS THE MOST GLORIOUS THING THAT COULD EVER POSSIBLY HAPPEN TO ME!
MY PLOT'S WORKING OUT EXACTLY AS I PLANNED!
AFTER SUPERMAN ANNOUNCES ME TO THE WORLD AS SUPER-GIRL, THE REAL SUPERGIRL WHOSE IDENTITY I'VE STOLEN WILL SPEND THE REST OF HER LIFE IN KANDOR, MISTAKENLY BELIEVING SHE'S LESLA-LAR!
THE GLORY, THE FAME, THAT WOULD HAVE RIGHTFULLY BEEN HERS, WILL NOW BE MINE!... --I'LL ARRANGE TO "ACCIDENTALLY" KILL LUTHOR WHILE CAPTURING HIM AFTER HE DESTROYS SUPERMAN WITH THE KRYPTONITE RAY...
A DEAD LUTHOR WON'T BE ABLE TO REVEAL THE TRUTH ABOUT ME! AND WITH SUPERMAN OUT OF THE WAY, I'LL BE THE MIGHTIEST PERSON ON EARTH, FREE TO CONQUER OR DESTROY EARTH, AS I PLEASE! HA, HA, HA!
END
SEE THE NEXT CHAPTER FOR THE SENSATIONAL CLIMAX OF THIS PLOT!
12

SUPERGIRL

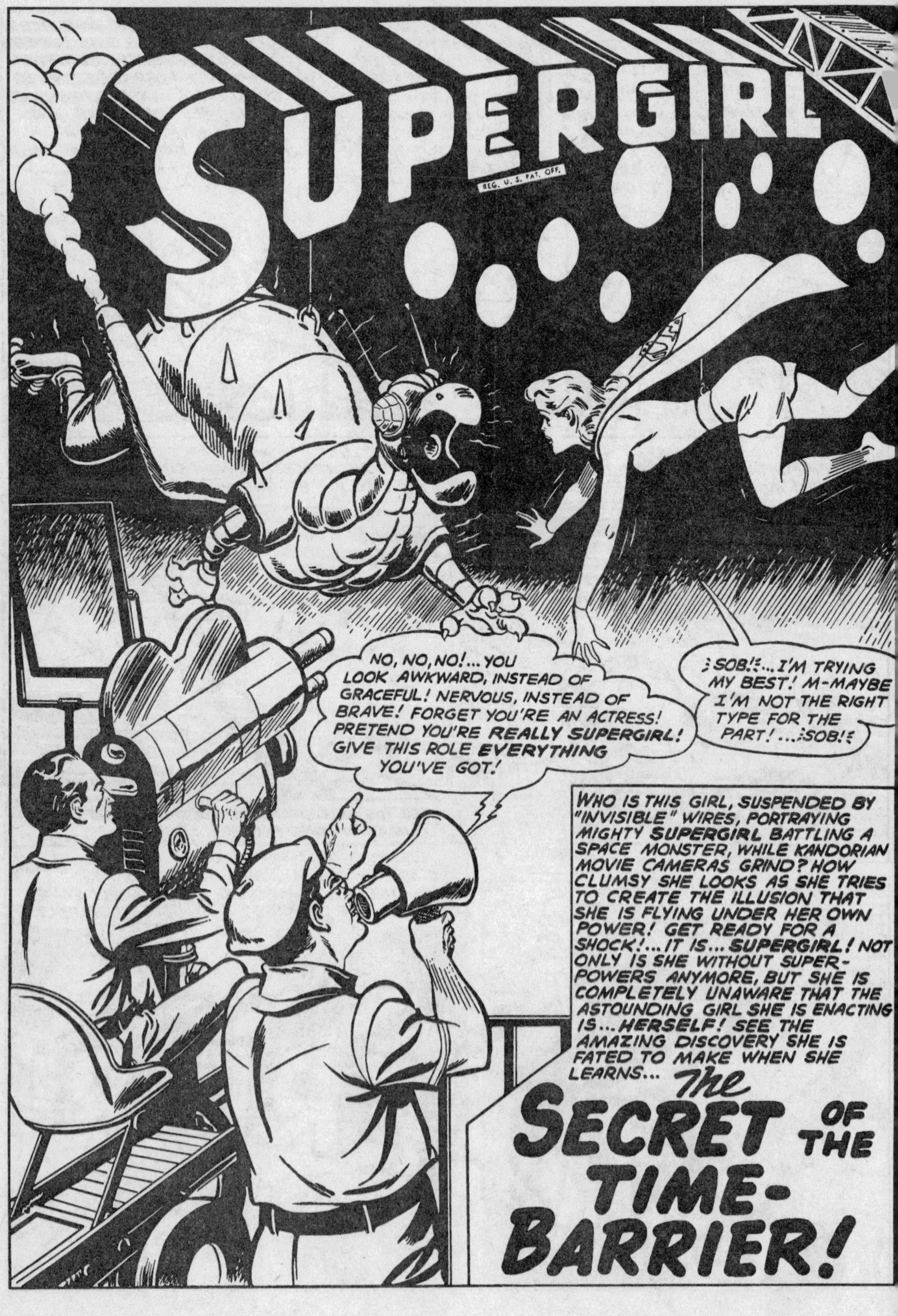
SUPERGIRL
REG. U.S. PAT. OFF.
NO, NO, NO!... YOU LOOK AWKWARD, INSTEAD OF GRACEFUL! NERVOUS, INSTEAD OF BRAVE! FORGET YOU'RE AN ACTRESS! PRETEND YOU'RE REALLY SUPERGIRL! GIVE THIS ROLE EVERYTHING YOU'VE GOT!
;SOB!;... I'M TRYING MY BEST! M-MAYBE I'M NOT THE RIGHT TYPE FOR THE PART! ...;SOB!;
WHO IS THIS GIRL, SUSPENDED BY "INVISIBLE" WIRES, PORTRAYING MIGHTY SUPERGIRL BATTLING A SPACE MONSTER, WHILE KANDORIAN MOVIE CAMERAS GRIND? HOW CLUMSY SHE LOOKS AS SHE TRIES TO CREATE THE ILLUSION THAT SHE IS FLYING UNDER HER OWN POWER! GET READY FOR A SHOCK!... IT IS... SUPERGIRL! NOT ONLY IS SHE WITHOUT SUPER-POWERS ANYMORE, BUT SHE IS COMPLETELY UNAWARE THAT THE ASTOUNDING GIRL SHE IS ENACTING IS... HERSELF! SEE THE AMAZING DISCOVERY SHE IS FATED TO MAKE WHEN SHE LEARNS...
The SECRET OF THE TIME-BARRIER!

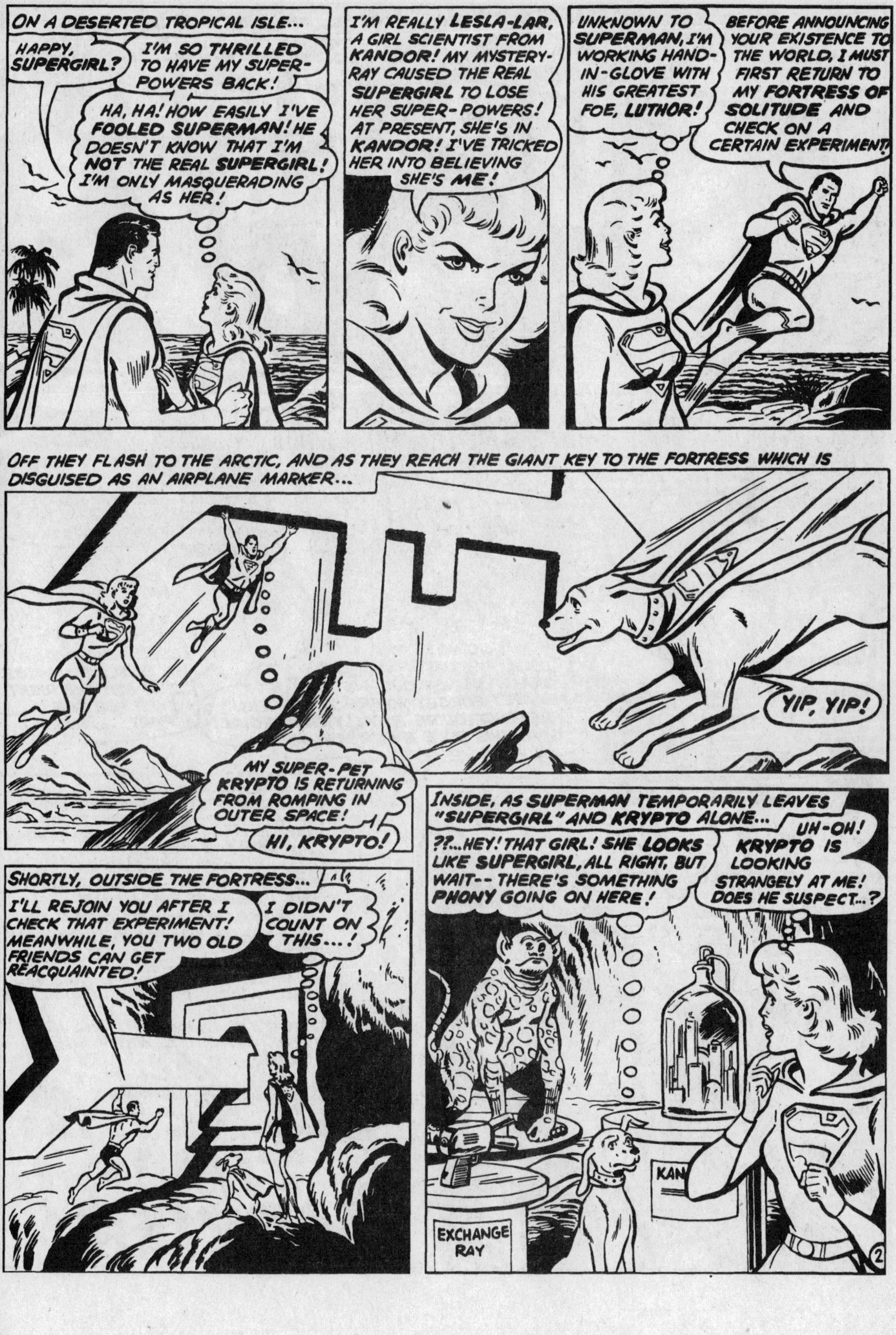
ON A DESERTED TROPICAL ISLE...
HAPPY, SUPERGIRL?
I'M SO THRILLED TO HAVE MY SUPER-POWERS BACK!
HA, HA! HOW EASILY I'VE FOOLED SUPERMAN! HE DOESN'T KNOW THAT I'M NOT THE REAL SUPERGIRL! I'M ONLY MASQUERADING AS HER!
I'M REALLY LESLA-LAR, A GIRL SCIENTIST FROM KANDOR! MY MYSTERY-RAY CAUSED THE REAL SUPERGIRL TO LOSE HER SUPER-POWERS! AT PRESENT, SHE'S IN KANDOR! I'VE TRICKED HER INTO BELIEVING SHE'S ME!
UNKNOWN TO SUPERMAN, I'M WORKING HAND-IN-GLOVE WITH HIS GREATEST FOE, LUTHOR!
BEFORE ANNOUNCING YOUR EXISTENCE TO THE WORLD, I MUST FIRST RETURN TO MY FORTRESS OF SOLITUDE AND CHECK ON A CERTAIN EXPERIMENT!
OFF THEY FLASH TO THE ARCTIC, AND AS THEY REACH THE GIANT KEY TO THE FORTRESS WHICH IS DISGUISED AS AN AIRPLANE MARKER...
MY SUPER-PET KRYPTO IS RETURNING FROM ROMPING IN OUTER SPACE!
HI, KRYPTO!
YIP, YIP!
SHORTLY, OUTSIDE THE FORTRESS...
I'LL REJOIN YOU AFTER I CHECK THAT EXPERIMENT! MEANWHILE, YOU TWO OLD FRIENDS CAN GET REACQUAINTED!
I DIDN'T COUNT ON THIS...!
INSIDE, AS SUPERMAN TEMPORARILY LEAVES "SUPERGIRL" AND KRYPTO ALONE...
??...HEY! THAT GIRL! SHE LOOKS LIKE SUPERGIRL, ALL RIGHT, BUT WAIT-- THERE'S SOMETHING PHONY GOING ON HERE!
UH-OH! KRYPTO IS LOOKING STRANGELY AT ME! DOES HE SUSPECT...?
EXCHANGE RAY
KAN
2

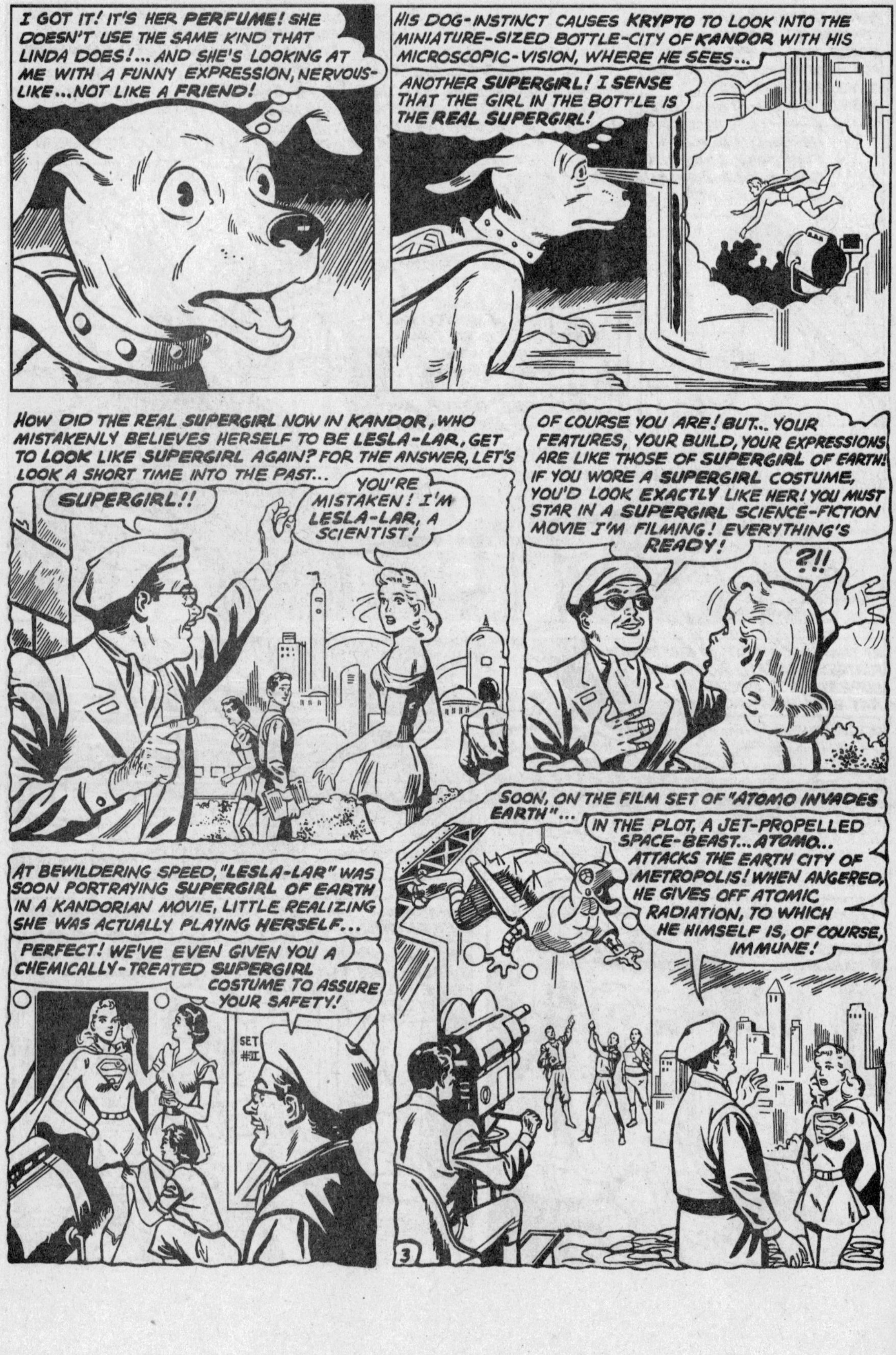
I GOT IT! IT'S HER PERFUME! SHE DOESN'T USE THE SAME KIND THAT LINDA DOES!... AND SHE'S LOOKING AT ME WITH A FUNNY EXPRESSION, NERVOUS-LIKE... NOT LIKE A FRIEND!
HIS DOG-INSTINCT CAUSES KRYPTO TO LOOK INTO THE MINIATURE-SIZED BOTTLE-CITY OF KANDOR WITH HIS MICROSCOPIC-VISION, WHERE HE SEES...
ANOTHER SUPERGIRL! I SENSE THAT THE GIRL IN THE BOTTLE IS THE REAL SUPERGIRL!
HOW DID THE REAL SUPERGIRL NOW IN KANDOR, WHO MISTAKENLY BELIEVES HERSELF TO BE LESLA-LAR, GET TO LOOK LIKE SUPERGIRL AGAIN? FOR THE ANSWER, LET'S LOOK A SHORT TIME INTO THE PAST...
SUPERGIRL!!
YOU'RE MISTAKEN! I'M LESLA-LAR, A SCIENTIST!
OF COURSE YOU ARE! BUT... YOUR FEATURES, YOUR BUILD, YOUR EXPRESSIONS ARE LIKE THOSE OF SUPERGIRL OF EARTH! IF YOU WORE A SUPERGIRL COSTUME, YOU'D LOOK EXACTLY LIKE HER! YOU MUST STAR IN A SUPERGIRL SCIENCE-FICTION MOVIE I'M FILMING! EVERYTHING'S READY!
?!!
AT BEWILDERING SPEED, "LESLA-LAR" WAS SOON PORTRAYING SUPERGIRL OF EARTH IN A KANDORIAN MOVIE, LITTLE REALIZING SHE WAS ACTUALLY PLAYING HERSELF...
PERFECT! WE'VE EVEN GIVEN YOU A CHEMICALLY-TREATED SUPERGIRL COSTUME TO ASSURE YOUR SAFETY!
SET #II
SOON, ON THE FILM SET OF "ATOMO INVADES EARTH"...
IN THE PLOT, A JET-PROPELLED SPACE-BEAST... ATOMO... ATTACKS THE EARTH CITY OF METROPOLIS! WHEN ANGERED, HE GIVES OFF ATOMIC RADIATION, TO WHICH HE HIMSELF IS, OF COURSE, IMMUNE!
3

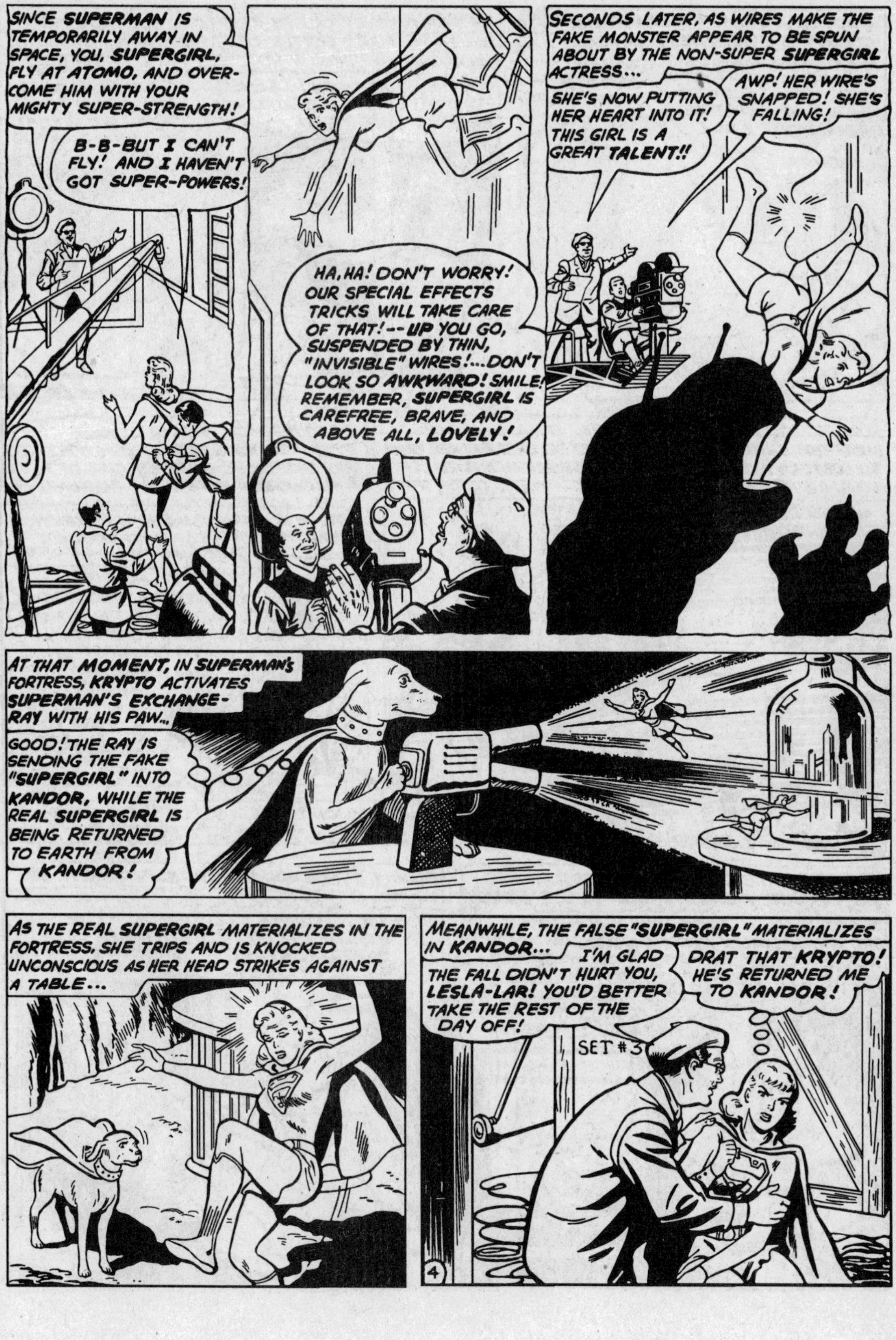
SINCE SUPERMAN IS TEMPORARILY AWAY IN SPACE, YOU, SUPERGIRL, FLY AT ATOMO, AND OVERCOME HIM WITH YOUR MIGHTY SUPER-STRENGTH!
B-B-BUT I CAN'T FLY! AND I HAVEN'T GOT SUPER-POWERS!
HA, HA! DON'T WORRY! OUR SPECIAL EFFECTS TRICKS WILL TAKE CARE OF THAT!--UP YOU GO, SUSPENDED BY THIN, "INVISIBLE" WIRES!...DON'T LOOK SO AWKWARD! SMILE! REMEMBER, SUPERGIRL IS CAREFREE, BRAVE, AND ABOVE ALL, LOVELY!
SECONDS LATER, AS WIRES MAKE THE FAKE MONSTER APPEAR TO BE SPUN ABOUT BY THE NON-SUPER SUPERGIRL ACTRESS...
SHE'S NOW PUTTING HER HEART INTO IT! THIS GIRL IS A GREAT TALENT!!
AWP! HER WIRE'S SNAPPED! SHE'S FALLING!
AT THAT MOMENT, IN SUPERMAN'S FORTRESS, KRYPTO ACTIVATES SUPERMAN'S EXCHANGE-RAY WITH HIS PAW...
GOOD! THE RAY IS SENDING THE FAKE "SUPERGIRL" INTO KANDOR, WHILE THE REAL SUPERGIRL IS BEING RETURNED TO EARTH FROM KANDOR!
AS THE REAL SUPERGIRL MATERIALIZES IN THE FORTRESS, SHE TRIPS AND IS KNOCKED UNCONSCIOUS AS HER HEAD STRIKES AGAINST A TABLE...
MEANWHILE, THE FALSE "SUPERGIRL" MATERIALIZES IN KANDOR...
I'M GLAD THE FALL DIDN'T HURT YOU, LESLA-LAR! YOU'D BETTER TAKE THE REST OF THE DAY OFF!
DRAT THAT KRYPTO! HE'S RETURNED ME TO KANDOR!
SET #3
4

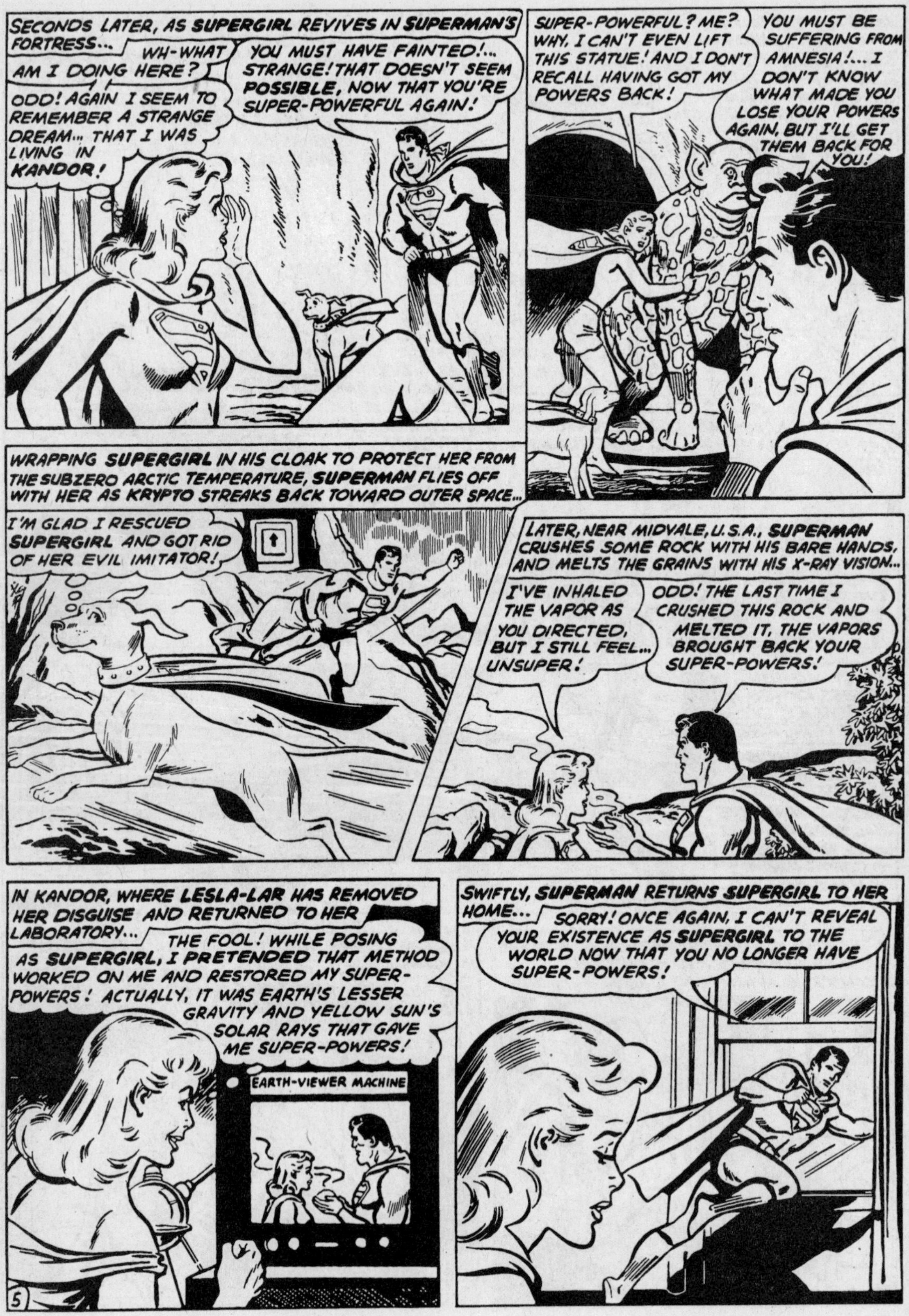
SECONDS LATER, AS SUPERGIRL REVIVES IN SUPERMAN'S FORTRESS...
WH-WHAT AM I DOING HERE?
ODD! AGAIN I SEEM TO REMEMBER A STRANGE DREAM... THAT I WAS LIVING IN KANDOR!
YOU MUST HAVE FAINTED!... STRANGE! THAT DOESN'T SEEM POSSIBLE, NOW THAT YOU'RE SUPER-POWERFUL AGAIN!
SUPER-POWERFUL? ME? WHY, I CAN'T EVEN LIFT THIS STATUE! AND I DON'T RECALL HAVING GOT MY POWERS BACK!
YOU MUST BE SUFFERING FROM AMNESIA!... I DON'T KNOW WHAT MADE YOU LOSE YOUR POWERS AGAIN, BUT I'LL GET THEM BACK FOR YOU!
WRAPPING SUPERGIRL IN HIS CLOAK TO PROTECT HER FROM THE SUBZERO ARCTIC TEMPERATURE, SUPERMAN FLIES OFF WITH HER AS KRYPTO STREAKS BACK TOWARD OUTER SPACE...
I'M GLAD I RESCUED SUPERGIRL AND GOT RID OF HER EVIL IMITATOR!
LATER, NEAR MIDVALE, U.S.A., SUPERMAN CRUSHES SOME ROCK WITH HIS BARE HANDS, AND MELTS THE GRAINS WITH HIS X-RAY VISION...
I'VE INHALED THE VAPOR AS YOU DIRECTED, BUT I STILL FEEL... UNSUPER!
ODD! THE LAST TIME I CRUSHED THIS ROCK AND MELTED IT, THE VAPORS BROUGHT BACK YOUR SUPER-POWERS!
IN KANDOR, WHERE LESLA-LAR HAS REMOVED HER DISGUISE AND RETURNED TO HER LABORATORY...
THE FOOL! WHILE POSING AS SUPERGIRL, I PRETENDED THAT METHOD WORKED ON ME AND RESTORED MY SUPER-POWERS! ACTUALLY, IT WAS EARTH'S LESSER GRAVITY AND YELLOW SUN'S SOLAR RAYS THAT GAVE ME SUPER-POWERS!
EARTH-VIEWER MACHINE
5
SWIFTLY, SUPERMAN RETURNS SUPERGIRL TO HER HOME...
SORRY! ONCE AGAIN, I CAN'T REVEAL YOUR EXISTENCE AS SUPERGIRL TO THE WORLD NOW THAT YOU NO LONGER HAVE SUPER-POWERS!

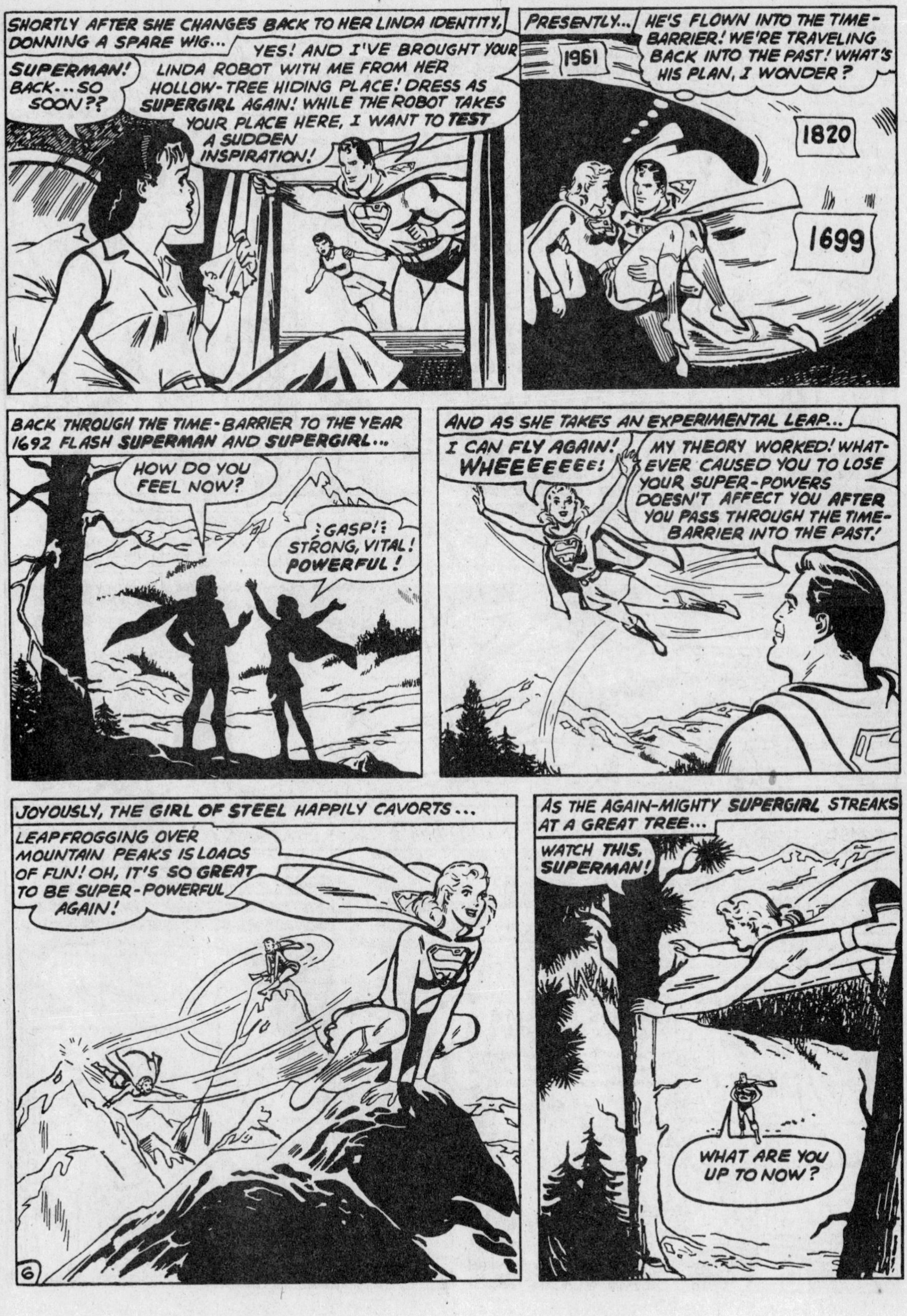
SHORTLY AFTER SHE CHANGES BACK TO HER LINDA IDENTITY, DONNING A SPARE WIG...
SUPERMAN! BACK... SO SOON??
YES! AND I'VE BROUGHT YOUR LINDA ROBOT WITH ME FROM HER HOLLOW-TREE HIDING PLACE! DRESS AS SUPERGIRL AGAIN! WHILE THE ROBOT TAKES YOUR PLACE HERE, I WANT TO TEST A SUDDEN INSPIRATION!
PRESENTLY...
HE'S FLOWN INTO THE TIME-BARRIER! WE'RE TRAVELING BACK INTO THE PAST! WHAT'S HIS PLAN, I WONDER?
1961
1820
1699
BACK THROUGH THE TIME-BARRIER TO THE YEAR 1692 FLASH SUPERMAN AND SUPERGIRL...
HOW DO YOU FEEL NOW?
:GASP!: STRONG, VITAL! POWERFUL!
AND AS SHE TAKES AN EXPERIMENTAL LEAP...
I CAN FLY AGAIN! WHEEEEEEE!
MY THEORY WORKED! WHATEVER CAUSED YOU TO LOSE YOUR SUPER-POWERS DOESN'T AFFECT YOU AFTER YOU PASS THROUGH THE TIME-BARRIER INTO THE PAST!
JOYOUSLY, THE GIRL OF STEEL HAPPILY CAVORTS...
LEAPFROGGING OVER MOUNTAIN PEAKS IS LOADS OF FUN! OH, IT'S SO GREAT TO BE SUPER-POWERFUL AGAIN!
6
AS THE AGAIN-MIGHTY SUPERGIRL STREAKS AT A GREAT TREE...
WATCH THIS, SUPERMAN!
WHAT ARE YOU UP TO NOW?

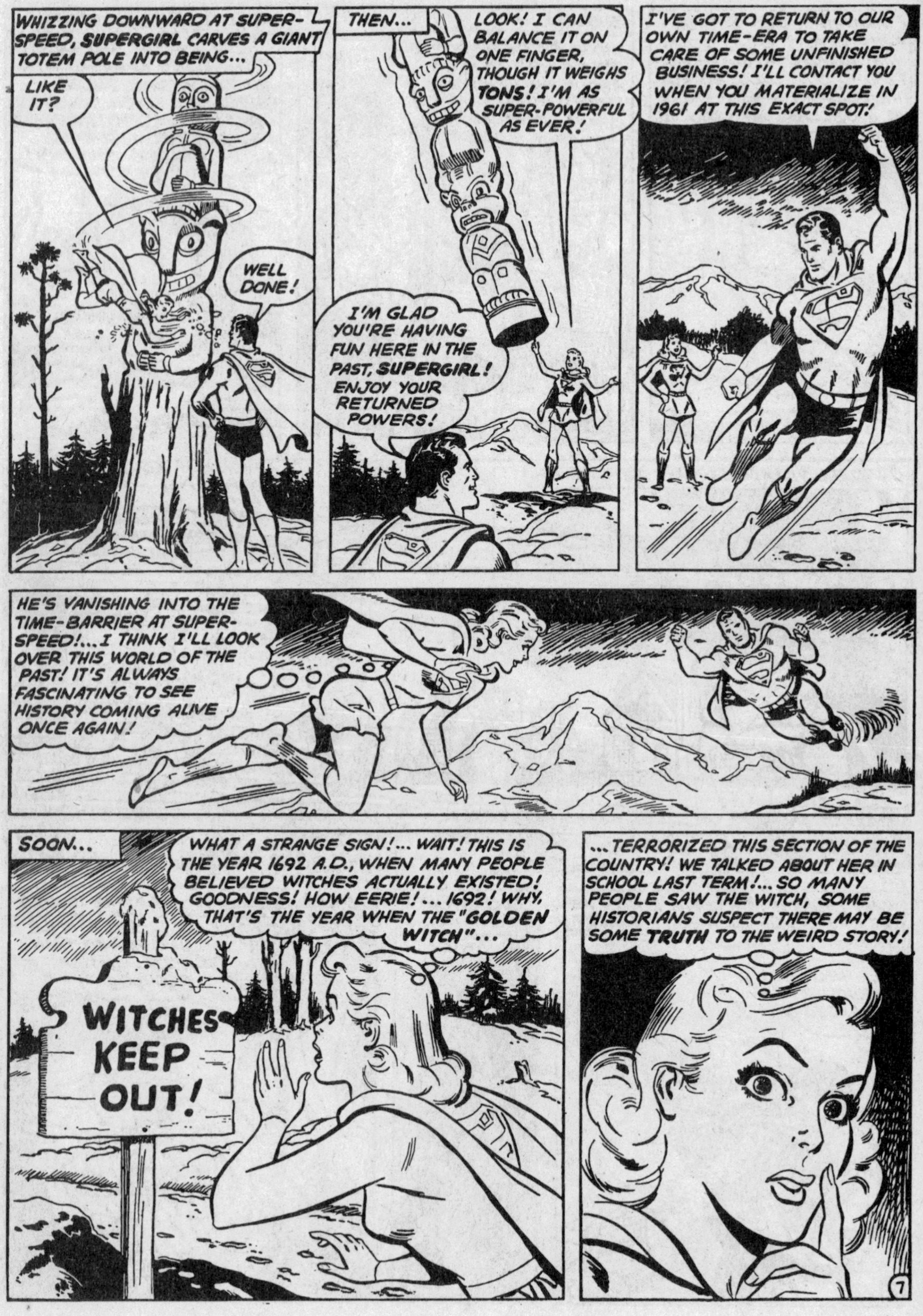
WHIZZING DOWNWARD AT SUPER-SPEED, SUPERGIRL CARVES A GIANT TOTEM POLE INTO BEING...
LIKE IT?
WELL DONE!
THEN...
LOOK! I CAN BALANCE IT ON ONE FINGER, THOUGH IT WEIGHS TONS! I'M AS SUPER-POWERFUL AS EVER!
I'M GLAD YOU'RE HAVING FUN HERE IN THE PAST, SUPERGIRL! ENJOY YOUR RETURNED POWERS!
I'VE GOT TO RETURN TO OUR OWN TIME-ERA TO TAKE CARE OF SOME UNFINISHED BUSINESS! I'LL CONTACT YOU WHEN YOU MATERIALIZE IN 1961 AT THIS EXACT SPOT!
HE'S VANISHING INTO THE TIME-BARRIER AT SUPER-SPEED!... I THINK I'LL LOOK OVER THIS WORLD OF THE PAST! IT'S ALWAYS FASCINATING TO SEE HISTORY COMING ALIVE ONCE AGAIN!
SOON...
WHAT A STRANGE SIGN!... WAIT! THIS IS THE YEAR 1692 A.D., WHEN MANY PEOPLE BELIEVED WITCHES ACTUALLY EXISTED! GOODNESS! HOW EERIE!... 1692! WHY, THAT'S THE YEAR WHEN THE "GOLDEN WITCH"...
WITCHES KEEP OUT!
...TERRORIZED THIS SECTION OF THE COUNTRY! WE TALKED ABOUT HER IN SCHOOL LAST TERM!... SO MANY PEOPLE SAW THE WITCH, SOME HISTORIANS SUSPECT THERE MAY BE SOME TRUTH TO THE WEIRD STORY!
7

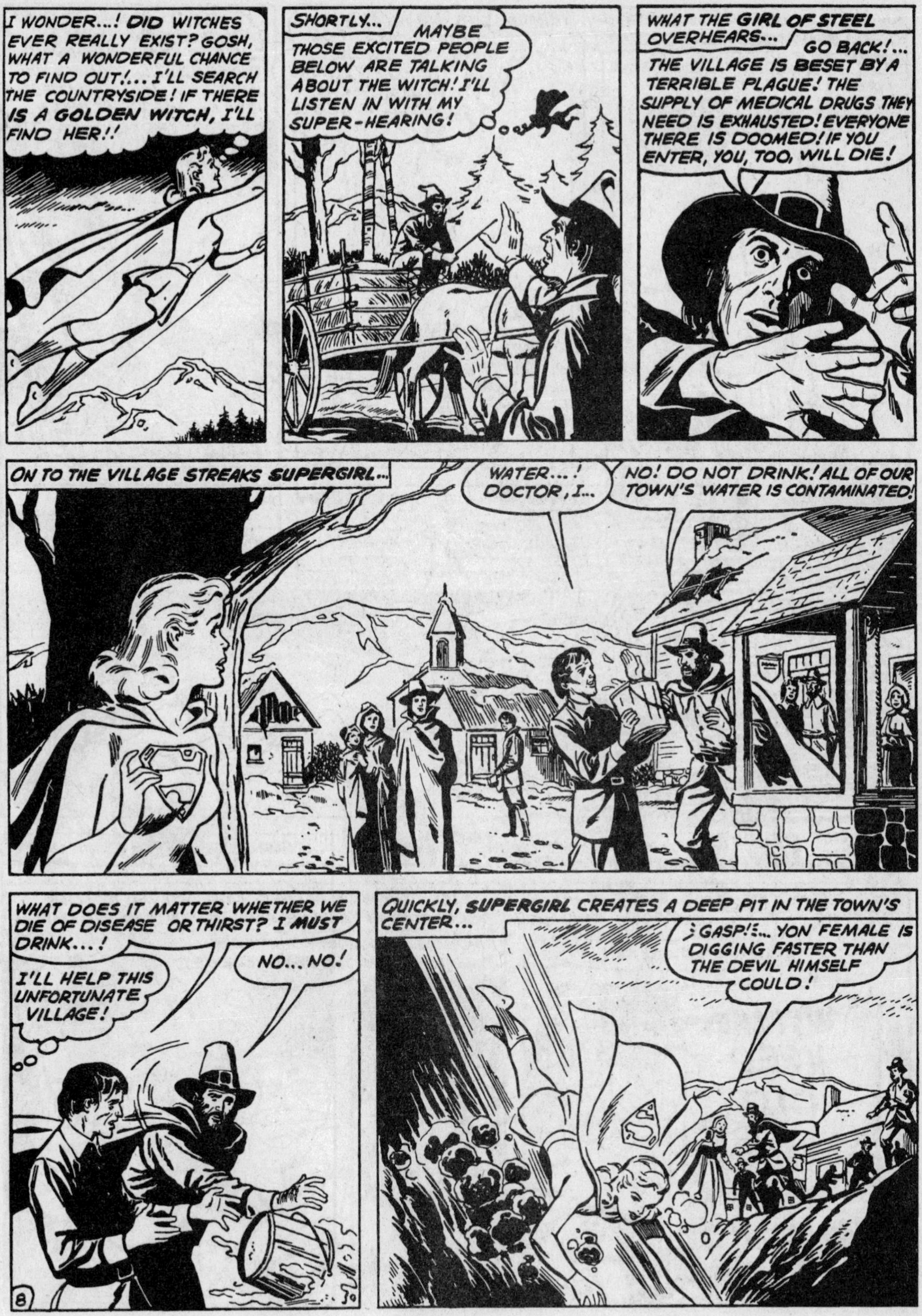
I WONDER...! DID WITCHES EVER REALLY EXIST? GOSH, WHAT A WONDERFUL CHANCE TO FIND OUT!... I'LL SEARCH THE COUNTRYSIDE! IF THERE IS A GOLDEN WITCH, I'LL FIND HER!!
SHORTLY...
MAYBE THOSE EXCITED PEOPLE BELOW ARE TALKING ABOUT THE WITCH! I'LL LISTEN IN WITH MY SUPER-HEARING!
WHAT THE GIRL OF STEEL OVERHEARS...
GO BACK!... THE VILLAGE IS BESET BY A TERRIBLE PLAGUE! THE SUPPLY OF MEDICAL DRUGS THEY NEED IS EXHAUSTED! EVERYONE THERE IS DOOMED! IF YOU ENTER, YOU, TOO, WILL DIE!
ON TO THE VILLAGE STREAKS SUPERGIRL...
WATER...! DOCTOR, I...
NO! DO NOT DRINK! ALL OF OUR TOWN'S WATER IS CONTAMINATED!
WHAT DOES IT MATTER WHETHER WE DIE OF DISEASE OR THIRST? I MUST DRINK...!
NO... NO!
I'LL HELP THIS UNFORTUNATE VILLAGE!
8
QUICKLY, SUPERGIRL CREATES A DEEP PIT IN THE TOWN'S CENTER...
GASP!... YON FEMALE IS DIGGING FASTER THAN THE DEVIL HIMSELF COULD!

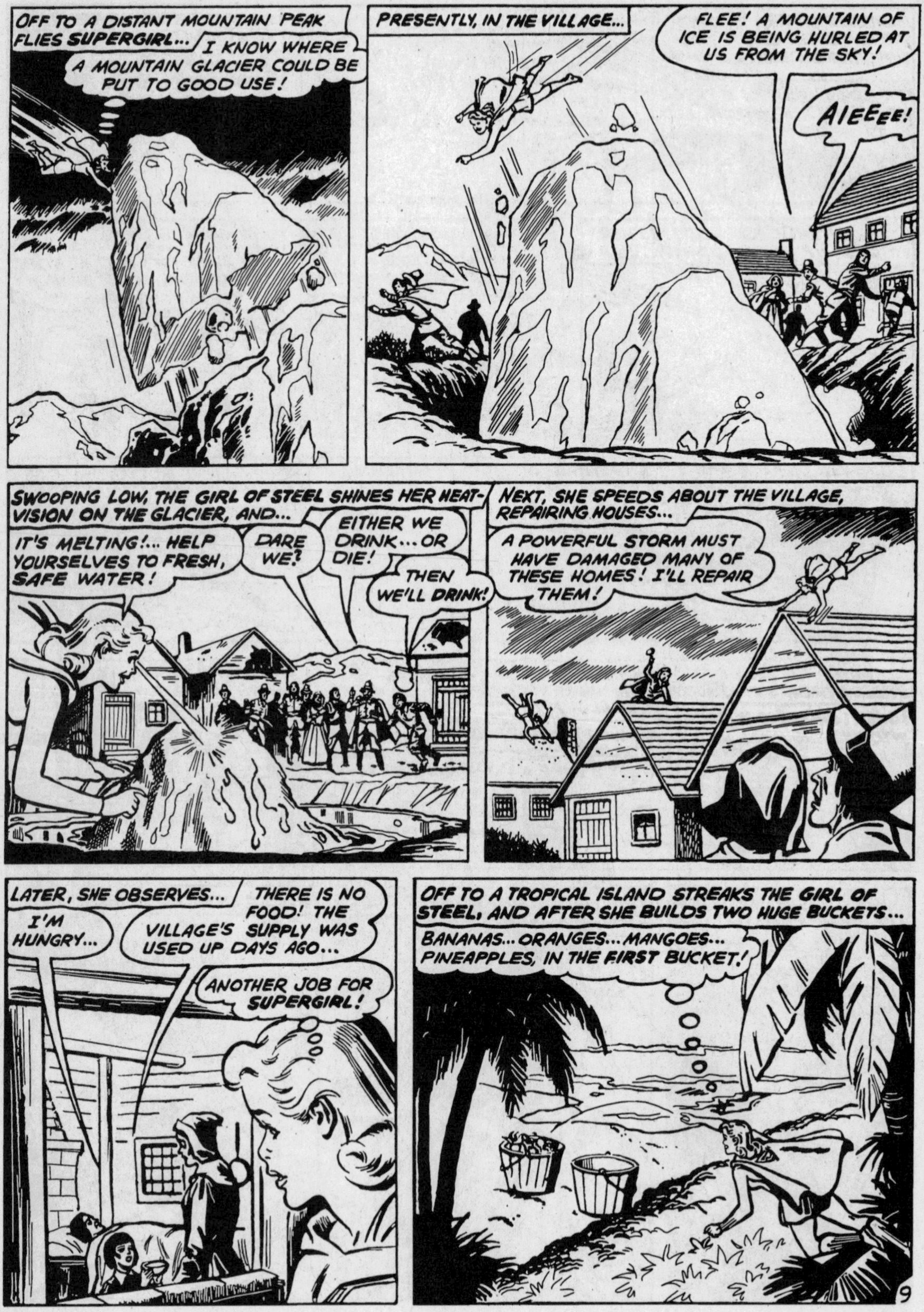
OFF TO A DISTANT MOUNTAIN PEAK FLIES SUPERGIRL...
I KNOW WHERE A MOUNTAIN GLACIER COULD BE PUT TO GOOD USE!
PRESENTLY, IN THE VILLAGE...
FLEE! A MOUNTAIN OF ICE IS BEING HURLED AT US FROM THE SKY!
AIEEEE!
SWOOPING LOW, THE GIRL OF STEEL SHINES HER HEAT-VISION ON THE GLACIER, AND...
IT'S MELTING!... HELP YOURSELVES TO FRESH, SAFE WATER!
DARE WE?
EITHER WE DRINK... OR DIE!
THEN WE'LL DRINK!
NEXT, SHE SPEEDS ABOUT THE VILLAGE, REPAIRING HOUSES...
A POWERFUL STORM MUST HAVE DAMAGED MANY OF THESE HOMES! I'LL REPAIR THEM!
LATER, SHE OBSERVES...
I'M HUNGRY...
THERE IS NO FOOD! THE VILLAGE'S SUPPLY WAS USED UP DAYS AGO...
ANOTHER JOB FOR SUPERGIRL!
OFF TO A TROPICAL ISLAND STREAKS THE GIRL OF STEEL, AND AFTER SHE BUILDS TWO HUGE BUCKETS...
BANANAS... ORANGES... MANGOES... PINEAPPLES, IN THE FIRST BUCKET!
9

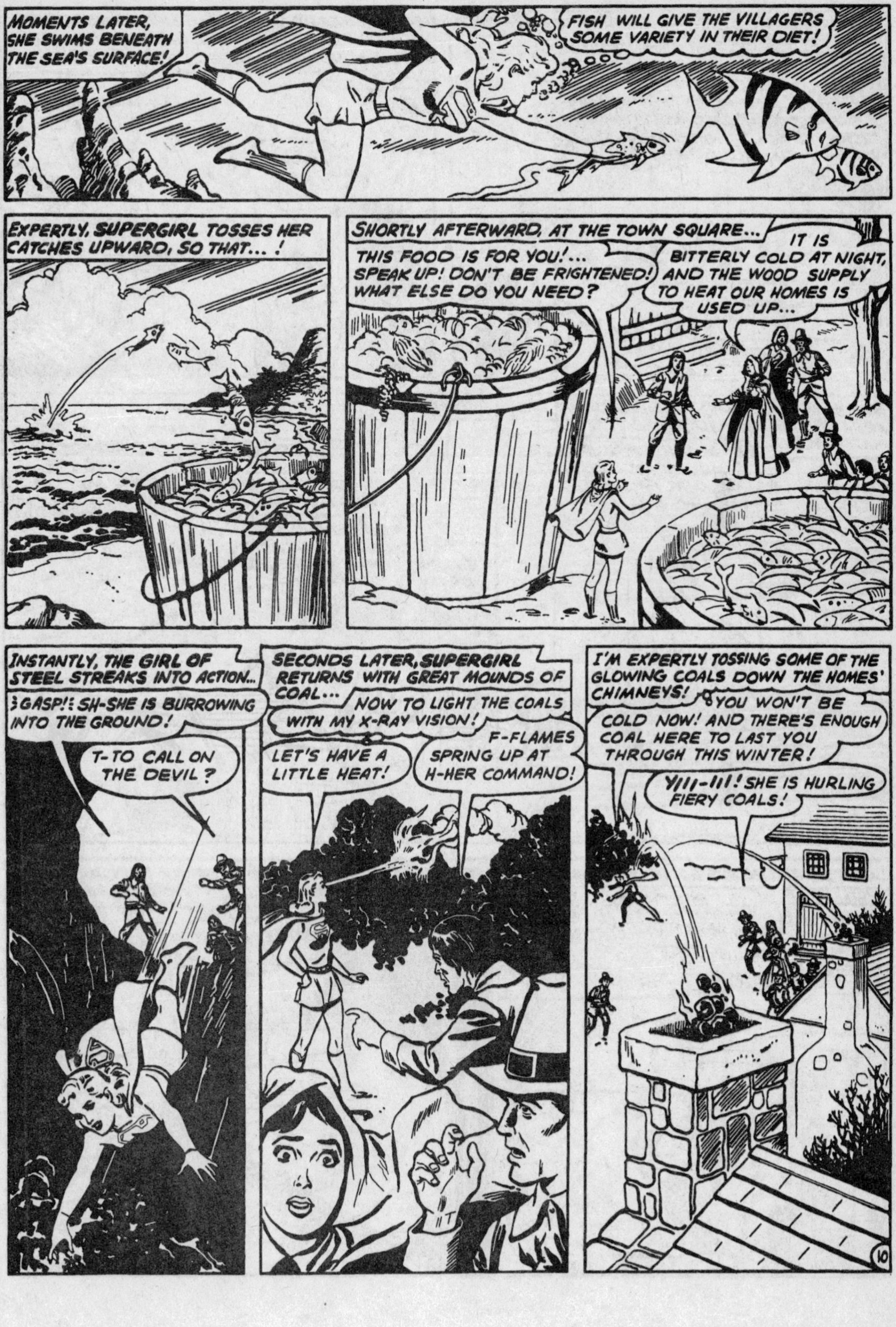
MOMENTS LATER, SHE SWIMS BENEATH THE SEA'S SURFACE!
FISH WILL GIVE THE VILLAGERS SOME VARIETY IN THEIR DIET!
EXPERTLY, SUPERGIRL TOSSES HER CATCHES UPWARD, SO THAT... !
SHORTLY AFTERWARD, AT THE TOWN SQUARE...
THIS FOOD IS FOR YOU!... SPEAK UP! DON'T BE FRIGHTENED! WHAT ELSE DO YOU NEED?
IT IS BITTERLY COLD AT NIGHT, AND THE WOOD SUPPLY TO HEAT OUR HOMES IS USED UP...
INSTANTLY, THE GIRL OF STEEL STREAKS INTO ACTION...
GASP!! SH-SHE IS BURROWING INTO THE GROUND!
T-TO CALL ON THE DEVIL?
SECONDS LATER, SUPERGIRL RETURNS WITH GREAT MOUNDS OF COAL...
NOW TO LIGHT THE COALS WITH MY X-RAY VISION!
LET'S HAVE A LITTLE HEAT!
F-FLAMES SPRING UP AT H-HER COMMAND!
I'M EXPERTLY TOSSING SOME OF THE GLOWING COALS DOWN THE HOMES' CHIMNEYS!
YOU WON'T BE COLD NOW! AND THERE'S ENOUGH COAL HERE TO LAST YOU THROUGH THIS WINTER!
YIII-III! SHE IS HURLING FIERY COALS!
10

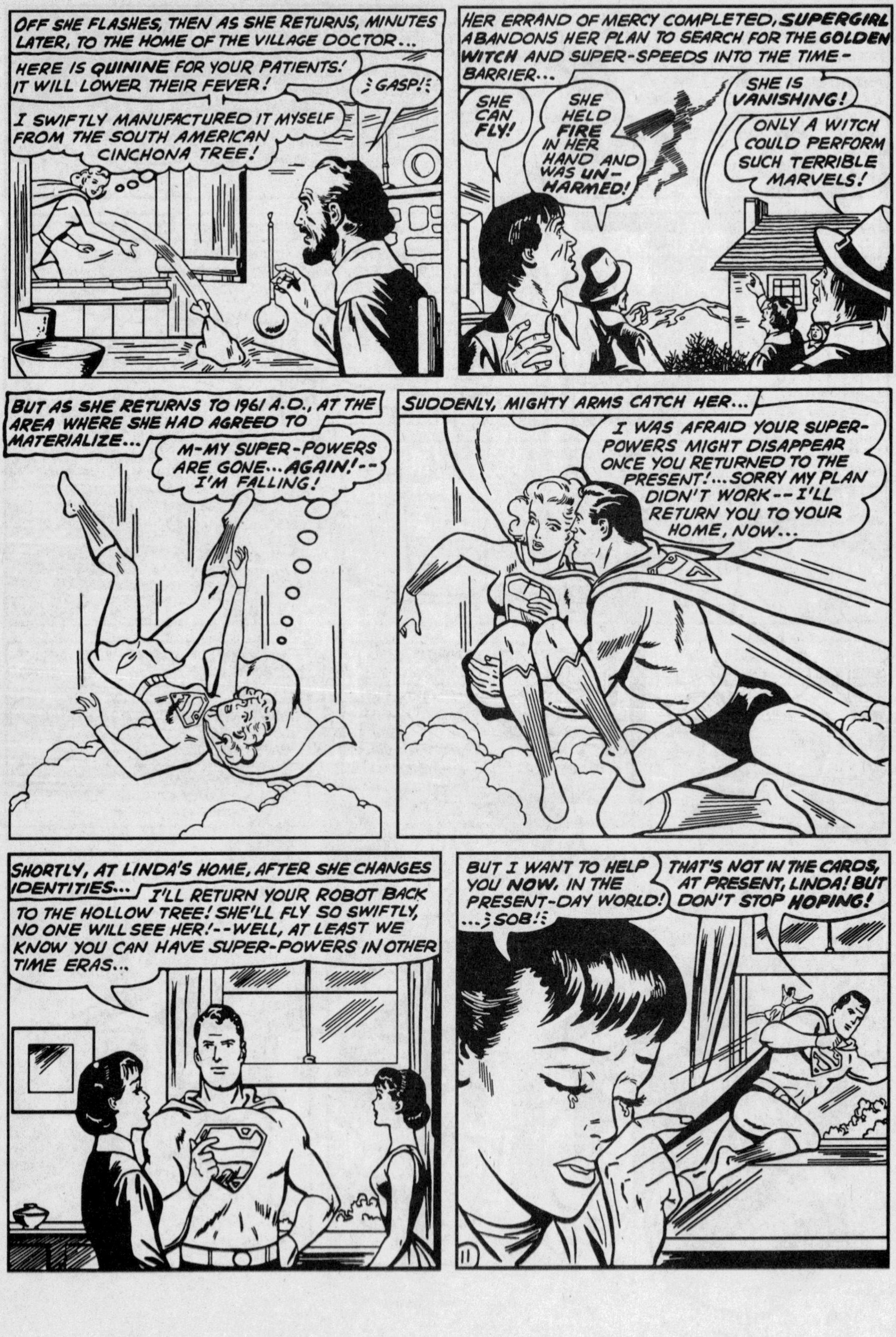
OFF SHE FLASHES, THEN AS SHE RETURNS, MINUTES LATER, TO THE HOME OF THE VILLAGE DOCTOR...
HERE IS QUININE FOR YOUR PATIENTS! IT WILL LOWER THEIR FEVER!
GASP!
I SWIFTLY MANUFACTURED IT MYSELF FROM THE SOUTH AMERICAN CINCHONA TREE!
HER ERRAND OF MERCY COMPLETED, SUPERGIRL ABANDONS HER PLAN TO SEARCH FOR THE GOLDEN WITCH AND SUPER-SPEEDS INTO THE TIME-BARRIER...
SHE CAN FLY!
SHE HELD FIRE IN HER HAND AND WAS UN-HARMED!
SHE IS VANISHING!
ONLY A WITCH COULD PERFORM SUCH TERRIBLE MARVELS!
BUT AS SHE RETURNS TO 1961 A.D., AT THE AREA WHERE SHE HAD AGREED TO MATERIALIZE...
M-MY SUPER-POWERS ARE GONE...AGAIN!--I'M FALLING!
SUDDENLY, MIGHTY ARMS CATCH HER...
I WAS AFRAID YOUR SUPER-POWERS MIGHT DISAPPEAR ONCE YOU RETURNED TO THE PRESENT!...SORRY MY PLAN DIDN'T WORK--I'LL RETURN YOU TO YOUR HOME, NOW...
SHORTLY, AT LINDA'S HOME, AFTER SHE CHANGES IDENTITIES...
I'LL RETURN YOUR ROBOT BACK TO THE HOLLOW TREE! SHE'LL FLY SO SWIFTLY, NO ONE WILL SEE HER!--WELL, AT LEAST WE KNOW YOU CAN HAVE SUPER-POWERS IN OTHER TIME ERAS...
BUT I WANT TO HELP YOU NOW, IN THE PRESENT-DAY WORLD! ...SOB!
THAT'S NOT IN THE CARDS, AT PRESENT, LINDA! BUT DON'T STOP HOPING!
11

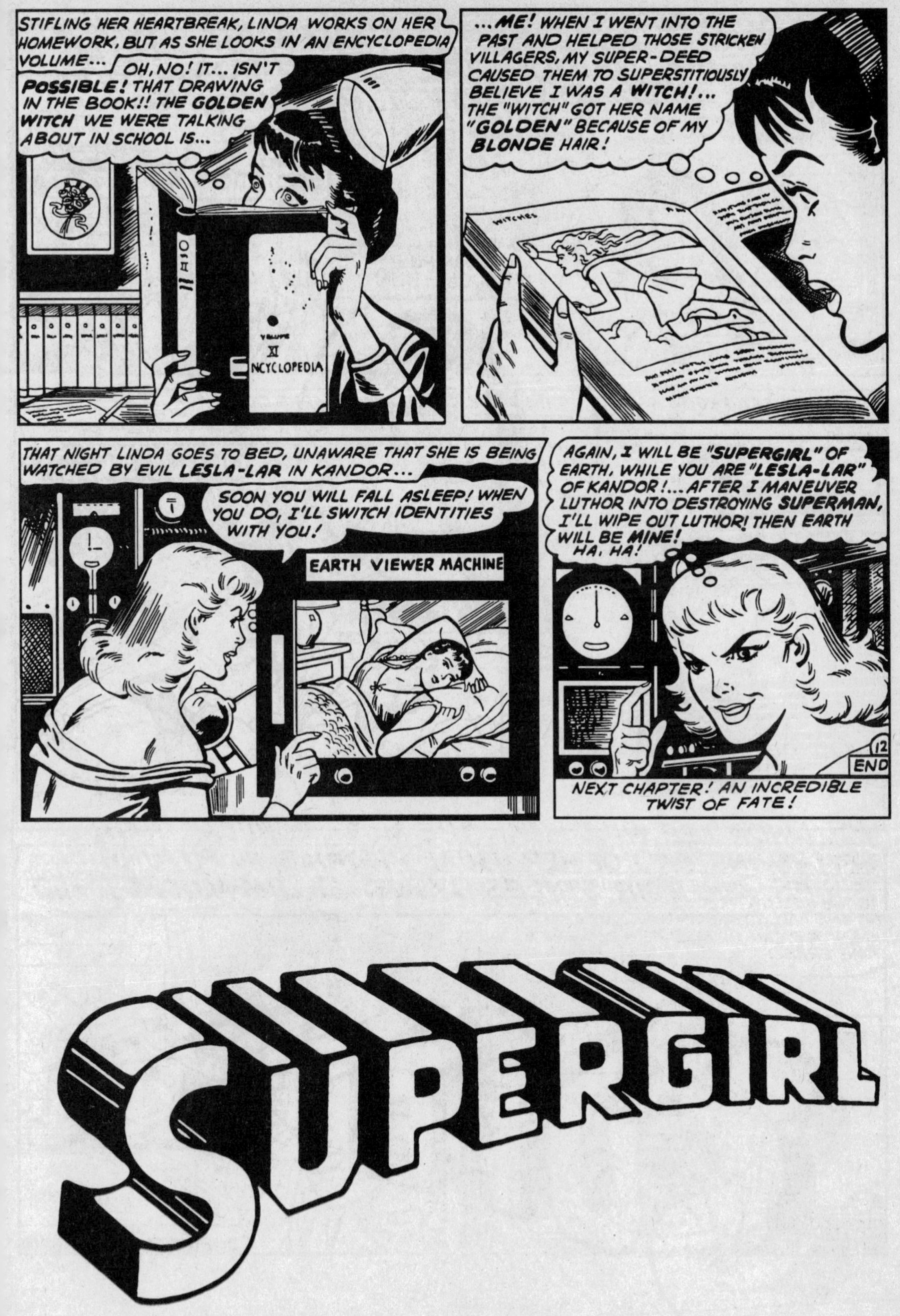
STIFLING HER HEARTBREAK, LINDA WORKS ON HER HOMEWORK, BUT AS SHE LOOKS IN AN ENCYCLOPEDIA VOLUME...
OH, NO! IT... ISN'T POSSIBLE! THAT DRAWING IN THE BOOK!! THE GOLDEN WITCH WE WERE TALKING ABOUT IN SCHOOL IS...
XI
NCYCLOPEDIA
...ME! WHEN I WENT INTO THE PAST AND HELPED THOSE STRICKEN VILLAGERS, MY SUPER-DEED CAUSED THEM TO SUPERSTITIOUSLY BELIEVE I WAS A WITCH!... THE "WITCH" GOT HER NAME "GOLDEN" BECAUSE OF MY BLONDE HAIR!
WITCHES
THAT NIGHT LINDA GOES TO BED, UNAWARE THAT SHE IS BEING WATCHED BY EVIL LESLA-LAR IN KANDOR...
SOON YOU WILL FALL ASLEEP! WHEN YOU DO, I'LL SWITCH IDENTITIES WITH YOU!
EARTH VIEWER MACHINE
AGAIN, I WILL BE "SUPERGIRL" OF EARTH, WHILE YOU ARE "LESLA-LAR" OF KANDOR!... AFTER I MANEUVER LUTHOR INTO DESTROYING SUPERMAN, I'LL WIPE OUT LUTHOR! THEN EARTH WILL BE MINE! HA, HA!
12
END
NEXT CHAPTER! AN INCREDIBLE TWIST OF FATE!

SUPERGIRL

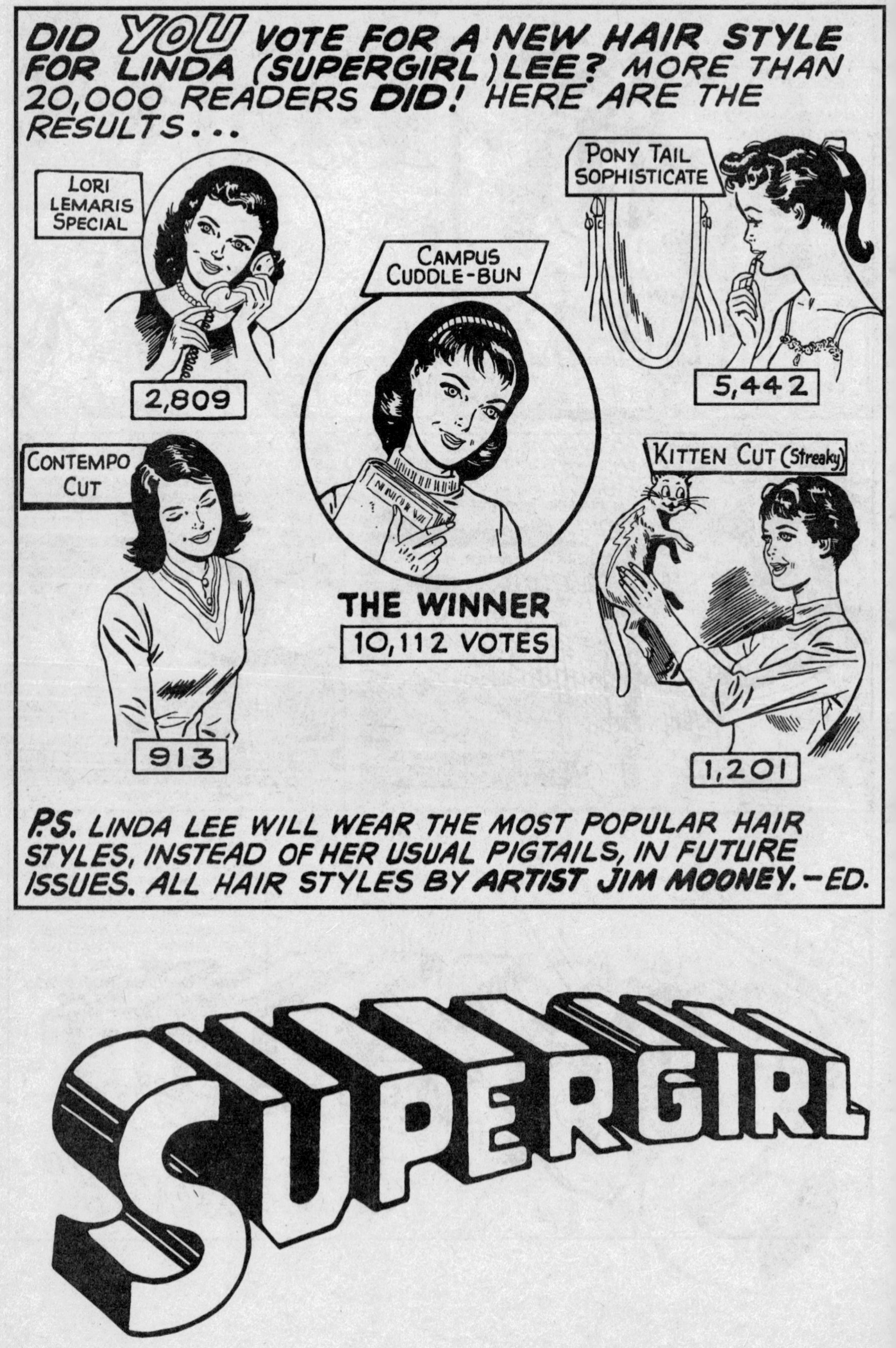
DID YOU VOTE FOR A NEW HAIR STYLE FOR LINDA (SUPERGIRL) LEE? MORE THAN 20,000 READERS DID! HERE ARE THE RESULTS...
LORI LEMARIS SPECIAL
2,809
CAMPUS CUDDLE-BUN
PONY TAIL SOPHISTICATE
5,442
CONTEMPO CUT
913
THE WINNER
10,112 VOTES
KITTEN CUT (Streaky)
1,201
P.S. LINDA LEE WILL WEAR THE MOST POPULAR HAIR STYLES, INSTEAD OF HER USUAL PIGTAILS, IN FUTURE ISSUES. ALL HAIR STYLES BY ARTIST JIM MOONEY. —ED.

SUPERGIRL

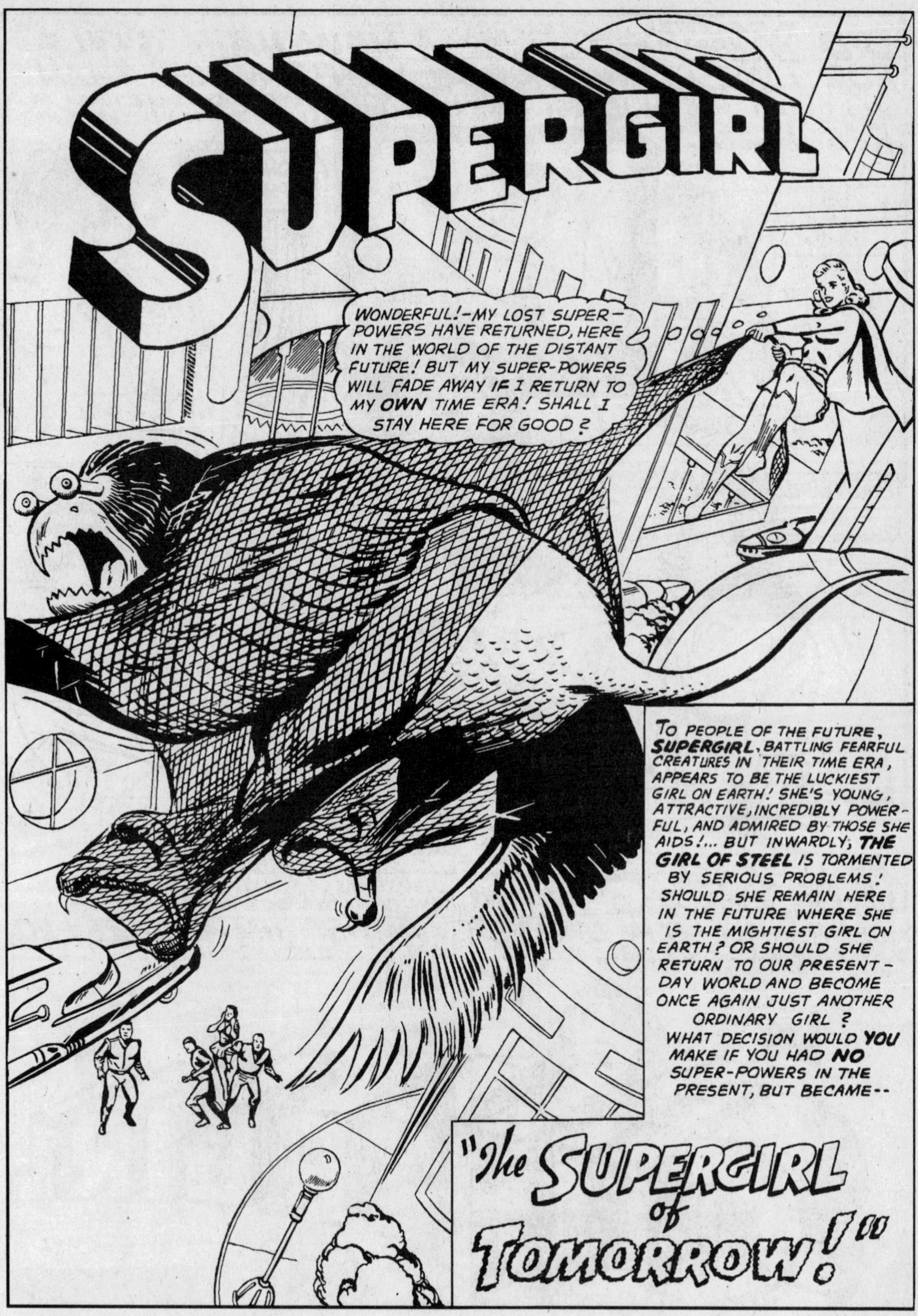
SUPERGIRL
WONDERFUL!-MY LOST SUPER-POWERS HAVE RETURNED, HERE IN THE WORLD OF THE DISTANT FUTURE! BUT MY SUPER-POWERS WILL FADE AWAY IF I RETURN TO MY OWN TIME ERA! SHALL I STAY HERE FOR GOOD?
TO PEOPLE OF THE FUTURE, SUPERGIRL, BATTLING FEARFUL CREATURES IN THEIR TIME ERA, APPEARS TO BE THE LUCKIEST GIRL ON EARTH! SHE'S YOUNG, ATTRACTIVE, INCREDIBLY POWERFUL, AND ADMIRED BY THOSE SHE AIDS!... BUT INWARDLY, THE GIRL OF STEEL IS TORMENTED BY SERIOUS PROBLEMS! SHOULD SHE REMAIN HERE IN THE FUTURE WHERE SHE IS THE MIGHTIEST GIRL ON EARTH? OR SHOULD SHE RETURN TO OUR PRESENT-DAY WORLD AND BECOME ONCE AGAIN JUST ANOTHER ORDINARY GIRL? WHAT DECISION WOULD YOU MAKE IF YOU HAD NO SUPER-POWERS IN THE PRESENT, BUT BECAME--
"The SUPERGIRL of TOMORROW!"

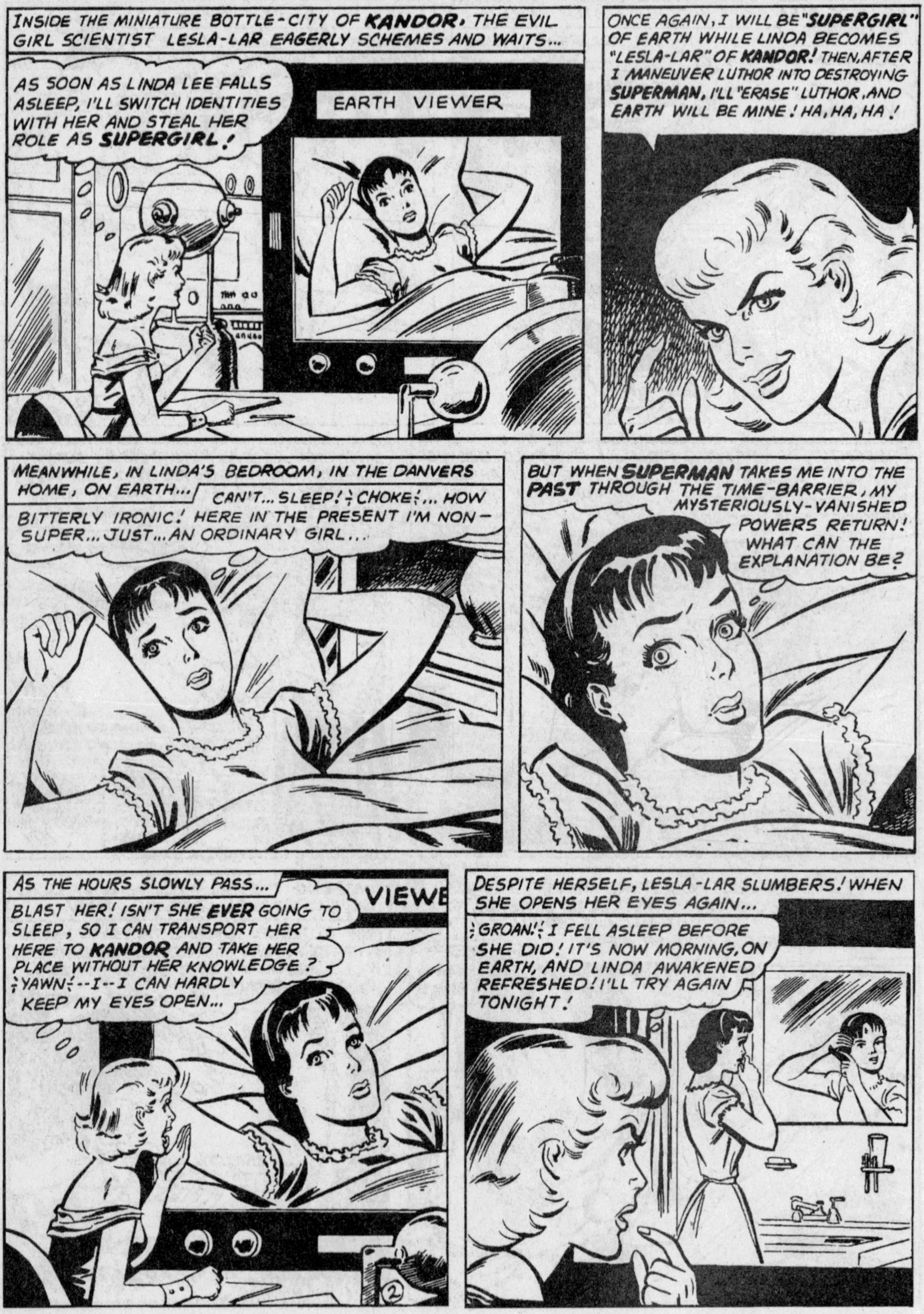
INSIDE THE MINIATURE BOTTLE-CITY OF KANDOR, THE EVIL GIRL SCIENTIST LESLA-LAR EAGERLY SCHEMES AND WAITS...
AS SOON AS LINDA LEE FALLS ASLEEP, I'LL SWITCH IDENTITIES WITH HER AND STEAL HER ROLE AS SUPERGIRL!
EARTH VIEWER
ONCE AGAIN, I WILL BE "SUPERGIRL" OF EARTH WHILE LINDA BECOMES "LESLA-LAR" OF KANDOR! THEN, AFTER I MANEUVER LUTHOR INTO DESTROYING SUPERMAN, I'LL "ERASE" LUTHOR, AND EARTH WILL BE MINE! HA, HA, HA!
MEANWHILE, IN LINDA'S BEDROOM, IN THE DANVERS HOME, ON EARTH...
CAN'T... SLEEP! ;CHOKE;... HOW BITTERLY IRONIC! HERE IN THE PRESENT I'M NON-SUPER... JUST... AN ORDINARY GIRL...
BUT WHEN SUPERMAN TAKES ME INTO THE PAST THROUGH THE TIME-BARRIER, MY MYSTERIOUSLY-VANISHED POWERS RETURN! WHAT CAN THE EXPLANATION BE?
AS THE HOURS SLOWLY PASS...
VIEWE
BLAST HER! ISN'T SHE EVER GOING TO SLEEP, SO I CAN TRANSPORT HER HERE TO KANDOR AND TAKE HER PLACE WITHOUT HER KNOWLEDGE? ;YAWN;--I--I CAN HARDLY KEEP MY EYES OPEN...
2
DESPITE HERSELF, LESLA-LAR SLUMBERS! WHEN SHE OPENS HER EYES AGAIN...
;GROAN!; I FELL ASLEEP BEFORE SHE DID! IT'S NOW MORNING, ON EARTH, AND LINDA AWAKENED REFRESHED! I'LL TRY AGAIN TONIGHT!

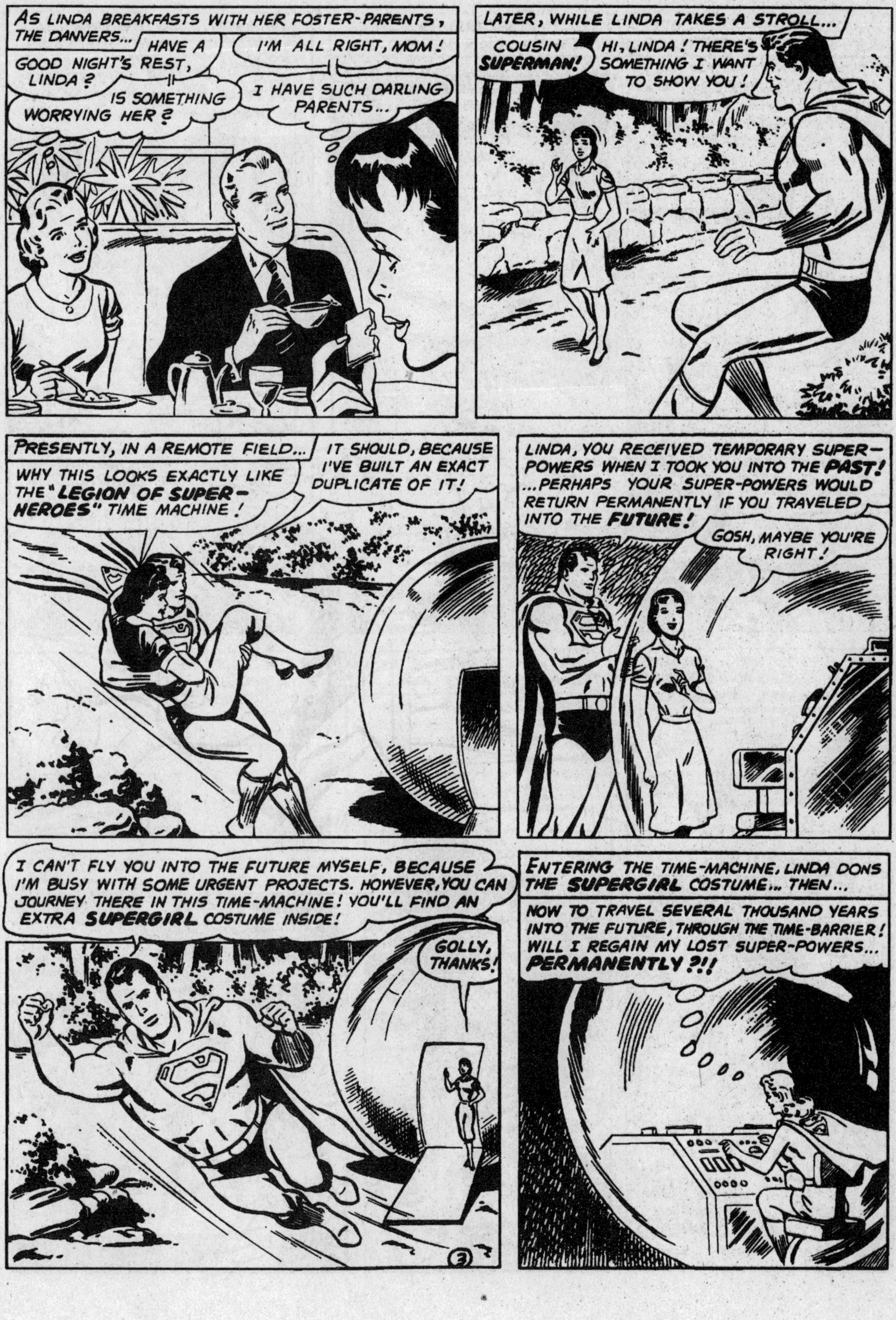
AS LINDA BREAKFASTS WITH HER FOSTER-PARENTS, THE DANVERS...
HAVE A GOOD NIGHT'S REST, LINDA?
IS SOMETHING WORRYING HER?
I'M ALL RIGHT, MOM!
I HAVE SUCH DARLING PARENTS...
LATER, WHILE LINDA TAKES A STROLL...
COUSIN SUPERMAN!
HI, LINDA! THERE'S SOMETHING I WANT TO SHOW YOU!
PRESENTLY, IN A REMOTE FIELD...
WHY THIS LOOKS EXACTLY LIKE THE "LEGION OF SUPER-HEROES" TIME MACHINE!
IT SHOULD, BECAUSE I'VE BUILT AN EXACT DUPLICATE OF IT!
LINDA, YOU RECEIVED TEMPORARY SUPER-POWERS WHEN I TOOK YOU INTO THE PAST! ...PERHAPS YOUR SUPER-POWERS WOULD RETURN PERMANENTLY IF YOU TRAVELED INTO THE FUTURE!
GOSH, MAYBE YOU'RE RIGHT!
I CAN'T FLY YOU INTO THE FUTURE MYSELF, BECAUSE I'M BUSY WITH SOME URGENT PROJECTS. HOWEVER, YOU CAN JOURNEY THERE IN THIS TIME-MACHINE! YOU'LL FIND AN EXTRA SUPERGIRL COSTUME INSIDE!
GOLLY, THANKS!
3
ENTERING THE TIME-MACHINE, LINDA DONS THE SUPERGIRL COSTUME... THEN...
NOW TO TRAVEL SEVERAL THOUSAND YEARS INTO THE FUTURE, THROUGH THE TIME-BARRIER! WILL I REGAIN MY LOST SUPER-POWERS... PERMANENTLY ?!!

MEANWHILE, IN LESLA-LAR'S KANDORIAN LABORATORY...

SHE'S SLIPPING AWAY, IN THAT ACCURSED TIME-MACHINE! DRAT! MY TIME-VIEWER CAN *ONLY* SEE INTO THE *PAST*, NOT THE FUTURE! --WHEN SHE RETURNS... I'LL BE... WAITING.!!

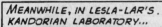

EARTH VIE

INTO THE FAR DISTANT FUTURE TRAVELS THE VEHICLE, AND AFTER THE *GIRL OF STEEL* EMERGES FROM IT...

GREAT *KRYPTON!* I CAN EASILY LIFT THE SHIP, THOUGH IT WEIGHS *TONS!* I *DO HAVE* SUPER-POWERS IN THIS FUTURE ERA!

A MOMENT AFTERWARD...

UH-OH! A GIANT, WINGED CREATURE OF PREY HUNTING DOWN HUMANS! THIS IS A JOB FOR *SUPERGIRL!!*

SWIFTLY FASHIONING A GREAT NET OF STRONG VINES, *SUPER-GIRL* FLASHES INTO ACTION...

TRAPPED IT!

;GASP.!; WE'VE BEEN SAVED BY A SUPER-STRONG FLYING GIRL!

SOON, AS SHE SPEAKS TO THE AWED FUTURE-MEN...

I'VE TRAVELED HERE FROM THE PAST!... WHAT A STRANGE CREATURE! WHERE DID IT COME FROM?

IT'S AN *ANGARK*, FROM... THE PLANET *MARS!*

"A FEW YEARS AGO, EARTH WAS ATTACKED BY A TASK FORCE FROM MARS! THE INVADERS BROUGHT THEIR WAR-BIRDS ALONG TO HARASS OUR DEFENSE FORCES...

ANGARKS ARE SNATCHING OUR TANKS HIGH INTO THE AIR, THEN *DROPPING* THEM TO DESTRUCTION!

4

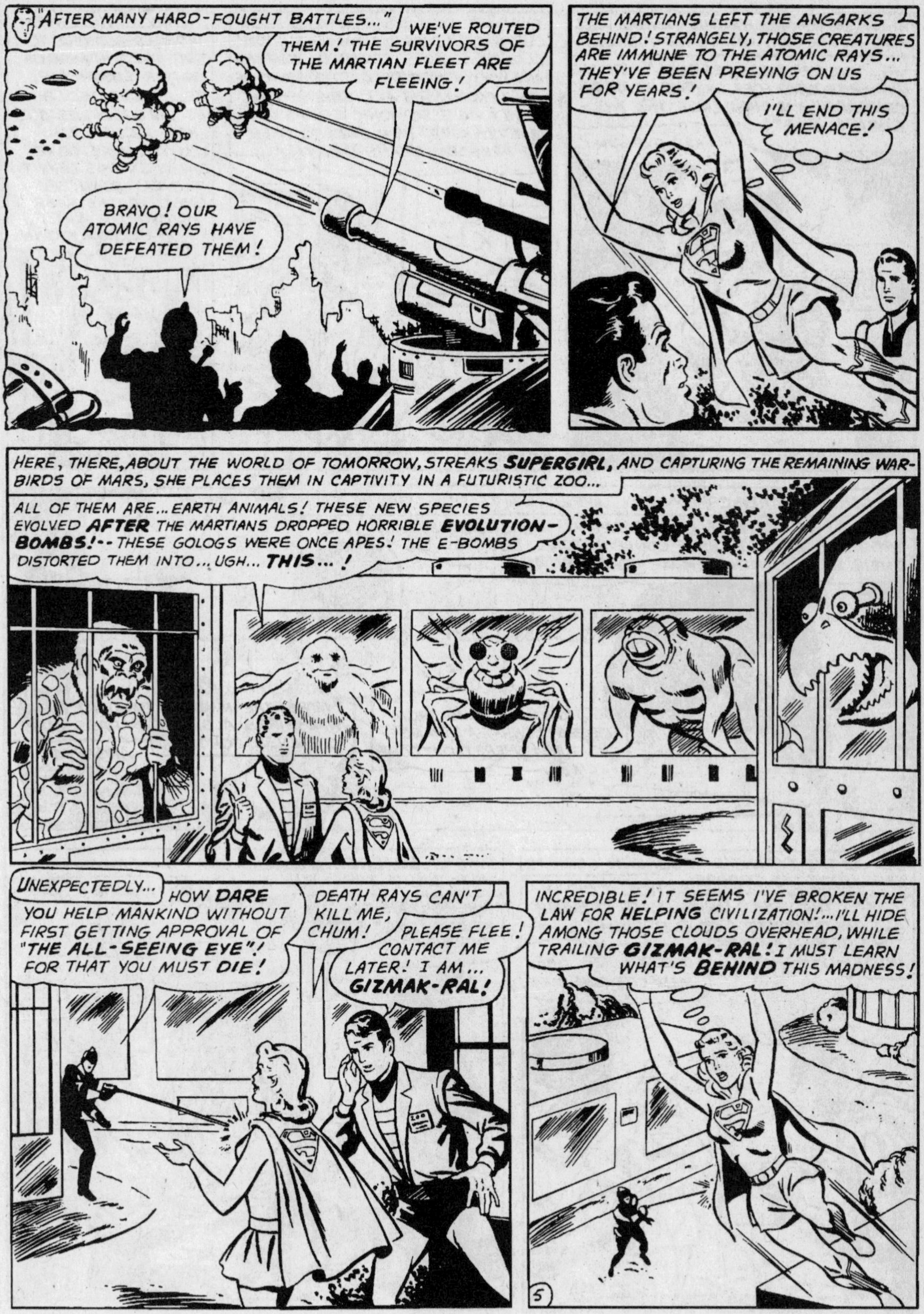
"AFTER MANY HARD-FOUGHT BATTLES..."
WE'VE ROUTED THEM! THE SURVIVORS OF THE MARTIAN FLEET ARE FLEEING!
BRAVO! OUR ATOMIC RAYS HAVE DEFEATED THEM!
THE MARTIANS LEFT THE ANGARKS BEHIND! STRANGELY, THOSE CREATURES ARE IMMUNE TO THE ATOMIC RAYS... THEY'VE BEEN PREYING ON US FOR YEARS!
I'LL END THIS MENACE!
HERE, THERE, ABOUT THE WORLD OF TOMORROW, STREAKS SUPERGIRL, AND CAPTURING THE REMAINING WAR-BIRDS OF MARS, SHE PLACES THEM IN CAPTIVITY IN A FUTURISTIC ZOO...
ALL OF THEM ARE... EARTH ANIMALS! THESE NEW SPECIES EVOLVED AFTER THE MARTIANS DROPPED HORRIBLE EVOLUTION-BOMBS!-- THESE GOLOGS WERE ONCE APES! THE E-BOMBS DISTORTED THEM INTO... UGH... THIS...!
UNEXPECTEDLY...
HOW DARE YOU HELP MANKIND WITHOUT FIRST GETTING APPROVAL OF "THE ALL-SEEING EYE"! FOR THAT YOU MUST DIE!
DEATH RAYS CAN'T KILL ME, CHUM!
PLEASE FLEE! CONTACT ME LATER! I AM... GIZMAK-RAL!
INCREDIBLE! IT SEEMS I'VE BROKEN THE LAW FOR HELPING CIVILIZATION!... I'LL HIDE AMONG THOSE CLOUDS OVERHEAD, WHILE TRAILING GIZMAK-RAL! I MUST LEARN WHAT'S BEHIND THIS MADNESS!
5

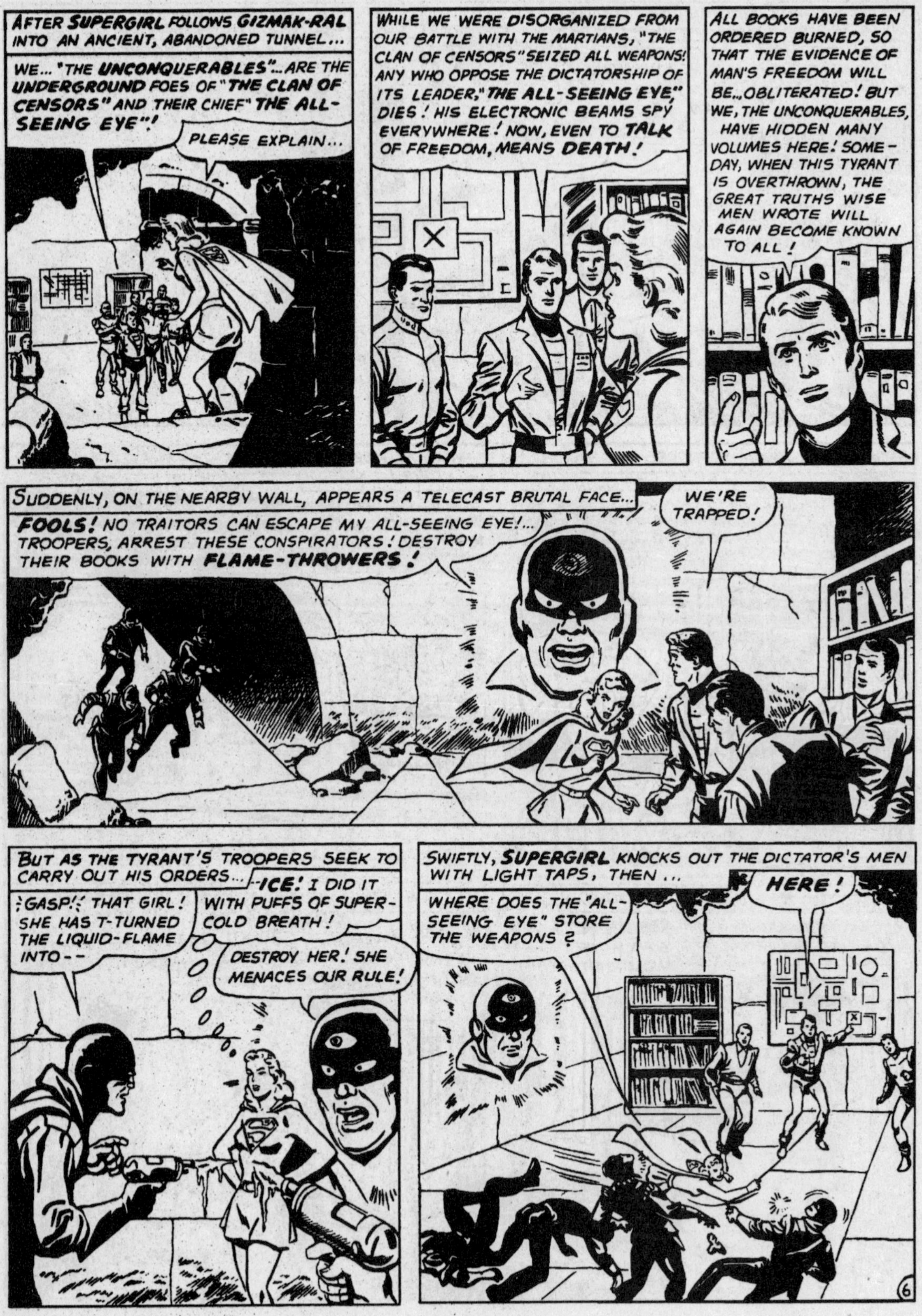
AFTER SUPERGIRL FOLLOWS GIZMAK-RAL INTO AN ANCIENT, ABANDONED TUNNEL...
WE... "THE UNCONQUERABLES"... ARE THE UNDERGROUND FOES OF "THE CLAN OF CENSORS" AND THEIR CHIEF "THE ALL-SEEING EYE"!
PLEASE EXPLAIN...
WHILE WE WERE DISORGANIZED FROM OUR BATTLE WITH THE MARTIANS, "THE CLAN OF CENSORS" SEIZED ALL WEAPONS! ANY WHO OPPOSE THE DICTATORSHIP OF ITS LEADER, "THE ALL-SEEING EYE," DIES! HIS ELECTRONIC BEAMS SPY EVERYWHERE! NOW, EVEN TO TALK OF FREEDOM, MEANS DEATH!
ALL BOOKS HAVE BEEN ORDERED BURNED, SO THAT THE EVIDENCE OF MAN'S FREEDOM WILL BE... OBLITERATED! BUT WE, THE UNCONQUERABLES, HAVE HIDDEN MANY VOLUMES HERE! SOME-DAY, WHEN THIS TYRANT IS OVERTHROWN, THE GREAT TRUTHS WISE MEN WROTE WILL AGAIN BECOME KNOWN TO ALL!
SUDDENLY, ON THE NEARBY WALL, APPEARS A TELECAST BRUTAL FACE...
FOOLS! NO TRAITORS CAN ESCAPE MY ALL-SEEING EYE!... TROOPERS, ARREST THESE CONSPIRATORS! DESTROY THEIR BOOKS WITH FLAME-THROWERS!
WE'RE TRAPPED!
BUT AS THE TYRANT'S TROOPERS SEEK TO CARRY OUT HIS ORDERS...
GASP! THAT GIRL! SHE HAS T-TURNED THE LIQUID-FLAME INTO--
ICE! I DID IT WITH PUFFS OF SUPER-COLD BREATH!
DESTROY HER! SHE MENACES OUR RULE!
SWIFTLY, SUPERGIRL KNOCKS OUT THE DICTATOR'S MEN WITH LIGHT TAPS, THEN...
WHERE DOES THE "ALL-SEEING EYE" STORE THE WEAPONS?
HERE!
6

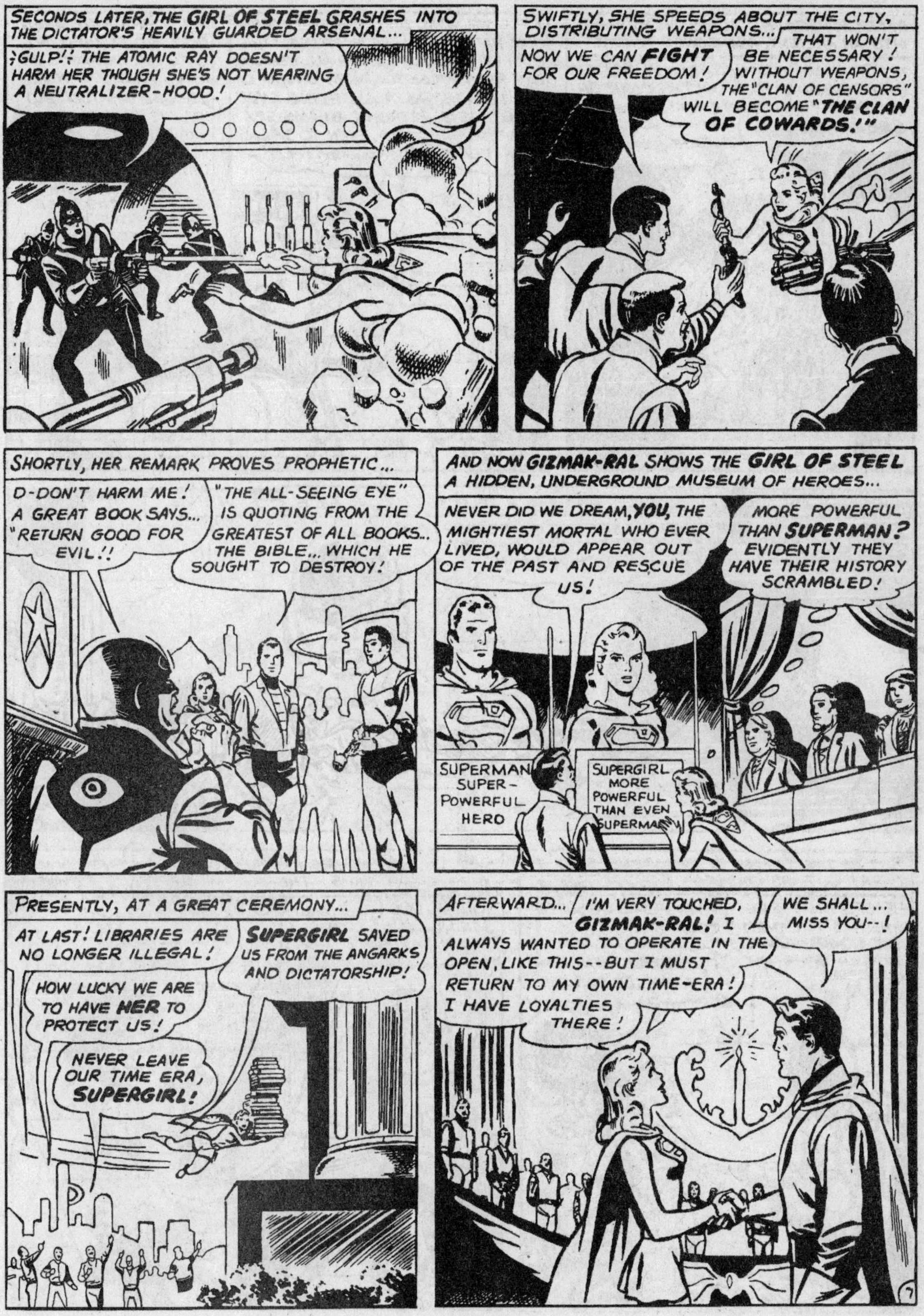
SECONDS LATER, THE GIRL OF STEEL CRASHES INTO THE DICTATOR'S HEAVILY GUARDED ARSENAL...
GULP! THE ATOMIC RAY DOESN'T HARM HER THOUGH SHE'S NOT WEARING A NEUTRALIZER-HOOD!
SWIFTLY, SHE SPEEDS ABOUT THE CITY, DISTRIBUTING WEAPONS...
NOW WE CAN FIGHT FOR OUR FREEDOM!
THAT WON'T BE NECESSARY! WITHOUT WEAPONS, THE "CLAN OF CENSORS" WILL BECOME "THE CLAN OF COWARDS!"
SHORTLY, HER REMARK PROVES PROPHETIC...
D-DON'T HARM ME! A GREAT BOOK SAYS... "RETURN GOOD FOR EVIL!"
"THE ALL-SEEING EYE" IS QUOTING FROM THE GREATEST OF ALL BOOKS.. THE BIBLE... WHICH HE SOUGHT TO DESTROY!
AND NOW GIZMAK-RAL SHOWS THE GIRL OF STEEL A HIDDEN, UNDERGROUND MUSEUM OF HEROES...
NEVER DID WE DREAM, YOU, THE MIGHTIEST MORTAL WHO EVER LIVED, WOULD APPEAR OUT OF THE PAST AND RESCUE US!
MORE POWERFUL THAN SUPERMAN? EVIDENTLY THEY HAVE THEIR HISTORY SCRAMBLED!
SUPERMAN SUPER-POWERFUL HERO
SUPERGIRL MORE POWERFUL THAN EVEN SUPERMAN
PRESENTLY, AT A GREAT CEREMONY...
AT LAST! LIBRARIES ARE NO LONGER ILLEGAL!
SUPERGIRL SAVED US FROM THE ANGARKS AND DICTATORSHIP!
HOW LUCKY WE ARE TO HAVE HER TO PROTECT US!
NEVER LEAVE OUR TIME ERA, SUPERGIRL!
AFTERWARD...
I'M VERY TOUCHED, GIZMAK-RAL! I ALWAYS WANTED TO OPERATE IN THE OPEN, LIKE THIS--BUT I MUST RETURN TO MY OWN TIME-ERA! I HAVE LOYALTIES THERE!
WE SHALL... MISS YOU--!
7

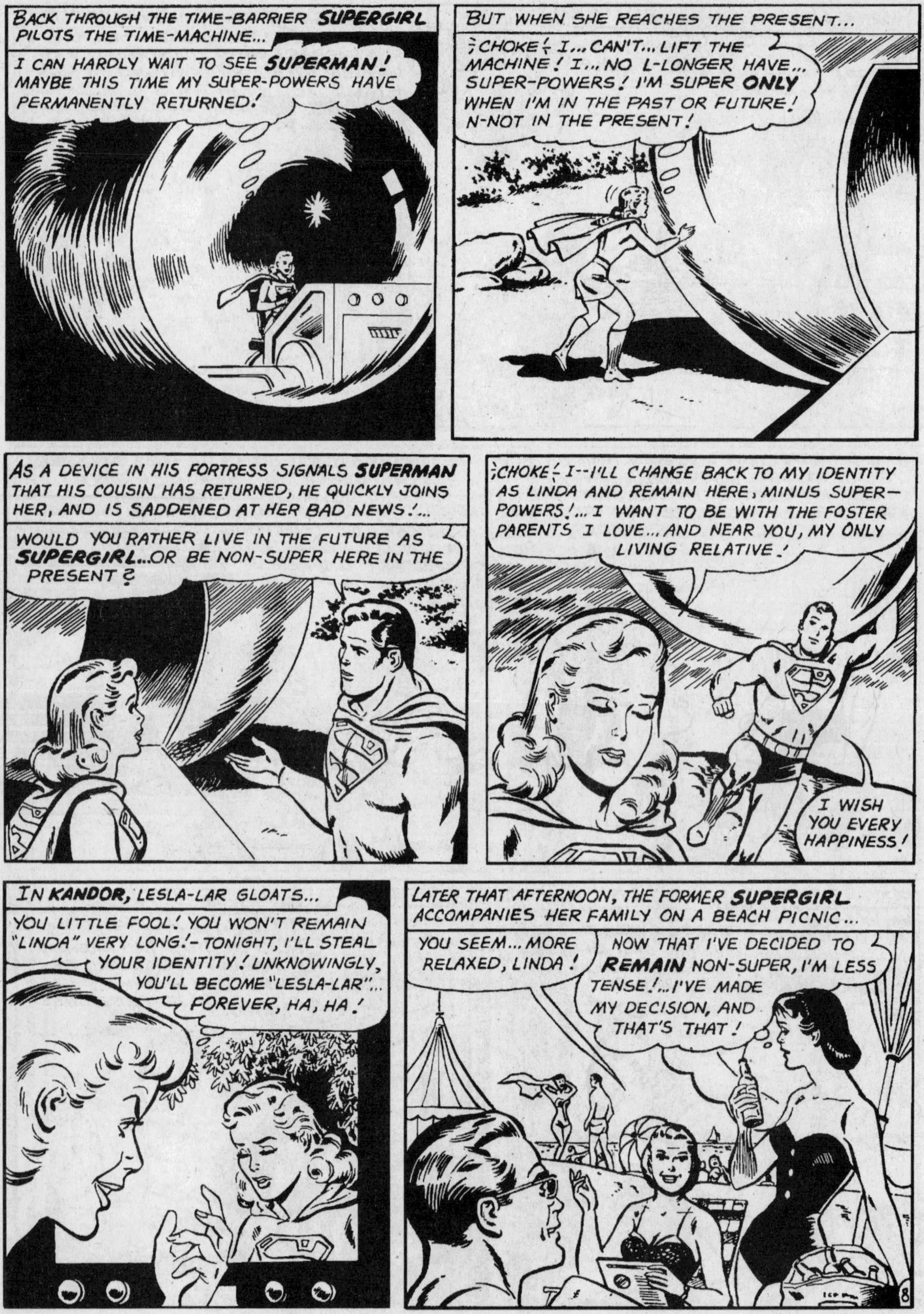
BACK THROUGH THE TIME-BARRIER SUPERGIRL PILOTS THE TIME-MACHINE...
I CAN HARDLY WAIT TO SEE SUPERMAN! MAYBE THIS TIME MY SUPER-POWERS HAVE PERMANENTLY RETURNED!
BUT WHEN SHE REACHES THE PRESENT...
¿CHOKE¿ I... CAN'T... LIFT THE MACHINE! I... NO L-LONGER HAVE... SUPER-POWERS! I'M SUPER ONLY WHEN I'M IN THE PAST OR FUTURE! N-NOT IN THE PRESENT!
AS A DEVICE IN HIS FORTRESS SIGNALS SUPERMAN THAT HIS COUSIN HAS RETURNED, HE QUICKLY JOINS HER, AND IS SADDENED AT HER BAD NEWS!...
WOULD YOU RATHER LIVE IN THE FUTURE AS SUPERGIRL...OR BE NON-SUPER HERE IN THE PRESENT?
¿CHOKE¿ I--I'LL CHANGE BACK TO MY IDENTITY AS LINDA AND REMAIN HERE, MINUS SUPER-POWERS!... I WANT TO BE WITH THE FOSTER PARENTS I LOVE... AND NEAR YOU, MY ONLY LIVING RELATIVE!
I WISH YOU EVERY HAPPINESS!
IN KANDOR, LESLA-LAR GLOATS...
YOU LITTLE FOOL! YOU WON'T REMAIN "LINDA" VERY LONG!- TONIGHT, I'LL STEAL YOUR IDENTITY! UNKNOWINGLY, YOU'LL BECOME "LESLA-LAR"... FOREVER, HA, HA!
LATER THAT AFTERNOON, THE FORMER SUPERGIRL ACCOMPANIES HER FAMILY ON A BEACH PICNIC...
YOU SEEM... MORE RELAXED, LINDA!
NOW THAT I'VE DECIDED TO REMAIN NON-SUPER, I'M LESS TENSE!... I'VE MADE MY DECISION, AND THAT'S THAT!
8

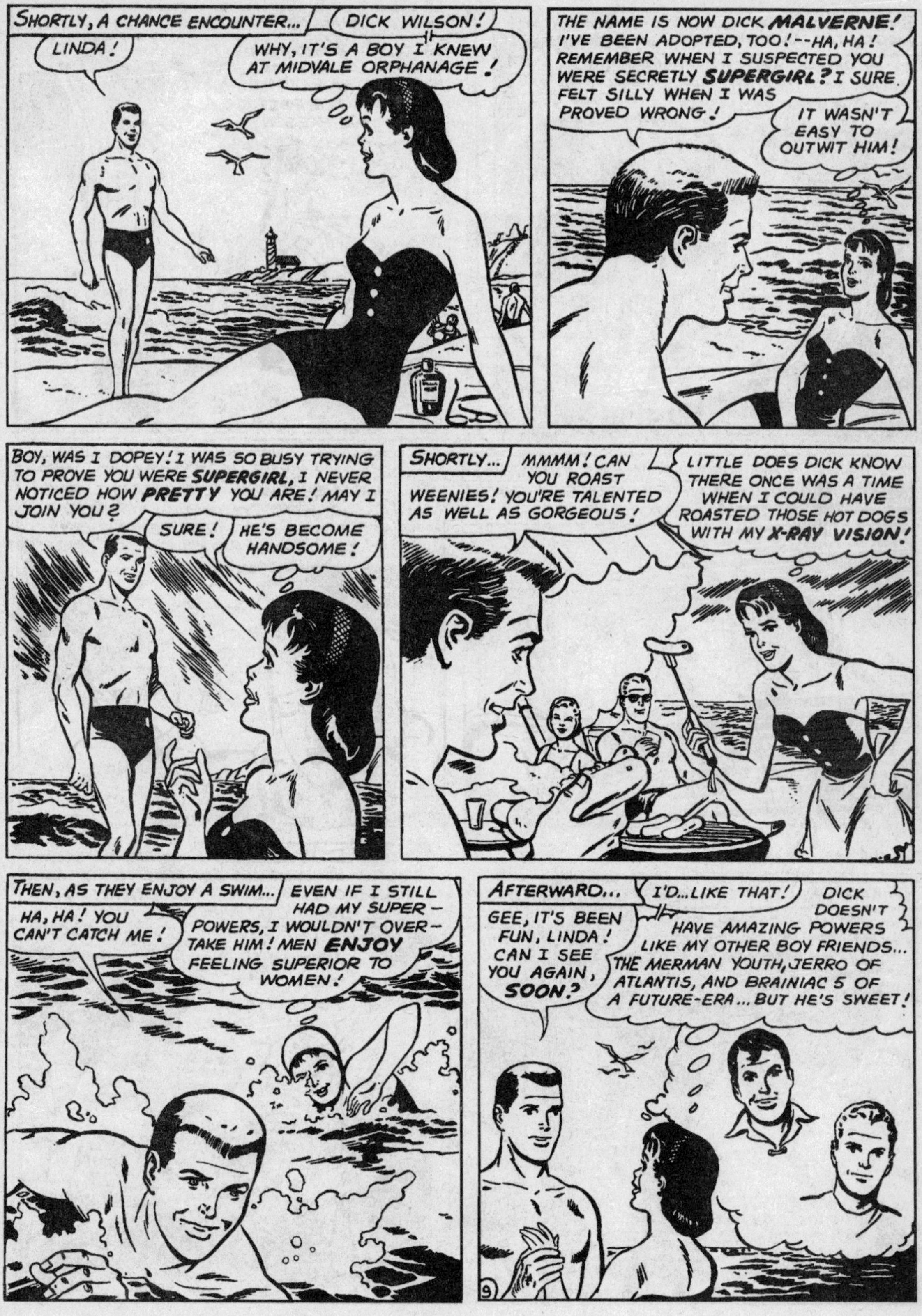
SHORTLY, A CHANCE ENCOUNTER...
LINDA!
DICK WILSON!
WHY, IT'S A BOY I KNEW AT MIDVALE ORPHANAGE!
THE NAME IS NOW DICK MALVERNE! I'VE BEEN ADOPTED, TOO!--HA, HA! REMEMBER WHEN I SUSPECTED YOU WERE SECRETLY SUPERGIRL? I SURE FELT SILLY WHEN I WAS PROVED WRONG!
IT WASN'T EASY TO OUTWIT HIM!
BOY, WAS I DOPEY! I WAS SO BUSY TRYING TO PROVE YOU WERE SUPERGIRL, I NEVER NOTICED HOW PRETTY YOU ARE! MAY I JOIN YOU?
SURE!
HE'S BECOME HANDSOME!
SHORTLY...
MMMM! CAN YOU ROAST WEENIES! YOU'RE TALENTED AS WELL AS GORGEOUS!
LITTLE DOES DICK KNOW THERE ONCE WAS A TIME WHEN I COULD HAVE ROASTED THOSE HOT DOGS WITH MY X-RAY VISION!
THEN, AS THEY ENJOY A SWIM...
HA, HA! YOU CAN'T CATCH ME!
EVEN IF I STILL HAD MY SUPER-POWERS, I WOULDN'T OVERTAKE HIM! MEN ENJOY FEELING SUPERIOR TO WOMEN!
AFTERWARD...
GEE, IT'S BEEN FUN, LINDA! CAN I SEE YOU AGAIN, SOON?
I'D...LIKE THAT!
DICK DOESN'T HAVE AMAZING POWERS LIKE MY OTHER BOY FRIENDS... THE MERMAN YOUTH, JERRO OF ATLANTIS, AND BRAINIAC 5 OF A FUTURE-ERA... BUT HE'S SWEET!
9

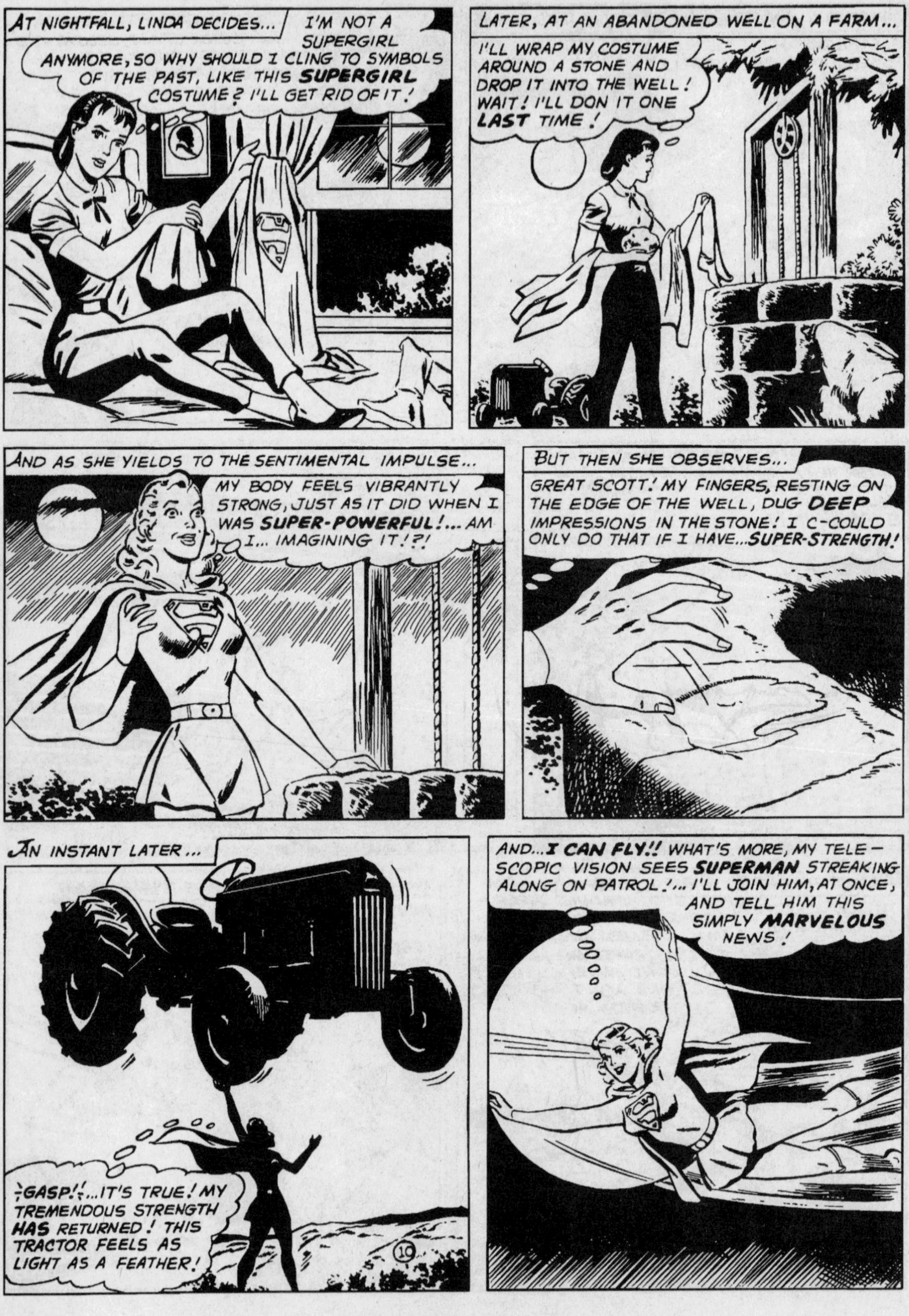
AT NIGHTFALL, LINDA DECIDES...
I'M NOT A SUPERGIRL ANYMORE, SO WHY SHOULD I CLING TO SYMBOLS OF THE PAST, LIKE THIS SUPERGIRL COSTUME? I'LL GET RID OF IT!
LATER, AT AN ABANDONED WELL ON A FARM...
I'LL WRAP MY COSTUME AROUND A STONE AND DROP IT INTO THE WELL! WAIT! I'LL DON IT ONE LAST TIME!
AND AS SHE YIELDS TO THE SENTIMENTAL IMPULSE...
MY BODY FEELS VIBRANTLY STRONG, JUST AS IT DID WHEN I WAS SUPER-POWERFUL!... AM I... IMAGINING IT!?!
BUT THEN SHE OBSERVES...
GREAT SCOTT! MY FINGERS, RESTING ON THE EDGE OF THE WELL, DUG DEEP IMPRESSIONS IN THE STONE! I C-COULD ONLY DO THAT IF I HAVE...SUPER-STRENGTH!
AN INSTANT LATER...
¡GASP!¡...IT'S TRUE! MY TREMENDOUS STRENGTH HAS RETURNED! THIS TRACTOR FEELS AS LIGHT AS A FEATHER!
10
AND...I CAN FLY!! WHAT'S MORE, MY TELE-SCOPIC VISION SEES SUPERMAN STREAKING ALONG ON PATROL!... I'LL JOIN HIM, AT ONCE, AND TELL HIM THIS SIMPLY MARVELOUS NEWS!

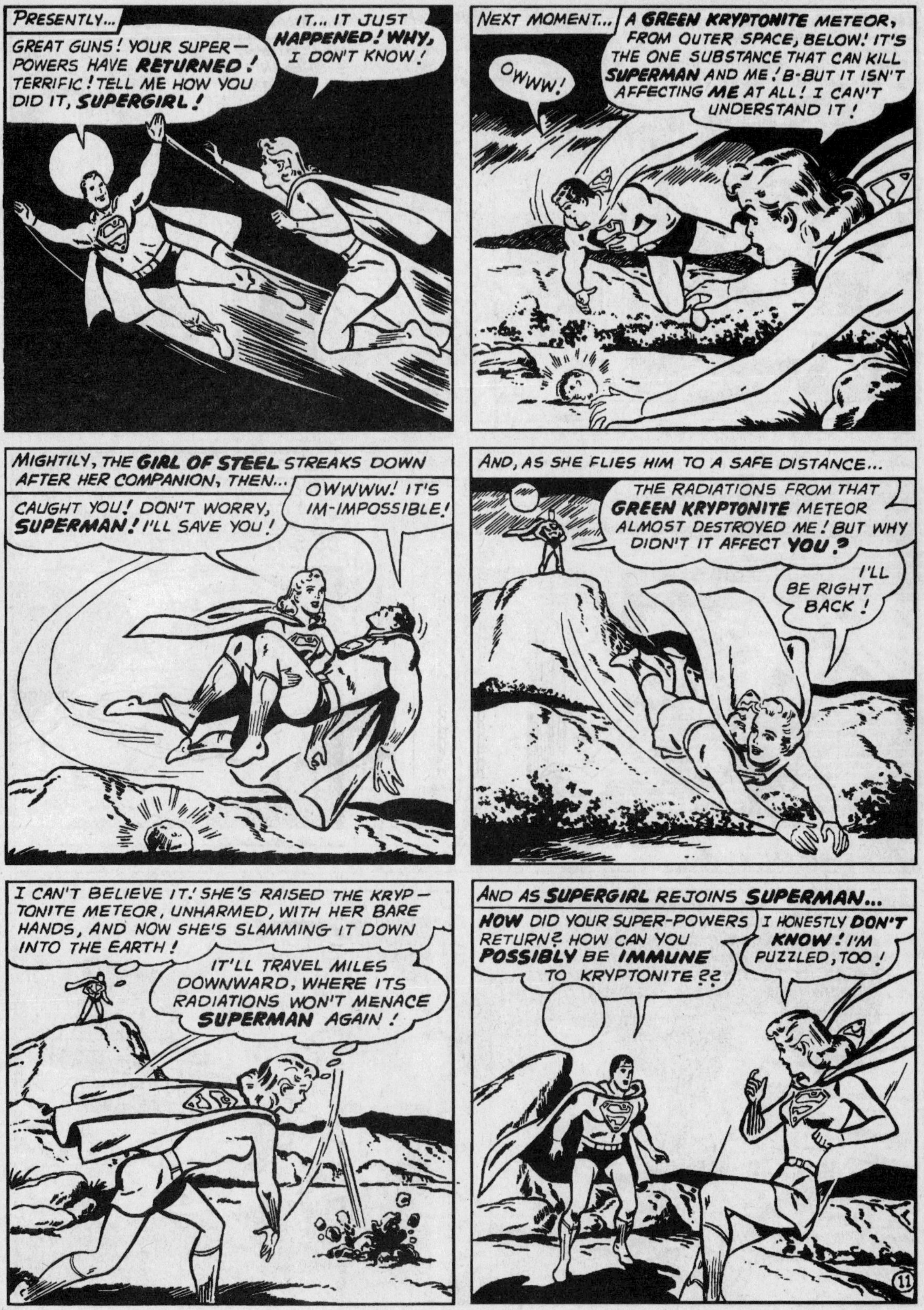
PRESENTLY...
GREAT GUNS! YOUR SUPER-POWERS HAVE RETURNED! TERRIFIC! TELL ME HOW YOU DID IT, SUPERGIRL!
IT... IT JUST HAPPENED! WHY, I DON'T KNOW!
NEXT MOMENT...
A GREEN KRYPTONITE METEOR, FROM OUTER SPACE, BELOW! IT'S THE ONE SUBSTANCE THAT CAN KILL SUPERMAN AND ME! B-BUT IT ISN'T AFFECTING ME AT ALL! I CAN'T UNDERSTAND IT!
OWWW!
MIGHTILY, THE GIRL OF STEEL STREAKS DOWN AFTER HER COMPANION, THEN...
CAUGHT YOU! DON'T WORRY, SUPERMAN! I'LL SAVE YOU!
OWWWW! IT'S IM-IMPOSSIBLE!
AND, AS SHE FLIES HIM TO A SAFE DISTANCE...
THE RADIATIONS FROM THAT GREEN KRYPTONITE METEOR ALMOST DESTROYED ME! BUT WHY DIDN'T IT AFFECT YOU?
I'LL BE RIGHT BACK!
I CAN'T BELIEVE IT! SHE'S RAISED THE KRYPTONITE METEOR, UNHARMED, WITH HER BARE HANDS, AND NOW SHE'S SLAMMING IT DOWN INTO THE EARTH!
IT'LL TRAVEL MILES DOWNWARD, WHERE ITS RADIATIONS WON'T MENACE SUPERMAN AGAIN!
AND AS SUPERGIRL REJOINS SUPERMAN...
HOW DID YOUR SUPER-POWERS RETURN? HOW CAN YOU POSSIBLY BE IMMUNE TO KRYPTONITE??
I HONESTLY DON'T KNOW! I'M PUZZLED, TOO!
11

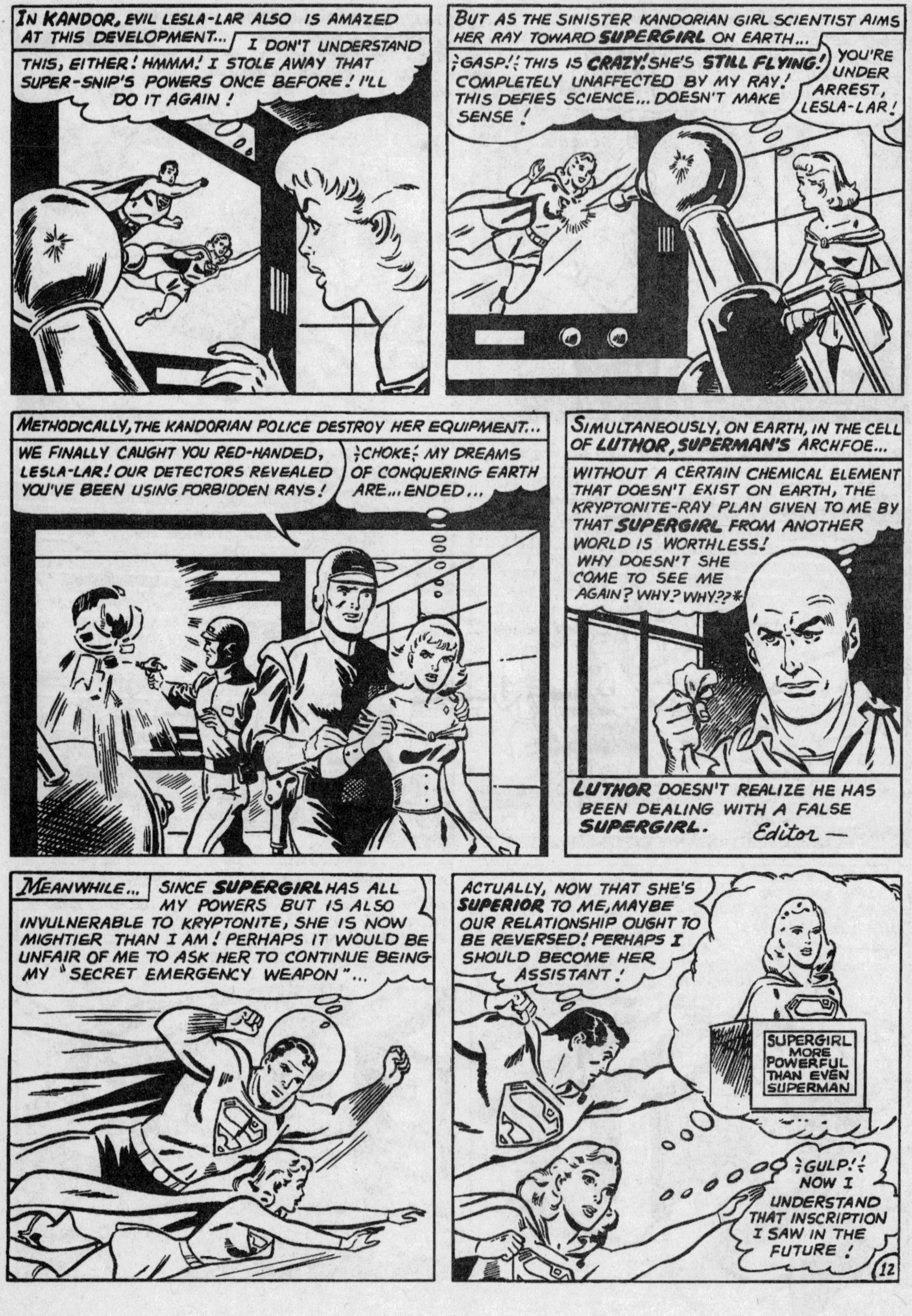
IN KANDOR, EVIL LESLA-LAR ALSO IS AMAZED AT THIS DEVELOPMENT...
I DON'T UNDERSTAND THIS, EITHER! HMMM! I STOLE AWAY THAT SUPER-SNIP'S POWERS ONCE BEFORE! I'LL DO IT AGAIN!
BUT AS THE SINISTER KANDORIAN GIRL SCIENTIST AIMS HER RAY TOWARD SUPERGIRL ON EARTH...
-GASP!- THIS IS CRAZY! SHE'S STILL FLYING! COMPLETELY UNAFFECTED BY MY RAY! THIS DEFIES SCIENCE... DOESN'T MAKE SENSE!
YOU'RE UNDER ARREST, LESLA-LAR!
METHODICALLY, THE KANDORIAN POLICE DESTROY HER EQUIPMENT...
WE FINALLY CAUGHT YOU RED-HANDED, LESLA-LAR! OUR DETECTORS REVEALED YOU'VE BEEN USING FORBIDDEN RAYS!
-CHOKE- MY DREAMS OF CONQUERING EARTH ARE... ENDED...
SIMULTANEOUSLY, ON EARTH, IN THE CELL OF LUTHOR, SUPERMAN'S ARCHFOE...
WITHOUT A CERTAIN CHEMICAL ELEMENT THAT DOESN'T EXIST ON EARTH, THE KRYPTONITE-RAY PLAN GIVEN TO ME BY THAT SUPERGIRL FROM ANOTHER WORLD IS WORTHLESS! WHY DOESN'T SHE COME TO SEE ME AGAIN? WHY? WHY??*
LUTHOR DOESN'T REALIZE HE HAS BEEN DEALING WITH A FALSE SUPERGIRL. Editor —
MEANWHILE...
SINCE SUPERGIRL HAS ALL MY POWERS BUT IS ALSO INVULNERABLE TO KRYPTONITE, SHE IS NOW MIGHTIER THAN I AM! PERHAPS IT WOULD BE UNFAIR OF ME TO ASK HER TO CONTINUE BEING MY "SECRET EMERGENCY WEAPON"...
ACTUALLY, NOW THAT SHE'S SUPERIOR TO ME, MAYBE OUR RELATIONSHIP OUGHT TO BE REVERSED! PERHAPS I SHOULD BECOME HER ASSISTANT!
SUPERGIRL MORE POWERFUL THAN EVEN SUPERMAN
-GULP!- NOW I UNDERSTAND THAT INSCRIPTION I SAW IN THE FUTURE!
12

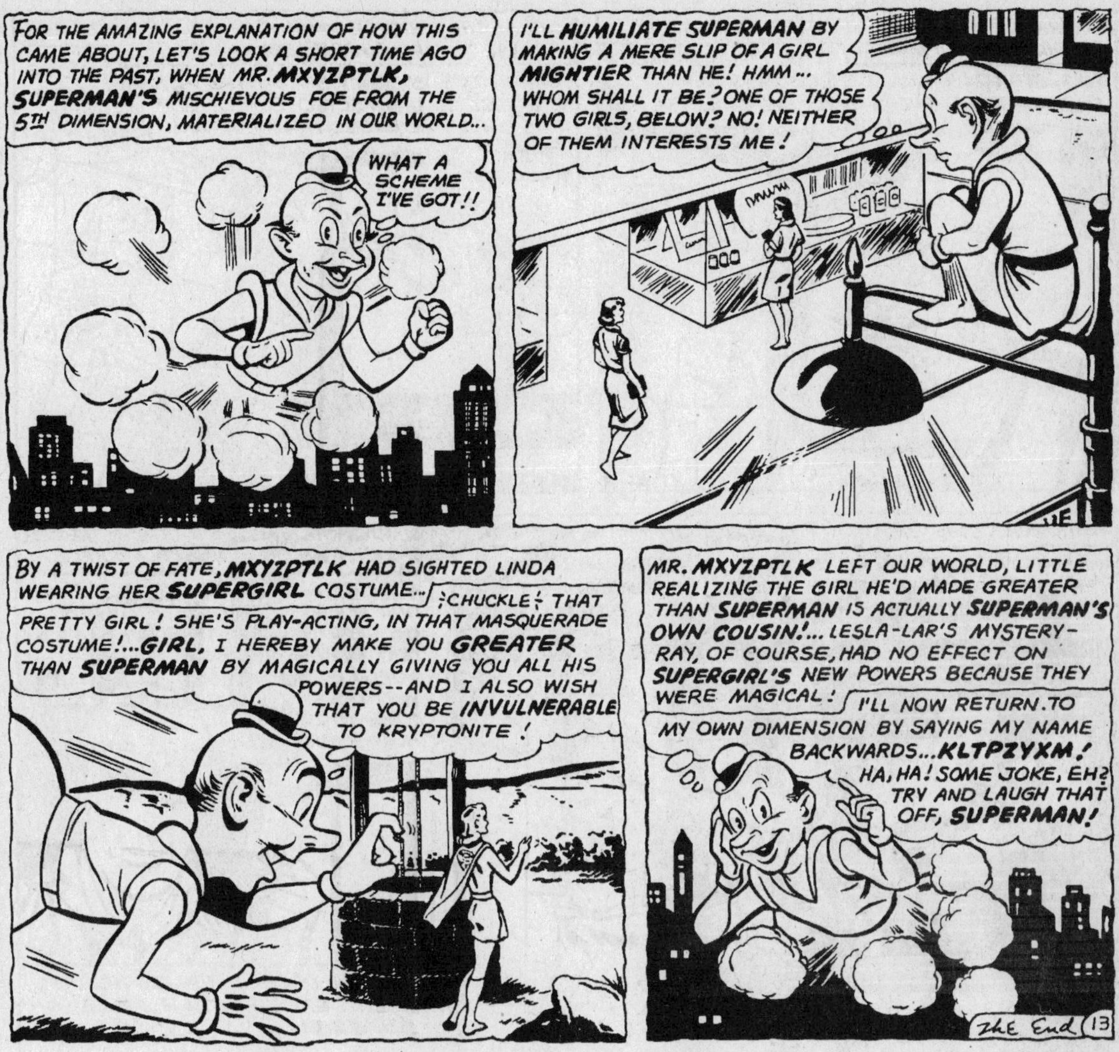
FOR THE AMAZING EXPLANATION OF HOW THIS CAME ABOUT, LET'S LOOK A SHORT TIME AGO INTO THE PAST, WHEN MR. MXYZPTLK, SUPERMAN'S MISCHIEVOUS FOE FROM THE 5TH DIMENSION, MATERIALIZED IN OUR WORLD...
WHAT A SCHEME I'VE GOT!!
I'LL HUMILIATE SUPERMAN BY MAKING A MERE SLIP OF A GIRL MIGHTIER THAN HE! HMM... WHOM SHALL IT BE? ONE OF THOSE TWO GIRLS, BELOW? NO! NEITHER OF THEM INTERESTS ME!
BY A TWIST OF FATE, MXYZPTLK HAD SIGHTED LINDA WEARING HER SUPERGIRL COSTUME...
-CHUCKLE- THAT PRETTY GIRL! SHE'S PLAY-ACTING, IN THAT MASQUERADE COSTUME!...GIRL, I HEREBY MAKE YOU GREATER THAN SUPERMAN BY MAGICALLY GIVING YOU ALL HIS POWERS--AND I ALSO WISH THAT YOU BE INVULNERABLE TO KRYPTONITE!
MR. MXYZPTLK LEFT OUR WORLD, LITTLE REALIZING THE GIRL HE'D MADE GREATER THAN SUPERMAN IS ACTUALLY SUPERMAN'S OWN COUSIN!... LESLA-LAR'S MYSTERY-RAY, OF COURSE, HAD NO EFFECT ON SUPERGIRL'S NEW POWERS BECAUSE THEY WERE MAGICAL!
I'LL NOW RETURN TO MY OWN DIMENSION BY SAYING MY NAME BACKWARDS...KLTPZYXM! HA, HA! SOME JOKE, EH? TRY AND LAUGH THAT OFF, SUPERMAN!
THE End
13

SUPERGIRL

SUPERGIRL

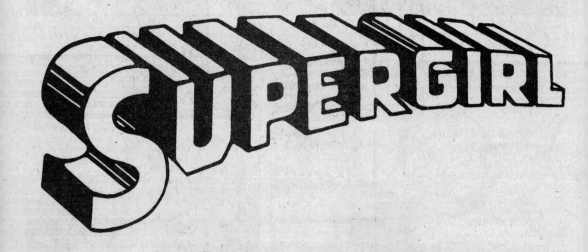

SHOWCASE PRESENTS

OVER 500 PAGES OF DC'S CLASSIC HEROES AND STORIES PRESENTED IN EACH VOLUME!

**GREEN LANTERN
VOL. 1**

**SUPERMAN
VOL. 1**

**SUPERMAN
VOL. 2**

**SUPERMAN FAMILY
VOL. 1**

**JONAH HEX
VOL. 1**

**METAMORPHO
VOL. 1**